THE COMPLETE HA

GAELIC G

FULL GAA RECORDS FROM 1887 TO 2009 INCLUSIVE

DBA

© Foilsithe ag:
DBA PUBLICATIONS LIMITED,
56 Carysfort Avenue, Blackrock, Co. Dublin.
Telephone: (01) 2887247. Facsimile: (01) 2883583.

THE COMPLETE HANDBOOK OF GAELIC GAMES

A comprehensive Record of Results and Teams (1887-2009)

Edited by
DES DONEGAN
with messages from
Criostóir Ó Cuana, Uachtarán
and
Pauric Ó Dufaigh, Ard Stiúrthóir,
Cumann Lúthchleas Gael

DUBLIN 2009

THE COMPLETE HANDBOOK OF
GAELIC GAMES

Previous editions: 1988, 1993, 1999 and 2005.

ISBN: 0-9551115-4-4

DBA

Published by:
DBA PUBLICATIONS LIMITED,
56 Carysfort Avenue, Blackrock, Co. Dublin.
Telephone: (01) 2887247. Facsimile: (01) 2883583.

Printed by: Naas Printing Limited.

CONTENTS

FOOTBALL RECORDS

COLLEGES RECORDS

HIGHER EDUCATION RECORDS

CAMOGIE RECORDS

PUBLISHER'S NOTE

When we published this statistical record five years ago, taking up the mantle of the late Raymond Smith, we were unprepared for the reception which this work would receive.

The numbers of the general public who are interested in the minutiae of the information contained herein is, naturally, limited. However, it has been generally accepted that this resource is an absolute necessity for an organisation such as the GAA. If this work had not initially been undertaken by Raymond Smith and his team back in the nineteen-eighties, much of the statistical record of the diverse and wide-ranging organisation would possibly have been lost for posterity. That it has not, is down to the huge effort put in by many people and it is fitting that they should be acknowledged here again: Mick Dunne, Jim Cronin, Tom Ryall, Jack Mahon, Seamus King and John Clarke. Others who contributed with specialist knowledge include Jerome Quinn, Cliona Foley, Donal Keenan, Seamus Ó Ceallaigh, Dónal McAnallen and P.J. Fulham.

Current contributors include Alan Clarke, Owen McCann, Dónal McAnallen and Patrick Doherty.

This edition, the fifth since 1988, marks the culmination of 125 years of the GAA. This is an auspicious moment in the history of what's often referred to as "the greatest amateur sporting organisation in the world" and we trust that this record forms a fitting part of its legacy into the future.

Des Donegan,
Publisher.

Message from Uachtarán, CLG

Is cúis mhór áthais dom cúpla focal a scríobh ar fhoilsiú an leabhar tábhachtach seo.

Táimid go léir an-bhródúil as stair an Chumainn agus is rud iontach é go bhfuil torthaí na gcluichí bailithe le chéile in aon cnuasach amháin go hairithe sa bhliain stairiúil seo.

The GAA's remit is a wide one but our games are, and will always remain, central to everything that we stand for.

To that end the work undertaken to update this volume of results is to be lauded especially in this our 125th Anniversary year.

There is something here for GAA supporters in every county ranging from schools, club and county results to information on our grounds, All-Ireland referees and other interesting miscellany and noteworthy achievements.

Having an updated record of winning counties, teams and captains provides us and those who cover and follow our games with an invaluable resource and a well maintained record of statistics is something that we should strive to keep intact.

The results collated in this publication evoke many memories for me of great games and superb occasions and touch upon numerous memorable days at some of our top venues around the country.

I would like to acknowledge everyone involved with this project but also the players, officials and volunteers who have made our games what they are since the foundation of the Association 125 years ago.

Ar aghaidh len ár gcluichí.

Christóir Ó Cuana,
Uachtarán.

Message from Ard Stiúrthóir, CLG

Is onóir mór domsa na focail seo a leanas a scríobh don foilseacháin is déanaí le torthaí ár gcluichí agus ba mhaith liom mo bhuíochas a gabháil do gach éinne as an sár obair a rinne siad.

Renowned journalist Raymond Smith did the Association a service many years ago when he and a dedicated group of journalists took on the job of compiling and maintaining a reliable record of our competition winners across so many grades in both codes.

A vital back up for any part of a sporting association is the provision of a bank of statistics for those who comment and write on our games and bring them to the wider public.

While the latest edition of this publication will undoubtedly be an aid to them, it also provides our members and followers with an extremely useful reference point and it is sure to serve as a final port of call in endless debates and arguments based on which of our counties or teams won different competitions and when.

Everyone will look through the volume in search of the results they cherish most and therein lies the importance of the work that has been undertaken to update a project that was last completed back in 2005.

A special word of thanks is due to DBA for their work on the latest edition of results and I look forward to future editions recording our winners and high achievers in the years ahead.

Rath Dé ar an obair,

Pauric Ó Dufaigh,
Ard Stiúrthóir.

CHANGE A REGULAR COMPANION OF GAELIC GAMES

by Owen McCann

Change has been a regular companion on the Gaelic Games scene over the years that mark the second half of the first decade of this new century.

Change like that which further enhanced Croke Park's standing as one of the best sports stadia in the world. That happened on the 3rd February 2007 with the official switching on of the floodlights there. Tyrone and Dublin met subsequently in the opening game of that season's Allianz National Football League before an attendance of 81,678.

Diarmuid Connolly, of Dublin, earned a place in folklore by recording the first score under lights at headquarters. The game was six minutes and twenty seconds old when he sent over the bar. Tyrone won by 0-11 to 0-10.

NEW ERA

Change again a week later at Croke Park. A proposal adopted at the 2005 Annual Congress that the stadium be made available for Rugby and Soccer internationals while Lansdowne Road was being re-developed was turned into a reality.

The new era that dawned at the famed stadium was ushered in when Ireland and France met in the Rugby Six Nations with a New Zealander as referee. Internationalism on a grand scale as Croke Park was brought to a new audience world-wide through live television coverage.

Then it was the turn of Soccer when Wales were visitors at the end of March 2007.

FLOODLIGHTS

Over recent years many other grounds throughout the country have installed floodlights and Saturday games under lights are becoming a growing trend in the early rounds of the National Leagues, with live television coverage also a feature.

The floodlight era at Croke Park at All-Ireland finals level arrived in March 2007 with the playing of deciders in the then comparatively recently launched club intermediate and junior championships. Greencastle, Tyrone, and Ardfert, Kerry, beat Duagh, Kerry, and Eoghan Rua, Derry, in junior and intermediate football respectively.

Croke Park was again to the forefront on 31st January 2009 with the launching there of year long celebrations to mark the 125th Anniversary of the Association's foundation in Thurles in 1884.

A classic game between Tyrone and Dublin in the opening round of the Allianz National Football League, a bumper attendance of 79,126, and a wonderful fireworks display got the celebrations off on the best possible note.

Not only that, but live television coverage of the entire programme helped to win new respect for the Association nationwide among non-Gaelic Games followers.

On the filed of play Stephen O'Neill competed with the floodlights by dazzling Croke Park with a majestic display, highlighted by excellent finishing that yielded eight points, two from frees. His contribution to Tyrone's 1-18 to 1-16 win was immense.

FIRST FINALS

August 2005 marked the playing of the first finals in two new intercounty hurling competitions—the Christy Ring Cup and the Nicky Rackard Cup. The competitions came about as a result of changes to the format of the senior hurling championship. The series was run off in three tiers or groups. Tier one was for the Liam MacCarthy Cup, tier two for the Ring Cup and tier three for the Rackard Cup.

First of the new finals was for the Christy Ring Cup. The competition commemorates one of the greatest hurlers of all time, Christy Ring, of Cork, and ten counties competed in the inaugural event.

Westmeath and Down qualified for the Croke Park final. An entertaining game appeared to be heading for a replay with the teams level at the end of normal time. But in added time midfielder Enda Loughlin and captain and centre half forward John Shaw each pointed to clinch a 1-23 to 2-8 win for Westmeath. Left half forward Andrew Mitchell (Westmeath) led the scoring review with nine points, eight from frees and one from a 65.

A week later came the Nicky Rackard Cup decider. Rackard, of Wexford, carved out a legendary reputation as a leader and forward with a flair for recording big scores.

Eleven counties, plus London and Warwickshire, started out on the road to glory that climaxed with a final between London and Louth at Croke Park. Left full forward Kevin McMullan did much to send London on the way to a comfortable 5-8 to 1-5 win. He scored two goals and a point. Right full forward Dave Bourke was also to the fore in the scoring returns, finishing with 1-4.

LONG WAITS ENDED

The old saying "that it is a long road that has no turning" came to mind when Waterford and Kilkenny lined out at Thurles in the 2007 Allianz National Hurling League final.

Waterford were bidding for their first title since 1963 and the lengthy wait was ended in style as they played their part in contributing to a grand game when forging out a hard-earned but merited 0-20 to 0-18 win.

Michael Walsh captained the side in fine style from midfield, while centre half forward Eoin Kelly, with eight points, was another to the fore in the success story.

An even longer spell out of the honours list came to an end for Roscommon in minor football in 2006. A first All-Ireland title in 55 years looked to be slipping away as they trailed Kerry by a point as a thrilling final moved close to the final whistle.

However, David O'Gara kept hopes alive by scoring the equaliser from play, 0-15 each, to send the first final between the counties to a replay.

The replay at Cusack Park, Ennis, attracted a bumper attendance of 17,282. A tight defence, marshalled by Neil Carty and team captain David Flynn, midfielders David Keenan and top scoring Donal Shine (he hit six points) and forwards O'Gara and Conor Devaney, powered Roscommon to a 1-10 to 0-9 win.

The Westerners did not concede a goal in their six-game campaign and maintained the county's unbeaten record in four All-Ireland final appearances—1939, 1941, 1952 and 2006, the only title won in a replay. Their success also ended a lengthy wait for Connacht as Roscommon brought the Tom Markham Cup back to the province after a lapse of 20 years.

PERSONNEL CHANGES

Changing of the guard as well a Croke Park in 2008—and on a grand scale.

Early in 2009 Liam Mulvihill bowed out as Director General of the GAA and was succeeded by Pauric Duffy (Monaghan).

Tom Walsh (Wicklow) ended his three year term of office as President of the Handball Council in 2008 and was succeeded by Tony Hannon, a native of Sligo, but resident in Roscommon for many years.

Later in the year Síle Wallace stepped down after twenty-two years as Ard Stiurthóir of the Camogie Association and Sinéad O'Connor, who was previously the Association's finance and sponsorship manager, succeeded to the position.

In September 2008 Danny Lynch ended a tenure of over 20 years as Public Relations Officer, and subsequently Lisa Clancy, then outgoing head of Corporate Communications for the Health Service Executive (HSE), was appointed Director of Communications at Croke Park.

The year 2008 bowed out with news of the retirements of two more long serving officials — Lorcán Ó Ruairc, National Administrator of the Irish Handball Council, and Seán Ó Laoire, Ard Stiurthóir na gCluichí, after almost 40 years at Croke Park.

Early in 2009 Chris Curran (Tyrone), who has been involved in handball for three decades as a player and administrator, took over as National Handball Manager.

Then in April 2009 Nicky Brennan handed over the reins of office as President of the GAA to Christy Cooney, who became the first Cork man to hold the position since the late Con Murphy in 1976 to 1979.

New Presidents as well in 2009 in Camogie and Ladies football. Joan O'Flynn, a native of Cork, who has spent a lot of time involved with the sport in Kildare, succeeded to the position in Camogie. Pat Quill returned to the position he filled in Ladies football from 1985 to 1988.

FAMOUS FIRSTS

Famous Firsts? Declan O'Sullivan carved out a special niche for himself when he led Kerry to a successful defence of the All-Ireland senior football title in 2007.

That was his second successive year to lead the Kingdom to the title. As a result he became the first footballer to be twice presented with the new Sam Maguire Cup, which was first awarded for the 1998 championship, won by Meath.

Brian Dooher equalled O'Sullivan's feat in 2008 when he led Tyrone to glory. He first captained the O'Neill County to the All-Ireland senior title in 2005.

Neil Gallagher led Donegal into the history books when he captained the side from midfield to victory over Mayo at Croke Park in 2007 for a first ever National Football League title.

Kerry and Cork, who are such famed Munster football rivals, chartered their way into new waters when they provided the first all-Munster All-Ireland senior final in 2007. The Kingdom powered to a resounding 3-13 to 1-9 win, with right full forward Colm Cooper an ace in their pack. He scored 1-5.

A long, long wait ended for Wicklow in May 2008 when they beat Kildare by 0-13 to 0-9 in a preliminary round Leinster senior football championship game. Hard to credit that the win was the Garden County's first at Croke Park in the championship in 124 years.

Right half forward Tony Hannon, who scored six points, and midfielder James Stafford starred for the Mick O'Dwyer managed side.

On the refereeing front another first was achieved by Jimmy White when he lined out as the man-in-the middle as the 2008 Ulster senior football final between Armagh and Fermanagh at Clones. He became the first "knight of the whistle" from Donegal to take charge of the showpiece game in the province. The final ended in a draw.

UNDER AGE GAMES

The drawing power of under-age football was put firmly into the spotlight—and not for the first time—in a big way in September 2008 by the All-Ireland minor football final replay between Tyrone and Mayo at Pearse Park, Longford.

The game was an all ticket affair and drew a bumper attendance of 15,056. The teams provided a classic match that went to extra time and was brimful of good football and top class individual displays.

Right half back Ronan McNabb played a real captain's part with his quality play as the Ulster side triumphed by 1-20 to 1-15 to become the first Northern county to win the Tom Markham Cup (minor) and Sam Maguire Cup in the same year.

INTERNATIONAL SCENE

Contrasting fortunes for the International Test series in football between Ireland and Australia. The second game in the 2006 series at Croke Park drew the largest attendance at any game in the series at 82,127. However, rough play in the opening quarter brought much criticism and eventually led to the suspension of the series for a time. Australia won that series on an aggregate of 109 to 79.

Relations were renewed in 2008 when the Test was revived with Ireland visiting Australia. The visitors won in Perth in the first game by 45-44, and clinched the series and the Cormac McAnallen Cup with a 57-53 win at Melbourne for an aggregate success of 102 to 97. Seán Cavanagh (Tyrone) captained Ireland and Sean Boylan (Meath) was the team manager.

Leighton Glynn (Wicklow) celebrated his debut in the Ireland colours earning the man-of-the match award at Perth, and Graham Canty (Cork) was named the man-of-the-series.

Still on the international theme and a noteworthy milestone in the history of the Hurling-Shinty international series between Ireland and Scotland.

In 2006 Scotland returned to Croke Park after a four year absence—games in Ireland were played at other venues—and were striving for a first win at the Stadium. The game was a curtain-raiser to the International Rules Test between Ireland and Australia.

Scotland made it a memorable day with a 2-13 to 2-5 win. They might well have finished with a bigger margin but for the brilliance in the Irish goal of Graham Clarke (Down), who brought off some superb saves.

They led at the interval by 1-7 to 1-1. Ireland, with a team composed of hurlers who competed in the Christy Ring and Nicky Rackard Cups, did better in the second half, but the visitors finished strongly for a well-deserved historic success.

That year, too, was marked by the inauguration of an International Rules series in Ladies Football between Ireland and Australia. The opening game was played at Kingspan Breffni Park, where Ireland won in impressive style by 130 to 15. The second game a Parnell Park, Dublin, was a much closer affair, with the hosts triumphing by 39 to 18 to take the title convincingly on an aggregate score of 169 to 33.

Ireland were captained by Sara O'Connor, of the Southern Gaels club and Kerry, and the team was managed by Jarlath Burns, the former Armagh footballer.

GREATEST TEAM PERFORMANCE

Greatest team performance in the annals of the All-Ireland senior hurling championship finals? That is a difficult question to answer. However, a very strong challenger for that mighty ranking must undoubtedly be Kilkenny's performance when retaining their All-Ireland title against Waterford in 2008.

A sparkling array of skills, craft, teamwork and scoring power added up to what was as close to the perfect performance as made little difference. Kilkenny scored three goals and thirty points to finish with twenty three points to spare—3-30 to 1-13.

There could not have been a better way than that for Kilkenny to equal their only other sequence of three All-Ireland titles in succession—1911, 1912 and 1913.

In 2009 Kilkenny beat Tipperary by 2-22 to 0-23 to become only the second county to win four All-Ireland senior hurling finals in succession. They played eighteen games—an outstanding achievement. Cork set the standard from 1941 to 1944 inclusive.

Much credit for Kilkenny's modern success story must go to Brian Cody, a former All-Ireland senior medal winner. The 2009 win marked his seventh time to manage an All-Ireland senior hurling title-winning team.

On the field of play Henry Shefflin made a wonderful contribution. He played in all eighteen games and scored 6-149 (167 points) and scored in every game. He also captained the Noresiders in 2007 and 2009.

INTERPROVINCIALS
The M. Donnelly interprovincial hurling and football tests of 2009 continued the system introduced in 2003 of charting new horizons. Abu Dhabi was the venue for the first time when the hurling decider was played there at the start of the St. Patrick's Day holiday period. Then, in November, the football final was played in London.

The policy of playing finals abroad was ushered in with the playing of the 2003 hurling final between Leinster and Connacht in Rome.

Back again to change—and at a Special Congress at Croke Park in early October 2008 Galway and Antrim,gained entry to the Leinster senior hurling championship from 2009 to 2011.

Experimental Disciplinary Playing Rules were introduced on a trial basis in January 2009 in pre-National Leagues competitions and followed on in the Leagues in football and hurling.

UNUSUAL TREBLES
Unusual trebles? What about the achievements of Paul Brady (Cavan) and Fiona Shannon (Antrim) in the World Handball Championships in Portland, Oregan, in October?

Brady became the first to win the Men's Open senior singles title for the third successive championship. His achievement was all the more noteworthy because he played with a damaged quad muscle. Shannon kept in step with Brady by becoming the first to win the Women's Open senior singles title for the third consecutive time.

As for the 125 Year celebrations in 2009, an ambitious programme of events was arranged to celebrate the occasion.

Lá na gClub in early May was a particularly successful highlight. So, too, was a Garden Party hosted by Uachtarán na hÉireann at Áras an Uachtarán

Other features included the launching at Croke Park in October of THE GAA: A PEOPLE'S HISTORY, a mammoth book telling how the GAA has carved out a unique place in Irish life, and a Central Council meeting in Thurles and a Coiste Bainistí meeting at Cusack Cottage in November to mark the date of the foundation of the GAA on 1st November, 1884.

RECORD EQUALLING FEAT
In October Henry Shefflin joined a select band of record-makers in the annals of the All Stars teams. He joined D. J. Carey (Kilkenny) and Pat Spillane (Kerry) on nine awards when chosen at centre half forward in the Vodafone Hurling team.

Shefflin won his first award in 2000 and his second in 2002 to start a run of eight awards in succession.

HURLING CAPTAINS

2008 James 'Cha' Fitzpatrick
(Cill Chainnigh)

2009 Michael Fennelly
(Cill Chainnigh)

2007 Henry Shefflin
(Cill Chainnigh)

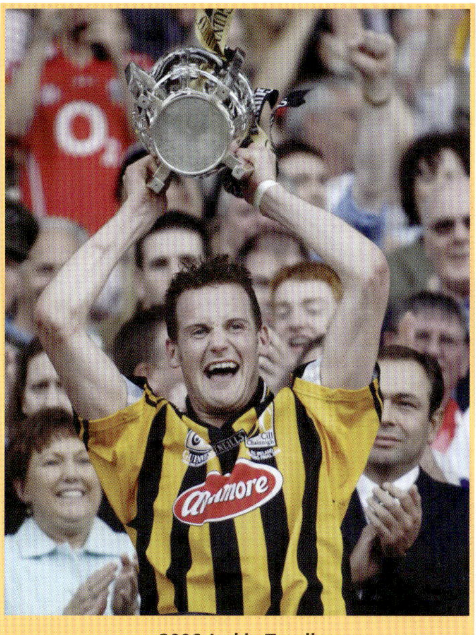

2006 Jackie Tyrell
(Cill Chainnigh)

HURLING

CILL CHAINNIGH 2006 GAA HURLING ALL-IRELAND SENIOR CHAMPIONS

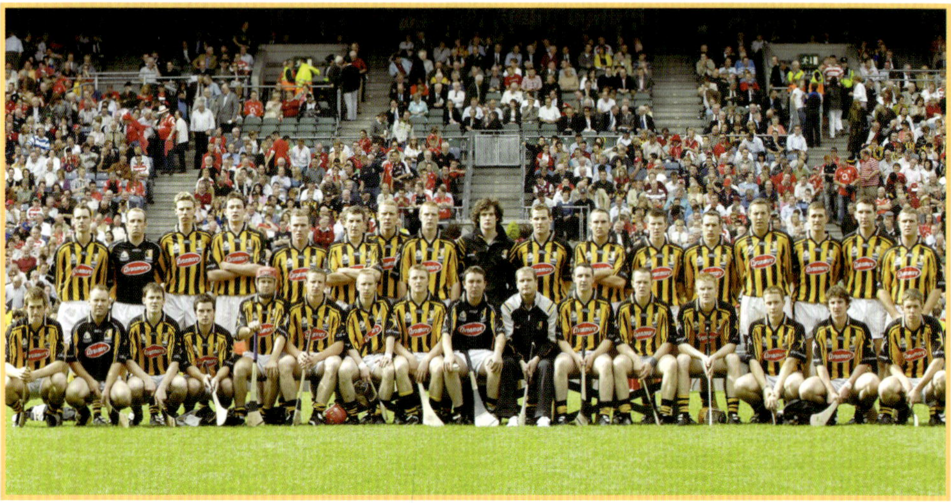

The Kilkenny squad which defeated Cork in the Guinness All-Ireland Hurling Final
Back row (l-r): Seaghan O'Neill, Richie O'Neill, Brian Hogan, Martin Comerford, Noel Hickey, Derek Lyng, James Ryall, Henry Shefflin, Donnacha Cody, Jackie Tyrell, Eddie Brennan, Michael Rice, Willie O'Dwyer, Peter Cleere, Richie Mullally, P.J. Delaney, Stephen Maher.
Front row (l-r): Sean Cummins, P.J. Ryan, Eoin Reid, Eoin McCormack, Tommy Walsh, John Tennyson, James 'Cha' Fitzpatrick, Aidan Fogarty, James McGarry, J.J. Delaney, Eoin Larkin, Michael Kavanagh, Richie Power, John Dalton, Austin Murphy, Michael Fennelly.

CILL CHAINNIGH 2007 GAA HURLING ALL-IRELAND SENIOR CHAMPIONS

The Kilkenny team which defeated Limerick in the All-Ireland Hurling Final
Back row (l-r): James Ryall, Peter Cleere, Canice Hickey, Noel Hickey, Jackie Tyrrell, Derek Lyng, Brian Hogan, Henry Shefflin, Michael Rice, Eddie Blackmore, P.J. Delaney, Donnacha Cody, Sean Cummins, Richie O'Neill, Richie Mullally, John Tennyson, Martin Comerford, T.J. Reid.
Front row (l-r): Richie Power, Michael Fennelly, Eoin Larkin, Michael Kavanagh, Tommy Walsh, Darragh McGarry (mascot), James 'Cha' Fitzpatrick, P.J. Ryan, J.J. Delaney, Willie O'Dwyer, Aidan Fogarty, Eoin Reid, Eoin McCormack, Richie Hogan, Michael Murphy, John Dalton, James McGarry.

HURLING

CILL CHAINNIGH 2008 GAA HURLING ALL-IRELAND SENIOR CHAMPIONS

The Kilkenny squad which defeated Waterford in the All-Ireland Hurling Final
Back row (l-r): Richie Mullally, Donnacha Cody, Martin Comerford, James Ryall, Canice Hickey, Noel Hickey, Derek Lyng, J¨ackie Tyrrell, Brian Hogan, PJ Delaney, Damien Fogarty, Willie O'Dwyer, Michael Rice, Sean Cummins, TJ Reid, John Dalton, Eddie Brennan.
Front row (l-r): Henry Shefflin, John Tennyson, David Herity, Richie Hogan, James McGarry, Eoin Larkin, Richie Power, James Fitzpatrick, Michael Kavanagh, JJ Delaney, PJ Ryan, Aidan Fogarty, Eoin Reid, Michael Fennelly, Eoin McGrath, Darragh McGarry, Tommy Walsh.

CILL CHAINNIGH 2009 GAA HURLING ALL-IRELAND SENIOR CHAMPIONS

The Kilkenny squad which defeated Tipperary in the All-Ireland Hurling Final
Back row (l-r): Richie O'Neill, Sean Cummins, Willie O'Dwyer, James Ryall, Noel Hickey, Canice Hickey, Brian Hogan, Michael Grace, Jackie Tyrrell, Derek Lyng, Michael Fennelly, Henry Shefflin, P.J. Delaney, T.J. Reid, Michael Rice, Eddie Brennan, John Dalton, Damien Fogarty, Martin Comerford, John Tennyson.
Front row (l-r): David Herity, Aidan Fogarty, Michael Kavanagh, Richie Hogan, P.J. Ryan, Richie Power,J.J. Delaney, Eoin Larkin, Tommy Walsh, Eoin McGrath, Eoin Reid, James 'Cha' Fitzpatrick.

HURLING ACTION

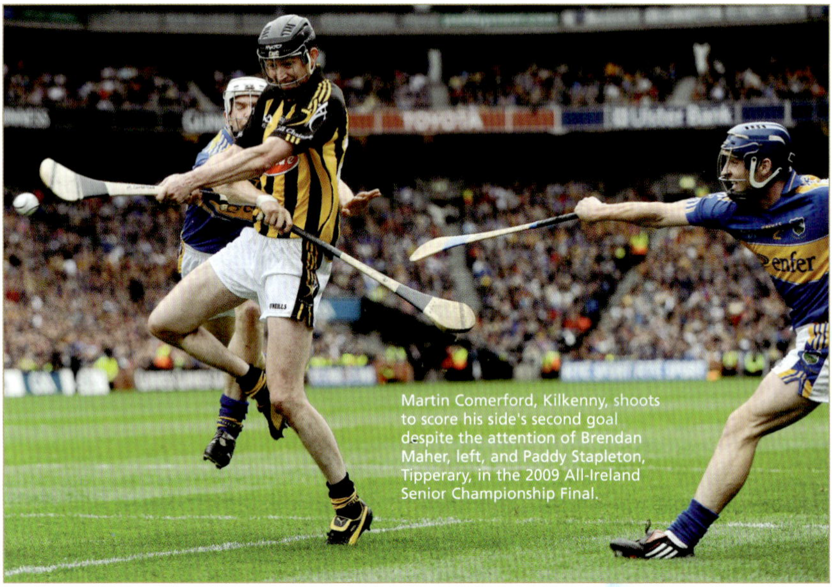

Martin Comerford, Kilkenny, shoots to score his side's second goal despite the attention of Brendan Maher, left, and Paddy Stapleton, Tipperary, in the 2009 All-Ireland Senior Championship Final.

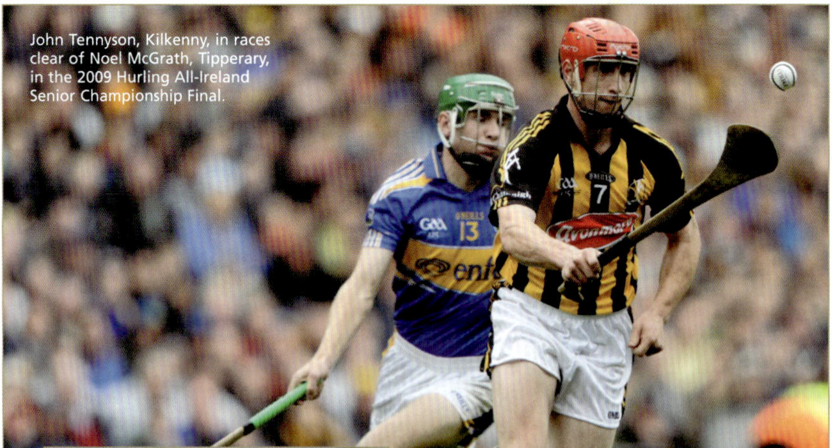

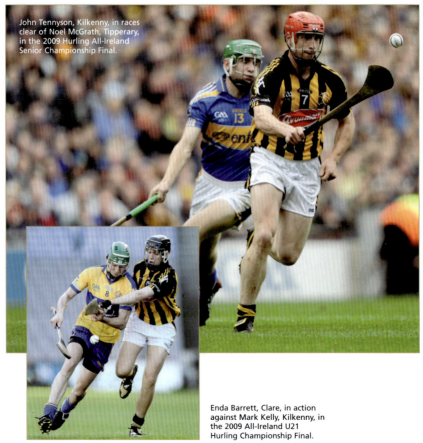

John Tennyson, Kilkenny, in races clear of Noel McGrath, Tipperary, in the 2009 Hurling All-Ireland Senior Championship Final.

Enda Barrett, Clare, in action against Mark Kelly, Kilkenny, in the 2009 All-Ireland U21 Hurling Championship Final.

HURLING ACTION

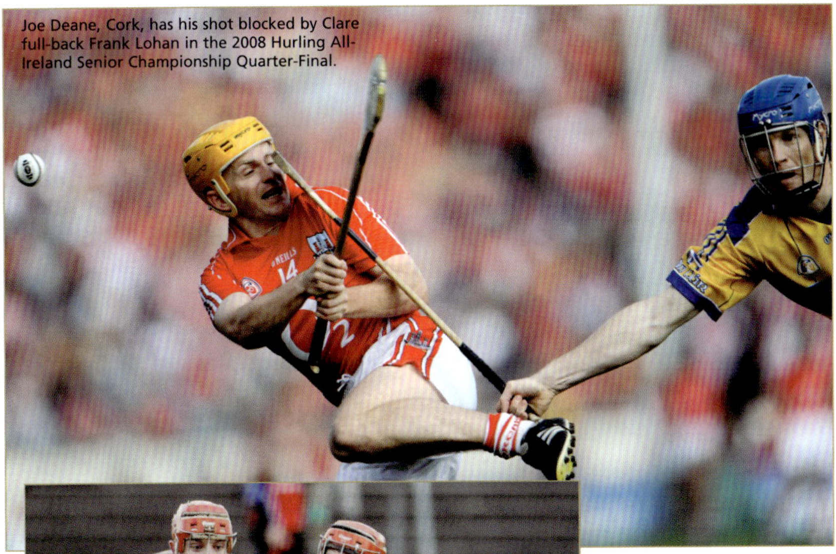

Joe Deane, Cork, has his shot blocked by Clare full-back Frank Lohan in the 2008 Hurling All-Ireland Senior Championship Quarter-Final.

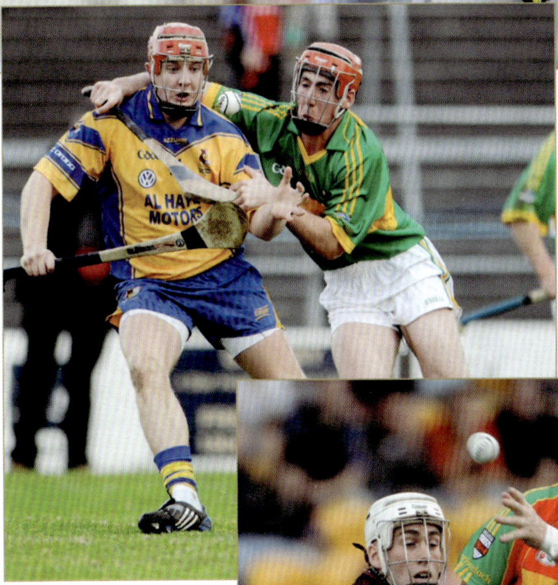

Joe Canning, Portumna, in action against Brian Regan, Gort, in the 2008 Galway Senior Hurling Final.

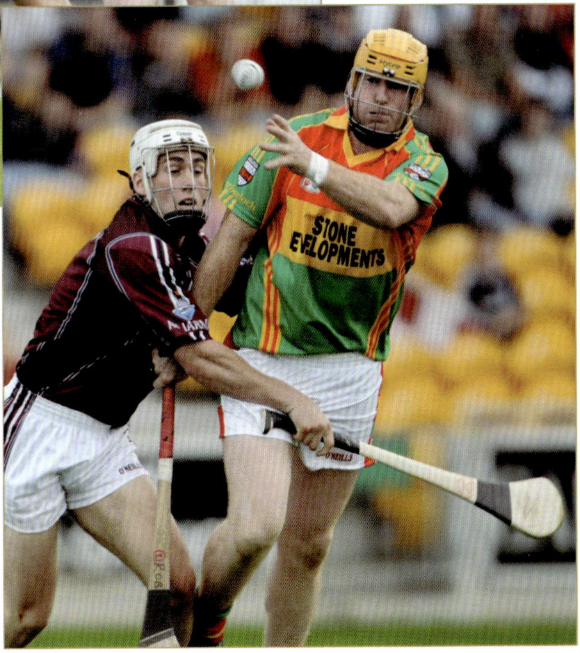

Robert Foley, Carlow, gets his pass away despite the attention of Adam Price, Westmeath, in the 2008 Christy Ring Cup Final at O'Connor Park, Tullamore.

HURLING ACTION

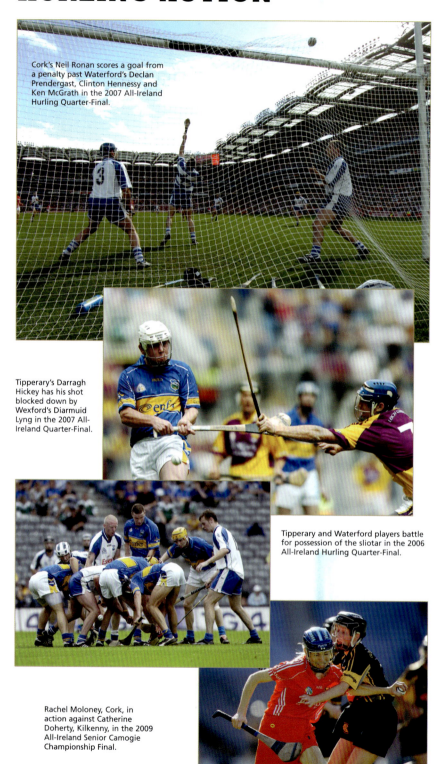

Cork's Neil Ronan scores a goal from a penalty past Waterford's Declan Prendergast, Clinton Hennessy and Ken McGrath in the 2007 All-Ireland Hurling Quarter-Final.

Tipperary's Darragh Hickey has his shot blocked down by Wexford's Diarmuid Lyng in the 2007 All-Ireland Quarter-Final.

Tipperary and Waterford players battle for possession of the sliotar in the 2006 All-Ireland Hurling Quarter-Final.

Rachel Moloney, Cork, in action against Catherine Doherty, Kilkenny, in the 2009 All-Ireland Senior Camogie Championship Final.

GAA 125 ANNIVERSARY

The year 2009 will be fondly remembered for the usual quota of on-field highs and lows, drama, controversy and talking points in football and hurling at a variety of competitions across different levels and grades.

While there were familiar sightings of green and gold and black and amber on the steps of the Hogan Stand in September after memorable championships in both codes, the 125th Anniversary celebrations ensured that the 2009 calendar year will also be remembered for more than just the games.

While the century and a quarter celebrations were well flagged before 2009 was upon us the events of January 31 at Croke Park well and truly underlined the start of the celebrations on a night to remember for a crowd of more than 80,000.

Brian Dooher, Tyrone, centre, in the company of 4 rival team captains representing the 4 provincial winners from 2008 from left, Ciaran McKeever, Armagh, Damien Burke, Galway, Graham Canty, Cork, and Paul Griffin, Dublin.

Although Dublin and Tyrone provided the fireworks on the field of a play in an excellent opening round league encounter – illuminated by Stephen O'Neill from the winning team – the post match lights and fireworks and extravaganza confirmed to the nation that 2009 was very much a year of note for the Association.

A specially commissioned 'Iconic Moments' DVD presentation complete with commentary from Micheál Ó Muircheartaigh was played as part of the exhibition and the presence of the bumper attendance after the game until the end of the event was a ringing endorsement of proceedings.

Following such a high profile and well received launch event for the celebrations was always going to be a tall order but it was never the intention of the GAA to organise a series of events of this scale or magnitude and a carefully choreographed schedule was organised for the remainder of the year.

While clubs and various other units organised their own events to mark the year in their

President Mary McAleese, her husband Dr. Martin McAleese, with Cuthbert Donnelly, Tyrone, Ulster GAA President Tom Daly with the Sam Maguire cup and Tom Markham cup, during the GAA 125 Years History Conference.

own way, the next stand out event was Lá na gClub which took place on a fixtures-free weekend on May 10.

Hundreds of clubs rose to the occasion by organising a host of different games and culture based events and parades and marching bands featured prominently across the country on what was a day to remember for the Association.

To mark the special Anniversary the GAA were invited soon after to a specially convened Garden Party in Áras an Uachtaráin by Uachtarán na hÉireann Mary McAleese to celebrate the 125 celebrations.

Association officials, players and volunteers were all present to hear a special speech from the President which outlined the contribution of the GAA to Irish society.

The 1984 All-Ireland finals - and the hurling decider which was moved to Thurles in particular - were fondly remembered and it was hoped that the 2009 finals would be viewed in a similar light in years to come.

To that end special post match arrangements were made before both finals based on special pageantry and entertainment focussing on the colours of all our counties amongst a specially commissioned giant 125 banner occupying centre stage when the hurlers of Kilkenny and

Members of Carricmore GFC, Co. Tyrone, patricipate in a parade as part of the 2009 Lá na gClub activities.

Tipperary and the footballers of Kerry and Cork took to the field on two memorable September Sundays.

While Kerry once again reigned supreme against their Munster rivals Cork – on a day when they actually took to the field as underdogs after what was a circuitous route to the final – Kilkenny marked the 125 year in style by capturing their fourth consecutive GAA Hurling Championship title in a final was widely proclaimed as a classic.

After the camogie and football finals, which were both won by Cork, the curtain came down on the inter-county season allowing club finals across the country to resume centre stage.

Before the year inched towards December however there were still a number of other events that officially drew the anniversary commemorations to a close.

Uachtarán CLG Criostóir Ó Cuana with An Taoiseach Brian Cowen T.D., and Páraic Duffy, Ard Stiúrthóir of the GAA, at the launch of 'The GAA - A People's History'.

As part of the Oral History Project commissioned by the Association, 'The GAA; A People's History' was published in October before launches around the country and another in London unveiled a magnificent collection of photographs and reproduced documents.

The new book underlined the scale and importance of a project that is the largest of its kind ever undertaken by a sporting organisation.

The Central Bank followed the earlier release of a specially designed unused currency coin set by releasing a limited edition 125 coin complete with the 125 logo and a hurler included to portray our indigenous games.

However it was right and fitting that the official celebrations should return to Liberty Square Thurles honouring the founding fathers who gathered in that town in 1884

Tipperary legend Jimmy Doyle presents the torch to Jimmy O'Gorman, Chairman of the Munster Council, on the pitch at Semple Stadium to commemorate the 125th arriversary of the GAA

without an inkling of the force that they were about to unleash on the country.

November 1 1884 was the day it all began in Lizzy Hayes' Hotel in the Tipperary Town and in a twist of fate the anniversary of this date fell on a Sunday – a day synonymous with our games - as representatives from the four provinces descended on Thurles for the official end to the year's celebrations.

Archbishop Clifford celebrated a special mass at which former presidents offered up GAA gifts and Uachtarán Chumann Lúthchleas Gael Criostóir Ó Cuana and Ard Stiúrthóir Páraic Ó Dufaigh read readings.

Afterwards a procession, led by the Artane Band, led marchers from the Cathedral to Dr Croke's statue in Liberty Square, stopping at Hayes Hotel in acknowledgement before formalities began.

Readings were made before proceedings ended with the playing of Amhrán na bhFiann and the Munster club clash of Thurles Sarsfields and Newtownshandrum saw the focus return to the games.

It was a year that had something for everyone and one that is unlikely to be matched until 2034 the 150th Anniversary of the Association.

In the meantime the memories of 2009 will abide.

Flag bearers during the 125th Celebrations at half time of the GAA Hurling All-Ireland Senior Championship Final.

31 January 2009
Flag bearers parade around the pitch before the Dublin v Tyrone game to mark the start of the 125th Anniversary Celebrations of the founding of the GAA in 1884 in the Allianz GAA National Football League, Division 1, Round 1 at Croke Park, Dublin

FOOTBALL CAPTAINS

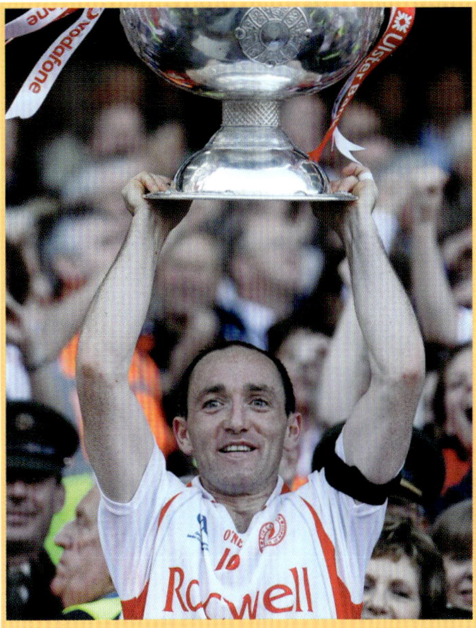

2008 Brian Dooher
(Tír Eoghain)

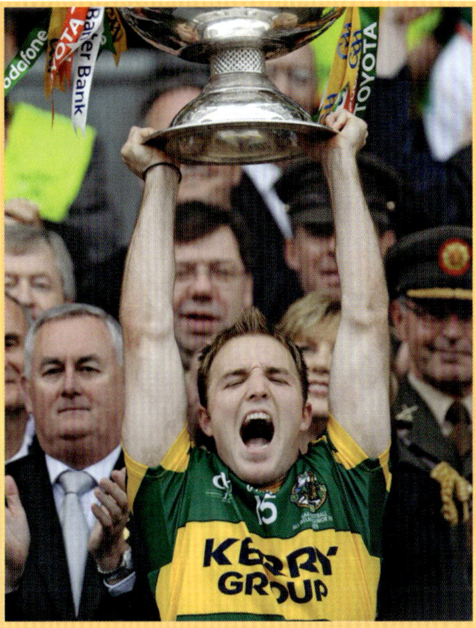

2009 Darran O'Sullivan
(Ciarraí)

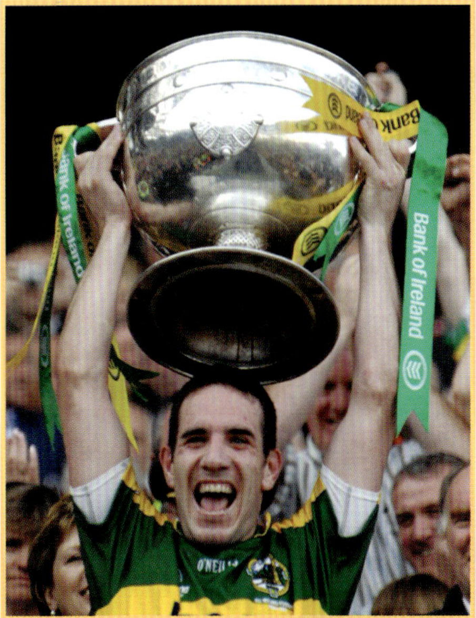

2007 Declan O'Sullivan
(Ciarraí)

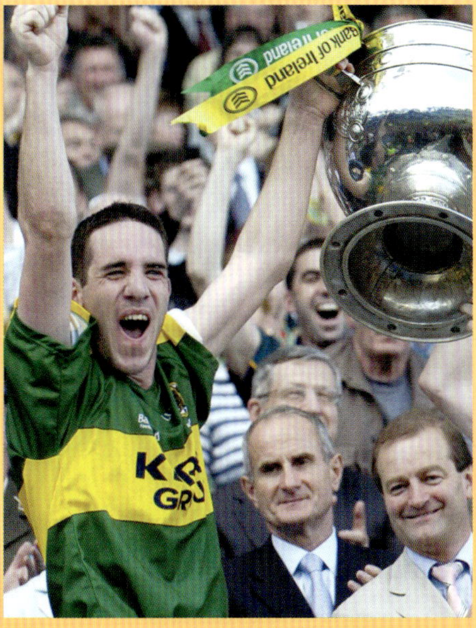

2006 Declan O'Sullivan
(Ciarraí)

FOOTBALL

CIARRAÍ 2006 GAA FOOTBALL ALL-IRELAND SENIOR CHAMPIONS

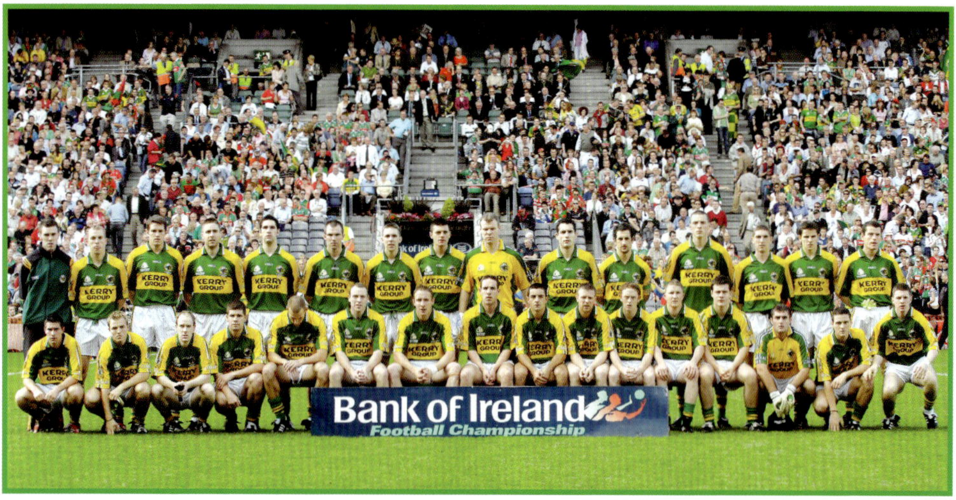

The Kerry squad which defeated Mayo in the All-Ireland Football Final
Back row (l-r): Daniel Bohane, Ronan Hussey, Eoin Brosnan, Darragh Ó Sé, Bryan Sheehan, Michael McCarthy, Marc Ó Sé, Aodán Mac Gearailt, Diarmuid Murphy, Tom O'Sullivan, Paul Galvin, Kieran Donaghy, Killian Young, Ronan O'Connor, Brendan Guiney.
Front row (l-r): Paul O'Connor, Darren O'Sullivan, Mossy Lyons, Eamon Fitzmaurice, Sean O'Sullivan, Seamus Moynihan, Tommy Griffin, Declan O'Sullivan, Aidan O'Mahony, Tomás Ó Sé, Colm Cooper, Mike Frank Russell, Padraig Reidy, Kieran Cremin, Adrian O'Connell, Kieran O'Leary.

CIARRAÍ 2007 GAA FOOTBALL ALL-IRELAND SENIOR CHAMPIONS

The Kerry squad which defeated Cork in the All-Ireland Football Final.
Back row (l-r): Daniel Bohan, Tommy Walsh, Ronan Hussey, Darragh Ó Sé, Paul Galvin, Kieran Donaghy, Marc Ó Sé, Tom O'Sullivan, Diarmuid Murphy, Seamus Scanlon, Killian Young, Mícheál Quirke, Declan Quill, Donncha Walsh, Rónán Ó Flatharta.
Front row (l-r): Mike Frank Russell, Mossy Lyons, Paul O'Connor, Darren O'Sullivan, Sean O'Sullivan, Eoin Brosnan, Padraig Reidy, Bryan Sheehan, Declan O'Sullivan, Aidan O'Mahony, Tomás Ó Sé, Colm Cooper, Tommy Griffin, Kieran O'Leary, Kieran Cremin.

FOOTBALL

TÍR EOGHAIN 2008 GAA FOOTBALL ALL-IRELAND SENIOR CHAMPIONS

The Tyrone squad which defeated Kerry in the All-Ireland Football Final.
Back row (l-r): Raymond Mulgrew, Damian McCaul, Justin McMahon, Colm Cavanagh, Owen Mulligan, Jonathan Curran, Sean Cavanagh, Pascal McConnell, Colin Holmes, Shaun O'Neill, Cathal McCarron, Peter Donnelly, Paul Quinn, Kevin Hughes, Brian McGuigan, Stephen O'Neill
Front row (l-r): Conor Gormley, Joe McMahon, Niall Gormley, Davy Harte, Tommy McGuigan, Enda McGinley, Philip Jordan, Brian Dooher (Capt.), Ryan Mellon, Martin Penrose, Colm McCullagh, Michael McGee, Ciaran Gourley. On the grass (l. to r.): PJ Quinn, Ryan McMenamin, Dermot Carlin.
Missing from the photo: John Devine

CIARRAÍ 2009 GAA FOOTBALL ALL-IRELAND SENIOR CHAMPIONS

The Kerry squad which defeated Cork in the All-Ireland Football Final.
Back row (l-r): Tadhg Kennelly, Ger Reidy, Daniel Bohan, Darragh Ó Sé, Bryan Sheehan, Paul Galvin, Aidan O'Mahony, Tom O'Sullivan, Mark Ó Sé, Seán O'Sullivan , Diarmuid Murphy, Séamus Scanlon, Aidan O'Shea, Donnacha Walsh, Tommy Walsh, Michéal Quirke, Maurice Corridan, Kieran Donaghy, Anthony Maher, David Moran, Rónán Ó Flatharta, Kieran Quirke,
Front row (l-r): Paul O'Connor. Mike McCarthy, Declan O'Sullivan, Killian Young , Darran O'Sullivan, Tomás Ó Sé, Tommy Griffin, Colm Cooper, Padraig Reidy, Barry John Walsh.

FOOTBALL ACTION

Daniel Goulding, Cork, prevents the ball from going out of play ahead of Tom O'Sullivan, Kerry in the 2009 Football All-Ireland Senior Championship Final.

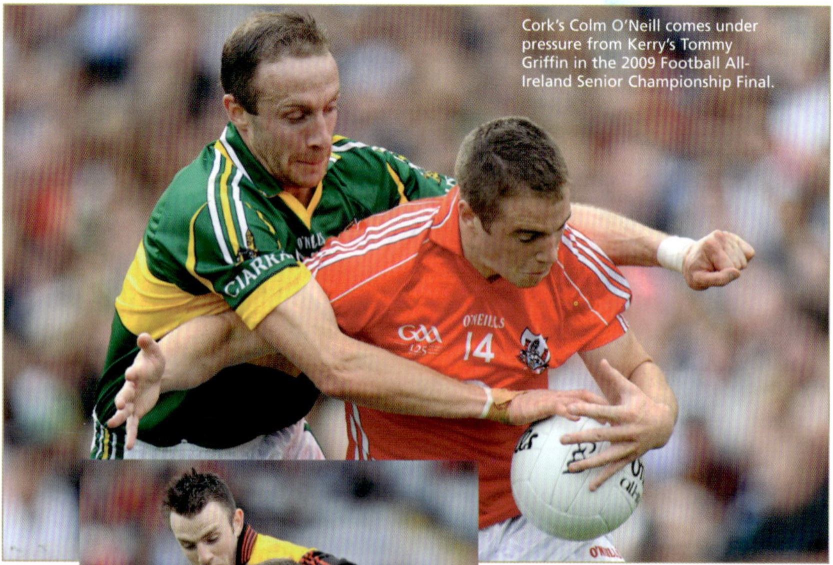

Cork's Colm O'Neill comes under pressure from Kerry's Tommy Griffin in the 2009 Football All-Ireland Senior Championship Final.

Mark Collins, Cork, in action against John Fitzpatrick, Down in the 2009 Under-21 All-Ireland Football Championship Final.

FOOTBALL ACTION

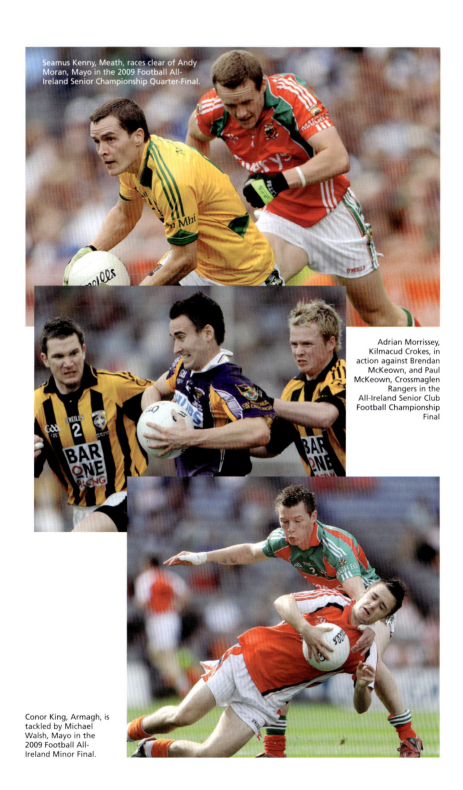

Seamus Kenny, Meath, races clear of Andy Moran, Mayo in the 2009 Football All-Ireland Senior Championship Quarter-Final.

Adrian Morrissey, Kilmacud Crokes, in action against Brendan McKeown, and Paul McKeown, Crossmaglen Rangers in the All-Ireland Senior Club Football Championship Final

Conor King, Armagh, is tackled by Michael Walsh, Mayo in the 2009 Football All-Ireland Minor Final.

FOOTBALL ACTION

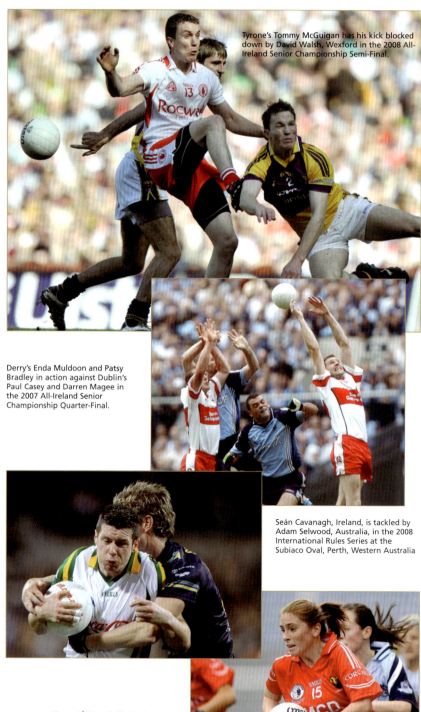

Tyrone's Tommy McGuigan has his kick blocked down by David Walsh, Wexford in the 2008 All-Ireland Senior Championship Semi-Final.

Derry's Enda Muldoon and Patsy Bradley in action against Dublin's Paul Casey and Darren Magee in the 2007 All-Ireland Senior Championship Quarter-Final.

Seán Cavanagh, Ireland, is tackled by Adam Selwood, Australia, in the 2008 International Rules Series at the Subiaco Oval, Perth, Western Australia

Rhona Nì Bhuachalla, Cork,w in action against Dublin in the 2009 All-Ireland Ladies Football Senior Championship Final.

THE COMPLETE HANDBOOK OF

GAELIC GAMES

HURLING
Records

HURLING

RESULTS OF ALL-IRELAND CHAMPIONSHIPS 1887- 2009

The distribution of Championship Honours to date is as follows:

SENIOR HURLING

Kilkenny (32) — 1904, 1905, 1907, 1909, 1911, 1912, 1913, 1922, 1932, 1933, 1935, 1939, 1947, 1957, 1963, 1967, 1969, 1972, 1974, 1975, 1979, 1982, 1983, 1992, 1993, 2000, 2002, 2003, 2006, 2007, 2008, 2009.
Cork (30) — 1890, 1892, 1893, 1894, 1902, 1903, 1919, 1926, 1928, 1929, 1931, 1941, 1942, 1943, 1944, 1946, 1952, 1953, 1954, 1966, 1970, 1976, 1977, 1978, 1984, 1986, 1990, 1999, 2004, 2005.
Tipperary (25) — 1887, 1895, 1896, 1898, 1899, 1900, 1906, 1908, 1916, 1925, 1930, 1937, 1945, 1949, 1950, 1951, 1958, 1961, 1962, 1964, 1965, 1971, 1989, 1991, 2001.
Limerick (7) — 1897, 1918, 1921, 1934, 1936, 1940, 1973.
Dublin (6) — 1889, 1917, 1920, 1924, 1927, 1938.
Wexford (6) — 1910, 1955, 1956, 1960, 1968, 1996.
Galway (4) — 1923, 1980, 1987, 1988.
Offaly (4) — 1981, 1985, 1994, 1998.
Clare (3) — 1914, 1995, 1997.
Waterford (2) — 1948, 1959.
Kerry (1) — 1891.
London (1) — 1901.
Laois (1) — 1915.

MINOR HURLING

Kilkenny (19) — 1931, 1935, 1936, 1950, 1960, 1961, 1962, 1972, 1973, 1975, 1977, 1981, 1988, 1990, 1991, 1993, 2002, 2003, 2008.
Cork (18) — 1928, 1937, 1938, 1939, 1941, 1951, 1964, 1967, 1969, 1970, 1971, 1974, 1978, 1979, 1985, 1995, 1998, 2001.
Tipperary (18) — 1930, 1932, 1933, 1934, 1947, 1949, 1952, 1953, 1955, 1956, 1957, 1959, 1976, 1980, 1982, 1996, 2006, 2007.
Galway (8) — 1983, 1992, 1994, 1999, 2000, 2004, 2005, 2009.
Dublin (4) — 1945, 1946, 1954, 1965.
Wexford (3) — 1963, 1966, 1968.
Limerick (3) — 1940, 1958, 1984.
Offaly (3) — 1986, 1987, 1989.
Waterford (2) — 1929, 1948.
Clare (1) — 1997.

UNDER-21 HURLING

Cork (11) — 1966, 1968, 1969, 1970, 1971, 1973, 1976, 1982, 1988, 1997, 1998.
Kilkenny (11) — 1974, 1975, 1977, 1984, 1990, 1994, 1999, 2003, 2004, 2006, 2008.
Galway (9) — 1972, 1978, 1983, 1986, 1991, 1993, 1996, 2005, 2007.
Tipperary (8) — 1964, 1967, 1979, 1980, 1981, 1985, 1989, 1995.
Limerick (4) — 1987, 2000, 2001, 2002.
Wexford (1) — 1965.
Waterford (1) — 1992.
Clare (1) — 2009.

JUNIOR HURLING

Cork (11) — 1912, 1916, 1925, 1940, 1947, 1950, 1955, 1958, 1983, 1987, 1994.
Tipperary (9) — 1913, 1915, 1924, 1926, 1930, 1933, 1953, 1989, 1991.
Kilkenny (9) — 1928, 1946, 1951, 1956, 1984, 1986, 1988, 1990, 1995.
Meath (6) — 1927, 1948, 1970, 1998, 1999, 2004.
London (5) — 1938, 1949, 1959, 1960, 1963.
Limerick (4) — 1935, 1941, 1954, 1957.
Dublin (3) — 1932, 1937, 1952.
Warwickshire (3) — 1968, 1969, 1973.
Armagh (3) — 1978, 1979, 2000.
Roscommon (3) — 1965, 1974, 2001.
Mayo (3) — 1980, 1981, 2003.
Offaly (2) — 1923, 1929.
Waterford (2) — 1931, 1934.
Kildare (2) — 1962, 1966.
Wicklow (2) — 1967, 1971.
Kerry (2) — 1961, 1972.
Louth (2) — 1976, 1977.
Derry (2) — 1975, 1982.
Wexford (2) — 1985, 1992.
Clare (2) — 1914, 1993.
Galway (2) — 1939, 1996.
Westmeath (1) — 1936.
Down (1) — 1964.
Monaghan (1) — 1997.
Antrim (1) — 2002.

SENIOR "B" HURLING

London (5) — 1985, 1987, 1988, 1990, 1995.
Antrim (3) — 1978, 1981, 1982.
Kerry (3) — 1976, 1983, 1986.
Kildare (3) — 1974, 1980, 1989.
Westmeath (3) — 1975, 1984, 1991.
Laois (2) — 1977, 1979.
Carlow (1) — 1992.
Meath (1) — 1993.
Roscommon (1) — 1994.
Derry (1) — 1996.
Wicklow (1) — 2003.

INTERMEDIATE HURLING

Cork (7) — 1965, 1997, 2001, 2003, 2004, 2006, 2009.
Tipperary (5) — 1963, 1966, 1971, 1972, 2000.
Wexford (4) — 1961, 1964, 2005, 2007.
Kilkenny (2) — 1973, 2008.
London (2) — 1967, 1968.
Galway (2) — 1999, 2002.
Carlow (1) — 1962.
Kildare (1) — 1969.
Antrim (1) — 1970.
Limerick (1) — 1998.

ALL-IRELAND SENIOR HURLING CHAMPIONSHIP

Note: There were no semi-finals until 1896. In the early years of the GAA competitions frequently ran behind time, so provincial councils would nominate a team to represent the province in the All-Ireland series. This team would play their provincial final at a later date; e.g. in 1912 Limerick defeated Antrim in the All-Ireland semi-final on August 25, but later lost to Cork in the Munster semi-final on September 1. Cork next beat Tipperary on October 27 in the provincial final and went on to play in the All-Ireland final.

Teams 21-aside
Goal outweighed any number of points

1887—Open draw. Counties represented by county champions.
Birr, August 1, 1 888 (21 -aside). Final: Tipperary (Thurles) 1-1; Galway (Meelick) nil. Actual score Tipperary, 1 goal, 1 point and 1 forfeit point.
1888—Championship unfinished owing to U.S.A. invasion by G.A.A. athletes.
1889—Inchicore, November 3. Final:
Dublin (Kickhams) 5-1; Clare [Tulla) 1-6.
1890—Clonturk Park, November 16. Final unfinished. Cork (Aghabullogue) awarded title. When play terminated (following Cork's withdrawal on the grounds of alleged excessively rough play by the opposition), Wexford (Castlebridge) were leading by 2-2 to 1-6 (a goall at this time exceeded any number of points).
1891—Clonturk Park, February 28, 1892.
Kerry (Ballyduff) 2-3; Wexford (Crossbeg) 1-5. (After 30 minutes extra time. Scores at end of normal time Kerry 1-1; Wexford 1-1.)

Teams reduced to 17-aside
Goal made equal to 5 points from 1892

1892—County champions permitted to select players from other clubs within county.
Clonturk Park, March 26, 1893.
Final unfinished. When play terminated Cork were leading Dublin by 2-4 to 1-1. Cork awarded title as Dublin left the pitch with ten minutes remaining.
1893—Phoenix Park, June 24, 1894. Final:
Cork (Blackrock) 6-8;
Kilkenny (Confederation) 0-2.
1894—Clonturk Park, March 24, 1895. Final:
Cork (Blackrock) 5-20; Dublin (Rapparees) 2-0.
1895—Jones's Road, March 15, 1896. Final:
Tipperary (Tubberadora) 6-8;
Kilkenny (Tullaroan) 10.

Goal made equal to three points from 1896

1896— Jones's Road, March 27, 1898.
Final: Tipperary (Tubberadora) 8-14; Dublin (Commercials) 0-4.
1897—Jones's Road, October 30, 1898.
Semifinal: Kilkenny 3-4; Galway 0-4.
Tipperary, November 20, 1898. Final: Limerick (Kilfinane) 3-4; Kilkenny (Tullaroan) 2-4.
1898—Athenry, December 17,1899.
Semi-final: Tipperary 3-14; Galway 1-3.
Jones's Road, March 25, 1900. Final: Tipperary (Tubberadora) 7-13; Kilkenny (Three Castles) 310.
1899—No semi-final.
Jones's Road, March 24, 1901. Final: Tipperary (Moycarkey) 3-12; Wexford (Blackwater) 1-4. Unfinished. Tipperary awarded title.
1900—Carrick-on-Suir, June 29, 1902.
Semi-final: Tipperary 1-11; Kilkenny 1-8.
Terenure, July 20, 1902. Semi-final: Galway 3-17; Antrim 0-1. (Note: This was actually the halftime score. The game was so one-sided that reporters present did not bother to record the exact final score given later in some records as 3-44 to 0-1, as Antrim failed to raise a flag in the second half.)
Terenure, September 21, 1902. Home Final: Tipperory 6-13; Galway 1 -5.
Jones's Road, October 26, 1902. Final: Tipperary (Two-Mile-Borris) 2-5; London (Desmonds) 0-6.
1901—Jones's Road, April 12, 1903.
Semi-final: Wexford 4-9; Antrim 1-2.
Limerick, May 17, 1903. Semi-final:
Cork 7- 12; Galway 1 -3.
Carrick-on-Suir, June 14, 1903. Home Final:
Cork 2-8; Wexford 0-6.
Jones's Road, August 2,1903. Final: London (Selection) 1-5; Cork (Redmonds) 0-4.
1902—Tipperary, March 20, 1904. Semi-final:
Cork 10-13; Galway 0-0.
Drogheda, June 5, 1904. Semi-final:
Dublin 6-19; Derry 0-6.
Tipperary, July 3,1904. Home Final:
Cork 1-7; Dublin 1-7.
Tipperary, July 1 7, 1904. (Replay):
Cork 2-6; Dublin 0-1.
Cork, September 11, 1904. Final: Cork (Dungourney) 3-13; London (Brian Boru) 0-0.

1903—Limerick, May 7, 1905. Semi-final:
Cork w.o. from Galway.
Jones's Road, June 18, 1905. Semi-final:
Kilkenny 6-29; Antrim 3-2.
Dungarvan, July 16, 1905. Home Final: Cork (Blackrock) 8-9; Kilkenny (Threecastles) 0-8.
Jones's Roacl, November 12, 1905. Final: Cork 3-16; London (Hibernians) 1-1.
1904—Jones's Road, May 6, 1906. Semi-final:
Cork 4- 18; Antrim 2-3.
Athlone, May 13, 1906. Semi-final:
Kilkenny 2-8; Galway 1-7.
Carrick-on-Suir, June 24, 1906. Final:
Kilkenny (Tullaroan) 1-9;
Cork (St. Finbarr's) 1-8.
1905—Jones's Road, August 5, 1906.
Kilkenny 2-21; Lancashire 0-5 (quarter-final).
Belfast, August 5, 1906.
Antrim 3-13; Glasgow 3-11 (quarter-final).
Limerick, September 2, 1906. Semi-final:
Cork 5- 13; Galway 0-4.
Jones's Road, September 30,1906. Semi-final:
Dublin 5-8; Antrim 1-9.
(Kilkenny qualified for All-Ireland final by beating Dublin in the Leinster final on October 21).
Tipperary, April 14, 1907. Final:
Cork 5-10; Kilkenny 3-13. (Objection and counter-objection. Replay ordered).
Dungarvan, June 30, 1907. (Replay): Kilkenny (Erin's Own) 7-7; Cork (St. Finbarr's) 2-9.
1906—Belfast, May 19, 1907.
Kilkenny 7-21; Antrim 1-3 (quarter-final).
Wexford, August 4, 1907. Semi-Final:
Dublin 4-10; London 2-2 (Note: Two different versions of Dublin's score appear in old newspaper files).
Limerick, September 8, 1907. Semi-final:
Tipperary 7- 14; Galway 0-2.
(Dublin qualified for All-Ireland semi-final by beating Kilkenny in Leinster final, played on July 14, 1907.)
Kilkenny, October 27, 1907. Final:
Tipperary (Thurles) 3-16; Dublin (Faughs) 3-8.
1907—Dundalk, March 15, 1908.
Dubiin 5-10; Antrim 2-5 (semi-final).
Limerick, May 10, 1908. Cork 2-8; Galway 1-7.
(Unfinished. Cork awarded game).
(Kilkenny qualified for the All-Ireland final by beating Dublin in the Leinster final on May 24, 1908.)
Dungarvan, June 21, 1908. Final: Kilkenny (Mooncoin) 3-12; Cork (Dungourney) 4-8.
1908—Limerick, February 14, 1909. Semi-final:
Tipperary 5-15; Galway 1 -0.
Jones's Road, February 21, 1909. Semi-final:
Dublin 4-12; Cavan 0-3.
Jones's Road, April 25, 1909. Final:
Tipperary 2-5; Dublin 1-8.
Athy, June 27, 1909. (Replay): Tipperary (Thurles) 3-15; Dublin (Kickhams) 1-5.
1909—Limerick, October 17. Semi-final:
Tipperary 6-7; Galway 5-7.
Jones's Road, November 14. Semi-final:
Kilkenny 3-17; Derry 0-3.
Cork, December 12. Final: Kilkenny (Mooncoin) 4-6; Tipperary (Thurles) (0-12).
1910—Belfast, July 31.
Glasgow 1-13; Antrim 0-7 (quarter-final).
Waterford, September 4. Kilkenny 5-11; London 0-3 (quarter-final).
(Note: Kilkenny, as reigning All-Ireland champions nominated to represent Leinster in quarter-final.)
Tuam, August 21. Semi-final:
Cork 7-3; Galway 1-0.
Jones's Road, October 2. Semi-final:
Dublin 6-6; Glasgow 5-1.
(Note: Cork nominated to represent Munster in All-Ireland semi-final but then beaten in Munster final by Limerick, who contested All-Ireland final.)
(Wexford qualified for the All-Ireland final by beating Dublin Provincial semi-final victors over Kilkenny, in the Leinster final on October 23.)
Jones's Road, November 20. Final: Wexford (Castlebridge) 7-0; Limerick (Castleconnell) 6-2.
1911—Jones's Road, November 26. Semi-final:
Kilkenny 5-5; Antrim 1-1.
Portlaoise, December 3. Semi-final:
Limerick 8-1; Galway 2-0.
[Limerick, Munster champions, refused to replay the final match which was postponed on February 18, 1912 in Cork owing to state of pitch. The final fixture was made for May 12, 1912. In a substitute contest, played at Dungarvan on July 28, 1912, Kilkenny beat Tipperary (nominated by Munster Councii) by 3-3 to 2-1, and were awarded the championship.]
1912—Jones's Road, August 25. Semi-final:
Limerick 11-3; Antrim 2-0.
Jones's Road, September 29. Semi-final:
Kilkenny 8-3; Galway 2-2.
(Cork defeated Limerick in Munster championship on September 1 and Tipperary in Munster final on October 27 to qualify for All-Ireland final.)
Jones's Road, November 17. Final: Kilkenny (Tullaroan) 2-1; Cork (Blackrock) 1 -3.

Teams reduced to 15-aside from 1913

1913—Glasgow, June 21.
Kilkenny 10-6; Glasgow 5-2 (quarter-final).
Liverpool, August 4. Semi-final:
Kilkenny 4-4; Lancashire 1-4.
Jones's Road, October 19. Semi-final:
Tipperary 10-0; Roscommon 0-1.
Croke Park, November 2. Final: (15-aside)
Kilkenny (Mooncoin) 2-4;
Tipperary (Toomevara) 1-2.
(Note: Ulster did not compete, their

champions going into the Junior Championship).
1914—Portlaoise, September 6. Semi-final:
Cork 6-6; Galway 0-0.
Croke Park, October 18. Final:
Clare (Quin) 5-1; Laois (Kilcotton) 1-0.
(Note: Cork nominated to represent Munster in All-Ireland semi-final but they subsequently lost the Munster final to Clare.)
1915—Gort, August 8. Semi-final:
Clare 2-1; Galway 1-1.
Croke Park, October 24. Final: Laois (Ballygeehan) 6-2; Cork (Redmonds) 4-1 .
(Note: Clare nominated to represent Munster in All-Ireland semi-final but subsequently failed to Cork in the Munster final.)
1916—Athlone, October 22. Semi-final:
Tipperary 8-1; Galway 0-0. Unfinished. Galway did not resume for second half.
Croke Park, January 21, 1917. Final: Tipperary (Boherlahan) 5-4; Kilkenny (Tullaroan) 3-2.
1917—No Semi-Final
Croke Park, October 28. Final: Dublin (Collegians) 5-4; Tipperary (Boherlahan) 4-2.
1918—Croke Park, January 26, 1919. Final:
Limerick (Newcastle West) 9-5;
Wexford (Selection) 1-3.
1919—Limerick, August 31. Semi-final:
Cork 3-8; Galway 0-2.
Croke Park, September 21. Final:
Cork (Selection) 6-4; Dublin (Collegians) 2-4.
1920—Croke Park, October 24. Semi-final:
Dublin 6-3; Galway 1-4.
Croke Park, May 14, 1922. Final: Dublin (Faughs) 4-9; Cork (Selection) 4-3.
1921—Limerick, June 25, 1922. Semi-final:
Limerick 6-0; Galway 2-2.
Croke Park, March 4, 1923. Final:
Limerick 8-5; Dublin (Faughs) 3-2.
1922—Galway, August 26, 1923. Semi-final:
Tipperary 3-2; Galway 1-3.
Croke Park, September 9, 1923. Final:
Kilkenny 4-2; Tipperary 2-6.
1923—Croke Park, April 27, 1924.
Limerick 7-4; Donegal 0-1.
Croke Park, May 18. 1924.
Galway 5-4; Kilkenny 2-0.
Croke Park, September 14, 1924. Final:
Galway 7-3; Limerick 4-5.
1924—Croke Park, November 9. Semi-final:
Dublin 8-4; Antrim 3-1.
Croke Park, November 23. Semi-final:
Galway 3-1; Tipperary 2-3.
Croke Park, December 14. Final:
Dublin 5-3; Galway 2-6.
1925—Croke Park, July 26. Semi-final:
Tipperary 12-9; Antrim 2-3.
Croke Park, August 9. Semi-final:
Galway 9-4; Kilkenny 6-0.
Croke Park, September 6. Final:
Tipperary 5-6; Galway 1-5.
1926—Croke Park, August 29. Semi-final:
Kilkenny 6-2; Galway 5-1.
Croke Park, October 24. Final:
Cork 4-6; Kilkenny 2-0.
1927—Thurles, August 21. Semi-final:
Cork 5-6; Galway 0-2.
Croke Park, September 4. Final:
Dublin 4-8; Cork 1-3.
1928—Kilkenny, August 26. Semi-final:
Cork 5-3; Dublin 0-2.
Croke Park, September 9. Final:
Cork 6-12; Galway 1 -0.
1929—Birr, August 11. Semi-final:
Galway 7-7; Kilkenny 7-1.
Croke Park, September 1. Final:
Cork 4-9; Galway 1-3.
1930—Birr, August 17. Semi-final:
Tipperary 6-8; Galway 2-4.
Croke Park, September 7. Final:
Tipperary 2-7; Dublin 1-3.
1931—Croke Park, August 16. Semi-final:
Kilkenny 7-2; Galway 3-1.
Croke Park, September 6. Final:
Cork 1-6; Kilkenny 1-6.
Croke Park, October 11. Replay:
Cork 2-5; Kilkenny 2-5.
Croke Park, November 1. Replay:
Cork 5-8; Kilkenny 3-4.
1932—Limerick, August 14. Semi-final:
Clare 9-4; Galway 4-14.
Croke Park, September 4. Final:
Kilkenny 3-3; Clare 2-3.
1933—Birr, August 13. Semi-final:
Kilkenny 5-10; Galway 3-8.
Croke Park, September 3. Final:
Kilkenny 1-7; Limerick 0-6.
1934—Roscrea, August 5. Semi-final:
Limerick 4-4; Galway 2-4.
Croke Park, September 2. Final:
Limerick 2-7; Dublin 3-4.
Croke Park, September 30. Replay:
Limerick 5-2; Dublin 2-6.
1935—Birr, August 4. Semi-final:
Kilkenny 6-10; Galway 1-8.
Croke Park, September 1. Final:
Kilkenny 2-5; Limerick 2-4.
1936—Roscrea, August 16. Semi-final:
Limerick 4-9; Galway 2-4. (Match unfinished. Limerick awarded game.)
Croke Park, September 6. Final:
Limerick 5-6; Kilkenny 1-5.
1937—Birr, August 8. Semi-final:
Kilkenny 0-8; Galway 0-6.
Killarney, September 5. Final:
Tipperary 3-11; Kilkenny 0-3.
1938—Ennis, August 7. Semi-final:
Waterford 4-8; Galway 3-1.
Croke Park, September 4. Final:
Dublin 2-5; Waterford 1-6.
1939—Roscrea, August 6. Semi-final:
Kilkenny 1-16; Galway 3-1.
Croke Park, September 3. Final:
Kilkenny 2-7; Cork 3-3.

1940—Ennis, August 11. Semi-final:
Limerick 3-6; Galway 0-5.
Croke Park, September 1. Final:
Limerick 3-7; Kilkenny 1-7.
1941—Roscrea, September 14. Semi-final:
Dublin 2-4; Galway 2-2.
Croke Park, September 28. Final:
Cork (nominated) 5-11; Dublin 0-6.
1942—Limerick, July 26. Semi-final:
Cork 6-8; Galway 2-4.
Croke Park, September 6. Final:
Cork 2-14; Dublin 3-4.
1943—Corrigan Park, Belfast, July 4.
Quarter-final: Antrim 7-0; Galway 6-2.
Corrigan Park, August 1. Semi-final:
Antrim 3-3; Kilkenny 1-6.
Croke Park, September 5. Final:
Cork 5-16; Antrim 0-4.
1944—Ennis, August 13. Semi-final:
Cork 1-10; Galway 3-3.
Corrigan Park, Belfast, August 13. Semifinal:
Dublin 6-12; Antrim 3-1.
Croke Park, September 3. Final:
Cork 2-13; Dublin 1-2.
1945—Birr, July 29. Semi-final:
Kilkenny 5-3; Galway 2-11.
Croke Park, August 5. Semi-final:
Tipperary 5-9; Antrim 1-6.
Croke Park, September 2. Final:
Tipperary 5-6; Kilkenny 3-6.
1946—Birr, July 28. Semi-final:
Cork 2-10; Galway 0-3.
Croke Park, August 4. Semi-final:
Kilkenny 7-11; Antrim 0-7.
Croke Park, September 1. Final:
Cork 7-5; Kilkenny 3-8.
1947—Birr, July 27. Semi-final:
Kilkenny 2-9; Galway 1-11.
Croke Park, August 3. Semi-final:
Cork 7-10; Antrim 0-5.
Croke Park, September 7. Final:
Kilkenny 0-14; Cork 2-7.
1948—Croke Park, August 1. Semi-final:
Dublin 8-13; Antrim 2-6.
Croke Park, August 15. Semi-final:
Waterford 3-7; Galway 1-6.
Croke Park, September 5. Final:
Waterford 6-7; Dublin 4-2.
1949—Croke Park, July 31. Semi-final:
Tipperary 6-18; Antrim 1-4.
Croke Park, August 7. Semi-final:
Laois 4-6; Galway 3-5.
Croke Park, September 4. Final:
Tipperary 3-11; Laois 0-3.
1950—Tuam, August 13. Semi-final:
Tipperary 4-7; Galway 2-6.
Croke Park, September 3. Final:
Tipperary 1-9; Kilkenny 1-8.
1951—Croke Park, July 29. Semi-final:
Wexford 3-11; Galway 2-9.
Croke Park, September 2. Final:
Tipperary 7-7; Wexford 3-9.
1952—Limerick, July 27. Semi-final:
Cork 1-5; Galway 0-6.
Croke Park, September 7. Final:
Cork 2-14; Dublin 0-7.
1953—Croke Park, August 16. Semi-final:
Galway 3-5; Kilkenny 1-10.
Croke Park, September 6. Final:
Cork 3-3; Galway 0-8.
1954—Croke Park, August 8. Semi-finals:
Wexford 12-17; Antrim 2-3.
Cork 4-13; Galway 2-1.
Croke Park, September 5. Final:
Cork 1-9; Wexford 1-6.
1955—Croke Park, August 7. Semi-final:
Wexford 2-12; Limerick 2-3.
Croke Park, September 4. Final:
Wexford 3-13; Galway 2-8.
1956—Croke Park, July 29. Semi-final:
Wexford 5-13; Galway 1-8.
Croke Park, September 23. Final:
Wexford 2-14; Cork 2-8.
1957—Croke Park, July 28. Semi-final:
Waterford 4-12; Galway 0-11.
Croke Park, September 1. Final:
Kilkenny 4-10; Waterford 3-12.
1958—Croke Park, August 10. Semi-final:
Tipperary 1-13; Kilkenny 1-8.
Croke Park, September 7. Final:
Tipperary 4-9; Galway 2-5.
Note: After the 1958 Final Galway made their debut in the Munster championship where they remained until 1969. Accordingly, the semi-final sequence was suspended until 1969 when London returned to the championships.
1959—Croke Park, September 6. Final:
Waterford 1-17; Kilkenny 5-5.
Croke Park, October 4. Replay:
Waterford 3-12, Kilkenny 1-10.
1960—Croke Park, September 4. Final:
Wexford 2-15; Tipperary 0-11.
1961—Croke Park, September 3. Final:
Tipperary 0-16; Dublin 1 -12.
1962—Croke Park, September 2. Final:
Tipperary 3- 10; Wexford 2-11.
1963—Croke Park, September 1. Final:
Kilkenny 4-17; Waterford 6-8.
1964—Croke Park, September 6. Final:
Tipperary 5-13; Kilkenny 2-8.
1965—Croke Park, September 5: Final:
Tipperary 2-16; Wexford 0-10.
1966—Croke Park, September 4: Final:
Cork 3-9; Kilkenny 1-10.
1967—Croke Park, Septermber 3. Final:
Kilkenny 3-8; Tipperary 2-7.
1968—Croke Park, September 1. Final:
Wexford 5-8; Tipperary 3-12.
1969—Croke Park, August 17. Semi-final:
Kilkenny 3-22; london 1-10.
Croke Park, September 7. Final:
Kilkenny 2-15; Cork 2-9
1970—Croke Park, August 16. Semi-final:
Cork 4-20; London 2-9.

Athlone, August 16. Semi-final:
Wexford 3-17; Galway 5-9.
Croke Park, September 6. Final:
Cork 6-21; Wexford 5-10.
(Note: First 80-minute Final)
1971—Castlebar, July 25. Quarter-final:
Galway 7-24; Antrim 1-8.
Croke Park, August 15. Semi-final:
Kilkenny 2-23; London 2-8.
Birr, August 15. Semi-final:
Tipperary 3-26; Galway 6-8.
Croke Park, September 5. Final:
Tipperary 5-17; Kilkenny 5-14.
1972—Ballycastle, July 23. Quarter-final:
Galway 7-16; Antrim 4-7.
Croke Park, August 6. Semi-final:
Kilkenny 5-28; Galway 3-7.
Cork, August 6. Semi-final:
Cork 7-20; London 1-12.
Croke Park, September 3. Final:
Kilkenny 3-24; Cork 5-11.
1973—Ballinasloe, July 29. Quarter-final.
London 4-7; Galway 3-5.
Ennis, August 5. Semi-final:
Limerick 1-15; London 0-7.
Croke Park, September 2. Final:
Limerick 1-21; Kilkenny 1-14.
1974—Athlone, July 7. Preliminary round:
Galway 3-19; Kildare 4-10.
Athlone, July 21. Quarter-final:
Galway 3- 13, London 0-6.
Birr, August 4. Semi-final:
Kilkenny 2-32; Galway 3-17.
Croke Park, September 1. Final:
Kilkenny 3-19; Limerick 1-13.
(Note: The All-Ireland 'B' Champions were allowed into the All-Ireland series in 1974.)
1975—Athlone, July 6. Quarter-final:
Galway 6-14; Westmeath 1-8.
Croke Park, August 17. Semi-final:
Galway 4-15; Cork 2-19.
Croke Park, September 7. Final:
Kilkenny 2-22; Galway 2-10.
(Note: The 70-minute Final was introduced in 1975)
1976—Limerick, July 18. Quarter-final:
Galway 3-12; Kerry 3-9.
Pairc Ui Chaoimh, August 15. Semi-final:
Wexford 5-14; Galway 2-23 (Draw).
Pairc Ui Chaoimh, August 22. Semi-final:
Wexford 3-14; Galway 2-14 (Replay).
Croke Park, September 5. Final:
Cork 2-21; Wexford 4-11.
1977—Birr, July 17. Quarter-final:
Galway 2-12; Laois 0-8.
Croke Park, August 7. Semi-final:
Cork 3- 14; Galway 1 - 15.
Croke Park, September 4. Final:
Cork 1-17; Wexford 3-8.
1978—Croke Park, July 23. Quarter-final:
Galway 4-19; Antrim 3-10.
Croke Park, August 6. Semi-final:
Kilkenny 4-20; Galway 4- 13.
Croke Park, September 3. Final:
Cork 1-15; Kilkenny 2-8.
1979—Birr, July 1. Quarter-final:
Galway 1-23; Laois 3-10.
Croke Park, August 5. Semi-final:
Galway 2-14; Cork 1-13.
Croke Park, September 2. Final:
Kilkenny 2-12; Galway 1-8.
1980—Croke Park, July 20. Quarter-final:
Galway 5-15; Kildare 1-11.
Croke Park, August 3. Semi-final:
Galway 4-9; Offaly 3-10.
Croke Park, September 7. Final:
Galway 2-15; Limerick 3-9.
1981—Croke Park, July 19. Quarter-final:
Galway 6-23; Antrim 3-11.
Croke Park, August 2. Semi-final:
Galway 1-8; Limerick 0-11 (Draw).
Croke Park, August 16. Semi-final:
Galway 4-16; Limerick 2-17 (Replay).
Croke Park, September 6. Final:
Offaly 2-12; Galway 0-15.
1982—Croke Park, July 18. Quarter-final:
Galway 6-19; Antrim 3-12.
Croke Park,. August 8. Semi-final:
Kilkenny 2-20; Galway 2-10.
Croke Park, September 5. Final:
Kilkenny 3-18; Cork 1 -13.
1983—O'Toole Park, July 10.
Preliminary round: Antrim 3-13; Kerry 2-10.
Mullingar, July 24. Quarter-final:
Galway 3-22; Antrim 2-5.
Croke Park, August 7. Semi-final:
Cork 5- 14; Galway 1-16.
Croke Park, September 4. Final:
Kilkenny 2-14; Cork 2-12.
1984—Birr, July 22. Quarter-final:
Galway 2-17; Westmeath 2-8.
Thurles, August 5. Semi-final:
Offaly 4-15; Galway 1-10.
Croke Park, August 5. Semi-final:
Cork 3-26; Antrim 2-5.
Thurles, September 2. Final:
Cork 3-16; Offaly 1-12.
1985—Casement Park, July 21. Quarter-final:
Antrim 3-12; London 1-15.
Croke Park, August 4. Semi-final:
Galway 4-12; Cork 5-5.
Armagh, August 4. Semi-final:
Offaly 3-17; Antrim 0-12.
Croke Park, September 1. Final:
Offaly 2-11; Galway 1-12.
1986—Ennis, July 19. Quarter-final:
Galway 4-24; Kerry 1-3.
Thurles, August 10. Semi-final:
Galway 4-12; Kilkenny 0-13.
Croke Park, August 10. Semi-final:
Cork 7-11; Antrim 1-24.
Croke Park, September 7. Final:
Cork 4-13; Galway 2-15.
1987—Casement Park, July 19. Quarter-final:

Antrim 3-14; London 1-15.
Croke Park, August 9. Semi-final:
Galway 3-20; Tipperary 2-17.
Dundalk, August 16. Semi-final:
Kilkenny 2-18; Antrim 2-11.
Croke Park, September 6. Final:
Galway 1-12; Kilkenny 0-9.
1988—Athenry, July 16. Quarter-final:
Galway 4-30; London 2-8.
Croke Park, August 7. Semi-final:
Tipperary 3-15; Antrim 2-10.
Croke Park, August 7. Semi-final:
Galway 3-18; Offaly 3-11.
Croke Park, September 4. Final:
Galway 1-15; Tipperary 0-14.
1989—Dundalk, July 23. Quarter-final:
Antrim 4-14; Kildare 0-7.
Croke Park, August 6. Semi-final:
Antrim 4-15; Offaly 1-15.
Croke Park, August 6. Semi-final:
Tipperary 1-17; Galway 2-11.
Croke Park, September 3. Final:
Tipperary 4-24; Antrim 3-9.
1990—Ballinasloe, July 22. Quarter-final:
Galway 1-23; London 2-11.
Croke Park, August 5. Semi-final:
Cork 2-20; Antrim 1-13.
Croke Park, August 5. Semi-final:
Galway 1-16; Oftaly 2-7.
Croke Park, September 2. Final:
Cork 5-15; Galway 2-21.
1991—Dundalk, July 21. Quarter-final:
Antrim 5-11; Westmeath 1-5.
Croke Park, August 4. Semi-final:
Tipperary 3-13; Galway 1-9.
Croke Park, August 4. Semi-final:
Kilkenny 2-18; Antrim 1-19.
Croke Park, September 1. Final:
Tipperary 1-16; Kilkenny 0-15.
1992—Carlow, July 26. Quarter-final.
Galway 4-19; Carlow 3-9.
Croke Park, August 9. Semi-final:
Cork 2-17;Down 1-11.
Croke Park, August 9. Semi-final:
Kilkenny 2-13, Galway 1-12.
Croke Park, September 6. Final:
Kilkenny 3-10; Cork 1-12.
1993—Castleblayney, July 25. Quarter-final:
Antrim 3-27; Meath 4-10.
Croke Park, August 8. Semi-final:
Galway 1-16; Tipperary 1-14.
Croke Park, August 8. Semi-final:
Kilkenny 4-18; Antrim 1-9.
Croke Park, September 5. Final:
Kilkenny 2-17; Galway 1-15.
1994—Athleague, July 17. Quarter-final:
Galway 2-21; Roscommon 2-6.
Croke Park, August 7. Semi-final:
Limerick 2-23; Antrim 0-11.
Croke Park, August 7. Semi-final:
Offaly 2-13; Galway 1-10.
Croke Park, September 4. Final:
Offaly 3-16; Limerick 2-13.
(Note: Guinness commenced sponsorship of championship from 1995.)
1995—Ruislip July 23. Quarter-final:
Down 0-16; London 0-9.
Croke Park, August 6. Semi-final:
Clare 3-12; Galway 1-13.
Croke Park, August 6. Semi-final:
Offaly 2-19; Down2-8.
Croke Park, September 3. Final:
Clare 1-13; Offaly 2-8.
1996—Gaelic Park (New York), June 16.
Preliminary round:
New York 1-16; London 0-14.
Gaelic Park (New York), July 7. Preliminary round: New York 4-16, Derry 0-13.
Athenry, July 20. Quarter-final:
Galway 4-22; New York 0-8.
Croke Park, August 4. Semi-final:
Limerick 1-17; Antrim 0-13.
Croke Park, August 4. Semi-final:
Wexford 2-13; Galway 3-7.
Croke Park, September 1. Final
Wexford 1-13; Limerick.0-14.
(Note: Beaten Munster and Leinster finalists allowed back into championship at quarter-final stage from 1997.)
1997—Clones, July 26. Quarter-final:
Tipperary 3-24; Down 3-8.
Thurles, July 27. Quarter-final:
Kilkenny 4-15; Galway 3-16.
Croke Park, August 10.
Semi-final: Clare 1-17; Kilkenny 1-13.
Croke Park, August 17. Semi-final:
Tipperary 2-16; Wexford 0-15.
Croke Park, September 14. Final:
Clare 0-20; Tipperary 2-13.
1998—Croke Park, July 26. Quarter-final:
Waterford 1-20; Galway 1-10.
Croke Park, July 26. Quarter-final:
Offaly 2-18; Antrim 2-9.
Croke Park, August 9. Semi-final:
Offaly 1-13; Clare 1 -13 (draw).
Croke Park, August 16. Semi-final:
Kilkenny 1-11; Waterford 1-10.
Croke Park, August 22. Replay:
Clare 1-16; Offaly 2-10. (NB: Referee played short time, refixture ordered.)
Thurles, August 29. Refixture:
Offaly 0-16; Clare 0-13.
Croke Park, September 13. Final:
Offaly 2-16; Kilkenny 1-13.
1999—Croke Park, July 25. Quarter-final:
Offaly 4-22, Antrim 0-12.
Croke Park, July 25. Quarter-final:
Clare 3-15, Galway 2-18 (draw).
Croke Park, August 2.
Clare 3-18, Galway 2-14 (replay).
Croke Park, August 8. Semi-final:
Cork 0-19, Offaly 0-16.
Croke Park, August 15. Semi-final:
Kilkenny 2-14, Clare 1-13.

Croke Park, September 12. Final:
Cork 0-13, Kilkenny 0-12.
2000 — Croke Park, July 23. Quarter-final:
Galway 1-14, Tipperary 0-15.
Croke Park, July 23. Quarter-final:
Offaly 2-23, Derry 2-17.
Croke Park, August 6. Semi-final:
Offaly 0-19, Cork 0-15.
Croke Park, August 13. Semi-final:
Kilkenny 2-19, Galway 0-17.
Croke Park, September 10. Final:
Kilkenny 5-15, Offaly 1-14.
2001 — Croke Park, July 29.Quarter-final:
Wexford 4-10, Limerick 2-15.
Croke Park, July 29. Quarter-final:
Galway 4-23, Derry 1-11.
Croke Park, August 12. Semi-final:
Tipperary 1-16, Wexford 3-10.
Croke Park, August 18. Replay:
Tipperary 3-12, Wexford 0-10.
Croke Park, August 19. Semi-final:
Galway 2-15, Kilkenny 1-13.
Croke Park, September 9. Final:
Tipperary 2-18, Galway 2-15.
2002 — Croke Park, July 28. Quarter-final:
Tipperary 1-25, Antrim 2-12.
Croke Park, July 28. Quarter-final:
Clare 1-15, Galway 0-17.
Croke Park, August 11. Semi-final:
Clare 1-16, Waterford 1-13.
Croke Park, August 18. Semi-final:
Kilkenny 1-20, Tipperary 1-16.
Croke Park, September 8. Final:
Kilkenny 2-20, Clare 0-19.
2003 — Croke Park, July 27. Quarter-final:
Tipperary 2-16, Offaly 2-11.
Croke Park, July 27. Quarter-final:
Wexford 2-15, Antrim 2-12.
Croke Park, August 10. Semi-final:
Cork 2-20, Wexford 3-17.
Croke Park, August 16. Replay:
Cork 3-17, Wexford 2-7.
Croke Park, August 17. Semi-final:
Kilkenny 3-18 Tipperary 0-15.
Croke Park, September 14. Final:
Kilkenny 1-14, Cork 1-11.
2004 — Croke Park, July 25. Quarter-final:
Cork 2-26, Antrim 0-10.
Croke Park, July 25. Quarter-final:
Kilkenny 1-13, Clare 1-13.
Thurles, July 31. Replay:
Kilkenny 1-11, Clare 0-9.
Croke Park, August 8. Semi-final:
Kilkenny 3-12, Waterford 0-18.
Croke Park, August 15. Semi-final:
Cork 1-27, Wexford 0-12.
Croke Park, September 12. Final:
Cork 0-17, Kilkenny 0-9.
2005 — Croke Park, July 24. Quarter-final:
Cork 1-18, Waterford 1-13.
Croke Park, July 24. Quarter-final:
Clare 1-20, Wexford 0-12.
Croke Park, July 31. Quarter-final:
Galway 2-20, Tipperary 2-18.
Croke Park, July 31. Quarter-final:
Kilkenny 0-18, Limerick 0-13.
Croke Park, August 14. Semi-final:
Cork 0-16, Clare 0-15.
Croke Park, August 21. Semi-final:
Galway 5-18, Kilkenny 4-18.
Croke Park, September 11. Final:
Cork 1-21, Galway 1-16.
2006 — Thurles, July 22. Quarter-final:
Cork 0-19, Limerick 0-18.
Thurles, July 22. Quarter-final:
Kilkenny 2-22, Galway 3-14.
Croke Park, July 23. Quarter-final:
Clare 1-27, Wexford 1-15.
Croke Park, July 23. Quarter-final:
Waterford 1-22, Tipperary 3-14.
Croke Park, August 6. Semi-final:
Cork 1-16, Waterford 1-15.
Croke Park, August 13. Semi-final:
Kilkenny 2-21, Clare 1-16.
Croke Park, September 3. Final:
Kilkenny 1-16, Cork 1-13.
2007 — Croke Park, July 28. Quarter-final:
Kilkenny 3-22, Galway 1-18.
Croke Park, July 28. Quarter-final:
Wexford 3-10, Tipperary 1-14.
Croke Park, July 29. Quarter-final:
Limerick 1-23, Clare 1-16.
Croke Park, July 29. Quarter-final:
Waterford 3-16, Cork 3-16 (draw).
Croke Park, August 5.
Waterford 2-17, Cork 0-20 (replay).
Croke Park, August 5. Semi-final:
Kilkenny 0-23, Wexford 1-10.
Croke Park, August 12. Semi-final:
Limerick 5-11, Waterford 2-15.
Croke Park, September 2. Final:
Kilkenny 2-19, Limerick 1-15.
2008 — Thurles, July 27. Quarter-final:
Cork 2-19, Clare 2-17.
Thurles, July 27. Quarter-final:
Waterford 2-19, Wexford 3-15.
Croke Park, August 10. Semi-final:
Kilkenny 1-23, Cork 0-17.
Croke Park, August 17. Semi-final:
Waterford 1-20, Tipperary 1-18.
Croke Park, September 7. Final:
Kilkenny 3-30, Waterford 1-13.
2009 — Thurles, July 26. Quarter-final:
Waterford 1-16, Galway 0-18.
Thurles, July 26. Quarter-final:
Limerick 2-18, Dublin 1-17.
Croke Park, August 9. Semi-final:
Kilkenny 2-23, Waterford 3-15.
Croke Park, August 16. Semi-final:
Tipperary 6-19, Limerick 2-7.
Croke Park, September 6. Final:
Kilkenny 2-22, Tipperary 0-23.

ALL-IRELAND S.H. FINALISTS

Author's note: Despite checking with a number of sources, allowances must still be made for possible errors in early teams, as records are not reliable from these times. It must be noted too that teams were not given in line-out order until the thirties.

1887

Tipperary—J. Stapleton (capt.), M. Maher, T. Maher, A. Maher, T. Burke, Martin McNamara, Ed. Murphy, Jer Dwyer, Tom Stapleton, Ned Bowe, Tom Healy, Dan Ryan, Jer. Ryan, Pat Leahy, Tim Dwyer, Jack Mockler, Jack Dunne, Tom Carroll, John Leamy, M. Carroll, P. Lambe.

Galway—Patk. Larkin, John Mannion, Owen Griffin, John Sa unders, Thos Foley, Ml. Conway, Ml. Kelly, John Mannion, Darby Mannion, Pat Haverty, James Haverty, Martin Griffin, Owen Griffin, John Cosgrave, A. Cosgrave, Ml. Cullen, Thos. Hanly, P. Madden, Ml. Kelly, Ml. Mannion, John Mannion. Non-playing captain: Jas. Lynam.

Referee—P. White (Offaly).

1888

No final played owing to visit of a team of hurlers and athletes to the USA.

1889

Dublin—N. O'Shea (capt.), Frank Coughlan, T. Butler, John Lambe, Dan Kerwick, J. D. O'Byrne, Thos. McKenna, W. J. Spain, James Harper, Chos. Hackett, Thos. Maher, J. Bishop, T. Belton, Polk. Ryan, J. Cahill, Ed. Gilligan, F. Palmer, S. Riordan, Patk. O'Shea, Patk. Riordan, Ml. Madigan.

Clare—Thos. Coughlan, D. McKenna, Daniel McNamara, John McNamara, D. Quilney, Daniel Moroney, M. O'Dea, Wm. Moroney, Ml. Corry, Ed. Corry, Patk. O'Neill, T. O'Connell, Ml. Flynn, P. Vaughan, John McKenna, Martin Russell, Patk. McGrath, T. Donnellan, J. Moloney, J. King, M. Kinnery. Non-playing captain: John Considine.

Referee—P. Tobin (Dublin).

1890

Cork—Dan Lane (capt.), J. Henchion, John Buckley, D. Lenihan, Dan Looney, Dan Drew, Tom O'Connor, Tom Twomey, M. Horgan, Pat Buckley, J. Reilly, Tim Kelleher, John Kelleher, P. O'Riordan, Dan O'Sullivan, Tom Good, D. Horgan, John Lenihan, Jer O'Sullivan, E. Reilly, Pad O'Riordan.

Wexford—Nick Daly (capt.), E. Leacy, L. Leacy, T. Devereaux, O. Daly, J. Murphy, W. Neville, J. Murphy, P. McDonald, J. Rossiter, W. Furlong, J. O'Leary, W. Doran, G. Sinnott, P. Furlong, P. Devereaux, W. Fortune, G. Browne, M. Browne, J. Fogart, W. O'Leory.

Referee—J. Sheehy (Limerick).

1891

Kerry—J. Mahony (capt.), M. Kelly, M. McCarthy, P. Carroll, P. Wynne, M. J. O'Sullivan, R. Kissane, F. Crowley, J. Crowley, J. O Sullivon, T. Dunne, J. Murphy, M. Fitzmourice, J. McDonnell, T. D. McCarthy, T. E. McCarthy, M. Riordan, P. Quane, J. Quane, P. Rourke, P. Kirby. Sub: J. Murphy (Dromartin) for T. Murphy.

Wexford—N. Daly (capt.), J. Leary, E. Leacy, L. Leacy, M. Lacy, James Murphy, John Murphy, T. Murphy, N. Murphy, M. Browne, G. Browne, P. Quirke, P. Byrne, M. Kirwan. M. Redmond, P. Harpur, N. Moher, O. Daly, P. McDonnell, T. Devereaux, M. Horpur.

Referee—P. Tobin (Dublin).

1892

(Teams reduced to 17 a side)

Cork—W. O'Callaghan (capt.), J. Kenneally, M Casserly, J. Keegan, J. Leaby, M. Sheehan, C. O'Callaghan, D. Halloran. T. Irwin, J. Conway, J. O'Connor, W. O'Connor, D. Scannell, J. Cashman, D. Coughlan, D. Drew, P. Buckley.

Dublin—P. Egan (capt.), A. Carroll, J. Dooley, A. Maher, T. Meagher, C. Kennedy, W. Hinton, J. Kavanagh, T. Belton, R. Stakelum, M. Kennedy, E. Gilligan, J. Ryan, P. Whelan, D. Murphy, N. Murphy, D Healy.

Referee—D. Fraher (Waterford).

1893

Cork—John Murphy (capt.), Jer. Norbeg, D. Scannell, Ml. Murphy, D. Hayes, P. Coughlan, Jas. Young, S. Hegarty, Ml. Cronin, Patk. O'Keeffe, J. Cullinane, John O'Leary, Jas. Delea, J. O'Connor, John Cashman, W. J. O'Connell, Patk. Flaherty.

Kilkenny—D. Whelan (capt.), J. Delany, J. Grace, J. Lalor, P. Maher, E. Teehan, J. Walsh, M. Coogan, M. Berry, M. Morrissey, J. McCarthy, R. Grace, J. King, J. Doheny, P. Brennan J. De Loughrey, P. Malone.

Referee—J. J. Kenny (Dublin).

1894

Cork—S. Hayes (capt.), D. Hayes, P. Coughlan, J. O'Leary, M. Murphy, J. Cashman, J. Kidney, J. Delea, M. Cronin, D. Coughlan, J. Kelleher, J. Norberg, S. Hegarty, J. Cullinane, J. O'Connor, J. Young, W. J. O'Connell.

Dublin—John McCabe (capt.), John Greene, M. Brady, L. Byrne, M. Connor, J. Lawler, L. Lawler, Dan Gillis, S. Donovan, J. Quigley, D. Cregan, Ed. McCabe, M. Kelly, N. Harding, P. O'Toole, P Lawlor, J. O'Mullane.

Referee—J. J. Kenny (Dublin).

1895

Tipperary—M. Maher (capt.), E. Maher, Phil Byrne, W. Kerwick, John Maher, D. Walsh,

John Walsh, Peter Maher, T. Flanagan, Jas. Flanagan, P. Riordon, Jas. Gleeson, Fergus Moriarty, John Connolly, J. Maher (F), E. Brennan, W. Devane.

Kilkenny—M. Dalton, P. Maher, J. Lalor, E. Teehon, E. Dunne, P. Egan, P. Ryon, M. Coogan, M. Meagher, J. Walsh, W. Walsh, J. Dunne, P. Malone, J. Grace (capt.), J. Doheny, T. Grace, J. Doheny.

Referee—J. J. Kenny (Dublin).

1896

Tipperary—M. Maher (capt.), J. Maher (F), P. Byrne, W. Devane. M. Wall, E. Maher, E. Brennan, J. Walsh, T. Condon, J. Connolly, J. Flanagan, T. Ryan, P. Scanlon, T. Flanagan, E. D. Ryan, P. Doherty, D. Walsh.

Dublin—P. Buckley (capt.), W. Carroll, P. Egan, J. Hill, D. Ryan, J. O'Dwyer, J. Donohue, M. Hackett, E. Hackett, J. Delany, Joseph Ryan, D. Ryan, Jerry Ryan, John Eviston, T. O'Dwyer, P. Purcell, W. O'Connell.

Referee—D. Wood (Dublin).

1897

Limerick—D. Grimes (capt.), J. ("Seán Óge") Hanly, M. Flynn, P. Flynn, M. Finn, P. O'Brien, T. Brazill, J. Condon, J. Catterall, J. Hynes, P. Butler, J. Flood, P. Mulcahy, M. Downes, J. Reidy, John Finn, P. Buskin.

Kilkenny—J. Walsh (capt.), J. Doheny, P. Maher, M. Dalton, E. Teehan, M. Lawlor, John Lawlor, James Lawlor, John Grace, M. Malone, J. Walsh, M. Merry, J. Quinn, P. Fielding, P. Ryan, E. Dunne, P. Malone.

Referee—J. J. McCabe (Dublin).

1898

Tipperary—M. Maher (capt.), E. Maher, E. Brennan, J. Walsh, J. Connolly, T. Ryan, W. Devane, E. Ryan, P. Byrne, W. Dunne, T. Condon, J. O'Keeffe, J. Maher (N.), D. Walsh, J. Maher (F.), Dick O'Keeffe, John Ryan.

Kilkenny—E. Hennessy (capt.}, J. Ryan, John Lalor, M. Dalton, T. Murphy, P. Maher, T. Grace, Jer. Doheny, P. Malone, M. Malone, P. Young, E. Teehan, Jas. Lawlor, John Lowlor, John Quinn, Martin Lawlor, Jas. Quinn.

Referee—J. J. McCabe (Dublin).

1899

Tipperary—T. Condon (capt.), Joe O'Keeffe, "Big Bill" Gleeson, J. Gleeson, R. O'Keeffe, Jas. O'Keeffe, D. Walsh, M. Maher, J. Walsh, J. Flanagan, J. Ryan, M. Wall, W. Dunne, P. Byrne, J. Maher, "Little Bill" Gleeson, T. Ryan.

Wexford—Jas. Furlong (capt.), J. Corrigan, T. Byrne, John Shiel, Martin Murphy, T. Cullen, A. Dempsey, Con Dempsey, M. Byrne, M. Brien, D. Whelan (snr.), D. Whelan (jnr.), J. Shiel (jnr.), M. Coughlan, A. Deloney, M. Murphy, Jack Shiel.

Referee—A. McKeogh (Dublin).

1900

Tipperary—E. Hayes, (capt.), P. Hayes, M. Ryan, M. Purcell, T. Allen, P. Maher, W. Maher, M. Maher, J. Walsh, T. Ryan, E. Maher, "Big Bill" Gleeson, "Little Bill" Gleeson, J. O'Keeffe, M. Wall, T. Semple, Jack Gleeson.

London—Dan Horgan (capt), M. Horgan, Jer. Connell, J. Lynch, Jer. Healy, Tim Doody, Sean Óg Hanly, James Grimes, D. Roche, John Coughlan, James Keogh, M. L. McMahon, John O'Brien, Patrick McNamara, Denis McNamara, John Leary, Michael Cofler.

Referee—J. McCarthy (Kilkenny).

HOME FINAL

Tipperary—E. Hayes (capt.), P. Hayes, M. Ryan, M. Purcell, T. Allen, W. Maher, J. Walsh, T. Ryan, E. Maher, W. Gleeson (2), M. Wall, J. O'Keeffe, P. Maher, J. Gleeson, T. Semple, M. Maher.

Galway—J. Mitchel (capt.), M. Keighery, J. Coy, M. Cunningham, M. Stankard, J. Sylver, M. Holland, T. Leary, T. Connors, P. Taylor, M. Leary, T. Larkin, P. Burke, J. Larkin, W. Fallon, J. Quinn, D. Farrell.

1901

London—J. Coughlan (capt.), P. King, J. King, P. Crowe, J. Fitzgerald, J. O'Brien, T. Barry, Jas. Barry, Jer. Connell, D. Horgan, M. Horgan, Seamus Lynch, Tim Doody, M. McMahon, E. Barrett, Jer. Kelleher, J. Crowley.

Cork—P. Cantillon (capt.), J. Ronayne, J. Leonard, D. McGrath, J. Kelleher, T. Hallahan, J. O'Neill, D. O'Keeffe, T. Powell, M. O'Reilly, J. Barrett, W. Sheehan, P. Sullivan, J. O'Leary, D. Daly, C. Young, J. Delea.

Referee—J. McCarthy (Kilkenny).

HOME FINAL

Cork—P. Cantillon (capt.), J. Delea, D. McGrath, T. Irwin, J. Leonard, D. O'Keeffe, T. Powell, J. Kelleher, J. Ronayne, J. O'Neill, T. Hallinan, C. Young, P. Sullivan, J. O'Leary, D. Daly, W. Sheehan, M. O'Reilly.

Wexford—J. Furlong (capt.), J. Corrigan, J. Murphy, M. O'Brien, Ml. O'Brien, M. Cummins, T. Dempsey, Con Dempsey, S. Donohue, T. Byrne, M. Byrne, P. Rath, O. Synnott, D. Crean, B. Murphy, J. Shiel, T. Cullen.

1902

Cork—J. Kelleher (capt.), J. Ronayne, J. Desmond, J. O'Shea, W. Daly, J. Daly, T. Mahony, T. Lynch, P. Leaky, T. Coughlan, W. Parfrey, S. Riordan, J. Leahy, W. Fitzgibbon, D. McGrath, D. O'Keeffe, M. O'Shea.

London—J. Nestor, J. Herbert, M. McMahon, J. Burke, T. Doody, P. Flanagan, T. Barry, J. Barry, T. Ryan, C. Sugrue, J. O'Leary, T. Donohue, T. Cummins, E. Barrett, P. D. Mehigan, J. Crowley, P. Clancy.

Referee—L. J. O'Toole (Dublin).

HOME FINAL REPLAY

Cork—J. Kelleher (capt.), J. Ronayne, J. Desmond, J. O'Shea, W. Doly, J. Daly, T. Mahony, M. O'Shea, P. Leahy, T. Coughlan, D. Coughlan, S. Riordan, W. Parfey, W. Fitzgibbon, D. McGrath, D. O'Keeffe, J. O'Leary. Sub: W. O'Neill.

Note: W. Moloney, C. Young, T. Lynch and P. Cantillon played in drawn game instead of M. O'Shea, D. Coughlan, S. Riordan and W. Fitzgibbon.

Dublin—D. McCormack (capt.), J. O'Brien, J. Cleary, P. Mahony, A. Harty, M. Callaghan, J. Callaghan, J. Conway, C. Dillon, W. P. Allen, J. Quinlan, P. Flynn, J. Kennedy, J. Grace, W. Connolly, J. Delaney, T. Gleeson.

Note: P. Mulcahy, J. Gleeson and W. Scanlon played for Dublin in the drawn game instead of P. Mahony, P. Flynn and J. Delaney.

1903

Cork—S. Riordan (capt.), T. Coughlan, J. Coughlan, D. Kidney, L. Flaherty, J. Kelleher, J. Desmond, J. O'Leary, W. Mackessy, A. Buckley, D. Buckley, W. Hennessy, W. O'Neill, P. O'Sullivan, M. O'Leary, D. O'Keeffe, D. McGrath.

London—P. King (capt.), J. Nestor, C. Sugrue, W. Power, D. Roche, P. J. Crotly, I. Kelleher, D. Horgan, J. O'Brien, J. Barry, M. J. O'Halloran, Sean Óg Hanly, P. McMahon, J. Bleech, J. O'Farrell, T. Doody, M. Larkin.

Referee—J. McCarthy (Kilkenny).

HOME FINAL

Cork—Same as above.

Kilkenny—M. Dalton (capt.), Jas Lalor, T. Murphy, M. Shortall, D. Grace. P. Maher, J. Doheny, S. Walton, J. Hoyne, P. Saunders, J. Kerwick, J. Fielding, P. Fielding, E. Doyle, J. Synnott, J. Quinn, J. Rochford.

1904

Kilkenny—J. Doheny (capt.), P. Maher, S. Walton, J. Hoyne, P. Saunders, J. Lawlor, R. Doyle, E. Doyle, P. Fielding. R. Walsh, J. Rochford, D. Grace, R. Brennan, D. Stapleton, P. Lanigan, J. Anthony, M. Lawlor. Sub: Jim Dunne for D Stapleton.

Cork—D. Harrington (capt.), W. O'Neill, D. Sheehan, M. O'Leary, D. Linehan, W. Moloney, P. O'Sullivan, D. McCarthy, J. Kelleher, W. Hennessy, J. Desmond, J. Ronayne, T. Coughlan, S. Riordan, D. O'Keeffe. D. McGrath W. Sheehan.

Referee—M. F. Crowe (Limerick).

1905

Kilkenny—D. J. Stapleton (capt.), J. Hoyne, T. Kenny, D. Kennedy, J. Anthony, J. J. Brennan, R. Walsh, J. Glennon, M. Gargan, S. Walton, J. Kelly, P. Lanigan, E. Doyle, J. Lawlor, R. Doyle, J. Rochford, M. Lawlor.

Cork—Jas. Kelleher (capt.), W. Hennessy, J. Ronayne, W. Mackessy, A. Buckley, D. McGrath, M. O'Leary, J. A. Beckett, W. Moloney, John Kelly, D. O'Leary, Chris Nolan, J. Harrington, D. McCarthy,P. O'Sullivan, W. O'Neill, "Sonny" Jim McCarthy. Sub: C. Young.

Referee—M. F. Crowe (Limerick).

Note: The above teams took part in disputed final on 14/4/1907. The following teams contested the refixed final on 30/6/1907:

Kilkenny—D. J. Stapleton (capt.), J. Hoyne, T. Kenny, D. Kennedy, J. Anthony, J. J. Brennan, R. Walsh, E. Teehan, Dan Grace, S. Walton, J. Kelly, P. Lanigan, E. Doyle, M. Lawlor, J. Lawlor, R. Doyle, J. Rochford. Sub: Tom Murphy for D. Stapleton.

Cork—J. Kelleher, W. Hennessy, J. Ronayne, W. Mackessy, A. Buckley, D. McGrath, M O'Leary, J. A. Beckett, W. Moloney, C. Young (capt.), John Kelly, D. O'Leary, Chris Nolan, P. D. Mehigan, ("Carbery"), D. Linehan, P. Leahy, W. O'Neill.

1906

Tipperary—Tom Semple (capt.), J. Hayes, J. O'Brien, P. Burke, M. O'Brien, T. Kerwick, P. Brolan, H. Shelley, J. Mockler, T. Kenna, P. Riordan, T. Allen, P. Maher, J. Burke, J. Gleeson, J. O'Keeffe, T. Gleeson.

Dublin—D. McCormack (capt.), A. C. Harty, P. Hogan, J. Cleary, J. O'Riordan, M. Murphy, J. Quinlan, J. O'Dwyer, P. Kennedy, W. Leonard, W. Murphy, T. Warner, B. O'Brien, M. O'Callaghan, J. Grace, M. Quinn, W. O'Callaghan.

Referee—T. Irwin (Cork).

1907

Kilkenny—R. "Drug" Walsh (capt.), R. Doyle, M. Doyle, E. Doyle, R. Doherty, J. Kelly, T. Kenny, M. Gargan, D. Stapleton, D. Kennedy, J. Keoghan, J. Rochford, D. Grace, P. Lanigan, J. Power, J. Anthony, S. Walton.

Cork—Jim Kelleher (capt.), J. Roynane, J. Desmond, W. Hennessy, T. Mahony, P. Leahy, J. O'Shea, T. Lynch, G. Buckley, J. Kelleher, T. Coughlan, S. Riordan, W. Parfrey, W. Kidney, D. O'Keeffe, J. A. Beckett, W. O'Neill.

Referee—M. F. Crowe (Limerick).

1908

Tipperary—Tom Semple (capt.), T. Kerwick, J. Mockler, J . O'Brien, H. Shelley, A. Corew, J. Mooney, T. Kenna, P. Burke, P. Brolan, J. Moloughney, J. Burke, T. Gleeson, M. O'Dwyer, J. Fitzgerald, P. Fitzgerald, Martin O'Brien.

Note: Jack Gleeson, Joe O'Keeffe, Bob Mockler and William Harris played in drawn game for Tipperary. Michael O'Dwyer, John Fitzgerald, Pat Fitzgerald and Jimmy Burke came on for replay.

Dublin—J. Grace, A. Fitzgerald, D. McCormack, W. Connolly, W. O'Callaghan, W. Leonard, R. O'Brien, J. O'Brien, J. Callaghan, D. Kelleher, P. Grace, J. Lynch, M. Quinn, T. Quane, J. McDonald, D. Doyle, J. Nolan. Sub: P.

Neville for R. O'Brien.
Note: P. O'Meara, W. Dillane, J. Collison, H. Boland and R. White played in drawn game. P. Grace, D. McCormack, R. O'Brien, D. Doyle and J. Nolan came on for replay.
Referees—Draw, T. Irwin (Cork); Replay, J. McCarthy (Cork).

1909

Kilkenny—R. "Drug" Walsh (capt.), E. Doyle, M. Doyle, R. Doherty, J. Kelly, W. Hennebry, J. Delahunty, J. Dunphy, D. Kennedy, J. Keoghan, S. Walton, J. Rochford, M. Gargan, M. Shortall, J. Ryan, P. Lanigan, R. Doyle, Sub: R. Grace for R. Doherty.
Tipperary—Tom Semple (capt.), J. O'Brien, T. Kerwick, P. P. Burke, J. Fitzgerald, J. Mockler, J. Moloughney, A. Carew, M. O'Brien, P. Fitzgerald, J. Mooney, R. Mockler, H. Shelly, T. Gleeson, J. Burke, P. Brolan J. Hackett. Sub: E. Hayes. Referee—M. F. Crowe (Limerick).

1910

Wexford—R. Doyle (capt.), R. Fortune, M. Cummins, P. Mackey, M. Parker, J. Mythen, A. Kehoe, J. Shortall, Sean Kennedy, S. Donohue, P. Roche, D. Kavanagh, J. Fortune, W. McHugh, P. Corcoran, M. Neville, W. Devereux.
Limerick—J. Mackey (capt.), J. Burke, M. Mangan, M. Fehilly, T. Mangan, C. Scanlon, M. Harrington, Egan Clancy, E. Treacy, T. O'Brien, T. Hayes, J. Madden, P. Flaherty, M. Danagher, J. Carroll, D. Conway, M. Sweeney.
Referee—M. F. Crowe (Limerick).
No Final: Kilkenny awarded walk-over from Limerick. The Kllkenny team that played Tipperary in lieu of final was the same team as played in 1912, so effectively comprised the 1911 All-lreland champion side.

1912

Kilkenny—S. Walton (capt.), J. T. Power, P. Grace, D. Kennedy, J. J. Brennan, P. Lanigan, J. Keoghan, R. Walsh, R. Grace, J. Rochford, E. Doyle, T. McCormack, R. Doyle, M. Doyle, M. Gargan, J. Kelly, R. Doherty.
Cork—A. Fitzgerald, D. Barry, P. Mahony, W. Mackessy, B. Murphy (capt.), M. Dorney, D. Kennefick, C. Sheehan, J. Murphy, M. Kidney, J. Kelleher, M. Byrne, J. Kennedy, W. Walsh, P. O'Brien L. Flaherty, T. Nagle.
Referee—M. F. Crowe (Limerick).

1913

(Teams reduced to 15 aside)
Kilkenny—R. "Drug" Walsh (capt.), J. Power, J. Keoghan, J. Rochford, J. Lennon, D. Kennedy, R. Grace, M. Gargan, J. J. Brennan, P. Grace, R. Doherty, R. Doyle, S. Walton, M. Doyle, J. Kelly.
Tipperary—P. "Wedger" Meagher (capt.), J. O'Meara, F. McGrath, S. Hackett, R. Mockler, J. Raleigh, T. Gleeson, J. Harty, E. Gilmartin, E. Cawley, P. Brolan, H. Shelley, J. Murphy, W. Kelly, E. O'Keeffe. Sub: J. McKenna for W. Kelly.
Referee—M. F. Crowe (Limerick).

1914

Clare—A. Power (capt.), J. Power, M. Flanagan, E. Grace, T. McGrath, P. McInerney, J. Shalloo, W. Considine, B. Considine, M. Moloney, R. Doherty, J. Fox, J. Clancy, J. Guerin, S. Spellisey. Subs: J. Rogers for S. Spellisey; P. Moloney for J. Fox.
Laois—Jack Carroll (capt.), R. O'Keeffe, Jim Carroll, W. Lenihan, J. Jones, T. Hyland, R. Reilly, T. Higgins, P. Goulding, J. Daly, E. P. McEvoy, F. Killeen, T. Jones, J. Hiney, T. Finlay.
Referee—J. Lalor (Kilkenny).

1915

Laois—J. Finlay (capt.), J. Walsh, T. Finlay, Jas. Carroll, John Carroll, Jos. Carroll, J. Daly, P. Campion, Joe Phelan, J. Hiney, John Phelan, E. McEvoy, R. O'Keeffe, J. Dunphy, P. Ryan.
Cork—C. Sheehan (capt.), "Bowler" Walsh, L. Flaherty, W. Fitzgerald, Seán Hyde, J. Ramsell, M. Byrne, F. Buckley, J. Kennedy, T. O'Riordan, P. Halloran, T. Nagle, Seán Óg Murphy, J. Murphy, B. Murphy.
Referee—W. Walsh (Waterford).

1916

Tipperary—J. Leaby (capt.), T. Dwan, J. Doherty, W. Dwyer, T. Shanahan, J. Power, J. Fitzpatrick, J. Collison, P. Leahy, H. Shelly, J. Murphy, R. Walsh, D. Walsh, W. Dwyer, A. O'Donnell.
Kilkenny—S. Walton (capt.), J. Kerwick, J. Walsh, T. Hanrahan, J. Ryan, D. Kennedy, J. Holohan, R. Grace, J. Whelan, P. Clohosey, J. Byrne, W. Finn, R. Tobin, M. Kennedy, P. Walsh.
Referee—W. Walsh (Waterford).

1917

Dublin—T. Daly, John Ryan (capt.), Seán Hyde, Sean O'Donovan, H. Burke, C. Stuart, J. Phelan, R. Mockler, T. Moore, J. Cleary, F. Burke, M. Neville, M. Hackett, M. Hayes, P. Kenefick. Sub: B. Considine came on shortly after start of match.
Tipperary—J. LeaLy (capt.), J. Power, W. Dwyer, J. Nagle, P. Leary, J. Doherty, R. Walsh, W. Dwyer, H. Shelly, M. Leaby, T. Shanahan, S. Hackett, J. O'Meara, J. Collison, J. Fitzpatrick.
Referee—W. Walsh (Waterford).

1918

Limerick—W. Hough (capt.), P. McInerney, D. Lanigan, R. McConkey, W. Gleeson, J. Keane, M. Rochford, D. Troy, T. McGrath, M. Murphy, P. Barry, W. Ryan, R. Ryan, J. Humpheries, P. Kennedy.
Wexford—M. Cummins (capt:), M. Stafford, C. Hyland, D. Kavanagh, P. Roche, L. Leary, J. Fortune, R. Walsh, N. Leary, J. Synnott, J. Fogarty, M. Neville, M. Murphy, P. Fagan, R. Lambert.
Referee—W. Walsh (Waterford).

1919

Cork—J. Kennedy (capt.), E. Gray, J. O'Keeffe, S. Óg Murphy, P. Aherne, C. Lucy, J. J. Hassett, T. Nagle, P. O'Halloran, M. Murphy, F. Kelleher, D. Ring, C. Sheehan, R. Gorman, J. B. Murphy.

Dublin—C. Stuart (capt.), R. Mockler, Seán Hyde, F. Burke, B. Considine, M. Murphy, M. Hayes, T. Moore, T. Daly, J. Ryan (Grocers), J. Cleary, J. Phelan, M. Neville, T Hayes, Dr. J. Ryan (U.C.D.).

Referee—W. Walsh (Waterford).

1920

Dublin—R. Mockler (capt.), M. Hayes, M. Neville, T. Moore, T. Hayes, Jas. Cleary, E. Tobin, R. Doherty, Jas. Walsh, T. Daly (goal), F. Burke, J. J. Callanan, Joseph Phelan, John Ryan (Grocers), J. Clune.

Cork—R. O'Gorman (capt.), J. Kennedy, E. Gray, J. O'Keeffe, J. Hassett, C. Lucey, P. Halloron, P. ("Balty") Aherne, Seán Óg Murphy, E. Coughlan, M. Murphy, F. Kelleher, C. Sheehan, Denis Ring, Dannix Ring.

Referee—T. McGrath (Clare).

1921

Limerick—R. McConkey (capt.), M. Murphy (goal), W. Gleeson, J. Humphreys, D. Lanigan, D. Murnane, W. Houch, J. Keane, W. Ryan, G. Howard, P. McInerney, T. Mangan, M. Mullane, C. Ryan, T. McGrath.

Dublin—R. Mockler (capt.), Martin Hayes, Tom Hayes, M. Neville, Tom Moore, Jas. Walsh, R. Doherty, J. Clune, F. Burke, J. J. Callanan, T. Daly (goal), E. Tobin, M. Darcy, J. Cleary, Jos. Bannon. Sub: J. Kennedy for T. Hayes.

Referee—W. Walsh (Waterford).

1922

Kilkenny—Walter Dunphy (capt.), Ed. Dunphy, M. McDonald (goal), John Holohan, Jas. Tobin, Thos. Carroll, Richard Grace, Wm. Kenny, Patk. Glendon, Pat Aylward, Martin Lawlor, John Roberts, Pat Donohoe, Matty Power, Richard Tobin.

Tipperary—J. Leahy, (capt.), J. Power, A. O'Donnell, P. Power, P. Browne, J. Cleary, M. Kennedy, S. Hackett, J. O'Meara, J. J. Hayes, P. Spillane, J. Fitzpatrick, T. Dwan, W. Dwan, J. Darcy.

Referee—P. Dunphy (Laois).

1923

Galway—M. Kenny (capt.), J. Mahony (goal), M. Derivan, Ignatius Harney, J. Power, A. Kelly, B. Gibbs, E. Gilmartin, J. Morris, Martin King, T. Fleming, R. Morrissey, L. McGrath, M. Gill, J. Garvey.

Limerick—P. McInerney (capt.), J. Hanley (goal), D. Murnane, W. Hough, D. Lanigan, W. Gleeson, Jas. Humphries, M. Neville, J. J. Kinnane, J. Keane, T. McGrath, M. Cross, R. McConkey, J. O'Grady, M. Fitzgibbon. Subs: S. Shanny for J. J. Kinnane; J. O'Shea for R. McConkey.

Referee—P. Kennifick (Cork).

1924

Dublin—T. Daly (goal), Joe Bannon, W Small, T. Kelly, M. Gill, Jas. Walsh, R. Mockler, P. Aylward, R. Doherty, M. Holland, D. O'Neill, G. Howard, Tom Barry, W. Banim, T. Finlay. Note: Frank Wall, non-playing captain.

Galway—M. Kenny (capt.), J. Mahony (goal), M. Derivan, Ignatius Harney, J. Power, A. Kelly, B. Gibbs, E. Gilmartin, J Morris, Martin King, T. Fleming, R. Morrissey, L. McGrath, J. Garvey, J Keogh.

Referee—P. O Caoimh (Cork).

1925

Tipperary—Johnny Leahy (capt.), A. O'Donnell (goal), M. Mockler, M. D'Arcy, J. J. Hayes, M. Kennedy, S. Hackett, J. Power, P. Leahy, P. Cahill, T. Duffy, J. D'Arcy, W. Ryan, P. Power, P. O'Dwyer. Sub: S. Kenny for M. Mockler.

Galway—A. Kelly (capt.), J. Mahony (goal), J. Stanford, J. Fallon, Mick Derivan, M. Broderick, P. J. Morrissey, I. Harney, Ml. King, P. O'Donnell, M. Connaire, M. Houlihan, Richard Morrissey, J. Shaughnessy, P. Rooney. Sub: P. Finn for J. Shaughnessy.

Referee—P. McCullagh (Wexford).

1926

Cork—Sean Óg Murphy (capt.), J. Coughlan (goal), Mce. Murphy, E. O'Connell, D. B. Murphy, Ml. Murphy, J. O'Regan, J. Hurley, Eudie Coughlan, Wm. Higgins, P. Delea, J. Kearney, Matt Murphy, M. Ahearne, P. Ahearne.

Kilkenny—Richard Grace (capt.), R. Cantwell (goal), Wm. Meagher, P. O'Reilly, T. Carroll, E. Doyle, W. Barry, W. Dunphy, Martin Power, L. Meagher, J. Carroll, Martin Brennan. E. Dunphy, H. Meagher, J. Roberts.

Referee—P. McCullagh (Wexford).

1927

Dublin—M. Gill (capt.), P. McInerney, W. Phelan, E. Tobin, J. Gleeson, T. O'Rourke, G. Howard, M. Power, E. Faky, T. Daly, T. Barry, J. Walsh, D. O'Neill, J. Bannon, M. Hayes.

Cork—Seán Óg Murphy (capt.), E. O'Connell, D. B. Murphy, M. Murphy, J. Hurley, E. Coughlan, M. Leary, P. Ahearne, M. Ahearne, P. Delea, J. O'Regan, P. Daly, Maurice Murphy, W. Higgins, J. Burke (goal).

Referee—D. Lanigan (Limerick).

1928
Cork—Seán Óg Murphy (capt.), E. O'Connell, J. Hurley, E. Coughlan, P. Ahearne, P. Delea, M. Ahearne, M. LeaLy, M. Burke, M. Madden, D. B. Murphy, J. O'Regan, T. Barry, P. O'Grady, M. O'Connell.

Galway—J. Power (capt.), M. Derivan, I. Harney, J. Mahony, P. Green, R. McCann, J. Shaughnessy, R. Morrissey, P. Gilligan, M. Broderick, F. Kealy, M. Cunningham, W. Curran, Mick King, T. Mullins. Sub. J. Deely for Mick King.

Referee—John Roberts (Kilkenny).

1929
Cork—D. Barry Murphy (capt.), J. Burke (goal), M. Madden, P. Collins, T. Barry, J. O'Regan, M. O'Connell, J. Kenneally, M. Ahearne, P. Ahearne, P. Delea, J. Hurley, E. Coughlan, P. O'Grady, E. O'Connell. Subs: D. McCarthy for P. Aherne.

Galway—J. Mahony (goal), P. Clarke, T. Fleming, J. Shaughnessy, W. Keane, L. Geoghegan, F. Keely, M. Cunningham, Ignatius Harney, C. Cooney, P. Corcoran, J. Derivan, R. Morrissey W. Derivan, J. Deely. Subs: M. Broderick for J. Shaughnessy; A. Furey for W. Derivan.

Referee—S. Robbins (Offaly).

1930
Tipperary—J. J. Callanan (capt.), J. O'Loughlin, J. Maher, M. Ryan, J. Harney, J. Lanigan, T. O'Meara (goal), M. Kennedy, P. McKenna, P. Purcell, P. Cahill, M. F. Cronin, T. Butler, T. Leahy, T. Treacy. Sub: J. Heeney.

Dublin—Jas. Walsh (capt.), John Dwyer (goal), T. O'Meara, E. Campion, M. Gill, C. Griffin, C. MacMahon, P. Mcinerney, M. Finn, T. Quinlan, T. Burke, Matt Power, E. Byrne, T. Teehan, J. Gleeson. Subs: H. Quirke, M. Daniels.

Referee—S. Jordan (Galway).

1931
Cork—J. Coughlan, M. Madden, E. O'Connell, P. "Fox" Collins, D. Barry Murphy, J. Regan, T. Barry, J. Hurley, M. O'Connell, E. Coughlan (capt.), M. Aherne, P. O'Grady, P. Delea, P. Aherne, W. Clancy.

The above team played in all three matches. George Garrett (Blackrock) come on as a sub in the first and second replay.

Kilkenny—J. Dermody, P. Phelan, P. O'Reilly, D. Treacy, T. Carroll, P. Byrne, E. Doyle, E. Byrne, Tommy Leaby, J. Duggan, J. LeaLy, Matty Power, D. Dunne, M. Larkin, P. Walsh. Sub: Martin Murphy.

Lory Meagher (capt.), Paddy Larkin and Billy Dalton played in the first and second games.

Martin White and Dick Morrissey played in the first game.

Jack Duggan came on as a sub in the first game for Dick Morrisssey. He played in second game. Paddy Walsh played in second game. Tommy Leahy came on as a sub in second game for Lory Meagher.

Referees—two games, S. Robbins (Offaly); 3rd game, W. Walsh (Waterford).

1932
Kilkenny—J. Dermody, P. Larkin, P. O'Reilly, J. Carroll, P. Phelan, P. Byrne, E. Doyle, E. Byrne, L. Meagher, J. Walsh (capt.), Mar. Power, Tom Leahy, J. Dunne, M. White, Mattie Power.

Clare—Tom Daly, J. Higgins, P. Mclnerney, J. J. Doyle (capt.), J. Houlihan, J. Hogan, L. Blake, J. Gleeson, T. Mclnerney, M. Falvey, M. Connery, Michael O'Rourke, J. Mullane, T. Burnell, T. Considine.

Referee: S. Robbins (Offaly).

1933
Kilkenny—E. Doyle (capt.), John Dunne, J. Dermody (goal), L. Meagher, P. Phelan, P. Larkin, M. White, P. O'Reilly, P. Byrne, J. Walsh, J. Fitzpatrick, E. Byrne, Tommy Leahy, Martin Power, Matty Power. Subs: J. Duggan for M. White; J. O'Connell for J. Dermody.

Limerick—M. Fitzgibbon {capt.), P Scanlan (goal), T. Ryan, J. Mackey, M. Mackey, M. Cross, T. McCarthy, P. Clohessy, D. Clohessy, E. Cregan, M. Ryan, P. Ryan, J. Roche, G. Howard, C. O'Brien. Sub: W. O'Donoghue.

Referee—S. Jordan (Galway).

1934 (REPLAY)
Limerick—T. Shinny (goal), E. Cregan, T. McCarthy, M Kennedy, M. Cross, P. Clohessy, G. Howard, T. Ryan (capt.), M. Ryan, J. Mackey, M. Mackey, J. Roche, J. O'Connell, D. Clohessy, J. Close.

Note: Paddy Scanlon and Bob McConkey played in drawn game. Tom Shinny and Jackie O'Connell came on for replay. M. Condon came on as sub. in drawn game.

Dublin—C. Forde (goal), A. Murphy, J. Bannon, T. Teehan, J. Walsh, D. Canniffe, P. Roche, Ed. Wade, M. Daniels, S. Hegarty, T. Treacy, S. Muldowney, S. Feeney (capt.), D. O'Neill, J O'Connell. Subs: C. McMahon for A. Murphy; J. Culleton for C. Forde.

C. Boland (capt.) played in drawn game. S. Feeney (capt.) came on for replay. F. McCormack and J. Culleton came on as subs in drawn game.

Referee—S. Jordan (Galway) draw and replay.

1935
Kilkenny—J. O'Connell (goal), P. Larkin, P. O'Reilly, P. Blanchfield, E. Byrne, P. Byrne, P. Phelan, L. Meagher (capt.), Tommy Leahy, J. Walsh, J. Duggan, M. White, J. Dunne, L.

Byrne, Matty Power. Subs: L. Duggan for J. Dunne; J. Dunne for Duggan.

Limerick—P. Scanlan (goal), E. Cregan, T. McCarthy, M. Kennedy, M. Cross, P. Clohessy, G. Howard, T. Ryan (capt.), M. Ryan, J. Mackey, M. Mackey, J. Roche, J. O'Connell, P. McMahon, J. Close.

Referee: T. Daly (Clare).

1936

Limerick—P. Scanlan (goal), T. McCarthy, P. O'Carroll, M. Kennedy, M. Cross, P. Clohessy, G. Howard, T. Ryan, M. Ryan, J. Mackey, M. Mackey (capt.), J. Roche, D. Clohessy, P. McMahon, J. Power.

Kilkenny—J. O'Connell (goal), P. Larkin (capt.), P. O'Reilly, P. Blanchfield, P. Byrne, L. Byrne, P. Phelan, L. Meagher, Tom Leahy, J. Walsh, M. White, J. Duggan, J. Dunne, L. Byrne, Matty Power. Sub: W. Burke for P. Blanchfield.

Referee—J. O'Regan (Cork).

1937

Tipperary—T. Butler (goal), D. O'Gorman, G. Cornally, J. Lanigan (capt.), J. Ryan, J. Maher, W. Wall, J. Cooney, J. Gleeson, Jim Coffey, T. Treacy, T. Doyle, W. O'Donnell, D. Murphy, P. "Sweeper" Ryan. Subs: D. Mackey for J. Gleeson; T. Kennedy for W. Wall.

Kilkenny—J. Duggan (capt.), J. O'Connell (goal), P. Larkin, P. Byrne, P. Blanchfield, E. Byrne, W. Burke, P. Phelan, T. Leahy, V. Madigan, J. Morrissey, P. Obbins, L. Duggan, M. White, Matt Power. Sub: L. Meagher for Tommy Leahy.

Referee—J. Flaherty (Offaly).

1938

Dublin—M. Daniels (capt.), C. Forde, T. Teehan, M. Butler, C. McMahon, M. Gill, P. Farrell, J. Byrne, H. Gray, R. Ryan, M. McDonnell, P. Doody, M. Brophy, M. Flynn, W. Loughnane. Sub: J. Gilmartin.

Waterford—M. Hickey (capt.), M. Curley, C. Ware J. Fanning, W. Walshe, J. Keane, J. Mountain, C. Moylon S. Feeney, W. Barron, T. Greaney, P. Sheehan, J. Halpin, L. Byrne, D. Goode.

Referee—I. Harney {Galway).

1939

Kilkenny—J. O'Connell (goal), P. Grace, P. Larkin, P. Blanchfield, R. Hinks, W. Burke, P. Phelan, J. Walsh (capt.), J. Kelly, J. Langton, Ter. Leahy, J. Gargan, J. Mulcahy, J. O'Brien, J. Phelan. Sub: R. Brannagan for J. Gargan.

Cork—J. Buttimer, A. Lotty, Batt Thornhill, W. Murphy, W. Campbell, J. Quirke, J. Young, J. Lynch (capt.), J. Barrett, C. Buckley, R. Dinneen, W. Tabb, J. Ryng, T. O'Sullivan, M. Brennan.

Referee—J. Flaherty {Offaly).

1940

Limerick—P. Scanlan, J. McCarthy, M. Hickey, M. Kennedy, T. Cooke, P. Clohessy, P. Cregan, T. Ryan, J. Roche, J. Mackey, M. Mackey (capt.), R. Stokes, E. Chawke, P. McMahon, J. Power. Sub: A. Herbert for P. Clohessy.

Kilkenny—J. O'Connell, P. Grace, P. Larkin, P. Blanchfield, R. Hinks, W. Burke, P. Phelan, J. Walsh, J. Kelly, J. Langton (capt.), Terry Leahy, J. Gargan, J. Mulcahy, S. O'Brien, Jas. Phelan.

Referee—J. J. Callanan (Tipperary).

1941

Cork—J. Buflimer, W. Murphy, B. Thornhill, A. Lotty, W. Campbell, C. Cottrill, D. J. Buckley, S. Barrett, J. Lynch, C. Ring, C. Buckley (capt,), J. Young, J. Quirke, T. O'Sullivan, M Brennan. Subs: P. O'Donovan for J. Lynch; J. Ryng for M. Brennan.

Dublin—C. Forde, D. Nicholls, M. Connolly, C. McMahon, M. Gill (jnr.), P. Farrell, J. Byrne, H. Gray, F. White, M. McDonnell, E. Wade (capt.), G. Glenn, E. O'Boyle, P. McSweeney, C. Downes. Sub: D. Conway for C. Forde.

Referee—W. O'Donnell (Tipperary).

1942

Cork—E. Porter, W. Murphy, B. Thornhill, C. Murphy, A. Lotty, D. J. Buckley, J. Young, J. Lynch (capt.), P. O'Donovan, C. Ring, Seán Condon, M. Kennefick, C. Tobin, J. Quirke, D. Beckett. Sub: J. Buttimer Ifor E. Porter).

Dublin—Jim Donegan, C. O'Dwyer, M. Butler, P. McCormack, E. O'Brien, F. White, (capt.), Jim Byrne, E. Wade, H. Gray, M. Ryan, M. McDonnell, J. Roche, D. Devitt, P. Kennedy, J. Mullane. Subs: S. Skehal for J. Roche; M. Griffin for S. Skehal.

Referee—M. Hennessy (Clare).

1943

Cork—T. Mulcahy, W. Murphy, B. Thornhill, C. Murphy, A. Lotly, D. J. Buckley, J. Young, J. Lynch, C. Cottrell, S. Condon, C. Ring, M. Kenefick (capt.), J. Quirke, T. O'Sullivan, M. Brennan. Subs: P. O'Donovan for S. Condon; B. Murphy for T. Sullivan.

Antrim—J. Hurl, J. Currie, K. Murphy, W. Graham, P. McGarry, J. Walsh (capt.), P. McKeown, J. Bateson, N. Campbell, D. McKillop, J. Butler, Joe Mullan, K. Armstrong, D. McAlister, S. Mulholland. Sub: S. McNeill for J. Walsh.

Referee—J. J. Stuart (Dublin).

1944

Cork—T. Mulcaby, W. Murphy, B. Thornhill, D. J. Buckley, P. O'Donovan, C. Murphy, A. Lotly, J. Lynch, C. Cottrell, C. Ring, S. Condon (capt.), J. Young, J. Quirke, J. Morrison, J. Kelly. Sub: P. Healy for C. Murphy.

Dublin—Jim Donegan, J. O'Neill, M. Butler

(capt.), P McCormack, F. White, C. Flanogan, J. Egan, M. Hassefl, H. Gray, T. Leahy, E. Wade, J. Byrne, P. Maher, C. Downes, M. Ryan. Sub: M. Gill for J. Egan.

Referee M. Hennessy (Clare).

1945

Tipperary—Jim Maher, J. Devitt, G. Cornally, F. Coffey, M. Murphy, John Maher (capt.), T. Purcell, H. Goldsboro, T. Wall, "Mutt" Ryan, T. Doyle, E. Gleeson, John Coffey, A. Brennan, P. "Sweeper" Ryan.

Kilkenny—J. Walsh, P. Grace, M. Kelly, P. Blanchfield (capt.), J. Heffernan, W. Burke, J. Meagher, D. Kennedy, T. Murphy, J. Gargan, J. Langton, T. Maher, T. Walton. S. O'Brien, J. Mulcahy. Subs: W. Walsh for W. Burke, J. Kelly for D. Kennedy.

Referee—V. Baston (Waterford).

1946

Cork—T. Mulcahy, W. Murphy, C. Murphy, D. J. Buckley, P. O'Donovan A. Lotty, J. Young, J. Lynch, C. Cottrell, P. Healy, C. Ring (capt.), C. Murphy, M. O'Riordan, G. O'Riordan, J. Kelly.

Kilkenny—Jim Donegan, P. Grace, M. Butler, W. Walsh, J. Kelly, S. Downey, J. Mulcahy (capt.), D. Kennedy, T. Leahy, J. Gargan, J. Langton, L. Reidy, T. Walton, S. O'Brien, P. O'Brien. Subs: T. Murphy, M. Kelly (Mooncoin).

Referee—J. Flaherty (Offaly).

1947

Kilkenny—Jim Donegan, P. Grace, P. ("Diamond") Hayden, M. Marnell, J. Kelly, P. Prendergast, J. Mulcahy, D. Kennedy (capt.), J. Heffernan, T. Walton, Terry Leahy, J. Langton, Shem Downey, W. Cahill, L. Reidy. Sub: E. Kavanagh for P. Prendergast.

Cork—T. Mulcahy, W. Murphy, C. Murphy, D. J. Buckley, P. Donovan, A. Lotty, J. Young, J. Lynch, C. Cottrell, S. Condon (capt.), C. Ring, C. Murphy, M. O'Riordan, G. O'Riordan, J. Kelly.

Referee—P. Purcell (Tipperary).

1948

Waterford—J. Ware (capt.), A. Fleming, J. Cusack, J. Goode, M. Hickey, V. Baston M. Hayes, J. O'Connor, E. Carew, K. O'Connor, J. Keane, C. Moylan, W. Galvin, E. Daly, T. Curran.

Dublin—K. Matthews, E. Dunphy, D. Walsh, S. Cronin, A. Herbert, J. Butler, P. Donnelly, M. Hassett, L. Donnelly, J. Kennedy, D. Cantwell, S. Óg O'Callaghan, M. Williams, J. Prior, F. Cummins (capt.).

Referee—C. Murphy (Cork).

1949

Tipperary—A. Reddan, M. Byrne, A. Brennan, J. Doyle, P. Stakelum (capt.), F. Coffey, T. Doyle, S. Kenny, P. Shanahan, Tommy Ryan, Mick Ryan, J. Kennedy, J. Ryan, "Sonny" Maher, S. Bannon, Sub: P. Kenny for F. Coffey.

Laois—T. Fitzpatrick, L. White, J. Bergin, P. McCormack, J. Murray, T. Byrne, P. Rustchitzko (capt.), J. Styles, W. Bohane, P. Hogan, H. Grey, P. O'Brien, P. Lalor, D. Forde, P. Kelly. Subs: W. Dargan for P. O'Brien; A. Dunne for P. Rustchitzko).

Referee—M. J. Flaherty (Galway).

1950

Tipperary—A. Reddan, M. Byrne, A. Brennan, J. Doyle, J. Finn, P. Stakelum, T. Doyle, S. Bannon, P. Shanahan, E. Ryan, Mick Ryan, S. Kenny (capt.), P. Kenny, "Sonny" Maher, J. Kennedy. Sub: Tommy Ryan for "Sonny" Maher.

Kilkenny—R. Dowling, J. Hogan, P. "Diamond" Hayden, M. Marnell, J. Kelly, P. Prendergast, W. Walsh, D. Kennedy, Shem Downey, J. Heffernan, M. Kenny (capt.), J. Langton, W. Costigan, J. Mulcahy, L. Reidy. Sub: T. Walton for Costigan.

Referee—C. Murphy.(Cork).

1951

Tipperary—A. Reddan, M. Byrne, A. Brennan, J. Doyle, J. Finn (capt.), P. Stakelum, T. Doyle, P. Shanahan, J. Hough, E. Ryan, Mick Ryan, Tim Ryan, P. Kenny, "Sonny" Maher, S. Bannon. Sub: S. Kenny for P. Kenny.

Wexford—R. Brennan, M. Byrne, N. O'Donnell, M. O'Hanlon, S. Thorpe, R. Rackard, W. Rackard, E. Wheeler, J. Morrissey, Padge Kehoe, J. Cummins, T. Russell, T. Flood, N. Rackard (capt), Paddy Kehoe.

Referee—W. O'Donoghue (Limerick).

1952

Cork—D. Creedon, G. O'Riordan, J. Lyons, A. O'Shaughnessy, M. Fouhy, V. Twomey, S. O'Brien, J. Twomey, G. Murphy, W. Griffin, W. J. Daly, C. Ring, L. Abernethy, L. Dowling, P. Barry (capt.). Subs: M. O'Riordan for Griffin; J. Lynam for Abernethy.

Dublin—K. Matthews, S. Cronin, P. Ryan, J. O'Callaghan, D. Ferguson, J. Prior (capt.), T. Fahy, C. Murphy, N. Allen, G. Kelly, R. McCarthy, S. Kennedy, J. Finan, A. O'Brien, A. Herbert. Subs: M. Wilson for Finan; M. Williams for Kennedy.

Referee—W. O'Donoghue (Limerick).

1953

Cork—D. Creedon, G. O'Riordan, J. Lyons, A. O'Shaughnessy, M. Fouhy, D. Hayes, V. Twomey, J. Twomey G. Murphy, W. J. Daly, J. Hartnett, C. Ring (capt.), T. O'Sullivan, L. Dowling, P. Barry.

Galway—S. Duggan, C. Corless, W. O'Neill, J. Brophy, M. Burke (capt.), J. Molloy, E. Quinn, J. Salmon, W. Duffy, J Duggan, H. Gordon, J. Killeen, M. Mclnerney, J. Gallagher, P Nolan. Subs: M. J. Flaherty for Nolan; P. Duggan for J. Duggan.

Referee—P. Connell (Offaly).

1954

Cork—D. Creedon, G. O'Riordan, J. Lyons, A. O'Shaughnessy, M. Fouhy, V. Twomey, D. Hayes, G. Murphy, W. Moore, W. J. Daly, J. Hartnett, C. Ring (Capt.), J. Clifford, E. Goulding, P. Barry. Sub: Tom O'Sullivan for Paddy Barry.

Wexford—A. Foley, W. Rackard, N. O'Donnell, M. O'Hanlon, J. English, R. Rackard, E. Wheeler, J. Morrissey, S. Hearne, Paddy Kehoe, T. Flood, Padge Kehoe (capt.), T. Ryan, N. Rackard, R. Donovan. Subs: T. Bolger for O'Donnell; D. Aherne for Paddy Kehoe. Referee—J. Mulcahy (Kilkenny).

1955

Wexford—A. Foley, R. Rackard, N. O'Donnell (capt.), M. O'Hanlon, J. English, W. Rackard, M. Morrissey, J. Morrissey, S. Hearne, Paddy Kehoe, E. Wheeler, Padge Kehoe, T. Ryan, N. Rackard, T. Flood. Subs: O. Gough for Wheeler; Wheeler for Gough, D. Aherne for Ryan.

Galway—T. Boland, J. Fives, B. Power, W. O'Neill, M. Burke, J. Molloy, T. Kelly, J. Salmon, W. Duffy, J. Duggan (capt.), J. Young, P. Duggan, P. Egan, J. Burke, T. Sweeney. Subs: H. Gordon for Power; M. Elwood for Sweeney.

Referee—R. Stakelum (Tipperary).

1956

Wexford—A. Foley, R. Rackard, N. O'Donnell, M. Morrissey, J. English (capt.), W. Rackard, J. Morrissey, S. Hearne, E. Wheeler, Padge Kehoe, M. Codd, T. Flood, T. Ryan, N. Rackard, T. Dixon.

Cork—M. Cashman, J. Brohan, J. Lyons, A. O'Shaughnessy (capt.), M. Fouhy, W. J. Daly, P. Philpott, E. Goulding, P. Dowling, M. Regan, J. Hartnett, P. Barry, C. O'Shea, T. Kelly, C. Ring. Subs: V. Twomey for O'Shaughnessy; G. Murphy for Hartnet.

Referee T. O'Sullivan (Limerick).

1957

Kilkenny—O. Walsh, T. Walsh, J. Walsh, J. Maher, P. Buggy, M. Walsh, J. McGovern, M. Brophy, J. Sutton, D. Heaslip, M. Kenny, M. Kelly (capt.), R. Rocket, W. Dwyer, S. Clohessy. Sub: W. Walsh for Sutton.

Waterford—R. Roche, T. Cunningham, A. Flynn, J. Barron, M. O'Connor, M. Óg Morrissey, S. Power, J. O'Connor, P. Grimes (capt.), M. Flannelly, T. Cheasty, L. Guinan, F. Walsh, J. Kiely, D. Whelan.

Referee—S. Gleeson (Limerick).

1958

Tipperary—J. O'Grady, M. Byrne, M. Maher, K. Carey, J. Finn, A. Wall (capt.), John Doyle, J. Hough, T. English, D. Nealon, T. Larkin, Jimmy Doyle, L. Keane, L. Devaney, L Connolly.

Galway—M. Sweeney, F. Spillane, P. Burke, S. Cullinane (capt.), J. Duggan, J. Fives, F. Benson, J. Salmon, P. J. Lally, T. Sweeney, J. Young, T. Kelly, P. J. Lawless, W. O'Neill, T. Conway. Subs: E. Dervan for Spillane; M. Fox for Young.

Referee—Matt Spain {Offalyl.

1959 REPLAY

Waterford—E. Power, J. Harney, A. Flynn, J. Barron, M. Lacey, M. Óg Morrissey, Jackie Condon, S. Power, P. Grimes, M. Flannelly, T. Cheasty, F. Walsh (capt.), L. Guinan, T. Cunningham, J. Kiely. Subs: M. O'Connor for Lacey; D. Whelan for Cunningham.

D. Whelan and C. Ware (Waterford) who played in the drawn game were replaced by T. Cunningham and M. Flannelly who retained their places for the replay.

Kilkenny—O. Walsh, T. Walsh, J. Walsh, J. Maher, P. Buggy, T. Kelly, J. McGovern, P. Kelly, M. Walsh, D. Heaslip, M. Fleming, S. Clohosey (capt.), R. Carroll, W. Dwyer, T. O'Connell. Sub: E. Keher for McGovern; M. Kelly for M. Fleming.

Mick Brophy played in drawn game. Tim Kelly came on for replay. Subs in drawn game: Tim Kelly for J. McGovern, John Sutton for Mick Fleming; Mick Fleming for John Sutton.

Referee—draw and replay, G. Fitzgerald (Limerick).

1960

Wexford—P. Nolan, J. Mitchell, N. O'Donnell (capt.), T. Neville, J. English, W. Rackard, J. Nolan, E. Wheeler, J. Morrissey, J. O'Brien, Padge Keogh, S. Quaid, O. McGrath, J. Harding, T. Flood. Subs: Seán Power for Quaid; M. Morrissey for Power.

Tipperary—T. Moloney, M. Hassett, M. Maher, K. Carey, M. Burns, A. Wall (capt.), John Doyle, T. English, Tom Ryan (Killenaule), Jimmy Doyle, L. Devaney, D. Nealon. L. Connolly, Tom Moloughney, S. McLoughlin. Subs: W. Moloughney for McLoughlin; N. Murphy for English.

Referee—J. Dowling (OfFaly).

1961

Tipperary—D. O'Brien, M. Hassett (capt.), M. Maher. K. Carey, M. Burns, A. Wall, John Doyle, M. O'Gara, T. English, Jimmy Doyle, L. Devaney, D. Nealon, J. McKenna, W. Moloughney, T. Moloughney. Subs: T. Ryan (Killenaule) for McKenna;, J. Hough for O'Gara, S. McLoughlin for Wall.

Dublin—J. Grey, D. Ferguson, N. Drumgoole (capt.), L. Foley, L. Ferguson, C. Hayes, S. Lynch, D. Foley, F. Whelan, A. Boothman, M. Bohan, L. Shannon, B. Boothman, P. Croke, W. Jackson. Sub: E. Malone for Bohan.

Referee—G. Fitzgerald (Limerick).

1962

Tipperary—D. O'Brien, John Doyle, M. Maher, K. Carey, M. O'Gara, A. Wall, M. Burns, T. English, L. Devaney, Jimmy Doyle (capt.), J. McKenna, T. Ryan (Killenaule), D. Nealon, T. Moloughney, S. McLoughlin. Subs: L. Connolly for O'Gara; T. Ryan {Toomevara) for Jimmy Doyle.

Wexford—P. Nolan, T. Neville, N. O'Donnell, E. Colfer, J. English, W. Rackard (capt.), J. Nolan, P. Wilson, M. Lyng, J. O'Brien, Padge Kehoe, P. Lynch, O. McGrath, E. Wheeler, T. Flood.

Referee—J. Dowling (Offaly).

1963

Kilkenny—O. Walsh, P. Larkin, C. Whelan, M. Treacy, S. Cleere (capt.), T. Carroll, M. Coogan, P. Moran, S. Clohosey, D. Heaslip, J. McGovern, E. Keher, T. Walsh, W. Dwyer. T. Murphy. Sub: O. Gough for McGovern.

Waterford—E. Power, T. Cunningham, A. Flynn, J. Byrne, L. Guinan, M. Óg Morrissey, J. Irish, M. Dempsey, Joe Condon (capt.), M. Flannelly, T. Cheasty, F. Walsh, S. Power, J. Barron. P. Grimes. Subs: P. Flynn for E. Power; J. Meaney for Condon; M. Walsh for Byrne.

Referee—J. Hatton (Wicklow).

1964

Tipperary—J. O'Donoghue, John Doyle, M. Maher, K. Carey, M. Burns, A. Wall, M. Murphy (capt.), T. English. M. Roche, Jimmy Doyle, L. Kiely, M Keating, D. Nealon. J. McKenna, S. McLoughlin. Subs: M. Lonergan for Maher; L. Devaney for Kiely.

Kilkenny—O. Walsh, C. Whelan, P. Dillon, P. Larkin, P. Henderson, T. Carroll, M. Coogan, P. Moran, S. Buckley (capt.), S. Cleere, J. Teehan, E. Keher, T. Walsh, T. Forrestal, T. Murphy. Subs: W. Murphy (Carrickshock) for Coogan; D. Heaslip for T. Murphy.

Referee—A. Higgins (Golway).

1965

Tipperary—J. O'Donoghue, John Doyle, M. Maher, K. Carey, M. Burns, A. Wall, L. Gaynor, T. English, M. Roche, Jimmy Doyle (capt.), L. Kiely, L. Devaney, D. Nealon, J. McKenna, S. McLoughlin.

Wexford—P. Nolan, W O'Neill, D. Quigley, E. Colfer, V. Staples, T. Neville (capt.), W. Murphy, P. Wilson, M. Byrne, J. O'Brien, J. Nolan, R. Shannon, P. Quigley, M. Codd, J. Foley. Subs: E. Wheeler for J. Nolan; O. McGrath for P. Quigley.

Referee—M. Hayes (Clare).

1966

Cork—P. Barry, P. Doolan, T. O'Donoghue, D. Murphy, A. Connolly, J. O'Sullivan, P. Fitzgerald, J. McCarthy, M. Waters, S. Barry, J. O'Halloran, G. McCarthy (capt.), C. McCarthy, C. Sheehan, J. Bennett.

Kilkenny—O. Walsh, P. Henderson, J Lynch (capt.), J. Treacy, S. Cleere, T. Carroll, M. Coogan, P. Moran, J. Teehan, E. Keher, C. Dunne, S. Buckley, J. Dunphy, P. Dillon, T. Walsh. Subs: T. Murphy for P. Dillon; P. Carroll for T. Murphy.

Referee—J. Hatton tWicklow).

1967

Kilkenny—O. Walsh, T. Carroll, P. Dillon, J. Treacy (capt.), S. Cleere, P. Henderson, M. Coogan, P. Moran, J. Teehan, E. Keher, T. Walsh, C. Dunne, J. Bennett, J. Lynch, Martin Brennan. Subs: R. Blanchfield for E. Keher; J. Kinsella for J. Bennett; P. Carroll for T. Walsh.

Tipperary—J. O'Donoghue, J. Doyle, K. Carey, N. O'Gorman, M. Burns, A. Wall, L. Gaynor, T. English, M. Roche (capt.), D. Nealon, J. Flanagan, L. Devaney, Jimmy Doyle, M. Keating, S. McLoughlin. Subs: L. Kiely for S. McLoughlin; M. Lonergan for M. Burns; P. J. Ryan for T. English.

Referee M. Hayes (Clare).

1968

Wexford—P. Nolan, T. Neville, E. Kelly, E. Colfer, V. Staples, D. Quigley (capt.), W. Murphy, P. Wilson, D. Bernie, P. Lynch, A. Doran, C. Jacob, J. O'Brien, S. Whelan, J. Berry. Sub: J. Quigley for S. Whelan.

Tipperary—J. O'Donoghue, J. Costigan. N. O'Gorman, J. Gleeson, M. Burns, M. Roche (capt.), L. Gaynor, P. J. Ryan, D. Nealon, M. Keating, J. Ryan, J. Doyle, L. Devaney, J. McKenna, S. McLoughlin. Sub: F. Loughnane for Jimmy Doyle.

Referee—J. Dowling (Offaly).

1969

Kilkenny—O. Walsh, T. Carroll, P. Dillon, J. Treacy, W. Murphy (Rower-Inistioge), P. Henderson, M. Coogan, F. Cummins, M. Lawler, C. Dunne, P. Delaney, E. Keher (capt.), J. Millea, Martin Brennan, T. Murphy. Subs: P. Kavanagh for Dunne, P. Moran for Delaney; S. Buckley for Murphy.

Cork—P. Barry, A. Maher, T. O'Donoghue, D. Murphy (capt.), D. Clifford, W. Walsh, G. McCarthy, D. Coughlan, R. Tuohy, T. Ryan, C. Cullinane, P. Hegarty, J. McCarthy, R. Cummins, Eddie O'Brien. Subs: J. O'Halloron for O'Brien; J. Murphy for Tuohy; S. Looney for Ryan.

Referee—S. O'Connor (Limerick).

1970

Cork—P. Barry (capt.), A. Maher, P. McDonnell, J. Horgan, D. Clifford, P. Hegarty, C. Roche, G. McCarthy, S. Looney, T. Ryan, W. Walsh, C. Cullinane, C. McCarthy, R. Cummins, Eddie O'Brien. Subs: S. Murphy for Clifford.

Wexford—P. Nolan, E. Colfer, M. Collins (capt.), T. Neville, M. Browne, D. Quigley, T. O'Connor, D. Bernie, M. Jacob, M. Quigley, P Quigley, J. Quigley, M. Butler, A. Doran, J. Berry. Subs: T. Byrne for Butler; J. Russell for Neville.
Referee: J. Hatton (Wicklow).

1971

Tipperary—P. O'Sullivan, L. King, J. Kelly, J. Gleeson, T. O'Connor (capt.), M. Roche, L. Gaynor, P. J. Ryan, S. Hogan, F. Loughnane, N. O'Dwyer, D. Ryan, J. Flanagan, R. Ryan, M. Keating. Subs: Jimmy Doyle for Hogan; P. Byrne for Flanagan.
Kilkenny—O. Walsh, P. Larkin, P. Dillon, J. Tracey, W. Murphy (Rower-Inistioge), P. Henderson (capt.), M. Coogan, F. Cummins, P. Lalor, M. Murphy, P. Delaney, E. Keher, Mick Brennan, K. Purcell, E. Byrne. Subs: P. Moran for W. Murphy; P. Cullen for Brennan; T. Carroll for Larkin.
Referee—F. Murphy (Cork).

1972

Kilkenny—N. Skehan (capt.), P. Larkin, P. Dillon, J. Treacy, P. Lawlor, P. Henderson, E. Morrissey, F. Cummins, L. O'Brien, M. Crotty, P. Delaney, J. Kinsella, E. Byrne, K. Purcell, E. Keher. Subs: M. Murphy for Byrne; M. Coogan for Larkin; P. Moran for Kinsella.
Cork—P. Barry, A. Maher, P. McDonnell, B. Murphy, F. Norberg (capt.), S. Looney, C. Roche, J. McCarthy, D. Coughlan, G. McCarthy, M. Malone, P. Hegarty, C. McCarthy, R. Cummins, S. O'Leary. Subs: Ted O'Brien for Norberg; D. Collins for Hegarty.
Referee—M. Spain (Offaly).

1973

Limerick—S. Horgan, W. Moore, P. Hartigan, J. O'Brien, P. Bennis, E. Cregan, S. Foley, R. Bennis, E. Grimes (capt.), B. Hartigan, M. Dowling, L. O'Donoghue, F. Nolan, E. Rea, J. McKenna. Subs: T. Ryan for B. Hartigan.
Kilkenny—N. Skehan, P. Larkin, N. Orr, P. Cullen, P. Lawlor, P. Henderson, B. Cody, F. Cummins, L. O'Brien, C. Dunne, P. Deloney (capt.), P. Broderick, M. Crotty, J. Lynch, Mick Brennan. Subs: K. Purcell for Broderick; W. Harte for Cummins; J. Kinsella for Lynch.
Referee—M. Slattery (Clare}.

1974

Kilkenny—N. Skehan, P. Larkin, N. Orr (capt.), J. Treacy, P. Lawlor, P. Henderson, T. McCormack, L. O'Brien, F. Cummins, M. Crotty, P. Delaney, W. Fitzpatrick, Mick Brennan, K. Purcell, E. Keher.
Limerick—S. Horgan, W. Moore, P. Hartigan, J. O'Brien, T. Ryan, E. Cregan, S. Foley (capt.}, B. Hartigan, E. Grimes, J. McKenna, R. Bennis, M. Ruth, L. O'Donoghue, E. Rea. F. Nolan. Subs: P. Bennis for Ryan; P. Kelly for B. Hartigan; P. Fitzmaurice for McKenna.
Referee—J. Moloney (Tipperaryl.

1975

Kilkenny—N. Skehan, P. Larkin, N. Orr, B. Cody, P. Lawlor, P. Henderson, T. McCormack, L. O'Brien, F. Cummins, M. Crotty, P. Delaney, W. Fitzpatrick (capt.), Mick Brennan, K. Purcell, E. Keher.
Galway—M. Conneely, N. Mclnerney, J. Clarke, P. Lally. J. McDonagh, S. Silke, I. Clarke, S. Murphy, John Connolly (capt.), G. Cooney, F. Burke, P. J. Molloy, M. Barrett, P. J. Qualter, P. Faby. Subs: M. Connolly for Barrett; Ted Murphy for Lally; J. Grealish for Murphy.
Referee—S. O'Connor (Limerick).

1976

Cork—M. Coleman, B. Murphy, P. McDonnell, M. Doherty, P. Barry, J. Crowley, D. Coughlan, G. McCarthy, P. Moylan, M. Malone, B. Cummins, J. Barry Murphy, C. McCarthy, R. Cummins (capt.), S. O'Leary. Subs: E. O'Donoghue for O'Leary, J. Horgan for Barry.
Wexford—J. Nolan, T. O'Connor, W. Murphy, J. Prendergast, L. Bennett, M. Jacob, C. Doran, E. Buggy, W. Rowesome, J. Murphy, M. Quigley, J. Quigley, M. Butler, A. Doran (capt.), C. Keogh. Subs: D. Rowesome for Keogh; M. Casey for W. Rowesome.
Referee—P. Johnson (Kilkenny).

1977

Cork—M. Coleman, B. Murphy, M. Doherty (capt.), J. Horgan, D. McCurtain, J. Crowley, D. Coughlan, T. Cashman. T. Crowley, M. Malone, G. McCarthy, J. Barry Murphy, C. McCarthy, R. Cummins, S. O'Leary. Subs: P. Moylan for Malone; Tadgh Murphy for G. McCarthy.
Wexford—J. Nolan, T. O'Connor, W. Murphy, J. Prendergast, L. Bennett. M. Jacob, C. Doran, D. Bernie, E. Buggy, C. Keogh, M. Quigley, M. Butler, J. Quigley, A. Doran (capt.), J. Murphy. Subs: J. Russell for Prendergast; M. Casey for J. Murphy; E. Walsh for Bernie.
Referee—S. O'Grady (Limerick).

1978

Cork—M. Coleman, B. Murphy, M. O'Doherty, J. Horgan, D. McCurtain, J. Crowley, D. Coughlan, T. Cashman, P. Moylan, J. Barry Murphy, G. McCarthy, T. Crowley, C. McCarthy (capt.), R. Cummins, S. O'Leary. Subs: J. Allen for Cashman; E. O'Donoghue for O'Leary.
Kilkenny—N. Skehan, P. Prendergast, P. Larkin, D. O'Hara, J. Hennessy, G. Henderson (capt.), R. Reid, F. Cummins, L. O'Brien, K. Fennelly, M. Crotty, W. Fitzpatrick, Mick Brennan, B. Cody, M. Ruth. Subs T. Malone for Fennelly; P. Henderson for O'Brien.
Referee—J. Rankins (Laois).

1979

Kilkenny—N. Skehan, P. Larkin, P. Prendergast, J. Henderson, R. Reid, G. Henderson, N. Brennan. J. Hennessy, F. Cummins, G. Fennelly (capt.), W. Fitzpatrick, L. O'Brien, Mick Brennan, M. Crotty, M. Ruth. Subs: K. Fennelly for Crotty; D. O'Hara for Prendergast.

Galway—S. Shinnors, N. Mclnerney, C. Hayes, A. Fenton, J. McDonagh (capt.), S. Silke, I. Clarke, John Connolly, S. Mahon. B. Forde, F. Burke, Joe Connolly, P. J. Molloy, N. Lane. F. Gantley. Subs: S. Linnane for Forde; M. Whelan for Burke.

Referee—G. Ryan (Tipperary).

1980

Galway—M. Conneely, C. Hayes, N. Mclnerney, Jimmy Cooney, S. Linnane, S. Silke, S. Coen, M. Connolly, S. Mahon, F. Burke, Joe Connolly (capt.), P. J. Molloy, B. Forde, John Connolly, N. Lane. Subs: F. Gantley for M. Connolly; J. Ryan for Molloy.

Limerick—T. Quaid, D. Murray, L. Enright, Dom Punch, L. O'Donoghue, M. Carroll, S. Foley (capt.), J. Carroll, David Punch, P. Fitzmaurice, J. Flanagan, W. Fitzmaurice. O. O'Connor, J. McKenna, E. Cregan. Subs: B. Carroll for Flanagan; P. Herbert for M. Carroll; E. Grimes for W. Fitzmaurice.

Referee—N. O'Donophue (Dublin).

1981

Offaly—D. Martin, T. Donoghue, E. Coughlan, P. Fleury, A. Fogarty, P. Delaney, G. Coughlan, J. Kelly, L. Currams, P. Kirwan, B. Bermingham, M. Corrigan, P. Carroll, P. Horan (capt.), J. Flaherty. Subs: B. Keeshan for O'Donoghue; D. Owens for Kirwan.

Galway—M. Conneely, S. Coen, N. Mclnerney, Jimmy Cooney, S. Linnane, S. Silke (capt.), I. Clarke, M. Connolly, S. Mahon, F. Gantley, Joe Connolly, P. J. Molloy, B. Forde, John Connolly, N. Lane. Subs: F. Burke for Gantley; P. Ryan for Forde.

Referee—F. Murphy (Cork).

1982

Kilkenny—N. Skehan, J. Henderson, B. Cody (capt.), D. O'Hara; N. Brennan, G. Henderson, P. Prendergast, J. Hennessy, F. Cummins, R. Power, G. Fennelly, K. Brennan, W. Fitzpatrick, C. Heffernan, L. Fennelly.

Cork—G. Cunningham, B. Murphy, M. O'Doherty, J. Blake, J. Buckley, J. Crowley, D. MacCurtain, T. Cashman, T. Crowley A. O'Sullivan, P. Horgan, J. Barry Murphy (capt.), S. O'Leary, R. Cummins, E. O'Donoghue. Subs: B. Óg Murphy for Buckley; K. Hennessy for O'Sullivan; F. Collins for MacCurtain.

Referee: N. O'Donoghue (Dublin).

1983

Kilkenny—N. Skehan, J. Henderson, B. Cody, D. O'Hara, J. Hennessy, G. Henderson, P. Prendergast, F. Cummins, G. Fennelly, R. Power, K. Brennan, L. Fennelly (capt.), W. Fitzpatrick, C. Heffernan, H. Ryan. Sub: P. Lannon for Power.

Cork—G. Cunningham, B. Murphy, D. O'Grady, D. MacCurtain, P. Horgan, J. Crowley, T. Cashman, J. Buckley, J. Fenton, B. Óg Murphy, K. Hennessy, T. Crowley, T. Mulcahy, J. Barry Murphy (capt.), E. O'Donoghue. Subs: F. Collins for Fenton; A. O'Sullivan for Mulcahy; S. O'Leary for B. Óg Murphy.

Referee—N. Duggan (Limerick).

1984

Cork—G. Cunningham, D. Mulcahy, D. O'Grady, J. Hodgins, T. Cashman, J. Crowley, D. MacCurtain, J. Fenton (capt.), P. Hartnett, K. Hennessy, T. Crowley, A. O'Sullivan, T. Mulcahy, J. Barry Murphy' S. O'Leary.

Offaly—D. Martin, L. Carroll, E. Coughlan, P. Fleury (capt.), A. Fogarty, P. Delaney, G. Coughlan, T. Conneely, J. Kelly, M. Corrigan, B. Bermingham, P. Carroll, D. Fogarty, P. Horan, Joe Dooley. Subs: P. Corrigan for Bermingham; P. Kirwan for Dooley.

Referee: P. Long (Kilkenny).

1985

Offaly—J. Troy, A. Fogarty, E. Coughlan, P. Fleury (capt.), T. Conneely, P. Delaney, G. Coughlan, D. Owens, J. Kelly, P. Corrigan, B. Bermingham, M. Corrigan, P. Cleary, P. Horan, J. Dooley. Subs: D. Fogarty for Owens; B. Keeshan for Conneely.

Galway—P. Murphy, O. Kilkenny, C. Hayes, S. Linnane, P. Finnerty, A. Keady, A. Kilkenny, M. Connolly (capt.), S. Mahon, M. McGrath, B. Lynskey, Joe Cooney, B. Forde, N. Lane, P. J. Molloy. Subs: J. Murphy for McGrath; A Cunningham for Fcrde; M. Haverty for Connolly.

Referee: G. Ryan (Tipperary).

1986

Cork—G. Cunningham, D. Mulcahy, R. Brown, J. Crowley, P. Hartnett, T. Cashman (capt.), D. Walsh, J. Fenton, J. Cashman, T. McCarthy, T. Mulcahy, A. O'Sullivan, G. Fitzgerald, J. Barry Murphy, K. Hennessy. Subs: K. Kingston for Fenton.

Galway—J. Commins, S. Linnane, C. Hayes, O. Kilkenny, P. Finnerty, A. Keady, G. Mclnerney, S. Mahon, P. Piggott, A. Kilkenny, B. Lynskey, M. Naughton, A. Cunningham, Joe Cooney, N. Lane (capt.). Subs: P. J. Molloy for Piggott; M. Connolly for Mahon; P. Murphy for Cunnningham.

Referee: J. F. Bailey (Dublinl.

1987

Galway—J. Commins, S. Linnane, C. Hayes (capt.), O. Kilkenny, P. Finnerty, A. Keady, G. McInerney, S. Mahon, P. Malone, M. McGrath, J. Cooney, M. Naughton, E. Ryan, B. Lynskey, A. Cunningham. Subs. N. Lane for Naughton; P. J. Molloy for Cunningham; A. Kilkenny for McGrath.

Kilkenny—K. Fennelly, J. Hennessy, P. Prendergast (capt.), J. Henderson, L. Walsh, G. Henderson, S. Fennelly, G. Fennelly, L. Ryan, K. Brennan, C. Heffernan, R. Power, P. Walsh, L. Fennelly, H. Ryan. Subs: T. Lennon for P. Walsh; L. McCarthy for Power.

Referee: T. Murray (Limerick).

1988

Galway—J. Commins, S. Linnane C. Hayes (capt.), O. Kilkenny, P Finnerty, A. Keady, G. McInerney, M. Coleman, P. Malone, A. Cunningham, B. Lynskey, M. Naughton, M. McGrath, Joe Cooney, E. Ryan. Subs: N. Lane for Cunningham; A. Kilkenny for Naughton; G. Burke for Lynskey.

Tipperary—K. Hogan, P. Delaney, C. O'Donovan, J. Heffernan, B. Ryan, N. Sheehy, J. Kennedy, Colm Bonnar, D. Ryan, D. O'Connell, J. Leary, P. Fox, N. English (capt.), A. Ryan, J. Hayes. Sub: Cormac Bonnar for J. Hayes.

Referee—G. Kirwan (Offaly)

1989

Tipperary—K. Hogan, J. Heffernan, C. O'Donovan, N. Sheehy, Conal Bonnar, B. Ryan (Capt.}, J. Kennedy, Colm Bonnar, D. Carr, J. Leahy, D. Ryan, M. Cleary, P. Fox, Cormac Bonnar, N. English. Subs: J. Hayes for Cormac Bonnar, D. O'Connell for Leary, A. Ryan for Cleary.

Antrim—N. Patterson, G. O'Kane, T. Donnelly, D. Donnelly, J. McNaughton, D. McKinley, L. McKeegan, P. McKillen, D. McMullan, C. Barr (Capt.), A. McCarry, O. McFetridge, D. Armstrong, B. Donnelly, T. McNaughton. Subs: D. McNaughton for McMullan, D. McKillop for O'Kane, M. Sullivan for McKinley.

Referee—P. Delaney (Laois).

1990

Cork—G. Cunningham, J. Considine, D. Walsh, S. O'Gormon, S. McCarthy, J. Cashman, K. McGuckian, B. O'Sullivan, T. McCarthy, G. Fitzgerald, M. Foley, Tony O'Sullivan, T. McCarthy, T. Mulcaby (Capt.), K. Hennessy, J. Fitzgibbon. Subs: D. Quirke for McGuckian, C. Casey for B. O'Sullivan.

Galway—J. Commins, D. Fahy, S. Treacy, O. Kilkenny, P. Finnerty, T. Keady, G. McInerney, M. Coleman, P. Malone, A. Cunningham, Joe Cooney (Capt.), M. Naughton, M. McGrath, N. Lane, E. Ryan. Subs: T. Monaghan for Malone, B. Lynskey for Cunningham.

Referee—J. Moore (Waterford).

1991

Tipperary—K. Hogan, P. Delaney, N. Sheedy, M. Ryan, Colm Bonnar, B. Ryan, Conal Bonnar, D. Carr (Capt.), A. Ryan, M. Cleary, D. Ryan, J. Leahy, P. Fox, Cormac Bonnar, N. English. Subs: C. Stakelum for Cormac Bonnar, D. O'Connell for N. English.

Kilkenny—M. Walsh, W. Hennessy, J. Henderson, L. Simpson, L. Walsh, P. Dwyer, E. O'Connor, R. Power, M. Phelan, J. Power, C. Heffernan (Capt.), D. J. Carey, E. Morrissey, L. Fennelly, L. McCarthy. Subs: A. Ronan for McCarthy, L. Ryan for Power.

Referee—Willie Horgan (Cork).

1992

Kilkenny—M. Walsh, E. O'Connor, P. Dwyer, L. Simpson, L. Walsh, P. O'Neill, W. O'Connor, M. Phelan, W. Hennessy, L. McCarthy, J. Power, D. J. Carey, E. Morrissey, L. Fennelly (Capt.), J. Brennan. Subs: C. Heffernan for Brennan, A. Ronan for Morrissey.

Cork—G. Cunningham, S. O'Gorman, D. Mulcahy, B. Corcoran, C. Casey, J. Cashman, D. Walsh, P. Buckley, S. McCarthy, Teddy McCarthy, T. Mulcahy, A. O'Sullivan, G. Fitzgerald (Capt.), J. Fitzgibbon, K. Hennessy. Subs: P. Hartnett for Walsh, G. Manley for Fitzgerald, M. Foley for Buckley.

Referee—D. Murphy (Wexford).

1993

Kilkenny—M. Walsh, E. O'Connor (Capt.), P. Dwyer, L. Simpson, L. Keoghan, P. O'Neill, W. O'Connor, W. Hennessy, M. Phelan, L. McCarthy, J. Power, D. J. Carey, E. Morrissey, P. J. Delaney, A. Ronan. Subs: J. Brennan for Morrissey, T. Murphy for Phelan, C. Heffernan for Delaney.

Galway—R. Burke, P. Cooney, S. Treacy, M. Killilea, T. Helebert, G. McInerney, P. Kelly, M. Coleman, P. Malone, B. Keogh, J. McGrath, J. Cooney, M. McGrath (Capt.), J. Rabbitte, L. Burke. Subs: J. Campbell for J. McGrath, P. Finnerty for Keogh.

Referee—T. Murray (Limerick).

1994

Offaly—Jim Troy, S. McGuckian, K. Kinahan, M. Hanamy (Capt.), B. Whelahan, H. Rigney, K. Martin, J. Pilkington, D. Regan, Johnny Dooley, John Troy, Joe Dooley, B. Dooley, B. Kelly, D. Pilkington. Subs: P. O'Connor for Joe Dooley.

Limerick—J. Quaid, S. McDonagh, M. Nash, J. O'Connor, D. Clarke, G. Hegarty, D. Nash, C. Carey, M. Houlihan, F. Carroll, G. Kirby (Capt.), M. Galligan, T. J. Ryan, P. Heffernan, D. Quigley. Sub: L. O'Connor for Galligan.

Referee—W. Barrett (Tipperary).

1995

Clare—D. Fitzgerald, M. O'Halloran, B. Lohan, F. Lohan, L. Doyle, S. McMahon, A. Daly (Capt.), J. O'Connor, O. Baker, F. Tuohy, P. J. O'Connell, F. Hegarty, S. McNamara, C. Clancy, G. O'Loughlin. Subs: E. Taaffe for McNamara, C. Lyons for Clancy, A. Neville for Taaffe.

Offaly—D. Hughes, S. McGuckian, K. Kinahan, M. Hanamy, B. Whelahan, H. Rigney, K. Martin, J. Pilkington (Capt.), D. Regan, Johnny Dooley, John Troy, M. Duignan, B. Dooley, P. O'Connor, Joe Dooley. Subs: D. Pilkington for O'Connor, B. Kelly for Joe Dooley.

Referee—D. Murphy (Wexford).

1996

Wexford—D. Fitzhenry, C. Kehoe, G. Cushe, J. O'Connor, R. Guiney, L. Dunne, L. O'Gorman, A. Fenlon, G. O'Connor, R. McCarthy, M. Storey (Capt.), L. Murphy, T. Dempsey, G. Laffan, E. Scallan. Subs: B. Byrne for Murphy, P. Finn for Guiney, P. Codd for Laffan.

Limerick—J. Quaid, S. McDonagh, M. Nash, D. Nash, D. Clarke, C. Carey (Capt.), M. Foley, M. Houlihan, S. O'Neill, F. Carroll, G. Kirby, B. Foley, O. O'Neill, D. Quigley, T. J. Ryan. Subs: P. Tobin for O. O'Neill, B. Tobin for Ryan, T. Herbert for B. Foley.

Referee—P. Horan (Offaly).

1997

Clare—D. Fitzgerald, M. O'Halloran, B. Lohan, F. Lohan, L. Doyle, S. McMahon, A. Daly (Capt.), O. Baker, C. Lynch, J. O'Connor, C. Clancy, P. J. O'Connell, N. Gilligan, G. O'Loughlin, F. Tuohy. Subs: F. Hegarty for Tuohy, D. Forde for O'Connell, B. Murphy for Hegarty.

Tipperary—B. Cummins, P. Shelly, N. Sheehy, M. Ryan, L. Sheedy, Colm Bonnar, Conal Bonnar, T. Dunne, C. Gleeson (Capt.), L. McGrath, D. Ryan, J. Leahy, M. Cleary, E. O'Neill, B. O'Meara. Subs: A. Ryan for McGrath, L. Cahill for Cleary.

Referee—D. Murphy (Wexford).

1998

Offaly—S. Byrne, S. Whelahan, K. Kinahan, M. Hanamy, B. Whelahan, H. Rigney (Capt.), K. Martin, J. Pilkington, Johnny Dooley, M. Duignan, John Troy, G. Hannify, B. Dooley, J. Errity, Joe Dooley. Subs: P. Mulhaire for G. Hannify, D. Hannify for B. Dooley, J. Ryan for Johnny Dooley.

Kilkenny—J. Dermody, T. Hickey (Capt.), P. O'Neill, W. O'Connor, M. Kavanagh, C. Brennan, L. Keoghcn, P. Larkin, P. Barry, D. J. Carey, A. Comerford, B. McEvoy, K. O'Shea, P. J. Delaney, C. Carter. Subs: N. Moloney for O'Shea, S. Ryan for Comerford, J. Costelloe for Kavanagh.

Referee—D. Murphy (Wexford).

1999

Cork—D. Óg Cusack, F. Ryan, D. O'Sullivan, J. Browne, W. Sherlock, B. Corcoron, S. Óg Ó hAilpín, M. Landers (Capt.), M. O'Connell, T. McCarthy, F. McCormack, N. Ronan, S. McGrath, J. Deane, B. O'Connor. Subs: A. Browne for Ronan, K. Murray for Landers.

Kilkenny—J. McGarry, P. Larkin, C. Brennan, W. O'Connor, M. Kavanagh, P. O'Neill, P. Barry, A. Comerford, D. Byrne (Capt.), D.J. Carey, J. Power, B. McEvoy, K. O'Shea, H. Sheflin, C. Carter. Subs: P. J. Delaney for Power, N. Moloney for Carter.

Referee—Pat O'Connor (Limerick).

2000

Kilkenny – J.McGarry, M.Kavanagh, N.Hickey, W.O'Connor (Capt.), P.Larkin, E.Kennedy, P.Barry, A.Comerford, B.McEvoy, D.Byrne, J.Power, J.Hoyne, C.Carter, D.J.Carey, H.Shefflin. Subs – C.Brennan for McEvoy, E.Brennan for C.Brennan.

Offaly – S.Byrne, S.Whelahan, K.Kinahan, N.Claffey, B.Whelahan, J.Errity, K.Martin, Johnny Dooley, G.Oakley, J.Pilkington, G.Hanniffy, B.Murphy, M.Duignan, J.Ryan, Joe Dooley. Subs – D.Franks for Claffey, J.Troy for Ryan, P.Mulhare for Murphy.

Referee – W.Barrett (Tipperary)

2001

Tipperary – B.Cummins, T.Costello, P.Maher, P.Ormonde, E.Corcoran, D.Kennedy, P.Kelly, T.Dunne (Capt.), E.Enright, M.O'Leary, J.Carroll, P.Corbett, E.Kelly, D.Ryan, E.O'Neill. Subs – D.Fahy for Costello, P.O'Brien for O'Neill, M.Ryan for P.Kelly, C.Gleeson for Kennedy.

Galway – M.Crimmins, G.Kennedy, M.Healy, O.Canning, D.Hardiman, L.Hodgins, C.Moore, D.Tierney, R.Murray, J.Rabbitte, M.Kerins, K.Broderick, A.Kerins, E.Cloonan, F.Healy. Subs – B.Higgins for Hardiman, O.Fahy for Rabbitte.

Referee – P.O'Connor (Limerick)

2002

Kilkenny – J.McGarry, M.Kavanagh, N.Hickey, P.Larkin, R.Mullally, P.Barry, J.J.Delaney, A.Comerford (Capt.), D.Lyng, J.Hoyne, H.Shefflin, J.Coogan, E.Brennan, M.Comerford, D.J.Carey. Subs – C.Carter for Coogan, B.McEvoy for Hoyne, J.Power for Brennan.

Clare – D.Fitzgerald, B.Quinn, B.Lohan, F.Lohan, D.Hoey, S.McMahon, G.Quinn, J.Reddan, C.Lynch, J.O'Connor, T.Grifin, A.Markham, T.Carmody, N.Gilligan, D.Forde. Subs – O.Baker for Reddan, G.Considine for Forde, A.Quinn for Markham, C.Plunkett for Baker.

Referee – A.MacSuibhne (Dublin)

2003

Kilkenny – J.McGarry, M.Kavanagh, N.Hickey, J.Ryall, S.Dowling, P.Barry, J.J.Delaney, D.Lyng, P.Mullally, H.Shefflin, J.Hoyne, T.Walsh, D.J.Carey (Capt.), M.Comerford, E.Brennan. Subs – C.Phelan for Walsh, A.Comerford for Ryall, R.Mullally for P.Mullally, J.Coogan for Brennan.

Cork – D.Óg Cusack, W.Sherlock, D.O'Sullivan, P.Mulcahy, T.Kenny, R.Curran, Seán Óg Ó hAilpín, J.Gardiner, M.O'Connell, B.O'Connor, N.McCarthy, T.McCarthy, Setanta Ó hAilpín, J.Deane, A.Browne. Subs – J.O'Connor for O'Connell, S.McGrath for B.O'Connor.

Referee – P.O'Connor (Limerick)

2004

Cork – D.Óg Cusack, W.Sherlock, D.O'Sullivan, B.Murphy, JGardiner, R.Curran, S.Óg Ó hAilpín, T.Kenny, J.O'Connor, B.O'Connor (Capt.), N.McCarthy, T.McCarthy, K.Murphy, B.Corcoran, J.Deane. Sub – J.Browne for B.Murphy.

Kilkenny – J.McGarry, M.Kavanagh, N.Hickey, J.Ryall, T.Walsh, P.Barry, J.J.Delaney, D.Lyng, K.Coogan, H.Shefflin, J.Hoyne, D.J.Carey, J.Fitzpatrick, M.Comerford, E.Brennan. Subs – C.Phelan for Fitzpatrick, S.Dowling for Coogan.

Referee – A.MacSuibhne (Dublin).

2005

Cork – D.Óg Cusack, B.Murphy, D.O'Sullivan, P.Mulcahy, J.Gardiner, R.Curran, S.Óg Ó hAilpín (Capt.), T.Kenny, J.O'Connor, K.Murphy (Sarsfields), N.McCarthy, T.McCarthy, B.O'Connor, B.Corcoran, J.Deane. Subs – N.Ronan for K.Murphy (Sarsfields), K.Murphy (Erin's Own) for N.McCarthy.

Galway – L.Donoghue, D.Joyce, T.Óg Regan, O.Canning, D.Hardiman, S.Kavanagh, D.Collins, F.Healy, D.Tierney, R.Murray, D.Forde, A.Kerins, G.Farragher, N.Healy, D.Hayes. Subs – K.Broderick for N.Healy, K.Hayes for Forde.

Referee – S.Roche (Tipperary).

2006

Kilkenny – J.McGarry, M.Kavanagh, N.Hickey, J.Tyrrell, T.Walsh, J.Tennyson, J.Ryall, D.Lyng, J.Fitzpatrick, E.Brennan, M.Comerford, E.Larkin, R.Power, H.Shefflin, A.Fogarty. Subs – W.O'Dwyer for Larkin, R.Mullally for Lyng.

Cork – D.Óg Cusack, P.Mulcahy, D.O'Sullivan, B.Murphy, J.Gardiner, R.Curran, S.Óg Ó hAilpín, T.Kenny, J.O'Connor, T.McCarthy, N.McCarthy, N.Ronan, B.O'Connor, B.Corcoran, J.Deane. Subs – K.Murphy (Sarsfields) for Ronan, W.Sherlock for Mulcahy, C.Naughton for T.McCarthy, C.O'Connor for K.Murphy, C.Cusack for Kenny.

Referee – B.Kelly (Westmeath).

2007

Kilkenny – P.J.Ryan, M.Kavanagh, N.Hickey, J.Tyrrell, T.Walsh, B.Hogan, J.J.Delaney, D.Lyng, J.Fitzpatrick, W.O'Dwyer, M.Comerford, E.Larkin, E.Brennan, H.Shefflin, A.Fogarty. Subs – J.Tennyson for Hickey, R.Power for O'Dwyer, M.Fennelly for Shefflin.

Limerick – B.Murray, D.Reale, S.Lucey, S.Hickey, P.Lawlor, B.Geary, M.Foley, D.O'Grady, M.O'Brien, M.Fitzgerald, O.Moran, S.O'Connor, A.O'Shaughnessy, B.Begley, D.Ryan. Subs – N.Moran for M.O'Brien, J.O'Brien for O'Connor, P.Tobin for Fitzgerald, K.Tobin for Ryan, M.O'Riordan for Lawlor.

Referee – D.Kirwan (Cork).

2008

Kilkenny – P.J.Ryan, M.Kavanagh, N.Hickey, J.Tyrrell, T.Walsh, B.Hogan, J.J.Delaney, J.Fitzpatrick, D.Lyng, H.Shefflin, M.Comerford, E.Larkin, E.Brennan, R.Power, A.Fogarty. Subs – T.J.Reid for Comerford, J.McGarry for Ryan.

Waterford – C.Hennessy, A.Kearney, D.Prendergast, E.Murphy, T.Browne, K.McGrath, K.Moran, M.Walsh, J.Nagle, D.Shanahan, S.Molumphy, S.Prendergast, E.McGrath, J.Mullane, E.Kelly. Subs – S.O'Sullivan for Nagle, J.Kennedy for S.Prendergast, P.Flynn for E.McGrath, T.Feeney for D.Prendergast, D.Bennett for Shanahan.

Referee – B.Kelly (Westmeath).

2009

Kilkenny – P.J.Ryan, M.Kavanagh, J.J.Delaney, J.Tyrrell, T Walsh, B.Hogan, J.Tennyson, D.Lyng, M.Rice, E.Brennan, E.Larkin, R.Power, R.Hogan, H.Shefflin, A.Fogarty. Subs – T.J.Reid for Fogarty, M.Fennelly for Lyng, M.Comerford for R.Hogan.

Tipperary – B.Cummins, P.Stapleton, P.Maher, P.Curran, D.Fanning, C.O'Mahony, B.Maher, J.Woodlock, S.McGrath, N.McGrath, J.O'Brien, S.Callanan, P.Kerwick, E.Kelly, L.Corbett. Subs – B.Dunne for O'Brien, W.Ryan for Kerwick, M.Webster for Woodlock.

Referee – D.Kirwan (Cork).

CAPTAINS OF WINNING ALL-IRELAND SENIOR HURLING TEAMS

1887—J. Stapleton (Tipperary).
1888—No final
1889—N. O'Shea (Dublin).
1890—D. Lane (Cork).
1891—J. Mahony (Kerry).
1892—W. O'Callaghan (Cork).
1893—J. Murphy (Cork).
1894—S. Hayes (Cork).
1895—M. Maher (Tipperary).
1896—M. Maher (Tipperary).
1897—D. Grimes (Limerick).
1898—M. Maher (Tipperary).
1899—T. Condon (Tipperary).
1900—E. Hayes (Tipperary).
1901—J. Coughlan (London).
1902—J. Kelleher (Cork).
1903—S. Riordan (Cork).
1904—J. Doheny (Kilkenny).
1905—D. J. Stapletoin (Kilkenny).
1906—T. Semple (Tipperary).
1907—R. "Drug" Walsh (Kilkenny).
1908—T. Semple (Tipperary).
1909—R. "Drug" Walsh (Kilkenny).
1910—R. Doyle (Wexford).
1911—No Final
1912—S. Walton (Kilkenny).
1913—R."Drug" Walsh (Kilkenny).
1914—A. Power (Clare).
1915—J. Finlay (Laois).
1916—J. Leahy (Tipperary).
1917—J. Ryan (Dublin).
1918—W. Hough (Limerick).
1919—J. Kennedy (Cork).
1920—R. Mockler (Dublin).
1921—R. McConkey (Limerick).
1922—W. Dunphy (Kilkenny).
1923—M. Kenny (Galway).
1924—F. Wall (Dublin). Non playing captain.
1925—J. Leahy (Tipperary).
1926—S. Óg Murphy (Cork).
1927—M. Gill (Dublin).
1928—S. Óg Murphy (Cork).
1929—D. Barry-Murphy (Cork)
1930—J. J. Callanan (Tipperary).
1931—E. Coughlan (Cork).
1932—J. Walsh (Kilkenny).
1933—E. Doyle (Kilkenny).
1934—T. Ryan (Limerick).
1935—L. Meagher (Kilkenny).
1936—M. Mackey (Limerick).
1937—J. Lanigan (Tipperaryh).
1938—M. Daniels (Dublin).
1939—J. Walsh (Kilkenny).
1940—M. Mackey (Limerick)
1941—C. Buckley (Cork).
1942—J. Lynch (Cork).
1943—M. Kennefick (Cork).
1944—S. Condon (Cork).
1945—J. Maher (Tipperary).
1946—C. Ring (Cork).
1947—D. Kennedy (Kilkenny).
1948—J. Ware (Waterford).
1949—P. Stakelum (Tipperary).
1950—S. Kenny (Tipperary).
1951—J. Finn (Tipperary).
1952—P. Barry (Cork).
1953—C. Ring (Cork).
1954—C. Ring (Cork).
1955—N. O'Donnell (Wexford)
1956—J. English (Wexford).
1957—M. Kelly (Kilkenny).
1958—A. Wall (Tipperary).
1959—F. Walsh (Waterford).
1960—N. O'Donnell (Wexford).
1961—M. Hassett (Tipperary).
1962—Jimmy Doyle (Tipperary).
1963—S. Cleere (Kilkenny).
1964—M. Murphy (Tipperary).
1965—Jimmy Doyle (Tipperary).
1966—G. McCarthy (Cork).
1967—J. Treacy (Kilkenny).
1968—D. Quigley (Wexford).
1969—E. Keher (Kilkenny).
1970—P. Barry (Cork).
1971—T. O'Connor (Tipperary).
1972—N. Skehan (Kilkenny).
1973—E. Grimes (Limerick).
1974—N.Orr (Kilkenny).
1975—W. Fitzpatrick (Kilkenny).
1976—R. Cummins (Cork).
1977—M. O'Doherty (Cork).
1978—C. McCarthy (Cork).
1979—K. Fennelly (Kilkenny).
1980—Joe Connolly (Galway).
1981—P. Horan (Offaly).
1982—B. Cody (Kilkenny).
1983—L. Fennelly (Kilkenny).
1984—J. Fenton (Cork).
1985—P. Fleury (Offaly).
1986—T. Cashman (Cork).
1987—C. Hayes (Galway).
1988—C. Hayes (Galway).
1989—B. Ryan (Tipperary).
1990—T. Mulcahy (Cork).
1991—D. Carr (Tipperary).
1992—L. Fennelly (Kilkenny).
1993—E. O'Connor (Kilkenny).
1994—M. Hanamy (Offaly).
1995—A. Daly (Clare).
1996—M. Storey (Wexford).
1997—A. Daly (Clare).
1998—H. Rigney (Offaly).
1999—M. Landers (Cork).
2000—W. O'Connor (Kilkenny).
2001—T. Dunne (Tipperary).
2002—A. Comerford (Kilkenny).
2003—D. J. Carey (Kilkenny).
2004—B. O'Connor (Cork).
2005—S. Óg Ó hAilpín (Cork)
2006—J. Tyrrell (Kilkenny)
2007—H. Shefflin (Kilkenny)
2008—J. Fitzpatrick (Kilkenny)
2009—M.Fennelly (Kilkenny)

MUNSTER SENIOR HURLING FINALS

1887—Open Draw
1888—Cork/Clare (unfinished due to American "Invasion")
1889—Clare w.o. Kerry
1890—Cork 2-0, Kerry 0-1
1891—Kerry 2-4, Limerick 0-1 (replay)
Limerick 1-2, Kerry 1-1 (objection)
1892—Cork 5-3, Kerry 2-5
1893—Cork 5-3, Limerick 0-0
1894—Cork 3-4, Tipperary 1-2
1895—Tipperary 7-8, Limerick 0-2
1896—Tipperary 7-9, Cork 2-3 (replay)
Tipperary 1-3, Cork 1-3
(unfinished, replay ordered).
1897—Limerick 4-9, Cork 1-6
1898—Tipperary 1-13, Cork 1 -2 (replay)
Tipperary 3-0, Cork 2-3 (draw)
(unfinished owing to fading light)
1899—Tipperary 5-16, Clare 0-8
1900—Tipperary 6-11, Kerry 2-1
1901—Cork 3-10, Clare 2-6
1902—Cork 2-9, Limerick 1-5
1903—Cork 5-16, Waterford 1-1
1904—Cork 3-10, Tipperary 3-4
1905—Cork 7-12, Limerick 1-4
1906—Tipperary 3-4, Cork 0-9
1907—Cork 1-6, Tipperary 1-4
1908—Tipperary, w.o., Kerry, scr.
1909—Tipperary 2-10, Cork 2-6
1910—Limerick 5-1, Cork 4-2
1911—Limerick 5-3, Tipperary 4-3
1912—Cork 5-1, Tipperary 31
1913—Tipperary 8-1, Cork 5-3
1914—Clare 3-2, Cork 3-1
1915—Cork 8-2, Clare 2-1
1916—Tipperary 5-0, Cork 1-2
1917—Tipperary 6-4, Limerick 3-1 (replay)
Tipperary 3-4, Limerick 3-4 (draw)
1918—Limerick 11-3, Clare 1-2
1919—Cork 3-5, Limerick 1-6
1920—Cork 3-4, Limerick 0-5
1921—Limerick 5-2, Cork 1-2
1922—Tipperary 4-2, Limerick 1-4 (replay)
Tipperary 2-2, Limerick 2-2 (draw)
1923—Limerick 2-3, Tipperary 1-0
1924—Tipperary 3-1, Limerick 2-2
1925—Tipperary 6-6, Waterford, 1-2
1926—Cork 3-6, Tipperary 2-4 (third game)
Cork 4-1, Tipperary 3-4 (second game)
Tipperary 1-2, Cork 0-0
(first game abandoned)
1927—Cork 5-3, Clare 3-4
1928—Cork 6-4, Clare 2-2 (replay)
Cork 2-2, Clare 2-2 (draw)
1929—Cork 4-6, Waterford 2-3
1930—Tipperary 6-4, Clare 2-8
1931—Cork 5-4, Waterford 1 -2 (replay)
Cork 1-9, Waterford 4-0 (draw)
1932—Clare 5-2, Cork 4-1
1933—Limerick 3-7, Waterford 1-2
(unfinished Limerick awarded game)
1934—Limerick 4-8, Waterford 2-5
1935—Limerick 5-5, Tipperary 1 -4
1936—Limerick 8-5, Tipperary 4-6
1937—Tipperary 6-3, Limerick 4-3
1938—Waterford 3-5, Clare 2-5
1939—Cork 4-3, Limerick 3-4
1940—Limerick 3-3, Cork 2-4 (replay)
Limerick 4-3, Cork 3-6 (draw)
1941—Tipperary 5-4, Cork 2-5
(played in Oct. after All-Ireland Final)
1942—Cork 4-15, Tipperary 4-1
1943—Cork 2-13, Waterford 3-8
1944—Cork 4-6, Limerick 3-6 (replay)
Limerick 4-13, Cork 6-7 (draw)
1945—Tipperary 4-3, Limerick 2-6
1946—Cork 3-8, Limerick 1-3
1947—Cork 2-6, Limerick 2-3
1948—Waterford 4-7, Cork 3-9
1949—Tipperary 1 -16, Limerick 2-10
1950—Tipperary 2-17, Cork 3-11
1951—Tipperary 2-11, Cork 2-9
1952—Cork 1-11, Tipperary 2-6
1953—Cork 3-10, Tipperary 1-11
1954—Cork 2-8, Tipperary 1-8
1955—Limerick 2-16, Clare 2-6
1956—Cork 5-5, Limerick 3-5
1957—Waterford 1-11, Cork 1-6
1958—Tipperary 4-12, Waterford 1-5
1959—Waterford 3-9, Cork 2-9
1960—Tipperary 4-13, Cork 4-11
1961—Tipperary 3-6, Cork 0-7
1962—Tipperary 5-14, Waterford 2-3
1963—Waterford 0-11, Tipperary 0-8
1964—Tipperary 3-13, Cork 1-5
1965—Tipperary 4-11, Cork 0-5
1966—Cork 4-9, Waterford 2-9
1967—Tipperary 4-12, Clare 2-6
1968—Tipperary 2-13, Cork 1-7
1969—Cork 4-6, Tipperary 0-9
1970—Cork 3-10, Tipperary 3-8
(First 80-minute Final)
1971—Tipperary 4-16, Limerick 3-18
1972—Cork 6-18, Clare 2-8
1973—Limerick 6-7, Tipperary 2-18
1974—Limerick 6-14, Clare 3-9
1975—Cork 3-14, Limerick 0-12
(70-minute Final introduced)
1976—Cork 3-15, Limerick 4-5
1977—Cork 4-15, Clare 4-10
1978—Cork 0-13, Clare 0-11
1979—Cork 2-14, Limerick 0-9
1980—Limerick 2-14, Cork 2-10
1981—Limerick 3-12, Clare 2-9
1982—Cork 5-31, Waterford 3-6
1983—Cork 3-22, Waterford 0-12
1984—Cork 4-15, Tipperary 3-14
1985—Cork 4-17, Tipperary 4-11
1986—Cork 2-18, Clare 3-12
1987—Tipperary 1-18, Cork 1-18 (draw)
Tipperary 4-22, Cork 1-22
(after extra time) (replay)

1988—Tipperary 2-19, Cork 1-13
1989—Tipperary 0-26, Waterford 2-8
1990—Cork 4-16, Tipperary 2-14
1991—Tipperary 2-16, Cork 4-10 (draw)
Tipperary 4-19, Cork 4-15 (replay)
1992—Cork 1-22, Limerick 3-11
1993—Tipperary 3-27, Clare 2-12
1994—Limerick 0-25, Clare 2-10
1995—Clare 1-17, Limerick 0-11
1996—Limerick 0-19, Tipperary 1-16 (draw)
Limerick 4-7, Tipperary 0-16 (replay)
1997—Clare 1-18, Tipperary 0-18
1998—Clare 1-16, Waterford 3-10 (draw)
Clare 2-16, Waterford 0-10
1999—Cork 1-15, Clare 0-14
2000—Cork 0-23, Tipperary 3-12.
2001—Tipperary 2-16, Limerick 1-17.
2002—Waterford 2-23, Tipperary 3-12.
2003—Cork 3-16, Waterford 3-12.
2004—Waterford 3-16, Cork 1-21.
2005—Cork 1-21, Tipperary 1-16.
2006—Cork 2-14, Tipperary 1-14.
2007—Waterford 3-17, Limerick 1-14.
2008—Tipperary 2-21, Clare 0-19.
2009—Tipperary 4-14, Waterford 2-16.

LEINSTER SENIOR HURLING FINALS

1887—Open Draw
1888—Kilkenny 0-7, Dublin 0-3
1889—Dublin w o from Laois
(Louth only other county to compete)
1890—Wexford 2-9, Laois 0-3
1891—Wexford w.o. from Laois
1892—Dublin unopposed
1893—Kilkenny w.o. from Dublin
1894—Dublin unopposed
1895—Kilkenny 1-5, Dublin 0-5
1896—Dublin 4-6, Kilkenny 0-0 (replay)
Dublin 1-8, Kilkenny 0-6
(replay ordered, objection)
1897—Kilkenny w.o. from Wexford
1898—Kilkenny 4-12, Dublin 3-2
1899—Wexford 2-12, Dublin 1-4
1900—Kilkenny 4-11, Dublin 4-10
1901—Wexford 7-6, Offaly 1-3
1902—Dublin 0-8, Kilkenny 1-4
1903—Kilkenny 1-5, Dublin 1-5
(Kilkenny awarded title; Dublin
goal disputed)
1904—Kilkenny 2-8, Dublin 2-6
1905—Kilkenny 2-8, Dublin 2-2
1906—Dublin 1-14, Kilkenny 0-5
1907—Kilkenny 4-14, Dublin 1-9
1908—Dublin w.o. Kilkenny (scratched)
1909—Kilkenny 5-16, Laois 2-7
1910—Wexforcl 3-3, Dublin 1-1
1911—Kilkenny 4-6, Dublin 3-1
1912—Kilkenny 6-6, Laois 2-4
1913—Kilkenny 7-5, Dublin 2-1 (replay)
Kilkenny 0-3, Dublin 1-0 [draw)
1914—Laois 3-2, Kilkenny 2-4
1915—Laois 3-2, Dublin 0-5
1916—Kilkenny 11-3, Wexforcl 2-2
1917—Dublin 5-1, Kilkenny 4-0
1918—Wexford 2-3, Dublin 1-2
1919—Dublin 1-5, Kilkenny 1-2
1920—Dublin 4-5, Kilkenny 2-2
1921—Dublin 4-4, Kilkenny 1-5
1922—Kilkenny 3-4, Dublin 1-2
1923—Kilkenny 4-1, Dublin 1-1
1924—Dublin 4-4, Offaly 3-1
1925—Kilkenny awarded title on objection
(Dublin "won" at Croke Park 6-4 to 4-7)
1926—Kilkenny 3-8, Offaly 1-4
1927—Dublin 7-7, Kilkenny 4-6
1928—Dublin 9-7, Offaly 4-3
1929—Declared void (both teams
disqualified for being late on
field after Kilkenny had beaten Dublin
by 3-5 to 2-6 in the final)
1930—Dublin 4-7, Laois 2-2
1931—Kilkenny 4-7, Laois 4-2
1932—Kilkenny 4-6, Dublin 3-5
1933—Kilkenny 7-5, Dublin 5-5
1934—Dublin 3-5, Kilkenny 2-2 (replay)
Dublin 2-8, Kilkenny 4-2 (draw)
1935—Kilkenny 3-8, Laois 0-6
1936—Kilkenny 4-6, Laois 2-5
1937—Kilkenny 5-3, Westmeath 2-4
1938—Dublin 4-9, Kilkenny 3-5 (replay)
Dublin 2-3, Kilkenny 2-3 (draw)
1939—Kilkenny 2-12, Dublin 4-3
1940—Kilkenny 3-6, Dublin 2-5
1941—Dublin 2-8, Kilkenny 1-8
1942—Dublin 4-8, Kilkenny 1-4
1943—Kilkenny 3-9, Dublin 2-6
1944—Dublin 4-7, Wexford 3-3
1945—Kilkenny 5-12, Dublin 3-4
1946—Kilkenny 3-8, Dublin 1-12
1947—Kilkenny 7-10, Dublin 3-6
1948—Dublin 5-9, Laois 3-3
1949—Laois 3-8, Kilkenny 3-6
1950—Kilkenny 3-11, Wexford 2-11
1951—Wexford 3-12, Laois 4-3
1952—Dublin 7-2, Wexford 3-6
1953—Kilkenny 1-13, Wexford 3-5
1954—Wexford 8-5, Dublin 1-4
1955—Wexford 5-6, Kilkenny 3-9 (replay)
Wexford 2-7, Kilkenny 2-7 (draw)
1956—Wexford 4-8, Kilkenny 3-10
1957—Kilkenny 6-9, Wexford 1-5
1958—Kilkenny 5-12, Wexford 4-9
1959—Kilkenny 2-9, Dublin 1-11
1960—Wexford 3-10, Kilkenny 2-11
1961—Dublin 7-5, Wexford 4-8
1962—Wexford 3-9, Kilkenny 2-10
1963—Kilkenny 2-10, Dublin 0-9
1964—Kilkenny 4-11, Dublin 1-8
1965—Wexford 2-11, Kilkenny 3-7
1966—Kilkenny l-15, wexford 2-6

1967—Kilkenny 4-10,Wexford 1-12
1968—Wexford 3-13, Kilkenny 4-9
1969—Kilkenny 3-9, Offoly 0- 16
1970—Wexford 4-16, Kilkenny 3-14
(First 80-minute final)
1971—Kilkenny 6-16, Wexford 3- 16
1972—Kilkenny 3-16, Wexford 1-14 (replay)
Kilkenny 6-13, Wexford 6-13 (draw)
1973—Kilkenny 4-22, Wexford 3-15
1974—Kilkenny 6-13, Wexford 2-24
1975—Kilkenny 2-20, Wexford 2-14
(70-minute final introduced)
1976—Wexford 2-20, Kilkenny 1-6
1977—Wexford 3-17, Kilkenny 3-14
1978—Kilkenny 2-16, Wexford 1-16
1979—Kilkenny 2-21, Wexford 2-17
1980—Offaly 3-17, Kilkenny 5-10
1981—Offaly 3-12, Wexford 2-13
1982—Kilkenny 1-11, Offaly 0-12
1983—Kilkenny 1-17, Offaly 0-13
1984—Offaly 1-15, Wexford 2-11
1985—Offaly 5-15, Laois 0-17
1986—Kilkenny 4-10, Offaly 1-11
1987—Kilkenny 2-14, Offaly 0-17
1988—Offaly 3-12, Wexford 1-14
1989—Offaly 3-15, Kilkenny 4-9
1990—Offaly 1-19, Dublin 2-11
1991—Kilkenny 1-13, Dublin 1-11
1992—Kilkenny 3-16, Wexford 2-9
1993—Kilkenny 2-12, Wexford 0-11 (replay)
Kilkenny 2-14, Wexford 1-17 (draw)
1994—Offaly 1-18, Wexford 0-14
1995—Offaly 2-16, Kilkenny 2-5
1996—Wexford 2-23, Offaly 2-15
1997—Wexford 2-14, Kilkenny 1-11
1998—Kilkenny 3-10, Offaly 1-11
1999—Kilkenny 5-14, Offaly 1-16
2000—Kilkenny 2-21, Offaly 1-13.
2001—Kilkenny 2-19, Wexford 0-12.
2002—Kilkenny 0-19, Wexford 0-17.
2003—Kilkenny 2-23, Wexford 2-12.
2004—Wexford 2-12, Offaly 1-11.
2005—Kilkenny 0-22, Wexford 1-16.
2006—Kilkenny 1-23, Wexford 2-12.
2007—Kilkenny 2-24, Wexford 1-12.
2008—Kilkenny 5-21, Wexford 0-17.
2009—Kilkenny 2-18, Dublin 0-18.

ULSTER SENIOR HURLING FINALS

1900—Antrim unopposed
1901—Antrim bt. Derry by 41 pts. to 12.
(Exact score not given.)
1902—Derry 2-7, Antrim 2-5
1903—Antrim 2-4, Donegal 0-5
1904—Antrim
1905—No record
1906—Donegal 5-21, Antrim 0-1
1907—Antrim 4-17, Derry 1 -6
1908—Derry 2-8, Cavan 0-2
1909—Antrim beat Monaghan
1910—Antrim beat Donegal
1911—Antrim w.o. Monaghan scr.
1912—Antrim beat Monaghan
1913—Antrim 3-3, Monaghan 0-0
1914—Monaghan 2-0, Antrim 2-0 (draw)
Monaghan 4-3, Antrim 1-0 (replay)
1915—Monaghan 1-5, Antrim 1-2
1916—Antrim 3-1, Monaghan 1-1
1917-22—Abandoned
1923—Donegal 7-1, Antrim 3-0
1924—Antrim 5-3, Donegal 4-0
1925—Antrim 5-4, Donegal 4-5
1926—Antrim 4-3, Cavan 3-1
1927—Antrim 5-4, Cavan 3-3
1928—Antrim 4-5, Cavan 1-1
1929—Antrim declared champions.
Donegal disqualified
1930—Antrim 10-4, Down 2-0
1931—Antrim 4- 10, Derry 0-1
1932—Donegal 5-4, Antrim 4-5
1933—Antrim 1-7, Donegal 2-1
1934—Antrim 3-4, Donegal 2-2
1935—Antrim 7-9, Donegal 0-3
1936—Antrim 2-10, Cavan 3-2
1937—Antrim 6-7, Donegal 3-2
1938—Antrim 3-5, Donegal 2-2
1939—Antrim 9-8, Down 4-2
1940—Antrim 4-4, Down 1 -3
1941—Down 5-3, Antrim 2-5
1942—Abandoned
1943—Antrim 6-8, Down 2-0
1944—Antrim 5-7, Monaghan 6-4 (draw)
Antrim 7-3, Monaghan 0-1 (replay)
1945—Antrim 8-2, Donegal 2-4
1946—Antrim 6-3, Armagh 2-1
1947-49—Antrim unopposed
1950-88—No final
1989—Antrim 2-16, Down 0-9
1990—Antrim 4-11, Down 2-11
1991—Antrim 3-14, Down 3-10
1992—Down 2- 16, Antrim 0-11
1993—Antrim 0-24, Down 0-11
1994—Antrim 1-19, Down 1-13
1995—Down 3-7, Antrim 1-13 (draw)
Down 1-19, Antrim 2-10 (replay)
1996—Antrim 1-20, Down 2-12
1997—Down 3-14, Antrim 0-19
1998—Antrim 1-19, Derry 2-13
1999—Antrim 2-19, Derry 1-9
2000—Derry 4-8, Antrim 0-19.
2001—Derry 1-17, Down 3-10.
2002—Antrim 3-16, Down 1-18.
2003—Antrim 3-21, Derry 1-12.
2004—Antrim 1-15, Down 1-15.
Antrim 3-14, Down 0-18. (replay)
2005—Antrim 2-22, Down 1-18.
2006—Antrim 2-20, New York 1-14.
2007—Antrim 2-24, Down 0-4.
2008—Antrim 3-18, Down 2-16.
2009—Antrim 3-20, Down 4-15.

CONNACHT SENIOR HURLING FINALS

1897-98—Galway unopposed
1900—Galway 4-2, Sligo 1-2
1901—Galway 4-10, Roscommon 2-0
1902—Galway 0-5, Roscommon 0-3
1903—Galway bt Roscommon
1904—Galway 2-4, Roscommon 0-2
1905—Galway 3-15, Mayo 1-0
1906—Galway w o. Sligo scr.
1907—Galway 3-5, Roscommon 1-2
1908—Galway bt Roscommon
1909—Mayo 10-1, Galway 4-1
1910—Galway 5-3, Roscommon 1-3
1911—Galway 4-2, Roscommon 1-0
1912—Galway 4-2, Roscommon 3-3
1913—Roscommon w.o. Mayo scr. (Roscommon beat Galway 3-4 to 3-2 in semi-final)
1914—Galway 5-1, Roscommon 2-1
1915—Galway unopposed
1916—Galway 2-3, Roscommon 3-0 (No record of replay but Galway figured in All-Ireland series)
1917—Galway 1-4, Roscommon 1-0
1918—1921—Galway unopposed
1922—Galway 12-8, Roscommon 1-0
1923—1958—Galway unopposed
1959-1969—Galway played in Munster
1979-1994—Galway unopposed
1995—Galway 2-21, Roscommon 2-12
1996—Galway 3-19 Roscommon 2-10
1997—Galway 6-24, Roscommon 0-5
1998—Galway 2-27, Roscommon 3-13
1999—Galway 4-26, Roscommon 2-8

CHRISTY RING CUP

2005—Westmeath 1-23, Down 2-18.
2006—Antrim 5-13, Carlow 1-7.
2007—Westmeath 2-15, Kildare 0-13.
2008—Carlow 3-22, Westmeath 4-16. (aet)
2009—Carlow 1-15, Down 0-14.

CHRISTY RING CUP FINALISTS

2005

Westmeath – M.Briody, M.Williams, C.Murtagh, C.Jordan, B.Murtagh, D.McCormack, B.Connaughton, R.Whelan, E.Loughlin, G.Gavin, J.Shaw, A.Mitchell, B.Kennedy, K.Cosgrove, J.Clarke. Subs – D.Curley for Connaughton, P.Greville for Williams.

Down – Graham Clarke, L.Clarke, S.Murray, C.Coulter, Gabriel Clarke, G.Savage, S.Wilson, G.Adair, A.Savage, E.Clarke, P.Braniff, B.McGourty, M.Coulter, G.Johnson, S.Clarke.

2006

Antrim – D.Quinn, B.McAuley, J.McKeague, J.Campbell, M.Molloy, K.McKeegan, C.Herron, C.Cunning, M.Scullion, J.Scullion, K.Kelly, M.Dallas, J.McIntosh, P.Richmond, B.McFall. Subs – D.McKillop for Scullion, P.McGill for Cunning, B.Delargy for Scullion, J.McKernan for Campbell.

Carlow – F.Foley, E.Nolan, T.Doyle, A.Gaule, E.Coady, S.Kavanagh, L.Kenny, C.Hughes, D.Roberts, P.Coady, D.Murphy, A.Brennan, P.Kehoe, R.Foley, S.McMahon. Subs – D.Shaw for Kenny, M.Keating for Brennan, S.McMahon for Kehoe, J.Waters for Hughes.

2007

Westmeath – M.Briody, N.Gavin, P.Greville, C.Jordan, P.Dowdall, D.McCormack, B.Connaughton, J.Shaw, P.Clarke, R.Whelan, B.Murtagh, A.Mitchell, B.Kennedy, D.McNicholas, D.Carty. Subs – E.Loughlin for Whelan, A.Price for Gavin, J.Clarke for P.Clarke, B.Smyth for Murtagh.

Kildare – C.Cunningham, T.Finnerty, P.Reidy, R.Tynan, D.Harney, D.Kennedy, M.Moloney, C.Buggy, B.White, K.Divilly, T.Spain, P.O'Brien, B.Byrne, A.McAndrew, O.Lynch. Subs – J.Doran for Tynan, B.Coulston for Byrne, M.Dowd for Spain, D.Nolan for O'Brien, R.Hoban for Moloney.

2008

Carlow – D.Miley, A.Gaule, D.Shaw, J.Rodgers, E.Coady, S.Kavanagh, R.Coady, D.Roberts, A.Brennan, R.Dunbarr, C.Hughes, M.Brennan, J.Coady, R.Foley, C.Doyle. Subs – J.Hickey for A.Brennan, K.English for Dunbarr, D.Murphy for Foley, B.Lawler for J.Coady, S.Murphy for Roberts, J.Doran for R.Coady, R.Foley for Hughes, R.Dunbarr for Murphy.

Westmeath – M.Briody, G.Gavin, P.Greville, A.Price, B.Connaughton, D.McCormack, P.Dowdall, L.Smyth, P.Clarke, A.Mitchell, B.Murtagh, E.Price, R.Jackson, D.McNicholas, J.Shaw. Subs – B.Smyth for Jackson, C.Jordan for Greville, N.Gavin for G.Gavin, P.Gilsenan for Jordan, P.Greville for Mitchell, C.Flanagan for L.Smyth.

2009

Carlow – F.Foley, W.Hickey, S.Kavanagh, D.Shaw, E.Coady, J.Rodgers, D.Byrne, J.Hickey, D.Roberts, R.Dunbar, M.Brennan, C.Doyle, A Gaule, R.Foley, P.Kehoe. Subs – E.Byrne for Dunbar, J.Coady for Kehoe.

Down – G.Clarke, F.Conway, S.Murray, S.Ennis, R.McGratton, K.Courtney, M.Ennis, A.Savage, C.Woods, C.O'Prey, P.Braniff, S.Wilson, J.Coyle, G.Johnston, O.Clarke. Subs – A.Higgins for Clarke, M.Coulter for Coyle.

CAPTAINS OF WINNING CHRISTY RING CUP TEAMS

2005 – J.Shaw (Westmeath)
2006 – K.McKeegan (Antrim)
2007 – D.McCormack (Westmeath)
2008 – E.Coady (Carlow)
2009 – M.Brennan (Carlow)

CHRISTY RING CUP FINAL REFEREES

2005 – D. Richardson (Limerick)
2006 – J.McGrath (Westmeath)
2007 – J.Sexton (Cork)
2008 – N.Cosgrove (Tipperary)
2009 – T.Ryan (Tipperary)

NICKY RACKARD CUP

2005 – London 5-8, Louth 1-5.
2006 – Derry 5-15, Donegal 1-11.
2007 – Roscommon 1-12, Armagh 0-13.
2008 – Sligo 3-19, Louth 3-10.
2009 – Meath 2-18, London 1-15.

NICKY RACKARD CUP FINALISTS

2005

London – J.J.Burke, E.Phelan, T.Simms, B.Forde, J.Dillon, F.McMahon, B.Foley, M.Harding, M.O'Meara, D.Smyth, J.Ryan, J.McGaughan, D.Bourke, B.Shorthall, K.McMullan. Subs – G.Fenton for O'Meara, E.Kinlon for Smyth, S.Quinn for Shorthall, P.Doyle for Phelan, P.Finnegan for McMullan.

Louth – S.Smith, D.Black, A.Carter, S.Darcy, D.Mulholland, P.Dunne, R.Byrne, D.McCarthy, S.Callan, T.Hilliard, J.Carter, D.Byrne, G.Smith, D.Dunne, N.McEneaney. Subs – S.Conroy for Black, G.Collins for R.Byrne, S.Byrne for J.Carter, A.Mynes for McEneaney, N.Byrne for Darcy.

2006

Derry – K.Stevenson, S.McCullagh, M.Conway, E.McKeever, C.Brunton, L.Hinphey, P.Sweeney, R.Kennedy, P.O'Kane, R.Convery, G.Biggs, D.McGrellis, S.McBride, K.Hinphey, J.O'Dwyer. Subs – R.McCloskey for Sweeney, P.Hearty for O'Dwyer, A.Rafferty for L.Hinphey, C.Quinn for Biggs, Biggs for McGrellis.

Donegal – G.Grindle, M.McGrath, C.Dowds, J.Callaghan, J.Donnelly, A.Begley, J.McGee, M.McCann, E.Organ, K.Campbell, C.Breathnach, A.McDaid, D.Cullen, G.Dwyer, N.Campbell. Subs – C.McLaughlin for Callaghan, P.Tooher for Dwyer, J.Dolan for McDaid.

2007

Roscommon – D.Connell, N.Cunniffe, C.Moran, M.Keaveney, A.Cunniffe, M.Kelly, L.Murray, M.Connaughton, T.Lennon, J.Moran, Gerry Fallon, T.Reddington, Cathal Kelly, Colm Kelly, S.Sweeney. Subs – Gary Fallon for Reddington, B.Kelly for Gerry Fallon.

Armagh – J.Burke, T.McCann, E.McDonnell, P.Kirk, P.McArdle, P.McCormack, B.McCormack, B.McCann, C.Christie, R.Gaffney, C.McCann, G.Enright, D.Coulter, C.McAlinden, F.Bradley. Subs – C.Carville for C.McCann, K.McCreevy for Enright.

2008

Sligo – C.Brennan, F.Coyne, W.Gill, R.Cox, D.Clarke, M.Burke, L.Reidy, J.Mullins, D.Colleary, M.Gilmartin, D.Burke, P.Seevers, L.Cadden, K.Raymond, J.Bannerton. Subs – C.Herity for Cadden, M.Shelley for Bannerton, C.O'Mahony for Gilmartin.

Louth – S.Smith, C.Kerrigan, T.Teefy, B.Hassett, D.Callan, A.Carter, J.Carter, T.Hilliard, S.Kerrigan, S.Fennell, R.Byrne, G.Smith, S.Conroy, S.Callan, D.Murphy. Subs – M.Kirwan for Teefy, D.Dunne for Smith, E.McCarthy for Kerrigan, C.Connolly for Fennell, P.Dunne for Conroy.

2009

Meath – S.Quinn, C.Burke, E.Fitzgerald, M.Foley, M.Horan, P.Fagan, D.Kirby, J.Boyle, P.Garvey, P.Durnin, N.Hackett, M.Cole, J.Keena, N.Horan, K.Fagan. Subs – G.O'Neill for Cole, R.Masse for Durnin.

London – P.Gannon, S.Fox, C.Burke, E.Phelan, K.Forde, N.Healy, K.Kennedy, K.Downes, F.McMahon, M.Mythen, C.O'Dwyer, T.Twomey, H.Vaughan, M.Finn, K.McMullan. Subs – E.Morrisey for Forde, F.Tierney for Twomey, N.Coady for McMahon.

CAPTAINS OF WINNING NICKY RACKARD CUP TEAMS

2005 – F.McMahon (London)
2006 – M.Conway (Derry)
2007 – M.Connaughton (Roscommon)
2008 – D.Burke (Sligo)
2009 – N.Hackett (Meath)

NICKY RACKARD CUP FINAL REFEREES

2005 – T.Mahon (Fermanagh)
2006 – D.Connolly (Kilkenny)
2007 – J.Kelly (Wexford)
2008 – S.Whelan (Wexford)
2009 – O.Elliott (Antrim)

LORY MEAGHER CUP FINALS

2009 – Tyrone 5-11, Donegal 3-16.

LORY MEAGHER CUP FINALISTS

2009

Tyrone – D.McCabe, S.P.Begley, D.Maguire, M.Kelly, T.McIntosh, S.Donnelly, C.Gallagher, J.Kelly, T.Hughes, D.Lavery, P.O'Connor, S.McKiver, C.Grogan, R.O'Neill, G.Fox. Subs – P.McMahon for Fox, A.Kelly for O'Connor.

Donegal – R.Scanlon, M.McGrath, J.Boyle, W.Scanlon, J.Donnelly, C.Breathnach, C.McLaughlin, D.Cullen, S.Boyle, C.Matthewson, S.McVeigh, K.Campbell, L.Henderson, G.O'Dwyer, N.Campbell. Subs – M.McCann for O'Dwyer, P.Hannigan for Matthewson, M.McGee for McVeigh.

CAPTAINS OF WINNING LORY MEAGHER CUP TEAMS

2009 – S.Donnelly (Tyrone)

LORY MEAGHER CUP FINAL REFEREES

2009 – T.Carroll (Offaly)

ALL-IRELAND MINOR HURLING FINALS

1928—Cork 7-6, Dublin 4-0 (replay)
Cork 1-8, Dublin 3-2 (draw)
1929—Waterford 5-0, Meath 1-1
1930—Tipperary 4-1, Kilkenny 2-1
1931—Kilkenny 4-7 Galway 2-3
1932—Tipperary 8-6, Kilkenny 5-1
1933—Tipperary 4-6, Galway 2-3
1934—Tipperary 4-3, Laois 3-5
1935—Kilkenny 4-2, Tipperary 3-3
1936—Kilkenny 2-4, Cork 2-3
1937—Cork 8-5, Kilkenny 2-7
1938—Cork 7-2, Dublin 5-4
1939—Cork 5-2, Kilkenny 2-2
1940—Limerick 6-4, Antrim 2-4
1941—Cork 3-11, Galway 1-1
1942—Suspended
1943—Suspended
1944—Suspended
1945—Dublin 3-14, Tipperary 4-6
1946—Dublin 1-6, Tipperary 0-7
1947—Tipperary 9-5, Galway 1 -5
1948—Waterford 3-8, Kilkenny 4-2
1949—Tipperary 6-5, Kilkenny 2-4
1950—Kilkenny 3-4, Tipperary 1-5
1951—Cork 4-5, Galway 1-8
1952—Tipperary 9-9, Dublin 2-3
1953—Tipperary 8-6 Dublin 3-6
1954—Dublin 2-7, Tipperary 2-3
1955—Tipperary 5-15, Galway 2-5
1956—Tipperary 4-16, Kilkenny 1-5
1957—Tipperary 4-7, Kilkenny 3-7
1958—Limerick 5-8, Galway 3-10
1959—Tipperary 2-8, Kilkenny 2-7
1960—Kilkenny 7-12, Tipperary 1-11
1961—Kilkenny 3-13, Tipperary 0-15
1962—Kilkenny 3-6, Tipperary 0-9
1963—Wexford 6-12, Limerick 5-9
1964—Cork 10-7, Laois 1 -4
1965—Dublin 4-10, Limerick 2-7
1966—Wexford 4-1, Cork 1-8 (replay)
Wexford 6-7, Cork 6-7 (draw)
1967—Cork 2-15, Wexford 5-3
1968—Wexford 2-13, Cork 3-7
1969—Cork 2-15, Kilkenny 3-6
1970—Cork 5- 19, Galway 2-9
1 971—Cork 2-11, Kilkenny 1 -11
1972—Kilkenny 8-7 Cork 3-9
1973—Kilkenny 4-5, Galway 3-7
1974—Cork 1-10, Kilkenny 1-8
1975—Kilkenny 3-19, Cork 1-14
1976—Tipperary 2 20, Kilkenny 1-7
1977—Kilkenny 1-8, Cork 0-9 (replay)
Kilkenny 4-8 Cork 3-11 (draw)
1978—Cork 1-15, Kilkenny 1-8
1979—Cork 2-11, Kilkenny 1-9
1980—Tipperary 2- 15, Wexford 1-10
1981—Kilkenny 1 -20, Galway 3-9
1982—Tipperary 2-7, Galway 0-4
1983—Galway 0-10, Dublin 0-7
1984—Limerick 1-14, Kilkenny 3-8 (draw)
Limerick 2-5, Kilkenny 2-4 (replay)
1985—Cork 3-10, Wexford 0-12
1986—Offaly 3-12, Cork 3-9
1987—Offaly 2-8, Tipperary 0-12
1988—Kilkenny 3-13, Cork 0-12
1989—Offaly 2-16, Clare 1-12
1990—Kilkenny 3-14, Cork 3-14 (draw)
Kilkenny 3-16, Cork 0-11 (replay)
1991—Kilkenny 0-15, Tipperary 1-10
1992—Galway 1-13, Waterford 2-4
1993—Kilkenny 1-17, Galway 1-12
1994—Galway 2-10 Cork 1-11
1995—Cork 2-10, Kilkenny 1-2
1996—Tipperary 0-20, Galway 3-11 (draw)
Tipperary 2- 14, Galway 2-12 (replay)
1997—Clare 1-11, Galway 1-9
1998—Cork 2-15, Kilkenny 1-9
1999—Galway 0-3, Tipperary 0-10
2000—Galway 2-19, Cork 4-10
2001—Cork 2-10, Galway 1-8
2002—Kilkenny 3-15, Tipperary 1-7
2003—Kilkenny 2-16, Galway 2-15
2004—Galway 3-12, Kilkenny 1-18 (draw)
Galway 0-16, Kilkenny 1-12. (replay)

2005—Galway 3-12, Limerick 0-17
2006—Tipperary 2-18, Galway 2-7.
2007—Tipperary 3-14, Cork 2-11.
2008—Kilkenny 3-6, Galway 0-13.
2009—Galway 2-15, Kilkenny 2-11.

ALL-IRELAND MINOR HURLING FINAL TEAMS

1928

Cork—L. Horgan, J. Glavin, F. Cronin, D. Coughlan, C. Sheehan, J. Lee, Der Cogan, C. Murphy, Dan Lynch Denis Lynch, M. Lewis, M. Moloney, M. Finn, G. O'Connor, J. Ryng.

Note: C. Duggan, J. Mannix, J. Healy, J. O'Connor played in drawn game. Dan Lynch, Denis Lynch, J. Ryng and C. Murphy were on for replay.

Dublin—M. Gleeson, J. Lloyd, G. Hughes, M. Kinsella, B. Reynolds, P. Melinn, R. Kavanagh, W. Kells, J. Hannon, M. Collins, G. O'Toole, F. Whelan, P. McHenry, P. Carton, K. O'Toole.

Note: Same team played in drawn game.

1929

Waterford—P. Rellis, F. Pinkert, L. Byrne, D. Wyse, P. Ryan, P. Donnelly (capt.), J. Butler, N. Noonan, J. Dwyer, N. Fardy, P. Sheehan, D. Goode, J. Goode, F. Houlihan, J. Murphy.

Meath—S. O Dalaigh, M. Trabbers, S. O'Gibne, P. O Lionaird, P. O'Fearghaill, P. MacOireachtaig, P. Donnellain, P. Plunceed, T. Ceinnide, S. Morain, R. MacNamee, S. Gearoid, G. O'Dare, N. de Bernett, P. Briain.

1930

Tipperary—E. Maher, J. Russell (capt.), Jack Coffey, W. O'Neill, L. Burke, G. Heavey, J. Lanigan, Jimmy Coffey, J. Dunne, J. Semple, E. Wade, P. Ryan, J. Close, T. Harney, J. Quinlan.

Kilkenny—A. Cullen, M. Tyrrell, J. Buggy, W. Burke, T Deneiffe, Milo Kennedy (capt.), W. Ayres, J. Morrissey, J. Shortall, F. Minogue, P. Kelly, M. Byrne, J. Maher, M. Shortall, P. Leahy.

1931

Kilkenny—M. Doyle, D. Hughes, A. Cullen, M. Tyrrell T. Shortall, M. Brennan, J. Murphy, J. Phelan, P. Kelly, J. Shortall (capt.), J. Dwyer, C. Barry, W. Walsh, W. Ayres, P. Shortall.

Galway—P. Comer, M. TuoLy, M. Kelly, M. Loughnane, R. Brogan, M. Donnellan, M. Lane, J. Moore, J. Barrett, J. Killilea, J. J. Darcy, A. Strong, P. J. Walsh, M. Hanniffy (capt.), A. Burke. Sub: J. Kinlen.

1932

Tipperary—T. O'Keeffe, J. Looby, J. O'Dwyer, M. Burke, P. Leahy, C. Downes, J. Cooney, P. Bowe, Ned Barry, P. Purcell, T. Burke, J. Fletcher, D. Gorman (capt.), W. Nolan, J. Maher.

Kilkenny—M. Doyle, W. Wyse, J. McCarthy, J. Dunne, J. Fielding, M. Frisby, R. Teehan, E. Langton, M. Gargan, E. O'Gorman, E. Shortall, D. Roche, M. Foley, P. Larkin, W. Guilfoyle.

1933

Tipperary—J. Moloney, J. Mooney, T. Doyle, Mutt Ryan, M. Condon, M. Everard, P. Duggan, P. Dwyer, Tony Brennan, P. Frazer, M. Burke, J. Farrell, P Callaghan, Tim Maher, Joe Fletcher (capt.)

Galway—J. Keller, M. Loughnane, P. Brogan, F Brogan, T. Molloy, M. Hennessy, T. Coughlan, M. Donnellan, P. J. Walshe, P. Fahy, T B. Murphy, C. Murphy, F. Lahiffe, J. Cox, B. Noone.

1934

Tipperary—C. Maher (capt.), T. Lanigan, J. Noonan, J. Mooney, J. Moloney, Jerry Coffey, Denis Ryan, Tom English, J. Moloney, Tony Brennan, P. Callaghan, Martin Loughnane, M. Mockler, Tom Cawley, P O'Dwyer.

Laois—J. McCabe, P. O'Connor, W. Brophy, W. O'Neill, A. Bergin, J. Ring, F Moloney, P. Rustchitzko, J. Kelly, T. Carroll, J. Hyland, M. Cahill, W. Delaney, P. Farrell, P. Carroll (capt.) Subs: J. Conroy and F. Matthews.

1935

Kilkenny—Tom Delaney, R. Hinks, P. Grace, (capt.), W. Holohan, P. Boyle, P. Walsh, M. McEvoy, T. Leahy, J. Cahill, E. Tallent, R. Brannigan, J. Langton, J. Mulcahy, T. Prendergast, S. O'Brien. Sub: P. Long.

Tipperary—P Morris, P O'Neill, C. Maher (capt.), T. Walsh, R. Ryan, J. O'Dwyer, T. Leahy, W. Brussels, J. Hennessy, P. Kearns, D. Ryan, M. Loughnane, T. Lanigan, P. Leaby, John Coffey.

1936

Kilkenny—T. Delaney, R. Hinks, P. Kavanagh, E. Fitzpatrick, N. Hyland, J. O'Neill, T. Waldron, R. Brannigan, P. Giles, J. Langton, T. Mahon, E. Tallent (capt.), J. Mulcahy, M. Grace, S. O'Brien.

Cork—M. O'Donovan, M. Healy, R. Murphy, D. Coughlan, M. Goggin, C. Atkinson, P. O'Callaghan, M. Prenderville, P. J. O'Riordan, C. McSweeney, W. Campbell, M. Cahill, R. Dineen, W. Buckley, D. McCarthy.

1937

Cork—D. Coughlan, R. Murphy, R. Dineen, D. O'Sullivan, A. Slattery, J. O'Shea, D. Lynch, J. Burrows, M. Goggin (capt.), M. Warner, D. Hackett, J. P. Creedon, J. O'Mahony, K. McMahon, M. Emphy.

Kilkenny—E. Brett, P. Kavanagh, E. O'Connor, N. Dollard, J. O'Neill, T. Waldron, P. Hennessy, P. Savage, M. Heffernan, P. Burke, J. Dwyer, T. Larkin, T. Murphy, P. Fahy, S. O'Brien.

1938

Cork—P. J. Quinn, J. O'Mahony, A. Lotty, G. Sadlier, C. Ring, P. Hogan, W. Cummins, E. Young, J. Looney, K. O'Keeffe, T. Foley, Luke O'Sullivan, T. Ryan, K. McGrath (capt.), Ted O'Sullivan.

Dublin—C. McCarthy, P Collins, E. Dunphy (capt.), C. Nicholson, M. Hickey, F Flynn, F. Fagan, P. Rafferty, D. Keane, G. Glenn, E. Walsh, M. Keane, R. Molumby, C. Jenkinson, J. Bradley.

1939

Cork—T. McGrath, W. Cummins, D. O'Driscoll, W. Holton P. Hayes, G. Sadlier, S. Murphy, E. Young, T. Crowley, M. Cody, T. Barry (capt.), J. White, P Keohane, D. Cahalane, K. McGrath. Subs: D. Keating for J. White.

Kilkenny—A. Roberts, E. Quinlan, R. Dowling, P. O'Brien, J. Murphy, K. Grogan, M. Holden, P. O'Neill (capt.), J. Walsh, A. Murray, M. Andrews, K. Ruth, M. Walsh, S. Downey, S. Kelly.

1940

Limerick—P. Healy, K. O'Donoghue, J. Crotty, P. Murphy, M. Culhane, T. Hogan, T. Cregan, M. Fenton, P. McCarthy (Newcastlewest) (capt.), P. McCarthy (Mungret), J. Hayes, W. Deere A. O'Rourke, C. Birrane, J. Blackwell.

Antrim—W. Webb, E. Dick, W. Feeney, M. Flynn, J. Lougheed, F. Fleming, J. Butler, J. Cormican, S. Quinn, W. McGowan, J. Gallagher, T. Lennon, P. Carmichael, J. McCallin, S. Mulholland.

1941

Cork—T. Mulcahy, J. Murphy, J. Looney, D. Lyons, T. Aherne, M. Murphy, C. Flaherty, P. Hill,
S. Condon (capt.), D. Twomey, M. Kennefick, P. O'Leary, D. McCarthy, J. Morrison, J. Kelly.

Galway—P. Doyle, P. Murphy, W. Fahy, P. Brady, W. Coen, C. Creane, S. Murphy, R. Beahan, V. Keane, G. McNamee, K. Kennelly, D. Solan, D. Quigley, T. Neary, M. Nestor.

1945

Dublin—J. Copeland, P Whelan, S. McLoughlin, G. Jennings, J. Prendergast, T. McLysaght, B. Clancy, S. McEntaggert, D. Healy (capt.), P. Donnelly, L. Donnelly, N. Maher, F. Tormey, P. McCarthy, P. Lynch. Sub: S. O'Neill tor P McCarthy.

Tipperary—N. Egan, D. Ryan, S. Bannon, T. Tynan, M. Cormack, P Stakelum (capt.), M. Shaughnessy, Jim O'Grady, W. Carroll, J. Harris, M. Maher (Boherlahan), P. Kenny, W. Molloy, J. Byrne, M. Ryan. Sub: W. O'Brien for N. Egan, N. Egan for Jim O'Grady.

1946

Dublin—G. Sutton (capt.), P. Whelan, J. Lavin, S. McLoughlin, J. Butler, N. Fingleton, B. Clancy, J. Guinea, C. McHale, N. Maher, L. Donnelly, J. Finnon, A. Young, C. Kavanagh, W. Fletcher. Sub: S. Molumby for C. McHale.

Tipperary—W. O'Brien, J. Doyle, J. Nolan, H. Sheehy, C. Dalton, J. Ryan, B. McGrath, Jim O'Gracly, P. Shanahan, M. Ryan (Éire Óg), M. Shaughnessy, P Kenny, T. OtMeara, M. Maher, V. Steiglitz. Sub: D. McNulty for C. Dalton.

1947

Tipperary—John O'Gracly, J. Doyle, J. J. McCormack, B. Mockler, C. Keane, J. Ryan, S. Twomey, M. Ryan (Éire Óg), J. Farrell, D. Butler, D. McNulty, P. Kenny (capt.), T. O'Meara, M. Butler, S. McDonnell. Sub: M. Maher (Holycross) for D. McNulty.

Galway—J. Leaper, D. O'Sullivan, P. Daly, S. McGrath, M. McGrath, P. Conroy, M. Power, T. Murphy, J. Salmon, M. Egan, P. Rooney, K. McNamee (capt.), D. Mullaly, S. Marmion, Jimmy Duggan. Sub: S. O Coileoin for J. McGrath.

1948

Waterford—S. O'Flynn, M. Morrissey, S. Hayden, M. Hogan, V. Walsh, M. Kelleher, T. Cunningham, J. Conlon, T. Gallagher, W. Conway, M. Flannelly (capt.), M. O'Connor, M. McHugh, P. O'Connor, M. Browne.

Kilkenny—S. Tobin, W. Doyle, K. Crotty, P. Dalton, T. O'Connor, D. Galavan, H. Ryan, M. O'Loughlin, W. Maher, T. Connolly, M. Roche, R. Carroll (capt.), W. Bennett, W. Ronan, R. O'Neill. Sub: W. Hoban for W. Ronan.

1949

Tipperary—John O'Gracly (capt.), Jim Moloney, Joe Moloney, S. Browne, D. Maher, J. Finn, S. McGrath, R. Holclen, W. Perkins, A. McDonnell, L. Keane, T Aherne, M. Buckley, M. Ryan (Moyne), G. Doyle. Sub: J. Maher.

Kilkenny—J. Murphy, J. Dobbyn, D. Maher, T. Walton (Capt.), T. O'Connor, M. O'Shaughnessy, J. McGovern, H. Ryan, P. Fitzgerald, T. Dowling, R. O'Neill, T. Prendergast, R. Mahony, P. Horgan, M. Cuggy.

1950

Kilkenny—J. Murphy, J. Doherty, J. Maher, P. Lyng, P. Lennon (capt.), Jim Walsh, J. McGovern,
P. Johnston, D. Gorey, M. Gardiner, M. Brophy, T. O'Hanrahan, S. O'Brien, J. Brennan, R. Brennan. Sub: C. Gough for J. Walsh.

Tipperary—G. Butler, P. Mockler, S. Power, M.Hynes, P. Croke, A. Wall, P McGrath, S. Cunningham, G. Doyle (capt.), D. Ryan, D. Nolan, L. McDonnell, W. Moloughney, S. Keaty, D. O'Brien. Subs: W. Quinn, S. Walsh.

1951

Cork—J. Dempsey, J. Coffey, M. Sheehan, P. Dreivers, P. Gaffney, S. O'Regan, F O'Regan, F. O'Mahony, P. Duggan, P. Crowley, J. O'Donoghue, J. Clifford (capt.), T. Kelly, S. O'Sullivan, E. Goulding. Sub: V. Dorgan for S. O'Regan.

Galway—D. Corrigan, B. Hoare, T. Tarpey, P Callanan, K. Sexton, W. Duffy, J. Larkin, E. Fallon, S. Cullinane, A Hansberry, J. McDonagh, M. Murphy, M. Cullinane, P Finn, S. Trayers. Sub: P. Creaven for S. Cullinane.

1952

Tipperary—E. McLoughney, D. Quinn, E. J. McGrath, E Burke, F. Dyer, W. Hayes, L. Quinn, P Hennessy, W. Quinn, L Devaney, A. Wall (capt.), S. McLoughlin, M. Butler, D. Browne, P. Cleary. Sub: S. McGovern for E. Burke.

Dublin—S. O'Neill, S. Hall, B. Campbell, L. Horan, M. Boylan, P. Higgins, S. Doyle, K. McLaughlin, Roger Feeley, O. Haughey, B. Boothman, C. Dolan, M. Doyle, M. O'Connor, V.Bell. Sub: S. Hennessy.

1953

Tipperary—T. McCormack, M. Cleary, T. Kelly, P. Barry, L. Quinn, R. Reidy, S. Kenny, W. Quinn (capt.), M. Kennedy, L. Devaney, J. Murphy, S. McLoughlin, S. Corcoran, M. Stapleton, L. Connolly. Sub: R. Ryan for R. Reidy.

Dublin—M. Meagher, T. Toner, T. O'Neill, S. Murphy, M. Bohan, B. Boothman, S. D'Art, T. Bracken, R. Feely, A. Kavanagh, V. Bell, T. Synott, L. Rowe, E. Clarke, C. Feely. Sub: P. McGuirk for L. Rowe.

1954

Dublin—S. O'Neill, K. Moore, T. O'Neill, M. Bohan, M. Meagher, B. Boothman (capt.), F. Whelan, T. Bracken, P. McGuirk, A. Kavanagh, V. Bell, P. Delaney, P. Hyland, E. Kelly, P. Farnan.
Sub: M. Mannion for T. Bracken.

Tipperary—J. Doyle, M. Cleary, D. O'Shea, C. Moloney, R. Ryan, R. Reidy, L. Quinn (capt.), L. Mahony, M. Burns, J. Murphy, T. Gouldsboro, W. O'Donovan, S. Kenny, C. Ahearne, L. Connolly. Subs: K. Dermody for S. Kenny, P. Ryan for Gouldsboro.

1955

Tipperary—S. Ryan, T Gleeson, R. O'Donnell, M. Craddock, D. Ryan, R. Reidy (capt.), S. Warren, C. Foyle, M. Burns, J. Doyle, A. Leahy, M. Gilmartin, W. O'Grady, P. Ryan, P. Dorney. Subs: J. Small for M. Burns, M. O'Gara for J. Small.

Galway—K. Croke, S. Naughton, T. Broderick, S. Keane, P. Davis, A. O'Dwyer, S. Murray, M. Fox, P. J. Lally, N. Murray, T. Ryan, L. Marmion, T. Flanagan, E. Newell, S. Gannon.
Sub: N. O'Neill for T Ryan.

1956

Tipperary—A. Tierney, T. Gleeson, M. Dorney, B. Maher, M. Craddock, P. Reynolds, J. Mulooly, S. Warren, S. Mackey, J. Doyle, P. Ryan (capt.), W. O'Grady, T. Flynn, J. Scott, S. Dalton.

Kilkenny—W. Barry, J. Blanchfield, P. Dillon, H. Hickey, J. Cormack, P. Moran, T. Carroll, S. Buckley, T. Brennan, T. Molloy, P. Driscoll, B. Buckley, M. Dunne, S. Leahy, J. Cullinane. Subs: A. Comerford for T. Brennan, R. Dowling for Hickey.

1957

Tipperary—T. Moloney, M. Craddock, M. Lonergan, P. Kearns, M. Stapleton, P Reynolds, A. Croke, M. Murphy, P Kennedy, S. Ryan, L. Kiely, J. Doyle (capt.), P. Doyle, M. Hogan, P. Butler. Subs: W. Hogan for S. Ryan, P. Woodlock for L. Kiely.

Kilkenny—W. Barry, P Moran, J. O'Donnell, H. Hickey, L. O'Brien, T. Carroll, N. Hanrahan, L. McCarthy, A. Comerford, P. Maher, R. Walsh (Thomastown) (capt.), E. Keher, T. Bowe, J. Doherty, M. Dunne. Sub: T. O'Connell for A. Comerford.

1958

Limerick—T. Hanley, J. McDonagh, J. Guinane, C. O'Connell, J. J. Bresnihan, J. Leonard, M. Hanrahan, B. Kelleher, P. Hartnett, P. Cobbe (capt.), L. Canty, P. Murphy, E. Carey, J. Hayes, S. Sexton. Sub: D. Dillane for J. J. Bresnihan.

Galway—P. Fahy, D. Robinson, A. McDonnell, S. Francis, S. Corcoran, J. Lyons, P J. Cormican, S. Kelly, C. Stanley, G. Egan, S. Devlin, J. Spillane, P. Jorclan, H. Conway, F. Glynn. Sub: G. Loughnane for C. Stanley.

1959

Tipperary—J. O'Donoghue, P. Griffin, G. Kinnane, W. Lonergan, J. Carroll, A. Croke, R. Slevin, T. Ryan (Killenaule), T. Ryan (Toomevara), P. Doyle, W. Carey, M. Duggan, M. Nolan, L. Kiely (capt), J. Ryan. Sub: J. Gleeson for W. Carey, P. Crampton for L. Kiely.

Kilkenny—E. Fitzpatrick, P. Larkin, P. Brett, S. Rafferty, P Grace, A. McGrath, N. Hanrahan, T. Barry, M. Murphy (capt.), J. Ayres, T. Brennan, E. Keher, R. Walsh (Thomastown), J. Nyhan, M. Walsh. Subs: D. Lannon for T. Barry, E. Connolly for P. Larkin.

1960

Kilkenny—P. Dempsey, W. Grace (capt.), P. Brett, N. Rohan, S. O'Brien, A. McGrath, O. Ryan, J. Barry, J. Ayres, R. Walsh (Slieverue), D. Kinsella,

P Freaney, P. Ryan, J. Nyhan, T. Murphy.
Tipperary—J. O'Donoghue, J. Kennedy, Christy O'Dwyer, L. Cummins, J. Cummins, Conor Dwyer, W. Greene, P. O'Connell, J. Ryan, W. Nolan, M. Keating, A. McGovern, M. O'Connor, M. Ryan, W. Ryan. Sub: W. Burke for W. Nolan.

1961

Kilkenny—P. Foley, J. McGrath, N. Forrestal, P. Cullen, S. O'Brien, P. Henderson, S. Hanrahan, T. Barry, J. Murphy, T. Walsh, D. Kinsella, P. Freaney, J. Dunphy (capt.), M. Aylward, J. Delaney.
Tipperary—P. O'Sullivan, J. Dillon, L. White, W. Eakins, D. Ryan, N. Lane, P. O'Dwyer, Conor Dwyer, M. Roche, W. Nolan, M. Keating, W. Ryan, N. Hogan (capt.), G. Ryan, T. Brennan.

1962

Kilkenny—N. Skehan, S. Treacy, T. Phelan, J. Walsh, S. Hanrahan, P. Drennan, W. Burke, J. Byrne, S. Muldowney, S. Cooke, T. Walsh, J. Delaney, J. Dunphy (capt.), P. Walsh, M. Aylward. Sub: T. Ryan for P. Walsh.
Tipperary—P Fleming, W. Smith, P. O'Rourke, M. O'Meara, O. Killoran, L. Gaynor, E. Loughnane, P. Delaney, M. O'Brien, W. Nolan, M. Keating (capt.}, F. Loughnane, D. Moloney, R. Buckley, T. Brennan. Subs: P. Hayes for D. Moloney, S. Dermody for E. Loughnane, S. Nash for T. Brennan.

1963

Wexford—L. Byrne, J. Hartley, M. Nolan, E. O'Connor, J. Murphy, M. Kinsella, V. Staples, W. Bernie (capt.), C. Rafferty, C. Dowdall, A. Doran, F. Swords, W. Carley, S. Barron, P. Quigley. Sub: B. Gaule for J. Hartley.
Limerick—A. Dunworth, S. O'Brien, J. Egan, S. O'Shaughnessy, P Heffernan, T. McAuliffe, P. O'Brien, A. Roche, E. Cregan, C. Danagher, B. Savage, M. Graham, S. Geary, G. Cosgrove, B. Cobbe. Subs: E. Grimes for C. Danagher, P Nash for A. Dunworth, W. O'Gorman for S. O'Shaughnessy.

1964

Cork—H. O'Brien, T. Murphy, G. Aherne, P. O'Sullivan, J. O'Callaghan, B. Wylie, W. Murphy, P. O'Riordan, C. Roche, D. Clifford, L. McAuliffe, K. Cummins (capt.), C. McCarthy, A. O'Flynn, M. Kenneally.
Laois—E. Bergin, L. Moore, M. McDonnell, F. Byrne, W. Phelan (capt.), L. Purcell, W. Delaney, M. Fennell, P. Dowling, B. Delaney, P. Dillon, P. Payne, D. Conlon, S. Kavanagh, P. Keyes. Subs: S. Sheppard for W. Phelan, P. Kavanagh for P Keyes.

1965

Dublin—P. Cunningham, A. Fletcher, L. Deegan, C. Brennan, W. Markey, P. Kennedy, L. Martin (capt.), H. Dalton, F. McDonald, J. Fetherston, E. Davey, T. Grealish, T. McCann, B. Whelan, N. Kinsella. Sub: P Cassels for C. Brennan, C. Brennan for E. Davey.
Limerick—T. Brennan, M. O'Flaherty (capt.), D. Manning, A. Cronin, S. Toomey, E. Boland, J. O'Hehir, P. Doherty, D. Foley, E. Grimes, C. Shanahan, N. Hayes, M. Grace, B. Murnane, S. Burke. Subs: J. Moynihan for N. Hayes, M. Hennessy for B. Murnane.

1966

Wexford—H. Butler, J. Quigley, E. Murphy, W. Butler, E. McDonald, E. Buggy, M. Fitzpatrick, D. Howell, T. Kavanagh, T. Furlong, L. Bent, P. Byrne, T. Royce, M. Browne, P. Bernie (capt.). Subs: J. Nangle for M. Fitzpatrick, J. Ryan for P. Byrne.
Note: M. Butler played in drawn game. Tom Kavanagh came on for replay. Subs in drawn game: T. Kavanagh for D. Howell, J. Ryan for T. Royce, T. Royce for M. Butler.
Cork—B. Hurley, D. Carroll, P. Geary, N. Norberg, Joe Aherne, J. Horgan, R. Cummins, P. Moylan, W. Walsh, B. Meade, S. Murphy, P. Ring, F. Keane, G. O'Riordan, M. Curley. Subs: L. Comer for G. O'Riordan, C. Kelly for F. Keane. D. Clifford, L. Comer and C. Kelly played in drawn game. P. Ring, G. O'Riordan and M. Curley were on for replay. Subs in drawn game: F. Hogan for W. Walsh, W. Walsh for F. Hogan.

1967

Cork—W. Glavin, M. McCarthy, B. Tobin, M. Bohane, Ted O'Brien, J. Horgan, M. Aherne, P. Moylan (capt.), J. Barrett, S. Murphy, M. Malone, C. Kelly, T. Buckley, B. O'Connor, P. Ring. Subs: M. Ryan for M. Malone, K. Fitzgerald for M. Ryan.
Wexford—P. Cox, J. Quigley, J. Royce, E. McDonald, E. Walsh (capt.), L. Byrne, L. Bennett, A. Kavanagh, P. Walsh, James Murphy, M. Butler, P. Byrne, M. Quigley, M. Casey, John Murphy. Sub: D. Lawlor for A. Kavanagh.

1968

Wexford—P. Cox, G. O'Connor, J. Russell, P. O'Brien, A. Kerrigan, L. Byrne, L. Bennett, P. Kennedy, T. Byrne (capt.), M. Quigley, P. Walsh, James Murphy, M. Butler, M. Casey, M. Byrne. Subs: L. Kinsella for L. Bennett, T. Walsh for P. Walsh; L. BenneH for M. Byrne.
Cork—M. Coleman, J. Horgan, B. Cummins, M. Bohane, B. Coleman, S. Looney, T. O'Shea, K. McSweeney, G. O'Sullivan, M. Ryan, P. Ring, T. Buckley, D. McCarthy (capt.), J. Rothwell, M. Malone. Sub: P. Kavanagh for M. Ryan.

1969

Cork—P. Lawton, P. Casey, J. Rothwell, D. O'Sullivan, K. Murray, M. O'Doherty, S. Collins (capt.), N. Crowley, S. O'Farrell, P. Kavanagh, T. Crowley, T. Sheehan, F. Coughlan, G. Hanley, S. O'Leary. Sub: J. Buckley for K. Murray.

Kilkenny—A. Condon, P. Boran, P. Butler, T. Teehan, D. McCormack (capt.), G. Burke, G. McCarthy, T. Phelan, T. Waters, P. Bollard, M. O'Shea, M. Buggy, T. Neary, M. Carroll, D. Corcoran. Subs: R. O'Shea for T. Neary, J. O'Brien for D. Corcoran.

1970

Cork—D. O'Brien, B. Murphy, L. Kelly, M. Corbett, V. Twomey, M. O'Doherty, J. Buckley, P. Kavanagh (capt.), N. Crowley, G. Hanley, S. O'Farrell, T. Sheehan, D. Relihan, T. Crowley, S. O'Leary.

Galway—E. Campbell, S. Cloonan, C. Maher, S. Fahy, I. Clarke, A. Fenton, S. Healy, S. Donoghue, S. Hynes (capt.), M. Donoghue, Joe McDonagh, D. Campbell, P. J. Molloy, C. Fitzgerald, G. Holland. Subs: W. Cummins for I. Clarke, B. Brennan for J. McDonagh, J. Hanniffy for M. Donoghue.

1971

Cork—F. O'Sullivan, M. Corbett, L. McNally, D. J. Foley, D. Coakley, J. Buckley, D. O'Keeffe, T. Canavan, D. O'Dwyer, P. Buckley, A. Creagh, V. Twomey (Na Piarsaigh), T. Fogarty, J. BarryMurphy, E. O'Sullivan. Subs: S. Coughlan for J. Barry Murphy; B. Cotter for P. Buckley; S. Ring for D. O'Keeffe.

Kilkenny—K. Fennelly, N. Brennan, A. Teehan, S. Brophy, M. Hogan, B. Cody, T. McCormack, T. Barry, J. McCormack, P. Kearney, N. Minogue, E. Holohan, P. Butler (Dunnamaggin), P. Butler (James Stephens), R. Sweeney. Subs: W. Fitzpatrick for R. Sweeney.

1972

Kilkenny—K. Fennelly, J. Ryan, J. Burke, P O'Brien, K. Robinson, B. Cody, J. Dowling, G. Woodcock, G. Fennelly, S. O'Brien, M. Tierney, W. Fitzpatrick, P. Butler (James Stephens), M. McCarthy, R. Sweeney. Sub: J. O'Sullivan for S. O'Brien.

Cork—F. O'Sullivan, J. Kennefick, L. McNally, J. Barrett, B. Manley, F. Delaney, S. O'Farrell, R. Wilmot, K. Collins, R. Fitzgerald, T. O'Sullivan, B. Óg Murphy, T. Collins, J. Barry-Murphy, E. O'Sullivan. Subs: J. Norberg for F. Delaney, B. Gallagher for J. Barrett.

1973

Kilkenny—P. Dunphy, R. O'Hara, G. Doheny, K. Robinson (capt.), J. Hennessy, J. Marnell, O. Bergin, G. Devane, B. Waldron, P. Lannon, P. Mulhall, J. Lyng, P. Treacy, S. O'Brien, M. Lyng. Subs: J. Purcell for M. Lyng, M. Lanigan for J. Lyng.

Galway—F. Larkin, H. Silke. G. Maher. G. Murphy, J. Dervan (capt.), T Murphy, G. Lohan, G. Holian, S. Linnane, M. Hanniffy, J. Donoghue, Brian Kelly, F Power, G. Burke, E. Dooley.

1974

Cork—J. Cronin, P. Coughlan, W. Geaney (capt.), J. Crowley, C. Brassil, T. Cashman, D. McCurtain, R. O'Mahony, F. Delaney, K. O'Driscoll, D. Ryan, G. McEvoy, T. Murphy, T. Cullinane, D. Buckley. Subs: D. Keane for K. O'Driscoll, D. Murphy for G. McEvoy, Pat Horgan for D. Murphy.

Kilkenny—A. Murphy, R. O'Hara, J. Marnell (capt.), G. Stapleton, J. Hennessy, G. Devane, J. Costelloe, B. Waldron, P. Lannon, M. Lyng, J. Walsh, K. Brennan, A. Driscoll, G. Tyrell, B. Fennelly. Subs: M. Kennedy for A. Driscoll, J. Henderson for J. Walsh.

1975

Kilkenny—E. Mahon, R. Power, P. Prendergast, J. Henderson, H. Ryan (Capt.), R. O'Hara, G. Stapleton, P. Lannon, J. O'Brien, K. Brennan, J. Wall, K. O'Shea, S. Hennessy, P. Brennan, J. Ryan.

Cork—J. Hayes, M. Cronin, F. Walsh, Jerry Murphy, B. Dineen, T. Cashman (capt.), D. McCurtain, D. Herlihy, Padraig Crowley, Paul Crowley, P. Horgan, J. O'Sullivan, F. Tobin, John Murphy, D. Buckley. Subs: Peter Hogan for D. Herlihy, T Lyons for John Murphy.

1976

Tipperary—V. Mullins, P. Loughnane, P. J. Maxwell, A. Slattery, M. Stapleton, G. Stapleton, J. O'Dwyer, J. Hogan (capt.), P. Ryan, E. O'Shea, M. Doyle, T. Grogan, M. Murphy, J. Stone, P. Power. Sub: P. Looby for J. Stone.

Kilkenny—E. Mahon (capt.), G. Stapleton, P. Holden, T. Lennon, J. Byrne, P. Prendergast, P. Murphy, S. Hennessy, J. Brennan, L. Fennelly, J. Wall, J. Heffernan, J. Ryan, P. Brennan, J. Waters. Subs: J. Carroll for J. Waters, J. Power for J. Heffernan, E. Deegan for L. Fennelly.

1977

Kilkenny—L. Ryan, C. Mackey, M. Meagher, Bill O'Hara, T. Lennon, S. Fennelly (capt.), D. Connolly, G. Ryan, J. Mulcaby, E. Deegan, R. Murphy, E. Crowley, M. Nash, E. Wallace, W. McEvoy. Subs: J. Heffernan for M. Nash, M. Nash For E. Wallace

Note: J. Heffernan played in drawn game. R. Murphy came on for replay. Sub. in drawn game J. Waters for E. Crowley.

Cork—J. Hegarty, J. Murphy, S. O'Mahony, S.

O'Brien, W. Cashman, S. Hayes (capt.), J. Whooley, A. O'Connell, Tadgh McCarthy, J. Hartnett, R. O'Connor, J. Monaghan, S. O'Gorman, J. Keane, T. Aherne. Sub: D. Murphy for A. O'Connell.

Note: J. Walsh played in clrawn garne. S. O'Mahony was on for replay. Sub in drawn game S. O'Mahony for J. Walsh.

1978

Cork—G. Cunningham, W. Cashman, P. Murphy (capt.), J. Hodgins, B. O'Driscoll, J. Murphy, T. McCarthy, D. Walsh, J. Hartnett, L. Lynch, Tom Aherne, G. O'Regan, D. Murphy, S. O'Gorman, S. Cashman.

Kilkenny—W. Walton, R. Maloney, W. O'Hara, P. Crowley, L. Hennessy, P. Gannon, M. Cleere, W. Walsh, J. Moriarty, E. Crowley, W. McEvoy, J. Holland, P. Phelan (capt.), M. Heffernan, W. Purcell. Subs: J. J. Long for J. Holland, P. Heffernan for M. Heffernan.

1979

Cork—G. Cunningham, W. Cashman, C. O'Connor, J. Hodgins, C. Marshall, K. O'Driscoll, C. Coughlan (capt.), D. Scanlon, D. Walsh, A. O'Sullivan, K. Hennessy, J. Greally, A. Coyne, M O'Sullivan, T. Coakley. Sub: R. Hegarty for J. Greally.

Kilkenny—M. Walsh, P. Ryan, E. Aylward, J. Holden, L. Hennessy, P. Heffernan, M. Gaffney, J. Moriarty, J. Mahon W. Purcell, J. O'Dwyer, S. Tyrell (capt.), P Phelan, J. Murphy, T. Moylan. Subs: W. Walton for T. Moylan, M. Walsh (Mooncoin) for M. Gaffney, M. Byrne for J. Murphy.

1980

Tipperary—K. Hogan, M. Conway, P Maher, E. Hogan, I. Conroy, J. Maher (capt.), D. Finnerty, J. Hayes, P. Kenny, G. O'Neill M. McGrath, J. Darcy, A. Browne, W. Peters, N. English. Subs: V. Dooley for M. McGrath, J. Treacy for N. English.

Wexford—T. Doyle, W. Keeling, P. Gahan. D. Sheehan, J. Roche (capt.), E. Cleary, J. Grannells, G. Coady, A. Gahan, J. Byrne J. Codd, T. Morrissey, M. FitzLenry, J. Barnwell, E. Murphy.

1981

Kilkenny—D. Burke, G. O'Neill, E. Kennedy (capt.), E. Wall, D. Hoyne, M. Morrissey, J. O'Hara, P. Ryan, T. Bawle, J McDonalcl, D. Carroll, R. Heffernan, L. McCarthy, S Delahunty, M. Rafter. Subs: S. Whearty for E. Kennedy, P. Cleere for M. Rafter, J. Donnelly for J. O'Hara.

Galway—T. Coen, S. Moylan, P. Finnerty, K. Flannery, J. Grealish, G. Fallon (capt.), T. Helebert, J. Burke, P. Winters, M. McGrath, A. Keady, J. Leahy, P. Burke, E. Ryan, A. Cunningham. Subs: M. Coleman for K. Flannery, S. Brody for J. Burke.

1982

Tipperary—J. Leamy, J. Flannery, J. Bergin, Colm Bonnar, B. Everard, D. Kealy, W. Hayes, J. Kennedy (capt.), G. Bradley, N. Sheehy, M. Cunningham, S. Slattery, J. Cormack, L. Stokes M Scully. Subs: M. Corcoran for B. Everard, G Ryan for L. Stokes, A. Ryan for N. Sheehy.

Galway—T. Kenny, S. Murphy, P. Finnerty, P Malone, P. Lynch, T. Helebert, G. Mclnerney, J. Byrne, M. Kenny, J. Noone, J. Burke, S. Connolly, G. Brehony, T. Moloney, A. Cunningham. Subs: G. Waldron for M. Kenny, D. Murphy for T. Helebert.

1983

Galway—J. Commins, M. Killeen, P. Dervan, S. Treacy, P. Brehony, P. Malone, G. Mcinerney, D. Jennings, J. J. Broderick, T. Monaghan, T. Moloney, J. Cooney, S. Keane, A. Cunningham (capt.), P. Higgins. Subs: M. Shiel for J. J. Broderick, G. Elwood for P. Higgins, N. Brody for T. Monaghan.

Dublin—T. O'Riordan, N. O'Carroll, E. Clancy, J. P. Byrne, D. Byrne, J. Murphy (capt.), S. Cullen, P. Williams, D. Foley, M. Hayes, R. Collins, P. Confrey, N. Quinn, S. Dalton, B. Gavin. Subs: P. Kearns for D. Foley, A. Spellman for M. Hayes.

1984

Limerick—V. Murnane, A. Madden, P. Carey, J. Fitzgerald, G. Hegarty, A. O'Riordan, A. Cunneen, A. Carmody, M. Reale, T. Byrnes, G. Kirby, G. Ryan, J. O'Neill, P. Davern, B. Stapleton. Subs: D. Marren for T. Byrnes, C. Coughlan for J. O'Neill

Note: D. Flynn played in drawn game. J. Fitzgerald was on for replay. Sub. in drawn game M. O'Brien for J. O'Neill.

Kilkenny—A. McCormack, W. Dwyer, B. Bryan, F. Morgan, L. O'Brien, J. Power, D. Mullen, G. Drennan, P. Phelan, P McEvoy, T. Lennon (capt.), W. Ayres, W. Purcell, M. Frisby, L. Dowling. Subs: L. Egan for G. Drennan, A. Byrne for W. Dwyer, J. Farrell for W. Purcell.

Note: J. Farrell, L. Egan, P. Fennelly and W. Cleere played in drawn game. M. Frisby, W. Purcell, W. Ayres and P. Phelan came on for replay. Subs. in drawn game W. Purcell for W. Cleere, P. Phelan for L. Dowling and W. Ayres for P. Fennelly.

1985

Cork—T. Kingston, C. Connery, P. Cahalane, B. Coutts, C. Casey, B. Murphy, K. McGuckian, M. O'Mahony (capt.), L. Kelly, G. O'Riordan, B. Harte, J. Fitzgibbon, G. Manley, M. Foley, M. Mullins.

Wexford—P. Nolan, L. O'Gorman, J. Redmond, S. Flood, J. Codd, Ger Cushe, V. Reddy, J. Bolger, J. O'Connor, E. Broders, V. Murphy, P. O'Callaghan, E. SynnoH, B. Moran,

P. Carton. Subs: S. wickham for E. Broders, J. Quirke for B. Moran.

1986

Offaly—J. Errity, P. Nallen, R. Mannion, D. Sherlock, J. Kilmartin, M. Hogan (Birr) (capt.), B. Kelly, D. Geoghegan, A. Kelly, G. Cahill, D. Regan, R. Byrne, T. Moylan, M. Duignan, D. Pilkington. Sub: B. Dooley for D. Sherlock.

Cork—P. Barry, N. Hackeh, D. Irwin, K. Keane, R. O'Connor, P. Kenneally, Tony O'Keeffe, J. O'Mahony, J. Corcoran, R. Sheehan, J. Walsh, M. Mullins, B. Cunningham, D. O'Connoll, G. Manley. Subs: D. Walsh for G. Manley, P. O'Brien for Tony O'Keeffe.

1987

Offaly—John Troy, B. Whelehan, D. Geoghegan, B. Hennessy, Johnny Dooley, J. Errity, A. Cahill, J. Pilkington, T. Dooley, S. Morkam, B. Dooley, K. Egan, T. Moylan (capt.), J. Troy (Kilcormac-Killoughey), D. Pilkington.

Tipperary—P. Kearns, L. Sheedy, M. O'Meara (capt.), N. Keane, M. Ryan, Conal Bonnar, B. Corcoran, M. Perdue, J. Quinlan, J. Leahy, S. Bohan, G. Dealey, D. Lyons, Colm Egan, B. Hogan. Subs. S. Quinn for M. Perdue, D. O'Meara for M. Ryan.

1988

Kilkenny—J. Conroy, G. Henderson, P. J. O'Connor, D. Roche, P. O'Neill, P. Brophy (capt.), J. Conlon, R. Dooley, D. Bradley, W. O'Keeffe, B. Ryan, P. O'Grady, A. Ronan, C. Carter, D. J. Carey. Subs: P. Treacy for O'Keeffe, J. Buggy for O'Grady.

Cork—I. Lynam, T. Twomey, D. Holland, L. Callinan, T. Dineen, D. Quirke, M. Noonan, T. Kelleher, B. Corcoran, T. Hurley, K. Roche, M. Sheehan, P. O'Brien (capt.), B. Cunningham, J. Dillon. Subs: S. Guitheen for Hurley (injured), P. Murray for Dillon.

1989

Offaly—John Troy, M. Hogan (Coolderry), F Cullen, H. Rigney, D. Barron, B. Whelahan (capt.), Donal Franks, A. Cahill, R. Dooley, Johnny Dooley, S. Grennan, O. O'Neill, R. McNamara, N. Hand, K. Flynn. Sub: R. Deegan for R. Dooley.

Clare—D. Fitzgerald, D. McInerney, P. Lee (capt.), F. Corey, P. Markham, J. O'Gorman, G. Cahill, C. Chaplin, S. Power, P. O'Rourke, G. Moroney, P. Minogue, P. McNamara, C. Clancy, P. Keary. Subs: J. O'Connor for Moroney, K. McNamara for Keary.

1990

Kilkenny—A. Behan, M. Holohan, L. Mahony, J. Carroll, D. O'Neill, C. Brennan, P. Larkin, J. McDermott (capt.), P. Long, A. Comerford, J. Shefflin, P. Farrell, P. J. Delaney, S. Ryan, D. Lawlor. Subs: A. Cleere for Long, B. Power for O'Neill.

Note: S. Meally, D. Beirne and A. Cleere played in drawn game. J. Carroll, C. Brennan and P. Long were on for replay. Subs in drawn game B. Power for D. Beirne, C. Brennan for A. Cleere, J. Carroll for S. Meally.

Cork—D. O'Mahony, F. Ryan, A. Murphy, A. White, C. Buckley, P. Smith (capt.), B. Sheehan, C. Dillon, R. O'Connell, B. Egan, B. Walsh, L. Meaney, K. Murray, M. Landers, D. Fleming. Subs: B. Corcoran for Buckley, M. Quirke for Ryan, R. Lewis for O'Connell.

Note: B. Corcoran, N. O'Donnell and C. Walsh played in drawn game. A. White, C. Dillon and D. Fleming were on for replay. Subs in drawn game C. Dillon for C. Buckiey, M. Quirke for N. O'Donnell and D. Fleming for C. Walsh.

1991

Kilkenny—M. Carey, S. Meally, L. Mahony, B. Power, A. O'Sullivan, E. Dwyer, D. O'Neill (capt.), D. Maher, J. Hickey, S. Dollard, P. J. Delaney, G. Walsh, D. Byrne, M. Owens, R. Shortall. Sub: P. Davis for Walsh.

Tipperary—M. Ferncombe, S. O'Donoghue, M. Rabbitte, M. Gleeson, P. Shanahan, B. Gaynor, T. Gleeson, A. Shelly, M. Leonard, T. Dunne, B. O'Meara, A. Hogan (capt.), L. Barrett, T. Fogarty, G. Maguire. Sub: Conor Egan for Barrett.

1992

Galway—L. Donoghue, T. Healy, M. Spellman, C. Moore, N. Shaughnessy, C. Donovan (capt.), M. Donoghue, F. Forde, S. Walsh, M. Lynskey, D. Coen, Peter Kelly, S. Corcoran, C. O'Doherty, D. Walsh. Subs: J. Murray for Lynskey, J. Kerins for O'Doherty.

Waterford—P. Haran, T. Morrissey, P. O'Donnell (capt.), J. O'Connor, A. Kirwan, G. Harris, T. Feeney, T. Kiely, F. O'Shea, J. P. Fitzpatrick, D. McGrath, J. J. Ronayne, R. Ryan, P. Foley, P. Flynn. Sub: B. McCarthy for Kiely.

1993

Kilkenny—O. Blanchfield, T. Hickey, S. Doyle (capt.), J. Ayres, V. O'Brien, B. Lonergan, B. Bolger, K. Grogan, S. Kealy, D. Cleere, L. Smith, E. Mackey, B. Dalton, D. Buggy, O. O'Connor. Sub: J. Young for Kealy.

Galway—K. Broderick, I. Linnane, T. Healy, R. Fahy, G. Kennedy, C. Moore, N. Linnane, O. Canning, S. Walsh, M. Conroy, D. Coen (capt.), K. Donoghue, S. Corcoran, D. Walsh, O. Fahy. Subs: M. Lynskey for I. Linnane, F. Healy for Corcoran, L. Madden for N. Linnane.

1994

Galway—A. Kerins, G. Kennedy (capt.), P. Huban, O. Canning, M. Healy, F. Gantley, L. Madden, L. Hogan, G. Glynn, K. Broderick, R. Farrell, F. Healy, E. Brady, R. Gantley, D. Fahy.

Subs: M. Cullinane for Hogan, B. Carr for Madden, P. Forde for Faby.

Cork—B. Hurley (capt.), P. O'Keeffe, S. Óg Ó hAilpín, P. Walsh, C. Collins, K. Egan, B. McSweeney, A. Cahill, G. Shaw, B. O'Driscoll, J. O'Flynn, A. Walsh, K. Kelleher, D. Ronan, P. Mullaney. Sub: P. O'Connor for A. Walsh.

1995

Cork—D. Óg Cusack, A. Kelleher, B. Kidney, P. Walsh, D. Barrett, S. Óg Ó hAilpín, J. O'Dwyer, D. Murphy, A. Walsh, P. Mullaney, T. McCarthy, M. O'Connell, S. O'Farrell, J. Deane, B. O'Keeffe (capt.). Subs: A. Coughlan for P. Mullaney, D. Cott for J. Dwyer.

Kilkenny—P. J. Ryan, M. Kavanagh, S. Dowling, A. Hickey, P. Hoyne (capt.), M. Dunphy, D. Carroll, P. J. Coady, R. Mullally, E. Behan, M. Hoyne, G. Kirwan, R. Cahill, T. O'Dowd, S. Millea. Subs: J. Drea for Kirwan, M. Gordan for Behan.

1996

Tipperary—F. Horgan, T. Costello, F Heaney, W. Hickey, T. Keane, J. Carroll, J. Teehan, W. Maher (capt.), M. Ryan, D. Browne, D. Fahey, P. Kelly, A. Doyle, E. O'Neill, M. Kennedy. Subs: P Lonergan for Ryan, P. O'Brien for Kelly, E. Carey for Doyle.

Note: N. Cleere and S. Ryan played in the drawn game. T. Keane and D. Browne were on for replay. Subs in drawn game E. Carey for S. Ryan, T. Keane for N. Cleere, D. Browne for E. Carey.

Galway—N. Murray, E. Tannian, M. Healy (capt.), K. Coy, R. Brady, C. O'Reilly, D. Shaughnessy, E. McEntee, C. Coen, R. Cullinane, A. Poinard, D. Loughrey, R. Gantley, E. Cloonan, M. Kerins. Subs: S. McClearn for Coen, E. Donoghue for McEntee.

Note: A. Walsh and P. Kennedy played in the drawn game. R. Gantley and M. Kerins were on for replay. Subs in drawn game M. Kerins for A. Walsh, R. Gantley for P Kennedy and M. Blake for D. Shaughnessy.

1997

Clare—G. O'Connell, W. Kennedy, K. Kennedy, D. Duggan, B. McMahon (Newmarketon-Fergus), J. Reddan (capt.), G. Malone, S. Fitzpatrick, G. Considine, P. Moroney, C. Earley, C. Mullen, M. Lennon, D. Madden, B. McMahon (Kilmaley). Subs: Joe O'Meara for Earley, John O'Meara for Lennon.

Galway—C. Callanan, E. McDonagh (capt.), D. Cloonan, E. Donoghue, J. Cannon, S. Morgan, A. Walsh, N. Lawlor, J. Hession, D. O'Donoghue, D. Tierney, G. Hurney, O. Deeley, K. Hayes, C. Coen. Subs: E. Hyland for Hession, K. Daniels for Tierney, G. Keary for Hurney.

1998

Cork—M. Morrissey, E. O'Sullivan, J. Olden, D. McNannara, B. Murphy, R. Curran, A. Fitzpatrick, A. O'Connor, J. Barrett, J. Egan, G. McCarthy, E. Fitzgerald, C. McCarthy (capt.), B. Lombard, W. Deasy. Subs: N. McCarthy for Deasy, V. Cusack for G. McCarthy, P. Murphy for Fitzgerald.

Kilkenny—J. Power, P Shefflin (capt.), N. Hickey, C. Hickey, C. Herity, J. Morgan, J. Ryall, J. Coogan, K. Moore, K. Power, B. Phelan, D. Walsh, G. Cleere, K. Raher, J. Murray. Subs: E. Walsh for Herity, H. Gannon for Moore.

1999

Galway—J. O'Loughlin, B. O'Mahoney, J. Culkin, R. Reilly, F. Moore, C. Dervan, M. J. Quinn, H. Whiriskey, G. Farragher, R. Murray, M. Coughlan, K. Brady, D. Hayes, D. Forde, C. Coen. Subs: B. Gantley for Coen, S. Tierney for Brady.

Tipperary—D. Young, C. Everard, P. Curran, D. Maher, C. Ryan, K. Mulryan, L. Kearney, T. King, S. Mason, D. Shelly, Dermot Gleeson, E. Brisbane, J. O'Brien, E. Kelly, K. Cummins. Subs:M. Maher for D. Maher, L. BreH for Cummins, Damien Gleeson for King.

2000

Galway – Aidan Diviney, B.O'Mahoney, T.Regan, N.Corcoran, S.Kavanagh, Adrian Diviney, A.Cullinane, G.Farragher, B.Coen, R.Murray, P.Garvey, K.Brady, D.Hayes, T.Kavanagh, D.Greene. Subs – J.Gantley for Brady, F.Moore for Corcoran, J.P.O'Connell for Gantley, K.Brady for Garvey.

Cork – Kieran Murphy (Erins' Own), C.Sullivan, J.O'Brien, B.Murphy, J.O'Neill, P.Tierney, G.Calnan, M.O'Connor, B.Carey, G.McLoughlin, C.Brosnan, T.O'Leary, S.Ó hAilpín, E.Collins, Kieran Murphy (Sarsfields). Subs – D.Cashman for McLoughlin, K.Foley for Brosnan, S.O'Sullivan for Carey, R.McCarthy for Calnan.

2001

Cork – M.Coleman, J.O'Mahony, C.O'Connor, K.Goggin, M.Prout, J.Gardiner, S.Murphy, K.Hartnett, B.Smiddy, J.O'Connor, Kieran Murphy (Erin's Own), T.O'Leary, F.Murphy, S.Ó hAilpín, Kieran Murphy (Sarsfields). Subs – T.Healy for C.O'Connor, D.O'Riordan for Smiddy.

Galway – P.Dullaghan, C.Dervan, T.Óg Regan, C.Finnerty, E.Lynch, S.Kavanagh, J.O'Leary, T.Tierney, G.Farragher, B.Lucas, K.Hayes, A.Cullinane, J.Gantley, J.Maher, K.Burke. Subs – K.Briscoe for O'Leary, A.Smith for Lucas, N.Healy for Hayes.

2002

Kilkenny – C.Grant, P.Holden, J.Tennyson, D.Prendergast, K.Nolan, C.Hoyne, P.J.Delaney, M.Rice, S.Maher, R.Power, W.O'Dwyer, S.Coonan, J.Fitzpatrick, E.Reid, A.Healy. Subs – R.Dowling for O'Dwyer, P.Kennedy for Delaney, S.Cadigan for Prendergast.

Tipperary – P.McCormack, M.Treacy, D.Bourke, M.Bergin, J.Boland, D.Morrisey, D.Kennedy, W.Cully, C.O'Mahoney, P.Shortt, F.Devanney, W.Ryan, E.Sweeney, T.Scroope, T.Ivors. Subs – D.Sheppard for Sweeney, T.Fitzgerald for Ivors, B.O'Sullivan for Cully, D.Corcoran for Boland, P.Ryan for Morrisey.

2003

Kilkenny – C.Grant, J.Dalton, J.Tennyson, S.Cadigan, D.Cody, D.Prendergast, P.O'Donovan, P.Hartley, M.Fennelly, E.McGrath, R.Power, A.Healy, M.Nolan, J.Fitzpatrick, E.Guinan. Subs – A.Murphy for McGrath, R.Wall for Healy, D.McCormack for Hartley.

Galway – A.Ryan, T.Linnane, G.Mahon, D.Kennedy, D.Ryan, J.Lee, R.Whyte, C.Burke, D.Kelly, N.Callanan, D.Garvey, N.Coleman, D.Reilly, A.Callanan, N.Healy. Subs – E.Fenton for Burke, K.Hynes for Coleman.

2004

Galway – M.Herlihy, P.Loughnane, G.Mahon, C.O'Donovan, M.Ryan, J.Lee, J.Hughes, A.Keary, D.Kennedy, K.Kilkenny, K.Hynes, F.Coone, K.Wade, J.Canning, B.Hanley. Sub – D.White for Ryan.
(J.Hughes, a sub in the drawn game was retained for the final at the expense of D.White. Other subs used in the drawn game were E.Collins, K.Coen and P.Madden).

Kilkenny – L.Tierney, J.Maher, K.Joyce, P.Cahill, N.Prendergast, R.Maher, S.Prendergast, P.Hartley, P.Hogan, G.Nolan, M.Nolan, N.Kenny, R.Hogan, E.Guinan, M.Ruth. Sub – E.O'Donoghue for Kenny. (P.Cahill for E.Walsh and M.Ruth for E.O'Donoghue were changes from the drawn final. Ruth and N.Delahunty were subs in the drawn final).

2005

Galway – J.Skehill, A.Leech, P.Loughnane, P.Callanan, J.Hughes, C.O'Donovan, K.Kilkenny, A.Keary, K.Coen, S.Glynn, J.Greene, A.Callanan, B.Murphy, C.Kavanagh, J.Canning. Subs – F.Kerrigan for Coen, S.Howley for O'Donovan, T.Flannery for Callanan, J.Gilsen for Murphy, B.Kenny for Leech.

Limerick – G.Flynn, S.Brown, L.Hurley, T.Condon, J.Kelly, D.Moloney, G.O'Mahoney, D.Moore, S.Hickey, D.Hanley, J.Ryan, B.O'Sullivan, M.Ryan, E.Ryan, D.O'Sullivan. Subs – G.Allis for D.O'Sullivan, G.Collins for Moore, D.O'Connor for Allis.

2006

Tipperary – J.Ryan, M.Cahill, P.Maher, B.Maher, E.Hogan, T.Stapleton, J.O'Keeffe, J.McLoughney, G.Ryan, S.Hennessy, T.McGrath, N.Bergin, P.Bourke, T.Dunne, T.Dalton. Subs – M.Gleeson for Bergin, S.Callinan for Dunne.

Galway – J.Skehill, J.Ryan, M.McMahon, A.Moylan, D.Burke, K.Keane, S.Quinn, E.Forde, G.Lally, A.Harte, M.Corcoran, L.Tully, S.Cohen, J.Canning, G.Hennelly. Subs – E.Concannon for Corcoran, K.Killilea for Lally, G.Burke for Harte, N.Lynch for Hennelly.

2007

Tipperary – J.Logue, K.O'Gorman, Padraig Maher, S.O'Brien, J.Barry, J.Coughlin, M.Cahill, B.Maher, N.McGrath, S.Hennessy, C.Lorigan, S.Carey, J.O'Neill, Patrick Maher, M.Heffernan. Subs – P.Murphy for Patrick Maher, J.Gallagher for O'Gorman, D.O'Brien for Lorigan.

Cork – D.McCarthy, C.Hurley, A.Kearney, K.Murphy, L.McLoughlin, J.Herlihy, C.O'Donovan, S.Farrell, D.O'Sullivan, P.Gould, M.Bowles, M.O'Mahony, L.O'Farrell, R.White, R.Clifford. Subs – S.McDonnell for Farrell, G.O'Connor for Kearney, D.Stack for Bowles, C.McCarthy for Stack, E.McCarthy for O'Sullivan.

2008

Kilkenny – E.Murphy, D.Healy, M.Walsh, A.Cuddihy, M.Moloney, R.Doyle, C.Fogarty, C.Kenny, J.Gannon, J.Brennan, T.Breen, R.Hickey, P.McCarthy, W.Walsh, M.Gaffney. Subs – M.O'Dwyer for Gaffney, D.Purcell for Gannon, C.Maher for Hickey.

Galway – F.Flannery, D.Connolly, R.Burke, G.O'Halloran, N.Donoghue, D.Cooney, R.Foy, D.Burke, D.Glennon, N.Quinn, N.Burke, D.Fox, R.Cummins, A.Dolan, B.Burke. Subs – B.Flaherty for Foy, M.Dolphin for Glennon, J.Cannon for Quinn, L.Madden for Fox.

2009

Galway – F.Flannery, J.Coen, D.Burke, C.Burke, M.Keating, B.Flaherty, J.Cooney, J.Regan, D.Glennon, D.Fox, N.Burke, J.Grealish, R.Cummins, R.Badger, S.Maloney. Subs – M.Horan for Keating, T.Horan for Badger, N.Keary for Grealish.

Kilkenny – J.Power, J.Lyng, D.Kenny, I.Duggan, J.Gannon, R.Doyle, L.Harney, C.Kenny, O.Walsh, G.Brennan, S.Kehoe, C.Buckley, M.Gaffney, W.Walsh, C.Maher. Subs – S.Phelan for Kehoe, G.Aylward for W.Walsh, P.Walsh for Brennan.

CAPTAINS OF WINNING ALL-IRELAND MINOR HURLING TEAMS

1928—L. Horgan (Cork)
1929—P. Donnelly (Waterford)
1930—J. Russell (Tipperary)
1931—J. Shortall {Kilkenny)
1932—D. O'Gorman (Tipperary)
1933—J. Fletcher (Tipperary)
1934—C. Maher (Tipperary)
1935—P. Grace (Kilkenny)
1936—E. Tallent (Kilkenny)
1937—M. Goggin (Cork)
1938—K. McGrath (Cork)
1939—T. Barry (Cork)
1940—P. McCarthy (Limerick)
1941—S. Condon {Cork)
1942-44—Abandoned
1945—D. Healy (Dublin)
1946—L. Donnelly (Dublin)
1947—P. Kenny (Tipperary)
1948—M. Flannelly (Waterford)
1949—J. O'Grady (Tipperary)
1950—P. Lennon (Kilkenny)
1951—J. Clifford (Cork)
1952—A. Wall (Tipperary)
1953—B. Quinn (Tipperary)
1954—B. Boothman (Dublin)
1955—R. Reidy (Tipperary)
1956—P. Ryan (Tipperary)
1957—J. Doyle (Tipperary)
1958—P. Cobbe (Limerick)
1959—L. Kiely (Tipperary)
1960—W. Grace (Kilkenny)
1961—J. Dunphy (Kilkenny)
1962—J. Dunphy (Kilkenny)
1963—W. Bernie (Wexford)
1964—K. Cummins (Cork)
1965—L. Martin (Dublin)
1966—P. Bernie (Wexford)
1967—P. Moylan (Cork)
1968—T. Byrne (Wexford)
1969—S. Collins (Cork)
1970—P. Kavanagh (Cork)
1971—J . Buckley (Cork)
1972—B. Cody (Kilkenny)
1973—K. Robinson (Kilkenny)
1974—L. Geaney (Cork)
1975—H. Ryan (Kilkenny)
1976—J. Hogan (Tipperary)
1977—S. Fennelly (Kilkenny)
1978—P. Murphy (Cork)
1979—C. Coughlan (Cork)
1980—J. Maher (Tipperary)
1981—E. Kennedy (Kilkenny)
1982—J. Kennedy (Tipperary)
1983—A. Cunningham (Galway)
1984—A. O'Riordan (Limerick)
1985—M. O'Mahony (Cork)
1986—M. Hogan (Offaly)
1987—T Moylan (Offaly)
1988—P. Brophy (Kilkenny)
1989—B. Whelahan (Offaly)
1990—J. McDermott (Kilkenny)
1991—D. O'Neill (Kilkenny)
1992—C. Donovan (Galway)
1993—S. Doyle (Kilkenny)
1994—G. Kennedy (Galway)
1995—B. O'Keeffe (Cork)
1996—W. Maher (Tipperary)
1997—J. Reddan (Clare)
1998—C. McCarthy (Cork)
1999—J. Culkin (Galway)
2000—R.Murray (Galway)
2001—T.O'Leary (Cork)
2002—M.Rice (Kilkenny)
2003—R.Power (Kilkenny)
2004—J.Lee (Galway)
2005—A.Keary (Galway)
2006—J.McLoughney (Tipperary)
2007—B.Maher (Tipperary)
2008—T.Breen (Kilkenny)
2009—R.Cummins (Galway)

ALL-IRELAND MINOR HURLING FINAL REFEREES

1928—Willie Walsh (Waterforcl)
1929—Jim Walsh (Dublin)
1930—Stephen Jordan (Galway)
1931—Paddy McNamee {Antrim)
1932—P. O'Donnell (Waterford)
1933—Tull Considine (Clare)
1934—Sean Robbins (Offaly)
1935—Jim O'Regan 1Cork)
1936—Ignatius Harney (Galway)
1937—Dan Ryan (Kerry)
1938—Eugene Kelly (Galway)
1939—Mick Hennessy (Clare)
1940—Dr. Joe Stuart (Dublin)
1941—Dr. Joe Stuart (Dublin)
1945—Jim Barry (Cork)
1946—M. J. Flaherty {Galway)
1947—John Conroy (Laois)
1948—Gerry Rosengrave (Dublin)
1949—Gerry Rosengrave (Dublin)
1950—J. Howard {Dublin)
1951—M. Feeney (Dublin)
1952—John Conroy (Laois)
1953—John Conroy (Laois)
1954—Charlie Conway (Cork)
1955—M. Leahy (Dublin)
1956—C. McLoughlin (Dublin)
1957—C. McLoughlin (Dublin)
1958—G. Rosengrave (Dublin)
1959—P. Kelly (Laois)
1960—Paddy Cronin (Cork)
1961—Clem Foley (Dublin)
1962—Paddy Cronin (Cork)
1963—Aubrey Higgins (Galway)
1964—Jimmy Duggan (Galway)
1965—Aubrey Higgins (Galway)

1966—Tom Foran (Tipperary) (draw)
J. Hatton (Wicklow) (replay)
1967—P. Johnson (Kilkenny)
1968—Mick Slattery (Clare)
1969—Jimmy Rankins (Laois)
1970—Clem Foley (Dublin)
1971—Mick Spain (Offaly)
1972—John Moloney (Tipperary)
1973—Sean O'Connor (Limerick)
1974—Mick Spain (Offaly)
1975—Jimmy Rankins (Loois)
1976—Paddy Cronin (Cork)
1977—Gerry Kirwan (Offaly)
1978—Jim Joe Landers (Waterford)
1979—Noel O'Donoghue (Dublin)
1980—Noel Dalton (Waterford)
1981—Michael Kelleher (Kildare)
1982—Willie Horgan (Cork}
1983—Pascal Long (Kilkenny)
1984—Frank Murphy (Cork)
1985—Seamus Brennan (Galway)
1986—John Moore (Waterford)
1987—Pascal Long (Kilkenny)
1988—Pat Delaney (Laois)
1989—Willie Horgan (Cork)
1990—Willie Barrett (Tipperary)
1991—Pat Horan (Offaly)
1992—Terence Murray (Limerick)
1993—Sean McMahon (Clare)
1994—A. MacSuibhne {Dublin)
1995—Pat O,Connor (Limerick)
1996—Joe O'Leary (Cork)
1997—Michael Wadding (Waterford)
1998—Gerry Devlin (Armagh)
1999—Pat Aherne (Carlow)
2000—B.Kelly (Westmeath)
2001—T.McIntyre (Antrim)
2002—D.Kirwan (Cork)
2003—D.Kirwan (Cork)
2004—J.Sexton (Limerick) (draw)
B.Gavin (Offaly) (replay)
2005—E.Morris (Dublin)
2006—D.Connolly (Kilkenny)
2007—J.Owens (Wexford)
2008—C.McAllister (Cork)
2009—J.McGrath (Westmeath)

MUNSTER MINOR HURLING FINALS

1928—Cork 3-4, Waterforcl 3-2
1929—Waterford 7-5, Tipperary 0-2
1930—Tipperary 4-3, Cork 3-0
1931—Tipperary 6-5, Waterford 6-3
1932—Tipperary 7-8, Clare 3-0
1933—Tipperary 3-1, Cork 2-2
1934—Tipperary 3-6, Waterford 0-5
1935—Tipperary 4-3, Cork 2-1
1936—Cork 6-5, Tipperary 1-4
1937—Cork 8-4, Limerick 3-2
1938—Cork 9-3, Kerry 0-0
1939—Cork 8-3, Clare 0-2
1940—Limerick 8-3, Clare 0-4
1941—Cork 4-6, Tipperary 3-3
1942-44 (inclusive)—No championship
1945—Tipperary 8-10, Clare 0-2
1946—Tipperary 5-6, Cork 4-2
1947—Tipperary 2-4, Waterford 1-2
1948—Waterford 3-6, Tipperary 0-3
1949—Tipperary 5-6, Clare 5-5
1950—Tipperary 12-3, Clare 2-0
1951—Cork 5-11, Limerick 1-3
1952—Tipperary 10-7, Clare 1-2
1953—Tipperary 3-11, Limerick 3-3
1954—Tipperary 3-5, Limerick 2-3
1955—Tipperary 8-11, Waterford 2-5
1956—Tipperary 10-10, Waterford 4-4
1957—Tipperary 3-8, Limerick 1-4
1958—Limerick 8-9, Waterford 2-5
1959—Tipperary 5-8, Limerick 1-4
1960—Tipperary 6-7, Galway 4-3
1961—Tipperary 7-11, Cork 1 -6
1962—Tipperary 4-11, Cark 4-1
1963—Limerick 4-12, Tipperary 5-4
1964—Cork 2-14, Tipperary 2-9
1965—Limerick 5-5, Tipperary 3-9
1966—Cork 6-7, Galway 2-8
1967—Cork 4-10, Limerick 0-3
1968—Cork 7-8, Waterford 4-2
1969—Cork 1-12, Tipperary 2-4
1970—Cork 3-8, Tipperary 4-4
1971—Cork 6-13, Clare 3-5
1972—Cork 4-11, Limerick 0-3
1973—Tipperary 5-12, Limerick 5-4
1974—Cork 3-7, Tipperary 2- 10 (draw)
Cork 2-11, Tipperary 2-7 (replay)
1975—Cork 3-16, Tipperary 1-7
1976—Tipperary 5-10, Limerick 5-6
1977—Cork 2-8, Limerick 2-7
1978—Cork 1-14, Tipperary 3-6
1979—Cork 3-17, Limerick 4-4
1980—Tipperary 1-17, Limerick 1-4
1981—Clare 3-13, Tipperary 3-11
1982—Tipperary 1-10, Limerick 1-7
1983—Tipperary 3-15, Limerick 2-8
1984—Limerick 3-6, Tipperary 2-7
1985—Cork I-13, Tipperary 1-8
1986—Cork 3-10, Tipperary 2-13 (draw)
Cork 2-11, Tipperary 1-11 (replay)
1987—Tipperary 2- 1, Cork 1-9
1988—Cork 5-7, Tipperary 1-2
1989—Clare 2-13, Limerick 2-12
1990—Cork 1-9, Clare 0-9
1991—Tipperary 3-13, Limerick I-5
1992—Waterford 4-7, Tipperary 3-10 (draw)
Waterford 2-10, Tipperary 0-14 (replay)
1993—Tipperary 1-12, Cork 1-9
1994—Cork 2-15, Waterford 0-9
1995—Cork 3-18, Waterforcl 0-10
1596—Tipperary 2-19, Waterford 1-11
1997—Tipperary 2-13, Clare 1-13
1998—Cork 3-13, Clare 0-8
1999—Tipperary 1-13, Clare 2-7

2000—Cork 2-19, Limerick 1-10.
2001—Tipperary 1-13, Cork 1-6.
2002—Tipperary 3-7, Cork 2-7.
2003—Tipperary 2-12, Cork 0-16.
2004—Cork 2-13, Tipperary 3-8.
2005—Cork 2-18, Limerick 1-12.
2006—Cork 2-20, Tipperary 1-15.
2007—Tipperary 0-18, Cork 1-11.
2008—Cork 0-19, Tipperary 0-18.
2009—Waterford 0-18, Tipperary 1-13.

LEINSTER MINOR HURLING FINALS

1928—Dublin 6-6, Offaly 3-2
1929—Meath 10-1, Kilkenny 6-1
1930—Kilkenny 6-3, Laois 3-5
1931—Kilkenny 4-9, Meath 0-3
1932—Kilkenny 9-6, Dublin 6-1
1933—Kilkenny 5-8, Dublin 2-6
1934—Laois 8-4, Dublin 2-0
1935—Kilkenny 7-8, Laois 1-1
1936—Kilkenny 3-13, Dublin 1-1
1937—Kilkenny 6-12, Dublin 2-4
1938—Dublin 5-4, Laois 1-3
1939—Kilkenny 3-8, Dublin 2-2
1940—Dublin 10-5, Laois 3-3
(Laois awarded title on objection)
1941—Laois 3-5, Kilkenny 2-4
1942—Kilkenny 3-10, Dublin 0-4
1943-1944—Championship suspended
1945—Dublin 5-4, Kilkenny 3-1
1946—Dublin 7-5, Laois 0-1
1947—Dublin 1-5, Kilkenny 2-2 (draw)
Dublin 3-2, Kilkenny 2-4 (replay)
1948—Kilkenny 5-2, Offaly 3-6
1949—Kilkenny 4-6, Dublin 0-4
1950—Kilkenny 4-2, Offaly 3-2
1951—Kilkenny 5- 11, Dublin 2-2
1952—Dublin 4-7, Kilkenny 4-5
1953—Dublin 2-6, Laois 1-4
1954—Dublin 4-12, Kilkenny 4-7
1955—Kilkenny 3-10, Wexford 5-4 (draw)
Kilkenny 0-11, Wexford 0-8 (replay)
1956—Kilkenny 4-7, Wexford 3-7
1957—Kilkenny 5-10, Offaly 4-2
1958—Kilkenny 5-11, Laois 1-7
1959—Kilkenny 7-9, Wexford 3-4
1960—Kilkenny 6-14, Wexford 5-5
1961—Kilkenny 4-12, Dublin 0-7
1962—Kilkenny 5-7, Wexford 5-4
1963—Wexford 6-10, Kilkenny 6-8
1964—Laois 4-9, Kilkenny 3-8
1965—Dublin 4-7, Wexford 1-6
1966—Wexford 7-6, Laois 1-7
1967—Wexford 6-7, Dublin 2-3
1968—Wexford 4-11, Kilkenny 4-4
1969—Kilkenny 3-9, Dublin 2-7
1970—Wexford 3-10, Kilkenny 1-10
1971—Kilkenny 7-18, Wexford 3-5
1972—Kilkenny 7-10, Wexford 0-4
1973—Kilkenny 3-10, Wexford 2-9
1974—Kilkenny 8-19, Dublin 3-5
1975—Kilkenny 2-18, Dublin 3-4
1976—Kilkenny 2-14, Wexford 1-8
1977—Kilkenny 5-10, Wexford 3-6
1978—Kilkenny4-19, Laois 2-6
1979—Kilkenny 5-13, Antrim 1-9
1980—Wexford 1-10, Dublin 2-6
1981—Kilkenny 3-10, Wexford 3-9
1982—Kilkenny 3-16, Offaly 3-4
1983—Dublin 5-14, Wexford 4-12
1984—Kilkenny 2-10, Wexford 1-11
1985—Wexford 0-12, Kilkenny 0-8
1986—Offaly 4-7, Wexford 1 -5
1987—Offaly 2-13, Kilkenny 0-12
1988—Kilkenny 2-16, Offaly 0-6
1989—Offaly 0-14, Kilkenny 0-14 (draw)
Offaly 4-13, Kilkenny 0- 13 (replay)
1990—Kilkenny 3-15, Laois 0-15
1991—Kilkenny 1-20, Laois 0-4
1992—Kilkenny 1-9, Wexford 0-11
1993—Kilkenny 4-14, Dublin 0-11
1994—Kilkenny 2-13, Offaly 3-6
1995—Kilkenny 4- 16, Offaly 2-6
1996—Kilkenny 1-16, Dublin 1-11
1997—Kilkenny 3-16, Offaly 0-10
1998—Kilkenny 1-11, Wexford 1-11 (draw)
Kilkenny 2-15, Wexford 0-6 (replay)
1999—Kilkenny 0-13, Wexford 0-13 (draw)
Kilkenny 2-13, Wexford 1-11 (replay)
2000—Offaly 0-13, Dublin 0-8.
2001—Kilkenny 3-16, Wexford 1-9.
2002—Kilkenny 2-15, Wexford 2-8.
2003—Kilkenny 0-18, Offaly 0-13.
2004—Kilkenny 1-15, Dublin 1-4.
2005—Dublin 0-17, Wexford 0-12.
2006—Kilkenny 4-22, Carlow 1-5.
2007—Dublin 2-14, Kilkenny 1-10.
2008—Kilkenny 1-19, Wexford 0-12.
2009—Kilkenny 1-19, Wexford 0-11.

CONNACHT MINOR HURLING

1931—Galway 7-2, Roscommon 1-1
1932—Galway 9-5, Roscommon 0-0
1933—Galway. No other team entered.
1934—Galway. No other team entered.
1935—Galway 9-4, Mayo 1-3
1936—Galway 7-7, Roscommon 1-1
1937—Galway 4-6, Roscommon 0-2
1938—Galway 7-3, Roscommon 3-0
1939—Galway 5-5, Roscommon 2-2
1940—Galway 7-5, Roscommon 1-2
1941—Galway. No other team entered.
1942-1944—No competition.
1945—Galway. No other team entered.
1946—Galway 5-9, Roscommon 0-1
1947—Galway 9-6, Roscommon 1-1
1948—Galway 4-6, Roscommon 5-2
1949—Galway 2-7, Roscommon 3-4 (draw)

Galway 6-5, Roscommon 4-4 (replay)
1950—Galway 8-7, Roscommon 2-0
1951—Galway 6-9, Roscommon 2-1
1952—Galway 3-7, Mayo 2-0
1953—Galway 12-10, Roscommon 1-0
1954—Galway 9-9, Roscommon 1-1
1955— Galway 12-11, Roscommon 2-1
1956—Galway 11-20, Roscommon 1-1
1957—Galway w.o., Roscommon scr.
1958—Galway 12-10, Roscommon 1-1
N.B.: Galway competed in Munster (1959-1969)
1959—Roscommon 3-8, Mayo 3-2
1960—Roscommon 2-8, Mayo 2-5
1961—No championship
1962—Roscommon.
1963—Roscommon 1-7, Mayo 3-0
1964—Mayo —, Roscommon —
1965—Leitrim 8-5, Mayo 0-0
1966—Roscommon
1967—Roscommon, Leitrim
(competed in 'B' minor championship)
1968—Roscommon
(competed in 'B' minor championship)
1969—Roscommon
(competed in 'B' minor championship)
1970-1988—Galway represented Province in All-Ireland series.
1989—Galway 2-14, Roscommon 0-6
1990-to date—Galway represented Province in All-Ireland series.

ULSTER MINOR HURLING FINALS

1930—Down 9-7, Monaghan 0-6
1931—Antrim 5-0, Down 3-1
1932—Down 3-5, Antrim 2-1
1933—Antrim 5-4, Donegal 4-5
1934—Down 8-8, Donegal 0-1
1935—Antrim 7-7, Down 3-1
1936—Antrim 6-3, Down 3-0
1937—Antrim 5-7, Donegal 2-2
1938—Antrim w.o.
Note: Donegal, the other finalists, were disqualified for being late taking the field in the semi-final against Derry.
1939—Antrim 11-2, Down 0-0
1940—Antrim beat Derry
1941—Antrim only team to compete
1942-44—Abandoned
1945—Antrim 11-6, Donegal 1-1
1946—Antrim 8-7, Donegal 0-2
1947—Antrim 10-5, Down 0-0
1948—Antrim 15-6, Donegal 0-0
1949—Antrim 13-6, Donegal 1-1
1950—Antrim 4-3, Armagh 1-3
1951—Antrim 12-2, Down 0-1
1952—Antrim 8-8, Down 1-1
1953—Antrim 11-14, Donegal 1-0
1954—Antrim 9-9, Down 1 -3
1955—Antrim 5-4, Armagh 2-2
1956—Antrim 7-4, Down 1-3
1957—Down 4-1, Antrim 3-3
1958—Antrim 10-5, Down 0-2
1959—Antrim 12-6, Donegal 0-2
1960—Antrim 16-4, Donegal 1-0
1961—Antrim 11-5, Donegal 4-4
1962—Antrim 12-7, Donegal 2-3
1963—Antrim 6-12, Donegal 1-1
1964—Antrim 11-11, Armagh 0-0
1965—Antrim 7-3, Armagh 0-1
1966—Antrim 6-6, Tyrone 1-3
1967—Down 5-2, Tyrone 4-2
Note: Special final Down took part in All-Ireland "B" championship in 1967 while Antrim competed in All-Ireland "A" championship.
1968—Antrim only team in "A" championship.
Note: Down won Special Minor Hurling title and went on to win All-Ireland.
1969—Antrim 2-11, Down 4-3
1970 Antrim 4- 12, Down 0-5
1971—Down 5-11, Derry 4-4
1972—Down 4-8, Armagh 2-4
1973—None
1974—Derry 3-6, Armagh 2-8
1975—Armagh 3-8, Down 3-6
1976—Down 5- 12, Tyrone 1-3
1977—None
1978—Down 4-9, Derry 1-11
1979—Derry 3-8, Monaghan 2-4
1980—Derry 1-5, Armogh 1 -4
1981—Derry 3-6, Armagh 1 -4
1982—Derry 3-14, Armagh 2-2
1983—Derry 5-10, Monaghan 0-6
Note: From 1971-83 the Ulster championship was for the weaker counties and winners played in Minor "B" All-Ireland series. Antrim played in Leinster in 1971 and also 1977-83. They represented Ulster in the All-Ireland "A" championship from 1972-76. After winning the All-Ireland "B" championship in 1978 Down also competed in Leinster from 1979-83.

1984—Down 3-6, Antrim 1-11
1985—Down 5-4, Antrim 2-9
1986—Antrim 2-9, Derry 1-10
1987—Antrim 5-9, Down 0-6
1988—Antrim 2-10, Down 2-9
1989—Down 2-11, Antrim 3-8 (draw)
Down 3-8, Antrim 2-8 (replay)
1990—Derry 4-11, Antrim 1 -8
1991—Derry 3-10, Antrim 2-11
1992—Antrim 0-12, Down 0-7
1993—Antrim 2-13, Down 1-9
1994—Down 3-11, Antrim 3-10
1995—Antrim 2-17, Derry 1-4
1996—Antrim 3- 13, Derry 2-10
1997—Antrim 3-14, Down 1-10
1998—Antrim 3-9, Derry 0-8
1999—Antrim 2-1 3, Down 0-3
2000—Antrim 2-11, Derry 1-9.
2001—Derry 0-13, Antrim 2-5.
2002—Antrim 1-11, Derry 0-4.
2003—Antrim 2-11, Derry 2-9.
2004—Antrim 5-15, Down 3-7.

2005—Antrim 3-18, Derry 2-7.
2006—Antrim 8-18, Derry 2-5.
2007—Antrim 2-14, Down 3-8.
2008—Antrim 3-18, Down 0-5.
2009—Antrim 4-16, Derry 0-9.

ALL-IRELAND UNDER-21 HURLING FINALS

1964—Tipperary 8-9, Wexford 3-1
1965—Wexford 3-7, Tipperary 1-4
1966—Cork 3-12, Wexford 5-6 (first game)
Cork 4-9, Wexford 4-9 (replay)
Cork 9-9, Wexford 5-9 (second replay)
1967—Tipperary 1-8, Dublin 1-7
1968—Cork 2-18, Kilkenny 3-9
1969—Cork 5-13, Wexford 4-7
1970—Cork 3-8, Wexford 2-11 (draw)
Cork 5-17, Wexford 0-8 (replay)
1971—Cork 7-8, Wexford 1 -11
1972—Galway 2-9, Dublin 1-10
1973—Cork 2-10, Wexford 4-2
1974—Kilkenny 3-8, Waterford 3-7
1975—Kilkenny 5-13, Cork 2-19
1976—Cork 2-17, Kilkenny 1-8
1977—Kilkenny 2-9, Cork 1-9
1978—Galway 3-5, Tipperary 2-8 (draw)
Galway 3-15, Tipperary 2-8 (replay)
1979—Tipperary 2-12, Galway 1-9
1980—Tipperary 2-9, Kilkenny 0-14
1981—Tipperary 2-16, Kilkenny 1-10
1982—Cork 0-12, Galway 0-11
1983—Galway 0-12, Tipperary 1-6
1984—Kilkenny 1-12, Tipperary 0-11
1985—Tipperary 1-10, Kilkenny 2-6
1986—Galway 1-14, Wexford 2-5
1987—Limerick 2-15, Galway 3-6
1988—Cork 4-11, Kilkenny 1-5
1989—Tipperary 4-10, Offaly 3-11
1990—Kilkenny 2-11, Tipperary 1-11
1991—Galway 2-17, Offaly 1-9
1992—Waterford 4-4, Offaly 0-16 (draw)
Waterford 0-12, Offaly 2-3 (replay)
1993—Galway 2-14, Kilkenny 3-11 (draw)
Galway 2-9, Kilkenny 3-3 (replay)
1994—Kilkenny 3-10, Galway 0-11
1995—Tipperary 1-14, Kilkenny 1-10
1996—Galway 1-14, Wexford 0-7
1997—Cork 3-11, Galway 0-13
1998—Cork 2-15, Galway 2-10
1999—Kilkenny 1-13, Galway 0-14
2000—Limerick 1-13, Galway 0-13.
2001—Limerick 0-17, Wexford 2-10.
2002—Limerick 3-17, Galway 0-8.
2003—Kilkenny 2-13, Galway 0-12.
2004—Kilkenny 3-21, Tipperary 1-6.
2005—Galway 1-15, Kilkenny 1-14.
2006—Kilkenny 2-14, Tipperary 2-14. (draw)
Kilkenny 1-11, Tipperary 0-11. (replay)
2007—Galway 5-11, Dublin 0-12.
2008—Kilkenny 2-13, Tipperary 0-15.
2009—Clare 0-15, Kilkenny 0-14.

ALL-IRELAND UNDER-21 HURLING FINALISTS

1964

Tipperary—P. O'Sullivan, W. Smith, N. O'Gorman, M. O'Meara, O. Killoran, C. Dwyer, L. Gaynor, M. Roche, J. Fogarty, N. Lane, M. Keating, F. Loughnane (capt.), J. Dillon, T. J. Butler, T. Brennan. Sub: P. J. Ryan for M. O'Meara.

Wexford—M. Jacob, J. Dunne, D. Quigley, B. Doyle, V. Staples, Jim Berry (capt.), W. Murphy, M. Byrne, J. Doran, C. Dowdall, C. Jacob, O. Cullen, S. Barron, A. Maher, P. Quigley. Subs: M. Kinsella for J. Dunne, B. Murray for M. Byrne, P. O'Connor for A. Maher.

1965

Wexford—M. Jacob, W. O'Neill (capt.), D. Quigley, A. Somers, V. Staples, M. Kinsella, W. Murphy, E. Ryan, J. Doran, C. Dowdall, P. Quigley, S. Barron, A. Maher, A. Doran, Jack Berry. Sub: C. Jacob.

Tipperary—S. Shinnors, M. Flanagan, J. Costigan, D. Burke, O. Killoran, N. O'Gorman, L. Gaynor, P J. Ryan, J. Quinlan, F. Loughnane, M. Keating, P. Ryan, T. Brennan, T. J. Butler, J. Ryan. Sub: M. O'Meara.

1966

Cork—J. Mitchell, W. Murphy, T. Falvey, P. O'Sullivan, C. Roche, J. Russell, D. Coughlan, J. McCarthy, G. McCarthy (capt.), S. Barry, T. Browne, P. Curley, C. McCarthy, A. O'Flynn, Eddie O'Brien. Subs: A. Maher, B. McKeown. (B. McKeown, K. Farrell, D. Clifford and P. O'Riordan played in first drawn game. T. Falvey, D. Coughlan, G. McCarthy and A. O'Flynn were in for second game. Subs in first game: T. Falvey for B. McKeown, G. McCarthy for J. Russell. Sub in second game: T. Browne for Eddie O'Brien. T. Browne played in third game in place of B. Wylie.)

Wexford—H. Butler, W. O'Neill, M. Nolan, A. Somers, W. Bowe, M. Kinsella, V. Staples, M. Jacob, C. Dowdall, S. Barron, P. Quigley, J. Quigley, P. Butler, A. Doran, E. Cousins. Sub: M. Gardiner. (J. Murphy and T. Murphy played in first drawn game. P. O'Brien and B. Ronan were on for second game. Sub in first game: B. Ronan for T. Murphy. Subs in second game: N. Rochford for B. Ronan, B. Ronan for N. Rochford. H. Butler, W. Bowe and P Butler came on for third game in place of P. O'Brien, B. Ronan and M. Gardiner.)

1967

Tipperary—H. Condron, S. Ryan, J. Kelly, D. Grady, M. Esmonde. T. O'Connor, S. Hogan, P. J. Ryan (capt.), C. Davitt, P. Lowry, N. O'Dwyer, J. Ryan, J. Walsh, P O'Connor, J. Flanagan. Subs: M. Nolan, T. Delaney.

Dublin—M. Behan, M. Hannick, P. Martin, C. Brennan, W. Markey, F. Cooney, G. O'Driscoll, H. Dalton, F. McDonnell, E. McGrath, E. Davey, L. Hennebry, T. Grealish, C. Moran, N. Kinsella. Sub: M. Kennedy.

1968

Cork—B. Hurley, W. Murphy, B. Tobin, F Norberg, N. Dunne, W. Walsh, R. Cummins, D. Clifford, P. Moylan, B. Meade, S. Murphy, P. Hegarty (capt.), H. O'Sullivan, P. Curley, P. Ring. Subs: M. McCarthy, R. Lehane, J. Murphy.

Kilkenny—J. Nolan, L. Byrne, C. O'Brien, M. Leahy, J. O'Shea, N. Morrissey, P. Kealy, F. Cummins, P. Lawlor, W. Harte, F. Farrell, J. Kinsella, P. Dowling, P. Keyes, B. O'Sullivan. Subs: T. Grant, S. Brennan, S. Kearney.

1969

Cork—B. Hurley, M. McCarthy (capt.), B. Tobin, F. Norberg, S. Looney, D. Clifford, Ted O'Brien, S. Murphy, P Moylan, B. Meade, W. Walsh, N. Dunne, F. Keane, R. Cummins, B. Cummins. Sub: P. McDonnell for S. Looney.

Wexford—P. Cox, E. McDonald, E. Murphy, B. Butler, E. Walsh, J. Russell, L. Bennett, M. Dalton, E. Buggy, T. Royce, M. Quigley, M. Browne, J. Quigley, M. Butler, C. Doran. Subs: T. Byrne for C. Doran, M. Casey.

1970

Cork—M. Coleman, M. McCarthy, P. McDonnell, B. Tobin, S. Murphy, J. Horgan, Ted O'Brien (capt.), S. Looney, P Moylan, C. Kelly, B. Cummins, K. McSweeney, S. O'Leary, J. Barrett, P. Ring.

(M. Malone and J. Nodwell played in drawn game. S. O'Leary and C. Kelly were on for replay. Subs in drawn game: S. O'Leary for M. Malone, C. Kelly for J. Nodwell.)

Wexford—P. Cox, J. Prendergast, J. Russell, E. McDonald, G. Collins, L. Byrne, L. Bennett (capt.), T. Byrne, C. Doran, B. Murphy M. Quigley, E. Murphy, M. Butler, M. Casey, P. Byrne. Subs: A. Kerrigan for B. Murphy, M. Byrne for P. Byrne, E. Walsh for E. Murphy Subs in drawn game: A. Kerrigan for P. Byrne, P. Byrne for B. Murphy.

(Wexford same team in draw and replay).

1971

Cork—M. Coleman, J. Horgan, P. McDonnell (capt.), B. Murphy, Seamus O'Farrell, M. O'Doherty, B. Coleman, S. Looney, N. Crowley, E. Fitzpatrick, M. Malone, K. McSweeney, B. Cummins, J. Rothwell, S. O'Leary. Subs: P. Casey for S. O'Farrell, D. Collins for E. Fitzpatrick, P. Kavanagh for S. Looney.

Wexford—P. Cox, J. Higgins, G. O'Connor, P. O'Brien, A. Kerrigan, L. Kinsella, L. Bennett, M. Quigley (capt.), A. Dwyer, B. Dunne, T. Byrne, S. Kinsella, P. Flynn, M. Casey, M. Butler. Subs: J. Russell for A. Dwyer, B. Murphy for J. Higgins.

1972

Galway—E. Campbell, L. Glynn, G. Kelly, L. Shields, I. Clarke (capt.), F. Donoghue, A. Brehony, G. Glynn, F. Burke, M. Coen, A. Fenton, M. Donoghue, M. Barrett, T. O'Donoghue, G. Holland. Subs: P. J. Molloy for M. Coen, J. McDonagh for M. Barrett.

Dublin—M. Holden, M. Leonard, N. Quinn, V. Lambe, G. Ryan, J. Brennan, E. Rheinisch, P. J. Holden, M. Greally, P. Lee, V. Holden, J. Kealy (capt.), C. Hennebry, B. Sweeney, J. Whelan. Sub: G. O'Connor for M. Greally, D. O'Donovan for P. Lee.

1973

Cork—F. O'Sullivan, M. Corbett, L. Kelly, B. Murphy, M. O'Doherty (capt.), J. Buckley, D. Burns, T. Crowley, B. Cotter, P. Kavanagh, Seamus O'Farrell, Tony Murphy, D. Relihan, T. Fogarty, S. O'Leary. Subs: T. Sheehan, J. Barry Murphy.

Wexford—J. Nolan, M. Hickey, S. Byrne, M. Dempsey, J. Moloney, E. Breen, R. Lambert, R. Kinsella, P. J. Harris, J. Murphy, A. Dwyer, C. Keogh, N. Walsh, J. Allen, S. Storey. Subs: M. Carty, S. Murphy.

1974

Kilkenny—K. Fennelly, T. McCormack, M. Hogan, J. Dunne, G. Henderson, B. Cody, M. Tierney, J. Dowling, S. Brophy, N. Brennan, G. Woodcock, G. Fennelly (capt.), P. Kearney, A. Teehan, W. Fitzpatrick. Subs: R. Sweeney for A. Teehan, P. Mulcahy for N. Brennan.

Waterford—W. Ryan, F. McCarthy, M. Flynn, K. Ryan, L. O'Brien, J. Galvin, E. Ryan, P. Egan, P. McGrath, B. Mansfield, L. Power, T. Casey, P. O'Keeffe, M. McNamara, P. Moore. Subs: L. Ahearne for P. Moore, E. Kehoe for M. Moore.

1975

Kilkenny—K. Fennelly (capt.), J. Marnell, J. Moran, Dick O'Hara, G. Henderson, B. Cody, J. Grace, J. Dowling, G. Fennelly, J. Hennessy, M. Tierney, J. Lyng, Terry Brennan, R. Sweeney, W. Fitzpatrick. Subs: K. Robinson, J. O'Sullivan, G. Woodcock.

Cork—F. O'Sullivan, J. Kennefick, D. Hurley, J. O'Herlihy, C. Brassil, K. Murphy, J. Crowley, J. Fenton, F. Delaney, B. Óg Murphy, Seán O'Farrell, Tadhg Murphy, E. O'Sullivan, J. Barry Murphy, Tom Collins. Sub: Tadhg O'Sullivan for T. Collins.

1976

Cork—J. Cronin, J. Crowley, W. Geaney, D. McCurtain, J. Fenton, T. Cashman, F. Delaney, S. O'Mahony, C. Brassil, J. Allen, R. McDonnell,

P. Horgan, Tadhg Murphy (capt.), K. Murphy, D. Buckley. Sub: W. Reidy.

Kilkenny—K. Fennelly, J. Marnell, D. Tyrell, D. O'Hara, H. Ryan, J. Moran, R. Reid, J. Hennessy, K. Robinson, J. Lyng, M. Lyng, K. Brennan, B. Fennelly, G. Tyrell, O. Bergin. Subs: B. Waldron, P. Dunphy, M. Kennedy.

1977

Kilkenny—E. Mahon, J. Lennon, J. Henderson, P. Prendergast, J. Hennessy, D. O'Hara, R. Reid, P. Lannon, M. Kennedy, R. Power, M. Lyng (capt.), B. Waldron, B. Fennelly, G. Tyrell, J. Wall. Sub: K. Brennan.

Cork—J. Cronin, J. Murphy, J. Crowley, F. Delaney, C. Brassil, T. Cashman, D. McCurtain, D. O'Herlihy, J. O'Brien, P. Horgan, T. Lyons, Paul Crowley, T. Murphy, R. McDonnell, D. Buckley. Subs: D. Keane, G. McEvoy, D. Ryan.

1978

Galway—G. Smith, C. Hayes, M. Headd, P. J. Burke, J. Greaney, M. Earls, S. Coen, S. Mahon, M. Kilkenny, G. Kennedy, J. Goode, P. Ryan, B. Forde (capt.), Matty Conneely, J. Ryan. Subs in drawn game: T. Brehony, J. Coen and S. Forde. G. Linnane played in drawn game. Gerry Kennedy came on for replay.

Tipperary—V. Mullins, J. Doyle, J. O'Dwyer, P. Loughnane, M. Stapleton, P. Fitzelle, G. Stapleton, J. Grace, P. Ryan, T. Walsh, M. Doyle, E. O'Shea, T. Ryan, S. Burke, T. Grogan. Subs: Enda Hogan, K. Fox, A. Slattery, J. Minogue played in drawn game. M. Stapleton was on for replay. Subs in drawn game: K. Fox, M. Murphy, and E. Hogan.

1979

Tipperary—V. Mullins, P. Loughnane, J. Ryan, E. Hogan, A. Slattery, J. O'Dwyer, G. Stapleton, G. O'Connor, P. Fox, M. Murphy, E. O'Shea, T. Grogan, B. Mannion, M. Doyle (capt.), P. Looby. Sub: P. Ryan for T. Grogan.

Galway—A. Carr, T. Brehony, M. Headd, C. Hayes (capt.), S. Coen M. Earls, E. Reilly, S. Davoren, M. Donoghue, J. Coen, G. Linnane, P. Ryan, S. Dolan, D. Burke, J. Ryan. Subs: G. Dempsey for M. Donoghue, J. Hanlon for G. Linnane, V. Kelly For M. Headd.

1980

Tipperary—V. Mullins, M. Ryan, Cormac Bonnar, P. Fox, B . Heffernan, J. O'Dwyer, P. McGrath, M. Kennedy, P. Kennedy (capt.), M. Murphy, B. Ryan, A. Buckley, J. Kennedy, D. O'Connell, P. Power. Sub: A. Kinsella for M. Kennedy.

Kilkenny—M. Walsh, M. Morrissey, M. Meagher, W. O'Hara, T. Lennon, W. Doherty, S. Fennelly, E. Wallace, G. Ryan, J Mulcahy, R. Murphy, M. Nash, W. McEvoy, L. Ryan, W. Purcell. Sub: J. Heffernan for R. Murphy.

1981

Tipperary—J . Farrell, M . Ryan, P . Brennan, P. Fox, I. Conroy, J. McIntyre, P. McGrath, A. Kinsella, P. Kennedy (capt.), N. English, B. Ryan, M. McGrath, G. O'Neill, D. O'Connell, A. Buckley.

Kilkenny—M. Walsh, P. Ryan, E. Aylward, J. Holden, S. Norris, W. O'Hara, M. Cleere, P. Gannon, M. Byrne, W. McEvoy, M. J. Ryan, W. Walton, J. Murphy, J. O'Dwyer, W. Purcell. Subs: S. Tyrell for J. Holden, E. Crowley for J. Murphy.

1982

Cork—G. Cunningham, M. McCarthy (capt.), M. Boylan, J. Hodgins, W. Cashman, K. O'Driscoll, Colm O'Connor, K. Hennessy, D. Curtin, Tony O'Sullivan, Tony Coyne, D. Walsh, E. Brosnan, M. O'Sullivan, Ger Motherway. Subs: P. Deasy for K. O'Driscoll, T. Mulcahy for G. Motherway, Gabriel McCarthy for M. O'Sullivan.

Galway—T. Coen, M. Mooney, P. Casserly, D. Burke, P. Healy, T. Nolan, O. Kilkenny, A. Staunton, J. Boland, M. Haverty, P Piggott, P. Murphy, J. Murphy, M. Grealish, M. McGrath. Subs: N. Morrissey for John Boland, A. Keady for M. Grealish.

1983

Galway—T. Coen, B. Dervan, P. Casserly (capt.), M. Donoghue, P. Finnerty, A. Keady, O. Kilkenny, A. Moylan, P. Healy, A. Staunton, M. Coleman, M. Costelloe, G. Burke, J. Murphy, M. McGrath. Subs: E. Ryan for G. Burke, C. Hennebry for M. Costelloe, M. Kenny for C. Hennebry.

Tipperary—K. Hogan, Colm Bonnar, P. Maher, E. Hogan, I. Conroy, N. English, D. Finnerty (capt.), J. Hayes, L. Bergin, P. Kenny, C. Donovan, M. McGrath, G. O'Neill, W. Peters, A. Browne. Subs: J. Kennedy for W. Peters, J. Maher for P. Kenny, V. Dooley for J. Hayes.

1984

Kilkenny—D. Burke, E. Wall, E. O'Connor, B. Young, D. Hoyne, L. Cleere, L. Walsh, T. Phelan, R. Heffernan, D. Carroll, P. Walsh, J. McDonald, L. McCarthy, R. McCarthy, S. Delahunty (capt.). Subs: P. Ryan for D. Carroll, M. Rafter for D. Carroll.

Tipperary—K. Hogan, J. McKenna, Eddie Hogan, Colm Bonnar, R. Stakelum, D. Kealy, J. Leahy, J. Kennedy, J. Hayes, A. Ryan, N. Sheehy, P. Kenny, A. Waters, D. Fogarty, M. Scully. Subs: W. Peters for P. Kenny, M. Cuningham for M. Scully.

1985

Tipperary—J. Leamy, N. McDonnell, P. O'Donoghue, Colm Bonnar, M. Corcoran, D.

Kealy, P. Delaney, J. Kennedy, A. Ryan, M. Cunningham, J. McGrath, N. Sheehy, J. Cormack, L. Stokes, M. Scully (capt.). Sub: M. Bryan for L. Stokes.

Kilkenny—R. Dunne, K. Ryan (capt.), E. O'Connor, P. Healy, T. Lannon, L. Cleere, L. O'Brien, T. Phelan, J. Scott, R. Moran, S. Delahunty, E. Morrissey, M. Dunne, M. Rafter, J. Walsh. Subs: P. Cleere for M. Rafter, T. Bawle for T. Phelan, P. Barron for J. Scott.

1986

Galway—J. Commins, P. Dervan, M. Kelly, M. Flaherty, M. Helebert, P. Malone, G. McInerney, T. Monaghan, D. Jennings, M. Connolly, A. Cunningham (capt.), A. Davoren, P. Nolan, Joe Cooney, P. Higgins. Subs: G. Elwood for P. Higgins, S. Keane for T. Monaghan.

Wexford—P. Nolan, J. Doyle, M. Foley, P. Bridges, L. O'Gorman, T. Dempsey, K. Murphy, Matt Foley, P. Barden, E. Sinnott, V. Murphy, D. Prendergast, M. Morrissey, P. Carton, R. Murphy. Subs: N. McDonald for M. Foley, J. Murray for D. Prendergast, C. Whelan for L. O'Gorman.

1987

Limerick—V. Murnane, A. Madden, P. Carey, D. Flynn, D. Nash, A. O'Riordan, M. Reale, G. Hegarty, J. O'Neill, G. Kirby, A. Carmody, G. Ryan (capt.), P. Barrett, J. O'Connor, L. O'Connor. Sub: D. Marren for P. Barrett.

Galway—M. Finnerty, B. Cawley, S. Dolphin, B. Cooney, T. Broderick, J. Burke, T. King, D. Cox, G. Coyne, M. Connolly (capt.), K. Coen, H. Davoren, M. Greaney, E. Burke, R. Duane. Subs: E. Lyons for M. Greaney, P. Killilea for T. Broderick, B. Hurney for K. Coen.

1988

Cork—T. Kingston, C. Connery (capt.), D. Irwin, S. O'Leary, C. Casey, P. Kenneally, A. Kealy, P. Delaney, J. Kennedy, A. Ryan, M. Cunningham, J. McGrath, N. Sheehy, J. Cormack, L. Stokes, M. Scully (capt.). Sub M. Bryan for L. Stokes.

Kilkenny—R. Dunne, K. Ryan (Capt.), E. O'Connor, P Healy, T. Lannon, L. Cleere, L. O'Brien, T. Phelan, J. Scott, R. Moran, S. Delahunty, E. Morrissey, M. Dunne, M. Rafter, J. Walsh. Subs: P. Cleere for M. Rafter, T. Bawle for T. Phelan, P. Barron for J. Scott.

1986

Galway—J. Commins, P. Dervan, M. Kelly, M. Flaherty, M. Helebert, P. Malone, G. McInerney, T. Monaghan, D. Jennings, M. Connolly, A. Cunningham (capt.), A. Davoren, P. Nolan, Joe Cooney, P. Higgins. Subs: G. Elwood for P. Higgins, S. Keane for T. Monaghan.

Wexford—P. Nolan, J. Doyle, M. Foley, P. Bridges, L. O'Gorman, T. Dempsey, K. Murphy, Matt Foley, P. Barden, E. Synnott, V. Murphy, D. Prendergast, M. Morrissey, P. Carton, R. Murphy. Subs: N. McDonald for M. Foley, J. Murray for D. Prendergast, C. Whelan for L. O'Gorman.

1987

Limerick—V. Murnane, A. Madden, P. Carey, D. Flynn, D. Nash, A. O'Riordan, M. Reale, G. Hegarty, J. O'Neill, G. Kirby, A. Carmody, G. Ryan (capt.), P. Barrett, J. O'Connor, L. O'Connor. Sub: D. Marren for P Barrett.

Galway—M. Finnerty, B. Cawley, S. Dolphin, B. Cooney, T. Broderick, J. Burke, T. King, D. Cox, G. Coyne, M. Connolly (capt.), K. Coen, H. Davoren, M. Greaney, E. Burke, R. Duane. Subs: E. Lyons for M. Greaney, P. Killilea for T. Broderick, B. Hurney for K. Coen.

1988

Cork—T. Kingston, C. Connery (capt.), D. Irwin, S. O'Leary, C. Casey, P. Kenneally, A. O'Keeffe, L. Kelly, T. Cooney, J. Corcoran, G. Manley, F. Horgan, D. O'Connell, M. Foley, J. Fitzgibbon.

Kilkenny—T. Phelan, F. Morgan (capt.), W. O'Connor, L. Drennan, R. Minogue, L. Keoghan, W. Hennessy, T. Fogarty, L. Egan, T. O'Keeffe, M. Phelan, J. Feehan, P. Hoban, S. O'Mahoney, J. Larkin. Subs: P. Carroll for Drennan; T. Murphy for Larkin; L. Dowling for T. Fogarty.

1989

Tipperary—B. Bane, L. Sheedy, M. Ryan, G. Frend, J. Madden, Conal Bonnar, S. Maher, J. Leahy, Declan Ryan (capt.), P. Hogan, C. Stakelum, Dinny Ryan, M. Nolan, D. Quirke, T. Lanigan. Subs: J. Cahill for Maher, D. Lyons for Lanigan, K. Ryan for Cahill.

Offaly—John Troy, B. Whelehan, D. Geoghegan, B. Hennessy, R. Mannion, B. Kelly, G. Cahill, J. Pilkington, A. Cahill, B. Dooley, D. Regan, Johnny Dooley, R. Byrne, D. Pilkington, M. Duignan. Sub: J. Kilmartin for Byrne.

1990

Kilkenny—J. Conroy, J. Holohan, P. O'Neill, D. Carroll, P. Brophy, T. Murphy, J. Conlon, J. Brennan (capt.), B. McGovern, A. Ronan, J. Lawlor, T. Shefflin, D. J. Carey, P. Treacy, C. Carter. Subs: P. O'Grady for Shefflin, J. Walton for McGovern.

Tipperary—B. Bane, L. Fallon, M. Ryan, G. Frend, E. Maher, N. Keane, B. Corcoran, J. Leahy (capt.), Conal Bonnar, C. Egan, L. Sheedy, G. Deely, D. Lyons, P. O'Brien, A. Wail. Subs: M. O'Meara for Egan, K. McCormack for Lyons.

1991

Galway—R. Burke, C. Helebert, B. Feeney (capt.), M. Killilea, G. McGrath, P. Hardiman, N. Power, B. Keogh, N. Larkin, L. Burke, J. Campbell, T. O'Brien, B. Larkin, J. Rabbitte, C. Moran. Subs: P. Egan for Hardiman, M. Curtin for Larkin.

Offaly—Damien Franks, M. Hogan, K. Kinahan, Donal Franks, D. Dooley, H. Rigney, B. Whelehan, J. Pilkington, P. Temple, Johnny Dooley, S. Grennan, A. Cahill, John Troy, J. Brady, E. Mulhare. Subs: O. O'Neill for Cahill, D. Barron for Brady.

1992

Waterford—R. Barry, K. O'Gorman, O. Dunphy, M. O'Sullivan, A. Browne (capt.), P. Fanning, F. Hartley, T. Fives, J. Brenner, A. Fitzgerald, M. Hubbard, Kevin McGrath, N. Dalton, S. Daly, P. Flynn. Sub: P Power for Dalton.

(Note: P Power played in drawn game. P. Flynn was on for replay. Subs in drawn game: M. Geary for P Power, P. Flynn for M. Geary.)

Offaly—Damien Franks, H. Kilmartin, K. Kinahan, Donal Franks, D. Barron, H. Rigney, B. Whelehan (capt.), S. Óg Farrell, M. Hogan, Johnny Dooley, S. Grennan, John Troy, M. Gallagher, N. Hand. O. O'Neill. Sub: A. Cahill for Hogan.

(K. Martin played in drawn game. D. Barron was on for replay. Sub in drawn game: B. Gath for M. Hogan.)

1993

Galway—M. Darcy. A. Headd, W. Burke, D. Canning, R. Walsh, N. Shaughnessy, M. Donoghue, L. Burke (capt.), Michael Kearns, F. Forde, J. McGrath, A. Kirwan, Peter Kelly, D. Coleman, M. Headd. Subs: C. O'Donovan for Coleman, C. O'Doherty for Kirwan, M Kilkelly for P. Kelly.

(M. Kilkelly played in drawn game. Michael Kearns was on for replay. Subs in drawn game: C. O'Doherty for N. Shaughnessy, P. Coyne for P. Kelly and N. O'Shaughnessy for P. Kelly.)

Kilkenny—J. Dermody, D. Beirne (capt.), M. Holohan, J. Carroll, D O'Neill, E. Kennedy, P. Larkin, A. Comerford, C. Brennan, P Farrell, J. McDermott, D. Maher, P. J. Delaney, S. Ryan, D Lawlor. Subs: M. Owens for McDermott, P. Hennessy for Ryan.

(J. Shefflin played in drawn game, J. McDermott was on for replay. Subs in drawn game: J. McDermott for J. Shefflin, M. Dowling for D. Maher, M. Owens for S. Ryan.)

1994

Kilkenny—M. Carey, S. Meally, E. Drea, B. Power, A. O'Sullivan, E. Dwyer, P. Larkin (capt.), B. McEvoy, D. Maher, S. Dollard, P. Barry, P. J. Delaney, B. Ryan, D. Byrne, R. Shortall. Subs: O. O'Connor for Barry, D. O'Neill for McEvoy.

Galway—L. O'Donoghue, D. Canning, W. Burke, M. Spellman, P. Diviney, N. Shaughnessy, M. Donoghue, C. O'Doherty, C. O'Donovan, F. Forde, J. McGrath, D. Coen, Peter Kelly, O. Fahy, M. Headd. Subs: D. Coleman for Fahy, C. Moore for Headd.

1995

Tipperary—B. Cummins, L. Barron, P. Shelly, P. Shanahan, B. Horgan (capt.), K. Slevin, B. Flannery, A. Butler, Terry Dunne, Thomas Dunne, L. McGrath, E. Enright, K. Tucker, D. O'Connor, D. Bourke. Sub: P. O'Dwyer for Enright.

Kilkenny—M. Carey, B. Lonergan, E. Drea, T. Hickey, V. O'Brien, J. Costelloe, E. Dwyer, D. Maher, P. Barry (capt.), D. Cleere, L. Smith, B. McEvoy, B. Ryan, D. Byrne, D. Buggy. Subs: M. Owens for Buggy, O. O'Connor for Smith.

1996

Galway—E. Cloonan, G. Kennedy, P Huban (capt.), L. Hodgins, B. Higgins, C. Moore, M. Healy, G. Glynn, O. Fahy, D. Moran, V. Maher, F. Healy, A. Kerins, D. Coen, K. Broderick.
Subs: M. Cullinane for Higgins, D. Walsh For F Healy.

Wexford—M. J. Cooper, J. Hegarty, E. Doyle, T. Radford, D. Ruth, J. Purcell, M. O'Leary, R. McCarthy, M. Byrne, J. Lawlor, S. Colfer, E. Cullen, P. Codd, G. Laffan, M. Jordan. Subs: D. Kent for Jorclon, D. O'Connor for Laffan, P. J. Carley for Colfer.

1997

Cork—D. Óg Cusack, J. Browne; D. O'Sullivan, W. Sherlock, D. Barrett, D. Murphy (capt.), S. Óg hAilpin, P Ryan, A. Walsh, B. O'Driscoll, T. McCarthy, M. O'Connell, J. O'Flynn, D. Ronan, J. Deane. Subs: S. O'Farrell for O'Flynn, B. Coleman for McCarthy.

Galway—N. Murray, G. Kennedy, P. Huban, F. Gantley, V. Maher, M. Healy, L. Hodgins, R. Gantley, G. Glynn, F Healy, M. Cullinane, K. Broderick, A. Kerins, E. Cloonan, O. Canning. Subs: D. Shaughnessy for Broderick, B. Higgins for Huban, M. Kerins for O. Canning.

1998

Cork—D. Óg Cusack, M. Prendergast, D. O'Sullivan, W. Sherlock, D. Barrett, D. Murphy (capt.), S. Óg Ó hAilpin, A. Walsh, L. Mannix, N. Ronan, T. McCarthy, M. O'Connell, B. O'Keeffe, S. O'Farrell, J. Deane. Subs: J. Anderson for Mannix, B. O'Connor for O'Farrell.

Galway—T. Grogan, V. Maher, J. Feeney, L. Madden, F. Healy, M. Healy, G. Lynskey, P. Walsh, A. Kerins, R. Gantley, C. Connaughton, M. Cullinane, K. Broderick, M. Kerins, E. Cloonan. Subs: D. Shaughnessy for Connaughton, R. Cullinane for Gantley.

1999

Kilkenny—J. Power, A. Walpole, N. Hickey, M. Kavanagh, A. Cummins, S. Dowling, R. Mullally, J. O'Neill, J. P. Corcoran, M. Gordon, J. Coogan, K. Power, A. Geoghegan, H. Shefflin, E. Brennan. Subs: P. Delaney for A. Geoghegan, J. Barron for E. Brennan.

Galway—N. Murray, E. McDonagh, D. Cloonan, S. McClearn, E. Linnane, R. Gantley, D. O'Shaughnessy, E. Tannian, E. Donoghue, D. Tierney, M. Kerins, D. Loughrey, A. Poniard, E. Cloonan, D. Donoghue. Subs: S. Lawless for A. Poniard, R. Cullinane for D. Loughrey, J. Culkin for E. Donoghue.

2000

Limerick – T.Houlihan, D.Reale, E.Mulcahy, P.Reale, P.O'Reilly, B.Geary, W.Walsh, J.Meskell, S.Lucey, P.O'Grady, S.O'Connor, D.Stapleton, D.Sheehan, B.Begley, M.Keane. Sub – K.Tobin for O'Connor.

Galway – K.Callanan, E.McDonagh, D.Cloonan, J.Cannon, D.Hardiman, C.Dervan, S.Morgan, J.Culkin, S.Donoghue, D.Forde, E.Hyland, E.Donoghue, D.Joyce, D.Huban, D.Donoghue. Subs – D.Tierney for Joyce, B.Cunningham for Hyland, M.Greaney for Huban, G.Keary for E.Donoghue.

2001

Limerick – T.Houlihan, D.Reale, B.Carroll, E.Mulcahy, M.O'Riordan, B.Geary, M.O'Brien, P.Lawlor, S.Lucey, E.Foley, K.Tobin, P.Tobin, C.Fitzgerald, N.Moran, M.Keane. Sub – A.O'Shaughnessy for P.Tobin.

Wexford – M.White, N.Maguire, D.O'Connor, R.Kirwan, R.Mallon, B.McGee, T.Kelly, N.Lambert, D.Stamp, R.Barry, G.Coleman, R.Jacob, B.Lambert, M.Jacob, D.Lyng. Subs – P.Donoghue for Kirwan, P.Carley for N.Lambert, N.Lambert for Barry.

2002

Limerick – T.Houlihan, D.Reale, E.Mulcahy, M.Cahill, E.Foley, P.O'Dwyer, M.O'Brien, P.Lawlor, N.Moran, C.Fitzgerald, J.O'Brien, K.Tobin, A.O'Shaughnessy, P.Kirby, M.Keane. Subs – P.Tobin for Fitzgerald, B.Carroll for O'Dwyer, R.Hayes for M.O'Brien.

Galway – A.Diviney, B.O'Mahony, S.Kavanagh, J.Culkin, F.Moore, C.Dervan, D.Forde, T. Óg Regan, G.Farragher, R.Murray, M.Coughlan, K.Brady, F.Hayes, A.Cullinane, D.Green. Subs – J.P.O'Connell for Regan, M.J.Quinn for Coughlan, K.Burke for Green.

2003

Kilkenny – D.Herity, G.Joyce, C.Hickey, M.Phelan, K.Coogan, J.Tyrell, J.J.Delaney, S.Hennessy, T.Walsh, C.Phelan, P.Cleere, W.O'Dwyer, A.Fogarty, M.Rice, B.Dowling. Subs – S.O'Neill for Dowling, E.McCormack for Cleere.

Galway – A.Diviney, D.Collins, T.Óg Regan, F.Moore, S.Kavanagh, E.Lynch, A.Cullinane, K.Brady, B.Mahony, D.Hayes, T.Tierney, R.Murray, K.Burke, G.Farragher, D.Greene. Subs – N.Healy for Burke, J.P.O'Connell for Greene, W.Donnellan for Tierney.

2004

Kilkenny – D.Herity, S.Maher, J.Tennyson, M.Fennelly, T.Walsh, P.J.Delaney, C.Hoyne, S.Hennessy, P.Cleere, S.O'Neill, W.O'Dwyer, E.Reid, J.Fitzpatrick, C.Phelan, R.Power. Subs – M.Wright for Fitzpatrick, B.Dowling for Cleere, E.Larkin for Reid, J.Phelan for O'Neill, N.Doherty for Delaney.

Tipperary – P.McCormack, A.Morrisey, C.O'Mahony, D.Walton, E.Hanley, D.Fitzgerald, H.Moloney, J.Caesar, W.Cully, P.Buckley, S.Sweeney, F.Devanney, E.Sweeney, T.Scroope, M.Farrell. Subs – W.Ryan for A.Morrisey, D.Sheppard for Buckley, D.Morrisey for E.Sweeney, T.Fitzgerald for S.Sweeney, P.Shortt for Cully.

2005

Galway – A.Ryan, P.Flynn, A.Gaynor, K.Briscoe, G.Mahon, B.Cullinane, D.Collins, B.Lucas, A.Garvey, J.Gantley, A.Callanan, E.Ryan, N.Healy, K.Burke, K.Wade. Subs – F.Coone for Ryan, C.Dervan for Gantley, D.Kelly for Cullinane.

Kilkenny – D.Fogarty, S.Maher, J.Tennyson, D.Cody, J.Dalton, P.J.Delaney, C.Hoyne, M.Fennelly, M.Rice, E.Larkin, A.Murphy, W.O'Dwyer, E.Reid, J.Fitzpatrick, R.Power. Sub – D.McCormack for Murphy.

2006

Kilkenny – L.Tierney, K.Joyce, J.Tennyson, S.Cummins, P.Hartley, J.Dalton, D.Fogarty, J.Fitzpatrick, M.Fennelly, T.J.Reid, A.Murphy, P.Hogan, R.Hogan, R.Power, D.McCormack. Sub – A.Healy for McCormack.

Tipperary – G.Kennedy, P.Stapleton, A.Byrne, C.O'Brien, D.Young, J.B.McCarthy, S.Horan, J.Woodlock, S.Lillis, R.O'Dwyer, N.Teehan, D.Sheppard, R.Ruth, D.O'Hanlon, D.Egan. Subs – P.Austin for Sheppard, K.Lanigan for Horan, D.Hickey for Teehan, K.Quinlan for Lillis.

**In the drawn encounter for Kilkenny A.Healy started for R.Hogan while for Tipperary R.McLoughney started for D.O'Hanlon. Subs in the drawn match were; Kilkenny – R.Hogan for Healy, M.Nolan for P.Hogan, B.Beckett for Murphy. Tipperary – D.O'Hanlon for McLoughney, D.Hickey for Ruth, K.Quinlan for McCarthy.*

2007

Galway – J.Skehill, A.Leech, G.Mahon, C.O'Donovan, M.Ryan, J.Lee, A.Keary, D.Kennedy, K.Kilkenny, S.Glynn, K.Hynes, F.Coone, C.Cavanagh, J.Canning, K.Wade. Subs – B.Hanley for Glynn, A.Harte for Kennedy, J.Greene for Coone, N.Kelly for Kavanagh, P.Loughnane for Leech.

Dublin – P.Curtin, R.Drumgoole, P.O'Callaghan, D.Webster, K.Dunne, T.Brady, J.Boland, J.McCaffrey, A.McCrabbe, E.Moran, R.O'Carroll, D.Connolly, P.Carton, D.O'Dwyer, S.Durkin. Subs – M.McGarry for Webster, I.Fleming for O'Carroll, S.Lehane for Connolly.

2008

Kilkenny – C.McGrath, P.Murphy, K.Joyce, E.O'Shea, L.Ryan, P.Hogan, N.Prendergast, J.Dowling, N.Walsh, C.Fennelly, J.Mulhall, T.J.Reid, M.Ruth, N.Cleere, R.Hogan. Subs – J.J.Farrell for Cleere, J.Maher for Dowling, M.Bergin for Farrell.

Tipperary – M.Ryan, M.Cahill, P.Maher, K.Maher, K.Lanigan, T.Stapleton, B.Maher, G.Ryan, S.Hennessy, P.Maher, S.Callinan, T.McGrath, P.Bourke, M.O'Meara, S.Bourke. Subs – J.O'Keeffe for Lanigan, D.O'Hanlon for O'Meara, P.Ivors for S.Bourke, J.Ryan for McGrath.

2009

Clare – D.Tuohy, E.Glynn, C.Dillon, C.O'Doherty, D.O'Donovan, N.O'Connell, J.Gunning, E.Barrett, C.O'Donovan, C.Morey, J.Conlon, S.Collins, C.Tierney, D.Honan, C.Ryan. Subs – C.McGrath for Tierney, P.O'Connor for Morey, E.Hayes for Gunning.

Kilkenny – C.McGrath, P.Murphy, P.Nolan, C.Fogarty, M.Walsh, D.Langton, Lester Ryan, M.Kelly, Liam Ryan, C.Fennelly, M.Bergin, J.Mulhall, R.Hogan, J.J.Farrell, J.Nolan. Sub – N.Cleere for Bergin.

CAPTAINS OF WINNING ALL-IRELAND UNDER-21 HURLING TEAMS

1964—Francis Loughnane (Tipperary)
1965—W. O'Neill (Wexford)
1966—G. McCarthy (Cork)
1967—P J. Ryan (Tipperary)
1968—P. Hegarty (Cork)
1969—M. McCarthy (Cork)
1970—T. O'Brien (Cork)
1971—P. McDonnell (Cork)
1972—I. Clarke (Galway)
1973—M. O'Doherty (Cork)
1974—G. Fennelly (Kilkenny)
1975—K. Fennelly (Kilkenny)
1976—T. Murphy (Cork)
1977—M. Lyng (Kilkenny)
1978—B. Forde (Galway)
1979—M. Doyle (Tipperary)
1980—Philip Kennedy (Tipperary)
1981—Philip Kennedy (Tipperary)
1982—M. McCarthy (Cork)
1983—P. Casserly (Galway)
1984—S. Delahunty (Kilkenny)
1985—M. Scully (Tipperary)
1986—A. Cunningham (Galway)
1987—G. Ryan (Limerick)
1988—C. Connery (Cork)
1989—Declan Ryan (Tipperary)
1990—J. Brennan (Kilkenny)
1991—B. Feeney (Galway)
1992—A. Browne (Waterford)
1993—L. Burke (Galway)
1994—P. Larkin (Kilkenny)
1995—B. Horgan (Tipperary)
1996—P. Huban (Galway}
1997—D. Murphy (Cork)
1998—D. Murphy (Cork)
1999—Noel Hickey (Kilkenny)
2000—D.Sheehan (Limerick)
2001—T.Houlihan (Limerick)
2002—P.Lawlor (Limerick)
2003—J.Tyrell (Kilkenny)
2004—J.Fitzpatrick (Kilkenny)
2005—K.Burke (Galway)
2006—M.Fennelly (Kilkenny)
2007—K.Hynes (Galway)
2008—J.Dowling (Kilkenny)
2009—C.O'Doherty (Clare)

ALL-IRELAND UNDER 21 HURLING REFEREES 1964-2009

1964—Aubrey Higgins (Galway)
1965—Jimmy Duggan (Galway)
1966—Donie Nealon (Tipperary) draw
1966—G. Fitzgerald (2nd/3rd games)
1967—Aubrey Higgins (Galway)
1968—Seamus Power (Waterford)
1969—Paddy Johnson (Kilkenny)
1970—Jim Dunphy (Waterford)
1971—Paddy Buggy (Kilkenny)
1972—Sean O'Grady (Limerick)
1973—John Moloney (Tipperary)
1974—Sean O'Grady (Limerick)
1975—Sean O'Meara (Tipperary)
1976—Gerry Kirwan (Offaly)
1977—Jimmy Rankins (Laois)
1978—Noel O'Donoghue (Dublin)
1979—Noel Dalton (Waterford)
1980—John Denton (Wexford)
1981—Nealie Duggan (Limerick)
1982—Gerry Kirwan (Offaly)
1983—Michael Kelieher (Kildare)
1984—Kevin Walsh (Clare)
1985—John Denton (Wexford)
1986—Gerry Long (Tipperary)

1987—Paschal Long (Kilkenny)
1988—John Moore (Waterford)
1989—Pascal Long (Kilkenny)
1990—Pat Delaney (Laois)
1991—Terence Murray (Limerick)
1992—Willie Barrett (Tipperary)
1993—John McDonnell (Tipperary)
1994—Pat Horan (Offaly)
1995—Terence Murray (Limerick}
1996—Pat O'Connor (Limerick)
1997—Pat Horan (Offaly)
1998—Dickie Murphy (Wexford)
1999—Ger Harrington (Cork)
2000—P.Horan (Offaly)
2001—A.MacSuibhne (Dublin)
2002—D.Murphy (Wexford)
2003—M.Wadding (Waterford)
2004—B.Kelly (Westmeath)
2005—J.Sexton (Limerick)
2006—M.Haverty (Galway)
B.Gavin (Offaly) (replay)
2007—J.Ryan (Tipperary)
2008—J.Owens (Wexford)
2009—C.McAllister (Cork)

MUNSTER UNDER-21 HURLING FINALS

1964—Tipperary 8-9, Waterford 3-1
1965—Tipperary 4-9, Galway 3-3
1966—Cork 5-12, Limerick 2-6
1967—Tipperary 3-9, Galway 3-5
1968—Cork 4-10, Tipperary 1 - 13
1969—Cork 3-11, Tipperary 1-5
1970—Cork 3-11, Tipperary 2-7
1971—Cork 5-11, Tipperary 4-9
1972—Tipperary 4-10, Clare 3- 10
1973—Cork 4-11, Limerick 2-7
1974—Waterford 2-5, Clare 1 -3
1975—Cork 3-12, Limerick 2-6
1976—Cork 2-11, Clare 3-6
1977—Cork 5-9, Limerick 1 -8
1978—Tipperary 3-13, Cork 4-10 (draw)
Tipperary 3-8, Cork 2-9 (replay)
1979—Tipperary 1-13, Cork 2-7
1980—Tipperary 4-11, Cork 2-9
1981—Tipperary 1-15, CorkO-10
1982—Cork 1-14, Limerick 1-4
1983—Tipperary 2-17, Clare 3-8
1984—TipperaryO-12, Limenck 1-8
1985—Tipperary 1-16, Clare 4-5
1986—Limerick 3-9, Clare 3-9 (draw)
Limerick 2-10, Clare 0-3 (replay)
1987—Limerick 3-14, Cork 2-9
1988—Cork 4-12, Limerick 1 -7
1989—Tipperary 5-16, Limerick 1-6
1990—Tipperary 2-21, Limerick 1-11
1991—Cork 0-17, limerick 1-7
1992—Waterford 0-17, Clare 1-12
1993—Cork 1-18, Limerick 3-9
1994—Waterford 1-12, Clare 0-12
1995—Tipperary 1-17, Clare 0-14
1996—Cork 3-16, Clare 2-7
1997—Cork 1-11, Tipperary 0-13
1998—Cork 3-18, Tipperary 1-10
1999—Tipperary 1-18, Clare 1-15
2000—Limerick 4-18, Cork 1-6.
2001—Limerick 3-14, Tipperary 2-16.
2002—Limerick 1-20, Tipperary 2-14.
(after extra time)
2003—Tipperary 2-14, Cork 0-17.
(after extra time)
2004—Tipperary 1-16, Cork 1-13.
2005—Cork 4-8, Tipperary 0-13.
2006—Tipperary 3-11, Cork 0-13.
2007—Cork 1-20, Waterford 0-10.
2008—Tipperary 1-16, Clare 2-12.
2009—Clare 2-17, Waterford 2-12.

LEINSTER UNDER-21 HURLING FINALS

1964—Wexford 4-7, Laois 2-2
1965—Wexford 7-9, Dublin 1 -5
1966—Wexford 7-10, Laois 2-8
1967—Dublin 2-10, Offaly 2-9
1968—Kilkenny 4-10, Dublin 5-4
1969—Wexford 3-16, Kilkenny 4-3
1970—Wexford 2-15, Kilkenny 5-4
1971—Wexford 2-16, Kilkenny 2-9
1972—Dublin 2-11, Offaly 0-15
1973—Wexford 2-13, Offaly 2-10
1974—Kilkenny 3-8, Wexford 1 -5
1975—Kilkenny 3-14, Wexford 0-8
1976—Kilkenny 3-21, Wexford 0-5
1977—Kilkenny 3-11, wexford 1-10
1978—Offaly 2-14, Laois 2-7
1979—Wexford 0-14, Kilkenny 2-8 (draw)
Wexford 1-8, Kilkenny 0-10 (replay)
1980—Kilkenny 2-14, Wexford 2-9
1981—Kilkenny 6-1 l, Wexford 2-10
1982—Kilkenny 5-20, Offaly 2-6
1983—Laois 3-13, Wexford 4-8
1984—Kilkenny 0-18, Wexford 1 - 10
1985—Kilkenny 4-18, Wexford 1 -4
1986—Wexford 2-9, Offaly 2-9 (draw)
Wexford 1-16, Offaly 0- 10 (replay)
1987—Wexford 4-11, Offaly 0-5
1988—Kilkenny 3-13, Offaly 2-5
1989—Offaly 3-16, Kilkenny 3-9
1990—Kilkenny 2-9, Laois 1-10
1991—Offaly 2-10, Kilkenny 0-12
1992—Offaly 1-15, Kilkenny 2-10
1993—Kilkenny 4-13, Wexford 2-7
1994—Kilkenny 1-14, Wexford 0-15
1995—Kilkenny 2-11, Wexford 1-12
1996—Wexford 1-9, Offaly 0-12 (draw)
Wexford 2-16, Offaly 2-5 (replay)
1997—Wexford 2-13, Offaly 0-15
1998—Kilkenny 2-10, Dublin 0-12
1999—Kilkenny 1-17, Offaly 1-6
2000—Offaly 3-14, Kilkenny 2-14.

2001—Wexford 0-10, Kilkenny 1-5.
2002—Wexford 1-15, Dublin 0-15 (aet)
2003—Kilkenny 0-12, Dublin 1-4.
2004—Kilkenny 1-16, Wexford 2-3.
2005—Kilkenny 0-17, Dublin 1-10.
2006—Kilkenny 2-18, Dublin 2-10.
2007—Dublin 2-18, Offaly 3-9.
2008—Kilkenny 2-21, Offaly 2-9.
2009—Kilkenny 2-20, Dublin 1-19.

ULSTER UNDER-21 HURLING FINALS

1964—Antrim only team entered
1965—Antrim 5-8, Down 4-7
1966—Antrim 4-5, Down 0-8
1967—Antrim 3-8, Down 2-7
1968—Down 7-6, Armagh 2-9
Note: This was Roinn 'B' final. Antrim represented Province in All-Ireland series.
1969—Down 5-17, Antrim 2-11
1970—Antrim 6-12, Down 2-10
1971—Down 5-11, Antrim 2-9
1972—Antrim 4-9, Down 1-11
1973—Antrim 1-6, Down 1-6 (draw)
Antrim 3-19, Down 3-3 (replay)
1974—Antrim 3-8, Down 0-3
1975—Down 3-10, Antrim 1-3
1976—Antrim 1-9, Down 0-4
1977—Down 3-7, Antrim 0-9
1978—Antrim 5-18, Down 3-9
1979—Antrim 9-13, Armagh 2-2
1980—Antrim 4-16, Down 0-9
1981—Antrim 2-9, Down 1-5
1982—Antrim 9-14, Down 4-5
1983—Down 2-7, Antrim 0-7
1984—Down 1-14, Antrim 0- 15
1985—Down 1-12, Antrim 1-10
1986—Derry 2-9, Down 2-9 (draw)
Derry 3-9, Down 1-2 (replay)
1987—Down 3-12 Derry 2-9
1988—Antrim 6-11, Down 1-4
1989—Antrim 4-18, Derry 0-4
1990—Down 2-9, Antrim 2-6
1991—Antrim 2-19, Down 2-6
1992—Antrim 3-11, Down 3-4
1993—Derry 2-13, Antrim 1-8
1994—Antrim 1 -20, Down 1-4
1995—Antrim 2-18, Derry 1-7
1996—Antrim 1-13, Down 1-12
1997—Derry 2-11, Antrim 0-1 7 (draw)
Derry 0-22, Antrim 1-16 (replay)
Note: After extra time.
Scores at the end of normal time:
Derry 0-15, Antrim 1-12.
1998—Antrim 3-20, Down 4-8
1999—Antrim 2-14, Derry O-12
2000—Antrim 2-14, Derry 0-3.
2001—Antrim 2-17, Derry 1-18.
2002—Antrim 2-13, Down 0-6.
2003—Down 3-12, Derry 1-12.
2004—Down 5-8, Derry 4-7.
2005—No Final
2006—Antrim 2-15, Down 3-11.
2007—Derry 2-16, Antrim 1-18.
2008—No Final.
2009—Antrim 1-18, Derry 0-9.

ALL-IRELAND JUNIOR HURLING FINALS

1912—Cork 3-6, Westmeath 2-1
1913—Tipperary 2-2, Kilkenny 0-0
1914—Clare 6-5, Laois 1-1
1915—Tipperary 1 -6, Offaly 2-2
1916—Cork 4-6, Kilkenny 3-4
1917-1922—Suspended
1923—Offaly 3-4, Cork 3-2
1924—Tipperary 5-5, Galway 1-2
1925—Cork 5-6, Dublin 1-0
1926—Tipperary 6-2, Galway 2-3
1927—Meath 2-3, Britain 1-1
Home Final: Meath 1-8; Galway 3-2 (draw)
Meath 5-4; Galway 3-2 (replay)
1928—Kilkenny 4-6, Tipperary 4-4
1929—Offaly 6-1, Cork 2-3
1930—Tipperary 6-8, Kilkenny 3-2
1931—Waterford 10-7, Lancashire 1-2
Home Final: Waterford 6-7, Antrim 0-3
1932—Dublin 8-4, London 2-0
Home Final: Dublin 6-5, Galway 3-3
1933—Tipperary 10-1, London 1 -4
Home Final Tipperary 8-3, Galway 1-3
1934—Waterford 3-5, London 3-3
Home Final: Waterford 5-8, Kildare 1-3
1935—Limerick 4-9, London 3-3
Home Final: Limerick 2-5, Galway 1-2
1936—Westmeath 2-5, Waterford 3-1
Note: Britain did not compete. Instead there was a Junior "International" between Ireland and England.
1937—Dublin 7-8, London 3-6
Home Final: Dublin 6-6, Galway 3-3
1938—London 4-4, Cork 4-1
Home Final: Cork 6-5, Antrim 2-4
1939—Galway 2-6, London 2-2
Home Final: Galway 3-8, Kilkenny 3-8 (draw);
Galway 4-6, Kilkenny 4-3 (replay)
1940—Cork 3-3, Galway 3-1
1941—Limerick 8-2, Galway 4-1
1942-45—Suspended
1946—Kilkenny 5-4, London 2-2
Home Final: Kilkenny 4-2, Galway 2-3
1947—Cork 3-10, London 2-3
Home Final: Cork 4-10, Dublin 2-5
1948—Meath 3-5, London 3-5 (draw)
Meath 2-7, London 2-5 (replay)
Home Final: Meath 5-9, Limerick 2-1
1949—London 3-7, Clare 3-6
Home Final: Clare 3-5, Kilkenny 3-3
1950—Cork 5-5, London 1-4

Home Final: Cork 3-4, Dublin 2-5
1951—Kilkenny 3-9, London 3-5
Home Final: Kilkenny 4-9, Galway 4-3
1952—Dublin 3-4, London 2 o
Home Final: Dublin 4-10. Antrim 2-5
1953—Tipperary 4- 10, Warwickshire 3-3
Home Final: Tipperary 1-7, Offaly 1-2
1954—Limerick 4-6, London 2-4
Home Final: Limerick 3-5, Antrim 1-8
1955—Cork 6- 10, Warwickshire 0-5
Home Final: Cork 3- 10, Galway 4-5
1956—Kilkenny 5-2, London 2-8
Home Final: Kilkenny 4-8, Kerry 2-4
1957—Limerick 5-12, London 2-5
Home Final: Limerick 7-15, Galway 5-8
1958—Cork 7-10, Warwickshire 4-2
Home Final: Cork 3-16, Antrim 2-5
1959—London 5-10, Antrim 2-10
Home Final: Antrim 3-4, Cork 2-3
1960—London 2-4, Carlow 2-4 (draw)
London 4-8, Carlow 2-11 (replay)
Home Final: Carlow 2-15, Cork 3-5
1961—Kerry4-14, London 2-5
Home Final: Kerry 4-9, Meath 5-3
1962—Kildare 4-7, London 2-4
Home Final: Kildare 7-15, Kerry 5-2
1963—London 4-7, Antrim 3-6
Home Final: Antrim 8-8, Westmeath 6-3
1964—Down 3-2, London 1 -3
Home Final: Down 9-5, Kerry 2-7
1965—Roscommon 3-10, Warwickshire 2-11
Home Final: Roscommon 6-8, Armagh 1-3
1966—Kildare 4-6, Warwickshire 2-9
Home Final: Kildare 3-12, Kerry 2-3
1967—Wicklow 3-15, London 6-6 (draw)
Wicklow 3-14, London 4-7 (replay)
Home Final: Wicklow 3-7, Kerry 1-2
1968—Warwickshire 1-14, Kerry 1-9
Home Final: Kerry 6-9, Sligo 5-9
1969—Warwickshire 3-6, Kerry 0-11
Home Final: Kerry 6-11, Antrim 2-10
1970—Meath 1 - 15, Hertfordshire 4-6 (draw)
Meath 3-14, Hertfordshire 3-7 {replay)
Home Final: Meath 3-19, Leitrim 1-7
1971—Wicklow 3-9, Hertfordshire 2-12 (draw)
Hertfordshire 4-9, Wicklow 3-11
(Dispute, replay ordered)
Wicklow 4-6, Hertfordshire 3-8 (second replay)
Home Final: Wicklow 2-18, Roscommon 1-12
1972—Kerry 5-5, Warwickshire 2-9
Home Final: Kerry 6-16, Meath 3-7
1973—Warwickshire 6-9, Louth 3-8
Home Final: Louth 4-11, Kerry 3-11
1974—Roscommon 2-11, Derry 2-9
1975—Derry 5-12, Louth 3-5
1976—Louth 6-8, Mayo 4-9
1977—Louth 1-14, Fermanagh 2-4
1978—Armagh 5-15, Mayo 2-6
1979—Armagh 2-13, Derry 2-1
1980—Mayo 2-13, Monaghon 0-7
1981—Mayo 2-13, Louth 1-8
1982—Derry 1-10, Monaghan 0-6
Resumed in original format in 1983
1983—Cork 3-14, Galway 2-15
1984—Kilkenny 0-13, Galway 2-5
1985—Wexford 3-9, Tipperary 1-13
1986—Kilkenny 1-17, Limerick 0-15
1987—Cork 3-11, Wexford 2-13
1988—Kilkenny 1-12, Tipperary 0-10
1989—Tipperary 0-12, Galway 0-8
1990—Kilkenny 4-21, Tipperary 2-11
1991—Tipperary 4-17, London 1 -5
Home Final: Tipperary 2-13, Kilkenny 0-10
1992—Wexford 2-7, Cork 0-13 (draw)
Wexford 0-13, Cork 1-8 (replay)
1993—Clare 3-10, Kilkenny 0-8
1994—Cork 2-13, Kilkenny 2-11
1995—Kilkenny 1-20, Clare 1-6
1996—Galway 1-14, Kilkenny 2-9
1997—Monaghan 3-11, Meath 0-11
1998—Meath 1-14, Monaghan 1-9
1999—Meath 2-11, Tyrone 0-9
2000—Armagh 1-11, Meath 1-4.
2001—Roscommon 1-18, Donegal 2-3.
2002—Antrim 2-7, Meath 1-6.
2003—Mayo 1-8, Donegal 0-9.
2004—Meath 1-10, Down 1-6.

Confined to weaker counties from 1961 to 1973. Stronger counties played in Intermediate Championship. Run in conjunction with Division 3 of National Hurling League 1974-82. Original format restored in 1983. But from 1997 confined to counties graded junior.

Note: There were no Home Finals in 1936, 1940 and 1941.

ALL-IRELAND JUNIOR HURLING FINALISTS

1912

Cork—C. Hallahan (capt.), J. Long, J. Hallahan, W. Finn, D. Aherne, P. Prior, J. Murphy, W. Lombard, C. Salmon, J. O'Brien, T. O'Riordan, J. Cahill, D. McDonnell, D. Singleton, W. Fitzgerald, P. Vaughan, C. O'Connell.

Westmeath—B. Murphy (capt.), J. Buckley, M. Byrne, F. Larkin, J. Blaney, M. Reilly, J. Martin, P. Malynn, H. Hanley, M. Boylan, T. Carty, M. Duffy, F Nee, M. Kelleghan, H. Grattan, P. Tormey, J. Kearney.

1913

Tipperary—Jack Ryan-Lanigan (capt.), Tom Ryan-Lanigan, T. Delaney, J. Hammonds, T. Dwyer, T. Dwan, Pierce Purcell, M. Hammonds, Ned McGrath, P. Leahy, A. O'Donnell, Dick Walsh, J. Power, J. Fitzpatrick, T. Shanahan, Subs: P. Dargan, J. Murphy.

Kilkenny—Jim Walton (capt.), T Cummins (goal), J. Holmes, Ned Hally, P. Meighan, P. O'Brien, J. O'Connor, Justin McGrath, Nick

Mullins, T. Murphy, Tom Hanrahan, Larry Dunphy, John Foskin, Matt Corr, Nick Fennelly Sub: Mick Corr.

1914

Clare—D. Minogue (capt.), S. Minogue, D. Flannery, P. Hannon, M. Bolton, T. Daly, J. Quinn, E. Lucid, J. Spellacy, P. Jorcdon, M. Baker, A. Gleeson, D. Crowe, J. Marrinan, P. Connell.

Laois—J. Finlay (capt.), J. Phelan, T. Costigan, J. Phelan, J. Walsh, J. Dunphy, M. Drennan, M. Begadon, M. Carroll, W. Quigley, J. Loughman, J. Dunphy, M. Sheppard, J. Deegan, P. Ryan.

1915

Tipperary—T. Dwan (capt.), W. Quinn, M. Leahy, Joe Fitzpatrick, J. Campbell, J. Kennedy, J. Hammonds, W. Dwyer, T. Shanahan, W. Horan, D. Walsh, F. Cronin, M. Leahy, T. Donovan, J. Doore.

Offaly—J. Corrigan (capt.), T. O'Donnell, J. Madden, P. Cummins, J. Carroll, F. Reddin, P. Sullivan, M. Cordial, J. O'Meara, H. Corrigan, M. Whelan, M. Kelly, J. Hogan, John Carroll, J. Murphy.

1916

Cork—Michael Brophy (capt.), A. Buckley (Cobh), G. Finn, D. Long, C. Neenan, P. Carton, P. Healy, J. O'Driscoll, R. Hunter, D. O'Sullivan, H. Atkins, John Barry-Murphy, Eugene O'Connell, A. Buckley, M. Scannell. Sub: Buckley for J. O'Driscoll.

Kilkenny—W. Power, P. Power, J. Sullivan, M. Dermody, E. Donoghue, E. Fennelly, R. Purcell, J. Roberts, J. Walsh, J. Coyne, R. Rockett, T. Mullins, R. Kenneally, J. Hanrahan, J. Whelan.

1923

Offaly—M. Cordial, W. Cordial, A. Cordial, J. Halligan (capt.), E. Hayes, P. Lyons, W. Fox, P. Fox, W. Ryan, M. Whelan, N. White, M. Carroll, J. Murphy, J. Horan, J. Carroll. Sub: R. Conway.

Cork—R. Canniffe, M. Murphy (capt.), J. Barry, T. Aherne, D. O'Donovan, S. Keane, J. Barry-Murphy, Matt Murphy, M. Ryan, S. Noonan, J. Crotty, F Kelleher, P. McCarthy, D. Barry-Murphy, J. Kenny.

1924

Tipperary—P. Purcell (capt.), W. O'Brien, J. O'Loughlin, Stephen Dwan, J. Costelloe, J. Gleeson, T. O'Meara, M. Flanagan, J. Hickey, M. Ryan, T. F. Meagher, P. Kennedy, Martin Kennedy, Rody Nealon, Martin Aherne. Sub: W. O'Meara.

Galway—J. Stanford (capt.), J. Fallon, P. Rooney, P. Kelly, M. Tierney, M. Broderick, J. Morrissey, M. Connaire, J. Cleary, W. Fahy, T. O'Donnell, P. Morgan, M. Houlihan, P. Gilligan, J. Shaughnessy.

1925

Cork—M. Kenny (capt.), J. Seymour (goal), E. Lynch, Joe Kearney, Christy Cronin, J. Desmond, J. Barry, D. Barry-Murphy, Dick Geaney, S. Noonon, J. Burke, M. Aherne, J. Hurley, Leo Brady, Jack Egan. Subs: J. Clarke, P. Healy, M. Daly (capt.).

Dublin—J. Hyland, W. Higgins, B. Muldoon, P. Cusack, D. McHugh (goal), T. Hennessy, J. Roche, P. McInerney, M. Murphy, E. Dwyer, E. Byrne, M. Treacy, J. Walsh, M. Healy, T. Costigan.

1926

Tipperary—T. Butler (goal), J. Moylan, P. Hogan, T. Crowe, P. Harty, J. Hayes, M. Ryan (Newport), M. Ryan (Boherlahan), T. Leahy, T. Treacy (capt.), E. Browne, A. Cleary, E. Walsh, J. O'Gorman, M. F. Cronin.

Galway—P. Sheary, M. Cunningham, Conway, T. Fury, Crowe, Griffin, J. Derivan, M. Connaire, J. Deely, T Tierney, T Hackett, M. Nestor, W. Curran, F. Keely, P. Larkin (capt.).

1927

Meath—L. Mitchell (capt.), R. Collins, M. Cluskey, T. Irwin, J. Loughran, J. Doherty, E. Giles, M. Madden, W. Smith, T. Browne, S. Finn, C. Doran, T. Loughran, J. Griffin, T. Carrigy. (C. Curley and M. Doherty played in drawn game. J. Loughran and T. Carrigy were on for replay.)

Britain—J. Ryan (capt.), T. King, J. Butterly, P. Landy, M. Redmond, J. Burke, J. O'Leary, J. Connolly, H. O'Donnell, M. Houlihan, E. Lambert, S. Donoghue, P. Costello, J. Shalloe, G. Moriarty.

1928

Kilkenny—M. Bergin, J. Carroll, T. Mullins (capt.), P. Kelly, J. McNamara, T. Grace, P. Butler, T. Cronin, J. Walsh, D. Duggan, M. Brennan, P. Dowling, P. Walsh, P. Dwan, J. Fitzpatrick.

Tipperary—A. Foley (capt.), P. O'Keeffe, E. Walsh, P. Guiry, T. Butler, J. Maher, T. Coffey, J. Stapleton, D. Max, R. Dwan, J. Heeney, T. Lowry, W. Matthews, D. Gleeson, Tony McLoughlin.

1929

Offaly—M. Corrigan (goal), E. Nolan, J. Kinnarney, W. Guinan, M. Dooley, J. Dooley, T. Dooley, T. Carroll, J. Verney, M. Coughlan, J. Holligan, J. Carroll, P. J. Grogan (capt.), J. King, W. Cordial.

Cork—E. O'Connor (capt.), J. Kinsley, D. Cogan, R. Madden, A. Caulfield, S. O'Leary, J. Riordan, P. Dorgan, C. Sheehan, J. Hurley (goal), J. Dermody, J. Callaghan, J. Desmond, J. Quirke M. Walsh.

1930

Tipperary—P. Harty (capt.), T. Harty, W. Ryan, T. Connolly, M. McGann, M. Browne, E. Wade, M. Ryan (Clonoulty), J. Dwyer, M. Ryan (lleigh), D. Looby, P. Furlong, W. Gorman, J. Fletcher, S. Harrington.

Kilkenny—Peter O'Reilly, M. Larkin, W. Dalton, Tommy Leahy, M. White, J. Leahy, R. Morrissey, D. Treacy, W. ("Lynch") Walsh, J. Malone, Milo Kennedy, W. Meagher, T. Wyse, W. Keane, T. Grace.

1931

Waterford—M. Curley (goal), J. O'Donnell, R. Condon (capt.), E. Flynn, G. Kehoe, A. Sandford, W. Sheehan, T. Greaney, P Hannigan, P. Gough, D. Goode, R. Morrissey, S. Ormond, J. Hunt, N. Condon.

Lancashire—T Collins (goal), M. Campbell, G. Moriarity, J. Connolly, B. Kennelly, M. Redmond, P Campbell, H. Davis, T. Ward, E. Brennan, T. Hannon, P. Lynch, P. Connnolly, S. Donohue, M. Holohan.

1932

Dublin—M. O'Hara (capt.), T. O'Brien, M. Gleeson, J. Kavanagh, B. Reynolds, F. Aherne, C. Sheehan, P. Sexton, W. Flanagan, T. Flanagan, J. Flanagan, J. Moran, T. Dwyer, W. Higgins, D. Sherry.

London—M. Walsh, J. Kearns, M. Cremins (capt.), P Duggan, T. Pyne, W. Scanlon, J. Butterly, P. Nash, M. Collins, J. Ryan, J. Cronin, J. McCarthy, D. O'Brien, J. Holohan, C. O'Neill.

1933

Tipperary—D. Roche, W. Roche, Pat O'Mahony, P. O'Toole, J. Dunne, E. Eade (capt.), P. O'Keeffe, Dave Looby, Dick Hayes, J. Tynan, J. Duggan, D. Gorman, D. Murphy, W. Ryan, D. Gleeson. Subs: M. O'Toole, J. Cooney.

London—J. Desmond, F. Johnson, J. Kinsley, S. Kiely, M. Madden, J. McCarthy, R. Sloan, J. Kearns, P. Duggan, F Trimm, J. Lyons, T. Grant, W. O'Hara, P. Hurney, J. Butterley. Sub: P. Nash for J. McCarthy.

1934

Waterford—M. Curley, W. Hennebry, J. Keane, J. Whelan, J. O'Gorman, M. Ryan, J. Healy, G. Kehoe (capt.), W. Sheehan, B. Doyle, M. Creed, P Sheehan, J. Murphy, J. Walsh, D. Mahony.

London—D. Hoyne, J. Butterly, P Hogan, J. Mahon, G. Pyne, M. Madden, S. Kiely, D. O'Keeffe, H. Burrows, J. Kinsley, M. Cremin, P. McCarthy, E. Foulds, W. Downey, T. Grant.

1935

Limerick—J. McCarthy, J. Curtin, P. O'Carroll, J. Ryan, T. McCarthy, M. Power, M. Cross (capt.), P. McCarthy (Feenagh), J. Sullivan, T. McCarthy, M. Butler, W. Daly, P McSweeney, W. Curtin, Jim O'Sullivan.

London—D. Hoyne, G. Pyne, M. Madden, S. Kiely, J. Hardiman, J. O'Keeffe, W. Galligan, D. O'Keeffe, T. Rainey, T. Grant, A. Noonan, J. Kinsley, E. Foulds, E. Kiely, M. Hynes.

1936

Westmeath—P. Fahy, W. Doyle, J. Mulligan, F. Monaghan, Todd Nugent, F. White (capt.), T. Gavigan, E. Moynihan, P. Lenihan, T. Morgan, M. McCarthy (capt.), S. Skehal, T. McNeice, Tim McGrath, Colm Boland, Sub.: Joe Leonard.

Waterford—M. Curley (goal), P. Fanning, D. Hogan, J. O'Gorman, M. Skehan, J. Shortall, J. Plunkett, J. Phelan, P. Greene, J. Murphy, J. Halpin, D. Mahony, P. Gough, M. Hickey, J. Mountain.

1937

Dublin—J. Hennessy, P. Tolan, M. Butler, P. Crowley, P. Horan, D. Hurley, S. Barrett, T. Leahy, R. Ryan, M. Fletcher, P. McCormack, J. Byrne, J. Maher/ P. McMahon (capt.), P. Doody.

London—D. Hoyne, D. Waters, B. Hickey, E. Fox (capt.), J. Hardiman, P. Grant, T. Rainey, P Foley, L. Moran, E. Foulds, M. Doolan, J. Long, P. McDonald, C. Curtin, M. Morris. Sub: P. McCarthy for P. McDonald.

1938

London—E. Shaughnessy, J. Dunne, T. Walker, E. Eade, J. Hickey, E. Foulds, L. Moran, J. Dwyer (capt.), J. Farrell, Mick Regan, J. Hardiman, T Rainey, B. Hickey, N. Noonan, D. Hoyne. Sub: R. Hogan for E. Shaughnessy.

Cork—J. Lynch (capt.), C. Madden, J. Hyde, J. P Creedon, B. Thornhill, Dan Coughlan, D. J.Buckley, R. Dineen, J. Tobin, P. Corbett, D. Cotter, W. Horgan, W. Twomey, T. O'Connell, J. O'Callaghan, Subs.: J. O'Mahony for W. Horgan, M. Lucey for J. Tobin.

1939

Galway—T. Nolan, W. Donnellan, J. Fahy, J. Curley, J. Hanney, W. O'Connor, M. Lowry, Joe Costello (capt.), T. Lambert, J. Hanniffy, E. Hogan, T. Cunningham, R. Forae, L. Connaire, M. Mulryan. Subs: P. Fahy for T. Nolan, R. McTigue for M. Mulryan.

London—J. Farrell (goal), J. Heffernan, B. Hickey, P. Walsh, E. O'Brien, K. Odlum, J. Hardiman, W. Galligan, J. Dwyer (capt.), J. Maher, M. Doolan, N. Noonan, J. Dunne, J. Smith, J. Hickey. Subs: P Grant for J. Hardiman, M. Noonan for W. Galligan.

1940

Cork—E. Porter, T. O'Connell, C. Kelly, W. Holton, H. O'Callaghan, G. Sadlier, R. Walsh, P. Aherne, J. Barry-Murphy, E. Riordan, P. J. Rioroan, L. Tully, C. Radley, D. Lynch (capt.), P. Corbett.

Galway—A. Reddan, D. Flynn, N. O'Connor, D. Diviney, R. Quinn, T. Fahy, J. Brophy, T. Barry, M. O'Leary, F. Fallon, W. Lambert, P. Thornton, K. Costello, D. Finn, P Robinson. Sub: P. Clarke for W. Lambert.

1941

Limerick—H. Wilson, J. O'Donoghue, S. O'Riordan (capt.), A. O'Donoghue, P Walsh, J. McCarthy, P. McCarthy (Mungret), J. Tobin, T. Toomey, O. O'Brien, T. Murphy, J. Foley, J. Madden, P. McCarthy (Feenagh), K. Foley. Sub: P. Aherne

Galway—S. Duggan, W. O'Connor, P. Ickham, P. Fahy, J. Power, W. Lambert, M. Lowry, J. Brogan, J. Ryan, P. Forde, P. Diviney, C. Corless, B. Mooney, V. McNamee, P. Daly.

1946

Kilkenny—J. Egan, M. Marnell, P. Hayden, P. O'Connor, P. Cahill, P. Prendergast, E. Power, P. Stapleton, P. Dack (capt.), H. Giles, M. Kenny, E. Doyle, P. McEvoy, D. Maher, W. Cahill. Sub: E. Purcell for J. Egan.

London—N. Egan, T. Hayes, M. Regan, S. Murphy, P. O'Brien, M. Ward, S. Fogarty, S. Costelloe, J. Somers, M. Doolan, P. Fouhy, J. Duggan, D. Doyle, W. Guilfoyle, M. Wade (capt.). Sub: J. Dower for M. Wade.

1947

Cork—W. Barry, B. Murphy, W. Holton, D. O'Donovan, D. Lyons, M. Nestor, J. O'Mahony, S. Twomey, J. Thornhill, J. West, M. O'Toole (capt.), W. J. Daly, M. Kearney, T. O'Sullivan, P. Abernethy, Sub.: J. O'Grady.

London—E. Maher (goal), T. Hayes, S. Riordan, M. Delaney, M. Ward, M. Regan, S. Fogarty, J. Costelloe, P. Fouhy, N. Egan, J. Donnelly, J. Duggan, D. Doyle, J. Aherne, M. Fletcher, Sub.: S. O'Mullane.

1948

Meath—R. Grogan, P. Kane, O. Reilly, N. Collier, S. Kelly, A. Donnelly (capt.), M. Kane, D. Mulligan, P. Donnelly, D. O'Mahony, P. Kelly, A. Foran, L. Wright, M. O'Brien, B. Smyth. Sub: T. Gerrard for L. Wright.

(T. Gerrard and J. Loughran played in drawn game. P. Kelly and D. O'Mahony were on for replay. Subs in drawn game: P. Kelly for L. Wright, P. Mitchell for B. Smith.)

London—W. Ryan, T. Hayes, G. Aherne, T. Tennyson, W. Miller, E. Wilson, S. Fogarty, J. Costelloe, S. Corcoran, N. Egan, P. Fitzpatrick, J. Duggan, J. Doyle, D. Doyle, M. Fletcher. Sub: R. Ronan for S. Corcoran.

(S. Riordan, M. Tuohy, M. Delaney, W. Flanagan, J. Lyons and M. Walsh played in drawn game. T. Hayes, J. Aherne, T. Tennyson, E. Wilson, S. Corcoran and J. Doyle were on for replay.)

1949

London—W. Ryan, T. Hayes, T. O'Mahony, S. O'Riordan, H. O'Shea, W. Brophy, S. Fogarty (capt.), Sean Costelloe, B. Hoban, P. Fitzpatrick, F. Hogan, J. Duggan, D. Doyle, P. Madden, J. Lawton, Subs.: P. Connors for T. O'Shea, J. Lewis for F. Hogan, C. Burke for P. Madden.

Clare—M. O'Keeffe, R. McNamara, W. Hogan, T. Casey, Ed. Doyle, P. McNamara, P. Halpin, D. O'Grady, J. Meaney, J. Smith (capt.), P. Greene, P. Leahy, Jas Kenneally, Ed. Hickey, D. Keane. Subs: W. Shanahan for J. Kenneally.

1950

Cork—F. Daly, D. Barry, J. Walsh, V. Twomey, P. Walsh, W. O'Neill (capt.), M. Cashman, G. Power, C. O'Neill, D. O'Driscoll, P. Healy, S. Fleming, A. Aherne, M. O'Donoghue, P. O'Riordan.

London—W. Ryan, P. McCarthy, T. Mahony, G. O'Brien, Seamus O Ceallachain, W. Brophy (capt.), M. Butler, B. Hoban, S. Costelloe, J. Goggin, C. Burke, J. Duggan, D. Doyle, R. Carew, R. Leahy, Subs: J. Maher for W. Brophy, W. Brophy for J. Maher, J. Maher for G. O'Brien, W. Lewis for R. Leahy, J. Lawton for C. Burke.

1951

Kilkenny—R. Rockett, J. Lynch, S. Hokey (capt.), W. Bolger, T. Walsh, P Fitzgerald, J. McGovern, J. Sutton, P. Stapleton, P. Johnson, P. Hennebry, M. Gardiner, T. Ryan, R. Burke, J. Barron.

London—E. Moloney, P. McCarthy, A. O'Brien, T. Gleeson, M. Butler, W. Brophy (capt.), P. Connors, S. Costelloe, J. Duggan, J. Goggin, B. Hoban, T. Bergin, C. McDonagh, J. Doyle, J. Lawton Subs: J. Maher for J. Doyle, J. O'Brien for T. Gleeson, S. Costelloe for E. Moloney.

1952

Dublin—S. Murphy, J. Duggan, W. Holmes, J. Young, J. Manton, C. Hayes, D. Kelly, L. Skelly (capt.), L. Harding, J. Rodgers, T. Ryan, M. Ryan, W. Fletcher, J. Griffin, S. Daly.

London—E. Moloney, M. Fitzpatrick, E. O'Brien, P. Murphy, M. Butler, W. Flanagan, W. Brophy, J. Wade, J. Duggan, D. Bransfield, S. McEntaggart, W. Murphy, E. O'Sullivan, T. Morrissey, T. Murphy, Sub.: P. Costelloe for S. McEntaggart.

1953

Tipperary—M. Fogarty, T. Kennedy, M. Doheny, S. Kelly, J. Callanan, S. Organ, T. Sweeney, J. Ryan, M. Conway, T. English, M. Kenny (capt.), J. Hannon, T. Foran, E. Hayes, K. McKenna.

Warwickshire—M. Leahy, J. Holmes, G. Creighton, P. Walsh, J. Barcoe, P Crowley, T. Ryan, M. Marnell, W. Harkins, S. Collins, D.

Fitzgerald, J. Byrne, P. Conway (capt.), W. Hayes, B. Graham. Subs: J. Walsh for W. Harkins, M. O'Mahony for D. Fitzgerald, W. Harkins for P. Walsh, J. McCarthy for J. Byrne.

1954

Limerick—P. Cunneen (goal), J. O'Sullivan, Jim Keogh, P. O'Neill, J. Dooley, S. Murphy, Jim Quaid, Jack Quaid, W. Dooley, A. Raleigh, M. Carmody (capt.), V. Cobbe, M. Sheehan, C. Daly, J. Barry.

London—E. Moloney, P. Murphy, K. Naughton, M. Butler, M. Lyons, W. Brophy (capt.), M. Fortune, S. Costelloe, Joe Duggan, T. Morrissey, S. O'Sullivan, D. Bransfield, M. Conway, P. Stapleton, S. Marmion. Subs: P. Cleary for M. Fortune, J. Barry for S. Marmion.

1955

Cork—L. O'Tuama, N. Looney, G. Mulcahy, L. Young, S. O'Mahony, C. Moynihan (capt.), P. Dowling, C. Cooney, J. Deasy, J. Browne, M. O'Toole, C. O'Shea, M. Quane, J. Cooney, P. O'Leary.

Warwickshire—P. Purcell, P. Foley, P. O'Meara, J. McCarthy, J. Barcoe, T. Ryan, M. Maher, E. Maher, J. Byrne, B. Boothman, J. Jordan, T. Kelly, D. Danagher, J. J. Nevin, B. Graham.

1956

Kilkenny—J. Murphy, Tom Walsh, J. "Link" Walsh, S. Tyrell (capt.), Phil Murphy, R. O'Neill, J. Burke, F. McCarthy, D. Gorey, D. Heaslip, Dick Bolger, J. Dunne, M. Fleming, W. Costigan, D. Hogan, Sub: J. Coyne.

London—M. Hickey, P Murphy, M. Kersse, M. Kelly, M. Lyons, W. Brophy, P. Ryan, P. Hourigan, J. Ryan, W. Dargan, S. O'Sullivan, E. Murphy, T. Morrissey, M. O'Neill, D. Shanahan (capt.). Subs: M. Fortune for P. Ryan, A. Casey for D. Shanahan.

1957

Limerick—G. Casey (goal), T. O Donnell (capt.), P. O'Connor, T. O'Dwyer, D. McCarthy, J. Dooley, J. Nealon, L. Hogan, M. Savage, M. O'Shea, J. Shanahan, M. Sheehan, P. Ryan, J. Enright, J. Barry, Sub.: Dick McGrath.

London—G. Sutton, P. Murphy, M. Kersse, M. Shanahan, T. Martin, J. Naughton, L. Friday, W. Dargan, M. O'Connell, E. Murray, W. Brophy, T. Morrissey, M. O'Neill, P. Hourigan, T. Morrissey.

1958

Cork—J. Dempsey, S. French, F Maxwell, A. O'Regan, J. Browne, N. Lynam, M. Thompson, C. Cooney, N. Gallagher, W. Galligan, M. O'Brien, S. Kelly, L. McGrath, F. Daly, M. Quane (capt.)

Warwickshire—J. Malone, M. Moore, G. Creighton, T. Ryan, M. Maher, M. Cunningham, P. Dalton, D. Curtin, J. Byrne (capt.), P. Thornhill, M. Galvin, B. Finnerty, W. SheeLy, J. J. Nevin, P. O'Connell. Sub: J. Mullins for M. Galvin.

1959

London—A. Morrissey, J. Kearns, M. Kersse, P. Murphy, M. Carmody, P. Dwyer, M. Kelly, E. Murray, W. Dargan, S. Sullivan, W. Duffy (capt.), D. Dillon, S. Healy, J. Rabbitte, C. Hickey, Subs.: V. O'Halloran for M. Carmody, W. Ryan for S. Healy, J. Hickey for J. Rabbitte, P. Ryan for S. O'Sullivan.

Antrim—D. O'Neill, E. Gallagher, G. Walsh, V. Kerr, J. Gibson, S. Wright (capt.), L. McGarry, S. Gallagher, A. Forsythe, P. Mullaney, R. Elliott, O. Campbell, E. McMullan, S. McGuinness, R. McMullan.

1960

London—A. Morrisey, J. Kearns, M. Kersse, P. Murphy, F. Spillane, P. Dwyer, A. Moloney, W. Dargan, E. Murray, P. Wilson, W. Duffy, P. Ryan, N. Murphy, J. Hickey, L. Healy. Sub: S. Somers for N. Murphy.

(M. O'Connell, J. Fitzgerald and J. Redmond played in drawn game. A. Moloney, P. Ryan and N. Murphy came on for replay. Subs in drawn game W. Ryan for M. O'Connell, Jim Redmond for John Redmond.)

Carlow—B. Hayden, J. Dermody, P. Somers, W. Walsh, W. Hogan, E. Gladney, T. Nolan, M. O'Brien, M. Morrissey, L. Walsh, W. Walsh (capt.), P. McGovern, J. McCarthy, M. Hogan, E. Long.

1961

Kerry—J. O'Donovan, N. Sheehy, N. Quill, T. Kirby, M. Hennessy (capt.), R. McElligott, K. Dermody, S. Lovett, S. Healy, J. Barry, T. Hennessy, P. Sullivan, J. Culloty, W. McCarthy, E. Sullivan.

London—W. Barnaville, J. Dermody, J. Twomey, M. O'Dwyer, M. Craddock, P. O'Dwyer, V. O'Halloran, P. Hourigan, T. Delaney, J. Dorgan, J. Tiernan, P. Spillane, W. Barron, S. Somers, C. Hickey, Subs: J. Naughton for J. Dermody, J. Organ for W. Barron, M. O'Connor for P. Hourigan.

1962

Kildare—P. Dunny, P. Morris, A. Whelan, P. Sharpe, D. Noonan, T. Connell (capt.), A. Sullivan, P Curley, F. Fogarty, K. O'Malley, M. Wall, J. Barker, M. Leahy, L. Kiely, S. Schwer, Sub.: P. Cummins for J. Barker.

London—M. Butler, J. Dermody, J. Twomey, M. Butler, M. Craddock, P. Hourigan, L. Murphy, E. Cullen, T. Sheehan, J. Fox, J. Sinnott, T. Delaney, J. J. Dillane, D. Croke, E. Mitchell, Subs.: M. O'Connor for L. Murphy, M. Belraine for M. Butler, M. Corcoran for T. Sheehan.

1963

London—A. Fayard, T. Connolly, M. Butler, M. O'Brien, M. O'Connor, M. Connolly, V. O'Halloran, T. Sheehan (capt.), M. Murphy, J. J. Browne, E. Murray, J. Barrett, P. Carmody, J. Hickey, J. O'Reilly, Sub: M. Diggins for Carmody.

Antrim—J. Kearns, J. Carberry, A. McIntosh, G. Walsh, S. McMullan, D. McNeill, S. Burns, C. Barrett, S. Richmond, C. Brogan, L. McGarry (capt.), P. McShane, B. McGarry, R. Elliott, S. Shannon. Subs: B. Elliott for L. McGarry, J. Hughes For C. Brogan.

1964

Down—A. Falloona, Paddy Branniff, H. O'Prey, D. Gilmore, F. Gilmore, H. Dorrian, W. Smith, E. Falloona, Podge Branniff, S. Savage, C. McMullan (capt.), D. Crawford, S. Fitzgerald, H. Sloan, J. McGivern, Subs: G. Gilmore for S. Savage, P. McGratton for Paddy Branniff.

London—M. Butler, W. Croke, P. Wiley, T. Morrissey, T. Delaney, C. Hughes, T. Gallagher, D. Henry, L. Murphy, P. O'Donoghue, C. Burke, M. Dunne, T. Barron, J. Dorgan, A. Gordon, Subs.: M. Treacy for C. Burke, G. Ryan for A. Gordon.

1965

Roscommon—Tony Gavin, T. Moylette, P Lyons, T. Murphy, B. Mitchell, J. Kenny, M. J. Keane, S. Cormican, M. Laffey, G. O'Malley, J. Boland, R. Fallon, M. Hoare (capt.), T. Boyle, J. McDonnell. Sub: M. Glennon for T. Boyle.

Warwickshire—J. O'Leary, P. Cullen, M. O'Leary, J. Shine, J. Nolan, J. Burke, T. Ryan, D. Dunne, E. Hanlon, M. Conway, P. Hallinan, W. Hogan, T Buckley, H. Shefflin, M. Murphy.

1966

Kildare—J. Curran, C. O'Malley, P. Sharpe, J. Wall, F. Fogarty, P. Dunny (capt.), T. Carew, R. Burke, T. Christian, J. Lalor, D. O'Keeffe, M. Dwane, N. Behan, W. Quinn, M. O'Brien, Sub.: L. O'Rourke for J. Lalor.

Warwickshire—E. O'Brien, J. Dineen, J. Burke, R. Hayes, T. Ryan, D. Dillane, P. Cullen, E. Hanlon, M. O'Sullivan, R. Dunne, P. Hallinan, W. Hogan, K. Phelan, M. O'Leary, T. Buckley, Subs.: P. Gillman for E. O'Brien, J. Byrne for K. Phelan, L. Cullinane for M. O'Leary.

1967

Wicklow—J. Torpey, T. Collins, J. Fogarty, Liam Collins, J. Kearns (capt.), T Kelly, Rory O'Shea, S. Doyle, Tony Doyle, P O'Dwyer, L. Jordan, T. Morrissey, M. Jordan, T. Scott, W. Hilliard, Sub.: C. Keddy for T. Kelly.

Note: A. Byrne played in drawn game. L. Collins came on for replay. Sub in drawn game C. Keddy for J. Fogarty.

London—M. Butler, W. Croke, T. Morrissey, E. Roche, W. Twomey, T. Allen, L. Murphy, M. Dunne, P. O'Neill, N. Peacock, J. Tiernan, J. Barrett, M. Butler, P Spillane, P. Delaney, Sub.: T Delaney for L. Murphy.

Note: T. Regan, P. Doherty, J. Holohan, M. Devereaux and K. Dunne played in drawn game. T. Morrissey, E. Roche, P. Delaney, L. Murphy and M. Butler came on for replay. Subs in drawn game: P. Flynn for P Doherty, L. Murphy for J Holohan.

1968

Warwickshire—D. Breen, J. Dineen, J. Quinn, R. Hayes, R. Timmons, D. Dillane, P. Cullen, S. O'Keeffe, C. Danagher, W. Hogan, T. Ryan, M. O'Sullivan, C. Crowe, J. Cronin, D. Dunne. Sub: T. Murphy for J. Cronin.

Kerry—J. Breen, Tadgh O'Sullivan, D. Kelleher, W. Kenny, T. Lyons, N. Power, T. Leen, R. O'Sullivan, G. Scollard, Theo O'Sullivan, T Cronin, J O'Sullivan, C. Flaherty, W. McCarthy (capt.), B. Twomey, Sub: M. Griffin for P O'Sullivan.

1969

Warwickshire—M. McCarthy, J. O'Brien, P. Grimes, P. Heffernan, M. Hanley, L. Dalton, L. Moore, T. Crowley, L. Moloney, W. Collins, M. Brennan, J. Gilligan, J. McLaughlin, J. Browne (capt.), V. Coffey, Sub: P. Hallinan for J. Gilligan.

Kerry—J. Breen, M. J. Quinlan, D. Kelleher, W. Kenny, N. Power, T. Cronin (capt.), P. J. McIntyre, T. B. McCarthy, P Finnegan, P McCarthy, P. Sullivan, J. O'Sullivan, C. Flaherty W. McCarthy, J. Gannon, Subs: B Twomey for C Flaherty T. Fleming for P McCarthy.

1970

Meath—P . McGovern T. Troy, T. Reilly, M Doherty, E. Cosgrove, G. Baugh, P. Priest, F. McGann, P. Christie, R. Melia, M. McCabe, S. Carney, F. Gleeson, S. Gohery, N. Costello, Subs: J. Curtis for P. Christie, W. Eiffe for M. Doherty ancd John Doherty.

(J. Harty and J Doherty played in drawn game. F Gleeson and S. Gohery were on for replay. Subs in drawn game: F. Gleeson for M. McCabe, S. Goherty for J. Doherty.

Hertsfordshire—P Waters, V. Donoghue, N. Kennedy, J. Burke, M. Doherty, T. Cleary, S. McGarry, M. Waters, M. Cuddy (capt.), M. Dollard, J. Cuddy, M. Howley, T. Garret, M. Fennessy, P. Waters, Subs: S. Moriarty for M Howley, S. Burke for M. Dollard, J. Byrne for V. O'Donoghue.

Note. J. Tobin played in drawn game M. Dollard came in for replay. Subs in drawn game: S Carroll for W. Fennessy; J. Byrne for J. Tobin.

1971

Wicklow—J. Byrne, L. O'Loughlin, Tony Reilly, J. O'Shaughnessy, J. Doyle, F. Byrne, M. O'Neill, P. Reilly (capt.), P. Berkerry, P. Sheehan, T. McCarthy, T. Kennedy, G. Delaney, E. Murray, G. Gibbons, Subs: A. Byrne for G. Delaney, D. O'Sullivan for A. Byrne, P O'Connell for G. Gibbons.

(P. Doyle and D. O'Sullivan played in first game. G Gibbons and T. Kennedy came on for disputed game and retained their places for third game.)

Hertsfordshire—P. Waters, M. Doherty, E. Kennedy, Joe Burke, James Burke, T. Cleary, S. McGarry, Peter Waters, M. Fitzgerald, J Cuddy (capt.), E. Walsh, M. Waters, T. Garrett. C. Murphy, J. Carroll. Subs: J. Kennedy for M. Waters, D. Kelly for James Burke, K. Sheridan for J. Cuddy, W. Fennessv for P. Kelly.

(K. Sheridan, M. Allen and W. Fennessy played in first game. E. Walsh came on as a sub for K. Sheridan and retained his place for second and third games. C. Murphy for W. Fennessy and M. Fitzgerald for M. Allen came on as subs in second game and retained their places for third game.)

1972

Kerry—A. Casey, B. Fitzgerald, E. B. Fitzgerald, W. Kenny, E. Canty, T. Cronin, T. Hussey, J. Bunyan, P. Finnegan, C. Nolan, T. Kenny, P. Costello, J. McCarthy, P. Donegan, J. Flanagan (capt.), Sub: M. Fitzgerald for T. Hussey.

Warwickshire—D. Breen, J. O'Brien, V. McKenna, T. Conroy, M. Hanley, D. Dillane, J. Scanlon, D. Crowley, L. Moloney, L. Moore, N. McLean, J. Moynihan, C. Danagher, L. Dalton, R. Walsh, Subs: C. Crowe for J. O'Brien, M. Griffin for L. Dalton.

1973

Warwickshire—O. Cuddy, V. McKenna, T. Conroy, P. Doherty, L. Dalton, D. Dillane, J. Scanlon, J. Madden, N. McLean (capt.), M. Murphy, L. Moloney, C. Crowe, E. Bergin, J. Ryan, J. Cronin, Subs.: T. Crowley for M. Murphy, T. Timmons for J. Scanlan.

Louth—P Mulholland, S. Walsh, J. Delaney (capt.), A. Farrelly, D. Callan, L. Toal, J. McGuinness, P. Murphy, M. Rice, P. Rice, T. Rice, S. McEneaney, A. Kinsh, F. Kerrigan, P. Fahy. Subs: T Lowry for P. Fahy, A. Melia for A. Kinsh.

1974

Roscommon—P Dolan, T. Healy, O. Hanley, T. Shaughnessy, C. McConn, S. Farrell, J. Dolan, J. Coyne, F. Mitchell, H. Cox, B. Tansey, D. Cox, B. Mitchell, M. Murphy, R. Fallon (capt.). Sub: J. Kilroy.

Derry—A. Crawford, T. McGill, L. Hinphey, Phonsie Boyle, J. O'Kane, S. Stevenson (capt.), A. O'Hara, P. Mellon, P. Stevenson, F. McCluskey, J. McGurk, D. Higgins, C. Ferris, F. Kennedy, B. O'Kane, Sub: C. Hinphey for B. O'Kane, P. Murphy for D. Higgins.

1975

Derry—Billy Taylor, T. McGill, L. Hinphey, A. O'Hara, J. O'Kane, S. Stevenson (capt.), P. Stevenson, M. McCloskey, S. Kealy, J. McGurk, P. Mellon, C. Hinphey, F. Kennedy, C. Ferris, L. Moore.

Louth—T. Lowry, J. Delaney, A. Byrne, A. Melia, D. O'Gorman, P. Fahy, T. Ryan, M. Rice, L. Geraghty, P. Rice, S. Mulcairns, P. Wright, A. Kerrigan, J. McGuinness, S. McEneaney.

1976

Louth—P. Hartnett, J. McGuinness, J. Delaney, S. Walsh, D. Callan, P. Fahy, A. Byrne, L. McKillian, L. Toal, S. McEneaney, T. Rice, P. Murphy, A. Melia, T. Lowry, S. Mulcairns. Subs: M. McGarry for A. Byrne, D. Hegarty for L. McKillian.

Mayo—M. Nolan, M. Robinson, M. Keane, E. Freeman, M. Walsh, D. Delaney, M. Molloy, A. Henry, M. Murphy, J. Henry, S. O'Keeffe, V. Henry, M. Connolly, M. Higgins, M. Kenny. Subs.: P Clarke for M. Walsh, J. Clarke for D. Delaney.

1977

Louth—P. Hartnett, M. Begley, J. Delaney, C. McGinley, D. Callan, P. Fahy, S. Walsh, P. Murphy, A. Kerrigan, T. Ryan, T. Rice, A. Melia, S. Mulcairns, T. Lowry, O. Reilly. Sub: J. McGuinness for C. McGinley.

Fermanagh—L. McLoughlin, E. Gallagher, R. Gallagher, O. O'Donnell, T. Rehill, C. Cullen, J. McGoldrick, J. Doran, A. Corrigan, G. Cleary, C. Rehill, B. Corrigan, G. McLoughlin, T. Daly, M. Hughes. Sub: F Baker for G. McLoughlin.

1978

Armagh—P Lavery, S. King, L. McKenna, I. Beattie, G. Devlin, M. Smith, E. Kinsella, C. Casey, B. McNally, J. McCormack, P. Devlin, J. Short, E. Mallon, C. McKeown, J. Corvon.

Mayo—M. Nolan, E. Freeman, M. Keane, B. Crowley, M. Robinson, P. Clarke, M. Walsh, M. Murphy, A. Henry, W. Loughnane, J. Henry, V. Henry, J. Hopkins, P. Malone, W. Kelly. Subs: R. Donoghue for J. Hopkins, M. Henry for B. Crowley.

1979

Armagh—P. Lavery, S. King (capt.), D. McBride, I. Beattie, G. Devlin, M. Smith, E. Kinsella, C. Casey, B. McNally, J. McCormack, P. Devlin, J. Short, J. Christie, F. Mallon, C. McKeown.

Derry—A. Treacy, T. McGill, G. McCullagh, M. McCloskey, J O'Kane, S. Stevenson, P. Murphy, P. Stevenson, J. McCullagh, P. O'Donoghue, E. Hassan, J. McGurk, D. Kealy, C Hinphy, P. Mellon. Sub: P Boyle for G. McCullagh.

1980

Mayo—M. Nolan, E. Freernan, M. Keane, M. Walsh, P. Clarke, A. Henry, P. Lynskey, J. Cunnane, V Henry, J. J. Hoban, C. Conlon, C. Murphy, J. Henry, M. Ryan, W. Kelly.

Monaghan—L. Freeman, D. Ryan, A. O'Reilly, M. Evans, N. McGuigan, G. Maher, J. Power, W. Connolly, J. Downey, P. Kerr, L. Lenihan, M. O'Dowd (snr.), N. Mullaney; O. Connell, P Bolger.

1981

Mayo—D Synnott, M. Walsh, M. Kenny, T. Phillips, P Clarke, A. Henry, P Lynskey, V. Henry, J. Cunnane, C. Conlon, J. Henry, C. Murphy; J. J. Hoban, D. Healy, P Delaney.

Louth—P. Hartnett, D. Callan, P. Moran, J. McGuinness, S. Mclnerney, A. Kerrigan. C. McGinley, P Murphy, C. Ross, A. Melia, O. Reilly, T. Murphy, W. Piper, T. Giles, M. McGarry. Subs: S. Mulcairns for P. Hartnett, S. French for W. Piper.

1982

Derry—A. Treacy, J. McCullagh, A. O'Hara (capt.), G. McCullagh, C. Kelly, P. Stevenson, D. O'Hara, G. Murphy, B. McGilligan, D. Kealy, S. McCloskey, D. Kealy, P. O'Donoghue, P Murphy, J. A. Mullan. Sub: E. Kealy for S. McCloskey.

Monaghan—L. Freeman, D. Ryan, A. O'Reilly, M. Giblin, N. McGuigan, L. Lenihan, B. Lynch, J. Downey, W. Connolly, M. O'Dowd Jnr., P. Egan, P Curran, J. J. Sullivan (capt.), O. Connell, M. O'Dowd Snr. Subs: N. Mullaney for P Curran, P. Hughes for M. O'Dowd Snr., S. O'Gorman for M. Giblin.

1983

Cork—J. Cronin, F Walsh, E. Flynn, Dan Relihan, Brendan Coleman, P. Madigan, N. Crowley, W. Walsh, M. Fitzgibbon (capt.), P O'Connell, D. Walsh, Ned Brosnan, Ray O'Connor, S. O'Gorman, G. Hanley. Subs: A. Jagoe for F. Walsh, M. McDonnell for P. O'Connell.

Galway—T. Carr, M. O'Donoghue, P. Finnerty (capt.), T. Riordan, S. Davoren, T. Nolan, T Brehony, N. Uniacke, E. Hanny, J. Murphy, M. Coleman, D. Glennon, J. Kelly, J. Coen, D. Connolly. Subs: E. McLarnan for A. Carr, Mattie Kenny for N. Uniacke, T. Uniacke for J. Kelly.

1984

Kilkenny—J. Brennan (capt.) W. O Hara, M. Galway, T. Whelan, P. Power, J Marnell, M. Cleere, D. Hoyne, S. Tyrrell, R. Walsh, P. Walsh, J. McDonald, M. Doyle, J. O'Dwyer, M. Rafter. Subs: John Lawler, J. Kinsel!a.

Galway—M. Gannon, K. Flannery, M. O'Donoghue, S. Treacy, P. Malone, M. Minton, M. Conway, E. Hanny, T. Helebert N. O'Halloran, M. Coleman, R. Haverty, N. Earls. L. Craven, G. Stankard. Subs: T. Moloney, Mattie Kenny, N. Uniacke.

1985

Wexford—S. Dunne, J. Prendergast, W. Dunphy, B. Bernie, L. Finn, J. Furlong, J. Weafer, J. Barron, P. Owley, R. Murphy, J. Walsh, M. Murphy, S. Murphy, B. O'Connor, T. Byrne. Subs.: P. Barden, P. Daly, V. Murphy.

Tipperary—P. McLoughney, J. McLoughney, P. Larkin, M. Burke, N. McDonald, J. O'Dwyer, M. Ryan, Colm Bonnar, M. Murphy, J. McGrath, G. O'Brien, D. Darcy, L. Stokes, L. McGrath (capt.), S. Burke, Subs: M. Ryan, D. Aherne

1986

Kilkenny—M. Walsh, J. Lannon, D. Dunne, E. Wall, J. Power, M. Cleere, G. Kenny, M. Morrissey (capt.), K. Hennessy, T. Bawle, T. Lannon, D. Carroll, R. Walsh, L. McCarthy, J. Meaney, Sub.: L. Cleere for M. Cleere.

Limerick—J. Cagney, M. Barrett, B. Ryan, M. Keogh, A. Galvin, G. Boyle, J. Burns, P. O'Connor, L. O'Brien, M. O'Brien, T. Burke, M. Ryan, T. Dunne, M. O'Connor (capt.), E. Farrell, Subs.: M. J. Coffey for M. Barrett, M. Woulfe for A. Galvin.

1987

Cork—T. Kingston, B. O'Sullivan, P. Redmond, D. Murphy, S. McCarthy, L. Lynch, J. Moynihan, D. Sheehan, M. Fitzpatrick (capt.), T Burke, L. Kelly, T Barry-Murphy, M. Foley, P Cahill, P. Crowley, Subs.: D. McCarthy, D. Relihan, R O'Connor.

Wexford—B. Murphy, J. Weafer, S. Ruth, P. Byrne, L. Finn, A. Fenlon, J. O'Leary, C. Jevans, G. Cody, J. Murphy,. J. Byrne, J. Barron (capt.), P. Cleary, S. Murphy, T. Byrne, Sub.: J. Higgins.

1988

Kilkenny—D. Burke, J. Marnell, P Holden, J. Lannon, S. Caulfield, P. Dwyer, T. McCluskey, G. Ryan, P. Ryan, T. Bawle, J. Walsh, D. Carroll, M. Rafter, J. O'Dwyer, J. Ronan (capt.). Subs: P Gannon for J. O'Dwyer, D. McCarthy for D. Carroll.

Tipperary—B. Bane, M. Stapleton. M. Bourke (capt.), D. Quinlan, F. McGrath, G. O'Brien, M. Corcoran, M. Kelly, E. Kelly, M. Cunningham, P Delaney, J. Harrington, M. McCormack, J. Sheedy, S. Bourke. Sub: P. Cahill for P. Delaney.

1989

Tipperary—J. Grace, M. Stapleton, Mick Ryan (Ballinahinch), D. Quinlan, G. O'Brien, R. Quirke, L. Sheedy, E. Kelly, K. Laffan (capt.), Dinny Ryan, P. Everard, D. Flannery, M. McCormack J. Sheedy, S. Nealon. Sub: Colm Egan for S. Nealon.

Galway—R. Burke, P Healy, P. Donoghue, B. Cooney, G. Spellman, S. Treacy, J. Noone (capt.), S. Mahon, P. Killilea, M. Connolly, O. Deely, Mattie Kenny, S. Ruane, T. Grealish, V. Treacy. Subs: P Keane for M. Kenny, D. Flanagan for S. Ruane, E. Keogh for V. Treacy.

1990

Kilkenny—M. Walsh, A. Byrne, P Holden (capt.), L. Simpson, J. Murphy, P. Walsh, J. Mahon, T. Bawle, P. Ryan, M. Dunphy, T. Murphy, C. Carter, M. Rafter, J. Lannon, M. Walsh (Slieverue). Subs: M. Walsh (Mooncoin) for M. Rafter, P Hoban for Lannon.

Tipperary—C. Egan, S. McManus, D. O'Brien, S. Brett, M. Ryan (Fethard), T. Crowe, T. O'Meara, O. Cummins, C. Bryan, L. Stokes, P. O'Brien, E. Maher, J. Harrington, M. Grace, G. Bradley (capt.). Subs: T. Murray for M. Grace, P. Kelly for T. O'Meara, B. Burke for T. Crowe.

1991

Tipperary—J. Leamy, M. Ryan (Fethard), M. Stapleton, D. Quinlan, P. Maguire, G. O'Brien (capt.), S. McManus, O. Cummins, C. Bryan, P. O'Keeffe, L. Sheedy, E. Maher, J. Harrington, E. Kelly, S. Nealon. Sub: M. Ryan (Ballinahinch) for M. Ryan.

London—T. Fahy, G. Maher, L. Weir, P. Maher, A. Fanning, M. Cahill, T. Bergin, G. Ryan, D. O'Hanlon, E. Fanning, J. Scott, P. Lonergan, D. Murphy, M. Rafferty, F. O'Donoghue. Subs: D. Hynes for T. Bergin, J. Hogan for P. Lonergan, F. Dwyer for E. Fanning.

1992

Wexford—M. Quigley, D. Morris, P. McGrath, J. Furlong, P. Nolan, G. Cody (capt.), D. Guiney, P. Owley, R. Guiney, R. O'Callaghan, P. Byrne, R. Quigley, J. Byrne, J. Bolger, S. Conroy. Sub: E. Scallan for R. Quigley.

(B. Kavanagh, M. Reck and E. Scallan played in drawn game. P. Owley, R. Guiney and R. Quigiey were on for replay. Subs in drawn game: P. Walsh for B. Kavanagh, P. J. Kavanagh for E. Scallan)

Cork—T. O'Donovan, D. Lucey, D. Holland, D. Motherway, M. Treacy, P. Kenneally, W. Long (capt.), J. O'Mahony, M. Sheehan, A. O'Driscoll, D. O'Leary, M. Mullins, K. Murray, B. Walsh, C. Clancy. Sub: B. Harte for M. Mullins.

(B. Sheehan and M. Downing played in drawn game. D. Lucey and M. Mullins were on for replay. Subs in drawn game: M. Mullins for M. Sheehan, B. Harte for M. Downing, P Cahill for J. O'Mahony).

1993

Clare—N. Considine, L. Doyle, F. Corey, B. Lynch, S. Power, T. Kennedy, N. Romer (capt.), D. Considine, C. Chaplin, P. O'Rourke, C. O'Neill, B. Quinn, V. Donnellan, B. McNamara, G. Rogers. Subs: C. Lynch for G. Rogers, J. McKenna for C. Chaplin.

Kilkenny—J. McGarry, J. Holohan, J. Mahon, D. Roche, J. Murphy, D. Shelly, C. Phelan, W. O'Keeffe, Paddy Farrell, T. O'Keeffe, C. Brennan, A. Comerford, C. Carter (capt.), P. Treacy, M. Walsh (Mooncoin). Subs: R. Dooley for J. Murphy, S. Ryan for A. Comerford.

1994

Cork—T. O'Donovan, A. White, J. O'Driscoll, J. Walsh, J. O'Sullivan, J. O'Mahoney, V. Murray (capt.), M. Downing, G. Cummins, M. Sheehan, P. Kenneally, F. McCormack, A. O'Driscoll, K. Morrisson, D. O'Connell. Subs: R. Sheehan for M. Sheehan, B. Sheehan for G. Cummins.

Kilkenny—J. McGarry, J. Holohan, J. Mahon, S. Mealy, J. Murphy, J. Conlon, P. Hennessy, A. Cleere, W. O'Keeffe, Paddy Farrell, B. McGovern, P. Treacy, M. Walsh (Mooncoin), D. Roche (capt.), O. O'Connor. Subs: T. Hickey for J. Holohan, O. Blanchfield for M. Walsh.

1995

Kilkenny—J. McGarry, J. Murphy (capt.), E. Drea, S. Meally, P. Hogan, E. Kennedy, T. Murphy, W. O'Keeffe, A. Cleere, Paddy Farrell, P. Treacy, D. Maher, D. Lawler, S. Ryan, O. O'Connor. Sub: B. McGovern for W. O'Keeffe.

Clare—Leo Doyle, S. Doyle, P. Hayes, S. O'Donnell, L. Hassett, E. Flynn, P. Sheehy, R. O'Halloran (capt.), B. Moloney, D. Forde, D. O'Riordan, F. Flynn, J. McKenna, G. Gleeson, B. Healy. Subs: B. O'Neill, P. McGuane, B. Fitzgerald.

1996

Galway—N. Murphy, K. Rabbitte, W. Burke, J. Feeney, J. Walsh, N. Larkin (capt.), N. Power, B. Carr, L. Hogan, B. Larkin, F. Gantley, F. Healy, A. Kerins, M. Connolly, M. Lynskey. Subs: F. O'Brien for L. Hogan, P. Diviney for J. Walsh, E. Caulfield for F. Gantley.

Kilkenny—J. Dunphy, J. Hickey, M. Holohan, C. Connery, A. Aherne, P. Hoban, M. Fitzgerald, R. Moore, B. Treacy, P. O'Grady, B. Barcoe, B. Phelan, R. Kelly, K. O'Shea (capt.), R. Shortall. Subs: P. Hickey for M. Holohan, M. Moran for B. Treacy, P. Cahill for M. Fitzgerald.

1997

Monaghan—O. Connell, D. Connolly, Jim Hayes, T. Gillanders, P. Ward, D. Hanrahan, J. Harding, P. Walsh, B. McShane, R. Healy, C. Connolly (capt.), D. Lennon, M. O'Dowd (jnr.), Joe Hayes, H. Cullen. Subs: P. Cunningham for H. Cullen, D. Reilly for P. Ward, J. O'Rourke for J. Harding.

Meath—N. Reilly, A. Heavin, C. Ferguson, D. Maguire, T Shine, C. Connell, P. Tansey, P. Coone, D. Reilly, R. Ferguson, M. Healy, F. Smith, D. Fitzsimons, M. Dineen, E. Dixon. Subs: E. McManus for D. Maguire, V. Maguire for F. Smith.

1998

Meath—T. Donoghue, J. Battersby, A. Connell, F. Dunne, E. Dixon, D. Connell (capt.), V. Maguire, F. O'Higgins, J. Burke, P. Coone, M. Healy, F. Smith, N. Reilly, N. McKeague, K. Murray. Subs: A. Snow for F. Smith, O. Gilsenan for F. O'Higgins.

Monaghan—O. Connell, N. McGuigan, D. Reilly, C. Curley, P Kelly, D. Connolly, D. Hanrahan, C. Connolly, J. Harding, H. Cullen, P O'Connell, R. Healy, P. Ward, K. Lavelle, P. Cunningham. Subs: M. O'Dowd (jnr.) for J. Harding, C. McEntee for R. Healy, T. Gillanders for P. Cunningham.

1999

Meath—D. Bannon, J. Horan, C. Ferguson, J. Curtis, B. Perry, J. Gorry, M. Mullen, D. Reilly, B. Gilsenan, T. McKeown, D. Byrne, S. Myles, M. Smith, P. Kelly, P. J. Walsh. Subs: D. Donnelly for Gilsenan, P. Ferguson for Byrne.

Tyrone—M. Ward, S. O'Neill, P. Sweeney, D. Molloy, P. Hughes, E. Hughes, K. Cunningham, N. Hurson, D. McCallion, P. Levery, V. Owens, T. Colton, T. McGowan, E. Devlin, P. Doyle. Subs: P. Hughes for P. Doyle, D. O'Neill for Colton.

2000

Armagh – B.McCormack, P.C.Gormley, E.McKee, S.Hughes, M.Fox, N.Traynor, P.Harvey, P.McCormack, M.Lennon, P.McKirk, P.McArdle, G.Enright, M.Grimes, P.McKernan, A.Hatzer. Subs – P.Burke for Grimes, R.Murray for McCann.

Meath – R.Flanagan, M.Horan, D.Gaughan, F.Fagan, P.Gannon, B.Ferguson,, M.Brennan, V.Maguire, D.McGuinness, F.Smith, M.Hanly, J.O'Connor, D.Smith, A.Doherty, W.Smyth. Subs – J.Flood for O'Connor, N.Watters for Doherty, D.Moran for Flood.

2001

Roscommon – D.Casey, M.Keaveney, N.Connolly, M.Flynn, K.Doyle, E.Browne, D.Fallon, T.Lennon, A.Beades, C.Fallon, S.O'Brien, P.Glennon, K.Regan, E.Gormley, B.Mannion. Subs – R.Donohoe for Glennon, F.Carr for Mannion, S.Donohoe for Fallon.

Donegal – P.O'Brien, F.Grant, C.Dowds, N.McGavigan, J.M.Wallace, D.McDermott, D.Campbell, A.Wallace, R.McLaughlin, N.Campbell, H.McDermott, M.McCann, S.Murphy, R.Durak, B.Friel. Subs – J.McGrath for Durak, K.McDermott for Friel.

2002

Antrim – A.McIlhatton, K.McCann, D.Rooney, J.Friel, C.Turley, P.Nugent, S.McGuiness, S.O'Kane, D.McToal, G.Turley, J.Caulfield, G.McIlhatton, N.McCann, T.Maguire, B.McCann. Subs – S.Burke for McToal, R.Edrahin for Friel, L.Burke for O'Kane.

Meath – C.Suher, L.O'Flynn, D.Gaughan, S.Fagan, A.McManus, B.Ferguson, D.Wright, C.Ferguson, M.Geraghty, T.Shine, J.Gorry, J.Mitchell, B.Doherty, E.Duignan, P.Hanley. Subs – C.Doherty for Mitchell, P.Fagan for Duignan, D.Geraghty for B.Doherty, G.Galvin for Gorry.

2003

Mayo – M.Walsh, D.Walsh, P.Healy, B.Delaney, D.McDonnell, P.Barrett, G.Whyte, D.McConn, K.Healy, A.Healy, J.Duffy, S.Broderick, O.Shaughnessy, P.Broderick, A.Hession. Subs – C.Ryan for Hession, K.Higgins for Shaughnessy.

Donegal – P.McDermott, J.M.Wallace, K.Dowds, M.McGrath, G.Boyle, D.McDermott, A.McDermott, A.Wallace, B.Friel, N.Campbell, E.McDermott, D.Greene, M.McCann, R.McLaughlin, P.O'Brien. Subs – J.Donnelly for Greene, J.O'Brien for E.McDermott.

2004

Meath – T.Donoghue, S.Duignan, E.Clancy, B.Flynn, C.Doyle, D.Troy, J.P.Ryan, J.Melia, D.Geraghty, M.Scanlon, P.Donnelly, S.Moran, D.Kirby, P.Tobin, R.Flanagan. Sub – B.Higgins for E.Clancy.

Down – G.McMullan, A.McGuinness, B.McAleenan, F.Murray, J.Brown, D.McCuskar, P.McCuskar, J.Murphy, T.Jennings, T.McMahon, K.Courtney, D.McGovern, J.McCuskar, J.McCrickard, A.Brown. Subs – D.Morgan for McGovern, N.Burns for Courtney.

ALL-IRELAND JUNIOR HURLING FINAL REFEREES

1912—M. F. Crowe (Dublin)
1913—Fred Cooney (Dublin)
1914—J. Kirwan (Dublin)
1915—Pat Dunphy (Laois)
1916—M. F. Crowe (Dublin)
1923—P. Kenefick (Dublin)
1924—P. McCullagh (Wexford)
1925—Tim Humphries (Limerick)
1926—Tom Hayes (Limerick)

1927—S. O'Neill (Dublin)
1928—Willie Walsh (Waterford)
1929—J. J. Callanan (Tipperary)
1930—Sean Hogan (Waterford)
1931—Jim Walsh (Dublin}
1932—J. Curran (Meath)
1933—Tom McGrath (Dublin)
1934—S. O'Neill (Dublin)
1935—Liam Murphy (Dublin)
1936—T. McGrath (Dublin)
1937—M. O'Neill (Wexford)
1938—J. Ryan (Liverpool)
1939—E. McMahon (Dublin)
1940—J. Madigan (Ennis)
1941—Mick Hennessy (Clare)
1946—Phil Purcell (Tipperary)
1947—Willie Murphy (Wexford)
1948—G. Kelly (Dublin)
1949—Con Murphy (Galway)
1950—J. Phelan (Kilkenny)
1951—Hubie Hogan (Tipperary)
1952—J. Keane (Waterford)
1953—Jack Mulcahy (Kilkenny)
1954—M. Leahy (Dublin)
1955—Moss Pollard (Waterford)
1956—C. McLoughlin (Dublin)
1957—Mick O'Mahony (Cork)
1958—F. Sheehan (Wexford)
1959—E. Conroy (Laois)
1960—Paddy Cronin (Cork)
1961—C. Conway (Cork)
1962—C. McLoughlin (Dublin)
1963—Clem Foley (Dublin)
1964—Clem Foley (Dublin)
1965—Jimmy Duggan (Galway)
1966—Clem Foley (Dublin)
1967—P. Johnson (Kilkenny)
1968—Clem Foley (Dublin)
1969—Pat Rankins (Laois)
1970—Mick Slattery (Clare)
1971—D. Doody (Dublin)
1972—P. Byrnes (Gloucestershire)
1973—E. Devlin (Tyrone)
1974—E. Farrell (Donegal)
1975—M. Clarke (Westmeath)
1976—Gerry Kirwan (Offaly)
1977—Clem Foley (Dublin)
1978—Noel O'Donoghue (Dublin)
1979—Noel O'Donoghue (Dublin)
1980—Seamus Brennan (Galway)
1981—Clem Foley (Dublin)
1982—Clem Foley (Dublin)
1983—Pat Delaney (Laois)
1984—John Moore (Waterford)
1985—Jim Joe Landers (Waterford)
1986—Jim Joe Landers (Waterford)
1987—Noel O'Donoghue (Dublin)
1988—Seamus Brennan (Galway)
1989—Pat Delaney (Laois)
1990—M Quinn (Clare)
1991—Pat Horan (Offaly)
1992—Pat Delaney (Laois)
1993—M. Darcy (Galway)
1994—Sean O'Meara (Offaly)
1995—John McDonnell (Tipperary)
1996—M. Wadding (Waterford)
1997—G. Devlin (Armagh)
1998—P. Aherne (Carlow)
1999—E. Morris (Dublin)
2000—M.Bodkin (Galway)
2001—J. McGrath (Westmeath)
2002—D.O'Donovan (Dublin)
2003—J.McGrath (Westmeath)
2004—G.Devlin (Armagh)

MUNSTER JUNIOR HURLING CHAMPIONSHIP FINALS

1910—Tipperary 5-0, Clare 2-0
(Unfinished. Replay ordered.)
Tipperary 5-1, Clare 1-0 (Refixture)
1911—Tipperary 6-4, Limerick 2-2
1912—Cork 4-5, Tipperary 3-1
1913—Tipperary 3-3, Cork 1-6
1914—Clare 6-2, Cork 5-2
1915—Tipperary 9-1, Clare 2-1
1916—Cork 6-0, Tipperary 4-1
1917-1922—Suspended
1923—Cork 8-4, Tipperary 5-1
1924—Tipperary 4-3, Limerick 2-2
1925—Cork 6-3, Clare 4-2
1926—Tipperary 3-7, Cork 2-3
1927—Limerick 4-4, Clare 2-2
1928—Tipperary 4-3, Waterford 0-3
1929—Cork 3-3, Waterford 2-4
1930—Tipperary 7-4, Clare 1-2
1931—Waterford 7-3, Tipperary 4-5
1932—Cork 1-4, Clare 1-2
1933—Tipperary 4-2, Cork 1-2
1934—Waterford 7-10, Cork 5-2
1935—Limerick 6-8, Waterford 2-0
1936—Waterford 3-1, Cork 1-1
1937—Cork 5-5, Limerick 3-1
1938—Cork 2-3, Clare 1-6 (draw)
Cork 7-5, Clare 4-0 (replay)
1939—Waterford 4-2, Limerick 2-4.
Limerick awarded title on an objection.
1940—Cork 5-3, Tipperary 3-3
1941—Limerick 4-8, Waterford 0-4
1942-1945—Suspended
1946—Limerick 6-6, Cork 5-6
1947—Cork 11-8, Waterford 1-3
1948—Limerick 4-7, Cork 4-5
1949—Clare 3-3, Cork 0-6
1950—Cork 3-7, Tipperary 3-6
1951—Tipperary 4-8, Limerick 3-2
1952—Limerick 6-6, Cork 2-6
1953—Tipperary 4-8, Cork 5-5 (draw)
Tipperary 4-7, Cork 4-6 (replay)
1954—Limerick 5-4, Tipperary 1-7
1955—Cork 5-10, Clare 4-4

1956—Kerry 6-7, Waterford 0-3
1957—Limerick 2-10, Cork 1-10
1958—Cork 6-9, Waterford 3-5
1959—Cork 3-9, Kerry 4-3
1960—Cork 4-5, Kerry 3-4
1961-1973—Kerry represented Province in All-Ireland series.
1974-1982—No team in All-Ireland junior from Munster.
1983—Cork 4-19, Tipperary 3-8
1984—Cork 0-14, Tipperary 0-10
1985—Tipperary 3-6, Limerick 1-10
1986—Limerick—, Cork—
1987—Cork 2-16, Tipperary 1-9
1988—Tipperary 5-9, Cork 0- 15
1989—Tipperary 2-14, Clare 2-8
1990—Tipperary 0-18, Cork 2-6
1991—Tipperary 4-13, Cork 5-10 (draw)
Tipperary 2-20, Cork 0-11
1992—Cork 1-12, Clare 1-10
1993—Clare 2-15, Waterford 0-10
1994—Cork 1-10, Clare 1-9
1995—Clare 4-11, Waterford 1-9
1996—Cork 2-15, Tipperary 2-10
1997-1999—No Munster team in All-Ireland Junior Hurling Championship.

LEINSTER JUNIOR HURLING CHAMPIONSHIP FINALS

1905—Kildare 3-8, Westmeath 3-5
1906—Kildare 2-6, Meath 1-8
1907—Carlow 2-9, Meath 0-9
1908—Dublin 1-7, Offaly 1-3
(Unfinished. Dublin awarded title.)
1909—Kilkenny 4-7, Dublin 3-3
1910—Laois 12-2, Meath 2-1
1911—Kilkenny 5-l, Dublin 5-1 (draw)
Kilkenny 3-2, Dublin 1-3 (replay)
1912—Westmeath 4-3, Offaly 2-1
1913—Kilkenny 7-3, Wexford 3-3
1914—Laois 16-4, Kildare 0-0
1915—Offaly 6-2, Meath 3-5
1916—Kilkenny 12-2, Westmeath 1-1
1917-1921—Suspended
1922—Offaly 4-3, Kilkenny 0-3
1923—Offaly 4-1, Laois 3-2
1924—Offaly 7-4, Dublin 5-5
1925—Dublin 4-4, Kilkenny 4-4 (draw)
Dublin 4-4, Kilkenny 4-2 (replay)
1926—Wexford 4-1, Laois 3-1
1927—Meath 3-4, Dublin 3-4 (draw)
Meath 4-6, Dublin 2-2 (replay)
1928—Kilkenny 3-2, Laois 0-2
1929—Offaly 7-3, Dublin 1-5
1930—Kilkenny 7-3, Laois 2-2
1931—Kilkenny 2-9, Dublin 1 -5
Declared null and void following an objection and counter objection.
1932—Dublin 6-2, Kildare 4-5
1933—Laois 3-8, Kilkenny 4-2
1934—Kildare 3-7, Kilkenny 3-7 (draw)
Kildare 1-8, Kilkenny 1-7 (replay)
1935—Kilkenny 5-5, Dublin 1-5
1936—Westmeath 4-8, Laois 5-2
1937—Dublin 11-8, Offaly 5-4
1938—Offaly 3-8, Kilkenny 1-8
1939—Kilkenny 6-9, Dublin 4-3
1940—Wexford 4-6, Dublin 2-7
1941—Kilkenny 6-3, Wexford 2-2
1942-1945—Suspended
1946—Kilkenny 4-5, Dublin 1-1
1947—Dublin 5-5, Meath 1-5
1948—Meath 2-10, Kilkenny 3-5
1949—Kilkenny 4-3, Dublin 3-2
1950—Dublin 3-7, Kilkenny 3-3
1951—Kilkenny 2-11, Dublin 2-6
1952—Dublin 4-5, Wicklow 2-7
1953—Offaly 3-7, Kilkenny 2-2
1954—Wicklow 4-15, Westmeath 1-3
1955—Dublin 4-12, Kilkenny 4-9
1956—Kilkenny 6-11, Laois 1-8
1957—Wexford 3-11, Dublin 3-4
1958—Kilkenny 2-10, Meoth 1-5
1959—Wexford 6-10, Offaly 0-1
1960 Carlow 6-8, Wexford 3-8
(1961-1973 Competition confined to weaker counties)
1961—Meath 1-11, Wicklow 3-3
1962—Kildare 4-10, Wicklow 2-8
1963—Westmeath 4-10, Wicklow 4-7
1964—Wicklow 4-8, Kildare 2-6
1965—Wicklow 3-14, Kildare 5-8 (draw)
Wicklow 4-5, Kildare 2-8 (replay)
1966—Kildare 4-10, Wicklow 4-6
1967—Wicklow 4-13, Meath 0-8
1968—Louth 4-12, Kildare 5-8
1969—Louth 5-8, Kildare 2-5
1970—Meath 6-13, Wicklow 5-9
1971—Wicklow 3-12, Kildare 0-7
1972—Meath 6-9, Kildare 4-11
1973—Louth 8-7, Meath 6-5
1974-1975—Louth represented Province in All Ireland series.
1976-1982—No competition in Leinster.
1983—Kilkenny 3-13, Wexford 1-7
1984—Kilkenny 2-13, Wexford 0-7
1985—Wexford 4-14, Dublin 2-6
1986—Kilkenny 2-18, Westmeath 0-6
1987—Wexford 6-15, Dublin 0-9
1988—Kilkenny 4-6, Carlow 3-3
1989—Kilkenny 5-12, Westmeath 0-9
1990—Kilkenny 1-9, Wexford 0-12 (draw)
Kilkenny 3-10, Wexford 1-10 (replay)
1991—Kilkenny 3-12, Wexford 2-6
1992—Wexford 2-11, Laois 1-12
1993—Kilkenny 1-15, Wexford 0-10
1994—Kilkenny 2-18, Wexford 3-8
1995—Kilkenny 2-14, Wexford 4-5
1996—Kilkenny 1-13, Wexford 1-7

1997-2002—No Competition
2003—Meath 0-11, Longford 0-9.
2004—Meath 4-14, Longford 2-7.

Note: Leinster teams took part in an Open Draw series.

CONNACHT JUNIOR HURLING CHAMPIONSHIP FINALS

1913-1915—Galway represented Province in All-Ireland series
1916-1922—No competition
1923-1924—Galway represented Province in All-Ireland series
1925—Galway 7-5, Roscommon 1-3
1926—Galway 7-8, Roscommon 2-3
1927-1928—Galway represented Province in All-Ireland series
1929—Galwoy 10-4, Sligo 1-1
1930—Galway 5-7, Sligo 3-2
1931—Galway beat Roscommon by 37 points to ten (exact score not given)
1932—West & South Galway 2-4, East & North Galway 1-0
1933—Galway represented Province in All-Ireland series
Special Final: Roscommon 3-5, Mayo 2-1
1934—Galway 7-4, Mayo 1-2
1935—Galway 4-2, Mayo 1-2
1936—Mayo 0-14, Galway 0-13
1937—Galway 5-7, Roscommon 3-2
1938—Galway 8-3, Roscommon 2-1
1939—Galway 7-6, Moyo 1-3
1940—Galway 6-5, Roscommon 1-4
1941—Galway represented Province in All-Ireland series
1942-1945—No competition
1946—Galway 6-6, Roscommon 3-6
1947—Galway 4-8, Roscommon 1-9
1948—Galway 4-8, Roscommon 0-0
1949—Galway 6-8, Roscommon 1-7
1950—Galway 6-6, Mayo 5-4
1951—Galway 6-12, Roscommon 4-4
1952—Roscommon 4-5, Galway 2-3
1953—Roscommon 2-5, Galway 3- 1.
Galway awarded title on an objection
1954—Galway beat Sligo
1955—Galway 6-8, Roscommon 4-4
1956—Galway 3-9, Roscommon 3-7
1957—Galway 5-13, Roscommon 1-5
1958—Roscommon 4-6, Galway 3-5
Galway competed in Munster 1959-1960
1959—Roscommon 3-5, Mayo 0-6
1960—Roscommon 9-18, Mayo 2-2
1961—Roscommon 5-15, Leitrim 5-1
1962—Roscommon 7-5, Leitrim 4-1
1963—Roscommon 2-14, Sligo 2-1
1964—Roscommon 1-9, Mayo 0-4
1965—Roscommon 1-6, Mayo 0-5
1966—Roscommon 6-6, Leitrim 1-4
1967—Mayo 5-8, Sligo 0-8
1968—Sligo
1969—Leitrim
1970—Leitrim
1971—Roscommon
1972—Roscommon 7-9, Mayo 0-4
1973—Sligo
1974—Roscommon 5-6, Leitrim 0-6
1975—Leitrim 1-8, Mayo 2-5 (draw)
Leitrim beat Mayo (replay)
1976—Leitrim 2-13, Sligo 2-1
1977-1982—No competition
1983-1996—Galway represented Province in All-Ireland series
1997-2001—No competition
2002—Mayo 4-11, Sligo 0-9.
2003—Mayo 4-12, Leitrim 0-11.
2004—Mayo 1-10, Sligo 2-3.

ULSTER JUNIOR HURLING CHAMPIONSHIP FINALS

1947—Donegal 6-2, Armagh 2-3
1948—Donegal 3-3, Down 3-1
1949—Armagh 4-7, Down 3-3
1950—Antrim 8-8, Donegal 2-3
1951—Antrim 7-1, Tyrone 2-1
1952—Antrim 4-6, Down 0-2
1953—Antrim 2-11, Donegal 1-3
1954—Antrim 7-3, Down 1-3
1955—Antrim 5-6, Down 4-6
(Unfinished. Refixed)
Antrim 4-15, Down 0-4 (Refixture)
1956—Down 4-6, Donegal 3-5
1957—Antrim 7-11, Down 3-5
1958—Antrim 3-4, Down 1-3
1959—Antrim 8-7, Donegal 2-2
1960—Down 5-2, Antrim 1-7
1961—Antrim 4-7, Down 1-3
1962—Down 3-7, Donegal 2-2
1963—Antrim 6-12, Armagh 2-4
1964—Down 9-7, Antrim 4-7
1965—Armagh 3-7, Down 4-2
1966—Antrim 3-13, Down 6-3
1967—Down 6-6, Monaghon 1-5
1968—Antrim 5-8, Donegal 0-3
1969—Antrim 5-16, Donegol 3-8
1970—No record of a championship. Ulster were not represented in All- Ireland series.
1971—Played on a league system. Won by Monaghan
1972—Donegal 5-3, Monaghan 5-1
1973—Armagh 3-10, Down 1-6
1974—Derry 3-5, Armagh 1-7
1975—Derry 0-4, Armagh 0-3
1976-1982—No competition
1983—Cavan 2-11, Donegal 2-6
1984—Derry 2-12, Monaghan 1-7
1 985—Cavan 4-7, Derry 0-5
1986—Monaghan 1-14, Fermanagh 1-10

1987—Monaghan 5-9, Fermanagh 2-10
1988—Monaghan 2-12, Cavan 2-8
1989—Donegal 3- 12, Monaghan 0-9
1990—Armagh 0-9, Fermanagh 0-9 (draw)
Armagh 3-7, Fermanagh 1-10 (replay)
1991—Armagh 2-7, Fermanagh 1-4
1992—Down 1-9, Fermanagh 0-8
1993—Down 2-9, Tyrone 1-11
1994—Fermanagh 4-20, Cavan 3-2
1995—Tyrone 5-11, Monaghan 5-9
1996—Tyrone 4-15, Donegal 2-13
1997—Monaghan 3-12, Fermanagh 3-8
1998—Monaghan 3-16, Donegal 1 -5
1999—Tyrone 1 -15, Dcwn 0-6
2000—Armagh 1-15, Down 3-7.
2001—Donegal 1-10, Antrim 1-9.
2002—Antrim 2-10, Down 1-11.
2003—Donegal 5-13; Down 2-10
2004—Down 1-11, Fermanagh 1-9.

HURLING "B" CHAMPIONSHIP FINALS

1974—Croke Park, June 23.
Kildare 1-26, Antrim 3-13.
1975—Croke Park, June 15.
Westmeath 4-16, Loncdon 3-19.
Croke Park, June 22. Replay:
Westmeath 3-23, London 2-7.
1976—Croke Park, June 27:
Kerry 0-15, London 1-10.
1977—Croke Park, June 26.
Laois 3-21, London 2-9.
1978—Croke Park, June 25.
Antrim 1-16, London 3-7.
1979—Tullamore, June 17.
Laois 2-13, London 3-10.
Athy, June 24. Replay:
Laois 1-20, London 0-17.
1980—Croke Park, July 6.
Kildare 2-20, London 2-14.
1981—Loughgiel, July 5.
Antrim 3-17, London 3-14.
1982—Ruislip, July 4.
Antrim 2-16, London 2-14.
1983—Tralee, June 26.
Kerry 2-8, London 1-7.
1984—Ruislip, July 8.
Westmeath 4-10, London 1-16.
1985—Trim, July 7.
London—1-8, Meath 1-6.
1986—Ruislip, June 29.
Kerry 3-10, London 1-9.
1987—Carlow, July 5.
London 0-20, Carlow 1-15.
1988—Ruislip, July 3.
London 2-6, Down 1-7.
1989—Newhridge, July 2
Kildare 1-13, London 1-12.
1990—Ruislip, July 8.
London 1-15, Kildare 5-2.
1991—Mullingar, July 7.
Westmeath 2-12, London 2-6.
1992—Ruislip, July 12.
Carlow 2-15, London 3-10.
1993—Ruislip, July 11.
Meath 2-16, London 1-16.
1994—Ruislip, July 3.
Roscommon 1-10, London 1-9.
1995—Portlaoise, July 2.
London 2-7, Wicklow 0-8.
1996—Croke Park, June 23.
Derry 1-14, Wicklow 0-10.
1997-2001—No competition
2002—Laois 2-20, Wicklow 2-7.
2003—Wicklow 4-16, Roscommon 2-13.
2004—Kildare 3-14, Mayo 3-7.

(Note: The All-Ireland "B" winners played in the quarter-final of the Championship proper.)

ALL-IRELAND INTERMEDIATE HURLING FINALS

1961—Wexford, September 17.
Wexford 3-15, London 4-4.
Home final: Kilkenny, August 13.
Wexford 5-6, Tipperary 5-6 (draw)
Replay: Kilkenny, August 20.
Wexford 4-11, Tipperary 3-9.
1962—Croke Park, September 9.
Carlow 6-15, London 3-3.
Home final: Birr, August 26.
Carlow 3-9, Galway 2-5
1963—Thurles, September 8.
Tipperary 1-10, London 1-7.
Home final: Waterford, August 18.
Tipperary 0- 17, Wexford 2-3
1964—Enniscorthy, September 20.
Wexford 4-7, London 1-11.
Home final: Waterford, August 16.
Wexford 2-8, Cork 1-5
1965—Cork, September 19.
Cork 2-20, London 5-5.
Home final: Enniscorthy, August 15.
Cork 3-7, Wexford 2-6.
1966—Enniscorthy, September 18.
Tipperary 4-11, Dublin 2-12.
Note: 1966-1973. British winners came in at the semi-final stage.
1967—Limerick, September 17.
London 1-9, Cork 1-5.
1968—Croke Park, September 29.
London 4-15, Dublin 0-3.
1969—Thurles, October 12.
Kildare 2-8, Cork 3-4.
1970—Croke Park, October 4.
Antrim 4- 18, Warwickshire 3-6.
1971—Kilkenny, September 19.
Tipperary 3-16, Wicklow 3-13.
1972—Birr, September 17.

Tipperary 2-13. Galway 1-9.
1973—Waterford, September 16.
Kilkenny 5-15, London 2-9.
(Discontinued 1974-'97)
1997—Limerick, October 11.
Cork 2-11, Galway 1-12
1998—Thurles, October 10.
Limerick 4-16, Kilkenny 2-17.
1999—Birr, September 25.
Galway 3-13, Kilkenny 2-10
2000—Tipperary 2-17, Galway 1-10.
2001—Cork 2-17, Wexford 2-8.
2002—Galway 2-15, Tipperary 1-10.
2003 – Cork 1-21, Kilkenny 0-23.
(after extra time)
2004—Cork 2-11, Kilkenny 2-11.
Cork 1-16, Kilkenny 1-10. (replay)
2005—Wexford 1-15, Galway 0-16.
2006—Cork 3-15, Kilkenny 1-18. (aet)
2007—Wexford 1-11, Waterford 1-9.
2008—Kilkenny 1-16, Limerick 0-13.
2009—Cork 2-23, Kilkenny 0-16.

ALL-IRELAND INTERMEDIATE HURLING FINALISTS (1961-73 & 1997-2009)

1961

Wexford—J. O'Neill, J. Hyland, W. Ryan, M. Collins, W. Doran, J. Creane, P Sullivon, L. Byrne (capt.), P. Lynch, J Walsh, N. Newport, T. Hawkins, L. Creane, J. Coady, S. Whelan. Sub: J. Kehoe for J. Coady.

London—A. Morrissey, P Murphy, M. Kerrse, A. Moloney, J. Kearns, D. Dillane, M. Cormody, W. Dorgan (capt.), J. Redmond, E. Murray, J. Kiely, P. Egan, L. Healy, W. Duffy, J. Hickey. Subs: P. Ryan for J. Hickey, R. O'Leary for D. Dillane.

1962

Carlow—J. O'Connell, W. Walsh, M. Hogan, A. Fortune, P. McGovern, P. Somers, T. Nolan, M. Morrissey, M. O'Brien, L. Walsh, W. Hogan, P. O'Connell, W. Walsh, E. Gladney, C. Hynes.
London—W. Barnaville, J. Kearns, C. Whelan, B. Neville, P. Dwyer, P Ryan, M. Carmody, J. Daly, R. O'Leary, J. Tiernan, T Cleary, W. Dargan, P. Harney, T. Morrissey, M. Devereaux. Subs M. Collins for P. Dwyer, P. Spillane for W. Dargan, P. Dwyer for M. Collins.

1963

Tipperary—P. O'Sullivan, T. Burke, M. Barry, P. Crampton, W. Boyle, G. Gleeson, P. Dawson, M. Roche, J. Fogarty, M. Kearns, J. Collison, M. Keating, T. Flynn, T. Larkin, J. Lanigon (capt.). Sub: P. J. Grace for T. Flynn.

London—W. Barnaville, J. Kearns, P Dwyer, B. Neville, M. Collins, P. Ryan, M. Carmody, P. Fahy, W. Dargan, J. Tiernan, T. Cleary, M. Devereaux, T. Morrissey, L. Furlong, P. Spillane. Subs: J. Daly for W. Dargan, P. Hourigan for M. Devereaux, M. Craddock for M. Carmody.

1964

Wexford—S. Boggan, N. O'Gorman, E. O'Brien, A. Carty, L. Butler, O. Hearne, J. Murphy, M. Delaney, B. Murray, O. Cullen, S. Whelan, P. Murphy, L. Delaney, L. Kehoe, N. O'Brien, Subs: J. Mannion for P. Murphy, T. Hassey for B. Murray, J. Dunne for J. Mannion.

London—W. Barnaville, J. Kearns, P. Dwyer, B. Neville, M. Collins, P Ryan, M. Carmody, M. Connolly, T. Cleary, E. Murray, T. Connolly, J. J. Browne, J. Barrett, T. Morrissey, L. Furlong. Sub: M. Devereaux for J. J. Browne.

1965

Cork—T. Monaghan/ D. Murphy (capt.), John Ryan, M. Garde, J. O'Keeffe, S. Barry-Murphy, F. Sheehan, O. O'Keeffe, J. Hogan, S. Barry, W. Galligan, J. K. Coleman, D. O'Brien, D. O'Keeffe, W. Fitton.

London—W. Barnoville, H. Hickey, B. Neville, M. McGrath, M. Collins, P. Fahy, V. O'Halloran, M. Connolly, W. Dargan, T. Cleary, T. Connolly, M. Devereaux, E. Murray, T. Morrissey, M. Ryan. Subs: J. Curtin for T. Connolly, T. Allen for B. Neville.

1966

Tipperary—S. Shinnors, P. Kennedy, E. Ryan, A. Burke, J. Drohan, N. O'Gorman, P. Dawson, W. O'Grady, J. Fogarty, S. Kenny, M. O'Grady, M. Jones, L. Connolly, S. Noonan, T. Brennan. Subs: D. Dunne for P. Dawson, P. McLoughlin for M. O'Grady.

Dublin—D. Massey, P. Moyles, P Corcoran, B. Dunne, S. Armstrong, T. Burke, S. Moyles, H. Dalton, T. McGrath, N. Kinsella, T. Woods, E. Flynn, T. Cunninghom, B. Sunderland, D. Doody. Sub: W. Markey for S. Armstrong.

1967

London—W. Barnaville, M Hassett, L. Walsh, E. Leary, R. Cashin, M. Connolly, M. Kirwan, P. Fahy, S. Lambe, T. Connolly, T Cleary, F. Condon, J. Organ, D. O'Keeffe, E. Murray.

Cork—T. Monoaghan, D. Murphy, P Dunne, S. Barry, P. Hegarty, J. Hogan, P. O'Sullivon, M. Meaney, J. Keating, Tomas Ryan, J. K. Coleman, M. Kenneally, D. Coleman, J. O'Connell, D. Doly. Subs: P. Murphy, P. Curley.

1968

London—W. Barnaville, M. Hassett, L. Walsh, C. Wylie, P. Fahy, M. Connolly, R. Cashin, M. Meaney, P. O'Neill, S. Lambe, F. Condon, T. Connolly, M. Loughnane, M. Kirwan, T. Cleary.

Dublin—P Cunningham, W. Devitt, K. Crooks, J. Doody, W. Markey, T. Woods, P. Murphy, T. Flynn, J. Kenny, J. Hackett, C. Ryan, J. Doran, L. Heneberry, W. Lee, D. Doody. Subs: J. Byrne for L. Heneberry, P McCabe for C. Ryan.

1969

Kildare—P. Connolly, S. Malone, C. O'Malley, N. Burke, A. Carew, P. Dunny, M. O'Brien, B. Burke (capt.), J. O'Connell, T. Christian, T. Carew, M. Dwane, N. Behan, M. Mullins, J. Wall. Subs: E. Walsh for T. Carew, P. Connolly for M. Dwane, T. Carew for E. Walsh.

Cork—T. Monaghan, J. Twomey, J. Ryan, J. O'Connell, O. O'Keeffe, J. Hogan, P. McDonnell, Jack Russell, Jim Russell, S. Gillen, M. Malone, F. Kelleher, T. Meaney, D. Daly, D. Coleman. Subs: N. Gallagher For M. Malone, T. O'Mahony for F. Kelleher.

1970

Antrim—J. Coyles, C. Elliott, K. Donnelly, E. Hamill, N. Wheeler, T. Connolly, A. McCamphill, S. Burns (capt.), S. Collins, S. Richmond, E. Donnelly, A. Hamill, B. McGarry, P. McShane, A. McCallin. Subs: A. Connolly for T. Connolly, J. P. McFadden for A. Connolly.

Warwickshire—D. Breen, J. O'Brien, P. Grimes, L. Moore, M. Hanley, L. Dalton, T. Ryan, J. Moynihan, D. Dillane, C. Crowe, F. Gantley, W. Hogan, C. Danagher, J. Quinn, V. Coffey. Subs: J. Byrne for J. Quinn, S. O'Keeffe for C. Crowe, P. Shields for V. Coffey.

1971

Tipperary—W. Barnaville, J. Dunlea, P. Kennedy, G. Kehoe, D. Crowe, P. Quinlan, B. Teehan, O. Quinn, J. P. McDonnell, S. Power, J. Noonan, M. Brennan, J. Barry, P. Lowry, E. Butler (capt.).

Wicklow—S. O'Brien, R. O'Shea, W. O'Reilly, J. Kearns, C. Keddy, L. Collins, P. Barry, S. Doyle, S. Brennan, M. O'Brien (capt.), M. Delaney, T. Morrissey, M. Jordan, T. Scott, W. Hilliard. Subs: P. Kennedy for C. Keddy, W. Hilliard for B. Hilliard.

1972

Tipperary—S. Cahalane, J. Costigan, J. Keogh, S. Fitzpatrick, M. Fitzgibbon, N. Seymour, J. Keane, W. Ferncombe, T. Moloney, J. Connors, J. Kennedy, M. Ruth, O. Killeen, J. Seymour, S. Mackey. Subs: J. Darcy for T. Moloney, T. Moloney for W. Ferncombe.

Galway—E. Campbell, P Hobbs, T. Lynch, T. Cloonan, L. Glynn, P. O'Brien, O. Parnell, P. Fahy, P. Ryan, G. Coone, E. Muldoon, M. Barrett, K. Hanniffy, P. Egan, T. O'Hara. Subs: M. Q'Connor for P. O'Brien, K. Lucas for 0. Parnell, T. Lane for K. Hanniffy.

1973

Kilkenny—P. Grace (capt.), M. Mason, K. Mahon, M. Hoyne, J. Dunne, T. Murphy, T. Foley, P. Kavanagh, D. Burke, J. Doyle, P. Holden, J. O'Connor, F. Cleere, J. Walsh, S. Muldowney.

London—M. Butler, C. O'Leary, J. Houlihan, M. Ryan, J. Roche, J. Hughes, J. Casey, S. Coughlan, M. Murphy, D. Hallissey, F. Birrane, A. Dwyer, D. McCarthy, P. Fahy, J. McNamara. Subs: C. Danagher for M. Murphy, M. Quinlan for J McNamara, J. Hanley for J. Houlihan.

1974 TO 1996 – NO COMPETITION

1997

Cork—D. Óg Cusack, S. Barrett, P. Mulcahy (capt.), J. Walsh, J. O'Sullivan, M. Landers, D. Murphy, G. Cummins, D. Barrett, T. McCarthy, R. Dwane, A. Walsh, D. Maher, S. O'Farrell, J. Smiddy. Subs: P. Cahill for S. Barrett, B. O'Driscoll (Killavullen) for T. McCarthy.

Galway—N. Murphy, P. Diviney, R. Burke, D. Turley, S. Forde, N. Larkin, N. Power (capt.), M. Kenny, L. Hogan, P. Forde, N. Kenny, F. Healy, B. Larkin, M. Connolly (Craughwell), R. Gantley. Subs: K. Rabbitte for P. Diviney, M. Forde for P. Forde, K. Gavin for B. Larkin.

1998

Limerick—P. Horgan, N. Murphy, W. O'Brien, J. Kiely, P. Neenan, G. Galvin, P Cahill, D. Carroll, P. Keyes, D. Murphy, A. Ryan, J. Cormican (capt.), M. O'Brien, O. O'Neill, J. Butler. Sub: M. Quaide for D. Murphy.

Kilkenny—M. Carey, D. Roche, P. Farrell (capt.), J. Walsh, M. Bookle, P. Brophy, S. Moran, D. Maher, J. Bolger, H. Shefflin, A. Cleere, B. Phelan, T. Shefflin, B. Barcoe, R. Shortall. Subs: C. Connery for D. Roche, R. Moore for S. Moran, O. O'Connor for B. Barcoe.

1999

Galway—N. Murphy, P. Diviney, W. Burke, D. Turley, E. Linnane, N. Larkin, N. Power, J. Donnelly, D. O'Brien, G. Glynn, L. Hogan, F. Healy, D. Joyce, M. Connolly, N. Kelly. Subs: D. Donoghue for Kelly, S. Lawless for Donnelly, E. Tannier for O'Brien.

Kilkenny—M. Tyler, S. Kealy, E. Drea, B. Joyce, D. Lyng, M. Bookle, S. Moran, B. O'Keeffe, D. Maher, J. Bolger, J. Carey, P. Farrell, R. Shortall, A. Prendergast, O. O'Connor. Subs: B. Phelan for Bolger, A. Cleere for Corey.

2000

Tipperary - S.Butler, B.Hogan, M.Ryan, M.Gleeson, D.Hackett, C.Bonar, D.Gleeson, S.Maher, J.Teehan, D.O'Connor, C.Morrisey, D.Corcoran, R.Killeen, P.Maguire, D.Browne.

Galway - K.Boyle, R.Brady, E.McEntee, R.Reilly, S.Forde, E.Hyland, S.McClernan, K.Carr, J.Cummins, G.McGlacin, B.Cunningham, S.Tierney, M.Fahy, M.Greaney, M.Headd. Subs - B.Connolly for Fahy, A.Connolly for McClernan, M.Corcoran for Cummins, M.Curtin for Corcoran, M.Lynskey for Curtin.

2001

Cork - B.Rochford, D.Lynch, L.Hayes, B.Lombard, J.Hughes, M.Daly, M.Prendergast, A.O'Connor, R.Dwyer, J.O'Callaghan, T.O'Mahony, S.Hayes, N.Murphy, N.McCarthy, E.Collins. Subs - J.Barrett for Hayes, D.Moher for Murphy.

Wexford - P.Carley, A.Murphy, D.Stafford, T.Walsh, S.Carley, W.Carley, C.Kehoe, J.Simpson, P.Redmond, J.Kenny, M.Murphy, E.Cullen, R.Murphy, M.J.Reck, F.Simpson. Subs - R.Barry for Redmond, J.Maguire for Murphy, M.Jacob for Kenny, B.Redmond for J.Simpson, K.Rooney for Kehoe.

2002

Galway - N.Murphy, S.McClearn, T. Óg Regan, R.Fahy, E.Tannion, C.Dervan, Adrian Diviney, J.Donnelly, G.Glynn, B.Cunningham, J.Campbell, K.Brady, C.Ryan, J.Conroy, B.Lawless. Subs - Aidan Diviney for Lawless, D.Hayes for Tannion, J.Gantley for Glynn, R.Reilly for Adrian Diviney.
(Adrian Diviney, S.Tierney and T.Kavanagh played in the drawn game and were replaced by T. Óg Regan, J.Campbell and C.Ryan for the replay. Subs in the drawn encounter were J.Campbell for Kavanagh, R.Devanney for Aidan Diviney, C.,Ryan for S.Tierney, R.Reilly for McClearn.)

Tipperary - F.Horgan, G.Griffin, M.Peters, B.Gaynor, C.Ryan, C.Morrisey, C.Everard, S.Maher, J.Teehan, B.Hogan, B.Stritch, P.Buckley, G.Maguire, D.Hackett, S.Everard. Subs - T.Connors for Hackett, S.Maher for Teehan, D.Browne for Buckley, P.Morrisey for Hogan. (Subs in the drawn encounter were M.Keeshan for Hackett, T.Connors for S.Everard, K.Hogan for C.Everard, P.Morrisey for Maguire).

2003

Cork - M.Coleman, M.Prout, J.O'Brien, B.Murphy, J.Hughes, B.Lombard, K.Hartnett, A.O'Connor, J.Barrett, J.O'Callaghan, B.Coleman, R.Dwyer, J.Murphy, D.O'Riordan, J.Quinlan. Subs - V.Morrisey for Dwyer, M.Daly for Lombard, V.Hurley for O'Connor, D.Moher for Quinlan, Quinlan for Murphy, Dwyer for Hughes, Lombard for Coleman, Murphy for Quinlan.

Kilkenny - R.O'Neill, P.Costello, S.Lanigan, G.Joyce, E.Mackey, A.Lawlor, J.O'Neill, J.Power, P.Buggy, A.Fogarty, P.Maher, J.Maher, D.Mackey, N.Moloney, P.Sheehan. Subs - D.Lawlor for Buggy, J.P.Corcoran for Sheehan, E.Walsh for P.Maher, N.Doherty for Power.

2004

Cork - A.Nash, J.Crowley, L.Hayes, R.McCarthy, B.Walsh, T.Lorden, D.Fitzgerald, T.Healy, J.Olden, J.Russell, D.Dineen, B.O'Dwyer, S.Hayes, R.Doherty, E.Conway. Subs - J.Masters for Healy, D.McSweeney for Walsh, N.Murphy for Dineen.

Kilkenny - R.O'Neill, J.Tennyson, S.Lanigan, P.Costelloe, S.Kealey, J.Costelloe, J.O'Neill, B.Phelan, C.Herity, D.Mackey, R.Power, J.Power, M.Grace, D.Buggy, E.Walsh. Subs - J.P.Corcoran for Mackey, J.Phelan for B.Phelan.

2005

Wexford - M.White, D.Guiney, B.O'Leary, P.Roche, K.Kavanagh, M.O'Leary, A.Kavanagh, L.Gleeson, C.Kenny, P.Nolan, M.Byrne, S.Doyle, P.Carley, G.Coleman, M.Furlong. Subs - M.Kelly for Coleman, R.Stafford for Gleeson, S.O'Neill for Guiney.

Galway - M.Herlihy, R.Whyte, N.Corcoran, P.Flynn, A.Garvey, E.Tannian, N.Earls, B.Gantley, D.McEvoy, B.Lucas, J.Gantley, E.Ryan, B.Lawless, N.Kenny, K.Burke. Subs - T.Kavanagh for McEvoy, K.Hooban for B.Gantley, J.Fordham for Garvey, R.Reilly for Whyte.

2006

Cork – A.Nash, J.Hughes, W.Twomey, T.Jordan, B.Lombard, D.McSweeney, V.Hurley, M.O'Callaghan, K.Hartnett, R.O'Dwyer, D.Dineen, J.Russell, M.O'Sullivan, R.Doherty, R.Conway. Subs – B.Coleman, S.Hayes, F.O'Leary, M.O'Donovan, B.Dwyer.

Kilkenny – D.Brennan, S.Cummins, G.Joyce, K.Joyce, P.Hartley, D.Carroll, A.McCarthy, P.Hogan, B.Phelan, E.O'Donoghue, A.Murphy, C.O'Loughlin, G.Nolan, M.Murphy, A.Hickey. Subs – E.Walsh, D.Kelly, J.P.Corcoran, D.O'Gorman, R.Hogan.

2007

Wexford – D.Flynn, C.Lawler, B.Kenny, D.Morton, J.O'Connor, B.Malone, L.Prendergast, R.Barry, D.Redmond, J.Roche, J.Breen, P.Doran, N.Kirwan, S.Banville, C.Lyng. Subs – E.Martin for Kirwan, B.O'Connor for Breen, C.O'Connor for Martin, A.Kavanagh for Banville.

Waterford – I.O'Regan, B.Wall, J.O'Leary, T.Molumphy, K.Stafford, S.Kearney, W.Hutchinson, G.Power, E.Bennett, P.Fitzgerald, C.Carey, M.Molumphy, P.Kearney, S.Casey, S.Barron. Subs – D.Power for Bennett, N.Jacob for Carey, J.Hartley for M.Molumphy, B.Foley for Power.

2008

Kilkenny – L.Tierney, M.Phelan, S.Cummins, S.Prendergast, P.Lonergan, P.Hartley, K.Joyce, N.Walsh, D.Fogarty, B.Beckett, C.Phelan, P.Hogan, M.Grace, P.Cleere, Noel Doherty. Subs – Niall Doherty for Walsh, E.Hennebry for Lonergan, J.Nolan for Grace, A.Healy for Noel Doherty, D.Prendergast for Fogarty.

Limerick – B.Hennessy, T.Condon, C.Carey, G.O'Leary, R.O'Neill, M.Keane, S.Walsh, A.Brennan, P.O'Brien, David Moloney, P.O'Reilly, M.McKenna, D.O'Neill, P.McNamara,

A.O'Connor. Subs – D.Stapleton for O'Brien, P.Harty for McKenna, P.Browne for David Moloney, N.Maher for D.O'Neill, Damien Moloney for Brennan.

2009

Cork – A.Nash, B.Coleman, D.McSweeney, B.Murphy, J.Carey, R.Cashman, J.Jordan, E.Dillon, L.Desmond, R.Dwyer, Mark O'Sullivan, L.McLoughlin, Maurice O'Sullivan, L.Farrell, S.Moylan. Subs – E.Collins for Maurice O'Sullivan, A.Mannix for Moylan, J.O'Leary for Carey, P.O'Leary for Coleman.

Kilkenny – T.Brophy, K.Mooney, P.Murphy, P.O'Donovan, J.Cottrell, R.Cody, W.Burke, C.Fogarty, N.Kennedy, E.Brennan, J.J.Farrell, B.Lannon, M.Boran, E.Kavanagh, E.Guinan. Subs – J.Cahill for Boran, C.Dunne for Lannon, E.Hickey for Cottrell, N.Cleere for Kavanagh, M.Murphy for Brennan.

INTERMEDIATE HURLING FINAL REFEREES

1961-73; 1997-2009

1961—Clem Foley (Dublin)
1962—Gerry Fitzgerald (Limerick)
1963—Paddy Johnson (Kilkenny)
1964—Paddy Buggy (Kilkenny)
1965—Gerry Fitzgerald
1966—Paddy Buggy (Kilkenny)
1967—Jimmy Hatton (Wicklow)
1968—John Dowling (Offaly)
1969—Donie Nealon (Tipperary)
1970—Jimmy Hatton (Wicklow)
1971—Noel Dalton (Waterford)
1972—Noel Dalton (Waterford
1973—Noel Dalton (Waterford
1997—Sean McMahon (Clare)
1998—Jimmy Cooney (Galway)
1999—Seán McMahon (Clare)
2000—T.McIntyre (Antrim)
2001—M.Bodkin (Galway)
2002—P.Neary (Kilkenny)
E.Morris (Dublin) (replay)
2003—T.McIntyre (Antrim)
2004—P.Ahern (Carlow)
2005—M.Wadding (Waterford)
2006—M.Wadding (Waterford)
2007—E.Morris (Dublin)
2008—J.McGrath (Westmeath)
2009—S.McMahon (Clare)

MUNSTER INTERMEDIATE HURLING FINALS

1961—Tipperary 3-10, Cork 2-12
1962—Galway 5-4, Cork 4-6
1963—Tipperary 6-10, Clare 0-4
1964—Cork 4-13, Galway 1-10
1965—Cork 1-15, Waterford 3-2
1966—Tipperary 4-2, Galway 1-7
1967—Cork 5-14, Limerick 2-12
1968—Limerick 3-8, Cork 1-6
1969—Cork 4-14, Galway 0-6
1970—Kerry 2-13, Cork 2-10
1971—Tipperary 1-11, Limerick 2-4
1972—Tipperary 4-16, Kerry 3-12
1973—Kerry represented Munster
No competition from 1974-1996
1997—Cork 1-15, Limerick 1-12
1998—Limerick 2-11, Tipperary 0-15
1999—Cork 2-9, Tipperary 1-7
2000—Tipperary 1-19, Cork 0-15.
2001—Cork 1-20, Clare 1-11.
2002—Tipperary 4-8, Waterford 2-7.
2003—Cork 2-12, Waterford 0-11.
2004—Cork 0-18, Tipperary 1-9.
2005—Cork 2-17, Tipperary 2-11.
2006—Cork 2-18, Tipperary 2-13.
2007—Waterford 5-11, Limerick 1-12.
2008—Limerick 2-16, Tipperary 2-12.
2009—Cork 5-24, Waterford 3-9.

LEINSTER INTERMEDIATE HURLING FINALS

1961—Wexford 3-11, Dublin 2-10
1962—Carlow 2-11, Kilkenny 2-3
1963—Wexford 3-8, Kilkenny 3-6
1964—Wexford 1-9, Kilkenny 2-5
1965—Wexford 4-16, Antrim 3-8
1966—Dublin 2-9, Wexford 1-8
1967—Kilkenny 6-8, Kildare 2-8
1968—Dublin 2- 14, Carlow 2-12
1969—Kildare 3-16, Wicklow 4-6
1970—Dublin 4-9, Wicklow 3-10
1971—Wicklow 1-15, Dublin 2-9
1972—Dublin 3-13, Wexford 3-4
1973—Kilkenny 11-15, Meath 1-3
1997—Kilkenny 5-15, Carlow 2-11
1998—Kilkenny 3-13, Wexford 0-11
1999—Kilkenny 2-15, Laois 0-9
2000—Kilkenny 2-12, Wexford 1-13.
2001—Wexford 5-13, Laois 1-9.
2002—Wexford 2-16, Kilkenny 0-19.
2003—Kilkenny 4-20, Dublin 1-10.
2004—Kilkenny 3-17, Wexford 1-10.
2005—Wexford 0-14, Kilkenny 0-13.
2006—Kilkenny 2-20, Wexford 0-8.
2007—Wexford 2-11, Kilkenny 1-12.
2008—Kilkenny 4-26, Dublin 3-15. (aet)
2009—Kilkenny 0-12, Wexford 0-11.

CONNACHT INTERMEDIATE HURLING FINALS

1966-1967—Roscommon represented Province
1968—Roscommon 4-4, Mayo 3-7 (draw)
Roscommon 7-11, Mayo 3-5 (replay)

1969—Mayo
(Note: 1970-1972 Galway represented Province. Galway competed in Munster (1961-1969).
1973-1996—No competition
1997—Galway 7-19, Roscommon 1-7
1998—Galway 2-22, Roscommon 1-11
1999—*Galway represented Province in All-Ireland series. Roscommon took part in Open Draw section. They qualified for All-Ireland semi-final in which they lost to Galway.*

ULSTER INTERMEDIATE HURLING FINALS

1966—Antrim 3-11, Down 4-5
1967—Antrim 6-13, Down 2-7
1968—Down 4-5, Antrim 2-9
1969—Antrim 5-6, Down 3-9
1970—Antrim 5-10, Down 3-13
1971—Down 5-8, Antrim 1-12
1972—Down 3-13, Antrim 5-7 (draw)
Down 2-9, Antrim 1-10 (replay)
1973—Antrim 3-11, Down 1-6
No competition from 1974-1996
1997—Derry 6-18, Armagh 1-6
1998—Down 3-11, London 2-12
(Note. Antrim competed in Leinster from 1961-'65.)
1999—No competition.
Down and London took part in Open Draw Section.

NATIONAL HURLING LEAGUE

1925-26—Cork 3-7, Dublin 1-5.
1926-27—None.
1927-28—Tipperary winners on points system: 14 points (from eight games). Draws with Dublin and Laois. Runners-up: Galway (with 12 points)
1928-29—Dublin 7-4, Cork 5-5.
1929-30—Cork 3-5, Dublin 3-0.
Semi-final: Dublin 8-6, Clare 1-0
1931-32—Galway 4-5, Tipperary 4-4.
Semi-final: Galway 7-7, Laois 3-5
1931-32—None.
1932-33—Kilkenny 3-8, Limerick 1-3 (Final at Kilkenny).
1933-34—Limerick 3-6, Dublin 3-3
(Final at Limerick).
1934-35—Limerick: winners on points system: 15 points (from eight games).
Runners-up: Kilkenny (with 14 points).
1935-36—Limerick: winners on on points system: 15 points (from eight games).
Runners-up: Cork with 12 points).
1936-37—Limerick: winners on points system: 13 points (from eight games).
Runners-up: Tipperary with 12 pts.
1937-38—Limerick 5-2, Tipperary 1-1.
1938-39—Dublin 1-8, Waterford 1-4.
Semi-final: Waterford 5-7, Wexford 3-4.
Dublin a bye.
1939-40—Cork 8-9, Tipperary 6-4.
1940-41—Cork 4-11, Dublin 2-7.
Suspended 1942-'45
1945-46—Clare 2-10, Dublin 2-5 (replay).
Clare 1-6, Dublin 1-6 (draw.)
Semi-final: Clare 6-2, Galway 2-7.
Dublin a bye.
1946-47—Limerick 3-8, Kilkenny 1-7 (replay).
Limerick 4-5, Kilkenny 2-11 (draw).
Semi-finals: Limerick 5-6, Laois 4-4;
Kilkenny 3-12, Tipperary 2-6
1947-48—Cork 3-3, Tipperary 1-2.
1948-49—Tipperary 3-5, Cork 3-3.
1949-50—Tipperary 1-12, New York 3-4 (in New York). Home Final: Tipperary 3-8, Kilkenny 1-10.
Semi-finals: Tipperary 9-3, Meath 0-6;
Kilkenny 5-6, Westmeath 4-6.
1950-51—Galway 2-11, New York 2-8 (in New York). Home final: Galway 6-7, Wexford 3-4.
Semi-finals: Wexford 6-4, Meath 2-1;
Galway 5-14, Offaly 0-4.
1951-52—Tipperary 6-14, New York 2-5 (in Croke Park). Home final: Tipperary 4-7 Wexford 4-6.
1952-53—Cork 2-10, Tipperary 2-7.
1953-54—Tipperary 3-10, Kilkenny 1-4
1954-55—Tipperary 3-5, Wexford 1-5.
1955-56—Wexford 5 9, Tipperary 2-14.
1956-57—Tipperary 3-11, Kilkenny 2-7.
1957-58—Wexford 5-7, Limerick 4-8.
1958-59—Tipperary 0-15, Waterford 0-7.
1959-60—Tipperary 2-15, Cork 3-8.
1960-61—Tipperary 6-6, WaterFord 4-9.
1961-62—Kilkenny 1-16, Cork 1-8.
Semi-final: Cork 6-12, Dublin 1-6.
Kilkenny a bye.
1962-63—Waterford 3-10, New York 1-10 (in replay at Kilkenny). Drawn game at Croke Park: Waterford 3-6, New York 3-6. Home final: Waterford 2-15, Tipperary 4-7.
Semi-finals: Waterford 0-9, Galway 0-7.
Tipperary 2-12, Kilkenny 2-9.
1963-64—Tipperary 4-16, New York 6-6 (in New York). Home final: Tipperary 5-12, Wexford 1 -4.
Semi-finals: Tipperary 3-16, Limerick 2-5;
Wexford 2-9, Cork 2-7.
1964-65—Tipperary 4-10, New York 2-11 (first leg). New York 3-9, Tipperary 2-9 (second leg). Aggregate: Tipperary 6-19, New York 5-20. Tipperary winners by two points on aggregate (both games in New York). Home final: Tipperary 3-14, Kilkenny 2-8.

Semi-finals: Kilkenny 5-9, Wexford 1-3; Tipperary 2-18, Waterford 1-9.

1965-66—Kilkenny 3-10, New York 2-7 (first leg in Croke Park). Kilkenny 7-5, New York 0-8 (second leg in Nowlan Park). Aggregate: Kilkenny 10-15, New York 2-15. Home Final: Kilkenny 0-9, Tipperary 0-7.

Semi-finals: Tipperary 3-14, Clare 4-7; Kilkenny 4-11, Cork 1-8.

1966-67—Wexford 3-10, Kilkenny 1-9.

Semi-finals: Wexford 6-12, Limerick 1-11; Kilkenny 3-10, Clare 2-3.

1967-68—New York 2-14, Tipperary 2-13 (first leg). Tipperary 4-14, New York 2-8. (second leg). Aggregate: Tipperary 6-27, New York 4-22 (both games in New York). Home Final: Tipperary 3-9, Kilkenny 1-13.

Semi-finals: Tipperary 1-15, Cork 2-7; Kilkenny 2-10, Clare 2-10 (draw); Kilkenny 3-8, Clare 3-8 (replay); Kilkenny 1-11, Clare 1-7 (second replay).

1968-69—Cork 3-12, Wexford 1-14.

Semi-finals: Cork 2-12, Tipperary 3-8; Wexford 2-5, Limerick 1-6.

1969-70—Cork 4-11, New York 4-8 (first leg). New York 2-8, Cork 1-10 (second leg). Aggregate: Cork 5-21 (36 points), New York 6-16 (34 points). Both games in New York. Semi-finals: April 12. Cork: Cork 2-10, Tipperary 2-7. April 19, Thurles: Limerick 4-15, Offaly 2-8. Home Final May 3 at Croke Park: Cork 2-17, Limerick 0-7. League Re-arranged into Two Groups wlth promotion and relegation):

1970-71—Semi-finals: May 9 (Limerick): Tipperary 2-12, Cork 2-10. May 16, Thurles: Limerick 1-11, Clare 2-6. Final: May 23 in Cork: Limerick 3-12 Tipperary 3-11. Division Two Promotion Play-off August 22 (Ennis): Clare 4-9, Kildare 3-9.

1971-72—Semi-finals: April 16 at Limerick: Cork 5-12 (27) Tipperary 4-8 (20). April 23 at Thurles: Limerick 3-13 (22), Kilkenny 2-13 (19).

Final: May 7 at Thurles: Cork 3-14 (23), Limerick 2-14 (20).

1972-73—Semi-finals: April 15, at Kilkenny: Limerick 2-11, Tipperary, 2-11 (draw). April 22, at Birr: Limerick, 5-10 (25) Tipperary, 3-14 (23), after extra time. April 29, at Waterford: Wexford, 2-10; Kilkenny, 2-9.

Final: May 13, 1973, at Croke Park: Wexford, 4-13 (25); Limerick, 3-7 (16).

1973-74—Semi-finals: April 21, at Limerick: Limerick,1-16 (19); Tipperary, 3-8 (17). April 7, at Croke Park: Cork, 0-18; Dublin 1-11 (14).

Final: May 5, 1974, at Limerick: Cork, 6-15 (33), Limerick, 1-12 (15).

1974-75—Semi-finals: April 27, at Limerick: Tipperary, 1-9, Clare, 0-10. May 4, at Thurles: Galway, 1-9; Kilkenny, 1-6.

Final: May 25, 1975, at Limerick: Galway, 4-9, Tipperary, 4-6.

1975-76—Semi-finals: April 4, at Thurles: Cork, 2-11, Kilkenny, 3-8 (Draw). April 25, at Thurles: Kilkenny, 2-17, Cork, 3-10. April 11, at Thurles: Wexford, 2-9, Clare, 3-6 (draw). April 25, at Thurles: Clare 3-24 (33), Wexford 4-16 (28).

Final: May 9, at Thurles: Clare 2-10, Kilkenny 0-16 (draw). June 20, at Thurles: Kilkenny 6-14, Clare 1-14.

1976-77—Semi-finals: April 10, Thurles: Clare 2-15, Offaly 0-7. Kilkenny 3-12, Tipperary 2-9.

Final: April 24, Thurles: Clare, 2-8; Kilkenny, 0-9.

1977-78—Semi-finals: April 9, Thurles: Clare, 2-16 Limerick 3-6. April 9, Carlow: Kilkenny 3-5, Wexford 2-8 (draw). April 16, Carlow: Kilkenny 5-15, Wexford. 5-14 (replay after extra time).

Final: April 30, Thurles: Clare 3-10, Kilkenny, 1-10.

1978-79—Semi-finals: April 15, Thurles: Galway 1-15, Limerick 4-5. April 16, Limerick: Tipperary 2-13, Clare 2-12. Final: May 6, Limerick: Tipperary 3-15, Galway 0-8.

1979-80—Semi-finals: April 21, Limerick: Cork 1-12; Galway, 0-12. Limerick 2-13; Tipperary 1-11.

Final: May 4, Cork: Cork 2-10, Limerick, 2-10 (draw). May 18, Cork: Cork 4-15, Limerick 4-6 (replay).

1980-81—Semi-finals: April 19, Kilkenny: Offaly 2-13, Laois 4-6. April 19, Thurles: Cork 1-19, Waterford 2-10. Final: May 3, Thurles: Cork 3-11, Offaly 2-8.

1981-82—Semi-finals: April 4, Thurles: Wexford 2-17, Cork, 1-16. Kilkenny, 2-14; Waterford, 1-17 (draw). April 11, Thurles: Kilkenny 5-14, Waterford 4-6 (Replay).

Final: April 18, Croke Park: Kilkenny, 2-14; Wexford, 1-11.

1982-83—Semi-finals: April 3, Thurles: Kilkenny 5-11, Laois, 1-17. April 10, Thurles: Limerick 3-10, Wexford, 2-6.

Final: April 24, Thurles: Kilkenny 2-14, Limerick 2-12.

1983-84—Semi-finals: April 1, Thur!es: Limerick 2-10, Tipperary 1-10. Wexford 4-9, Cork 114. Final: April 8, Thurles:

Limerick 3-16, Wexford, 1-9.
1984-85—Semi-finals: March 31, Thurles: Limerick 0-15, Offaly 1-9. Clare 1-14, Galway 0-11.
Final: April 14, Thurles: Limerick, 3-12; Clare,1-7.
1985-86—Semi-finals: April 27, Thurles: Kilkenny 2-15, Cork, 1-8. Galway 1-16, Wexford, 3-10 (draw) May 4, Thurles: Galway 3-11, Wexford 2-5 (replay).
Final: May 11, Thurles: Kilkenny 2-10, Galway 2-6.
1986-87—Semi-finals: April 19, Portlaoise: Galway 5-16, Waterford 1-12. April 19, Cork: Clare 211, Tipperary 1-11.
Final: May 3, Thurles: Galway 3-12, Clare 3-10.
1987-88—Semi-Finals: April 10, 1988, Croke Park: Tipperary 4-19, Waterford 1-8. Offaly 2-16, Wexford 3-11.
Final: April 24, 1988, Croke Park: Tipperary 3-15; Offaly 2-9.
1988-89—Semi-finals: April 16,1989, at Croke Park: Tipperary 0-15, Kilkenny 1-11. Galway 2-13, Dublin 1-9.
Final: April 30, 1989, at Croke Park: Galway 2-16, Tipperary 4-8.
1989-90—Semi-finals: April 8,1990, at Thurles: Wexford 2-12, Cork 2-12 (draw); Kilkenny 2-16, Dublin 1-9. April 16, 1990 at Kilkenny: Wexford 1-9, Cork 0-6 (replay).
Home Final: April 22, 1990 at Croke Park: Kilkenny 3-12, Wexford 1-10. Final: May 6, 1990 at Gaelic Park (New York) Kilkenny 0-18, New York 0-9.
1990-91—Semi-finals: April 28,1991, at Croke Park: Wexford 2-12, Kilkenny 2-12 (draw); at Limerick: Offaly 1-7, Tipperary 0-7. May 5, at Thurles: Wexford 2-14, Kilkenny 1-12 (replay).
Final: May 12, 1991, at Croke Park: Offaly 2-6, Wexford 0-10.
1991-92—Semi-finals: April 19, 1992 at Ennis: Tipperary 1-15, Galway 1-8. April 26, 1992 at Limerick: Limerick 2-11, Cork 1-4.
Final: May 10, 1992 at Limerick: Limerick 0-14, Tipperary 0-13.
1992-93—Semi-finals: April 25, 1993 at Thurles: Cork 2-11, Tipperary 1-13. Wexford 3-14, Limerick 1-11.
Final: May 9, 1993 at Thurles: Cork 2-11, Wexford 2-11 (draw). May 16 1993 at Thurles: Cork 018, Wexford 3-9 (after extra time: 1st replay): May 22, 1993 at Thurles: Cork 3-11, Wexford 1-12 (2nd replay).
1993-94—Semi-finals: April 24, 1994, at Limerick: Galway 1-13, Clare 0-10. April 30, 1994 at Pairc Ui Caoimh: Tipperary 2-13, Cork 1-13.
Final: May 8, 1994 at Limerick: Tipperary 2-14, Galway 0-12.
1994-95—Semi-finals. April 23, 1995, at Thurles: Clare 2-14, Waterford 0-8. Kilkenny 4-8, Offaly 0-14.
Final: May 7, 1995 at Thurles: Kilkenny 2-12, Clare 0-9.
1995-96—Semi-finals: April 28, 1996 at Kilkenny: Tipperary 1-13, Laois 1-11; at Limerick: Galway 2-15, Wexford 1-10.
Final: May 12, 1996 at Limerick: Galway 2-10, Tipperary 2-8.
1997—Semi-finals: August 23, 1997 at Ennis Galway 1-14, Tipperary 0-6. August 24,1997, at Kilkenny: Limerick 1-17, Kilkenny 0-10.
Final: October 5, 1997 at Ennis: Limerick 1-12, Galway 1-9.
1998—Semi-Finals: May 3, 1998 at Thurles: Cork 2-15, Clare 0-10. Waterford 2-17, Limerick 1-11.
Final: May 17, 1998 at Thurles: Cork 2-14, Waterford 0-13.
1999—Semi-finals: May 2, at Limerick: Galway 2-15, Kilkenny 1-15.
Tipperary 0-19, Clare 1-15.
Final: May 16, 1999, at Ennis: Tipperary 1-14, Galway 1-10.
2000—Semi-finals – April 30 at Thurles:
Galway 2-15, Waterford 1-15.
Tipperary 2-18, Limerick 0-17.
Final – May 14 at Limerick:
Galway 2-18, Tipperary 2-13.
2001—Semi-finals – April 28 at Ennis:
Tipperary 2-19, Galway 1-15.
April 29 at Thurles:
Clare 2-21, Kilkenny 3-8.
Final – May 6 at Limerick:
Tipperary 1-19, Clare 0-17.
2002—Semi-finals – April 21 at Pairc UiChaoimh:
Cork 0-21, Tipperary 1-10.
April 21 at Limerick:
Kilkenny 2-14, Limerick 0-15.
Final – May 5 at Thurles:
Kilkenny 2-15, Cork 2-14.
2003—Final – May 5 at Croke Park:
Kilkenny 5-14, Tipperary 5-13.
2004—Final – May 9 at Limerick:
Galway 2-15, Waterford 1-13.
2005—Final – May 2 at Thurles:
Kilkenny 3-20, Clare 0-15.
2006—Semi-final – April 23 at Thurles:
Limerick 3-23, Clare 2-23. (aet)
Semi-final – April 23 at Thurles:
Kilkenny 3-20, Tipperary 2-11.
Final – April 30 at Thurles:
Kilkenny 3-11, Limerick 0-14.

2007—Semi-final – April 15 at Thurles:
Kilkenny 2-22, Wexford 2-7.
Semi-final – April 15 at Thurles:
Waterford 1-19, Cork 1-16.
Final – April 29 at Thurles:
Waterford 0-20, Kilkenny 0-18.
2008—Semi-final – April 13 at Nowlan Park:
Tipperary 1-15, Kilkenny 1-10.
Semi-final – April 13 at the Gaelic Grounds:
Galway 2-22, Cork 0-24.
Final – April 20 at the Gaelic Grounds:
Tipperary 3-18, Galway 3-16.
2009—Final – May 3 at Thurles:
Kilkenny 2-26, Tipperary 4-17. (aet)

Roll of Honour – Tipperary (19), Cork (14), Kilkenny (14), Limerick (11), Galway (8), Wexford (4), Clare (3), Dublin (2), Waterford (2), Offaly (1).

Note: Sponsorship of the National Leagues was taken up by the Ford Motor Company in 1986, Royal Liver Assurance took over in 1988 and Church & General Insurance became sponsors in 1994, later to be known as Allianz.

NATIONAL HURLING LEAGUE FINALISTS

1925/26

Cork—J. Coughlan, Maurice Murphy, S. Óg Murphy (capt.), Mick Murphy, D. Barry Murphy, J. O'Regan, E. O'Connell, J. Hurley, W. Higgins, Matt Murphy, P Aherne, E. Coughlan, D. Aherne, M. Aherne, T. O'Brien.

Dublin—E. Tobin (capt.), P. Mcinerney, M. Gill, M. Finn, G. Howard, J. Kirwan, P. Browne, W. Phelan, J. Walsh (Faughs), R. Doherty, T. Barry, J. Bannon, T. Kelly, D. O'Neill, T. Daly.

1926/27
NO COMPETITION.

1927/28

Tipperary—T. Butler (Sarsfields), S. Moloney, J. Leahy (capt.), M. Ryan, W. Small, J. J. Hayes, P. Purcell, M. Flanagan, T. Treacy, P. Cahill, P. Leahy, P Dwyer, J. J. Callanan, M. Kennedy, M. Cronin.

(Played on a league system. The above team played in final game against Laois and clinched the title.)

1928/29

Dublin—M. Gill (capt.), T. Lawless, T. Burke, G. Howard, M. Power, P. Mcinerney, T. Quinlan, M. Finn, J. Walsh (Faughs), T. Barry, T. O'Meara, C. McMahon, E. Byrne, J. Leeson, S. Tumpane.

Cork—M. Casey, M. Madden, W. Donnelly, P. Collins, D. Barry Murphy (capt.), J. O'Regan, T Barry, J. Hurley, M. O'Connell, E. Coughlan, P. O'Grady, J. Kenneally, P. Aherne, P. Delea, M. Aherne.

1929/30

Cork—J. Coughlan, M. Madden, W. Donnelly, J. O'Regan, P. Collins, T. Barry, D. Barry Murphy, E. Coughlan (capt.), J. Hurley, P. Delea, M. O'Connell, S. O'Sullivan, W. Clancy, M. Aherne, W. Stanton. Sub: P O'Grady for M. O'Connell.

Dublin—J. O'Dwyer, T. O'Meara, P. Mclnerney, C. McMahon, E. Campion, T. Teehan, J. Walsh (Faughs), M. Gill (capt.), J. Leeson, T. Quinlan, M. Daniels, S. Hegarty, S. Tumpane, C. Griffin, M. Power. Sub: J. O'Connoll for M. Gill.

1930/31

Galway—M. Keating, H. Hodgins, W. Donnelly, M. Broderick, P. Clarke, M. Finn, W. Keane, M. Gill, I. Harney (capt.), R. Donoghue, M. King, M. Cunningham, W. Curran, J. Deely, G. O'Reilly.

Tipperary—T. O'Meara, P Byrne, G. Howard, J. Gleeson, T. Treacy, P. Purcell, P. Cahill, J. Donovon, J. O'Loughlin, T. Leahy, T. Harty, W. O'Meara, M. Cronin, M. Kennedy (capt.), M. S. Cronin.

1931/32
NO COMPETITION.

1932/33

Kilkenny: J. Dermody, P. Larkin, P. O'Reilly, J. Carroll, P. Phelan, P. Byrne, E. Doyle (capt.), E. Byrne, L. Meagher, J. Walsh, Tommy Leahy, Martin Power, J. Fitzpatrick, J. Dunne, Matty Power.

Limerick—P. Scanlan, E. Cregan, T. McCarthy, M. Fitzgibbon, D. O'Malley, P. Clohessy, M. Cross, T. Ryan (capt.), M. Quinlivan, J. Mackey, M. Mackey, Martin Ryan, D. Clohessy, C. O'Brien, M. Hough. Subs: P. Joyce for M. Cross, J. J. Moloney for M. Fitzgibbon.

1933/34

Limerick—P. Scanlan, E. Cregan, M. Hickey, M. Kennedy (capt.), M. Cross, G. Howard, W. O'Donoghue, T. Ryan, Mick Ryan, J. Mackey, M. Mackey, J. Roche, P. Ryan, C. O'Brien, M. Sexton.

Dublin—C. Forde, A. Murphy, J. Bannon, P. Kealy, J. Walsh (Civil Service), D. Canniffe, P. Roche, C. McMahon, E. Wade, S. Hegarty, S. Muldowney, T. Delaney, M. Hough, P Browne, J. O'Connor. Subs: H. Quirke for J. Bannon, T. Quinlan for T. Delaney.

1934/35

Limerick—P. Scanlan, E. Cregan, T. McCarthy, M. Kennedy, M. Cross, P. Clohessy, G. Howord,

T. Ryan (capt.), Mick Ryan, J. Mackey, M. Mackey, J. Roche, J. O'Connell, P. McMahon, J. Close.

(Played on a league system. The above team played in final game against Laois and clinched the title.)

1935/36

Limerick—T. Shinny, P. Carroll, T. Mccarthy, M. Kennedy, M. Cross, P. Clohessy, G. Howard, T. Ryan (capt.), J. Roche, J. Mackey, M. Mackey, J. Power, D. Clohessy, P McMahon, J. Close.

(Played on a league system. The above team played in final game against Dublin and clinched the title.)

1936/37

Limerick—P. Scanlan, P. Carroll, T. McCarthy, M. Kennedy, M. Cross, P. Clohessy, J. Power, T. Ryan, Mick Ryan, D. Givens, M. Mackey (capt.), J. Roche, D. Clohessy, P. McMahon, J. McCarthy.

(Played on a league system. The above team played in final game against Cork and clinched the title.)

1937/38

Limerick: P. Scanlan, M. Power, T. McCarthy, M. Kennedy, P. Carroll, P. Clohessy, J. Power, T. Ryan, P. Walsh, J. Mackey, M. Mackey (capt.), P. Cregan, D. Givens, J. McCarthy, J. Roche.

Tipperary: G. Doyle, D. O'Gorman, G. Cornally, J. Lanigan, Johnny Ryan, J. Maher, T. Kennedy, M. Burke, W. Barry, Jim Coffey, T. Treacy, T. Doyle, W. O'Donnell, D. Murphy, P. Ryan (capt.).

1938/39

Dublin—C. Forde, T. Teehan, P. Crowley, C. McMahon, M. Gill (Jnr), J. Gilmartin, J. Byrne, H. Gray, M. Daniels (capt.), P. Flanagan, M. McDonnell, P. Doody, M. Brophy, M. Flynn, W. Loughnane.

Waterford—M. Curley, J. Manning, C. Ware, J. Fanning, A. Fleming, J. Keane (capt.), J. Mountain, T. Greaney, C. Moylan, W. Barron, L. Byrne, P. Sheehan, W. Lynch, D. Goode, E. Daly. Sub: J. Butler for P Sheehan.

1939/40

Cork—J. Buttimer, W. Murphy, B. Thornhill, A. Lotty, W. Campbell, J. Lynch (capt.), D. J. Buckley, S. Barrett, C. Buckley, C. Ring, J. Quirke, J. Young, R. Ryng, T. O'Sullivan, M. Brennan.

Tipperary—W. Ryan, D. O'Gorman, G. Cornally, J. Lanigan, Johnny Ryan, J. Maher (capt.), W. O'Donnell, J. Cooney, D. Mackey, T. Doyle, J. Looby, T Kennedy, P. Maher, T. Treacy, D. Murphy. Sub: P Dwyer for D. Mackey.

1940/41

Cork—J. Buttimer, W. Murphy, B. Thornhill, A. Lotty, W. Campbell, J. Quirke, D. J. Buckley, S. Barrett, C. Buckley (capt.), C. Ring, J. Lynch, J. Young, R. Ryng, T. O'Sullivan, M. Brennan.
Dublin: C. Forde, C. McMahon, M. Butler, R. O'Brien, M. Prenderville, P. Farrell, J. Byrne, E. Wade (capt.), H. Gray, D. Devitt, C. Downes, P Maher, M. Brophy, P. McSweeney, E. O'Boyle. Sub: G. Glenn for P. Maher.

1942/1945 NO COMPETITION.

1945/46

Clare—J. Daly, D. McInerney, P. O'Callaghan, T. Byrnes, D. Carroll, D. Solan, B. McMahon, A. Hannon, J. Solan, M. Nugent, R. Frost, M. Daly (capt.), M. O'Halloran, J. Whelan, P. J. Quane. Subs: J. Minogue for M. O'Halloran, P. Lyons for J. Minogue.

G. Frost, P. Byrnes, P. Lyons and A. O'Brien played in drawn game. T. Byrnes, B. McMahon, J. Solan and M. O'Halloran were on for replay.

Dublin—M. Banks, Seamus O'Ceallachain, E. Dunphy, A. O'Dwyer, G. O'Leary, M. Maher, S. Coughlan, H. Gray, P. O'Brien, E. Wade (capt.), A. Herbert, Sean Óg O'Ceallachain, M. McDonnell, E. Daly, J. Prior. Subs: D. Cantwell for M. McDonnell, M. Gill (Jnr) for E. Wade, D. Devitt for M. Maher.

J. O'Neill, P. Flanagan, F. Cummins and D. Cantwell played in drawn game. Seamus O'Ceallachain, A. Herbert, M. McDonnell and J. Prior were on for replay. Sub in drawn game: Seamus O'Ceallachain for J. O'Neill.

1946/47

Limerick—P. Collopy, J. Sadlier, M. Herbert, T. Cregan, S. Herbert, J. Power, T. O'Brien, M. Ryan (Kilteely), P. Fitzgerald (St Patrick's), J. Mulcahy, R. Stokes, M. Dooley, P. Fitzgerald (Askeaton), D. Flanagan, J. Barry. Subs: J. Mackey for M. Dooley, J. O'Donoghue for D. Flanagan.

J. Creamer, T. Murphy, J. Mackey and C. Birrane played in drawn game. M. Ryan, M. Dooley, D. Flanagan and J. Barry were on for replay. Subs in drawn game: C. Crowley for C. Birrane, J. Barry for T. Murphy.

Kilkenny—R. Dowling, P. Grace, P. Hayden, M. Marnell, J. Kelly, P. Prendergast, W. Walsh, D. Kennedy (capt.), J. Heffernan, J. Langton, Terry Leahy, L. Reidy, T. Walton, J. Mulcahy, S. Downey. Sub: P. Kenny for P. Prendergast.

Same team played in drawn game. Sub in drawn game: P. O'Brien for D. Kennedy.

1947/48

Cork—T. Mulcahy, W. Murphy, C. Murphy, A. Lotty, M. Fouhy, P. O'Donovan, J. Young (capt.), B. Murphy, S. Twomey, M. O'Toole, J.

Lynch, W. J. Daly, J. Hartnett, D. Twomey, P. Barry.

Tipperary—A. Reddin, Johnny Ryan, W. Wall (capt.), T. Purcell, J. Devitt, P. Furlong, P. Stakelum, Tom Wall, Mick Ryan, R. Stakelum, Jack Ryan, T. Doyle, P. Fahy, P. Kenny, W. Hogan. Sub: John Doyle for Mick Ryan.

1948/49

Tipperary—A. Reddin, J. Devitt, A. Brennan, F. Coffey, M. Byrne, P. Furlong, T. Purcell, P. Shanahan, P. Stakelum (capt.), R. Stakelum, W. Carroll, Mick Ryan, Mutt Ryan, S. Maher, Jim Ryan. Sub: Tommy Ryan for Mutt Ryan.

Cork—T. Mulcahy, W. Murphy, C. Murphy, J. Young (capt.), M. Fouhy, P. O'Donovan, J. Hartnett, B. Murphy, S. Twomey, C. Ring, J. Lynch, W. J. Daly, M. O'Riordan, G. O'Riordan, D. Twomey. Sub: S. Condon for D. Twomey.

1949/50

Tipperary—A. Reddin, M. Byrne, A. Brennan, John Doyle, J. Finn, P. Stakelum, T. Doyle, P. Shanahan, S. Bannon, E. Ryan, Mick Ryan, S. Kenny (capt.), P. Kenny, S. Maher, J. Kennedy.

New York—P. Leamy, M. O'Rourke, P. Murphy, J. Looney, T. Flynn, J. Smee (capt.), P. Naughton, P. Grimes, S. Craven, D. Doorley, T. Leahy, B. O'Donoghue, S. Gallagher, J. Kennedy, S. Kelly.

HOME FINAL

Tipperary—Same as played in final except Tommy Ryan and Jack Ryan in place of J. Finn and E. Ryan. Sub: J. Finn for P. Stakelum.

Kilkenny—R. Dowling, J. Hogan, P. Hayden, M. Marnell, J. Keane (capt.), P. Prendergast, W. Walsh, W. Costigan, S. Downey, J. Heffernan, M. Kenny, L. Reidy, T. Walton, D. Kennedy, P. J. Garvan. Subs: J. Langton for T. Walton, P. Crowley for J. Langton.

1950/51

Galway—S. Duggan, C. Corless, F. Flynn, J. Brophy, H. Gordon, Tadgh Kelly, J. Molloy, J. Salmon, T. Moroney, K. McNamee, J. Gallagher, F. Duignan, M. Burke, M. J. Flaherty (capt.), M. Glynn. Sub: John Killeen for F. Duignan.

New York—P. Leamy, M. O'Neill, A. Fitzpatrick, P. Murphy, P. Naughton, M. O'Rourke, J. Looney, P. Hoarty, D. Doorley, S. Gallagher, T. Leahy (capt.), M. Loughlin, J. Kennedy, J. Smee, P. Devaney. Subs: S. Craven for M. Loughlin, T. O'Connor for D. Doorley, J. Barrett for S. Craven.

HOME FINAL

Galway—Same as played in final. Sub: M. McInerney for M. Glynn.

Wexford—A. Foley, W. Rackard, M. Byrne, M. Hanlon, S. Thorpe, R. Rackard, E. Wheeler, M. Codd, J. Morrissey, Podge Kehoe, Paddy Kehoe, T. Russell, D. Aherne, N. Rackard, T. Flood (capt.). Subs: M. Flood for S. Thorpe, P. Shannon for A. Foley, R. Donovan for M. Codd, J. Quinn for T. Russell.

1951/52

Tipperary—A. Reddin, Michael Maher, A. Brennan, John Doyle, J. Finn, P. Stakelum (capt.), T. Doyle, P. Shanahan, J. Hough, E. Ryan, Mick Ryan, P. Kenny, Jim Ryan, S. Maher, P. Maher Sub: R. Mockler for A. Brennan.

New York—P. Leamy, M. O'Neill, P. Murphy, J. Looney, P. Moylan, M. O'Rourke, P. Naughton, D. Doorley, A. Galvin, T. Leahy, S. Gallagher (capt.), P. Hoarty, J. Whelan, J. Kennedy, C. O'Leary. Subs S. Craven for J. Kennedy, A. Fitzpatrick for T. Leahy, T. Leahy for C. O'Leary.

HOME FINAL

Tipperary—Same as played in final except S. Bannon and Tim Ryan for J. Finn and P. Kenny.

Wexford—A. Foley, S. Thorpe, N. O'Donnell, M. Hanlon, Paddy Kehoe, R. Rackard, W. Rackard, J. Morrissey, E. Wheeler, Podge Kehoe, J. Cummins, M. Flood, D. Aherne, N. Rackard (capt.), T. Flood. Sub: M. Byrne for N. Rackard.

1952/53

Cork—D. Creedon, G. O'Riordan, J. Lyons, A. O'Shaughnessy, M. Fouhy, D. O'Leary (capt.), V. Twomey, G. Murphy, J. Twomey, J. Lynam, J. Hartnett, W. J. Doly, C. Ring, L. Dowling, P. Barry. Sub: M. Cashman for D. O'Leary.

Tipperary—A. Reddin, M. Byrne, J. Finn, John Doyle, S. Bannon, P. Stakelum, T. Doyle (capt.), P. Shanahan, J. Hough, E. Ryan, A. Wall, Tim Ryan, P. Kenny, P. Maher, Mick Ryan. Subs: Jim Ryan for P. Maher, S. O'Meara for Tim Ryan, Tommy Ryan for Mick Ryan.

1953/54

Tipperary—A. Reddin, M. Byrne, J. Finn (capt.), John Doyle, M. Kenny, P. Stakelum, C. Keane, J. Hough, T. English, E. Ryan, Mick Ryan, P. Kenny, M. Seymour, W. Quinn S. Bannon.

Kilkenny—M. Rowe, J. Maher, P. Hayden, M. Marnell, P. Buggy, J. Hogan, J. McGovern, J. Sutton, D. Kennedy (capt.), S. Clohosey, P. J. Garvan, M. Kelly, J. Langton, P. Fitzgerald, S. Downey. Sub: R. Carroll for M. Kelly.

1954/55

Tipperary—A. Reddin, M. Byrne, Michael Maher, John Doyle (capt.), C. Keane, J. Finn, J. McGrath, J. Hough, T. English, L. Devaney, P. Stakelum, G. Doyle, S. Bannon, L. Keone, T. Barrett.

Wexford—A. Foley, W. Wickham, N. O'Donnell (capt.), M. Hanlon, J. English, J. Morrissey, T. Bolger, E. Wheeler, S. Hearne,

Podge Kehoe, T. Dixon, D. Aherne, Paddy Kehoe, T. Ryan, T. Flood. Subs: M. Codd for E. Wheeler, E. Wheeler for M. Codd.

1955/56

Wexford—A. Foley, R. Rackard, N. O'Donnell, M. Hanlon, J. English (capt.), W. Rackard, M. Morrissey, J. Morrissey, S. Hearne, Podge Kehoe, E. Wheeler, T. Flood, T. Ryan, N. Rackard, T. Dixon.

Tipperary—A. Reddin, M. Byrne (capt.), Michael Maher, John Doyle, J. Finn, P. Stakelum, A. Wall, J. Hough, S. O'Meara, L. Devaney, L. Skelly, T. English, P. Kenny, W. Quinn, S. Bannon.

1956/57

Tipperary—M. Keane, M. Byrne, Michael Maher, John Doyle, J. Finn, P. Stakelum, A. Wall, J. Hough, T. English, Mick Ryan, L. Devaney, Jimmy Doyle, P. Kenny, S. O'Meara, L. Skelly.

Kilkenny—O. Walsh, T. Walsh (Dunna - maggin), J. Walsh, J. Maher, P. Buggy, J. Sutton, J. McGovern, W. Walsh, M. Brophy, D. Heaslip, M. Kenny, J. Murphy, R. Rockett, W. Dwyer, S. Clohosey.

1957/58

Wexford—P. Nolan, W. Rackard, N. O'Donnell, J. Redmond, J. English, J. Morrissey, M. Morrissey, E. Wheeler, S. Hearne, H. O'Connor (capt.), Podge Kehoe, O. Gough, M. Lyng, T. Flood, M. Codd. Subs: J. O'Brien for H. O'Connor, O. McGrath for M. Lyng.

Limerick—G. Casey, D. Kelly (capt.), J. Enright, J. Keogh, T. McGarry, Jim Quaide, S. Quaide, T. Casey, D. Moylan, L. Hogan, N. Stokes, V. Cobbe, J. Shanahan, M. Tynan, L. Moloney. Subs: W. Hogan for M. Tynan, M. Tynan for L. Moloney, L. Moloney for W. Hogan.

1958/59

Tipperary—T. Moloney, M. Byrne, Michael Moher, K. Carey, J. Finn, A. Wall (capt.), John Doyle, T. English, D. Nealon, L. Devaney, J. McDonnell, Jimmy Doyle, T. Larkin, Martin Maher, L. Connolly. Sub: P. Hennessy for T. Larkin.

Waterford—E. Power, J. Harney, A. Flynn, J. Barron, M. Óg Morrissey, P. Grimes, Jackie Condon, M. Lacey, S. Power, L. Guinan, T. Cheasty, F. Walsh (capt.), P. Troy, J. Kiely, D. Whelan. Subs: J. Flavin for P. Troy, W. Dunphy for S. Power.

1959-60

Tipperary—T. Moloney, M. Byrne, Michael Maher, K. Carey, M. Burns, A. Wall (capt.), John Doyle, T. English, T. Ryan (Killenaule), Jimmy Doyle, L. Devaney, D. Nealon, L. Connolly, W. Moloughney, T. Moloughney. Sub: G. McCarthy for T. Moloughney.

Cork—M. Cashman, J. Brohan, D. O'Riordan, S. French, D. Murphy, J. O'Sullivan, M. McCarthy, N. Gallagher, E. Goulding (capt.), P. Harte, T. Kelly, P. Fitzgerald, P. Barry, L. Dowling, C. Ring. Subs: A. Connolly for D. Murphy, M. Horgan for A. Connolly.

1960/61

Tipperary—D. O'Brien, M. Hassett (capt.), Michael Maher, K. Carey, M. Burns, A. Wall, John Doyle, T. English, L. Devaney, Jimmy Doyle, D. Nealon, T. Ryan (Killenaule), J. McKenna, W. Moloughney, T. Moloughney. Subs: T. Shanahan for K. Carey, K. Carey for T. Shanahan.

Waterford—E. Power, T. Cunningham, A. Flynn, J. Barron, M. Flannelly, M. Óg Morrissey (capt.), Joe Condon, S. Power, P. Grimes, M. Murphy, T. Cheasty, F. Walsh, L. Guinan, T. Walsh, D. Whelan. Sub: M. Lacey for D. Whelan.

1961/62

Kilkenny—O. Walsh, T. Walsh (Dunnamaggin), J. Walsh, M. Walsh, S. Cleere, A. Hickey (capt.), M. Coogan, A. Comerford, N. Power, E. Keher, R. Carroll, W. Murphy (Carrickshock), D. Heaslip, S. Clohosey, W. Dwyer.

Cork—M. Cashman (capt.), J. Brohan, D. Brennan, P. Duggan, J. O'Sullivan, D. Murphy, S. Kennefick, T. Kelly, P. Fitzgerald, P. Harte, D. Sheehan, M. Mortell, L. Dowling, C. Ring, M. Quane. Subs: J. Bennett for M. Mortell, R. Browne for P. Harte.

1962/63

Waterford—E. Power, T. Cunningham, A. Flynn, M. Óg Morrissey, L. Guinan, J. Byrne, J. McGrath, Joe Condon, J. Kirwan, J. Meaney (capt.), M. Flannelly, F. Walsh, S. Power, J. Barron, P. Grimes. Sub: J. Irish for J. McGrath.

J. Irish and C. Ware played in drawn game. J. McGrath and Joe Condon came on for replay. Sub in drawn game: Joe Condon for C. Ware.

New York—K. Croke, P. Dowling, C. O'Connell, M. Morrissey, J. Murphy, M. Sweeney, J. O'Donnell, B. Hennessy, J. Keating, S. Ryall, J. Carey (capt.), B. Kelleher, W. Carey, M. Donovan, P. Kirby. Subs: B. McCann for M. Sweeney, J. Naughton for M. Donovan.

D. O'Brien, P. Hennessy and J. Quarry played in drawn gome. K. Croke, J. O'Donnell and M. Donovan came on for replay. Subs in drawn game: J. Donoghue for J. Quarry, S. Lakes for J. Murphy, M. Donovan for P Hennessy.

HOME FINAL

Waterford—Same as played in final except P. Flynn, M. Dempsey and T. Cheasty for E. Power, J. McGrath and J. Meaney. Subs: J. Meaney .or M. Dempsey, E. Power for P. Flynn.

Tipperary—R. Mounsey, John Doyle, Michael Maher, K. Carey, M. Burns, A. Wall, M. Murphy, S. English, T. English, Jimmy Doyle, J. McKenna T. Ryan (Killenaule), D. Nealon, L. Devaney, S. McLoughlin (Capt). Sub: T. Moloughney for S. English.

1963/64

Tipperary—J. O'Donoghue, John Doyle, Michael Maher, K. Carey, M. Burns, A. Wall, M. Murphy, T. English, M. Roche, Jimmy Doyle, L. Kiely, M. Keating, D. Nealon, T. Ryan (Killenaule), P. Ryan.

New York—D. O'Brien, P. Dowling, C. O'Connell, M. Morrissey, J. Murphy, B. Hennessy, P. Hennessy, J. Keating, P. Kelleher, S. Ryall, J. Carney, B. Kelleher, J. Donoghue, J. Carey, P. Kirby.

HOME FINAL

Tipperary—Same as played in final except J. McKenna and S. McLoughlin (capt.) for Tom Ryan Killenaule) and M. Keating.

Wexford—P. Nolan (capt.), T. Neville, D. Quigley, E. Colfer, P. Wilson, W. Rackard, J. Nolan, J. Kennedy, E. Wheeler, J. O'Brien, R. Shannon, P. Lynch, O. McGrath, Podge Kehoe, J. Foley.

1964/65

Tipperary—J. O'Donoghue, John Doyle, Michael Maher, K. Carey, M. Burns, A. Wall, L. Gaynor, T. English, M. Roche, Jimmy Doyle (capt.), T. Ryan (Toomevara), L. Kiely, D. Nealon, L. Devaney, S. McLoughlin. Sub: P. Doyle for T. English.

M. Keating played in first leg. Tom Ryan (Toomevara) was on for second leg. Sub in first leg: T. Ryan (Toomevara) for M. Keating.

New York—K. Croke, S. Custy, J. Maher, M. Morrissey, P. Hennessy, P. Dowling, J. Murphy, B. Hennessy, P. Donoghue, M. Curtin (capt.), P. Kirby, D. Long, J. Donoghue, J. Naughton, P. Egan. Subs: W. Carey for P. Donoghue, J. Kelly for W. Carey, M. Butler and P. Kelleher played in first leg. S. Custy and J. Naughton came on for second leg.

Subs in first leg B. Kelleher for M. Butler, M. Butler for J. Murphy, B. Aherne for B. Kelleher.

HOME FINAL

Tipperary—Same as played in final except J. McKenna for T. Ryan (Toomevara).

Kilkenny—O. Walsh, P. Henderson, P. Dillon, J. Treacy, P. Drennan, S. Cleere, M. Coogan, P. Moran (capt.), S. Buckley, T. Forristal, P. Carroll, E. Keher, J. Dunphy, J. Lynch, T. Walsh (Thomastown). Subs: J. Teehan for P. Carroll, C. Dunne for T. Walsh.

1965/66

Kilkenny—O. Walsh, T. Carroll, J. Lynch (capt.), J. Treacy, S. Cleere, P. Henderson, M. Coogan, P. Moran, J. Teehan, S. Buckley, J. Bennett, C. Dunne, T. Walsh (Thomastown), P. Dillon, J. Dunphy. Subs: P. Carroll for J. Dunphy, J. Dunphy for S. Buckley.

P. Carroll played in first leg. P. Dillon was on for second leg.

New York—K. Croke, P. Donoghue, J. Maher, M. Morrissey, P. Hennessy, P. Dowling, J. Murphy, B. Hennessy, B. Aherne, B. Kelleher, J. Donoghue, M. Curtin, D. Long, E. England, S. Forde. Subs: J. Doherty for M. Curtin, M. Curtin For B. Kelleher, J. Kelly for D. Long.

J. Kelly (Capt) and P. Kelleher played in first leg. E. England and S. Forde were on for second leg. Subs in first leg: A. English for J. Kelly, J. Doherty for P. Hennessy.

HOME FINAL

Kilkenny—Same as played in final except E. Keher and P. Carroll for J. Bennett and C. Dunne.

Tipperary—P O'Sullivan, John Doyle, K. Carey, J. Gleeson, M. Burns, A. Wall (capt.), L. Gaynor, T English, M. Roche, Jimmy Doyle, L. Devaney, L. Kiely, D. Nealon, M. Keating, T. Ryan (Toomevara). Subs: J. McKenna For L. Kiely, P. J. Ryan for M. Roche.

1966/67

Wexford—P. Nolan, D. Ouigley, M. Collins, E. Colfer, V. Staples, T. Neville, W. Murphy, Joe Murphy, R. Shannon, J. O'Brien, P Lynch, P. Wilson, F. Duff, A. Doran, S. Whelan. Subs: C. Jacob for F. Duff, M. Kinsella for W. Murphy.

Kilkenny—O. Walsh, J. Lynch, P. Dillon, J. Treacy, S. Cleere, P. Henderson, M. Coogan, P. Moran, C. Dunne, T. Walsh (Thomastown), J. Teehan, E. Keher, R. Blanchfield, J. Bennett, Martin Brennan. Sub: F. Cummins for J. Teehan.

1967/68

Tipperary—J. O'Donoghue, J. Costigan, N. O'Gorman, J. Gleeson, M. Burns, M. Roche (capt.), L. Gaynor, J. Flanagan, P. J. Ryan, M. Keating, Jimmy Ryan, Jimmy Doyle, D. Nealon, P. Lowry, S. McLoughlin. Sub: M. Stapleton for N. O'Gorman.

P. Rowland played in first leg. P. Lowry was on for second leg.

New York—K. Croke, P. Donoghue, J. Maher, S. Custy, P. Kirby, P. Dowling, J. Murphy, B. Hennessy, H. McCabe, M. Curtin, M. Mortell, S. Lakes, J. Donoghue, C. O'Connoll, M. Bermingham. Subs: P. Egan for M. Mortell, D. Long for S. Lakes.

P. Egan and B. Kelleher played in first leg. M. Mortell and C. O'Connoll were on for second leg.

HOME FINAL

Tipperary—Same as played in final except L. Devaney for P. Lowry. Sub: J. McKenna for S. McLoughlin.

Kilkenny—O. Walsh, T. Carroll, P. Dillon, J. Treacy, S. Cleere, P. Henderson, M. Coogan, P. Moran, F. Cummins, J. Bennett (capt.), J. Kinsella, C. Dunne, E. Keher, J. Lynch, Martin Brennan. Sub: R. Blanchfield for Martin Brennan.

1968/69

Cork—Paddy Barry, A. Maher, T. O'Donoghue, D. Murphy (capt.), D. Clifford, J. McCarthy, C. Roche, G. McCarthy, R. Touhy, T. Ryan, W. Walsh, P. Hegarty, C. McCarthy, C. Cullinane, E. O'Brien.

Wexford—P. Nolan, T. Neville, J. Furlong, E. Colfer, V. Staples, D. Quigley, W. Murphy, M. Jacob, D. Bernie, J. Quigley, P. Lynch, P. Wilson, A. Doran, S. Whelan, J. Berry.

1969/70

Cork—Paddy Barry, A. Maher, P. McDonnell, J. Horgan, S. Murphy, P. Hegarty, C. Roche, G. McCarthy (Capt), S. Looney, T. Ryan, W. Walsh, D. Clifford, C. McCarthy, R. Cummins, E. O'Brien. Subs: J. O'Sullivan for G. McCarthy, G. McCarthy for J. O'Sullivan.

C. Cullinane played in first leg. D. Clifford came on for second leg.

New York—H. Condron, M. Reynolds, J. Maher, J. O'Neill, P. Donoghue, P. Dowling, P. Dwyer, J. Firth, M. Curtin, T. Corbett, J. Carney, S. Lakes, D. O'Brien, B. Hennessy, P. Kirby. Subs: J. Foley for P. Kirby, J. Harte for J. Foley, B. Kelleher for J. Carney.

S. Custy played in first leg. M. Reynolds came on for second leg. Subs in first leg: B. Kelleher for J. Carney, J. Harte for P. Dwyer.

HOME FINAL

Cork—Same as played in final except J. O'Sullivan (Capt) and C. Cullinane for S. Murphy and D. Clifford.

Limerick—J. Hogan, J. McDonagh, P. Hartigan, J. O'Brien, Phil Bennis, J. O'Donnell, A. O'Brien, P. J. Keane, B. Hartigan, E. Grimes, R. Bennis, E. Cregan, P. O'Brien, T. Bluett, Peter Bennis. Subs: A. Dunworth for E. Grimes, T. Ryan for P. O'Brien.

1970/71

Limerick—J. Hogan, A. O'Brien (capt.), P. Hartigan, J. O'Brien, C. Campbell, J. O'Donnell, Phil Bennis. S. Foley, M. Graham, R. Bennis, B. Hartigan, E. Grimes, D. Flynn, M. Cregan, E. Cregan. Sub: E. Prenderville for C. Campbell.

Tipperary—P. O'Sullivan, N. Lane, J. Kelly, W. Ryan, J. Fogarty, T. O'Connor, L. Gaynor, M. Roche, M. Jones, F. Loughnane (capt.), J. Flanagan, Jack Ryan, R. Ryan, M. Keating, P. Byrne. Subs: Jimmy Doyle for R. Ryan, J. Gleeson for W. Ryan, M. Nolan for J. Flanagan.

1971/72

Cork—Paddy Barry, B. Murphy, P. McDonnell, Paddy Crowley, F Norberg (capt.), S. Looney, C. Roche, J. McCarthy, D. Coughlan, D. Collins, M. Malone, P. Hegarty, C. McCarthy, R. Cummins, S. O'Leary. Subs: S. Murphy for C. Roche.

Limerick—J. Hogan (capt.), A. O'Brien, P. Hartigan, J. Allis, Phil Bennis, J. O'Brien, M. Graham, S. Foley, B. Hartigan, F. Nolan, R. Bennis, E. Grimes, D. Flynn, W. Moore, E. Cregan. Subs: C. Campbell for Phil Bennis, S. Burke for E. Cregan.

1972/73

Wexford—P. Nolan, J. Prendergast, E. Murphy, J. Quigley (capt.), C. Doran, M. Jacob, W. Murphy, D. Bernie, E. Buggy, C. Keogh, M. Quigley, T. Byrne, H. Gough, A. Doran, J. Berry. Subs: P. Kehoe for J. Prendergast, J. Purcell for H. Gough.

Limerick—S. Horgan, P. Hartigan, E. Rea, J. O'Brien, M. Dowling, J. O'Donnell, S. Foley, B. Hartigan, E. Grimes, R. Bennis, E. Cregan, M. Graham, L. O'Donoghue, W. Moore, F. Nolan. Subs: A. Dunworth for M. Graham, Phil Bennis for A. Dunworth, L. Enright for Jim O'Donnell.

1973/74

Cork—Paddy Barry, A. Maher, M. O'Doherty, J. Horgan (capt.), Pat Barry, J. Buckley, C. Roche, P. Hegarty, D. Coughlan, T. O'Brien, W. Walsh, G. McCarthy, S. O'Leary, M. Malone, E. O'Donoghue. Sub: C. McCarthy for W. Walsh.

Limerick—S. Horgan, P. Herbert, P. Hartigan, J. O'Brien, T. Ryan, E. Cregan, S. Foley, W. Fitzmaurice (capt.), E. Grimes, L. O'Donoghue, R. Bennis, M. Ruth, J. McKenna, E. Rea, F. Nolan. Subs: B. Hartigan for W. Fitzmaurice, M. Dowling for J. McKenna, P. Fitzmaurice for M. Ruth.

1974/75

Galway—M. Conneely, N. McInerney, J. Clarke, P Lally, J. McDonagh, S. Silke, I. Clarke, S. Murphy, John Connolly (capt.), G. Coone, F. Burke, P. J. Molloy, M. Barrett, P. J. Qualter, P. Fahy.

Tipperary—J. Duggan (capt.), L. King, J. Keogh, J. Bergin, T O'Connor, N. O'Dwyer, J. Dunlea, J. Kehoe, S. Hogan, F. Loughnane, T. Butler, F. Murphy, J. Flanagan, R. Ryan, P. Quinlan.

1975/76

Kilkenny—N. Skehan, P. Larkin (capt.), N. Orr, B. Cody, P. Lawlor, P. Henderson, G.

Henderson, L. O'Brien, F. Cummins, M. Crotty, M. Ruth, W. Fitzpatrick, Mick Brennan, P. Delaney, E. Keher. Sub: J. Lyng for E. Keher.

T. McCormack and K. Purcell played in drawn game. N. Orr and W. Fitzpatrick were on for replay. Subs in drawn game: W. Fitzpatrick for L. O'Brien, M. Fennelly for K. Purcell, J. Hennessy for T. McCormack.

Clare—S. Durack, M. McKeogh, J. Power (capt.), J. McMahon, G. Loughnane, S. Hehir, J. O'Gorman, M. Moroney, S. Stack, J. Callanan, J. McNamara, C. Honan, T. Crowe, N. Casey, E. O'Connor. Sub: C. Woods for S. Hehir.

C. Woods played in drawn game. J. O'Gorman was on for replay.

1976/77

Clare—S. Durack, J. McMahon, J. Power, J. O'Gorman, G. Loughnane, G. Lohan, S. Stack, M. Moroney, C. Honan, J. McNamara (capt.), E. O'Connor, J. Callanan, T. Crowe, N. Casey, P. O'Connor.

Kilkenny—N. Skehan, P. Larkin, P. Henderson, D. O'Hara, P. Lawlor, B. Cody, G. Henderson, J. Hennessy, F. Cummins, L. O'Brien, M. Ruth, M. Crotty, Mick Brennan, P Delaney, E. Keher.

1977/78

Clare—S. Durack, J. O'Gorman, J. Power, J. McMahon, G. Loughnane, S. Hehir, S. Stack (capt.), M. Moroney, J. Callanan, J. McNamara, N. Casey, C. Honan, P. O'Connor, M. McKeogh, E. O'Connor.

Kilkenny—N. Skehan, P. Larkin, D. O'Hara, P. Henderson, J. Hennessy, G. Henderson, R. Reid, L. O'Brien, F. Cummins, Mick Brennan, M. Ruth, K. Brennan, M. Crotty, T. Malone, W. Fitzpatrick.

1978/79

Tipperary—P. McLoughney, P. Williams (capt.), J. Keogh, T. O'Connor, K. O'Connor, N O'Dwyer, P. Fitzelle, M. Doyle, G. Stapleton, E. O'Shea, J. Williams, P. Queally, F. Loughnane, J. Kehoe, S. Power. Sub. T. Butler for J. Kehoe.

Galway—F. Larkin, N. Mcinerney, J. McDonagh (capt.), I. Clarke, J. Greaney, S. Silke, Jimmy Cooney, John Connolly, S. Mahon, Michael Connolly, Joe Connolly, P. J. Molloy, N. Lane, F Burke, P. Ryan. Subs: M. Earls for S. Silke, F Gantley for M. Connolly.

1979/80

Cork—T. Murphy, D. Burns, B. Murphy, J. Crowley, D. Coughlan, T. Cashman, D. McCurtain (capt.), J. Fenton, P. Moylan, T. Crowley, P. Horgan, D. Buckley, S. O'Leary, R. Cummins, E. O'Donoghue. Sub: J. Barry Murphy for D. Buckley.

J. Horgan, J. Barry Murphy and C. McCarthy played in drawn game. P. Moylan, S. O'Leary and J. Fenton were on for replay. Sub in drawn game: S. O'Leary for C. McCarthy.

Limerick—T. Quaide, D. Murray, L. Enright, D. Punch, L. O'Donoghue, M. Carroll, S. Foley (capt.), J. Carroll, P. Fitzmaurice, E. Grimes, J. Flanagan, B. Carroll, O. O'Connor, J. McKenna, E. Cregan. Sub: G. Mulcahy for B. Carroll.

G. Mulcahy played in drawn game. S. Foley was on for replay. Sub in drawn game: S. Foley for G. Mulcahy.

1980/81

Cork—G. Cunningham, B. Murphy, D. O'Grady (capt.), J. Horgan, D. McCurtain, T. Cashman, N. Kennefick, J. Fenton, P. Moylan, T. Crowley, P. Horgan, Padraig Crowley, S. O'Leary, J. Barry Murphy, E. O'Donoghue. Sub: D. Mulcaby for T. Cashman.

Offaly—C. King, B. Keeshan, E. Coughlan, P. Fluery, T. Conneely, P. Delaney, G. Coughlan, J. Kelly, L. Currams, M. Corrigan, B. Bermingham, P Carroll, P. Kirwan, P. Horan (capt.), D. Owens. Sub T. Donoghue for T. Conneely.

1981/82

Kilkenny—N. Skehan, J. Henderson, B. Cody (capt.), D. O'Hara, N. Brennan, G. Henderson, P. Prendergast, J. Hennessy, F. Cummins, R. Power, G. Fennelly, K. Brennan, Mick Brennan, L. Fennelly, W. Fitzpatrick. Subs: M. Ruth for R. Power, W. Walton for K. Brennan.

Wexford—J. Nolan, B. Murphy, J. Russell, L. Bennett, J. Conran, M. Jacob, C. Doran, P. Courtney, G. O'Connor, J. Fleming, J. Holohan, M. Quigley, S. Kinsella, A. Doran, Johnny Murphy. Sub: E. Walsh for J. Russell.

1982/83

Kilkenny—N. Skehan, J. Henderson, D. O'Hara, P. Neary, N. Brennan, G. Henderson, P. Prendergast, F. Cummins, S. Fennelly, R. Power, G. Fennelly, H. Ryan, W. Fitzpatrick, C. Heffernan, L. Fennelly (Capt). Subs: T. McCormack for J. Henderson, P. Lannon for R. Power.

Limerick—T. Quaide, P. Fitzmaurice, L. Enright (capt.), P. Herbert, L. O'Donoghue, S. Foley, P. Foley, J. Carroll, D. Fitzgerald, P. Kelly, J. Flanagan, M. J. Coffey, O. O'Connor, J. McKenna, M. Rea. Subs: N. Leonard for P. Fitzmaurice, F. Nolan for S. Foley.

1983/84

Limerick—T. Quaide, P. Fitzmaurice, L. Enright (capt.), P. Herbert, M. Lonergan, M. Carroll, P. Foley, J. Carroll, B. Carroll, L. O'Donoghue, D. Fitzgerald, P. Kelly, O. O'Connor, J. McKenna, M. Rea. Sub: J. Flanagan for 0. O'Connor.

Wexford—J. Nolan, E. Cleary, A. Walsh, P. Kenny, J. Conran, G. O'Connor, M. Jacob, P. Courtney, B. Byrne, J. Jordan, James O'Connor, J. McDonald, E. Mythen, M. Quigley, T. Harrington. Subs: J. Walker for E. Mythen, M. O'Connor for J. Conran, Johnny Murphy for B. Byrne.

1984/85

Limerick—T. Quaide, P. Fitzmaurice, L. Enright (capt.), P. Herbert, L. O'Donoghue, M. Carroll, P. Foley, J. Carroll, B. Carroll, P. Kelly, D. Fitzgerald, R. Sampson, O. O'Connor, P. McCarthy, S. Fitzgibbon.

Clare—D. Corry, J. Minogue, S. Hehir, T. Keane, G. Loughnane, M. Meagher, S. Stack, A. Cunningham, D. Coote, C. Lyons, J. Shanahan, J. Callanan, S. Dolan, P. Morey, M. Guilfoyle. Subs: A. Nugent for M. Guilfoyle, P. Lynch for S. Dolan.

1985/86

Kilkenny—K. Fennelly, P. Prendergast, J. Henderson, F. Holohan (capt.), J. Hennessy, G. Henderson, S. Fennelly, G. Fennelly, R. Power, P. Walsh, K. Brennan, J. O'Hara, L. Ryan, L. Fennelly, C. Heffernan. Sub: J. Mulcahy for J. O'Hara.

Galway—P. Murphy, S. Coen, C. Hayes, S. Linnane, O. Kilkenny, P. Piggott, A. Kilkenny, B. Lynskey, S. Mahon, M. Naughton, A. Cunningham, Joe Cooney, B. Forde, N. Lane, P. J. Molloy. Subs: A. Keady for P. Piggott, M. McGrath for B. Forde, M. Connolly (Craughwell) for P. J. Molloy.

1986/87

Galway—P. Murphy, S. Linnane, C. Hayes (capt.), P. Piggott, O. Kilkenny, A. Keady, A. Kilkenny, M. Coleman, S. Mahon, M. McGrath, Joe Cooney, M. Naughton, E. Ryan, B. Lynskey, A. Cunningham. Subs: N. Lane for M. Coleman, M. Coen for S. Mahon.

Clare—E. McMahon, J. Russell, J. Moroney, M. Glynn, G. Loughnane, S. Stack, J. Lee, J. Shanahan, J. Callanan (capt.), G. O'Loughlin, V. O'Loughlin, M. Guilfoyle, C. Lyons, T. Guilfoyle, G. McInerney. Subs: S. Dolan for G. O'Loughlin, A. Cunningham for M. Glynn, V. Donnellan for A. Cunningham.

1987/88

Tipperary—K. Hogan, C. O'Donovan, N. Sheehy, S. Gibson, B. Ryan, J. Kennedy, P. Delaney, J. Hayes, Colm Bonnar, D. Ryan, D. O'Connell, P. O'Neill (capt.), P. Fox, N. English, A. Ryan. Subs: C. Stakelum for D. O'Conneil, J. Leahy for A. Ryan, M. Corcoran for S. Gibson.

Offaly—Jim Troy, J. Miller, A. Fogarty, M. Hanamy, B. Keeshan, M. Coughlan, G. Coughlan, J. Kelly, Joe Dooley, P. O'Connor, D. Fogarty, M. Corrigan, P. Cleary, E. Coughlan, P. Corrigan. Subs: P. J. Martin for M. Coughlan, M. Duignan for P. Corrigan, G. Cahill for P. O'Connor.

1988/89

Galway—J. Commins, S. Linnane, C. Hayes (capt.), O. Kilkenny, P. Finnerty, A. Keady, S. Treacy, M. Coleman, P. Malone, M. McGrath, B. Lynskey, M. Naughton, G. Burke, Joe Cooney, E. Ryan. Subs: N. Lane for B. Lynskey, P. Higgins for P. Finnerty, A. Kilkenny for P. Malone.

Tipperary—K. Hogan, B. Ryan, C. O'Donovan, P. Delaney, R. Stakelum, N. Sheehy, Conal Bonnar, D. Carr, Colm Bonnar, D. Ryan, J. Hayes, J. Leahy, M. Cleary, Cormac Bonnar, P. McGrath (Capt). Subs: J. Cormack for C. O'Donovon, D. O'Connell for J. Hayes.

1989/90

Kilkenny—K. Fennelly (capt.), W. Hennessy, J. Henderson, P. Phelan, J. Power, P. Dwyer, M. Cleere, M. Phelan, L. Ryan, D. J. Carey, R. Power, J. McDonald, E. Morrissey, C. Heffernan, L. Fennelly. Sub: L. McCarthy for L. Fennelly.

New York—J. Duggan, J. Lyons, T. Canty, M. Cosgrove, B. Keeshan, J. Fleming, S. Collison, A. Nugent, S. Donoghue, L. Bergin, I. Conroy, R. Sampson, H. Ryan, W. Lowry, J. McInerney. Sub: M. McCarthy for W. Lowry.

HOME FINAL

Kilkenny—Same as played in final except S. Fennelly (Capt) and W. O'Connor in place of P. Phelan and L. Ryan. Subs: P. Phelan for W. O'Connor, L. Ryan for S. Fennelly.

Wexford—T. Morrissey, N. McDonald, E. Cleary, J. Conran, D. Prendergast, G. O'Connor, L. Dunne, B. Byrne, G. Coady, M. Storey, R. Coleman, James O'Connor, T. Dempsey (capt.), J. Holohan, M. Reck. Subs: M. Fitzhenry for James O'Connor, L. O'Gorman for D. Prendergast.

1990/91

Offaly—Jim Troy, B. Hennessy, S. McGuckian, M. Hanamy, H. Rigney, R. Mannion, B. Whelahan, J. Pilkington, J. Kelly, Johnny Dooley, D. Regan, Joe Dooley, D. Owens (capt.), M. Duignan, M. Corrigan. Subs: B. Dooley for M. Corrigan, B. Kelly for Joe Dooley.

Wexford—T. Morrissey, N. McDonald, G. Cushe, P. Bridges, S. Flood, L. Dunne, L. O'Gorman, B. Byrne, G. O'Connor, M. Storey, E. Synnott, D. Prendergast, T. Dempsey, J. Holohan, S. Wickham. Subs: J. Conran for S. Wickham, D. Guiney for B. Byrne.

1991/92

Limerick—T. Quaid, B. Finn, P. Carey, D. Nash, M. Houlihan, C. Carey, A. Garvey, M. Reale, G. Hegarty, M. Galligan, A. Carmody, G. Kirby, L. Garvey, J. O'Connor, S. Fitzgibbon. Subs – R. Sampson for L. Garvey, P. Davoren for Galligan.

Tipperary—K. Hogan, P. Delaney, N. Sheehy, G. Frend, B. Ryan, C. Bonnar, R. Ryan, D. Carr, E. Ryan, M. Cleary, J. Hayes, C. Stakelum, P. Fox, D. Ryan, N. English.
Sub – J. Leahy for Hayes.

1992/93

Cork—G. Cunningham, J. Considine, S. O'Gorman, L. Forde, D. Walsh, J. Cashman, B. Corcoran (capt.), C. Casey, S. McCarthy, T. McCarthy, P. Buckley, T. Mulcahy, G. Manley, P. O'Callaghan, B. Egan. Subs: A. O'Sullivan for J. Cashman, M. Foley for P. O'Callaghan, J. Fitzgibbon for T. Mulcahy.

T. Kingston and K. Hennessy played in first and second games. P. Buckley played in first and third games. P. Hartnett played in first game. G. Cunningham was on for third game. L. Forde and P. O'Callaghan played in second and third games. Subs in second game P. Buckley for P. O'Callaghan, G. Cunningham for T. Kingston, G. Fitzgerald for K. Hennessy.

Wexford—D. Fitzhenry, S. Flood, G. Cushe, N. McDonald, John O'Connor, L. Dunne, T. Dunne, G. O'Connor, T. Dempsey, M. Storey, J. Bolger, L. O'Gorman, E. Scallan, E. Cleary, L. Murphy. Subs: C. McBride for J. Bolger, B. Byrne for E. Cleary.

Wexford played the same team in all three games. Subs in first game: D. Guiney for N. McDonald, B. Byrne for T. Dempsey. Subs in the second game: B. Byrne for J. Bolger, E. Synnott for E. Scallan, C. McBride for E. Synnott, D. Prendergast for L. O'Gorman.

1993/94

Tipperary—J. Grace, G. Frend, N. Sheehy, M. Ryan, R. Ryan, M. O'Meara, Conal Bonnar, P. King, J. Hayes, J. LeaLy, L. McGrath, A. Ryan, D. Ryan, A. Crosse, M. Cleary. Sub: T. Dunne for A. Ryan.

Galway—R. Burke, P. Cooney, S. Treacy, N. Power, P. Kelly, G. McInerney, T. Helebert, M. Coleman, P. Malone, J. Campbell, B. Keogh, J. McGrath, N. Shaughnessy, J. Rabbitte, L. Burke. Subs: M. McGrath for J. McGrath, M. Donoghue for T. Helebert, F Forde for J. Campbell,

1994/95

Kilkenny—M. Walsh, E. O'Connor, P. Dwyer, L. Simpson, L. Keoghan, E. Dwyer, W. O'Connor, M. Phelan, W. Hennessy (capt.), A. Ronan, J. Power, P. J. Delaney, E. Morrissey, D. J. Carey, D. Byrne. Subs: C. Brennan for M. Phelan, D. Gaffney for J. Power.

Clare—D. Fitzgerald, M. O'Halloran, B. Lohan, F. Lohan, L. Doyle, S. McMahon, A. Daly (capt.), K. Morrissey, S. Sheehy, P. J. O'Connell, C. Clancy, J. O'Connor, J. McInerney, E. Taaffe, G. O'Loughlin. Subs: F. Touhy for C. Clancy, F Hegarty for K. Morrissey, C. Lyons for J. McInerney.

1995/96

Galway—M. Darcy, T. Helebert, P. Cooney, G. McInerney, C. O'Donovan, N. Shaughnessy, M. Donoghue, M. Coleman (capt.), B. Keogh, J. Rabbitte, C. Moore, L. Burke, K. Broderick, Joe Cooney, F. Forde. Subs: S. Treacy for P. Cooney, P. Kelly for C. O'Donovon.

Tipperary—B. Cummins, G. Frend, P. Shelly, M. Ryan, Conal Bonnar, Colm Bonnar, B. Carroll, C. Gleeson, G. O'Meara, R. Ryan, E. Tucker, J. Leahy, M. Cleary, N. English, L. Cahill. Subs: A. Ryan for E. Tucker, K. Tucker for M. Cleary.

1997

Limerick—J. Quaid, S. McDonagh, M. Nash, D. Nash, D. Clarke, T. J. Ryan, J. Foley, C. Carey, S. O'Neill, M. Galligan, M. Foley, B. Foley, J. Moran, O. Moran, G. Kirby (Capt).

Galway—P. Costelloe, G. Kennedy, L. Hodgins, V. Maher, B. Keogh, C. Moore, M. Donoghue, L. Burke, N. Shaughnessy, J. Campbell, M. Coleman, J. McGrath, D. Coen, J. Rabbitte, O. Fahy. Subs: A. Kerins for N. Shaughnessy, F. Forde for J. McGrath.

1998

Cork—G. Cunningham, F. Ryan, J. Browne, D. O'Sullivan (capt.), M. Landers, B. Corcoron, S. Óg Ó hAilpín, P. Ryan, M. Daly, S. McGrath, F. McCormack, K. Morrison, S. O'Farrell, A. Browne, J. Deane. Sub: B. Egan for M. Daly.

Waterford—B. Landers, T. Feeney; S. Cullinane, M. O'Sullivan, S. Frampton (capt.), F. Hartley, B. Greene, A. Browne, P. Queally, D. Shanahan, K. McGrath, D. Bennett, B. O'Sullivan, A. Kirwan, P Flynn. Sub: M. White for B. O'Sullivan.

1999

Tipperary—B. Cummins; D. Fahy, F. Heaney, L. Sheedy; B. Horgan, D. Kennedy, E. Corcoran; E. Enright, D. Carr; T. Dunne (capt.), D. Ryan, B. O'Meara, L. Cahill, P. Shelly, J. Leahy. Subs: Conal Bonner for B. Horgan, C. Gleeson for E. Enright, G. Maguire for P. Shelly.

Galway—D. Howe; P. Huban, B. Feeney, L.

Hodgins; N. Shaughnessy, F. Flynn, P. Hardiman; T. Kavanagh, L. Burke, A. Kerins, C. Moore (capt.), K. Broderick; O. Fahy, M. Kerins, E. Cloonan. Subs: N. Kenny for T. Kavanagh, F. Healy for C. Moore.

2000

Galway – M.Crimmins, L.Hodgins, B.Feeney, V.Maher, F.Gantley, C.Moore, P.Hardiman, A.Kerins, R.Gantley, J.Rabbitte, M.Kerins, D.Tierney, O.Canning, O.Fahy, F.Healy.

Tipperary – B.Cummins, L.Sheedy, P.Maher, M.Ryan, P.Ormonde, D.Kennedy, E.Corcoran, J.Carroll, B.O'Meara, M.O'Leary, D.Ryan, T.Dunne, P.O'Brien, P.Shelley, G.Maguire. Subs – D.Fahy for Sheedy, E.O'Neill for Maguire, J.Leahy for O'Meara.

2001

Tipperary – B.Cummins, T.Costello, P.Maher, P.Ormonde, J.Leahy, E.Corcoran, M.Ryan, C.Gleeson, T.Dunne, M.O'Leary, E.Enright, L.Cahill, E.Kelly, D.Ryan, L.Corbett. Subs – B.O'Meara for Cahill, E.O'Neill for D.Ryan.

Clare – D.Fitzgerald, C.Forde, B.Lohan, F.Lohan, L.Doyle, J.Reddan, G.Quinn, O.Baker, C.Lynch, T.Griffin, J.O'Connor, G.Considine, D.Forde, N.Gilligan, B.Murphy. Subs – A.Markham for Considine, S.McMahon for Doyle, P.J.O'Connell for Griffin.

2002

Kilkenny – J.McGarry, M.Kavanagh, N.Hickey, P.Larkin, R.Mullally, P.Barry, J.J.Delaney, D.Lyng, P.Tennyson, J.Hoyne, H.Shefflin, A.Comerford, E.Brennan, M.Comerford, S.Grehan. Subs – K.Power for Grehan, S.Dowling for Tennyson, B.Dowling for Power.

Cork – D. Óg Cusack, W.Sherlock, D.O'Sullivan, F.Ryan, D.Barrett, J.Browne, S. Óg Ó hAilpín, A.Cummins, J.Gardiner, J.O'Connor, K.Murphy, N.McCarthy, E.Collins, A.Browne, B.O'Connor. Subs – T.McCarthy for Gardiner, K.Murray for N.McCarthy, P.Ryan for Murphy.

2003

Kilkenny – P.J.Ryan, M.Kavanagh, N.Hickey, P.Larkin, R.Mullally, P.Barry, J.J.Delaney, D.Lyng, P.Tennyson, J.Hoyne, H.Shefflin, T.Walsh, D.J.Carey, M.Comerford, E.Brennan. Subs – J.Coogan for Tennyson, A.Cummins for Larkin, C.Carter for Hoyne.

Tipperary – B.Cummins, M.Maher, P.Maher, B.Dunne, B.Horgan, D.Kennedy, P.Kelly, T.Dunne, N.Morris, J.Carroll, C.Gleeson, L.Cahill, E.Kelly, G.O'Grady, L.Corbett. Subs – E.Brislane for Morris, J.Devane for P.Maher, E.O'Neill for O'Grady.

2004

Galway – L.Donoghue, D.Joyce, D.Cloonan, O.Canning, D.Hardiman, David Hayes, D.Collins, F.Healy, T. Óg Regan, A.Cullinane, D.Forde, A.Kerins, Damien Hayes, E.Cloonan, K.Broderick. Subs – F.Moore for Regan, R.Gantley for Collins, D.Tierney for Cullinane, O.Fahy for Damien Hayes.

Waterford – S.Brenner, J.Murray, T.Feeney, E.McGrath, B.Phelan, T.Browne, K.McGrath, M.Walsh, D.Bennett, D.Shanahan, A.Moloney, E.Kelly, S.Prendergast, P.Flynn, J.Mullane. Subs – J.Kennedy for Moloney, P.O'Brien for Kennedy, E.Murphy for Bennett.

2005

Kilkenny – J.McGarry, J.Ryall, N.Hickey, J.Tyrell, R.Mullally, P.Barry, J.J.Delaney, B.Barry, D.Lyng, M.Comerford, E.Larkin, T.Walsh, R.Power, D.J.Carey, H.Shefflin. Subs – E.Brennan for Power, M.Kavanagh for Ryall.

Clare – D.Fitzgerald, F.Lohan, B.Lohan, G.O'Grady, A.Markham, S.McMahon, G.Quinn, B.O'Connell, C.Lynch, C.Plunkett, D.McMahon, T.Carmody, T.Griffin, N.Gilligan, A.Quinn. Subs – B.Quinn for F.Lohan, B.Nugent for Plunkett, D.O'Connell for A.Quinn, D.Clancy for B.O'Connell.

2006

Kilkenny – J.McGarry, M.Kavanagh, J.J.Delaney, N.Hickey, J.Tyrrell, J.Tennyson, T.Walsh, D.Lyng, R.Mullally, R.Power, M.Comerford, E.Larkin, J.Fitzpatrick, H.Shefflin, A.Fogarty. Subs – W.O'Dwyer for Power, M.Fennelly for Lyng.

Limerick – B.Murray, D.Reale, T.J.Ryan, M.Foley, O.Moran, B.Geary, D.Moloney, D.Ryan, D.O'Grady, M.O'Brien, S.Lucey, C.Fitzgerald, A.O'Shaughnessy, B.Begley, B.Foley. Subs – N.Moran for O'Brien, S.Hickey for M.Foley, P.O'Grady for D.O'Grady.

2007

Waterford – C.Hennessy, A.Kearney, E.Murphy, D.Prendergast, T.Browne, K.McGrath, J.Murray, M.Walsh, J.Kennedy, D.Shanahan, E.Kelly, S.Molumphy, S.Walsh, S.Prendergast, J.Mullane. Subs – P.Ryan for S.Walsh, E.McGrath for Murray, S.O'Sullivan for Kennedy.

Kilkenny – P.J.Ryan, N.Hickey, B.Hogan, J.J.Delaney, J.Tyrrell, P.J.Delaney, T.Walsh, D.Lyng, W.O'Dwyer, E.Brennan, M.Comerford, R.Power, H.Shefflin,

J.Fitzpatrick, A.Fogarty. Subs – E.Larkin for Fitzpatrick, E.McCormack for Fogarty.

2008

Tipperary – B.Cummins, E.Buckley, P.Curran, C.O'Brien, E.Corcoran, C.O'Mahony, S.Maher, B.Dunne, S.McGrath, S.Butler, R.O'Dwyer, J.Woodlock, E.Kelly, L.Corbett, W.Ryan. Subs – S.Callinan for O'Dwyer, J.O'Brien for Dunne, A.Byrne for Corcoran, D.Hickey for Ryan.

Galway – J.Skehill, C.Dervan, T.Óg Regan, F.Moore, S.Kavanagh, J.Lee, A.Cullinane, K.Hynes, R.Murray, G.Farragher, F.Healy, D.Hayes, N.Healy, I.Tannian, J.Canning. Subs – A.Kerins for N.Healy, D.Forde for Farragher, A.Callanan for Murray, K.Wade for Tannian.

2009

Kilkenny – P.J.Ryan, M.Kavanagh, J.J.Delaney, J.Tyrrell, T.Walsh, B.Hogan, J.Ryall, J.Tennyson, M.Rice, R.Hogan, H.Shefflin, E.Larkin, E.Brennan, T.J.Reid, A.Fogarty. Subs – M.Comerford for Hogan, M.Grace for Comerford, J.Fitzpatrick for Shefflin, S.Cummins for Kavanagh.

Tipperary – B.Cummins, P.Stapleton, P.Curran, C.O'Brien, D.Fanning, Padraic Maher, S.Maher, T.Stapleton, S.McGrath, J.Woodlock, S.Callanan, J.O'Brien, N.McGrath, M.Webster, L.Corbett. Subs – B.Maher for Fanning, H.Maloney for S.Maher, B.Dunne for Maloney, S.Hennessy for Woodlock, D.Fitzgerald for T.Stapleton, Patrick Maher for Webster, E.Buckley for Padraic Maher.

INTERPROVINCIAL HURLING CHAMPIONSHIP 1927-2009

Munster (45) - 1928, 1929, 1930, 1931, 1934, 1935, 1937, 1938, 1939, 1940, 1942, 1943, 1944, 1945, 1946, 1948, 1949, 1950, 1951, 1952, 1953, 1955, 1957, 1958, 1959, 1960, 1961, 1963, 1966, 1968, 1969, 1970, 1976, 1978, 1981, 1984, 1985, 1992, 1995, 1996, 1997, 2000, 2001, 2005, 2007.
Leinster (26) - 1927, 1932, 1933, 1936, 1941, 1954, 1956, 1962, 1964, 1965, 1967, 1971, 1972, 1973, 1974, 1975, 1977, 1979, 1988, 1993, 1999, 2002, 2003, 2006, 2008, 2009.

Connacht (11) - 1947, 1980, 1982, 1983, 1986, 1987, 1989, 1991, 1994, 1998, 2004.

No competition in 1990.

1927—November 21, 1926, Portlaoise:
Leinster 7-6, Connocht 3 -5.
March 17, 1927, Croke Park:
Final: Leinster 1-11, Munster 2-6.
1928—February 12, Tuam:
Munster 7-3, Connacht 2-4.
March 17, Croke Park:
Final: Munster 2-2, Leinster 1-2.
1929—Ulster not competing, Leinster had a bye, and Connacht being struck out, Munster got a wolk-over.
March 17, Croke Park:
Final: Munster 5-3, Leinster 3-1.
1930—March 17, Croke Park:
Final: Munster 4-6, Leinster 2-7.
1931—February 8, Birr:
Semi-final: Munster 10-9, Connacht 1-2.
March 17, Croke Park:
Final: Munster 1-12, Leinster 2-6.
1932—February 28, Birr:
Semi-final: Leinster 6-8, Connacht 2-4.
March 17, Croke Park:
Final: Leinster 6-8; Munster 4-4.
1933—February 19, Portumna:
Munster 4-5, Connacht 3-7.
March 17, Croke Park:
Final: Leinster 4-6, Munster 3-6.
1934—February 25, Roscrea:
Leinster 7-6, Connacht 4-6.
March 17, Croke Park:
Final: Munster 6-3, Leinster 3-2.
1935—February 24, Portumna:
Munster 7-5, Connacht 4-4.
March 17, Croke Park:
Final: Munster 3-4, Leinster 3-0.
1936—February 16, Roscrea:
Leinster 2-7, Connacht 2-4.
March 17, Croke Park:
Final: Leinster 2-8, Munster 3-4.
1937—February 14, Ennis:
Munster 4-5, Connocht 3-1.
March 17, Croke Park:
Final: Munster 1-9, Leinster 3-1.
1938—February 20, Ballinasloe:
Connacht 3-6, Leinster 3-6.
Replay, February 27, Tullamore:
Leinster 4-5, Connacht 0-3.
March 17, Croke Park:
Final: Munster 6-2, Leinster 4-3.
1939—February 26, Birr:
Munster 8-5, Connacht 0-2.
March 17, Croke Park:
Final: Munster 4-4, Leinster 1-6.
1940—February 25, Birr:
Leinster 4-5, Connacht 1-4.
March 17, Croke Park:
Final: Munster 4-9, Leinster 5-4.
1941—February 16, Golway:
Munster 7-5, Connacht, 0-6.
March 16, Croke Park:

Final: Leinster 2-5, Munster 2-4.
1942—February 15, Ballinasloe:
Leinster 7-8, Connacht 4-7.
March 17, Croke Park:
Final: Munster 4-9, Leinster 4-5.
1943—February 14, Nenagh:
Munster 3-5, Connacht 3-2.
March 17, Croke Park:
Final: Munster 4-3, Leinster 3-5.
1944—February 13, Birr:
Connacht 4-5, Leinster 1-5.
February 20, Croke Park:
Munster 9-3, Ulster 3-1.
March 17, Croke Park:
Final: Munster 4-10, Connacht 4-4.
(Note: The year 1944 represented Ulster's first appearance in the competition.)
1945—February 11, Belfast:
Ulster 3-1, Leinster 2-3.
February 11, Galway:
Munster 2-5, Connacht 2-5.
Replay, March 4, Limerick:
Munster 4-8, Connacht 3-7.
March 17, Croke Park:
Final: Munster 6-8, Ulster 2-0.
1946—February 17, Croke Park:
Connacht 4-14, Ulster 1-7.
February 17, Waterford:
Munster 0-6, Leinster 1-2.
March 17, Croke Park:
Final: Munster 3-12, Connacht 4-8.
1947—March 9, Croke Park:
Connacht 2-6, Leinster 2-5.
March 16, Croke Park:
Munster 9-7, Ulster, 0-0.
April 6, Croke Park:
Final: Connacht 2-5, Munster 1-1.
1948—February 15, Lurgan:
Leinster 5-5, Ulster 4-2.
February 15, Ballinasloe:
Munster 6-5, Connacht 1-4.
March 17, Croke Park:
Final: Munster 3-5, Leinster 2-5.
1949—February 13, Croke Park:
Munster 2-8, Leinster 1-8. Connacht 5-7, Ulster 2-7.
March 17, Croke Park:
Final: Munster 5-3, Connacht 2-9.
1950—February 12, Croke Park:
Munster 9-4, Ulster 3-2.
February 12, Ballinasloe:
Leinster 3-10, Connacht 2-6.
March 17, Croke Park:
Final: Munster 0-9, Leinster 1-3.
1951—February 18, Croke Park:
Leinster 7-9, Ulster 0-2. Munster 6-7, Connacht 2-7.
March 17, Croke Park
Final: Munster 4-9, Leinster 3-6.
1952—February 17, Cork:
Munster 4-8, Leinster 3-5.
February 17, Corrigan Park:
Connacht 7-6, Ulster 3-0.
March 17, Croke Park:
Final: Munster 5-11, Connacht 4-2.
1953—February 8, Croke Park
Munster 8-6, Ulster 1-5.
February 22, Portlaoise:
Leinster 7-9, Connacht 4-3.
March 17, Croke Park:
Final: Munster 5-7, Leinster 5-5.
1954—February 21, Croke Park:
Munster 4-12, Connacht 3-7. Leinster 8-7, Ulster 1-1.
March 17, Croke Park:
Final: Leinster 0-9, Munster 0-5.
1955—March 13, Casement Park:
Connacht 5-10, Ulster 2-4.
March 17, Croke Park:
Munster 3-10, Leinster, 2-9.
April 3, Croke Park:
Final: Munster 6-8, Connocht 3-4.
1956—February 19, Casement Park:
Munster 5-13, Ulster 2-6.
February 26, Ballinasloe:
Leinster 5-7, Connacht 2-9.
March 17, Croke Park:
Final: Leinster 5-11, Munster 1 -7.
1957—February 1 7, Limerick:
Munster 3-11, Connacht 3-11 (draw)
Replay: March 3, Limerick:
Munster 6-6, Connacht 0-10.
February 1 7, Casement Park:
Leinster 7-7, Ulster 2-5.
March 17, Croke Park:
Final: Munster 5-7, Leinster 2-5.
1958—February 16, Casement Park:
Leinster 8-10, Ulster 3-3.
March 2, Galway:
Munster 2-15, Connacht 1-8.
March 17, Croke Park:
Final: Munster 3-7, Leinster 3-5.
1959—March 17, Croke Park:
Connacht 2-14, Leinster 3-7.
June 7, Croke Park:
Final: Munster 7-11, Connacht 2-6.
Note: Ulster did not compete.
1960—February 21, Limerick:
Munster 5-12, Connacht 1-9.
February 21, Croke Park:
Leinster 8-6, Ulster 5-3.
March 1 7, Croke Park:
Final: Munster 6-6, Leinster 2-7.
1961—February 19, Ballinasloe:
Leinster 5-8, Connacht 3-7.
February 19, Casement Park:
Munster 3-13, Ulster 1-2.
March 17, Croke Park:
Final: Munster 4-12, Leinster 3-9.
1962—February 18, Ballinsoloe:
Munster 6-11, Connacht 1-3.
February 25, Cavan:
Leinster 11-4, Ulster 6-3.
March 17, Croke Park:

Final: Leinster 1-11, Munster 1-9.
1963—February 24, Croke Park:
Munster 9-7, Ulster 3-5. Leinster 5-14, Connacht 3-3.
March 17, Croke Park:
Final: Munster 5-5, Leinster 5-5.
Replay, 14 April, Croke Park:
Munster 2-8, Leinster 2-7.
1964—February 16, Limerick:
Munster 4-9, Connacht 3-5.
February 16, Croke Park:
Leinster 8-9, Ulster 1-4.
March 17, Croke Park:
Final: Leinster 3-7, Munster, 2-9.
1965—February 28, Casement Park:
Munster 3-11, Ulster 3-2.
February 21, Galway:
Leinster 4-9, Connacht 2-3.
March 17, Croke Park:
Final: Leinster 3-11, Munster 0-9.
1966—February 27, Ballinasloe:
Munster 6-10, Connacht 3-3.
March 6, Ballybay:
Leinster 6-14, Ulster 3-7.
March 17, Croke Park:
Final: Munster 3-13, Leinster 3-11.
1967—February 26, Croke Park:
Leinster 10-10, Connacht 3-2.
Munster 6-11, Ulster 2-6.
March 17, Croke Park:
Final: Leinster 2-14, Munster 3-5.
1968—February 25, Thurles:
Munster 3-15, Connacht 1-5.
February 25, Navan:
Leinster 5-10, Ulster 3-8.
March 17, Croke Park:
Final: Munster 0-14, Leinster 0-10.
1969—February 23, Casement Park:
(Preliminary Round):
Connacht 3-9, U~ster 3-8.
March 2, Ballinasloe:
Connacht 1-11, Leinster 2-6.
March 17, Croke Park:
Final: Connacht 2-9, Munster 2-9.
Replay, April 6, Galway:
Munster 3-13, Connacht 4-4.
1970—February 8, Galway
(Preliminary Round): Ulster 3-6, Connacht 2-6.
February 22, Croke Park:
Semi-final: Munster 6-14, Ulster 3-6.
March 17, Croke Park:
Final: Munster 2-15, Leinster 0-9.
1971—February 21, Casement Park:
(Preliminary Round): Connacht 4- 11 , Ulster 1-4.
February 28, Athlone. Semi-final:
Leinster 5-13, Connacht 4-14.
March 17, Croke Park:
Final: Leinster 2-17, Munster 2-12.
1972—January 30, Croke Park:
(Preliminary Round): Combined Universities 0-5, Ulster, 1-1. Abandoned owing to snow.
February 6, Croke Park:
Refixture: Combined Universities 0-14, Ulster 1-7.
February 20, Croke Park:
Semi-final: Leinster 3-12, Universities of Ireland 2-13.
February 20, Portumna:
Semi-final: Munster 2-10 Connacht 2-8.
March 17, Croke Park:
Final: Leinster 3-12, Munster 1-10.
1973—January 28, Croke Park:
(Preliminary Round): Combined Universities 6-13, Ulster 1-7.
February 18, Croke Park:
Semi-final: Leinster 4-13, Combined Universities 0-9.
February 18, Cork:
Semi-final: Munster 3-10, Connacht 2-7.
March 17, Croke Park:
Final: Leinster 1-13, Munster 2-8.
1974—January 27, Croke Park:
(Preliminory Round): Combined Universities 4-10, Ulster 2-7
February 17, Kilkenny:
Semi-final: Leinster 3-13, Connacht 3-6.
February 17, Limerick:
Semi-final: Munster 5-11, Combined Universities 2-7.
March 18, Croke Park:
Final: Leinster 2-15, Munster 1-13.
1975—February 16, Parnell Park:
Semi-final: Munster 4-16, Ulster 2-5.
February 16, Ballinasloe:
Semi-final: Leinster 1-11, Connacht 1 -7.
March 17, Croke Park:
Final: Leinster 2-9, Munster 1-11.
1976—February 15, Croke Park:
Semi-final: Leinster 6-15, Ulster 0-12.
February 15, Ballinasloe:
Semi-final: Munster 2-10, Connacht 3-6.
March 17, Croke Park:
Final: Munster 4-9, Leinster 4-8.
1977—February 13, Enniscorthy:
Semi-final: Leinster 1-12, Connacht 2-5.
February 13, Croke Park:
Semi-final: Munster 3-17, Ulster 3-6.
March 17, Croke Park:
Final: Leinster 2-17, Munster 1-13.
1978—April 16, Pairc Ui Caoimh:
Semi-final: Munster 0-20, Connacht. 1-11.
April 23, Corrigan Park:
Semi-finai: Leinster 3-17, Ulster 1-13.
May 7, Pairc Ui Caoimh:
Final: Munster 2-13, Leinster 1-11.
1979—March 11, Ballinasloe:
Semi-final: Connacht 4-9, Munster 2-7.
March 11, Croke Park, Semi-final:
Leinster 1-19, Ulster 0-11.
April 1, Thurles:

Final: Leinster 1-13, Connacht 1-9.
1980—February 17, Ballinsaloe:
Semi-final: Connacht 1-13, Leinster 1-10 (after extra time).
February 17, Croke Park:
Semi-final: Munster 4-16, Ulster 1-10.
March 17, Croke Park:
Final: Connacht 1-5, Munster 0-7.
1981—March 1, Birr:
Semi-final: Leinster 0-11, Connacht 0-6.
March 1, Newbridge. Semi-final: Munster 5-13, Ulster 1-8.
March 17, Ennis:
Final: Munster 2-16, Leinster 2-6.
1982—February 14, Galway:
Semi-final: Connacht 1-1 3, Munster 2-8.
February 14, Casement Park:
Semi-final: Leinster 3-15, Ulster 2-5.
March 17, Tullamore:
Final: Connacht 3-8, Leinster 2-9.
1983—February 6, Croke Park:
Semi-final: Leinster 3-16, Ulster 1-8.
February 6, Limerick:
Semi-final: Connacht 1-9, Munster 0-9.
March 17, Cavan:
Final: Connacht 0-10, Leinster 1-5.
1984—March 17, Ballinasloe:
Semi-final: Leinster 2-10, Connacht O-5.
March 17, Limerick:
Semi-final: Munster 3-21, Ulster 1-7.
March 18, Ennis:
Final Munster 1-18, Leinster 2-9.
1985—January 27, Birr:
Semi-final: Connacht 1-12, Leinster 2-6.
January 27, Newcastle:
Semi-final: Munster 3-16, Ulster 2-6.
March 18: Thurles: Final: Munster 3-6, Connacht 1-11.
1986—February 16, Galway.
Semi-final: Connacht 1-10, Leinster 1-9.
February 16, Croke Park:
Semi-final: Munster 1-19, Ulster 0-11.
March 17, Ballinasloe:
Final: Connacht 3-11, Munster 0-11.
1987—October 3, Ennis:
Semi-finals: Connacht 5-13, Ulster 0-15. Leinster 1-16, Munster 1-11.
October 4, Ennis:
Final: Connacht 2-14, Leinster 1-14.
1988—October 15, Corrigan Park:
Semi-finals: Connacht 4-13, Munster 2-11. Leinster 1-13, Ulster 1-8.
October 16, Casement Park:
Final: Leinster 2-14, Connacht 1-12.
1989—October 7, Wexford:
Semi-final: Munster 3-31, Ulster 1-22 (after extra time).
October 7, Wexford:
Semi-final: Connacht 1-19, Leinster 2-15.
October 8, Wexford:
Final: Connacht 4-16, Munster 3-17.
1990—No competition.
1991—March 10, Pairc Ui Chaoimh:
Semi-final: Munster 2-19, Leinster 1-10.
March 10, Athenry:
Semi-final: Connacht 1-11, Ulster I -6.
April 7, Croke Park:
Final: Connacht 1-13, Munster 0-12.
1992—March 14, Kilkenny:
Semi-finals: Munster 1-12, Leinster 0-10. Ulster 2-6, Connacht 0-7.
March 15, Kilkenny:
Final: Munster 3-12, Ulster 1-8.
1993—October 10, Tullamore:
Semi-final: Leinster 3-13, Connacht 1-9.
October 10, Casement Park:
Semi-final: Ulster 0-21, Munster 0-18.
November 7, Final: Leinster 1-15, Ulster 2-6.
1994—February 6, Kilkenny:
Semi-final: Leinster 2-17, Ulster 0-8.
February 6, Tulla:
Semi-final: Connacht 1-10, Munster 0-9.
February 20, Thurles:
Final: Connacht 1-11, Leinster 1-10.
1995—February 5, Ballinasloe:
Semi-final: Ulster 2-10, Connacht 0-14.
February 5, Limerick
Semi-final: Munster 2-25, Leinster 5-12 (after extra time).
April 2, Croke Park:
Final: Munster 0-13, Ulster 1-9.
1996—February 25, Ballinasloe:
Semi-final: Leinster 2-16, Connacht 0-18 (after extra time).
February 25, Ennis:
Semi-final: Munster 5-13, Ulster 0-7.
March 18, Ennis:
Final: Munster 2-20, Leinster 0-10.
1997—November 8, Ballinasloe:
Semi-Finals: Leinster 2-16, Ulster 1-9. Munster 1-19, Connacht 2-15.
November 9, Ballinasloe:
Final: Munster 0-14, Leinster 0-10.
1998—November 8, Kilkenny:
Semi-final: Leinster 2-15, Munster 0-9.
November 8, Corrigan Park:
Semi-final: Connacht 3-18, Ulster 1-12.
November 22, Kilkenny:
Final: Leinster 0-16, Connacht 2-9.
1999—November 7, Casement Park:
Semi-final: Munster 0-29, Ulster 3-14.
November 7, Birr:
Semi-final: Connacht 1-14, Leinster 1-10
November 25, Semple Stadium, Thurles:
Final: Connacht 2-13, Munster 1-15.
2000—November 11 at Dicksboro:
Semi-finals – Leinster 1-15, Ulster 1-7.
November 11 at Freshford:
Munster 1-19, Connacht 3-7.
Final – November 12 at Nowlan Park:
Munster 3-15, Leinster 2-15.
2001—November 10 at Templemore:
Semi-finals – Connacht 4-16, Ulster 1-9.

November 10 at Nenagh:
Munster 2-20, Leinster 3-12.
Final – November 11 at Nenagh:
Munster 1-21, Connacht 1-15.

2002—November 2 at Nowlan Park:
Semi-finals –
Leinster 3-18, Connacht 2-13.
November 2 at Nowlan Park:
Munster 5-18, Ulster 0-10.
Final – November 3 at Nowlan Park:
Leinster 4-15, Munster 3-17.

2003—October 18 at Limerick:
Semi-finals –
Connacht 1-20, Munster 1-16.
October 19 at Casement Park:
Leinster 5-16, Ulster 2-10.
Final – November 8 at Rome:
Leinster 4-9, Connacht 2-12.

2004—October 23 at Casement Park:
Semi-finals – Connacht 2-24, Ulster 2-11.
October 24 at Croke Park:
Munster 1-21, Leinster 0-13.
Final – December 5 at Salthill:
Connacht 1-15, Munster 0-9.

2005—Semi-final – October 23 at Loughrea:
Leinster 1-25, Connacht 0-10.
Semi-final – October 23 at Casement Park:
Munster 0-25, Ulster 1-13.
Final – November 6 at Boston:
Munster 1-21, Leinster 2-14.

2006—Semi-final – October 14 at Parnell Park:
Leinster 2-19, Ulster 0-12.
Semi-final – October 15 at Ennis:
Connacht 2-17, Munster 1-16.
Final – October 28 at Salthill:
Leinster 1-23, Connacht 0-17.

2007—Semi-final– October 13 at Fermoy:
Munster 1-21, Leinster 1-13.
Semi-final – October 20 at Ballybofey:
Connacht 1-28, Ulster 4-13.
Final – October 27 at Croke Park:
Munster 2-22, Connacht 2-19.

2008—Semi-final– October 25 at Fermoy:
Munster 2-14, Ulster 1-12.
Semi-final – October 25 at Kiltoom:
Leinster 2-11, Connacht 1-10.
Final – November 1 at Portlaoise:
Leinster 1-15, Munster 1-12.

2009—Semi-final – February 21 at Salthill:
Connacht 2-20, Munster 2-18.
Semi-final – February 21 at Casement Park: Leinster 4-14, Ulster 0-8.
Final – March 14 at Abu Dhabi:
Leinster 3-18, Connacht 1-17.

INTERPROVINCIAL HURLING TEAMS 1927-2009

1927

Leinster—Dr. T. Daly (goal), Ed. Tobin, P. Mclnerney, G. Howard, M. Gill, D. O'Neill, E. Fahy, Jas. Walsh, M. Power (Dublin), J. Byrne (Laois), W. Dunphy, E. Doyle, L. Meagher, J. Roberts, H. Meagher (Kilkenny).

Munster—Seán Óg Murphy, E. Coughlan, E. O'Connell, M. Murphy, J. Regan, J. Hurley, P. Aherne, M. Aherne (Cork), M. Murphy (goal), J. J. Kinnane, M. Cross, W. Gleeson {Limerick), M. D'Arcy, P. Cahill, M. Kennedy (Tipperary).

1928

Munster—Seán Óg Murphy, E. O'Connell, D. B. Murphy, J. Hurley, E. Coughlan (Cork), T. Shinny (goal), J. J. Kinnane, M. Fitzgibbon, T. Conway (Limerick), P. Cahill, M. Kennedy, J. J. Callanan, P. Purcell, M. Cronin (Tipperary), T. Considine (Clare). Sub.: M. Leahy (Cork).

Leinster—M. Gill, T. Daly (goal), P. Mclnerney, J. Walsh, E. Tobin, G. Howard, D. O'Neill, M. Power, E. Fahey, T. Barry (Dublin), W. Dunphy, E. Doyle, H. Meagher (Kilkenny), J. Byrne, P. Kelly (Laois).

1929

Munster—Seán Óg Murphy, D. B. Murphy, J. O'Regan, M. O'Connell, E. Coughlan, M. Aherne (Cork), T. Shinny (goal), M. Fitzgibbon, T. Conway, M. Cross (Limerick), J. J. Doyle, T. Considine (Clare), P. Purcell, P. Cahill, M. Kennedy (Tipperary). Sub.: C. Keane (Tipperary) for T. Conway.

Leinster—M. Gill, G. Howard, T. Barry, P. Mclnerney, J. Walsh, M. Power (Dublin), R. Collins (goal) (Meath), J. Byrne, E. Tobin, D. O'Neill, J. Murphy (Laois), P. Byrne, P. Kealy, L. Meagher (Kilkenny), W. Cordial (Offaly).

1930

Munster—D. B. Murphy, J. O'Regan, J. Hurley, M. O'Connell (Cork), T. Shinny (goal), M. Cross, M. Fitzgibbon, T. Conway (Limerick), P. Cahill, P. Purcell, M. Kennedy, T. Treacy (Tipperary), J. J. Doyle, T. Considine (Clare), C. Ware (Waterford).

Leinster—W. Dunphy, P. Phelan (goal), Martin Power, P. Byrne, L. Meagher, P. Walsh (Kilkenny), T. Burke, C. McMahon, E. Byrne, Jim Walsh, M. Gill, M. Power, M. Finn, S. Tumpane (Dublin), E. Giles (Meath). Sub: P. Kelly (Laois).

1931

Munster—T. O'Meara, P. Purcell, P. Cahill, T. Treacy, M. Kennedy (Tipperary), C. Ware (Waterford), J. J. Doyle, T. Considine (Clare), P.

Collins, J. Hurley, D. B. Murphy, E Coughlan, P. Aherne (Cork), M. Cross, G. Howard (Limerick).
Leinster—Jas. Walsh, John O'Dwyer (goal), P. Mclnerney, Chas. McMahon, T. Teehan, M. Gill, S. Tumpane, T. Quinlan, S Hegarty, M. Power (Dublin), P. Byrne, E. Doyle, P. Phelan, J. Roberts, Ecl. Byrne (Kilkenny). Subs: C. Griffin (Dublin) for T. Quinlan, J. O'Meara (Dublin) for T. Teehan.

1932

Leinster—J. Dermody (goal), P. O'Reilly, P. Larkin, P. Phelan, D. Dunne, T. Leahy, M. Power, E. Byrne (Kilkenny), T. Teehan, C. McMahon, J. Walsh, S. Hegarty, D. O'Neill (Dublin), P. Drennan, E. Tobin (Laois). Sub: Jim Grace {Kilkenny) for P. Larkin.
Munster—E. Coughlan, P. Collins, G. Garrett, W. Clancy, D. B. Murphy, M. Aherne (Cork), T. O'Meara (goal), P. Purcell, T. Treacy, P. Cahill, M.. Kennedy (Tipperary), J. J. Doyle (Clare), C. Ware, P. Browne (Waterford), M. Cross (Limerick). Sub: P. Clohessy (Limerick) for P. Browne.

1933

Leinster—J. Dermody, P. Larkin, P. O'Reilly, P. Phelan, P. Byrne, E. Doyle, E. Byrne, L. Meagher, J. Walsh, D. Dunne, M. Power (Kilkenny), C. McMahon, E. Wade, J. Walsh, D. O'Neill (Dublin). Subs: Tommy Leahy and Johnny Dunne (Kilkenny) for J. Walsh (Kilkenny) and D. Dunne.
Munster—Tom Daly, J. J. Doyle, J. Houlihan, L. Blake (Clare), G. Garrett, P. Collins, D. B. Murphy, T. McCarthy, W Clancy (Cork), T. McCarthy, P. Clohessy, Tim Ryan (Limerick), P. Purcell, M. Kennedy (Tipperary), D. Wyse (Waterford). Sub: M. Cross (Limerick) for L. Blake.

1934

Munster—P. Scanlan, E. Cregan, T. McCarthy, M. Cross, P. Clohessy, Tim Ryan, Ml. Mackey (Limerick), G. Garrett, D. B. Murphy, J. Kennealy (Cork), P. Purcell, T. Treacy, M. Kennedy (Tipperary), L. Blake (Clare), D. Wyse (Waterford).
Leinster—C. Forde, C. McMahon, Ed. Wade, S. Hegarty (Dublin), P. Larkin, P. Byrne, P. Phelan, E. Byrne, Tommy Leahy, L. Meagher, Martin Power, J. Walsh, J. Fitzpatrick, J. Dunne, Matty Power (Kilkenny). Sub: J. Cashin (Laois) for P. Larkin.

1935

Munster—T. Ryan, P. Scanlan (goal), T. McCarthy, M. Kennedy, John Mackey, M. Mackey, P. Clohessy (Limerick), C. Ware (Waterford), G. Garrett, J. Barrett, M. Brennan (Cork), L. Blake, M. Hennessy, J. Harrington (Clare), M. Kennedy (Tipperary).
Leinster—C. McMahon, C. Forde (goal), A. Murphy, D. Canniffe, S. Hegarty, E. Wade, J. O'Connell (Dublin), P. Larkin, P. Phelan, Tommy Leahy, E. Byrne, L. Meagher, Matt Power, L. Byrne, J. Dunne (Kilkenny). Subs: T. Treacy (Dublin) for D. Canniffe, J. Walsh (Kilkenny) for S. Hegarty.

1936

Leinster—J. O'Connell (goal), P. Larkin, P. Byrne, P. Blanchfield, Tommy Leahy, Ed. Byrne, P. Phelan, J. Walsh, J. Dunne, M. Power (Kilkenny), T. Teehan, D. Canniffe, C. McMahon, M. Daniels, Ed. Wade (Dublin).
Munster—P. Scanlan (goal), T. McCarthy, M. Kennedy, M. Cross, P. Clohessy, T. Ryan, J. Mackey, M. Mackey, P. McMahon (Limerick), J. Maher, P. Purcell (Tipperary), S. Barrett, M. Brennan (Cork), L. Blake, M. Hennessy (Clare). Subs: J. Cooney (Tipperary) for P. Purcell, J. Quirke (Cork) for P. Clohessy, P. Clohessy for M. Hennessy.

1937

Munster—M. Mackey, P. Scanlan (goal), T. McCarthy, M. Kennedy, P. Clohessy, T. Ryan, J. Mackey, P. McMahon (Limerick), J. Maher, J. Cooney, (Tipperary), J. Keane, C. Moylan (Waterford), J. Quirke, M. Brennan (Cork), L. Blake (Clare).
Leinster—J. O'Connell (goal), P. Larkin, P. Byrne, Tommy Leahy, E. Byrne, P. Phelan, M. White (Kilkenny), T. Teehan, C. McMahon, E. Wade, C. Downes, D. Canniffe (Dublin), A. Bergin, H. Gray, P. Farrell (Laois).

1938

Munster—J. Lanigan, J. Coffey, D. O'Gorman, W. O'Donnell (Tipperary), P. Scanlan (goal), T. McCarthy, P. Clohessy, T. Ryan, M. Mackey, J. Mackey (Limerick), J. Keane, C. Moylan (Waterford), L. Blake (Clare), S. Barrett, J. Quirke (Cork). Sub: J. Lynch (Cork) for L. Blake.
Leinster—P. Larkin, J. O'Connell (goal), W. Burke, P. Blanchfield, Terry Leahy, P. Phelan (Kilkenny), T. Teehan, P. Farrell, C. McMahon, E. Wade, P. MacCormack, M. Daniels (Dublin), J. Brophy (Kilkenny), F. Monaghan (Westmeath), W. Delaney (Laois). Subs: A. Bergin (Laois) for P. Blanchfield, C. Boland (Westmeath) for F. Monaghan.

1939

Munster—M. Curley, J. Keane, C. Moylan, L. Byrne (Waterford), P. Carroll, P. Clohessy, T. Ryan, J. Mackey, M. Mackey (Limerick), S. Barrett, M. Brennan (Cork), D. O'Gorman, E. Wade (Tipperary), T. Loughnane, J. Mullane (Clare).
Leinster—J. O'Connell, P. Larkin, W. Burke, P. Blanchfield, Terry Leahy, P. Phelan, J. Walsh (Kilkenny), M. Gill, P. Farrell, J. Byrne, H. Gray,

M. McDonnell, M. Flynn, P. Doody (Dublin), F. White (Westmeath).

1940

Munster—P. Scanlan (goal), P. Clohessy, J. Power, J. Mackey, M. Mackey, P. McMahon (Limerick), W. Murphy, W. Campbell, Sean Barrett, J. Quirke, M. Brennan (Cork), G. Cornally, W. O'Donnell (Tipperary), J. Mullane (Clare), C. Moylan (Waterford). Sub: J. Keane (Waterford) for P. Clohessy.

Leinster—J. O'Connell (goal), P. Grace, W. Burke, P. Blanchfield, R. Hinks, J. Walsh, J. Langton, P. Phelan, J. Kelly, J. Phelan (Kilkenny), A. Bergin, P. Farrell (Laois), M. Gill, H. Gray, M. Brophy (Dublin). Subs: J. Byrne (Dublin) for M. Gill, F. White (Westmeath) for P. Grace, Sean O'Brien (Kilkenny) for A. Bergin.

1941

Leinster—J. O'Connell, P. Grace (Kilkenny), M. Butler (Dublin), P. Blanchfield, R. Hinks (Kilkenny), F. White (Westmeath), P. Phelan (Kilkenny), E. Wade, H. Gray, (Dublin), J. Langton (Kilkenny), P. McSweeney, M. McDonnell (Dublin), J. Mulcahy, S. O'Brien (Kilkenny), Jimmy Phelan (Kilkenny). Sub: J. Kelly (Kilkenny) for M. McDonnell.

Munster—P. Scanlan (Limerick), W. Murphy (Cork), J. Maher (Tipperary), A. Lotty, W. Campbell (Cork), J. Keane (Waterford), P. Cregan, T Ryan (Limerick), C. Buckley (Cork), J. Power (Limerick), J. Lynch (Cork), R. Stokes (Limerick), J. Mullane (Clare), J. Quirke (Cork), P. Flanagan (Tipperary).

1942

Munster—J. McCarthy (Limerick), D. O'Gorman (Tipperary), B. Thornhill, W. Murphy (Cork), J. Ryan (Tipperary), J. Keane (Waterford), P. Cregan (Limerick), J. Lynch (Cork), C. Moylan (Waterford), W. Barron (Waterford), C. Ring (Cork), R. Stokes (Limerick), J. Quirke (Cork), W. O'Donnell {Tipperary), J. Power (Limerick).

Leinster—D. Conway (Dublin), P. Larkin (Kilkenny), Mick Butler (Dublin), P. Blanchfield (Kilkenny), F. White (Westmeath), W. Burke, P. Phelan, J. Walsh (Kilkenny), H. Gray (Dublin), J. Langton (Kilkenny), M. McDonnell, J. Byrne (Dublin), J. Mulcahy, Jimmy Phelan (Kilkenny), C. Downes (Dublin).

1943

Munster—J. Maher (Tipperary), W. Murphy, B. Thornhill (Cork), P. Cregan (Limerick), A. Fleming, J. Keane (Waterford), J. Young, J. Lynch (Cork), R. Stokes (Limerick), C. Ring (Cork), J. Power (Limerick), T. Doyle (Tipperary), J. Quirke (Cork), W. O'Donnell (Tipperary), M. Mackey (Limerick). Sub: J. Mackey (Limerick) for W. O'Donnell.

Leinster—J. Donegan (Dublin), P. Grace (Kilkenny), M. Butler (Dublin), Joe Bailey (Wexford), F. White (Dublin), W. Burke (Kilkenny), J. Byrne (Dublin), J. Kelly (Kilkenny), D. Dooley (Offaly), M. Ryan (Dublin), N. Rackard (Wexford), J. Farrell (Laois), J. Langton, J. Walsh, Jimmy Phelan (Kilkenny). Sub: Jack Phelan (Kilkenny) for W. Burke, H. Gray (Dublin) for Jack Phelan.

1944

Munster—J. Ware (Waterford), W. Murphy, B. Thornhill (Cork), P. Cregan (Limerick), A. Fleming (Waterford), J. Power (Limerick), C. Cottrell, J. Lynch, S. Condon (Cork), R. Stokes (Limerick), C. Ring, J. Young, J. Quirke (Cork), J. Mackey (Limerick), P. J. Quane (Clare).

Connacht—(All Galway). S. Duggan, P. Forde, M. Forde, P. Brogan, M. Lynch, J. Brophy, D. Flynn, P. Thornton, R. Forde, T. Ryan, M. J. Flaherty, J. Gallagher, M. Nestor, A. Brennan, M. Fennessy. Subs: R. Quinn for P. Brogan, W. Fahy for J. Gallagher.

1945

Munster—J. Ware, A. Fleming (Waterford), W. Murphy (Cork), P. Cregan (Limerick), P. O'Donovan (Cork), J. Power (Limerick), J. Young (Cork), P. McCarthy (Limerick), C. Cottrell (Cork), T. Purcell (Tipperary), C. Ring (Cork), R. Stokes (Limerick), M. Mockey (Limerick), J. Quirke (Cork), P. J. Quane (Clare).

Ulster—M. McKeown, W. Feeney (Antrim), J. Butler, E. O'Toole (Monaghan), P. McKeown (Antrim), B. Denvir (Down), M. Butler (Antrim), O. Keenan (Down), N. Campbell, D. Cormican, K. Armstrong, L. McGrady (Antrim), J. White (Down) C. Mullan, S. Mulholland (Antrim). Subs: T. McAllister (Antrim) for E. O'Toole, J. Butler (Antrim) for J. White.

1946

Munster—J. Maher (Tipperary), W. Murphy (Cork), G. Cornally (Tipperary), A. Fleming (Waterford), J. Devitt (Tipperary), P. Lyons (Clare), M. Hayes (Waterford), R. Stokes, J. Power, S. Herbert (Limerick), C. Ring, J. Young (Cork), P. Fitzgerald (Limerick), A. O'Brien (Clare), T. Doyle (Tipperary).

Connacht—(All Galway). S. Duggan, James Killeen, R. Quinn, D. Flynn, M. J. Flaherty, J. Brophy, W. Faby, John Killeen, P. Gantley, J. Gallagher, P. Jordan, S. Gallagher, M. Doyle, T. Flynn, M. Nestor. Sub: T. Doyle for M. Doyle.

1947

Connacht—(All Galway). S. Duggan, D. Flynn, P. Forde, W. FaLy, M. J. Flaherty, J. Brophy, B. Power, J. Killeen, P. Gantley, J. Gallagher, H. Gordon, P. Jordan, M. Nestor, Tadgh Kelly, S. Gallagher.

Munster—T. Mulcahy, W. Murphy (Cork), J. Keane (Waterford), P. Cregan (Limerick), M. Maher (Tipperary), A. Lotty (Cork), A. Fleming, V. Baston, M. Hayes (Waterford), C. Ring (Cork), J. Power (Limerick), J. Young, M. O'Riordan, G. O Riordan (Cork), T. Doyle (Tipperary). Subs: M. Ryan (Limerick) for M. Hayes and D. Solon (Clare for A. Lotly.

1948

Munster—T. Mulcahy, W. Murphy, C. Murphy (Cork), J. Goode (Waterford), J. Devitt (Tipperary), P. Donovan (Cork), D. Solon (Clare), V. Baston, M. Hayes (Waterford), S. Herbert, J. Power (Limerick), C. Ring (Cork), M. Daly (Clare), E. Daly (Waterford), T. Doyle (Tipperary). Subs: M. Riordan (Cork) for S. Herbert, J. Sadlier (Limerick) for D. Solon.

Leinster—R. Dowling, P. Grace, P. Hayden, M. Marnell, J. Kelly (Kilkenny), P. Brennan (Dublin), J. Mulcahy (Kilkenny), M. Hassett (Dublin), J. Heffernan, J. Langton, Terry Leahy (Kilkenny), A. Herbert (Dublin), N. Rackard (Wexford), J. Prior (Dublin), S. Downey (Kilkenny).

1949

Munster—J. Ware, A. Fleming (Waterford), C. Murphy (Cork), T. Cregan (Limerick), J. Devitt (Tipperary), P. Donovan (Cork), T. Purcell (Tipperary), V. Baston (Waterford), M. Ryan (Limerick), C. Ring (Cork), J. Keane (Waterford), S. Herbert (Limerick), M. Daly (Clare) E. Daly (Waterford), W. O'Carroll (Tipperary). Sub. P. Fitzgerald (Limerick) for W. O'Carroll.

Connacht—S. Duggan, M. Badger, R. Quinn, W. Fahy, M. McInerney, C. Corless, M. J. Flaherty, T. Boyle, J. Killeen, F. Duignan, H. Gordon, T. Moroney, Tadgh Kelly, B. Power, J. Gallagher. Sub: J. Solmon for W. Fahy.

Note: All Galwav with exception of T. Boyle (Roscommon).

1950

Munster—A. Reddan (Tipperary), A. Fleming (Waterford), G. O'Riordan (Cork), J. Sadlier (Limerick), P. Stakelum, (Tipperary), V. Baston (Waterford), M. Fouhy (Cork), S. Bannon, P. Shanahan, J. Kennedy, M. Ryan, S. Kenny (Tipperary), M. Riordan (Cork), W. McAllister (Clare), C. Ring (Cork).

Leinster—T. Fitzpatrick (Laois), S. Cronin (Dublin), P. Hayden, M. Marnell (Kilkenny), J. Murray, T. Byrne (Laois), R. Rackard (Wexford), J. Styles (Laois), W. Walsh (Kilkenny), A. Dunne (Laois), A. Herbert (Dublin), J. Langton, S. Downey (Kilkenny), N. Rackard (Wexford), L. Reidy (Kilkenny). Subs: P. Prendergast (Kilkenny) for J. Murray, M. Lyons (Dublin) for N. Rackard.

1951

Munster—A. Reddan (Tipperary), A. Fleming, D. Walsh (Waterford), D. McInerney (Clare), S. Bannon, P. Stakelum (Tipperary), J. Goode (Waterford), M. Fouhy (Cork), S. Kenny (Tipperary), M. Nugent (Clare), M. Ryan (Tipperary), E. Stokes (Limerick), P. Kenny (Tipperary), D. McCarthy (Limerick), C. Ring (Cork). Subs. John Doyle for D. McInerney, P. Shanahan (Tipperary) for S. Kenny, W. J. Daly (Cork) for M. Ryan.

Leinster—R. Dowling (Kilkenny), S. Cronin (Dublin), P. Hayden, M. Marnell (Kilkenny), R. Rackard (Wexford), P. Prendergast, W. Walsh, D. Kennedy (Kilkenny), J. Morrissey, Padge Kehoe (Wexford), J. Prior (Dublin), J. Langton, S. Downey (Kilkenny), N. Rackard, T. Flood (Wexford). Subs.: N. Allen for D. Kennedy, P. Donnelly (Dublin) for W. Walsh, J. Hogan (Kilkenny) for S. Cronin, D. Kennedy for N. Allen.

1952

Munster—A. Reddan (Tipperary), J. Goode, D. Walsh (Waterford), J. Doyle (Tipperary), S. Herbert (Limerick), P. Stakelum (Tipperary), M. Fouhy (Cork), P. Shanahan (Tipperary), J. Kiely (Waterford), M. Nugent (Clare), M. Ryan, S. Bannon, P. Kenny (Tipperary), D. McCarthy (Limerick), C. Ring (Cork).

Connacht—(All Galway). S. Duggan, C. Corless, F. Flynn, J. Brophy, J. Molloy, Tadgh Kelly, H. Gordon, J. Salmon, J. Killeen, F. Duignan, M. Burke, P. Nolan, P. Manton, M. J. Flaherty, J. Gallagher. Subs: T. Moroney for F. Flynn, M. Glynn for F. Dulgnan.

1953

Munster—A. Reddan (Tipperary), J. Goode (Waterford), J. Doyle (Tipperary), A. O'Shaughnessy (Cork), S. Herbert (Limerick), P. Stakelum (Tipperary), D. O'Grady (Clare), G. Murphy (Cork), P. Shanahan (Tipperary), M. Nugent (Clare), W. J. Daly (Cork), S. Bannon, P. Kenny (Tipperary), D. McCarthy (Limerick), C. Ring (Cork). Subs: M. Queally (Waterford) for A. O'Shaughnessy, P. Barry (Cork) for C. Ring.

Leinster—K. Matthews (Dublin), J. Hogan, P. Hayden, M. Marnell (Kilkenny), D. Ferguson (Dublin), R. Rackard (Wexford), W. Walsh (Kilkenny), C. Murphy, N. Allen (Dublin), Paddy Kehoe, E. Wheeler (Wexford), T. Maher (Laois), M. Kelly (Kilkenny), N. Rackard, T. Flood (Wexford). Sub: W. Rackard (Wexford) for Tim Maher, Jim Prior (Dublin) for M. Kelly.

1954

Leinster—K. Matthews (Dublin), J. Hogan, P. Hayden (Kilkenny), M. Hanlon (Wexford), P. Buggy (Kilkenny), E. Wheeler (Wexford), J. McGovern (Kilkenny), N. Allen (Dublin), J. Sutton (Kilkenny), M. Ryan (Dublin), D. Carroll

(Kilkenny), T. Flood (Wexford), J. Langton, P. Fitzgerald, M. Kelly (Kilkenny). Subs: J. Morrissey for M. Ryan, W. Rackard (Wexford) M. Hanlon.

Munster—A. Reddan (Tipperary), G. O'Riordan, J. Lyons (Cork), J. Doyle, J. Finn, P. Stakelum (Tipperary), M. Fouhy (Cork), J. Hough (Tipperary), J. Kiely (Waterford), W. J. Daly (Cork), J. Hartnett (Cork), S. Bannon (Tipperary), J. Smith (Clare), D. McCarthy (Limerick), C. Ring (Cork).

1955

Munster—A. Reddan (Tipperary), G. O'Riordan, J. Lyons (Cork), J. Doyle, P. Stakelum (Tipperary), D. O'Grady (Clare), V. Twomey (Cork), J. Smith (Clare), J. Hough (Tipperary), W. J. Daly (Cork), D. Dillon (Clare), J. Hartnett (Cork), S. Power (Waterford), J. Greene (Clare), C. Ring (Cork).

Connacht—(All Galway). T. Boland, F. Spillane, B. Power, H. Gordon, M. Murphy, W. Duffy, Tommy Kelly, J. Salmon, J. Duggan, P. Duggan, E. Monahan, M. Cullinane, P. Manton, M. Elwood, J. Fives. Subs: S. Cullinane for Boland, T. Glynn for Murphy.

1956

Leinster—A. Foley (Wexford), D. Ferguson (Dublin), N. O'Donnell, R. Rackard, J. English, W. Rackard (Wexford), W. Walsh (Kilkenny), J. Morrissey (Wexford), J. McGrath (Westmeath), S. Clohosey (Kilkenny), E. Wheeler, T. Flood (Wexford), L. Cashin (Dublin), N. Rackard (Wexford), R. Rackett (Kilkenny). Sub.: S. Hearne (Wexford) for McGrath.

Munster—A. Reddan, M. Byrne (Tipperary), J. Lyons, A. O'Shaughnessy, V. Twomey (Cork), J. Finn, J. Doyle, P. Stakelum (Tipperary), J. O'Connor (Waterford), J. Carney (Clare), D. Kelly (Limerick), J. Smith (Clare), S. Power (Waterford), J. Hartnett, C. Ring (Cork). Sub: T. Casey (Limerick) for O'Shaughnessy.

1957

Munster—M. Cashman, J. Brohan, J. Lyons, A. O'Shaughnessy (Cork), M. O'Connor (Waterford), J. Finn (Tipperary), P. Philpott (Cork), M. Ryan (Tipperary), J. O'Connor (Waterford), D. Kelly (Limerick), T. Kelly (Cork), F. Walsh (Waterford), P. Kenny (Tipperary), C. Ring, P. Barry (Cork).

Leinster—A. Foley, R. Rackard, N. O'Donnell (Wexford), D. Ferguson (Dublin), J. English, W. Rackard (Wexford), J. McGovern, W. Walsh (Kilkenny), E. Wheeler (Wexford), S. Clohosey, M. Kenny (Kilkenny), T. Flood (Wexford), R. Rockett (Kilkenny), N. Rackard (Wexford), W. Dwyer (Kilkenny). Subs.: O. Walsh (Kilkenny) for Foley, L. Cashin (Dublin) for Rockett.

1958

Munster—M. Cashman (Cork), J. Finn (Tipperary), J. Lyons (Cork), J. Barron (Waterford), T. McGarry (Limerick), M. Óg Morrissey (Waterford), A. Wall (Tipperary), S. Power, P. Grimes (Waterford), J. Smith (Clare), L. Moloney (Limerick), J. Doyle (Tipperary), P. Barry, C. Ring (Cork), D. Whelan (Waterford). Subs: M. Maher (Tipperary) for Finn, T. Cheasty (Waterford) for Moloney.

Leinster—O. Walsh (Kilkenny), N. Drumgoole (Dublin), N. O'Donnell (Wexford), J. Maher (Kilkenny), J. English (Wexford), P. Buggy, J. McGovern, M. Brophy, J. Sutton, D. Heaslip (Kilkenny), E. Wheeler (Wexford), C. O'Brien (Laois), M. Kenny, W. Dwyer, S. Clohosey (Kilkenny). Sub. W. Rackard (Wexford) for Buggy.

1959

Munster—M. Cashman, J. Brohan (Cork), M. Maher (Tipperary), J. Barron (Waterford), T. McGarry (Limerick), A. Wall (Tipperary), M. Óg Morrisey (Waterford), T. English (Tipperary), T. Casey (Limerick), D. Nealon (Tipperary), S. Power (Waterford), J. Doyle (Tipperary), J. Smith (Clare), C. Ring (Cork), L. Guinan (Waterford). Sub: T. Kelly (Cork) for Power.

Connacht—(All Galway). F. Benson, R. Stanley, P. Burke, S. Cullinane, J. Duggan, J. Fives, M. Sweeney, Tommy Kelly, P. J. Lally, T. Sweeney, P. J. Lawless, S. Gohery, P. Egan, T. Conway, M. Fox. Subs: J. Lyons for Fives, G. Cahill for Kelly.

1960

Munster—M. Cashman, J. Brohan (Cork), A. Flynn, J. Barron (Waterford), T. McGarry (Limerick), M. Óg Morrissey (Waterford), John Doyle (Tipperary), S. Power, P. Grimes (Waterford), Jimmy Doyle (Tipperary), T. Cheasty, F. Walsh (Waterford), J. Smith (Clare). C. Ring, P. Barry (Cork). Sub. D. Kelly (Limerick) for McGarry.

Leinster—O. Walsh, T. Walsh (Kilkenny), N. O'Donnell (Wexford), P. Croke (Dublin), J. English (Wexford), M. Bohan (Dublin), J. McGovern (Kilkenny), L. Shannon (Dublin), E. Wheeler (Wexford), D. Heaslip, S. Clohosey (Kilkenny), Padge Kehoe (Wexford), C. O'Brien (Laois), W. Dwyer, T. O'Connell (Kilkenny). Subs: J. Byrne (Dublin) for O'Connell, R. Carroll (Kilkenny) for Byrne.

1961

Munster—M. Cashman, J. Brohan (Cork), M. Maher (Tipperary), J. Barron (Waterford), T. McGarry (Limerick), A. Wall (Tipperary), M. Morrissey (Waterford), T. English (Tipperary), S. Power (Waterford), Jimmy Doyle (Tipperary), T. Kelly (Cork), F. Walsh (Waterford), J. Smith (Clare), C. Ring (Cork), L. Devaney {Tipperary).

Subs: T. Cheasty (Waterford) for Ring, P. Duggan (Cork) for Morrissey.

Leinster—O. Walsh, T. Walsh (Kilkenny), N. O'Donnell, T. Neville, J. English, E. Wheeler, J. Nolan (Wexford), D. Foley (Dublin), S. Clohosey (Kilkenny), J. O'Brien, Padge Kehoe (Wexford), E. Keher (Kilkenny), O. McGrath (Wexford), W. Dwyer (Kilkenny), T. Flood (Wexford). Subs.: M. Walsh (Kilkenny) for Keher, S. Quaid (Wexford) for Dwyer, O. Fennell (Laois) for Clohosey.

1962

Leinster—O. Walsh (Kilkenny), D. Ferguson, N. Drumgoole, L. Foley (Dublin), J. English, W. Rackard (Wexford), O. Fennell (Laois), D. Foley, M. Kennedy, A. Boothman (Dublin), C. O'Brien (Laois), F. Whelan. (Dublin), O. McGrath (Wexford), W. Dwyer (Kilkenny), W. Jackson (Dublin). Sub.: D. Heaslip (Kilkenny) for Jackson.

Munster—M. Cashman, J. Brohan (Cork), M. Maher, K. Carey (Tipperary), J. O'Sullivan (Cork), M. Óg Morrissey (Waterford), M. Burns, T. English, L. Devaney, Jimmy Doyle (Tipperary), T. Kelly (Cork), D. Nealon (Tipperary), J. Smith (Clare), C. Ring (Cork), S. Power (Waterford). Subs: P. J. Keane (Limerick) for Kelly, A. Wall (Tipperary) for English, F. Walsh (Waterford) for Devaney.

1963 REPLAY

Munster—M. Cashman, J. Brohan (Cork), M. Maher, John Doyle (Tipperary), T. McGarry (Limerick), A. Wall (Tipperary)J, J. Byrne (Waterford), P. J. Keane (Lirnerick), J. Condon (Waterford), Jimmy Doyle (Tipperary), T. Cheasty (Waterford), D. Nealon (Tipperary), J. Smith (Clare), C. Ring (Cork), L. Devaney (Tipperary). Subs: F. Walsh (Waterford) for Ring, T. English (Tipperary) for Walsh.
[Note: T. English (Tipperary) played in drawn game. T. Cheasty came on for replay. M. Burns and Tom Ryan (Tipperary) came on as subs in drawn game for T. English and D. Nealon.]

Leinster—O. Walsh (Kilkenny), T. Neville (Wexford), J. Walsh (Kilkenny), L. Foley (Dublin), S. Cleere (Kilkenny), W. Rackard, J. Nolan (Wexford), D. Foley (Dublin), P. Wilson, J. O'Brien (Wexford), C. O'Brien (Laois), F. Whelan (Dublin), W. Hogan (Carlow), E. Wheeler (Wexford), D. Heaslip (Kilkenny). Subs: J. English (Wexford) for Cleere, E. Keher (Kilkenny) for Hogan, O. McGrath (Wexford) for Heaslip.
[Note: E. Keher (Kilkenny) and M. Kennedy (Dublin) played in drawn game. P. Wilson and J. O'Brien came on for replay. O. McGrath (Wexford) for W. Hogan, O. Fennell (Laois) for M. Coogan (Kilkenny), M. Coogan for M. Kennedy.]

1964

Leinster—O. Walsh (Kilkenny), T. Neville, D. Quigley (Wexford), L. Foley (Dublin), S. Cleere (Kilkenny), W. Rackard (Wexford), O. Fennell (Laois), P. Wilson (Wexford), P. Moran (Kilkenny), F. Whelan (Dublin), E. Wheeler (Wexford), E. Keher, T. Walsh (Kilkenny), C. O'Brien (Laois), M. Bermingham (Dublin). Subs.: M. Coogan (Kilkenny) for Fennell, Martin Hogan (Carlow) for Foley, D. Foley (Dublin) for Bermingham.

Munster—J. Hogan (Limerick), John Doyle (Tipperary), A. Flynn (Waterford), D. Murphy (Cork), L. Guinan (Waterford), A. Wall (Tipperary), P. Fitzgerald, J. O'Sullivan (Cork), T. English, Jimmy Doyle (Tipperary), T. Cunningham (Waterford), P. Cronin (Clare), L. Devaney (Tipperary), J. Smith (Clare), P. Grimes (Waterford). Sub: A. O'Brien (Limerick) for Wall.

1965

Leinster—O. Walsh (Kilkenny), T. Neville (Wexford), P. Dillon (Kilkenny), E. Colfer (Wexford), S. Cleere, T. Carroll (Kilkenny), P. Molloy (Offaly), P. Wilson (Wexford), P. Moran (Kilkenny), J. O'Brien (Wexford), D. Foley (Dublin), E. Keher, T. Walsh (Kilkenny), C. O'Brien (Laois), M. Bermingham (Dublin).

Munster—J. O'Donoghue, John Doyle (Tipperary), A. Flynn (Waterford), K. Carey (Tipperary), L. Guinan (Waterford), A. Wall (Tipperary), P. Fitzgerald (Cork), T. English, M. Roche, Jimmy Doyle (Tipperary), P. J. Keane (Limerick), M. Keating (Tipperary), J. Bennett (Cork), L. Devaney, S. McLoughlin (Tipperary). Subs: N. Gallagher (Cork) for English, K. Long (Limerick) for Carey.

1966

Munster—E. Power (Waterford), A. O'Brien (Limerick), A. Flynn (Waterford), D. Murphy, D. O'Riordan (Cork), A. Wall (Tipperary) L. Guinan (Waterford), M. Roche (Tipperary), B. Hartigan (Limerick), L. Danaher (Clare), L. Kiely (Tipperary), F. Walsh (Waterford), D. Nealon, J. McKenna, S. McLoughlin (Tipperary). Subs: P. Fitzgerald (Cork) for O'Riordan, L. Devaney (Tipperary), for Danagher, P. Cronin (Clare) for Nealon.

Leinster—O. Walsh (Kilkenny), T. Neville (Wexford), J. Lynch (Kilkenny), E. Colfer (Wexford), S. Cleere (Kilkenny), D. Quigley, W. Murphy (Wexford), B. Cooney (Dublin), P. Molloy (Offaly), W. Walsh (Carlow), T. Forrestal, E. Keher, T. Walsh, P. Dillon (Kilkenny), J. O'Brien (Wexford). Subs: P. Moran (Kilkenny) for Quigley, J. Foley (Wexford) for Molloy.

1967

Leinster—O. Walsh (Kilkenny), D. Quigley, T. Neville, E. Colfer (Wexford), S. Cleere, P. Henderson, M. Coogan, P. Moran (Kilkenny),

H. Dalton (Dublin), E. Keher, J. Teehan, C. Dunne (Kilkenny), P. Molloy (Offaly), J. Bennett, T. Walsh (Kilkenny). Subs: N. Kinsella (Dublin) for Teehan, M. Browne (Wexford) for Dunne.

Munster—P. Barry (Cork), V. Loftus (Clare), A. Flynn (Waterford), D. Murphy (Cork), A. O'Brien, K. Long (Limerick), P. Fitzgerald (Cork), M. Roche (Tipperary), B. Hartigan (Limerick), S. Barry, J. O'Halloran (Cork), P. Cronin (Clare), D. Nealon, J. McKenna (Tipperary), T. Bluett (Limerick).

1968

Munster—M. Foley (Waterford), P. Doolan, T. O'Donoghue (Cork), N. O'Gorman (Tipperary), A. O'Brien (Limerick), J. Cullinane (Clare), L. Gaynor, M. Roche (Tipperary), J. McCarthy (Cork), B. Hartigan (Limerick), L. Guinan (Waterford), E. Cregan (Limerick), S. Barry (Cork), M. Keating, D. Nealon (Tipperary). Subs: C. McCarthy (Cork) for Nealon, P. Cronin (Clare) for Cregan.

Leinster—O. Walsh (Kilkenny), D. Quigley (Wexford), P. Dillon, J. Treacy, S. Cleere, P. Henderson (Kilkenny), W. Murphy (Wexford), P. Moran (Kilkenny), D. Foley (Dublin), E. Keher, C. Dunne (Kilkenny), P. Wilson, J. O'Brien, A. Doran (Wexford), P. Molloy (Offaly). Subs: P. Lynch (Wexford) for Wilson, T. Carroll (Kilkenny) for Murphy.

1969 REPLAY

Munster—J. O'Donoghue (Tipperary), A. O'Brien (Limerick), T. O'Donoghue, D. Murphy (Cork), J. Cullinane (Clare), J. McCarthy (Cork), L. Gaynor, P. J. Ryan (Tipperary), E. Cregan (Limerick), N. Pyne (Clare), N. O'Dwyer (Tipperary), G. McCarthy (Cork), Jimmy Doyle (Tipperary), C. Cullinane (Cork), J. Flanagan (Tipperary).

[Note J. Kirwan (Waterford) and N. O'Gorman (Tipperary) played in drawn game. N. Pyne (Clare) and C. Cullinane (Cork) came on for replay. C. Cullinane came on as a sub in drawn game for E. Cregan.]

Connacht—(All Galway unless stated). A. Gavin, M. Howley, T. Bohan, S. Francis, M. Burke (Sligo), M. McTigue, T. Murphy, J. Connolly, S. Stanley, P. Fahy, B. O'Connor, P. Mitchell, W. Murphy (Sligo), M. O'Connor, D. Coen. Subs: B. Mitchell (Roscommon) for P. Mitchell, C. Muldoon for W. Murphy.

[Note: B. Mitchell (Roscommon) played in drawn game. P. Fahy on for replay.]

1970

Munster—J. O'Donoghue (Tipperary), A. Maher (Cork), M. Considine (Clare), J. O'Brien (Limerick), D. Clifford (Cork), M. Roche, L. Gaynor (Tipperary), G. McCarthy (Cork), B. Hartigan (Limerick), N. O'Dwyer (Tipperary), W. Walsh (Cork), P. Enright (Waterford), Jimmy Doyle (Tipperary), R. Cummins (Cork), M. Keating (Tipperary). Sub: A. O'Brien (Limerick) for Roche.

Leinster—O. Walsh, T. Carroll, P. Dillon (Kilkenny), P. Spellman (Offaly), P. Henderson (Kilkenny), D. Quigley (Wexford), M. Coogan, P. Moran (Kilkenny), D. Haniffy, J. J. Healion (Offaly), P. Wilson (Wexford), E. Keher (Kilkenny), P. Molloy (Offaly), L. Lawlor (Dublin), A. Doran (Wexford). Subs.: P. Delaney (Kilkenny) for Healion, F. Cummins (Kilkenny) for Haniffy.

1971

Leinster—P. Nolan, D. Quigley, P. Kavanagh (Wexford), J. Treacy (Kilkenny), M. Browne (Wexford), P. Dunny (Kildare), H. Dalton (Dublin), D. Bernie (Wexford), F. Cummins (Kilkenny), J. Quigley (Wexford), P. Delaney, E. Keher, J. Millea (Kilkenny), A. Doran (Wexford), M. Bermingham (Dublin). Subs: D. Martin (Offaly) for Nolan, P. Henderson (Kilkenny) for Dunny.

Munster—P. O'Brien (Clare), A. Maher (Cork), J. Kelly (Tipperary), J. Horgan, C. Roche (Cork), M. Roche, L. Gaynor (Tipperary), B. Hartigan (Limerick), P. J. Ryan, F. Loughnane, N. O'Dwyer (Tipperary), P. Hegarty (Cork), J. Flanagan (Tipperary), R. Cummins (Cork), E. Cregan (Limerick). Subs: G. McCarthy (Cork) for P. J. Ryan; Ryan for Loughnane.

1972

Leinster—D. Martin (Offaly), P. Larkin, P. Dillon J. Treacy (Kilkenny), M. Browne (Wexford), P. Dunny (Kildare), M. Coogan, F. Cummins (Kilkenny), H. Dalton (Dublin), B. Moylan (Offaly), P. Delaney, E. Keher, Mick Brennan (Kilkenny), A. Doran (Wexford), K. Purcell (Kilkenny). Subs.: M. Bermingham (Dublin) for Brennan, P. Wilson (Wexford) for Dalton.

Munster—P. O'Sullivan, L. King (Tipperary), P. Hartigan, J. O'Brien (Limerick), C. Roche (Cork), J. Kirwan (Waterford), J. O'Gorman (Clare), M. Roche (Tipperary), S. Foley (Limerick), F. Loughnane, N. O'Dwyer (Tipperary), P. Hegarty (Cork), E. Grimes (Limerick), R. Ryan (Tipperary), E. Cregan (Limerick). Subs.: J. Flanagan (Tipperary) for Grimes, C. McCarthy (Cork) for Hegarty.

1973

Leinster—N. Skehan (Kilkenny), T. O'Connor (Wexford), P. Horan (Offaly), J. Treacy, P. Lawlor, P. Henderson (Kilkenny), M. Mahon (Laois), F. Cummins (Kilkenny), M. Jacob, M. Quigley (Wexford), P. Delaney, K. Purcell {Kilkenny), M. Bermingham (Dublin), A. Doran (Wexford), E. Keher (Kilkenny). Subs: L. O'Brien (Kilkenny) for Cummins, B. Moylan (Offaly) for Bermingham.

Munster—S. Durack (Clare), A. Maher (Cork), P. Hartigan (Limerick), J. Gleeson (Tipperary), S. Foley (Limerick), T. O'Connor, L. Gaynor (Tipperary), D. Coughlan (Cork), E. Grimes (Limerick), F. Loughnane, J. Flanagan, N. O'Dwyer (Tipperary), M. Malone, R. Cummins, S. O'Leary (Cork). Subs: J. O'Brien (Limerick) for Grimes, C. McCarthy (Cork) for N. O'Dwyer.

1974

Leinster—N. Skehan, P. Larkin (Kilkenny), P. Horan (Offaly), P. Dunny (Kildare), P. Lawlor, P. Henderson (Kilkenny), C. Doran, C. Kehoe (Wexford), F. Cummins (Kilkenny), M. Quigley (Wexford), P. Delaney (Kilkenny), P. Quigley (Dublin), K. Purcell (Kilkenny), A. Doran (Wexford), E. Keher (Kilkenny).

Munster—S. Durack (Clare), B. Murphy (Cork), P. Hartigan, J. O'Brien (Limerick), T. O'Connor (Tipperary), E. Cregan (Limerick), C. Roche (Cork), S. Hogan {Tipperary), S. Foley (Limerick), F. Loughnane (Tipperary), A. Heffernan (Waterford), E. Grimes, L. O'Donoghue, E. Rea, F. Nolan (Limerick). Subs: G. McCarthy (Cork) for Heffernan, M. Hickey {Waterford) for Nolan, P. McGrath (Waterford) for Rea.

1975

Leinster—N. Skehan, P. Larkin (Kilkenny), P. Horan (Offaly), P. Dunny (Kildare), P. Lawlor, P. Henderson (Kilkenny), M. Jacob (Wexford), L. O'Brien, F. Cummins (Kilkenny), M. Quigley (Wexford), P. Delaney (Kilkenny), P. Quigley (Dublin), K. Purcell (Kilkenny), A. Doran (Wexford), E. Keher (Kilkenny). Subs: C. Doran (Wexford) for Jacob, J. Quigley (Wexford) for P. Quigley.

Munster—S. Durack (Clare), L. King (Tipperary), P. Hartigan (Limerick), S. Hannon (Waterford), G. Loughnane (Clare), E. Cregan (Limerick), P. McGrath (Waterford), G. McCarthy (Cork), S. Hogan, F. Loughnane, N. O'Dwyer, J. Kehoe (Tipperary), E. O'Connor (Clare), W. Walsh (Cork), J. McKenna (Limerick). Sub J. Barry-Murphy (Cork) for McKenna.

1976

Munster—S. Shinnors (Tipperary), P. McDonnell (Cork), P. Hartigan (Limerick), S. Hannon (Waterford), T. O'Connor, N. O'Dwyer (Tipperary), P McGrath (Waterford), G. McCarthy (Cork), J. McKenna (Limerick), F. Loughnane (Tipperary), M. Hickey (Waterford), J. Callinan (Clare), L. O'Donoghue (Limerick), R. Cummins, E. O'Donoghue (Cork). Sub: G. Loughnane (Clare) for O'Connor.

Leinster—N. Skehan, P. Larkin (Kilkenny), P. Horan (Offaly), P. Dunny (Kildare), P. Lalor, P. Henderson (Kilkenny), C. Doran, M. Quigley (Wexford), F. Cummins, M. Crotty, M. Ruth (Kilkenny), J. Quigley (Wexford), Mick Brennan (Kilkenny), A. Doran (Wexford), E. Keher (Kilkenny). Subs. B. Cody (Kilkenny) for Dunny. M. Holden (Dublin) for J. Quigley.

1977

Leinster—J. Nolan (Wexford), P. Larkin (Kilkenny), W. Murphy (Wexford), P. Henderson, P. Lawlor (Kilkenny), M. Jacob, C. Doran (Wexford), F. Cummins (Kilkenny), N. Buggy (Wexford), L. O'Brien (Kilkenny), M. Quigley (Wexford), M. Ruth, Mick Brennan (Kilkenny), A. Doran (Wexford), E. Keher (Kilkenny).

Munster—S. Durack (Clare), N. Cashin (Waterford), P. Hartigan (Limerick), J. Horgan (Cork), G. Loughnane (Clare), N. O'Dwyer (Tipperary), D. Coughlan, G. McCarthy, P. Moylan (Cork), E. O'Connor (Clare), J. Kehoe (Tipperary), J. Callinan (Clare), L. O'Donoghue (Limerick), N. Casey (Clare), P. Moriarty (Kerry). Subs: C. Honan (Clare) for Moriarty, M. Hickey (Waterford) for O'Donoghue.

1978

Munster—S. Durack (Clare), N. Cashin (Waterford), M. Doherty, J. Horgan (Cork), G. Loughnane (Clare), P. Hartigan (Limerick), P. McGrath (Waterford), J. Callinan (Clare), T. Cashman (Cork), T. Butler (Tipperary), G. McCarthy (Cork), C. Honan (Clare), C. McCarthy (Cork), J. McKenna (Limerick), N. Casey (Clare).

Leinster—N. Skehan, P. Larkin, R. O'Hara (Kilkenny), W. Murphy (Wexford), G. Henderson (Kilkenny), M. Jacob, C. Doran E. Buggy (Wexford), F. Cummins (Kilkenny), M. Walsh (Laois), M. Quigley, M. Butler (Wexford), W. Fitzpatrick (Kilkenny), A. Doran (Wexford), M. Ruth (Kilkenny). Subs: L. O'Brien (Kilkenny) for M. Butler, C. Keogh (Wexford) for M. Ruth.

1979

Leinster—N. Skehan. P. Larkin (Kilkenny), W. Murphy, J. Prendergast (Wexford), J. Hennessy (Kilkenny), P. Carton (Dublin), C. Doran (Wexford), G. Henderson (Kilkenny) P. Quirke (Carlow), J. Kelly (Offaly), M. Holden (Dublin), M. Walsh (Laois), W. Fitzpatrick (Kilkenny), A. Doran, E. Buggy (Wexford).

Connacht—(All Galway, except where stated) F. Larkin, N. Mclnerney, J. McDonagh, J. Lucas, J. Greaney, C. Hayes, Jimmy Cooney, S. Mahon, John Connolly, N. Lane, Joe Connolly, P. J. Molloy, A. Fenton, F. Gantley, J. Henry (Mayo). Subs: M. Coen for Molloy, F. Burke for Gantley, Molloy for Lucas.

1980

Connacht—(All Galway), S. Shinnors, N. Mclnerney, C. Hayes, Jimmy Cooney, S. Linnane, S. Silke, I. Clarke, S. Mahon John Connolly, M. Kilkenny, Joe Connolly, P. J.

Molloy, N. Lane, G. Curtin, F. Gantley.

Munster—P. McLoughney (Tipperary), B. Murphy (Cork), J. Keogh, T. O'Connor (Tipperary), D. McCurtain (Cork), M. Carroll (Limerick), G. Loughnane (Clare), T. Cashman (Cork), P. McGrath, M. Walsh (Waterford), J. McKenna (Limerick), J. Callinan (Clare), J. Barry Murphy, R. Cummins (Cork), P. O'Connor (Clare.). Subs: O. O'Connor (Limerick) for Barry Murphy, E. O'Donoghue (Cork) for P. O'Connor, T. Crowley (Cork) for McGrath.

1981

Munster—P. McLoughney (Tipperary), G. Loughnane (Clare), B. Murphy (Cork), T. O'Connor (Tipperary), D. McCurtain (Cork), S. Hehir (Clare), L. O'Donoghue (Limerick), J. Fenton, T. Cashman (Cork), J. Callinan (Clare), P. Horgan (Cork), M. Walsh (Waterford), E. O'Donoghue (Cork), J. McKenna, E. Cregan (Limerick). Subs: O. O'Connor (Limerick) for E. O'Donoghue, T. Crowley (Cork) for O'Connor.

Leinster—N. Skehan (Kilkenny), C. Doran (Wexford), E. Coughlan, P. Fleury (Offaly), P. Carton (Dublin), P. Delaney (Offaly), C. Jones (Laois), J. Murphy tWexford), J. Kelly, M. Corrigan (Offaly), P. Quirke (Carlow), P. Carroll (Offaly), Martin Cuddy (Laois), P. Horan (Offaly), M. Walsh (Laois). Subs: J. Hennessy (Kilkenny) for M. Walsh.

1982

Connacht—All Galway except where stated): D. Synnott (Mayo), S. Coen, N. Mclnerney, J. McDonagh, S. Linnane, S. Silke, I. Clarke, M. Connolly, S. Mahon, J. Henry (Mayo), Joe Connolly, P. Piggott, F. Gantley, B. Lynskey, P. J. Molloy. Subs. Jimmy Cooney for McDonagh, B. Forde for Gantley, N. Lane or Piggott.

Leinster—J. Nolan, L. Bennett (Wexford), J. Bohane (Laois) P. Fleury, A. Fogarty, P. Delaney (Offaly), J. Hennessy (Kilkenny), G. O'Connor (Wexford), G. Henderson (Kilkenny), M. Brophy (Laois), B. Bermingham, M. Corrigan, P. Carroll (Offaly), P. J. Cuddy (Laoisl, W. Fitzpatrick (Kilkenny).

1983

Connacht—All Galway, except where stated). D. Synnott (Mayo), N. Mclnerney, C. Hayes, S. Coen, S. Linnane, S. Mahon, J. McDonagh, M. Connolly, I. Clarke, A. Staunton, F. Burke, B. Lynskey, B. Forde, N. Lane. P. J. Molloy.

Leinster—N. Skehan, J. Henderson (Kilkenny), E. Coughlan (Offaly), L. Bennett (Wexford), A. Fogarty, P. Delaney (Offaly), G. Henderson, G. Fennelly (Kilkenny), J. Kelly, P. Carroll (Offaly), M. Cuddy (Laois), L. Fennelly, W. Fitzpatrick, C. Heffernan (Kilkenny), S. Kinsella (Wexford). Subs: F. Cummins (Kilkenny) for G. Fennelly, J. Conran (Wexford) for Delaney.

1984

Munster—G. Cunningham (Cork), S. Hehir (Clare), L. Enright, P. Herbert, L. O'Donoghue (Limerick), S. Stack (Clare) P. Ryan (Waterford), J. Fenton (Cork), J. Carroll (Limerick), N. English (Tipperary), D. Fitzgerald (Limerick), B. Ryan (Tipperary), K. Hennessy (Cork), J. McKenna (Limerick), G. Mclnerney (Clare). Sub: T. Mulcahy (Cork) for Hennessy.

Leinster—N. Skehan, J. Henderson (Kilkenny), E. Coughlan, P. Fleury (Offaly), J. Conran (Wexford), J. Delaney (Laois), A. Fogarty (Offaly), F. Cummins, J. Hennessy (Kilkenny), P. Critchley, M. Cuddy (Laois), G. Fennelly (Kilkenny), P. J. Cuddy (Laois), C. Heffernan, W. Fitzpatrick (Kilkenny). Subs: P. Courtney (Wexford) for Critchley, M. Cosgrove (Westmeath) for Fitzpatrick.

1985

Munster—G. Cunningham, (Cork), S. Hehir (Clare), L. Enright, P. Herbert (Limerick), T. Cashman (Cork), S. Stack (Clare), D. MacCurtain (Cork), J. Carroll (Limerick), P. Hartnett (Cork), N. English, D. O'Connell (Tipperary), J. Fenton, T. Mulcahy, K. Hennessy, A. O'Sullivan (Cork). Subs: J. Callinan (Clare) for A. O'Sullivan, S. Power for D. O'Connell, R. Ryan (Tipperary) for N. English.

Connacht—(All Galway): P. Murphy, P. Finnerty, C. Hayes, S. Linnane, T. Keady, M. Mooney, Ollie Kilkenny, S. Mahon, T. Kilkenny, M. Haverty, P. Piggott, Joe Cooney, M. McGrath, N. Lane, A. Cunningham. Subs: A. Staunton for A. Kilkenny, B. Forde for M. McGrath.

1986

Connacht—(All Galway) P. Murphy, A. Kilkenny, C. Hayes, S. Linnane, P. Finnerty, T. Keady, A. Kilkenny, P. Malone, S. Mahon, M. McGrath, A. Cunningham, Joe Cooney, P. J. Molloy, M. Connolly, N. Lane.

Munster—G. Cunningham (Cork), P. Fitzmaurice (Limerick), D. Mulcahy (Cork), T. Keane (Clare), D. Foran (Woterford), J. Carroll (Limerick), B. Ryan (Tipperary), J. Fenton, P. Hartnett (Cork), N. English (Tipperary), K. Hennessy (Cork), C. Lyons (Clare), D. Fitzgerald, P. McCarthy (Limerick), D. O'Connell (Tipperary). Subs: P. Kelly for K. Hennessy, L. O'Donoghue (Limerick) for D. Foran.

1987

Connacht (all Galway)—J. Commins, S. Linnane, C. Hayes, O. Kilkenny, P. Malone, P. Piggott, T. Monaghan, S. Mahon, A. Kilkenny, M. Naughton, A. Cunningham, Joe Cooney, M. McGrath, B. Lynskey, E. Ryan. Subs: P. J. Molloy for Naughton: N. Lane for Mahon.

Leinster—J. Troy (Offaly), J. Bohane (Laois), P. Prendergast (Kilkenny), J. Henderson (Kilkenny), B. Keeshan (Offaly), G. Henderson

(Kilkenny), J. Taylor (Laois), G. Fennelly (Kilkenny), J. Kelly (Offaly) P. Critchley (Laois), B. Byrne (Wexford), L. Ryan (Kilkenny), P. Cleary (Offaly), H. Ryan (Kilkenny), D. Fogarty (Offaly). Subs: R. Power (Kilkenny) for Kelly; T. Dempsey (Wexford) for B. Byrne.

1988

Leinster—J. Troy (Offaly), E. Cleary (Wexford), A. Fogarty (Offaly), J. Henderson (Kilkenny), J. O'Connor (Wexford), M. Cleere (Kilkenny), J. Power (Kilkenny), L. Ryan (Kilkenny), S. Dalton (Dublin), V. Teehan (Offaly), B. McMahon (Dublin), M. Corrigan (Offaly), P. J. Cuddy (Laois), C. Heffernan (Kilkenny), D. Kilcoyne (Westmeath).

Connacht (all Galway)—J. Commins, S. Linnane, C. Hayes, M. Helebert, R. Duane, B. Lynskey, T. Monaghan, P. Malone, Joe Cooney, M. Connolly (Craughwell), A. Cunningham, M. Naughton, M. McGrath, E. Dervan, G. Burke, Subs: P. Nolan for Burke (45th minute).

1989

Connacht (all Galway)—J. Commins, D. Fahy, S. Treacy, S. Dolphin, P. Finnerty, M. Coleman, P. Higgins, J. Hardiman, T. Monaghan, A. Cunningham, J. Cooney, M. Kenny, G. Burke, S. Dolan, E. Ryan. Subs: P. Malone for Hardiman R. Duane for Monaghan.

Munster—T. Quaid (Limerick), G. Fitzpatrick (Waterford), C. O'Donovan (Tipperary), J. Heffernan (Tipperary); Conal Bonnar (Tipperary), L. O'Connor (Waterford), B. Finn (Limerick), S. Ahearne (Waterford), A. O'Sullivan (Cork), S. Fitzgibbon (Limerick), G. Kirby (Limerick), M. Cleary (Tipperary), T. Guilfoyle (Clare), Cormac Bonnar (Tipperary), N. English (Tipperary). Subs: C. Stakelum (Tipperary) for O'Sullivan, Colm Bonnar (Tipperary) for Fitzpatrick.

1990
NO COMPETITION

1991

Connacht (all Galway)—R. Burke, B. Dervan, P. Finnerty, D. Fahy, A. Keady, M. Coleman, G. Keane, A. Cunningham, P. Malone, M. McGrath, J. Cooney, M. Naughton, G. Burke, B. Lyaskey, J. Rabbitte. Subs: D. Curley for Burke, P. Higgins for Cunningham.

Munster—G. Cunningham (Cork), D. Byrne (Waterford), P. Carey (Limerick), J. O'Connell (Clare), J. Cashman (Cork), D. Ryan (Tipperary), B. Ryan (Tipperary), M. Houlihan (Limerick) G. Hegarty (Limerick); C. Carey (Limerick), T. Guilfoyle (Clare), J. Leahy (Tipperary), B. O'Sullivan (Waterford), G. Fitzgerald (Cork), M. Cleary (Tipperary). Subs: C. Casey (Cork) for Hegarty, Conal Bonnar (Tipperary) for Cashman, C. Stakelum (Tipperary) for Guilfoyle.

1992

Munster—G. Cunningham (Cork), D. Byrne (Waterford), N. Sheehy (Tipperary), P. Delaney (Tipperary), J. O'Connell (Clare), J. Cashman (Cork), D. Walsh (Cork), M. Houlihan (Limerick), D. Carr (Tipperary), M. Cleary (Tipperary), J. Leahy (Tipperary), A. Ryan (Tipperary), B. O'Sullivan (Waterford), G. Kirby (Limerick), C. Carey (Limerick). Subs: C. Walsh (Kerry) for Leahy, B. Ryan (Tipperary) for Delaney, L. Garvey (Limerick) for Cleary.

Ulster—P. Gallagher (Antrim), K. Coulter (Down), D. McKinley (Antrim), P. Braniff (Down), M. Mallon (Down), P. Jennings (Antrim), P. McMullan (Down), D. Hughes (Down), C. Mageen (Down), J. Carson (Antrim), A. McCarry (Antnm), S. Downey (Derry), O. McFetridge (Antrim), C. Barr (Antrim), N. Sands (Down). Subs: N. Keith (Down) for Gallagher, M. Baillie (Down) for Carson, G. O'Kane (Antrim) for Coulter, D. McKillop (Antrim) for McCorry.

1993

Leinster—J. Troy (Offaly), M. Hanamy (Offaly), C. Duggan (Laois), L. Simpson (Kilkenny), L. Dunne (Wexford), P. O'Neill (Kilkenny), W. O'Connor (Kilkenny), L. O'Gorman (Wexford), M. Phelan (Kilkenny), M. Storey (Wexford), J. Power (Kilkenny), P. Potterton (Meath), E. Morrissey (Kilkenny), D. J. Carey (Kilkenny), A. Ronan (Kilkenny). Sub: T. Dempsey (Wexford) for Storey.

Ulster—N. Keith (Down), S. McMullen (Antrim), G. Coulter (Down), P. Branniff (Down), M. Mallon (Down), D. McKinley (Antrim), R. Donnelly (Antrim), P. McKillen (Antrim), C. Mageen (Down), P. O'Prey (Down), Gary O'Kane (Antrim), J. Carson (Antrim), A. Elliott (Antrim), M. Bailie (Down), N. Sands (Down). Sub: S. P. McKillop (Antrim) for Bailie.

1994

Connacht (all Galway)—R. Burke, P. Cooney, S. Treacy, D. Fahy, N. Power, G. Mclnerney, M. Donoghue, M. Coleman, P. Malone, F. Forde, N. Shaughnessy, B. Keogh, L. Turley, J. Rabbitte, L. Burke. Sub: D. Colemon for Forde.

Leinster—J. Troy (Offaly), E. O'Connor (Kilkenny), C. Duggan (Laois), L. Simpson (Kilkenny), L. O'Gorman (Wexford), B. Maher (Laois), L. Keoghan (Kilkenny), T. Dempsey (Wexford), M. Phelan (Kilkenny), M. Storey (Wexford), J. Power (Kilkenny), Johnny Dooley (Offaly), D. J. Carey (Kilkenny), E. Morrissey (Kilkenny), P. Potterton (Meath). Sub: A. Ronan (Kilkenny) for Dooley.

1995

Munster—J. Quaid (Limerick), S. McDonagh (Limerick), M. Nash (Limerick), A. Daly (Clare), D. Clarke (Limerick), M. Ryan (Tipperary), D. Nash (Limerick), Colm Bonnar (Tipperary), C. Carey (Limerick), M. Cleary (Tipperory), A. Browne (Waterford), B. Egan (Cork), K. Murray (Cork), G. Kirby (Limerick), D. Quigley (Limerick). Subs: P. Flynn (Waterford) for Browne, J. O'Connor (Clare) for Quigley, J. Brenner (Waterford) for Egan.

Ulster—N. Keith (Down), K. Coulter (Down), O. Colgan (Antrim), P. Brannif (Down), M. Mallon (Down), G. Savage (Down), S. P. McKillop (Antrim), P. McKillen (Antrim), C. McCambridge (Antrim), T. McNaughton (Antrim), O. Collins (Derry), D. O'Prey (Down), V. Owens (Tyrone), H. Gilmore (Down), N. Sands (Down). Subs: B. Coulter (Down) for Owens, R. Donnelly (Antrim) for Gilmore.

1996

Munster—D. Fitzgerald (Clare), S. McDonagh (Limerick), B. Lohan (Clare), D. Nash (Limerick), A. Browne (Waterford), S. McMahon (Clare), A. Daly (Clare), O. Baker (Clare), C. Carey (Limerick), M. Cleary (Tipperary), D. Ryan (Tipperary), T. Dunne (Tipperary), J. O'Connor (Clare), G. Kirby (Limerick), D. Quigley (Limerick). Subs: L. Doyle (Clare) for McDonagh, B. Corcoran for Dunne, G. Manley (Cork) for Cleary.

Leinster—D. Hughes (Offaly), B. Maher (Laois), K. Kinahan (Offaly), M. Hanamy (Offaly), B. Whelahan (Offaly), L. Dunne (Wexford), N. Rigney (Laois), A. Fenlon (Wexford), D. Conroy (Laois), Joe Dooley (Offaly), J. Power (Kilkenny), D. J. Carey (Kilkenny), E. Morrissey (Dublin), J. Troy (Offaly), D. Byrne (Kilkenny). Subs: S. Power (Dublin) for Kinahan, L. Keoghan (Kilkenny) for Conroy, D. Martin (Meath) for Power.

1997

Munster—D. Fitzgerald (Clare), S. McDonagh (Limerick), B. Lohan (Clare), M. Ryan (Tipperary), D. Clarke (Limerick), L. Doyle (Clare), A. Browne (Waterford), O. Moran (Limerick), C. Lynch (Clare), T. Dunne (Tipperary), K. McGrath (Waterford), M. Galligan (Limerick), M. Cleary (Tipperary), N. Gilligan (Clare), S. McGrath (Cork). Subs: C. Bonnar (Tipperary) for Moran, D. Forde (Clare) for Cleary.

Leinster—R. Cashin (Laois), B. Maher (Laois), S. Power (Dublin), L. Simpson (Kilkenny), N. Rigney (Laois), C. Byrne (Kildare), R. Boland (Dublin), A. Comerford (Kilkenny), O. Dowling (Laois), Johnny Dooley (Offaly), D. Rooney (Laois), C. McCann (Dublin), R. McCarthy (Wexford), C. Brennan (Kilkenny), C. Carter (Kilkenny). Sub: G. Ennis (Dublin) for McCann, C. Cassidy (Offaly) for Byrne, John Troy (Offaly) for Rooney.

1998

Leinster—S. Byrne (Offaly), S. Whelahan (Offaly), J. Errity (Offaly), W. O'Connor (Kilkenny), L. Walsh (Dublin), B. Whelahan (Offaly), L. Keoghan (Kilkenny), L. O'Gorman (Wexford), A. Fenlon (Wexford), D. Cuddy (Laois), M. Storey (Wexford), B. McEvoy (Kilkenny), D. J. Carey (Kilkenny), John Troy (Offaly), C. Carter (Kilkenny). Subs: N. Rigney (Laois) for Walsh, N. Moloney (Kilkenny) for O'Gorman).

Connacht—(all Galway except where stated)—K. Devine, G. Kennedy, B. Feeney, V. Maher, R. Walsh, N. Shaughnessy, P. Hardiman, T. Kavanagh, M. Cunniffe (Roscommon), J. Rabbitte, C. Moore, N. Kenny, O. Fahy, A. Kelly (Roscommon), K. Broderick. Sub: A. Kerins for Cunniffe.

1999

Connacht—(All Galway): M. Crimmins, L. Hodgins, B. Feeney, C. Moore, P. Walsh, N. Larkin, P. Hardiman, R. Gantley, A. Kerins, O. Fahy, J. Rabbitte, O. Canning, E. Cloonan, M. Kerins, K. Broderick.

Munster—B. Cummins (Tipperary), F. Ryan (Cork), D. O'Sullivan (Cork), B. Corcoran (Cork), L. Doyle (Clare), O. Moran (Limerick), S. Óg Ó hAilpín (Cork), M. O'Connell (Cork), T. Dunne (Tipperary), A. Markham (Clare), F. McCormack (Cork), K. McGrath (Waterford), L. Cahill (Tipperary), N. Gilligan (Clare), S. McGrath (Cork). Subs: D. Shanahan (Waterford) for T. Dunne, D. Kennedy (Tipperary) for B. Corcoran.

2000

Munster – B.Cummins (Tipperary), F.Ryan, D.O'Sullivan (Cork), B.Lohan (Clare), J.Carroll (Tipperary), O.Moran (Limerick), E.Corcoran (Tipperary), P.Queally (Waterford), J.Leahy (Tipperary), A.Markham (Clare), A.Browne (Cork), B.O'Meara (Tipperary), S.McGrath (Cork), P.Flynn (Waterford), J.Deane (Cork). Subs – T.J.Ryan (Limerick) for Markham, D.Barrett (Cork) for Queally, D.Forde (Clare) for Flynn.

Leinster – J.McGarry, M.Kavanagh (Kilkenny), K.Kinahan (Offaly), W.O'Connor (Kilkenny), B.Whelahan (Offaly), L.Dunne (Wexford), P.Barry, A,Comerford (Kilkenny), A.Fenlon (Wexford), G.Hanniffy (Offaly), J.Power (Kilkenny), N.Horan (Meath), C.Carter, D.J.Carey, H.Shefflin (Kilkenny). Subs – E.Kennedy (Kilkenny) for Dunne, L.Murphy (Wexford) for Horan, P.Larkin (Kilkenny) for Fenlon.

2001

Munster – B.Cummins (Tipperary), T.J.Ryan (Limerick), P.Maher (Tipperary), F.Lohan (Clare), D.Reale, O.Moran (Limerick), P.Kelly (Tipperary), C.Carey (Limerick), P.Queally (Waterford), D.Forde (Clare), K.McGrath (Waterford), S.McGrath (Cork), E.Kelly (Tipperary), A.Browne (Cork), N.Gilligan (Clare). Subs – D.Barrett (Cork) for Queally, Queally for Barrett, B.O'Meara (Tipperary) for S.McGrath, N.Ronan (Cork) for Forde.

Connacht (all Galway) – L.Donoghue, G.Kennedy, M.Healy, C.Moore, P.Walsh, L.Hodgins, D.Hardiman, R.Murray, A.Kerins, N.Hayes, M.Kerins, K.Broderick, D.Coen, O.Fahy, F.Healy. Subs – B.Higgins for Walsh, J.Culkin for Murray, D.Hayes for Healy.

2002

Leinster – J.McGarry, M.Kavanagh, N.Hickey (Kilkenny), D.O'Connor (Wexford), R.Mullally, J.J.Delaney (Kilkenny), L.Ryan (Dublin), D.Lyng, A.Comerford, J.Hoyne, H.Shefflin (Kilkenny), C.Keaney (Dublin), J.Coogan, E.Brennan (Kilkenny), B.Murphy (Offaly). Subs – S.Byrne (Offaly) for McGarry, C.Kehoe (Wexford) for O'Connor.

Munster – B.Cummins, (Tipperary), B.Greene (Waterford), D.O'Sullivan (Cork), P.Maher (Tipperary), D.Hoey (Clare), E.Corcoran (Tipperary), S. Óg Ó hAilpín (Cork), P.Queally (Waterford), T.Dunne (Tipperary), T.Griffin (Clare), K.McGrath (Waterford), B.O'Connor (Cork), E.McGrath (Waterford), B.Begley (Limerick), J.Deane (Cork). Subs – D.Reale (Limerick) for Greene, A.O'Shaughnessy (Limerick) for Deane, O.Moran (Limerick) for O'Sullivan, E.Kelly (Waterford) for Begley, P.O'Connell (Kerry) for Hoey.

2003

Leinster – J.McGarry, M.Kavanagh, N.Hickey (Kilkenny), D.Franks (Offaly), L.Dunne (Wexford), B.Whelahan (Offaly), S.Hiney, C.Keaney (Dublin), D.Lyng, T.Walsh, J.Hoyne (Kilkenny), R.Hanniffy (Offaly), R.Jacob (Wexford), H.Shefflin (Kilkenny), B.Carroll (Offaly). Subs – G.Hanniffy (Offaly) for Jacob, B.Murphy (Offaly) for Carroll, D.O'Connor (Wexford) for Franks, P.Cuddy (Laois) for Whelahan.

Connacht (all Galway) – L.Donoghue, D.Joyce, D.Cloonan, F.Moore, F.Healy, T. Óg Regan, D.Tierney, O.Canning, J.Conroy, A.Kerins, M.Kerins, K.Broderick, D.Forde, E.Cloonan, R.Gantley. Sub – R.Murray for Regan.

2004

Connacht (all Galway) – L.Donoghue, D.Joyce, S.Kavanagh, O.Canning, F.Healy, L.Hodgins, F.Moore, D.Collins, D.Tierney, A.Kerins, M.Kerins, K.Broderick, D.Hayes, O.Fahy, D.Donoghue. Subs – T. Óg Regan for Hodgins, G.Farragher for Collins, N.Healy for A.Kerins, K.Higgins for D.Donoghue.

Munster – B.Cummins, P.Curran, P.Maher (Tipperary), J.Murray (Waterford), E.Corcoran (Tipperary), R.Curran, J.Gardiner (Cork), T.Browne (Waterford), O.Moran (Limerick), D.Shanahan (Waterford), N.Gilligan (Clare), N.Moran (Limerick), J.Mullane (Waterford), E.Kelly, (Tipperary), J.Deane (Cork). Subs – C.Lynch (Clare) for Browne, K.Murphy (Cork) for Deane, P.O'Brien (Tipperary) for Gilligan.

2005

Munster – D.Fitzgerald (Clare), E.Murphy (Waterford), P.Curran (Tipperary), P.Mulcahy (Cork), J.Gardiner (Cork), R.Curran (Cork), D.Fitzgerald (Tipperary), O.Moran (Limerick), P.Kelly (Tipperary), E.Kelly (Waterford), S.Prendergast (Waterford), D.McMahon (Clare), B.O'Connor (Cork), M.Webster (Tipperary), N.Gilligan (Clare). Subs – A.Markham (Clare) for Murphy, D.Óg Cusack (Cork) for Fitzgerald, S.Butler (Tipperary) for Webster, T.Carmody (Clare) for Prendergast.

Leinster – J.McGarry (Kilkenny), R.Mullally (Kilkenny), D.Ryan (Wexford), J.Tennyson (Kilkenny), R.Hanniffy (Offaly), D.Ruth (Wexford), J.J.Delaney (Kilkenny), J.Ryall (Kilkenny), B.Barry (Kilkenny), T.Walsh (Kilkenny), R.Power (Kilkenny), J.Young (Laois), E.Brennan (Kilkenny), G.Hanniffy (Offaly), B.Carroll (Offaly). Subs – B.Murphy (Offaly) for Ryall, J.Hoyne (Kilkenny) for Power, M.Comerford (Kilkenny) for Murphy, D.Lyng (Wexford) for Barry, E.Quigley (Wexford) for Carroll.

2006

Leinster – B.Mullins (Offaly), R.Mullally (Kilkenny), J.Tennyson (Kilkenny), J.Ryall (Kilkenny), Diarmuid Lyng (Wexford), R.Hanniffy (Offaly), T.Walsh (Kilkenny), Derek Lyng (Kilkenny), G.Hanniffy (Offaly), E.Larkin (Kilkenny), R.Power (Kilkenny), D.Franks (Offaly), E.Brennan (Kilkenny), J.Bergin (Offaly), A.Fogarty (Kilkenny). Subs – M.Jacob (Wexford) for Franks, M.Travers (Wexford) for Mullally, D.McCormack (Westmeath) for Diarmuid Lyng, J.Young (Laois) for Derek Lyng, J.McCormack (Dublin) for Larkin.

Connacht (all Galway) – L.Donoghue, D.Joyce, G.Mahon, T.Óg Regan, D.Collins, D.Cloonan, J.Lee, R.Murray, D.Tierney, I.Tannian, M.Kerins, A.Kerins, K.Burke, E.Cloonan, F.Healy. Subs – D.Hayes for Burke, M.J.Quinn for Mahon, N.Healy for A.Kerins, K.Broderick for Murray, G.Farragher for M.Kerins.

2007

Munster – B.Murray (Limerick), E.Murphy (Waterford), D.Fanning (Tipperary), G.Quinn (Clare), J.Gardiner (Cork), T.Browne (Waterford), S.Hickey (Limerick), D.O'Grady (Limerick), B.O'Connell (Clare), S.McGrath (Tipperary), O.Moran (Limerick), E.Kelly (Waterford) J.Mullane (Waterford), D.Shanahan (Waterford), L.Corbett (Tipperary). Subs – S.Óg Ó hAilpín (Cork) for O'Connell, N.Gilligan (Clare) for McGrath, G.O'Grady (Tipperary) for Murphy, N.Moran (Limerick) for O.Moran, M.O'Brien (Limerick) for Shanahan.

Connacht (all Galway) – J.Skehill, F.Moore, C.Dervan, G.Mahon, D.Collins, J.Lee, A.Keary, F.Healy, R.Murray, A.Kerins, I.Tannian, S.Glynn, D.Hayes, N.Healy, A.Callanan. Subs – D.Joyce for Collins, T.Óg Regan for Mahon, K.Hynes for Glynn, K.Higgins (Mayo) for A.Kerins, G.Kennedy for Moore.

2008

Leinster – P.J.Ryan (Kilkenny), J.Dalton (Kilkenny), J.Tyrrell (Kilkenny), D.Franks (Offaly), T.Walsh (Kilkenny), R.Fallon (Dublin), J.O'Connor (Wexford), R.Hanniffy (Offaly), E.Coady (Carlow), M.Rice (Kilkenny), B.Murtagh (Westmeath), E.Larkin (Kilkenny), E.Brennan (Kilkenny), R.Power (Kilkenny), R.Hogan (Kilkenny). Subs – B.Hogan (Kilkenny), A.Fogarty (Kilkenny), D.Horan (Offaly), T.Fitzgerald (Laois).

Munster – B.Cummins (Tipperary), C.O'Brien (Tipperary), P.Curran (Tipperary), S.Hickey (Limerick), J.Gardiner (Cork), G.Quinn (Clare), S.Óg Ó hAilpín (Cork), T.Kenny (Cork), B.O'Connell (Clare), P.Kelly (Tipperary), T.Carmody (Clare), B.O'Connor (Cork), A.O'Shaughnessy (Limerick), E.Kelly (Waterford), N.Gilligan (Clare). Subs – D.Óg Cusack (Cork), L.Corbett (Tipperary), D.Fanning (Tipperary), S.Callanan (Tipperary).

2009

Leinster – P.J.Ryan (Kilkenny), D.Franks (Offaly), D.Kenny (Offaly), J.Tyrrell (Kilkenny), T.Walsh (Kilkenny), J.J.Delaney (Kilkenny), M.Jacob (Wexford), R.Hanniffy (Offaly), E.Quigley (Wexford), M.Rice (Kilkenny), H.Shefflin (Kilkenny), D.Lyng (Wexford), D.O'Callaghan (Dublin), J.Bergin (Offaly), E.Brennan (Kilkenny). Subs – A.Fogarty (Kilkenny) for O'Callaghan, S.Hiney (Dublin) for Tyrrell, C.Farrell (Wexford) for Hanniffy, A.McCrabbe (Dublin) for Rice, S.Clynch (Meath) for Lyng.

Connacht (all Galway unless stated) – C.Callanan, M.Ryan, G.McLearn, C.O'Donovan, A.Coen, B.Costello, G.Mahon, A.Cullinane, K.Raymond (Sligo), P.Killilea, M.Kerins, K.Hooban, N.Healy, R.Murray, A.Callanan. Subs – B.Burke for O'Donovan, C.Donnellan for Killilea, F.Healy for Raymond, J.Gantley for Hooban, M.Keaveney (Roscommon) for Mahon.

CAPTAINS OF WINNING INTERPROVINCIAL HURLING TEAMS

1927—Watty Dumphy (Kilkenny)
1928—Sean Óg Murphy (Cork)
1929—Sean Óg Murphy (Cork)
1930—Dinny Barry Murphy (Cork)
1931—Philip Purcell (Tipperary)
1932—Jim Dermody (Kilkenny)
1933—Eddie Doyle (Kilkenny)
1934—Timmy Ryan (Limerick)
1935—Timmy Ryan (Limerick)
1936—Paddy Larkin (Kilkenny)
1937—Mick Mackey (Limerick)
1938—Jim Lanigan (Tipperary)
1939—John Keane (Waterford)
1940—Sean Barret (Cork)
1941—Bobby Hinks (Kilkenny)
1942—Willie O'Donnell (Tipperary)
1943—Jack Lynch (Cork)
1944—Sean Condon (Cork)
1945—Johnny Quirke (Cork)
1946—Ger Cornally (Tipperary)
1947—Sean Duggan (Galway)
1948—Willie Murphy (Cork)
1949—Jim Ware (Waterford)
1950—Pat Stakelum (Tipperary)
1951—Sean Kenny (Tipperary)
1952—Pat Stakelum (Tipperary)
1953—Christy Ring (Cork)
1954—Johnny McGovern (Kilkenny)
1955—Christy Ring (Cork)
1956—Nick O'Donnell (Wexford)
1957—Mick Cashman (Cork)
1958—Phil Grimes (Waterford)
1959—Tony Wall (Tipperary)
1960—Frankie Walsh (Waterford)
1961—Tony Wall (Tipperary)
1962—Noel Dromgoole (Dublin)
1963—Jimmy Doyle (Tipperary)
1964—Seamus Cleere (Kilkenny)
1965—Paddy Moran (Kilkenny)
1966—Jimmy Doyle (Tipperary)
1967—Ollie Walsh (Kilkenny)
1968—Mick Roche (Tipperary)
1969—Len Gaynor (Tipperary)
1970—Gerald McCarthy (Cork)
1971—Tony Doran (Wexford)
1972—Jim Treacy (Kilkenny)
1973—Pat Delaney (Kilkenny)
1974—Pat Henderson (Kilkenny)
1975—Pat Delaney (Kilkenny)
1976—Eamon O'Donoghue
1977—Tony Doran (Wexford)
1978—Charlie McCarthy (Cork)
1979—Phil "Fan" Larkin (Kilkenny)

1980—Joe Connolly (Galway)
1981—Joe McKenna (Limerick)
1982—Sean Silke (Galway)
1983—Sylvie Linnane (Galway)
1984—John Fenton (Cork)
1985—Ger Cunningham (Cork)
1986—Noel Lane (Galway)
1987—Conor Hayes (Galway)
1988—Aidan Fogarty (Offaly)
1989—Joe Cooney (Galway)
1990—No competition
1991—Pete Finnerty (Galway)
1992—Declan Carr (Tipperary)
1993—John Power (Kilkenny)
1994—Michael Coleman (Galway)
1995—Gary Kirby (Limerick)
1996—Anthony Daly (Clare)
1997—Brian Lohan (Clare)
1998—Willie O'Connor (Kilkenny)
1999—Brian Feeney (Galway)
2000—Fergal Ryan (Cork)
2001—Brendan Cummins (Tipperary)
2002—Andy Comerford (Kilkenny)
2003—Michael Kavanagh (Kilkenny)
2004—Ollie Fahy (Galway)
2005—John Gardiner (Cork)
2006—Eddie Brennan (Kilkenny)
2007—John Mullane (Waterford)
2008—Tommy Walsh (Kilkenny)
2009—Henry Shefflin (Kilkenny)

OIREACHTAS TOURNAMENT (HURLING)

1939—Croke Park, November 5. Final:
Limerick 4-4, Kilkenny 2-5.
1940—Croke Park, October 27. Final:
Kilkenny 7-11, Cork 1-6.
1941-43—Run as football tournament.
1941—Dublin 3-3, Kildare 2-6 (draw)
Newbridge: Dublin 1-8, Kildare 1-5 (replay)
1942—Dublin 1-6, Cavan 1-3
1943—Roscommon 1-6, Cavan 0-6
1944—Dublin 6-6, Galway, 3-6.
1945—Croke Park, October 21. Final:
Tipperary 4-6, Galway, 4-3
1946—Croke Park. Final:
Antrim 2-7, Laois 0-10
1947—Croke Park, November 23. Final:
Kilkenny 2-12, Galway 2-6
1948—Croke Park, October 17. Final:
Dublin, 3-6, Waterford, 2-6
1949—Croke Park, October 16. Final:
Tipperary 2-8, Laois 1-6
1950—Croke Park, October 15. Final:
Galway 2-9, Wexford, 2-6
1951—Croke Park, October 21. Final:
Wexford 4-7, Kilkenny, 3-7
1952—Croke Park, October 19. Final:
Galway 3-7, Wexford, 1-10
1953—Croke Park, October 25. Final:
Wexford 5-11, Clare 4-5
1954—Croke Park, October 24. Final:
Clare 2-8, Wexford 2-8
Croke Park, November 21. Replay:
Clare 3-6, Wexford 0-12
1955—Croke Park, October 23. Final:
Wexford 3-11, Kilkenny, 3-4.
1956—Croke Park, October 21. Final:
Wexford 0-16, Kilkenny 1-9
1957—Croke Park, October 20. Final:
Kilkenny 4-10, Waterford 3-5.
1958—Thurles, October 19: Final:
Galway 5-16, Wexford 2-4
1959—Croke Park, October 18. Final:
Kilkenny 6-6, Galway 5-8
1960—Croke Park, October 23. Final:
Tipperary 4-11, Cork 2-10
1961—Croke Park, October 22. Final:
Tipperary 3-6, Wexford, 2-9 (draw)
Croke Park, November 5. Replay:
Tipperary 2-13, Wexford 3-4
1962—Croke Park, October 21. Final:
Waterford 4-12, Tipperary 3-9
1963—Croke Park, October 20. Final:
Tipperary, 4-15; Wexford 3-12.
1964—Croke Park, October 18. Final:
Tipperary 5-7; Kilkenny, 4-8.
1965—Croke Park, October 18. Final:
Tipperary 2-12, Kilkenny 2-7
1966—Croke Park, December 4. Final:
Kilkenny 4-7, Wexford 1-7
1967—Croke Park, October 17. Final:
Kilkenny 4-4, Clare 1-8
1968—Thurles, October 27. Final:
Tipperary 1-9, Cork 1-6.
1969—Croke Park, November 2. Final:
Kilkenny 4-14, Cork 3-10
1970—Thurles, December 13. Final:
Tipperary 1-12, Cork 0-8
1971—Croke Park, October 17. Final:
Limerick 4-12, Wexford 3-8
1972—Croke Park, October 15. Final:
Tipperary 2-13, Wexford 2-13 (draw)
Kilkenny, November 26. Replay:
Tipperary 2-13, Wexford 1-8
1973—Cork, December 16. Final:
Cork 1-8, Kilkenny 1-6
1974—Mardyke (Cork), November 3. Final:
Cork 3-15. Waterford 1-5
1975—Croke Park, October 26. Final:
Cork 3-13, Wexford 2-7.
1976—Croke Park, October 24. Final:
Galway 1-15, Cork 2-9
1977—Ballinasloe, March 19, 1978. Final:
Galway. 2-8, Cork 2-8
Replay did not rake place
1978—Wexford, October 22. Final:
Wexford 0-18, Galway 1-10.
1979—Croke Park, September 23. Final:

Wexford 3-17, Offaly, 5-8
1980—Birr, October 5. Final:
Wexford 1-19, Offaly 3-5.
1981—Loughrea, October 18. Final:
Galway 1-15, Wexford 1-7
1982—Ennis, November 7. Final:
Clare 3-9, Limerick 2-9
1983—Ennis, November 6. Final:
Clare 1-12, Kilkenny 1-11
1984—Callan, December 2. Final:
Kilkenny 1-11, Cork 1-7
1985—Pairc Ui Caoimh, November 10. Final:
Cork 2-11, Galway 1-10
1986—Athenry, May 31, 1987. Final:
Wexford 3-17, Galway 1-22 (after extra time).
Scores at normal time Wexford 1-14,
Galway 0-17
1987—No competition.
1988—Enniscorthy, April 3. Final:
Galway 4-15, Wexford 3-11
1989—Ennis, March 4, 1990. Final:
Galway 1-19, Tipperary 0-8
1990—Ennis, November 11. Final:
Tipperary 1-15, Galway 0-7
1991—Ballinasloe, November 23. Final:
Galway 2-12, Wexford 3-5
1992—Dingle, November 1. Final:
Galway 1-13, Waterford 0-10
1993—Athenry, October 25. Final:
Galway 2-1 9, Clare 3-9 (after extra time).
Scores at end of normal time
Galway 1-10, Clare 3-4.
1994—Dungarvan, December 4. Final:
Wexford 2-7, Cork 1-8
1995—Wexford, November 25. Final:
Offaly 2-13, Wexford 0-9
1996—Ennis, December 1. Final:
Clare 0-11, Kilkenny 1-4
1997—Ballinasloe, February 29, 1998. Final:
Galway 0- 14, Cork 0-8
1998—Páirc Uí Rinn (Cork), March 14, 1999.
Final: Cork 0-15, Galway 0-10
1999—December 3, 2000. Final:
Kilkenny 4-6, Galway 0-12.

WALSH CUP

Kilkenny (17)—1955, 1957, 1958, 1959, 1961, 1962, 1963, 1970, 1973, 1974, 1988, 1989, 1992, 2005, 2006, 2007, 2009.
Wexford (15)—1954, 1956, 1965, 1967, 1968, 1969, 1987, 1995, 1996, 1997, 1998, 1999, 2000, 2001, 2002.
Offaly (5)—1977, 1981, 1990, 1993, 1994.
Dublin (4)—1960, 1964, 1966, 2003.
Laois (2)—1980, 1991.
Westmeath (1)—1982.
U.C.D. (1)—2004.
Antrim (1)—2008.

Note: No competition 1971,1972, 1975, 1976, 1978, 1979, 1983-1986.

KEHOE CUP

Wicklow (6)—1989, 1991, 1998, 2001, 2002, 2003.
Carlow (6)—1986, 1990, 1992, 1999, 2005, 2006.
Westmeath (6)—1978, 1983, 1994, 1995, 2000, 2009.
Meath (5)—1993, 1996, 1997, 2004, 2008.
London (2)—1987, 1988.
Wexford (1)—1977.
Kilkenny (1)—1980.
Dublin (1)—1981.
Laois (1)—1982.
D.I.T. (1)—2007.

Note: No competition 1979, 1984, 1985.

THOMOND FEIS

Limerick (14)—1913, 1920,1922, 1925, 1928, 1932, 1933, 1934, 1935, 1937, 1940, 1944, 1945, 1947.
Tipperary (8)—1915,1916,1924,1927,1930, 1931, 1949, 1951.
Cork (7)—1914, 1926, 1936, 1941, 1948, 1952, 1954.
Clare (3)—1929, 1946, 1956.
Note: No competition 1917-1919, 1921, 1923, 1938, 1939, 1 942, 1943, 1950 (Unfinished. Cork and Tipperary in final.) 1953, 1955. Discontinued after 1956.

CROKE CUP FINALS 1896-1915

HURLING

1896—Jones's Road, June 27, 1897.
Clare 6-16, Wexford 0-2
1897—Thurles, July 9, 1899.
Limerick 3-8, Kilkenny 1-4
1898-1901—Cup presented to All-Ireland winners
1902—Jones's Road, February 19, 1905.
Cork 5-10, London 0-3
1903—Dungarvan, May 27, 1906.
Cork 6-9, Wexford 0-5
Note: After the finals of 1896 and 1897 the competition restarted on October 2, 1904. The All Ireland competition had finished on September 11, 1904. It was the 1902 competition with Dungourney having the Cork selection. The following year Blackrock as 1903 champions had the Cork selection.
1904-1906—None
1907—Loughrea, October 13, 1907.
Galway 4-5, Clare 1-8
1908—Jones's Road, November 22, 1908.
Clare 3-14, Galway 1-4
1909—Limerick, October 24.
Laois 3-11, Kerry 3-7

1910—Cork, April 23, 1911.
Cork 12-1, Galway 3-1
1911—Thurles, April 21, 1912.
Tipperary 6-3, Dublin 4-3
1912—Portlaoise, March 30, 1913.
Tipperary 5-3, Laois 3-2
1913—Tullamore, May 17, 1914.
Cork 7-8, Galway 1-1
1914—Dungarvan, December 18.
Cork 9-1, Kilkenny 5-1
1915—Athlone, April 9, 1916.
Dublin 6-5, Clare 2-0
From 1909-1915 the beaten Provincial Finalists played the semi-finals.

RAILWAY SHIELD FINALS

1905—Limerick, 11 November, 1905. Leinster (Kilkenny) 4-10, Connacht (Galway) 4-5
1906—Ennis, 17 February, 1907. Munster (Tipperary) 9-14, Connacht (Galway) 1-5
1907—Jones' Road, 29 September, 1907. Leinster (Selected) 0-14, Munster (Tipperary) 1-8
1908—St. James Park, Kilkenny. 19 July, 1908. Leinster (Kilkenny) 0-14, Munster (Tipperary) 2-5
(Leinster won outright in 1908)

ALL-IRELAND CLUB CHAMPIONSHIPS 1970/71 to 2004/09

ROLL OF HONOUR

SENIOR HURLING

4 —Birr (Offaly) – 1995, 1998, 2002, 2003.
Ballyhale Shamrocks (Kilkenny) – 1981, 1984, 1990, 2007.
3— Blackrock (Cork) – 1972, 1974, 1979.
Athenry (Galway) – 1997, 2000, 2001.
James Stephens (Kilkenny) – 1976, 1982, 2005.
Portumna (Galway) – 2006, 2008, 2009.
2— Glen Rovers (Cork) – 1973, 1977.
St.Finbarr's (Cork) – 1975, 1978.
Sarsfields (Galway) – 1993, 1994.
1— Roscrea (Tipperary) – 1971.
Borris-Ileigh (Tipperary) – 1987.
Buffer's Alley (Wexford) – 1989.
Castlegar (Galway) – 1980.
Glenmore (Kilkenny) – 1981.
Loughgeil Shamrocks (Antrim) – 1983.
St.Martin's (Kilkenny) – 1985.
Kilruane McDonaghs (Tipperary) – 1986.
Midleton (Cork) – 1988.
Kiltormer (Galway) – 1992.
Sixmilebridge (Clare) – 1996.
St.Joseph's Doora-Barefield (Clare) – 1999.
Newtownshandrum (Cork) – 2004.

1970/71 PROVINCIAL FINALS

Connacht: Athleague, 28 March 1971. Liam Mellowes (Galway) 4- 10; Roscommon Gaels 2-5.
Ulster: Loughgiel, 18 July 1971. Loughgiel Shamrocks (Antrim) 6-14; Ballygalget (Down) 2-5.
Munster: Limerick, 18 August 1971. Roscrea {Tipperary) 4-11; Clarecastle (Clare) 1-6.
Leinster: Croke Park, 1 August 1971. St. Rynagh's (Offaly) 4-10; Rathnure (Wexford) 2-9.

1970/71 SEMI FINALS

Loughgiel: 14 November 1971. Roscrea 6-10; Loughgiel Shamrocks 2-8.
St. Rynagh's W.O. Liam Mellowes.

1970/71 FINAL

Birr: 19 December 1971. Roscrea 4-5; St. Rynagh's 2-5.

1971/72 PROVINCIAL FINALS

Connacht: Ballyforan, 26 March 1972. Tommy Larkin's (Galway) 7-14; Four Roads (Roscommon) 0-6.
Ulster: Portaferry, —. Loughgiel Shamrocks (Antrim) 3-8; Portaferry (Down) 1-12.
Munster: Kilmallock, 25 April 1972. Blackrock (Cork) 4-10; Moyne-Templetuohy (Tipperary) 3-1.
Leinster: Carlow, 2 April 1972. Rathnure (Wexford) 2-12; Bennettsbridge (Kilkenny) 1-8.

1971/72 SEMI FINALS

New Ross: 30 April 1972. Rathnure 5-26; Loughgiel Shamrocks 2-4.
Ballinasloe: 30 April 1972. Blackrock 3-7; Tommy Larkin's (Galway) 2-8.

1971/72 FINAL

Waterford: 14 May 1972.
Blackrock 5-13; Rathnure 6-9.

1972/73 PROVINCIAL FINALS

Connacht: Athleague, 18 March 1973.
Castlegar (Galway) 7-12; Tremane (Roscommon) 2-7.
Ulster: Waterfoot, 8 April 1973. O'Donovan Rossas (Antrim) 2-8; Ballycran (Down) 3-2.
Munster: Limerick, 22 April 1973. Glen Rovers (Cork) 2-9; Roscrea (Tipperary) 1-10.
Leinster: Carlow, 6 May 1973. St. Rynagh's (Offaly) 5-5; Rathnure (Wexford) 2-13.

1972/73 SEMI FINALS
Cork: 6 May 1973.
Glen Rovers 6-9; Castlegar 1-7.
Waterfoot: 20 May 1973. St. Rynagh's 5-9; O'Donovan Rossas 2-8.

1972/73 FINAL
Croke Park: 9 December 1973. Glen Rovers 2-18; St. Rynagh's 2-8.

1973/74 PROVINCIAL FINALS
Connacht: Knockcroghery, 3 March 1974. Castlegar (Galway) 7-8; Tremane (Roscommon) 1-7.
Ulster: Dunloy, 9 December 1973. St. John's {Antrim) w.o.; Dungiven (Derry) scr.
Munster: Bruff, 17 February 1974. Blackrock (Cork) 1-13; Newmarket-on-Fergus (Clare) 0-14.
Leinster: Kilkenny, 3 March 1974. Rathnure (Wexford) 1-18; St. Rynagh's (Offaly) 2-9.

1973/74 SEMI FINALS
Cork: 3 March 1974. Blackrock 5-12; St. John's (Antrim) 1-5.
Enniscorthy: 10 March 1974. Rathnure 1-15; Castlegar 1-6.

1973/74 FINAL
Croke Park: 17 March 1974. Blackrock 2-14; Rathnure 3-11 (Draw)
(Replay): Dungarvan, 28 April 1974. Blackrock 3-8; Rathnure 1-9.

1974/75 PROVINCIAL FINALS
Connacht: Ballyhaunis, 2 February 1975. Ardrahan (Galway) 9-12; Tooreen (Mayo) 1-6.
Ulster: Corrigan Park (Belfast), 8 December 1974. Ballycran (Down) 3-5; Sarsfields (Antrim) 3-2.
Munster: Limerick, 19 January 1975. St. Finbarr's (Cork) 0-7; Newmarket-on-Fergus (Clare) 0-3.
Leinster: Croke Park, 26 January 1975. Fenians (Kilkenny) 2-6; St. Rynagh's (Offaly) 1-6.

1974/75 SEMI FINALS
Ballinasloe: 23 February 1975. The Fenians 2-13; Ardrahan 1-8.
Ballycran: 23 February 1975. St. Finbarr's 8-8; Ballycran 3-10.

1974/75 FINAL
Croke Park: 16 March 1975. St. Finbarr's 3-8; Fenians 1-6.

1975/76 PROVINCIAL FINALS
Connacht: Athleague, 7 March 1976. Ardrahan (Galway) 2-14; Athleague (Roscommon) 1-4.
Ulster: Glenariffe, 14 December 1975. Ballygalget (Down) 4-6; Ballycastle McOuillans (Antrim) 1-9.
Munster: Emly, 7 December 1975. Blackrock (Cork) 8-12; Mount Sion (Waterford) 3-8.
Leinster: Carlow, 25 January 1976. James Stephens (Kilkenny) 1-14; St. Rynagh's (Offaly) 2-4.

1975/76 QUARTER FINAL
Ballinosloe: 1 February 1976. Ardrahan 0-7; Brian Boru's (London) 0-5.

1975/76 SEMI FINALS
Ballinasloe: 22 February 1976. Blackrock 2-15; Ardrahan 1-12.
Kilkenny: 22 February 1976. James Stephens 4-15; Ballygalget (Down) 1-7.

1975/76 FINAL
Thurles: 14 March 1976. James Stephens 2-10; Blackrock 2-4.

1976/77 PROVINCIAL FINALS
Connacht: Tremane, 6 February,1977. Tremane (Roscommon) 2-7; Kiltormer (Galway) 1-9.
Ulster: Ballycran, 21 November,1976. Ballycran (Down) 0-8; O'Donovan Rossa (Antrim) 0-7.
Munster: Limerick, 19 December 1976. Glen Rovers (Cork) 2-8; South Liberties (Limerick) 2-4.
Leinster: Carlow, 6 February 1977. Camross (Laois) 3-9; James Stephens (Kilkenny) 1-14.

1976/77 QUARTER FINAL
Páirc Uí Chaoimh: 6 February 1977. Glen Rovers 1 -13; St. Gabriel's (London) 1 -6.

1976-77 SEMI FINALS
Mardyke (Cork): 6 March 1977.
Glen Rovers 7-10; Tremane 0-3.
Ballycran: 6 March 1977.
Camross 3-12; Ballycran 0-7.

1976/77 FINAL
Thurles: 27 March 1977.
Glen Rovers 2-12; Camross 0-8.

1977/78 PROVINCIAL FINALS
Connacht: Four Roads (Roscommon) w.o.; Kiltormer {Suspended).
Ulster: Casement Park, 6 November, 1977. O'Donovan Rossa (Antrim) 1-13; Ballycran (Down) 2-6.
Munster: Tulla,18 December 1977. St. Finbarr's (Cork) 3-5; Sixmilebriclge (Clare) 3-5 (Draw)
(Replay): Tipperary, 22 January 1978. St. Finbarr's 2-8; Sixmilebridge 0-6.
Leinster: Carlow, 5 March 1978. Rathnure (Wexford) 0-16; Fenians (Kilkenny) 1-10.

1977/78 QUARTER FINAL
Corrigan Park: 5 February 1978. O'Donovan Rossa's 2-11; St. Gabriel's (London) 1-9.

1977/78 SEMI FINALS
Togher: 26 March 1978. St. Finbarr's 6-12; O'Donovan Rossa 1-16.
Wexford: 26 March 1978. Rathnure 2-20; Four Roads 2-8.

1977/78 FINAL
Thurles: 27 March 1978. St. Finbarr's 2-7; Rathnure 0-9.

1978/79 PROVINCIAL FINALS
Connacht: Athleague, 3 December 1978. Ardrahan (Galway) 2-9; Tooreen (Mayo) 1-7.
Ulster: Portaferry, 22 October 1978. Ballycastle McQuillans (Antrim) 2-14; Portaferry (Down) 2-7.
Munster: Páirc Uí Chaoimh (Cork), 3 February 1978. Blackrock (Cork) 3-8; Newmarket-on-Fergus (Clare) 1-8.
Leinster: Carlow, 3 December 1978. Ballyhale Shamrocks (Kilkenny) 1-13; Crumlin (Dublin) 1-6.

1978-79 QUARTER FINAL
Galway: 28 January 1979. St. Gabriel's (London) 2-5; Ardrahan 1-8 (Draw)
(Replay): Athlone, 18 February 1979. St. Gabriel's 2-9; Ardrahan 0-10.

1978/79 SEMI FINALS
Kilkenny: 4 March 1979. Ballyhale Shamrocks 4-10; St. Gabriel's 1-7.
Ballycastle: 4 March 1979. Blackrock 5-12; Ballycastle McQuillan's 2-6.

1978/79 FINAL
Thurles: 25 March 1979. Blackrock 5-7; Ballyhale Shamrocks 5-5.

1979/80 PROVINCIAL FINALS
Connacht: Athleague, 30 March 1980. Castlegar (Galway) 1-16; Tremane (Roscommon) 1-9.
Ulster: Carey, 11 November 1979. Ballycastle McQuillans (Antrim) 0-11; Ballycran (Down) 0-8.
Munster: Pairc Ui Chaoimh, 9 December 1979. Blackrock (Cork) 0-13; Dunhill (Waterford) 1-8.
Leinster: Athy, 23 March 1980. Crumlin (Dublin), 3-5; Camross (Laois) 0-11.

1979/80 QUARTER FINAL
Pairc Ui Chaoimh: 6 April 1980. Blackrock (Cork) 4-15; Brian Boru's (London) 1-10.

1979/80 SEMI FINALS
Croke Park: 27 April 1980. Ballycastle McQuillans 3-9; Crumlin 0-8.
Athenry: 25 May 1980. Castlegar 2-9; Blackrock 0-9.

1979/80 FINAL
Navan: 1 June 1980. Castlegar 1-11; Ballycastle McQuillans 1-8.

1980/81 PROVINCIAL FINALS
Connacht: Athleague, 12 April 1981. Sarsfields (Galway) 4-12; Tremane (Roscommon) 0-5.
Ulster: Ballycran, 26 October 1980. Ballycastle McQuillans (Antrim) 1-20; Ballycran (Down) 0-13.
Munster: Fermoy, 30 November 1980. St. Finbarr's (Cork) 2-12; Roscrea (Tipperary) 1-14.
Leinster: Athy, 14 December 1980. Ballyhale Shamrocks (Kilkenny) 3-10; Coolderry (Offaly) 1-8.

1980/81 QUARTER FINAL
Ballycastle: 12 April 1981. Ballycastle McQuillans 1-14; Brian Boru's (London) 2-4.

1980/81 SEMI FINALS
Ballycastle: 26 April 1981. Ballyhale Shamrocks 2-11; Ballycastle McQuillans 0-12.
Páirc Uí Chaoimh: 26 April 1981. St. Finbarr's 2-11; Sarsfields 1-3.

1980/81 FINAL
Thurles: 17 May 1981. Ballyhale Shamrocks 1-15; St. Finbarr's 1-11.

1981/82 PROVINCIAL FINALS
Connacht: Athleague, 28 March 1982. Gort (Galway) 8-13; Tooreen (Mayo) 0-3.
Ulster: Cushendall, 18 October 1981. Cushendall (Antrim) 4-17; Portaferry (Down) 0-9.
Munster: Waterford, 29 November 1981. Mount Sion (Waterford) 3-9; South Liberties (Limerick) 1-4.
Leinster: Athy, 21 March 1982. James Stephens (Kilkenny) 0-13; Faythe Harriers (Wexford) 1-9.

1981/82 QUARTER FINAL
Ballinasloe: 11 April 1982. Gort 4-12; St. Gabriel's (London) 0-9.

1981/82 SEMI FINAL
Kilkenny: 25 April 1982. James Stephens 1-13; Gort 1-8.
Waterford: 25 April 1982. Mount Sion 1-14; Cushendall 1-8.

1981/82 FINAL
Thurles: 16 May 1982. James Stephens 3-13; Mount Sion 3-8.

1982/83 PROVINCIAL FINALS
Connacht: Athleague, 23 January 1983. Kiltormer (Galway) 3-14; Four Roads

(Roscommon) 0-6.
Ulster: Ballygalget, 24 October 1982.
Loughgiel Shamrocks (Antrim) 1-9; Ballygalget (Down) 0-9.
Munster: Nenagh, 12 December 1982.
Moycarkey-Borris (Tipperary) 1-9; Patrickswell (Limerick) 0-11.
Leinster: Kilkenny, 21 November 1982.
St. Rynagh's (Offaly) 1-16; Buffers Alley (Wexford) 2-10.

1982/83 QUARTER FINAL
Thurles: 6 February 1983. Moycarkey-Borris 3-5; Brian Boru's (London) 0-5.

1982/83 SEMI FINALS
Ballinasloe: 13 February 1983. St. Rynagh's 2-8; Kiltormer 0-8.
Loughgiel: 13 February 1983. Loughgiel Shamrocks 2-7; Moycarkey-Borris 1-6.

1982/83 FLNAL
Croke Park: 17 April 1983. Loughgiel Shamrocks 1-8; St. Rynagh's 2-5 (Draw).
(Replay): Casement Park, Belfast, 24 April 1983. Loughgiel Shamrocks 2-12; St. Rynagh's 1-12.

1983/84 PROVINCIAL FINALS
Connacht: Ballyhaunis, 6 November 1983.
Gort (Galway) 3-13; Tooreen (Mayo) 1-5.
Ulster: Ballycastle, 23 October 1983.
Ballycastle McQuillans (Antrim) 4-12; Ballygalget (Down) 2-3.
Munster: Kilmallock, 20 November 1983.
Midleton (Cork) 3-6; Borris-lleigh (Tipperary) 1-12 (Draw).
(Replay): Kilmallock, 4 December 1983.
Midleton 1-14; Borris-lleigh 1-11.
Leinster: Athy, 4 December 1983. Ballyhale Shamrocks (Kilkenny) 3-6; Kinnity (Offaly) 0-9.

1983/84 QUARTER FINAL
Ballyvoy: 5 February 1984. Ballycastle McQuillans 3-7; Desmonds (London) 0-8.

1983/84 SEMI FINALS
Limerick: 14 April 1984.
Gort 1-11; Midleton 2-4.
Navan: 14 April 1984.
Ballyhale Shamrocks 3-14; Ballycastle McQuillans 2-10.

1983/84 FINAL
Birr: 15 April 1984. Ballyhale Shamrocks 1-10; Gort 1-10 (Draw).
(Replay): Thurles, 3 June 1984. Ballyhale Shamrocks 1-10; Gort 0-7.

1984/85 PROVINCIAL FINALS
Connacht: Aughamore, 25 November 1984.
Castlegar (Galway) 2-14; Tooreen (Mayo) 2-7.
Ulster: Ballycran, 14 October 1984.
Ballycastle McQuillans (Antrim) 1-14; Ballycran (Down) 1-3.
Munster: Thurles, 16 December 1984.
Sixmilebridge (Clare) 4-10; Patrickswell (Limerick) 2-6.
Leinster: Athy, 2 December 1984. St. Martin's (Kilkenny) 2-11; Kinnity (Offaly) 0-12.

1984/85 QUARTER FINAL
Galway: 16 December 1984. Castlegar 4-12; St. Gabriel's (London) 0-3.

1984/85 SEMI FINALS
Callan: 3 March 1985.
St. Martin's 3-15; Ballycastle McQuillans 2-7.
Galway: 3 March 1985.
Castlegar 3-5; Sixmilebridge 1-5.

1984/85 FINAL
Croke Park: 17 March 1985. St. Martin's 2-9; Castlegar 3-6 (Draw).
(Replay): Thurles, 24 March 1985. St. Martin's 1-13; Castlegar 1-10.

1985/86 PROVINCIAL FINALS
Connacht: Athleague, 24 November 1985.
Turloughmore (Galway) 1-8; Ballygar (Roscommon) 2-4.
Ulster: Cushendall, 13 October 1985.
Cushendall (Antrim) 0-19; Ballycran (Down) 0-10.
Munster: Limerick, 24 November 1985.
Kilruane McDonaghs (Tipperary) 1-8; Blackrock (Cork) 1-8 (Draw).
(Replay): Limerick, 1 December 1985.
Kilruane McDonaghs 0-12; Blackrock 0-6.
Leinster: Kilkenny, 24 November 1985. Buffers Alley (Wexford) 3-9; Kinnity (0ffaly) 0-7.

1985/86 QUARTER FINAL
Cloughjordan: 19 January 1986. Kilruane McDonaghs 2-9; Desmonds (London) 0-4.

1985/86 SEMI FINALS
Nenagh: 2 February 1986.
Kilruane McDonaghs 3-9; Turloughmore 0-9.
Cushendall: 2 February 1986.
Buffers Alley 1-10; Cushendall 0-5.

1985/86 FINAL
Croke Park: 16 March 1986. Kilruane McDonaghs 1-15; Buffers Alley 2-10.

1986/87 PROVINCIAL FINALS
Connacht: Aughamore, 16 November 1986.
Killimordaly (Galway) 6-16; Tooreen (Mayo) 1-4.
Ulster: Gulladuff, 19 October 1986. Ballycastle

McQuillans (Antrim) 1-13; Lavey (Derry) 1-8.
Munster: Limerick, 30 November 1986.
Borrisoleigh (Tipperary) 1-13; Clarecastle (Clare) 1-9.
Leinster: Croke Park, 30 November 1986.
Rathnure (Wexford) 2-16; Camross (Laois) 3-9.

1986/87 QUARTER FINAL
Dunloy: 1 February 1987. Ballycastle McQuillans 4-14; St. Gabriel's (London) 1-6.

1986/87 SEMI FINALS
Wexford: 8 February 1987.
Rathnure 0-11; Killimordaly 0-9.
Thurles: 8 February 1987.
Borris-lleigh 3-16; Ballycastle McQuillans 3-8.

1986/87 FINAL
Croke Park: 17 March 1987.
Borrisoleigh 2-9; Rathnure 0-9.

1987/88 PROVINCIAL FINALS
Connacht: Woodmount, 13 December 1987.
Athenry (Galway) 4-18; Padhraic Pearses (Roscommon) 0-7.
Ulster: Ballycran, 8 November 1987. Cushendall (Antrim) 3-10; Ballycran (Down) 1-6.
Munster: Kilmallock, 5 December 1987.
Midleton (Cork) 1-12; Cappawhite (Tipperary) 1-11.
Leinster: Kilkenny, 6 December, Rathnure (Wexford) 3-8; Portlaoise (Laois) 1-13.

1987/88 QUARTER FINAL
Ballinasloe: 31 January 1988.
Athenry 2-14; Glen Rovers (Hertfordshire) 0-5.

1987/88 SEMI FINALS
Ballinasloe: 14 February 1988.
Athenry 3-12; Rathnure 1-4.
Cushendall: 14 February 1988.
Midleton 3-11; Cushendall 2-5.

1987/88 FINAL
Croke Park: 17 March 1988.
Midleton 3-8; Athenry 0-9.

1988/89 PROVINCIAL FINALS
Connacht: Ballyforan, 20 November 1988.
Four Roads (Roscommon) 3-5; Abbeyknockmoy (Galway) 1-8.
Ulster: Shaws Rd., Belfast, 23 October 1988.
O'Donovan Rossa (Antrim) 0-13; Lavey (Derry) 0-11.
Munster: Thurles, 4 December 1988.
Patrickswell (Limerick) 3-13; Mount Sion (Waterford) 2-13.
Leinster: Carlow, 4 December 1988.
Buffers Alley (Wexford) 1-12; Ballyhale Shamrocks (Kilkenny) 1-9.

1988/89 QUARTER FINAL
Limerick: 29 January 1989.
Patrickswell 2-15; Desmonds (London) 0-7.

1988/89 SEMI FINALS
Wexford: 12 February 1989.
Buffers Alley 2-19; Four Roads 0-9.
Kilmallock: 12 February 1989.
O'Donovan Rossa 2-9; Patrickswell 2-8.

1988/89 FINAL
Croke Park: 17 March 1989.
Buffers Alley 2-12; O'Donovan Rossa 0- 12.

1989/90 PROVINCIAL FINALS
Connacht: Athleague, 5 November 1989.
Sarsfields (Galway) 5-14; Tooreen (Mayo) 0-0.
Ulster: Portaferry, 22 October 1989.
Loughgiel Shamrocks {Antrim) 1-14; Portaferry (Down) 2-9.

Munster: Limerick, 19 November 1989.
Ballybrown (Limerick) 2-12; Sixmilebridge (Clare) 1-8.
Leinster: Athy, 9 December 1989.
Ballyhale Shamrocks (Kilkenny) 2-11; Cuala (Dublin) 0-7.

1989/90 QUARTER FINAL
Carey: 28 January 1990.
Loughgiel Shamrocks 3-12; Desmonds (London) 2-10.

1989/90 SEMI FINALS
Ballinasloe: 11 February 1990.
Ballyhale Shamrocks 2-8; Sarsfields 0-12.
Loughgiel: 11 February 1990.
Ballybrown 0-9; Loughgiel Shamrocks 0-8.

1989/90 FINAL
Croke Park: 17 March 1990.
Ballyhale Shamrocks 1-16; Ballybrown 0-16.

1990/-91 PROVINCIAL FINALS
Connacht: Athleague, 25 November 1990.
Kiltormer (Galway) 5-11; Oran (Roscommon) 0-6.
Ulster: Casement Park, 11 November 1990.
Dunloy (Antrim) 0-17; Ballygalget (Down) 2-4.
Munster: Ennis 25 November 1990. Patrickswell (Limerick) 0-8; Eire Óg (Clare) 0-6.
Leinster: Athy, 25 November 1990. Glenmore (Kilkenny) 0-15; Camross (Laois) 1-9.

1990/91 QUARTER FINAL
Athenry: 9 December 1990. St. Gabriel's (London) 2-11; Kiltormer 1 -12 (after extra time). Draw after 60 minutes: St. Gabriel's: 0-8; Kiltormer 1-5.

1990/91 SEMI FINALS
Kilkenny: 24 February 1991.
Glenmore 1-18; Dunloy 1-10.
Limerick: 24 February 1991.
Patrickswell 8-12; St. Gabriel's 3-6.

1990/91 FINAL
Croke Park: 17 March 1991.
Glenmore 1-13; Patrickswell 0- 2.

1991/92 PROVINCIAL FINALS
Connacht: Ballyforan, 10 November 1991.
Kiltormer (Galway) 2-9; Four Roads (Roscommon) 1-6.
Ulster: Casement Park, 13 October 1991.
Cushendall (Antrim) 1-16; Portaferry (Down) 0-5.
Munster: Mitchelstown, 8 December 1991.
Cashel King Cormacs (Tipperary) 0-9; Midleton (Cork) 0-6.
Leinster: Portlaoise, 24 November 1991. Birr (Offaly) 2-14; Ballyhale Shamrocks (Kilkenny) 0-3.

1991/92 QUARTER FINAL
Ruislip (London): 9 February 1992.
Cashel King Cormacs 0-23; Sean Treacys (London) 0-6.

1991/92 SEMI FINALS
Cushendall: 8 March 1992.
Birr 2-9; Cushendall 1-6.
Cashel: 23 February 1992. Kiltormer 1-10; Cashel King Cormacs 2-7 (Draw).
(Replay): Ballinasloe, 8 March 1992. Kiltormer 1-14, Cashel King Cormacs 2-11 (after extra time). Kiltormer 0-11; Cashel King Cormacs 2-5 (end of normal time).
(2nd Replay): Croke Park, 17 March 1992.
Kiltormer 2-8; Cashel King Cormacs 1-8.

1991/92 FINAL
Thurles: 29 March 1992.
Kiltormer 0-15; Birr 1-8.

1992/93 PROVINCIAL FINALS
Connacht: Athleague, 29 November 1992.
Sarsfields (Galway) 2-15; Oran (Roscommon) 0-7.
Ulster: Casement Park, 11 October 1992.
Cushendall (Antrim) 2-12; Ballygalget (Down) 1-10.
Munster: Limerick, 29 November 1992.
Kilmallock (Limerick) 3-11; Sixmilebridge (Clare) 2-11.
Leinster: Croke Park, 29 November 1992.
Buffers Alley (Wexford) 2-13; St. Rynagh's (Offaly) 0-13.

1992/93 QUARTER FINAL
Ruislip (London): 6 December 1992.
Desmonds (London) 2-7; Cushendall 1-8.

1992/93 SEMI FINALS
Kilmallock: 28 February 1993.
Kilmallock 1-16; Desmonds 0-6.
Wexford: 28 February 1993.
Sarafields 4-13; Buffers Alley 1-10.

1992/93 FINAL
Croke Park: 17 March 1993.
Sarsfields 1-17; Kilmallock 2-7.

1993/94 PROVINCIAI FINALS
Connacht: Ballyforan, 21 November 1993.
Sarsfields (Galway) 5-15; Four Roads (Roscommon) 0-7.
Ulster: Casement Park, 24 October 1993.
Ballycran (Down) 2-10; Cushendall (Antrim) 0-12.
Munster: Limerick, 21 November 1993.
Toomevara (Tipperary) 0-15; Sixmilebridge (Clare) 0-7.
Leinster: Portlaoise, 5 December 1993. St. Rynagh's (Offaly) 1-14; Dicksboro Kilkenny) 2-10.

1993/94 QUARTER FINAL
Ruislip (London): 5 December 1993. Sarsfields 2-14; Sean Treacys (London) 0-5.

1993/94 SEMI FINALS
Croke Park: 20 February 1994.
Toomevara 1-13; Ballycran 1-5.
Thurles: 20 February 1994.
Sarsfields 1-11; St. Rynagh's 1-7.

1993/94 FINAL
Croke Park: 17 March 1994.
Sarsfields 1-14; Toomevara 3-6.

1994/95 PROVINCIAL FINALS
Connacht: Athleague, 13 November 1994.
Athenry (Galway) 3-20; St. Dominic's (Roscommon) 2-3.
Ulster: Casement Park, 16 October 1994.
Dunloy (Antrim) 3-9; Lavey (Derry) 1-12.
Munster: Thurles, 27 November 1994.
Kilmallock (Limerick) 2-11; Toomevara (Tipperary) 1-11.
Leinster: Kilkenny, 27 November 1994.
Birr (Offaly) 0-10; Oulart-The-Ballagh (Wexford) 1-7 (Draw).
(Replay): Kilkenny, 4 December 1994.
Birr 3-7; Oulart-The-Ballagh 2-5.

1994/95 QUARTER FINAL
Ruislip (London): 11 December 1994.
Kilmallock 1-16; Sean Treacy's (London) 0-10.

1994/95 SEMI FINALS
Thurles: 19 February 1995.
Birr 2-8; Kilmallock 0-9.
Clones: 19 February 1995. Dunloy 2-10;
Athenry 1-11.

1994/95 FINAL
Croke Park: 17 March 1995.
Birr 0-9; Dunloy 0-9 (Draw).
(Replay): Croke Park, 2 April 1995.
Birr 3-13; Dunloy 2-3.

1995/96 PROVINCIAL FINALS
Connacht: Ballyhaunis, 26 November 1995.
Sarsfields (Galway) 2-17; Tooreen (Mayo) 0-5.
Ulster: Casement Park, 15 October 1995.
Dunloy (Antrim) 2- 18; Ballycran (Down) 0-9.
Munster: Limerick, 26 November 1995.
Sixmilebridge (Clare) 2-18; Eire Óg Nenagh (Tipperary) 1-7.
Leinster: Carlow, 26 November 1995.
Glenmore (Kilkenny) 2-13; Oulart-The-Ballagh (Wexford) 2-10.

1995/96 QUARTER FINAL
Ruislip (London): 26 November 1995.
Dunloy 1-16; St. Gabriel's (London) 0-9.

1995/96 SEMI FINALS
Thurles: 11 February 1996.
Sixmilebridge 5-11; Sarsfields 1-12.
Croke Park: 11 February 1996.
Dunloy 2-13; Glenmore 0-7.

1995/96 FINAL
Croke Park: 17 March 1996.
Sixmilebridge 5-10; Dunloy 2-6.

1996/97 PROVINCIAL FINALS
Connacht: Ballyforan, 8 December 1996.
Athenry (Galway) 1-15; Four Roads (Roscommon) 1-8.
Ulster: Casement Park, 27 October 1996.
Cushendall (Antrim) 3-9; Portaferry (Down) 2-8.
Munster: Thurles, 24 November 1996. Wolfe Tones (Clore) 4-9; Ballygunner (Waterford) 4-8.
Leinster: Kilkenny, 1 December 1996. Camross (Laois) 1-12; O'Tooles (Dublin) 2-5.

1996/97 QUARTER FINAL
Ruislip (London): 15 December 1996. Athenry 3-15; St. Gabriel's (London) 1-8.

1996/97 SEMI FINALS
Parnell Park (Dublin):16 February 1997. Wolfe Tones 2-8; Cushendall 1-10.
Thurles: 16 February 1997. Athenry 4-17; Camross 3-3.

1996/97 FINAL
Croke Park: 17 March 1997. Athenry 0-14; Wolfe Tones 1-8.

1997/98 PROVINCIAL FINALS
Connacht: Ballinlough, 6 December 1997.
Sarsfields (Galway) 5-15; Tooreen (Mayo) 1 -5.
Ulster: Casement Park, 5 October 1997. Dunloy (Antrim) 3-16; Lavey (Derry) 4-10.
Munster: Thurles, 7 December 1997.
Clarecastle (Clare) 2-11;
Patrickswell (Limerick) 0-15.
Leinster: Kilkenny, 30 November 1997.
Birr (Offaly) 0-11; Castletown (Laois) 0-5.

1997/98 QUARTER FINAL
Ruislip (London): 14 December 1997.
Clarecastle 2-24; St. Gabriel's (London) 1-7.

1997/98 SEMI FINALS
Thurles: 15 February 1998. Birr 1-15;
Clarecastle 3-9 (Draw).
(Replay): Thurles, 28 February 1998.
Birr 0-12; Clarecastle 0-11 (after extra time).
Birr 0-7; Clarecastle 0-7 (end of normal time).
Mullingar: 15 February 1998.
Sarsfields 3-14; Dunloy 4-11 (Draw).
(Replay): Mullingar, 1 March 1998.
Sarsfields 1-15; Dunloy 1-11.

1997/98 FINAL
Croke Park: 17 March 1998.
Birr 1-13; Sarsfields 0-9.

1998/99 PROVINCIAL FINALS
Connacht: Aughamore, 15 November 1998.
Athenry (Galway) 6-24; Tooreen (Mayo) 0-5.
Ulster: Corrigan Park (Belfast), 1 November 1998. Ballygalget (Down) 1-13; Bollycastle McQuillans (Antrim) 3-7.
(Replay): Corrigan Park (Belfast), 15 **November 1998. Ballygalget (Down)** 1-14; Ballycastle McQuillans (Antrim) 1-12 (after extra time). Ballygalget 1-8; Ballycastle McQuillans 1-8 (end of normal time).
Munster: Limerick, 6 December 1998. St. Joseph's Doora-Barefield (Clare) 0-12; Toomevara (Tipperary) 0-8.
Leinster: Kilkenny,13 December 1998.
Rathnure (Wexford) 1-13; Portlaoise (Laois) 1-6.

1998/99 QUARTER FINAL
Ruislip (London): 6 December 1998.
Ballygalget 1-9; Bros. Pearse (London) 0-4.

1998/99 SEMI-FINALS
Thurles: 21 February, 1999. St. Joseph's Doora-Barefield 1-13, St. Mary's Athenry 1-12.
Parnell Park (Dublin): 28 February, 1999.
Rathnure 2-19, Bollygalget 1-8.

1998/99 FINAL
Croke Park: 17 March, 1999. St. Joseph's Doora-Barefield 2-14, Rathnure 0-8.
Note: Allied Irish Banks (AIB) began sponsorship of the All-Ireland Club Championship in 1992.

1999/2000 PROVINCIAL FINALS
Connacht: Garrymore, 28 November 1999.
Athenry (Galway) 1-13 Tooreen (Mayo) 1-6.
Ulster: Casement Park, 3 October 1999.
Cushendall (Antrim) 1-12, Ballygalget (Down) 1-8.
Munster: Thurles, 28 November 1999.
St.Joseph's Doora-Barefield (Clare) 4-9, Ballygunner (Waterford) 3-8.
Leinster: Kilkenny, 28 November 1999.
Birr (Offaly) 1-16, Castletown (Laois) 0-11.

1999/2000 QUARTER-FINAL
Ruislip (London): 5 December 1999.
Athenry 2-20, St.Gabriel's (London) 1-9.

1999/2000 SEMI-FINALS
Thurles: 13 February 2000.
Athenry 2-9, Birr 1-10.
Parnell Park: 13 February 2000.
St.Joseph's Doora-Barefield 0-12, Cushendall 0-12. Replay
Parnell Park: 19 February 2000.
St.Joseph's Doora-Barefield 1-14, Cushendall 1-8.

1999/2000 FINAL
Croke Park: 17 March 2000.
Athenry 0-16, St.Joseph's Doora-Barefield 0-12.

2000/01 PROVINCIAL FINALS
Connacht: Athleague, 3 December 2000.
Athenry (Galway) 2-16, Four Roads (Roscommon) 1-7.
Ulster: Casement Park, 22 October 2000.
Dunloy (Antrim) 4-14, Slaughtneil (Derry) 0-9.
Munster: Thurles 26 November 2000.
Sixmilebridge (Clare) 2-17, Mount Sion (Waterford) 3-8.
Leinster: Kilkenny, 26 November 2000.
Graigue-Ballycallan (Kilkenny) 0-14, U.C.D. (Dublin) 1-8.

2000/01 QUARTER-FINAL
Ruislip (London): 3 December 2000.
Sixmilebridge 2-11, Fr.Murphy's (London) 0-6.

2000/01 SEMI-FINALS
Parnell Park: 25 February 2001.
Athenry 3-20, Dunloy 1-10.
Thurles: 25 February 2001.
Graigue-Ballycallan 1-16, Sixmilebridge 2-13.
Replay
Thurles: 31 March 2001.
Graigue-Ballycallan 1-13, Sixmilebridge 1-12.

2000/01 FINAL
Croke Park: 16 April 2001.
Athenry 3-24, Graigue-Ballycallan 2-19.
after extra time

2001/02 PROVINCIAL FINALS
Connacht: Athleague, 18 November 2001.
Clarinbridge (Galway) 2-18, Four Roads (Roscommon) 1-6.
Ulster: Casement Park, 21 October 2001.
Dunloy (Antrim) 3-11, Lavey (Derry) 1-6.
Munster: Thurles, 2 December 2001.
Ballygunner (Waterford) 2-14, Blackrock (Cork) 0-12.
Leinster: Kilkenny, 2 December 2001.
Birr (Offaly) 0-10, Castletown (Laois) 1-7.
Replay: Kilkenny, 16 December 2001.
Birr 2-10, Castletown 0-5.

2001/02 QUARTER-FINAL
Ruislip (London): 2 December 2001.
Dunloy 6-12, Fr.Murphy's (London) 1-6.

2001/02 SEMI-FINALS
Thurles: 17 February 2002.
Clarinbridge 1-15, Ballygunner 2-8.
Clones: 17 February 2002.
Birr 2-12, Dunloy 1-11.

2001/02 FINAL
Thurles: 17 March 2002.
Birr 2-10, Clarinbridge 1-5.

2002/03 PROVINCIAL FINALS
Connacht: Ballyforan, 17 November 2002.
Athenry (Galway) 1-19, Four Roads (Roscommon) 0-9.
Ulster: Loughgeil, 27 October 2002.
Dunloy (Antrim) 0-12, Portaferry (Down) 1-6.
Munster: Thurles, 1 December 2002.
Mount Sion (Waterford) 0-12, Sixmilebridge (Clare) 0-10.
Leinster: Portlaoise, 1 December 2002.
Birr (Offaly) 2-5, Young Irelands (Kilkenny) 1-2.

2002/03 QUARTER-FINAL
Ruislip (London): 24 November 2002.
Athenry 4-15, Sean Treacy's (London) 0-5.

2002/03 SEMI-FINALS
Mullingar: 16 February 2003.
Dunloy 1-14, Mount Sion 1-13.
Ennis: 16 February 2003.
Birr 0-15, Athenry 0-6.

2002/03 FINAL
Croke Park: 17 March 2003.
Birr 1-19, Dunloy 0-11.

2003/04 PROVINCIAL FINALS
Connacht: Athleague, 16 November 2003.
Portumna (Galway) 0-17, Athleague (Roscommon) 0-5.
Ulster: Casement Park, 9 November 2003.
Dunloy (Antrim) 3-19, Dungiven (Derry) 0-9.
Munster: Thurles, 30 November 2003.

Newtownshandrum (Cork) 2-18, Patrickswell (Limerick) 2-9.
Leinster: Portlaoise, 30 November 2003.
O'Loughlin Gaels (Kilkenny) 0-15, Birr (Offaly) 0-9.

2003/04 QUARTER-FINAL
Ruislip (London): 6 December 2003.
Newtownshandrum 1-14, Fr.Murphy's (London) 1-5.

2003/04 SEMI-FINALS
Clones: 15 February 2004.
Dunloy 2-13, Portumna 2-10.
Thurles: 15 February 2004.
Newtownshandrum 1-16, O'Loughlin Gaels 0-19.
Replay Thurles: 21 February 2004.
Newtownshandrum 0-14, O'Loughlin Gaels 1-8.

2003/04 FINAL
Croke Park: 17 March 2004.
Newtownshandrum 0-17, Dunloy 1-6.

2004/05 PROVINCIAL FINALS
Connacht: Charlestown, 14 November 2004.
Athenry (Galway) 2-16, Ballyhaunis (Mayo) 0-7.
Ulster: Casement Park, 31 October 2004.
O'Donovan Rossa (Antrim) 0-16, Ballygalget (Down) 0-14.
Munster: Thurles, 21 November 2004.
Toomevara (Tipperary) 1-14, Mount Sion (Waterford) 1-13.
Leinster: Portlaoise, 28 November 2004.
James Stephens (Kilkenny) 1-13, U.C.D. (Dublin) 1-12.

2004/05 SEMI-FINALS
Ennis: 12 February 2005.
Athenry 3-12, Toomevara 1-11.
Parnell Park: 13 February 2005.
James Stephens 0-17, O'Donovan Rossa 1-6.

2004/05 FINAL
Croke Park: 17 March 2005.
James Stephens 0-19, Athenry 0-14.

2005/06 PROVINCIAL FINALS
Connacht: Athleague, 20 November 2005.
Portumna (Galway) 2-22, Four Roads (Roscommon) 0-6.
Ulster: Casement Park, 30 October 2005.
Ballygalget (Down) 1-18, Cushendall (Antrim) 3-8.
Munster: Thurles, 4 December 2005.
Newtownshandrum (Cork) 0-16, Ballygunner (Waterford) 1-12.
Leinster: Portlaoise, 27 November 2005.
James Stephens (Kilkenny) 2-13, U.C.D. (Dublin) 1-12.

2005/06 SEMI-FINALS
Thurles: 12 February 2006.
Portumna 2-17, James Stephens 0-11.
Portlaoise: 12 February 2006.
Newtownshandrum 0-14, Ballygalget 1-10.

2005/06 FINAL
Croke Park: 17 March 2006.
Portumna 2-8, Newtownshandrum 1-6.

2006/07 PROVINCIAL FINALS
Connacht: Athleague, 19 November 2006.
Loughrea (Galway) 2-16, Athleague (Roscommon) 2-3.
Ulster: Casement Park, 12 November 2006.
Cushendall (Antrim) 1-15, Dungiven (Derry) 1-7.
Munster: The Gaelic Grounds, 3 December 2006.
Toomevara (Tipperary) 2-9, Erin's Own (Cork) 2-8.
Leinster: Portlaoise, 26 November 2006.
Ballyhale Shamrocks (Kilkenny) 1-20, Birr (Offaly) 1-8.

2006/07 SEMI-FINALS
Portlaoise: 10 February 2007.
Ballyhale Shamrocks 2-20, Toomevara 3-14.
Mullingar: 11 February 2007.
Loughrea 1-11, Cushendall 0-9.

2006/07 FINAL
Croke Park: 17 March 2007.
Ballyhale Shamrocks 3-12, Loughrea 2-8.

2007/08 PROVINCIAL FINALS
Connacht: Athleague, 18 November 2007.
Portumna (Galway) 6-23, James Stephens (Mayo) 0-7.
Ulster: Casement Park, 28 October 2007.
Dunloy (Antrim) 2-14, Dungiven (Derry) 2-8.
Munster: The Gaelic Grounds, 2 December 2007.
Loughmore/Castleiney (Tipperary) 1-6, Tulla (Clare) 0-7.
Leinster: Tullamore, 2 December 2007.
Birr (Offaly) 1-11, Ballyboden St.Enda's (Dublin) 0-13.

2007/08 SEMI-FINALS
The Gaelic Grounds: 24 February 2008.
Portumna 2-13, Loughmore/Castleiney 2-8.
Clones: 24 February 2008.
Birr 0-17, Dunloy 0-9.

2007/08 FINAL
Croke Park: 17 March 2008.
Portumna 3-19, Birr 3-9.

2008/09 PROVINCIAL FINALS
Connacht: Portumna (Galway) unopposed.
Ulster: Casement Park, 19 October 2008.
Cushendall (Antrim) 1-14, Ballygalget (Down) 1-13.

Munster: Thurles, 30 November 2008.
De La Salle (Waterford) 1-9, Adare (Limerick) 0-10.
Leinster: Nowlan Park, 30 November 2008.
Ballyhale Shamrocks (Kilkenny) 2-13, Birr (Offaly) 1-11.

2008/09 SEMI-FINALS

Thurles: 22 February 2009.
Portumna 5-11, Ballyhale Shamrocks 1-16.
Parnell Park: 22 February 2009.
De La Salle 1-21, Cushendall 1-19. (aet)

2008/09 FINAL

Croke Park: 17 March 2009.
Portumna 2-24, De La Salle 1-8.

ALL-IRELAND CLUB HURLING FINAL TEAMS (1971-2009)

1971

Roscrea—T. Murphy, M. Hogan, K. Carey, B. Maher, P. Rowland, T. O'Connor, J. Crampton, M. Minogue, D. Moloney (capt.), F. Loughnane, J. Hannon, J. Cunningham, J. Tynan M. Nolan, W. Stapleton.

St. Rynagh's—D. Martin, N. Gallagher, F. Whelehan, A. Horan, P. Moylan, P Horan, S. Moylan, R. Horan, B. Johnson, B. Lyons, P. J. Whelehan, H. Dolan, G. Burke, B. Moylan, P. Mulhare.

1972

Blackrock—B Hurley, P. Casey, P. Geary, J. Horgan (capt), S. Murphy, F. Cummins, F. Norberg, M. Murphy, P. Kavanagh, D. Collins, R. Cummins, P Moylan, B. Cummins, J. Rothwell, D. Prendergast.

Rathnure—M. Foley, J. Quigley, A. Somers, M. Mooney, J. O'Connor, T. O'Connor, J. Quigley, M. Byrne, J. Mooney, J. Higgins, M. Quigley, J. Murphy, P Flynn, J. English, D. Quigley. Sub: S. Barron for P Flynn.

1973

Glen Rovers—F. O'Neill, D. O'Riordan, M. O'Doherty, P Barry, J. O'Sullivan, D. Coughlan, M. O'Halloran, J. J. O'Neill P. O'Doherty, P. Harte, R. Crowley, T. Buckley, M. Ryan, T. Collins, J. Young. Sub: M. Corbett for D. O'Riordan.

St. Rynagh's—D. Martin, J. Dooley, F. Whelehan, A. Horan, P Moylan, P. Horan, H. Dolan, P. J. Whelehan, B. Johnson, B. Lyons, B. Moylan, J. Horan, R. Horan, P. Mulhare, S. Moylan.

1974

Blackrock—T. Murphy, J. Rothwell, P. Geary, J. Horgan (capt.), F. Cummins, C. O'Brien, F Norberg, J. Russell, P Moylan, P. Kavanagh, J. O'Halloran, D. Collins, D. Prendergast, R. Cummins, E. O'Donoghue. Subs: S. Kearney for P Kavanagh, D. Buckley for S. Kearney. (Note: B. Cummins played in dlrawn game. C. O'Brien was on for replay.)

Rathrure—M. Foley, P. Quigley, Jim Quigley, M. Mooney, J. O'Connor, T. O'Connor, S. Murphy, M. Qulgley, J. Higgins, P Flynn, J. Murphy, M. Byrne, John Qulgley, A. Somers, D. Qulgley. (Note: J. Mooney, V. Fenlon played in drawn game. J. Higgins, A. Somers in replay.) Subs: J. Higgins for M. Byrne, S. Murphy for J. Mooney in drawn game. Sub: J. Mooney for J. Higgins in replay.

1975

St. Finbarrs—J. Power (capt.), A. Maher, S. Canty, C. Barrett, B. O'Brien, D. O'Grady, T. Butler, G. McCarthy, C. Roche, E. Fitzpatrick, J. Barry Murphy, S. Gillen, C. McCarthy, S. Looney, J. O'Shea. Sub: C. Cullinane for S. Long.

The Fenians—P. J. Ryan, S. Delaney, N. Orr, M. Fitzpatrick, G. Murphy, P Henderson, G. Henderson, F. Hawkes, M. Garrett, J. Moriarty, P. Delaney, J. Ryan, W. Fitzpatrick, W. Watson, P Fitzpatrick. Sub: P Murphy for F Hawks.

1976

James Stephens—M. Moore, P. Neary, P. Larkin. N. Morrissey, T. McCormack, B. Cody, J. O'Brien, D. McCormack, M. Taylor, J. Hennessy, L. O'Brien, J. McCormack, M. Crotty, M. Leahy, G. Tyrell. Sub: M. Neary for J. O'Brien.

Blackrock—T. Murphy, F Norberg, C. O'Brien, D. McCurtain, A. Creagh, J. Horgan, J. Murphy, F. Cummins, J. Rothwell, P. Moylan, D. Collins, P. Kavanagh, E. O'Sullivon, R. Cummins, E. O'Donoghue. Subs: T. Lyons for D. Collins, D. Prendergast for P. Moylan.

1977

Glen Rovers—F. O'Neill (capt.), J. O'Sullivan, M. O'Doherty, T. O'Brien, F. O'Sullivan, D. Clifford, D. Coughlan, R. Crowley, J. J. O'Neill, P Harte, P. Horgan, P O'Doherty, M. Ryan, T. Collins, V. Marshall. Subs: L. McAuliffe, T. O'Neill, F. Cunningham.

Camross—J. Carroll, J. Dooley, T. Cuddy, R. Maloney, J. Doran, J. Fitzpatrick, O. Cuddy, P. Dowling, P. J. Cuddy, Martin Cuddy, G. Cuddy M. Carroll, Michael Cuddy, F. Keenan, S. Cuddy. Subs: Tim Keenan for Michael Cuddy, S. Bergin for P. Dowling, S. Collier for R. Moloney.

1978

St. Finbarr's—J. Power, C. Barrett, A. Maher, D. Burns, D. O'Grady, N. Kennefick, G. Murphy, G. McCarthy, J. Cremin, J. Allen, J. Barry Murphy, B. Wiley, E. Fitzpatrick, C. Ryan, C. McCarthy. Sub: B. Meade for G. Murphy.

Rathnure—M. Foley, A. Somers, D. Quigley, T. O'Connor, J. O'Connor, M. Codd, S. Murphy, J. Conran, J. Houlihan, D. O'Connor, M. Quigley, J. Murphy, P. Flynn, J. Quigley, P. Quigley. Sub: L. Byrne for P. Qulgley.

1979

Blackrock—T. Murphy, F. Norberg, C. O'Brien, J. Horgan (capt.), D. McCurtain, F. Cummins, A. Creagh, T. Cashman, J. O'Grady, P. Moylan, T. Lyons, D. Collins, E. O'Sullivan, R. Cummins, E. O'Donoghue. Sub: D. Buckley for A. Creagh.

Ballyhale Shamrocks—O. Harrington, D. Shefflin, L. Dalton, R. Reid, W. Phelan, M. Mason, F. Holohan, J. Walsh, S. Fennelly, M. Fennelly, P. Holden, G. Fennelly, L. Fennelly, B. Fennelly, K. Fennelly. Sub: M. Healy for L. Dalton.

1980

Castlegar—T. Grogan, Ted Murphy, Padraic Connolly, J. Coady, G. Glynn, John Connolly, M. Glynn, T. Murphy, S. Fahy, J. Francis, Joe Connolly, P. O'Connor, Gerry Connolly, Michael Connolly (capt.), L. Mulryan. Sub: P. Burke for P. O'Connor.

Ballycastle—P. Smith, K. Boyle, K. Donnelly (capt.), G. McAuley S. Donnelly, T. Donnelly, D. Donnelly, T. Barton, S. Boyle, B. Donnelly, P. Watson, P. Boyle, P. Dallat, E. Donnelly, O. Laverty.

1981

Ballyhale Shamrocks—K. Fennelly, W. Phelan, L. Dalton, R. Reid (capt.), F. Holohan, M. Mason, D. Connolly, J. Walsh, S. Fennelly, M. Fennelly, P. Holden, G. Fennelly, B. Fennelly, L. Fennelly, M. Kelly. Sub: D. Fennelly for W. Phelan.

St. Finbarr's—G. Cunningham, A. Maher, D. O'Grady, J. Blake, D. Burns, B. O'Brien (capt.), N. Kennefick, J. Cremin, J. Meyler, C. Ryan, T. Maher, E. Fitzpatrick, J. Barry Murphy, C. McCarthy, J. Allen. Subs: G. O'Shea for E. Fitzpatrick, F. Scannell for D. Burns, G. Murphy for A. Maher.

1982

James Stephens—M. Moore, P. Neary, B. Cody, P. Larkin, J. Hennessy, M. Hennessy, J. O'Brien (capt.), T. McCormack, D. McCormack, A. Egan, E. Kelly, W . Walton, J. McCormack, M. Crotty, J. J. Cullen. Sub: D. Collins for A. Egan.

Mount Sion—S. Greene, B. Knox, E. Keogh D. Shefflin, P. O'Grady, P. McGrath, P. Ryan, L. Slevin, D. Connolly, A. Cooney, T. Butler, K. Heffernan, M. Geary, P. Kelly, J. Greene. Subs: J. Dalton for K. Heffernan, K. Ryan for P. O'Gracly P. O'Grady for M. Geary.

1983

Loughgiel Shamrocks—N. Patterson (capt.), M. Carey, P. J. Mullen, S. Carey, E. Connolly, P. Mcllhatton, A. McNaughton, M. O'Connell, G. McKinley, P. Carey (junior), D. McKinley, B. Laverty, P. Carey (senior), A. McCarry, S. McNaughton. (Note: M. Coyle and B. McCarry played in drawn game; P. Carey (senior) and (junior) subs in drawn match for M. Coyle and B. McCarry, retained for replay.)

St. Rynagh's—D. Martin, M. Whelehan, J. Dooley, W. Keane, T. White, A. Fogarty, T Conneely, A. Horan, S. White (capt.), J. Kirwan, P. Horan, D. Devery, J. Horan, F. Kenny, H. Dolan. Subs: G. O'Mahony for A. Horan (draw). J. Cannon for F. Kenny, G. Dolan for J. Kirwan (replay).

1984

Ballyhale Shamrocks—O. Harrington, F. Holohan, L. Dalton, W. Phelan, M. Fennelly, M. Mason, S. Fennelly, J. Walsh, T. Phelan, B. Fennelly, G. Fennelly, M. Kelly, D. Fennelly, K. Fennelly, L. Fennelly. Sub: L. Long for L. Fennelly. (Note: L. Long, D. Connolly played in drawn game; L. Fennelly and T. Phelan were on for replay. Subs in drawn match, T. Phelan for S. Fennelly, R. Keneally for D. Connolly, L. Fennelly for B. Fennelly.)

Gort—J. Commins, S. Linnane, J. Nolan, J. Regan, J. Harte (capt.), P. Piggott, P. Neylon, C. Rock, M. Cahill, P. Hehir, B. Brennan, G. Lally, G. Linnane, K. Fahy, J. Crehan. Subs: M. Murphy for B. Brennan, M. Linnane for M. Murphy, M. Mulcairns for G. Linnane. M. Brennan played in draw. J. Regan came on for replay. Subs in drawn game M. Murphy for P. Hehir, M. Mulcairns for B. Brennan.

1985

St. Martin's—B. Shore, J. Kelly, A. Maher, J. J. Dowling, T. Walsh, Jim Moran, M. Maher, P Lawlor, John Moran, J. Morrissey, J. Brennan (capt.), P Moran, D. Coonan, T Moran, R. Moloney. Sub: E. Morrissey for John Moran (draw), and E. Morrissey for P. Lawlor (replay).

Castlegar—T. Grogan, P. Connolly, Ted Murphy, M. Glynn, T. McCormack, S. Murphy, G. Glynn, Tom Murphy, M. Connolly, M. O'Shea, S. Fahy, M. Costelloe, M. Murphy, John Connolly, G. Connolly. (Note: J. O'Connor and J. Coyne played in drawn game. M. Costelloe for J. Coyne, and M. Glynn for Tom Murphy came on as subs in drawn match and retained their places for replay.)

Subs in replay: J. Coyne for S. Fahy, Joe Connolly for G. Connolly, J. O'Connor for T. McCormack.

1986

Kilruane McDonaghs—A. Sheppard (capt.), J. Cahill, D. O'Meara, S. Gibson, J. Banaghan, J. O'Meara, G. Williams, E. Hogan, D. Cahill, Jerry Williams, Jim Williams, E. O'Shea, Pat Quinlan, P. Williams, Philip Quinlan. Sub: S. Hennessy

for E. Hogan.
Buffers Alley—H. Butler, B. Murphy, P. Kenny, C. Doran, J. Donobue, P. Gahan, S. Whelan (capt.), M. Casey, G. Sweeney, T. Dempsey, T. Dwyer, M. Foley, M. Butler, A. Doran, S. O'Leary. Subs: P. Donohue for G. Sweeney, E. Sinnott for M. Foley.

1987

Borris-lleigh—N. Maher, F. Spillane, T. Stapleton, M. Ryan (capt.), R. Stakelum, G. Stapleton, B. Ryan, T. Ryan, F. Collins, C. Stakelum, N. O'Dwyer, J. McGrath, M. Coen, P. Kenny, A. Ryan. Sub: B. Kenny for T. Ryan.
Rathnure—T. Morrissey, M. Codd, M. Qulgley, J. Doyle, D. Sheehan, J. O'Connell (capt.), J. Conran, J. Holohan, L. Ronan, J. Codd, J. Redmond, N. Hearne, P Codd, J. Murphy, M. Morrissey. Sub: J. Quigley for J. Codd.

1988

Midleton—G. Power, D. Mulcahy, M. Boylan, S. O'Mahony, E. Cleary, S. O'Brien, P. Hartnett, Tadhg McCarthy, M. Crotty, J. Fenton, J. Hartnett, J. Boylan, G. Fitzgerald, C. O'Neill, K. Hennessy. Subs: G. Glavin for M. Crotty, C. O'Neill for J. Boylan, G. Smyth for S. O'Mahony.
Athenry—M. Gannon, D. Monaghan, B. Caulfield, A. Jennings, P Hardiman, M. Cahill, G. Keane, J. Hardiman, P. Healy, G. Dempsey, S. Keane, P. J. Molloy, S. Kearns, P Higgins, D. Higgins. Subs: M. Donoghue for D. Higgins, B. Feeney for S. Keane, J. Rabbitte for G. Dempsey.

1989

Buffers Alley—H. Butler, B. Murphy, P. Kenny (capt.), J. O'Leary, P. Gahan, M. Foley, C. Whelan, E. Sinnott, S. Whelan, T. Dempsey, M. Casey, P. Donoghue, M. Butler, A. Doran, S. O'Laoire.
O'Donovan Rossa—P. Quinn, G. Rogan, D. Murray (capt.), M Barr, A. Murray, M. Reynolds, S. Collins, J. Fagan, J. Close, D. Armstrong, C. Barr, P. Ward, N. Murray, J. Reilly, C. Murphy. Subs: S. Shannon for Ward, P. Rogan for Close, C. Condon for Collins.

1990

Ballyhale Shamrocks—K. Fennelly, M. Fennelly, F. Holohan, W. Phelan, R. Walsh, P. Phelan, S. Fennelly, G. Fennelly, T. Shefflin, T. Phelan, J. Lawlor, D. Fennelly, B. Fennelly, L. Fennelly, B. Mason.
Ballybrown—F O'Reilly, J. Coughlan, J. Kenny, S. Adams, P. O'Connor, J. O'Connor, A. Hall, J. Mann, C. Coughlan, O. O'Connor, P Mulqueen, P. Davoren, C. Keyes, T Kenny, S. Hayes. Subs: E. Cliff for Hayes, G. O'Reilly for Mann.

1991

Glenmore—M. Deady, E. O'Connor; E. Aylward, P. J. O'Connor, L. Walsh, W. O'Connor, D. Ennett, R. Heffernan (capt.), D. Heffernan, D. Mullally, M. Phelan, P. Barron, J. Heffernan, C. Heffernan, J. Flynn. Subs: S. Dollard for Ennett, M. "Foxy" Phelan for Flynn, M. Aylward for P. J. O'Connor.
Patrickswell—J. Murphy, Philip Foley, Paul Foley, E. Kelleher, David Punch, P. Carey, Pa Foley, S. Carey, A. Carmody, C. Carey, G. Kirby, S. Kirby, N. Carey, S. Foley, L. Enright. Sub: Dom Punch for Kelleher.

1992

Kiltormer—S. McKeigue, B. McManus, C. Hayes, K. Tierney, F. Curley, P. Dervan, G. Kelly, T. Larkin, A. Staunton (capt.), J. Campbell, A. Kilkenny, D. Curley, D. Cox, M. Staunton, S. Kelly. Subs: T. Furey for Dervan, T. Hanrahan for McManus.
Birr—P Kirwan, M. Hogan, D. Geoghegan, B. Hennessy, B. Whelahan (capt.), J. Errity, G. Cahill, J. Pilkington, M. Finnane, D. Regan, P Murphy, D. Pilkington, M. Errity, R. Landy, O. O'Neill. Subs: N. Hogan for M. Errity, J. Carroll for Finnane.

1993

Sarsfields—T. Kenny, Pakie Cooney, B. Cooney, M. Cooney, Padraic Kelly, D. Keane, W. Earls, N. Morrissey, Joe Cooney, M. McGrath, J. McGrath, A. Donohue, Peter Kelly, M. Kenny, Peter Cooney.
Kilmallock—G. Hanly, S. Burchill, J. J. O'Riordan, S. O'Grady, D. Barry, D. Clarke, G. O'Riordan, M. Houlihan, S. Barrett, P. Barrett, M. Nelligan, P. Kelly, P. Tobin, B. Hanley, D. Hanley. Sub: T. Nelligan for M. Nelligan.

1994

Sarsfields—T. Kenny; Pakie Cooney, B. Cooney, M. Cooney; P. Kelly, D. Keane, W. Earls; N. Morrissey, J. Cooney; M. McGrath, J. McGrath, A. Donohue; P. Kelly, M. Kenny, Peter Cooney. Sub: J. Keone for Morrissey.
Toomevara—J. Grace; P. Meagher, R. Brislane, D. O'Meara; G. Frend, M. O'Meara, P. Shanahan; T. Delaney, P. King; M. Nolan, M. Murphy, L. Flaherty; T. Carroll, K. Kennedy, Thomas Dunne. Subs. Terry Dunne for Kennedy; L. Nolan for Flaherty.

1995

Birr—R. Shields; M. Hogan, J Errity, B. Hennessy; B. Whelahan, G. Cahill, N. Hogan; J. Pilkington, D. Regan; O. O'Neill, C. McGlone, D. Pilkington; S. Whelahan, P. Murphy, A. Cahill. Subs: M. Finnane for O'Neill; L. Vaughan for C. McGlone; R. Landy for M. Hogan. Sub in drawn game R. Landy for S. Whelahan.

Dunloy—S. Elliott; B. Óg Cunning, S. McMullan, S. McIlhatton; F. McMullan, Gary O'Kane, S. Mullan; T. McGrath, C. McGuckian; N. Elliott, P. Molloy, J. Elliott; E. McKee, Gregory O'Kane, A. Elliott. Sub: J. Cunning for Molloy. (Subs in drawn game: Note: L. Richmond for J. Elliott, S. Boyle for E. McKee, J. Cunning for P. Molloy.)

Note: Same teams fielded by both clubs in drawn game and replay.

1996

Sixmilebridge—C. Fitzgerald; M. Halloran, K. McInerney; M. Toomey, C. Chaplin, J. O'Connell, P. Hayes; J. Chaplin, N. Earley; David Chaplin, F. Quilligan, M. Conlon: D. McInerney, Danny Chaplin, G. McInerney. Subs: N. Gilligan for Quilligan; N. O'Gorman for Hayes.

Dunloy—S. Elliott; N. McCamphill, P. Molloy, S. McIlhatton; S. McMullan, Gary O'Kane, S. Mullan; F. McMullan, C. McGuckian; N. Elliott, T. McGrath, A. Elliott; E. McKee, Gregory O'Kane, J. Elliott. Subs: B. Óg Cunning for McCamphill; M. Molloy for J. Elliott; L. Richmond for S. McMullan.

1997

St. Mary's, Athenry—M. Crimmins; E. Keogh, G. Keane, J. Feeney; B. Higgins, B. Feeney, P. Hardiman; P. Healy, B. Keogh, J. Rabbitte, P. Higgins, B. Hanley, A. Poinard, E. Cloonan, C. Moran. Subs: E. Brady for Hanley; J. Hardiman for Healy.

Wolfe Tones, Shannon—D. Garrihy; G. McIntyre, B. Lohan, M. Hartigan; F. Lohan, S. Power, P. Meaney; D. Riordan, Pat O'Rourke; F. Carrig, J. McPhilips, P. Lee; Paul O'Rourke, D. Collins, P. Keary. Subs: C. O'Neill for Riordan; J. Riordan for Pat O'Rourke.

1998

Birr—B. Mullins; S. Whelehan, J. Errity, G. Doorley; Barry Whelahan, Brian Whelahan, N. Claffey; J. Pilkington, C. Hanniffy; D. Hanniffy, C. McGlone, D. Pilkington; G. Cahill, D. Regan, P. Carroll. Subs: O. O'Neill for Carroll; L. Power for McGlone.

Sarsfields—T. Kenny; Padraig Kelly, B. Cooney, G. McGrath; M. Stratford, M. Ward, W. Earls; N. Morrissey, Joe Cooney; P. Forde, M. McGrath, A. Donohue; Peter Kelly, J. McGrath, Peter Cooney. Subs: C. Murray for G. McGrath; M. Kenny for Stratford; C. Hynes for Morrissey.

1999

St. Joseph's Doora-Barefield—C. O'Connor, G. Hoey, D. Cahill, K. Kennedy, D. O'Driscoll, S. McMahon, D. Hoey, O. Baker, J. Considine, J. O'Connor, N. Brodie, L. Hassett, G. Baker, C. O'Neill, A. Whelan. Subs: C. Mullen for G. Baker, F. O'Sullivan for J. Considine.

Rathnure—J. Morrissey, S. Somers, J. Conran, D. Guiney, L. Somers, Joe Mooney, R. Guiney, M. Redmond, M. O'Leary, A. Codd, M. Byrne, P. Codd, M. Morrissey, C. Byrne, B. O'Leary. Subs: N. Higgins for L. Somers, R. Codd for M. Morrissey, J. Holohan for C. Byrne.

2000

Athenry – M.Crimmins, E.Keogh, G.Keane, J.Feeney, B.Higgins, B.Feeney, P.Hardiman, B.Keogh, B.Hanley, J.Rabbitte, P.Higgins, D.Moran, C.Moran, E.Cloonan, D.Donohue. Subs – A.Poniard for C.Moran, P.Healy for Higgins, D.Higgins for Donohue.

St. Joseph's Doora-Barefield – C.O'Connor, G.Hoey, D.Cahill, K.Kennedy, D.Hoey, S.McMahon, D.O'Driscoll, O.Baker, J.Considine, J.O'Connor, N.Brodie, L.Hassett, G.Baker, C.O'Neill, A.Whelan. Subs – C.Mullen for Brodie, F.O'Sullivan for Whelan, P.Fahy for O'Neill.

2001

Athenry – M.Crimmins, E.Keogh, G.Keane, J.Feeney, B.Higgins, B.Feeney, P.Hardiman, B.Keogh, B.Hanley, J.Rabbitte, P.Higgins, D.Moran, C.Moran, E.Cloonan, D.Donohue. Subs – D.Burns for C.Moran, S.Donohue for Hanley, D.Cloonan for D.Donohue, D.Donohue for B.Feeney, D.Higgins for P.Higgins.

Graigue-Ballycallan – J.Ronan, J.Butler, P.O'Dwyer, J.Ryall, P.McCluskey, T.Comerford, A.Hoyne, James Young, E.O'Dwyer, D.Byrne, J.Hoyne, M.Hoyne, E.Brennan, T.Dermody, A.Ronan. Subs – D.Hoyne for McCluskey, Joe Young for Dermody, J.Lynch for A.Hoyne.

2002

Birr – B.Mullins, G.Cahill, J.Errity, J.P.O'Meara, N.Claffey, Brian Whelahan, D.Franks, R.Hanniffy, Barry Whelahan, J.Pilkington, G.Hanniffy, L.Power, S.Browne, S.Whelahan, D.Pilkington. Sub – P.Molloy for Power.

Clarinbridge – L.Donoghue, M.Spellman, A.Quinn, G.Spellman, J.Cannon, M.Donoghue, L.Madden, D.Coen, B.Carr, P.Coen, M.Kerins, A.Kerins, C.Coen, D.Forde, D.Donoghue.

2003

Birr – B.Mullins, G.Cahill, J.Errity, J.P.O'Meara, N.Claffey, Brian Whelahan, D.Franks, Barry Whelahan, J.Pilkington, R.Hanniffy, G.Hanniffy, L.Power, P.Molloy, S.Whelahan, D.Pilkington. Sub – S.Browne for Power.

Dunloy – G.McGhee, D.McMullan, S.Mullan, F.McMullan, M.Molloy, Gary O'Kane, P.McMullan, C.Cunning, C.McGuckian, L.Richmond, Gregory O'Kane, N.Elliott, P.Richmond, A.Elliott, M.Curry. Sub – E.McKee for Cunning.

2004

Newtownshandrum – P.Morrisey, J.McCarthy, B.Mulcahy, G.O'Mahony, I.Kelleher, P.Mulcahy, P.Noonan, A.T.O'Brien, Jerry O'Connor, D.Mulcahy, B.O'Connor, J.P.King, J.Bowles, D.O'Riordan, M.Farrell. Subs – John O'Connor for Farrell, D.Naughton for King, A.G.O'Brien for O'Mahony.

Dunloy – G.McGhee, S.Mullan, Gary O'Kane, F.McMullan, M.Molloy, M.McClements, D.McMullan, C.Cunning, P.McMullan, P.Richmond, C.McGuckian, L.Richmond, M.Curry, Gregory O'Kane, A.Elliott. Sub – D.Quinn for Curry.

2005

James Stephens – F.Cantwell, D.Cody, M.Phelan, D.Grogan, J.Tyrell, P.Larkin, P.Barry, P.O'Brien, B.McEvoy, J.Murphy, E.Larkin, G.Whelan, E.McCormack, R.Hayes, D.McCormack. Sub – J.Murray for Murphy.

Athenry – M.Crimmins, T.Kelly, P.Hardiman, J.Feeney, B.Higgins, B.Feeney, S.Donohue, L.Howley, B.Hanley, J.Rabbitte, M.J.Quinn, E.Caulfield, D.Moran, E.Cloonan, D.Donohue. Subs – D.Burns for Caulfield, D.Carroll for Hanley, C.O'Donovan for S.Donohue.

2006

Portumna – I.Canning, M.Gill, E.McEntee, O.Canning, G.Heagney, M.Ryan, A.O'Donnell, L.Smith, E.Lynch, D.Canning, K.Hayes, A.Smith, D.Hayes, N.Hayes, J.Canning.

Newtownshandrum – P.Morrisey, M.Farrell, B.Mulcahy, D.Gleeson, A.T.O'Brien, P.Mulcahy, P.Noonan, J.P.King, J.O'Connor, D.Mulcahy, B.O'Connor, J.O'Connor, W.O'Mahony, J.Bowles, C.Naughton.

2007

Ballyhale Shamrocks – J.Connolly, P.Shefflin, E.Walsh, P.Holden, K.Nolan, A.Cummins, B.Aylward, J.Fitzpatrick, M.Fennelly, E.Fitzpatrick, H.Shefflin, T.J.Reid, E.Reid, P.Reid, M.Aylward. Sub – D.Hoyne for E.Fitzpatrick.

Loughrea – N.Murray, T.Regan, D.McLearn, D.Melia, B.Mahony, G.Kennedy, J.Dooley, G.Keary, R.Regan, E.Coen, J.Maher, V.Maher, B.Dooley, J.Loughlin, K.Colleran. Subs – M.Haverty for Loughlin, Loughlin for Dooley, K.Daniels for Coen.

2008

Portumna – I.Canning, M.Gill, E.McEntee, O.Canning, G.Heagney, M.Ryan, P.Smith, L.Smith, E.Lynch, A.Smith, K.Hayes, N.Hayes, D.Hayes, J.Canning, D.Canning. Subs – A.O'Donnell for P.Smith, C.Ryan for D.Canning.

Birr – B.Mullins, J.P.O'Meara, N.Claffey, M.Verney, B.Watkins, P.Cleary, D.Hayden, R.Hanniffy, Barry Whelahan, G.Hanniffy, Brian Whelahan, S.Ryan, P.O'Meara, S.Whelahan, S.Brown. Subs – M.Dwane for Ryan, P.Molloy for P.O'Meara, B.Harding for Hayden.

2009

Portumna – I.Canning, M.Dolphin, E.McEntee, O.Canning, G.Heagney, M.Ryan, A.O'Donnell, E.Lynch, L.Smith, N.Hayes, K.Hayes, A.Smith, D.Hayes, J.Canning, C.Ryan. Subs – D.Canning for C.Ryan, M.Gill for Heagney, P.Smith for L.Smith, P.Treacy for O'Donnell, J.O'Flaherty for McEntee.

De La Salle – S.Brenner, A.Kelly, K.Moran, M.Doherty, D.Russell, I.Flynn, S.Daniels, B.Phelan, C.Watt, P.Nevin, J.Mullane, L.Hayes, D.Twomey, D.McGrath, D.Greene. Subs – B.Farrell for Hayes, T.Kearney for McGrath, J.Quirke for Farrell, A.O'Neill for Watt, D.Dooley for Twomey.

CAPTAINS OF WINNING ALL-IRELAND CLUB HURLING TEAMS

1971—D . Moloney (Roscrea)
1972—J. Horgan (Blackrock)
1973—D. Coughlan (Glen Rovers)
1974—J. Horgan (Blockrock)
1975—J. Power (St. Finbarr's)
1976—P. Larkin (James Stephens)
1977—M. Doherty (Glen Rovers)
1978—D. Burns (St. Finbarr's)
1979—J. Horgan (Blackrock)
1980—M. Connolly (Castlegar)
1981—R. Reid (Ballyhale Shamrocks)
1982—J. O'Brien (James Stephens)
1983—N. Patterson (Loughgiel Shamrocks)
1984—K. Fennelly (Ballyhale Shamrocks)
1985—J. Brennan (St. Martin's)
1986—T. Sheppard (Kiluane McDonagh's)
1987—M. Ryan (Borris-Ileigh)
1988—G. Power (Midleton)
1989—P. Kenny (Buffer's Alley)
1990—W. Phelan (Ballyhale Shamrocks)
1991—R . Heffernan (Glenmore)
1992—A. Staunton (Kiltormer)
1993—P. Cooney (Sarsfields)
1994—P. Cooney (Sarsfields)
1995—J. Pilkington (Birr)
1996—G. McInerney (Sixmilebridge)
1997—B. Feeney (Athenry)
1998—J. Errity (Birr)
1999—L. Hassett (St. Joseph's Doora-Barefield)
2000—J.Rabbitte (Athenry)
2001—J.Rabbitte (Athenry)
2002—S.Whelahan (Birr)
2003—G.Hanniffy (Birr)
2004—J.McCarthy (Newtownshandrum)
2005—P.Barry (James Stephens)

2006—E.McEntee (Portumna)
2007—T.Coogan (Ballyhale Shamrocks)
2008—O.Canning (Portumna)
2009—O.Canning (Portumna)

ALL-IRELAND CLUB HURLING REFEREES 1971-2009

1971—Frank Murphy (Cork)
1972—Noel Dalton (Waterford)
1973—Sean O'Grady (Limerick)
1974—Paddy Johnson (Kilkenny)
1975—Mick Spain (Offaly)
1976—Jimmy Rankins (Laois)
1977—John Moloney (Tipperary)
1978—Noel O'Donoghue (Dublin)
1979—Seamus Brennan (Galway)
1980—Nealie Duggan (Limerick)
1981—Noel O'Donoghue (Dublin)
1982—George Ryan (Tipperary)
1983—N. O'Donoghue/J. Rankins
1984—George Ryan (Tipperary)
1985—George Ryan (Tipperary)
1986—Terence Murray (Limerick)
1987—Gerry Kirwan (Offaly)
1988—Gerry Kirwan (Offaly)
1989—Willie Horgan (Cork)
1990—Willie Horgan (Cork)
1991—Willie Barrett (Tipperary)
1992—Dickie Murphy (Wexford)
1993—Pat Horan (Offaly)
1994—Pat Horan (Offaly)
1995—Pat O'Connor (Limerick)
1996—Dickie Murphy (Wexford)
1997—Dickie Murphy (Wexford)
1998—Willie Barrett (Wexford)
1999—Pat O'Connor (Limerick)
2000—M Wadding (Waterford)
2001—J McDonnell (Tipperary)
2002—G Harrington (Cork)
2003—S McMahon (Clare)
2004—B Kelly (Westmeath)
2005—S Roche (Tipperary)
2006—B.Gavin (Offaly)
2007—D.Kirwan (Cork)
2008—J.Sexton (Cork)
2009—J.McGrath (Westmeath)

ALL-STARS HURLING TEAMS

1971—D. Martin (Offaly), A. Maher (Cork), P. Hartigan (Limerick), J. Treacy (Kilkenny), T. O'Connor (Tipperary), M. Roche (Tipperary), M. Coogan (Kilkenny), F. Cummins (Kilkenny), John Connolly (Galway), F. Loughnane (Tipperary), M. Keating (Tipperary), E. Keher (Kilkenny), M. Bermingham (Dublin), R. Cummins (Cork), E. Cregan (Limerick).

1972—N. Skehan (Kilkenny), A. Maher (Cork), P. Hartigan (Limerick), J. Treacy (Kilkenny), P. Lawlor (Kilkenny), M. Jacob (Wexford), C. Roche (Cork), F. Cummins (Kilkenny), D. Coughlan (Cork), F. Loughnane (Tipperary), P. Delaney (Kilkenny), E. Keher (Kilkenny), C. McCarthy (Cork), R. Cummins (Cork), E. Cregan (Limerick).

1973—N. Skehan (Kilkenny), P. Larkin (Kilkenny), P. Hartigan (Limerick), J. O'Brien (Limerick), C. Doran (Wexford), P. Henderson (Kilkenny), S. Foley (Limerick), R. Bennis (Limerick), L. O'Brien (Kilkenny), F. Loughnane (Tipperary), P. Delaney (Kilkenny), E. Grimes (Limerick), M. Quigley (Wexford), K. Purcell (Kilkenny), E. Keher (Kilkenny).

1974—N. Skehan (Kilkenny), P. Larkin (Kilkenny), P. Hartigan (Limerick), J. Horgan (Cork), G. Loughnane (Clare), P. Henderson (Kilkenny), C. Roche (Cork), L. O'Brien, (Kilkenny), J. Galvin (Waterford), J. McKenna (Limerick), M. Quigley (Wexford), M. Crotty (Kilkenny), J. Qulgley (Wexford), K. Purcell (Kilkenny), E. Keher (Kilkenny).

1975—N. Skehan (Kilkenny), N. Mclnerney (Galway), P. Hartigan (Limerick), B. Cody (Kilkenny), T. O'Connor (Tipperary), S. Silke (Galway), I. Clarke (Galway), L. O'Brien (Kilkenny), G. McCarthy (Cork), M. Quigley (Wexford), J. McKenna (Limerick), E. Grimes (Limerick), M. Brennan (Kilkenny), K. Purcell (Kilkenny), E. Keher (Kilkenny).

1976—N. Skehan (Kilkenny), P. Larkin (Kilkenny), W. Murphy (Wexford), J. McMahon (Clare), J. McDonagh (Galway), M. Jacob (Wexford), D. Coughlan (Cork), F. Burke (Galway), P. Moylan (Cork), M. Malone (Cork), M. Quigley (Wexford), J. Barry Murphy (Cork), M. Brennan (Kilkenny), A. Doran (Wexford), S. O'Leary (Cork).

1977—S. Durack (Clare), J. McMahon (CLare), M. O'Doherty (Cork), J. Horgan (Cork), G. Loughnane (Clare), M. Jacob (Wexford), D. Coughlan (Cork), T. Cashman (Cork), M. Moroney (Clare), C. Keogh (Wexford), J. Barry Murphy (Cork), P. J. Molloy (Galway), C. McCarthy (Cork), R. Cummins (Cork), S. O'Leary (Cork).

1978—S. Durack (Clare), P. Larkin (Kilkenny), M. O'Doherty (Cork), J. Horgan (Cork), J. Hennessy (Kilkenny), G. Henderson (Kilkenny), D. Coughlan (Cork), T. Cashman (Cork), I. Clarke (Galway), J. Barry Murphy (Cork), N. Casey (Clare), C. Honan (Clare), C. McCarthy (Cork), J. McKenna (Limerick), T. Butler (Tipperary).

1979—P. McLoughney (Tipperary), B. Murphy (Cork), M. O'Doherty (Cork), T. O'Connor (Tipperary), D. McCurtain (Cork), G. Henderson (Kilkenny), I. Clarke (Galway), John Connolly

(Gaiway), J. Hennessy (Kilkenny), J. Callinan (Clare), F. Burke (Galway), L. O'Brien (Kilkenny), M. Brennan (Kilkenny), J. McKenna (Limerick), E. Buggy (Wexford).

1980—P. McLoughney (Tipperary), N. Mclnerney (Galway), L. Enright (Limerick), Jimmy Cooney (Galway), D. McCurtain (Cork), S. Silke (Galway), I. Clarke (Galway), J. Kelly (Offaly), M. Walsh (Waterford), Joe Connolly (Galway), P. Horgan (Cork), P Carroll (Offaly), B. Forde (Galway), J. McKenna (Limerick), E. Cregan (Limerick).

1981—S. Durack (Clare), B. Murphy (Cork), L. Enright (Limerick), Jimmy Cooney (Galway), L. O'Donoghue (Limerick), S. Stack (Clare), G. Coughlan (Offaly), S. Mahon (Galway), L Currams (Offaly), J. Callinan (Clare), G. O'Connor (Wexford) M Corrigan (Offaly), P. Carroll (Offaly), J. McKenna (Limerick), J Flaherty (Offaly).

1982—N. Skehan (Kilkenny), J. Galvin (Waterford), B. Cody (Kilkenny), P. Fleury (Offaly), A. Fogarty (Offaly), G. Henderson (Kilkenny), P. Prendergast (Kilkenny), T. Crowley (Cork), F. Cummins (Kilkenny), A. O'Sullivan (Cork), P. Horgan (Cork), R. Power (Kilkenny), W. Fitzpatrick (Kilkenny), C. Heffernan (Kilkenny), J Greene (Waterford).

1983—N. Skehan (Kilkenny), J. Henderson (Kilkenny), L. Enright (Limerick), D. O'Hara (Kilkenny), J. Hennessy (Kilkenny), G. Henderson (Kilkenny), T. Cashman (Cork), F. Cummins (Kilkenny), J. Fenton (Cork), N. English (Tipperary), G. Fennelly (Kilkenny), N. Lane (Galway), W. Fitzpatrick (Kilkenny), J. Barry Murphy (Cork), L. Fennelly (Kilkenny).

1984—G. Cunningham (Cork), P. Fitzmaurice (Limerick), E. Coughlan (Offaly), P. Fleury (Offaly), J. Hennessy (Kilkenny), J. Crowley (Cork), D. MacCurtain (Cork), J. Fenton (Cork), J. Kelly (Offaly), N. English (Tipperary), K. Brennan (Kilkenny), P. Kelly (Limerick), T. Mulcahy (Cork), N. Lane (Galway), S. O'Leary (Cork).

1985—G. Cunningham (Cork), S. Coen (Galway), E. Coughlan (Offaly), S. Linnane (Galway), P. Finnerty (Galway), P. Delaney (Offaly), G. Coughlan (Offaly), P. Critchley (Laois), J Fenton (Cork), N. English (Tipperary), B. Lynskey (Galway), Joe Cooney (Galway), P. Cleary (Offaly), P. Horan (Offaly), L. Fennelly (Kilkenny).

1986—G. Cunningham {Cork), D. Mulcahy (Cork), C. Hayes (Galway), S. Linnane (Galway), P Finnerty (Galway), A. Keady (Galway), B. Ryan (Tipperary), R. Power (Kilkenny), J. Fenton (Cork), A. O'Sullivan (Cork), T. Mulcahy (Cork), Joe Cooney (Galway), D. Kilcoyne (Westmeath), J. Barry Murphy (Cork), K. Hennessy (Cork).

1987—K. Hogan (Tipperary), J. Hennessy (Kilkenny), C. Hayes (Galway), O. Kilkenny (Galway), P. Finnerty (Galway), G. Henderson (Kilkenny), J. Conran (Wexford), S. Mohan (Galway), J. Fenton (Cork), M. McGrath (Galway), Joe Cooney (Galway), A. Ryan (Tipperary), P. Fox (Tipperary), N. English (Tipperary), L. Fennelly (Kilkenny).

1988—J. Commins (Galway), S. Linnane (Galway), C. Hayes (Galway), M. Hanamy (Offaly), P. Finnerty (Galway), A. Keady (Galway), B. Ryan (Tipperary), Colm Bonnar (Tipperary), G. O'Connor (Wexford), D. Ryan (Tipperary), C. Barr (Antrim), M. Naughton (Galway), M. McGrath (Galway), N. English (Tipperary), A. O'Sullivan (Cork).

1989—J. Commins (Galway), A. Fogarty (Offaly), E. Cleary (Wexford), D. Donnelly (Antrim), Conal Bonnar (Tipperary), B. Ryan (Tipperary), S. Treacy (Galway), M. Coleman (Galway), D. Carr (Tipperary), E. Ryan (Galway), Joe Cooney (Galway), O. McFetridge (Antrim), P Fox (Tipperary), Cormac Bonnar (Tipperary), N. English (Tipperary).

1990—G. Cunningham (Cork), J. Considine (Cork), N. Sheehy (Tipperary), S. O'Gorman (Cork), P. Finnerty (Galway), J. Cashman (Cork), L. Dunne (Wexford), M. Coleman (Galway), J. Pilkington (Offaly), M. Cleary (Tipperary), Joe Cooney (Galway), A. O'Sullivan (Cork), E. Morrissey (Kilkenny), B. McMahon (Dublin), J. Fitzgibbon (Cork).

1991—M. Walsh (Kilkenny), P. Delaney (Tipperary), N. Sheehy (Tipperary), S. Treacy (Galway), Conal Bonnar (Tipperary), J. Cashman (Cork), C. Casey (Cork), T. McNaughten (Antrim), J. Leahy (Tipperary), M. Cleary (Tipperary), G. Kirby (Limerick), D. J. Carey (Kilkenny), P. Fox (Tipperary), Cormac Bonnar (Tipperary), J. Fitzgibbon (Cork).

1992—T. Quaid (Limerick), B. Corcoran (Cork), P. Dwyer (Kilkenny), L. Simpson (Kilkenny), B. Whelehan (Offaly), C. Carey (Limerick), W. O'Connor (Kilkenny), M. Phelan (Kilkenny), S. McCarthy (Cork), G. McGrattan (Down), J. Power (Kilkenny), A. O'Sullivan (Cork), M. Cleary (Tipperary), L. Fennelly (Kilkenny), D. J. Carey (Kilkenny).

1993—M. Walsh (Kilkenny), E. O'Connor (Kilkenny), S. O'Gorman (Cork), L. Simpson (Kilkenny), L. Dunne (Wexford), P. O'Neill (Kilkenny), P. Kelly (Galway), P. Malone (Galway), P. McKillen (Antrim), M. Storey (Wexford), J. Power (Kilkenny), D. J. Carey (Kilkenny), M. Cleary (Tipperary), J. Rabbitte (Galway), B. Egan (Cork).

1994—Joe Quaid (Limerick), A. Daly (Clare), K. Kinahan (Offaly), M. Hanamy (Offaly), D. Clarke (Limerick), H. Rigney (Offaly), K. Martin (Offaly), C. Carey (Limerick), M. Houlihan (Limerick), Johnny Dooley (Offaly), G. Kirby (Limerick), J. Leahy (Tipperary), B. Dooley (Offaly), D. J. Carey (Kilkenny), D. Quigley (Limerick).

1995—D. Fitzgerald (Clare), K. Kinahan (Offaly), B. Lohan (Clare), L. Doyle (Clare), B. Whelehan (Offaly), S. McMahon (Clare), Anthony Daly (Clare), O. Baker (Clare), M. Coleman (Galway), Johnny Dooley (Offaly), G. Kirby (Limerick), J. O'Connor (Clare), B. Dooley (Offaly), D. J. Carey (Kilkenny), G. O'Loughlin (Clare).

1996—Joe Quaid (Limerick), T. Helebert (Galway), B. Lohan (Clare), L. O'Gorman (Wexford), L. Dunne (Wexford), C. Carey (Limerick), M. Foley (Limerick), A. Fenlon (Wexford), M. Houlihan (Limerick), R. McCarthy (Wexford), M. Storey (Wexford), L. Murphy (Wexford), L. Cahill (Tipperary), G. Kirby Limerick), T. Dempsey (Wexford).

1997—D. Fitzhenry (Wexford), P Shelly (Tipperary), B. Lohan (Clare), W. O'Connor (Kilkenny), L. Doyle (Clare), S. McMahon (Clare), L. Keoghan (Kilkenny), C. Lynch (Clare), T. Dunne (Tipperary), J. O'Connor (Clare), D. Ryan (Tipperary), J. Leahy (Tipperary), K. Broderick (Galway), G. O'Loughlin (Clare), D. J. Carey (Kilkenny).

1998—S. Byrne (Offaly), W. O'Connor (Kilkenny), K. Kinahan (Offaly), M. Hanamy (Offaly), A. Daly (Clare), S. McMahon (Clare), K. Martin (Offaly), Tony Browne (Waterford), O. Baker (Clare), M. Duignan (Offaly), M. Storey (Wexford), J. O'Connor (Clare), Joe Dooley (Offaly), B. Whelahan (Offaly), C. Carter (Kilkenny).

1999—Donal Óg Cusack (Cork), Fergal Ryan (Cork), Diarmuid O'Sullivan (Cork), Frank Lohan (Clare), Brian Whelahan (Offaly), Brian Corcoran (Cork), Peter Barry (Kilkenny), Andy Comerford (Kilkenny), Tommy Dunne (Tipperary), DJ Carey (Kilkenny), John Troy (Offaly), Brian McEvoy (Kilkenny), Sean McGrath (Cork), Joe Deane (Cork), Niall Gilligan (Clare).

2000—Brendan Cummins (Tipperary), Noel Hickey (Kilkenny), Diarmuid O'Sullivan (Cork), Willie O'Connor (Kilkenny), John Carroll (Tipperary), Eamonn Kennedy (Tipperary), Peter Barry (Kilkenny), Johnny Dooley (Offaly), Andy Comerford (Kilkenny), Denis Byrne (Kilkenny), Joe Rabbitte (Galway), Henry Shefflin (Kilkenny), Charlie Carter (Kilkenny), DJ Carey (Kilkenny), Joe Deane (Cork).

2001—Brendan Cummins (Tipperary), Darragh Ryan (Wexford), Philip Maher (Tipperary), Ollie Canning (Galway), Eamonn Corcoran (Tipperary), Liam Hodgins (Galway), Mark Foley (Limerick), Thomas Dunne (Tipperary), Eddie Enright (Tipperary), Mark O'Leary (Tipperary), James O'Connor (Clare), Kevin Broderick (Galway), Charlie Carter (Kilkenny), Eugene Cloonan (Galway), Eoin Kelly (Tipperary).

2002—David Fitzgerald (Clare), Michael Kavanagh (Kilkenny), Brian Lohan (Clare), Philip Larkin (Kilkenny), Fergal Healy (Waterford), Peter Barry (Kilkenny), Paul Kelly (Tipperary), Colin Lynch (Clare), Derek Lyng (Kilkenny), Eoin Kelly (Waterford), Henry Shefflin (Kilkenny), Ken McGrath (Waterford), Eoin Kelly (Tipperary), Martin Comerford (Kilkenny), DJ Carey (Kilkenny).

2003—Brendan Cummins (Tipperary), Michael Kavanagh (Kilkenny), Noel Hickey (Kilkenny), Ollie Canning (Galway), Seán Óg Ó hAilpín (Cork), Ronan Curran (Cork), JJ Delaney (Kilkenny), Derek Lyng (Kilkenny), Tommy Walsh (Kilkenny), John Mullane (Waterford), Henry Shefflin (Kilkenny), Eddie Brennan (Kilkenny), Setanta Ó hAilpín (Cork), Martin Comerford (Kilkenny), Joe Deane (Cork).

2004—Damien Fitzhenry (Wexford), Wayne Sherlock (Cork), Diarmuid O'Sullivan (Cork), Tommy Walsh (Kilkenny), JJ Delaney (Kilkenny), Ronan Curran (Cork), Seán Óg Ó hAilpín (Cork), Ken McGrath (Waterford), Jerry O'Connor (Cork), Dan Shanahan (Waterford), Niall McCarthy (Cork), Henry Shefflin (Kilkenny), Eoin Kelly (Tipperary), Brian Corcoran (Cork), Paul Flynn (Waterford).

2005 – Davy Fitzgerald (Clare), Pat Mulcahy (Cork), Diarmuid O'Sullivan (Cork), Ollie Canning (Galway), Derek Hardiman (Galway), John Gardiner (Cork), Sean Óg Ó hAilpín (Cork), Jerry O'Connor (Cork), Paul Kelly (Tipperary), Ben O'Connor (Cork), Henry Shefflin (Kilkenny), Tommy Walsh (Kilkenny), Ger Farragher (Galway), Eoin Kelly (Tipperary), Damien Hayes (Galway).

2006 – Donal Óg Cusack (Cork), Eoin Murphy (Waterford), J.J.Delaney (Kilkenny), Brian Murphy (Cork), Tony Browne (Waterford), Ronan Curran (Cork), Tommy Walsh (Kilkenny), Jerry O'Connor (Cork), James Fitzpatrick (Kilkenny), Dan Shanahan (Waterford), Henry Shefflin (Kilkenny), Eddie Brennan (Kilkenny), Eoin Kelly (Tipperary), Martin Comerford (Kilkenny), Tony Griffin (Clare).

2007 – Brian Murray (Limerick), Michael Kavanagh (Kilkenny), Declan Fanning (Tipperary), Jackie Tyrrell (Kilkenny), Tommy Walsh (Kilkenny), Ken McGrath (Waterford), Tony Browne (Waterford), Michael Walsh (Waterford), James Fitzpatrick (Kilkenny), Dan Shanahan (Waterford), Ollie Moran (Limerick), Stephen Molumphy (Waterford), Andrew O'Shaughnessy (Limerick), Henry Shefflin (Kilkenny), Eddie Brennan (Kilkenny).

2008 – Brendan Cummins (Tipperary), Michael Kavanagh (Kilkenny), Noel Hickey (Kilkenny), Jackie Tyrrell (Kilkenny), Tommy Walsh (Kilkenny), Conor O'Mahony (Tipperary), J.J.Delaney (Kilkenny), James Fitzpatrick (Kilkenny), Shane McGrath (Tipperary), Ben O'Connor (Cork), Henry Shefflin (Kilkenny), Eoin Larkin (Kilkenny), Eddie Brennan (Kilkenny), Eoin Kelly (Waterford), Joe Canning (Galway).

2009 – P J Ryan (Kilkenny), Ollie Canning (Galway), Padraig Maher (Tipperary), Jackie Tyrrell (Kilkenny), Tommy Walsh (Kilkenny), Michael Walsh (Waterford), Conor O'Mahony (Tipperary), Michael Rice (Kilkenny), Alan McCrabbe (Dublin), Lar Corbett (Tipperary), Henry Shefflin (Kilkenny), Eoin Larkin (Kilkenny), Noel McGrath (Tipperary), Joe Canning (Galway), John Mullane (Waterford).

LEADING AWARD WINNERS

D. J. Carey (Kilkenny) 9 – 1991-1995, 1997, 1999, 2000, 2002.
Henry Shefflin (Kilkenny) 9 – 2000, 2002, 2003, 2004, 2005, 2006, 2007, 2008, 2009.
Noel Skehan (Kilkenny) 7 – 1972-1976, 1982, 1983.
Tommy Walsh (Kilkenny) 7 – 2003, 2004, 2005, 2006, 2007, 2008, 2009.
Joe McKenna (Limerick) 6 – 1974, 1975, 1978, 1979, 1980, 1981
Nicholas English (Tipperary) 6 – 1983-1985, 1987-1989.

ALL-TIME HURLING ALL-STAR AWARD WINNERS

1980—Mick Mackey (Limerick)
1981—Jack Lynch (Cork)
1982—Garrett Howard (Limerick)
1983—Fowler Mclnerney (Clare)
1984—Jim Langton (Kilkenny)
1985—Eudie Coughlan (Cork)
1986—Tommy Doyle (Tipperary)
1987—Christy Moylan (Waterford)
1988—Paddy "Fox" Collins (Cork)
1989—M. J. "Inky" Flaherty (Galway)
1990—John Joe Doyle (Clare)
1991—Jackie Power (Limerick)
1992—Bobby and Billy Rackard (Wexford)
1993—Pat Stakelum (Tipperary)
1994—Martin White (Kilkenny)
Discontinued

HURLER OF THE YEAR AWARD

The following are the Hurling stars who have been awarded Texaco Trophies by the Sports Editors since the inauguration of the award in 1958 by the sponsors Texaco. Also listed are the Hall of Fame winners in hurling since the introduction of this category in 1960.

1958—Tony Wall, Tipperary.
1959—Christy Ring, Cork.
1960—Nick O'Donnell, Wexford.
1961—Liam Devaney, Tipperary.
1962—Donie Nealon, Tipperary.
1963—Seamus Cleere, Kilkenny.
1964—John Doyle, Tipperary.
1965—Jimmy Doyle, Tipperary.
1966—Justin McCarthy, Cork.
1967—Ollie Walsh, Kilkenny.
1968—Dan Qulgley, Wexford.
1969—Ted Carroll, Kilkenny.
1970—Pat McDonnell, Cork.
1971—Michael Keating, Tipperary.
1972—Eddie Keher, Kilkenny.
1973—Eamonn Grimes, Limerick.
1974—Pat Henderson, Kilkenny.
1975—Liam O'Brien, Kilkenny.
1976—Tony Doran, Wexford.
1977—Denis Coughlan, Cork.
1978—John Horgan, Cork.
1979—Ger Henderson, Kilkenny.
1980—John Connolly, Galway.
1981—Pat Delaney, Offaly.
1982—Noel Skehan, Kilkenny.
1983—Frank Cummins, Kilkenny.
1984—John Fenton, Cork.
1985—Eugene Coughlan, Offaly.
1986—Ger Cunningham, Cork.
1987—Joe Cooney (Galway).
1988—Tony Keady (Galway).
1989—Nicholas English (Tipperary).
1990—Tony O'Sullivan (Cork).
1991—Pat Fox (Tipperary).
1992—Brian Corcoran (Cork).
1993—D. J. Carey (Kilkenny).
1994—Brian Whelehan (Offaly).
1995—Sean McMahon (Clare).
1996—Larry O'Gorman (Wexford).
1997—Jamesie O'Connor (Clare).
1998—Brian Whelehan (Offaly).
1999—Brian Corcoran (Cork).
2000—D. J. Carey (Kilkenny).
2001—Thomas Dunne (Tipperary).
2002—Henry Shefflin (Kilkenny).
2003—J. J. Delaney (Kilkenny).
2004—Seán Óg Ó hAilpín (Cork).
2005—Jerry O'Connor (Cork)
2006—Henry Shefflin (Kilkenny)
2007—Dan Shanahan (Waterford)
2008—Eoin Larkin (Kilkenny)
2009—Tommy Walsh (Kilkenny)

HALL OF FAME

1961—Mick Mackey, Limerick.
1971—Christy Ring, Cork.
1992—John Doyle, Tipperary.
2001—Willie Rackard, Wexford.

THOSE HONOURED BETWEEN 1963 AND 1967

Before the All-Star Awards were officially formalised in 1971 and took on a new importance, the now-defunct Gaelic Weekly sponsored the selection of All-Star teams from 1963 to 1967 (inclusive) in both hurling and football. Here are the hurling teams:

1963—O. Walsh (Kilkenny), T. Neville (Wexford), A. Flynn (Waterford), John Doyle (Tipperary), S. Cleere (Kilkenny), Billy Rackarcl (Wexford), L. Guinan (Waterford), T. English (Tipperary), D. Foley (Dublin), Jimmy Doyle (Tipperary), M. Flannelly (Waterford), E. Keher (Kilkenny), L. Devaney (Tipperary), J. Smith (Clare), P. Grimes (Waterford).

1964—O. Walsh (Kilkenny), John Doyle (Tipperary), P. Dillon (Kilkenny), T. Neville (Wexford), S. Cleere (Kilkenny), Tony Wall (Tipperary), P. Henderson (Kilkenny), M. Roche (Tipperary), P. Moran (Kilkenny), Jimmy Doyle (Tipperary), M. Keating (Tipperary), E. Keher (Kilkenny), T. Walsh (Kilkenny), J. McKenna (Tipperary), D. Nealon (Tipperary).

1965—J. O'Donoghue (Tipperary), T. Neville (Wexford), A. Flynn (Waterford), K. Carey (Tipperary), D. O'Riordan (Cork), Tony Wall (Tipperary), J. Duggan (Galway), P. Wilson (Wexford), M. Roche (Tipperary), Jimmy Doyle (Tipperary), P. Carroll (Kilkenny), P. Cronin (Clare), D. Nealon (Tipperary), John McKenna (Tipperary), S. McLoughlin (Tipperary).

1966—P. Barry (Cork), P. Henderson (Kilkenny), A. Flynn (Waterford), D. Murphy (Cork), S. Cleere (Kilkenny), K. Long (Limerick), M. Coogan (Kilkenny), B. Hartigan (Limerick), T. English (Tipperary), S. Barry (Cork), E. Keher (Kilkenny), P. Cronin (Clare), P. Molloy (Offaly), John McKenna (Tipperary), M. Fox (Galway).

1967—O. Walsh (Kilkenny), P. Henderson (Kilkenny), P. Dillon (Kilkenny), J. Treacy (Kilkenny), S. Cleere (Kilkenny), J. Cullinan (Clare), L. Gaynor (Tipperary), M. Roche (Tipperary), P. Moran (Kilkenny), E. Keher (Kilkenny), T. Walsh (Kilkenny), P. Cronin (Clare), D. Nealon (Tipperary), Tony Doran (Wexford), M. Keating (Tipperary).

1968-1970 No All-Star Teams

ATTENDANCE FIGURES — ALL-IRELAND FINALS

2009—Kilkenny v Tipperary	82,104
2008—Kilkenny v Waterford	82,186
2007—Kilkenny v Limerick	82,127
2006—Kilkenny v Cork	82,275
2005—Cork v Galway	81,136
2004—Cork v Kilkenny	78,212
2003—Kilkenny v Cork	79,383
2002—Kilkenny v Clare	76,254
2001—Tipperary v Galway	68,512
2000—Kilkenny v Offaly	61,493
1999—Cork v. Kilkenny	62,989
1998—Offaly v. Kilkenny	65,491
1997—Clare v. Tipperary	65,575
1996—Wexford v. Limerick	65,849
1995—Clare v. Offaly	65,092
1994—Offaly v. Limerick	56,458
1993—Kilkenny v. Galway	63,460
1992—Kilkenny v. Cork	64,354
1991—Tipperary v. Kilkenny	64,500
1990—Cork v. Galway	63,954
1989—Tipperary v. Antrim	65,496
1988—Galway v. Tipperary	63,545
1987—Galway v. Kilkenny	59,550
1986—Cork v. Galway	43,451
1985—Offaly v. Galway	61,814
1984—Cork v. Offaly	58,814
1983—Kilkenny v. Cork	58,381
1982—Kilkenny v. Cork	59,550
1981—Offaly v. Galway	71,384
1980—Galway v. Limerick	64,384
1979—Kilkenny v. Galway	63,711
1978—Cork v. Kilkenny	64,155
1977—Cork v. Wexford	63,168
1876—Cork v. Wexford	62,071
1975—Kilkenny v. Galway	63,711
1974—Kilkenny v. Limerick	62,071
1973—Limerick v. Kilkenny	58 009
1972—Kilkenny v. Cork	66,135
1971—Tipperary v. Kilkenny	61,393
1970—Cork v. Wexford	65,062
1969—Kilkenny v. Cork	66,844
1968—Tipperary v. Wexford	63,461
1967—Tipperary v. Kilkenny	64,241
1966—Cork v. Kilkenny	68,249
1965—Tipperary v. Wexford	67,498
1964—Tipperary v. Kilkenny	71,282
1963—Kilkenny v. Waterford	73,123
1962—Tipperary v. Wexford	75,039
1961—Tipperary v. Dublin	67,866
1960—Wexford v. Tipperary	77,154
1959—Waterford v. Kilkenny	73,707
1959—Waterford v. Kilkenny (replay)	77,285
1958—Tipperary v. Galway	47,276
1957—Kilkenny v. Waterford	70,594
1956—Wexford v. Cork	83,096
1955—Wexford v. Galway	77,854
1954—Cork v. Wexford	84,856
1953—Cork v . Galway	71,195
1952—Cork v. Dublin	64,332
1951—Tipperary v. Wexford	68,515
1950—Tipperary v. Kilkenny	67,629
1949—Tipperary v. Laois	67,168
1947—Kilkenny v. Cork	61,510
1946—Cork v. Kilkenny	64,415
1945—Tipperary v. Kilkenny	69,459
1944—Cork v. Dublin	26,896
1943—Cork v. Antrim	48,843

1942—Cork v. Dublin	27,313
1941—Cork v. Dublin	26,150
1940—Limerick v. Kilkenny	39,260
1939—Kilkenny v. Cork	39,302
1938—Dublin v. Waterford	37,129
1937—Tipperary v. Kilkenny	43,638
1936—Limerick v. Kilkenny	51,235
1935—Kilkenny v. Limerick	46,591
1934—Limerick v. Dublin	34,867
1934—Limerick v. Dublin (replay)	30,250
1933—Kilkenny v. Limerick	45,176
1932—Kilkenny v. Clare	34,372
1931—Cork v. Kilkenny	26,460
1931—Cork v. Kilkenny (1st replay)	33,124
1931—Cork v. Kilkenny (2nd replay)	31,935

Note: The first Cusack Stand was officially opened on August 21, 1938, with 5,000 upper - deck seats. In 1966 seating to accommodate a further 9,000 was installed on the terraces underneath to form a lower deck reducing the capacity of Croke Park to 75,000. The new Hogan Stand was officially opened on 7 June 1959 with accommodation for 16,000, replacing the much smaller 900-seat structure which had been built in 1924. The first phase of the modernisation of the stadium began in October 1993 with the demolition of the Cusack Stand. The replacement was a 40,000-seat structure, which was the first in Irish sport to offer corporate boxes and premier seats; it was first used on July 31, 1994 for the Leinster football final and was officially opened on 5 June 1996. Phase 2 of the redevelopment – a new stand at the Canal end – commenced in October 1998. This and the new Hogan Stand were officially opened in March 2003 and the redevelopment was completed in 2005 with the opening of the new HIll 16. This brings the capacity to 83,000.

LEINSTER FINAL ATTENDANCES

1950—Kilkenny v. Wexford	36,494
1951—Wexford v. Laois	29,692
1952—Dublin v. Wexford	30,500
1953—Kilkenny v. Wexford	37,533
1954—Wexford v. Dublin	28,592
1955—Wexford v. Kilkenny (draw)	41,226
Wexford v. Kilkenny (replay)	37,079
1956—Wexford v. Kilkenny	52,077
1957—Kilkenny v. Wexford	52,272
1958—Kilkenny v. Wexford	41,729
1959—Kilkenny v. Dublin	31,312
1960—Wexford v. Kilkenny	42,332
1961—Dublin v. Wexford	27,446
1962—Wexford v. Kilkenny	45,303
1963—Kilkenny v. Dublin	33,438
1964—Kilkenny v. Dublin	30,103
1965—Wexford v. Kilkenny	28,000
1966—Kilkenny v. Wexford	35,000
1967—Kilkenny v. Wexford	25,242
1968—Wexforcd v. Kilkenny	25,000
1969—Kilkenny v. Offaly	24,800
1970—Wexford v. Kilkenny	19,306
1971—Kilkenny v. Wexford	19,344
1972—Kilkenny v. Wexford (draw)	18,611
Kilkenny v. Wexford (replay)	22,745
1973—Kilkenny v. Wexford	24,000
1974—Kilkenny v. Wexford	20,742
1975—Kilkenny v. Wexford	26,228
1976—Wexford v. Kilkenny	23,500
1977—Wexford v. Kilkenny	30,614
1978—Kilkenny v. Wexford	27,371
1979—Kilkenny v. Wexford	24,991
1980—Offaly v. Kilkenny	9,613
1981—Offaly v. Wexford	29,053
1982—Kilkenny v. Offaly	32,093
1983—Kilkenny v. Offaly	35,707
1984—Offaly v. Wexford	30,016
1985—Offaly v. Laois	32,123
1986—Kilkenny v. Offaly	28,635
1987—Kilkenny v. Offaly	29,133
1988—Offaly v. Wexford	28,234
1989—Offaly v. Kilkenny	24,519
1990—Offaly v. Dublin	20,383
1991—Kilkenny v. Dublin (S.F.C.: Meath v. Wicklow on same programme).	41,215
1992—Kilkenny v. Wexford	41,097
1993—Kilkenny v. Wexford (draw)	37,715
Kilkenny v. Wexford (replay)	41,833
1994—Offaly v. Wexford	32,141
1995—Offaly v. Kilkenny	31,950
1996—Wexford v. Offaly	34,365
1997—Wexford v. Kilkenny	55,492
1998—Kilkenny v. Offaly	32,490
1999—Kilkenny v. Offaly	38,310
2000—Kilkenny v Offaly	32,802
2001—Kilkenny v Wexford	41,146
2002—Kilkenny v Wexford	37,567
2003—Kilkenny v Wexford	50,000
2004—Wexford v Offaly	46,820
2005—Kilkenny v Wexford	35,010
2006—Kilkenny v Wexford	44,081
2007—Kilkenny v Wexford	34,872
2008—Kilkenny v Wexford	18,855
2009—Kilkenny v Dublin	29,427

MUNSTER FINAL ATTENDANCES

1950—Tipperary v. Cork, Killarney	38,733
1951—Tipperary v. Cork, Limerick	42,337
1952—Cork v. Tipperary,Limerick	42,326
1953—Cork v. Tipperary, Limerick	46,265
1954—Cork v. Tipperary, Limerick	50,071
1955—Limerick v. Clare, Limerick	23,125
1956—Cork v. Limerick, Thurles	47,017
1957—Waterford v. Cork, Thurles	40,368

1958—Tipperary v. Waterford,Thurles	41,384
1959—Waterford v. Cork, Thurles	55,174
1960—Tipperary v. Cork, Thurles	49,670
1961—Tipperary v. Cork, Limerick	61,175
1962—Tipperary v. Waterford, Limerick	31,000
1963—Waterford v. Tipperary, Limerick	36,000
1964—Tipperary v. Cork, Limerick	44,245
1965—Tipperary v. Cork, Limerick	40,687
1966—Cork v. Waterford, Limerick	31,352
1967—Tipperary v. Clare, Limerick	34,940
1968—Tipperary v. Cork, Limerick	43,238
1969—Cork v. Tipperary, Limerick	43,569
1970—Cork v. Tipperary, Limerick	33,900
1971—Tipperary v. Limerick, Killarney	31,118
1972—Cork v. Clare, Thurles	25,048
1973—Limerick v. Tipperary, Thurles	41,723
1974—Limerick v. Clare, Thurles	36,446
1975—Cork v. Limerick, Limerick	46,851
1976—Cork v. Limerick, Thurles	46,800
1977—Cork v. Clare, Thurles	44,586
1978—Cork v. Clare, Thurles	54,981
1979—Cork v. Limerick, Thurles	47,849
1980—Limerick v. Cork, Thurles	43,090
1981—Limerick v. Clare, Thurles	40,205
1982—Cork v. Waterford, Thurles	38,558
1983—Cork v. Waterford, Thurles	20,816
1984—Cork v. Tipperary,Thurles	50,093
1985—Cork v. Tipperary, Cork	49,691
1986—Cork v. Clare, Killarney	39,975
1987—Tipperary v. Cork (draw) Thurles	56,005
Tipperary v.Cork (replay) Killarney	45,000
1988—Tipperary v. Cork (all ticket) Cork	50,000
1989—Tipperary v. Waterford, Cork	30,241
1990—Cork v. Tipperary, Thurles	45,000
1991—Tipperary v Cork (draw) Cork	47,500
Tipperary v. Cork (replay) Thurles	55,600
1992—Cork v. Limerick, Thurles	48,036
1993—Tipperary v. Clare, Limerick	41,557
1994—Limerick v. Clare, Thurles	43,638
1995—Clare v. Limerick, Thurles	46,361
1996—Limerick v. Tipperary (draw) Limerick	43,525
Limerick v Tipperary (replay) Cork	40,000
1997—Clare v. Tipperary, Cork	43,560
1998—Clare v Waterford (draw) Thurles	51,417
Clare v.Waterford (replay) Thurles	51,731
1999—Cork v. Clare, Thurles	54,000
2000—Cork v Tipperary, Thurles	54,586
2001—Tipperary v Limerick, Cork	43,500
2002—Waterford v Tipperary, Cork	40,276
2003—Cork v Waterford, Thurles	52,833
2004—Waterford v Cork, Thurles	53,000
2005—Cork v Tipperary, Cork	43,500
2006—Cork v Tipperary, Thurles	53,286
2007—Waterford v Limerick, Thurles	48,371
2008—Tipperary v Clare, Limerick	48,076
2009—Tipperary v Waterford	40,330

THE COMPLETE HANDBOOK OF

GAELIC GAMES

FOOTBALL
Records

FOOTBALL

RESULTS OF ALL-IRELAND CHAMPIONSHIPS 1887-2009

The distribution of Championship Honours to date is as follows:

ROLL OF HONOUR

SENIOR FOOTBALL

Kerry (36) — 1903, 1904, 1909, 1913, 1914, 1924, 1926, 1929, 1930, 1931, 1932, 1937, 1939, 1940, 1941, 1946, 1953, 1955, 1959, 1962, 1969, 1970, 1975, 1978, 1979, 1980, 1981, 1984, 1985, 1986, 1997, 2000, 2004, 2006, 2007, 2009.
Dublin (22) — 1891, 1892, 1894, 1897, 1898, 1899, 1901, 1902, 1906, 1907, 1908, 1921, 1922, 1923, 1942, 1958, 1963, 1974, 1976, 1977, 1983, 1995.
Galway (9) — 1925, 1934, 1938, 1956, 1964, 1965, 1966, 1998, 2001.
Meath (7) — 1949, 1954, 1967, 1987, 1988, 1996, 1999.
Cork (6) — 1890, 1911, 1945, 1973, 1989, 1990.
Wexford (5) — 1893, 1915, 1916, 1917, 1918.
Cavan (5) — 1933, 1935, 1947, 1948, 1952.
Down (5) — 1960, 1961, 1968, 1991, 1994.
Tipperary (4) — 1889, 1895, 1900, 1920.
Kildare (4) — 1905, 1919, 1927, 1928.
Louth (3) — 1910, 1912, 1957.
Mayo (3) — 1936, 1950, 1951.
Offaly (3) — 1971, 1972, 1982.
Tyrone (3) — 2003, 2005, 2008.
Limerick (2) — 1887, 1896.
Roscommon (2) — 1943, 1944.
Tyrone (3) — 2003, 2005, 2008.
Donegal (1) — 1992.
Derry (1) — 1993.
Armagh (1) — 2002.
Note: No Championship in 1888, U.S. Invasion

MINOR FOOTBALL

Kerry (11) — 1931, 1932, 1933, 1946, 1950, 1962, 1963, 1975, 1980, 1988, 1994.
Dublin (10) — 1930, 1945, 1954, 1955, 1956, 1958, 1959, 1979, 1982, 1984.
Cork (10) — 1961, 1967, 1968, 1969, 1972, 1974, 1981, 1991, 1993, 2000.
Tyrone (7) — 1947, 1948, 1973, 1998, 2001, 2004, 2008.
Mayo (6) — 1935, 1953, 1966, 1971, 1978, 1985.
Galway (6) — 1952, 1960, 1970, 1976, 1986, 2007.
Derry (4) — 1965, 1983, 1989, 2002.
Down (4) — 1977, 1987, 1999, 2005.
Roscommon (4) — 1939, 1941, 1951, 2006.
Meath (3) — 1957, 1990, 1992.
Laois (3) — 1996, 1997, 2003.
Cavan (2) — 1937, 1938.
Louth (2) — 1936, 1940.
Armagh (2) — 1949, 2009.
Clare (1) — 1929.
Tipperary (1) — 1934.
Offaly (1) — 1964.
Westmeath (1) — 1995.
Note: Suspended 1942-1944 (inclusive).

UNDER-21 FOOTBALL

Cork (11) — 1970, 1971, 1980, 1981, 1984, 1985, 1986, 1989, 1994, 2007, 2009.
Kerry (10) — 1964, 1973, 1975, 1976, 1977, 1990, 1995, 1996, 1998, 2008.
Tyrone (4) — 1991, 1992, 2000, 2001.
Mayo (4) — 1967, 1974, 1983, 2006.
Galway (3) — 1972, 2002, 2005.
Roscommon (2) — 1966, 1978.
Donegal (2) — 1982, 1987.
Derry (2) — 1968, 1997.
Kildare (1) — 1965.
Antrim (1) — 1969.
Down (1) — 1979.
Offaly (1) — 1988.
Meath (1) — 1993.
Westmeath (1) — 1999.
Armagh (1) — 2004.

JUNIOR FOOTBALL

Cork (15) — 1951, 1953, 1955, 1964, 1972, 1984, 1987, 1989, 1990, 1993,1996, 2001, 2005, 2007, 2009.
Kerry (14) — 1913, 1915, 1924, 1928, 1930, 1941, 1949, 1954, 1963, 1967, 1983, 1991, 1994, 2006.
London (6)—1938, 1966, 1969, 1970, 1971, 1986.
Dublin (6) — 1914, 1916, 1939, 1948, 1960, 2008.
Mayo (5) — 1933, 1950, 1957, 1995, 1997.
Meath (5) — 1947, 1952, 1962, 1988, 2003.
Louth (4) — 1925, 1932, 1934, 1961.
Galway (4) — 1931, 1958, 1965, 1985.
Tipperary (3) — 1912, 1923, 1998.
Roscommon (2) — 1940, 2000.
Wicklow (2) — 1936, 2002.
Waterford (2) — 1999, 2004.
Armagh (1) — 1926.
Cavan (1) — 1927.
Westmeath (1) — 1929.
Sligo (1) — 1935.
Longford (1) — 1937.
Down (1) — 1946.
Monaghan (1) — 1956.
Fermanagh (1) — 1959.
Tyrone (1) — 1968.
Laois (1) — 1973.
Wexford (1) — 1992.
Note: Junior Football suspended in 1917-1922 and 1974-1982 (inclusive).

SENIOR "B" FOOTBALL

Leitrim (1) — 1990. Clare (1) 1991, Wicklow (1) 1992, Laois (1) 1993, Carlow (1) 1994, Tipperary (1) 1995, Fermanagh (1) 1996, Louth (1) 1997, Monaghan (1) 1998.

ALL-IRELAND SENIOR FOOTBALL CHAMPIONSHIP

Teams 21-aside
Goal outweighted any number of points

1887—Open draw.
Counties represented by county champions.
Inchicore, August 28. Louth (Dundalk Young Irelands) 0-7, Wexford (Castlebridge) 0-4.
Limerick Junction, October 22. Tipperary (Templemore) 0-3; Limerick (Commercials) 0-3.
Tipperary Town, March 11, 1888. Replay: Limerick (Commercials) 1-9; Tipperary (Templemore) 0-4.
Clonskeagh, April 29, 1888. Final: Limerick (Commercials) 1-4; Louth (Dundalk Young Irelands) 0-3.
1888—Championship unfinished owing to U.S.A. invasion by G.A.A. athletes.
1889—No semi-finals.
Inchicore, October 20. Final: Tipperary (Bohercrowe) 3-6; Laois (Maryborough) 0-0.
1890—Clonturk Park, November 16.
Cork (Midleton) 1-15; Armagh (Harps) 0-0.
Wexford (Blues & Whites) W.O. from Galway (Cahirlistrane).
Clonturk Park, June 26, 1892. Final: Cork (Midleton) 2-4; Wexford (Blues & Whites) 0-1.
1891—No Connacht representatives.
Clonturk Park, February 28, 1892. Dublin (Young Irelands) 3-7, Cavan (Slashers) 0-3.
Clonturk Park, February 28,1892. Final: Dublin (Young Irelands) 2-1; Cork (Clondrohid) 1-9.

Teams reduced to 17-aside Goal made equal to 5 Points from 1892

1892—At the Annual Congress county champions were granted permission to select players from other clubs within the county. No Ulster representatives.
Clonturk Park, March 19, 1893. Dublin 1-9; Roscommon 1-1.
Clonturk Park, March 26, 1893. Final: Dublin (Young Irelands)1-4; Kerry (Laune Rangers)0-3.

(With no representation from Ulster and Connacht there were no semi-finals from 1893 to 1899)

1893—Phoenix Park, June 24, 1894. Final:
Wexford (Young Irelands) 1-1; Cork (Dromtariffe) 0-1.
(Game unfinished. Wexford declared champions).
1894—Clonturk Park, March 24, 1895. Final:
Dublin (Young Irelands) 0-6; Cork (Nils) 1-1 (draw).
Thurles, April 21, 1895. Replay: Cork 1-2, Dublin 0-5. Unfinished. Dublin awarded title.
Note: The final was replayed at Thurles on 21 May 1895. Cork were leading 1-2 to 0-5 when a dispute arose and Dublin walked off before the finish. When Cork refused to play a third time the title was awarded to Dublin.

1895—Jones's Road, March 15, 1896. Final:
Tipperary (Arravale Rovers) 0-4; Meath (Pierce O'Mahony's) 0-3.
Goal made equal to 3 Points from 1896 and the parallelogram introduced.
1896—Jones's Road, February 6, 1898. Final:
Limerick (Commercials) 1-5; Dublin (Young Irelands) 0-7.
1897—Jones's Road, February 5, 1899. Final:
Dublin (Kickhams) 2-6; Cork (Dunmanway) 0-2.
1898—Tipperary Town, April 8, 1900. Final: Dublin (Geraldines) 2-8; Waterford (Erin's Hope) 0-4.
1899—Jones's Road, February 10, 1901. Final:
Dublin (Geraldines) 1-10; Cork (Nils) 0-6.
1900—Galway W.O. from Antrim.
Carrick-on-Suir, June 30, 1902. Kilkenny 1-6; Tipperary 0-7.
(An objection by Tipperary resulted in the Central Council ordering a replay. Kilkenny refused to replay the game which was awarded to Tipperary.)
Terenure, September 21, 1902. Home Final:
Tipperary 2-17; Galway (Krugers, Tuam) 0-1.
Jones's Road, October 26, 1902. Final: Tipperary (Clonmel Shamrocks) 3-7; London (Hibernians) 0-2.
1901—Jones's Road, April 1 2, 1903.
Dublin 1-12; Antrim 0-3.
Limerick, May 17, 1903.
Cork 4-16; Mayo 0-1.
Tipperary, July 5, 1903. Home Final:
Dublin 1-2 (Isles of the Sea); Cork (Nils) 0-4.
Jones's Road, August 2, 1903. Final:
Dublin 0-14; London (Hibernians) 0-2.
1902—Athenry, April 24, 1904.
Tipperary 2-5; Galway 0-4.
Drogheda, June 11, 1904.
Dublin 4-16; Armagh 1-6.
Kilkenny, July 24, 1904. Home Final:
Dublin 0-6; Tipperary 0-5.
Cork, September 11, 1904. Final: Dublin (Bray Emmets) 2-8, London (Hibernians) 0-4.
1903—Limerick, May 7, 1905.
Kerry 2-7; Mayo 0-4.
Jones's Road, June 18, 1905.
Kildare 0-8;Cavan 0-0.
Tipperary, July 23, 1905. Home Final:
Kerry 1-4; Kildare (Clane) 1-3. (Disputed.)
Cork, August 27, 1905. Replay:
Kerry 0-7, Kildare, 1-4
Cork, October 13, 1905. 2nd Replay:
Kerry 0-8; Kildare 0-2.
Jones's Road, November 12,1905. Final:
Kerry (Tralee Mitchels) 0-11;
London (Hibernians) 0-3.
1904—Jones's Road, May 6, 1 906. Kerry 4-10; Cavan 0-1.
Athlone, May 13, 1906. Dublin 0-8; Mayo 1-4.
Cork, July 1, 1906. Final: Kerry (Tralee Mitchels) 0-5; Dublin (Kickhams) 0-2.
1905—Jones's Road, August 5, 1906.
Dublin 1-9; London, 1-4.
Limerick, September 2, 1906.
Kerry 2-10 Roscommon 1-3.
Jones's Road, September 30.
Kildare 4-15; Cavan 1-6.

[Kildare qualified for All-Ireland final by beating Dublin and Louth (final) in Leinster championship.]
Thurles, June 16, 1907. Final:
Kildare (Roseberry) 1-7; Kerry 0-5.
1906—Belfast, May 19, 1907.
Kildare 2-10; Monaghan 1-3.
Wexford, August 4, 1907.
Dublin 2-7; London 0-3.
Limerick, September 8, 1907.
Cork 0-10; Mayo 0-6.
(Dublin qualified for All-Ireland final by beating Kildare in Leinster final).
Athy, October 20, 1907. Final:
Dublin (Kickhams) 0-5; Cork (Fermoy) 0-4.
1907—Jones's Road, March 15, 1908. Dublin 1-5; Monaghan 0-2.
Limerick, May 10, 1908.
Cork 2-10; Mayo 0-2.
Cork, June 7, 1908.
Cork 1-14; London 1 5.
Tipperary, July 5, 1908. Final:
Dublin (Kickhams) 0-6; Cork (Lees) 0-2.
1908—Jones's Road, February 21,1909.
Dublin 1-8; Antrim 0-2.
Limerick, February 14, 1909.
Kerry 2-4; Mayo 0-1.
Thurles, May 9, 1909. Home Final:
Dublin 0-10; Kerry (Mitchels) 0-3.
Jones's Road, August 1, 1909. Final: Dublin (Geraldines) 1-10; London (Hibernians) 0-4.
1909—Ennis, November 21, 1909.
Kerry 2-12; Mayo 0-6.
Belfast, October 10, 1909.
Louth 2-13; Antrim 0-15.
Jones's Road, December 5. Final:
Kerry (Tralee Mitchels) 1-9; Louth (Tredaghs) 0-6.
1910—Tuam, August 21, 1910.
Kerry 1-7; Mayo 0-4.
Dundalk, September 11, 1910.
Louth 3-4; London 2-2.
Jones's Road, October 2, 1910.
Dublin 3-5, Antrim 0-2.
(Louth qualified for the final by beating Dublin in the Leinster championship).
Final fixed for Jones's Road. Louth (Tredaghs) W.O. from Kerry (Tralee Mitchels) who refused to travel.
1911—Jones's Road, December 10.
Antrim 3-1; Kilkenny 1-1.
Portlaoise, December 3. Cork 3-4; Galway 0-2.
Jones's Road, January 14, 1912. Final: Cork (Lees) 6-6; Antrim (Shauns) 1-2.
1912—Jones's Road, August 25, 1912. Antrim 3-5; Kerry 0-2.
Jones's Road, September 29, 1912. Dublin 2-4; Roscommon 1-1.
(Louth qualified by beating Dublin in the Leinster championship).
Jones's Road, November 3. Final: Louth (Tredaghs) 1-7; Antrim (Mitchels) 1-2.

Teams reduced to 15-aside from 1913.
1913—London, August 4, 1913.
Louth 3-6; London 1-2.
(Wexford qualified by beating Louth in the Leinster final).
Jones's Road, October 5, 1913.
Wexford 4-4; Antrim 0-1.
Portlaoise, November 9, 1913.
Kerry 1-8; Galway 0-1.
Croke Park, December 14, 1913. Final:
Kerry (Killarney) 2-2; Wexford (Raparees) 0-3.
1914—Portlaoise, September 6, 1914.
Kerry 2-4; Roscommon 0-1.
Croke Park, September 13, 1914.
Wexford 2-6; Monaghan 0-1.
Croke Park, November 1, 1914. Final:
Kerry 1-3; Wexford 2-0.
Croke Park, November 29, 1914. Replay: Kerry (Killarney) 2-3; Wexford (Blues & Whites) 0-6.
1915—Portlaoise, September 19, 1915.
Kerry 2-3; Roscommon 1-1.
Croke Park, October 17, 1915.
Wexford 3-7; Cavan 2-2.
Croke Park, November 7, 1915. Final: Wexford (Blues & Whites) 2-4; Kerry (Selection) 2-1.
1916—Carrickmacross, October 22, 1916.
Wexford 0-9; Monaghan 1-1.
Athlone, October 22, 1916.
Mayo 1-2; Cork 0-2.
(Objection replay ordered.)
Croke Park, November 19, 1916.
Mayo 1-2; Cork 1-1.
Croke Park, December 17, 1916. Final:
Wexford (Blues & Whites) 3-4; Mayo (Stephenites, Ballina) 1-2.
1917—Athlone, November 18, 1917.
Clare 2-1: Galway 0-4.
Wexford, November 18, 1917.
Wexford 6-6; Monaghan 1-3.
Croke Park, December 9, 1917. Final: Wexford (Blues & Whites) 0-9; Clare (Selection) 0-5.
1918—Croke Park, January 12, 1919.
Tipperary 2-2; Mayo 1-4.
Belturbet, October 20, 1918:
Louth 2-4; Cavan 0-4.
(Wexford qualified for final by beating Louth in Leinster final.)
Croke Park, February 16, 1919. Final: Wexford (Blues & Whites) 0-5; Tipperary (Fethard) 0-4.
1919—Croke Park, August 24, 1919.
Galway 2-6; Kerry 3-3.
Croke Park, September 14, 1919.
Replay: Galway 4-2; Kerry 2-2.
Navan, September 14, 1919.
Kildare 3-2; Cavan 1-3.
Croke Park, September 28, 1919. Final:
Kildare (Caragh) 2-5; Galway (Selection) 0-1.
1920—Navan, September 26, 1920.
Dublin 3-6; Cavan 1-3.
Croke Park, May 7, 1922.
Tipperary 1-5; Mayo 1-0.
Croke Park, June 11, 1992. Final:
Tipperary 1-6; Dublin (O'Toole's) 1-2.
1921—Dundalk, June 18, 1922.
Dublin 2-8; Monaghan 2-2.
Mayo W.O. from Tipperary.
Croke Park, June 17, 1923. Final: Dublin (St. Mary's) 1-9; Mayo (Stephenites, Ballina) 0-2.
1922—Dundalk, July 15, 1923.
Dublin 2-5; Monaghan 0-0.

Croke Park, September 9, 1923.
Sligo 1-8; Tipperary 0-7.
(Galway qualified by beating Sligo in replay of Connacht final.)
Croke Park, October 7,1923. Final:
Dublin (O'Toole's) 0-6; Galway (Ballinasloe) 0-4.
1923—Croke Park, April 27, 1924. Semi-Final:
Kerry 1-3; Cavan 1-2.
Croke Park, May 18. 1924, Semi-Final:
Dublin 1-6; Mayo 1-2.
Croke Park, September 28. 1924 Final:
Dublin 1-5; Kerry 1-3.
1924—Croke Park, December 7. Semi-final.
Kerry 1-4; Mayo 0-1.
Croke Pork, January 18, 1925. Semi-final:
Dublin 0-6; Cavan 1-1.
Croke Park, April 26, 1925. Final:
Kerry 0-4; Dublin 0-3.
1925—Galway declared champions.
Games in lieu of Championship:
Croke Park, December 6, 1925.
Galway 3-4; Wexford 1-1.
Croke Park, January 10, 1926.
Galway 3-2; Cavan 1-2.
(Kerry, Munster Champions, refused to compete.)
The results of the Championship semi-finals were:
Tralee, August 23.
Kerry 1-7; Cavan 2-3.
Croke Park, August 30.
Mayo 2-4; Wexford 1-4.
1926—Croke Park, August 8. Semi-final:
Kerry 1-6; Cavan 0-1.
Croke Park, August 22. Semi-fina!:
Kildare 2-5; Galway 0-2.
Croke Park, September 5. Final:
Kerry 1-3; Kildare 0-6.
Croke Park, October 17. Replay:
Kerry 1-4; Kildare 0-4.
1927—Tuam, August 28. Semi-final:
Kerry 0-4; Leitrim 0-2.
Drogheda, August 28. Semi-final:
Kildare 1-7; Monaghan 0-2.
Croke Park, September 25. Final:
Kildare 0-5; Kerry 0-3.
1928—Cavan, August 26. Semi-final:
Cavan 2-5; Sligo 0-4.
Cork, September 2. Semi-final:
Kildare 3-7; Cork 0-2.
Croke Park, September 30. Final:
Kildare 2-6; Cavan 2-5.
1929—Roscommon, August 18. Semi-final:
Kerry 3-8; Mayo 1-1.
Croke Park, August 25. Semi-final:
Kildare 0-9; Monaghan 0-1.
Croke Park, September 22. Final:
Kerry 1-8; Kildare 1-5.
1930—Croke Park, August 24. Semi-final:
Monaghan 1-6; Kildare 1-4.
Roscommon, August 24. Semi-final:
Kerry 1-9; Mayo 0-4.
Croke Park, September 28. Final:
Kerry 3-11; Monaghan 0-2.
1931—Tuam, August 30. Semi-final:
Kerry 1-6; Mayo 1-4.
Cavan, August 30. Semi-final:
Kildare 0-10; Cavan 1-5.
Croke Park, September 27. Final:
Kerry 1-11; Kildare 0-8.
1932—Croke Park, August 21. Semi-final:
Mayo 2-4; Cavan 0-8.
Croke Park, August 21. Semi-final:
Kerry 1-3; Dublin 1-1.
Croke Park, September 25. Final:
Kerry 2-7; Mayo 2-4.
1933—Mullingar, August 20. Semi-final:
Galway 0-8; Dublin 1-4.
Cavan, August 27. Semi-final:
Cavan 1-5; Kerry 0-5.
Croke Park, September 24. Final:
Cavan 2-5; Galway 1-4.
1934—Tuam, August 12. Semi-final:
Galway 1-8; Cavan 0-8.
Tralee, September 9. Semi-final:
Dublin 3-8; Kerry 0-6.
Croke Park, September 23. Final:
Galway 3-5; Dublin 1 -9.
1935—Croke Park, August 18. Semi-final:
Cavan 1-7; Tipperary 0-8.
Croke Park, August 25. Semi-final:
Kildare 2-6; Mayo 0-7.
Croke Park, September 22. Final:
Cavan 3-6; Kildare 2-5.
1936—Roscommon, August 9. Semi-final:
Mayo 1-5; Kerry 0-6.
Croke Park, August 23. Semi-final:
Laois 2-6; Cavan 1-5.
Croke Park, September 27. Final:
Mayo 4-11; Laois 0-5.
1937—Cork, August 15. Semi-final:
Kerry 2-3; Laois 1-6.
Mullingar, August 22. Semi-final:
Cavan 2-5; Mayo 1-7.
Waterford, August 29. Replay:
Kerry 2-2; Laois 1-4.
Croke Park, September 26. Final:
Kerry 2-5; Cavan 1-8.
Croke Park, October 17. Replay:
Kerry 4-4; Cavan 1-7.
1938—Mullingar, August 14. Semi-final:
Galway 2-10; Monaghan 2-3.
Croke Park, August 21. Semi-final:
Kerry 2-6; Laois 2-4.
Croke Park, September 25. Final:
Galway 3-3; Kerry 2-6.
Croke Park, October 23. Replay:
Galway 2-4; Kerry 0-7.
1939—Croke Park, August 13. Semi-final:
Kerry 0-4; Mayo 0-4.
Croke Park, August 20. Semi-final:
Meath 1-9; Cavan 1-1.
Croke Park, September 10. Replay:
Kerry 3-8; Mayo 1-4.
Croke Park, September 24. Final:
Kerry 2-5; Meath 2-3.
1940—Croke Park, August 18. Semi-final:
Galway 3-8; Meath 2-5.
Croke Park, August 18. Semi-final:
Kerry 3-4; Cavan 0-8.
Croke Park, September 22. Final:
Kerry 0-7; Galway 1-3.
1941—Croke Park, August 10. Semi-final:
Kerry 0-4; Dublin 0-4.

Tralee, August 17. Replay:
Kerry 2-9; Dublin 0-3.
Croke Park, August 17. Semi-final: Galway 1-12; Cavan 1-4.
Croke Park, September 7. Final: Kerry 1-8; Galway 0-7.
1942—Croke Park, August 2. Semi-final:
Dublin 1-6; Cavan 1-3.
Croke Park, August 9. Semi-final:
Galway 1-3; Kerry 0-3.
Croke Park, September 20. Final:
Dublin 1-10; Galway 1-8.
1943—Croke Park, August 8. Semi-final:
Roscommon 3-10; Louth 3-6.
Croke Park, August 15. Semi-final:
Cavan 1-8; Cork 1-7.
Croke Park, September 26. Final: Roscommon 1-6; Cavan 1-6.
Croke Park, October 10. Replay: Roscommon 2-7; Cavan 2-2.
1944—Croke Park, August 20. Semi-final:
Roscommon 5-8; Cavan 1-3.
Croke Park, August 27. Semi-final: Kerry 3-3; Carlow 0-10.
Croke Park, September 24. Final: Roscommon 1-9; Kerry 2-4.
1945—Croke Park, August 12. Semi-final: Cork 2-12; Galway 2-8.
Croke Park, August 19. Semi-final: Cavan 1-4; Wexford 0-5.
Croke Park, September 23. Final: Cork 2-5; Cavan 0-7.
1946—Croke Park, August 18. Semi-final:
Kerry 2-7; Antrim 0-10.
Croke Park, August 25. Semi-final: Roscommon 3-5; Laois 2-6.
Croke Park, October 6. Final:
Kerry 2-4; Roscommon 1-7.
Croke Park, October 27. Replay:
Kerry 2-8; Roscommon 0-10.
1947—Croke Park, August 3. Semi-final:
Cavan 2-4; Roscommon 0-0.
Croke Park, August 10. Semi-final:
Kerry 1-11; Meath 0-5.
Polo Grounds, New York, September 14. Final:
Cavan 2-11; Kerry 2-7.
1948—Croke Park, August 22. Semi-final:
Cavan 1-14; Louth 4-2.
Croke Park, August 29. Semi-final:
Mayo 0-13; Kerry 0-3.
Croke Park, September 26. Final:
Cavan 4-5; Mayo 4-4.
1949—Croke Park, August 14. Semi-final:
Meath 3-10; Mayo 1-10.
Croke Park, August 21. Semi-final:
Cavan 1-9; Cork 2-3.
Croke Park, September 25. Final:
Meath 1-10; Cavan 1-6.
1950—Croke Park, August 13. Semi-final:
Mayo 3-9; Armagh 0-6.
Croke Park, August 20. Semi-final:
Louth 1-7; Kerry 0-8.
Croke Park, September 24. Final:
Mayo 2-5; Louth 1-6.
1951—Croke Park, August 12. Semi-final:
Kerry 1-5; Mayo 1-5.
Croke Park, August 19. Semi-final:
Meath 2-6; Antrim 1-7.
Croke Park, September 9. Replay:
Mayo 2-4; Kerry 1-5.
Croke Park, September 23. Final: Mayo 2-8; Meath 0-9.
1952—Croke Park, August 3. Semi-final:
Meath 1-6; Roscommon 0-7.
Croke Park, August 17. Semi-final:
Cavan 0-10; Cork 2-3.
Croke Pork, September 28. Final:
Cavan 2-4; Meath 1-7.
Croke Park, October 12. Replay:
Cavan 0-9; Meath 0-5.
1953—Croke Park, August 9. Semi-final:
Armagh 0-8; Roscommon 0-7.
Croke Park, August 23. Semi-final:
Kerry 3-6; Louth 0-10.
Croke Park, September 27. Final:
Kerry 0-13; Armagh 1-6.
1954—Croke Park, August 1. Semi-final:
Meath 1-5; Cavan 0-7.
Croke Park, August 15. Semi-final:
Kerry 2-6; Galway 1-6.
Croke Park, September 26. Final:
Meath 1-13; Kerry 1-7.
1955—Croke Park, August 14. Semi-final:
Kerry 2-10; Cavan 1-13.
Croke Park, August 21. Semi-final:
Dublin 0-7; Mayo 1-4.
Croke Park, September 11. Replays:
Kerry 4-7; Cavan 0-5. Dublin 1-8; Mayo 1-7.
Croke Park, September 25. Final
Kerry 0-12; Dublin 1-6.
1956—Croke Park, August 5. Semi-final:
Cork 0-9; Kildare 0-5.
Croke Park, August 12. Semi-final:
Galway 0-8; Tyrone 0-6.
Croke Park, October 7: Final:
Galway 2-13; Cork 3-7.
1957—Croke Park, August 11. Semi-final:
Cork 2-4; Galway 0-9.
Croke Park, August 18. Semi-final:
Louth 0-13; Tyrone 0-7.
Croke Park, September 22. Final:
Louth 1-9; Cork 1-7.
1958—Croke Park, August 17. Semi-final:
Dublin 2-7; Galway 1-9.
Croke Park, August 24. Semi-final:
Derry 2-6; Kerry 2-5.
Croke Park, September 28. Final:
Dublin 2-12; Derry 1-9.
1959—Croke Park, August 16. Semi-final:
Kerry 1-10; Dublin 2-5.
Croke Park, August 23. Semi-final:
Galway 1-11; Down 1-4.
Croke Park, September 27. Final:
Kerry 3-7; Galway 1-4.
1960—Croke Park, August 7. Semi-final:
Kerry 1-8; Galway 0-8.
Croke Park, August 21. Semi-final:
Down 1-10; Offaly 2-7.
Croke Park, September 11. Replay:
Down 1-7; Offaly 1-5.
Croke Park, September 25. Final:
Down 2-10; Kerry 0-8.
1961—Croke Park, August 6. Semi-final:
Down 1-12; Kerry 0-9.

Croke Park, August 20. Semi-final:
Offaly 3-6; Roscommon 0-6.
Croke Park, September 24. Final:
Down 3-6; Offaly 2-8.
1962—Croke Park, August 5. Semi-final:
Kerry 2-12; Dublin 0-10.
Croke Park, August 19. Semi-final:
Roscommon 1-8; Cavan 1-6.
Croke Park, September 23. Final:
Kerry 1-12; Roscommon 1-6.
1963—Croke Park, August 4. Semi-final:
Galway 1-7; Kerry 0-8.
Croke Park, August 1 8. Semi-final:
Dublin 2-11; Down 0-7.
Croke Park, September 22. Final:
Dublin 1-9; Galway 0-10.
1964—Croke Park, August 9. Semi-final:
Galway 1-8; Meath 0-9.
Croke Park, August 23. Semi-final:
Kerry 2-12; Cavan 0-6.
Croke Park, September 27. Final:
Galway 0-15; Kerry 0-10.
1965—Croke Park, August 8. Semi-final:
Kerry 4-8; Dublin 2-6.
Croke Park, August 22. Semi-final:
Galway 0-10; Down 0-7.
Croke Park, September 26. Final:
Galway 0-12; Kerry 0-9.
1966—Croke Park, August 7. Semi-final:
Galway 1-11; Cork 1-9.
Croke Park, August 21. Semi-final:
Meath 2-16; Down 1-9.
Croke Park, September 25. Final:
Galway 1-10; Meath 0-7.
1967—Croke Park, August 6. Semi-final:
Cork 2-7; Cavan 0-12.
Croke Park, August 20. Semi-final:
Meath 3- 14; Mayo 1-14.
Croke Park, September 24. Final:
Meath 1-9; Cork 0-9.
1968—Croke Park, August 4. Semi-final:
Kerry 2-13; Longford 2-11.
Croke Park, August 18. Semi-final:
Down 2-10; Galway 2-8.
Croke Park, September 22. Final:
Down 2-12; Kerry 1-13.
1969—Croke Park, August 10. Semi-final:
Kerry 0-14; Mayo 1-10.
Croke Park, August 24. Semi-final:
Cavan 1-9; Offaly 0-12.
Croke Park, September 14. Replay:
Offaly 3-8; Cavan 1-10.
Croke Park, September 28. Final:
Kerry 0-10; Offaly 0-7.
1970—Croke Park, August 9. Semi-final:
Meath 0-15; Galway 0-11.
Croke Park, August 23. Semi-final:
Kerry 0-23; Derry 0-10.
Croke Park, September 27. Final:
Kerry 2-19; Meath 0-18.

(Note: First 80-minute Final was introduced in 1970)

1971—Croke Park, August 8. Semi-final:
Galway 3-11; Down 2-7.
Croke Park, August 22. Semi-final:
Offaly 1-16; Cork 1-11.
Croke Park, September 26. Final:
Offaly 1-14; Galway 2-8.
1972—Croke Park, August 13. Semi-final:
Kerry 1-22; Roscommon 1-12.
Croke Park, August 20. Semi-final:
Offaly 1-17; Donegal 2-10.
Croke Park, September 24. Final:
Offaly 1-13; Kerry 1-13.
Croke Park, October 15. Replay:
Offaly 1-19; Kerry 0-13.
1973—Croke Park, August 12. Semi-final:
Galway 0-16; Offaly 2-8.
Croke Park, August 19. Semi-final:
Cork 5-10; Tyrone 2-4.
Croke Park, September 23. Final:
Cork 3-17; Galway 2-13.
1974—Croke Park, August 11. Semi-final:
Dublin 2-11; Cork 1-8.
Croke Park, August 18. Semi-final:
Galway 3-13; Donegal 1-14.
Croke Park, September 22. Final:
Dublin 0-14; Galway 1-6.

Note: The 70-minute Final was introduced in 1975)

1975—Croke Park, August 10. Semi-final:
Kerry 3-13; Sligo 0-5.
Croke Park, August 24. Semi-final:
Dublin 3-13; Derry 3-8.
Croke Park, September 28. Final:
Kerry 2-12; Dublin 0-11.
1976—Croke Park, August 8. Semi-final:
Kerry 5-14; Derry 1-10.
Croke Park, August 29. Semi-final:
Dublin 1-8; Galway 0-8.
Croke Park, September 26. Final:
Dublin 3-8; Kerry 0-10.
1977—Croke Park, August 14. Semi-final:
Armagh 3-9; Roscommon 2-12 (draw).
Croke Park, August 28. Replay:
Armagh 0-15; Roscommon 0-14.
Croke Park, August 21. Semi-final:
Dublin 3-12; Kerry 1-13.
Croke Park, September 25. Final:
Dublin 5- 12; Armagh 3-6.
1978—Croke Park, August 13. Semi-final:
Kerry 3-11; Roscommon 0-8.
Croke Park, August 20. Semi-final:
Dublin 1-16; Down 0-8.
Croke Park, September 24. Final:
Kerry 5-11; Dublin 0-9.
1979—Croke Park, August 12. Semi-final:
Kerry 5-14; Monaghan 0-7.
Croke Park, August 19. Semi-final:
Dublin 0-14; Roscommon 1-10.
Croke Park, September 16. Final:
Kerry 3-13; Dublin 1-8.
1980—Croke Park, August 10. Semi-final:
Roscommon 2-20; Armagh 3-11.
Croke Park, August 24. Semi-final:
Kerry 4-15; Offaly 4-10.
Croke Park, September 21. Final:
Kerry 1-9; Roscommon 1-6.
1981—Croke Park, August 9. Semi-final:
Kerry 2-19; Mayo 1-6.

Croke Park, August 23. Semi-final:
Offaly 0-12; Down 0-6.
Croke Park, September 20. Final:
Kerry 1-12; Offaly 0-8.
1982—Croke Park, August 15. Semi-final:
Kerry 3-15; Armagh 1-11.
Croke Park, August 22. Semi-final:
Offaly 1-12; Galway 1-11.
Croke Park, September 19. Final:
Offaly 1-15; Kerry 0-17.
1983—Croke Park, August 14. Semi-final:
Galway 1-12; Donegal 1-11.
Croke Park, August 21. Semi-final:
Dublin 2-11; Cork 2-11 (draw).
Pairc Ui Chaoimh, August 28. Replay:
Dublin 4-15; Cork 2-10.
Croke Park, September 18. Final:
Dublin 1-10; Galway 1-8.
1984—Croke Park, August 12. Semi-final:
Kerry 2-17; Galway 0-11.
Croke Park, August 19 Semi-final:
Dublin 2-11; Tyrone 0-8.
Croke Park, September 23. Final:
Kerry 0-14; Dublin 1-6.
1985—Croke Park, August 11. Semi-final:
Kerry 1-12; Monaghan 2-9 (draw).
Croke Park, August 18. Semi-final:
Dublin 1-13; Mayo 1-13 (draw).
Croke Park, August 25. Replay:
Kerry 2-9; Monaghan 0-10.
Croke Park, September 8. Replay:
Dublin 2-12; Mayo 1-7.
Croke Park, September 22. Final:
Kerry 2-12; Dublin 2-8.
1986—Croke Park, August 17. Semi-final:
Tyrone 1-12; Galway 1-9.
Croke Park, August 24. Semi-final:
Kerry 2-13; Meath 0-12.
Croke Park, September 21. Final:
Kerry 2-15; Tyrone 1-10.
1987—Croke Park, August 16. Semi-final:
Cork 1-11; Galway 1-11 (draw).
Croke Park, August 23. Semi-final:
Meath 0-15; Derry 0-8.
Croke Park, August 30. Replay:
Cork 0-18; Galway 1-4.
Croke Park, September 20. Final:
Meath 1-14; Cork 0-11.
1988—Croke Park, August 14. Semi-final:
Cork 1-14; Monaghan 0-6.
Croke Park, August 21. Semi-final:
Meath 0-16; Mayo 2-5.
Croke Park, September 18. Final:
Meath 0-12; Cork 1-9 (draw).
Croke Park, October 9. Replay:
Meath 0-13; Cork 0-12.
1989—Croke Park, August 13. Semi-final:
Mayo 0-12; Tyrone 1-6.
Croke Park, August 20. Semi-final:
Cork 2-10; Dublin 1-9.
Croke Park, September 17. Final:
Cork 0-17; Mayo 1-11.
1990—Croke Park, August 12. Semi-final:
Cork 0-17; Roscommon 0-10.
Croke Park, August 19. Semi-final:
Meath 3-9; Donegal 1-7.
Croke Park, September 16. Final:
Cork 0-11; Meath 0-9.
1991—Croke Park, August 11. Semi-final:
Down 2-9; Kerry 0-8.
Croke Park, August 18. Semi-final:
Meath 0-15; Roscommon 1-11.
Croke Park, September 15. Final:
Down 1-16; Meath 1-14.
1992—Croke Park, August 16. Semi-final:
Donegal 0-13; Mayo 0-9.
Croke Park, August 23. Semi-final:
Dublin 3-14; Clare 2-12.
Croke Park, September 20. Final:
Donegal 0-18; Dublin 0-14.
1993—Croke Park, August 15. Semi-final:
Cork 5-15; Mayo 0-10.
Croke Park, August 22. Semi-final:
Derry 0-15; Dublin 0-14.
Croke Park, September 19. Final:
Derry 1-14; Cork 2-8.
1994—Croke Park, August 14. Semi-final:
Down 1-13; Cork 0-11.
Croke Park, August 21. Semi-final:
Dublin 3-15; Leitrim 1-9.
Croke Park, September 18. Final:
Down 1-12; Dublin 0-13.
1995—Croke Park, August 13. Semi-final:
Tyrone 1-13; Galway 0-13.
Croke Park, August 20. Semi-final:
Dublin 1-12; Cork 0-12.
Croke Park, September 17. Final:
Dublin 1-10; Tyrone 0-12.
1996—Croke Park, August 11. Semi-final:
Mayo 2-13; Kerry 1-10.
Croke Park, August 18. Semi-final:
Meath 2-15; Tyrone 0-12.
Croke Park, September 15. Final:
Meath 0-12; Mayo 1-9 (draw).
Croke Park, September 29. Replay:
Meath 2-9; Mayo 1-11.
1997—Croke Park, August 24. Semi-final:
Kerry 1-17; Cavan 1-10.
Croke Park, August 31. Semi-final:
Mayo 0-13; Offaly 0-7.
Croke Park, September 28. Final:
Kerry 0-13; Mayo 1-7.
1998—Croke Park, August 23. Semi-final:
Galway 0-16; Derry 1-8.
Croke Park, August 30. Semi-final:
Kildare 0-13; Kerry 1-9.
Croke Park, September 27. Final:
Galway 1-14; Kildare 1-10.
1999—Croke Park, August 22.
Semi-final: Cork 2-12; Mayo 0-12.
Croke Park, August 29. Semi-final:
Meath 0-15; Armagh 2-5.
Croke Park, September 26. Final:
Meath 1-11; Cork 1-8.
2000—Croke Park, August 20. Semi-final:
Kerry 2-11, Armagh 2-11.
Croke Park, August 27. Semi-final:
Galway 0-15, Kildare 2-6.
Croke Park, September 2. Replay:
Kerry 2-15, Armagh 1-15. (after extra time)
Croke Park, September 24. Final:
Kerry 0-14, Galway 0-14.

Croke Park, October 7. Replay:
Kerry 0-17, Galway 1-10.
2001—Thurles, August 4. Quarter-final:
Kerry 1-14, Dublin 2-11.
Castlebar, August 4. Quarter-final:
Galway 0-14, Roscommon 1-5.
Croke Park, August 5. Quarter-final:
Meath 2-12, Westmeath 3-9.
Clones, August 5. Quarter-final:
Derry 1-9, Tyrone 0-7.
Thurles, August 11. Replay:
Kerry 2-12, Dublin 1-12.
Croke Park, August 11. Replay:
Meath 2-10, Westmeath 0-11.
Croke Park, August 26. Semi-final:
Galway 1-14, Derry 1-11.
Croke Park, September 2. Semi-final:
Meath 2-14, Kerry 0-5.
Croke Park, September 23. Final:
Galway 0-17, Meath 0-8.
2002—Croke Park, August 4. Quarter-final:
Kerry 2-17, Galway 1-12.
Croke Park, August 4. Quarter-final:
Armagh 2-9, Sligo 0-15.
Croke Park, August 5. Quarter-final:
Cork 0-16, Mayo 1-10.
Croke Park, August 5. Quarter-final:
Dublin 2-8, Donegal 0-14.
Croke Park, August 17. Replay:
Dublin 1-14, Donegal 0-7.
Navan, August 18. Replay:
Armagh 1-16, Sligo 0-17.
Croke Park, August 25. Semi-final:
Kerry 3-19, Cork 2-7.
Croke Park, September 1. Semi-final:
Armagh 1-14, Dublin 1-13.
Croke Park, September 22. Final:
Armagh 1-12, Kerry 0-14.
2003—Croke Park, August 3. Quarter-final:
Armagh 0-15, Laois 0-13.
Croke Park, August 3. Quarter-final:
Tyrone 1-21, Fermanagh 0-5.
Croke Park, August 4. Quarter-final:
Kerry 1-21, Roscommon 3-10.
Croke Park, August 4. Quarter-final:
Donegal 0-14, Galway 1-11.
Castlebar, August 10. Replay:
Donegal 0-14, Galway 0-11.
Croke Park, August 24. Semi-final:
Tyrone 0-13, Kerry 0-6.
Croke Park, August 31. Semi-final:
Armagh 2-10, Donegal 1-9.
Croke Park, September 28. Final:
Tyrone 0-12, Armagh 0-9.
2004— Croke Park, August 7. Quarter-final:
Fermanagh 0-12, Armagh 0-11.
Croke Park, August 7. Quarter-final:
Mayo 0-16, Tyrone 1-9.
Croke Park, August 14. Quarter-final:
Derry 2-9, Westmeath 0-13.
Croke Park, August 14. Quarter-final:
Kerry 1-15, Dublin 1-8.
Croke Park, August 22. Semi-final:
Mayo 0-9, Fermanagh 0-9.
Croke Park, August 28. Replay:
Mayo 0-13, Fermanagh 1-8.
Croke Park, August 29. Semi-final:
Kerry 1-17, Derry 1-11.
Croke Park, September 26. Final:
Kerry 1-20, Mayo 2-9.
2005—Croke Park, August 7. Quarter-final:
Cork 2-14, Galway 2-11.
Croke Park, August 7. Quarter-final:
Kerry 2-15, Mayo 0-18.
Croke Park, August 13. Quarter-final:
Tyrone 1-14, Dublin 1-14.
Croke Park, August 20. Quarter-final:
Armagh 2-17, Laois 1-11.
Croke Park, August 27. Replay:
Tyrone 2-18, Dublin 1-14.
Croke Park, August 28. Semi-final:
Kerry 1-19, Cork 0-9.
Croke Park, September 4. Semi-final:
Tyrone 1-13, Armagh 1-12.
Croke Park, September 25. Final:
Tyrone 1-16, Kerry 2-10.
2006—Croke Park, August 5. Quarter-final:
Kerry 3-15, Armagh 1-13.
Croke Park, August 5. Quarter-final:
Cork 1-11, Donegal 1-10.
Croke Park, August 12. Quarter-final:
Dublin 1-12, Westmeath 0-5.
Croke Park, August 13. Quarter-final:
Mayo 0-15, Laois 0-15.
Croke Park, August 20. Replay:
Mayo 0-14, Laois 0-11.
Croke Park, August 20. Semi-final:
Kerry 0-16, Cork 0-10.
Croke Park, August 27. Semi-final:
Mayo 1-16, Dublin 2-12.
Croke Park, September 17. Final:
Kerry 4-15, Mayo 3-5.
2007—Croke Park, August 4. Quarter-final:
Cork 1-11, Sligo 0-8.
Croke Park, August 4. Quarter-final:
Meath 1-13, Tyrone 2-8.
Croke Park, August 11. Quarter-final:
Dublin 0-18, Derry 0-15.
Croke Park, August 12. Quarter-final:
Kerry 1-12, Monaghan 1-11.
Croke Park, August 19. Semi-final:
Cork 1-16, Meath 0-9.
Croke Park, August 26. Semi-final:
Kerry 1-15, Dublin 0-16.
Croke Park, September 16. Final:
Kerry 3-13, Cork 1-9.
2008—Croke Park, August 9. Quarter-final:
Wexford 1-14, Armagh 0-12.
Croke Park, August 9. Quarter-final:
Kerry 1-21, Galway 1-16.
Croke Park, August 10. Quarter-final:
Cork 2-11, Kildare 1-11.
Croke Park, August 16. Quarter-final:
Tyrone 3-14, Dublin 1-8.

Croke Park, August 24. Semi-final:
Kerry 1-13, Cork 3-7.
Croke Park, August 31. Replay:
Kerry 3-14, Cork 2-13.
Croke Park, August 31. Semi-final:
Tyrone 0-23, Wexford 1-14.
Croke Park, September 21. Final:
Tyrone 1-15, Kerry 0-14.
2009—Croke Park, August 2. Quarter-final:
Tyrone 0-16, Kildare 1-11.
Croke Park, August 2. Quarter-final:
Cork 1-27, Donegal 2-10.
Croke Park, August 3. Quarter-final:
Kerry 1-24, Dublin 1-7.
Croke Park, August 9. Quarter-final:
Meath 2-15, Mayo 1-15.
Croke Park, August 23. Semi-final:
Cork 1-13, Tyrone 0-11.
Croke Park, August 30. Semi-final:
Kerry 2-8, Meath 1-7.
Croke Park, September 20. Final:
Kerry 0-16, Cork 1-9.

ALL-IRELAND FOOTBALL TEAMS

Author's note. Despite checking with a number of sources, allowance must still be made for possible errors in early teams, as records are not reliable from these times. It must be noted too that teams were not given in line-out order until the nineteen-thirties.

1887
Limerick—Denis Corbett (capt.), P. Reeves, J. Mulqueen, M. Slattery, T. McNamara, T. Fitzgibbon, P. Kelly, P. J. Corbett, T. Kennedy, E. Nicholas, J. Hyland, M. O'Brien, E. Casey, R Normoyle, T. Keeting, W. J. Spain, J. R. Kennedy, W. Gunning, P. Keating, W. Cleery, R. Breen.

Louth—M. J. Carroll (capt.), E. Goodman, J. Dowdall, N. Fagan, R. Clarke, T. McGrane, T. O'Connor, P. McGuinness, J. McGuire, A. O'Hagan, T. Campbell, R. Morgan, P. Jackson, J. Keating, T. Murphy, E. Murphy, W. Wheetley, P. McGuinn, E. Fealy, T. O'Rourke, T. Lowry.

Referee—J. Cullinane (Tipperary)

1888
No final played owing to visit of hurlers and athletes to the USA, known as "The American Invasion".

1889
Tipperary—Gil Kavanagh (capt.), J. Cranley, P. Glasheen, T. Dwyer, P. Finn, W. O'Shea, P. Buckley, D. Whelan, J. Daly, J. Ronan, P. Hall, J. Carey, M. Wade, B. O'Brien, L. Fox, W. Ryan, Joe Ryan, Jack Ryan, Wm. Ryan, P. Ryan, J. Keating.

Laois—J. Delaney (capt.), J. Whelan, J. Fleming, J. Walsh, J. Murphy, N. Maher, P. Brady, D. Drennan, T. McDonnell, M. Culleton, J. Troy, D. Teehan, J. Conroy, J. Dunne, J. Teehan, J. O'Connor, Tom Cushion, Tim Cushion, P. Cushion, D. Cushion, M. Cushion.

Referee F. T. O'Driscoll (Cork).

1890
Cork—Jim Power (capt.), J. Downey, P. Moore, J. Leahy, R. Kelleher, M. Coleman, T. Lucey, Jack Fitzgerald, Jim Fitzgerald, M. Riordan, T. Downey, R. Power, J. D. O'Brien, M. Hennessy, M. Egan, J. Aherne, M. Murphy, M. Buckley, W. Buckley, W. Hennessy, P. O'Sullivan.

Wexford—P. Keating (capt.), J. McGrath, J. French, J. Meyler, D. Phillips, T. Gaffney, P. Byrne, T. Byrne, A. Furlong, T. Hayes, J. Kenny, M. Clancy, M. Murphy, J. Monaghan, M. O'Neill, J. Keegan, J. Doyle, P. Curran, J. O'Connor, J. Hayes, N. Meyler.

Referee—J. J. Kenny (Dublin).

1891
Dublin—John Kennedy (capt.), G. Charlemont (gl.), G. Roche, J. Scully, T. Lyons, J. Roche, J. Silke, P. Heslin, J. Mahony, A. O'Hagan, P. O'Hagan, Dick Curtis, S. Hughes, S. Flood, T. Murphy, J. Geraghty, T. Halpin, M. Cooney, P. Kelly, R. Flood, M. Condon.

Cork—Con O'Leary (capt.), Denis O'Leary, J. O'Leary, Dan O'Leary, D. J. Kelleher, J. Kelleher, Con Kelleher, Jer Kelleher, C. Duggan, J. Duggan, A. Desmond, P. Desmond T. O'Riordan, M. O'Riordan, M. Quill, J. O'Sullivan, J. Murphy, D. O'Sullivan, T. O'Shea, J. Ahern, M. Kelleher.

Referee—F. J. Whelan (Laois).

1892
Dublin—John Kennedy (capt.), G. Roche, G. Charlemont, J. Roche, J. Geraghty, R. Flood, S. Flood, S. Hughes, F. O'Malley, T. Doran, L. Kelly, P. Kelly, P. Heslin, M. Byrne, J. Silke, T. ("Darby") Errity, R. Curtis.

Kerry—J. P. O'Sullivan (capt.), J. J. O'Sullivan, J. Curran, T Curran, J. Murphy, P. Sugrue, F. Doherty, D. P. Murphy, M. O'Brien, W. O'Sullivan, M. Flynn, W. Fleming, M. Hayes, J. O'Reilly, P. O'Regan, D. Clifford, P. Teahan.

Referee—D. Fraher (Waterford).

1893
Wexford—Thomas Hayes (capt.), James Maloney Redmond, T. ("Hoey") Redmond, P. Curran, M. Curran, J. McGinn, J. Doyle, N. Leahy, J. Bolger, J. O'Neill, W. O'Leary, A. Furlong, T. O'Connor, J. O'Connor, P. O'Connor, F. Boggan, J. Phelan.

Cork—Jack ("Fox") O'Keeffe (capt.), D. O'Hanlon, T. Burton, T. Forrest, D. Doherty T. Irwin, J. O'Leary, J. Mulcahy, M. Buckley, M. O'Keeffe, T. Healy, J. Vaughan, J. Riordan, J. Coughlan, J. O'Sullivan, E. Mulcahy, W. Riordan.

Referee—T. Gilligan (Dublin).

1894
Dublin—John Kennedy (capt.), G. Charlemont, Dick Curtis, G. Roche, P. Heslin, T. Lyons, J. Geraghty, L. Kelly, P. Kelly, T. Hughes,

T. O'Mahony, M. Condon, M. Byrne, T. ("Darby") Errity, P. O'Toole, J. Kirwan, F. O'Malley.

Cork—J. O'Leary (capt.), J. Mulcahy, P. J. Walsh, D. Kelleher, T. Houlihan, D. McSweeney, M. Coleman, M. McCarthy, W. Riordan, D. Coughlan, F. Joyce, W. Burgess, P. Coughlan, D. O'Connell, M. Downey, T. Irwin, J. Riordan.

Referee—R. T. Blake (Meath).

1895

Tipperary—Paddy Finn (capt.), Willie Ryan, R. Quane, J. Riordan, M. Finn, P. Glasheen, M. ("Terry") McInerney, J. Carew, M. Conroy, J. Carey, D. Butler, W. P. Ryan, J. Heffernan, P. Daly, J. O'Brien, B. Finn, P. Dwyer.

Meath—M. Murray (capt.), H. Pendleton, P. Clarke, J. Hegarty, J. Russell, J. W. Toombe, J. A. Shaw, M. McCabe, P. Fox, J. Elliott, M. Rogers, C. Curtis, J. Sharkey, P. Daly, J. Quinn, V. McDermott, J. Fitzpatrick.

Referee—J. Kenny (Dublin).

1896

Limerick—Con Fitzgerald (capt.), D. Birrane, W. Guiry, J. O'Riordan, L. Roche, J. O'Riordan, L. Sheehan, P. Roche, A. Quillinan, J. Buttimer, T. Campion, J. Dalton, B. Murphy, W. McNamara, J. Murphy, J. Nash, M. Ryan. Sub: J. Griffin.

Dublin—George Roche (capt.), J. Kirwan, L. Kelly, W. Conlon, J. Teeling, T. Hession, J. Gannon, Dick Curtis, S. Mooney, R. Graham, P. O'Toole, J. Brady, T. Doran, T. ("Darby") Errity, P. Heslin, M. Byrne, J. Ledwidge.

Referee—T. Dooley (Cork).

1897

Dublin—P. J. Walsh (capt.), W. Guiry, R. Scanlon, L. Kelly, W. Callaghan, E. Downey, Dick Curtis, D. O'Donnell, M. Chambers, V. Kelly, C. Cannon, P. O'Donoghue, R. O'Brien, P. Redmond, J. Matthews, W. Flynn, J. O'Brien.

Cork—D. O'Donovan (capt.), F. J. Crowley, J. Fuller, J. O'Kelly-Lynch, D. Crowley, T. Lordan, P. Lordan, T. Coughlan, C. Coughlan, D. Bernard, F. Searles, T. Twohill, T. Crowley, T. Mullane, D. Coughlan, J. Murphy, J. Aherne.

Referee—D. S. Lyons (Limerick).

1898

Dublin—Matt Rea (capt.), J. J. Keane, T. H. Redmond, W. Sherry, J. Heslin, D. O'Callaghan, P. Levey, C. Sargent, P. Redmond, P. McCann, T. Norton, T. ("Darby") Errity, P. Fitzsimmons, P. Smith, J. Ryan, J. Ledwidge.

Waterford—M Cullinan, J. Nagle, W. Meade, P. Sullivan, J. Nestor J. C. Heelan, P. Kirwan, J. Hogan, J. F. Flynn, J. Power, T. Power, J. Kennedy, R. Rockett, D. F. Flynn, S. Curran, M. Dunworth, G. Cummin. Sub W. O'Brien for T. Power.

Referee—J. McCarthy (Kilkenny).

1899

Dublin—Matt Rea (capt.), J. Lane, P. McCann, D. Smith, W. Sherry, T. ("Darby") Errity, G. Brady, John Ryan, J. Norton, J. J. Keane, J. Farrelly, P. Leary, P. Fitzsimons, D. O'Callaghan, J. Heslin, J. Ledwidge, T. H. Redmond.

Cork—R. Coughlan (capt.), W. Mackessy, S. Murphy, J. Clifford, D. Coughlan, W. O'Neill, J. Long, J. Cronin, M. Howard, Tom Irwin, M. Aherne, M. Sullivan, J. Collins, C. Walsh, J. Murphy, J. Kelleher, M. Barrett.

Referee—L. Stanley (Louth).

1900

Tipperary—J. Tobin (capt.), P. Moloney, W. McReil, J. Dwan, D. Myers, M. Walsh, J. O'Brien, R. Quane, R. Hourigan, P. Wall, W. O'Toole, D. Harney, J. O'Shea, J. Cooney, D. Smyth, P. Cox, J. Hayes.

London—M. J. Hayes, S. Maguire, J. Maguire, J. Hooper, D. Donovan, M. Reidy, T. Corcoran, J. Gaffney, T. J. Quilter, J. Crowley, P. J. Crotty, F. Collins, M. J. O'Grady, T. Lyons, D. Cronin, J. Hayes, T. Brown.

Referee—T. H. Redmond (Dublin).

Home Final: Tipperary—J. Tobin (capt.), P. Moloney, J. Long, R. Hourigan, M. Kiely, D. Smith, P. Cox, J. Hayes, P. Sweeny, M. Alyward, J. Dwan, D. Myers, M. Walsh, J. O'Brien, R. Quane, L. Tobin, P. Moroney.

Galway—J. Hosty, W. Kennedy, S. Bourke, T. Hannon, F. Walsh (capt.), M. Farrell, J. Kilkenny, T. Handlebury, M. Connor, J. O'Brien, C. Whyte, D. Hession, S. Barry, M. (Tom) Connolly, J. Ridge, J. O'Brien, M. Muldowney.

1901

Dublin—J. Darcy (capt.), J. McCullagh, J. Fahy, D. Holland, T. Doyle, J. O'Brien, B. Connor, P. Daly, M. Madigan, L. Kelly, J. Grace, P. Redmond, M. O'Brien P. McCann, J. Whelan, T. Lawless, V. Harris.

London—S. Maguire (capt.), J. Maguire, D. Donovan, J. Hooper, M. J. Hayes, J. O'Driscoll, W. Morrissey, T. Corcoran, J. O'Dwyer, J. Griffin, M. Roddy, J. Scanlon, J. Fitzgerald, T. Twomey, M. J. O'Grady, D. Cronin, J. Shouldice.

Referee—J. McCarthy (Kilkenny).

Home Final: Dublin—J. Darcy (capt.), M. McCullagh, D. Brady, P. McCann, J. Fahy, J. O'Brien, M. Madigan, J. Grace, T. Doyle, J. Whelan, T. Lawless, M. O'Brien, L. Kelly, V. Harris, P. McCann, P. Redmond, P. Daly.

Cork—J. Murphy (capt.), Gus Groegor, T. Hartigan, S. Murphy, J. McCarthy, J. Long, C. Walsh, J. Morrissey, W. Mackessy, C. McCarthy, J. McCarthy, W. O'Neill, P. Spillane, P. Daly, M. O'Connor, J. Desmond, T. Mahony.

1902

Dublln—J. Dempsey (capt.), S. Mulvey, D. Brady, W. Casey, W. Sherry, A. Wall, J. Brennan, P. Weymess, P. D. Breen, J. McCann, T. Errity, J. Fahy, J. Grace, J. Keane, P. Brady, E. Brady, P. Daly.

London—J. Maguire, M. Hayes, D. Donovan, J. O'Driscoll, J. Fitzpatrick, P. Sheehan, J. Heffernan, J. Heffernan, M. Roddy, J. Shouldice, C. Shine, J. Kavanagh, J. Dwyer, J. Griffin, D. O'Leary, J. O'Grady, J. Fitzgerald.

Referee—T. F. O'Sullivan (Kerry).

Home Final: Dublin—J. Dempsey, S. Mulvey, D. Brady, M. Casey, W. Sherry, J. McCann, T. Errity, J. Keane, J. Grace, C. Brady, P. Daly, J. Brennan, P. Weymess, P. Archdeacon, P. D. Breen, - Dunne.

Tipperary—R. Quane (capt.), W. P. Ryan, R. Butler, D. Quane, J. Noonan, J. Wyse, J. Butler, J. Bohan, J. Ryan, D. Smith, D. Myers, W. Barrett, P. Moloney, E. Kelly, P. Wall, J. O'Shea, J. Hayes.

1903

Kerry—T. O'Gorman (capt.), J. O'Gorman, D. Curran, Mce. McCarthy, J. Buckley, C. Healy, A. Stack, R. Fitzgerald, P. Dillon, W. Lynch, D. McCarthy, J. Myers, D. Kissane, F. O'Sullivan, R. Kirwan, D. Breen, J. T. Fitzgerald.

London—S. Maguire (capt.), D. Donovan, J. O'Driscoll, A. Leary, T. Doody, T. Quilter, J. Griffin, J. Shouldice, M. J. Collins, J. Heffernan, J. Walsh, J. P. McKeever, C. Shine, J. Dwyer, T. O'Neill, M. Sheehan, J. Scanlan.

Referee—J. McCarthy (Kilkenny).

Home Final: Kerry—(Third match) Same as above, except that E. O'Neill played instead of F. O'Sullivan. C. Duggan played instead of F. O'Sullivan in first two games.

Kildare—Jos. Rafferty (capt.), W. Merriman, L. Cribben, W. Losty, J. Wright, J. Dunne, W. Bracken, J. Murray, M. Murray, M. Kennedy, J. Scott, M. Donnelly, F. "Joyce" Conlon, J. Gorman, M. Fitzgerald, J. Fitzgerald, E. Kennedy.

1904

Kerry—A. Stack (capt.), M. McCarthy, J. T. Fitzgerald, J. O'Gorman, T. O'Gorman, C. Healy, P. J. Cahill, J. Buckley, D. Curran, J. O'Sullivan, P. Dillon, J. Myers, D. McCarthy, R. Fitzgerald, W. Lynch, F. O'Sullivan, D. Breen.

Dublin—J. Lynch (capt.), P. McCann, M. Kelly, P. Daly, J. Brennan, J. Dempsey, D. Brady, J. Grace, M. Keane, P. O'Callaghan, T. Murphy, M. Barry, J. Chadwick, L. Sheehan, T. Walsh, P. Casey, J. Fahy.

Referee—J. Fitzgerald (Cork).

1905

Kildare—J. Murray (capt.), M. Murray, J. Fikgerald, M. Kennedy, J. Rafferty, J. Gorman, T. Keogh, F. "Joyce" Conlon, J. Scott, W. Merriman, L. Cribben, W. Bracken, W. Losty, J. Connolly, E. Kennedy, T. Kelly, M. Fitzgerald.

Kerry—M. McCarthy (capt.), P. J. Cahill, J. T. Fitzgerald, T. O'Gorman, J. O'Gorman, J. O'Sullivan, C. Healy, T. Costello, D. Curran, R. Fitzgerald, P. Dillon, J. Myers, C. Murphy, J. Spillane, R. Kirwan, D. Breen, J. Wrenn.

Referee—M. F. Crowe (Limerick).

1906

Dubllin—J. Grace (capt.), D. Brady, J. Dempsey, D. Kelleher, J. Brennan, M. Kelly, M. Keane, M. Curry, M. Barry, P. O'Callaghan, P. Casey, H. Hilliard, M. Madigan, T. Quane, T. Walsh, P. Grace, L. Sheehan.

Cork—M. O'Connor (capt.), P. Daly, P. Lenihan, C. Paye, J. Kent, R. O'Sullivan, W. Mackessy, M. Mehigan, M. Twomey, T. Breen, T. O'Donoghue, J. McCarthy, J. Morrissey, C. McCarthy, J. Murphy, F. Searles, R. Flavin.

Referee—John Fitzgerald (Kildare).

1907

Dublin—D. Kelleher, D. Brady, J. Brennan, J. Grace (capt.), J. Lynch, H. Hilliard, T. Quane, J. Dempsey, P. Casey, M. Curry, M. Barry, M. Madigan, P. O'Collaghan, T. Walsh, M. Kelly, D. Kavanagh, P. Grace.

Cork—W. Mackessy (capt.), J. McCarthy, J. Morrissey, M. Mehigan, P. O'Neill, J. Ryan, T. Breen, J. Beckett, J. Shorten, C. O'Shea, J. Driscoll, J. Lehane, J. Kelleher, J. Kent, R. O'Sullivan, Jerh. Murphy, R. Flavin.

Referee—John Fitzgerald (Kildare).

1908

Dublin—D. Kelleher (capt.), J. Grace, H. Hilliard, T. Walsh, J. Lynch, D. Cavanagh, J. S. Brennan, T. Healy, F. Cooney, J. Brennan, P. Daly, T. McAuley, P. Whelan, P. Fallon, M. Collins, M. Power, J. Shouldice.

London—E. O'Sullivan (capt.), J. Kerin, D. Daly, J. B. Kavanagh, D. P. Cremin, M. Hickey, W. O'Brien, S. Black, T. Ambrose, C. Shine, J. Griffin, J. Walsh, J. Maguire, E. O'Leary, P. M. Attridge, C. Tobin, M. O'Donoghue.

Referee—M. Conroy (Dublin).

Home Final: Dublin—Same as final.

Kerry—J. T. Fitzgerald (capt.), P. Dillon, R. Fitzgerald, J. Sullivan, J. O'Riordan, J. Lawlor, M. Mahony, P. Mullane, B. O'Connor, C. Murphy, F. Cronin, E. Spillane, J. McCarthy, C. Healy, T. Costello, D. Breen, J. Casey. Sub: J. Condon for J. O'Riordan.

1909

Kerry—T. Costello (capt.), M. McCarthy, C. Healy, T. Rice, J. O'Sullivan, D. Breen, M. J. Quinlan, R. Fitzgerald, C. Murphy, E. Spillane, J. Skinner, P. Mullane, J. Kennelly, B. O'Connor, J. McCarthy, F. J. Cronin, P. Dillon.

Louth—J. Carvin (capt.), W. Byrne, Joe Quinn, C. Clarke, Joe Donnelly, Jim Clarke, E. Burke, Joe Mulligan, J. Brennan, J. Hanlon, Joe Matthews, O. Markey, J. Bannon, L. McCormack, J. Hand, J. Donegan, T. Morgan.

Referee—M. F. Crowe (Limerick).

1910

No final: Louth awarded walk-over from Kerry. (The following is the Louth team that beat Dublin in the Leinster final and would no doubt have contested the All-Ireland final if it had gone ahead: M. Byrne, J. Mulligan, J. Donnelly, J. Brennan, O. Markey, T. Matthews, L. McCormack, J. Bannon, M. Hand, P. O'Reilly, J. McDonnell, J. Clarke, J. Quinn, E. Burke, J. Smith, J. Carvin, T. Morgan).

1911

Cork—M. Mehigan (capt.), M. O'Shea, E. Barrett, J. A. Beckett, J. O'Driscoll, J. Donovan, W. Mackessy, M. Cotter, T. Murphy, J. Lehane, W. Lehane, J. Lynch, C. Kelleher, J. Young, P. Connell, C. Paye, J. O'Neill. Subs: P. McSweeney for J. O'Neill, T. Breen for C. Paye.

Antrim—H. Sheehan (capt.), H. Kane, J. Murphy, P. Barnes, J. Mulvihill, P. Moylan, P. L. Kelly, J. M. Darby, C. McCurry, J. Fegan, J. Mullen, E. Gorman, J. Healy, J. Coburn, W. Manning, P. Meany, W. Williams.

Referee—M. O'Brennan (Roscommon).

1912

Louth—J. Smith (capt.), M. Byrne, J. Clarke, J. Quinn, J. Fitzsimmons, J. Mulligan, E. Burke, L. McCormack, J. Reilly, J. Bannon, D. Warren, J. Johnstone, O. Markey, T. Matthews, J. Campbell, J. Brennan, S. Fitzsimons.

Antrim—J. Coburn (capt.), J. Monaghan, P. Moylan, T. Meany, H. Sheehan, P. L. Kelly, W. Manning, J. Murphy, M. Goggan, L. Waters, J. Mulvihill, E. Ward, J. Mullen, J. Gorman, P. Barnes, M. Maguire, J. Gallagher.

Referee—T. Irwin (Cork).

1913

Kerry—R. Fitzgerald (capt.), J. Skinner, D. Doyle, C. Murphy, P. Healy, J. O'Mahony, C. Clifford, T. Rice, J. J. Rice, M. McCarthy, T. Costelloe, J. Lawlor, D. Mullins, P. O'Shea, P. Kennelly.

Wexford—T. Doyle (capt.), T. Mernagh, A. Doyle, J. Cullen (goal), E. Black, T. Murphy, J. Doyle, J. Kennedy, P. Mackey, G. Kennedy, J. Mullally, R. Reynolds, F. Furlong, J. Byrne, J. Rossiter.

Referee—M. F. Crowe (Limerick).

1914 REPLAY

Kerry—R. Fitzgerald (capt.), M. McCarthy, D. Doyle, J. Skinner, J. Mahony, C. Murphy, P. Healy, C. Clifford, P. Breen, T. Rice, J. J. Rice, J. Lawlor, D. Mullins (goal), T. Costelloe, P. O'Shea. (H. Murphy and W. Keating played in drawn game. M. McCarthy and J. J. Rice came in For replay.)

Wexford—Sean Kennedy (capt.), T. McGrath (goal), T. Murphy, P. Mackey, J. Byrne, P. D. Breen, T. Doyle, T. Mernagh, P. Murphy, J. Doyle, J. Mullally, R. Reynolds, A. Doyle, G. Kennedy, J. Rossitor.

Referee—Draw and replay, H. Boland (Dublin).

1915

Wexford—Sean Kennedy (capt.), Gus Kennedy, P. Mackey, T. Murphy, F. Furlong, J. Wall, Fr. E. Wheeler, T. Mernagh, T. Doyle, E. Black, A. Doyle, James Byrne, M. Howlett, R. Reynolds, T. McGrath (goal).

Kerry—R. Fitzgerald (capt.), M. McCarthy, J. Lawlor, T. Costelloe, T. Rice, H. Murphy, P. Healy, C. Clifford, Con Murphy, P. O'Shea, M. Donovan, J. Rice, D. Doyle, M. Carroll, D. Mullins (goal).

Referee—P. Dunphy (Laois).

1916

Wexford—Sean Kennedy (capt.), T. McGrath (goal), P. Mackey, Fr. E. Wheeler, Jas. Byrne, T. Murphy, T. Mernagh, M. Howlett, F. Furlong, Tom Doyle, J. Crowley, R. Reynolds, J. Wall, A. Doyle, Gus Kennedy.

Mayo—P. Loftus, T. Gibson, J. Waldron, J. E. McEllin, G. Delaney, P. Robinson, J. Lydon, H. Hession, D. F. Courell, M. Murray, T. Boshell, P. Kelly, J. Reilly, A. Lyons, P. Smith.

Referee—P. Dunphy (Laois).

1917

Wexford—Sean Kennedy (capt.), G. Kennedy, P. Mackey, A. Doyle, T. Mernagh, T. McGrath (goal), T. Murphy, W. Hodgins, J. Quinn, J. Byrne, J. Crowley, F. Furlong, M. Howlett, T. Doyle, R. Reynolds.

Clare—M. Conole, P. Hennessy, J. Foran, E. McNamara, P. O'Brien, M. McMahon, J. Fitzgerald, M. McNamara, J. Marrinan, P. O'Donoghue, J. Spellissy, E. Carroll, M. Malone, E. Roche, T. Considine.

Referee—P. Dunphy (Laois).

1918

Wexford—T. McGrath (goal), N. Stuart, P. Mackey, J. Byrne (capt.), T. Murphy, T. Doyle, M. Howlett, W. Hodgins, J. Doran, J. Crowley, R. Reynolds, T. Pierse, A. Doyle, G. Kennedy, J. Redmond.

Tipperary—A. Carroll, J. McNamara, E. O'Shea, J. Shelly, W. Ryan, E. Egan, T. Powell, J. Quinlan, J. Ryan, W. Grant, J. Skinner, R. Heffernan, G. McCarthy, J. O'Shea.

Referee—P. Dunphy (Laois).

1919

Kildare—L. Stanley (capt.), L. Cribben, J. Conlon, J. Moran, T. Goulding, M. Buckley, J. O'Connor, P Doyle, M. Sammon, G. Magan, J. Stanley, C. Flynn, B. McGlade, James O'Connor, F. "Joyce" Conlon.

Galway—T. Egan (capt.), D. Egan, J. Egan, Peter Higgins, M. "Knacker" Walsh, P. Roche, J. Hanniffy, G. Jennings, L. Rahery, M. Flannelly, H. Burke, G. Feeney, M. Walsh, T. McDonnell, M. Cawley.

Referee—P. Dunphy (Laois).

1920

Tipperary—A. Carroll (goal), J. McNamara, Edwd. O'Shea, R. Lanigan, Bill Ryan, J. Shelly (capt.), W. Grant, W. Barrett, M. Tobin, J. Ryan, J. Doran, G. McCarthy, V. Vaughan, M. Arrigan, T. Powell.

Dublin—J. McDonnell (goal), W. Robbins, Joe Joyce, P. Carey, Joe Synott, Joe Norris, John Reilly, J. Murphy, W. Donovan, J. Carey, P. McDonnell, Ger Doyle, John Synnod, F. Burke, S. Synnott.

Referee—W. Walsh (Waterford).

1921

Dublin—E. Carroll (capt.), John Reilly, Joe Norris, P. Carey, John Synnott, P. Kirwan, W. Donovan, P. Fallon (goal), John Murphy,

Thomas Pierse, F. Burke, C. McDonald, A. Belmain, J. O'Grady, W. Fitzsimons.

Mayo—B. Durkin (capt.), J. White, Geo. Delaney, M. Barrett, W. Boshell, P. McLean, J. Lavin, P. Robinson, F. Doherty, J. E. McEllin, P. O'Beirne, M. McNicholas, K. Dillon (goal), J. Forde, P. Colleran. Sub: P. Moran for B. Durkin.

Referee—W. Walsh (Waterford).

1922

Dublin—P. Carey (capt.), J. McDonnell (goal), P. McDonnell, W. Robbins, A. Gibbons, Joe Synnott, John Synnott, Joe Norris, John Reilly, W. Rooney, C. McDonald, Wm. Donovan, P. Kirwan, F Burke, Tom Pierse.

Galway—M. Walsh (capt.), W. Flanagan (goal), D. Egan, J. Egan, T. Molloy, T. Hession, J. Hanniffy, L. McGrath, J. Kirwan, P. Roche, G. Jennings, P. Jennings, Wm. Walsh, M. Donnellan, P. Kilroy.

Referee—P. Dunphy (Laois).

1923

Dublin—John Reilly, P. McDonnell (capt.), John Murphy, Joseph Norris, Joe Synnott, Patk. Carey, P. Kirwan, J. Stynes, Frank Burke, John McDonnell (goal), John Synnott, M. Shanahan, J. Sherlock, P. O'Beirne, L. Stanley.

Kerry—J. Sheehy (goal), J. Barrett, P. Sullivan, E. Moriarty, P. Russell, T. Kelleher, J. Moriarty (capt), C. Brosnan, P. McKenna, John Ryan, John J. Sheehy, D. Donoghue, John Baily, Jas. Baily, W. Landers.

Referee—J. Byrne (Wexford).

1924

Kerry—J. Moriarty, John Sheehy (goal), Phil Sullivan (capt.), Joe Barrett, John Murphy, Paul Russell, Jack Walsh, Con Brosnan, R. Stack, John Ryan, John J. Sheehy, R. Prenderville, John Baily, Jas. Baily, W. Landers.

Dublin—P. McDonnell (capt.), J. McDonnell (goal), P. Carey W. O'Reilly, Joe Synnott, Joe Norris, John Reilly, Peter Synnott, M. O'Brien, P. O'Beirne, John Murphy, M. Shanahan, F. Burke, G. Madigan, P. J. Kirwan.

Referee—T. Shevlin (Roscommon).

1925

N.B.—No Football Final played. Kerry and Cavan being declared illegal, Mayo, nominated by Connacht Council, beat Wexford, and then lost the Connacht final to Galway, who were declared champions. The Galway team which beat Mayo was: M. Walsh (capt.), T. Molloy, J. Egan, D. Egan, H. Burke, F. Benson, W. Smyth, T Leech, M. Bannerton, Leonard McGrath, P. Roche, G. Jennings, P. Ganley, Lar McGrath, M. Donnellan.

1926

Kerry—John J. Sheehy (capt.), John Riordan (goal), P. Clifford, Joe Barrett, Jack Walsh, Paul Russell, J. Moriarty, John Slattery, Con Brosnan, Robt. Stack, John Ryan, D. O'Connell, Tom Mahony, Jas. Baily, Wm. Gorman.

Kildare—Jos. Loughlin (capt.), Jas. Cummins (goal), Ml. Buckley, Matt. Goff, B. Graham, F. Malone, Jack Higgins, John Hayes, P. Martin, Gus Fitzpatrick, L. Stanley, Paul Doyle, Wm. Gannon, T. Donoghue, Joe Curtis.

The Kerry and Kildare players given are those who did duty in the replay. D. O'Connell, J. Slattery and P. Clifford replaced J. Murphy, Joe O'Sullivan and Phil O'Sullivan on the Kerry side, while T. Donoghue and Gus Fitzpatrick replaced A. O'Neill and G. Higgins on the Kildare side.

J. Slattery and P. Clifford came on as subs in drawn game.

Referee—Draw and replay, T. Shevlin (Roscommon).

1927

Kildare—M. Buckley (capt.), M. Walsh (goal), Gus Fitzpatrick, F. Malone, J. Higgins, J. Hayes, J. Loughlin, W. Gannon, J. Curtis, P. Martin, P. Doyle, W. Mangan, P. Loughlin, T. Keogh, M. Goff. Sub: P. Ryan.

Kerry—J. J. Sheehy (capt.), J. O'Riordan (goal), D. O'Connor, J. Barrett, J. Walsh, D. O'Connell, P. O'Sullivan, J. Slattery, C. Brosnan, R. Stack, J. Ryan, E. Fitzgeraid, T. Mahony, Jas. Baily, J. J. Landers.

Referee—T. Shevlin (Roscommon).

1928

Kildare—W. ("Squires") Gannon (capt.), M. Walshe, M. Buckley, M. Goff, Gus Fitzpatrick, F. Malone, J. Higgins, J. Hayes, Joe Loughlin, P. Martin, P. Loughlin, P. Doyle, W. Mangan, J. Curtis, T. Keogh.

Cavan—J. Smith (capt.), J. Morgan, T. Campbell, H. Clegg, J. J. Clarke, H. Mulvany, P. Lynch, H. O'Reilly, P. Devlin, Jas. Murphy, A. Conlon, J. Farrell, W. Young, W. A. Higgins, G. Malcolmson. Sub: T. Crowe.

Referee—T. Burke (Louth).

1929

Kerry—J. Riordan (goal), D. O'Connor, Joe Barrett (capt.), Jack Walsh, Paul Russell, Joe O'Sullivan, T. O'Donnell, Con Brosnan, R. Stack, J. Ryan, M. Doyle, J. J. Landers, E. Sweeney, Jas. Baily, J. J. Sheehy.

Kildare—J. Higgins (capt.), J. O'Reilly (goal), J. Hayes, M. Goff, Gus Fitzpatrick, M. Fenerall, F. Malone, P. Loughlin, Joe Loughlin, P. Martin, Wm. Hynam, Paul Doyle, T. Wheeler, P. Pringle, W. Gannon.

Referee—P. O'Farrell (Roscommon).

1930

Kerry—J. J. Sheehy (capt.), J. Riordan (goal), D. O'Connor, J. Barrett, Jack Walsh, P. Russell, J. O'Sullivan, T. O'Donnell, C. Brosnan, R. Stack, J. Ryan, M. Doyle, E. Fitzgerald, E. Sweeney, J. J. Landers.

Monaghan—P. Kilroy (capt.), T. Bradley (goal), T. Shevlin, J. Farrell, P. Duffy, P. Heeran, J. Duffy, P. Lambe, W. Mason, M. McAleer, C. Fisher, J. O'Carroll, P. McConnon, J. Sexton, H. Brannigan. Sub: P. J. Duffy.

Referee—J. Byrne (Wexford).

1931

Kerry—Con Brosnan (capt.), D. O'Keeffe (goa), D. O'Connor, J. Barrett, Jack Walsh, P. Russell, J. O'Sullivan, T. Landers, R. Stack, J. J. Landers, M. Doyle, E. Fitzgerald, J. Ryan, P. Whitty, M. Regan.

Kildare—M. Walsh (capt.) (goal), J. Meany, M. Goff, F. Malone, P. Miles, J. Higgins, W. Hynam, P. Watters, P. Loughlin, J. Maguire, P. Martin, P. Byrne, H. Burke, D. Burke, P. Doyle.

Referee—T. Keating (Tipperary).

1932

Kerry—D. O'Keeffe, D. O'Connor, Joe Barrett (capt), Jack Walsh, P. Russell, Joe O'Sullivan, P. Whitty, R. Stack, J. Walsh, C. Geaney, M. Doyle, T. Landers, J. Ryan, C. Brosnan, J. J. Landers. Sub: W. Landers for C. Geaney.

Mayo—T. Burke, J. Gannon, P. Quinn, P. Kelly, T. Tunney, S. O'Malley, G. Ormsby, M. Mulderrig, M. Ormsby, P. Munnelly, T. Hanley, P. Flannelly, G. Courell, P. Moclair, J. Forde.

Referee—M. O'Neill (Wexford).

1933

Cavan—J. Smith (capt.), W. Young (goal), M. Denneny, P. Phair, T. O'Reilly, P. Lynch, H. O'Reilly, W. Connolly, T. Coyle, L. Blessing, P. Devlin, D. Morgan, J. Smallhorn, V. McGovern, M. J. Magee. Subs: T. Crowe, P. W. Connolly, T. O'Reilly (Mullahoran).

Galway—M. Donnellan (capt.), F. Fox, B. Nestor, M. Brennan (goal), H. Carey, M. Connaire, J. Dunne, J. Kelleher, M. Kelly, T. McCarthy, F. Burke, M. Higgins, D. O'Sullivan, T. Hughes, D. Mitchell.

Referee—M. O'Neill (Wexford).

1934

Galway—M. Higgins (capt.), M. Brennan (goal), P. J. McDonnell, M. Ferriter, H. Carey, D. O'Sullivan, T. Hughes, T. McCarthy, F. Fox, J. Dunne, M. Connaire, R. Griffin, M. Kelly, D. Mitchell, B. Nestor.

Dublin—J. McDonnell (goal), G. Comerford, M. O'Brien, D. Brennan, M. Casey, F. Cavanagh, P. Cavanagh, P. Hickey, W. Dowling, R. Beggs, M. Wellington, G. Fitzgerald, M. Kelly, M. Keating (capt.), E. McCann.

Referee—J. McCarthy (Kerry).

1935

Cavan—W. Young, W. Connolly, J. Smith, M. Denneny, T. Dolan, T. O'Reilly (Mullahoran), P. Phair, H. O'Reilly (capt.), T. O'Reilly, D. Morgan, P. Devlin, J. Smallhorn, P. Boylan, L. Blessing, M. J. Magee.

Kildare—J. Maguire (goal), W. Mangan, M. Goff, J. Byrne, P. Watters, J. Higgins, F. Dowling, P. Mathews, C. Higgins, T. Mulhall, P. Byrne, P. Martin, J. Dowling, M. Geraghty, T. Keogh. Sub: J. Dalton for C. Higgins.

Referee—S. Jordan (Galway).

1936

Mayo—T. Burke (goal), J. McGowan, P. Quinn, "Purty" Kelly, T. Regan, S. O'Malley (capt.), G. Ormsby, P. Flannelly, H. Kenny, J. Carney, P. Laffey, T. Grier, J. Munnelly, P. Moclair, P. Munnelly.

Laois—J. McDonnell (capt.), T. Delaney (goal), T. Delaney, J. Brennan, T. O'Brien, P. Swayne, D. Walsh, C. Delaney, W. Delaney, D. Douglas, J. Delaney, M. Delaney, T. Keogh, J. Keating, J. O'Reilly. Sub: J. Moran for D. Walsh.

Referee—J. McCarthy (Kerry).

1937 REPLAY

Kerry—D. O'Keeffe (goal), W. Kinnerk, J. Keohane, W. Myers, T. O'Donnell, W. Dillon, T. Healy, J. Walsh, S. Brosnan, J. Flavin, C. O'Sullivan, T. Landers, J. J. Landers, M. Doyle (capt.), T. O'Leary. Sub: T. O'Connor for T. O'Donnell.

Gearóid Fitzgerald and Paddy Kennedy played in drawn game. J. Flavin and T. O'Leary came in for replay. Sub: S. McCarthy.

Cavan—W. Young (goal), E. Finnegan, J. Smith, M. Denneny, D. Kerrigan, T. O'Reilly (capt.), J. J. O'Reilly, V. White, P. Smith, D. Morgan, P. Deviin, J. Smallhorn, P. Boylan, L. Blessing, M. Magee. Subs: T. O'Reilly (Mullahorn), J. White, W. Carroll, J. Mitchell.

W. Carroll and J. White played in drawn game. D. Kerrigan and J. Smallhorn were on for replay.

Referee—Draw and replay, M. Hennessy (Clare).

1938 REPLAY

Galway—J. McGauran (goal), M. Raftery, M. Connaire, D. O'Sullivan, F. Cunniffe, R. Beggs, C. Connolly, J. Burke, J. Dunne (capt.), J. Flavin, M. Higgins, R. Griffin, E. Mulholland, M. Kelly, B. Nestor. Subs: M. Ryder for E. Mulholland, P. McDonagh for J. Burke.

Kerry—W. Kinnerk (capt.), D. O'Keeffe, P. B. Brosnan, W. Myers, W. Dillon, W. Casey, T. O'Connor, J. Walsh, S. Brosnan, P. Kennedy, A. McAuliffe, C. O'Sullivan, M. Regan, M. Doyle, T. O'Leary. Sub: J. J. Landers for J. Walsh.

J. J. Landers and Joe Keohane played in drawn game. P. B. Brosnan and M. Regan came on for replay.

Referees—draw, T. Culhane (Limerick); replay, P. Waters (Kildare).

1939

Kerry—D. O'Keeffe, W. Myers, J. Keohane, T. Healy, W. Dillon, W. Casey, E. Walsh, P. Kennedy, J. O'Gorman, M. Kelly, T. O'Connor (capt.), J. Walsh, C. O'Sullivan, D. Spring, T. Landers.

Meath—H. McEnroe, P. Beggan, T. McGuinness, P. Donnelly, T. Meade, C. O'Reilly, J. Kearney, M. O'Toole, J. Loughran, M. Gilsenan (capt.), A. Donnelly, J. Clarke, W. Brien, J. Cummins, K. Devin. Subs: H. Lynch for W. Brien, M. Clinton for M. O'Toole.

Referee—J. Flaherty (Offaly).

1940

Kerry—D. O'Keeffe, W. Myers, J. Keohane, T. Healy, W. Dillon, W. Casey, E. Walsh, S. Brosnan, J. Walsh, J. O'Gorman, T. O'Connor, P. Kennedy, M. Kelly, D. Spring (capt.), C. O'Sullivan. Sub: P. B. Brosnan.

Galway—J. McGauran, M. Raftery, M. Connaire, D. O'Sullivan, F. Cunniffe, R. Beggs, C. Connolly, J. Dunne (capt.), J. Duggan, J. Flavin, J. Burke, J. Canavan, M. Higgins, E. Mulholland, B. Nestor.

Referee—S. Burke (Kildare).

1941

Kerry—D. O'Keeffe, W. Myers, Joe Keohane, T. Healy, W. Dillon (capt.), W. Casey, E. Walsh, S. Brosnan, P. Kennedy, J. Walsh, T. O'Connor, P. B. Brosnan, J. O'Gorman, M. Kelly, C. O'Sullivan. Subs: T. Landers for W. Myers, M. Lyne for J. Walsh.

Galway—J. McGauran, M. Raftery, P. McDonagh, D. O'Sullivan (capt.), F. Cunniffe, R. Beggs, J. Duggan, C. Connolly, D. Kavanagh, J. Hanniffy, J. Dunne, J. Canavan, E. Mulholland, P. McDonagh, J. Burke. Sub: P. Thornton for J. Canavan.

Referee—P. McKenna (Limerick).

1942

Dublin—C. Kelly, R. Beggs, P. Kennedy, C. Crone, P. Henry, P. O'Reilly, B. Quinn, M. Falvey, Joe Fitzgerald (capt.), J. Joy, P. Bermingham, Gerry Fitzgerald, M. Fletcher, P. O'Connor, T. Banks.

Galway—J. McGauran, F. Cunniffe, M. Connaire, P. McDonagh, J. Duggan, J. Casey, Tom O'Sullivan, D. Kavanagh, C. Connolly (capt.), J. Clifford, M. Fallon, J. Canavan, J. Flavin, P. Thornton, Sean Thornton. Subs: E. Mulholland (for Clifford); Sean Walsh for J. Flavin).

Referee—S. Kennedy (Donegal).

1943 REPLAY

Roscommon—F. Glynn, L. Cummins, J. P. O'Callaghan, W. Jackson, B. Lynch, W. Carlos, O. Hoare, E. Boland, L. Gilmartin, P. Murray, J. Murray (capt.), D. Keenan, D. McDermott, J. McQuillan, F. Kinlough.

Cavan—J. D. Benson, E. Finnegan, B. Cully, P. P. Galligan, G. Smith, T. O'Reilly (capt.), J. J. O'Reilly, S. Deignan, T. P. O'Reilly, D. Morgan, P. Smith, M Higgins, P. Boylan, Joe Stafford, H. Rogers. Sub: J. Keegan for H. Rogers.

W. Heavey, Roscommon, who played in the drawn game, was replaced by O. Hoare for replay. J. Maguire, Cavan, who played in drawn was replaced by H. Rogers for replay.

Referees—Draw, P. McKenna (Limerick); replay, P. Mythen (Wexford).

1944

Roscommon—O. Hoare, W. Jackson, J. P. O'Callaghan, J. Casserly, B. Lynch, W. Carlos, P. Murray, E. Boland, L. Gilmartin, F. Kinlough, J. Murray (capt.), D. Keenan, H. Gibbons, J. McQuillan, J. J. Nerney. Sub: D. McDermott for J. J. Nerney.

Kerry—D. O'Keeffe, T. Healy, J. Keohane, T. Brosnan, W. Dillon, M. McCarthy, E. Walsh, P. Kennedy, S. Brosnan, J. Clifford, J. Lyne, P. B. Brosnan (capt.), D. Lyne, M. Kelly, E. Dunne Subs: D. Kavanagh for P. Kennedy; J. Walsh for P. B. Brosnan.

Referee—P. Mythen (Wexford).

1945

Cork—M. O'Driscoll, D. Magnier, P. A. Murphy, C. Crone, P. Cronin, T. Crowley (capt.), D. O'Connor, F. O'Donovan, E. Young, E. Casey, H. O'Neill, M. Tubridy, J. Lynch, J. Cronin, D. Beckett. Sub: J. Ahern for E. Casey.

Cavan—B. Kelly, T. O'Reilly (capt.), B. Cully, P. P. Galligan, J. Wilson, J. J. O'Reilly, P. Smith, A. Tighe, S. Deignan, A. Commiskey, J. Boylan, T. P. O'Reilly, J. Stafford, P. Donohue, P. J. Duke.

Referee—J. Dunne (Galway).

1946 REPLAY

Kerry—D. O'Keeffe, D. Lyne, J. Keohane, P. B. Brosnan, J. Lyne, W. Casey, E. Walsh, Teddy O'Connor, P. Kennedy (capt.), J. Falvey, Tom O'Connor, B. Grvey, F. O'Keeffe, P. Burke, D. Kavanagh.

Note: Gus Cremins (capt.) and Willie O'Donnell played in drawn game. F. O'Keeffe and J. Falvey came on for replay. Gus Cremin replaced J. Falvey as sub during replay.

Subs in drawn game: E. Dowling for P. Kennedy, B. Kelleher for J. Lyne.

Roscommon—G. Dolan, W. Jackson, J. Casserly, O. Hoare, B. Lynch, W. Carlos, T. Collins, P. Murray, E. Boland, F. Kinlough, J. Murray (capt.), D. Keenan, J. McQuillan, J. J. Fallon, J. J. Nerney. Sub: D. McDermott for B. Lynch.

Vincent Beirne came on as a sub in drawn game for J. Murray.

Referees—Draw, W. Delaney (Laois): Replay, P. Mythen (Wexford).

1947

Cavan—V. Gannon, W. Doonan, B. O'Reilly, P. Smith, J. Wilson, J. J. O'Reilly (capt.), S. Deignan, P. J. Duke, P. Brady, A. Tighe, M. Higgins, C. McDyer, J. Stafford, P. Donohoe, T. P. O'Reilly.

Kerry—D. O'Keeffe, D. Lyne (capt.), J. Keohane, P. Brosnan, J. Lyne, W. Casey, E. Walsh, E. Dowling, E. O'Connor, E. O'Sullivan, D. Kavanagh, B. Garvey, F. O'Keeffe, T. O'Connor, P. Kennedy. Subs: W. O'Donnell for E. Dowling; M. Finucane for E. Walsh; T. Brosnan for W. O'Donnell; G. Teehan for P. Kennedy.

Referee—M. O'Neill (Wexford).

1948

Cavan—J. D. Benson, W. Doonan, B. O'Reilly, P. Smith, P. J. Duke, J. J. Reilly (capt.), S. Deignan, P. Brady, V. Sherlock, A. Tighe, M. Higgins, J. J. Cassidy, J. Stafford, P. Donohoe, E. Carolan. Sub: O. R. McGovern for J. J. O'Reilly.

Mayo—T. Byrne, P. Quinn, P. Prendergast, S. Flanagan J. Forde (capt.), P. McAndrew, Jn. Gilvarry, E. Mongey, P. Carney, W. Kenny, T. Langan, Joe Gilvarry, T. Acton, P. Solon, S. Mulderrig.
Referee—J. Flaherty (Offaly).

1949
Meath—K. Smith, M. O'Brien, P. O'Brien, K. McConnell, S. Heery, P. Dixon, C. Hand, P. Connell, J. Kearney, F. Byrne, B. Smyth (capt.), M. McDonnell, P. Meegan, W. Halpenny, P. McDermott. Sub: P. Carolan for F. Byrne.
Cavan—J. Morris, J. McCabe, P. Smith, O. R. McGovern, P. J. Duke, J. J. O'Reilly (capt.), S. Deignan, P. Brady, V. Sherlock, A. Tighe, M. Higgins, J. J. Cassidy, J. Stafford, P. Donohoe, E. Carolan.
Referee—D. Ryan (Kerry).

1950
Mayo—W. Durkin, J. Forde, P. Prendergast, S. Flanagan (capt.), P. Quinn, H. Dixon, J. McAndrew, P. Carney, E. Mongey, M. Flanagan, W. Kenny, J. Gilvarry, M. Mulderrig, T. Langan, P. Solon. Subs: S. Wynne for W. Durkin; M. Caulfield for W. Kenny; S. Mulderrig for M. Caulfield.
Louth—S. Thornton, M. Byrne, T. Conlon (capt.), J. Tuft, S. Boyle, P. Markey, P. McArdle, J. Regan, F. Reid, J. McDonnell, N. Roe, S. White, R. Lynch, H. Reynolds, M. Reynolds. Subs: R. Mooney for N. Roe; M. McDonnell for P. McArdle.
Referee—S. Deignan (Cavan),

1951
Mayo—S. Wynne, J. Forde, P. Prendergast, S. Flanagan (capt.), J. Staunton, H. Dixon, P. Quinn, E. Mongey, J. McAndrew, P. Irwin, P. Carney, S. Mulderrig, M. Flanogan, T. Langan, J. Gilvarry. Sub: L. Hastings for H. Dixon.
Meath—K. Smyth, M. O'Brien, P. O'Brien, K. McConnell, S. Heery (capt.), C. Kelly, C. Hand, D. Taaffe, P. Connell, F. Byrne M. McDonnell, P. Meegan, B. Smyth, J. Reilly, P. McDermott. Subs: P. Dixon for C. Hand; C. Hand for S. Heery.
Referee—W. Delaney (Laois).

1952 REPLAY
Cavan—S. Morris, J. McCabe, P. Brady, D. Maguire, P. Carolan, L. Maguire, B. O'Reilly, V. Sherlock, T. Hardy, S. Hetherton, M. Higgins (capt.), E. Carolan, J. J. Cassidy, A. Tighe, J. Cusack.
Note: P. Fitzsimons played in drawn game. J. Cusack came on for replay. P. Fitzsimmons was introduced as sub for J. J. Cassidy in replay.
Meath—K. Smyth, M. O'Brien, P. O'Brien, K. McConnell, T. O'Brien, C. Kelly, C. Hand, B. Maguire, D. Taaffe, D. Brennan, B. Smith, P. Meegan (capt.), M. McDonnell, J. Reilly, P. McDermott.
Note: P. McGearty and P. Connell played in drawn game. T. O'Brien and D. Brennan came on for replay.
Referee—Draw and replay, S. Hayes (Tipperary).

1953
Kerry—J. Foley, J. Murphy (capt.), E. Roche, D. Murphy, C. Kennelly, J. Cronin, J. M. Palmer, Seán Murphy, D. Hanifin, J. Brosnan, J. J. Sheehan, T. Lyne, T. Ashe, S. Kelly, J. Lyne. Sub: G. O'Sullivan for Hannifin.
Armagh—E. McMahon, E Morgan, J. Bratten, J. McKnight, F. Kernan, P. O'Neill, S. Quinn (capt.), M. O'Hanlon, M. McEvoy, J. Cunningham, B. Seeley, W. McCorry, P. Campbell, A. O'Hagan, G. O'Neill. Subs: G. Wilson for McMahon; G. Murphy for Wilson; J. O'Hare for Quinn.
Referee—P. McDermott (Meath).

1954
Meath—P. McGearty, M. O'Brien, P. O'Brien, K. McConnell, K. Lenehan, J. Reilly, E. Durnin, P. Connell, T. O'Brien, M. Grace, B. Smyth, M. McDonnell, P. Meegan, T. Moriarty, P. McDermott. (capt.).
Kerry—G. O'Mahony, J. M. Palmer, E. Roche, D. Murphy, Sean Murphy, J. Cronin, C. Kennelly, John Dowling (capt.), T. Moriarty, R. Buckley, J. J. Sheehan, P. Sheehy, J. Brosnan, S. Kelly, T. Lyne.
Referee—S. Deignan (Cavan).

1955
Kerry—G. O'Mahony, J. O'Shea, E. Roche, J. M. Palmer, Sean Murphy, J. Cronin, T. Moriarty, J. Dowling (capt.), D. O'Shea, P. Sheehy, T. Costelloe, T. Lyne, J. Culloty, M. Murphy, J. Brosnan. Sub: J. J. Sheehan for Moriarty.
Dublin—P. O'Flaherty, D. Mahony (capt.), J. Lavin, M. Moylan, Maurice Whelan, J. Crowley, N. Maher, J. McGuinness, C. O'Leary, D. Ferguson, O. Freaney, J. Boyle, P. Haughey, K. Heffernan, C. Freaney. Subs: T. Jennings for McGuinness; W. Monks for Jennings.
Referee—W. Goodison (Wexford).

1956
Galway—J. Mangan (capt.), J. Keeley, G. Daly, T. Dillon, J. Kissane, J. Mahon, M. Greally, F. Evers, Matly McDonagh, J. Coyle, S. Purcell, W. O'Neill, J. Young, F. Stockwell, G. Kirwan. Sub: A. Swords for Young.
Cork—P. Tyres, P. Driscoll, D. O'Sullivan (capt.), D. Murray, P. Harrington, D. Bernard, M. Gould, S. Moore, E. Ryan, D. Kelleher, C. Duggan, P. Murphy, T. Furlong, N. Fitzgerald, J. Creedon. Sub: E. Goulding for Murphy.
Referee—P. McDermott (Meath).

1957
Louth—S. Flood, O. Reilly, T. Conlon, J. Meehan, P. Coleman, P. Smith, S. White, K. Beahan, D. O'Neill, S. O'Donnell, D. O'Brien (capt.), F. Lynch, S. Cunningham, J. McDonnell, J. Roe.
Cork—L. Power, M. Gould, D. Bernard, D. Murray, P. Harrington, P. O'Driscoll, J. J. Henchion, E. Ryan, S. Moore, J. O'Sullivan, N. Fitzgerald, T. Furlong, E. Goulding, C. Duggan (capt.), D. Kelleher. Sub: F. McAuliffe for J. O'Sullivan.
Referee—P. Geraghty (Galway).

1958

Dublin—P. O'Flaherty, L. Foley, M. Wilson, Joe Timmons, C. O'Leary, J. Crowley, J. Boyle, John Timmons, S. Murray, P. Haughey, O. Freaney, D. Ferguson, P. Farnan, J. Joyce, K. Heffernan (capt.). Subs: Maurice Whelon for Murray; P. Downey for John Timmons.

Derry—P. Gormley, P. McLarnon, H. F. McGribben, T. Doherty, P. Breen, C. Mulholland, P. Smith, J. McKeever (capt.), P. Stuart, S. O'Connell, B. Murray, D. McKeever, B. Mullan, O. Gribben, C. Higgins. Subs: R. Gribben for Higgins; L. O'Neill for Mullan; C. O'Neill for Breen.

Referee—S. Deignan (Cavan).

1959

Kerry—J. Culloty, J. O'Shea, N. Sheehy, T. Lyons, Sean Murphy, K. Coffey, M. O'Dwyer, M. O'Connell (capt.), Seamus Murphy, D. McAuliffe, T. Long, P. Sheehy, D. Geaney, John Dowling, T. Lyne. Subs: Jack Dowling for Lyons; Moss O'Connell for Mick O'Connell; G. McMahon for Geaney.

Galway—J. Farrell, J. Kissane, S. Meade, M. Greally, M. Garrett, J. Mahon, S. Colleran, F. Evers, Matty McDonagh, J. Young, S. Purcell (capt), Ml. McDonagh, M. Laide, F. Stockwell, J. Nallen. Subs: J. Keeley for Nallen, P. Dunne for Greally.

Referee—J. Dowling (Offaly).

1960

Down—E. McKay, G. Lavery, L. Murphy, P. Rice, K. Mussen (capt.), D. McCartan, K. O'Neill, J. Lennon, J. Carey, S. O'Neill, J. McCartan, P. Doherty, A. Hadden, P. O'Hagan, B. Morgan. Sub: K. Denvir for Lennon.

Kerry—J. Culloty, J. O'Shea, N. Sheehy, T. Lyons, Seán Murphy, K. Coffey, M. O'Dwyer, M. O'Connell, J. D. O'Connor, Seamus Murphy, T. Long, P. Sheehy (capt.), G. McMahon, John Dowling, T. Lyne. Subs: Jack Dowling for John Dowling; J. Brosnan for McMahon; D. McAuliffe for Lyne.

Referee—J. Dowling (Offaly).

1961

Down—E. McKay, G. Lavery, L. Murphy, P. Rice, P. O'Hagan, D. McCartan, J. Smith, J. Carey, J. Lennon, S. O'Neill, J. McCartan, P. Doherty (capt.), A. Hadden, P. J. McIlroy, B. Morgan. Subs: K. O'Neill for P. Rice; Rice for G. Lavery.

Offaly—W. Nolan (capt.), P. McCormack, G. Hughes, J. Egan, P. O'Reilly, M. Brady, C. Wrenn, S. Brereton, S. Ryan, T. Cullen, P. Daly, T. Greene, M. Casey, D. O'Hanlon, H. Donnelly. Subs: F. Weir for M. Casey, S. Foran for S. Ryan, F. Higgins for P. O'Reilly.

Referee—L. Maguire (Cavan).

1962

Kerry—J. Culloty, Seamus Murphy, N. Sheehy, T. Lyons, S. Óg Sheehy (capt.), N. Lucey, M. O'Dwyer, M. O'Connell, J. Lucy, D. McAuliffe, T. O'Sullivan, J. O'Riordan, G. McMahon, T. Long, P. Sheehy. Subs: J. J. Barrett for T. Lyons, K. Coffey for D. McAuliffe.

Roscommon—A. Brady, J. J. Breslin, J. Lynch, J. O. Moran, R. Creaven, G. O'Malley (capt.), G. Reilly, B. Kyne, J. Kelly, G. Geraghty, E. Curley, A. Whyte, Don Feely, C. Mahon, Des Feely. Subs: T. Turley for G. Reilly, A. Kenny for T. Turley.

Referee—E. Moules (Wicklow).

1963

Dublin—P. Flynn, L. Hickey, L. Foley, W. Casey, D. McKane, P. Holden, M. Kissane, D. Foley (capt.), John Timmons, B. McDonald, Mickie Whelan, G. Davey, S. Behan, D. Ferguson, N. Fox. Sub: P. Downey for P. Holden.

Galway—M. Moore, E. Colleran, N. Tierney, S. Meade, J. B. McDermott, J. Donnellan, M. Newell, M. Garrett (capt.), M. Reynolds, C. Dunne, Matly McDonagh, P. Donnellan, J. Keenan, S. Cleary, S. Leydon. Sub: B. Geraghty for S. Cleary.

Referee—E. Moules (Wicklow).

1964

Galway—J. Geraghty, E. Colleran, N. Tierney, J. B. McDermott, J. Donnellan (capt.), S. Meade, M. Newell, M. Garrett, M. Reynolds, C. Dunne, M. McDonagh, S. Leydon, C. Tyrrell, S. Cleary, J. Keenan.

Kerry—J. Culloty, M. Morris, N. Sheehy (capt.), P. Donoghue, Denis O'Sullivan, Seamus Murphy, J. D. O'Connor, M. Fleming, Donie O'Sullivan, P. Griffin, M. O'Dwyer, M. O'Connell, F. O'Leary, T. Long, J. J. Barrett. Subs: J. McCarthy for J. D. O'Connor, B. O'Callaghan for F. O'Leary, K. Coffey for J. McCarthy.

Referee—J. Hatton (Wicklow).

1965

Galway—J. Geraghty, E. Colleran (capt.), N. Tierney, J. B. McDermott, J. Donnellan, S. Meade, M. Newell, P. Donnellan, M. Garrett, C. Dunne, Matty McDonagh, S. Leydon, C. Tyrrell, S. Cleary, J. Keenan. Sub: M. Reynolds.

Kerry—J. Culloty, Donie O'Sullivan, N. Sheehy, M. Morris, Seamus Murphy, P. O'Donoghue, J. D. O'Connor (capt.), Denis O'Sullivan, M. O'Connell, V. Lucey, P. Griffin, D. O'Shea, B. O'Callaghan, M. O'Dwyer, J. J. Barrett. Subs: D. Geaney for V. Lucey, J. O'Shea for J. J. Barrett.

Referee—M. Loftus (Mayo).

1966

Galway—J. Geraghty, E. Colleran (capt.), N. Tierney, J. B. McDermott, C. McDonagh, S. Meade, M. Newell, J. Duggan, P. Donnellan, C. Dunne, Matty McDonagh, S. Leydon, L. Sammon, S. Cleary, J. Keenan. Sub: J. Donnellan for S. Meade.

Meath—S. McCormack, D. Donnelly, J. Quinn, P. Darby, P. Collier, B. Cunningham, P. Reynolds, P. Moore, T. Brown, A. Brennan, M.

O'Sullivan, D. Carty (capt.), G. Quinn, N. Curran, O. Shanley. Subs: M. White for D. Donnelly, J. Fagan for D. Carty, M. Quinn for J. Fagan.
Referee—J. Hatton (Wicklow).

1967
Meath—S. McCormack, M. White, J. Quinn, P. Darby (capt.), P. Collier, B. Cunningham, P. Reynolds, P. Moore, T. Kearns, A. Brennan, M. Kerrigan, M. Mellett, P. Mulvaney, N. Curran, O. Shanley.
Cork—W. Morgan, B. Murphy, J. Lucey, J. O'Mahony, F. Cogan, D. Coughlan, K. Dillon, M. Burke, M. O'Loughlin, E. Philpott, E. McCarthy, B. O'Neill, E. Ryan, C. O'Sullivan, F. Hayes. Subs: J. Carroll for M. Burke, J. Downing for E. McCarthy, J. J. Murphy for J. Downing.
Referee—J. Moloney (Tipperary).

1968
Down—D. Kelly, B. Sloan, D. McCartan, T. O'Hare, R. McConville, W. Doyle, J. Lennon (capt.), J. Milligan, C. McAlarney, M. Cole, P. Doherty, J. Murphy, P. Rooney, S. O'Neill, J. Purdy. Subs: L. Powell for J. Lennon, G. Glynn for L. Powell.
Kerry—J. Culloty, Seamus Murphy, P. O'Donoghue, S. Burrows, Denis O'Sullivan, M. Morris, Donie O'Sullivan, M. O'Connell, M. Fleming, B. Lynch, P. Griffin (capt.), E. O'Donoghue, T. Prendergast, D. J. Crowley, M. O'Dwyer. Subs: P. Moynihan for T. Prendergast, S. Fitzgerald for S. Burrows.
Referee—M. Loftus (Mayo).

1969
Kerry—J. Culloty (capt.), Seamus Murphy, P. O'Donoghue, S. Fitzgerald, T. Prendergast, M. Morris, M. O'Shea, M. O'Connell, D. J. Crowley, B. Lynch, P. Griffin, E. O'Donoghue, M. Gleeson, L. Higgins, M. O'Dwyer.
Offaly—M. Furlong, P. McCormack, G. Hughes, J. Egan (capt.), E. Mulligan, N. Clavin, M. Ryan, L. Coughlan, W. Bryan, P. Keenan, A. Hickey, A. McTague, S. Kilroy, S. Evans, J. Cooney. Subs: F. Costelloe for A. Hickey, K. Kilmurray for P. Keenan, P. Monaghan for S. Kilroy.
Referee—J. Moloney (Tipperary).

1970
Kerry—J. Culloty, Seamus Murphy, P. O'Donoghue, Donie O'Sullivan (capt.), T. Prendergast, J. O'Keeffe, M. O'Shea, M. O'Connell, D. J. Crowley, B. Lynch, P. Griffin, E. O'Donoghue, M. Gleeson, L. Higgins, M. O'Dwyer. Sub: S. Fitzgerald for Donie O'Sullivan.
Meath—S. McCormack, M. White, J. Quinn (capt.), B. Cunningham, O. Shanley, T. Kearns, P. Reynolds, V. Foley, V. Lynch, A. Brennan, M. Kerrigan, M. Mellett, K. Rennicks, J. Murphy, M. Fay. Subs: P. Moore for M. Mellette, W. Bligh for T. Kearns.
Referee—P. Kelly (Dublin).

1971
Offaly—M. Furlong, M. Ryan, P. McCormack, M. O'Rourke, E. Mulligan, N. Clavin, M. Heavey, W. Bryan (capt.), K. Claffey, J. Cooney, K. Kilmurray, A. McTague, J. Gunning, S. Evans, Murt Connor. Subs: J. Smith for N. Clavin; P. Fenning for J. Gunning.
Galway—P. J. Smyth, B. Colleran, J. Cosgrove, N. Colleran, L. O'Neill, T. J. Gilmore, C. McDonagh, L. Sammon (capt.), W. Joyce, P. Burke, J. Duggan, M. Rooney, E. Farrell, F. Canavan. S. Leydon. Subs: T. Divilly for M. Rooney; M. Feerick for P. Burke.
Referee—P. Kelly (Dublin).

1972 (REPLAY)
Offaly—M. Furlong, M. Ryan, P. McCormack, L. Coughlan, E. Mulligan, S. Lowry, M. Heavey, W. Bryan, S. Evans, J. Cooney, K. Kilmurray, A. McTague (capt.), S. Darby, J. Smith, P. Fenning. Subs: Murt Connor for J. Cooney; N. Clavin for E. Mulligan; M. Wright for L. Coughlan.
Note: Murt Connor played in drawn game. Seamus Darby came on for replay. Jody Gunning came on as a sub in drawn game for E. Mulligan.
Kerry—E. Fitzgerald, Donie O'Suillvan, P. O'Donoghue, S. Fitzgerald, T. Prendergast (capt.), M. O'Shea, P. Lynch, M. O'Connell, J. O'Keeffe, B. Lynch, D. Kavanagh, E. O'Donoghue, M. Gleeson, L. Higgins, M. O'Dwyer. Subs: Derry Crowley for S. Fitzgerald; P. Griffin for M. Gleeson; J. Walsh for B. Lynch.
Referee—P. Devlin (Tyrone).
Note: Kerry fielded same team in both games. Derry Crowley and Pat Griffin came on as subs in drawn game for S. Fitzgerald and L. Higgins.
Referee F. Tierney (Cavan).

1973
Cork—W. Morgan (capt.), F. Cogan, H. Kelleher, B. Murphy (Nemo Rangers), K. J. O'Sullivan, J. Coleman, C. Hartnett, D. Long, D. Coughlan, E. Kirby, D. Barron, D. McCarthy, J. Barry Murphy, R. Cummins, J. Barrett. Subs: S. Coughlan for J. Coleman; D. Hunt for McCarthy; M. Scannell for D. Kelleher.
Galway—G. Mitchell, J. Waldron, J. Cosgrove, B. Colleran, L. O'Neill, T. J. Gilmore, J. Hughes, W. Joyce, J. Duggan, M. Burke, L. Sammon (capt.), M. Rooney, J. Coughlan, T. Naughton, M. Hughes. Subs: F. Canavan for J. Coughlan; C. McDonagh for M. Burke.
Referee—J. Moloney (Tipperary).

1974
Dublin—P. Cullen, G. O'Driscoll, S. Doherty (capt.), R. Kelleher, P. Reilly, A. Larkin, G. Wilson, S. Rooney, B. Mullins, B. Doyle, A. Hanahoe, D. Hickey, J. McCarthy, J. Keaveney, A. O'Toole.
Galway—G. Mitchell (capt.), J. Waldron, J. Cosgrove, B. Colleran, L. O'Neill, T. J. Gilmore, J. Hughes, W. Joyce, M. Rooney, T. Naughton, J. Duggan, P. Sands, C. McDonagh, L. Sammon, J. Tobin. Sub: J. Burke for C. McDonagh.
Referee—P. Devlin (Tyrone).

1975

Kerry—P. O'Mahony, G. O'Keeffe, J. O'Keeffe, J. Deenihan, P. Ó Sé, T. Kennelly, G. Power, P. Lynch, P. McCarthy, B. Lynch, D. "Ogie" Moran, M. O'Sullivan (capt.), J. Egan, M. Sheehy, P. Spillane. Subs: G. O'Driscoll for M. O'Sullivan.

Dublin—P. Cullen, G. O'Driscoll, S. Doherty (capt.), R. Kelleher, P. Reilly, A. Larkin, G. Wilson, B. Mullins, B. Brogan, A. O'Toole, A. Hanahoe, D. Hickey, J. McCarthy, J. Keaveney, P. Gogarty. Subs: B. Doyle for B. Brogan; P. O'Neill for J. McCarthy; B. Pocock for P. Reilly.

Referee—J. Moloney (Tipperary).

1976

Dublin—P. Cullen, G. O'Driscoll, S. Doherty, R. Kelleher, T. Drumm, K. Moran, P. O'Neill, B. Mullins, B. Brogan, A. O'Toole, A. Hanahoe (capt.), D. Hickey, B. Doyle, J. Keaveney, J. McCarthy. Subs: F. Ryder for A. Hanahoe; P. Gogarty for B. Doyle.

Kerry—P. O'Mahony, G. O'Keeffe, J. O'Keeffe (capt.), J. Deenihan, P. Ó Sé, T. Kennelly, G. Power, P. Lynch, P. McCarthy, D. "Ogie" Moran, M. Sheehy, M. O'Sullivan, B. Lynch, J. Egan, P. Spillane. Subs: C. Nelligan for P. O'Mahony; S. Walsh for P. McCarthy; G. O'Driscoll for M. O'Sullivan.

Referee—P. Collins (Westmeath).

1977

Dublin—P. Cullen, G. O'Driscoll, S. Doherty, R. Kelleher, T. Drumm, K. Moran, P. O'Neill, B. Mullins, B. Brogan, A. O'Toole, A. Hanahoe (capt.), D. Hickey, B. Doyle, J. Keaveney, J. McCarthy. Subs: P. Reilly for P. O'Neill; A. Larkin for B. Brogan; J. Brogan for R. Kelleher.

Armagh—B. McAlinden, D. Stevenson, T. McCreesh, J. McKerr, K. Rafferty, P. Moriarty, J. Donnelly, J. Kernan, C. McKinistry, L. Kearns, J. Smyth (capt.), N. Marley, S. Devlin, P. Trainor, P. Loughran. Subs: J. Loughran for J. Donnelly; S. Daly for N. Marley; F. Toman for J. McKerr.

Referee—J. Moloney (Tipperary).

1978

Kerry—C. Nelligan, J. Deenihan, J. O'Keeffe, M. Spillane, P. Ó Sé, T. Kennelly, P. Lynch, J. O'Shea, S. Walsh, G. Power, D. "Ogie" Moran (capt.), P. Spillane, M. Sheehy, E. Liston, J. Egan. Sub: P. O'Mahony for J. Deenihan.

Dublin—P. Cullen, G. O'Driscoll, S. Doherty, R. Kelleher, T. Drumm, K. Moran, P. O'Neill, B. Mullins, B. Brogan, A. O'Toole, A. Hanahoe (capt.), D. Hickey, B. Doyle, J. Keaveney, J. McCarthy.

Referee—S. Aldridge (Kildare).

1979

Kerry—C. Nelligan, J. Deenihan, J. O'Keeffe, M. Spillane, P. Ó Sé, T. Kennelly (capt.), P. Lynch, J. O'Shea, S. Walsh, T. Doyle, D. "Ogie" Moran, P. Spillane, M. Sheehy, E. Liston, J. Egan. Subs: V. O'Connor for J. O'Keeffe.

Dublin—P. Cullen, M. Kennedy, M. Holden, D. Foran, T. Drumm, F. Ryder, P. O'Neill, B. Mullins, B. Brogan, A. O'Toole, A. Hanahoe (capt.), D. Hickey, M. Hickey, B. Doyle, J. McCarthy. Subs: J. Ronayne for M. Hickey; G. O'Driscoll for McCarthy; B. Pocock for A. O'Toole.

Referee—H. Duggan (Armagh).

1980

Kerry—C. Nelligan, J. Deenihan, J. O'Keeffe, P. Lynch, P. Ó Sé, T. Kennelly, G. O'Keeffe, J. O'Shea, S. Walsh, G. Power (capt.), D. "Ogie" Moran, P. Spillane. M. Sheehy. T. Doyle, J. Egan. Subs: G. O'Driscoll for G. Power.

Roscommon—G. Sheerin, H. Keegan, P. Lindsay, G. Connellan, G. Fitzmaurice, T. Donlon. D. Murray (capt.), D. Earley, S. Hayden, J. O'Connor, J. O'Gara, A. Dooley, M. Finneran, A. McManus, E. McManus. Subs: M. Dolphin for A. Dooley, M. McDermott for S. Hayden.

Referee—S. Murray (Monaghan).

1981

Kerry—C. Nelligan, J. Deenihan (capt.). J. O'Keeffe. P. Lynch, P. Ó Sé, T. Kennelly, M. Spillane, S. Walsh, J. O'Shea, G. Power, D. "Ogie" Moran, T. Doyle, M. Sheehy, E. Liston, J. Egan. Subs: P. Spillane for J. Egan, G. O'Keeffe for M. Spillane.

Offaly—M. Furlong, M. Fitzgerald, L. Connor, C. Conroy, P. Fitzgerald, R. Connor (capt.), L. Currams, T. Connor, P. Dunne, V. Henry, G. Carroll, A. O'Halloran, Matt Connor, S. Lowry, B. Lowry. Subs: J. Mooney for T. Connor, J. Moran for V. Henry.

Referee—P. Collins (Westmeath).

1982

Offaly—M. Furlong, M. Lowry, L. Connor, M. Fitzgerald, P. Fitzgerald, S. Lowry, L. Currams, T. Connor, P. Dunne, J. Guinan, R. Connor (capt.), G. Carroll, J. Mooney, Matt Connor, B. Lowry. Subs: Stephen Darby for M. Lowry; Seamus Darby for J. Guinan.

Kerry—C. Nelligan, G. O'Keeffe, J. O'Keeffe, P. Lynch, P. Ó Sé, T. Kennelly, T. Doyle, J. O'Shea, S. Walsh, G. Power, T. Spillane, D. "Ogie" Moran, M. Sheehy, E. Liston, J. Egan (capt.). Subs: P. Spillane for D. Moran.

Referee—P. J. McGrath (Mayo).

1983

Dublin—J. O'Leary, M. Holden, G. Hargan, R. Hazley, P. Canavan, T. Drumm (capt.), P. J. Buckley, J. Ronayne, B. Mullins, B. Rock, T. Conroy, C. Duff, J. Caffrey, A. O'Toole, J. McNally. Subs: J. Kearns for T. Conroy; K. Maher for J. Caffrey.

Galway—P. Coyne, J. Hughes, S. Kinneavy, M. Coleman, P. O'Neill, P. Lee, S. McHugh (capt.), B. Talty, R. Lee, B. Brennan, V. Daly, B. O'Donnell, T. Tierney, G. McManus, S. Joyce. Subs: M. Brennan for B. Talty; W. Joyce for P. Lee; J. Tobin for J. Hughes.

Referee—J. Gough (Antrim).

1984

Kerry—C. Nelligan, P. Ó Sé, S. Walsh, M. Spillane, T. Doyle, T. Spillane, G. Lynch, J. O'Shea, A. O'Donovan (capt.), J. Kennedy, D. "Ogie" Moran, P. Spillane, G. Power, E. Liston, J. Egan. Sub: T. O'Dowd for J. Egan.

Dublin—J. O'Leary, M. Holden, G. Hargan, M. Kennedy, P. Canavan, T. Drumm (capt.), P. J. Buckley, J. Ronayne, B. Mullins, B. Rock, T. Conroy, K. Duff, J. Kearns, A. O'Toole J. McNally. Subs: M. O'Callaghan for J. McNally; C. Sutton for J. Ronayne.

Referee—Paddy Collins (Westmeath).

1985

Kerry—C. Nelligan, P. Ó Sé (capt.), S. Walsh, M. Spillane, T. Doyle, T. Spillane, G. Lynch, J. O'Shea, A. O'Donovan, T. O'Dowd, D. "Ogie" Moran, P Spillane, M. Sheehy, E. Liston, G. Power. Sub: J. Kennedy for G. Power.

Dublin—J. O'Leary, M. Kennedy, G. Hargan, R. Hazley, P. Canavan, N. McCaffrey, D. Synnott, J. Roynane, B. Mullins (capt.), B. Rock, T. Conroy, C. Redmond, J. Kearns, J. McNally, K. Duff. Subs: T. Carr for Redmond; P. J. Buckley for B. Mullins.

Referee—P. Kavanagh (Meath).

1986

Kerry—C. Nelligan, P. Ó Sé, S. Walsh, M. Spillane, T. Doyle (capt.), T. Spillane, G. Lynch, J. O'Shea, A. O'Donovan, W. Maher, D. "Ogie" Moran, P. Spillane, M. Sheehy, E. Liston, G. Power. Sub: T. O'Dowd for A. O'Donovan.

Tyrone—A. Skelton, J. Mallon, C. McGarvey, J. Lynch, K. McCabe, N. McGinn, P. Ball, P. Donaghy, H. McClure, M. McClure, E. McKenna (capt.), S. McNally, M. Mallon, D. O'Hagan, P. Quinn. Subs: S. Conway for J. Lynch; S. Rice for E. McKenna; A. O'Hagan for M. Mallon.

Referee—J. Dennigan (Cork).

1987

Meath—M. McQuillan, R. O'Malley, M. Lyons (capt.), T. Ferguson, K. Foley, L. Harnan, M. O'Connell, L. Hayes, G. McEntee, D. Beggy, J. Cassells, P. J. Gillic, C. O'Rourke, B. Stafford, B. Flynn. Subs: C Coyle for J. Cassells; P. Lyons for M. O'Connell.

Cork—J. Kerins, A. Davis, C. Corrigan, D. Walsh, A. Nation, C. Counihan (capt.), N. Cahalane, S. Fahy, T. McCarthy, J. O'Driscoll, L. Tompkins, J. Kerrigan, C. O'Neill, C. Ryan, J. Cleary. Subs: J. Evans for C. Corrigan; T. Leahy for S. Fahy; P. Hayes for C. Ryan.

Referee—P. Lane (Limerick).

1988 (REPLAY)

Meath—M. McQuillan, R. O'Malley, M. Lyons, T. Ferguson, C. Coyle, L. Harnan, M. O'Connell, L. Hayes, G. McEntee, D. Beggy, J. Cassells (capt.), P. J. Gillic, C. O'Rourke, B. Stafford, B. Flynn. Sub: M. McCabe for Gillic.

Note: Paraic Lyons, Kevin Foley and Mattie McCabe played in drawn game when Colm Coyle (for M. McCabe), Terry Ferguson (for K. Foley) and Joe Cassells (for B. Flynn) came on as subs and were on the team for the replay. Mick Lyons was captain in the drawn game.

Cork—J. Kerins, N. Cahalane, C. Corrigan, S. O'Brien, A. Davis, C. Counihan, A. Nation (capt.), S. Fahy, T. McCarthy P. McGrath, L. Tompkins, B. Coffey, D. Allen. D. Barry, M McCarthy. Subs: C O'Neill for McCarthy; J. O'Driscoll for McGrath.

Note: Stephen O'Brien, who came on as a sub for Denis Walsh in the first half of the drawn game retained his place for the replay.

Referee—T. Sugrue (Kerry).

1989

Cork—J. Kerins, N. Cahalane, S. O'Brien, J. Kerrigan, M. Slocum, C. Counihan, A. Davis, T. McCarthy, S. Fahy, D. Barry, L. Tompkins, B. Coffey, P. McGrath, D. Allen (capt.), J. Cleary. Subs: J. O'Driscoll for Coffey; M. McCarthy for S. Fahy; Danny Culloty for J. Cleary.

Mayo—G. Irwin, J. Browne (capt.). P. Forde, D. Flanagan, M. Collins, T. J. Kilgallon, J. Finn, S. Maher, L. McHale, G. Maher, W. J. Padden, N. Durkin, M. Fitzmaurice, J. Burke, K. McStay. Subs: A. Finnerty for J. Burke; R. Dempsey for S. Maher; B. Kilkelly for G. Maher.

Referee—P. Collins (Westmeath).

1990

Cork—J. Kerins, A. Nation, S. O'Brien, N. Cahalane, M. Slocum, C. Counihan, B. Coffey, S. Fahy, D. Culloty, D. Barry, L. Tompkins (capt.), T. McCarthy, P. McGrath, C. O'Neill, M. McCarthy. Subs: J. O'Driscoll for M. McCarthy; P. Hayes for D. Barry; J. Cleary for P. McGrath.

Meath—D. Smyth, R. O'Malley, M. Lyons, T. Ferguson, B. Reilly, K. Foley, M. O'Connell, L. Hayes, G. McEntee, D. Beggy, P. J. Gillic, C. Brady, C. O'Rourke (capt.), B. Stafford, B. Flynn. Subs: C. Coyle for C. Brady; J. Cassells for G. McEntee; T. Dowd for D. Beggy

Referee—P. Russell (Tipperary).

1991

Down—N. Collins, B. McKernan, C. Deegan, P. Higgins, P. O'Rourke (capt.), J. Kelly, D. J. Kane, B. Breen, E. Burns, R. Carr, G. Blaney, G. Mason, M. Linden, P. Withnell, J. McCartan. Subs: L. Austin for B. Breen, A. Rodgers for P. Withnell.

Meath—M. McQuillan, B. Reilly, M. Lyons, T. Ferguson, K. Foley, L. Harnan, M. O'Connell, L. Hayes (capt.), G. McEntee, D. Beggy, T. Dowd, C. Coyle, P. J. Gillic, B. Stafford, B. Flynn. Subs: C. O'Rourke for C. Coyle; A. Browne for M. Lyons; M. McCabe for P. J. Gillic.

Referee—S. Prior (Leitrim).

1992

Donegal—G. Walsh, B. McGowan, M. Gallagher, N. Hegarty, D. Reid, M. Gavigan, J. J. Doherty, A. Molloy (capt.), B. Murray, J. McHugh, M. McHugh, J. McMullan, D. Bonner, T. Boyle, M. Boyle, Sub: B. Cunningham for B. Murray.

Dublin—J. O'Leary, M. Deegan, G. Hargan, T. Carr (capt.), P. Curran, K. Barr, E. Heery, P. Clarke, D. Foran, C. Redmond, J. Sheedy, N. Guiden, D. Farrell, V. Murphy, M. Galvin. Sub: P. Bealan for D. Foran.

Referee—T. Sugrue (Kerry).

1993

Derry—D. McCusker, K. McKeever, A. Scullion, F. McCusker, J. McGurk, H. Downey (capt.), G. Coleman, A. Tohill, B. McGilligan, D. Heaney, D. Barton, D. Cassidy, J. Brolly, S. Downey, E. Gormley. Subs: D. McNicholl for D. Cassidy; E. Burns for S. Downey.

Cork—J. Kerins, N. Cahalane, M. O'Connor, B. Corcoran, C. O'Sullivan, S. O'Brien, A. Davis, S. Fahy, T. McCarthy, D. Davis, J. Kavanagh, B. Coffey, C. Corkery, J. O'Driscoll, M. McCarthy (capt.), Subs: D. Culloty for T. McCarthy; J. Cleary for M. McCarthy; C. Counihan for C. Corkery.

Referee—T. Howard (Kildare).

1994

Down—N. Collins, M. Magill, B. Burns, P. Higgins, E. Burns, B. Breen, D. J. Kane (capt.), G. McCartan, C. Deegan, R. Carr, G. Blaney, J. McCortan, M. Linden, A. Farrell, G. Mason. Sub: G. Colgan for C. Deegan.

Dublin—J. O'Leary (capt.), P. Moran, D. Deasy, P. Curran, P. Clarke, K. Barr, M. Deegan, B. Stynes, P. Gilroy, J. Sheedy, V. Murphy, N. Guiden, D. Farrell, M. Galvin, C. Redmond. Subs: P. Bealin for P. Gilroy, S. Cahill for M. Galvin, J. Barr for N. Guiden.

Referee—T. Sugrue (Kerry).

1995

Dublin—J. O'Leary (capt.), P. Moran, C. Walsh, K. Galvin, P. Curran, K. Barr, M. Deegan, P. Bealin, B. Stynes, J. Gavin, D. Farrell, P. Clarke, M. Galvin, J. Sherlock, C. Redmond. Subs: P. Gilroy for K. Galvin, R. Boyle for M. Galvin, V. Murphy for D. Farrell.

Tyrone—F. McConnell, P. Devlin, C. Lawn, F. Devlin, R. McGarrity, S. McCallan, S. McLoughlin, F. Logan, J. Gormley, C. Corr (capt), Pascal Canavan, C. Loughran, C. McBride, Peter Canavan, S. Lawn. Subs: M. McGlennon for C. Loughran, B. Gormley for S. Lawn, P. Donnolly for S. McCallan.

Referee—P. Russell (Tipperary).

1996

Meath—C. Martin, M. O'Reilly, D. Fay, M. O'Connell, C. Coyle, E. McManus, P. Reynolds, J. McGuinness, J. McDermott, T. Giles, T. Dowd (capt.), G. Geraghty, C. Brady, B. Reilly, B. Callaghan. Subs: J. Devine for B. Callaghan, O. Murphy for M. O'Reilly.

Evan Kelly played in drawn game. C. Brady came on for replay. Subs in drawn game C. Brady for E. Kelly, J. Devine for J. McGuinness, D. Curtis for P. Reynolds.

Mayo—J. Madden, D. Flanagan, K. Cahill, K. Mortimer, P. Holmes, J. Nallen, N. Connelly (capt.), L. McHale, D. Brady, M. Sheridan, C. McManamon, J. Horan, R. Dempsey, J. Casey, A. Finnerty. Subs: P. J. Loftus for R. Dempsey, P. Fallon for D. Flanagan, T. Reilly for A. Finnerty.

D. Nestor played in drawn game. A. Finnerty came on for replay. Subs in drawn game P. J. Loftus for D. Nestor, A. Finnerty for J. Casey, K. O'Neill for J. Horan.

Referee: P. McEnaney (Monaghan) for both draw and replay.

1997

Kerry—D. O'Keeffe, K. Burns, B. O'Shea, S. Stack, S. Moynihan, L. O'Flaherty, E. Breen, Darragh Ó Sé, W. Kirby, P. Laide, L. Hassett (capt.), D. O'Dwyer, B. O'Shea, D. Ó Cinnéide, M. Fitzgerald. Subs: J. Crowley for B. O'Shea, D. Daly for W. Kirby, M. F. Russell for D. Ó Cinnéide.

Mayo—P. Burke, P. Holmes, K. Mortimer, D. Flanagan, F. Costelloe, J. Nallen, N. Connelly (capt.), P. Fallon, D. Heaney, M. Sheridan, C. McManamon, J. Casey, K. McDonald, L. McHale, D. Nestor. Subs: J. Horan for D. Flanagan, D. Byrne for M. Sheridan, P. J. Loftus for D. Nestor.

Referee—B. White (Wexford).

1998

Galway—M. McNamara, T. Meehan, G. Fahy, T. Mannion, R. Silke (capt.), J. Divilly, S. Óg de Paor, K. Walsh, S. Ó Domhnaill, M. Donnellan, S. Walsh, J. Fallon, S. Walsh, D. Savage, P. Joyce, N. Finnegan. Sub: P. Clancy for S. Walsh.

Kildare—C. Byrne, B. Lacey, J. Finn, K. Doyle, S. Dowling, G. Ryan (capt.), A. Rainbow, N. Buckley, W. McCreery, E. McCormack, D. Kerrigan, D. Earley, M. Lynch, K. O'Dwyer, P. Gravin. Subs: P. Brennon for P. Gravin, B. Murphy for M. Lynch.

Referee: J. Bannon (Longford).

1999

Meath—C. O'Sullivan, M. O'Reilly, D. Fay, C. Murphy, P. Reynolds, E. McManus, H. Traynor, N. Crawford, J. McDermott, N. Nestor, T. Giles, D. Curtis, E. Kelly, G. Geraghty (capt.), O. Murphy. Subs: R. Kealy for N. Nestor, B. Callaghan for H. Traynor, T. Dowd for E. Kelly.

Cork—K. O'Dwyer, R. McCarthy, S. Óg Ó hAilpín, A. Lynch, C. O'Sullivan, O. Sexton, M. Cronin, N. Murphy, M. O'Sullivan, M. Cronin, J. Kavanagh, P. O'Mahony, P. Clifford (capt.), D. Davis, M. O'Sullivan. Subs: F. Murray for M. O'Sullivan, F. Collins for M. Cronin and M. Donovan for P. O'Mahony.

Referee: Mick Curley (Galway).

2000

Kerry – D.O'Keeffe, M.Hassett, S.Moynihan, M.McCarthy, T.Ó Sé, E.Fitzmaurice, T.O'Sullivan, D.Ó Sé, D.Daly, A.MacGearailt, L.Hassett, N.Kennelly, M.F.Russell, D.Ó Cinnéide, J.Crowley, Subs – M.Fitzgerald for Kennelly, T.Griffin for O'Sullivan.

(Kerry started with the same 15 as in the drawn encounter. Subs used in the drawn final were M.Fitzgerald for Crowley, D.Dwyer for Kennelly.)

Galway – M.McNamara, T.Meehan, G.Fahy, R.Fahy, D.Meehan, J.Divilly, S.Óg dePaor, K.Walsh, S.Ó Domhnaill, P.Clancy, M.Donnellan, T.Joyce, D.Savage, P.Joyce, N.Finnegan. Subs – J.Bergin for K.Walsh, K.Walsh for Ó Domhnaill, J.Donnellan for T.Joyce, S.Walsh for Clancy.
(R.Silke and J.Bergin started the drawn final but not the replay. Subs used in the drawn final were – K.Walsh for Bergin, R.Fahy for Silke, J.Donnellan for T.Joyce.)
Referee – B.White (Wexford)
Drawn game referee was P.McEnaney (Monaghan)

2001

Galway – A.Keane, K.Fitzgerald, G.Fahy, R.Fahy, D.Meehan, T.Mannion, S.Óg dePaor, K.Walsh, M.Donnellan, J.Bergin, P.Clancy, J.Fallon, P.Joyce, D.Savage, T.Joyce. Subs – A.Kerins for Bergin, K.Comer for dePaor.
Meath – C.Sullivan, M.O'Reilly, D.Fay, C.Murphy, D.Curtis, M.Nestor, H.Traynor, N.Crawford, J.McDermott, E.Kelly, T.Giles, R.Kealy, O.Murphy, G.Geraghty, R.Magee. Subs – P.Reynolds for Murphy, J.Cullinane for Kealy, N.Kelly for Murphy, A.Kenny for Magee.
Referee – M.Collins (Cork)

2002

Armagh – B.Tierney, E.McNulty, J.McNulty, F.Bellew, A.O'Rourke, K.McGeeney, A.McCann, J.Toal, P.McGrane, P.McKeever, J.McEntee, O.McConville, S.McDonnell, R.Clarke, D.Marsden. Subs – B.O'Hagan for J.McEntee, T.McEntee for McKeever.
Kerry – D.O'Keeffe, M.Ó Sé, S.Moynihan, M.McCarthy, T.Ó Sé, E.Fitzmaurice, J.Sheehan, D.Ó Sé, D.Daly, S.O'Sullivan, E.Brosnan, L.Hassett, M.F.Russell, D.Ó Cinnéide, C.Cooper. Subs – A.MacGearailt for O'Sullivan, T.O'Sullivan for M.Ó Sé, J.Crowley for Hassett, B.O'Shea for Daly.
Referee – J.Bannon (Longford)

2003

Tyrone – J.Devine, C.Gourley, C.McAnallen, R.McMenamin, C.Gormley, G.Devlin, P.Jordan, K.Hughes, S.Cavanagh, B.Dooher, B.McGuigan, G.Cavlan, E.McGinley, P.Canavan, O.Mulligan. Subs – S.O'Neill for McGuigan, McGuigan for Canavan, C.Holmes for Gourley, Canavan for Cavlan, C.Lawn for Gormley.
Armagh – P.Hearty, F.Bellew, E.McNulty, A.Mallon, A.O'Rourke, K.McGeeney, A.McCann, P.Loughran, P.McGrane, R.Clarke, J.McEntee, O.McConville, S.McDonnell, D.Marsden, T.McEntee. Subs – P.McKeever for Marsden, K.Hughes for Mallon, Marsden for Clarke, B.O'Hagan for J.McEntee.
Referee – B.White (Wexford)

2004

Kerry – D.Murphy, A.O'Mahony, M.McCarthy, T.O'Sullivan, M.Ó Sé, E.Fitzmaurice, T.Ó Sé, W.Kirby, E.Brosnan, L.Hassett, D.O'Sullivan, P.Galvin, C.Cooper, D.Ó Cinnéide, J.Crowley. Subs – S.Moynihan for Hassett, M.F.Russell for Crowley, R.O'Connor for Ó Cinnéide, P.Kelly for Galvin, B.Guiney for T.Ó Sé.
Mayo – P.Burke, D.Geraghty, D.Heaney, G.Ruane, P.Gardiner, J.Nallen, P.Kelly, R.McGarrity, F.Kelly, T.Mortimer, C.McDonald, B.Maloney, C.Mortimer, J.Gill, A.Dillon. Subs – D.Brady for F.Kelly, C.Moran for Geraghty, M.Conroy for Gill, A.Moran for C.Mortimer, P.Navin for Heaney.
Referee – P.McEnaney (Monaghan)

2005

Tyrone – P.McConnell, R.McMenamin, J.McMahon, M.McGee, D.Harte, C.Gormley, P.Jordan, E.McGinley, S.Cavanagh, B.Dooher, B.McGuigan, R.Mellon, P.Canavan, S.O'Neill, O.Mulligan. Subs – C.Homles for Canavan, C.Lawn for McMahon, Canavan for McGinley.
Kerry – D.Murphy, M.McCarthy, A.O'Mahony, T.O'Sullivan, T.Ó Sé, S.Moynihan, D.Ó Sé, W.Kirby, L.Hassett, E.Brosnan, P.Galvin, C.Cooper, Declan O'Sullivan, D.Ó Cinnéide. Subs – M.F.Russell for Hassett, Darren O'Sullivan for Ó Cinnéide, E.Fitzmaurice for Moynihan, B.Sheehan for Galvin.
Referee – M.Monahan (Kildare)

2006

Kerry – D.Murphy, M.McCarthy, T.O'Sullivan, A.O'Mahony, S.Moynihan, M.Ó Sé, T.Ó Sé, D.O'Se, T.Griffin, S.O'Sullivan, Declan O'Sullivan, P.Galvin, C.Cooper, K.Donaghy, M.F.Russell. Subs – E.Brosnan for T.O'Se, Darren O'Sullivan for S.O'Sullivan, B.Sheehan for Russell, E.Fitzmaurice for Griffin, B.Guiney for O'Mahony.
Mayo – D.Clarke, D.Geraghty, D.Heaney, K.Higgins, A.Higgins, J.Nallen, P.Gardiner, R.McGarrity, P.Harte, B.J.Padden, G.Brady, A.Dillon, K.O'Neill, C.Mortimer, C.McDonald. Subs – D.Brady for Nallen, T.Mortimer for Dillon, B.Moran for O'Neill, A.Kilcoyne for Padden, A.Moran for Gardiner.
Referee – B.Crowe (Cavan).

2007

Kerry – D.Murphy, M.Ó Sé, T.O'Sullivan, P.Reidy, A.O'Mahony, T.Ó Sé, K.Young, D.Ó Sé, S.Scanlon, P.Galvin, Declan O'Sullivan, E.Brosnan, C.Cooper, K.Donaghy, B.Sheehan. Subs – S.O'Sullivan for Galvin, Darren O'Sullivan for Brosnan, T.Griffin for Young, M.F.Russell for Sheehan, M.Lyons for Reidy.
Cork – A.Quirke, M.Shields, G.Canty, K.O'Connor, N.O'Leary, G.Spillane, J.Miskella, D.Kavanagh, N.Murphy, C.McCarthy, P.O'Neill, K.McMahon, J.Masters, M.Cussen, D.O'Connor. Subs – D.Goulding for Masters, A.Lynch for Miskella, F.Gould for McMahon, K.O'Sullivan for McCarthy.
Referee – D.Coldrick (Meath).

2008

Tyrone – P.McConnell, Joseph McMahon, Justin McMahon, C.Gormley, D.Harte, P.Jordan, R.McMenamin, C.Holmes, E.McGinley, B.Dooher, M.Penrose, R.Mellon,

T.McGuigan, S.Cavanagh, C.McCullagh. Subs – S.O'Neill for McCullagh, K.Hughes for Holmes, B.McGuigan for Penrose, O.Mulligan for Mellon, C.Cavanagh for T.McGuigan.

Kerry – D.Murphy, M.Ó Sé, T.O'Sullivan, P.Reidy, T.Ó Sé, A.O'Mahony, K.Young, D.Ó Sé, S.Scanlon, B.Sheehan, Declan O'Sullivan, E.Brosnan, C.Cooper, K.Donaghy, T.Walsh. Subs – Darren O'Sullivan for Brosnan, T.Griffin for Scanlon, P.Galvin for Walsh, D.Moran for Sheehan.

Referee – M.Deegan (Laois)

2009

Kerry – D.Murphy, M.Ó Sé, T.Griffin, T.O'Sullivan, T.Ó Sé, M.McCarthy, K.Young, D.Ó Sé, S.Scanlon, Darren O'Sullivan, T.Kennelly, P.Galvin, C.Cooper, Declan O'Sullivan, T.Walsh. Subs – D.Walsh for Kennelly, M.Quirke for D.Ó Sé, K.Donaghy for Darren O'Sullivan, D.Moran for T.Walsh, A.O'Mahony for Young.

Cork – A.Quirke, K.O'Connor, M.Shields, A.Lynch, N.O'Leary, G.Canty, J.Miskella, A.O'Connor, N.Murphy, P.Kelly, P.O'Neill, P.Kerrigan, D.Goulding, C.O'Neill, D.O'Connor. Subs – E.Cadogan for K.O'Connor, F.Goold for Kerrigan, D.Kavanagh for Lynch, J.Masters for Goulding, M.Cussen for A.O'Connor.

Referee – M.Duffy (Sligo)

CAPTAINS OF WINNING ALL-IRELAND SENIOR FOOTBALL TEAMS

1887—D. Corbett (Limerick).
1888—No Final Played.
1889—G. Kavanagh (Tipperary).
1890—J. Power (Cork).
1891—J. Kennedy (Dublin).
1892—J. Kennedy (Dublin).
1893—T. Hayes (Wexford).
1894—J. Kennedy (Dublin).
1895— P. Finn (Tipperary).
1896—C. Fitzgerald (Limerick).
1897—P. J. Walsh (Dublin).
1898—M. Rea (Dublin).
1899— M. Rea (Dublin).
1900—J. Tobin (Tipperary).
1901—J. Darcy (Dublin).
1902—J. Dempsey (Dublin).
1903—T. O'Connor (Kerry).
1904—A. Stack (Kerry).
1905—J. Murray (Kildare).
1906—J. Grace (Dublin).
1907—J. Grace (Dublin).
1908—D. Kelleher (Dublin).
1909—T. Costello (Kerry).
1910—No Final. Louth awarded walk-over from Kerry.
1911—M. Mehigan (Cork)
1912—J. Smith (Louth).
1913—R Fitzgerald (Kerry).
1914—R. Fitzgerald (Kerry).
1915—S. Kennedy (Wexford).
1916—S. Kennedy (Wexford).
1917—S. Kennedy (Wexford).
1918—J. Byrne (Wexford).
1919—L. Stanley (Kildare).
1920—J. Shelly (Tipperary).
1921—E. Carroll (Dublin).
1922—P. Carey (Dublin).
1923—P. McDonnell (Dublin).
1924—P. Sullivan (Kerry).
1925—No Final
1926—J. J. Sheehy (Kerry).
1927—M. Buckley (Kildare).
1928—W. "Squires" Gannon (Kildare).
1929—J. Barrett (Kerry).
1930—J. J. Sheehy (Kerry).
1931—C. Brosnan (Kerry).
1932—J. Barrett (Kerry).
1933—J. Smith (Cavan).
1934—M. Higgins (Galway).
1935—H. O'Reilly (Cavan).
1936—S. O'Malley (Mayo).
1937—M. Doyle (Kerry).
1938—J. Dunne (Galway).
1939—T. O'Connor (Kerry).
1940—D. Spring (Kerry).
1941—W. Dillon (Kerry)
1942—J. Fitzgerald (Dublin).
1943—J. Murray (Roscommon).
1944—J. Murray (Roscommon).
1945—T. Crowley (Cork).
1946—P. Kennedy (Kerry).
1947—J. J. O'Reilly (Cavan).
1948—J. J. O'Reilly (Cavan).
1949—B. Smyth (Meath)
1950—S. Flanagan (Mayo).
1951—S. Flanagan (Mayo).
1952—M. Higgins (Cavan).
1953—J. Murphy (Kerry).
1954—P. McDermott (Meath).
1955—J. Dowling (Kerry).
1956—J. Mangan (Galway).
1957—D. O'Brien (Louth).
1958— K. Heffernan (Dublin).
1959—M. O'Connell (Kerry).
1960—K. Mussen (Down).
1961—P. Doherty (Down).
1962—S. Óg Sheehy (Kerry).
1963—D. Foley (Dublin).
1964—J. Donnellan (Galway).
1965—E. Colleran (Galway).
1966—E. Colleran (Galway).
1967—P. Darby (Meath).
1968—J. Lennon (Down).
1969—J. Culloty (Kerry).
1970—D. O'Sullivan (Kerry).
1971—W. Bryan (Offaly).
1972—A. McTague (Offaly).
1973—W. Morgan (Cork).

1974—S. Doherty (Dublin).
1975—M. O'Sullivan (Kerry).
1976—T. Hanahoe (Dublin).
1977—T. Hanahoe (Dublin).
1978—D. "Ogie" Moran (Kerry).
1979—T. Kennelly (Kerry).
1980—G. Power (Kerry).
1981—J. Deenihan (Kerry).
1982—R. Connor (Offaly).
1983—T. Drumm (Dublin).
1984—A. O'Donovan (Kerry).
1985—P. Ó Sé (Kerry).
1986—T. Doyle (Kerry).
1987—M. Lyons (Meath).
1988—J. Cassells (Meath).
1989—D. Allen (Cork).
1990—L. Tompkins (Cork).
1991—P. O'Rourke (Down).
1992—A. Molloy (Donegal).
1993—H. Downey (Derry).
1994—D. J. Kane (Down).
1995—J. O'Leary (Dublin).
1996—T. Dowd (Meath).
1997—L. Hassett (Kerry).
1998—R. Silke (Galway).
1999—G. Geraghty (Meath).
2000—S. Moynihan (Kerry).
2001—G. Fahy (Galway).
2002—K. McGeeney (Armagh).
2003—P. Canavan (Tyrone).
2004—D. Ó Cinnéide (Kerry).
2005—B. Dooher (Tyrone).
2006—D.O'Sullivan (Kerry)
2007—P.Galvin (Kerry)
2008—B.Dooher (Tyrone)
2009—Darren O'Sullivan (Kerry)

MUNSTER SENIOR FOOTBALL FINALS

1888—Tipperary, w.o., Limerick (scratched)
1889—Tipperary 1-2, Cork 0-3
1890—Cork 1-4, Kerry 0-1
Cork 0-1, Kerry 0-0 (abandoned after 57 minutes when football burst)
1891—Cork 3-2, Waterford 1-1
1892—Kerry 0-12, Waterford 0-0
1893—Cork, w.o., Kerry
1894—Cork 2-4, Tipperary 0-1 (refixture)
Cork—0-6, Tipperary 0-2 (objection)
1895—Tipperary 0-5, Limerick 0-2
1896—Limerick 0-4, Waterford 0-1
(Unfinished. Title awarded to Limerick)
1897—Cork 0-5, Limerick 0-3
1898—Waterford 1-11, Cork 1-3
1899—Cork 3-11, Tipperary 0-1 (third match)
Cork 1-2, Tipperary 0-1 *(refixture, abandoned half time,dispute over score).*
Tipperary 2-1, Cork 0-1 (first game, abandoned half-time, no ball available)
1900—Tipperary 1-13, Kerry 1-4
1901—Cork 1-9, Limerick 1-6
1902—Tipperary 1-4, Kerry 1-4 (draw)
Tipperary 1-6, Kerry 1-5 (replay)
1903—Kerry 1-7, Cork 0-3
1904—Kerry 0-3, Waterford 0-3 (draw)
Kerry 2-3, Waterford 0-2 (replay)
1905—Kerry 2-10, Limerick 1-6
1906—Cork 1-10, Kerry 0-3
1907—Cork 1-7, Tipperary 0-1
1908—Kerry 0-7, Waterford 0-2
1909—Cork 2-8, Kerry 1-7 (objection)
Kerry 1-5, Cork 0-6 (replay)
1910—Kerry 0-4, Cork 0-2
1911—Cork 2-5, Waterford 0-1
1912—Kerry 0-3, Clare 0-1
1913—Kerry 1 -6, Cork 0-1
1914—Kerry 0-5, Cork 0-1
1915—Kerry 4-3, Clare 0-1
1916—Cork 2-2, Clare 1-4
1917—Clare 5-4, Cork 0-1
1918—Tipperary 1-1, Kerry 0-1
1919—Kerry 6-11, Clare 2-0
1920—Tipperary 2-2, Kerry 0-2
1921—No S.F. Championship
(Note: Tipperary nominated to represent Munster but gave a walk-over to Mayo in All-Ireland semi-final.)
1922—Tipperary 1-7, Limerick 0-1
1923—Kerry 0-5, Tipperary 0-3
1924—Kerry 5-8, Clare 2-2
1925—Kerry 5-5, Clare 0-0
1926—Kerry 0-11, Tipperary 1-4
1927—Kerry 4-4, Clare 1-3
1928—Cork 4-3, Tipperary, 0-4
1929—Kerry 1-14, Clare 1-2
1930—Kerry 3-4, Tipperary 1-2
1931—Kerry 5-8, Tipperary 0-2
1932—Kerry 3-10, Tipperary 1-4
1933—Kerry 2-8, Tipperary 1-4
1934—Kerry 1-14, Limerick 1-2
1935—Tipperary 2-8, Cork 1-2
1936—Kerry 1-11, Clare 2-2
1937—Kerry 4-9, Clare 1-1
1938—Kerry 4-14, Cork 0-6
1939—Kerry 2-11, Tipperary 0-4
1940—Kerry 1-10, Waterford 0-6
1941—Kerry 2-9, Clare 0-6
1942—Kerry 3-7, Cork 0-8
1943—Cork 1-7, Tipperary 1-4
1944—Kerry 1-6, Tipperary 0-5
1945—Cork 1-11, Kerry 1-6
1946—Kerry 2-15, Waterford 2-1
1947—Kerry 3-8, Cork 2-6
1948—Kerry 2-9, Cork 2-6
1949—Cork 3-6, Clare 0-7
1950—Kerry 2-5, Cork 1-5
1951—Kerry 1-6, Cork 0-4
1952—Cork 0-11, Kerry 0-2
1953—Kerry 2-7, Cork 2-3
1954—Kerry 4-9, Cork 2-3
1955—Kerry 0-14, Cork 2-6
1956—Cork 0-8, Kerry 2-2 (draw)
Cork 1-8, Kerry 1-7 (replay)
1957—Cork 0-16, Waterford 1-2
1958—Kerry 2-7, Cork 0-3
1959—Kerry 2-15, Cork 2-8
1960—Kerry 3-15, Waterford 0-8
1961—Kerry 0-10, Cork 1-7 (draw)
Kerry 2-13, Cork 1-4 (replay)

1962—Kerry 4-8, Cork 0-4
1963—Kerry 1-18, Cork 3-7
1964—Kerry 2-11, Cork 1-8
1965—Kerry 2-16, Limerick 2-7
1966—Cork 2-7, Kerry 1-7
1967—Cork 0-8, Kerry 0-7
1968—Kerry 1-21, Cork 3-8
1969—Kerry 0-16, Cork 1-4
1970—Kerry 2-22, Cork 2-9
1971—Cork 0-25, Kerry 0-14
1972—Kerry 2-21, Cork 2-15
1973—Cork 5-12, Kerry 1-15
1974—Cork 1-11, Kerry 0-7
1975—Kerry 1-14, Cork 0-7
1976—Kerry 0-10, Cork 0-10 (draw}
Kerry 3-20, Cork 2-19 (replay)
(after extra time)
1977—Kerry 3-15, Cork 0-9
1978—Kerry 3-14, Cork 3-7
1979—Kerry 2-14, Cork 2-4
1980—Kerry 3-13, Cork 0-12
1981—Kerry 1-11, Cork 0-3
1982—Kerry 0-9, Cork 0-9 (draw)
Kerry 2-18, Cork 0-12 (replay)
1983—Cork 3-10, Kerry 3-9
1984—Kerry 3-14, Cork 2-10
1985—Kerry 2-11, Cork 0-11
1986—Kerry 0-12, Cork 0-8
1987—Cork 1-10, Kerry 2-7 (draw)
Cork 0-13, Kerry 1-5 (replay)
1988—Cork 1-14, Kerry 0-16
1989—Cork 1-12, Kerry 1-9
1990—Cork 2-23, Kerry 1-11
1991—Kerry 0-23, Limerick 3-12
1992—Clare 2-10, Kerry 0-12
1993—Cork 1-16, Tipperary 1-8
1994—Cork 2-19, Tipperary 3-9
1995—Cork 0-15, Kerry 1-9
1996—Kerry 0-14, Cork 0-11
1997—Kerry 1-13, Clare 0-11
1998—Kerry 0-17, Tipperary 1-10
1999—Cork 2-10, Kerry 2-4
2000—Kerry 3-15, Clare 0-8.
2001—Kerry 0-19, Cork 1-13.
2002—Cork 2-11, Tipperary 1-14.
Cork 1-23, Tipperary 0-7. (replay)
2003—Kerry 1-11, Limerick 0-9.
2004—Kerry 1-10, Limerick 1-10.
Kerry 3-10, Limerick 2-9. (replay)
2005—Kerry 0-10, Cork 0-10.
Kerry 1-11, Cork 0-11.
2006—Cork 1-12, Kerry 0-9.
2007—Kerry 1-15, Cork 1-13.
2008—Cork 1-16, Kerry 1-11.
2009—Cork 2-6, Limerick 0-11.

LEINSTER SENIOR FOOTBALL FINALS

1887—No Final, open draw
1888—Kilkenny 1-4, Wexford 0-2
1889—Laois 0-3, Louth 0-2
1890—Wexford 1-3, Dublin 1-2
1891—Dublin w.o. Kildare (scratched)
1892—Dublin w.o. Louth (scratched)
1893—Kilkenny 0-5, Wexford 0-1 (unfinished – Wexford awarded title)
1894—Dublin 0-4, Meath 0-4 (draw)
Dublin 0-2, Meath 0-2 (replay)
Dublin 1-8, Meath 1-2 (second replay)
1895—Meath 0-6, Dublin 0-2
1896—Dublin 2-4, Meath 1-5
1897—Dublin 1-9, Wicklow 0-3
1898—Dublin 2-6, Wexford 0-0
1899—Dublin 1 -7, Wexford 0-3
1900—Kilkenny 0-12, Louth 0-0
1901—Dublin 1-9, Wexford 0-1
1902—Dublin 2-4, Wexford 0-2 (unfinished, replay ordered)
Dublin 1-5, Wexford 0-5 (replay)
1903—Kildare 1-2, Kilkenny 0-5 (draw)
Kildare 1-6, Kilkenny 1-5 (point disputed)
Kildare 0-9, Kilkenny 0-1 (2nd replay)
1904—Dublin 0-5, Kilkenny 0-1
1905—Kildare 0-12, Louth 1-7
1906—Dublin 1-9, Kildare 0-8
1907—Dublin 1-11, Offaly 0-4
1908—Dublin 1-7, Kildare 0-3
1909—Louth 2-9, Kilkenny 0-4
1910—Louth 0-3, Dublin 0-0
1911—Kilkenny 2-4, Meath 1- 1
1912—Louth 1-2, Dublin 1-1
1913—Wexford 2-3, Louth 2-2
1914—Wexford 3-6, Louth 0-1
1915—Wexford 2-2, Dublin 2-2 (draw)
Wexford 3-5, Dublin 1-3 (replay)
1916—Wexford 1-7, Kildare 1-0
1917—Wexford 1-3, Dublin 1-1
1918—Wexford 2-5, Louth 1-4
1919—Kildare 1-3, Dublin 1-2
1920 - Dublin 1-3, Kildare 0-3
1921—Dublin 0-6, Kildare 1-3 (draw)
Dublin 3-3, Kildare 1-2 (replay)
1922—Dublin 1-7, Kilkenny 0-2
1923—Dublin 3-5, Meath 0-0
1924—Dublin 1-4, Wexford 1-4 (draw)
Dublin 3-5, Wexford 2-3 (replay)
1925—Wexford 2-7, Kildare 0-3
1926—Kildare 2-8, Wexford 1-5
1927—Kildare 0-5, Dublin 0-3
1928—Kildare 0-10, Dublin 1-6
1929—Kildare 2-3, Laois 0-6
1930—Kildare 0-6, Meath 1-3 (draw)
Kildare 2-6, Meath 1-2 (replay)
1931—Kildare 2-9, Westmeath 1-6
1932—Dublin 0-8, Wexford 1-5 (draw)
Dublin 4-6, Wexford 1-5 (replay)
1933—Dublin 0-9, Wexford 1-4
1934—Dublin 1-2, Louth 0-5 (draw)
Dublin 3-2, Louth 2-5 (replay)
Dublin 2-9, Louth 1-10 (second replay)
1935—Kildare 0-8, Louth 0-6
1936—Laois 3-3, Kildare 0-8
1937—Laois 0-12, Louth 0-4
1938—Laois 2-8, Kildare 1-3
1939—Meath 2-7, Wexford 2-3
1940—Meath 2-7, Laois 1-7
1941—Dublin 4-6, Carlow 1-4
1942—Dublin 0-8, Carlow 0-6
1943—Louth 3-16, Laois 2-4
1944—Carlow 2-6, Dublin 1-6
1945—WexFord 1-9, Offaly 1-4

1946—Laois 0-11, Kildare 1-6
1947—Meath 3-7, Laois 1-7
1948—Louth 2-10, Wexford 2-5
1949—Meath 4-5, Westmeath 0-6
1950—Louth 1-3, Meath 1 -3 (draw)
Louth 3-5, Meath 0-13 (replay)
1951—Meath 4-9, Laois 0-3
1952—Meath 1-6, Louth 0-8
1953—Louth 1-7, Wexford 0-7
1954—Meath 4-7, Offaly 2-10
1955—Dublin 5-12, Meath 0-7
1956—Kildare 2-11, Wexford 1-8
1957—Louth 2-9, Dublin 1-7
1958—Dublin 1-11, Louth 1-6
1959—Dublin 1-18, Laois 2-8
1960—Offaly 0-10, Louth 1-6
1961—Offaly 1-13, Dublin 1-8
1962—Dublin 2-8, Offaly 1-7
1963—Dublin 2-11, Laois 2-9
1964—Meath 2-12, Dublin 1-7
1965—Dublin 3-6, Longford 0-9
1966—Meath 1-9, Klldare 1-8
1967—Meath 0-8, Offaly 0-6
1968—Longford 3-9, Laois 1-4
1969—Offaly 3-7, Kildare 1-8
1970—Meath 2-22, Offaly 5-12
1971—Offaly 2-14, Kildare 0-6
1972—Offaly 1-18, Kildare 2-8
1973—Offaly 3-21, Meath 2-12
1974—Dublin 1-14, Meath 1-9
1975—Dublin 3-13, Kildare 0-8
1976—Dublin 2-8, Meath 1-9
1977—Dublin 1-9, Meath 0-8
1978—Dublin 1-17, Kildare 1-6
1979—Dublin 1-8, Offaly 0-9
1980—Offaly 1-10, Dublin 1-8
1981—Offaly 1-18, Laois 3-9
1982—Offaly 1-16, Dublin 1-7
1983—Dublin 2-13, Offaly 1-11
1984—Dublin 2-10, Meath 1-9
1985—Dublin 0-10, Laois 0-4
1986—Meath 0-9, Dublin 0-7
1987—Meath 1-13, Dublin 0-12
1988—Meath 2-5 Dublin 0-9
1989—Dublin 2-12, Meath 1-10
1990—Meath 1-14, Dublin 0-14
1991—Meath 1-11, Laois 0-8
1992—Dublin 1-13, Kildare 0-10
1993—Dublin 0-11, Kildare 0-7
1994—Dublin 1-9, Meath 1-8
1995—Dublin 1-18, Meath 1-8
1996—Meath 0-10, Dublin 0-8
1997—Offoly 3-17, Meath 1-15
1998—Kildare 1-12, Meath 0-10
1999—Meath 1-14, Dublin 0-12
2000—Kildare 0-14, Dublin 0-14.
Kildare 2-11, Dublin 0-12. (replay)
2001—Meath 2-11, Dublin 0-14.
2002—Dublin 2-13, Kildare 2-11.
2003—Laois 2-13, Kildare 1-13.
2004—Westmeath 0-13, Laois 0-13.
Westmeath 0-12, Laois 0-10. (replay)
2005—Dublin 0-14, Laois 0-13.
2006—Dublin 1-15, Offaly 0-9.
2007—Dublin 3-14, Laois 1-14.
2008—Dublin 3-23, Wexford 0-9.
2009—Dublin 2-15, Kildare 0-18.

CONNACHT SENIOR FOOTBALL FINALS

1892—Roscommon represented Province in All-Ireland series.
1888-1891 and 1893-1899: No Connacht representatives in All-Ireland series.
1900—Galway, unopposed
1901—Mayo 2-4, Galway 0-3
1902—Mayo 2-2, Galway 0-6
1903—Roscommon 1-1, Mayo 0-3
1904—Mayo 3-6, Roscommon 0-1
1905—Roscommon 0-7, Mayo 0-5
1906—Mayo 2-13, Roscommon 0-5
1907—Mayo 3-9, Galway 0-1
1908—Mayo 1-4, Galway 0-3
1909—Mayo 1-4, Galway 0-5
1910—Galway 1-3, Roscommon 1-2
1911—Galway nominated
1912—Roscommon 0-2, Galway 0-0
1913—Galway 1-2, Mayo 0-3
1914—Roscommon 1-2, Leitrim 0-1
1915—Mayo 3-1, Roscommon 1-3
1916—Mayo 1-5, Roscommon 0-3
1917—Galway 1-4, Mayo 1-1
1918—Mayo 0-4, Galway 0-1
1919—Galway 1-6, Roscommon 0-5
1920—Mayo 2-3, Sligo 1-4
1921—Mayo 1-4, Roscommon 0-1
1922—Sligo 3-2, Galway 1-7
(objection, replay ordered)
Galway 2-4, Sligo 2-2 (replay)
1923—Mayo 0-3, Galway 0-2
1924—Mayo 0-1, Galway 0-1 (draw)
Mayo 2-6, Galway 0-5 (replay)
1925—Galway 1-5, Mayo 1-3
1926—Galway 3-2, Mayo 1-2
1927—Leitrim 2-4, Galway 0-3
1928—Sligo 1-4, Mayo 0-6
1929—Mayo 1-6, Galway 0-4
1930—Mayo 1-7, Sligo 1-2
1931—Mayo 2-10, Roscommon 3-2
1932—Mayo 2-6, Sligo 0-7
1933—Galway 1-7, Mayo 1-5
1934—Galway 2-4, Mayo 0-5
1935—Mayo 0-12, Galway 0-5
1936—Mayo 2-4, Galway 1-7 (draw)
Mayo 2-7, Galway 1-4 (replay)
1937—Mayo 3-5, Galway 0-8
1938—Galway 0-8, Mayo 0-5
1939—Awarded to Mayo (Mayo 2-6, Galway 0-3. Match unfinished.)
1940—Galway 1-7, Mayo 0-5
1941—Galway 0-8, Roscommon 1-4
1942—Galway 2-6, Roscommon 3-2
1943—Roscommon 2-6, Galway 0-8
1944—Roscommon 2-11, Mayo 1-6
1945—Galway 2-6, Mayo 1-7
1946—Roscommon 1-4, Mayo 0-6 (objection and counter-objection, replay ordered)
Roscommon 1-9, Mayo 1-2 (replay)
1947—Roscommon 2-12, Sligo 1-8
1948—Mayo 2-4, Galway 1-7 (draw)
Mayo 2-10, Galway 2-7 (replay)
(after extra time)
1949—Mayo 4-6, Leitrim 0-3
1950—Mayo 1-7, Roscommon 0-4

1951—Mayo 4-13, Galway 2-3
1952—Roscommon 3-5, Mayo 0-6
1953—Roscommon 1-6, Mayo 0-6
1954—Galway 2-10, Sligo 3-4
1955—Mayo 3-11, Roscommon 1-3
1956—Galway 3-12, Sligo 1 -5
1957—Galway 4-8, Leitrim 0-4
1958—Galway 2-10, Leitrim 1-11
1959—Galway 5-8, Leitrim 0-12
1960—Galway 2-5, Leitrim 0-5
1961—Roscommon 1-11, Galway 2-7
1962—Roscommon 3-7, Galway 2-9
1963—Galway 4-11, Leitrim 1-6
1964—Galway 2-12, Mayo 1-5
1965—Galway 1-12, Sligo 2-6
1966—Galway 0-12, Mayo 1-8
1967—Mayo 4-15, Leitrim 0-7
1968—Galway 2-10, Mayo 2-9
1969—Mayo 0-11, Galway 1-8 (draw)
Mayo 1-11, Galway 1-8 (replay)
1970—Galway 2-15, Roscommon 1-8
1971—Galway 2-15, Sligo 2-15 (draw)
Galway 1-17, Sligo 3-10 (replay)
1972—Roscommon 5-8, Mayo 3-10
1973—Galway 1-17, Mayo 2-12
1974—Galway 2-14, Roscommon 0-8
1975—Sligo 2-10, Mayo 1-13 (draw)
Sligo 2-10, Mayo 0-15 (replay)
1976—Galway 1-8, Roscommon 1-8 (draw)
Galway 1-14, Roscommon 0-9 (replay)
1977—Roscommon 1-12, Galway 2-8
1978—Roscommon 2-7, Galway 0-9
1979—Roscommon 3-15, Mayo 2-10
1980—Roscommon 3-13, Mayo 0-8
1981—Mayo 0-12, Sligo 0-4
1982—Galway 3-17, Mayo 0-10
1983—Galway 1-13, Mayo 1-10
1984—Galway 2-13, Mayo 2-9
1985—Mayo 2-11, Roscommon 0-8
1986—Galway 1-8, Roscommon 1-5
1987—Galway 0-8, Mayo 0-7
1988—Mayo 1-12, Roscommon 0-8
1989—Mayo 0-12, Roscommon 1-9 (draw)
Mayo 3-14, Roscommon 2-13
after extra time (replay)
1990—Roscommon 0-16, Galway 1-11
1991—Roscommon 0-14, Mayo 0-14 (draw)
Roscommon 0-13, Mayo 1-9 (replay)
1992—Mayo 1-14, Roscommon 0-10
1993—Mayo 1-5, Roscommon 0-7
1994—Leitrim 0-12, Mayo 2-4
1995—Galway 0-17, Mayo 1-7
1996—Mayo 3-9, Galway 1-11
1997—Mayo 0-11, Sligo 1-7
1998—Galway 0-11, Roscommon 0-11 (draw)
Galway 1-17, Roscommon 0-17 (replay)
after extra time.
1999—Mayo 1-14, Galway 1-10
2000—Galway 1-13, Leitrim 0-8.
2001—Roscommon 2-10, Mayo 1-12.
2002—Galway 1-11, Sligo 0-11.
2003—Galway 1-14, Mayo 0-13.
2004—Mayo 2-13, Roscommon 0-9.
2005—Galway 0-10, Mayo 0-8.
2006—Mayo 0-12, Galway 1-8.
2007—Sligo 1-10, Galway 0-12.
2008—Galway 2-12, Mayo 1-14.
2009—Mayo 2-12, Galway 1-14.

ULSTER SENIOR FOOTBALL FINALS

1887—No Ulster championship
1888—Monaghan 0-2, Cavan 0-2 (draw)
Monaghan 0-3, Cavan 0-1 (replay)
1889—No Ulster championship
1890—Armagh 2-8, Tyrone 1-2
1891—Cavan 1-11, Armagh 0-0 (replay)
(Note: First game unfinished, disputed goal).
1892-1900—No Ulster championship
Cavan played in Leinster in 1895.
1900—Antrim were to have represented Ulster
but gave walk-over to Galway.
1901—Antrim 3-5, Armagh 2-5
1902—Armagh 2-2, Antrim 1-4
1903—Cavan 0-5, Armagh 0-5 (draw)
Cavan 0-5, Armagh 0-5 (replay)
Cavan 0-8, Armagh 0-4 (2nd replay)
1904—Cavan 0-7, Monaghan 0-4
1905—Cavan 0-7, Monaghan 0-3
1906—Monaghan 2-10, Antrim 1-2
1907—No Final result in records
1908—Antrim 1-8, Cavan 0-4
1909—Antrim 1-9, Cavan 0-5
1910—Antrim 3-4, Cavan 0-1
1911—Antrim 2-8, Cavan 0-4
1912—Antrim 2-2, Armagh 0-1
1913—Antrim 2-1, Monaghan 1-2
1914—Monaghan 2-4, Fermanagh 0-2
1915—Cavan 3-2, Monaghan 2-5 (draw)
Cavan 0-4, Monaghan 0-3 (replay)
1916—Monaghan 2-3, Antrim 0-2
1917—Monaghan 4-2, Armagh 0-4
1918—Cavan 3-2, Antrim 0-0
1919—Cavan 5-6, Antrim 0-2
1920—Cavan 4-6, Armagh 1-4
1921—Monaghan 2-2, Derry 0-1
1922—Cavan 2-3, Monaghan 2-3 (draw)
Cavan 3-4, Monaghan 3-3 (replay)
1923—Cavan 5-10, Monaghan 1-1
1924—Cavan 1-3, Monaghan 0-6 (draw)
Cavan 2-3, Monaghan 1-3 (replay)
1925—Cavan 2-3, Antrim 3-0 (draw)
Cavan 3-6, Antrim 0-1 1replay)
1926—Cavan 5-3, Antrim 0-6
1927—Monaghan 3-5, Armagh 2-5
1928—Cavan 2-6, Armagh 1-4
1929—Monaghan 1-4, Cavan 1-4 (draw)
Monaghan 1-10, Cavan 0-7 (replay)
1930—Monaghan 4-3, Cavan 1-5
1931—Cavan 0-8, Armagh 2-1
1932—Cavan 2-4, Armagh 0-2
1933—Cavan 6-13, Tyrone 1-2
1934—Cavan 3-8, Armagh 0-2
1935—Cavan 2-6, Fermanagh 2-1
1936—Cavan 1 -7, Monaghan 0-7
1937—Cavan 0-13, Armagh 0-3
1938—Monaghan 2-5, Armagh 2-2
1939—Cavan 2-3, Armagh 1-3 (first game
unfinished. Replay ordered)
Cavan 2-3, Armagh 1-4 (replay)
1940—Cavan 4-10, Down 1-5
1941—Cavan 3-9 Tyrone 0-5
1942—Cavan 5-11, Down 1-3
1943—Cavan 2-3, Monaghan 0-5

1944—Cavan 1-9, Monaghan 1-6
1945—Cavan 4-10, Fermanagh 1-4
1946—Antrim 2-8, Cavan 1-7
1947—Cavan 3-4, Antrim 1-6
1948—Cavan 2-12, Antrim 2-4
1949—Cavan 1-7, Armagh 1-6
1950—Armagh 1-11, Cavan 1-7
1951—Antrim 1-7, Cavan 2-3
1952—Cavan 1-8, Monaghan 0-8
1953—Armagh 1-6, Cavan 0-5
1954—Cavan 2-10, Armagh 2-5
1955—Cavan 0-11, Derry 0-8
1956—Tyrone 3-5, Cavan 0-4
1957—Tyrone 1-9, DerryO-10
1958—Derry 1-11, Down 2-4
1959—Down 2-16, Cavan 0-7
1960—Down 3-7, Cavan 1-8
1961—Down 2-10, Armagh 1-10
1962—Cavan 3-6, Down 0-5
1963—Down 2-11, Donegal 1-4
1964—Cavan 2-10, Down 1-10
1965—Down 3-5, Cavan 1-8
1966—Down 1-7, Donegal 0-8
1967—Cavan 2-12, Down 0-8
1968—Down 0-16, Cavan 1-8
1969—Cavan 2-13, Down 2-6
1970—Derry 2-13, Antrim 1-12
1971—Down 4-15, Derry 4-11
1972—Donegal 2-13, Tyrone 1-11
1973—Tyrone 3-13, Down 1-11
1974—Donegal 1-14, Down 2-11 (draw)
Donegal 3-9, Down 1-12 (replay)
1975—Derry 1-16, Down 2-6
1976—Derry 1-8, Cavan 1-8 (draw)
Derry 0-22, Cavan 1-16 (replay)
(after extra time)
1977—Armagh 3-10, Derry 1-5
1978—Down 2-19, Cavan 2-12
1979—Monaghan 1-15, Donegal 0-11
1980—Armagh 4-10, Tyrone 4-7
1981—Down 3-12, Armagh 1-10
1982—Armagh 0-10, Fermanagh 1-4
1983—Donegal 1-14,Cavan 1-11
1984—Tyrone 0-15, Armagh 1-7
1985—Monaghan 2-9, Derry 0-8
1986—Tyrone 1-11, Down 0-10
1987—Derry 0-11, Armagh 0-9
1988—Monaghan 1-10, Tyrone 0-11
1989—Tyrone 0-11, Donegal 0-11 (draw)
Tyrone 2-13, Donegal 0-7 (replay)
1990—Donegal 0-15, Armagh 0-14
1991—Down 1-15, Donegal 0-10
1992—Donegal 0-14, Derry 1-9
1993—Derry 0-8, Donegal 0-6
1994—Down 1-17, Tyrone 1-11
1995—Tyrone 2-13, Cavan 0-10
1996—Tyrone 1-9, Down 0-9
1997—Cavan 1-14, Derry 0-16
1998—Derry 1-7, Donegal 0-8
1999—Armagh 3-12, Down 0-10
2000—Armagh 1-12, Derry 1-11.
2001—Tyrone 1-13, Cavan 1-11.
2002—Armagh 1-14, Donegal 1-10.
2003—Tyrone 1-17, Down 4-8.
Tyrone 0-23, Down 1-5. (replay)
2004—Armagh 3-15, Donegal 0-11.
2005—Armagh 2-8, Tyrone 0-14.
Armagh 0-13, Tyrone 0-11. (replay)
2006—Armagh 1-9, Donegal 0-9.
2007—Tyrone 1-15, Monaghan 1-13.
2008—Armagh 2-8, Fermanagh 1-11.
Armagh 1-11, Fermanagh 0-8. (replay)
2009—Tyrone 1-18, Antrim 0-15.

ALL-IRELAND MINOR FOOTBALL FINALS

1929—Clare 5-3, Longford 3-5
1930—Dublin 1-3, Mayo 0-5
1931—Kerry 3-4, Louth 0-4
1932—Kerry 3-8, Laois 1-3
1933—Kerry 4-1, Mayo 0-9
1934—Tipperary awarded title.
Note: Dublin and Tyrone, the semi-finalists, were disqualified.
1935—Mayo 1-6, Tipperary 1-1
1936—Louth 5-1, Kerry 1-8
1937—Cavan 1-11, Wexford 1-5
1938—Cavan 3-3, Kerry 0-8
1939—Roscommon 1-9, Monaghan 1-7
1940—Louth 5-5, Mayo 2-7
1941—Roscommon 3 6, Louth 0-7
1942—No competition
1943—No competition
1944—No competition
1945—Dublin 4-7, Leitrim 0-4
1946—Kerry 3-7, Dublin 2-3
1947—Tyrone 4-4, Mayo 4-3
1948—Tyrone 0-11, Dublin 1-5
1949—Armagh 1-7, Kerry 1-5
1950—Kerry3-6, Wexford 1-4
1951—Roscommon 2-7, Armagh 1-5
1952—Galway 2-9, Cavan 1-6
1953—Mayo 2-11, Clare 1-6
1954—Dublin 3-3, Kerry 1-8
1955—Dublin 5-4, Tipperary 2-7
1956—Dublin 5-14, Leitrim 2-2
1957—Meath 3-9, Armagh 0-4
1958—Dublin 2- 10, Mayo 0-8
1959—Dublin 0-11, Cavan 1-4
1960—Galway 4-9, Cork 1-5
1961—Cork 3-7, Mayo 0-5.
1962—Kerry 6-5, Mayo 0-7
1963—Kerry 1-10, Westmeath 0-2
1964—Offaly 0-15, Cork 1-11
1965—Derry 2-8, Kerry 2-4
1966—Mayo 1-12, Down 1-8
1967—Cork 5-14, Laois 2-3
1968—Cork 3-5, Sligo 1-10
1969—Cork 2-7, Derry 0-11
1970—Galway 1-8, Kerry 2-5 (draw)
Galway 1-11, Kerry 1-10 (replay)
1971—Mayo 2-15, Cork 2-7
1972—Cork 3-11, Tyrone 2-11
1973—Tyrone 2-11, Kildare 1-6
1974—Cork 1-10, Mayo 1-6
1975—Kerry 1-10, Tyrone 0-4
1976—Galway 1-10, Cork 0-6
1977—Down 2-6, Meath 0-4
1978—Mayo 4-9, Dublin 3-8
1979—Dublin 0-10, Kerry 1-6
1980—Kerry 3-12, Derry 0-11

1981—Cork 4-9, Derry 2-7
1982—Dublin 1-11, Kerry 1-5
1983—Derry 0-8, Cork 1-3
1984—Dublin 1-9, Tipperary 0-4
1985—Mayo 3-3, Cork 0-9
1986—Galway 3-8, Cork 2-7
1987—Down 1-12, Cork 1-5
1988—Kerry 2-5, Dublin 0-5
1989—Derry 3-9, Offaly 1-6
1990—Meath 2-11, Kerry 2-9
1991—Cork 1-9, Mayo 1-7
1992—Meath 2-5, Armagh 0-10
1993—Cork 2-7, Meath 0-9
1994—Kerry 0-16, Galway 1-7
1995—Westmeath 1-10, Derry 0-11
1996—Laois 2-11, Kerry 1-11
1997—Laois 3-11, Tyrone 1-14
1998—Tyrone 2-11, Laois 0-11
1999—Down 1-14, Mayo 0-14
2000—Cork 2-12, Mayo 0-13.
2001—Tyrone 0-15, Dublin 1-12.
Tyrone 2-11, Dublin 0-6. (replay)
2002—Derry 1-12, Meath 0-8.
2003—Laois 1-11, Dublin 1-11.
Laois 2-10, Dublin 1-9. (replay)
2004—Tyrone 0-12, Kerry 0-10.
2005—Down 1-15, Mayo 0-8.
2006—Roscommon 0-15, Kerry 0-15.
Roscommon 1-10, Kerry 0-9. (replay)
2007—Galway 1-10, Derry 1-9.
2008—Tyrone 0-14, Mayo 0-14.
Tyrone 1-20, Mayo 1-15. (aet) (replay)
2009—Armagh 0-10, Mayo 0-7.

ALI-IRELAND MINOR FOOTBALL FINAL TEAMS (1929-2009)

1929
Clare—T. Crowe, J. O'Leary, G. Comerford, E. Kelly, J. McMahon, D. Twomey, J. Keane, L. Conlon, J. Morgan, J. Kilmartin, J. Lucey, P. Keane, P. Lucey, P. Stack, J. Brown.

Longford—B. Phipps, A. Vaughan, J. Mulvey, J. Lyons, J. Quinn, J. Sheridan, P. Keenan, P. Farrell, J. Barden, W. Clarke, T. McHale, P. McLoughlin, M. Barden, W. Farrell, J. Smith.

1930
Dublin—B. Synott, G. McLoughlin, T. Sharkey, K. Barry, S. O'Toole, T. Markham, T. Lawless, J. Scott, P. Diffney, W. Fallon, W. Bastow, B. Murphy, M. Grimes, J. Pearse, P. Castian, F. Williams, J. Brady, P. Crummey.

Note: Only Dublin panel of 18 listed in media but not the final 15.

Mayo—John O'Gara, C. Gannon, C. Ward, G. Ormsby, C. McHale, John Acton, J. O'Donoghue, M. Flannery, C. O'Boyle, Jas. McGowan, T. Burke, W. Dever, P. McGoff, B. Scanlon, Martin O'Connor.

1931
Kerry—B. Reidy, F. O'Neill, P. Walsh, E. Mahony, D. J. McCarthy, J. O'Keeffe, T. O'Sullivan, J. O'Gorman, P. McMahon, T. Murphy, P. O'Sullivan, M. Buckley, T. Chute, C. O'Sullivan, B. Healy.

Louth—P. McDonnell, J. Tiernan, J. Hearty, J. Beirne, L. Dyas, G. Marley, J. Kelly, J. Caffrey, K. McArdle, P. Collier, Fearon, A. Dempsey, G. Watters, J. Harlin, A. Bradley.

1932
Kerry—B. Reidy, F. O'Neill, E. Healy, J. P. Doyle, P. McMahon, P. Ronan, S. McCarthy, J. O'Sullivan, T. Weir, P. McMahon (Listowel), T. Wrenn, P. Ferriter, M. Brosnan, T. Leary, C. O'Sullivan. Sub: P. Lawlor.

Laois—E. Roche, J. Hinchion, M. Hyland, W. Troy, J. Nolan, M. Fanning, S. Shortt, S. Harkins, M. McGough, W. Delaney, J. J. Delaney, J. J. Reilly, S. Meehan, M. Cahill, T. Kehoe.

1933
Kerry—B. Reidy, M. O'Gorman, M. McCarthy, L. Crowley, S. Sullivan, W. Myers, T. O'Leary, W. Dillon, S. Brosnan, E. Buckley, B. Cronin, D. Griffin, W. Fitzgibbon, P. Kennedy, J. Counihan.

Mayo—W. McHale, Joe Murphy, J. O'Neill, J. O'Donoghue, B. Duggan, J. Munnelly, J. Wright, P. Murphy, W. Mongey, M. Gallagher, J. Bracken, R. Winters, J. J. Kilroy, T Hoban, M. Griffin.

1934
Tipperary—A. Greensmith, J. O'Connor, W. Power, M. Byrne, H. O'Donnell, J. Hickey, M. Lawlor, H. McGrath, T. Kenny, C. Dillon, M. Gavin, J. Maher, M. Power, P. Blanchfield, B. Kissane.

No final. DUBLIN/TYRONE disqualified for illegalities. Tipperary beat Mayo 4-9 to 2-5 in semi-final.

1935
Mayo—T. Hannon, P. J. Irwin, D. Egan, M. J. Kearney, D. McNamara, W. Durkin, P. O'Malley, P. J. Judge, J. Galvin, J. McLoughlin, P. J. Roche, M. O'Malley, P. McNicholls, J. Keane, P. Quinn.

Tipperary—M. Gavin, E. O'Meara, W. Treacy, H. Greensmith, E. Smith, P. Quinn, M. Flynn, W. McCarthy, P. Dillon, J. Hickey, P. Rafferty, T. Kenny, W. Hennessy, W. O'Donoghue, W. Power.

1936
Louth—F. Rock, A. Lynn, P. Tuite, B. O'Dowda, L. Byrne, M. Cunningham, L. McEntee, L. Waller, J. O'Reilly, G. Hall, E. McGrath, D. Brady, K. O'DowHa, J. Cunningham, M. McArdle.

Kerry—G. Teahan, P. Dowling, P. Kennedy, T. Healy, J. Keohane, S. O'Sullivan, T. Lyne, T. O'Connor, D.J. Healy, T. O'Sullivan, P. Breen, P. Sexton, B. Scannell, T. Brosnan, W. Casey.

1937
Cavan—J. J. Brady, M. Argue, B. Cully, T. Cully, P. Clarke, M. O'Reilly, T. P. O'Reilly, P. O'Reilly, D. Brady, P. Conaty, H. Bouchier, P. McDonnell, J. McCormack, M. Farrell, P. Fay.

Wexford—M. Kehoe, J. Dwyer, M. Butler, H. Kenny, D. Hall, T. Hurley, J. Morris, J. Murphy, P. Foley, P. Dunbar, T. Redmond, W. Howlin, J. Williams, S. Roice, S. Thorpe.

1938
Cavan—J. D. Benson, W. Doonan, B. Cully, P. P. Galligan, M. Reilly, P. Coyle, S. Deignan, J. Maguire, J. McCormack, K. O'Reilly, P. Conaty, M. Fitzsimons, F. Coyle, J. Johnson, P. Doyle.

Kerry—P. O'Brien, P. Burke, E. Dunne, T. Long, P. O'Donnell, M. Farrell, D. Kavanagh, T. O'Connor, T. Flavin, D. Rice, M. O'Shea, J. Bailey, T. Lyne, P. Fitzgerald, M. Kennedy.

1939
Roscommon—S. Naughton, L. Cummins, W. Carlos, D. Boyd, T. Cox, L. Gilmartin, A. Murray, T. Lynch (Oran), S. Lavin, C. O'Beirne, J. Tiernan, J. McDermott, J. Bambrick, G. Kilduff, H. Winston. Sub: W. Penny for H. Winston.

Monaghan—P. Farrell, D. Hughes, Phil Donoghue, D. Marron, J. McGeogh, O. King, V. Flanagan, P. Ruttledge, D. Rice, F. McCormack, J. McGeogh, P. McCarney, J. Woods, P. McKenna, J. McHugh.

1940
Louth—C. Brown, B. Breen, B. Burke, M. Flanagan, B. Fretwell, E. Reay, O. Mohan, L. Murphy, P. J. Kelly, A. Cahill, S. McGivern, P. Corr, P. McCourt, J. Kiernan, G. Brennan.

Mayo—A. Breslin, M. Galvin, C. Long, J. McLaughlin, T. Acton, F. Mongey, S. Durkin, M. Langan, J. Forkin, J. Ralph, J. J. McGowan, A. McNally, J. Jennings, T. Byrne, D. Loughrey. Sub: P. Browne.

1941
Roscommon—G. Dolan, T. F. Bannon, T. J. Lynch (Boyle), L. Kelly, P. Donnelly, B. Lynch, P. Hoare, W. Carlos, E. Curran, B. O'Gara, P. Duignan, B. O'Rourke, C. Murray, G. Kilduff, P. Hannelly.

Louth—J. Allen, J. P. Grist, J. Mulligan, W. Pigott, J. Larkin, M. O'Grady, J. Clarke, B. O'Dowda, P. McCourt, P. Corr, J. MacArtain, A. Cahill, E. Boyle, M. Hardy, J. O'Reilly. Sub: P. Kelly.

1945
Dublin—C. Feeney, D. O'Mahony, J. Sharry, G. Jennings, N. Maher, D. Healy, T. Nolan, S. McEntaggert, S. Guinea, L. Donnelly, O. Freaney, J. Nugent, J. Copeland, P. McCarthy, C. Dignam.

Leitrim—P. Heeran, T. P. Reynolds, J. Bohan, M. Dolan, J. Brennan, S. Mulvey, T. Cryan, J. Heslin, R. O'Beirne, P. Dolan, M. Fallon, B. McTiernan, M. J. McKeon, K. Herity, C. Cassidy. Sub: F. Canning.

1946
Kerry—J. Ryan, S. McCarthy, B. O'Sullivan, D. Murphy, S. O'Sullivan, D. Sheehan, J. Fenton, T. Moriarty, T. Ashe, M. Lynch, D. O'Regan, P. O'Sullivan, J. O'Brien, J. Madden, P. Godley.

Dublin—C. Feeney, D. Mahony, P. Lawlor, P. Cloonan, J. Butler, J. Lavin, B. Clancy, N. Fingleton, N. Maher, L. Donnelly, O. Freaney, D. Stanley, K. Heffernan, A. Clohessy, C. Mehigan. Subs: P. Bates for P. Cloonan, T. Mulligan for Mahony.

1947
Tyrone—M. Bradley, L. Campbell, R. McNulty, V. Cullen, M. Vaughan, E. Devlin, M. Cushenan, S. McGrath, J. Poyntz, H. Hartop, M. Dargan, J. McConnell, D. McCafferty, T. Sullivan, P Donnelly

Mayo—A. O'Toole, M. Kinnane, P. Flanagan, M. Jordan, A. McMorris, P. Doherty, N. Keane, M. McDonnell, T. Walsh, M. Loughnane, P. Carroll, C. McHale, L. Flynn, P. Solan, M. O'Connell.

1948
Tyrone—J. McGahern, D. Donnelly, Mal Connolly, E. Knox, Louis Campbell, E. Devlin, P. O'Hanlon, S. McGrath, H. Hartop, J. O'Reilly, M. Dargan, B. Eastwood, Leo Devlin, J. J. O'Hagan, J. Twomey. Sub: S. Donnelly.

Dublin—P. King, P. Connolly, K. Lougheed, G. Brogan, W. Fleming, S. Page, P. McGahan, T. Jennings, C. Freaney, B. Conboy, D. Ferguson, J. Kelly, P. Ryan, D. Carney, B. Redmond. Sub: J. Guidon.

1949
Armagh—L. McCorry, E. McCann, J. Bratton, J. McKnight, F. Kernan, B. O'Neill, T. McConville, E. Mee, S. Collins, T. Connolly, S. Blaney, J. Cunningham, S. Smith, P. J. McKeever B. McGrane. Sub: M. McKnight for S. Collins.

Kerry—J. Foley, J. O'Shea, P. Colgan, M. Galway, M. Kerins, J. Moriarty, P. Costello, S. Murphy, D. Falvey, P. Coleman, P. O'Donnell, P. Sheehy, B. Galvin, C. Kennelly, R. Miller.

1950
Kerry—D. O'Neill, M. Galway, M. Brosnan, J. Collins, T. Murphy, P. O'Donnell, J. Kerins, S. Murphy, P. Sheehy, R. Millar, C. Kennelly, C. O'Riordan, B. Galvin, T. Lawlor, P. Fitzgerald.

Wexford—T. O'Sullivan, M. O'Donoghue, R. McCabe, M. Hyde, M. Culliton, A. Doyle, J. Synott, P. O'Kennedy, B. McGuinness, W. Bennett, L. Larkin, P. Sheehan, J. O'Sullivan, P. Jordan'J. Doran.

1951
Roscommon—P Muldoon, O. Murray, J. Lynch, E. O'Connor, B. Molloy, T. Finnegan, G. Healy, H. Connolly, J. Rafferty, J. O'Brien, J. Campbell, E. Duignan, L. Duffy, M. Shivnan, H. Penny. Sub: M. Kelly for E. Duignan.

Armagh—G. Murphy, G. Donnelly, B. Seeley, P. Moore, D. Skelton, E. Quinn, M. Grimley, B. O'Neill, S. McCresh, A. Dilllon, S. Hanratty, S. Crossey, P. Kierans, P. McArdle, D. McCorry. Sub. S. McMahon for A. Dillon.

1952

Galway—M. Ryan, B. Naughton, S. Kyne, S. Hoban, M. Lohan, E. Dunleavy, M. Hawkshaw, M. Kelly, B. Mahon, T. Brosnan, S. Mitchell, L. Manning, B. Waldron, G. Kirwan, M. Geraghty.

Cavan—S. Frawley, P. O'Hare, S. Farrelly, P. A. Farrell, D. Kelly, B. Brady, S. Keoghan, T. Maguire, G. Keyes, S. Farrelly, G. Smythe, V. Blythe, G. Fitzpatrick, M. McKenna, S. McDonnell.

1953

Mayo—S. Stewart, P. Gavin, S. Veldon, F. Fahy, W Joyce, J. Jennings, B. Keane, D. Keane, M. Stewart, E. Neilan, T. Treacy, V. Blyth, V. Kilcullen, C. McDonnell, E. Walsh. Sub: M. Tuohy for J. Jennings.

Clare—M. Garry, J. Carmody, T. Griffin, D. Fitzgerald, J. Power, T. Mangan, S. Barrett, P. O'Dea, M. Greene, P. Griffin, F. Cassidy, J. Drury, T. Flynn, C. Comer, M. McGrath. Sub: P. Daly for M. Greene.

1954

Dublin—R. Brady, M. Bohan, B. O'Boyle, D. Sweeney, T. Bracken, N. Boylan, M. Cronin, B. McLaughlin, P. Heron, V. Bell, P. Farnan, A. Kavanagh, G. O'Reilly, P. Feeney, D. Waters. Subs: E. Gilbert for P. Farnan, V. Lyons G. O'Reilly.

Kerry—M. Cournane, T. Barrett, J. Dowling, L. Cloghlan, B. Kennelly, P. Shea, F. O'Leary, T. Long, J. Foley, T. O'Dowd J. Cullotty, F. Lynch, T. Garvey, B. Sheehy, G. White. Sub: T. Foley for G. White.

1955

Dublin—S. Denigan, V. Murphy, D. Sweeney, D. Hearns, R. Doherty, S. Graham, C. Jones, P. Heron, L. Foley, E. Burgess, S. Linehan, C. McSweeney, J. Joyce, G. Wolfe, C. Leaney. Sub: L. Boyle for G. Wolfe.

Tipperary—S. Ryan, G. King, S. Condon, P. Burke, S. Connolly, T. Walsh, D. Stapleton, P. Tobin, L. Boland, A. Danagher, E. Casey, M. Moroney, M. Ryan, S. Ferris, S. Brennan. Sub: P. Nolan for S. Ryan.

1956

Dublin—D. Creed, A. Talbot, P. Lacey, D. Hearns, R. Doherty, D. Cashel, V. Kavanagh, L. Foley, S. Lenihan, J. Brogan, D. Foley, N. Fox, R. McCrea, G. Wolfe, C. Leaney. Sub: P. Dennis for G. Wolfe.

Leitrim—L. Feehily, S. Bredin, T. Fallon, P. McGloin, W. McWeeney, P. McGowan, S. Fallon, P. Heslin, J. Murray, L. Foran, J. O'Donnell, P. Dolan, P. McIntyre, F. Canning, P. Conboy. Sub: J. Clyne for S. Fallon.

1957

Meath—P. J. O'Reilly, T. Gibney, J. Kelleher, B. Cunningham, J. Fagan, T. Fitzsimons, M. Clerkin, J. Halpin, S. Clinch, P. Hanley, J. Grey, B. Cahill, T. Monaghan, M. Greville, L. Drumm.

Armagh—J. Finnegan, S. McConville, A. Bennett, B. Connolly, F. Toal, B. Donaghy, A. Casey, O. Agnew, R. Dowds, S. Mallon, S. Murphy, H. Loughran, B. McGeary, K. Halpenny, S. Toner. Subs: N. Greene for O. Agnew, C. McNiece for F. Toal.

1958

Dublin—K. Donnelly, N. Joyce, P. Holden, D. Mulligan, D. Jones, A. Whelan, M. Kissane, D. Foley, A. O'Reilly, P. Taylor, N. Fox, B. McDonald, J. Sweeney, J. Gilroy, B. Beggs. Sub: S. Behan for P. Taylor.

Mayo—K. Doherty, M. O'Boyle, M. Sweeney, M. Tighe, J. Rowe, L. Doherty, C. Maguire, T. Rochford, J. Rowe, J. Corcoran, T. Gibbons, J. Cosgrove, M. Lyons, J. Langan, P. Sheridan. Subs: A. O'Connell for M. Lyons, P. Griffin for J. Cosgrove.

1959

Dublin—P. Talbot, E. Grainger, A. Doran, F. McCourt, M. Campion, M. Kissane, F. Byrne, S. Behan, J. Levins, P. Delaney, B. McDonald, J. Dowling, J. McKettrick, G. McCabe, S. Coen. Subs: B. Cooney for T. McKettrick, P. Taylor for S. Behan.

Cavan—S. Boyle, F. Cafferty, F. McKiernan, F. O'Reilly, P. Flood, T. Morris, F. Kennedy, B. Morris, D. McCluskey, B. Sherlock, D. Brady, K. Blessing, L. McCluskey, K. McCormack, P. Murray. Subs: T. McKiernan for D. McCluskey, G. O'Reilly for L. McCluskey, L. McCluskey for G. O'Reilly.

1960

Galway—M. King, G. Lohan, N. Tierney, L. O'Brien, E. Colleran, A. Ryan, J. Smith, H. Anderson, S. Cleary, C. Tyrrell, G. Prendergast, S. Leydon, J. Gavin, E. Slattery, A. Donnelly.

Cork—T. Hegarty, J. Burke, J. McGrath, V. Cronin, P. Pyne, E. O'Connor, G. Harrington, M. O'Brien, P. Curley, J. Travers, B. Coughlan, B. Larkin, T. Burke, D. Moynihan, L. O'Hanrahan. Subs: D. Buckley for P. Pyne, D. Nangle for J. McGrath.

1961

Cork—R. Cawley, D. Nangle, J. McGrath, V. Cronin, G. Harrington, B. Larkin, J. O'Donoghue, F. Cogan, E. Coughlan, F. Hayes, D. Barrett, D. Philpott, T. Burke, M. Archer, T. Monaghan.

Mayo—H. O'Brien, C. Hanley, B. Reape, S. Murphy, E. Carroll, G. Nicholson, V. Nally, J. Langan, J. Madden, D. McSweeney, M. Connaughton, P. J. McLoughlin, J. Nealon, E. Maguire, J. Warde. Subs: D. Carroll for G. Nicholson, M. O'Malley for D. McSweeney.

1962

Kerry—S. Fitzgerald, D. Lovett, C. O'Connor, S. Burrowes, T. Fitzgerald, P. O'Donoghue, A. Burrowes, D. O'Sullivan, T. Doyle, S. O'Mahony, A. Barrett, D. O'Shea, S. Flavin, R. O'Donnell, T. Mulvihill. Subs: S. Corridon for T. Doyle, T. Kenneally for T. Mulvihill.

Mayo—L. McEllin, A. Brett, J. Early, D. O'Leary, N. Golden, M. Brennan, E. Carroll, M. Connaughton, M. O'Malley, F. McDonald, P. Costello, C. Dolan, N. Maguire, D. McSweeney, J. J. Cribben. Sub: T. Staunton for L. McEllin.

1963

Kerry—S. Fitzgerald, A. Behan, J. McCarthy, S. Burrowes, T. O'Shea, B. Burrowes, C. O'Riordan, D. O'Sullivan, G. Curran, T. O'Hanlon, A. Spring, J. Saunders, T. Kelleher, H. McKinney, C. Donnelly. Subs: M. O'Sullivan, S. O'Shea.

Westmeath—K. Higgins, B. Glynn, P. Malone, T. King, J. Murray, P. Bradley, R. Cornally, G. Frawley, R. Niland, P. Buckley, F. Connaughton, C. Kelly, J. V. Costello, K. Coffey, M. Fagan. Subs: T. Reeves, D. Hamm.

1964

Offaly—M. Furlong, S. Coughlan, J. Smith, M. Ryan, E. Mulligan, S. Grogan, L. Duffy, O. Kilmurray, F. Greene, W. Bryan, A. McTague, J. Gunning, E. Kennedy, D. Mcinlyre, M. Byrne. Sub: M. O'Rourke for W. Bryan.

Cork—T. Murphy, R. Kelly, J. Cawley, P. Lyne, B. O'Brien, N O'Donovan, Colman McCarthy, J. Cogan, J. Downing, E. Philpott, T. F. Hayes, C. Roche, B. O'Leary, L. McAuliffe, Charlie McCarthy. Sub: D. Bermingham for Charlie McCarthy.

1965

Derry—E. McCaul, A. Burke, T. Quinn, M. Kelly, C. Mullen, M. McAfee, A. McGuckian, T. Diamond, S. Lagan, B. Mullen, M. Niblock, E. Coleman, S. Kearney, S. McCluskey, P. Friel.

Kerry—B. Lynch, J. O'Sullivan, J. Coughlan, T. Crean, P. O'Donovan, M. Aherne, P. Scanlon, P. O'Connell, F. Moroney, R. Geaney, D. Moriarty, B. McCarthy, K. Griffin, G. O'Donnell, T. Kelleher. Sub: S. O'Connor for T. Crean.

1966

Mayo—E. Rooney, S. Hughes, T. Snee, B. Meenehan, G. Nevin, T. Cafferkey, B. McHale, S. O'Dowd, A. Joyce, J. Timoney, T. Fitzgerald, D. Griffith, P. Glavey, J. Smyth, A. Kelly. Sub: S. Kilbride for P. Glavey.

Down—J. Harte, S. Brennan, L. Sloan, H. Smith, B. Sloan, C. McAlarney, D. Curran, J. Murphy, D. Mooney, J. Purdy, N. Millar, M. Cole. M. Lavery, P. Rooney, J. Morgan. Sub: H. McGrath for N. Millar, N. Millar for M. Cole.

1967

Cork—M. Cotter, S. Looney, Ted Murphy, J. Fahy, Der Cogan, S. Murphy, K. Kehilly, Donal Aherne, D. Long, Jerry Horgan, D. Hunt, J. Barrett, D. Morley, N. Kirby, Ted O'Brien. Sub: David Aherne for S. Looney.

Laois—A. Burke, M. Murphy, P. Fingleton, J. Mangan, J. Kavanagh, W. Monaghan, C. Murphy, S. Fleming, I. Houlihan, S. Furey, R. Millar, S. Allen, E. Condron, J. Lawlor, T. Keane. Sub. C. McEvoy for C. Murphy.

1968

Cork—D. O'Mahony, Jerry Coleman, F. Cronin, S. Looney, D. Cogan, R. O'Sullivan, C. Hartnett, Donal Aherne, Barry Murphy, Tony Murphy, John Coleman, H. O'Sullivan, F. Twomey, M. O'Doherty, B. Cummins. Sub: D. McCarthy for H. O'Sullivan.

Sligo—P. McLoughlin, R. Lipsett, J. Brennan, N. Kellegher, J. Kilgallon, J. Gilmartin, K. Conway, G. Hegarty, A. Richardson, D. Kerins, R. Henry, H. Quinn, R. Sherlock, R. Boland, P. Kearins. Sub. J. Kilgallon for R. Sherlock.

1969

Cork—B. O'Brien, P. Barry, G. B. O'Sullivan, D. Moloney, Brian Murphy, M. O'Doherty, C. Hartnett, E. Hallinan, J. Coleman, D. Curran, E. Fitzparick, H. O'Sullivan, J. Courtney, D. Barron, P. Lonergan.

Derry—K. McGahon, P. Burke, L. Murphy, P. McGuckian, B. Kearney, M. Moran, R. Hasson, E. Laverty, H. McGoldrick, S. Mullan, B. Ward, T. McWilliams, M. O'Neill, S. McGeehan, G. O'Neill. Subs: M. Bradley for T. McWilliams, S. Coyle for E. Lavery.

1970

Galway—J. Higgins, S. Cloonan, A. Marren, J. Kemple, P. J. Burke, M. Geraghty, J. Corcoran, T. O'Connor, P. Silke, I. Barrett, M. Rooney, J. Lardner, M. Burke, S. Meehan, J. Tobin. Sub: M. Walsh who played in drawn game for S. Meehon. S. Meehan came on as sub in drawn game for M. Walsh.

Kerry—P. O'Mahony, B. O'Shea, S. Clifford, J. Deenihan, D. Healy, M. O'Sullivan, G. O'Keeffe, P. Lynch, J. Long, C. O'Connell, J. Egan, G. Power, P. B. Brosnan, S. Fitzgerald, A. Moore. Subs: M. O'Connor for D. Healy, R. Casey for G. O'Keeffe. T. McEllistrim and A. Moore came on as subs in drawn game. S. Fitzgerald and A. Moore were on for replay. J. Murphy and G. Dillon played in drawn game.

1971

Mayo—M. Griffin, J. O'Mahony, S. Reilly, A. Durkan, G. Feeney, C. Moynihan, J. Culkin, J. Quinn, R. McNicholas, M. Gannon, J. P. Kean, M. Higgins, G. Farragher, F. Harty, M. Maloney. Sub: M. Fahy for J. Quinn.

Cork—G. Stanton, K. Collins, J. O'Shea, K. Murphy, M. Corbett, C. Kelleher, R. Wilmot, J. Lynch, S. Fitzgerald, D. Crowley, S. Coughlan, S. Murphy, D. Philpott, J. Barry Murphy, A. Fahy. Subs: V. Twomey for S. Fitzgerald, D. O'Sullivan for R. Wilmot, G. Aherne for S. Murphy.

1972

Cork—T. O'Sullivan, D. Keohane, Conor Barrett, T. Creedon, S. O'Farrell, S. O'Sullivan, R. Wilmot, K. Murphy, K. Collins, L. Gould, D. O'Hare, G. Aherne, Liam Good, J. Barry Murphy, S. O'Shea. Sub: B. Og Murphy for S. O'Shea.

Tyrone—P. Kerlin, G. Goodwin, H. Mooney, D. Daly, P. O'Neill, C. McAleer, J. Doherty, F. McGuigan,

D. McKenna, M. Quinn, J. Hughes, B. O'Neill, T. Campbell, M. Harte, P. Quinn. Subs: D. Kennedy for T. Campbell, M. Coyle for P. Quinn.

1973

Tyrone—B. Campbell, G. Goodwin, M. Lennon, H. Mooney S. Gormley, C. McAleer, J. O'Doherty, P. Kerlin, D. McKenna S. O'Kane, E. McKenna, J. Cunningham, M. Quinn, B. O'Neill, K. Currie. Sub: S. Coyne for K. Currie.

Kildare—A. Dunne, J. Clancy, J. Grehan, S. Ryan, J. Jacob, P. Archibald, T. Browne, N. Fennelly, P. Winders, P. Mulhearn, J. Geoghegan, J. Delaney, E. Delahunt, N. Fahy, B. Whelan. Subs: P. Lyons, J. Dooley.

1974

Cork—F. Delaney, W. Lynch, J. Slattery, E. Desmond, B. Twomey, J. Crowley, T. Cashman, D. Good, R. Kenny, Declan Murphy, Diarmuid McCarthy, Don McCarthy, G. O'Sullivan, M. O'Regan, T. Murphy. Subs: M. Carey for J. Crowley, D. McCurtain for Don McCarthy, W. O'Driscoll for R. Kenny.

Mayo—J. Cuddy, S. Sweeney, D. Conway, J. Gallagher, E. Brett, V. Ryan, J. Brennan, P. Mohan, W. Nally, K. Geraghty, M. Burke, S. Moran, G. Hennigan, J. Burke, M. Mannion. Subs: J. Nally for S. Sweeney, G. Reilly for G. Hennigan, M. McCormack for M. Mannion.

1975

Kerry—C. Nelligan, V. O'Connor, M. O'Sullivan, M. Colgan, J. J. O'Connor, M. Spillane, G. Casey, S. Walsh, N. O'Donovan, F. Scannell, J. Mulvihill, R. Bunyan, C. O'Connor J. O'Shea, P. Sheehan.

Tyrone—A. Skelton, B. Campbell, K. McGarvey P. McCallan, P. J. Trainor, K. McCabe, J. J. Campbell, T. O'Rourke, G. McCallan, P. Teague, M. McCoy, P. Donnelly, D O'Hagan, M. McAnneny, S. Daly. Subs: S. Donnelly for T. O'Rourke, E. McCann for S. Daly.

1976

Galway—P. Coyne, M. Coleman, O. Burke, C. Ó Fatharta, J. Kelly, R. Bermingham, G. Forde, G. Burke, L. Higgins, B. Brennan, S. Ruane, P. Conroy, K. O'Sullivan, G. McManus, F. Rooney. Sub: K. Donnellan for B. Brennan.

Cork—S. Martin, T. Healy, J. Murphy, M. Moloney, D. Buckley, J. Cremin, J. Nolan, P. McCarthy, B. McSweeney, T. Dalton, M. Mullins, P. Smith, K. O'Leary, G. Mulcahy, J. O'Sullivan. Subs: M. Shinnick for K. O'Leary, J. Wilmot for T. Dalton.

1977

Down—P. Donnan, S. McNulty, A. McAulfield, Seán Brunker, P. O'Rourke, M. Sands, B. McGovern, John McCartan, P. Kennedy, E. Toner, A. Rogers, M. McCann, T. Bradley, B. Loughran, J. Digney. Subs: E. McGivern for T. Bradley, F. Rooney for B. McGovern.

Meath—M. McQuillan, L. Harnan, B. Cullen, C. O'Reilly, G. Gough, C. Brazil, M. Sheilds, A. Tormey, J. Butler, G. Cooney, N. O'Sullivan, P. Finnerty, J. McCluskey, F. O'Sullivan, B. Reddy. Sub: J. Tallon.

1978

Mayo—S. Warde, M. Maloney, G. Golden, M. Walsh, N. Heffernan, A. Garvey, E. Melvin, M. Joyce, T. J. Kilgallon, S. Clarke, J. Maughan, A. McNicholas, K. O'Malley, J. Lyons, E. Griffin. Subs: L. Lyons for S. Clarke, T. Byrne for J. Lyons, C. Gilmartin for M. Maloney.

Dublin—P. O'Toole, F. Walsh, P. Canavan, C. Finnegan, K. Byrne, S. Fleming, T. Mannion, J. Kelly, A. White, C. Duff, M. Loftus, C. Griffin, N. Gaffney, B. Rock, K. Barry. Sub: D. Deasy for J. Kelly.

1979

Dublin—J. O'Leary, J. Grace, V. Conroy, S. Wade, C. Eustace, C. Finnegan, Derek Murphy, B. Kavanagh, P. Boylan, B. Jordan, M. LoRus, C. Duff, Dermot Murphy, B. Rock, K. Barry. Subs: T. Kelly for J. Grace, P. McCabe Derek Murphy.

Kerry—N. Cronin, S. Keane, B. Lavin, C. Bambury, D. Keane, P. Sheehan, A. Shannon, A. O'Donovan, T. Dee, J. Chute, L. Kearns, D. Kennelly, W. O'Connor, T. Spillane, G. O'Donnell.

1980

Kerry—R. O'Brien, D. Keane, M. Crowley, M. Counihan, J. O'Sullivan, T. SheeLy, J. T. O'Sullivan, P. O'Donoghue, A. O'Donovan, T. Dee, J. Shannon, L. Kearns, T. Parker, W. Maher, M. McAuliffe. Sub: T. Spillane for L. Kearns.

Derry—J. Mackle, B. McNabb, M. O'Brien, M. Tully, M. Convery, O. McKee, D. McCluskey, D. Barton, D. O'Kane, L. McElhinny, B. McErlean, J. McErlean, P. McKiernan, T. McGuckian, R. McCusker. Subs: M. Bradley for M. O'Brien, D. McNicholl for T. McGuckian.

1981

Cork—M. Maguire, D. O'Brien, J. Murphy, N. Cahalane, C. Hannon, V. Hedderman, A. Davis, A. Leahy, T. Mannix, Tony O'Sullivan, E. O'Mahony, P. Fitzgerald, P. Healy, C. O'Neill, J. Cleary. Sub: T. Cole for T. Mannix.

Derry—L. Peoples, B. McNabb, K. Rafferty, E. Reilly, C. Kelly, B. McPeake, M. Tully, L. McElhinny, M. Bradley, Eunan Rafferty, D. O'Kane, T. McGuckian, Dermot McNicholl, J. McErlean, J. A. Mullen. Subs: J. McGrath for B. McNabb, P. McCormack for M. Bradley.

1982

Dublin—J. McNally, C. Sage, F. McGrath, L. O'Rourke, E. Heary, T. Delaney, M. Deegan, D. Sheehan, B. Cooke, M. Coffey, M. Egan, S. O'Brien, P. O'Carroll, T. McCormack, B. Redmond. Sub: T. Murphy for T. McCormack.

Kerry—D. O'Neill, D. Cremin, J. Keane, J. O'Connell, J. Moriarty, J. O'Donnell, J. Rice, T. Brosnan, S. Wight, D. O'Donoghue, M. Keating, P. Galvin, B. Keane, E. Fitzgerald, M. McAuliffe. Subs: P. J. O'Leary for P. Galvin, T. O'Connor for J. Keane, E. Marey for J. O'Connell.

1983

Derry—D. Kelly, P. O'Donnell, P. Bradley, J. McGurk, R. Conway, B. Kealy, N. Mullon, P. Young, C. Barton, C. McNicholl, D. McNicholl, E. McElhinny, E. Lynch, D. Cassidy, Tony McKiernan.

Cork—R. Duffy, M. Maguire, T. Minihane, K. Scanlon, M. Slocum, B. Searles, J. Moynihan, B. Coffey, B. Stack, M. McCarthy, Teddy McCarthy, D. Kennedy, J. Cashman, M. Kelleher; P. Harrington. Subs: I. Breen for J. Cashman, E. Kenneally for D. Kennedy, T. Power for P. Harrington.

1984

Dublin—M. Broderick, G. Walsh, J. Barry, Ciaran Walsh, A. Martin, J. Power, B. McKeon, J. Stynes, P. Clarke, D. de Lappe, A. McClean, J. Fahy, N. Clancy, M. Crowley, C. Crowley. Subs.: P. Daly for C. Walsh, D. Whelan for A. McClean.

Tipperary—G. Enright, D. Walsh, R. Quirke, D. Williams, J. Owens, F. Howlin, M. Holland, B. Burke, G. Ryan, M. Goonan, J. O'Meara, K. Farrelly, T. Sheehan, A. Crosse, S. Brett. Subs.: D. Pyke for K. Farrelly, J. Hackett for S. Brett.

1985

Mayo—J. Cummins, K. Beirne, E. Gilvarry, M. Coyle, D. Burke, D. Fitzgerald, J. French, M. Fitzmaurice, G. Maher, Tony Munnelly, P. Walsh, T. O'Grady, P. Kerrane, M. J. Mullen, J. Gallagher. Sub: M. MullagLy for Tony Munnelly.

Cork—J. O'Mahony, M. Murphy, D. Duggan, J. Allen, N. Creedon, B. Murphy, T. Griffin, K. Kiely, J. O'Driscoll, B. Harte, D. O'Connell, G. O'Regan, P Cahill, P. Collins, R. Sheehan. Sub: K. Nagle for R. Sheehan.

1986

Galway—A. Brennan, B. Silke, F. McWalter, G. Farrell, P. Fallon, A. Mulholland, M. Tarpey, J. Joyce, K. Walsh, T. Kilcommins, F. O'Neill, M. McDonagh, T. Mannion, P. Maher, T. Finnerty. Subs.: B. Walsh for B. Silke, N. Costelloe for T. Kilcommins, J. Mitchell for M. McDonagh.

Cork—P. Hayes S. O'Brien M. O'Connor S. O'Rourke, N. Murphy, M. Crowley, D. Burke, F. Corrigan, G. Lally, P. Davis, M. Mullins, P. Coleman, N. Twomey, D. Larkin, I. Aherne. Subs.: M. Farr for S. O'Rourke, R. Sheehan for G. Lally.

1987

Down—D. Hawkins, N. Caulfield, L. Duggan, M. McGivern, M. Quinn, C. Deegan, C. Mason, B. McCartan, P. Hannaway, C. Murray, R. Haughean, G. Breen, R. Fitzpatrick, T. Fagan, J. McCartan.

Cork—J. J. Sweeney, D. O'Callaghan, B. Cooney, M. Lyons, S. Coughlan, S. O'Brien, D. Burke, L. Honohan, S. Dineen, G. McPolin, M. Burke, D. Davis, J. J. Barrett, D. O'Sullivan, N. Twomey. Subs: F. Fitzgerald for G. McPolin, J. Corcoran for L. Honohan, S. Calnan for D. O'Sullivan.

1988

Kerry—P. O'Leary, P. Lenihan, N. Savage, J. B. O'Brien, L. Flaherty, V. Knightly, S. Walsh, E. Stack. F. Ashe, P. Laide, D. Cahill, S. O'Sullivan, C. Geaney, D. Farrell, B. O'Sullivan. Sub: F. Doherty for D. Farrell.

Dublin—D. O'Farrell, P. McManus, J. Jordan, C. Kavanagh, T. O'Boyle, B. Murray, G. O'Regan, D. Quinlivan, P. Cassells, D. Howard, B. Stynes, T. Keogh, D. Farrell, S. Moylan, B. Barnes. Subs: S. Cahill for Cassells, T. Gavigan for O'Boyle.

1989

Derry—M. O'Connor, J. Martin, P. McAllister, G. Simpson, B. McGonigle, G. Coleman, R. Skelly, J. Mulholland, A. Tohill, R. McEldowney, J. Lynn, E. Burns, E. O'Kane, D. Heaney, D. Boteson. Subs: K. Diamond for Martin, R. Murphy for Lynn J. O'Connor for E. O'Kane.

Offaly—D. Scully, K. Flynn, C. Maher, P. Dunne, B. Daly, F. Cullen, P. Moran, S. Grennan, B. O'Brien, A. Hogan, N. Hand, D. McKeon, W. Reynolds, S. Kellaghan, C. McTeague. Subs: F. Kinnally for Daly, J. Hiney for Reynolds, P. Carroll for Dunne.

1990

Meath—C. Martin, V. Ryan, E. McManus, N. Collier, R. McGrath, G. Geraghty, T. Hanley, J. Hendrick, J. McCarthy, T. Byrne, D. Martin, B. Kealy, H. Carolan, T. O'Connor, C. Sheridan. Sub: C. Macken for Ryan.

Kerry—D. O'Keeffe, F. Stack, J. Cronin, J. O'Driscoll, O. Joy, S. Moynihan, B. O'Shea, C. Kennedy, S. O'Driscoll, J. Bowler W. O'Donnell, K. O'Shea, C. O'Grady, J. WiebolUt, G. Farrell. Sub: S. Curtin for S. O'Driscoll.

1991

Cork—K. O'Dwyer, D. O'Callaghan, B. Corcoran, B. Murphy G. McCullagh, T. Lynch, A. McCarthy, F. Collins, P. Hegarty, S. Barrett, M. O'Sullivan, P. O'Mahony, K. Harrington, J. Kavanagh, P. O'Rourke. Subs: F. O'Mahony for O'Rourke, D. O'Neill for Barrett.

Mayo—B. Heffernan, T. Burke, J. McSharry, K. Mortimer, P. Cunney, D. Leyden, F. Costello, M. Smith, P. McNamara T. J. McHugh, K. O'Neill, R. Golding, D. Burke, T. Walkin, D. McDonagh. Subs: S. Brady for McDonagh, C. Deacy for McHugh.

1992

Meath—B. Murphy, K. Cantwell, J. Brady, J. Smith, P. Shankey, J. Tighe, B. Sheridan, D. Hunt, N. Dunne, K. Harten, C. Hall, G. Bell, P. Duff, P. O'Sullivan, T. Giles. Subs: P. Nestor for Duff, M. Farrelly for Harten.

Armagh—D. Whitmarsh, E. Fearon, E. Martin, E. Bratten, C. Wilson, M. Hanratty, K. O'Hagan, B. O'Hagan, P. McGrane, B. Hughes, D. Marsden, P. McNulty, D. Toner, D. Mackin, N. McGleenan. Subs: J. Rafferty for McGleenan, A. McCann for Fearon, K. Mallie for Braflen.

1993

Cork—D. McAuley; T. O'Mahony, K. O'Connell, J. Kingston; A. O'Shea, E. Sexton, S. Prendeville; J. O'Connell, D. Dempsey; M. Cronin, A. O'Regan,

FOOTBALL

J. Buckley; S. Collins, P. O'Flynn, B. CuthLert. Sub: J. McCarthy for Dempsey.

Meath—N. Craven, N. Kearney, C. Woods, H. Traynor; P. Reynolds, D. Fay, B. Sheridan; T. Giles, A. Finnegan; N. Farrelly, J. Lacy, N. Walsh; O. Murphy, B. Callaghan, P. Nestor. Subs: P. Duff for Nestor, N. Regan for Walsh, J. Farrelly for Finnegan.

1994

Kerry—B. Murphy, K. O'Driscoll, B. O'Shea, S. O'Mahony, T. Fleming, T. McCarthy, F. O'Connor, D. Dwyer, G. O'Keeffe, J. Ferriter (capt.), L. Brosnan, G. Lynch, J. O'Shea, P. Sullivan, G. Murphy. Sub: M. Russell for G. Murphy.

Galway—L. Kelly, R. Fahy, K. Keane, T. Meehan, J. Divilly, D. Meehon, J. Lardner, A. Donnellan (capt.), M. Higgins, P. Clancy, M. Donnellan, P. Joyce, D. Savage, J. Concannon, D. Reilly. Subs: M. Waldron for J. Lardner, T. Reilly for D. Savage.

1995

Westmeath—A. Lennon, D. Phelan, K. Hickey, F. Murray, M. Murtagh, K. McKinley, S. Deering, D. Gavin (capt.), J. Casey, J. Deehan, T. Cleary, T. Stuart-Trainor, D. Martin, C. Keane, J. Glennon. Sub: C. Lyons for D. Martin.

Derry—D. Hopkins, J. Heaney, M. Kelly, E. McGilloway, P. McFlynn, C. McNally, P. Diamond, J. McBride (capt.), G. Doyle, G. Coleman, E. Muldoon, A. McGuckin, G. Cushnehan, J. Cassidy, G. Cassidy. Subs: D. McGrillis for G. Coleman, P. Wilson for G. Doyle, E. Farren for G. Cushnahan.

1996

Laois—R. Darby, P. Langton, M. Buggy, D. O'Hara, N. Collins, D. Conroy, C. Parkinson, M. Delaney (capt.), N. Garvin, O. Delaney, C. Conway, S. Kelly, B. McDonald, D. Doogue, K. Fitzpatrick.

Kerry—K. O'Keeffe, K. Leen, M. McCarthy, O. O'Connell, P. McCarthy, T. O'Shea, P. Murphy, J. Lynch (capt.), J. Sugrue, N. Kenneally, B. O'Connor, L. Murphy, M. Cahill, G. Clifford, J. Twiss. Subs: A. Mac Gearailt for J. Lynch, M. Beckett for J. Sugrue, R. Lynch for M. Cahill.

1997

Laois—M. Leigh, P. McDonald, E. Bland, T. Mulligan, D. Mullins, J. Higgins, J. P. Kehoe, B. Fitzpatrick, D. Rooney, M. Lambe, S. Kelly, T. Kelly, K. Kelly (capt.), B. McDonald, M. Hovendon.

Tyrone—G. Maguire, K. O'Brien, G. Gourley, B. Donnelly, A. Ball, D. McCrossan (capt.), G. Hetherington, C. McAnallen, K. Hughes, J. Campbell, B. McGuigan, C. Martin, M. Harte, R. Thornton, S. O'Neill. Subs: B. O'Neill for C. Martink, C. McGinley for G. Hetherington.

1998

Tyrone—P. McConnell; G. Devlin, M. McGee, F. Loughran; C. Meenagh, D. O'Hanlon, P. O'Neill; C. McAnallen, K. Hughes; G. Wylie, M. Hughes, S. O'Neill; A. Lynch, E. McGinley, E. Mulligan. Subs: B. McGuigan for M. Hughes, R. O'Neill for K. Hughes.

Laois—J. Graham; R. Jones, B. Gaynor, C. Clear; A. Fennelly, P. Leonard, B. McCormack; B. Fitzpatrick, J. Behan; M. Dunne, B. McDonald, K. Kelly, J. M. McDonald, P. Clancy, M. Clancy. Subs: B. O'Connell for M. Clancy, J. Moran for J. M. McDonald, D. Walsh for M. Dunne.

1999

Down—J. Sloan, J. Clarke, B. Grant, M. Doran, B. Kearney, L. Doyle, C. Murtagh, L. Sloan, B. Coulter, D. McGrady, M. Walsh, R. Murtagh, P. J. McAlinden, J. Fegan, R. Sexton.

Mayo—J. O'Hara, M. J. Meenaghan, P. Kelly, J. Brogan, R. Keane, P. Coady, C. Moran, J. Gill, G. Duffy, R. Moran, B. J. Padden, B. Loftus, G. Dillon, A. Dillon, E. Gallagher. Subs: D. Costelloe for E. Gallagher, J. Moran for B. Loftus.

2000

Cork – Kevin Murphy, N.O'Donovan, P.Deane, E.Bourke, N.O'Leary, D.O'Hare, P.McCarthy, G.McLoughlin, Kieran Murphy, M.O'Connor, C.Murphy, J.Collins, J.Masters, K.McMahon, C.Brosnan. Subs – D.Barron for O'Connor, D.Burns for McLoughlin.

Mayo – D.Clarke, R.Keane, R.Walshe, D.Geraghty, D.Costello, E.Devenney, C.Moran, E.Barrett, A.Burke, P.Prenty, C.Mortimer, D.Flynn, P.Carey, A.Dillon, T.Geraghty. Subs – S.Drake for Devenney, J.Morrin for T.Geraghty.

2001

Tyrone – J.Devine, R.O'Neill, D.Carlin, N.McStravog, J.McMahon, K.McCrory, P.Quinn, P.Donnelly, S.Cavanagh, C.Donnelly, B.Mulligan, T.McGuigan, L.Meenan, M.Penrose, G.Toner. Sub – N.Gormley for Meenan.

(Tyrone started with the same 15 as in the drawn final. Subs used in the drawn final were – A.Donaghy for Mulligan, P.Rafferty for Toner.

Dublin – P.Copeland, D.McCann, M.Fitzpatrick, D.Galvin, P.Griffin, B.Cullen, B.Lyons, P.Brennan, D.O'Mahony, N.McAuliffe, G.Cullen, G.Brennan, D.O'Callaghan, D.Farrell, J.Noonan. Subs – M.Whelan for G.Brennan, N.Clarke for Galvin, M.Taylor for P.Brennan. (G.Dent and M.Taylor started the drawn final but not the replay. Subs used in the drawn final were – M.Whelan for P.Brennan, C.Corrigan for Taylor, D.McCann for Dent.

2002

Derry – E.McNicholl, M.McGoldrick, G.O'Kane, J.Keenan, C.McCallon, M.Lynch, P.O'Hea, P.Bradley, R.Convery, B.McGoldrick, C.O'Kane, C.Moran, J.Bateson, P.Young, C.Mullan.

Meath – M.Brennan, B.O'Reilly, T.O'Connor, D.O'Halloran, S.Stephens, C.King, E.Dunne,

J.Melia, F.Murphy, D.Murtagh, P.Murray, G.McCullagh, B.Regan, J.Sheridan, B.Farrell. Subs – R.Brennan for O'Halloran, M.Whearty for Regan, T.Farrelly for Murray, A.Reynolds for McCullagh, A.Johnson for Dunne.

2003

Laois – C.Gorman, C.Healy, C.Ryan, R.Stapleton, P.O'Leary, C.Begley, N.Donagher, B.Quigley, C.Rogers, D.Bergin, Colm Kelly (Stradbally), P.McNulty, M.Tierney, D.Brennan, Colm Kelly (St.Josephs). Subs – I.Fleming for C.Kelly (Stradbally), D.Murphy for Tierney. (Laois uses the same starting 15 in the drawn final. Subs in the drawn final were – B.Fitzgerald for C.Kelly (Stradbally), D.Murphy for McNulty)

Dublin – K.Walsh, A.Downes, K.Cleere, W.Lowry, C.Murtagh, G.Brennan, I.Ward, B.Phelan, J.Coughlan, M.Vaughan, F.Fitzgerald, G.O'Meara, J.O'Hara, K.Leahy, B.Kennedy. Subs – J.Brogan for O'Hara, D.Walsh for Downes, M.Hallows for Murtagh, W.Moore for Fitzgerald.
(D.Reilly, F.Fitzgerald and A.Relihan started in the drawn final, but not in the replay. Subs in the drawn final were – F.Fitzgerald for Brennan, J.O'Brien for Kennedy, C.Moore for O'Hara)

2004

Tyrone – J.Curran, N.McGinn, P.Marlow, D.Burke, J.Gilmore, N.Kerr, M.Murray, R.Mulgrew, S.O'Hagan, C.O'Neill, M.Cunningham, R.McRory, G.Devlin, C.Cavanagh, A.Cassidy. Subs – P.J.Quinn for Murray, C.McCarron for Cavanagh, J.Kelly for O'Neill, S.O'Neill for Burke, S.Donaghy for O'Hagan.

Kerry – B.Kealy, P.Reidy, L.Quinn, K.Young, D.Doyle, C.Kelliher, D.O'Connor, B.Moran, A.Kennelly, D.O'Sullivan, S.Murphy, M.O'Donoghue, M.Evans, R.Keating, P.O'Connor. Subs – P.Curran for Keating, E.Mangan for O'Donoghue, D.Culloty for Kelliher, B.Looney for Murphy.

2005

Down – M.McAllister, G.Magee, C.Garvey, H.Magee, G.McCartan, E.McConville, K.Duffin, J.Colgan, P.Fitzpatrick, D.Lavery, M.Clarke, S.Grant, C.Brannigan, R.Kelly, P.McCumiskey. Subs – R.Kerr for Grant, C.Murney for Duffin, C.Clerkin for Lavery, K.McKernan for Fitzpatrick, G.Joyce for McAllister.
vMayo – S.Nallen, J.Burke, G.Cafferkey, P.Healy, C.Barrett, T.Cuniff, D.Hughes, P.Collins, D.O'Connor, P.Hanley, A.Campbell, D.Kilcullen, R.O'Boyle, P.O'Connor, M.Sweeney. Subs – S.O'Shea for Burke, G.O'Boyle for P.O'Connor, K.Barnicle for Nallen, J.Noone for O'Boyle, S.Kelly for Kilcullen.

2006

Roscommon – M.Miley, P.Domican, P.Gleeson, S.Ormsby, N.Carty, D.Flynn, C.Garvey, D.Keenan, D.Shine, F.Cregg, D.O'Hara, C.Devaney, P.Garvey, J.McKeague, K.Waldron. Subs – C.McHugh for McKeague, A.O'Hara for P.Garvey.

Kerry – T.Mac an tSaoir, B.Russell, M.Maloney, D.Ó Sé, S.Enright, A.Greadey, B.Costello, T.Walsh, D.Moran, P.Curtin, G.O'Driscoll, J.Buckley, G.Sayers, P.Curran, E.Kennedy. Subs – D.O'Shea for Buckley, S.Browne for Costello, J.Doolan for Curtin.
*In the drawn encounter for Roscommon M.McLoughlin and K.Higgins started for N.Carty and K.Waldron while for Kerry D.O'Shea started for J.Buckley. Subs in the drawn match were; Roscommon – N.Carty for McLoughlin, K.Waldron for Higgins, A.O'Hara for P.Garvey, C.Smith for McKeague. Kerry – P.Curtin for Ó Sé, S.Brown for Russell, J.Doolan for Sayers, W.Devane for Buckley.

2007

Galway – O.Higgins, E.Glynn, C.Forde, K.Kelly, C.Doherty, D.O'Reilly, T.Fahy, P.Conroy, A.Griffin, J.J.Greaney, M.Martyn, J.O'Brien, J.Ryan, T.Walsh, D.Reddington. Subs – J.Burke for Ryan, O.O'Brien for Greaney.

Derry – A.Warnock, M.McKinney, C.McWilliams, D.Bell, N.Forrester, J.F.Bradley, B.Henry, C.McKaigue, C.O'Boyle, J.Kielt, S.Cleary, D.Mullan, A.Heron, G.McGeehan, L.Moore. Subs – D.Heavron for Forrester, C.McFeely for Cleary, L.Kennedy for Heron.

2008

Tyrone – T.Harney, S.McRory, G.Teague, F.McQuaid, R.McNabb, P.Harte, R.Tierney, N.McKenna, R.Keenan, C.Gervin, D.McNulty, M.Donnelly, K.Coney, P.McNiece, C.O'Neill. Subs – K.Mossey for McRory, S.Warnock for McNulty, B.McGarvey for Tierney.

Mayo – R.Hennelly, D.Dolan, K.Keane, J.Broderick, S.McHale, E.Reilly, S.Nally, J.Cafferty, G.McDonagh, C.Freeman, A.O'Shea, R.Geraghty, K.Charlton, A.Walsh, A.Corduff. Subs – D.O'Hara for Charlton, D.Gavin for Geraghty, J.Carney for McHale.

*In the drawn encounter for Tyrone R.Pickering and M.Rogers started for R.Tierney and R.Keenan. Mayo started with the same fifteen. Subs in the drawn match were; Tyrone – R.Tierney for McRory, S.Warnock for Rogers, B.McGarvey for McNabb. Mayo – D.Galvin for Charlton, D.O'Hara for Geraghty.

2009

Armagh – S.O'Reilly, K.Downey, R.Finnegan, D.McKenna, K.Nugent, N.Rowland, J.Morgan, P.Carragher, A.Murnin, R.Grugan, J.Donnelly, C.King, R.Tasker, E.McVerry, G.McPartland. Subs – C.McCafferty for Finnegan, T.McAlinden for McVerry.

Mayo – M.Schlingermann, D.Gavin, K.Rogers, M.Walsh, C.Charlton, S.McDermott, C.Crowe, D.Kirby, A.Walsh, D.Coen, A.Farrell, F.Durkan, B.Ruttledge, A.Corduff, C.O'Connor. Subs – J.Carney for Farrell, J.McDonnell for Coen.

CAPTAINS OF WINNING ALL-IRELAND MINOR FOOTBALL TEAMS

1929—G. Comerford (Clare)
1930—B. Synott (Dublin)
1931—J. O'Gorman (Kerry)
1932—C. O'Sullivan (Kerry)
1933—T. O'Leary (Kerry)
1934—A. Greensmith (Tipperary)
1935—W. Durkin (Mayo)
1936—L. McEntee (Louth)
1937—J. J. McCormack (Cavan)
1938—P. Conaty (Cavan)
1939—L. Gilmartin (Roscommon)
1940—B. Burke (Louth)
1941—W. Carlos {Roscommon)
1942'44—Abandoned
1945—S. McEntaggart (Dublin)
1946—T. Moriarty (Kerry)
1947—E. Devlin (Tyrone)
1948—E. Devlin (Tyrone)
1949—S. Blaney (Armagh)
1950—M. Brosnan (Kerry)
1951—B. Molloy (Roscommon)
1952—B. Mahon (Galway)
1953—E. Walsh (Mayo)
1955—P. Heron (Dublin)
1956—L. Foley (Dublin)
1957—B. Cahill (Meath)
1958—D. Foley (Dublin)
1959—M. Kissane (Dublin)
1960—S. Cleary (Galway)
1961—E. Coughlan (Cork)
1962—S. O'Mahony (Kerry)
1963—T. O'Hanlon (Kerry)
1964—S. Grogan (Offaly)
1965—T. Diamond (Derry)
1966—S. O'Dowd (Mayo)
1967—D. Aherne (Cork)
1968—D. Aherne (Cork)
1969—E. Fitzpatrick (Cork)
1970—J. Corcoran (Galway)
1971—J. P. Kean (Mayo)
1972—G. Aherne (Cork)
1973—D. McKenna (Tyrone)
1974—E. Desmond (Cork)
1975—R. Bunyan (Kerry)
1976—G. Burke (Galway)
1977—J. McCartan (Down)
1978—A. Garvey (Mayo)
1979—M. Loftus (Dublin)
1980—T. Dee (Kerry)
1981—V. Hedderman (Cork)
1982—L. O'Rourke (Dublin)
1983—D. McNicholl (Derry)
1984—P. Clarke (Dublin)
1985—M. Fitzmaurice (Mayo)
1986—J. Joyce (Galway)
1987—M. Quinn (Down)
1988—D. Cahill (Kerry)
1989—G. Coleman (Derry)
1990—E. McManus (Meath)
1991—A. McCarthy (Cork)
1992—P. O'Sullivan (Meath)
1993—Brian Cuthbert (Cork
1994—Jack Ferriter (Kerry)
1995—Damien Gavin (Westmeath)
1996—Martin Delaney (Laois)
1997—Kieran Kelly (Laois)
1998—Cormac McAnallen {Tyrone)
1999—Liam Doyle (Down)
2000—J.Masters (Cork)
2001—P.Donnelly (Tyrone)
2002—G.O'Kane (Derry)
2003—C.Rogers (Laois)
2004—M.Cunningham (Tyrone)
2005—J.Colgan (Down)
2006—D.Flynn (Roscommon)
2007—P.Conroy (Galway)
2008—R.Pickering (Tyrone)
2009—D.McKenna (Armagh)

ALL-IRELAND MINOR FOOTBALL REFEREES 1929-2009

1929—Seán Robbins (Offaly)
1930—Jack McCarthy (Kerry)
1931—Patsy Fearon (Armagh)
1932—Seán Robbins (Offaly)
1933—John Doyle (Dublin)
1934—Tipperary awarded
1935—P. J. Masterson (Cavan)
1936—Tom Shevlin (Roscommon)
1937—Stephen Synott (Dublin)
1938—P. Ratty (Meath)
1939—P. Ratty (Meath)
1940—P. J. Masterson (Cavan)
1941—Seán Kennedy (Dublinl
1945—P. J. Masterson {Cavan)
1946—Brendan Nestor (Galway)
1947—J. Dowling (Kildare)
1948—John Dunne (Galway)
1949—Gerald Courell (Mayo)
1950—J. Shanely (Leitrim)
1951—Peter McDermott (Meath)
1952—Seán Óg Ó Ceallacháin (Dublin)
1953—D. King (Down)
1954—Bill Jackson (Roscommon)
1955—Patsy Geraghty (Galway)
1956—Gus Cremins (Kerry)
1957—C. Costello (Galway)
1958—P. Silke (Galway)
1959—P. Geraghty (Galway)
1960—M. McArdle (Louth)
1961—Brian Smith (Meath)
1962—Jimmy Hatton (Wicklow)
1963—Jackie Martin (Tyrone)
1964—Mick Loftus (Mayo)
1965—Jimmy Hatton (Wicklow)
1966—Eamon Moules (Wicklow)
1967—Patsy Devlin (Tyrone)
1968—Liam Maguire (Monaghan)
1969—Brendan Louth (Dublin)
1970—P. Greene (Antrim)
1971—Fintan Tierney (Cavan)
1972—M. Hynes (Roscommon)
1973—P. O'Gorman (Sligo)

1974—Paddy Collins (Westmeath)
1975—P. J. McGrath (Mayo)
1976—Martin Meally (Kilkenny)
1977—Tommy Moran (Leitrim)
1978—Jimmy Dennigan (Cork)
1979—P. J. McGrath (Mayo)
1980—Seamus Murray (Monaghan)
1981—Tony Jordan (Dublin)
1982—J. Keaney (Tyrone)
1983—P. Kavanagh (Meath)
1984—J. Mullaney (Roscommon)
1985—Gerry McGlory (Antrim)
1986—Carthage Buckley (Offaly)
1987—Seamus Prior (Leitrim)
1988—Michael Greenan (Cavan)
1989—Paddy Russell (Tipperary)
1990—Damien Campbell (Fermanagh)
1991—Tommy McDermott (Cavan)
1992—Seamus Prior (Leitrim)
1993—Michael Cranny (Down)
1994—Pat Casserly (Westmeath)
1995—Michael Curley (Galway)
1996—Brian White (Wexford)
1997—John Bannon (Longford)
1998—Michael Curley (Galway)
1999—Seamus McCormack (Meath)
2000—M.Monaghan (Kildare)
2001—M.Daly (Mayo)
D.Joyce (Galway) (replay)
2002—M.Ryan (Limerick)
2003—J.Geany (Cork)
M.Hughes (Tyrone) (replay)
2004—T.Quigley (Wexford)
2005—M.Deegan (Laois)
2006—S.Doyle (Wexford).
P.Hughes (Armagh) (replay)
2007—D.Fahy (Longford).
2008—R.Hickey (Clare)
C.Reilly (Meath) (replay)
2009—E.Kinsella (Laois)

MUNSTER MINOR FOOTBALL FINALS

1929—Clare 1-6, Waterford 0-4
1930—Clare 2-3, Tipperary 1-3
1931—Kerry 3-6, Tipperary 0-7
1932—Kerry 4-5, Cork 2-5
1933—Kerry 2-9, Cork 3-4
1934—Tipperary 3-10, Waterford 0-5
1935—Tipperary 3-5, Cork 0-4
1936—Kerry 1-5, Tipperary 1-2
1937—Kerry 3-8, Clare 1-2
1938—Kerry 8-9, Cork 1-2
1939—Cork 3-3, Kerry 3-2
1940—Kerry 1-3, Clare 1-2
1941—Kerry 7-5, Waterford 2-1
1942-44—Championship abandoned
1945—Kerry 2-4, Cork 2-3
1946—Kerry 4-7, Tipperary 0-2
1947—Kerry 0-7, Cork 1-3
1948—Kerry 3-4, Cork 1-5
1949—Kerry 0-7, Cork 0-5
1950—Kerry 4-10, Limerick 1-5
1951—Kerry 0-7, Cork 1-3
1952—Cork 3-9, Clare 1-1
1953—Clare 0-7, Cork 0-2
1954—Kerry4-10, Cork 1-3
1955—Tipperary 0-9, Kerry 1-6 (draw)
Tipperary 0-9, Kerry 1-5 (replay)
1956—Limerick 1-7, Kerry 1-5
1957—Kerry 1 -5, Cork 0-5
1958—Kerry 3-11, Waterford 0-4
1959—Cork 2-7, Kerry 0-7
1960—Cork 3-8, Kerry 0-7
1961—Cork 2-12, Clare 0-2
1962—Kerry 2-9, Cork 0-9
1963—Kerry 0-8, Cork 0-8 (draw)
Kerry 0-11, Cork 0-4 (replay)
1964—Cork 4-11, Clare 0-5
1965—Kerry 3-11, Cork 1-5
1966—Cork 5-12, Kerry 1-7
1967—Cork 2-8, Kerry 0-3
1968—Cork 2-13, Kerry 0-2
1969—Cork 3-11, Kerry 0-12
1970—Kerry 4-9, Cork -11
1971—Cork 2-13, Kerry 1-2
1972—Cork 2-14, Kerry 1-14
1973—Cork 1-13, Kerry 3-5
1974—Cork 0-13, Kerry 1-6
1975—Kerry 3-7, Cork 1-11
1976—Cork 0-10, Kerry 1-5
1977—Cork 1-7, Kerry 1-3
1978—Kerry 1-4, Cork 0-6
1979—Kerry 3-6, Cork 2-9 (draw)
Kerry 1-11, Cork 1-5 (replay)
1980—Kerry 1-12, Cork 1-10
1981—Cork 0-9, Kerry 1-5
1982—Kerry 1-11, Cork 0-5
1983—Cork 1-11, Tipperary 1-5
1984—Tipperary 2-3, Kerry 0-8
1985—Cork 1-8, Kerry 0-4
1986—Cork 2-12, Kerry 0-4
1987—Cork 0-8, Kerry 0-8 (draw)
Cork—0-12, Kerry 1-8 (replay)
1988—Kerry 1-8, Cork 0-10
1989—Kerry 2-10, Cork 2-9
1990—Kerry 1-10, Cork 0-3
1991—Cork 0-10, Kerry 0-8
1992—Cork 0-11, Kerry 2-5 (draw)
Cork 3-6, Kerry 2-7 (replay)
1993—Cork 2-15, Tipperary 2-7
1994—Kerry 2-11, Clare 3-5
1995—Tipperary 2-6, Cork 0-10
1996—Kerry 3-9, Cork 2-6
1997—Kerry4-12, Limerick 1-7
1998—Kerry 2-11, Limerick 0-8
1999—Cork 2-16, Kerry 1-9
2000—Cork 1-13, Kerry 0-14.
2001—Kerry 0-15, Cork 0-12.
2002—Kerry 3-16, Tipperary 2-6.
2003—Kerry 1-14, Cork 0-10.
2004—Kerry 0-9, Cork 0-9.
Kerry 0-13, Cork 1-7. (replay)
2005—Cork 3-8, Kerry 1-11.
2006—Kerry 1-13, Tipperary 0-8.
2007—Cork 1-16, Kerry 2-8.
2008—Kerry 1-9, Tipperary 1-9.
Kerry 2-12, Tipperary 0-8. (replay)
2009—Kerry 0-12, Tipperary 0-6.

LEINSTER MINOR FOOTBALL FINALS

1929—Longford 3-4, Dublin 1-4
1930—Dublin 1-6, Longford 0-4
1931—Louth 1-5, Wexford 0-3
1932—Laois 3-2, Louth 1-7
1933—Dublin 3-7, Laois 0-6
1934—Dublin 0-5, Kildare 0-2
1935—Louth 1-7, Dublin 1-6
1936—Louth 3-6, Wexford 2-1
1937—Wexford 2-7, Louth 2-5
1938—Longford 3-6, Louth 2-8
1939—Westmeath 1-2, Louth 0-2
1940—Louth 3-5, Kildare 1-6
1941—Louth 4-4, Wexford 1-6
1942—Louth 5-10, Kildare 0-6
1943-1944—Championships suspended.
1945—Dublin 3-5, Wexford 1-0
1946—Dublin 4-6, Meath 0-3
1947—Offaly 1-7, Dublin 1-7 (draw)
Offaly 1-7, Dublin 1-5 (replay)
1948—Dublin 2-5, Offaly 1-6
1949—Dublin 3-10, Kildare 1-5
1950—Wexford 3-6, Dublin 2-8
1951—Louth 3-9, Westmeath 2-5
1952—Westmeath 3-14, Wicklow 3-3
1953—Louth 1-6, Kildare 0-6
1954—Dublin 2-7 Meath 0-11
1955—Dublin 2-11, Meath 1-4
1956—Dublin 1-10, Meath 1-9
1957—Meath 0-8, Offaly 0-5
1958—Dublin 2-10, Louth 1-6
1959—Dublin 3-13, Offaly 1-7
1960—Offaly 1-12, Louth 1-5
1961—Dublin 2-8, Offaly 1-8
1962—Offaly 2-8, Dublin 1-4
1963—Westmeath 2-14, Dublin 3-7
1964—Offaly 1-7, Laois 1-6
1965—Offaly 2-11, Kildare 1 -5
1966—Laois 1-10, Offaly 0-7
1967—Laois 1-8, Dublin 2-4
1968—Dublin 1-11, Laois 0-8
1969—Wexford 0-11, Dublin 0-7
1970—Dublin 2-8, Meath 0-13
1971—Dublin 2-7, Louth 0-4
1972—Meath 3-8, Dublin 1-10
1973—Kildare 4-11, Laois 0-10
1974—Wicklow 5-6, Longford 1-9
1975—Kildare 2-9, Meath 3-5
1976—Dublin 2-8, Offaly 0-13
1977—Meath 1-7, Dublin 0-9
1978—Dublin 3-12, Wexford 0-11
1979—Dublin 2-13, Meath 0-8
1980—Meath 1-12, Kildare 1-9
1981—Dublin 1-8, Meath 0-9
1982—Dublin 0-10, Westmeath 0-4
1983—Kildare 1-11, Meath 1-6
1984—Dublin 0-12, Westmeath 1-6
1985—Meath 0-11, Offaly 1-4
1986—Dublin 2-16, Meath 0-6
1987—Kildare 0-13, Dublin 2-5
1988—Dublin 4-6, Meath 0-8
1989—Offaly 2-11, Kildare 0-7
1990—Meath 1-19, Kildare 1-6
1991—Kildare 2-8, Dublin 0-12
1992—Meath 1-8, Westmeath 1-5
1993—Meath 1-16, Wicklow 3-3
1994—Dublin 2-12, Wexford 2-6
1995—Westmeath 0-12, Laois 1-9 (draw}
Westmeath 3-12, Laois 2-15 (1st replay) after extra time
Westmeath 1-10, Laois 0-9 (2nd replay)
1996—Laois 0-15, Dublin 2-9 (draw)
Laois 2-18, Dublin 1-8 (replay)
1997—Laois 2-11, Wicklow 0-10
1998—Laois 2-9, Dublin 0-12
1999—Dublin 1-13, Wexford 2-10 (draw)
Dublin 2-13, Wexford 1-12 (replay)
2000—Westmeath 2-9, Dublin 1-10.
2001—Dublin 1-17, Offaly 0-6.
2002—Longford 3-8, Meath 3-5.
2003—Dublin 1-11, Laois 1-9.
2004—Laois 0-10, Kildare 0-6.
2005—Laois 1-12, Offaly 1-7.
2006—Meath 1-16, Offaly 2-5.
2007—Laois 3-8, Carlow 1-12.
2008—Meath 1-14, Offaly 2-10.
2009—Dublin 1-10, Kildare 1-10.
Dublin 1-15, Kildare 1-10. (replay) (aet)

CONNACHT MINOR FOOTBALL FINALS

1930—Mayo 3-4, Sligo 1-1
1931—Mayo 2-7, Sligo 0-3
1932—Galway 2-5, Mayo 2-3
1933—Mayo 5-7, Roscommon 0-6
1934—Mayo 2-13, Galway 0-5
1935—Mayo 2-2, Sligo 1 -4
1936—Mayo 4-9, Sligo 1-8
1937—Galway 2-8, Mayo 1-3
1938—Galway 6-5, Leitrim 1-6
1939—Roscommon 1-10, Mayo 1-3
1940—Mayo 8-5, Leitrim 1-6
1941—Roscommon 2-6, Galway 0-6
1942-44—Competition suspended in war years
1945—Leitrim 1-5, Sligo 2-2 (draw)
Leitrim 2-6, Sligo 1-5 (replay)
1946—Mayo 4-9, Galway 1-5
1947—Mayo 3-6, Sligo 2-5
1948—Galway 3-6, Sligo 1-3
1949—Roscommon 2-4, Sligo 1-7 (draw)
Roscommon 3-10, Sligo 2-7 (replay)
(Sligo awarded title on objection)
1950—Mayo 3-7, Roscommon 1-4
1951—Galway 1-8, Roscommon 2-4
(Roscommon awarded title on objection).
1952—Galway 4-11, Sligo 0-3
1953—Mayo 1-9, Roscommon 1-3
1954—Mayo 9-16, Sligo 0-4
1955—Mayo 2-5, Galway 1-5
1956—Leitrim 2-7, Roscommon 1-6
1957—Mayo 4-4, Leitrim 2-5
1958—Mayo 1-8, Roscommon 1-4
1959—Galway 3-9, Mayo 1-8
1960—Galway 4-11, Roscommon 0-3
1961—Mayo 5-8, Sligo 0-5
1962—Mayo 7-8, Galway 0-10
1963—Mayo 3-5, Roscommon 1-5
1964—Mayo 2-7, Galway 1 -3
1965—Roscommon 2-10, Mayo 1-10

1966—Mayo 1-9, Roscommon 0-7
1967—Roscommon 2-5, Mayo 1-5
1968—Sligo 1-8, Galway 0-7
1969—Galway 3-3, Mayo 0-8
1970—Galway 2-11, Mayo 1-6
1971—Mayo 2-12, Roscommon 1-8
1972—Galway 4-11, Roscommon 1-11
1973—Mayo 3-7, Galway 0-3
1974—Mayo 4-12, Roscommon 2-3
1975—Roscommon 1-15, Galway 0-5
1976—Galway 6-16, Sligo 3-3
1977—Mayo 2-20, Leitrim 0-7
1978—Mayo 2-6, Galway 0-4
1979—Mayo 5-11, Galway 3-7
1980—Mayo 3-8, Roscommon 2-9
1981—Roscommon 2-8, Mayo 3-4
1982—Galway 1-7, Leitrim 0-7
1983—Galway 2-10, Roscommon 2-5
1984—Roscommon 1-11, Mayo 2-8 (draw)
Roscommon 3-9, Mayo 2-8 (replay)
1985—Mayo 0-6, Galway 1-1
1986—Galway 1-9, Mayo 2-1
1987—Galway 2-8, Mayo 2-4
1988—Galway 2-9, Mayo 3-4
1989—Galway 2-8, Roscommon 0-13
(Provincial Council decides to replay: disputed penalty goal).
Roscommon 2-11, Galway 0-15
(after extra time)
1990—Galway 1-18, Roscommon 2-3
1991—Mayo 4-9, Leitrim 0-6
1992—Roscommon 0-10, Mayo 0-9
1993—Galway 0-11, Mayo 1-8 (draw)
Galway 3-8, Mayo 1-10 (replay)
1994—Galway 2-11, Mayo 0-9
1995—Galway 2-14, Mayo 2-11
1996—Mayo 0-10, Sligo 0-10 (draw)
Mayo 2-3, Sligo 0-8 (replay)
1997—Mayo 0-13, Roscommon 0-9
1998—Leitrim 0-8, S1igo 0-7
1999—Mayo 3-3, Galway 1-6
2000—Mayo 1-12, Roscommon 1-8.
2001—Mayo 0-15, Galway 0-11.
2002—Galway 1-12, Leitrim 0-6.
2003—Galway 1-9, Mayo 0-9.
2004—Galway 3-10, Roscommon 2-10.
2005—Galway 0-10, Mayo 0-9.
2006—Roscommon 0-12, Mayo 0-9.
2007—Galway 2-7, Roscommon 0-9.
2008—Mayo 0-10, Roscommon 0-7.
2009—Mayo 1-5, Roscommon 0-8.
Mayo 1-8, Roscommon 0-5. (replay)

ULSTER MINOR FOOTBALL FINALS

1930—Armagh 3-4, Monaghan 0-10
1931—Tyrone 0-7, Armagh 0-4
1932—Antrim 2-7, Tyrone 1-2
1933—Antrim 2-7, Armagh 1-1
1934—Tyrone 1-4, Down 1-3
1935—Tyrone 2-2, Donegal 2-1
Objection and counter-objection
Competition declared null and void.
1936—Antrim 2-7, Tyrone 2-4
1937—Cavan 1-10, Armagh 0-3
1938—Cavan 2-7, Antrim 2-4
1939—Monaghan 0-5, Cavan 0-5 (draw)
Monaghan 1-8, Cavan 1-7 (replay)
1940—Monaghan 0-8, Antrim 0-4
1941—Antrim 2-5, Cavan 1-7
1942-44—Abandoned
1945—Monaghan 1-7, Down 0-7
1946—Tyrone 1-4, Monaghan 0-5
1947—Tyrone 3-6, Armagh 2-8
1948—Tyrone 5-7, Monaghan 2-3
1949—Armagh 4-6, Donegal 1-4
1950—Antrim 1-8, Armagh 1-8 (draw)
Antrim 1-9, Armagh 1-1 (replay)
1951—Armagh 3-1, Cavan 1-4
1952—Cavan 1-5, Down 1-3
1953—Armagh 2-15, Tyrone 3-2
1954—Armagh 2-8, Down 0-9
1955—Antrim 4-3, Cavan 2-6
1956—Donegal 2-5, Armagh 0-6
1957—Armagh 3-6, Donegal 0-10
1958—Down 3-9, Cavan 3-1
1959—Cavan 2-11, Antrim 2-7
1960—Down 2-7, Monaghan 1-4
1961—Armagh 3-8, Monaghan 1-4
1962—Down 2-5, Armagh 0-8
1963—Down 4-6, Donegal 2-11
1964—Antrim 2-10, Cavan 0-6
1965—Derry 3-11, Cavan 2-4
1966—Down 1-12, Derry 1-9
1967—Tyrone 0-16, Fermanagh 2-5
1968—Armagh 4-8, Derry 1-7
1969—Derry 1-9, Tyrone 0-5
1970—Derry 1-14, Fermanagh 0-11
1971—Tyrone 0-19, Fermanagh 0-7
1972—Tyrone 3-6, Cavan 1-6
1973—Tyrone 1-13, Down 0-9
1974—Cavan 3-9, Derry 1-4
1975—Tyrone 0-10, Cavan 0-7
1976—Tyrone 5-7, Cavan 1-9
1977—Down 0-8, Armagh 1-5 (draw)
Down 0-11, Armagh 1-6 (replay)
1978—Tyrone 3-11, Monaghan 2-9
1979—Down 1-7, Tyrone 0-6
1980—Derry 3-14, Armagh 1-2
1981—Derry 0-11, Armagh 1-2
1982—Antrim 2-10, Down 3-5
1983—Derry 3-9, Monaghan 0-4
1984—Derry 1-4, Armagh 0-3
1985—Donegal 2-11, Cavan 1-3
1986—Down 1-12, Derry 0-10
1987—Down 1-7, Armagh 0-4
1988—Tyrone 2-7, Cavan 0-3
1989—Derry 2-15, Armagh 2-3
1990—Derry 2-10, Down 2-8
1991—Donegal 1-10,Tyrone 1-9
1992—Armagh 0-13, Donegal 0-9
1993—Tyrone 1-9, Derry 1 -5
1994—Armagh 3-13, Down 1-7
1995—Derry 2-12, Down 1 -7
1996—Donegal 0-9, Derry 0-9 (draw)
Donegal 0-9, Derry 1-5 (replay)
1997—Tyrone 3-13, Antrim 2-10
1998—Tyrone 4-9, Antrim 2-2
1999—Down 0-10, Donegal 0-10 (draw)
Down 2-7, Donegal 0-9 (replay)
2000—Derry 2-11, Tyrone 1-11.
2001—Tyrone 2-13, Monaghan 0-13.

2002—Derry 0-12, Tyrone 0-11.
2003—Tyrone 3-9, Fermanagh 0-9.
2004—Tyrone 0-11, Down 0-11. (draw)
Tyrone 0-15, Down 0-8. (replay)
2005—Armagh 0-11, Down 0-10.
2006—Donegal 2-12, Antrim 1-5.
2007—Tyrone 0-10, Derry 1-6.
2008—Tyrone 0-13, Monaghan 0-10.
2009—Armagh 1-8, Down 1-5.

ALL-IRELAND UNDER-21 FOOTBALL FINALS

1964—Kerry 1-10, Laois 1-3
1965—Kildare 2-11, Cork 1-7
1966—Roscommon 2-10, Kildare 1-12
1967—Mayo 4-9, Kerry 1-7 (replay)
Mayo 2-10, Kerry 2-10 (draw)
1968—Derry 3-9, Offaly 1-9
1969—Antrim 1-8, Roscommon 0-10
1970—Cork, 2-11, Fermanagh 0-9
1971—Cork 3-10, Fermanagh 0-3
1972—Galway 2-6, Kerry 0-7
1973—Kerry 2-13, Mayo 0-13
1974—Mayo 2-10, Antrim 2-8 (replay)
Mayo 0-9, Antrim 0-9 (draw)
1975—Kerry 1-15, Dublin 0-10
1976—Kerry 0-14, Kildare 1-3
1977—Kerry 1-11, Down 1-5
1978—Roscommon 1 -9, Kerry 1-8
1979—Down 1-9, Cork 0-7
1980—Cork 2-8, Dublin 1-5
1981—Cork 2-9, Galway 1-6 (replay)
Cork 0-14, Galway 2-8 (draw)
1982—Donegal 0-8, Roscommon 0-5
1983—Mayo 1-8, Derry 1-5 (replay)
Mayo 2-5, Derry 1-8 (draw)
1984—Cork 0-9, Mayo 0-6
1985—Cork 0-14, Derry 1-8
1986—Cork 3-16, Offaly 0-12
1987—Donegal 1-12, Kerry 2-4 (replay)
Donegal 1-7, Kerry 0-10 (draw)
1988—Offaly 0-11, Cavan 0-9
1989—Cork 2-8, Galway 1-10
1990—Kerry 5-12, Tyrone 2-11
1991—Tyrone 4-16, Kerry 1-5
1992—Tyrone 1-10, Galway 1-7
1993—Meath 1-8, Kerry 0-10
1994—Cork 1-1 2, Mayo 1-5
1995—Kerry 2-12, Mayo 3-9 (draw)
Kerry 3-10, Mayo 1-12 (replay)
1996—Kerry 1-17, Cavan 2-10
1997—Derry 1-12, Meath 0-5
1998—Kerry 2-8, Laois 0-11
1999—Westmeath 0-12, Kerry 0-9
2000—Tyrone 3-12, Limerick 0-13.
2001—Tyrone 0-13, Mayo 0-10.
2002—Galway 0-15, Dublin 0-7.
2003—Dublin 0-12, Tyrone 0-7.
2004—Armagh 2-8, Mayo 1-9.
2005—Galway 6-5, Down 4-6.
2006—Mayo 1-13, Cork 1-11.
2007—Cork 2-10, Laois 0-15.
2008—Kerry 2-12, Kildare 0-11.
2009—Cork 1-13, Down 2-9.

ALL-IRELAND UNDER-21 FOOTBALL FINAL TEAMS (1964-2009)

1964

Kerry—S. Fitzgerald, M. Morris, P. O'Donoghue, D. Lovett, S. McCarthy, V. Lucey, Donie O'Sullivan, Denis O'Sullivan, P. Griffin, H. McKinney, A. Barrett, D. O'Shea, D. O'Donnell (capt.), J. J. Barrett, S. Burrowes. Subs: P. Cahill for M. Morris, T. Fitzgerald for P. Griffin.

Laois—T. Miller, E. Fennelly, A. Maher, J. Conway, G. Lawlor, J. Leonard, S. Harkins, G. Brennan, E. Mulhall, J. Fennell, M. Fennell, D. Brennan, C. O'Connor, P. Delaney, B. Delaney. Subs: R. Miller for C. O'Connor, J. Heenan for E. Mulhall, E. Mulhall for J. Heenan.

1965

Kildare—O. Crinnigan, D. Wynne, S. Cash, J. McTeague, S. Reilly, P. Nally, J. Millar, J. Donnelly, P. Mangan, T. Carew, P. Dunny (capt.), K. Kelly, T. Walsh, P. Newins, N. Behan. Subs: T. Keogh for M. Behan, P. Harman for P. Nally.

Cork—W. Morgan, D. Kehilly, J. Lucey, J. Crowley, D. Dineen, F. Cogan, J. Dunlea, D. Couglan, J. Dowling, E. Philpott, M. O'Loughlin, J. Cogan, Batt O'Keeffe, B. O'Neill, Brendan O'Keeffe. Sub: C. Roche for D. Coughlan.

1966

Roscommon—P. Reynolds, P. Clarke, P. Nicholson, C. Shine (capt.), G. Mannion, P. Moclair, T. Heneghan, M. J. Keane, J. O'Connor, J. Finnegan, D. Earley, J. Cox, M. Cummins, J. Keane, J. Kelly. Sub: M. O'Gara for M. Cummins.

Kildare—O. Crinnigan, D. Wynne, S. Cash, J. McTeague, J. O'Reilly, P. Nally, T. Keogh, P. Mangan, L. Casey, T. Carew, P. Dunny, T. Walsh, K. Kelly, M. Mullins, N. Behan. Sub: M. Mannion for L. Casey.

1967

Mayo—E. Rooney, J. Earley, C. Loftus, N. McDonald, J. Ryan, T. Cafferkey, M. Flatley, W. Loftus (capt.), T. Keane, S. O'Dowd, J. Gibbons, W. McGee, T. Fitzgerald, D. Griffith, J. Smith. Sub: J. Clark for N. McDonald. (Note: M. Nally played in drawn game.)

Kerry—J. O'Brien, P. Sweeney, G. McCarthy, C. O'Sullivan, D. Crowley, S. Burrowes, T. O'Callaghan, P. O'Connell, M. Aherne, B. McCarthy, P. Finnegan, P. O'Connor, E. O'Donoghue, W. Kennedy, B. Lynch. Subs: P. Joy for P. O'Connor, V. McDyer for B. McCarthy.

1968

Derry—J. Somers, M. Trolan, T. Quinn, M. P. Kelly, T. Diamond (capt.), M. McAfee, G. O'Loughlin, T. McGuinness, S. Lagan, E.

Coleman, M. Niblock, J. J. Kearney, A. McGuickan, S. McCloskey, K. Teague. Subs: A. McGurk for G. O'Loughlin, C. O'Donnell for J. J. Kearney.

Offaly—N. Kinnarney, L. Pender, J. Smith, P. Byrne, E. Mulligan, N. Clavin, P. Monaghan, W. Bryan, S. Evans, C. Daly, L. Flynn, G. Grehan, M. Feehan, S. Kilroy, P. Keegan. Subs: J. Dunne for L. Pender, P. Fenning for C. Daly.

1969

Antrim—R. McIlroy, D. Burns, S. Killough, M. McGranaghan, J. Mullan, L. Millar, M. Colbert, L. Boyle (capt.), T. Dunlop, A. Hamill, G. McCann, G. Mellis, A. McCallin, G. Dillon, D. McGrogan. Sub: G. Pollock for M. Colbert.

Roscommon—W. Gallagher, T. Mahon, E. Beades, W. Feeley, P. Tiernan, A. O'Sullivan, J. Kerrane, D. Earley (capt.), M. Cox, T. Hunt, J. Kelly, M. Freyne, M. O'Hara, J. Cox, M. O'Gara.

1970

Cork—D. O'Mahony, M. O'Doherty, M. Scannell, S. Looney, S. Murphy, K. Kehilly, C. Hartnett, D. Hunt (capt.), D. Long, Tony Murphy, E. Kirby, John Coleman, J. Barrett, D. Barron, T. O'Brien. Subs: F. Twomey for S. Murphy, Donal Aherne for D. Hunt.

Fermanagh—P. Sheridan, P. Reilly, C. Campbell, J. Courtney, M. McGarrity, S. Sheridan, S. Flanagan, D. Campbell, D. McKenna, T. McGrath, A. Campbell, E. McPartland (capt.), E. Treacy, G. Gallagher, P. McGinnitty. Sub: T. Boyle for E. McPartland, E. McPartland for T. Boyle, T. Boyle for D. McKenna.

1971

Cork—D. O'Mahony, P. Barry, M. O'Doherty, S. Looney (capt.), D. Cogan, B. Murphy, C. Hartnett, J. Coleman, D. Aherne, T. Murphy, B. Daly, F. Twomey, B. Cogan, D. Barron, D. Curran. Sub: J. Lynch for B. Daly.

Fermanagh—P. Sheridan, P. O'Reilly, C. Campbell, P. Burns, B. McGovern, S. Flanagan, G. Lynch, D. McKenna, C. Gallagher, P. McGinnitly, A. Campbell, M. Cassidy, E. Treacy, T. McGrath, B. O'Reilly. Subs: H. Kelly for A. Campbell, M. McGarritly for G. Lynch.

1972

Galway—M. Noonan, J. Waldron (capt.), J. Dillon, B. Costelloe, P. J. Burke, M. Geraghty, S. Stephens, M. Walsh, M. Rooney, P. Burke, T. Naughton, M. Burke, J. Lardner, F. Rushe, J. Tobin. Sub: E. Monaghan for J. Lardner.

Kerry—J. Crean, S. O'Donovan, J. Deenihan, D. O'Keeffe, M. Murphy, P. Lynch, G. O'Keeffe, N. O'Sullivan, J. O'Keeffe, M. McEllistrim, M. O'Sullivan, J. Walsh (capt.), P. Horan, M. Ferris, G. Power. Subs: J. Egan for M. Ferris, M. O'Connor for P. Horan.

1973

Kerry—P. O'Mahony, B. Harman, J. Deenihan, B. O'Shea, G. O'Keeffe, G. Power, K. O'Donoghue, J. Long, P. Lynch, J. Coffey (capt.), M. O'Sullivan, P. O'Shea, M. O'Shea, J. Egan, M. Sheehy. Subs: M. Ferris for M. O'Shea, N. Brosnan for P. Lynch.

Mayo—S. Langan, P. Cunningham, S. Reilly, J. O'Mahony, G. Feeney (capt.), C. Moynihan, J. Culkin, R. McNicholas, G. Farragher, M. Gannon, T. Webb, R. Bell, E. Ralph, S. McGrath, M. Flannery. Subs: S. Barrett for M. Flannery, S. Weir for E. Ralph.

1974

Mayo—I. Heffernan, A. Durkin, S. Reilly, J. O'Mahony, G. Feeney, C. Moynihan, J. Culkin (capt.), R. Bell, G. Farragher, M. Flannery, J. P. Kean, T. Webb, M. Moloney, D. McGrath, M. Higgins. Subs: D. McGrath for M. Flannery in draw game; J. Burke for M. Moloney, M. O'Malley for A. Durcan in replay; J. Burke played in drawn game. D. McGrath came in for replay.

Antrim—C. Moore, N. Madden, P. McKiernan, J. McAllister, G. McHugh, J. P. O'Kane, C. Smith, L. Jennings, J. McKiernan, K. Gough, P. Armstrong, B. Growcott, H. McRory, J. O'Hare, D. Cormican. Subs: J. McAllister, K. Young draw; K. Young replay; R. Carlin played in drawn game.

1975

Kerry—C. Nelligan, K. O'Donoghue (capt.), P. Ó Sé, G. Leahy, M. Spillane, T. Kennelly, D. (Ogie) Moran, G. O'Driscoll, S. Walsh, B. Walsh, M. Sheeby, D. Murphy, T. Doyle, J. O'Shea, P. Spillane.

Dublin—A. Fayne, B. Fitzpatrick, L. Egan, G. McCaul, K. Bruton J. Thompson, M. Holden, F. Ryder, J. Corcoran, P. Connellan, B. Mullins, P. J. Buckley, P. Reaney, C. Fitzpatrick, S. McCarthy. Subs: D. O'Reilly for J. Corcoran, A. Cunningham for K. Bruton, P. Rooney for P. Connellan.

1976

Kerry—C. Nelligan, M. Colgan, P. Ó Sé, G. Leahy, M. Spillane, D. "Ogie" Moran, V. O'Connor, S. Walsh, J. O'Shea, N. O'Donovan, P. Spillane, G. Murphy (capt.), B. Walsh, G. O'Sullivan, P. Foley.

Kildare—A. Dunne, C. Farrell, P. O'Donoghue, F. Mulligan, D. O'Reilly, J. Crofton, P. Kenny, J. Geoghegan, M. Fennelly, T. Shaw, M. Condon, P. Mulhern, N. Fahy, M. O'Gorman, B. Whelan. Subs: S. Ryan for C. Farrell, P. Lyons for N. Fahy, P. Carr for P. Mulhern.

1977

Kerry—C. Nelligan, M. Keane, V. O'Connor, M. Spillane, D. (Ogie) Moran (capt.), J. Mulvihill, G. Casey, J. O'Shea, E. Liston, T. Doyle, S. Walsh, P. Foley, D. Moran, T. Bridgman, D. Coffey. Sub: G. O'Sullivan for D. Moran.

Down—J. Carr, M. Sands, D. Carey, H. Trainor, J. McCartan, T. McGovern, P. O'Rourke, J. Wright, L. Austin, D. Watson, R.

Mathews, V. McGovern, B. Loughran, J. McCartan, M. McCann. Subs: E. McGivern for P. O'Rourke, A. McAulfield for B. Loughran.

1978

Roscommon—B. Kenny, D. Newton, P. Dolan, S. Tighe, G. Connellan, R. O'Beirne, E. Egan, S. Hayden (capt.), G. Fitzmaurice, M. Finneran, G. Emmett, C. Reynolds, A. McHugh, H. Crowley, T. McManus. Sub: A. Dooley for A. McHugh.

Kerry—C. Nelligan, M. Keane, V. O'Connor, M. Spillane, G. Lynch, J. Mulvihill, G. Casey, J. O'Shea, S. Walsh, T. Bridgman, D. Higgins, J. L. McElligot, P. Foley, E. Liston, P. Sheehan. Sub: D. Coffey for P. Sheehan.

1979

Down—Pat Donnan, E. King, A. McAulfield, M. Sands, G. Murdock, P. O'Rourke, B. McGovern, P. Kennedy, L. Austin, J. McCartan (capt.), M. Burns, G. Blaney, Peter Donnan, G. O'Hare, J. Digney. Sub: M. McCann for G. O'Hare.

Cork—B. O'Driscoll, T. Healy, M. Healy, J. Murphy, L. Forde, M. Moloney, J. Kerrigan, R. Lotty, D. O'Mahony, T. Dalton, M. Mullins, B. McSweeney, S. Hayes, G. Mulcahy, F. O'Mahony. Subs: D. Kelleher for D. O'Mahoney, D. Philpott for R. Lotty, J. Nolan for T. Healy.

1980

Cork—M. Creedon, J. Fouhy, M. Healy, C. Counihan, B. McSweeney, T. Hennebry, J. Kerrigan, D. Philpott, Brian Lotty, D. Barry, S. Hayes, T. Dalton (capt.), E. Fitzgerald, N. O'Connor, F. O'Mahony. Sub: M. Burns for B. McSweeney.

Dublin—J . O'Leary, F. Walsh, V. Conroy, D. Foran, P. Canavan, S. Wade, C. Eustace, J. Ronayne, P. Boylan, D. O'Brien, M. Loftus, C. Duff, W. Hughes, B. Rock, A. McCaul. Subs: S. Fleming for C. Eustace, V. Kearney for W. Hughes, G. O'Neill for A. McCaul.

1981

Cork—M. Creedon, J. Fouhy, M. Healy, P. Buckley, M. Hannon, M. Burns, C. Corrigan, Brian Lotty, D. Murphy, D. Barry, S. Hayes (capt.), M. Connolly, A. O'Sullivan, N. O'Connor, E. Fitzgerald.

(Note: C. Hartnett and D. Kelleher played in drawn game. P. Buckley and A. O'Sullivan came on for replay.) Subs: P. Buckley for C. Hartnett, T. Ross for D. Murphy in drawn game; T. Ross for D. Murphy, D. Kelleher for M. Connolly in replay.

Galway—P. Coyne, S. Cronin, P. Connolly, S. Rhattigan, H. Heskin, T. Tierney, M. Gleeson, A. Murphy, P. Kelly, V. Daly, M. McDonagh, M Brennan, P. O'Dea, C. O'Dea, C. Gibbons.

(Note: S. Kelly, P. Clancy, H. Blehein, B. O'Donnell played in drawn game. S. Rhattigan, G. Gibbons, P. Kelly and H. Heskin came on for replay.) Subs: H. Heskin for M. Gleeson, P. Kelly for C. McDonagh in drawn game; M. Sweeney for M. McDonagh, M. McDonagh for C. O'Dea in replay.

1982

Donegal—M. Kelly, M. McBrearty, S. Bonnar, M. Gallagher, E. McIntyre, T. McDermott, B. Tuohy (capt.), A. Molloy, D. Reid, M. McHugh, C. Mulgrew, J. McMullen, S. Meehan, P. Carr, P. McGroarty. Subs: P. Gallagher for S. Bonnar, S. Maguire for P. McGroarty.

Roscommon—G. Cunniffe, G. Wynne, G. Collins, M. Shanahan, P. McNeill, M. Tiernan, P. Rogers, E. Glancy, T. Corcoran, E. McManus, P. Hickey, J. Connellan, P. Earley, R. McPhillips, P. Doorey (capt.). Subs: J. Kelly for R. McPhillips, S. Killoran for E. Glancy.

1983

Mayo—G. Irwin, P. Forde, J. Maughan, E. Gibbons (capt.), J. McNabb, M. Feeney, J. Finn, G. Geraghty, S. Maher, P. Brogan, J. Lindsay, N. Durkin, B. Kilkelly, T. Grogan, P. Duffy.

(Note: M. Kerins played in draw and came on as a sub in replay for T. Grogan. Kevin McStay replaced P. Duffy in draw and J. Lindsay in replay. P. Brogan was on for replay.)

Derry—J. Mackle, K. Rafferty, F. Burke, T. Scullion, J . McErlean, B. McPeake, C. Keenan, C. Quinn, D. Barton, L. McIlhenny, D. McNicholl, P. McCann, T. McGuinness, R. McCusker, T. McGuckian.

(Note: E. Cassidy, B. McErlean played in drawn game.) Subs: R. McCusker for E. Cassidy, P. McCann for J. McErlean in drawn game (they retained their places for the replay). D. O'Kane for T. McGuinness, M. Tully B. McPeake, E. Cassidy for C. Quinn came subs in replay.

1984

Cork—M. Maguire, John Murphy (Passage), N. Cahalane (capt.), A. Davis, D. Cleary, M. Slocum, T. Nation, D. Cullotty, T. Leahy, B. Coffey, T. Mannix, M. McCarthy, K. McCarthy, C. O'Neill, A. O'Sullivan. Subs: T. McCarthy for A. O'Sullivan, J. Cleary for K. McCarthy, B. Stack for D. Culloty.

Mayo—G. Irwin, C. Dever, J. Gilmore, E. Gibbons, A. McGarry, J. McNabb, J. Finn, P. Brogan, S. Maher, J. Dooley, P. Duffy, N. Durkin, B. Kilkelly, L. McHale, P. O'Reilly. Sub: T. Morgan for P. O'Reilly.

1985

Cork—J. O'Mahony, K. Scanlon, A. Davis (capt.), D. Walsh, D. Cleary, B. Stack, M. Slocum, D. Cullotty, P. Hayes, M. McCarthy, T. McCarthy, B. Coffey, S. O'Donovan, C. O'Neill, P. McGrath. Sub: B. Lane for D. Cullotty.

Derry—D. McCusker, B. Young, F. Bourke, P. McCann, J. McGurk, B. McPeake, N. Mullen, D. O'Kane, D. Healy, Declan McNicholl, D. Cassidy, M. McGurk, Dermot McNicholl, Cathal McNicholl, T. McKiernan. Subs: P. Bradley for F. Bourke, C. Barton for M. McGurk, J. Mulholland for N. Mullen.

1986

Cork—J. O'Mahony, K. Scanlon, J. Murphy (Glanmire), D. Walsh, M. Slocum (capt.), M.

Maguire, A. Griffin, P. Hayes, T. McCarthy, C. O'Connell, M. McCarthy, B. Coffey, P. Harrington, J. O'Driscoll, P. McGrath. Subs: J. O'Brien for J. O'Mahony, A. McCarthy for M. Maguire, B. Stack for A. Griffin.

Offaly—A. Daly, J. Owens, C. Higgins, K. Corcoran, A. Stewart, K. Rigney, B. Scully, G. O'Brien, P. Brady, V. Claffey, D. Claffey, C. Ryan, R. Scully, M. Casey, V. Brady. Subs: G. Blong for J. Owens, K. Brasil for K. Rigney, G. Galvin for G. O'Brien.

1987

Donegal—D. Gallagher, J. J. Doherty, J. Connors, T. Maguire, P. Carr, J. Cunningham (capt.), D. Keon, B. Cunningham, J. Gallagher, P. Hegarty, T. Ryan, B. McGowan, D. Ward, M. Boyle, L. Gavigan. Sub: S. Ward for J. Gallagher in replay.

Note: Donegal played same team in drawn game. Subs in drawn game: C. White for P. Hegarty, J. McDermott for D. Ward.

Kerry—C. Moran, K. Savage, M. Brosnan, M. Nix, S. Stack, N. O'Leary, P. Coughlan, M. Galway, J. Brosnan, P. J. Gaine, G. Looney, D. McEvoy, G. Murphy, P. Hoare, M. Dennehy. (Note: M. Downey played in draw.) Subs: G. Murphy for M. Dennehy in drawn game (he retained his place for replay); D. Moynihan for G. Looney, T. Walsh for P. Coughlan, M. Downey for M. Dennehy in replay.

1988

Offaly—D. O'Neill, P. Moran, G. O'Brien (capt.), T. Coffey, J. Stewart, A. Bracken, P. O'Reilly, M. Plunkett, K. Kelleghan, G. Daly, V. Claffey, N. O'Shea, M. Casey, J. Mullan, B. Flynn. Subs: B. Scully for G. Daly, V. Daly for V. Claffey.

Cavan—J. Reilly, G. Smith, D. O'Reilly, B. Sweeney, J. Donnellan, J. Brady, P. Sharkey, L. Brady, M. Fegan, F. Cahill, S. Donoghue, D. Brady, V. Kelly, V. Dowd, F. Mooney. Sub: C. Murtagh for L. Brady.

1989

Cork—A. Cawley, M. Lyons, M. O'Connor, D. Burke, S. Coughlan, S. O'Brien (capt.), N. Murphy, D. Fitzgerald, L. Honohan, I. Ahearne, M. Mullins, D. Davis, J. Barrett, D. O'Sullivan, N. Twomey. Subs: S. Calnan for Ahearne, C. Corkerry for Barrett.

Galway—A. Brennan, J. Kilraine, F. McWalter, B. Walsh, P. Fallon, A. Mulholland, N. O Neachtain, B. Moylan, A. O'Connor, S. De Paor, T. Mannion, F. O'Neill, T. Kilcommins, K. Walsh, T. Finnerty. Subs: B. Silke for Kilraine, J. Joyce for de Paor, E. Geraghty for Mannion.

1990

Kerry—P. O'Leary, J. B. O'Brien, S. Burke, L. Flaherty, P. Slattery, V. Knightley (capt.), E. Breen, M. Fitzgerald, N. O'Mahony, P. Laide, P. McKenna, G. O'Driscoll, P. Dennehy, D. Farrell, W. O'Sullivan. Sub: P. Griffin for Dennehy.

Tyrone—C. Blee, F. Devlin. A. McGinn, P. Devlin, P. Donnelly, B. McGinn, A. Morris, A. Kilpatrick, D. Barr, A. Cush, M. Cummings, P. Canavan, L. Strain, C. McElduff, C. Loughran, Sub: E. McCaffrey for Cummings.

1991

Tyrone—C. Blee, D. Hagan, C. Lawn, F. Devlin, P. Donnelly, B. McGinn, T. O'Neill, A. Kilpatrick, D. Barr, A. Cush, E. McCaffrey, P. Canavan (capt.), C. Loughran, C. McBride, B. Gormley. Subs: S. Lawn for Donnelly, J. Cassidy for Blee.

Kerry—P. O'Leary, J. O'Brien, N. Savage, J. Cronin, L. Flaherty, V. Knightley, S. Walsh, F. Ashe, C. Kearney, P. Laide, G. O'Driscoll, S. O'Sullivan, G. Farrell, D. Farrell, W. O'Sullivan. Subs: E. Stack for Kearney, D. Cahill for Walsh, T. Byrnes for Laide.

1992

Tyrone—B. McConnell, E. Martin, C. Lawn, F. Devlin, S. Lawn, J. Gormley, C. Hughes, A. Kilpatrick, S. McCallan, E. McCaffrey, C. Donnelly, P. Canavan (capt.), K. Loughran, C. McBride, B. Gormley. Sub: M. Slevin for C. Lawn.

Galway—D. O Flaharta, K. Fallon, G. Fahy, E. Godwin, I. O'Donoghue, P. Crowley, D. Cronin, F. Gavin, P. Boyce, J. Wilson, C. McGauran, T. Wilson, B. Forde, J. Fallon, N. Finnegan. Subs: F. Keenan for Crowley, A. Feerick for Forde.

1993

Meath—C. Martin, V. Ryan, E. McManus, R. McGrath, J. McCarthy, G. Geraghty, T. Hanley (capt.), J. Hendrick, J. McGuinness, T. Shine, H. Carolan, T. Byrne, P. O'Sullivan, T. O'Connor, C. Sheridan. Subs: B. Kealy for Hendrick, T. Giles for O'Connor, N. Collier for McCarthy.

Kerry—D. O'Keeffe, M. Hassett, G. McGrath, N. Mangan, S. Curtin, F. Stack, J. O'Connell, S. Moynihan, J. Quirke, C. O'Grady, B. O'Shea, P. O'Driscoll, E. Hennessy, J. O'Shea, S. Culloty. Subs: D. O'Shea for Quirke, K. Scanlon For McGrath, S. O'Driscoll for J. O'Shea.

1994

Cork—K. O'Dwyer, D. O'Callaghan, B. Corcoran, T. Óg Lynch M. O'Donovan, B. Murphy, P. O'Regan, F. Collins, D. O'Neill, J. Buckley, J. Kavanagh, P. O'Mahony, J. Clifford, P. Hegarty, P. O'Rourke. Subs: M. O'Sullivan for Buckley, M. Moran for O'Rourke.

Mayo—B. Heffernan, F. Costello, K. Morley, J. Nallen, P. Cunney, K. Mortimer, J. Casey, P. McNamara, D. O'Loughlin, R. Ruane, D. Jennings, R. Golding, K. O'Neill, K. McDonald, M. Sheridan. Subs: D. Byrne for O'Loughlin, M. Smith for Jennings, J. McHugh for P. McNamara.

1995

Kerry—D. Murphy (capt.), N. Mangan, B. McCarthy, B. O'Shea, K. Burns, M. Hassett, C. McCarthy, D. Ó Sé, D. Daly, D. Dwyer, J.

Crowley, M. Moynihan, J. Ferriter, L. Hassett, D. Ó Cinnéide. Subs: K. O'Driscoll for O'Shea, C. Drummond for Mangan, D. Dennehy for Dwyer. W. Kirby went in as a sub in the drawn game for D. Ó Sé.) Note: Kerry played same team in both games.

Mayo—J. Madden, F. Costello, L. Moffat, R. Connelly, T. Corcoran, K. Mortimer (capt.), S. Moffat, D. Brady, J. Casey, D. O'Loughlin, J. Mitchell, E. McDonagh, M. Horan, D. Byrne, D. Nestor. Subs: D. Tierney for McDonagh, D. Sweeney for Mitchell, B. Forde for O'Loughlin.

(R. Connelly, E. McDonagh and M. Horan replaced D. Mulligan, P. Whitaker and K. McDonald who played in draw. M. Higgins, D. Sweeney and C. Deacy went on as subs in drawn fame for P. Whitaker, J. Mitchell and D. Mulligan.)

1996

Kerry—D. Murphy, K. O'Driscoll, B. McCarthy, M. O'Shea, K. Burns, C. Drummond, E. Fitzmaurice, D. Ó Sé, W. Kirby, D. Dwyer, L. Hassett (capt.), D. Ó Cinnéide, J. O'Shea, B. Clarke, M. F. Russell. Subs: J. Brennan for Clarke, R. O'Rahilly for Brennan, J. Ferriter for J. O'Shea.

Cavan—A. Donohoe, P. Murphy, M. Reilly, C. McCarey, P. Brady, P. Reilly, M. McGauran, D. McCabe, T. Farrelly, D. Fagan, R. Brennan, A. Forde, J. Reilly, L. Reilly, M. Graham. Sub: B. Mulvaney for Fagan.

1997

Derry—S. O'Kane, S. Donnelly, D. O'Neill, M. Kelly, P. McFlynn, S. M. Lockhart, E. McGillowey, E. Muldoon, G. Doyle, B. Murray, J. McBride, S. McGuckin, J. Cassidy, A. McGuckin, M. Gribbin.

Meath—C. O'Sullivan, S. Carolan, D. Fay, A. Meade, N. Kearney, M. Reilly, P. Reynolds, S. O'Rourke, J. Cullinane, B. Smyth, S. Dillon, K. Dowd, R. McGee, B. Callaghan, R. Farrelly. Subs: C. McGrath for Carolan, E. Grogan for Dowd, F. Owens for O'Rourke.

1998

Kerry—D. Moloney, M. McCarthy, T. O'Sullivan, K. Leen, J. Sheehan, T. Ó Sé, M. Beckett, T. Griffin, E. Fitzmaurice, A. Mac Gearailt, P. O'Sullivan, L. Brosnan, M. F. Russell, N. Kennelly, B. Scanlon. Subs: I. Twiss for Scanlon, M. Burke for Beckett.

Laois—D. O'Mahony, J. P. Kehoe, M. Buggy, J. Higgins, N. Collins, D. Conroy, C. Parkinson, M. Delaney, N. Garvan, G. Ramsbottom, I. Fitzgerald, C. Conway, B. McDonald, D. Doogue, K. Fitzpatrick. Subs: S. Kelly for Delaney, T. Kelly for Doogue.

1999

Westmeath—C. Mullin, P. Mullen, J. Galvin, F. Murray, B. Lambden, A. Canning (capt.), M. Burke, K. Burke, D. O'Shaughnessy, S. Deering, F. Wilson, R. Browne, J. Fallon, M. Ennis, D. Dolan. Sub: D. Heavin for J. Galvin.

Kerry—K. Cremin, S. O'Sullivan, T. O'Sullivan, M. McCarthy, S. Hegarty, T. Ó Sé, E. Galvin, T. Griffin, J. Sugrue, N. Kennelly (capt.), A. MacGearailt, T. Kennelly, P. Galvin, L. Murphy, I. Twiss. Subs: S. O'Sullivan for P. Galvin, M. D. Cahill for Twiss.

2000

Tyrone – P.McConnell, G.Devlin, D.O'Hanlon, M.McGee, C.McGinley, C.Gourley, D.McCrossan, C.McAnallen, K.Hughes, J.Campbell, B.McGuigan, S.O'Neill, M.Harte, R.Thornton, O.Mulligan. Subs – E.McGinley for McAnallen, A.Ball for McCrossan.

Limerick – M.Keogh, M.O'Riordan, P.Fitzgerald, B.Geary, C.Mullane, S.Lucey, T.Stack, J.Stokes, J.Galvin, P.Ahern, M.Culhane, T.Carroll, C.Fitzgerald, B.Begley, C.Hickey. Sub – S.Byrne for Culhane.

2001

Tyrone – P.McConnell, C.Gormley, D.O'Hanlon, M.McGee, C.Meenagh, G.Devlin, P.Jordan, P.Donnelly, C.McAnallen, R.Mellon, B.McGuigan, S.O'Neill, E.McGinley, K.Hughes, O.Mulligan. Sub – G.Wylie for Donnelly.

Mayo – D.Clarke, M.J.Meenaghan, P.Kelly, K.Deignan, E.Casey, B.Prendergast, G.Brady, J.Gill, S.Grimes, C.Lyons, A.Dillon, T.Mortimer, M.Keane, B.Maloney, C.Mortimer. Subs – M.McNicholas for Lyons, B.Padden for Dillon, R.Loftus for Grimes, R.Walsh for Meenagh.

2002

Galway – D.Morris, C.Monaghan, K.Fitzgerald, M.Comer, R.Murray, D.Blake, K.Brady, J.Bergin, K.Comer, M.Clancy, J.Devane, D.Burke, M.Meehan, D.O'Brien, N.Joyce. Sub – D.Hanley for Burke.

Dublin – S.Cluxton, N.Kane, D.Corcoran, P.Griffin, P.Casey, B.Cullen, N.O'Driscoll, D.Magee, C.Murphy, L. Óg Ó hEineacháin, C.Keaney, D.Lally, A.Brogan, G.Cullen, T.Quinn. Subs – D.O'Callaghan for Keaney, D.O'Mahony for G.Cullen, S.Walsh for Corcoran, M.Lyons for Lally, G.Smith for Murphy.

2003

Dublin – P.Copeland, N.Kane, M.Fitzpatrick, P.Griffin, N.Cooper, B.Cullen, C.Prenderville, D.O'Mahony, P.Brennan, C.Keaney, L. Óg Ó hEineacháin, D.Lally, A.Brogan, G.Cullen, J.Noonan. Subs – D.Murray for Cooper, M.Lyons for Ó hEineacháin, S.Walsh for G.Cullen.

Tyrone – J.Devine, S.Sweeney, K.McCrory, D.Carlin, O.Devine, M.Garry, P.O'Farrell, P.Donnelly, S.Cavanagh, K.Hughes, L.Meenan, J.McMahon, M.Penrose, A.McCarron, R.McCann. Subs – T.McGuigan for McCann, P.Armour for O'Farrell, D.McDermott for Penrose.

2004
Armagh – P.Wilson, G.Smyth, F.Moriarty, A.Mallon, A.Kernan, C.McKeever, B.McDonald, M.Mackin, G.Swift, G.Loughran, S.Kernan, P.Toal, M.McNamee, R.Austin, B.Mallon. Subs – P.Duffy for McDonald, B.Toner for Loughran, J.Murtagh for Austin, M.Moore for A.Kernan, S.O'Neill for Mackin.

Mayo – F.Ruddy, D.Geraghty, P.Navin, T.Howley, M.Carey, L.O'Malley, S.Drake, B.Moran, C.Barrett, A.Kilcoyne, R.McNamara, A.Moran, A.Costello, D.Munnelly, M.Conroy. Subs – P.Casey for Kilcoyne, P.Lydon for Drake, P.Doherty for Carey, J.Prenty for Munnelly, N.Lydon for Conroy.

2005
Galway – M.Killilea, A.Burke, F.Hanley, M.Flannery, D.Mullahy, N.Coyne, G.Sice, N.Coleman, B.Cullinane, B.Faherty, D.Dunleavy, F.Breathnach, M.Meehan, C.Blake, S.Armstrong. Subs – J.Murphy for Mullahy, A.Glynn for Coyne.

Down – D.Alder, N.McEvoy, M.Rooney, E.Henry, D.Neeson, J.Colgan, D.Cunningham, A.Rogers, M.McClean, C.Laverty, A.Carr, N.McArdle, M.Poland, J.McGovern, J.Brown. Subs – J.Ireland for Henry, M.Clarke for McGovern, J.Patterson for McArdle, N.Miskelly for Brown, G.Dobbin for Rooney.

2006
Mayo – K.O'Malley, T.Howley, G.Cafferkey, K.Higgins, C.Barrett, T.Cunniffe, C.Boyle, S.O'Shea, B.Moran, A.Campbell, J.Dillon, A.Kilcoyne, M.Ronaldson, M.Hannick, M.Conroy. Subs – S.Ryder for Boyle, K.Costello for Dillon, E.Varley for Hannick.

Cork – K.O'Halloran, R.Carey, C.Murphy, S.O'Donoghue, D.Limerick, M.Shields, E.Cadogan, A.O'Connor, F.Gould, P.Kelly, C.Keane, P.Kerrigan, D.Goulding, P.O'Flynn, J.Hayes. Subs – G.O'Shea for Hayes, F.Lynch for Kelly.

2007
Cork – K.O'Halloran, R.Carey, M.Shields, K.Harrington, S.O'Donoghue, D.Limerick, E.Cadogan, F.Gould, A.O'Sullivan, F.Lynch, C.Keane, P.Kerrigan, C.O'Neill, D.Goulding, S.Cahalane. Subs – R.Leahy for Cahalane, G.O'Shea for Keane, S.McCarthy for Lynch.

Laois – C.Munnelly, C.Healy, M.Timmons, B.Meredith, S.Lalor, J.O'Loughlin, N.Donoher, B.Quigley, C.Og Greene, D.Brennan, C.Rogers, S.O'Leary, M.Tierney, S.O'Neill, D.Conway. Subs – D.Kingston for O'Neill, I.Fleming for O'Leary.

2008
Kerry – T.Mac an tSaoir, C.O'Mahony, M.Maloney, S.Enright, Aidan O'Sullivan, K.Young, G.Duffy, D.Moran, Alan O'Sullivan, K.O'Leary, J.Buckley, M.O'Donoghue, P.Curran, T.Walsh, P.O'Connor. Subs – K.Brennan for Duffy, E.Hickson for Aidan O'Sullivan, B.Looney for Buckley, J.Doolan for Walsh, E.O'Neill for O'Donoghue.

Kildare – N.McConnell, C.Brophy, D.Brennan, S.Murphy, J.Browne, G.White, T.Byrne, M.Waters, N.Higgins, D.Whyte, E.O'Flaitheartaigh, K.Kelly, S.Fahy, A.Smith, G.Smullen. Subs – N.Clynch for Brophy, J.Fogarty for Kelly, J.Cocoman for Whyte, M.O'Sullivan for Fahy.

2009
Cork – A.Seymour, S.McLoughlin, L.Jennings, N.Galvin, Conor O'Driscoll, A.Walsh, B.Daly, C.O'Donovan, K.O'Driscoll, C.Sheehan, M.Collins, Colm O'Driscoll, C.O'Neill, D.Goold, P.Honohan. Subs – J.Fitzpatrick for Sheehan, B.Lombard for Jennings, B.O'Driscoll for Honohan, L.McLoughlin for K.O'Driscoll.

Down – G.Joyce, M.Digney, C.Murney, D.Turley, T.Hanna, J.Fitzpatrick, J.Murphy, M.Magee, O.Fitzpatrick, E.Toner, C.Maginn, J.O'Reilly, P.Devlin, P.McComiskey, C.Poland. Sub – N.Higgins for Digney.

CAPTAINS OF WINNING ALL-IRELAND UNDER-21 FOOTBALL TEAMS

1964—D. O'Donnell (Kerry)
1965—P. Dunny (Kildare)
1966—C. Shine (Roscommon)
1967—W. Loftus (Mayo)
1968—T. Diamond (Derry)
1969—L. Boyle (Antrim)
1970—D. Hunt (Cork)
1971—S . Looney (Cork)
1972—J. Waldron (Galway)
1973—J. Coffey (Kerry)
1974—J. Culkin (Mayo)
1975—K. O'Donoghue (Kerry)
1976—G. Murphy (Kerry)
1977—D. "Ogie" Moran (Kerry).
1978—S. Hayden (Roscommon)
1979—Ned King (Down)
1980—T. Dalton (Cork)
1981—S. Hayes (Cork)
1982—B. Tuohy (Donegal)
1983—E. Gibbons (Mayo)
1984—N. Cahalane (Cork)
1985—A. Davis (Cork)
1986—M. Slocum (Cork)
1987—J. Cunningham (Donegal)
1988—G. O'Brien (Offaly)
1989—S. O'Brien (Cork)
1990—V. Knightley (Kerry)
1991—Peter Canavan (Tyrone)
1992—Peter Canavan (Tyrone)
1993—Thomas Hanley (Meath)
1994—Damien O'Neill (Cork)
1995—Diarmuid Murphy (Kerry)
1996—Liam Hassett (Kerry)
1997—John McBride (Derry)
1998—Brian Scanlon (Kerry)

1999—Aiden Canning (Westmeath)
2000—C.McAnallen (Tyrone)
2001—C.McAnallen (Tyrone)
2002—J.Bergin (Galway)
2003—A.Brogan (Dublin)
2004—C.McKeever (Armagh)
2005—A.Burke (Galway)
2006—K.Higgins (Mayo)
2007—A.O'Sullivan (Cork)
2008—K.Young (Kerry)
2009—C.O'Neill (Cork)

ALL-IRELAND UNDER 21 FOOTBALL REFEREES 1964-2009

1964—Jimmy Martin (Roscommon)
1965—Jackie Martin (Tyrone)
1966—Jackie Martin (Tyrone)
1967—John Moloney (Tipperary)
1968—Jimmy Hatton (Wicklow)
1969—Brendan Lowth (Dublin)
1970—Paul Kelly (Dublin)
1971—S. Campbell (Kildare)
1972—Dick Barry (Meath)
1973—Mick Spain (Offaly)
1974—Gerry Hoey (Louth)
1975—Brendan Hayden (Carlow)
1976—Gerry Fagan (Armagh)
1977—Martin Meally (Kilkenny)
1978—Seamus Murray (Monaghan)
1979—G. McCabe (Tyrone)
1980—Weeshy Fogarty (Kerry)
1981—K. Campbell (Fermanagh)
1982—Tommy Moran (Leitrim)
1983—Padraig O'Gorman (Sligo)
1984—Paddy Kavanagh (Meath)
1985—Carthage Buckley (Offaly)
1986—John Gough (Antrim)
1987—Mickey Kearns (Sligo)
1988—Tommy Sugrue (Kerry)
1989—Pat Moran (Laois)
1990—Paddy Collins (Westmeath)
1991—Carthage Conlon (Westmeath)
1992—Tommy Howard (Kildare)
1993—Damien Campbell (Fermanagh)
1994—Pat McEnaney (Monaghan)
1995—Pat McEnaney (Monaghan)
1996—Pat Casserley (Westmeath)
1997—Michael Curley (Galway)
1998—Pat McEnaney (Monaghan)
1999—Brendan Gorman (Armagh)
2000—S.McCormack (Meath)
2001—A.Mangan (Kerry)
2002—M.McGrath (Donegal)
2003—G.Kinneavy (Roscommon)
2004—A.Mangan (Kerry)
2005—M.Deegan (Laois)
2006—J.McQuillan (Cavan)
2007—V.Neary (Mayo)
2008—M.Duffy (Sligo)
2009—C.Reilly (Meath)

MUNSTER UNDER-21 FOOTBALL FINALS

1962—Kerry 2-7, Cork 1-4
1963—Cork 2-3, Kerry 1-4
1964—Kerry 0-15, Tipperary 1-2
1965—Cork 2-14, Tipperary 1-6
1966—Kerry 3-8, Cork 0-14
1967—Kerry 2-12, Clare 1-7
1968—Kerry 5-7, Clare 2-9
1969—Cork 1-14, Kerry 1-11
1970—Cork 5-12, Clare 1-7
1971—Cork 1-10, Waterford 2-5
1972—Kerry 1-11, Cork 2-7
1973—Kerry 2-12, Cork 1-12
1974—Cork 3-5, Kerry 1-10
1975—Kerry 0-17, Waterford 1-5
1976—Kerry 2-16, Cork 1-6
1977—Kerry 2-8, Cork 0-8
1978—Kerry 0-14, Cork 0-9
1979—Cork 1-11, Clare 1-9
1980—Cork 3-15, Clare 0-4
1981—Cork 0-11, Kerry 0-6
1982—Cork 2-12, Kerry 0-4
1983—Kerry 1-10, Cork 0-12
1984—Cork 1-18, Limerick 0-4
1985—Cork 1-18, Clare 1-7
1986—Cork 0-8, Tipperary 0-7
1987—Kerry 0-7, Tipperary 0-7 (draw)
Kerry 0-15, Tipperary 1-11 (replay aet)
1988—Kerry 0-14, Clare 2-6
1989—Cork 3-15, Clare 1-7
1990—Kerry 2-9, Cork 0-9
1991—Kerry 1-8, Cork 0-10
1992—Kerry 3-12, Cork 1-8
1993—Kerry 1-21, Waterford 3-5
1994—Cork 2-11, Waterford 0-4
1995—Kerry 1-21, Waterford 2-5
1996—Kerry 3-14, Clare 0-6
1997—Kerry 2-11, Cork 3-8 (draw)
Kerry 0-12, Cork 1-7 (replay)
1998—Kerry 3-10, Tipperaray 1-11
1999—Kerry 1-10, Cork 0-7
2000—Limerick 0-7, Waterford 0-4.
2001—Cork 1-12, Limerick 0-8.
2002—Kerry 3-15, Clare 2-11.
2003—Waterford 2-8, Kerry 1-9.
2004—Cork 0-13, Kerry 0-12.
2005—Cork 1-14, Limerick 1-11.
2006—Cork 4-14, Waterford 1-6.
2007—Cork 3-19, Tipperary 3-12.
2008—Kerry 0-15, Tipperary 2-7.
2009—Cork 1-9, Tipperary 2-5.

LEINSTER UNDER-21 FOOTBALL FINALS

1964—Laois 1-8, Offaly 0-8
1965—Kildare 1-11, Offaly 0-10
1966—Kildare 4-14, Longford 2-5
1967—Kildare 3-11, Wicklow 0-4
1968—Offaly 2-13, Wexford 0-7
1969—Laois 2-7, Wicklow 2-6
1970—Louth 2-13, Offaly 3-9
1971—Offaly 1-9, Meath 0-11

1972—Kildare 0-14, Offaly 2-8 (draw)
Kildare 2-9, Offaly 0-6 (replay)
1973—Offaly 3-8, Kildare 3-6
1974—Dublin 1-10, Wexford 0-8
1975—Dublin 0-12, Laois 1-6
1976—Kildare 1-12, Dublin 0-9
1977—Offaly 0-12, Kildare 0-4
1978—Louth 2-8, Offaly 2-7
1979—Offaly 4-14, Louth 5-4
1980—Dublin 2-7, Kildare 1-10 (draw)
Dublin 0-10, Kildare 0-8 (replay)
1981—Louth 2-8, Longford 0-6
1982—Laois 2-11, Longford 0-3
1983—Kildare 1-13, Louth 1-8
1984—Dublin 0-9, Carlow 1-5
1985—Meath 2-7, Kildare 0-12
1986—Offaly 1-11, Laois 2-8 (draw)
Offaly 1-10, Laois 0-9 (replay)
1987—Laois 1-12, Meath 1-8
1988—Offaly 0-8, Wexford 1-5 (draw)
Offaly 0-12, Wexford 2-6
(first replay) after extra time
Offaly 1-12, Wexford 1-12
(second replay) after extra time
Offaly 2-7, Wexford 2-5 (third replay)
1989—Meath 2-5, Kildare 0-9
1990—Meath 1-14, Wicklow 0-6
1991—Meath 0-9, Wicklow 1-5
1992—Kildare 2-12, Dublin 0-9
1993—Meath 2-11, Dublin 2-9
1994—Laois 2-4, Meath 1-7 (draw)
Laois 1-17, Meath 1-13 after extra time
(replay)
1995—Offaly 0-14, Westmeath 0-8
1996—Meath 1-8, Louth 0-8
1997—Meath 1-11, Westmeath 0-7
1998—Laois 1-13, Dublin 1-7
1999—Westmeath 1-12, Laois 2-9 (draw)
Westmeath 1-9, Laois 0-10 (replay)
2000—Westmeath 0-7, Meath 0-6.
2001—Meath 0-10, Dublin 0-5.
2002—Dublin 1-17, Wicklow 2-4.
2003—Dublin 3-13, Longford 1-6.
2004—Kildare 0-7, Dublin 1-4. (draw)
Kildare 1-10, Dublin 0-12. (replay)
2005—Dublin 1-10, Kildare 1-10. (draw)
Dublin 0-13, Kildare 0-11. (replay)
2006—Laois 0-9, Longford 0-7.
2007—Laois 0-13, Offaly 1-7.
2008—Kildare 0-10, Wexford 0-6.
2009—Dublin 0-12, Laois 0-9.

CONNACHT UNDER-21 FOOTBALL FINALS

1964—Galway 3-6, Mayo 3-5
1965—Galway 3-9, Mayo 1-13
1966—Roscommon 1-15, Mayo 0-9
1967—Mayo 3-11, Roscommon 2-8
1968—Mayo 1-13, Roscommon 2-3
1969—Roscommon 1-9, Galway 0-12 (draw)
Roscommon 1-10, Galway 2-3
(replay after extra time)
1970—Mayo 0-14, Roscommon 1-10
1971—Mayo 5-10, Roscommon 0-8
1972—Galway 0-16, Roscommon 0-5
1973—Mayo 1-7, Galway 0-5
1974—Mayo 1-12, Roscommon 0-9
1975—Mayo 2-10, Galway 0-9
1976—Mayo 1-8, Galway 0-2
1977—Leitrim 1-3, Roscommon 0-5
1978—Roscommon 3-9, Galway 2-11
1979—Galway 0-12, Sligo 0-9
1980—Mayo 4-11, Galway 1-5
1981—Galway 0-9, Mayo 0-8
1982—Roscommon 1-10, Galway 0-5
1983—Mayo 1-19, Roscommon 1-6
1984—Mayo 2-7, Galway 2-4
1985—Mayo 2-6, Galway 0-7
1986—Mayo 0-12, Leitrim 0-5
1987—Galway 1-10, Roscommon 0-10
1988—Galway 0-10, Roscommon 0-6
1989—Galway 1-13, Roscommon 0-3
1990—Galway 0-9, Leitrim 0-5
1991—Leitrim 1-7, Galway 0-9
1992—Galway 1-10, Mayo 0-12
1993—Galway 0-14, Roscommon 0-9
1994—Mayo 0-12, Sligo 0-6
1995—Mayo 1-10, Sligo 1-10 (draw)
Mayo 1-16, Sligo 3-4 (replay)
1996—Galway 0-12, Mayo 0-5
1997—Mayo 0-7, Galway 0-6
1998—Galway 0-13, Leitrim 1-7
1999—Roscommon 1-12, Sligo 0-9
2000—Galway 1-12, Mayo 0-12.
2001—Mayo 0-15, Sligo 0-7.
2002—Galway 1-9, Mayo 1-8.
2003—Mayo 1-9, Galway 0-11.
2004—Mayo 0-16, Roscommon 0-13.
2005—Galway 1-13, Mayo 0-4.
2006—Mayo 0-15, Galway 1-5.
2007—Mayo 1-22, Roscommon 1-8.
2008—Mayo 1-14, Roscommon 0-14.
2009—Mayo 3-14, Sligo 1-8.

ULSTER UNDER-21 FOOTBALL FINALS

1963—Donega! 3-6, Cavan 1-3
1964—Donegal 2-14, Monaghan 0-4
1965—Down 0-9, Cavon 1-2
1966—Donegal 2-12, Down 1-6
1967—Derry 1-11, Monaghan 1-4
1968—Derry 4-9, Monaghon 2-4
1969—Antrim 2-8, Down 1-9
1970—Fermanagh 0-13, Cavan 0-8
1971—Fermanagh 2-12, Tyrone 1-8
1972—Derry 1-7, Tyrone 1-7
Tyrone 3-13, Derry 1-6 (replay)
1973—Tyrone 2-14, Monaghan 2-5
1974—Antrim 2-6, Tyrone 1-8
1975—Antrim 2-7, Tyrone 0-7
1976—Derry 1-6, Down 1-4
1977—Down 3-5, Cavan 0-10
1978—Down 0-11, Cavan 1-6
1979—Down 1-9, Tyrone 0-5
1980—Tyrone 4-4, Down 2-5
1981—Monaghan 0-8, Donegal 0-6
1982—Donegal 0-10, Derry 1-5
1983—Derry 3-13, Donegal 1-3

1984—Down 1-10, Antrim 1-8
1985—Derry 3-7, Tyrone 0-7
1986—Derry 4-7, Donegal 0-6
1987—Donegal 0-7, Monaghan 1-4 (draw)
Donegal 1-11, Monaghan 0-8 (replay)
1988—Cavan 3-10, Antrim 0-6
1989—Antrim 1-6, Down 1-5
1990—Tyrone 2-8, Down 0-11
1991—Tyrone 3-10, Down 0-8
1992—Tyrone 0-14, Monaghan 2-6
1993—Derry 1-9, Down 1-8
1994—Fermanagh 2-8, Derry 0-8
1995—Donegal 1-9, Cavan 1-9 (draw)
Donegal 3-11, Cavan 1-11 (replay)
1996—Cavan 1-11, Derry 1-5
1997—Derry 1-12, Fermanagh 1-6
1998—Armagh 1-8, Derry 0-10
1999—Monaghan 0-12, Donegal 1-8
2000—Tyrone 1-18, Donegal 1-4.
2001—Tyrone 1-19, Fermanagh 0-10.
2002—Tyrone 0-13, Cavan 1-7.
2003—Tyrone 2-8, Monaghan 0-11.
2004—Armagh 2-12, Derry 0-4.
2005—Down 2-14, Cavan 2-12. (after extra time)
2006—Tyrone 0-12, Derry 1-7.
2007—Armagh 1-16, Monaghan 1-9.
2008—Down 3-11, Derry 1-14.
2009—Down 1-14, Armagh 2-10.

ALL-IRELAND JUNIOR FOOTBALL FINALS 1912-2009

1912—Tipperary 1-4, Louth 1-3
1913—Kerry 0-7, Carlow 1-2
1914—Dublin 5-4, Mayo 1-6
1915—Kerry 0-6, Westmeath 1-2
1916—Dublin 6-4, Limerick 0-3 (replay)
Dublin 1-2, Limerick 1-2 (draw)
1917-1922—Suspended
1923—Tipperary 2-6, Carlow 1-1
1924—Kerry 1 -6, Longford 0-4
1925—Louth 2-6, Mayo 2-5
1926—Armagh 4-11, Dublin 0-4
1927—Cavan 4-1, Britain 1-1
Home Final: Cavan 0-7, Kildare 1-3
1928—Kerry 2-8, Louth 2-3
No Home Final.
London competed at semi-final stage.
1929—Westmeath 0-9, London 1-2
Home Final:
Westmeath 3-3, Limerick 0-3
1930—Kerry 2-2, Dublin 1-4
No Home Final. London competed at quarter-final stage.
1931—Galway 3-3, London 1-5
Home Final: Galway 1-8, Kildare 1-7
1932—Louth 0-6; London 0-4
Home Final: Louth 1-12, Roscommon 0-4
1933—Mayo 3-7, London 2-4
Home Final Mayo 2-15, Donegal 2-2
1934—Louth 1-3, London 0-3
Home Final: Louth 0-9, Kerry 1-4
1935—Sligo 5-8; London 0-3
Home Final: Sligo 4-2, Tipperary 2-5
1936—Wicklow 3-3, Mayo 2-5
No Home Final
1937—Longford 0-9 London 0-7
Home Final: Longford 1-7, Mayo 1-6
1938—London 5-7, Leitrim 2-9
Home Final: Leitrim 1-8, Kildare 0-5
1939—Dublin 2-14, London 0-4
Home Final: Dublin 2-9, Roscommon 1-9
1940—Roscommon 2-9, Westmeath 0-5
No Home Final
1941—Kerry 0-9, Cavan 0-4
No Home Final
1942-45—Suspended
1946—Down 2-10, Warwickshire 1-9
Home Final: Down 2-7, Leitrim 2-3
1947—Meath 2-11, London 2-6
Home Final: Meath 1-12, Kerry 3-3
1948—Dublin 2-11, London 1-5
Home Final: Dublin 2-6, Armagh 2-3 (unfinished). Replay ordered.
Dublin 3-8, Armagh 2-6.
1949—Kerry 2-14, Lancashire 0-6
Home Final: Kerry 3-11, Down 3-5
1950—Mayo 2-4, London 0-3
Home Final: Mayo 4-3, Derry 2-7
1951—Cork 5-11, Warwickshire 1-3
Home Final: Cork 1-5, Mayo 1-2
1952—Meath 3-9, London 0-4
Home Final: Meath 0-11, Leitrim 0-2
1953—Cork 1-11, Lancashire 1-4
Home Final: Cork 2-9, Longford 0-4
1954—Kerry 1-7, London 1-5
Home Final: Kerry 3-6, Donegal 1-6
1955—Cork 3-9, Warwickshire 1-5
Home Final: Cork 3-10, Derry 1-7
1956—Monaghan 3-7, London 2-6
Home Final: Monaghan 1-8, Kildare 0-5
1957—Mayo 2-7, Warwickshire 2-5
Home Final: Mayo 1-11, Cork 1-3
1958—Galway 4-5, Lancashire 3-1
Home Final: Galway 1-10, Meath 0-7
1959—Fermanagh 1-11, London 2-4
Home Final: Fermanagh 1-13, Kerry 2-3
1960—Dublin 2-5, London 0-5
Home Final: Dublin 1-12, Galway 0-9
1961—Louth 1-13, Yorkshire 1-10
Home Final: Louth 0-11, Galway 1-7
1962—Meath 1-13, London 3-5
Home Final: Meath 1-11, Cavan 3-4
1963—Kerry 3-5, Lancashire 2-5
Home Final: Kerry 1-12, Wexford 2-7
1964—Cork 1-8, London 2-4
Home Final: Cork 2-5, Meath 1-8 (draw)
Cork 2-9, Meath 0-10 (replay)
1965—Galway 1-8, Hertfordshire 0-4
Home Final: Galway 1-15, Kildare 2-4
1966—London 1-6, Cork 0-8
Home Final: Cork 2-12, Down 0-9
1967—Kerry 0-9, London 0-4
Home Final: Kerry 1-10, Mayo 1-3
1968—Tyrone 3-8, London 0-7.
Home Final: Tyrone 3-9, Mayo 2-11
1969—London 3-9, Wicklow 1-12
Home Final: Wicklow 0-12, Kerry 1-8
1970—London 1-12, Kildare 0-11
Home Final: Kildare 1-12, Cork 1-10

1971—London 1-9, Dublin 0-9
Home Final: Dublin 1-14, Cork 2-5
1972—Cork 5-16, Hertfordshire 0-3
Home Final: Cork 1-10, Galway 0-8
1973—Laois 0-12, London 1-8
Home Final: Laois 2-13, Sligo 1-5
1974-1982—Suspended
1983—Kerry 0-15, Yorkshire 0-2
Home Final: Kerry 1-9, Dublin 0-5
1984—Cork 3-20, Warwickshire 0-7
Home Final: Cork 1-10, Wexford 0-9
1985—Galway 4-17, Warwickshire 0-4
Home Final: Galway 0-9, Kerry 0-9 (draw)
Galway 0-11, Kerry 0-7 (replay)
1986—London 1-9, Cork 0-7
Home Final: Cork 0-9, Meath 1-6 (draw)
Cork 0-11, Meath 1-4 (replay)
1987—Cork 0-14, Warwickshire 0-3
Home Final: Cork 2-7, Dublin 0-8
1988—Meath 1-10, London 0-3
Home Final: Meath 1-9, Cork 1-5
1989—Cork 0-18, Warwickshire 0-3
Home Final: Cork 1-11, Kildare 0-3
1990—Cork 3-16, Warwickshire 0-8
Home Final: Cork 1-12, Meath 1-10
1991—Kerry 2-14, Lonclon 0-5
Home Final: Kerry 1-15, Meath 0-12
1992—Wexford 1-9, Cork 0-11
Semi-finals: Cork 1-19, London 1-4
Wexford 1-13, Mayo 0-12
1993—Cork 0-11, Laois 2-3
Semi-finals: Laois 1-19, Lancashire 2-6
Cork 0-15, Mayo 0-7
1994—Kerry 0-15, Galway 0-4
Semi-finals: Kerry 0-13, Dublin 1-7
Galway 1-13, Lancashire 0-8
1995—Mayo 3-9, London 0-10
Semi-finals: London 2-10, Kerry 1-12
Mayo 3-10, Meath 2-7
1996—Cork 4-11, Meath 0-10
Semi-finals: Meath 0-16, Yorkshire 2-6
Cork 0-12, Galway 1-5
1997—Mayo 2-8, Kerry 1-10
Semi-finals: Kerry 0-12, Meath 1-8
Mayo 2-10, Warwickshire 0-8
1998—Tipperary 2-9, Offaly 0-6
Semi-finals: Offaly 0-12, Sligo 1-6
Tipperary 4-22, Warwickshire 0-4
1999—Waterford 2-12, Meath 2-11
Semi-finals: Waterford 2-11, Roscommon 1-9
Meath 6-20, Warwickshire 0-6
2000—Roscommon 0-14, Kerry 0-11.
2001—Cork 1-15, Mayo 3-7.
2002—Wicklow 4-9, Kerry 2-12.
2003—Meath 0-16, Galway 1-7.
2004—Waterford 1-10, Leitrim 1-10. (draw)
Waterford 2-12, Leitrim 2-9. (replay)
2005—Cork 0-10, Meath 1-4.
2006—Kerry 1-9, Roscommon 0-10.
2007—Cork 1-14, Wexford 3-2.
2008—Dublin 0-13, Roscommon 0-7.
2009—Cork 0-15, Roscommon 0-12.

JUNIOR FOOTBALL FINALISTS

1912
Tipperary—Ned O'Shea, John O'Shea, L. Gorman, Ned Delahunty, F. O'Brien, Ned Egan, N. Vaughan, T. Connors, M. Devitt, H. Kennedy, J. Quinn, D. Stapleton, Dick Heffernan, P. Dwyer, J. Shelly, Bill Scully, P. Egan.
Louth—M. Carolan, M. Tinnelly, J. McGann, S. Reilly, J. Burke, P. Kirk, J. Naughton, E. McCormack, P. McLoughlin, T. Burke, J. Matthews, P. O'Hanlon, P. Mulholland, P. McGeogh, W. Wiley, M. Heeney, B. Lennon.

1913
Kerry—A. Callaghan (goal), P. Foley, J. Keating, J. McGaley, J. Kennedy, P. O'Donnell, J. Courtney, H. Murphy, E. Murphy, T. King, E. Hogan, M. Daly, J. Connell, J. Collins, J. McCarthy.
Carlow—W. Mulhall (capt.), M. Lawlor, D. Fitzpatrick, Millett, W. Cooney, F. Shaw, J. Murphy, A. Murphy, P. Haughney, P. Hogan, Hennessy, M. Haughney, M. Hogan, Tobin, W. Murphy.

1914
Dublin—P. Carey, S. Synott, T. Corr, M. Nolan, P. Smith, D. Kiely, D. Kelly, P. Kearns, F. Burke, F. McGann, J. Cromien, P. McDonnell, J. Coogan, J. McAdams, P. Whelan.
Mayo—J. O'Reilly, J. Gavin, J. Jordan, J. Robinson, Jas. Robinson, P. Cowley, T. Ruane, M. Murray, T. Gibson, J. Brennan, J. McNally, E. McEllin, J. Reilly, P. Galvin, J. McNulty.

1915
Kerry—R. Power, W. Sheehan, J. Cronin, M. Carroll, P. Sullivan, J. Dunne, T. Doherty, M. Moriarty, J. Connor, T King (capt.), P. Slattery, M. Daly, J. Walsh, B. Hickey, J. McGaley.
Westmeath—L. Leech, P Whelehan, J. McKeogh, M. McKeon, J. Cooney, R. O'Reilly, P. Arthur, J. Moran, Rochford, J. Reilly, Bob Reilly, J. McGuinness, Early, P. Ledwith, Mallory.

1916
Dublin—J. Maguire (capt.), F. McGann, H. O'Neill, N. Sheridan, J. O'Reilly, P. McDonnell, J. Molloy, P White, J. O'Donovan, P. McCarville, F. Burke, B. Joyce, J. Hayden, J. Treacy, J. Byrne.
Limerick—C. Kiely (capt.), P. O'Donnell, M. Walsh, M. Osborne (goal), M. Davoren, D. O'Grady, J. J. O'Keeffe, T. Butler, J. Lyons, M. McGrath, D. Breen, A. Dalton, J. O'Donovan, D. Casey, J. Crowley.

1923
Tipperary—Ned Cummins (capt.), T Hogan, P. Walsh, H. Dillon, Gus Dwyer, M. Barry, M. Nolan, D. Mullins, T Tubridy, G. McCarthy, J. Delaney, T. Dunne, J. Davy, T. Armitage, P. Dwan.

Carlow—B. Hennessy, M. Murray, B. Nolan, W. Cooney, W. Doyle, W. Hogan, W. Qulgley, M. Hogan, J. Moore, P. Haughney T. Nolan, E. Wall, M. Hanley, R. McDonnell, T. Dillon.

1924

Kerry—J. Riordan (goal), J. McCarthy (capt.), D. O'Connell, W. Riordan, J. Slattery, P. Clifford, T. Graham, M. Graham, T. Mahony, Paud Sullivan, T. O'Donnell, S. Kerins, E. Fitzgerald, D. O'Connor, T. O'Connor.

Longford—F. Gaffney (capt.), J. Brennan, P. Bates, F. Canning, P. McWade, C. Heuston, J. McWade, M. Deane, E. Gaffney, M. Grehan, P Reilly, M. Burke, M. Cawley, M. O'Toole, H. Greene. Subs: F. Beirne, J. Gavigan.

1925

Louth—S. Hughes, M. Tuite, J. Traynor, J. Lynch (capt.), M. Lynch, J. McMahon, W. Doyle, T. Rath, M. McKeown, J. Heaney, J. Halligan, E. Kane, J. Murray, F. Penthony, P Butterley.

Mayo—P. Hoban, J. Courell, R. Coleman, M. J. Moran, J. McGahern, J. Gallagher (capt.), M. Barrett, J. Carr, J. Burke, T. Carty, M. Chambers, J. Biggins, E. Hogan, C. Armstrong, M. J. Horan.

1926

Armagh—C. Morgan, H. Cumiskey, Gene Hanratty (capt.), J. Vallely, Joe Harney, J. Maguire, Owen Connolly, J. Corrigan, F. McAvinchey, F. Toner, P. Fearon, J. Kernan, H. Arthurs, J. Donaghy, J. McCusker. Sub: J. McEntee for F. McAvinchey.

Dublin—H. Kelly (goal), T. Kavanagh (capt.), E. Rice, D. Nolan, J. Rodgers, M. Langton, J. Corcoran, W. Finlay, S. Banim, A. Doyle, D. Murphy, Joe Sherlock, S. Nolan, J. Doran, M. Gill.

1927

Cavan—P. Lynch, J. Morgan, J.P. Dolan, T. Crowe, G. Malcolson, P. Leddy, F. Gilsenan, L. Mallon, P. Fox, H. O'Reilly, F. Fitzpatrick J. Young, P. Devlin, A. Conlon, P.J. O'Reilly.

Britain—P.J. Kane, P. Darby, E. O'Hourigan, M. Fitzgerald, P. O'Malley, M. Kelly, L. Hartnett, R. Mackey, J. Burns, G. Keevans, J. Farrell, J. Cox, P. Gallagher, L. Duffy, S. Marshall.

1928

Kerry—Billy McSweeney, R. O'Donoghue (capt), T. Barrett, M. Healy, J. Price, M. Doyle, J. Quill, J. Murphy, T. Landers, R. Savage, T. Curran, J. Horan, T. O'Donnell, R. Clifford, J. Sullivan.

Louth—Callaghan, Roche, Downey, Corroway, Cluskey, Bishop, Canavan, MaHhews, Connor, Byrne, Byrne, Hearty, Gunning, Mullan, Bailey.

1929

Westmeath—F. McGuinness (capt.), S. Bracken (goal), M. McCarthy, A. Mullen, T. Finneran, J. Dunican, A. Dunne, J. Austin, D. Breen, J. Byrne, P. Bracken, J. Guilfoyle, J. Smyth, J. Coughlan, T. Seery.

London—J. Farrell (capt.), C. Finnegan (goal), D. Fitzpatrick, R. Smith, J. Shalloe, J. Dillon, R. Tuite, L. Hartnett, G. Murphy, H. Murphy, P. Mulpeter, T. Morgan, L. Cunningham, J. Reilly, C. Traynor.

1930

Kerry—D. O'Keeffe, P. Murphy, D. O'Donoghue, J. O'Connor, S. Moynihan, J. O'Connor (Cahirciveen), L. Powell, C. Geaney, D. Spring, J. Flavin, J. Price, W. Quill, M. O'Regan, M. Healy, T. Landers.

Dublin—J. Begley, Hugh Kelly, P. Rogers, F. Kavanagh, P. Byrne, P. Hickey, J. O'Rourke, P. Kavanagh, C. Duffy, E. Lee, A. Dixon, G. O'Reilly. E. Hunston, Dr. S. Lavan, M. Brennan.

1931

Galway—J. O'Rourke, M. Connaire, W. Mannion, P. Morris, J. Mitchell, M. Mannion, P. Daly, F. Fox, J. Dunne, M. Stewart, J. Kelleher (capt.), W. Birrell, F. Morris, Martin Donnellan, B. Nestor.

London—C. Finnegan, D. Fitzpatrick, R. Smith, J. Murphy, J. Dillon, P. O'Malley (capt.), C. Murray, J. Fitzpatrick, G. Murphy, J. O'Brien, M. Lennon, P. Mulpeter, J. Power, M. Reilly, C. Traynor.

1932

Louth—P. Byrne (capt.), M. Leech, P. Dunne, W. Crilly, T. McArdle, V. Kerr, P. Cluskey, P. Martin, P. Devlin, J. Culligan, P. Moore, J. Mullan, T. Tiernan, P. Downey, J. Moonen. Sub: J. Byrne for P. Devlin.

London—D. Fitzpatrick (capt.), M. Murphy, M. Fitzpatrick, M. Lennon, C. Corpenter, C. Finnegan, J. Dillon, J. Fitzpatrick, J. Murphy, P. MulpeteQ G. Murphy, H. Murphy, D. Loughlin, J.J. Power, J. McGrath. Sub: Joe Murphy for C. Murray.

1933

Mayo—T. Grier (capt.), J. O'Gara, P. O'Loughtin, P. J. Coffey, B. Frazer, P. J. Walsh, M. Raftery, P. Collins, T. Regan, J. Carney, P. Conboy, P. Laffey, H. O'Brien, T. Kelly, T. Culkin.

London—C. Finnegan, L. Murphy, M. Murphy, G. Murphy, J. Roche, J.J. Keogh, P. Mulpeter, W. Kelly, T. Keyes, J. Dillon, J. Fitzpatrick (capt.), H. Murphy, J. O'Brien, C. Carpenter, J. Murphy. Sub: R. Smith for J. Fitzpatrick.

1934

Louth—H. Callan (goal), J. Doyle (capt.), P. Tuite, T. Tiernan, J. Collins, J. McKevitt, P. Cluskey, M. Callaghan, J. Beirne, P. Byrne, J. Clarke, P. Mullen, P. Moore, V. Kerr, P. McKevitt.

London—J. Smith, R. Kelly, H. Murphy, T. Behan, T. Shields, P. Mulpeter, G. Murphy, J. Roche, J. Fitzpatrick, Walsh, C. Carpenter, P. Buckley, P. Devlin, J. Murphy, P. Carroll.

1935
Sligo—J. Scanlon (capt.), S. Scanlon, P. McGovern, J. Carty, M. Kennedy, O. Harte, P. Tiernan, F. Henry, M. Waters, C. Curran, P. Brennan, M. Stenson, J. O'Donnell, S. Tansey, J. Quinn.

(Note: The Sligo team listed is the one that is on all the papers. However according to the photograph three of those listed, M. Kennedy, P. Brennan and J. Quinn were not on. The three players in the photograph were F. Cavanagh, M. Snee and M. O'Dowd.

London—D. Buckley (capt.), J. Smith, W. Higgins, P. Grant, K. Hughes, P. Hartley, T. Shiels, P. Carroll, G. Murphy, P. Mulpeter, L. Murphy, R. Murphy, J. O'Loughlin, J. Murtagh, J. Reilly.

1936
Wicklow—J. Kelly, T. Sullivan, P. Nolan, M. O'Brien, Bob Elliot, J. Dalton, J. Deering, M. Byrne, D. Kerrigan, M. Keating, P. Sullivan, T. Tyrell, M. O'Neill (capt.), Ned Byrne, G. Kealy. M. Frawley for M. Byrne, R. Walsh.

Mayo—J. Acton, A. Golden, W. Frazer, W. Durkin, J. Robinson, M. Collins, W. Mongey, P. Bennett, J. McLoughlin, T. Grier, D. Sullivan, M. O'Malley, P. O'Malley, P. Judge, M. Heaney.

1937
Longford—G. Marsden, J. Lyons, J. McDermott, J. Murphy, E. Reilly, J. Regan, B. Sheridan, J. McCarthy, J. Keenan, W. Keenan, H. Rogers, J. Rogers, F. Marsden, B. Reilly, J. Murphy.

London—J. Smith, C. Feeney, D. Larkin, T. Shields, J. Sweeney, D. Fitzmaurice, C. Murphy, P. McEnroe, J. O'Sullivan, H. Murphy, M. O'Sullivan, P. Conboy, P. Mulpeter, M. Moore, R. Baker, E. Stenson. Sub: J. Sweeney.

1938
London—J. Smith, C. Murphy, T. Shields, J. Sweeney, D. Fitzmaurice, J. Sullivan (capt.), J. Byrne, P. Conboy, H. Murphy, E. Stenson, W. Kelly, P. Rosney, O. McKeown, R. Baker, P. Mulpeter. Subs: J. Grennan, P. Burke, D. Larkin.

Leitrim—F. McGoldrick, P. Reynolds, E. O'Reilly, M. Kilkenny (capt.), F. Carter, J. F. McGuinness, P. Rogan, G. Shanley, M. Moran, J. Shanley, E. Dolan, J. Keegan, J. Molohan, J. Turbitt, J. Mitchell. Sub: H. Turbitt.

1939
Dublin—P. Dowling, B. Murphy, C. Donnellan, W. Rayburn, F. Harford, H. Donnelly, D. Smyth, R. Smyth, J. Farrell, T. Dowling, M. Richardson, M. Meehan, T. Markey, J. Sweeney, M. O'Reilly. Sub: P. Kennedy For J. Sweeney.

London—J. Smith, C. Murphy, T. Shiels, F. Feeney, E. Stenson, J. O'Sullivan, J. Kennedy, H. Murphy, J. Byrne, P. Burke, E. Monaghan, W. Williams, O. McKeown, R. Baker, P. Mulpeter.

1940
Roscommon—F. Glynn, J. F. Comer, J. P. O'Callaghan, O. Hoare, H. Connor, P. Kelly, W. Heavey, J. Murray, E. Boland, P. Kenny, K. Winston, D. Keenan, G. Beirne, H. Gibbons (capt.), P. McManus. Sub: P. Murray, K. Heavey.

Westmeath—S. Bracken, E. Martin, C. Fagan, A. Carr, P. J. O'Neill, J. Carbury (capt.), M. Dunne, J. Lawlor, J. Leech, V. Gillick, P. McCormack, M. Devaney, E. McCormack, P. Mullen, G. Wallace. Subs: M. Daly for J. Leech, A. Mullen for V. Gillick, M. Keogh.

1941
Kerry—J. Sheehy, T. Brosnan (capt.), T. O'Sullivan, T. Long, T. Barrett, D. Lyne, T. Lyne, J. Sexton, J. Murphy, M. McCarthy, D. J. Healy, J. Kennington, W. O'Donnell, P. Donoghue, P. McCarthy.

Cavan—J. D. Benson, T. Cahill, J. F. McGahern, M. Argue, J. O'Reilly, P. Coyle, J. Greenan, J. Maguire, W. Doonan, T. Hennessy, B. Hunt, J. Devlin, P. Coyle, J. Coyle, P. J. Clarke. Sub: J. J. Cassidy.

1946
Down—E. McGivern, P. O'Hagan, A. Murnin, H. Downey, G. Browne, E. Grant, Noel McCarthy, G. Carr (capt.), J. Haughian, G. Doherty, T. Brown, D. Downey, D. Kennedy, H. Brown, J. Heaney. Subs: K. O'Hare, M. Short.

Warwickshire—R. Tumulty, R. Green, P. J. Foran, J. Lonergan, T. Geraghty, W. Halton, M. Hartney, P. Hartnett, A. Green, P. Mooney, P. Judge, J. McDermott, J. Casey, M. O'Dowd, J. O'Neill.

1947
Meath—T. Tuite, E. McCabe, W. Rispin, J. Donegan, P. Connell, M. O'Brien, G. McArdle, D. Taaffe, E. Daly, W. Snow, J. Johnson, J. Sampson, J. Carolan, L. McGuinness (capt.), J. Hand. Subs: J. Casserley for J. Sampson, A. O'Reilly for T. Tuite, M. McCaffrey for W. Rispin.

London—F. Finnesson, J. Poppenwell, S. Melotte, S. Mulderrig, P. Casey, E. McQuillan, P. Dolan, M. Wrenn, F. Moore, R. Allen, D. Mulvihill, M. Kilcullen, F. Cummins, J. Farrelly, P. Traynor. Sub: D. O'Shea for J. Farrelly.

1948
Dublin—V. Russell, L. Ledwidge, G. Donoghue, N. Fingleton, M. Richardson, E. Lyons, M. Scanlon, S. Farrell, J. Tunney, P. Walsh (capt.), J. O'Toole, J. McDonnell, J.

Copeland, E. Kenneally, K. Heffernan.
London—F. Fennison, F. Cummins, E. McQuillan, T. Crean, P. Casey, J. Owens, D. Mulvihill, F. P. Forkin, C. Carroll, T. Dunne, P. Dolan, F. Bambrick, J. Murray, D. Curran, J. Moriarty.

1949

Kerry—L. Fitzgerald, J. O'Connor, T. Flynn, D. Dowling, M. Lynch, P. Shanahan, M. McElligott, Seán Murphy, J. Dowling, P. Murphy, P. McCarthy, T. Long (capt.), J. C. Cooper, M. J. Palmer, J. Kennedy.
Lancashire—J. Duffy, T. Heffernan, P. McDermott, J. Brett, J. Regan, Jas. Duffy, M. Kilkenny (capt.), J. Fitzgerald, R. Harrison, J. Keane, P. J. Wright, F. Flynn, J. Tiernan, P. Carroll, M. Mullally. Sub: R. O'Rafferty for J. Fitzgerald.

1950

Mayo—T. Byrne, P. Gilvarry, P. Doherty, T. Quinn, J. Staunton, J. O'Sullivan, C. Hegarty, S. Hennigan, P. Jordan, T. Canavan, S. Mellotte (capt.), M. Loftus, F. McGovern, M. McDonnell, J. J. McGowan. Sub: A. O'Toole for T. Canavan.
London—M. Minchin, J. Owens, T. Crean, J. Butler, F. Canavan, M. Lynch, P. Brennan, J. Leahy, P. McConnan, S. Shields, R. Murphy, M. Barry, F. Stockwell, P. Quinn, J. Barton. Sub: J. Griffin for F Canavan

1951

Cork—C. Kearney, W. Barry, Noel Fitzgerald, P. J. Kelly, S. O'Connell, D. Bernard, J. Downing, T. Moriarty, J. J. Henchion (capt.), Ted Kelleher, M. Galvin, G. Hurley, E. Prendergast, S. Condon, P. O'Regan Subs: M. O'Shea for J. Downing, F. Scanlan for T. Moriarty.
Warwickshire—F. Conroy, F. Daly, P. O'Reilly, P. Kinsella, A. O'Neill, J. Turner, T. O'Brien, H. Burke, D. Regan (capt.), P. Reynolds, W. Holton, P. Clarke, J. Johnson, P. O'Sullivan, P. Clarke. Subs: T. Skahill for F. Daly, M. Walsh for P. Clarke.

1952

Meath—P. Watters, P. McKeever, J. Donegan, E. Mee, F. Clare, K. Lenehan, B. Conlon, T. O'Brien, S. Duff, L. O'Brien, D. Brennan, S. O'Brien, P. Whelan (capt.), T. Moriarly, P. Ratty. Subs: J. Smith for B. Conlon, J. McHugh for J. Smith.
London—P. Fall, H. O'Donnell, J. O'Sullivan, T. Crean, P. Brennan, J. Butler, T. O'Connell, J. Walsh, J. Leahy, S. Boyle, J. Barton, S. Shiels, J. Moriarty, P. Fitzgerald, M. Lowrey. Sub: S. Henry for J. Butler.

1953

Cork—J. Lyons (capt.), J. Finnegan, G. Linehan, E. Downey, D. O'Herlihy, D. Murray, J. Lowney, J. Collins, D. Madden, T. Furlong, G. Brennan, J. O'Donovon, E. Goulding, J. Creedon, J. Barry. Sub: J. O'Keeffe for D. Madden.
Lancashire—E. McDermott, J. McCabe, P. McDermott, J. Cahill, J. Harrison, E. Bartley, S. Keane, J. Quirke, P. J. Wright, M. McDermott, J. Corr, J. Burns, T. Shiel, C. Johnson, V. Wymes. Sub: J. Flynn.

1954

Kerry—N. Hussey, T. Spillane, J. O'Connor, T. Healy, T. Costello, J. Spillone, D. Falvey, E. Fitzgerald, D. Dillon, J. Cullotly, T. Collins, S. Lovett, P. P. Fitzgerald, E. Dowling, B. Galvin.
London—P. Casey, J. McHugh, T. Crehan, P. Hinson, J. Glennon, E. Moran, C. Carroll, K. Mulderrig, J. Walsh, M. Lowry, P. McGlennon, M. O'Malley, J. Sugrue, J. Murrihy, S. Shields. Sub: J. McGurk for J. Murrihy.

1955

Cork—L. Power, T. Moynihan, Dermot O'Sullivan, T. O'Callaghan, T. Connolly, B. O'Sullivan, Paddy Murphy, J. Collins, T. Furlong, D. Murphy, Dermot O'Donovan, Bob Troy, D. J. O'Sullivan, R. Nutly, O. McAuliffe (capt.). Subs: P. J. Kelly for P. Murphy, P. Murphy for T. Moynihan.
Warwickshire—D. McMahon, J. Gately, J. Turner, T. Quinn, A. O'Neill, P. Duggan, P. Holton, W. Wynne, J. Wynne, P. O'Flynn, P. Murphy, P. Burke, J. Johnson, R. Malone, C. Deeney.

1956

Monaghan—T. McArdle, G. McArdle, O. O'Rourke, B. Hamill, D. McGuigan, D. Ward, P. McGuigan, J. Byrne, S. McElroy, S. Mulligan, T. Duffy, P. Murphy, P. Clarke (capt.), N. Ward, E. McCooey. Sub: E. Murphy for S. M. McElroy.
London—J. J. Minihan, J. McHugh, P. Dooley, J. Clarke, D. McCarthy, J. Spillane, A. Cunningham, J. Lynn (capt.), C. Greene, M. Lowry, P. McGlennon, M. Vesey, J. Lyons, S. Mulderrig, E. Nealon. Subs: W. Cantillon for D. McCarthy, A. McWade for J. M McHugh.

1957

Mayo—E. Waters, I. McCaffrey, C. O'Toole, J. Healy, T. Lyons, J. McAndrew, P. Gannon, T. Quigley, P. Maye, D. McManus, P. McManamon, J. Biesty, J. Munnelly, M. Lokus (capt), J McGrath. Sub: P. Fallon for P. Maye.
Warwickshire—M. Flaherty, R. Burke, J. Wynne, J. Gately, T. O'Donoghue, E. Conway, B. Kennecly, A. O'Neill, P. McMurrough, J. O'Malley, M. Wynne, M. West, C. McGuigan, L. Brogan, P. Burke. Sub: T. Quinn for B. Kennedy.

1958

Galway—K. Cummins, B. Naughton, P. Davin, S. Meade, J. Donnellan, F. Cloonan, P. Dunne, J. Mannion, J. Glavey, M. "Hauleen" McDonagh, P. Coyle, E. Sharkey, M. Walsh, L. Mannion (capt.), M. Costello.
Lancashire—P. McCabe, J. Harrison, E. Smith, S. Houricane, P. Fox, C. Smith, S. Harte, J. Gargan, M. Reynolds, P. O'Brien, S. Goff, P. Farrelly 1capt.), J. St. John, M. O'Connor, S. Keane. Sub: C. McLoughlin.

1959

Fermanagh—J. O'Neill, O. O'Callaghan, I. McQuillan (capt.), J. Collins, J. J. Treacy, J. Cassidy, L. McMahon, J. Maguire, M. Brewster, D. O'Rourke, P. T. Treacy, K. Sreenan, F. McGurn, O. Clerkin, D. Devanney. Sub: H. Murphy for H. McGurn.

London—M. Nolan, J. Jennings, S. Mulderrig, P. McDonnell, R. Doherty, M. Freyne, S. Murphy, S. O'Sullivan, A. Cunningham, L. McLoughlin, P. Whelan, S. Harrison, S. McCormack, T. O'Connell, D. Waters. Subs: J. Garvey for S. O'Sullivan, E. Barrett for P. McDonnell, S. Moran for M. Freyne, T. O'Sullivan for J. Garvey.

1960

Dublin—F. McPhillips, C. Kane, J. Farrell, F. McHugh, C. Carroll, D. Mulligan, O. Callaghan, S. Murray, P. Hallinan, P. Delaney, V. Murphy, S. Coen, B. McDonald, J. Kirwan, F. McCourt.

London—C. Galligan, F. Tiernan, S. Hendry, F. Hurley, T. Crohon, J. Jennings, S. Murphy, T. Egan, J. Moffatt, M. Vesey, P. Wilson, P. Kane, J. Myles, T. Connell, S. Harrison. Subs: S. Mulderrig for M. Vesey, M. Burke for J. Myles.

1961

Louth—J. Clifford, O. Coombes, J. Butterly, A. Kirwan, A. Sheelan (capt.), M. Kelly, P. Dixon, F. Fegan, P. Jordan, J. Sheelan, M. McKeown, J. Judge, S. Goodman, H. Donnelly, F. Kirk. Subs: J. Mallon for O. Coombes, L. Toal for P. Jordan.

Yorkshire—M. Courtney, D. Grennan, L. Daly, T. Fox, P. Donlon, P. Beirne, P. O'Hara, M. Jordan, J. Kelly, H. Marron, M. Keegan (capt.), M. Kelly, P. Burke, M. Neary, J. Shields.

1962

Meath—M. Clarke, S. McCormack, J. Ryan, J. Quinn, W. Eiffe, T. Gibney, P. Price, T. Muldoon, T. Monaghan, P. McCormack, P. Hanley, J. Walsh (capt.), P. Christie, O. Kealy, T. Mongey. Subs: G. Quinn for P. Hanly, J. Kane for T. Muldoon, P. Black for T. Monaghan.

London—J. Kelly, P. McLarnon, S. Hendry, S. Mulderrig, P. Russell, J. Jennings, W. Flaherty, S. McCowell, N. O'Reilly, R. Doherty, P. Long, D. Sheehan, D. Mullins, J. Ashe, F. Smith. Subs: J. Hughes for P. McLarnon, J. Sharkey for W. Flaherty, P. Burke for N. O'Reilly.

1963

Kerry—A. Guerin, P. Kerins, J. Dowling, P. Sayers, T. Sheehan, M. Morris, J. Driscoll, J. D. O'Connor, D. O'Sullivan, T. Burke, B. Sheehy, D. O'Shea, T. O'Dowd, J. Burke, D. O'Donnell.

Lancashire—M. O'Donoghue, R. Henderson, E. Smith, P. Osborne, B. Harrington, C. Smith, M. O'Connell, O. Agnew, S. Corridan, M. McGeaney, P. J. Gilmartin, E. Fullan, T. Brennan, S. Goff, E. Hogan. Subs: R. Reidy for P. J. Gilmartin, P. Farrelly for E. Fullan.

1964

Cork—B. Murphy, D. Kehilly, J. McGrath, D. Coughlan, J. Dunlea, F. Kehilly, J. Crowley, D. McCarthy, M. O'Loughlin, T. Burke, C. Kelliher (capt.), M. Coughlan, H. Casey, S. McCarthy, Dermot O'Donovan. Sub: R Honohan.

London—J. Kelly, T. Fox, S. Hendry, C. O'Connor, E. O'Connor, E. O'Driscoll, J. Madden, T. Dowling, S. McCowell, J. Devine, P. Fitzmaurice, R. Doherty, D. Mullins, D. O'Connor, M. Doran. Sub: F. Gaughan for D. Mullins, A. Heaphy for C. O'Connor, H. Sheehan for R. Doherty.

1965

Galway—Greg Higgins, K. O'Connor, M. Kane, M. Tarpey, Coleen McDonagh, T. Brennan, T. Kelly, F. Canavan, J. Glynn, T. Sands, F. Heaney, T. Keenan, B. Geraghty, E. Geraghty, P. Crisham.

Hertsfordshire—L. O'Leary, P. Forde, P. Davin, J. McNicholas, J. Fitzpatrick, J. Lonergan, H. Hegarty, J. Connors, N. Ging, A. Rothwell, M. Connors, M. Smith, M. Trainor, E. McCruaden, T. O'Rourke. Subs: M. Lonergan for P. Forde, S. Daly for J. Lonergan, M. Donoghue for E. McCrudden.

1966

London—M. Nally, N. Lucey, S. O'Sullivan, P. Flynn, J. Kilcommins, J. Harrison, J. Madden, N. O'Reilly, J. Langan, P. McKenna, T. O'Sullivan, E. Glennon, P. Grainger, R. Dowd, T. Roche. Sub: M. Moffatt for J. Langan.

Cork—G. McCarthy, J. O'Flynn, T. Bermingham, A. Burke, M. Healy, J. O'Halloran, J. O'Leary, P. J. O'Sullivan, R. Evans, T. Burke, D. Sheehan, R. Honohan, C. Kelleher, Denis McCarthy (Kilmurray), B. O'Keeffe. Sub: J. Downing, J. Allen.

1967

Kerry—A. Fogarty, D. Lovett, D. O'Sullivan, G. McCarthy, D. Crowley, M. Gleeson, P. Aherne, M. O'Shea, M. Aherne, P. O'Connor, P. O'Connell, W. Doran, P. Finnegan, B. Kennedy, P. J. McIntyre. Sub: B. McCarthy for P. O'Connor.

London—P. Patton, M. Moffatt, S. Hendry, E. O'Connor, A. McDonagh, S. Keane, M. O'Meara, B. Morris, J. Kelly, L. Octagen, C. O'Malley, N. Peacock, H. Sheehan, M. Cahill, M. Doran. Subs: J. Allen for H. Sheehan, P. Russell for J. Kelly.

1968

Tyrone—A. Gallagher, D. O'Neill, S. Graham, P. Coyle, M. Jordan, A. McRory, F. McCartan, P. O'Neill (capt.), C. O'Hagan, P. McGonagle, S. Donaghy, K. Teague, F. Donnelly, B. Dolan, J. Early.

London—M. Nally, E. O'Connor, J. McDonagh, M. Moffatt, A. McDonagh, J. Madden, T. McGovern, P. McKenna, J. Gallagher, C. O'Meara, G. Driscoll, E. Glennon, P. J. Fitzpatrick, E. Slattery, F. Doherty. Subs: K. Kelly, M. Doran, R. O'Hare.

1969

London—M. Nally, J. Madden, F. Tiernan, M. Doran, J. Fenton, J. Harrison, M. Newell, P. McKenna, T. Dowling, P. J. Fitzpatrick, J. Meeney, H. Sheehan, G. Driscoll, M. Cahill, T. Greene. Subs: J. Toner for Harrison, M. Cooney for Fenton.

Wicklow—P. Cronin, W. Whelan, C. Keogh, P. Hedderman, M. Behan, G. Moran, J. Cullen, T. Foley, M. Coffey, T. Humphries, M. O'Toole, J. McDonald, L. Keogh, N. Carthy (capt.), W. Wall. Subs: S. Doyle for J. Cullen, P. Carty for G. Moran.

1970

London—M. Nally, J. Madden, J. McDonagh, J. Fenton, A. McDonagh, J. Harrison, M. Doran, P. McKenna, W. McAuliffe, B. Haipin, G. Mahony, E. Glennon, G. Driscoll, M. Cahill, T. Dowds. Subs: J. Toner, M. Fennell for M. Cahill.

Kildare—J. Leahy, D. Dalton, M. Cullen, T. Foley, T. Brereton, S. Dowling, K. O'Brien, J. O'Connell, H. Hyland, M. Mannion, P. Kinihan, J. J. Walsh, J. O'Reilly, T. Christian, D. Flanagan. Sub: J. Goulding for J. J. Walsh.

1971

London—M. Nally, C. Kelly, J. McDonagh, J. Behan, M. McMenamin, J. Harrison, M. Doran (capt.), P. McKenna, G. O'Mahony, J. Fennell, I. Donnelly, John O'Mahony, T. Meany, M. Fennell, T. Dowd. Sub: J. Thompson for J. Behan.

Dublin—A. Milner, L. Hickey, J. O'Neill, S. O'Hare, D. O'Donovan, F. Kavanagh, P. Farran, P. Wilson, F. Farren, C. Hanley, A. O'Toole, W. McCabe, F. Hutchinson, B. Keenan, J. Clarke. Subs: M. McMenamon for J. O'Neill, J. Kelly for J. Clarke.

1972

Cork—N. Murphy, Ted Murphy, J. Fahy, M. O'Doherty, Der Cogan, D. Kehilly, N. Crowley, M. Mehigan, S. Daly, Tony Murphy, S. O'Connor, D. Curran, Colmon Twomey, M. Sloane, T. Monaghan.

Hertsfordshire—M. English, P. Murphy (capt.), B. Cahill, F. O'Connor, M. Lawlor, S. Daly, J. Sherry, J. Mulvaney, J. Kellett, J. McGinley, F. Tynan, R. Sherlock, M. J. O'Sullivan, B. Flynn, E. McNelis. Subs: T. Clifford for B. Cahill, P. J. Galligan for P. Murphy, N. Deane for M. J. O'Sullivan.

1973

Laois—S. Whelan, P. Lalor, E. Harte, D. Lutterel, T. Clancy, J. Miller, P. Dunne, E. Whelan (capt.), B. Nerney, N. Flynn, S. Fleming, M. Dooley, D. Doogue, A. Fennell, D. Booth. Sub: T Dowling for D. Doogue.

London—M. Nally, J. Freyne, J. Hickey, M. Whelan, C. Kelly, F. Dolan, A. Flavin, M. Carolan, P. McKenna, M. McManamon, J. O'Mahony, N. McCarthy, T. Meany, B. Devlin, B. O'Connell. Subs: S. Corridan for M. Carolan, R. Munnelly for P. McKenna, J. Donnelly for S. Corridan.

1983

Kerry—J. Kennelly, M. Colgan, B. O'Sullivan, P. Brosnan, P. Sheehan, D. Hartnett, J. Stack, Ger O'Driscoll, T. O'Connell, J. Walsh, R. O'Donoghue, P. O'Mahony, J. Doyle, J. O'Sullivan, P. Sheehan. Subs: G. Casey for J. O'Sullivan, D. Higgins for P. Sheehan.

Yorkshire—B. Grogan, A. Beggs, D. McGuigan, S. Kennedy, B. O'Carroll, B. Coleman, P. Kissane, P. J. O'Reilly, H. Ruane, T. Cormelly, D. Murphy, G. Mills, P. J. Cullen, M. O'Connor, G. Molloy.

1984

Cork—W. McCarthy, D. O'Sullivan, J. Murphy, C. Counihan, B. Stack, D. Mulcahy, A. Davis, C. Collins, D Culloty, T. Cole, C. O'Reilly (capt.), M. McCarthy, N. O'Connor, P. Barrett, G. O'Rourke. Subs: P. O'Connor for N. O'Connor, J. O'Sullivan for D. Culloty, B. Daly for A. Davis.

Warwickshire—F. Quinn, K. McEvoy, M. Cunningham, A. Cairns, B. Higgins, P. Moran (capt.), E. Dowd, T. Tolan, B. McDonnell, S. Dunne, N. McLean, D. Brennan, A. Smith, B. Nannery, A. Tolan. Subs: J. McDonagh for M. Cunningham, J. McKinney for B. Higgins, M. Cunningham for A. Smith.

1985

Galway—P. Coyne, T. Heavey, G. Dolan, C. Faherty, G. Daly, M. Melia, S. Glynn, P. Greaney, H. Bleahen, P. O'Dea, G. Burke, T. McHugh, S. Burke, C. O'Dea (capt.), F. Stockwell. Subs. P. Hynes for S. Burke, G. Kinneavy for P. Coyne, J. Morley for G. Dolan.

Warwickshire—F. Quinn, G. Dowd, J. McDonagh, C. Conway, P. Moran, T. Hourihane, P. Power, T. Tolan, G. Byrne, D. Brennan, S. Dunne, D. Cooke, E. Tolan, N. McLeane, A. Connellan. Subs: M. Cunningham for T. Hourihane, J. King for G. Byrne, E. Sheridan for A. Connellan.

1986

London—G. Doyle, F. Glynn, T. Finnerty, R. Harran, S. Hussey, A. Wolfe, A. Hanley, M. Duggan, T. Walsh, J. O'Sullivan, B. O'Herlihy, J. Sheridan, M. Gallagher, L. Hughes, T. Parker.

Cork—J. O'Brien, D. O'Sullivan, S. Bowes, D. O'Connor, G. O'Connell, Gene O'Driscoll, T. O'Callaghan, D. Creedon, M. Spillane, M. Hannon, L. O'Callaghan, C. O'Connell, W. O'Riordan, T. Murphy, D. J. O'Shea. Sub: B. O'Herlihy.

1987

Cork—N. Gallagher, M. Walsh, S. Bowes, D. O'Connor, K. Creed, G. O'Driscoll, T. O'Callaghan, M. Spillane, G. Lally, W. O'Riordan, M. Kelleher (capt.), C. O'Connell, P. Harrington, T. Murphy, J. Dennehy. Sub: B. Lotty.

Warwickshire—F. Quinn, K. Kerr, P. Walsh, B. Carolan, K. Brennan, T. Tolan, P. Cooke, P. McLoughlin, E. Sheridan, E. Tolan, P. Higgins, D. Cooke, J. Butler, J. O'Donoghue, R. Doherty. Subs: N. McLean, J. O'Hanlon, M. Corcoran.

1988
Meath—R. O'Connell, P. Mcintyre, P. Fay, D. Mullen, D. Lynch, J. McEnroe (capt.), L. McEnroe, T. Kane, J. Cunningham, P. Henry, P. Curran, J. Devine, M. Kirk, T. Mullen, N. Rennick. Sub: H. Gilsennan for T. Mullen.
London—P. J. Burke, M. Grant, D. Carville, R. Heraty, J. Breen, M. Somers, A. Hanley, P. Pidgeon, P. Dreelan, R. Haran, C. White, S. Cassidy, B. Murphy, J. Linden, M. Hession. Subs: P. Reynolds for B. Murphy, D. Duggan for J. Linden.

1989
Cork—M. Creedon, P. Kenneally G. O'Connell, D. O'Connor, K. Creed, P. Buckley, B. Herlihy, M. Murphy, M. O'Connor, J. Casey, T. Buckley, D. McCarthy (capt.), O. Riordan, N. O'Connor, N. Twomey. Subs: C. O'Connell for M. Murphy, G. Ring for N. O'Connor, O. O'Sullivan for K. Creed.
Warwickshire—F. Quinn, S. Quigley, G. Dowd, P. McLaughlin, B. Carolan, J. King, T. Rafferty, E. Sheridan, D. Sheridan, D. Cooke, E. O'Loughlin, C. Folan, T. Tolan, G. Butler, A. Connellan. Subs: E. Tolan, L. Dundass, P. McLoughlin.

1990
Cork—J. Collins (capt.), M. Lyons, M. Farr, A. Devoy, S. Coughlan, P. Coleman, D. Burke, D. Fitzgerald, C. O'Sullivan, G. McPolin, A. Barry, G. Manley, M. Lewis, T. O'Reilly, J. Caulfield. Subs: D. Lynch, Martin Kelleher.
Warwickshire—F. Quinn, S. Daly, D. Sheridan, P. Kinnally, P. O'Connor, A. Connellan, D. Cooke, N. McMenamin, M. Laverty, C. Folan, J. Mooney, E. Tolan, S. Crowe, J. O'Donoghue, T. Tolan. Sub: M. Corcoran.

1991
Kerry—K. Moran, T. Hanafin, L. Burns, T. Dennehy, R. O'Dwyer, V. Knightly, P. Dillane, F. Ashe, T. Harrington (capt.), D. Moynihan, G. O'Driscoll, J. Kennedy, M. McAuliffe, T. Brosnan, S. O'Sullivan. Subs: T. Evans, S. Tuohy, J. Murphy.
London—M. Kelly, P. Murray, G. McDaid, T. Rooney, J. Flaherty, M. Somers, G. McColgan, S. McLoughlin, S. O'Brien, P. Goggins, P. Dreelan, D. Murray, P. Coleman, S. McDonald, R. Haran. Subs: M. Lavery, V. O'Neill, P. Doyle.

1992
Wexford—J. Cooper, S. O'Neill, T. Gorman, M. Caulfield, J. Casey, J. Dunne, P. Courtney, P. Walsh, B. Kavanagh, J. Byrne, N. Guinan, N. Darcy, S. Dunne, M. Furlong, G. Byrne. Subs: M. Darcy for S. Dunne, M. Mahon for M. Darcy.
Cork—J. O'Brien, A. Devoy, P. Coleman, M. Farr, S. Coughlan, Niall Murphy, Mark O'Connor, C. O'Sullivan, D. Devoy, R. Sheehan, G. Manley, D. Lynch, N. O'Connor, E. O'Mahony, M. Lewis. Subs: A. Berry for R. Sheehan, G. Cooney for D. Lynch.

1993
Cork—J. O'Brien, D. Walsh, P. Hanley, D. Burke, O. O'Sullivan, B. Murphy, D. McIlhenny, F. Collins, G. Ring, D. Fitzgerald, G. McPolin, P. Buckley, M. Harrington, K. Harrington, R. Sheehan (capt.).
Laois—E. Burke, B. Kerwin, D. Cryan, K. Dennis, B. Keville, J. O'Reilly, J. Buggy, A. Phelan, P. J. Dempsey, T. Bowe, L. Ramsbottom, T. Gorman, P. Coffey, M. Behan, M. O'Brien. Subs: D. Sweeney, D. Delaney.

1994
Kerry—D. O'Keeffe, P. Lenihan, L. Burns, J. B. O'Brien, J. Stack, K. Scanlon, S. Stack, D. Daly, D. Ó Cinnéide, J. Crowley, M. Keating (capt.), D. Moynihon, S. Murphy, S. Fitzgerald, P. O'Donoghue. Subs: J. Daly for D. Daly, C. O'Donnell for Keating, J. Walsh for K. Scanlon.
Galway—C. McGinley, T. Ryder, P. Crowley, D. Geraghty, R. Doyle, D. Carr, F. Keenan, D. Cronin, D. Gilmartin, P. Duffy, K. Collins, L. Colleran, D. Ó Flatharta, T. Morgan, J. Dooley. Subs: N. Ó Neachtáin for K. Collins, T. Screen for F. Keenan, J. Donnellan for P. Duffy.

1995
Mayo—N. O'Brien, S. Grealish, K. Byrne, B. Henihan, P. Touhy, G. McNicholas, D. O'Loughlin, P. McNamara, J. Heshin, G. Butler, M. Butler, O. Walsh, W. Fitzpatrick, V. Keane, D. Nestor. Subs: N. Loftus, N. Jennings, J. Commins.
London—M. O'Connor, C. Byrne, M. Moclair, P. Sheehy, C. Murphy, J. Sharvin, G. Barrett, S. McLoughlin, P. Coleman, O. Joy, P. McNamee, M. Byrne, T. Coakley, P. Coggins, J. Coffey. Sub: G. O'Shea.

1996
Cork—K. Farr, K. Creed (capt.), R. Walsh, P. Murray, J. O'Leary, Donal Óg Liatháin, M. O'Donovan, P. Murphy, O. O'Sullivan, J. Clifford, J. McCarthy, M. Harrington, J. Whooley, P. Hayes, N. Twomey. Subs: E. Barrett for P. Murphy, J. Dennehy for N. Twomey.
Meath—J. O'Sullivan, A. Coffey, D. Lane, A. Kealy, N. Collier, N. Kearney, S. Murphy, N. Nestor, J. Henry, R. Keely, S. Duff, K. Barry, P. O'Sullivan, T. O'Connor, B. Healy. Subs: M. Kirk for K. Barry, L. Rennicks for N. Collier.

1997
Mayo—J. Dunne, D. Costello, J. McCallion, J. Fallon, F. Touhy, V. Keane, G. Ruane, J. Hession, K. Comer, D. O'Loughlin, J. Commins, O. Walsh, W. Fitzpatrick, M. Smith, A. Morley. Subs: S. Grealish, D. Jennings.
Kerry—D. Murphy, A. Morris, M. O'Donoghue, D. Moynihan, K. Scanlon, M. O'Connor, S. O'Mahony, J. Daly, G.

O'Connor, L. Brosnan, E. Fitzpatrick, J. J. Corduff, S. McElligott, J. Quirke, P. O'Donoghue. Subs: O. Doherty for Morris, D. Dennehy for Corduff.

1998

Tipperary—S. Delahunty, D. Byrne, F. Clifford, M. O'Mahony, P. J. Lanigan, D. Peters, W. Morrisssey, P. Ormond, M. Leonard, P. Cahill, M. O'Shea, B. Maguire, K. Coonan, A. Crosse, T. Sheehan. Subs: D. O'Brien for B. Maguire, J. McAuliffe for M. Leonard.

Offaly—K. Furlong, J. Hurst, A. Murphy, B. Wynne, M. Kennedy, P. Mulvihill, D. Quinn, D. Kelly, P. Connolly, G. Comerford, N. Bryant, C. Brazil, J. Kennedy, M. Keenaghan, D. Connolly. Subs: S. Manley for G. Comerford, K. Slattery for C. Brazil.

1999

Waterford—A. Kirwan (capt.), D. Ryan, R. Power, M. Byrne, N. Guiry, P. Walsh, A. Reynolds, S. Bergin, P. Queally, C. Power, K. Walsh, D. Wyse, P. Ferncombe, J. Kiely, D. Whelan. Subs: C. O'Keeffe for K. Walsh, G. Walsh for P. Ferncombe.

Meath—J. Curry, M. Briody, A. Coffey, N. Collier, P. Curran, N. Horan, D. Davis, J. Cullinane, E. Grogan, P. Nestor, J. Carey, M. Crampton, N. Walsh, S. Duff, F. McMahon. Subs: S. Murphy for M. Briody, J. Mitchell for N. Walsh, B. Shaw for P. Nestor.

2000

Roscommon – S.Curran, I.Daly, G.Mockler, N.Galvin, B.Mannion, P.Noone, A.McPadden, K.Keane, D.Gillooly, G.Cox, B.O'Brien, C.Lynch, J.Neary, K.Mannion, R.O'Donoghue. Sub – J.Heneghan for Lynch.

Kerry – D.Murphy, D.McNamara, M.O'Donoghue, L.Harty, N.Sheedy, K.Scanlon, S.O'Mahony, P.Somers, J.Daly, J.Shanahan, D.Moynihan, L.Murphy, J.Dennehy, J.Quirke, B.Scanlon. Subs – E.Hennessy for Murphy, L.Brosnan for J.Quirke, M.Quirke for Daly.

2001

Cork – P.Mackey, D.Duggan, M.Daly, J.Honohan, N.O'Leary, G.Spillane, T.Kenny, M.Kelleher, M.Monaghan, P.Connolly, B.Coleman, A.O'Driscoll, B.O'Sullivan, G.Kelleher, P.Dunlea. Subs – J.Buckley for Connolly, S.Levis for Daly.

Mayo – N.O'Brien, A.Costello, B.Heneghan, B.Burke, S.Grimes, J.Fallon, J.Rafter, D.O'Loughlin, P.Kelly, J.Mitchell, A.O'Malley, K.Malone, D.Quinn, B.Maloney, M.Horan. Subs – N.Dunne for Horan, D.McDonagh for Malone.

2002

Wicklow – K.Quirke, A.Byrne, H.Kenny, R.Doyle, C.Foley, A.Jameson, C.Davis, D.Doran, B.O'Keeffe, J.Doyle, D.McGillycuddy, J.P.Davis, W.O'Gorman, S.Byrne, K.O'Brien. Subs – S.Corrigan for Doran, J.Murphy for J.Doyle, S.Miley for J.P.Davis.

Kerry – K.Cremin, D.McNamara, S.O'Sullivan, Don Murphy, B.Fitzgerald, C.Scanlon, S.Flynn, P.Somers, E.O'Donoghue, A.Constable, J.Ferriter, M.Cooper, B.Scanlon, P.Kennedy, C.Foley. Subs – R.Donovan for Somers, N.Sheehy for McNamara, Damien Murphy for Don Murphy.

2003

Meath – J.Curry, C.McLoughlin, T.Bannon, P.Nugent, N.Horan, F.McMahon, B.Kieran, I.McManus, J.Gallagher, C.Sheridan, P.Duff, S.Bray, B.Farrell, B.Lynch, R.Russell. Subs – W.Byrne for Russell, S.Smith for Gallagher.

Galway – D.O'Dowd, C.Monaghan, R.Gibbons, P.Fahy, M.Conroy, J.Flaherty, D.O'Brien, P.Gilmore, B.Cullinane, S.Mannion, B.Moran, D.Ward, B.Colleran, M.Costello, C.Bane. Subs – C.McHugh for Ward, S.Cloherty for Gilmore, S.Kenny for Conroy.

2004

Waterford – A.Kirwan, D.Ryan, R.Power, M.Boyne, N.Barrie, L.Hurney, J.Phelan, D.Kirwan, M.O'Brien, K.Wheelan, M.Kiely, R.Hennessy, E.Doherty, P.Foley, J.Kiely. Subs – A.Power for A.Kirwan, T.Kirwan for Phelan, S.Dempsey for O'Brien, J.Power for J.Kiely, S.McGrath for J.Power.
(S.Dempsey started the drawn final. Subs in the drawn final were A.Ahern for Dempsey, J.Power for Hennessy)

Leitrim – K.Ludlow, K.Kennedy, O.McBride, B.Butler, F.Holohan, D.McHugh, D.Duignan, K.Scollan, J.Kilbane, J.Cullen, D.O'Donnell, B.McWeeney, S.Maguire, O.Maguire, J.Holohan. Subs – P.McGarry for McHugh, S.Foley for Scollan, G.McWeeney for O'Donnell, S.Doorigan for J.Cullen.
(S.Maguire started the drawn final. Subs in the drawn final were – B.McWeeney for Kennedy, S.Foley for Munnelly, P.McGarry for Scollan, G.McWeeney for S.Maguire)

2005

Cork – A.Quirke, C.Murphy, D.Wiseman, M.Prout, K.Kehilly, G.Spillane, E.Wiseman, A.O'Connor, S.O'Sullivan, J.Buckley, S.Hayes, J.Russell, D.Goulding, V.Hurley, P.Dunlea. Subs – D.O'Connor for Hurley, N.O'Riordan for Hayes.

Meath – J.Curry, T.Bannon, C.McLoughlin, P.Nugent, B.Kiernan, J.Donoghue, G.Hynes, B.Lynch, S.Dillon, P.Curran, I.McManus, G.McCullagh, J.McGee, J.Gallagher, R.Maguire. Subs – C.Brennan for McManus, W.Reilly for Curran.

2006

Kerry – S.Óg Ciardabháin, S.Hegarty, J.Costello, D.Doyle, D.O'Sullivan, B.Hickey, J.King, J.P.Brosnan, A.Garnett, N.Fleming, M.Murphy, C.Daly, R.McAuliffe, S.Wallace, J.Buckley. Subs – K.Foley for Fleming, F.O'Sullivan for Brosnan, F.Griffin for King.

Roscommon – David Moran, T.Bannon, D.Donnellan, A.Murtagh, B.Goode, N.Moran, G.Mockler, D.McNulty, R.O'Connor, R.Cox, P.Moran, S.Purcell, Derek Moran, M.Connolly, S.Heneghan. Subs – M.O'Keeffe for Bannon, S.Sharkey for Mockler, J.Callery for Heneghan, M.Killilea for O'Connor.

2007

Cork – K.Murphy, D.Wiseman, E.Wiseman, D.O'Riordan, P.Kissane, B.Cogan, M.Feehily, A.O'Sullivan, A.O'Connor, F.Lynch, V.Hurley, S.O'Sullivan, C.Brosnan, N.O'Sullivan, P.Dunlea. Subs – J.Russell for N.O'Sullivan, P.Cahill for Brosnan.

Wexford – A.Masterson, D.Walsh, M.Gahan, C.Molloy, T.Wall, J.Waters, S.Cousins, P.Murphy, B.Doyle, M.Flynn-O'Connor, D.Farrell, W.Hudson, J.O'Shaughnessy, D.Foran, P.Sinnott. Subs – P.Atkinson for Flynn-O'Connor, G.Jacob for O'Shaughnessy, K.Kennedy for Waters, P.Hughes for Hudson.

2008

Dublin – C.Clarke, D.Daly, M.Fitzsimons, C.Prenderville, M.White, A.Dennis, N.Brogan, D.Bastick, C.Daly, R.Joyce, K.Connolly, J.Cooper, W.Finnegan, E.O'Gara, A.Darcy. Subs – D.Homan for Joyce, C.Norton for Finnegan, N.Tormey for Connolly.

Roscommon – M.Miley, N.Carty, R.Cox, J.Whyte, E.Towey, J.Harte, C.Garvey, B.Higgins, M.Reynolds, D.Moran, J.McKeague, K.Higgins, F.Dolan, F.Cregg, P.Garvey. Subs – R.Brady for Whyte, M.O'Donoghue for P.Garvey, D.Ward for Towey, C.McHugh for K.Higgins, M.Killilea for McKeague.

2009

Cork – P.O'Shea, P.Gayer, E.Wiseman, J.McLoughlin, R.O'Sullivan, G.Healy, M.Fehilly, A.O'Sullivan, C.O'Donovan, D.O'Donovan, S.O'Sullivan, C.O'Driscoll, V.Hurley, R.O'Mahony, J.P.Murphy. Subs – M.Prout for Fehilly, P.O'Cahill for Hurley, N.O'Riordan for A.O'Sullivan.

Roscommon – M.Miley, K.Kilcline, M.McLoughlin, E.Towey, N.Carthy, D.McGarry, C.Dineen, P.Freeman, M.Reynolds, C.McCormack, D.Keenehan, R.Cox, P.Garvey, R.Kelly, D.McDermott. Subs – S.Ormsby, T.Mahon for McCormack, B.Mullen for Kelly.

ALL-IRELAND JUNIOR FOOTBALL FINAL REFEREES 1912-2009

1912—Tom Irwin (Cork)
1913—M. F. Crowe (Dublin)
1914—E. Tarrant (Laois)
1915—P. Dunphy (Laois)
1916—P. D. Breen (Wexford)/A. Rogers (Louth)
1923—Mick Sammon (Dublin)
1924—P. Kilduff (Kildare)
1925—M. Shanahan (Dublin)
1926—Tom Burke (Louth)
1927—Tom Burke (Louth)
1928—Tom Shevlin (Roscommon)
1929—Seán O'Connor (Dublin)
1930—W. P. Aherne (Cork)
1931—Seán O'Connor (Dublin)
1932—J. Giles (Meath)
1933—S. O'Neill (Dublin)
1934—P. Waters (Kildare)
1935—P. Waters (Kildare)
1936—D. Ryan (Kerry)
1937—John Ryan (Liverpool)
1938—D. Hamilton (Dublin)
1939—P. J. Masterson (Cavan)
1940—P. McKenna (Limerick)
1941—Jimmy Flaherty (Offaly)
1946—F. Brophy (Dublin)
1947—Paddy Mythen (Wexford)
1948—Paul Russell (Kerry)
1949—Simon Deignan (Cavan)
1950—J. Moran (Tuam)
1951—Moss Colbert (Limerick)
1952—P. McGooey (Monaghan)
1953—Capt. J. O'Boyle (Donegal)
1954—Seán Hayes (Tipperary)
1955—Simon Deignan (Cavan)
1956—Michael McArdle (Louth)
1957—Peter McDermott (Meath)
1958—Mick Higgins (Cavan)
1959—John Dowling (Offaly)
1960—Jimmy Martin (Roscommon)
1961—Brian Smith (Meath)
1962—Michael McArdle (Louth)
1963—Jimmy Martin (Roscommon)
1964—A. Coleman (Laois)
1965—Eamon Moules (Wicklow)
1966—Tom Cunningham (Galway)
1967—Tom Cunningham (Galway)
1968—Paul Kelly (Dublin)
1969—Fintan Tierney (Cavan)
1970—Mick Spain (Offaly)
1971—Jimmy Martin (Roscommon)
1972—Martin Meally (Kilkenny)
1973—Hugh McPoland (Antrim)
1974/1982—Suspended
1983—Ray Moloney (Limerick)
1984—Tommy Moran (Leitrim)
1985—Paddy Lane (Limerick)
1986—Tommy Moran (Leitrim)
1987—Tommy Sugrue (Kerry)
1988—Pat Egan (Leitrim)
1989—Michael Cranny (Down)
1990—Tommy Howard (Kildare)
1991—Joe Kearney (Roscommon)

1992—Seán McHale (Mayo)
1993—Joe Kearney (Roscommon)
1994—Tommy McDermott (Cavan)
1995—Muiris O'Sullivan (Kerry)
1996—Michael McGrath (Donegal)
1997—Martin McBrien (Tyrone)
1998—Des Joyce (Galway)
1999—Haulie Beirne (Roscommon)
2000—E.Murtagh (Longford)
2001—E.Whelan (Laois)
2002—M.Hughes (Tyrone)
2003—S.McGonigle (Donegal)
2004—E.Whelan (Laois) (draw)
P.Fox (Westmeath) (replay)
2005—P.Carney (Roscommon)
2006—F.Barrett (Kildare)
2007—B.Tyrell (Tipperary)
2008—M.Sludden (Tyrone)
2009—T.Quigley (Dublin)

MUNSTER JUNIOR FOOTBALL FINALS (1910-2009)

1910—Tipperary 1-1, Limerick 0-0
1911—Cork 3-1, Waterford 3-0
1912—Tipperary 0-5, Cork 0-2
1913—Kerry 1-3, Limerick 1-2 (first game)
(Note: Replay ordered following an objection.
Result: Kerry 1-4, Limerick 0-0.
1914—Kerry 0-7, Waterford 0-0
1915—Kerry 2-3, Waterford 1-5
1916—Limerick awarded title on an objection after Cork had won final 1-0 to 0-2.
1917-1922—Suspended
1923—Tipperary 2-5, Cork 1-3
1924—Kerry 2-2, Clare 1-1
1925—Clare 0-6, Cork 0-5
1926—Kerry 1-5, Tipperary 2-1
1927—Kerry 1-10, Clare 3-2
1928—Kerry 3-2, Waterford 0-4
1929—Limerick 2-6, Clare 0-3
1930—Kerry 2-2, Clare 1-1
1931—Kerry 2-5, Cork 2-3
1932—Cork 1-5, Kerry 1-3
1933—Cork 2-2, Kerry 1-3
1934—Kerry 2-12, Waterford 0-1
1935—Tipperary 4-10, Cork 0-3
1936—Kerry 4-14, Waterford 3-1
1937—Tipperary 3-6, Limerick 0-6
1938—Kerry 2-4, Limerick 1-0
1939—Limerick 1-7, Kerry 1-2
1940—Cork 1-6, Tipperary 0-3
1941—Kerry 1-10, Tipperary 0-3
1942-1945—Suspended
1946—Kerry 3-3, Cork 1-7
1947—Kerry 3-7, Limerick 3-5
1948—Waterford 2-8, Limerick 1-7
1949—Kerry 2-5, Waterford 0-6
1950—Limerick 3-6, Cork 1-6
1951—Cork 3-6, Kerry 1-4
1952—Tipperary 0-15, Kerry 2-9 (draw)
Tipperary 0-8, Kerry 0-6 (replay)
1953—Cork 1-10, Tipperary 0-10
1954—Kerry 1-9, Cork 2-2
1955—Cork 3-7, Limerick 0-5
1956—Kerry 4-10, Waterford 1-4
1957—Cork 1-7, Limerick 0-7
1958—Kerry 3-11, Waterford 2-4
1959—Kerry 3-8, Cork 0-6
1960—Kerry 2-6, Cork 1-8
1961—Kerry 2-4, Cork 0-6
1962—Cork 3-6, Limerick 0-8
1963—Kerry 2-4, Limerick 0-6
1964—Cork 2-5, Clare 1-4
1965—Kerry 3-13, Clare 0-6
1966—Cork 1-7, Clare 0-7
1967—Kerry 2-7, Cork 0-9
1968—Kerry 3-11, Clare 2-6
1969—Kerry 1-11, Tipperary 1-5
1970—Cork 2-10, Kerry 2-9
1971—Cork 2-7, Clare 1-5
1972—Cork 2-13, Kerry 0-9
1973-1982—Suspended
1983—Kerry 2-10, Cork 0-9
1984—Cork 1-12, Kerry 0-9
1985—Kerry 0-7, Tipperary 0-7 (draw).
Kerry 1-5, Tipperary 1-4 (replay)
1986—Cork 1-12, Tipperary 1-6
1987—Cork 1-12, Tipperary 1-5
1988—Cork v Tipperary
1989—Cork 0-10, Kerry 0-9
1990—Cork 1-9, Kerry 1-6
1991—Kerry 1-12, Waterford 3-4
1992—Cork 0-13, Clare 1-9
1993—Cork 1-10, Tipperary 0-9
1994—Kerry 1-6, Clare 0-8
1995—Kerry 1-21, Cork 0-19 (after extra time)
1996—Cork 1-10, Kerry 1-8
1997—Kerry 1-15, Clare 0-9
1998—Tipperary 0-6, Cork 0-5
1999—Waterford 0-9, Clare 0-7
2000—Kerry 1-15, Clare 1-6.
2001—Cork 0-17, Tipperary 0-11.
2002—Kerry 2-14, Tipperary 0-15.
2003—Kerry 2-9, Cork 0-14.
2004—Waterford 1-7, Cork 0-9.
2005—Cork 2-13, Kerry 0-8.
2006—Kerry 0-12, Cork 1-8.
2007—Cork 0-12, Clare 0-11.
2008—Kerry 1-11, Cork 1-9.
2009—Cork 1-21, Clare 0-13.

LEINSTER JUNIOR FOOTBALL FINALS (1905-2009)

1905—Westmeath 1-4, Carlow 1-3
1906—Wicklow 1-11, Westmeath 0-0
1907—Laois 2-11, Westmeath 0-5
1908—Dublin 1-8, Meath 0-3
1909—Wicklow 1-10, Westmeath 0-3
1910—Louth 1-5, Laois 1-1
1911—Wexford 3-1, Dublin 0-2
1912—Louth 3-1, Carlow 2-2
1913—Carlow 3-4, Meath 0-0
1914—Dublin 2-2, Kilkenny 0-3
1915—Westmeath 3-0, Wexford 2-1
1916—Dublin 2-7, Wexford 0-2
1917-1921—Suspended

1922—Dublin 0-3, Wicklow 0-3 (draw)
Dublin 2-2, Wicklow 0-3 (replay)
1923—Carlow 2-5, Dublin 1-1
1924—Meath 1-3, Longford 0-2. Longford awarded the title on an objection.
1925—Louth 1-3, Dublin 0-4
1926—Dublin 0-4, Kildare 0-3
1927—Kildare 3-3, Offaly 2-3
1928—Louth 1-5, Dublin 1-4
1929—Westmeath 1-2, Laois 0-2
1930—Dublin 3-3, Carlow 0-2
1931—Kildare 1-6, Dublin 1-4
1932—Louth 2-7, Carlow 1 -5
1933—Carlow 5-3, Wicklow 4-5
1934—Louth 2-4, Kildare 1-7 (draw)
Louth 1-7, Kildare 0-5 (replay)
1935—Offaly 1-6, Dublin 1 -6 (draw)
Offaly 2-3, Dublin 0-2 (replay)
1936—Wicklow 5-5, Kildare 0-3
1937—Longford 3-7, Offaly 4-1
1938—Kildare 1-3, Westmeath 0-5
1939—Dublin 2-4, Meath 1-7 (draw)
Dublin 2-12, Meath 0-7 (replay)
1940—Westmeath 5-7, Kildare 0-5
1941—Laois 2-7, Louth 2-5
1942-1945—Suspended
1946—Louth 3-5, Wexford 0-1
1947—Meath 2-3, Dublin 1-4
1948—Dublin 3-6, Wexford 4-3 (draw).
Dublin 6-3, Wexford 2-4 (replay)
1949—Wicklow 5-2, Meath 2-10
1950—Dublin 1-15, Wexford 2-8
1951—Dublin 5-7, Carlow 0-7
1952—Meath 2-6, Wicklow 0-1
1953—Longford 3-5, Kilkenny 1-5
1954—Dublin 0-10, Louth 0-10 (draw)
Dublin 2-11, Louth 2-4 (replay)
1955—Dublin 1-12, Meath 4-3 (draw)
Dublin 1-8, Meath 0-5 (replay)
1956—Kildare 2-8, Wexford 2-3
1957—Louth 2-6, Kilkenny 1-5
1958—Meath 1-5, Dublin 1-3
1959—Dublin 2-16, Longford 0-5
1960—Dublin 2-9, Meath 0-5
1961—Louth 2-4, Dublin 0-8
1962—Meath 2-11, Wexford 1-4
1963—Wexford 0-14, Westmeath 1-6
1964—Meath 3-10, Kildare 1-13
1965—Kildare 2-7, Laois 0-7
1966—Louth 3-14, Kildare 3-12 (after extra time)
1967—Kildare 0-11, Offaly 1-7
1968—Laois 2-7, Westmeath 3-4 (draw)
Laois 0-9, Westmeath 0-4 (replay)
1969—Wicklow 2-5, Meath 0-5
1970—Kildare 3-13, Dublin 1-11
1971—Dublin 2-9, Kilkenny 0-5
1972—Offaly 3-8, Wexford 1-3
1973—Laois 1-9, Meath 0-9
1974-1982—Suspended
1983—Dublin 2-8, Meath 0-5
1984—Wexford 0-8, Louth 0-6
1985—Dublin 3-16, Louth 2-4
1986—Meath 1-10, Kildcre 1-5
1987—Dublin 1-8, Meath 0-4
1988—Meath 0-10, Dublin 1-4
1989—Kildare 1-7, Louth 1-6
1990—Meath 0-15, Dublin 0-11
1991—Meath 1-10, Dublin 1-10 (draw)
Meath 1-14, Dublin 2-2 (replay)
1992—Wexford 1-16, Meath 2-10
1993—Laois 2-8, Carlow 0-11
1994—Dublin 0-9, Louth 0-5
1995—Meath 2-11, Offaly 1-5
1996—Meath 1-13, Laois 2-7
1997—Meath 0-16, Louth 1-8
1998—Offaly 1-18, Kildare 0-8
1999—Meath 1-9, Dublin 1-6
2000—Wexford 1-9, Dublin 1-5.
2001—Offaly 2-9, Meath 1-11.
2002—Wicklow 3-6, Kildare 0-9.
2003—Meath 1-15, Wexford 0-7.
2004—Kildare 0-9, Dublin 0-8.
2005—Meath 1-9, Louth 0-5.
2006—Meath 1-12, Louth 0-11.
2007—Wexford 1-10, Dublin 1-8.
2008—Dublin 1-13, Meath 1-9.
2009—Louth 1-8, Longford 0-11.
Louth 1-12, Longford 0-10. (replay)

CONNACHT JUNIOR FOOTBALL FINALS (1907-2009)

1907—Mayo 2-9, Galway 0-4
1908-1912—Suspended
1913—Mayo 2-6, Galway 0-0
1914—Mayo 1-3, Galway 1-2
1915—Galway 2-5, Mayo 1-4
1916-1918—Suspended
1919—Galway 5-0, Leitrim 1-2
1920-1923—Suspended
1924—Mayo 1-4, Galway 0-1
1925—Mayo 3-5, Leitrim 1-0
1926—Sligo 1-3, Roscommon 0-1
1927—Mayo 3-12, Leitrim 0-4
1928—Sligo 1-3, Mayo 0-1
1929—Galway 1-7, Roscommon 0-6. Refixture following an objection. Roscommon w.o. Galway scr.
1930—Mayo 2-9, Roscommon 3-2
1931—Galway 3-8, Leitrim 0-3
1932—Roscommon 4-6, Sligo 0-5
1933—Mayo 3-0, Galway 1-5
1934—Mayo 2-5, Roscommon 1-6
1935—Sligo 2-2, Mayo 1-4
1936—Mayo 3-7, Sligo 2-3
1937—Mayo 3-10, Galway 3-7
1938—Leitrim 0-9, Galway 1-5
1939—Roscommon 2-6, Mayo 1-4
1940—Roscommon 1-7, Mayo 2-1
1941—Leitrim 3-9, Galway 1-7
1942-1945—Suspended
1946—Leitrim 2-9, Galway 0-4
1947—Galway 4-10, Roscommon 2-6
1948—Galway 4-11, Sligo 1-4
1949—Galway 3-9, Mayo 1-9
1950—Mayo 4-7, Roscommon 1-5
1951—Mayo 3-4, Leitrim 2-4
1952—Leitrim 2-7, Mayo 1-3
1953—Mayo 6-7, Galway 1-1
1954—Galway 2-6, Roscommon 1-8

1955—Mayo 3-6, Galway 0-2
1956—Sligo 3-2, Mayo 2-3
1957—Mayo 2-8, Galway 2-6
1958—Galway 3-11, Sligo 0-2
1959—Roscommon 2-5, Galway 1-6
1960—Galway 3-5, Leitrim 0-10
1961—Galway 2-12, Mayo 0-9
1962—Leitrim 2-11, Mayo 2-7
1963—Mayo 3-4, Galway 1-5
1964—Roscommon 2-6, Galway 2-6 (draw)
Roscommon 0-8, Galway 0-7 (replay)
1965—Galway 6-17, Leitrim 0-1
1966—Galway 2-5, Roscommon 0-7
1967—Mayo 1-11, Galway 2-5
1968—Mayo 3-10, Roscommon 1-10
1969—Galway 2-8, Sligo 0-4
1970—Mayo 1-11, Roscommon 1-10
1971—Mayo 0-6, Leitrim 0-4
1972—Galway 1-9, Mayo 1-4
1973—Sligo 4-8, Leitrim 1-4
1974-1982—Suspended
1983—Galway 2-13, Leitrim 3-9
1984—Galway 2-7, Mayo 0-7
1985—Galway 1-9, Leitrim 0-6
1986-1991—Suspended
1992—Mayo represented province in All-Ireland series
1993—Mayo 1-9, Leitrim 0-11
1994—Galway 0-12, Mayo 1-9 (draw)
Galway 0-11, Mayo 0-8 (replay)
1995—Mayo 1-15, Galway 1-9
1996—Galway 1-10, Mayo 2-5
1997—Mayo 1-15, Roscommon 0-8
1998—Sligo 3-13, Roscommon 3-5
1999—Roscommon 2-7, Galway 0-10
2000—Roscommon 2-8, Leitrim 0-8.
2001—Mayo 1-16, Leitrim 0-9.
2002—Mayo 2-14, Leitrim 1-4.
2003—Galway 1-7, Roscommon 0-4.
2004—Leitrim 0-12, Roscommon 1-8.
2005—Sligo 0-12, Mayo 0-11.
2006—Roscommon 1-10, Mayo 0-11.
2007—Mayo 3-10, Sligo 2-7.
2008—Roscommon 2-10, Leitrim 0-13. (aet)
2009—Roscommon 2-9, Mayo 0-10.

ULSTER JUNIOR FOOTBALL FINALS (1914-1986)

1914—Cavan beat Antrim
1915—Cavan 2-3, Antrim 1-3
1916—Cavan 0-7, Monaghan 0-0
1917-1922—Suspended
1923—Antrim 1-3, Cavan 1-2
1924—Cavan 3-7, Antrim 2-0
1925—Armagh 2-3, Cavan 2-1
1926—Armagh 0-3, Tyrone 0-2
1927—Cavan 4-8, Armagh 1-2
1928—No competition
1929—Armagh 3-14, Derry 1-2
1930—Donegal w.o. Cavan scr.
1931—Down 1-3, Cavan 0-5
1932—Cavan 2-5, Down 1-1
1933—Donegal 3-7, Derry 1-3
1934—Donegal 0-9, Down 1-4. Replay ordered following an objection. Down 4-6, Donegal 3-5
1935—Armagh 3-6, Derry 3-2
1936—Cavan 4-7, Down 4-2
1937—Antrim 2-6, Tyrone 1-6
1938—Cavan 2-3, Armagh 2-1
1939—Donegal 2-8, Cavan 3-4
1940—Cavan 3-5, Antrim 1-8
1941—Cavan 2-7, Armagh 1-8
1942—Antrim 3- 10, Fermanagh 1-6
1943—Fermanagh 3-8, Antrim 2-6
1944—Cavan 0-10, Donegal 0-5
1945—Derry 4-2, Armagh 0-6
1946—Down 2-5, Donegal 0-7
1947—Down 5-4, Derry 0-7
1948—Armagh 1-12, Antrim 3-2
1949—Down 2-4, Fermanagh 1-3
1950—Derry 2-7, Antrim 1-4
1951—Armagh 3-6, Down 0-6
1952—Donegal 4-5, Tyrone 1-8
1953—Derry 3-6, Cavan 1-5
1954—Donegal 1-7, Tyrone 0-8
1955—Derry 0-13, Down 0-6
1956—Monaghan 0-10, Cavan 0-2
1957—Cavan 3-6, Donegal 2-2
1958—Down 0-10, Antrim 1-5
1959—Fermanagh 2-13, Antrim 1-4
1960—Antrim 1-7, Derry 1-6
1961—Monaghan 2-8, Antrim 1-6
1962—Cavan 0-8, Down 0-7
1963—Antrim 5-8, Donegal 1-3
1964—Derry 2-13, Antrim 0-8
1965—Down 3-8, Derry 2-8
1966—Down 2-6, Monaghan 0-8
1967—Derry 2-8, Cavan 0-4
1968—Tyrone 2-6, Armagh 0-3
1969—Derry 3-9, Down 2-5
1970—Antrim 3-8, Donegal 3-5
1971—Down 3-10, Fermanagh 1-1
1972—Antrim 3-8, Monaghan 1-6
1973-1982—Suspended
1983—Tyrone 5-7, Monaghan 1-8
1984—Cavan 2-7, Monaghan 0-10
1985—Armagh 2-9, Donegal 0-12
1986—Tyrone 1-7, Monaghan 0-4
1987-2009—No competition

ALL-IRELAND "B" FOOTBALL FINALS

1990—Roscommon, November 11
Leitrim 2-11, Sligo 0-2
1991—Ballinasloe, November 17
Clare 1-12, Longford 0-9 (extra time)
1992—Navan, December 6
Wicklow 1-5, Antrim 0-4
1993—Longford, November 14
Laois 0-17, Sligo 0-5
1994—Tullamore, November 20
Carlow 2-10, Westmeath 1-11
1995—Birr, August 27
Tipperary 2-12, Longford 2-5.
1996—Carrick-on-Shannon, November 17
Fermanagh 0-9, Longford 0-9 (draw)
Carrick-on-Shannon, December 8
Fermanagh 0-12, Longford 0-9 (replay)
1997—Ballinasloe, November 10
Louth 1-11, Clare 1-8

1998—Scotstown, November 22
Monaghan 2-11, Fermanagh 0-13
1999—Casement Park, December 5
Antrim 2-10, Fermanagh 1-10
2000—Navan, November 19
Fermanagh 3-15, Wicklow 2-6

TOMMY MURPHY CUP

2004 – Croke Park, August 22:
Clare 1-11, Sligo 0-11.
2005 – Croke Park, September 4:
Tipperary 3-10, Wexford 0-15.
2006 – Croke Park, August 27:
Louth 3-14, Leitrim 1-11.
2007 – Croke Park, August 4:
Wicklow 3-13, Antrim 1-17. (aet)
2008 – Croke Park, August 2:
Antrim 3-12, Wicklow 1-15.

NATIONAL FOOTBALL LEAGUE RESULTS
1925-2009

1925-26—Laois beat Sligo (replay 4-6 to 1-4), and Kerry (1-6 to 1-5) and Dublin (2-1 to 1-0) in Final.
No League in 1926-27
1927-28—Deciders: Kildare (0-8 to 0-5) and Kerry (0-6 to 0-4) beat Mayo, and Kerry beat Kildare (2-4 to 1-6) in Final.
1928-29—Deciders: Kildare (4-5) beat Monaghan (0-5); Sligo (1 -5) beat Westmeath (0-4); Kerry (1-5) beat Sligo (1-2) and in Final, Kildare (1-7 to 2-3).
1930-31—Final: Kerry (1-3) beat Cavan (1-2). Division II—Northern Donegal. Midiand A—Kilkenny. Midland B—Westmeath.
1931-32—Semi-final: Kerry 2-5, Mayo 1-6. Meath refused to meet Cork (at home). Final: Kerry 5-2, Cork 3-3.
1932-33—Final at Croke Park: Meath 0-10, Cavan 1-6. Special Division—Final: Wexford 3-5, Cork 1-8.
1933-34 Division 1—Inter-Group Test, May 13, 1934, at Castlebar: Mayo 2-3, Dublin 1-6. Replay, October 15, Croke Park. Mayo 2-4, Dublin 1-5. Division II Inter-Group Test, **October 14, 1934, at Tuam:** Offaly 3-6, Sligo 1-6.
1934-35—Division 1—Inter-Group Tests, June 9, 1935, Clonmel: Mayo 6-8, Tipperary 2-5. **August 4, 1935,** Castlebar: Mayo 5-8, Fermanagh 0-2. **Tipperary were winners of McGrath Cup in Munster and Fermanagh in Ulster tournaments. Division II—Final at Armagh, October 27, 1935:** Armagh 3-1, Westmeath 0-9.
1935-36—Division 1—Mayo (12 points from eight games). Runners-up: Dublin and Cavan (with 10 points). Division II— Final at **Mullingar, March 29, 1936:** Offaly 3-3, Longford 1-6.
1936-37—Division 1—Decider, April 11, 1937. Croke Park: Mayo 5-4, Meath 1-8. Division II—Decider, March 7, 1937, Ardara: Longford 1-7, Donegal 1-3.
1937-38—Division 1—Decider, Castlebar, July 3, 1938: Mayo 3-9, Wexford 1-3. Division II—Tipperary. Connacht League—Sligo.
1938-39—Final, at Ballina: Mayo 5-9, Meath 0-6. (Twenty-seven counties took part in this season's League).
1939-40—Final, at Croke Park: Galway 2-5, Meath 1-5. (Mayo (holders) did not compete. Twenty-three counties participated).
1940-41—Group Winners: Mayo and Dublin. Final, at Croke Park: Mayo 3-7, Dublin 0-7.
1941-42—National Leagues suspended. Substitute Competitions—South Leinster—Laois. Connacht—Roscommon. Ulster—Antrim. North Leinster—Dublin.
1943-44—Leinster League—Meath.
1944-45 Leinster League—Meath.
1944—Ulster Minor League—Armagh.
Connacht League—Galway.
1945—Connacht League—Sligo.
1945-46—Final: Meath 2-2, Wexford 0-6.
1946-47—Final: Derry 2-9, Clare 2-5.
1947-48—Final: Cavan 5-9, Cork 2-8 (replay). Cavan 2-11, Cork 3-8 (draw).
1948-49—Final: Mayo 1-8; Louth, 1-6.
1949-50—Final: New York 2-8, Cavan 0-12 (in Croke Park).
Home Final: Cavan 2-8, Meath 1-6.
1950-51 Final: Meath 1-10, New York 0-10 (in New York).
Home Final: Meath 0-6, Mayo 0-3.
1951-52 Final: Cork 1-12, New York 0-3 (in Croke Park).
Home Final: Cork 2-3, Dublin 1-5.
1952-53—Final: Dublin 4-6, Cavan 0-9.
1953-54—Final: Mayo 2-10, Carlow 0-3.
1954-55—Final: Dublin 2-12; Meath, 1-3.
1955-56—Final: Cork 0-8, Meath, 0-7.
1956-57—Final: Galway 1-8, Kerry 0-6.
1957-58—Final: Dublin 3-13, Kildare 3-8.
1958-59—Final: Kerry 2-8, Derry 1-8.
1959-60—Final: Down 0-12, Cavan 0-9.
1960-61—Final: Kerry 4-16, Derry 1-5.
1962—Final: Down 2-5, Dublin 1-7.
1963—Final: Kerry 1-18, New York 0-10 (in Croke Park).
Home Final: Kerry 0-9, Down 1-5.
1964—Final: New York 2-12, Dublin 1-13 (in New York).
Home Final: Dublin 2-9, Down 0-7.
1965—27/6/65. Galway 1-4, New York 0-8 (in New York). 4/7/65: Galway 3-8, New York 0-9 (in New York). Aggregate: Galway 4-12, New York 0-17.
Home Final: Galway 1-7, Kerry 0-8.
1966—2/10/66: Longford 1-9, New York 0-7 (in Longford). 9/10/66: Longford 0-9, New York 0-10 (at Croke Park). Aggregate: Longford 1-18, New York 0-17.
Home Final: Longford 0-9, Galway 0-8.
1967—14/5/67: New York 3-5, Galway 1-6 (in New York). 21/5/67: New York 4-3, Galway 0-10 (in New York). Aggregate: New York 7-8, Galway 1-16.

Home Final: Galway 0-12, Dublin 1-7.
1968—26/5/68. Down 2-14, Kildare 2-11 (at Croke Park).
1969—22/6/69: Kerry 0-12, New York 0-12 (in New York). 29/6/69: Kerry 2-21, New York 2-12 (after extra time). Aggregate: Kerry 2-33, New York 2-24.
Home Final: 18/5/69: Kerry 3-11, Offaly 0-8.
1970—Semi-finals: April 5, Croke Park. Mayo 0-10, Kerry 1-5. April 12, Croke Park. Down 1-11, Kildare 2-3.
Final: April 19, Croke Park. Mayo 4-7, Down 0-10.
1971—Semi-finals: May 16, Croke Park. Kerry 1-11, Derry 1-10. May 23, Croke Park. Mayo 19, Dublin 0-8.
Final: June 20, Croke Park. Kerry 0-11, Mayo 0-8.
1972—Semi-Finals: April 9, Croke Park. Kerry 0-17, Derry 0-13. April 16, Croke Park. Mayo 2-10, Offaly 0-16. Replay: April 30, Croke Park. Mayo 1-9, Offaly 0-6.
Final: May 14, Croke Park. Kerry 2-11, Mayo 1-9.
1973—Semi-finals: April 8, Croke Park. Kerry 0-11, Derry 2-5. No replay. Derry conceded walkover. April 15, Croke Park. Offaly 0-11, Sligo 0-6.
Final: May 6, Croke Park. Kerry 2-12, Offaly 0-14.
1974—Semi-finals: April 7, Croke Park. Kerry 2-14, Tyrone 0-12. April 28, Croke Park. Roscommon 0-12, Sligo 0-12. Replay: May 5, Castlebar. Roscommon 0-16, Sligo 0-10.
Final: May 19, Croke Park. Kerry 1-6, Roscommon 0-9. Replay: May 26, Croke Park. Kerry 0-14, Roscommon 0-8.
1975—Semi-finals: April 27, Croke Park. Meath 4-6, Mayo 0-8. May 4, Croke Park. Dublin 3-12, Tyrone 1-7.
Final: May 18, Croke Park. Meath 0-16, Dublin 1-9.
1976—Semi-finals: April 4, Croke Park. Dublin 1-11, Galway 0-12. April 11, Croke Park. Derry 17, Cork 1-6.
Final: May 2, Croke Park. Dublin 2-10, Derry 0-15.
1977—Semi-finals: March 27, Croke Park. Dublin 2-12, Mayo 0-5. April 3, Croke Park. Kerry 2-13, Roscommon 0-8.
Final: April 17, Croke Park. Kerry 1-8, Dublin 1-6.
1978—Semi-finals: April 2, Croke Park. Dublin 0-12, Laois 0-7. April 9, Croke Park. Mayo 0-10, Down 0-6.
Final: April 23, Croke Park. Dublin 2-18, Mayo 2-13.
1979—Semi-finals: April 15, Croke Park. Roscommon 1-14, Offaly 0-12. April 22, Croke Park, Cork 2-9, Kildare 0-4.
Final: May 13, Croke Park. Roscommon 0-15, Cork 1-3.
1980—Semi-finals: April 6, Croke Park. Kerry 1-11, Armagh 1-6. April 13, Croke Park. Cork 1-16, Galway 1-6.
Final: April 27, Pairc Ui Caoimh. Cork 0-11, Kerry 0-10.
1981—Semi-finals: April 26, Ennis. Galway 0-10, Kerry 0-8. April 26, Roscommon. Roscommon 1-11, Mayo 1-6.
Final: May 10, Croke Park. Galway 1-11, Roscommon 1-3.
1982—Semi-finals: April 11, Croke Park. Cork 1-15, Offaly 1-10. April 11, Croke Park. Kerry 3-4, Armagh 1-5.
Final: April 25, Killarney. Kerry 0-11, Cork 0-11.
Replay: May 9, Pairc Ui Caoimh: Kerry 1-9, Cork 0-5.
1983—Semi-finals: April 10, Croke Park. Down 1-9, Kildare 0-4. April 10, Croke Park. Armagh 28, Meath 1-7.
Final: April 24, Croke Park. Down 1-8, Armagh 0-8.
1983-84—Semi-finals: April 1, Croke Park. Kerry 0-12, Down 1-6. Galway 1-10, Meath 0-13 (draw). April 15, Croke Park—Galway 0-10, Meath 0-9 (replay).
Final: April 29, Limerick—Kerry 1-11, Galway 0-11.
1984-85—Semi-finals: March 24, Croke Park— Armagh 1-9, Down 0-6. Monaghan. 1-6, Tyrone 0-9 (draw). **March 31, Armagh—** Monaghan 1-8, Tyrone 0-8 (replay, after extra time).
Final: April 7, Croke Park—Monaghan 1-11, Armagh 0-9.
1985-86—Semi-finals: April 20, Croke Park— Laois 0-12, Dublin 1-7. Monaghan 0-10 Mayo 1-6.
Final: May 4, Croke Park—Laois 2-6, Monaghan 2-5.
1986-87—Semi-finals: April 12, Croke Park— Kerry 2-11, Monaghan 2-9. April 19, Croke Park—Dublin 1-8, Galway 0-8.
Final: April 26, Croke Park—Dublin 1-11 Kerry 0-11.
1987-88—Semi-finals: April 3, Croke Park—Dublin 4-12, Monaghan 1-8. Meath 0-13, Down 1-9.
Final: April 17, Croke Park—Meath 0-11, Dublin 1-8 (draw). Replay: May 22, Croke Park—Meath 2-13, Dublin 0-11.
1988-89—Semi-finals: April 9, 1989: Croke Park—Dublin 1-10, Cavon 1-9. **April 9, 1989: Páirc Uí Chaoimh**—Cork 0-10, Kerry 0-4.
Home Final: April 23, 1989: Croke Park—Cork 0-15, Dublin 0-12.
Final: May 7, 1989: Gaelic Park, New York—1st leg—Cork 1-12, New York 1-5; May 14, **1989: Gaelic Park,** New York—2nd leg— Cork 2-9, New York 1-9. Aggregate—Cork 3-21, New York 2-14.
1989-90—Semi-finals: April 15, 1990: Croke Park—Meath 0-14, Cork 0-10. Down 4-8, Roscommon 0-11.
Final: April 29, 1990: Croke Park—Meath 2-7, Down 0-11.
1990-91—Semi-finals: April 21, 1991: Croke Park—Kildare 0-14, Donegal 0-10. Dublin 1-18, Roscommon 0-11.
Final: May 5,1991: Croke Park—Dublin 1-9, Kildare 0-10.
1991-92—Semi-finals: April 19, 1992: Croke Park—Derry 0-12, Meath 1-8. Tyrone 0-13,

Dublin 1-9.
Final: May 3, 1992: Croke Park—Derry 1-10, Tyrone 1-8.
1992-93—Semi-finals: April 18, 1993: Croke Park—Donegal 1-12,Clare 1-7. Dublin 1-10, Kerry 0-11.
Final: May 2, 1993: Croke Park—Dublin 0-9, Donegal 0-9 (draw). May 9, 1993: Croke Park—Dublin 0-10, Donegal 0-6 (replay).
1993-94—Semi-finals: April 1 7, 1994: Croke Park—Armagh 3-11, Laois 1-9. Meath 0-15, Westmeath 0-11.
Final: May 1, 1994: Croke Park—Meath 2-11, Armagh 0-8.
1994-95—Semi-finals: April 30, 1995: Croke Park—Derry 1-8, Tyrone 2-3. Donegal 1-14, Laois 2-8.
Final: May 14, 1995: Croke Park—Derry 0-12, Donegal 0-8.
1995-96—Semi-finals: April 21, 1996: Croke Park—Derry 1-12, Mayo 0-7. Donegal 0-10, Cork 0-9.
Final: May 5, 1996: Croke Park—Derry 1-16, Donegal 1-9.
1996-97—Semi-finals: April 20, 1997: Croke Park—Kerry 2-13, Laois 1-10. Cork 2-10, Kildare 1-9.
Final: May 4, 1997: Páirc Uí Caoimh:
Kerry 3-7, Cork 1-8.
1997-98—Semi-finals: April 12, 1994:
Croke Park—Derry 1-12, Monaghan 0-8. Offaly 3-10, Donegal 1-14.
Final: April 26, 1998: Croke Park:
Offaly 0-9, Derry 0-7.
1998-99—Semi-finals: April 25, 1999:
Croke Park—Cork 0-6, Meath 0-3. Dublin 0-11, Armagh 0-11 (draw). May 2, 1999: Croke Park—Dublin 1-14, Armagh 0-12 (replay).
Final: May 9, 1999: Páirc Uí Chaoimh:
Cork 0-12, Dublin 1-7
1999-2000—Semi-final – April 23 at Clones:
Derry 0-15, Roscommon 0-8.
Semi-final – April 23 at Thurles:
Meath 4-11, Kerry 1-18.
Final – May 7 at Croke Park:
Derry 1-12, Meath 1-12.
Replay – May 20 at Clones:
Derry 1-8, Meath 0-9.
2000-2001—Semi-final – April 21 at Roscommon:
Galway 2-12, Sligo 0-11.
Semi-final – April 22 at Sligo:
Mayo 0-16, Roscommon 1-10.
Final – April 29 at Croke Park:
Mayo 0-13, Galway 0-12.
2002—Semi-final – April 14 at Enniskillen:
Tyrone 3-12, Mayo 0-11.
Semi-final – April 14 at Mullingar:
Cavan 5-13, Roscommon 3-12.
Final – April 28 at Clones:
Tyrone 0-16, Cavan 0-7.
2003—Semi-finals – April 20 at Croke Park:
Laois 1-14, Armagh 1-11.
Tyrone 4-11, Fermanagh 1-11.
Final – May 4 at Croke Park:
Tyrone 0-21, Laois 1-8.
2004—Semi-final – April 18 at Limerick:
Kerry 0-12, Limerick 0-10.
Semi-final – April 18 at Omagh:
Galway 1-16, Tyrone 1-16. (after extra time)
Replay – April 25 at Galway:
Galway 2-18, Tyrone 1-19.(after extra time)
Final – May 2 at Croke Park:
Kerry 3-11, Galway 1-16.
2005—Semi-final – April 17 at Portlaoise:
Wexford 1-8, Tyrone 1-7.
Semi-final – April 24 at Croke Park:
Armagh 0-19, Mayo 0-14.
Final – May 1 at Croke Park:
Armagh 1-21, Wexford 1-14.
2006—Semi-final – April 16 at Killarney:
Kerry 1-15, Laois 0-10.
Semi-final – April 16 at Castlebar:
Galway 1-11, Mayo 1-6.
Final – April 23 at the Gaelic Grounds:
Kerry 2-12, Galway 0-10.
2007—Semi-final – April 15 at Croke Park:
Donegal 1-13, Kildare 1-11.
Semi-final – April 15 at Croke Park:
Mayo 2-10, Galway 1-12.
Final – April 22 at Croke Park:
Donegal 0-13, Mayo 0-10.
2008—Final – April 27 at Parnell Park:
Derry 2-13, Kerry 2-9.
2009—Final – April 26 at Croke Park:
Kerry 1-15, Derry 0-15.

ROLL OF HONOUR

Kerry 19, Mayo 11, Dublin 8, Meath 7, Derry 6, Cork 5, Down 4, Galway 4, New York 3, Laois 2, Tyrone 2, Cavan 1, Longford 1, Roscommon 1, Offaly 1, Armagh 1, Monaghan 1, Donegal 1.

Note: Sponsorship of the National Leagues was taken up by the Ford Motor Company in 1986, Royal Liver Assurance took over in 1988 and Church & General Insurance became sponsors in 1994, later to be known as Allianz.

NATIONAL FOOTBALL LEAGUE FINALISTS

1925/26

Laois—R. Miller (capt.), W. Irwin, P. Bates, J. Browne, Matt Delaney, T. Cribben, J. Ward, C. Miller, W. Whelan, Jim Miller, P. Whelan, J. O'Shea, J. Delaney, John Miller, T. Costelloe.

Dublin—P. McDonnell, J. McDonnell, Joe Synnott, John Synnott, J. Reilly, J. Kirwan, M. Durnin, P. Molloy, Jim Norris, P. Carey, M. Lennon, P. Mohan, Joe Norris, C. McDonald, P. Stynes.

1926/27
NO COMPETITION.

1927/28

Kerry—J. Riordan, D. O'Connor, J. Barrett Jack Walsh, P. Russell, Joe O'Sullivan, James O'Sullivan, C. Brosnan, R. Stack, J. Ryan, J. J.

Sheehy (capt.), E. Fitzgerald, E. Sweeney, James Baily, J. J. Landers.

Kildare—M. Walsh, M. Buckley, M. Goff, A. Fitzpatrick, F. Malone, J. Higgins, J. Hayes, J. Loughlin, W. Gannon, J. Curtis, P. Martin, P. Doyle, W. Mangan, P. Loughlin, T. Keogh. Subs: A. O'Neill for J. Curtis.

1928/29

Kerry—J. Riordan, D. O'Connor, J. Barrett (capt.), Jack Walsh, P. Russell, Joe O'Sullivan, T. O'Donnell, C. Brosnan, R. Stack, J. Ryan, J. J. Sheehy, M. Doyle, E. Sweeney, James Baily, J. J. Landers.

Kildare—J. O'Reilly, M. Buckley, M. Goff, C. Graham, W. Hynan, J. Higgins (capt.), J. Hayes, P. Loughlin, F. Malone, P. Martin, P. Plant, P. Doyle, P. Byrne, P. Pringle, A. O'Neill.

1929/30

Kerry—J. Riordan (capt.), T. O'Donnell, P. Whitty, Jack Walsh, P. Russell, Joe O'Sullivan, E. Fitzgerald, C. Brosnan, R. Stack, C. Geaney, M. Doyle, J. Flavin, E. Sweeney, J. J. Landers, T. Landers. Sub: E. Barrett for R. Stack.

Cavan—W. Young, T. Campbell, T. Crowe, M. Dinneny, J. Molloy, P. Lynch, F. Fitzpatrick, J. Smith (capt.), H. O'Reilly, P. McNamee, O. Fay, J. Smallhorne, L. Blessing, T. J. Weymns, T. Coyle. Subs: T. O'Reilly (Cornafean) for W. Young, W. Young for T. Coyle.

1930/31

Kerry—D. O'Keeffe, D. O'Connor, P. Whitty, Jack Walsh, T. O'Donnell, W. Kinnerk, M. Healy, R. Stack, J. J. Landers, T. Landers, M. Doyle (capt.), J. Ryan, J. Quill, W. Landers, C. Brosnan.

Cork—P. J. Downing, C. Cronin, M. O'Flynn, D. Kiely, J. Lynch, J. Dunlea, T. Kiely, D. Burke, Tim Cotter, M. O'Connor, W. Lynch, L. Flanagan, G. Harrington, J. McKenna, J. O'Regan (capt.).

1931/32
NO COMPETITION.

1932/33

Meath—P. Browne, R. Cassidy, W. Dillon, W. Clynch, P. Geraghty, T. Meade, T. Smith, J. Loughran, R. Durnin, A. Donnelly, W. Shaw (capt.), M. Rogers, M. Brennan, P. McEnroe, P. Mooney.

Cavan—W. Young, W. Connolly, P. Lynch, M. Dinneny, T. Coyle, J. Smith (capt.), P. Phair, H. O'Reilly, T. O'Reilly (Cornafean), D. Morgan, P. Devlin, J Smallhorne, V. McGovern, L. Blessing, M. J. Magee. Sub: T. O'Reilly (Mullahoran) for M. J. Magee.

1933/34

Mayo—T. Burke, J. Gannon, P. Quinn, P. Kelly, T. Regan, H. Kenny, P. Brett, P. Flannelly, G. Ormsby, J. Carney, P. O'Malley, P. Laffey, G. Courell (capt.), P. Moclair, P. Munnelly. P. O'Loughlin, M. Raftery and P. Collins played in drawn game. J. Gannon, P. O'Malley and P. Brett came on for replay.

Dublin—J. McDonnell, D. Brennan, S. Lambe, F. Cavanagh, P. Hickey, E. McCann, P. Cavanagh, R. Beggs, M. Kelly, W. Dowling, G. Fitzgerald, M. O'Brien, M. Wellington, M. Keating (capt.), H. Farnan.

J. O'Shea, C. McMahon and P. Perry played in drawn game. S. Lambe, M. Kelly and H. Farnan came on for replay.

1934/35

Mayo—T. Burke, T. McNicholas, P. Quinn, P. Kelly, T. Regan, H. Kenny, P. Brett, P. Flannelly, G. Ormsby, J. Carney, J. Munnelly, P. Laffey, G. Courell (capt.), P. Moclair, P. Munnelly. Sub: J. Gannon for T. McNicholas.

Fermanagh—P. Donaghy, E. Lennon, W. Carty, P. Burns, H. Darcy, E. McDonnell, H. McPike, J. McCullagh, T. McDonnell, G. Magee, P. McGrane, J. Monaghan, C. McDonnell, W. Maguire, F. Johnston.

1935/36

Mayo—D. Acton, J. McGowan, P. Quinn, P. Kelly, T. Regan, G. Ormsby, P. Collins, P. Flannelly, H. Kenny, J. Carney, J. Munnelly, P Laffey, G. Courell (capt.), P. Moclair, P. Munnelly.

(Played on a league system. The above is the team which beat Cavan and clinchecl the title.)

1936/37

Mayo—T. Burke, J. McGowan, P. Quinn, P. Kelly, T. Regan, G. Ormsby, P. Robinson, P. Flannelly, H. Kenny, J. Carney, T. Grier, P. Laffey, J. Munnelly, P Moclair (capt.), P. Munnelly.

Meath—P. Browne, R. Cassidy, P. Beggan, H. McEnroe, P. Geraghty (capt.), K. Murray, P. Duffy, M. Casey, J. Cummins, T. Burns, A. Donnelly, M. Gilsenan, T. Coogan, T. McGuinness, M. Rogers.

1937/38

Mayo—T. Burke, J. McGowan, P. Quinn, P. Kelly, T. Regan, G. Ormsby, T. McNicholas, Patsy Flannelly, H. Kenny, J. Laffey, P. J. Judge, P. Laffey, J. Munnelly, P. Moclair (capt.), M. Hannon. Subs: M. O'Malley for T. McNicholas, S. Melody for T. Regan.

Wexford—P. Lynch, J. Furlong, P Hayes (capt.), F. Clancy, P. Boggan, D. Morris, P. Mythen, J. Donoghue, P. Quinn, J. Moriarty, J. Nolan, M. Roche, F. Walsh, T. Roche, W. Howlin.

1938/39

Mayo—T. Burke, J. McGowan, P. Quinn, J. Sammon, T. Regan, G. Ormsby, T. Robinson, C. O'Toole, H. Kenny, J. Carney, P. J. Judge, P. Laffey, J. Munnelly, P. Moclair (capt.), T. Hoban.

Meath—H. McEnroe, C. Coleman, M. O'Toole, M. Clinton, K. Johnston, C. O'Reilly, P Donnelly, J. Loughran, J. Kearney, J. Clarke, A Donnelly, M. Gilsenan (capt.), W. Brien, J. Cummins, H. Lynch.

1939/40

Galway—J. McGauran, M. Raftery, C. Connolly, P McDonagh, F. Cunniffe, R. Beggs, J. Casey, P. Mitchell, J. Dunne (capt.), J. Flavin, E. Mulholland, J. Burke, M. Higgins, C. McGovern, B. Nestor.

Meath—H. McEnroe, P. Beggan, M. O'Toole, P. Donnelly, K. Johnston, C. O'Reilly, J. Kearney, J. Loughran, P. Ward, P. McDermott, A. Donnelly, M. Gilsenan (capt.), W. Brien, T. McGuinness, K. Devin. Sub: J. Cummins for K. Devin.

1940/41

Mayo—D. Acton, J. McGowan, R. Winters, J. Laffey, T. Regan, G. Ormsby, T. Robinson, H. Kenny (capt.), J. Munnelly (Ballycastle), J. Carney, P. J. Judge, P. Laffey, M. O'Malley, J. Munnelly, T. Hoban.

Dublin—C. Kelly, T. Moore, G. McLoughlin, B. Murphy, P. O'Reilly, M. Falvey, B. Quinn, P. Holly (capt.), S. O Dubhda, J. Joy, G. Fitzgerald, T. Banks, M. Fletcher, P. Bermingham, J. Buckley.

1942/1945 NO COMPETITION.

1945/46

Meath—K. Smith, J. Kearney, M. O'Toole (capt.), J. Byrne, P. Gogan, A. Donnelly, C. Hand, M. O'Brien, P. O'Brien, F. Byrne, P. McDermott, V. Sherlock, P. Meegan, W. Halpenny, J. Clarke.

Wexford—M. Kehoe, T. Doyle, G. Kavanagh, J. Coady, J. Culleton, W. Goodison, J. Morris, D. Clancy, P. Kehoe, D. O'Neill, N. Rackard, T. Somers, S. Thorpe, T. O'Leary, J. O'Connor. Subs: M. Hanlon for G. Kavanagh, G. Kavanagh for M. Hanlon.

1946/47

Derry—C. Moran, S. Keenan, J. Convery, J. Hurley, J. Murphy, S. McCann, T. E. McCloskey, M. McNaught, R. Gribben, P. Keenan (capt.), F. Niblock, L. Higgins, P. McErlean, J. E. Mullan, J.Cassidy.

Clare—P. Gallagher, D. Hogan, F. Keane, M. Collins, D. Fitzgerald, J. Murrihy, R. Bradley, E.J.Carroll, P. Power, P. Daly, S. Guinnane, P.J. Griffin, J. Hill, R. Fitzpatrick, N. Crowley.

1947/48

Cavan—S. Morris, W. Doonan, B. O'Reilly, P. Smith, O. R. McGovern, J. J. O'Reilly (capt.), S. Deignan, P. J. Duke, P. Brady, A. Tighe, M. Higgins, J. J. Cassidy, J. Stafford, P. Donohoe, E. Carolan. Sub: T. P. O'Reilly for E. Carolan.

J. D. Benson, B. Cully and T. P. O'Reilly played in drawn game. S. Morris, B. O'Reilly and E. Carolan came on for replay.

Cork—M. O'Driscoll, D. O'Connor, P. A. Murphy, C. Crone, J. Hartnett, T. Crowley, T. O'Driscoll, C. McGrath, B. Murphy, D. O'Donovan, C. Duggan, T. Daly, J. Lynam, Jim Cronin, E. Young. Subs: F. O'Donovan for B. Murphy, H. O'Neill for C. Crone.

J. Murphy, C. Power, F. O'Donovan, N. Ryan and J. Aherne played in drawn game. J. Hartnett, T. O'Driscoll, B. Murphy, T. Daly and E. Young came on for replay. Subs in drawn game: J. Hartnett for N. Ryan, C. O'Connor for C. Power.

1948/49

Mayo—T. Byrne (capt.), P. Gilvarry, P. Prendergast, J. Forde, W. Kenny, E. Mongey, S. Mulderrig, P. Carney, H. Dixon, L. Hastings, T. Langan, Joe Gilvarry, T. Acton, P. Solan, M. Flanagan.

Louth—S. Thornton, J. Bell, J. Malone, T. Mulligan, S. Boyle, P. Markey, P. McArdle, J. Regan, H. Reynolds, F. Fegan, J. Quigley, S. White, H. O'Rourke, T. Walsh, M. Reynolds.

1949/50

New York—P. O'Reilly, J. Quinn, T. Gallagher, D. O'Connor, J. Redican, W. Carlos, E. Kenny, P. McAndrew, P. Ryan, M. O'Sullivan (capt.), J. Hughes, F. Quinn, P. Holly, S. Keane, J. Corcoran.

Cavan—S. Morris, S. Deignan, J. McCabe, P. Smith, P. Carolan, J. J. O'Reilly (capt.), J. J. Cassidy, P. Brady, V. Sherlock, A. Tighe, M. Higgins, T. Hardy, E. Carolan, P. Donohoe, J. Cusack.

HOME FINAL

Cavan—Same as played in final except L. Maguire in place of J. McCabe. Sub: J. Stafford for S. Morris.

Meath—K. Smith, M. O'Brien, P. O'Brien, K. McConnell, S. Heery, P. Dixon, C. Hand, D. Taaffe, P. Connell, F. Byrne, B. Smith (capt.), P. Meegan, P. Carolan, J. Meehan, M. McDonnell.

1950/51

Meath—K. Smith, M. O'Brien, P. O'Brien, K. McConnell, C. Kelly, P. Dixon, C. Hand, D. Taaffe, P. Connell, F. Byrne, M. McDonnell, P. Meegan (capt.), B. Smith, J. Reilly, P. McDermott. Subs: L. McGuinness for B. Smith, B. Smith for P. Connell.

New York—T. Sheehan, D. O'Connor, T. Gallagher, J. Foley, J. Redican, W. Carlos, E. Kenny, P. McAndrew, E. Austin, M. O'Sullivan, T. O'Connor (capt.), J. Hughes, F. Quinn, M. Culhane, J. Corcoran. Subs: F. Driscoll for E. Austin, D. Danagher for J. Corcoran.

HOME FINAL

Meath—Same as played in final except S. Heery in place of K. McConnell. Sub: K. McConnell for C. Hand.

Mayo—S. Wynne, J. Forde, P. Prendergast, S. Flanagan (capt.), J. Staunton, H. Dixon, J. McAndrew, E. Mongey, P. Irwin, M. Flanagan, S. Mulderrig, Joe Gilvarry, M. Mulderrig, T. Langan, P. Solan.

1951/52

Cork—D. O'Keeffe, C. Dineen, P. A. Murphy, J. O'Brien, D. O'Donovan, D. Bernard, M. Gould, D. Kelleher, C. Duggan, T. Moriarty, C.

McGrath, E. Young (capt.), M. Cahill, J. J. Henchion, Jim Cronin.

New York—T. Sheehan, D. O'Connor, T. Gallagher, J. Foley, J. Redican, W. Carlos, E. Kenny, P. McAndrew, F. Driscoll, M. O'Sullivan, J. Hughes, P. Ryan, F. Quinn, J. McElligott, T. O'Connor (capt.). Subs: J. Looney for J. Redican, E. Driscoll for W. Carlos, T. Conway for D. O'Connor, E. Lyons for J. Looney, W. Carlos for J. McElligoff

HOME FINAL

Cork—Same as played in final except P. O'Driscoll and John Cronin in place of D. Kelleher and Jim Cronin. Sub: D. Kelleher for M. Gould.

Dublin—G. O'Toole, M. Moylan, J. Lavin, N. Allen, S. Scally, D. Sullivan, F. McCready, J. Crowley, Mossy Whelan, C. O'Leary, O. Freaney, M. Murphy, D. Ferguson, A. Young, K. Heffernan. Subs: D. Mahony for F. McCready.

1952/53

Dublin—A. O'Grady, D. Mahony, M. Moylan, M. Wilson, J. Lavin, N. Allen, N. Maher, J. Crowley, Mossy Whelan (capt.), D. Ferguson, O. Freaney, C. Freaney, B. Atkins, A. Young, K. Heffernan.

Cavan—S. Morris, J. McCabe, P. Brady, V. Clarke, T. Hardy, L. Maguire, S. Keogan, P. Carolan, P. Fitzsimons, B. Gallagher, M. Higgins (capt.), E. Carolan, S. Deignan, A. Tighe, J. Cusack. Subs: G. Keyes for P. Carolan, D. Smith for V. Clarke, P. Carolan for S. Keogan, D. McCaffrey for J. McCabe.

1953/54

Mayo—S. Wynne, J. Forde, P. Prendergast, S. Flanagan, F. Fleming, J. McAndrew, E. Moriarty, J. Nallen, P. Irwin, S. O'Donnell, P. Carney (capt.), E. Mongey, M. Flanagan, T. Langan, D. O'Neill.

Carlow—A. Magee, L. Murphy, W. Canavan, P. Connolly, M. Molloy, A. Murphy, P. Delaney, J. Fogarty, E. Kehoe, W. Magill (capt.), E. Doogue, W. Whelan, W. Walsh, J. Hayes, L. Quigley. Subs: P. Metcalf for P. Delaney.

1954/55

Dublin—P. O'Flaherty, D. Mahony (capt.), J. Lavin, M. Moylan, W. Monks, N. Allen, N. Maher, J. Crowley, S. McGuinness, D. Ferguson, O. Freaney, C. O'Leary, P. Haughey, K. Heffernan, S. O'Boyle. Subs: Mossy Whelan for Seamus McGuinness.

Meath—P. McGearty, M. O'Brien, P. O'Brien, K. McConnell, K. Lenehan, J. Reilly, E. Durnin, T. O'Brien, P. Connell, M. Grace, B. Smith, W. Rattigan, M. McDonnell, T. Moriarty, P. Ratty (capt.). Subs: L. O'Brien for B. Smith, J. Ryan for P. O'Brien.

1955/56

Cork—P. Tyers, P. O'Driscoll, D. O'Sullivan (capt.), D. Murray, P. Harrington, D. Bernard, M. Gould, E. Ryan, S. Moore, D. Kelleher, C. Duggan, P. Murphy, T. Furlong, N. Fitzgerald, J. Creedon.

Meath—P. McGearty, K. Lenihan, J. Ryan, W. McGurk, T. O'Brien (capt.), P. McKeever, E. Durnin, M. Dunican, T. Duff, L. O'Brien, M. McDonnell, W. Rattigan, B. Smith, S. Duff, P. Ratty. Subs: M. Grace for L. O'Brien, T. Smith for W. Rattigan.

1956/57

Galway—J. O'Neill, S. Keeley, G. Daly, T. Dillon, J. Kissane, J. Mahon (capt.), M. Greally, F. Evers, M. McDonagh, J. Coyle, S. Purcell, W. O'Neill, J. Young, F. Stockwell G. Kirwan.

Kerry—D. O'Neill, J. O'Shea (capt.), E. Roche, T. Lyons, Sean Murphy, John Dowling, C. Kennelly, D. O'Shea, T. Long, P. Sheehy, T. Moriarty, T. Lyne, T. Collins, M. Murphy, D. McAuliffe. Sub: P. Fitzgerald for T. Collins.

1957/58

Dublin—P. O'Flaherty, M. Wilson, Joe Timmons, J. Brennan, C. O'Leary, J. Crowley, S. O'Boyle, S. Murray, P. Downey, P. Haughey, O. Freaney, D. Ferguson, P. Farnan, J. Joyce, K. Heffernan (capt.). Subs: L. Foley for P. Downey, C. Leaney for D. Ferguson.

Kildare—M. Nolan, S. McCormack, D. Flood, P. Connolly, P. Gibbons, M. Carolan, P. Maguire, P. Moore, T. Connolly, C. Kelly, L. McCormack (capt.), K. O'Malley, E. Treacy, J. Dowling, E. Hogan. Subs: P. Timmons for P. Maguire, M. Doyle for P. Connolly.

1958/59

Kerry—J. Culloty, J. O'Shea, Jack Dowling, T. Lyons, Sean Murphy, K. Coffey, M. O'Dwyer, M. O'Connell, Seamus Murphy, D. McAuliffe, T. Long, P. Sheehy, D. Geaney, John Dowling, J. Brosnan.

Derry—P. Gormley, P. McLarnon, H. F. Gribben, T. Doherty, P. Breen, C. Mulholland, P. Smith, J. McKeever, L. O'Neill, S. O'Connell, B. Murray, D. McKeever, B. Mullan, O. Gribben, P. Stuart.

1959/60

Down—E. McKay, G. Lavery, L. Murphy, P. Rice, K. Mussen (capt.), D. McCartan, K. O'Neill, P. J. McElroy, P. O'Hagan, S. O'Neill, J. Carey, P. Doherty, A. Hadden, J. McCartan, B. Morgan.

Subs: K. Denvir for J. Carey, E. Lundy for L. Murphy, L. Murphy for E. Lundy, E. Lundy for A.Hadden

Cavan—B. O'Reilly, N. O'Reilly, G. Kelly, M. Brady, H. Gaffney, T. Maguire (capt.), J. Meehan, J. McDonnell, H. B. O'Donoghue, C. Smith, T. Galligan, C. Gallagher, M. Shiels, J. Brady, J. Sheridan. Subs: S. Conaty for T. Galligan, T. Galligan for J. McDonnell.

1960/61

Kerry—J. Culloty, Jack Dowling, N. Sheehy (capt.), T. Lyons, K. Coffey, T. Long, M. O'Dwyer, M. O'Connell, Seamus Murphy, D. McAuliffe, B. Sheehy, J. Sheehy, T. O'Dowd, John Dowling, D. Geaney

Derry—P. Gormley, P. McLarnon, B. Devlin, H. F. Gribben, C. Mulholland, T. Scullion, P. Smith, P. Stuart, B. Murray, J. McKeever (capt.), S. O'Connell, L. O'Neill, D. McKeever, W. O'Kane, C. O'Connor. Subs: G. Magee for C. O'Connor, G. O'Neill for P. Stuart, C. O'Connor for P. Gormley.

1961/62

Down—E. McKay, G. Lavery, L. Murphy, P. Rice, K. Mussen, P. O'Hagan, K. O'Neill, J. Carey, J. Lennon, S. O'Neill, J. McCartan, P. Doherty (capt.), A. Hadden, D. McCartan, B. Morgan. Sub: P. Hamill for K. O'Neill.

Dublin—P. Flynn, L. Hickey, L. Foley, W. Casey, C. O'Leary, P. Holden, C. Kane, John Timmons, D. McKane, Micky Whelan, P. Farnan, A. Donnelly, E. Burgess, J. Joyce, K. Heffernan (capt.). Subs: N. Fox for J. Timmons, J. Timmons for P. Farnan.

1962/63

Kerry—S. Fitzgerald, K. Coffey, N. Sheehy (capt.), Donie O'Sullivan, J. J. Barrett, Seamus Murphy, J. D. O'Connor, J. O'Riordan, M. Fleming, B. O'Callaghan, M. O'Dwyer, Derry O'Shea, P. Aherne, T. Burke, Denis O'Sullivan.

New York—J. Duffy, J. Lowrey, D. Bernard, S. McElligott, P. Lynch, J. Foley, M. Foley, J. Halpin, T. Feighery, S. Kenna, G. McCarthy, M. Moynihan, P. Boyle, B. O'Donnell, P. Carey. Sub: P. Flood for P. Lynch.

HOME FINAL

Kerry—Same as played in final except J. Culloty, T. Lyons, M. O'Connell, J. Lucey, S. Og Sheehy, W. Doran and T. Long for S. Fitzgerald, J. J. Barrett, M. Fleming, D. O'Shea, P. Aherne, T. Burke and Denis O'Sullivan. Subs: D. Geaney for J. O'Riordan, P. Aherne for S. Og Sheehy, J. J. Barrett for T. Lyons.

Down—P. McAlinden, G. Lavery, L. Murphy, P. Rice, P. O'Hagan, D. McCartan, K. O'Neill, J. Lennon, A. Hadden, B. Morgan, B. Johnston, S. O'Neill, K. Mussen, P. J. McElroy, P. Doherty. Subs: P. Hamill for P. J. McElroy, T. O'Hare for K. Mussen.

1963/64

New York—J. Duffy, H. Coyle, P. Nolan, S. McElligott, B. Hennessy, E. McCarthy, P. Barden, M. Moynihan, D. Finn, P. Cummins, P. Casey, J. Foley, T. Hennessy (capt.), B. O'Donnell, E. McGuinness.

Dublin—P. Flynn, L. Hickey, L. Foley, C. Kane, D. McKane, P. Holden, M. Kissane, D. Foley, John Timmons, B. McDonald, Micky Whelan (capt.), N. Fox, G. Davey, W. Casey, D. Ferguson. Sub: M. Keane for L. Hickey.

HOME FINAL

Dublin—Same as played in final except E. Breslin and J. Gilroy for D. McKane and N. Fox.

Down—P. McAlinden, G. Lavery (capt.), L. Murphy, T. O'Hare, P. O'Hagan, D. McCartan, K. O'Neill, B. Johnston, L. Powell, S. O'Neill, J. McCartan, P. Doherty, J. Lennon, P. Rice, V. Kane. Subs: B. Morgan for J. Rice, P. Hamill for P. O'Hagan, J. Smith for L. Murphy.

1964/65

Galway—J, Geraghty, J. B. McDermott, N. Tierney, S. Meade, J. Donnellan (capt.), E. Colleran, M. Newell, M. Reynolds, P. Donnellan, C. Dunne, M. McDonagh, S. Leydon, C. Tyrrell, S. Cleary, J. Keenan. Subs: T. Sands for S. Meade, B. Geraghty for J. Keenan.

M. Garrett played in first leg. P. Donnellan was on for second leg. Subs in first leg: P. Donnellan for M. Garrett, M. Tarpey for S. Meade.

New York—J. Duffy, M. Foley, P. Nolan, K. Finn, D. Finn, G. McCarthy, P. Barden, T. Feighery, J. Halpin, P. Cummins, J. Foley, T. Foley, S. Nugent, B. O'Donnell, P. Casey. Subs: B. Tumulty for, D. Ryan, S. Kenna.

H. Coyle and M. Moynihan played in first leg. M. Foley and T. Furlong were on for second leg. Sub in first leg: T. Furlong.

HOME FINAL

Galway—Same as played in final except M. Garrett for P. Donnellan. Sub: P. Donnellan for M. Reynolds.

Kerry—J. Culloty, Donie O'Sullivan, P. O'Donoghue, M. Morris (capt.), Denis O'Sullivan, J. D. O'Connor, Seamus Murphy, J. Lucey, M. Fleming, B. O'Callaghan, M. O'Connell, P. Griffin, J. J. Barrett, V. Lucey, M. O'Dwyer.

1965/66

Longford—J. Heneghan, Seamus Flynn, L. Gillen, B. Gilmore, B. Barden (capt.), J. Donlon, P. Barden, Jimmy Flynn, T. Mulvihill, J. Devine, M. Hopkins, J. Hanniffy, S. Murray, R. Burns, S. Donnelly. Subs: T. McGovern for L. Gillen, L. Gillen for T. McGovern.

M. Burns played in first leg. T. Mulvihill was on for second leg. Sub in first leg T. Mulvihill for M. Burns.

New York—W. Nolan, P. Maguire, P. Nolan, K. Finn, D. Finn, S. Nugent, G. Driscoll, J. Foley, B. Tumulty, D. Byrne, M. Moynihan, K. McNamee, P. Cummins (capt.), S. Brogan, J. Halpin.

S. Kenna, B. O'Donnell and J. O'Brien played in first leg. D. Byrne, M. Moynihan and S. Brogan were on for second leg. Subs in first leg: G. McCarthy for B. O'Donnell, D. Ryan for J. O'Brien, T. Frawley for S. Kenna.

HOME FINAL

Longford—Same as played in final except T. McGovern and M. Burns for P. Barden and T. Mulvihill.

Galway—J. Geraghty, S. Meade, N. Tierney, J. B. McDermott, E. Colleran (capt.), J. Donnellan, M. Newell, T. Sands, M. Reynolds, C. Dunne, F. Canavan, S. Leydon, C. Tyrrell, M. McDonagh, J. Keenan.

1966/67

New York—W. Nolan, K. Finn (capt.), P. Nolan, P. Maguire, D. Finn, S. Nugent, S. Kenna, B. Tumulty, J. Foley, P. Cummins, M. Moynihan, P. Caulfield, T. Furlong, B. O'Donnell, J. Halpin.

Subs: T. Feighery for P. Caulfield, A. Brady for J. Halpin. T. Feighery and D. Ryan played in first leg. P. Cummins and P. Caulfield came on for second leg. Sub in first leg—P. Cummins for D. Ryan.

Galway—J. Geraghty, E. Colleran (capt.), S. Meade, J. B. McDermott, J. Donnellan, N. Tierney, C. McDonagh, J. Duggan, J. Glynn, C. Dunne, M. McDonagh, S. Leydon, L. Sammon, F. Canavan, P. Donnellan. Subs: J. Keenan for L. Sammon, M. Reynolds for J. Duggan.

J. Keenan played in first leg. M. McDonagh was on for second leg. Subs in first leg: M. McDonagh for F. Canavan, F. Canavan for L. Sammon.

HOME FINAL

Galway—Same as played in final except M. Newell, S. Cleary and J Keenan for S. Meade, M. McDonagh and F. Canavan. Subs: S. Meade for N. Tierney, M. McDonagh for S. Cleary.

Dublin—P. Cullen, W. Casey, L. Hickey, C. Kane, M. Kissane, M. Kelleher, G. Davey, S. O'Connor, A. Donnelly, Micky Whelan, J. Keaveney (capt.), M. Cranny, B. Dowling, J. Eivers, L. Deegan. Subs: S. Lee for M. Cranny, D. Foley for M. Kissane.

1967/68

Down—D. Kelly, B. Sloan, D. McCartan, T. O'Hare, R. McConville, L. Powell, J. Lennon (capt.), J. Milligan, C. McAlarney, M. Cole, P. Doherty, J. Murphy, P. Rooney, S. O'Neill, J. Purdy. Subs: R. Murphy for L. Powell.

Kildare—O. Crinnigan, J. McTeague, N. Ryan, J. Cummins, T. Keogh, P. Mangan, J. Doyle, K. Maguire, L. Casey, J. Donnelly, P. Dunny, T. Carew, K. Kelly, P. Connolly (capt.), M. Mullins. Subs: M. Carolan for K. Maguire, L. Gleeson for L. Casey.

1968/69

Kerry—J. Culloty (capt.), Seamus Murphy, P. O'Donoghue, S. Fitzgerald, Donie O'Sullivan, M. Morris, M. O'Shea, M. Fleming, D.J.Crowley, B. Lynch, C. O'Sullivan, E. O'Donoghue, T. Prendergast, L. Higgins, M. O'Dwyer. Subs: M. O'Connell for C. O'Sullivan, Derry Crowley for L. Higgins.

M. O'Connell and D. O'Donnell played in first leg. C. O'Sullivan and T. Prendergast were on for second leg. Subs in first leg: P. Moynihan for M. O'Connell, T. Prendergast for D. O'Donnell, C. O'Sullivan for P. Moynihan.

New York—W. Nolan, D. Finn, P. Nolan, P. Maguire, M. Moore, K. Finn, S. Nugent, T. Feighery, D. Duff, M. Gannon, J. Foley, M. Moynihan (capt.), D. Ryan, T. Furlong, J. Halpin. Subs: M. Fitzgerald for P. Nolan, B. O'Donnell for T. Furlong, P. Cummins for M. Gannon.

M. Fitzgerald played in first leg. J. Halpin was on For second leg. Subs in first leg: P. Cummins For M. Fitzgerald, J. Halpin for D. Duffy.

HOME FINAL

Kerry—Same as played in final except Denis O'Sullivan, M. O'Connell, P. Griffin (capt.) and D. O'Donnell for Seamus Murphy, Donie O'Sullivan, C. O'Sullivan and T. Prendergast.

Offaly—M. Furlong, M. Ryan, G. Hughes, P. McCormack, E. Mulligan, J. Smith, N. Clavin, L. Coughlan, A. Hickey, P. Monaghan (capt.), W. Bryan, A. McTague, M. O'Rourke, J. Cooney, S. Kilroy. Subs: J. Egan for N. Clavin, B. Guinan for W. Bryan, W. Bryan for A. Hickey.

1969/70

Mayo—E. Rooney, S. Hughes, R. Prendergast, R. Niland, J. Corey (capt.), J. Morley, J. Earley, P. J. Loftus, J. Langan, T. Fitzgerald, J. Gibbons, J. Corcoran, D. Griffith, W. McGee, J. J. Cribben. Sub: S. O'Grady for P. J. Loftus.

Down—D. Kelly, B. Sloan, D. McCartan, T. O'Hare (capt.), R. McConville, J. Fitzsimons, H. McGrath, J. Milligan, J. Lennon, J. Murphy, J. Morgan, M. Cole, P. Rooney, S. O'Neill, J. Purdy. Subs—C. McAlarney for J. Fitzsimons, N. Millar for H. McGrath.

1970/71

Kerry—J. Culloty, Donie O'Sullivan (capt.), P. O'Donoghue, S. Fitzgerald, T. Prendergast, J. O'Keeffe, M. O'Shea, P. Lynch, D. J. Crowley, B. Lynch, P. Griffin, E. O'Donoghue, M. Gleeson, L. Higgins, M. O'Dwyer. Sub: Derry Crowley for S. Fitzgerald.

Mayo—E. Rooney, S. Hughes, R. Prendergast, J. Earley, J. Carey, J. Morley, B. O'Reilly, S. Kilbride, P. J. Loftus, T. Fitzgerald, J. Gibbons, J. Corcoran, W. McGee, J. J. Cribben, D. Griffith.
Subs: S. O'Grady for S. Kilbride, R. Niland for B. O'Reilly.

1971/72

Kerry—E. Fitzgerald, Donie O'Sullivan, P. O'Donoghue, S. Fitzgerald, T. Prendergast, Derry Crowley, M. O'Shea, M. O'Connell, J. O'Keeffe, P. Lynch, D. Kavanagh, E. O'Donoghue, M. Gleeson (capt.), L. Higgins, M. O'Dwyer. Subs: B. Lynch for E. O'Donoghue, J. Walsh for Derry Crowley, M. O'Sullivan for S. Fitzgerald.

Mayo—J. J. Costelloe, M. Begley, R. Prendergast (capt.), T. Keane, M. Higgins, J. Morley, B. O'Reilly, S. O'Grady, S. Kilbride, T. Fitzgerald, J. Gibbons, J. Corcoran, T. O'Malley, W. McGee, J. J. Cribben. Subs: F. Burns for B. O'Reilly, D. Griffith for J. J. Cribben.

1972/73

Kerry—E. Fitzgerald, Donie O'Sullivan, P. O'Donoghue, J. Deenihan, G. O'Keeffe, Derry Crowley, M. O'Shea, D. Kavanagh, J. O'Keeffe,

B. Lynch (capt.), L. Higgins, E. O'Donoghue, J. Egan, M. O'Dwyer, J. Walsh. Subs: M. O'Sullivan for L. Higgins, G. Power for M. O'Shea.

Offaly—M. Furlong, S. Lowry, M. Ryan, M. O'Rourke, E. Mulligan, L. Coughlan, M. Wright, W. Bryan, S. Evans, P. Fenning, K. Kilmurray, A. McTague, Murt Connor, J. Smith, J. Cooney. Subs: N. Kelly for E. Mulligan, K. Claffey for Murt Connor.

1973/74

Kerry—P. O'Mahony, Donie O'Sullivan, P. O'Donoghue, Derry Crowley, P. Ó Sé, P. Lynch, G. O'Keeffe, J. O'Keeffe, J. Long, E. O'Donoghue, M. O'Sullivan, G. Power, J. Egan, S. Fitzgerald, M. Sheehy.

P. Spillane and J. Walsh played in drawn game. P. Ó Sé and E. O'Donoghue were on for replay. Subs in drawn game: E. O'Donoghue for P. Spillane, P. O'Shea for S. Fitzgerald.

Roscommon—J. McDermott, H. Keegan, P. Linsday, G. Mannion, A. Regan, D. Watson, J. Kerrane, M. Freyne, J. O'Gara, J. Kelly, D. Earley, J. Mannion, J. Finnegan, T. Heneghan, T. Donlon. Subs: G. Beirne for D. Watson, H. Griffin for J. Mannion.

P. White and M. McNamara played in drawn game. J. McDermott and J. Mannion were on for replay. Subs in drawn game: M. Griffin for J. Kelly, P. O'Callaghan for M. McNamara.

1974/75

Meath—R. Giles (capt.), M. Collins, J. Quinn, B. Murray, P. Smith, P. Reynolds, P. J. O'Halloran, J. Cassells, M. Ryan, E. O'Brien, K. Rennicks, P. Traynor, M. Kerrigan, C. Rowe, O. O'Brien.

Dublin—P. Cullen, G. O'Driscoll, S. Doherty, R. Kelleher, P. O'Reilly, A. Larkin, G. Wilson, B. Mullins, S. Rooney, R. Doyle, A. Hanahoe, D. Hickey, J. McCarthy, J. Keaveney, A. O'Toole. Sub P. Gogarty for D. Hickey.

1975/76

Dublin—P. Cullen, G. O'Driscoll, S. Doherty, R. Kelleher, B. Pocock, P. O'Neill, K. Synnott, B. Mullins, K. Moran, A. O'Toole, A. Hanahoe, D. Hickey, R. Doyle, J. Keaveney, P. Gogarty. Sub: B. Brogan for P. O'Neill.

Derry—M. McFeely, L. Murphy, T. Quinn, P. Stevenson, G. O'Loughlin, A. McGurk, M. Moran, T. McGuinness, S. Lagan, G. McElhinney, M. Lynch, G. Bradley, B. Kelly, S. O'Connell, J. O'Leary. Subs: F. McCloskey for S. Lagan, A. McGuckian for G. Bradley.

1976/77

Kerry—C. Nelligan, J. Deenihan, P. Lynch, G. O'Keeffe, P. Ó Sé, T. Kennelly, G. Power, J. O'Keeffe, J. O'Shea, S. Walsh, D. Moran, M. Sheehy, B. Walsh, P. Spillane, J. Egan.

Dublin—P. Cullen, G. O'Driscoll, S. Doherty, R. Kelleher, T. Drumm, K. Moran, P. O'Neill, B. Brogan, A. Larkin, A. O'Toole, A. Hanahoe, D. Hickey, R. Doyle, J. Keaveney, J. McCarthy. Subs: M. Hickey for B. Brogan, F. Ryder for A. Larkin.

1977/78

Dublin—P. Cullen, G. O'Driscoll, S. Doherty, R. Kelleher, F. Ryder, J. Brogan, P. O'Neill, B. Mullins, B. Brogan, A. O'Toole, A. Hanahoe, D. Hickey, R. Doyle, J. Keaveney, J. McCarthy.

Mayo—E. Lavin, S. Minogue, G. King, P. Burke, G. Feeney, S. Sweeney, H. Gavin, A. Egan, D. Dolan, J. P. Kean, W. Nally, L. Donoghue, T. O'Malley, W. J. Padden, W. Fitzpatrick. Subs: R. Bell for J. P. Kean, M. Gavin for P. Burke.

1978/79

Roscommon—J. McDermott, S. Tighe, P. Lindsay, T. Heneghan, G. Fitzmaurice, T. Donlon, D. Murray, D. Earley, S. Hayden, A. McManus, J. O'Gara, S. Kilbride, M. Finneran, M. Freyne, E. McManus. Sub: R. Beirne for T. Heneghan.

Cork—W. Morgan, S. O'Sullivan, K. Kehily, B. Murphy, J. Crowley, C. Ryan, J. Kerrigan, J. Courtney, V. Coakley, D. McCarthy, J. Barry Murphy, D. Allen, P. Kavanagh, D. Barron, C. Kearney. Subs: T. O'Reilly for V. Coakley, M. Mullins for D. McCarthy, J. Coleman for J. Crowley.

1979/80

Cork—W. Morgan, S. O'Sullivan, K. Kehily, J. Evans, J. O'Sullivan, C. Ryan, J. Kerrigan, T. Creedon, V. Coakley, S. Murphy, D. Allen, T. Dalton, J. Barry Murphy, J. Allen, D. Barron. Subs: A. Creagh for V. Coakley, C. Kearney for A. Creagh, J. Lynch for S. Murphy.

Kerry—P. O'Mahony, J. Deenihan, J. O'Keeffe, M. Spillane, P. Ó Sé, T. Kennelly, P. Lynch, J. Ó Sé, S. Walsh, D. Moran, T. Doyle, P. Spillane, G. Power, E. Liston, J. Egan. Sub: V. O'Connor for P. Spillane.

1980/81

Galway—P. Coyne, J. Hughes, S. Kinneavy, P. Moran, P. O'Neill, P. Lee, S. McHugh, B. Talty, W. Joyce, B. Brennan (capt.), D. Smith, S. Joyce, T. Naughton, T. J. Gilmore, G. McManus. Subs: G. Burke for T. J. Gilmore, P. Conroy for D. Smith,

Roscommon—G. Sheerin, H. Keegan, P. Lindsay, J. McManus, G. Connellan, T. Donlon, D. Murray, S. Hayden, J. O'Gara, E. McManus, A. McManus, D. Earley, J. O'Connor, M. Finneran, G. Emmett. Subs: M. McDermott for J. O'Gara, M. Dolphin for J. O'Connor.

1981/82

Kerry—C. Nelligan, J. Deenihan, J. O'Keeffe, G. O'Keeffe, P. Ó Sé, T. Kennelly. G. Lynch, J. O'Shea, S. Walsh, J. L McElligott, D. Moran, T. Doyle, G. Power, E. Liston, J. Egan.

V. O'Connor and M. Spillane played in drawn game. P. Ó Sé and T. Doyle were on for replay. Subs in drawn game: P. Ó Sé for V. O'Connor,

FOOTBALL

P. Spillane for M. Spillane.
Cork—M. Creedon, M. Healy, K. Kehily, J. Evans, M. Moloney, T. Creedon, J. Kerrigan, M. Burns, D. Creedon, D. Barry, D. Allen, T. O'Reilly, D. McCarthy, C. Ryan, E. Fitzgerald. Subs: T. Murphy for E. Fitzgerald.
M. Connolly played in drawn game. T. O'Reilly was on for replay. Subs in drawn game: T. Murphy for M. Connolly, S. Hayes for E. Fitzgerald.

1982/83
Down—J. McAleavy, E. King, T. McGovern, M. Turley (capt.), P. Kennedy, P. O'Rourke, B. McGovern, L. Austin, B. Toner, John McCartan, D. Bell, G. Blaney, M. Linden, A. Rogers, B. Mason.
Armagh—B. McAlinden, D. Stevenson, J. McKerr (capt.), K. McNally, B. Canavan, P. Moriarty, J. Donnelly, N. Marley, F. McMahon, J. Murphy, J. Kernan, S. Deviin, J. Corvan, B. McGeown, M. McDonald. Subs: D. McCoy for J. Kernan, K. McGurk for D. Stevenson, C. Harney for B. McGeown.

1983/84
Kerry—C. Nelligan, P. Ó Sé, V. O'Connor, M. Spillane, T. Doyle, J. Higgins, G. Power, J. O'Shea, S. Walsh, T. O'Dowd, D. Moran, P. Spillane, D. O'Donoghue, T. Spillane, M. Sheehy. Subs: E. Liston for T. O'Dowd, W. Maher for D. O'Donoghue.
Galway—P. Coyne, S. McHugh, S. Kinneavy, P. Lee, P. O'Neill, T. Tierney, M. Coleman, B. Talty, R. Lee, B. O'Donnell, G. McManus, S. Joyce, V. Daly, M. Brennan, K. Clancy. Subs: H. Bleahen for R. Lee, P. O'Dea for K. Clancy, L. Higgins for G. McManus.

1984/85
Monaghan—P. Linden, E. Sherry, G. McCarville, F. Caulfield, G. Hoey, C. Murray, Brendan Murray, H. Clerkin, D. Byrne, D. Flanagan, E. McEneaney, Bernie Murray, R. McCarron, E. Murphy, E. Hughes.
Armagh—B. McAlinden, D. Stevenson, T. Cassidy, J. Murphy, B. Canavan, K. McNally, J. Donnelly, J. McCorry, F. McMahon, A. Short, C. Harney, K. McGurk, J. Corvan, D. Seely, J. Cunningham. Subs: J. Kernan for J. Cunningham, P. Rafferty for K. McGurk, J. McKerr for B. Canavan.

1985/86
Laois—M. Conroy, P. Dunne, Martin Dempsey, E. Kelly, M. Aherne, P. Brophy, C. Browne (capt.), J. Costelloe, L. Irwin, G. Browne, W. Brennan, T. Prendergast, Michael Dempsey, E. Whelan, C.Maguire. Subs: N. Prendergast for C. Maguire, G. Lalor for W. Brennan, B. Nerney for N. Prendergast.
Monaghan—P. Linden, E. Sherry, G. McCarville, F. Caulfield, Brendan Murray, C. Murray, D. Loughman, H. Clerkin, K. Carragher, R. McCarron, M. O'Dowd, E. Hughes, M. Caulfield, E. Murphy, G. Hoey. Subs: E. McEneaney for M. O'Dowd, D. Byrne for D. Loughman.

1986/87
Dublin—J. O'Leary, D. Carroll, G. Hargan, M. Kennedy, D. Synnott, G. O'Neill, N. McCaffrey, J. Roynane, D. Bolger, B. Rock, J. McNally, K. Duff, D. De Lappe, M. Galvin, A. McCaul. Sub: D. Sheehan for D. De Lappe.
Kerry—C. Nelligan, P. Ó Sé, T. Spillane, M. Spillane, S. Stack, T. Doyle, G. Lynch, J. O'Shea, T. O'Dowd, J. Kennedy, D. Moran, P. Spillane, W. Maher, M. Sheehy, G. Power. Subs: J. Higgins for S. Stack, E. Liston for W. Maher.

1987/88
Meath—M. McQuillan, R. O'Malley, M. Lyons (capt.), P. Lyons, K. Foley, L. Harnan, M. O'Connell, L. Hayes, G. McEntee, B. Reilly, P. J. Gillic, M. McCabe, C. O'Rourke, B. Stafford, B. Flynn.
T. Ferguson, D. Beggy and J. Cassells played in drawn game. P. Lyons, B. Reilly and M. McCabe were on for replay. Subs in drawn game: M. McCabe for J. Cassells, P. Lyons for T. Ferguson.
Dublin—J. O'Leary, D. Carroll, G. Hargan, M. Kennedy, D. Synnott, N. McCaffrey, P. Clarke, J. Bissett, D. Bolger, V. Murphy, C. Redmond, K. Duff, D. De Lappe, J. McNally, B. Rock. Subs: T. O'Driscoll for D. Synnott, B. O'Hagan for D. Carroll, J. Prendergast for T. O'Driscoll.
E. Heery, T. Conroy and M. Galvin played in drawn game. P. Clarke, C. Redmond and B. Rock were on for replay. Sub in drawn game: P. Clarke for D. Bolger.

1988/89
Cork—J. Kerins, N. Cahalane, C. Corrigan, J. Kerrigan, M. Slocum, C. Counihan, A. Davis, L. Tompkins, B. Coffey, S. O'Brien, D. Barry, A. Nation (capt.), P. McGrath, D. Allen, J. Cleary. Subs: E. O'Mahony for C. Corrigan, D. Culloty for E. O'Mahony, M. Maguire for J. Kerins.
T. McCarthy and J. O'Driscoll played in first leg. C. Corrigan and D. Barry were on for second leg. Subs in first leg: C. Corrigan for J. O'Driscoll, C. O'Neill for P. McGrath.
New York—K. Nolan, A. Wiseman, V. Hatton, J. Donoghue, J. Owens, E. McNulty, E. McIntyre, P. Dunne (capt.), D. McSweeney, T. Connaughton, J. P. O'Kane, M. McEntee, M. Connolly, W. Doyle, W. Lowry. Subs: K. O'Reilly for W. Doyle, J. Cassidy for D. McSweeney, D. O'Connell for A. Wiseman.
J. Lyons and K. O'Reilly played in first leg. E. McNulty and W. Doyle were on for second leg. Subs in first leg: W. Doyle for K. O'Reilly, L. Molloy for T. Connaughton, P. O'Toole for D McSweeney.

HOME FINAL
Cork—Same as played in final except T. McCarthy for A. Nation.
Dublin—J. O'Leary, E. Heery, G. Hargan, M. Kennedy, N. McCaffrey, T. Carr, M. Deegan, J. Roynane, P. Bealin, V. Murphy, C. Redmond, K. Duff, B. Rock, M. Galvin, A. McNally. Sub: D. Carroll for P. Bealin.

1989/90

Meath—D. Smith, K. Foley, M. Lyons, T. Ferguson, B. Reilly, L. Harnan, M. O'Connell, L. Hayes, C. Brady, D. Beggy, C. Coyle, P. J. Gillic, C. O'Rourke (capt.), B. Stafford, B. Flynn. Subs J. Cassells for C. Coyle, S. Kelly for L. Harnan.

Down—N. Collins, P. Higgins, C. Deegan, B. Breen, J. Kelly, P. O'Rourke (capt.), D. J. Kane, R. Carr, E. Burns, A. Rogers, G. Blaney, C. Burns, C. Murray, M. Linden, James McCartan. Subs: B. Mason for A. Rogers. M. McCartan for C. Burns.

1990/91

Dublin—J. O'Leary, M. Deegan, C. Walsh, M. Kennedy, T. Carr (capt.), K. Barr, E. Heery, D. Foran, P. Clarke, C. Redmond, P. Curran, N. Guiden, J. Sheehy, V. Murphy, D. McCarthy. Subs: M. Galvin for D. McCarthy, K. Duff for N. Guiden.

Kildare—N. Connolly, D. Dalton, J. Crofton, S. Dowling, G. Ryan, P. O'Donoghue, W. Sex, M. Lynch, S. McGovern, D. Kerrigan, T. Harris, J. McDonald, P. McLoughlin, D. McKevitt, J. Gilroy. Subs: S. Ryan for W. Sex, N. Donlon for J. McDonald.

1991/92

Derry—D. McCusker, K. McKeever, D. Quinn, A. Scullion, H. Downey, C. Rafferty, G. Coleman, B. McGilligan, D. Heaney, A. Tohill, D. McNicholl, G. McGill, J. Brolly, F. McCusker, E. Gormley. Subs: S. Downey for D. McNicholl, J. McGurk for C. Rafferty, D. Bateson for G. McGill.

Tyrone—F. McConnell, S. Meyler, C. Lawn, P. Donnelly, F. Devlin, E. Kilpatrick, N. Donnelly, C. Corr, P. Donaghy, A. Cush, E. McCaffrey, B. Gormley, M. McGleenan, D. O'Hagan, Peter Canavan. Subs: P. Devlin for S. Meyler.

1992/93

Dublin—J. O'Leary (capt.), C. Walsh, D. Deasy, P. Moran, E. Heery, P. Curran, M. Deegan, J. Sheedy, P. Bealin, J. Gavin, T. Carr, N. Guiden, P. Clarke, V. Murphy, M. Doran.

J. Calvert and C. Redmond played in drawn game. J. Gavin and P. Clarke were on for replay. Subs in drawn game: K. Barr for J. Calvert, M. Galvin for M. Doran.

Donegal—G. Walsh, J. J. Doherty, M. Gallagher, B. McGowan, D. Reid, N. Hegarty, M. Shovlin, A. Molloy, B. Murray, J. McHugh, B. Cunningham, J McMullan, D. Bonner, A. Boyle, M. Boyle. Subs: S. Maguire for J. McMullan, M. Gavigan for M. Shovlin, M. McHugh for B. Cunningham.

M. Gavigan and M. McHugh played in drawn game. N. Hegarty and J. McMullan were on for replay. Sub in drawn game: N. Hegarty for M. Gavigan.

1993/94

Meath—D. Smith, R. O'Malley (capt.), M. O'Connell, T. Hanley, G. Geraghty, C. Murphy, B. Reilly, J. McGuinness, P. J. Gillic, N. Dunne, C. O'Rourke, T. Giles, B. Flynn, T. Dowd, J. Devine. Sub B. Stafford for N. Dunne.

Armagh—B. Tierney, D. Clarke, G. Hoey, J. Rafferty, D. Horish, K. McGeeney, M. McQuillan, N. Smith, J. Burns, C. O'Rourke, K. McGurk, D. Marsden, B. O'Hagan, G. Houlahan (capt.), J. McConville. Subs: J. Grimley for B. O'Hagan, D. Macken for D. Marsden, J. Toner for C. O'Rourke.

1994/95

Derry—D. McCusker, K. McKeever, A. Scullion, G. Coleman, J. McGurk, H. Downey, F. McCusker, A. Tohill, B. McGilligan, D. Heaney, D. Barton, E. Burns, J. Brolly, S. Downey, E. Gormley. Sub: D. Bateson for J. Brolly.

Donegal—G. Walsh, J. J. Doherty, M. Gallagher, B. McGowan, M. Crossan, M. Gavigan, M. Shovlin, M. McShane, B. Murray, P. Hegarty, N. Hegarty, J. McHugh, J. Duffy, A. Boyle, M. Boyle. Sub: D. Bonner for A. Boyle.

1995/96

Derry—J. Kelly, K. McKeever, G. Coleman, A. Scullion, K. Diamond, H. Downey, F. McCusker, A. Tohill, B. McGilligan, E. Burns, D. Barton, S. M. Lockhart, J. Brolly, S. Downey, E. Gormley. Subs: D. Dougan for E. Burns, G. McGill for S. Downey.

Donegal—G. Walsh, M. Gallagher, J. J. Doherty, M. Crossan, B. McGowan, J. Cunningham, M. Shovlin, J. Ruane, B. Murray, P. Hegarty, N. Hegarty, J. B. Gallagher, B. Roper, A. Boyle, M. Boyle. Subs: J. McHugh for J. B. Gallagher, D. McNamara for B. Roper.

1996/97

Kerry—D. O'Keeffe, K. Burns, B. O'Shea, M. Hassett (capt.), S. Moynihan, L. Flaherty, E. Breen, D. Ó Sé, W. Kirby, P. Laide, L. Hassett, D. O'Dwyer, D. Ó Cinnéide, B. Clarke, M. Fitzgerald. Subs: M. F. Russell for D. Ó Cinneide.

Cork—K. O'Dwyer, M. O'Connor, R. McCarthy, E. Sexton, S. Óg Ó hAilpin, N. Cahalane, M. O'Donovan, C. O'Sullivan, D. O'Neill, M. Cronin, B. Corcoran, O. O'Sullivan, C. Corkery, S. O'Brien, A. Dorgan. Subs: J. Kavanagh for C. Corkery, P. Griffin for B. Corcoran, B. Murphy for M. Cronin.

1997/98

Offaly—P. Kelly, C. Daly, J. Ryan, D. Foley, J. Kenny, F. Cullen (capt.), J. Brady, R. Mooney, James Grennan, C. Quinn, J. Stewart, C. McManus, V. Claffey, R. Malone, P. O'Reilly. Subs: Sean Grennan for R. Malone, B. Mooney for P. O'Reilly.

Derry—E. McCloskey, P. Diamond, S. M. Lockart, K. McKeever, P. McFlynn, H. Downey, J. McBride, A. Tohill, F. McCusker, G. McGill, G. Coleman, D. Dougan, J. Brolly, B. Murray, J. Cassidy. Sub: S. McLarnon for J. Cassidy.

FOOTBALL

1998/99

Cork—K. O'Dwyer; M. O'Donovan, S. Óg Ó hAilpín, A. Lynch; C. O'Sullivan, E. Sexton, M. Cronin; Michael O'Sullivan, N. Murphy; A. Dorgan, J. Kavanagh, P. O'Mahony; P. Clifford (capt.), Mark O'Sullivan, A. O'Regan. Subs: D. Davis for O'Regan, R. McCarthy for Murphy.

Dublin—D. Byrne; P. Moran, P. Christie, S. Ryan; T. Lynch, P. Curran, K. Galvin; C. Whelan, E. Sheehy; J. Gavin, D. Darcy, B. Stynes; B. O'Brien, D. Farrell (capt.), N. O'Donoghue. Subs: D. Homan for O'Donoghue, J. Sherlock for O'Brien.

2000

Derry – M.Conlon, G.Coleman, S.M.Lockhart, D.O'Neill, H.Downey, P.McFlynn, A.Tohill, D.Heaney, N.McOscar, D.Dougan, R.Rocks, P.Bradley, E.Muldoon, J.McBride. Subs – C.Gilligan for Rocks, G.McGonigle for Gilligan, S.McLarnon for Bradley.
(E.McCloskey, K.McKeever, B.Murray and E.Burns played in the drawn final, but didn't line out in the replay. Subs in the drawn encounter were G.McGonigle for McBride, R.Dougan for Coleman, S.Downey for Burns, F.McCusker for Murray.

Meath – C.Sullivan, M.O'Reilly, D.Fay, C.Murphy, N.Nestor, A.Moyles, R.Kealy, N.Crawford, J.McDermott, E.Kelly, T.Giles, D.Curtis, O.Murphy, R.Fitzsimons, J.Devine. Subs – B.Callaghan for Devine, T.Dowd for Curtis, S.Dillon for Kelly.
(H.Traynor, P.Reynolds and G.Geraghty played in the drawn final, but didn't line out in the replay. Subs in the drawn encounter were N.Nestor for Kealy, J.Devine for Fitzsimons.)

2001

Mayo – P.Burke, R.Connelly, T.Nallen, K.Cahill, F.Costello, A.Roche, N.Connelly, C.McManamon, D.Brady, J.Gill, D.McDonagh, S.Carolan, M.McNicholas, R.Loftus, T.Mortimer. Subs – M.Moyles for Mortimer, J.Nallen for Roche, M.Sheridan for Loftus, D.Nestor for Moyles.

Galway – P.Lally, M.Comer, K.Fitzgerald, M.Colleran, D.Meehan, J.Divilly, S. Óg de Paor, M.Donnellan, J.Bergin, M.Clancy, K.Comer, L.Colleran, D.Savage, P.Joyce, J.Donnellan. Subs – S.Walsh for Clancy, R.Fahy for M.Comer, T.Mannion for Colleran, J.Fallon for K.Comer, S. Ó Domhnaill for Bergin.

2002

Tyrone – P.Ward, C.Gormley, C.Lawn, B.Robinson, R.McMenamin, C.Gourley, P.Jordan, C.McAnallen, C.Holmes, B.Dooher, S.O'Neill, G.Cavlan, B.McGuigan, K.Hughes, Peter Canavan. Subs – S.Cavanagh for Hughes, Pascal Canavan for McGuigan, D.McCrossan for Jordan.

Cavan – A.Donohue, E.Reilly, T.Prior, C.Hannon, M.Brides, A.Forde, J.Doonan, P.McKenna, C.Collins, P.Galligan, P.Reilly, F.O'Reilly, L.Reilly, J.Reilly, M.Graham. Subs – E.Reilly for Graham, E.Jackson for Doonan, R.Rogers for L.Reilly.

2003

Tyrone – J.Devine, R.McMenamin, C.Holmes, M.McGee, C.Gormley, G.Devlin, P.Jordan, C.McAnallen, S.Cavanagh, B.Dooher, B.McGuigan, S.O'Neill, E.McGinley, P.Canavan, O.Mulligan. Subs – G.Cavlan for McGinley, R.Mellon for McGuigan, C.Lawn for McMenamin, D.McCrossan for Gormley.

Laois – F.Byron, T.Kelly, C.Byrne, J.Higgins, D.Rooney, K.Fitzpatrick, D.Conroy, P.Clancy, N.Garvan, C.Parkinson, I.Fitzgerald, M.Lawlor, B.McDonald, D.Delaney, S.Kelly. Subs – R.Munnelly for Lawlor, C.Conway for Delaney, D.Miller for Garvan, D.Sweeney for S.Kelly, A.Fennelly for Fitzgerald.

2004

Kerry – D.Murphy, T.O'Sullivan, M.McCarthy, A.O'Mahony, T.Ó Sé, E.Fitzmaurice, S.Moynihan, E.Brosnan, W.Kirby, P.Galvin, D.O'Sullivan, L.Hassett, C.Cooper, J.Crowley, M.F.Russell. Subs – D.O'Cinneide for Crowley, M.Ó Sé for Galvin.

Galway – A.Keane, K.Fitzgerald, G.Fahy, M.Comer, D.Meehan, P.Clancy, S.Óg de Paor, J.Bergin, S.Ó Domhnaill, M.Clancy, M.Donnellan, J.Devane, M.Meehan, P.Joyce, T.Joyce. Subs – N.Joyce for Devane, C.Monaghan for Comer, D.Savage for M.Clancy.

2005

Armagh – P.Hearty, A.Mallon, F.Bellew, P.McCormack, A.Kernan, K.McGeeney, C.McKeever, J.Toal, P.McGrane, M.O'Rourke, J.McEntee, O.McConville, S.McDonnell, R.Clarke, B.Mallon. Subs – P.McKeever for O'Rourke, A.McCann for Kernan, J.McNulty for Bellew, P.Loughran for McGrane, A.O'Rourke for McKeever.

Wexford – J.Cooper, C.Morris, P.Wallace, N.Murphy, D.Breen, D.Murphy, S.Cullen, D.Fogarty, N.Lambert, D.Kinsella, P.Colfer, J.Hegarty, R.Barry, J.Hudson, M.Forde. Subs – P.Forde for Hegarty, J.Darcy for Colfer, D.Foran for Darcy, P.Curtis for N.Murphy.

2006

Kerry – D.Murphy, A.O'Mahony, M.Ó Sé, T.O'Sullivan, S.Moynihan, T.Ó Sé, M.Lyons, D.Ó Sé, K.Donaghy, P.Galvin, E.Fitzmaurice, B.Sheehan, C.Cooper, Declan O'Sullivan, R.O'Connor. Subs – Darren O'Sullivan for O'Connor, E.Brosnan for Fitzmaurice, T.Griffin for O'Mahony, M.F.Russell for Cooper.

Galway – A.Keane, D.Meehan, K.Fitzgerald, D.Burke, A.Burke, D.Blake, M.Comer, P.Clancy, N.Coleman, M.Clancy, D.Savage, M.Donnellan, M.Meehan, P.Joyce, S.Armstrong. Subs – P.Geraghty for Armstrong, B.Cullinane for Savage, F.Hanley for D.Burke.

2007

Donegal – P.Durcan, N.McGee, K.Lacey, P.Campbell, B.Dunnion, B.Monaghan, P.McConagley, N.Gallagher, K.Cassidy, B.Roper, C.Bonner, C.Toye, C.McFadden, B.Devenney, M.Hegarty. Subs – K.McMenamin for Devenney, E.McGee for N.McGee, T.Donoghue for McConagley, R.Kavanagh for Gallagher, A.Sweeney for Bonner.

Mayo – D.Clarke, K.Higgins, J.Kilcullen, L.O'Malley, E.Devenney, B.J.Padden, P.Gardiner, D.Heaney, J.Nallen, P.Harte, G.Brady, A.Dillon, A.Moran, C.Mortimer, M.Conroy. Subs – A.Higgins for Kilcullen, K.O'Neill for Conroy, T.Howley for A.Higgins, A.Kilcoyne for Dillon, A.Campbell for Nallen.

2008

Derry – B.Gillis, K.McGuckin, N.McCusker, F.McEldowney, L.Hinphey, G.O'Kane, M.McIvor, F.Doherty, J.Diver, M.Lynch, B.McGoldrick, E.Muldoon, C.Gilligan, P.Bradley, E.Bradley. Subs – S.M.Lockhart for McEldowney, P.Murphy for E.Bradley, K.McCloy for Hinphey, J.Keenan for McIvor, C.Mullan for Gilligan.

Kerry – D.Murphy, P.Reidy, M.Ó Sé, T.O'Sullivan, T.O'Se, A.O'Mahony, R.Flaharta, D.Ó Sé, S.Scanlon, Declan O'Sullivan, D.Walsh, E.Brosnan, Darren O'Sullivan, K.Donaghy, M.F.Russell. Subs – C.Cooper for Declan O'Sullivan, M.Quirke for Scanlon, D.Bohane for O'Flaharta, A.Maher for Russell.

2009

Kerry – D.Murphy, P.Reidy, T.O'Sullivan, K.Young, T.Ó Sé, A.O'Mahony, T.Griffin, A.Maher, M.Quirke, Darren O'Sullivan, Declan O'Sullivan, D.Walsh, C.Cooper, K.Donaghy, T.Walsh. Subs – D.Ó Sé for Quirke, T.Kennelly for D.Walsh, D.Moran for Maher, B.Sheehan for Donaghy, D.Bohan for Griffin, S.O'Sullivan for Darren O'Sullivan.

Derry – B.Gillis, K.McGuckin, K.McCloy, G.O'Kane, C.McKaigue, B.McGuigan, S.L.McGoldrick, F.Doherty, J.Diver, E.Lynn, P.Murphy, B.Mullan, E.Bradley, P.Bradley, M.Lynch. Subs – J.Kielt for P.Bradley, P.Bradley for Mullan, D.McBride for O'Kane, S.Bradley for Murphy, R.Dillon for McKaigue.

INTERPROVINCIAL FOOTBALL CHAMPIONSHIP 1927-2009

ROLL OF HONOUR

Ulster (28) – 1942, 1943, 1947, 1950, 1956, 1960, 1963, 1964, 1965, 1966, 1968, 1970, 1971, 1979, 1980, 1983, 1984, 1989, 1991, 1992, 1993, 1994, 1995, 1998, 2000, 2003, 2004, 2007.
Leinster (28) – 1928, 1929, 1930, 1932, 1933, 1935, 1939, 1940, 1944, 1945, 1952, 1953, 1954, 1955, 1959, 1961, 1962, 1974, 1985, 1986, 1987, 1988, 1996, 1997, 2001, 2002, 2005, 2006.
Munster (15) – 1927, 1931, 1941, 1946, 1948, 1949, 1972, 1975, 1976, 1977, 1978, 1981, 1982, 1999, 2008.
Connacht (9) – 1934, 1936, 1937, 1938, 1951, 1957, 1958, 1967, 1969.
Combined Universities (1) – 1973.
Note: No competiton in 1990

1927—November 14, 1926, Cavan:
Munster 1-8, Ulster 3-1.
November 14, 1926, Ballinasioe:
Connacht 1-4, Leinster 1-3.
Final, March 17, Croke Park:
Munster 2-3, Connacht 0-5.
1928—Februory 19, Portlaoise:
Leinster 1-9, Connacht 1-5.
February 26, Croke Park:
Ulster 2-8, Munster 2-6 (unfinished).
Final, March 17, Croke Park:
Leinster 1-8, Ulster 2-4.
1929—February 10, Cavan:
Leinster 2-8, Ulster 1-2,
(Connacht was struck out and Munster got a bye.)
Final, March 17, Croke Park:
Leinster 1-7, Munster 1-3.
1930—February 23, Croke Park:
Leinster 0-8, Connacht 0-3.
Munster 2-13, Ulster 1-3.
Final, March 17, Croke Park:
Leinster 2-3, Munster 0-6.
1931—February 1, Athlone:
Munster 4-5, Connacht 1-7.
February 8, Navan:
Leinster 1-8, Ulster 1-2.
Final, March 17, Croke Park:
Munster 2-2, Leinster 0-6.
1932—February 14, Mardyke (Cork):
Munster 1-9, Connacht 0-5.
February 14, Drogheda:
Leinster 4-11, Ulster 1-3.
Final, March 17, Croke Park:
Leinster 2-10, Munster 3-5.
1933—February 12, Mardyke (Cork):
Leinster 2-4, Munster 1-2.
February 12, Monaghan:
Connacht 1-5, Ulster 0-5.
Final, March 17, Croke Park:
Leinster 0-12, Connacht 2-5.
1934—February 11, Mardyke (Cork):
Leinster 2-6, Munster 1-5.
February 18, Castlebar:
Connacht 0-8, Ulster 0-6.
Final, March 17, Croke Park:
Connacht 2-9, Leinster 2-8.
1935—February 17, Mullingar:
Leinster 1-6, Connacht 1-3.
February 24, Croke Park:
Munster 0-10, Ulster 1-5.
Final, March 17, Croke Park:
Leinster 2-9, Munster 0-7.
1936—February 9, Dundalk:
Leinster 0-2, Ulster 0-2.
February 9, Castlebar:
Connacht 1-7, Munster 2-2.
March 1, Cavan:

Replay, Ulster 1-7, Leinster 1-5.
Final, March 17, Croke Park:
Connacht 3-11, Ulster 2-3.
1937—February 7, Carrick-on-Shannon:
Connacht 4-6, Ulster 1-4.
February 21, Portlaoise:
Munster 5-6, Leinster 1-1.
Final March 17, Croke Park:
Connacht 2-4, Munster 0-5.
1938—February 13, Croke Park:
Munster 0-8, Leinster 1-4
February 13 Cavan:
Connacht 2-8, Ulster 0-3.
Final, March 17, Croke Park:
Connacht 2-6, Munster 1-5.
1939—February 19. Croke Park:
Ulster 2-8, Munster 1-6.
February 19, Ballinasloe:
Leinster 3-4, Connacht 2-5.
Final, March 17, Croke Park:
Leinster 3-8, Ulster 3-3.
1940—February 11, Ballinasloe:
Munster 3-4, Connacht 2-5.
February 11, Dundalk:
Leinster 2-4, Ulster 0-6.
Final, March 1 7, Croke Park:
Leinster 3-7, Munster 0-2.
1941—February 9, Killarney:
Munster 1-9, Connacht 0-6.
February 9, Cavan:
Ulster 1-9, Leinster 2-5.
Final, March 16, Croke Park:
Munster 1-8, Ulster 1-8.
Replay, April 14, Croke Park:
Munster 2-6, Ulster 1-6.
1942—February 22, Wexford:
Munster 2-7, Leinster 0-6.
February 22, Longford:
Ulster 3-7, Connacht 2-6.
Final, March 17, Croke Park:
Ulster 1-10, Munster 1-5.
1943—February 21, Croke Park:
Ulster 3-8, Connacht 0-8.
February 28, Tralee:
Leinster 1-3, Munster 0-4.
Final, March 17, Croke Park:
Ulster 3-7, Leinster 2-9.
1944—February 20, Croke Park:
Ulster 2-10, Munster 1-7.
February 27, Croke Park:
Leinster 2-11, Connacht 1-8.
Final, March 17, Croke Park:
Leinster 1-10, Ulster 1-3.
1945—February 18, Ballinasloe:
Connacht 2-8, Munster 1-6.
February 25, Croke Park:
Leinster 4-3, Ulster 2-9.
Replay, March 4, Croke Park:
Leinster 4-9, Ulster 3-6.
Final, March 17, Croke Park:
Leinster 2-5, Connacht 0-6.
1946—February 24, Cork:
Munster 1-6, Connacht 0-5.
February 24, Cavan:
Leinster 2-5, Ulster 1-5.
Final, March 17, Croke Park:
Munster 3-5, Leinster 1-9.
1947—February 16, Croke Park:
Ulster 0-11, Munster 1-3.
March 9, Croke Park:
Leinster 3-7, Connacht 1-7.
Final, March 17, Croke Park:
Ulster 1-6, Leinster 0-3.
1948—February 22, Tralee:
Munster 3-5, Connacht 2-6.
February 29, Croke Park:
Ulster 2-10, Leinster 1-12.
Final, March 17, Croke Park:
Munster 4-5, Ulster 2-6.
1949—February 20, Ballinasloe:
Munster 4-7, Connacht 1-11.
February 20, Clones:
Leinster 3-5, Ulster 2-2.
Final, March 17, Croke Park:
Munster 2-7, Leinster 2-7.
Replay, March 20, Croke Park:
Munster 4-9, Leinster 1-4.
1950—February 12, Croke Park:
Ulster 2-9, Connacht 2-6.
February 19, Navan:
Leinster 2-6, Munster 1-5.
Final, March 17, Croke Park:
Ulster 4-11, Leinster 1-7.
1951—February 25, Tralee:
Munster 2-8, Leinster 1-9.
February 25, Croke Park:
Connacht 3-6, Ulster 2-8.
Final, March 1 7, Croke Park:
Connacht 1-9; Munster 1-8.
1952—February 24, Croke Park:
Munster 1-7, Ulster 0-3.
February 24, Ballinasloe:
Leinster 1-8, Connacht 1-7.
Final, March 17, Croke Park:
Leinster 0-5, Munster 0-3.
1953—February 8, Croke Park:
Leinster 2-11, Connacht 2-7.
February 15, Croke Park:
Munster 2-5, Ulster 2-5 (draw).
Replay, February 22, Croke Park:
Munster 1-12, Ulster 2-7.
Final, March 17, Croke Park:
Leinster 2-9, Munster 0-6.
1954—February 14, Croke Park:
Leinster 3-14, Ulster 3-6.
February 14, Tralee:
Connacht 2-9, Munster 2-8.
Final, March 1 7, Croke Park:
Leinster 1-7, Connacht 1-5.
1955—February 13, Cavan:
Leinster 2-9, Ulster 2-4.
February 13, Castlebar:
Connacht 1-6, Munster 1-5.
Final, March 17, Croke Park:
Leinster 1-14, Connacht 1-10.
1956—February 19, Casement Park:
Ulster 3-8, Connacht 1-4.
March 4, Croke Park:
Munster 3-4, Leinster 0-9.
Final, March 17, Croke Park:
Ulster 0-12, Munster 0-4.
1957—February 10, Cork:
Munster 2-5, Leinster 0-9.
February 10, Markievicz Park:

Connacht 2-8, Ulster 0-8.
Final, March 17, Croke Park:
Connacht 2-9, Munster 1 -6.
1958—February 16, Ballinasloe:
Connacht 1-11, Leinster 0-7.
February 23, Cavan:
Munster 1-6, Ulster 0-8.
Final, March 17, Croke Park:
Connacht 2-7, Munster 0-8.
1959—February 15, Tullamore:
Leinster 0-10, Connacht 0-8.
March 8, Tralee:
Munster 2-1 2, Ulster 0-7.
Final, March 17, Croke Park:
Leinster 2-7, Munster 0-7.
1960—February 21, Croke Park:
Ulster 2-9, Leinster 1-5.
February 28, Tralee:
Munster 4-9, Connacht 2-3.
Final, March 17, Croke Park:
Ulster 2-12, Munster 3-8.
1961—February 19, Casement Park:
Leinster 2-5, Ulster 1-7.
February 26, Tuam:
Munster 0-6, Connacht 1-3.
Replay, March 12, Croke Park:
Munster 4-7, Connacht 1-6.
Final, March 17, Croke Park:
Leinster 4-5, Munster 0-4.
1962—February 18, Tullamore:
Leinster 2-17, Munster 0-6.
February 25, Cavan:
Ulster 5-6, Connacht 1-7.
(Jim McCartan scored 3-1).
Final, March 17, Croke Park:
Leinster 1-11, Ulster 0-11.
1963—February 17, Tralee:
Leinster 2-6, Munster 1-8.
(Des Foley, Leinster captain, scored winning goal two minutes from the end).
February 17, Sligo:
Ulster 2-8, Connacht 1-5.
Final, March 17, Croke Park:
Ulster 2-8, Leinster 1-9.
1964—February 16, Croke Park:
Ulster 3-6, Munster 0-11.
February 23, Ballinasloe:
Leinster 3-7, Connacht 0-9.
Final, March 17, Croke Park:
Ulster 0-12, Leinster 1-6.
1965—Febuary 21, Croke Park:
Ulster 0-14, Munster 0-9.
February 28, Navan:
Connacht 1-7, Leinster 0-8.
Final, March 17, Croke Park:
Ulster 0-19, Connacht 0-15.
(Paddy Doherty scored 0-11 for Ulster, four from play and Cyril Dunne 0-10, all from frees. Neither missed a shot at the posts from a free. A crowd of 30,734 saw Ulster record their first treble).
1966—February 27, Tralee:
Munster 0-11, Connacht 0-11.
Replay, March 13, Nenagh:
Munster 2-8, Connacht 2-6.
February 27, Croke Park:
Ulster 1-8; Leinster 1-4.
(Paddy Doherty 0-8, seven from frees and the eighth when he collected a rebound from the upright to send the ball over at the second attempt).
Final, March 17, Croke Park:
Ulster 2-5, Munster 1-5.
(Ulster recorded four-in-a-row before a 24,312 attendance).
1967—February 26, Galway:
Connacht 0-11, Munster 0-6.
February 26, Casement Park:
Ulster 0-9, Leinster 0-8.
(Seán O'Connell Derry, 0-6, five from frees.)
Final, March 17, Croke Park:
Connacht 1-9, Ulster 0-11.
(Ulster's five-in-a-row bid failed before 22,054 attendance. Vital Connacht goal scored by Mickey Kerins, Sligo, just before interval).
1968—February 25, Navan:
Leinster 0-11, Munster 0-6.
March 3, Cavan:
Ulster 4-8, Connacht 1-10.
(Seán O'Neill 3-0, Seán O'Connell 1-2)
Final, March 17, Croke Park:
Ulster 1-10, Leinster, 0-8.
(Before an attendance of 11,158, the lowest on record, Ulster won their fifth title in six years).
1969—February 16, Tuam:
Connacht 1-11, Ulster 2-4.
February 23 Killarney:
Munster 2-11, Leinster 1-9.
Final, March 17. Croke Park:
Connacht 1-12, Munster 0-6.
1970—February 22, Croke Park:
Ulster 2-12, Munster 0-6.
Februray 22, Crossmolina:
Connacht 1-11, Leinster 1-4.
Final, March 17, Croke Park:
Ulster 2-11, Connacht 0-10.
1971—February 21, Navan:
Connacht 1-9, Leinster 0-9.
February 28, Croke Park:
Ulster 2-7, Munster 1-7.
Final, March 17, Croke Park:
Ulster 3-11, Connacht 2-11.
(Before an attendance of 20,306, almost 4,000 more than in 1970, Ulster won their seventh title in nine years and Seán O'Neill set a record by winning his eighth Railway Cup medal and gave a classic display in the process).
1972—Roscommon, February 13:
Preliminary Round: Connacht 1-15, Combined Universities 1-9.
February 20, Cork:
Munster 1-9, Connacht 0-9.
February 20, Croke Park:
Leinster 0-13, Ulster 1-9.
Final: March 17, Croke Park:
Munster 1-15, Leinster 1-15.
Replay, April 23, Cork:
Munster2-14, Leinster 0-10.
1973—Cavan, January 28:
Preliminary Round: Combined Universities 2-7, Ulster 0-12.
February 18, Roscommon:
Connacht 3-10, Munster 2-10.

February 18, Croke Park:
Universities 0-11, Leinster 0-8.
Final, March 17, Croke Park:
Universities 2-12, Connacht 0-18 (draw).
Replay, April 23, Athlone:
Universities 4-9, Connacht 1-11.
1974—Mardyke, January 26:
Preliminary Round: Combined Univerities 1-7, Munster 1-4.
February 10, Tullamore:
Leinster 0-12, Universities 0-9.
February 10, Ballybay:
Connacht 2-11, Ulster 4-4.
Final, March 17, Croke Park:
Leinster 2-10, Connacht 1-7.
1975—February 16, Cork (Mardyke):
Munster 1-9, Leinster 0-8.
February 16, Carrick-on-Shannon:
Ulster 5-13, Connacht 1-12.
Final, March 17. Croke Park:
Munster 6-7, Ulster 0-15.
1976—February 15, Ballina:
Leinster 2-9, Connacht 1-10.
February 15, Croke Park:
Munster 3-7, Ulster 0-9.
Final, March 17, Croke Park:
Munster 2-15, Leinster 2-8.
1977—February 13, Croke Park:
Munster 0-14, Ulster 0-8.
February 13, Navan:
Connacht 2-13, Leinster 1-8.
Final, March 17, Croke Park:
Munster 1-14, Connacht 1-9.
1978—March 19, Sligo:
Munster 2-6, Connacht 0-7.
March 19, Cavan:
Ulster 1-7, Leinster 0-7.
Final, March 27, Croke Park:
Munster 2-7, Ulster 2-7 (draw).
Replay, April 16, Croke Park:
Munster 4-12, Ulster 0-19
(after extra time).
1979—March 11, Croke Park:
Ulster 5-8, Leinster 1-13.
March 11, Tralee:
Munster 4-7, Connacht 1-6.
Final, March 18, Croke Park:
Ulster 1-7, Munster 0-6.
1980—March 2, Newbridge:
Munster 2-10, Leinster 1-11.
March 2, Cavan:
Ulster 0-17, Connacht 1-3.
Final, March 17, Croke Park:
Ulster 2-10, Munster 1-9.
1981—March 8, Roscommon:
Connacht 2-19, Ulster 2-14
(after extra time).
March 8, Killarney:
Munster 2-12, Leinster 0-10.
Final, March 17, Ennis:
Munster 3-10, Connacht 1-9.
1982—February 14, Croke Park:
Munster 4-5, Ulster 0-10.
February 14, Galway:
Connacht 0-8, Leinster 0-2.
Final, March 17, Tullamore:
Munster 1-8, Connacht 0-10.
1983—February 6, Tullamore:
Leinster 1-9, Connacht 0-7.
February 6, Croke Park:
Ulster 2-10, Munster 2-4
Final, March 17, Cavan:
Ulster 0-24, Leinster 2-10
(after extra time)
1984—March 17, Ballinasloe:
Connacht 0-15, Leinster 1-9.
March 17, Limerick:
Ulster 0-12, Munster 0-7.
Final, March 18, Ennis:
Ulster 1-12, Connacht 1-7.
1985—January 27, Croke Park:
Leinster 2-8, Ulster 2-7.
January 27, Roscommon:
Munster 3-7, Connacht 0-12.
Final, March 17, Croke Park:
Leinster 0-9, Munster 0-5.
1986—February 16, Tralee:
Connacht 2-6, Munster 0-7.
February 16, Cavan:
Leinster 3-7, Ulster 1-9.
Final, March 17, Ballinasloe:
Leinster 2-8, Connacht 2-5.
1987—October 3, Newbridge:
Munster 3-12, Ulster 1-9.
Leinster 2-10, Connacht 1-9.
Final, October 4, Newbridge:
Leinster 1-13, Munster 0-9.
1988—October 15, Ballina:
Leinster 2-11, Munster 0-8.
Ulster 3-12, Connacht 1-10.
Final, October 16, Ballina:
Leinster 2-9, Ulster 0-12.
1989—October 7, Macroom:
Munster 0-8, Leinster 0-7.
October 7, Mitchelstown:
Ulster 4-8, Connacht 0-7.
Final, October 8, Pairc Ui Chaoimh:
Ulster 1-11, Munster 1-8.
1990—No competition.
1991—March 24, Ballybofey:
Ulster 1-15, Connacht 1-13
(after extra time)
March 24, Navan:
Munster 1-10, Leinster 0-11.
Final, April 7, Croke Park:
Ulster 1-11, Munster 1-8.
1992—March 1, Tralee:
Munster 2-7, Leinster 1-9.
March 1, Carrick-on-Shannon:
Ulster 0-11, Connacht 0-7.
Final, March 15, Newry:
Ulster 2-7, Munster 0-8.
1993—October 17, Newry:
Ulster 3-17, Munster 0-8.
October 17, Roscommon:
Leinster 3-11 Connacht 2-8.
Final, October 31, Longford:
Ulster 1-12, Leinster 0-12.
1994—February 13, Ballinasloe:
Munster 1-15, Connacht 0-10.
February 13, Armagh.
Ulster 0-9, Leinster 1-5.
Final, March 6, Ennis:
Ulster 1-6, Munster, 1-4.

1995—February 5, Newhridge:
Leinster 3-14, Munster 1-9.
February 5, Clones:
Ulster 0-16, Connacht 0-8.
Final, February 26, Clones:
Ulster 1-9, Leinster 0-8.
1996—February 18, Navan:
Leinster 1-8, Connacht 1-6.
March 10, Clones:
Munster 2-17, Ulster 1-20
after extra time (draw).
March 18, Ennis:
Munster 0-13, Ulster 0-12 (replay).
Final, April 14, Newbridge:
Leinster 1-13, Munster 0-9.
1997—January 26, Navan:
Leinster 3-14, Ulster 1-10.
January 26, Ennis:
Connacht 2-15, Munster 1-1 7
(after extra time)
Final, February 9, Castlebar:
Leinster 2-14, Connacht 0-12.
1998—January 25, Roscommon:
Ulster 0-15, Connacht 0-15
after extra time (draw).
February 1, Clones:
Ulster 0-20, Connacht 1-14
after extra time (replay).
January 25, Killarney:
Leinster 2-8, Munster 0-12.
Final, February 8, Clones:
Ulster 0-20, Leinster 0-17
(after extra time).
1999—April 4, Tuam:
Connacht 4-7, Leinster 1-8
April 4, Killarney:
Munster 1-20, Ulster 3-14
after extra time(draw)
April 18, Omagh:
Munster 2-19, Ulster 3-13
after extra time(replay)
Final, May 2, Tuam:
Munster 0-10, Connacht 0-6.
2000—Semi-finals - January 30 at Castlebar:
Connacht 2-10, Munster 1-3.
January 30 at Casement Park:
Ulster 1-14, Leinster 0-10.
Final - February 6 at Sligo:
Ulster 1-9, Connacht 0-3.
2001—Semi-finals - November 10 at Tralee:
Leinster 2-11, Munster 0-16.
(after extra time)
November 10 at Killarney:
Connacht 0-15, Ulster 1-10.
Final - November 11 at Killarney:
Leinster 1-10, Connacht 0-10.
2002—Semi-finals - November 2 at
Ballindereen: Ulster 0-17, Munster 0-15.
November 2 at Ballindereen:
Leinster 1-15, Connacht 2-9.
Final - November 3 at Galway:
Leinster 1-14, Ulster 2-9.
2003—Semi-finals - November 15 at
Enniskillen: Ulster 2-13, Leinster 0-16.
(after extra time)
November 15 at Enniskillen:
Connacht 1-13, Munster 1-9.
Final - November 16 at Enniskillen:
Ulster 0-14, Connacht 0-9.
2004—Semi-finals - October 31 at Portlaoise:
Leinster 1-10, Munster 1-9.
October 31 at Castlebar:
Ulster 0-15, Connacht 1-6.
Final - November 13 at Paris:
Ulster 1-13, Leinster 1-8.
2005—Semi-final – October 29 at Parnell Park:
Leinster 1-14, Connacht 3-7.
Semi-final – October 30 at Crossmaglen:
Ulster 2-13, Munster 0-9.
Final – November 12 at Parnell Park:
Leinster 0-20, Ulster 0-18. (aet)
2006—Semi-final – October 6 at Ballyforan:
Connacht 1-15, Munster 2-10. (aet)
Semi-final – October 7 at Breffni Park:
Leinster 2-13, Ulster 2-10.
Final – October 22 at Boston:
Leinster 2-14, Connacht 2-11.
2007—Semi-final – October 13 at Fermoy:
Munster 2-11, Leinster 0-12.
Semi-final – October 20 at Ballybofey:
Ulster 1-15, Connacht 2-9.
Final – October 27 at Croke Park:
Ulster 1-12, Munster 1-8.
2008—Semi-final – October 25 at Fermoy:
Munster 1-5, Ulster 0-5.
Semi-final – October 25 at Kiltoom:
Connacht 2-15, Leinster 0-11.
Final – November 1 at Portlaoise:
Munster 1-9, Connacht 0-7.
2009—Semi-final – October 24 at Crossmaglen:
Ulster 1-14; Leinster 1-10.
Semi-final - October 24 at Gaelic Grounds:
Munster 1-13; Connacht 1-10.

RAILWAY CUP FOOTBALL FINAL TEAMS

1927

Munster—J. Riordan (goal), John J. Sheehy, Joe Barrett, J. Walsh, Paul Russell, E. Fitzgerald, J. Slattery, C. Brosnan, R. Stack, J. Ryan, Joe Sullivan, T. Mahony, James Baily, Frank Sheehy, P. Clifford (all Kerry).

Connacnt—T. Molloy, M. Walsh, M. Bonnerton, T. Leech, T. Hegarty, Mick Donnellan (Galway), R. Creagh, John Forde, M. Mulderrig (Mayo), G. Higgins (goal), Thos. Shevlin, M. Murphy (Roscommon), P. Colleran (Sligo), W. Martin, M. Dolan (Leitrim).

1928

Leinster—M. Walsh (goal), M. Goff, J. Higgins, F. Malone, P. Martin, P. Doyle (Kildare), P. Russell, P. McDonnell (Dublin), M. O'Neill, N. Walsh (Wexford), M. McKeown, W. Lawless (Louth), P. Bates, W. Whelan (Laois), M. Keoghan (Meath). Sub: J. Delaney (Laois).

(Paul Russell selected for both Munster and Leinster, Central Council ruled that he play for Leinster).

Ulster—P. Kilroy, T. Bradley (goal), F. Farrell, J. Brannigan, J. Duffy, J. Treanor (Monaghan), G. Hanratty, J. Maguire, P. Fearon, J. McCusker

(Armagh), J. P. Murphy, J. Smith (Cavan), P. Cunning, J. C. McDonnell (Antrim), C. Fisher (Monaghan).

1929

Leinster—W. Gannon, M. Goff, A. Fitzpatrick, J. Higgins, P. Doyle, P. Martin (Kildare), J. McDonnell (goal), J. Norris, M. O'Brien, P. McDonnell (Dublin), P. Bates, J. Delaney (Laois), M. McKeown (Louth), N. Walsh, M. O'Neill (Wexford).

Munster—Dr. J. Kearney, M. Murphy, M. Donegan (Cork), J. Riordan (goal), J. Barrett, J. Walsh, P. Russell, J. O'Sullivan, C. Brosnan, E. Fitzgerald, J. J. Sheehy, J. Landers (Kerry), M. Keating (Limerick), T. Lee, C. Keane (Tipperary).

1930

Leinster—John Higgins, M. Goff, W. Hynan, F. Malone, P. Loughlin, P. Doyle, P. Martin (Kildare), John McDonnell (goal), P. McDonnell, M. O'Brien (Dublin), D. Walsh, D. Douglas, J. Delaney (Laois), P. Byrne (Wexford), M. Rogers (Meath). Sub: M. O'Neill (Wexford).

Munster—J. Barrett, J. Riordan (goal), J. Walsh, J. O'Sullivan, P. Russell, T. O'Donnell, C. Brosnan, R. Stack, J. Ryan, M. Doyle, E. Sweeney, J. J. Sheehy, M. O'Rourke, T. Barrett (Kerry), M. Donegan (Cork).

1931

Munster—J. O'Riordan, D. O'Connor, J. Barrett, J. Walsh, P. Russell, J. O'Sullivan, T. O'Donnell, C. Brosnan, R. Stack, E. Fitzgerald, M. Doyle, J. J. Landers, E. Sweeney, T. Landers, J. J. Sheehy (all Kerry).

Leinster—M. Goff, J. Hayes, F. Malone, J. Higgins, W. Hynan, P. Loughlin, P. Martin (Kildare), John McDonnell M. O'Brien, T. O'Dowd (Dublin), T. Nulty, M. Rogers (Meath), D. Walsh, D. Douglas, J. Delaney (Laois).

1932

Leinster—J. Higgins, M. Goff, P. Martin, P. Byrne, D. Burke (Kildare), J. McDonnell (goal), P. Hickey, T. O'Dowd (Dublin), M. Nulty, T. Meade, M. Rogers, T. McGuinness (Meath), D. Walsh, J. Delaney, D. Douglas (Laois).

Munster—D. O'Keeffe (goal), D. O'Connor, P. Whitty, John Walsh, P. Russell, T. Landers, C. Brosnan, R. Stack, M. Doyle J. Landers, J. Ryan, C. Geaney (Kerry), G. Comerford (Clare), J. Duggan (Limerick), P. Arrigan (Tipperary).

1933

Leinster—J. McDonnell, P. Hickey, C. McLoughlin, D. Brennan, E. McCann, T. O'Dowd (Dublin), T. Meade, W. Shaw (Meath), J. Higgins, P. Martin, P. Byrne (Kildare), N. Walsh, P. Splllane (Wexford), D. Douglas, J. Delaney (Laois).

Connacht—T. Burke, P. Kelly, P. Quinn, S. O'Malley, G. Courell, P. Moclair, J. Forde, M. Mulderrig (Mayo), H. Carey, Ml. Donnellan, Ml. Higgins, L. Colleran, M. Kilcoyne, M. Noone (Sligo), J. Creighton (Roscommon).

1934

Connacht—T. Burke (goal), P. Quinn, P. Kelly, P. Flannelly, G. Ormsby, J. Carney, G. Courell, P. Moclair (Mayo), H. Carey, M. Connaire, F. Fox, J. Dunne, M. Donnellan, M. Higgins, B. Nestor (Galway).

Leinster—J. McDonnell (goal), D. Brennan, P. Synnott, M. Kelly (Dublin), T. Meade, J. Loughran (Meath), M. McKeown (Louth), P. Fane, P. Mythen, N. Walsh (Wexford), J. Higgins, P. Martin, P. Byrne (Kildare), D. Douglas, J. Delaney (Laois).

1935

Leinster—J. McDonnell (goal), R. Beggs, P. Cavanagh, G. Comerford (Dublin), E. Boyle, J. Coyle (Louth), T. McGuinness, W. Shaw, A. Donnelly (Meath), J. Byrne, P. Watters, P. Byrne (Kildare), W. Delaney, John Delaney, D. Douglas (Laois).

Munster—P. Russell, T. O'Donnell, P. Whitty, P. O'Connor (Kerry), M. O'Sullivan (goal), J. Lonergan, T. O'Keeffe, R. Power, R. Allen B. McGann (Tipperary), M. Studdert (Clare), T. Greany, P. O'Donnell (Waterford), T. Culhane (Limerick), T. Cotter (Cork).

1936

Connacht—T. Burke (goal), P. Kelly, T. Regan, G. Ormsby, H. Kenny, P. Flannelly, J. Carney, P. Moclair (Mayo), M. Connaire, F. Fox, R. Beggs, M. Higgins, R. Griffin, B. Nestor (Galway), F. Cavanagh (Sligo). Sub: F. Cunniffe (Golway) for F. Cavanagh.

Ulster—W. Young (goal), T. Dolan, M. Denneny, T. O'Reilly, P. Phair, H. O'Reilly, T. O'Reilly, D. Morgan, P. Devlin, J. Smallhorn, P. Boylan, L. Blessing, M. J. Magee (Cavan), J. Vallely, J. McCullagh (Armagh).

1937

Connacht—T. Burke (goal), T. Regan, P. Quinn, P. Kelly, P. Flannelly, H. Kenny, J. Carney, P. Laffey, J. Munnelly, P. Moclair (Mayo), M. Connaire, J. Dunne, D. O'Sullivan, B. Nestor, R. Beggs (Galway). Sub: J. McGowan (Mayo) for P. Quinn.

Munster—D. O'Keeffe (goal), J. O'Gorman, J. Walsh, P. Kennedy, M. Doyle, G. Fitzgerald, T. Landers, M. Kelly (Kerry), W. McMahon, M. Casey, G. Comerford, J. Burke (Clare), W. Scott, R. Power (Tipperary), T. Culhane (Limerick). Sub: A. Slattery (Clare) for R. Power.

1938

Connacht—P. Moclair, T. Burke (goal), J. McGowan, T. Regan, H. Kenny, J. Carney, P. Laffey, J. Munnelly, P. Kelly (Mayo), M. Connaire, C. Connolly, D. O'Sullivan, J. Dunne, M. Higgins, B. Nestor (Galway). Sub: P. Flannelly (Mayo) for J. Carney.

Munster—J. Keohane, D. O'Keeffe (goal), W. Myers, W. Kinnerk, W. Dillon, T. Healy, J. Walsh, P. Kennedy, J. J. Landers, C. O'Sullivan (Kerry), T. Culhane (Limerick), G. Comerford, J. Burke, M. Casey (Clare), T. Cotter (Cork). Sub: A. Slattery (Clare) for M. Casey.

1939

Leinster—M. Farrell, D. Walsh, M. Delaney, J. Slator, W. Delaney, C. Delaney (Laois), E. Boyle, E. Callan, J. Coyle (Louth), T. McEvoy (Offaly), J. Loughran, A. Donneliy (Meath), P. Bermingham (Dublin), P. O'Sullivan (Wicklow), T. Mulhall (Kildare). Sub: J. Delaney (Laois).

Ulster—A. Lynn, R. Keelaghan, J. Crawley, V. Duffy (Monaghan), E. McMahon, E. McLoughlin, J. McCullagh, A. Murray, J. Fitzpatrick (Armagh), P. Smith, T. O'Reilly, J. J. O'Reilly, V. White (Cavan), J. Doherty (Donegal), E. Thornbury (Antrim).

1940

Leinster—P. Dowling (goal), P. Bermingham (Dublin), E. Boyle (Louth), T. McEvoy, W. Mulhall (Offaly), D. Walsh, M. Delaney, W. Delaney, T. Murphy, C. Delaney (Laois) J. Kearney, M. Gilsenan, A. Donnelly (Meath), P. O'Sullivan (Wicklow), T. Mulhall (Kildare).

Munster—D. O'Keeffe (goal), W. Myers, J. Keohane, T. Healy, W. Dillon, W. Casey, E. Walsh, P. Kennedy, T. O'Connor, M. Kelly, Sean Brosnan, J. Walsh, J. Gorman, D. Spring, T. Landers. Subs: P. B. Brosnan for W. Casey, C. O'Sullivan for E. Walsh (all Kerry).

1941 REPLAY

Munster—D. O'Keeffe, W. Myers, Joe Keohane, T. Healy (Kerry), R. Harnedy (Cork), W. Casey, E. Walsh, S. Brosnan, P. Kennedy, J. Walsh, T. O'Connor (Kerry), E. Young (Cork), M. Kelly, P. Brosnan, J. O'Gorman (Kerry).

Ulster—B. Kelly (Cavan), E. McLoughlin, E. McMahon (Armagh), J. McGlory (Down), G. Smith (Cavan), J. McCullagh (Armagh), T. O'Reilly, J. J. O'Reilly, P. Smith, D. Morgan (Cavan), A. Murray (Armagh), T. P. O'Reilly (Cavan), J. Carr, M. Lynch (Down), V. Duffy (Monaghan). Sub: B. Cully (Cavan) for E. McMahon.

(P. B. Brosnan (Kerry) replaced C. O'Sullivan (Kerry) on the Munster team, while T. P. O'Reilly (Cavan) and M. Lynch (Down) replaced P. Conaty (Cavan) and J. Gallagher (Donegal) on the Ulster team which played in the drawn game.)

1942

Ulster—B. Kelly (Cavan), E. McLoughlin (Armagh), B. Cully, T. O'Reilly, G. Smith (Cavan), J. McCullagh (Armagh), V. Duffy (Monaghan), C. McDyer (Donegal), J. J. O'Reilly (Cavan), K. Armstrong (Antrim), A. Murray (Armagh), T. P. O'Reilly (Cavan), B. Cullen (Tyrone), S. Deignan (Cavan), H. Gallagher (Donegal).

Munster—D. O'Keeffe, W. Myers, J. Keohane, T. Healy, W. Dillon, W. Casey, E. Walsh, S. Brosnan, P. Kenneoy, John Walsh, T. O'Connor (Kerry), E. Young (Cork), J. O'Gorman, M. Kelly, P. B. Brosnan (Kerry). Sub: R. Harnedy (Cork) for E. Walsh.

1943

Ulster—J. D. Benson (Cavan), E. McLoughlin (Armagh), B. Cully, T. O'Reilly, G. Smith (Cavan), J. McCullagh (Armagh), V. Duffy (Monaghan), J. J. O'Reilly (Cavan), C. McDyer (Donegal), K. Armstrong (Antrim). A. Murray (Armagh), P. Maguire (Derry), P. McCarney (Monaghan), S. Deignan (Cavan), H. Gallagher (Donegal). Sub: T. McCann (Down).

Leinster—P. Lynch (Wexford), J. Murphy, P. Kennedy, C. Crone, P. Henry, P. O'Reilly (Dublin), J. Clarke (Meath), J. Fitzgerald (Dublin), T. Murphy (Loois), J. Joy (Dublin), W. Delaney (Laois), P. Berminghom (Dublin), M. Gilsenan (Meath), P. O'Connor, T. Banks (Dublin).

1944

Leinster—P. Larkin (Louth), J. Archbold (Carlow), E. Boyle (Louth), C. Crone, P. O'Reilly (Dublin), J. Quigley (Louth), M. Geraghty (Kildare), W. Delaney (Laois), J. Thornton (Louth), D. O'Neill (Wicklow), O. Halpin (Louth), P. McDermott (Meath), P. Bermingham (Dublin), C. Delaney (Laois), J. Rea (Carlow).

Ulster—H. Vernon (Antrim), E. McLoughlin, J. McCullagh (Armagh), E. Finnegan, G. Smith (Cavan), E. McDonald (Monaghan), J. J. O'Reilly, L. McAlinden (Armagh), S. Deignan (Cavan), K. Armstrong (Antrim), A. Murray (Armagh), P. Maguire (Derry), P. McCarney (Monaghan), B. McAteer (Antrim), H. Gallagher (Donegal). Sub: F. Hamill (Antrim) for E. Finnegan.

1945

Leinster—P. Larkin, S. Boyle, E. Boyle (Louth), P. McIntyre (Dublin), P. Whelan (Carlow), P. O'Reilly (Dublin), M. Geraghty (Kildare), J. Morris (Carlow), J. Hanniffy (Longford), F. Byrne (Meath), W. Delaney (Laois), D. O'Neill (Wicklow), P. Meegan (Meath), C. Delaney (Laois), J. Rea (Carlow). Sub: T Murphy (Laois) for J. Hanniffy.

Connacht—T. Byrne (Mayo), W. Jackson (Roscommon), T. Dunleavy (Sligo), C. Connolly (Galway), B. Lynch, W. Carlos (Roscommon), T. O'Sullivan (Galway), E. Boland (Roscommon), C. McDyer (Sligo), M. Fallon (Galway), J. Murray, D. Keenan, P. Murray, J. McQuillan Roscommon), T. Hoban (Mayo). Subs: L. McAlinden (Leitrim) for C. McDyer, J. Munnelly (Mayo) for E. Boland.

1946

Munster—J. Williams (Tipperary), D. Magnier, P. Murphy, C. Crone, P. Cronin, T. Crowley (Cork), E. Walsh, P. Kennedy (Kerry), M. Cahill (Tipperary), M. Tubridy (Cork), W. O'Donnell (Kerry), E. Young (Cork), D. Kavanagh (Kerry), J. Cronin (Cork), J. Lyne (Kerry).

Leinster—P. Larkin, S. Boyle, E. Boyle (Louth), J. Cody, J. Culleton, W. Goodison (Wexford), M. Geraghty (Kildare), M.

O'Brien (Wicklow), J. Morris (Carlow), F. Byrne (Meath), W. Delaney (Laois), D. O'Neill (Wexford), P. Meegan (Meath), N. Rackard (Wexford), J. Rea (Carlow).

1947

Ulster—J. O'Hare (Down), W. Feeney, G. Watterson (Antrim), J. McCullagh (Armagh), E. McDonnell (Monaghan), J. J. O'Reilly, S. Deignan (Cavan), H. O'Neill, S. Gallagher, K. Armstrong (Antrim), M. Higgins (Cavan), F. Niblock (Derry), S. Gibson, B. McAteer, S. McCallin (Antrim). Sub: H. Brown (Down).

Leinster—K. Smyth (Meath), M. O'Brien (Kildare), E. Boyle (Louth), J. Cody (Wexford), P. O'Reilly (Dublin), W. Goodison (Wexford), M. Geraghty (Kildare), M. Haughney, D. Connolly (Laois), F. Byrne, P. McDermott (Meath), D. O'Neill (Wexford), P. Meegan (Meath), P. Lennon, R. Byrne (Wicklow).

1948

Munster—D. O'Keeffe (Kerry), P. A. Murphy (Cork), J. Keohane, P. B. Brosnan, J. Lyne (Kerry), T. Crowley (Cork), E. O'Connor, T. Spillane (Kerry), M. Cahill (Tipperary), C. McGrath (Cork), W. O'Donnell, B. Garvey (Kerry), N. Crowley (Clare), J. Cronin, J. Aherne (Cork).
Subs: T. O'Sullivan (Kerry) for T. Crowley and F. O'Keeffe (Kerry) for W. O 'Donnell.

Ulster—J. O'Hare (Down), W. Doonan (Cavan), G. Watterson (Antrim), P. Smith, P. J. Duke, J. J. O'Reilly, S. Deignan (Cavan), E. McDonald (Monaghan), S. Gallagher, K. Armstrong (Antrim), M. Higgins (Cavan), S. Gallagher (Donegal), S. Gibson (Antrim), P. Donohoe, A. Tighe (Cavan). Subs: H. O'Neill (Antrim) for M. Higgins and M. Higgins later for W. Doonan

1949 REPLAY

Munster—M. O'Driscoll (Cork), E. O'Connor (Kerry), P. A. Murphy (Cork), P. B. Brosnan, M. Finucane, J. Lyne (Kerry), M. Cahill (Tipperary), C. McGrath (Cork), E. Dowling (Kerry), D. O'Donovan, C. Duggan (Cork), B. Garvey (Kerry), N. Crowley (Clare), J. Cronin (Cork), P. Brennan (Tipperary). Sub: T. Spillane (Kerry) for E. O'Connor.

(Tom O'Connor (Kerry) played in drawn game. Packie Brennan (Tipperary) came on for replay.)

Leinster—K. Smith (Meath), J. Bell (Louth), A. Murphy (Carlow), J. Coady (Wexford), S. Boyle, P. Markey (Louth), S. Brennan (Kildare), J. Donegan (Offaly), P. O'Brien (Meath), F. Fegan (Louth), P. White (Kildare), D. Connolly (Laois), W. Halpenny (Meath), W. Kelly (Wexford), P. McDermott (Meath). Subs: A. Burke (Kildare), S. White (Louth) and J. Quigley (Louth) for A. Murphy, J. Donegan and W. Halpenny.

(Des Connolly (Laois) who came on as sub in first game for Kevin Heffernan (Dublin) retained his place for the replay.)

1950

Ulster—J. O'Hare (Down), J. J. O'Reilly (Cavan), M. Moyna (Monaghan), P. Smith, P. J. Duke (Cavan), P. O'Neill, S. Quinn (Armagh), P. Brady (Cavan), W. McCorry (Armagh), A. Tighe, M. Higgins, V. Sherlock (Cavan), K. Armstrong (Antrim), P. Donohue (Cavan), H. McKearney (Monaghan). Sub: S. Gallagher (Antrim) for V. Sherlock.

Leinster—K, Smith (Meath), J. Bell (Louth), N. Redmond (Wexford), K. McConnell (Meath), W. Geraghty (Kildare), W. Goodison (Wexford), C. Hand, P. Connell (Meath), J. McDonnell (Louth), F. Byrne, B. Smyth (Meath), S. White (Louth), W. Kelly, N. Rackard (Wexford), P. McDermott (Meath). Sub: S. Brennan (Kildare) for W. Geraghty.

1951

Connacht—J. Mangan (Galway), W. McQuillan (Roscommon), P. Prendergast, S. Flanagan (Mayo), E. Boland (Roscommon), H. Dixon, E. Mongey (Mayo), S. Purcell (Galway), G. O'Malley (Roscommon), E. Keogh (Galway), P. Carney, J. Gilvarry, M. Mulderrig, T. Langan, P. Solon (Mayo). Subs: M. Flanagan (Mayo) for P. Carney, F. White (Sligo) for M. Flanagan.

Munster—L. Fitzgerald, J. Murphy (Kerry), P. A. Murphy (Cork), P. B. Brosnan (Kerry), P. Driscoll (Cork), J. Lyne (Kerry), S. Cronin (Cork), S. Connolly (Clare), C. Duggan (Cork), T. McGrath (Waterford), C. McGrath (Cork), P. J. O'Dea (Clare), P. Brennan (Tipperary), J. M. Palmer (Kerry), D. O'Donovan (Cork). Sub: D. Murphy (Kerry) for S. Connolly.

1952

Leinster—T. Malone (Kildare), M. O'Brien (Meath), T. Conlon, J. Tuft (Louth), G. O'Reilly (Wicklow), P. Dunne (Laois), S. Brennan (Kildare), D. Taaffe (Meath), J. Rogers (Wicklow), P. Meegan (Meath), O. Freaney (Dublin), S. White (Louth), M. McDonnell (Meath), H. Reynolds (Louth), K. Heffernan (Dublin). Subs: K. McConnell (Meath) for Tuft, J. Crowley (Dublin) for Taaffe and C. O'Leary (Dublin) for McDonnell.

Munster—D. O'Keeffe (Cork), J. Murphy (Kerry), P. A. Murphy (Cork), P. B. Brosnan, S. Murphy (Kerry), J. Cronin (Cork), J. M. Palmer (Kerry), C. McGrath, C. Duggan (Cork), J. Brosnan (Kerry), E. Young (Cork), J. J. Sheehan (Kerry), T. Ashe (Kerry), M. Cahill (Cork), P. J. O'Dea (Clare). Sub: P. Sheehy (Kerry) for M. Cahill.

1953

Leinster—T. Malone (Kildare), M. O'Brien, P. O'Brien, K. McConnell (Meath), G. O'Reilly (Wicklow), P. Dunne (Laois), A. Murphy (Carlow), S. Brennan (Kildare), J. Rogers (Wicklow), P. Meegan (Meath), V. Tierney (Longford), S. White (Louth), O. Freaney (Dublin), J. McDonnell (Louth), K. Heffernan (Dublin).

Munster—D. Roche (Cork), J. Murphy, E.

Roche, J. O'Shea (Kerry), P. O'Driscoll (Cork), J. Cronin, C. Kennelly, B. O'Shea (Kerry), D. Kelleher, D. O'Donovan (Cork), T. Lyne (Kerry), W. Kirwan (Waterford), M. Cahill (Cork), S. Kelly (Kerry), P. Brennan (Tipperary). Sub: F.Meany (Clare) for B. O'Shea.

1954

Leinster—J. O'Neill (Wexford), M. O'Brien, P. O'Brien, K. McConnell (Meath), G. O'Reilly (Wicklow), P. Dunne (Laois), A. Murphy (Carlow), J. Rogers (Wicklow), S. White (Louth), J. Reilly (Meath), O. Freaney, C. O'Leary (Dublin), P. Meegan (Meath), J. McDonnell (Louth), K. Heffernan (Dublin).

Connacht—A. Brady, P. English (Roscommon), P. Prendergast, S. Flanagan (Mayo), B. Lynch (Roscommon), T. Dillon (Galway), F. Kelly, G. O'Malley (Roscommon), J. Nallen (Mayo), I. O'Dowd (Sligo), S. Purcell (Galway), E. O'Donohue (Roscommon), T. Hayden (Leitrim), T. Langan (Mayo), P. McGarty (Leitrim).

1955

Leinster—P. McGearty, M. O'Brien, P. O'Brien, K. McConnell (Meath), A. Murphy (Carlow), J. Fitzparick (Wicklow), S. White (Louth), J. Rogers (Wicklow), P. Casey (Offaly), J. McDonnell (Louth), O. Freaney, C. O'Leary (Dublin), M. McDonnell, T. Moriarty (Meath), K. Heffernan (Dublin).

Connacht—A. Brady (Roscommon), F. White (Sligo), P. Prendergast, S. Flanagan (Mayo), J. Mahon, T. Dillon (Galway), F. Kelly, G. O'Malley (Roscommon), I. O'Dowd (Sligo), P. Irwin (Mayo), S. Purcell, W. O'Neill (Galway), E. O'Donohue (Roscommon), M. Gaffney (Sligo), P. McGarty (Leitrim). Sub: T. Langan (Mayo) for O'Donohue.

1956

Ulster—S. Morris, N. O'Reilly (Cavan), J. Bratten, J. McKnight (Armagh), K. Mussen (Down), J. Rice (Monaghan), J. McDonnell (Cavan), J. McKeever (Derry), T. Maguire (Cavan), K. Denvir (Down), J. Taggart (Tyrone), J. Cunningham, P. Campbell (Armagh), V. Sherlock (Cavan), Rody Gribben (Derry).

Munster—P. Tyers (Cork), J. O'Shea (Kerry), D. O'Sullivan, P. Driscoll (Cork), T. Moriarty (Kerry), D. Bernard, D. Murray (Cork), J. Dowling (Kerry), E. Ryan (Cork), P. Sheehy (Kerry), C. Duggan (Cork), T. Lyne, J. Culloty, M. Murphy (Kerry), T. Cunningham (Waterford). Sub: Seán Murphy (Kerry) for Culloty.

1957

Connacht—J. Mangan (Galway), W. Casey (Mayo), I. O'Dowd (Sligo), T. Dillon (Galway), G. O'Malley (Roscommon), J. Mahon (Galway), E. Moriarty (Mayo), N. Blessing (Leitrim), J. Nallen (Mayo), F. Evers, S. Purcell (Galway), P. McGarty (Leitrim), J. Young, F. Stockwell (Galway), M. Christie (Sligo).

Munster—D. O'Neill (Kerry), P. O'Driscoll (Cork), E. Roche, J. O'Shea, S. Murphy (Kerry), D. Bernard, D. Murray, S. Moore (Cork), T. Long (Kerry), E. Ryan, C. Duggan (Cork), T. Lyne, J. Brosnan, M. Murphy (Kerry), D. Kelleher (Cork). Subs: N. Fitzgerald (Cork) for Brosnan, T. Moriarty (Kerry) for Long.

1958

Connacht—A. Brady (Roscommon), W. Casey (Mayo), I. O'Dowd (Sligo), T. Dillon, J. Mahon (Galway), G. O'Malley (Roscommon), M. Greally (Galway), J. Nallen (Mayo), F. Evers, M. McDonagh, S. Purcell (Galway), P. McGarty (Leitrim), G. Kirwan, F. Stockwell (Galway), C. Flynn (Leitrim).

Munster—L. Power (Cork), J. O'Shea, T. Lyons (Kerry), P. Driscoll, P. Harrington (Cork), T. Cunningham (Waterford), D. Murray (Cork), M. O'Connell (Kerry), S. Moore, N. Fitzgerald (Cork), J. Dowling (Kerry), E. Ryan (Cork), P. Sheehy, M. Murphy (Kerry), D. Kelleher (Cork).

1959

Leinster—S. Flood (Louth), G. Hughes (Offaly), A. Doyle (Wexford), J. Timmons, J. Boyle (Dublin), P. Nolan (Offaly), M. Grace (Meath), F. Walsh (Laois), C. O'Leary (Dublin), S. Brereton (Offaly), O. Freaney (Dublin), J. Kenna (Laois), P. Farnan, J. Joyce, K. Keffernan (Dublin).

Munster—L. Power (Cork), Jack Dowling, T. Lyons (Kerry), D. Murray (Cork), Sean Murphy, J. O'Shea, M. O'Dwyer (Kerry), P. Harrington (Cork), Seamus Murphy (Kerry), T. Mangan (Clare), N. Fitzgerald (Cork), P. Sheehy (Kerry), T. Furlong (Cork), John Dowling, T. Long (Kerry). Subs: E. Ryan (Cork) for Seamus Murphy.

1960

Ulster—T. Turbett (Tyrone), G. Kelly (Cavan), H. F. Gribben (Derry), P. Rice (Down), P. Breen (Derry), T. Maguire (Cavan) J. McDonnell (Cavan), J. Lennon (Down), J. O'Neill (Tyrone), S. O'Neill (Down), J. McKeever (Derry), P. Doherty (Down), J. Whan (Armagh), J. Brady (Cavan), A. Hadden (Down). Sub: K. Mussen (Down) for Breen.

Munster—L. Power (Cork), J. O'Shea (Kerry), C. O'Sullivan (Cork), N. Sheehy (Kerry), P. Harrington (Cork), K. Coffey, M. O'Dwyer, M. O'Connell, Seamus Murphy, D. McAuliffe (Kerry), E. Ryan (Cork), T. Long (Kerry), J. O'Sullivan (Cork), J. Dowling (Kerry), E. McCarthy (Cork).

1961

Leinster—W. Nolan, P. McCormack, G. Hughes, J. Egan, M. Brady (Offaly), P. Holden (Dublin), C. Wrenn (Offaly), M. Carley (Westmeath), S. Foran (Offaly), K. Beahan, F. Lynch (Louth), J. Kenna (Laois), S. Brereton (Offaly), J. Joyce, K. Heffernan (Dublin).

Munster—J. Culloty (Kerry), P. Harrington (Cork), T. Lyons, N. Sheehy, K. Coffey, T. Long,

FOOTBALL

M. O'Dwyer, Seamus Murphy (Kerry), C. O'Sullivan, E. McCarthy (Cork), J. Keating (Tipperary), P. Sheehy (Kerry), T. Power (Waterford), J. Dowling, G. McMahon (Kerry). Subs: D. McAuliffe (Kerry) for Power, J. O'Sullivan (Cork) for Keating.

1962

Leinster—A. Phillips (Wicklow), P. McCormack, G. Hughes (Offaly), M. Carolan (Kildare), B. Barden (Longford), P. Holden (Dublin), C. Wrenn (Offaly), D. Foley (Dublin), M. Carley (Westmeath), S. Brereton (Offaly), M. Whelan (Dublin), T. Greene (Offaly), P. Gearty (Longford), J. Timmons, K. Heffernan (Dublin). Sub: F. Lynch (Louth) for T. Greene.

Ulster—T. McArdle (Monaghan), G. Kelly (Cavan), L. Murphy, P. Rice (Down), B. Mone (Monaghan), D. McCartan (Down), J. McDonnell (Cavan), J. Carey (Down), E. Larkin (Armagh), S. O'Neill, J. McCartan, P. Doherty (Down), S. O'Connell (Derry), J. Whan (Armagh), B. Morgan (Down). Subs: T. Hadden (Down) for J. Carey, M. Donaghy (Tyrone) for S. O'Connell.

1963

Ulster—T. Turbett (Tyrone), G. Kelly (Cavan), L. Murphy, P. Rice (Down), P. J. Flood (Donegal), T. Maguire, J. McDonnell (Cavan), S. Ferriter (Donegal), R. Carolan (Cavan), S. O'Neill (Down), F. McFeeley (Donegal), P. Doherty (Down), J. Whan (Armagh), P. T. Treacy (Fermanagh), B. Morgan (Down). Subs: J. O'Neill (Tyrone) for S. Ferriter, J. McCartan (Down) for R. Carolan.

Leinster—A. Phillips (Wicklow), P. McCormack, G. Hughes (Offaly), P. Connolly (Kildare), W. Casey, P. Holden (Dublin), C. Wrenn (Offaly), M. Carley (Westmeath), M. Carolan (Kildare), F. Walsh (Laois), D. Foley, M. Whelan (Dublin), P. Cummins (Kildare), N. Delaney (Laois), S. Brereton (Offaly). Subs: L. Foley (Dublin) for M. Carley, F. Lynch (Louth) for D. Foley, T. Browne (Laois) for S. Brereton.

1964

Ulster—S. Hoare (Donegal), G. Kelly (Cavan), L. Murphy (Down), B. Brady (Donegal), D. McCartan (Down), T. Maguire J. McDonnell (Cavan), J. Lennon (Down), S. Ferriter (Donegal), S. O'Neill, J. McCartan, P. Doherty (Down), J. Whan (Armagh), P. Treacy (Fermanagh), F. Donnelly (Tyrone). Subs: C. Gallagher (Cavan) for F. Donnelly, J. O'Neill (Tyrone) for Joe Lennon.

Leinster—A. Phillips (Wicklow), P. McCormack, G. Hughes (Offaly), W. Casey, M. Kissane, P. Holden (Dublin), F. Lynch (Louth), D. Foley (Dublin), T. Browne (Laois), J. Mulroy (Louth), J. Timmons, M. Whelan (Dublin), S. Murray, B. Burns (Longford), G. Kane (Westmeath). Subs: L. Foley (Dublin) for G. Kane, M. Carley (Westmeath) for T. Browne, B. McDonald (Dublin) for J. Mulroy.

1965

Ulster—S. Hoare (Donegal), G. Kelly (Cavan), B. Brady (Donegal), A. Morris (Cavan), D. McCartan (Down), T. Maguire (Cavan), P. Kelly, S. Ferriter (Donegal), R. Carolan (Cavan), S. O'Connell (Derry), J. O'Neill (Tyrone), P. Doherty (Down), C. Gallagher (Cavan), S. O'Neill (Down), P. T. Treacy (Fermanagh). Sub: J. Carroll (Monaghan) for S. Ferriter.

Connacht—J. Geraghty, E. Colleran, S. Meade (Galway), J Murray (Leitrim), J. Donnellan (Galway), C. Cawley (Sligo), M Newell (Galway), J. Langan (Mayo), M. Reynolds, C. Dunne (Galway), P. McGarty (Leitrim), M. Kearins (Sligo), M. McDonagh, S. Cleary, S. Leydon (Galway).

1966

Ulster—S. Hoare, P. Kelly (Donegal), T. McCreesh (Armagh), T. O'Hare, P. O'Hagan, D. McCartan (Down), P. J. Flood (Donegal), R. Carolan (Cavan), J. O'Neill (Tyrone), J. Lennon J. McCartan, P. Doherty (Down), C. Gallagher (Cavan), S. O'Neill (Down), P. T. Treacy (Fermanagh). Subs: A. Morris (Cavan), S. O'Connell (Derry).

Munster—J. Culloty, Donie O'Sullivan (Kerry), S. Downes (Clare), M. Morris, Denis O'Sullivan (Kerry), A. Fitzgerald (Limerick), J. D. O'Connor, M. Fleming (Kerry), M. Burke (Cork), P. McMahon (Clare), P. Moynihan, D. Geaney, B. O'Callaghan (Kerry), C. O'Sullivan (Cork), M. Keating (Tipperary). Subs: M. Tynan (Limerick), J. Lucey (Cork).

1967

Connacht—J. Geraghty, E. Colleran, N. Tierney, J. B. McDermott, J. Donnellan (Galway), J. Morley (Mayo), R. Craven (Roscommon), P. Donnellan (Galway), J. Langan (Mayo), C. Dunne, J. Duggan (Galway), M. Kearins (Sligo), J. Keenan (Galway), J. Corcoran (Mayo), S. Leydon (Galway). Sub: D. Earley (Roscommon) for J. Langan.

Ulster—S. Hoare (Donegal), G. Kelly (Cavan), B. Brady (Donegal), T. O'Hare, D. McCartan (Down), P. J. Flood (Donegal), J. Lennon (Down), R. Carolan (Cavan), A. McAtamney (Antrim), M. Brewster (Fermanagh) J. McCartan (Down), S. O'Connell (Derry), M. McLoone (Donegal), S. O'Neill (Down), M. Griffin (Donegal). Subs: J. O'Neill (Tyrone) for A. McAtamney, S. Ferriter (Donegal) for M. Brewster.

1968

Ulster—S. Hoare (Donegal), G. Kelly (Cavan), B. Brady (Donegal), T. O'Hare, J. Lennon, D. McCartan (Down), P. Pritchard, R. Carolan (Cavan), C. McAlarney (Down), M. Niblock (Derry), J. J. O'Reilly (Cavan), N. Gallagher (Donegal), S. O'Connell (Derry), S. O'Neill (Down), C. Gallagher (Cavan). Sub: D. O'Carroll (Donegal).

Leinster—M. Furlong (Offaly), P. Cole

(Westmeath), L. Gillen (Longford), J. Smith (Offaly), J. Donlon (Longford), L. Toal (louth), G. Davey (Dublin), J. Donnelly (Kildare), L. Coughlan (Offaly), B. Gaughran (Louth), J. Hannify (Longford), A. McTague (Offaly), D. Dolan (Westmeath), M. Whelan (Dublin), S. Donnelly (Longford). Subs: J. Conway (Laois), W. Bryan (Offaly).

1969

Connacht—P. Brennan (Sligo), N. Colleran, N. Tierney (Galway), R. Craven (Roscommon), J. Morley, J. Carey (Mayo), L. Caffrey (Sligo), J. Duggan (Galway), D. Earley (Roscommon), H. O'Carroll (Leitrim), J. Colleary, M. Kearins (Sligo), J. Corcoran, W. McGee (Mayo), J. Keenan (Galway). Sub: S. Leydon (Galway) for M. Kearins.

Munster—W. Morgan, B. Murphy (Cork), S. Downes (Clare), Donie O'Sullivan (Kerry), F. Cogan (Cork), M. Morris (Kerry), B. Hartigan (Limerick), M. Fleming (Kerry), B. O'Neill (Cork) B. Lynch, P. Griffin (Kerry), M. Haugh (Clare), M. O'Connell (Kerry), R. Cummins (Cork), E. O'Donoghue (Kerry). Sub: P. McMahon (Clare) for M. Fleming.

1970

Ulster—A. Gallagher (Tyrone), A. McCabe (Cavan), T. McCreesh (Armagh), T. O'Hare (Down), B. McEniff (Donegal), M. McAfee (Derry), E. McGowan, R. Carolan (Cavan), A. McAtamney (Antrim), J. Murphy (Down), M. Niblock (Derry), S. Duggan, G. Cusack (Cavan), S. O'Neill (Down), S. O'Connell (Derry).

Connacht—E. Rooney, J. Carey, R. Prendergast (Mayo), N. Colleran (Galway), G. Mannion (Roscommon), J. Morley (Mayo), L. Caffrey (Sligo), D. Earley (Roscommon), J. Duggan (Galway), H. O'Carroll (Leitrim), J. Colleary, M. Kearins (Sligo), J. Kelly (Roscommon), W. McGee (Mayo), J. Keenan (Galway).

1971

Ulster—P. McCarthy (Monaghan), J. Burns (Antrim), H. Diamond (Derry), A. McCabe (Cavan), B. McEniff (Donegal), M McAfee (Derry), E. McGowan, R. Carolan (Cavan), F. Fitzsimmons (Antrim), S. O'Connell (Derry), C. McAlarney (Down), M. Niblock (Derry), G. Cusack (Cavan), S. O'Neill (Down), A. McCallin (Antrim). Subs: E. Coleman (Derry) for F. Fitzsimons, J. Murphy (Down) for G. Cusack.

Connacht—E. Rooney, J. Carey (Mayo), N. Colleran (Galway), T. Colleary (Sligo), G. Mannion (Roscommon), J. Morley (Mayo), L. O'Neill, J. Duggan (Galway), D. Earley (Roscommon), B. Wynne (Leitrim), J. Colleary, M. Kearins (Sligo), L. Sammon (Galway), W. McGee (Mayo), J. Corcoran (Mayo).

1972 REPLAY

Munster—B. Morgan (Cork), D. O'Sullivan (Kerry), J. Wall (Waterford), S. Fitzgerald, T. Prendergast, J. O'Keeffe (Kerry}, K. J. O'Sullivan (Cork), M. O'Connell (Kerry), F. Cogan, D. Hunt, D. Coughlan (Cork), E. O'Donoghue (Kerry), M. Keating (Tipperary), R. Cummins (Cork), M. O'Dwyer (Kerry). Sub: J Barrett (Cork) for O'Donoghue.

Leinster—M. Furlong, M. Ryan, P. McCormack (Offaly), J. Conway (Laois), E. Mulligan, N. Clavin (Offaly), P. Mangan (Kildare), W. Bryan (Offaly), B. Millar (Laois), K. Rennicks (Meath), K. Kilmurray, A. McTague, J. Cooney (Offaly), T. Carew (Kildare), M. Fay (Meath). Subs: Murt Connor (Offaly) for Fay. P. Reynolds (Meath) for Millar.

[Mick Scannell (Cork) came on as a sub in drawn game. Murt Connor (Offaly) played in drawn game. Mick Fay was selected for replay. Jim Mulroy (Louth) and John Smith (Offaly) came on as subs in drawn game.]

1973 REPLAY

Universities—N. Murphy (U.C.C. & Cork), J. Waldron (U.C.D. & Galway), S. Killough (Queens & Antrim), J. Stafford (U.C.D. & Cavan), G. McHugh (Queens & Antrim), P. O'Neill (U.C.D. & Dublin), T. Regan (U.C.G. & Roscommon), J. O'Keeffe (U.C.D. & Kerry), K. Kilmurray (U.C.D. & Offaly), B. Lynch (U.C.C. & Kerry), D. McCarthy (U.C.D. & Cork), M. Carney (U.C.G. & Donegal), P. Moriarty (Queens & Armagh), D. Kavanagh (U.C.C. & Kerry), A. McGuirk (Queens & Derry).

[Note: P. Lynch (U.C.C. & Kerry), J. Rainey (Queens and Antrim) and C. Hughes (Maynooth and Carlow) played in drawn game. J. Stafford, P. O'Neill and M. Carney came on for replay. Sub (drawn game) J. P. Kane (U.C.D. and Mayo).

Connacht—J. Neill, T. Heneghan (Roscommon), J. Brennan (Sligo), J. Morley (Mayo), B. Murphy (Sligo), T. J. Gilmore, L. O'Neill (Galway), D. Earley (Roscommon), S. Kilbride (Mayo), B. Wynne (Leitrim), L. Sammon (Galway), M. Kearins (Sligo), M. Burke (Galway), M. Freyne (Roscommon), J. Duggan (Galway). Subs: J. Kelly (Roscommon) for Burke; J. Gibbons (Mayo) for Wynne.

[Matty Brennan (Sligo) and John Kelly (Roscommon) played in drawn game. T. J. Gilmore and Jimmy Duggan came on for replay. Sub (drawn game) Jimmy Duggan.]

1974

Leinster—M. Furlong (Offaly), D. Dalton (Kildare), M. Ryan, M. O'Rourke, E. Mulligan, S. Lowry (Offaly), G. Wilson (Dublin), P. Mangan (Kildare), R. Millar (Laois), P. Fenning (Offaly), S. Allen (Laois), K. Rennicks (Meath), J. Cooney, W. Bryan (Offaly), B. Gaughran (Louth). Subs: D. Nugent (Louth) for Wilson, P. Dunny (Kildare) for Gaughran.

Connacht—N. Crossan (Leitrim), J. Waldron (Galway), J. Brennan (Sligo), H. Keegan, J. Kerrane (Roscommon), T. J. Gilmore (Galway), P. Henry (Sligo), D. Earley (Roscommon), S. Kilbride (Mayo), L. Sammon, J. Duggan (Galway), M. Kearins (Sligo), T. O'Malley (Mayo), M. Freyne (Roscommon), J. Tobin

FOOTBALL

(Galway). Subs: M. Brennan (Sligo) for Henry, J. Morley (Mayo) For Kilbride, M. Burke (Galway) for Tobin.

1975

Munster—W. Morgan (Cork), E. Webster (Tipperary), H. Kelleher (Cork), J. Deenihan (Kerry), K. J. O'Sullivan (Cork), J. O'Keeffe, G. Power (Kerry), D. Long, D. McCarthy (Cork), B. Lynch (Kerry), J. Barrett (Cork), M. O'Sullivan (Kerry), J. Barry-Murphy (Cork), S. Kearney (TipperaryJ, J. Egan (KerryJ. Sub: D. Hunt (Cork) for Long.

Ulster—L. Turbett (Tyrone), D. Monaghan, P. McShea (Donegal), P. Mulgrew (Tyrone), P. Kerr (Monaghan), J. P. O'Kane (Antrim), E. Tavey (Monaghan), T. McGuinness (Derry), P. McGinnity (Fermanagh), F. McGuigan (Tyrone), C. McAlarney (Down), M. Carney {Donegal), P. Rooney (Down), S. Bonner (Donegal), S. O'Neill (Down). Subs: A. Curran (Donegal) for Mulgrew, M. Slevin (Down) for Kerr, B. Donnelly (Tyrone) for Rooney.

1976

Munster—P. O'Mahoney (Kerry), E. Webster (Tipperary), B. Murphy (Cork), J. Deenihan, P. Ó Sé (Kerry), K. Kehily (Cork), G. Power (Kerry), D. Long (Cork), D. Moran (Kerry), D. Allen (Cork), M. Sheehy, M. O'Sullivan, J. Egan (Kerry), J. Barry-Murphy (Cork), P. Spillane (Kerry). Sub: G. O'Keeffe (Kerry) for Webster.

Leinster—P. Cullen, G. O'Driscoll (Dublin), J. Conway (Laois), R. Kelleher (Dublin), J. Balfe (Kildare), S. Lowry (Offaly), K. Brennan (Laois), B. Mullins (Dublin), K. Rennicks (Meath), R. Doyle, A. Hanahoe, D. Hickey (Dublin) P. Fenning (Offaly), J. Keaveney, A. O'Toole (Dublin). Subs: M. O'Rourke (Offaly) for Balfe. S. Doherty (Dublin) for O'Rourke.

1977

Munster—W. Morgan, K. Kehily (Cork), J. O'Keeffe (Kerry), B. Murphy (Cork), D. Moran, T. Kennelly, G. Power (Kerry), D. Long, D. McCarthy, S. O'Shea (Cork), M. Sheehy, P. Spillane (Kerry), J. Barry-Murphy (Cork), S. Walsh, J. Egan (Kerry). Subs: J. O'Shea (Kerry) for D. McCarthy (Cork), D. Allen (Cork) for S. O'Shea.

Connacht—G. Mitchell (Galway), G. Kirrane (Mayo), M. J. Judge, S. McHugh (Galway), G. Feeney (Mayo), J. Hughes (Galway), P. Henry (Sligo), T. J. Gilmore, W. Joyce (Galway), R. Bell, J. P. Kean (Mayo), M. Martin (Leitrim), T. O'Malley (Mayo), J. Duggan, L. Sammon (Galway). Subs: T. Naughton (Galway) for Gilmore, H. Keegan (Roscommon) for McHugh.

1978

Munster—B. Morgan, B. Murphy (Cork), J. O'Keeffe, J. Deenihan, P. Ó Sé, T. Kennelly (Kerry), M. Murphy (Clare), G. McGrath (Tipperary), M. Quish (Limerick), P. Spillane, M. Sheehy, G. Power (Kerry), J. Barry-Murphy (Cork), S. Walsh (Kerry), J. Hennessy (Waterford). Subs: J. O'Shea (Kerry) for Quish. G. O'Driscoll (Kerry) for Spillane. D. Moran (Kerry) for Hennessy

[K. Kehilly, D. Allen, D. McCarthy (all Cork) and Ger O'Driscoll (Kerry) played in drawn game. B. Murphy, M. Quish, J. B. Murphy and M. Sheehy came on for replay.]

Ulster—J. Somers (Derry), D. Stevenson (Armagh), P. Mulgrew (Tyrone), E. McGowan (Cavan), P. Moriarty (Armagh), A. McGurk, M. Moran (Derry), C. McAlarney (Down), P. McGinnity (Fermanagh), L. Austin (Down), E. McKenna (Tyrone), J. Kernan (Armagh), J. Byrne (Down), P. Rooney (Down), P. Traynor (Armagh). Subs: K. McCabe (Tyrone) for Moriarty. N. Marley (Armagh) for Traynor. B. Kelly (Derry) for Byrne, J. Smith (Armagh) for Austin. The game went to extra time.

[Kevin McCabe (Tyrone) and J. Smith (Armagh) played in drawn game. P. Moriarty and Joe Kernan came on for replay. Subs (drawn game) N. Marley (Armagh) for L. Austin, D. Watson (Down) for K. McCabe, J. Kernan (Armagh) for P. Traynor.]

1979

Ulster—B. McAlinden, D. Stevenson (Armagh), T. McGovern (Down), F. Ward (Donegal), K. McCabe (Tyrone), P. Moriarty (Armagh), M. Moran (Derry), P. McGinnity (Fermanagh), L. Austin, C. McAlarney (Down), J. Kernan (Armagh), B. Donnelly (Tyrone) P. Loughran (Armagh), P. Rooney (Down), S. Devlin (Armagh). Subs: C. Digney (Down) for Moran, P. McNamee (Cavan) for Loughran. J. Smyth (Armagh) for Donnelly.

Munster—C. Nelligan (Kerry), K. Kehily (Cork), J. O'Keeffe (Kerry), T. Creedon (Cork), P. Ó Sé, T. Kennelly, P. Lynch, J. O'Shea, S. Walsh (Kerry), P. Leahy (Limerick), M. Sheehy, G. Power (Kerry), J. Barry-Murphy (Cork), E. Liston, J. Egan (Kerry). Subs: P. Spillane (Kerry) for Leahy, D. Moran (Kerry) for Egan.

1980

Ulster—B. McAlinden (Armagh), E. Hughes (Monaghan), T. McGovern (Down), F. Ward (Donegal), K. McCabe (Tyrone), P. Moriarty (Armagh), S. McCarville (Monaghan), P. McGinnitty (Fermanagh), L. Austin, C. McAlarney (Down), J. Kernan (Armagh), E. Young (Derry), P. McNamee (Cavan), P. Rooney (Down), P. Loughran (Armagh). Sub: M. Moran (Derry) for Loughran.

Munster—C. Nelligan, J. Deenihan, J. O'Keeffe (Kerry), K. Kehily (Cork), P. Ó Sé, T. Kennelly (Kerry), T. Creedon (Cork), S. Walsh (Kerry), C. Ryan (Cork), G. Power, M. Sheehy, P. Spillane (Kerry), D. Allen (Cork), E. Liston, J. Egan (Kerry). Sub: J. Barry-Murphy (Cork) for Power.

1981

Munster—C. Nelligan, J. Deenihan, J. O'Keeffe (Kerry), K Kehily (Cork), P. Ó Sé, T. Kennelly, D. Moran, S. Walsh, J O'Shea, G.

Power (Kerry), D. Allen (Cork), P. Spillane, M Sheehy, E. Liston, J. Egan (Kerry).
Connacht—M. Webb (Mayo), J. Hughes (Galway), P. Lindsay, J. McManus (Roscommon), S. McHugh (Galway), T. Donnellan, D. Murray, S. Hayden (Roscommon), M. McCorrick (Sligo), B. Brennan (Galway), J. Kent (Sligo), D. Earley, M. Finneran, A. McManus (Roscommon), M. Carney (Mayo). Subs: H. Gavin (Mayo) for Hughes, G. McManus (Galway) for Finneran.

1982

Munster—C. Nelligan (Kerry), J. Evans (Cork), J. O'Keeffe (Kerry), K. Kehily (Cork), P. O'Shea, T. Kennelly (Kerry), M. Moloney (Cork), J. O'Shea, S. Walsh, G. Power (Kerry), C. Ryan (Cork), D. Moran (Kerry), S. Moloney (Clare), E. Liston (Kerry), D. Allen (Cork). Subs: J. Kerrigan (Cork) for M. Moloney, N. Normoyle (Clare) for Power.
Connacht—M. Webb, M. Gavin (Mayo), P. Lindsay (Roscommon), M. O'Toole (Mayo), P. O'Neill, M. Coleman, S. McHugh, B. Talty (Galway), J. Lyons (Mayo), D. Earley, A. McManus (Roscommon), J. Kent (Sligo), B. Brennan (Galway), J. Burke (Mayo), G. McManus (Galway). Subs: S. Hayden (Roscommon) for Lyons, M. Carney (Mayo) for Brennan.

1983

Ulster—B. McAlinden (Armagh), P. Kennedy (Down), G. McCarville (Monaghan), J. Irwin (Derry), E. Hughes (Monaghan), P. Moriarty (Armagh), J. Reilly (Cavan), L. Austin (Down), F. McMahon (Armagh), P. McGinnitty (Fermanagh), G. Blaney, J. McCartan (Down), J. Corvan (Armagh), E. McKenna (Tyrone), M. McHugh (Donegal). Subs: P. O'Rourke (Down) for McCarville, P. McNamee (Cavan) for McCartan, D. Stevenson (Armagh) for Hughes, G. McCarville for McHugh.
Leinster—M. Furlong (Offaly), T. Foley (Wexford), L. O'Connor, M. Fitzgerald, P. Fitzgerald (Offaly), P. O'Donoghue (Kildare), M. Casey (Longford), T. Connor (Offaly), T. O'Dwyer (Carlow), P. Dunne, R. Connor, G. Carroll (Offaly), C. O'Rourke (Meath), M. Connor (Offaly), S. Fahy (Kildare). Subs: L. Tompkins (Kildare) for O'Dwyer, G. McEntee (Meath) for T. Connor, B. Rock (Dublin) for O'Rourke, A. Wiseman (Louth) for O'Donoghue, T. Connor for McEntee, J. Crofton (Kildare) for P. Fitzgerald. This final went to extra time.

1984

Ulster—B. McAlinden (Armagh), P. Kennedy (Down), G. McCarville (Monaghan), J. Irwin (Derry), M. Carr, M. Lafferty (Donegal), J. Reilly (Cavan), L. Austin (Down), E. McKenna (Tyrone), P. McGinnity (Fermanagh), J. Kernan (Armagh), G. Blaney (Down), M. McHugh (Donegal), F McGuigan (Tyrone), E. Hughes (Monaghan). Subs: T. McDermott (Donegal) for Irwin, F. McMahon (Armagh) for Austin, P. O'Rourke (Down) for Carr.
Connacht—P. Coyne (Galway), H. Keegan (Roscommon), S. Kinneavy, S. McHugh, P. O'Neill, T. Tierney (Galway), D. Flanagan (Mayo), M. Quinn (Leitrim), M. McCarrick (Sligo), B. Talty (Galway), D. Earley (Roscommon), M. Martin (Leitrim), J. Kent (Sligo), S. Mulhern (Leitrim), S. Joyce (Galway). Subs: T. J. Kilgallon (Mayo) for Quinn, B. O'Donnell (Galway) for McCarrick

1985

Leinster—J. O'L.eary, M. Holden (Dublin), M. Lyons (Meath), M. Drennan (Laois), P. Canavan (Dublin), J. Cassells (Meath), C. Browne (Laois), B. Mullins (Dublin), P. Dunne (Offaly), L. Tompkins (Kildare), T. Conroy, C. Duff, B. Rock (Dublin), C. O'Rourke (Meath), J. Mooney (Offaly). Sub. S. Fitzhenry (Wexford) for B. Rock.
Munster—C. Nelligan, P. Ó Sé, T. Spillane, M. Spillane (Kerry), N. Roche (Clare), J. Kerrigan (Cork), G. Lynch, J. O'Shea, A. O'Donovan, J. Kennedy, G. Power (Kerry), C. O'Neill, E. O'Mahony (Cork), E. Liston (Kerry), F. Kelly (Tipperary). Subs: G. McGrath (Tipperary) for C. O'Neill, E. O'Brien (Waterford) for F. Kelly.

1986

Leinster—J. O'Leary (Dublin), P. Dunne (Laois), G. Hargan (Dublin), P. Lyons (Meath), C. Browne (Laois), N. McCaffrey, D. Synnott (Dublin), L. Hayes, J. Cassells (Meath), B. Rock (Dublin), K. O'Brien (Wicklow), G. Browne (Laois), J. Mooney (Offaly), T. Conroy, C. Duff (Dublin).
Connacht—G. Sheerin (Roscommon), M. Carney (Mayo), H. Keegan (Roscommon), S. McHugh (Galway), F. Noone (Mayo), V. Daly (Galway), D. Flanagan (Mayo), T. Tierney (Galway), T. J. Kilgallon (Mayo), P. Kelly (Galway), J. Kent (Sligo), N. Durkin, J. Burke (Mayo), P. Earley (Roscommon), M. Martin (Leitrim). Subs: K. McStay (Mayo) for J. Kent, P. Brogan (Mayo) for T. J. Kilgallon, M. McCarrick (Sligo) for P. Earley.

1987

Leinster—J. O'Leary (Dublin), R. O'Malley (Meath), G. Hargan (Dublin), S. Dowling (Kildare), C. Browne (Laois), L. Harnan (Meath), N. McCaffrey (Dublin), G. McEntee (Meath), L. Hayes (Meath), P. J. Gillic (Meath), J. McNally (Dublin), K. Duff (Dublin), B. Lowry (Offaly), B. Stafford (Meath), B. Flynn (Meath). Subs: G. Browne (Laois) for McNally; Mick Lyons (Meath) for G. Browne.
Munster—J. Kearns (Cork), A. Davis (Cork), A. Moloney (Clare), N. Roche (Clare), N. Cahalane (Cork), C. Counihan (Cork), G. Lynch (Kerry), A. Leahy (Cork), L. O'Connor (Waterford), T. Brown (Limerick), D. Fitzgibbon (Limerick), F. Griffin (Clare), J. Cleary (Cork), F. Ryan

(Limerick), J. McGrath (Waterford). Subs: M. McAuliffe (Kerry for McGrath, D. Culloty (Cork) for Brown, P. Ivers (Limerick) for Cahalane.

1988

Leinster—M. McQuillan (Meath), D. Synnott (Dublin), J. O'Gorman (Wexford), M. Kennedy (Dublin), D. Kelly (Offaly), L. Harnan (Meath), K. Foley (Meath), D. Kavanagh (Offaly), D. Bolger (Dublin), C. Coyle (Meath), V. Murphy (Dublin), C. Duff (Dublin), P. Brady (Offaly), B. Stafford (Meath), D. Barry (Longford). Subs: E. Heery (Dublin) for Synnott and M. McCabe (Meath) for Murphy.

Ulster—P. Linden (Monaghan), J. Lynch (Tyrone), E. Sherry (Monaghan), A. Scullion (Derry), C. Murray (Monaghan), D. Loughman (Monaghan), J. Reilly (Cavan), B. McGilligan (Derry), P. Donaghy (Tyrone), K. McCabe (Tyrone), G. Blaney (Down), D. McNicholl (Derry), N. Hughes (Monaghan), E. Murphy (Monaghan), M. McHugh (Donegal). Subs: F. Cahill (Cavan) for McNicholl.

1989

Ulster—P. Linden (Monaghan), C. Hamill (Antrim), E. Sherry (Monaghan), A. Scullion (Derry), M. McQuillan (Armagh), D. Loughman (Monaghan), J. Reilly (Cavan), M. Grimley (Armagh), P. Donaghy (Tyrone), J. McMullan (Donegal), D. O'Hagan (Tyrone), G. Blaney (Down), M. McHugh (Donegal), E. McKenna (Tyrone), J. McConville (Armagh). Subs: P McErlean (Antrim) for McMullan, A. Molloy (Donegal) for Donaghy.

Munster—C. Nelligan (Kerry), C. Murphy (Kerry), M. O'Connor (Cork), N. Roche (Clare), J. Costello (Tipperary), C. Counihan (Cork), A Davis (Cork), T. McCarthy (Cork), A. O'Donovan (Kerry), P. McGrath (Cork), M. McCarthy (Cork), B. Coffey (Cork), C. O'Neill (Cork), J. O'Driscoll (Cork), M. McAuliffe (Kerry). Subs: M. Fitzgerald (Kerry) for McAuliffe, D. Culloty 1Cork) for McCarthy, D. Fitzgibbon (Limerick) for McGrath.

1990
NO COMPETITION.

1991

Ulster—G. Walsh (Donegal), J. J. Doherty (Donegal), C. Deegan (Down), A. Scullion (Derry), M. McQuillan (Armagh), D. Loughman (Monaghan), M. Shovlin (Donegal), B. McGilligan (Derry), P. Donaghy (Tyrone), A. Cush (Tyrone), N. Smith (Armagh), D Bonner (Donegal), P. Canavan (Tyrone), G. Blaney (Down), J. McCartan (Down). Subs: D. McNicholl (Derry) for Cush, E. Kilpatrick (Tyrone) for Deegan, K. McGurk (Armagh) for Bonner.

Munster—J. Kerins (Cork), N. Roche (Clare), N. Cahalane (Cork), C. Murphy (Kerry), M. Slocum (Cork), C. Counihan (Cork), A. Davis (Cork), D. Culloty (Cork), N. O'Mahony (Kerry), D. Barry (Cork), J. Costello (Tipperary), S. O'Brien (Cork), C. O'Neill (Cork), F. McInerney (Clare), E. O'Brien (Waterford). Subs: D. Fitzgibbon (Limerick) for Costello, P. Vaughan (Clare) for O'Mahony.

1992

Ulster—N. Collins (Down), M. Gallagher (Donegal), C. Deegan (Down), T. Scullion (Derry), M. McQuillan (Armagh), E. Kilpatrick (Tyrone), B. Breen (Down), S. King (Cavan), P. Brogan (Donegal), R. Carr (Down), N. Smith (Armagh), A. Cush (Tyrone), M. Linden (Down), T. Boyle (Donegal), R. Carolan (Cavan). Subs: B. McGilligan (Derry) for Brogan, M. McHugh (Donegal) for Cush.

Munster—P. O'Leary (Kerry), N. Roche (Clare), P. Coleman (Cork), A. Davis (Cork), E. Breen (Kerry), C. Counihan (Cork), L. Flaherty (Kerry), D. Culloty (Cork), A. O'Donovan (Kerry), J. O'Driscoll (Cork), T. Fleming (Kerry), G. Killeen (Clare), J. Cronin (Kerry), D. Fitzgerald (Limerick), F. Kelly (Tipperary). Subs: D. Fitzgibbon (Limerick) for Killeen, A. Moloney (Clare) for Counihan, M. McCarthy (Cork) for Fitzgerald.

1993

Ulster—D. McCusker (Derry), K. McKeever (Derry), M. Gallagher (Donegal), A. Scullion (Derry), M. McQuillan (Armagh), N. Hegarty (Donegal), D. J. Kane (Down), A. Tohill (Derry), B. McGilligan (Derry), D. Heaney (Derry), M. McHugh (Donegal), N. Smyth (Armagh), J. McCartan (Down), G. Houlihan (Armagh), E. Gormley (Derry). Subs: F. Cahill (Cavan) for McHugh, F. Devlin (Tyrone) for McQuillan.

Leinster—J. O'Leary (Dublin), R. O'Malley (Meath), D. Deasy (Dublin), H. Kenny (Wicklow), G. Geraghty (Meath), G. Ryan (Kildare), S. Melia (Louth), F. Daly (Wicklow), P. Bealin (Dublin), M. Lynch (Kildare), R. Danne (Wicklow), V. Murphy (Dublin), S. White (Louth), K. O'Brien (Wicklow), C. Redmond (Dublin). Subs: P. O'Byrne (Wicklow) for Murphy, C. Hayden (Carlow) for White.

1994

Ulster—D. McCusker (Derry), J. J. Doherty (Donegal), M. Gallagher (Donegal), A. Scullion (Derry), M. McQuillan (Armagh), D. Loughman (Monaghan), D. J. Kane (Down), B. McGilligan (Derry), A. Tohill (Derry), J. McHugh (Donegal), N. Smyth (Armagh), R. Carr (Down), G. Houlihan (Armagh), D. Heaney (Derry), J. McCartan (Down). Subs: H. Downey (Derry) for Loughman, P. Canavan (Tyrone) for McHugh, B. Murray (Donegal) for Heaney.

Munster—P. O'Leary (Kerry), P. Coleman (Cork), M. O'Connor (Cork), A. Gleeson (Kerry), C. O'Sullivan (Cork), A. Moloney (Clare), J. Owens (Tipperary), J. Quane (Limerick), D. Culloty (Cork), J. Costello (Tipperary), W. O'Shea (Kerry), F. McInerney (Clare), M. Fitzgerald (Kerry), D. Fitzgibbon Limerick, J. O'Driscoll (Cork}. Sub: T. Morrissey (Clare) for Culloty.

1995

Ulster—F. McConnell (Tyrone), K. McKeever (Derry), A. Scullion (Derry), M. Gallagher (Donegal), M. McQuillan (Armagh), D. J. Kane (Down), F. Devlin (Tyrone), P. Brewster (Fermanagh), B. Murray (Donegal), R. Carolan (Cavan), G. Blaney (Down), J. McCartan (Down), M. Linden (Down), A. Boyle (Donegal), P. Canavan (Tyrone). Subs: H. Downey (Derry) for McQuillan, A. Tohill (Derry) for Brewster, R. Carr (Down) for Boyle.

Leinster—J. O'Leary (Dublin), D. Dalton (Kildare), H. Kenny (Wicklow), P. Moran (Dublin), D. Lalor (Laois), G. Ryan (Kildare), P. Curran (Dublin), P. Bealin (Dublin), A. Maher (Laois), H. Emerson (Laois), J. Sheedy (Dublin), N. Buckley (Kildare), D. Farrell (Dublin), T. Dowd (Meath), C. Kelly (Louth). Subs: S. Doran (Wexford) for Farrell, K. O'Brien (Wicklow) for Kelly.

1996

Leinster—C. Byrne (Kildare), G. O'Neill (Louth), H. Kenny (Wicklow), E. Heery (Dublin), P. Curran (Dublin), G. Ryan (Kildare), D. Lalor (Laois), P. Bealin (Dublin), J. McDermott (Meath), S. O'Hanlon (Louth), A. Maher (Laois), G. Geraghty (Meath), K. O'Brien (Wicklow), B. Stynes (Dublin), C. Kelly (Louth). Sub: N. Buckley (Kildare) for O'Hanlon.

Munster—K. O'Dwyer (Cork), B. Corcoran (Cork), M. O'Connor (Cork), B. Rouine (Clare), C. O'Sullivan (Cork), S. Burke (Kerry), S. Stack (Kerry), D. Foley (Tipperary), D. Ó Sé (Kerry), W. O'Shea (Kerry), J. Kavanagh (Cork), B. Burke (Tipperary), M. Daly (Clare), C. Corkery (Cork), D. Ó Cinnéide (Kerry). Subs: M. O'Sullivan (Cork) for Burke, D. Culloty (Cork) for Ó Sé.

1997

Leinster—C. Byrne (Kildare), D. Brady (Westmeath), H. Kenny (Wicklow), D. Lalor (Laois), P. Curran (Dublin), G. Ryan (Kildare), J. Donaldson (Louth), J. McDermott (Meath), A. Maher (Laois), S. O'Hanlon (Louth), B. Stynes (Dublin), J. McDonald (Kildare), G. Geraghty (Meath), T. Dowd (Meath), C. Kelly (Louth). Subs: C. Whelan (Dublin) for McDonald, G. O'Neill (Louth) for Brady, S. Doran (Wexford) for Geraghty.

Connacht—P. Comer (Galway), K. Mortimer (Mayo), G. Fahy (Galway), E. Gavin (Roscommon), N. Connelly (Mayo), D. Mitchell (Galway), S. de Paor (Galway), J. Nallen (Mayo), L. McHale (Mayo), E. O'Hara (Sligo), D. Darcy (Leitrim), T. Ryan (Roscommon), C. McManamon (Mayo), N. Dineen (Roscommon), N. Finnegan (Galway). Subs: J. Casey (Mayo) for Mitchell, J. Horan (Mayo) for McHale, P. Kenny (Leitrim) for Dineen.

1998

Ulster—F. McConnell (Tyrone), J. J. Doherty (Donegal), C. Lawn (Tyrone), P. Devlin (Tyrone), K. McGeeney (Armagh), H. Downey (Derry), N. Hegarty (Donegal), J. Burns (Armagh), A. Tohill (Derry), J. McGuinness (Donegal), G. Cavlan (Tyrone), P. McGrane (Armagh), D. McCabe (Cavan), A. Boyle (Donegal), P. Canavan (Tyrone). Subs: G. Coleman (Derry) for Lawn, P. Brewster (Fermanagh) for Burns, M. Linden (Down) for McGuinness. In extra time McGuinness for McGrane, D. Marsden (Armagh) for Boyle.

Leinster—C. Byrne (Kildare), C. Daly (Offaly), D. Fay (Meath), M. O'Reilly (Meath), D. Lalor (Laois), G. O'Neill (Louth), F. Cullen (Offaly), J. McDermott (Meath), N. Buckley (Kildare), C. Whelan (Dublin), B. Stynes (Dublin), T. Giles (Dublin), T. Dowd (Meath), D. Darcy (Dublin), K. O'Brien (Wicklow). Subs: Seán Grennan (Offaly) for Stynes, G. Geraghty (Meath) for Whelan, P. Brady for Darcy. In extra time K. Reilly (Louth) for Buckley, V. Claffey (Offaly) for Grennan, J. Kenny (Offaly) for M. O'Reilly.

1999

Munster—D. O'Keeffe (Kerry); M. O'Donovan, S. Óg Ó hAilpín (Cork), A. Malone (Clare); C. O'Sullivan (Cork), S. Moynihan, E. Breen; D. Ó Sé (Kerry), J. Quane (Limerick); P. O'Mahoney, J. Kavanagh (Cork), D. Ó Cinnéide (Kerry); P. Lambert (Tipperary), M. O'Sullivan, A. Dorgan (Cork). Subs: L. Hassett (Kerry) for D. Ó Cinnéide, A. Lynch (Cork) for M. O'Donovan.

Connacht—P. Burke (Mayo); R. Silke (Galway), D. Donlan (Roscommon), K. Mortimer (Mayo), M. Ryan (Roscommon), J. Nallen (Mayo), S. Óg de Paor (capt.); S. Ó Domhnaill (Galway), P. Fallon (Mayo); M. Donnellan (Galway), E. O'Hara (Sligo), P. Joyce (Galway); L. Dowd (Roscommon), P. Taylor (Sligo), N. Finnegan (Galway). Subs: J. Fallon (Galway) for P. Joyce, F. Costelloe (Mayo) for M. Ryan, D. Sloyan (Sligo) for P. Fallon.

2000

Ulster – F.McConnell (Tyrone), M.Crossan (Donegal), S.M.Lockhart, G.Coleman, P.McFlynn, H.Downey (Derry), M.Magill (Down), P.Brewster (Fermanagh), G.McCartan (Down), J.McGuinness (Donegal), S.Mulholland (Down), O.McConville (Armagh), B.Devenney (Donegal), E.Gormley, Peter Canavan (Tyrone). Subs – D.Heaney (Derry) for McGuinness, T.Blake (Donegal) for McConnell, Pascal Canavan (Tyrone) for McConville, B.Dooher (Donegal) for Gormley, R.Gallagher (Fermanagh) for Mullholland.

Connacht – P.Burke, K.Mortimer (Mayo), G.Fahy (Galway), D.Gavin (Roscommon), D.Heaney (Mayo), J.Divilly (Galway), M.Ryan (Roscommon), S.Ó Domhnaill (Galway), P.Fallon (Mayo), J.Fallon (Galway), D.Duggan (Roscommon), E.O'Hara, D.Sloyane (Sligo), P.Joyce, N.Finnegan (Galway). Subs – K.O'Neill (Mayo) for Finnegan, A.Higgins (Mayo) for Mortimer, S.Davey (Sligo) for P.Fallon.

2001

Leinster – C.O'Sullivan, M.O'Reilly (Meath), D.Mitchell (Westmeath), C.Daly (Offaly), D.Healy (Westmeath), N.Nestor, (Meath), K.Doyle (Kildare), R.O'Connell (Westmeath), N.Garvan (Laois), C.McManus (Offaly), P.Barden (Longford), E.Kelly (Meath), C.Quinn (Offaly), G.Geraghty (Meath), G.Heavin (Westmeath). Subs – J.Higgins (Laois) for Doyle, J.Hegarty Wexford) for Quinn, M.Stanfield (Louth) for Garvan, P.Conway (Laois) for Barden.

Connacht – A.Keane (Galway), D.Galvin (Roscommon), K.Fitzgerald, R.Fahy, T.Joyce (Galway), F.Grehan (Roscommon), M.Colleran, K.Walsh, J.Bergin (Galway), C.Connelly (Roscommon), E.O'Hara (Sligo), P.Clancy, D.Savage, P.Joyce (Galway), F.Dolan (Roscommon). Subs – S.O'Neill (Roscommon) for O'Hara, J.Dunning (Roscommon) for Dolan, T.Mortimer (Mayo) for Connelly.

2002

Leinster – E.Murphy, B.Lacey (Kildare), P.Christie (Dublin), A.Hoey (Louth), K.Slattery (Offaly), P.Andrews (Dublin), A.Rainbow (Kildare), C.McManus (Offaly), C.Whelan (Dublin), M.Farrelly (Louth), P.Barden (Longford), E.Kelly (Meath), J.P.Rooney (Louth), R.Cosgrove (Dublin), D.Dolan (Westmeath). Subs – T.Gill (Wicklow) for Rooney, M.Stanfield (Louth) for Farrelly, R.O'Connell (Westmeath) for Barden, T.Kelly (Laois) for Lacey.

Ulster – S.McGreevy (Antrim), E.McNulty (Armagh), C.Lawn, C.Gormley, R.McMenamin (Tyrone), C.McGeeney, A.McCann, P.McGrane (Armagh), J.McGuinness (Donegal), K.Hughes (Tyrone), R.Gallagher (Fermanagh), M.Hegarty, A.Sweeney (Donegal), R.Clarke, D.Marsden (Armagh). Subs – L.Doyle (Down) for McMenamin, T.Freeman (Monaghan) for Sweeney, M.Walsh (Down) for Hegarty, P.Reilly (Cavan) for Gallagher.

2003

Ulster – M.McVeigh (Down), E.McNulty (Armagh), N.McCusker (Derry), N.McCready (Donegal), A.Forde (Cavan), B.Monaghan (Donegal), R.McMenamin (Tyrone), G.McCartan (Down), P.McGrane (Armagh), T.Brewster (Fermanagh), S.Cavanagh (Tyrone), L.Doyle (Down), S.McDonnell (Armagh),

Connacht - S.Curran (Roscommon), K.Fitzgerald, G.Fahy (Galway), M.McGuinness (Leitrim), S.Og dePaor (Galway), F.Grehan (Roscommon), J.Nallen (Mayo), K.Walsh, J.Bergin (Galway), G.Cox (Roscommon), P.Joyce, D.Savage, M.Clancy (Galway), C.Mortimer (Mayo), F.Dolan (Roscommon). Subs - J.Gill (Mayo) for Cox, T.Mortimer (Mayo) for C.Mortimer, S.O'Neill (Roscommon) for Walsh, D.Casey (Roscommon) for Fitzgerald, G.McGowan (Sligo) for Gill.

2004

Ulster - M.McVeigh (Down), N.McCready, R.Sweeney (Donegal), E.McNulty (Armagh), P.McFlynn (Derry), B.Monaghan (Donegal), R.McMenamin (Tyrone), D.Gordon (Down), M.McGrath (Fermanagh), B.Dooher, B.McGuigan, S.Cavanagh, S.O'Neill (Tyrone), P.Bradley, E.Muldoon (Derry). Subs - P.Loughran (Armagh) for McGrath, R.Johnston (Fermanagh) for McFlynn, K.Madden (Antrim) for Bradley.

Leinster - G.Connaughton, D.O'Donoghue (Westmeath), T.Kelly (Laois), N.McKeigue (Meath), K.Fitzpatrick (Laois), B.Cullen (Dublin), K.Slattery (Offaly), N.Garvan (Laois), N.Crawford, E.Kelly (Meath), P.Barden (Longford), J.Doyle (Kildare), A.Brogan (Dublin), P.Kellaghan (Offaly), M.Forde (Wexford). Subs - P.Davis (Longford) for Forde, T.Walsh (Carlow) for Fitzpatrick, P.Keenan (Louth) for Kellaghan, T.Smullen (Longford) for Slattery.

2005

Leinster – F.Byron (Laois), M.Ennis (Westmeath), T.Kelly (Laois), D.Healy (Westmeath), B.Cahill (Dublin), C.Moran (Dublin), P.Andrews (Dublin), T.Walsh (Carlow), N.Garvan (Laois), A.Mangan (Westmeath), R.Munnelly (Laois), P.Clancy (Laois), D.Dolan (Westmeath), G.Geraghty (Meath), J.Sherlock (Dublin). Subs – M.Forde (Wexford) for Walsh, J.Doyle (Kildare) for Munnelly, B.Sheehan (Laois) for Mangan, S.Ryan (Dublin) for Garvan, Garvan for Sherlock, D.Regan (Meath) for Forde.

Ulster – J.Reilly (Cavan), K.McGuckin (Derry), K.McCloy (Derry), E.McNulty (Armagh), A.Kernan (Armagh), C.Gormley (Tyrone), A.Mallon (Armagh), D.Gordon (Down), S.Cavanagh (Tyrone), B.Dooher (Tyrone), C.Toye (Donegal), D.Clerkin (Monaghan), T.Freeman (Monaghan), P.Bradley (Derry), S.McDonnell (Armagh). Subs – A.O'Rourke (Armagh) for McCloy, D.Diver (Donegal) for Gormley, R.Mellon (Tyrone) for Bradley, P.Hearty (Armagh) for Reilly, R.Clarke (Armagh) for Mellon.

2006

Leinster – G.Connaughton (Westmeath), A.Fennelly (Laois), B.Cahill (Dublin), M.Ennis (Westmeath), C.King (Meath), C.Moran (Dublin), K.Slattery (Offaly), B.Quigley (Laois), P.Clancy (Laois), D.Lally (Dublin), J.Doyle (Kildare), M.Carpenter (Carlow), C.Keaney (Dublin), J.Sheridan (Meath), B.Kavanagh (Longford). Subs – A.Mangan (Westmeath) for Kavanagh, T.Walsh (Carlow) for Clancy, D.Clarke (Louth) for Lally.

Connacht – D.Clarke (Mayo), D.Burke (Galway), F.Hanley (Galway), S.McDermott (Roscommon), S.Daly (Roscommon), D.Blake (Galway), D.Heaney (Mayo), P.Harte (Mayo), D.Brady (Mayo), A.Kerins (Galway), G.Brady (Mayo), A.Dillon (Mayo), C.Mortimer (Mayo), M.Meehan (Galway), D.Savage (Galway). Subs – K.Mannion (Roscommon) for G.Brady, S.Davey (Sligo) for Harte, K.O'Neill (Mayo) for Kerins.

2007

Ulster – J.Reilly (Cavan), B.Owens (Fermanagh), K.McCloy (Derry), K.Lacey (Donegal), C.McKeever (Armagh), C.Gormley (Tyrone), K.Cassidy (Donegal), E.Lennon (Monaghan), D.Gordon (Down), D.Clerkin (Monaghan), S.Cavanagh (Tyrone), P.Finlay (Monaghan), T.Freeman (Monaghan), P.Bradley (Derry), E.Muldoon (Derry). Subs – B.Monaghan (Donegal) for McCloy, S.McDonnell (Armagh) for Bradley, J.Crozier (Antrim) for Lacey, B.Coulter (Down) for Gordon, S.Goan (Fermanagh) for McKeever.

Munster – A.Quirke (Cork), T.O'Gorman (Waterford), T.O'Sullivan (Kerry), K.O'Connor (Cork), T.O'Se (Kerry), M.Shields (Cork), G.Spillane (Cork), D.O'Se (Kerry), S.Scanlon (Kerry), E.Brosnan (Kerry), P.O'Neill (Cork), J.Miskella (Cork), M.F.Russell (Kerry), K.Donaghy (Kerry), D.O'Connor (Cork). Subs – G.Canty (Cork) for O'Gorman, F.Gould (Cork) for D.O'Se, M.D.O'Sullivan (Kerry) for Miskella, G.Hurney (Waterford) for Brosnan.

2008

Munster – P.Fitzgerald (Tipperary), D.Duggan (Cork), J.McCarthy (Limerick), P.Reidy (Kerry), T.Ó Sé (Kerry), S.Lavin (Limerick), T.O'Gorman (Waterford), J.Galvin (Limerick), N.Murphy (Cork), P.Kelly (Cork), D.O'Connor (Cork), M.O'Gorman (Waterford), D.Goulding (Cork), A.O'Connor (Cork), I.Ryan (Limerick). Subs – R.Costigan (Cork), J.Hayes (Cork), S.O'Donoghue (Cork), E.Rockett (Waterford).

Connacht – D.Clarke (Mayo), G.Bradshaw (Galway), T.Cunniffe (Mayo), C.Harrison (Sligo), P.Gardiner (Mayo), D.Blake (Galway), J.Nallen (Mayo), R.McGarrity (Mayo), M.Finneran (Roscommon), A.Moran (Mayo), P.Harte (Mayo), A.Dillon (Mayo), C.Mortimer (Mayo), D.Maxwell (Leitrim), E.Mulligan (Leitrim). Subs – J.Bergin (Galway), G.Heneghan (Roscommon), D.Kelly (Sligo).

CAPTAINS OF WINNING RAILWAY CUP FOOTBALL TEAMS

1927—John Joe Sheehy (Kerry)
1928—Matt Goff (Kildare)
1929—Bill Gannon (Kildare)
1930—John Higgins (Kildare)
1931—Joe Barrett (Kerry)
1932—John Higgins (Kildare)
1933—John McDonnell (Dublin)
1934—Mick Donnellan (Galway)
1935—John McDonnell (Dublin)
1936—Paddy Moclair (Mayo)
1937—Purty Kelly (Mayo)
1938—Paddy Moclair (Mayo)
1939—Bill Delaney (Laois)
1940—Matty Gilsenan (Meath)
1941—Danno Keeffe (Kerry)
1942—John J. O'Reilly (Cavan)
1943—John J. O'Reilly (Cavan)
1944—Jim Thornton (Louth)
1945—Peeny Whelan (Carlow)
1946—Tadgh Crowley (Cork)
1947—Kevin Armstrong (Antrim)
1948—Jackie Lyne (Kerry)
1949—Batt Garvey (Kerry)
1950—John J. O'Reilly (Cavan)
1951—Seán Flanagan (Mayo)
1952—Paddy Meegan (Meath)
1953—Paddy Meegan (Meath)
1954—Stephen White (Louth)
1955—Paddy O'Brien (Meath}
1956—Seamus Morris (Cavan)
1957—Jack Mangan (Galway)
1958—Seán Purcell (Galway)
1959—Kevin Heffernan (Dublin)
1960—Seán O'Neill (Down)
1961—Willie Nolan (Offaly)
1962—Greg Hughes (Offaly)
1963—Jim McDonnell (Cavan)
1964—Paddy Doherty (Down)
1965—Tom Maguire (Cavan)
1966—Jim McCartan (Down}
1967—Enda Colleran (Galway)
1968—Joe Lennon (Down)
1969—Noel Tierney (Galway)
1970—Ray Carolan (Cavan
1971—Mal McAfee (Derry)
1972—Donal Hunt (Cork)
1973—Brendan Lynch (U.C.C. and Kerry)
1974—Martin Furlong (Offaly)
1975—Billy Morgan (Cork)
1976—Michael O'Sullivan (Kerry)
1977—John O'Keeffe (Kerry)
1978—John O'Keeffe (Kerry)
1979—Colm McAlarney (Down)
1980—Peter McGinnitty (Fermanagh)
1981—Ger Power (Kerry)
1982—Tim Kennelly (Kerry)
1983—Peter McGinnitty (Fermanagh)
1984—Eugene McKenna (Tyrone)
1985—Brian Mullins (Dublin)
1986—John O'Leary (Dublin)
1987—Ger McEntee (Meath)
1988—Michael McQuillan (Meath)
1989—Jim Reilly (Cavan)
1990—No competition
1991—Tony Scullion (Derry)
1992—Greg Blaney (Down).
1993—Martin McHugh (Donegal)
1994—Brian McGilligan (Derry)
1995—Mickey Linden (Down)
1996—Paul Curran (Dublin)
1997—Tommy Dowd (Meath)
1998—Peter Canavan (Tyrone)
1999—Seamus Moynihan (Kerry)
2000—Henry Downey (Derry)
2001—Mark O'Reilly (Meath)
2002—
2003—Paul McGrane (Armagh)
2004—Michael McVeigh (Down)
2005—Ciarán Whelan (Dublin)
2006—Colin Moran (Dublin)
2007—Conor Gormley (Tyrone)
2008—Nicholas Murphy (Cork)

ALL-IRELAND CLUB CHAMPIONSHIPS 1970/71 - 2008/09

ROLL OF HONOUR

SENIOR FOOTBALL

7 **Nemo Rangers (Cork)** – 1973, 1979, 1982, 1984, 1989, 1994, 2003.
4 **Crossmaglen Rangers (Armagh)** – 1997, 1999, 2000, 2007.
3 **St.Finbarr's (Cork)** – 1980, 1981, 1987.
2 **U.C.D.** – 1974, 1975.
Burren (Down) – 1986, 1988.
St.Vincent's (Dublin) – 1976, 2008.
Kilmacud Crokes (Dublin) – 1995, 2009.
1 **East Kerry** – 1971.
Bellaghy (Derry) – 1972.
Austin Stacks (Kerry) – 1977.
Thomond College (Limerick) – 1978.
Portlaoise (Laois) – 1983.
Castleisland Desmonds (Kerry) – 1985.
Baltinglass (Wicklow) – 1990.
Lavey (Derry) – 1991.
Dr.Crokes (Kerry) – 1992.
O'Donovan Rossa (Cork) – 1993.
Laune Rangers (Kerry) – 1996.
Corofin (Galway) – 1998.
Crossmolina (Mayo) – 2001.
Ballinderry (Derry) – 2002.
Caltra (Galway) – 2004.
Ballina Stephenites (Mayo) – 2005.
Salthill-Knocknacarra (Galway) – 2006.

1970/71 - PROVINCIAL FINALS
Connacht: Galway, 28 February 1971. Fr. Griffin's (Galway) 2-9; Castlebar (Mayo) 1-10.
Ulster: Casement Park, 27 December 1970. Bryansford (Down) 0-6; Newbridge (Derry) 0-3.
Munster: Killarney, 17 March 1971. East Kerry (Kerry) 0-7; Muskerry (Cork) 0-6.
Leinster: Croke Park, 25 July 1971. Gracefield (Offaly) 0-12; Newtown Blues (Louth) 0-9.
1970-71 SEMI-FINALS
Tullamore: 5 September 1971. East Kerry 0-12; Gracefield 0-7.
Newry: 28 March 1971. Bryansford walk-over Fr. Griffin's. (Fr. Griffin's did not play because Liam Sammon was unavailable owing to San Francisco exhibition v. Kerry.)

1970/71 FINAL
Croke Park: 21 November 1971. East Kerry 5-9; Bryansford 2-7.

1971/72 PROVINCIAL FINALS
Connacht: Castlebar, 19 March 1972. Claremorris (Mayo) 0-10; Milltown (Galway) 1-5.
Ulster: Dungannon, 19 December 1971. Bellaghy (Derry) 1-11; Clan na Gael (Armagh) 0-5.
Munster: Mitchelstown, 19 April 1972. U.C.C. 2-9; Clonmel Commercials (Tipperary) 1-8.
Leinster: Carlow, 2 April 1972. Portlaoise (Laois) 2-11; Athlone (Westmeath) 2-9.

1971/72 SEMI-FINALS
Cork: 23 April 1972. U.C.C. 3-12; Claremorris 1-7.
Magherafelt: 23 April 1972. Bellagby 1-11; Portlaoise 1-10.

1971/72 FINAL
Croke Park: 12 May 1972. Bellaghy 0-15; U.C.C. 1-11.

1972/73 PROVINCIAL FINALS
Connacht: Galway, 11 February 1973. Fr. Griffin's (Galway) 1-8; Ballaghaderreen (Mayo) 0-6.
Ulster: Castleblaney, 31 December 1972. Clan na Gael (Armagh) 0-8; Ardboe (Tyrone) 1-3.
Munster: Kilmallock, 23 April 1973. Nemo Rangers (Cork) 3-9; Doonbeg (Clare) 0-5.
Leinster: Navan, 15 April 1973. St. Vincent's (Dublin) 6-10; The Downs (Westmeath) 2-5.

1972/73 SEMI-FINALS
Galway: 29 April 1973. Nemo Rangers (Cork) 0-17; Fr. Griffin's (Galway) 0-9.
Croke Park: 29 April 1973. St. Vincent's (Dublin) 2-8; Clan na Gael (Armagh) 0-7.

1972/73 FINAL
Portlaoise: 4 June 1973. Nemo Rangers 2-11; St. Vincent's 2-11 (Draw).
Thurles: 24 June 1973. Nemo Rangers 4-6; St. Vincent's 0-10 (Replay).

1973/74 PROVINCIAL FINALS
Connacht: Carrick-on-Shannon, 16 December 1973. Knockmore (Mayo) 4-10, Seán O'Heslin's (Leitrim) 0-8.
Ulster: Irvinestown, 2 December 1973. Clan na Gael (Armagh) 1-10; St. Joseph's (Donegal) 0-3.
Munster: Bruff, 20 January 1974. U.C.C. 2-8; Loughmore-Castleiney (Tipperary) 1-5.
Leinster: Drogheda, 3 March 1974. U.C.D. 1-6; Cooley Kickham's (Louth) 0-7.

1973/74 SEMI-FINALS
Lurgan: 10 March 1974. Clan na Gael 3-7; U.C.C.1-10.
Ballina: 10 March 1974. U.C.D. 4-13; Knockmore 0-4.

1973-74 FINAL
Croke Park: 18 March 1974. U.C.D. 1-6; Clan na Gael 1-6 (Draw).
Croke Park: 28 April 1974. U.C.D. 0-14; Clan na Gael 1-4 (Replay).

1974/75 PROVINCIAL FINALS
Connacht: Ballyhaunis, 9 February 1975. Roscommon Gaels (Roscommon) 0-11; Garrymore (Mayo) 0-11 (Draw).
(Replay): Castlerea, 16 February 1975. Roscommon Gaels 1-12; Garrymore 0-7.
Ulster: Omagh, 8 December 1974. Clan na Gael (Armagh) 1-7; Trillick (Tyrone) 1-4.

Munster: Limerick, 19 January 1975. Nemo Rangers (Cork) 2-6; Austin Stacks (Kerry) 1-7.
Leinster: Croke Park, 26 January 1975. U.C.D. 2-7; Ferbane (Offaly) 1-9.

1974/75 SEMI-FINALS
Roscommon: 23 February 1975. U.C.D. 0-12; Roscommon Gaels 1-2.
Mardyke (Cork): 23 February 1975. Nemo Rangers 1-3; Clan na Gael 1-3 (Draw)
(Replay): Lurgan: 9 March 1975. Nemo Rangers 2-5; Clan na Gael 0-6.

1974/75 FINAL
Croke Park: 16 March 1975. U.C.D. 1-11; Nemo Rangers 0-12.

1975/76 PROVINCIAL FINALS
Connacht: Roscommon, 30 November 1975. Roscommon Gaels (Roscommon) 0-6; Fr. Griffin's (Galway) 0-5.
Ulster: Omagh, 30 November 1975. St. Joseph's (Donegal) 3-6; Castleblaney Faughs (Monaghan) 1-8.
Munster: Limerick, 14 December 1975. Nemo Rangers (Cork) 2-7; Austin Stacks (Kerry) 2-7 (Draw).
(Replay): Limerick, 21 December 1975. Nemo Rangers 1-9; Austin Stacks 2-6 (Draw).
(2nd Replay): Limerick, 18 January 1976. Nemo Rangers 1-9. Austin Stacks 0-10.
Leinster: Athy, 18 January 1976. St. Vincent's (Dublin) 3-9; St. Joseph's (Laois) 1-8.

1975/76 QUARTER FINAL
Roscommon: 8 February 1976. Roscommon Gaels 1-7; Seán McDermott's (London) 0-8.

1975/76 SEMI-FINALS
Ballyshannon: 22 February 1976. Roscommon Gaels 1-7; St. Joseph's 0-3.
Mardyke (Cork): 22 February 1976. St. Vincent's 0-10; Nemo Rangers 0-3.

1975/76 FINAL
Portlaoise: 14 March 1976. St. Vincent's 4-10; Roscommon Gaels 0-5.

1976/77 PROVINCIAL FINALS
Connacht: Claremorris, 28 November 1976. Killererin (Galway) 3-8; Garrymore (Mayo) 0-5.
Ulster: Omagh, 28 November 1976. Ballerin (Derry) 2-8; Clan na Gael (Armagh) 2-3.
Munster: Tralee, 12 December 1976. Austin Stack's (Kerry) 1-7; St. Finbarr's (Cork) 0-8.
Leinster: Croke Park, 30 January 1977. Portlaoise 1-12; Cooley Kickham's (Louth) 0-8.

1976/77 QUARTER FINAL
Tralee: 30 January 1977. Austin Stack's 2-16; Kingdom (London) 0-7.

1976/77 SEMI-FINALS
Portlaoise: 20 February 1977. Austin Stack's 1-14; Portlaoise 2-6.
Tuam: 20 February 1977. Ballerin 5-9; Killererin1-4.

1976/77 FINAL
Croke Park: 13 March 1977. Austin Stack's 1-13; Ballerin 2-7.

1977/78 PROVINCIAL FINALS
Connacht: Sligo, 27 November 1977. St. Mary's (Sligo) 4-6; Corofin (Galway) 1-9.
Ulster: Castleblaney, 11 December 1977. St. John's (Antrim) 2-10; Cavan Gaels 2-2.
Munster: Páirc Uí Chaoimh, 5 February 1978. Thomond College (Limerick) 0-12; Nemo Rangers (Cork) 1-3.
Leinster: Newbridge, 11 December 1977. Summerhill (Meath) 5-4; St. Vincent's (Dublin) 0-6.

1977/78 QUARTER FINAL
Corrigan Park (Belfast): 29 January 1978. St. John's 4-9; Kingdom (London) 1-8.

1977/78 SEMI-FINALS
Limerick: 5 March 1978. Thomond College 1-12; St. Mary's 1-8.
Corrigan Park: 5 March 1978. St. John's 4-12; Summerhill 1-8.

1977/78 FINAL
Croke Park: 26 March 1978. Thomond College 2-14; St. John's 1-3.

1978/79 PROVINCIAL FINALS
Connacht: Tuam, 17 December 1978. Killererin (Galway) 1-11; Castlebar Mitchels (Mayo) 1-4.
Ulster: Dungannon, 12 November 1978. Scotstown (Monaghan) 1-8; St. John's (Antrim) 1-4.
Munster: Kilrush, 4 February 1979. Nemo Rangers (Cork) 0-8; Kilrush Shamrocks (Clare) 0-5.
Leinster: Croke Park, 26 November 1978. Walsh Island (Offaly) 2-9; St. Joseph's (Laois) 3-5.

1978/79 QUARTER FINAL
Killererin w.o, Kingdom (London).
Note: Kingdom withdrew because of a spate of injuries.

1978/79 SEMI-FINALS
Tuam: 4 March 1979. Nemo Rangers 3-6; Killererin 1-6.
Tullamore: 4 March 1979. Scotstown 3-4; Walsh Island 0-8.

1978/79 ALL-IRELAND FINAL
Croke Park: 17 March 1979. Nemo Rangers 2-9; Scotstown 1-3.

1979/80 PROVINCIAL FINALS
Connacht: Sligo, 2 December 1979. St. Grellan's (Galway) 0-4; St. Mary's (Sligo) 0-4 (Draw)
(Replay): Ballinasloe, 10 February 1980. St. Grellan's 0-9; St. Mary's 0-8.
Ulster: Coalisland, 9 March 1980. Scotstown (Monaghan) 0-9; Carrickcruppin (Armagh) 0-8.
Munster: Páirc Uí Chaoimh, 1 December 1979. St. Finbarr's (Cork) 0-10; Kilrush Shamrocks (Clare) 0-4.

Leinster: Athy, 23 March 1980. Walsh Island (Offaly) 3-2; Portlaoise (Laois) 1-6.

1979/80 QUARTER FINAL
Páirc Uí Chaoimh: 6 April 1980.
St. Finbarr's 3-17; Kingdom (London) 1-3.

1979/80 SEMI-FINALS
Ballinasloe: 4 May 1980. St. Grellan's, Ballinasloe 1-11; Walsh Island 1-8.
Clones: 11 May 1980
St. Finbarr's 0-7; Scotstown 0-4.

1979/80 FINAL
Tipperary: 25 May 1980.
St. Finbarr's 3-9; St. Grellan's, Ballinasloe 0-8.

1980/81 PROVINCIAL FINALS
Connacht: Sligo, 12 April 1981.
St. Mary's (Sligo) 3-6; St. Grellan's, Ballinasloe (Galway) 3-3.
Ulster: Armagh, 23 November 1980.
Scotstown (Monaghan) 1-4; St. John's (Antrim) 1-3.
Munster: Stradbally, 12 April 1981.
St. Finbarr's (Cork) 3-12; Stradbally (Waterford) 1-8.
Leinster: Newbridge, 22 February 1981.
Walterstown (Meath) 2-9; Éire Óg (Carlow) 2-8.

1980/81 QUARTER FINAL
Monaghan: 19 April 1981.
Scotstown 1-8; Tara (London) 0-5.

1980/81 SEMI-FINALS
Navan: 3 May 1981.
Walterstown 2-12; St. Mary's 1-5.
Páirc Ui Chaoimh: 24 May 1981.
St. Finbarr's 0-8; Scotstown 0-4.

1980/81 FINAL
Croke Park: 31 May 1981. St. Finbarr's 1-8; Walterstown 0-6.

1981/82 PROVINCIAL FINALS
Connacht: Hollymount, 28 March 1982.
Garrymore (Mayo) 0-9; St. Mary's (Sligo) 1-5.
Ulster: Lurgan, 18 April 1982.
Ballinderry (Derry) 2-3; Burren (Down) 0-5.
Munster: Páirc Uí Chaoimh, 6 March 1982.
Nemo Rangers (Cork) 3-9; Kilrush Shamrocks (Clare) 1-6.
Leinster: Athy, 4 April 1982.
Raheens (Kildare) 1-7; Portlaoise (Laois) 0-6.

1981/82 QUARTER FINAL
Hollymount: 11 April 1982.
Garrymore 0-9; Parnell's (London) 0-8.

1981/82 SEMI-FINALS
Páirc Ui Chaoimh: 18 April 1982.
Nemo Rangers 1-10; Raheens 0-7.
Bellaghy: 25 April 1982. Garrymore 0-8; Ballinderry 1-4.

1981/82 FINAL
Ennis: 16 May 1982.
Nemo Rangers 6-11; Garrymore 1-8.

1982/83 PROVINCIAL FINALS
Connacht: Johnstown (Athlone), 30 January 1983. Clann na nGael (Roscommon) 2-6; Tourlestrane (Sligo) 1-3.
Ulster: Coalisland,14 November 1982. St. Gall's (Antrim) 0-15; Roslea (Fermanagh) 2-5.
Munster: Bruff, 23 January 1983. St. Finbarr's (Cork) 0-11; Castleisland Desmonds (Kerry) 1-8 (Draw)
(Replay): Bruff, 30 January 1983. St. Finbarr's 2-6; Castleisland Desmonds 0-6.
Leinster: Carlow, 28 November 1982.
Portlaoise (Laois) 1-8; Ballymun Kickham's (Dublin) 0-7.

1982/83 QUARTER FINAL
Togher (Cork): 6 February 1983.
St. Finbarr's 5-21; Hugh O'Neill's (Yorkshire) 1-6.

1982/83 SEMI-FINALS
Portarlington: 6 March 1983.
Portlaoise 0-7; St. Finbarr's 0-6.
Johnstown (Athlone): 6 March 1983. Clann na nGael 3-6; St. Gall's 2-8.

1982/83 ALL-IRELAND FINAL
Cloughjordan: 20 March 1983.
Portlaoise 0-12; Clann na nGael 2-0.

1983/84 PROVINCIAL FINALS
Connacht: Sligo, 27 November 1983.
St. Mary's (Sligo) 1-7; Knockmore (Mayo) 0-5.
Ulster: Lurgan, 13 November 1983. Burren (Down) 0-7; St. Gall's (Antrim) 0-7 (Draw)
(Replay): Lurgan, 27 November 1983. Burren 1-4; St. Gall's 0-5.
Munster: Limerick, 22 January 1984. Nemo Rangers (Cork) 2-10; Doonbeg (Clare) 0-3.
Leinster: Newbridge, 11 December 1983.
Walterstown (Meath) 3-9; Walsh Island (Offaly) 2-11.

1983/84 QUARTER FINAL
Burren: 29 January 1984. Burren 3-12, Tír Conaill Gaels (London) 0-2.

1983/84 SEMI-FINALS
Kiltoom: 11 February 1984. Walterstown 3-6; Burren 0-8.
Johnstown (Athlone): 11 February 1984. Nemo Rangers 2-10; St. Mary's 1-7.

1983/84 FINAL
Athlone: 12 February 1984.
Nemo Rangers 2-10; Walterstown 0-5.

1984/85 PROVINCIAL FINALS
Connacht: Johnstown (Athlone), 4 November 1984. Clann na nGael (Roscommon) 1-6; St. Mary's (Sligo) 0-9 (Draw)

(Replay): Sligo, 9 December 1984. Clann na nGael 1-7; St. Mary's 0-9.
Ulster: Armagh, 9 December 1984. Burren (Down) 0-10; St. John's (Antrim) 2-2.
Munster: Bruff, 23 December 1984. Castleisland Desmonds (Kerry) 2-6; St. Finbarr's (Cork) 0-9.
Leinster: Newbridge, 9 December 1984. St. Vincent's (Dublin) 1-13; Tinahely (Wicklow) 1-3.

1984/85 QUARTER FINAL
Johnstown (Athlone): 16 December 1984. Clann na nGael 0-11; Parnell's (London) 0-5.

1984/85 SEMI-FINALS
Burren: 24 February 1985. St. Vincent's 2-5; Burren 0-8.
Castleisland: 24 February 1985. Castleisland Desmonds 1-4; Clann na nGael 0-7 (Draw)
(Replay): Johnstown (Athlone), 18 March 1985. Castleisland Desmonds 2-6; Clann na Gael 0-8.

1984/85 FINAL
Tipperary: 24 March 1985. Castleisland Desmonds 2-2; St. Vincent's 0-7.

1985/86 PROVINCIAL FINALS
Connacht: Ballina, 8 December 1985. Clann na Gael (Roscommon) 0-10; Ballina Stephenites (Mayo) 1-5.
Ulster: Armagh, 17 November 1985. Burren (Down) 0-6; Scotstown (Monaghan) 1-2.
Munster: Bruff, 22 December 1985. Castleisland Desmonds (Kerry) 1-11; St. Finbarr's (Cork) 0-5.
Leinster: Athy, 8 December 1985. Portlaoise (Laois) 1-8; Baltingloss (Wicklow) 1-8 (Draw)
(Replay): Athy, 15 December 1985. Portlaoise (Laois) 2-8; Baltinglass (Wicklow) 1-9.

1985/86 QUARTER FINAL
Castleisland: 9 February 1986. Castleisland Desmonds 5-12; Kingdom (London) 2-4.

1985/86 SEMI-FINALS
Portlaoise: 23 February 1986. Burren 2-13; Portlaoise 0-6.
Kiltoom: 23 February 1986. Castleisland Desmonds 0-11; Clann na nGael 1-8 (Draw)
(Replay): Castleisland, 1 March 1986. Castleisland Desmonds 2-9; Clann na Gael 1-6.

1985/86 FINAL
Croke Park: 16 March 1986. Burren 1-10; Castleisland Desmonds 1-6.

1986/87 PROVINCIAL FINALS
Connacht: Cloone, 23 November 1986. Clann na nGael (Roscommon) 2-9; Seán O'Heslin's (Leitrim) 2-4.
Ulster: Armagh, 23 November 1986. Castleblaney Faughs (Monaghan) 0-4; Burren (Down) 0-3.
Munster: Dungarvan, 23 November 1986. St. Finbarr's (Cork) 2-15; Kilrossanty (Waterford) 1-5.
Leinster: Newbridge, 6 December 1986. Ferbane (Offaly) 3-5; Portlaoise (Laois) 1-10.

1986/87 QUARTER FINAL
Castleblaney: 1 February 1987. Castleblaney Faughs 2-10; Kingdom (London) 0-7.

1986/87 SEMI-FINALS
Roscommon: 15 February 1987. Clann na nGael 0-13; Ferbane 1-5.
Castleblaney: 15 February 1987. St. Finbarr's 2-9; Castleblaney Faughs 1-12 (Draw)
(Replay): Páirc Uí Chaoimh, 1 March 1987. St. Finbarr's 3-5; Castleblaney Faughs 2-7.

1986/87 FINAL
Croke Park: 17 March 1987. St. Finbarr's 0- 10; Clann na nGael 0-7.

1987/88 PROVINCIAL FINALS
Connacht: Johnstown (Athlone), 15 November 1987. Clann na nGael (Roscommon) 0-9; Ballina Stephenites (Mayo) 0-8.
Ulster: Ballybay, 15 November 1987. Burren (Down) 0-8; Kingscourt (Cavan) 0-6.
Munster: Killarney, 20 December 1987. Nemo Rangers (Cork) 5-15; Newcastlewest (Limerick) 2-3.
Leinster: Newbridge, 29 November 1987. Portlaoise (Laois) 1-8; Parnell's (Dublin) 1-8 (Draw)
(Replay): Newhridge, 20 December 1987. Portlaoise 1-7; Parnell's 1-5.

1987/88 QUARTER FINAL
Kiltoom: 31 January 1988. Clann na nGael 0-16; Kingdom (London) 0-7.

1987/88 SEMI-FINALS
Midleton: 21 February 1988. Burren 1-5; Nemo Rangers 0-6.
Portlaoise: 21 February 1988. Clann na nGael 1-9; Portlaoise 0-9.

1987/88 FINAL
Croke Park: 17 March 1988. Burren 1-9; Clann na nGael 0-8.

1988/89 PROVINCIAL FINALS
Connacht: Castlebar, 27 November 1988. Clann na nGael (Roscommon) 1-8, Castlebar Mitchels (Mayo) 0-9.
Ulster: Ballybay, 13 November 1988. Burren (Down) 0-8; Pearse Óg (Armagh) 0-3.
Munster: Clonmel, 27 November 1988. Nemo Rangers (Cork) 1-6; Kilrossanty (Waterford) 1-2.
Leinster: Newbridge,11 December 1988. Parnell's (Dublin) 2-5; Ferbane (Offaly) 1-8 (Draw)
(Replay): Newbridge, 18 December 1988. Parnell's 1-4; Ferbane 0-6.

1988/89 QUARTER FINAL
Ballinlough (Cork): 17 December 1988. Nemo Rangers 3-15; John Mitchel's (Birmingham) 0-2.

1988/89 SEMI-FINALS
Burren: 19 February 1989.
Clann na nGael 1-6; Burren 1-5.
Ballygarvan (Cork): 19 February 1989.
Nemo Rangers 1-4; Parnell's 0-5.

1988/89 FINAL
Croke Park: 17 March 1989.
Nemo Rangers 1-13; Clann na nGael 1-3.

1989/90 PROVINCIAL FINALS
Connacht: Kiltoom, 10 December 1989.
Clann na nGael (Roscommon) 3-10; Knockmore (Mayo) 0-7.
Ulster: Armagh, 12 November 1989.
Scotstown (Monaghan) 2-9; Coalisland (Tyrone) 0-5.
Munster: Killarney, 10 December 1989.
Castlehaven (Cork) 0-13; St. Senan's, Kilkee (Clare) 1-8.
Leinster: Newbridge, 26 November 1989.
Baltinglass (Wicklow) 1-6; Thomas Davis (Dublin) 1-6 (Draw)
(Replay): Newbridge, 10 December 1989.
Baltinglass 1-9; Thomas Davis 0-11.

1989/90 QUARTER FINAL
Kiltoom: 28 January 1990.
Clann na nGael 2-9; Kingdom (London) 1-4.

1989/90 SEMI-FINALS
Kiltoom: 18 February 1990.
Clann na Gael 1-8; Scotstown 0-6.
Aughrim: 18 February 1990.
Baltinglass 1-5; Castlehaven 0-6.

1989/90 FINAL
Croke Park: 17 March 1990.
Baltinglass 2-7; Clann na nGael 0-7.

1990/91 PROVINCIAL FLNALS
Connacht: Athenry, 23 December 1990. Salthill (Galway) 0-11; Seán O'Heslin's (Leitrim) 0-5.
Ulster: Armagh, 18 November 1990. Lavey (Derry) 2-10; Kingscourt (Cavan) 0-4.
Munster: Fermoy, 9 December 1990. Dr. Crokes (Kerry) 0-8; Clonmel Commercials (Tipperary) 0-8 (Draw)
(Replay): Fermoy, 16 December 1990. Dr. Crokes 0-15; Clonmel Commercials 0-10 (after extra time). Dr. Crokes 0-9; Clonmel Commercials 0-9 (end of normal time).
Leinster: Newhridge, 23 December 1990.
Thomas Davis (Dublin) 0-8; Baltinglass (Wicklow) 1-5 (Draw)
(Replay): Newbridge, 27 January 1991.
Thomas Davis 1-8; Baltinglass 0-8.

1990/91 QUARTER FINAL
Ballinascreen: 9 December 1990. Lavey 2-11; Tir Conaill Gaels (London) 1-12 (after extra time). Lavey 2-6; Tir Conaill Gaels 1-9 (end of normal time)

1990/91 SEMI-FINALS
Killarney: 3 March 1991.
Salthill 3-9; Dr. Crokes 2-6.
Derry: 3 March 1991.
Lavey 2-6; Thomas Davis 0-10.

1990/91 FINAL
Croke Park: 17 March 1991.
Lavey 2-9; Salthill 0-10.

1991/92 PROVINCIAL FINALS
Connacht: Corofin, 17 November 1991.
Corofin (Galway) 2-5; Clann na nGael (Roscommon) 0-9.
Ulster: Omagh, 1 December 1991.
Castleblaney Faughs (Monaghan) 0-8; Killybegs (Donegal) 0-6.
Munster: Bruff, 1 December 1991.
Dr. Crokes (Kerry) 2-10; Doonbeg (Clare) 0-8.
Leinster: Newbridge, 15 December 1991.
Thomas Davis (Dublin) 1-7; Clara (Offaly) 1-5.

1991/92 QUARTER FINAL
Ruislip (London): 9 February 1992. Dr. Crokes (Killarney) 3-9; Parnell's (London) 1-7.

1991/92 SEMI-FINALS
Parnell Park (Dublin): 1 March 1992.
Thomas Davis 2-9; Castleblaney Faughs 1-7.
Tuam: 1 March 1992.
Dr. Crokes 3-4; Corofin 1-5.

1991/92 FINAL
Croke Park: 17 March 1992.
Dr. Crokes 1- 11; Thomas Davis 0-13.

1992/93 PROVINCIAL FINALS
Connacht: Aughawillan, 22 November 1992.
Knockmore (Mayo) 4-4; Aughawillan (Leitrim) 0-7.
Ulster: Armagh, 22 November 1992. Lavey (Derry) 0-10; Burrren (Down) 0-10 (Draw)
(Replay): Armagh, 6 December 1992. Lavey 0-11; Burren 1-5.
Munster: Killarney, 6 December 1992.
O'Donovan Rossa (Cork) 2-13; St. Senan's (Clare) 0-12.
Leinster: Newbridge, 24 January 1993.
Éire Óg (Carlow) 2-5; Ballyroan (Laois) 1-7.

1992/93 QUARTER FINAL
Ruislip (London): 13 December 1992.
Lavey 0-12; Tir Conaill Gaels 1-7.

1992/93 SEMI-FINALS
Knockmore: 21 February 1993.
Éire Óg 2-5; Knockmore 0-9.
Ballinascreen: 21 February 1993.
O'Donovan Rossa 2-10; Lavey 0-4.

1992/93 FINAL
Croke Park: 17 March 1993.
O'Donovan Rossa 1-12; Éire Óg 3-6 (Draw)
(Replay): Limerick, 28 March 1993.
O'Donovan Rossa 1-7; Eire Og 0-8.

1993/94 PROVINCIAL FINALS
Connacht: Castlebar, 28 November 1993.
Castlebar Mitchels (Mayo) 1-9; Clann na Gael (Roscommon) 0-12 (Draw)
(Replay): Kiltoom, 5 December 1993.
Castlebar Mitchels 1-7; Clann na nGael 0-9.
Ulster: Armagh, 5 December 1993. Errigal Chiarán (Tyrone) 3-7; Downpatrick (Down) 1-8.

Munster: Killarney, 12 December 1993. Nemo Rangers (Cork) 1-17; Kilmurray-Ibrickane (Clare) 0-4.
Leinster: Newbridge, 12 December 1993. Éire Óg (Carlow) 3-7; Erin's Isle (Dublin) 0-11.

1993/94 QUARTER FINAL
Ruislip (London): 12 December 1993. Castlebar Mitchels 0-11; Tir Conaill Gaels (London) 0-8.

1993/94 SEMI-FINALS
Longford: 27 February 1994.
Castlebar Mitchels 1-9; Éire Óg 1 -9 (Draw)
(Replay): Longford, 5 March 1994.
Castlebar Mitchels 0-8; Eire Og 0-7.
Newbridge: 5 March 1994.
Nemo Rangers 1-13; Errigal Chiarán 0-11 (after extra time). Nemo Rangers 0-8; Errigal Chiarán 0-8 (end of normal time).

1993/94 FINAL
Croke Park: 17 March 1994.
Nemo Rangers 3-11; Castlebar Mitchels 0-8.

1994/95 PROVINCIAL FINALS
Connacht: Aughawillan, 4 December 1994.
Tuam Stars (Galway) 2-9; Aughawillan (Leitrim) 1-8.
Ulster: Armagh, 11 December 1994.
Bellaghy (Derry) 0-11; Clontibret O'Neill's (Monaghan) 0-10.
Munster: Páirc Ui Rinn (Cork), 20 November 1994. Castlehaven (Cork) 2-14, CLonmel Commercials (Tipperary) 1-4.
Leinster: Newbridge, 4 December 1994.
Kilmacud Crokes (Dublin) 0-12; Seneschalstown (Meath) 1-8

1994/95 QUARTER FINAL
Castlehaven: 11 December 1994.
Castlehaven 3-18; Oisín (Manchester) 0-3.

1994/95 SEMI-FINALS
Thurles: 26 February 1995.
Kilmacud Crokes 1-11; Castlehaven 1-7.
Enniskillen: 26 February 1995.
Bellaghy 0-13; Tuam Stars 1-6.

1994/95 FINAL
Croke Park: 17 March 1995.
Kilmacud Crokes 0-8; Bellaghy 0-5.

1995/96 PROVINCIAL FINALS
Connacht: Corofin, 3 December 1995. Corofin (Galway) 2-11; St. Mary's (Leitrim) 0-10.
Ulster: Clones, 3 December 1995.
Mullaghbawn (Armagh) 1-11; Bailieboro (Cavan) 2-5.
Munster: Páirc Ui Rinn (Cork), 19 November 1995. Laune Rongers (Kerry) 3-19; Moyle Rovers (Tipperary) 2-4.
Leinster: Newbridge, 3 December 1995.
Éire Óg (Carlow) 2-9; An Tochar (Wicklow) 0-15 (Draw)
(Replay): Newbridge, 10 December 1995. Éire Óg 0-15; An Tóchar 1-6.

1995/96 QUARTER FINAL
Parnell Park (London): 10 December 1995.
Mullaghbawn 0-11; Tara (London) 0-5.

1995/96 SEMI-FINALS
Navan: 18 February 1996.
Éire Óg 0-12; Mullaghbawn 0-6.
Ennis: 18 February 1996.
Laune Rangers 0-8; Corofin 0-6.

1995/96 FINAL
Croke Park: 17 March 1996.
Laune Rangers 4-5; Éire Óg 0-11.

1996/97 PROVINCIAL FINALS
Connacht: Ballina, 23 November 1996.
Knockmore (Mayo) 1-5, Clann na nGael (Roscommon) 0-6.
Ulster: Clones, 1 December 1996. Crossmaglen Rangers (Armagh) 1-7; Bellaghy (Derry) 1-7 (Draw)
(Replay): Clones, 8 December 1996.
Crossmaglen Rangers 2-5; Bellaghy 0-8.
Munster: Killarney, 1 December 1996. Laune Rangers (Kerry) 0-13; Clonakilty (Cork) 0-10.
Leinster: Newbridge,1 December 1996. Éire Óg (Carlow) 1-10; St. Sylvester's (Dublin) 0-8.

1996/97 QUARTER FINAL
Ruislip (London): 8 December 1996.
Knockmore (Mayo) 1-11; Tir Conaill Gaels (London) 2-6.

1996/97 SEMI-FINALS
Mullingar: 23 February 1997.
Knockmore 3-14; Eire Og 0-5.
Portlaoise: 23 February 1997.
Crossmaglen Rangers 1-8; Laune Rangers 1-7.

1996/97 FINAL
Croke Park: 17 March 1997.
Crossmaglen Rangers 2-13; Knockmore 0-11.

1997/98 PROVINCIAL FINALS
Connacht: Carrick-on-Shannon, 7 December 1997. Corofin (Galway) 2-10; Allen Gaels (Leitrim) 0-11.
Ulster: Clones, 9 November 1997. Dungiven (Derry) 0-14; Errigal Chiarán (Tyrone) 1-8.
Munster: Fermoy, 14 December 1997.
Castlehaven (Cork) 1-14; Fethard (Tipperary) 1-8.
Leinster: Navan, 7 December 1997.
Erin's Isle (Dublin) 2-11; Clane (Kildare) 1-11.

1997/98 QUARTER FINAL
Ruislip (London): 8 February 1998. Castlehaven 0-15; Tír Conaill Gaels (London) 0-8.

1997/98 SEMI-FINALS
Ballyshannon: 22 February 1998.
Corofin (Galway) 0-11; Dungiven (Derry) 0-9.
Thurles: 22 February 1998.
Erin's Isle 2-12; Castlehaven 0-17.

1997/98 FINAL
Croke Park: 17 March 1998.
Corofin 0-15; Erin's Isle 0-10.

1998/99 PROVINCIAL FINALS

Connacht: Ballina, 13 December 1998.
Ballina Stephenites (Mayo) 1-10; Roscommon Gaels (Roscommon) 0-6.
Ulster: Clones, 22 November 1998.
Crossmaglen Rangers (Armagh) 1-11; Bellaghy (Derry) 1-10.
Munster: Limerick,13 December 1998.
Doonbeg (Clare) 1-8; Moyle Rovers (Tipperary) 2-5.
(Replay): Limerick, 20 December 1998.
Doonbeg 0-7; Moyle Rovers 0-4.
Leinster: Newbridge, 6 December 1998. Éire Óg (Carlow) 1-6; Kilmacud Crokes (Dublin) 0-9.
(Replay): Tullamore, 13 December 1998.
Éire Óg 0-7; Kilmacud Crokes 0-7.
(2nd Replay): Newbridge, 31 January 1999.
Éire Óg 1-11; Kilmacud Crokes 0-11.

1998/99 QUARTER FINALS

Ruislip (London): 13 December 1998.
Crossmaglen Rangers 1-18; Tír Conaill Gaels (London) 0-8.

1998/99 SEMI-FINALS

Navan: 21 February 1999.
Crossmaglen Rangers 1-10; Éire Óg 1-5.
Ballinasloe: 21 February 1999.
Ballina Stephenites 0-8, Doonbeg 0-4.

1998/1999 FINAL

Croke Park: 17 March.
Crossmaglen Rangers 0-9,
Ballina Stephenites 0-8.

1999/2000 PROVINCIAL FINALS

Connacht: Roscommon, 21 November 1999.
Crossmolina (Mayo) 0-9, Roscommon Gaels 0-9.
(Replay): Crossmolina, 27 November 1999.
Crossmolina 1-7, Roscommon Gaels 0-5.
Ulster: Clones, 21 November 1999.
Crossmaglen Rangers (Armagh) 0-10, Enniskillen Gaels (Fermanagh) 0-9.
Munster: Limerick, 12 December 1999. U.C.C. 1-17, Doonbeg (Clare) 0-7.
Leinster: Navan, 5 December 1999.
Na Fianna (Dublin) 1-11, Sarsfields (Kildare) 0-8.

1999/2000 QUARTER-FINAL

Leeds: 5 December 1999:
Crossmolina 8-15, Hugh O'Neill's (Yorkshire) 0-4.

1999/2000 SEMI-FINALS

Longford: 20 February 2000.
Na Fianna 1-10, Crossmolina 2-3.
Parnell Park: 20 February 2000.
Crossmaglen Rangers 2-16, U.C.C. 3-6.

1999/2000 FINAL

Croke Park: 17 March 2000.
Crossmaglen Rangers 1-14, Na Fianna 0-12.

2000/01 PROVINCIAL FINALS

Connacht: Crossmolina, 19 November 2000.
Crossmolina (Mayo) 1-10, Corofin (Galway) 0-5.
Ulster: Clones, 5 November 2000.
Bellaghy (Derry) 1-10, Errigal Ciaran (Tyrone) 1-4.
Munster: Limerick, 3 December 2000.
Nemo Rangers (Cork) 0-11, Glenflesk (Kerry) 0-7.
Leinster: Portlaoise, 3 December 2000.
O'Hanrahan's (Carlow) 1-7, Na Fianna (Dublin) 1-5.

2000/01 QUARTER-FINAL

Ruislip (London): 10 December 2000.
Nemo Rangers 2-8, Tir Chonaill Gaels (London) 0-6.

2000/01 SEMI-FINALS

Clonmel: 18 February 2001.
Nemo Rangers 0-12, O'Hanrahan's 1-7.
Enniskillen: 18 February 2001.
Crossmolina 1-8, Bellaghy 0-7.

2000/01 FINAL

Croke Park: 16 April 2001.
Crossmolina 0-16, Nemo Rangers 1-12.

2001/02 PROVINCIAL FINALS

Connacht: Tuam, 25 November 2001.
Charlestown (Mayo) 2-9, Annaghdown (Galway) 2-7.
Ulster: Casement Park, 25 November 2001.
Ballinderry (Derry) 1-10, Mayobridge (Down) 1-7.
Munster: Fethard, 25 November 2001.
Nemo Rangers (Cork) 1-11, Fethard (Tipperary) 0-10.
Leinster: Newbridge, 16 December 2001.
Rathnew (Wicklow) 0-9, Na Fianna (Dublin) 1-6.
(Replay): Newbridge, 23 December 2001.
Rathnew 2-16, Na Fianna 1-10.

2001/02 QUARTER-FINAL

Ruislip (London): 9 December 2001.
Ballinderry 2-14, Tir Chonaill Gaels (London) 0-6.

2001/02 SEMI-FINALS

Longford: 24 February 2002.
Ballinderry 1-9, Rathnew 0-7.
Nenagh: 2 March 2002.
Nemo Rangers 0-9, Charlestown 0-7.

2001-02 FINAL

Thurles: 17 March 2002.
Ballinderry 2-10, Nemo Rangers 0-9.

2002/03 PROVINCIAL FINALS

Connacht: Roscommon, 1 December 2002.
Crossmolina (Mayo) 1-11, Strokestown (Roscommon) 0-10.
Ulster: Clones, 1 December 2002.
Errigal Ciaran (Tyrone) 0-8, Enniskillen Gaels (Fermanagh) 1-3.
Munster: Killarney, 8 December 2002.
Nemo Rangers (Cork) 4-15, Monaleen (Limerick) 0-6.
Leinster: Navan, 22 December 2002.
Dunshaughlin (Meath) 0-13,
Mattock Rangers (Louth) 0-7.

2002/03 QUARTER-FINAL
Ruislip (London): 8 December 2002.
Crossmolina 1-11, St.Brendan's (London) 1-7.

2002/03 SEMI-FINALS
Roscommon: 23 February 2003.
Crossmolina 3-10, Dunshaughlin 1-12.
Portlaoise: 23 February 2003.
Nemo Rangers 1-12, Errigal Ciaran 0-11.

2002/03 FINAL
Croke Park: 17 March 2003.
Nemo Rangers 0-14, Crossmolina 1-9.

2003/04 PROVINCIAL FINALS
Connacht: Galway, 30 November 2003.
Caltra (Galway) 1-6, Curry (Sligo) 0-6.
Ulster: Clones, 30 November 2003.
Loup (Derry) 0-11, St.Gall's (Antrim) 1-5.
Munster: Limerick, 30 November 2003.
An Ghaeltacht (Kerry) 1-8, St.Senan's (Clare) 1-6.
Leinster: Navan, 7 December 2003.
St.Brigid's (Dublin) 3-11, Round Towers (Kildare) 1-10.

2003/04 QUARTER-FINAL
Ruislip (London): 7 December 2003.
An Ghaeltacht 3-12, Tara (London) 1-8.

2003/04 SEMI-FINALS
Thurles: 22 February 2004.
An Ghaeltacht 1-9, St.Brigid's 2-3.
Sligo: 22 February 2004. Caltra 2-9, Loup 0-9.

2003/04 FINAL
Croke Park: 17 March 2004.
Caltra 0-13, An Ghaeltacht 0-12.

2004/05 PROVINCIAL FINALS
Connacht: Ballina, 5 December 2004.
Ballina Stephenties (Mayo) 1-13, Killererin (Galway) 2-6.
Ulster: Casement Park, 28 November 2004.
Crossmaglen Rangers (Armagh) 0-14, Mayobridge (Down) 0-9.
Munster: Thurles, 5 December 2004.
Kilmurry-Ibrickane (Clare) 0-9, Stradbally (Waterford) 0-9.
(Replay): Kilmallock, 12 December 2004.
Kilmurry-Ibrickane 0-9, Stradbally 0-8.
Leinster: Newbridge, 5 December 2004.
Portlaoise (Laois) 1-11, Skryne (Meath) 2-4.

2004/05 QUARTER-FINAL
Ruislip (London); 5 December 2004.
Crossmaglen Rangers 2-10, Kingdom Kerry Gaels (London) 1-9.

2004/05 SEMI-FINALS
Galway: 20 February 2005.
Ballina Stephenites 0-10, Kilmurry-Ibrickane 0-8.
Parnell Park: 20 February 2005.
Portlaoise 0-8, Crossmaglen Rangers 0-7.

2004/05 FINAL
Croke Park: 17 March 2005.
Ballina Stephenites 1-12, Portlaoise 2-8.

2005/06 PROVINCIAL FINALS
Connacht: Salthill, 23 November 2005.
Salthill-Knocknacarra (Galway) 1-10, St.Brigid's (Roscommon) 0-5.
Ulster: Omagh, 27 November 2005.
St.Gall's (Antrim) 1-8, Bellaghy (Derry) 0-8.
Munster: The Gaelic Grounds, 11 December 2005.
Nemo Rangers (Cork) 2-12, St.Senan's (Clare) 1-6.
Leinster: Navan, 4 December 2005.
Kilmacud Crokes (Dublin) 0-10, Sarsfields (Kildare) 0-9.

2005/06 QUARTER-FINAL
Ruislip (London): 4 December 2005.
Salthill-Knocknacarra 0-9, Tir Chonaill Gaels (London) 0-5.

2005/06 SEMI-FINALS
Longford: 19 February 2006.
Salthill-Knocknacarra 1-9, Kilmacud Crokes 1-7.
Portlaoise: 19 February 2006.
St.Gall's 0-10, Nemo Rangers 1-6.

2005/06 FINAL
Croke Park: 17 March 2006.
Salthill-Knocknacarra 0-7, St.Gall's 0-6.

2006/07 PROVINCIAL FINALS
Connacht: Roscommon, 26 November 2006.
St.Brigid's (Roscommon) 1-10, Corofin (Galway) 3-3.
Ulster: Casement Park, 3 December 2006.
Crossmaglen Rangers (Armagh) 0-5, Ballinderry (Derry) 0-3.
Munster: Páirc Uí Chaoimh, 10 December 2006.
Dr.Crokes (Kerry) 2-5, The Nire (Waterford) 0-8.
Leinster: Portlaoise, 3 December 2006.
Moorefield (Kildare) 3-6, Rhode (Offaly) 0-8.

2006/07 QUARTER-FINAL
Ruislip (London): 28 January 2007.
Dr.Crokes 2-12, St.Brendan's (London) 0-5.

2006/07 SEMI-FINALS
Mullingar: 18 February 2007.
Crossmaglen Rangers 1-11, St.Brigid's 0-11.
The Gaelic Grounds: 18 February 2007.
Dr.Crokes 1-9, Moorefield 0-12.
(Replay) Nenagh: 24 February 2007.
Dr.Crokes 2-9, Moorefield 0-8.

2006/07 FINAL
Croke Park: 17 March 2007.
Crossmaglen Rangers 1-9, Dr.Crokes 1-9.
(Replay) Portlaoise: 1 April 2007.
Crossmaglen Rangers 0-13, Dr.Crokes 1-5.

2007/08 PROVINCIAL FINALS
Connacht: Ballina, 25 November 2007.
Ballina Stephenites (Mayo) 2-8, St.Brigid's (Roscommon) 0-12.
Ulster: Newry, 25 November 2007.
Crossmaglen Rangers (Armagh) 1-9, St.Gall's (Antrim) 1-6.
Munster: Killarney, 9 December 2007.

Nemo Rangers (Cork) 1-10, Ballinacourty (Waterford) 1-7.
Leinster: Mullingar, 16 December 2007.
St.Vincent's (Dublin) 2-8, Tyrrellspass (Westmeath) 0-7.

2007/08 QUARTER-FINAL
Ruislip (London): 27 January 2008.
Crossmaglen Rangers 0-10, Tír Chonaill Gaels (London) 0-6.

2007/08 SEMI-FINALS
Navan: 24 February 2008.
St.Vincent's 2-9, Crossmaglen Rangers 0-11.
Ennis: 24 February 2008.
Nemo Rangers 0-14, Ballina Stephenites 1-4.

2007/08 FINAL
Croke Park: 17 March 2008.
St.Vincent's 1-11, Nemo Rangers 0-13.

2008/09 PROVINCIAL FINALS
Connacht: Salthill, 23 November 2008.
Corofin (Galway) 0-11, Eastern Harps (Sligo) 0-6.
Ulster: Enniskillen, 30 November 2008.
Crossmaglen Rangers (Armagh) 1-10, Ballinderry (Derry) 1-10.
(Replay): Enniskillen, 14 December 2008.
Crossmaglen Rangers 0-12, Ballinderry 1-4.
Munster: The Gaelic Grounds, 7 December 2008.
Dromcollogher-Broadford (Limerick) 0-6, Kilmurry-Ibrickane (Clare) 0-5.
Leinster: Parnell Park, 7 December 2008.
Kilmacud Crokes (Dublin) 2-7, Rhode (Offaly) 1-7.

2008/09 QUARTER-FINAL
Ruislip (London): 18 January 2009.
Corofin 2-7, Tir Chonaill Gaels (London) 0-6.

2008/09 SEMI-FINALS
Mullingar: 21 February 2009.
Kilmacud Crokes 2-11, Corofin 0-11.
Longford: 21 February 2009.
Crossmaglen Rangers 4-11, Dromcollogher-Broadford 0-6.

2008/09 FINAL
Croke Park: 17 March 2009.
Kilmacud Crokes 1-9, Crossmaglen Rangers 0-7.

ALL-IRELAND CLUB FOOTBALL FINAL TEAMS 1971-2009

1971
East Kerry—E. Fitzgerald, D. O'Sullivan, D. Crowley, J. Gleeson, G. Cullinane, N. Power, J. O'Donoghue, P. Moynihan, P. Casey, P. O'Donoghue, D. O'Keeffe, D. Healy, D. Coffey, M. Gleeson, D. Kavanagh. Sub: T. Looney for P. Casey.

Bryansford—J. Boden, B. Cunningham, O. Burns, J. Neeson, D. McNamara, P. Cunningham, S. Cunningham, B. Ward, P. Neeson, W. Kane, M. Cunningham, K. Bailie, S. O'Hare, B. Neeson, E. Grant. Subs: F. McGinn for D. McNamara, J. McGinn for K. Bailie.

1972
Bellaghy—P. McTaggart, T. Scullion, A. Mulholland, F. Cassidy, T. Diamond, H. McGoldrick, C. Browne, L. Diamond, P. Doherty, F. Downey, B. Cassidy, F. O'Loane, H Donnelly, T. Quinn, K. Cassidy.

U.C.C.—N. Murphy, J. Gleeson, M. Keane, J. Coughlan, J. O'Grady, S. Looney, T. Looney, N. O'Sullivan, P. Lynch, B. Lynch, R. Bambury, D. Murray, D. Coffey, D. Kavanagh, N. Brosnan. Sub: S. Murphy for N. Brosnan.

1973
Nemo Rangers—B. Morgan, J. Corcoran, E. Brophy, B. Murphy, R. Twomey, F. Cogan, D. O'Driscoll, D. Barrett, M. O'Donoghue, K. Collins, S. Coughlan, B. Cogan, L. Good, J. Barrett, C. Murphy. (Note: D. Cogan played in drawn game.)

St. Vincent's—T. O'Byrne, L. Ferguson, G. O'Driscoll, M. Hannick, M. Behan, D. Billings, E. Brady, P. Hallinan, P. J. Reid, B. Doyle, T. Hanahoe, B. Mullins, C. Keaney, D. Foley, J. Keaveney. (Note: G. Keavey, S. Mullins played in drawn game.) Subs: L. Foley, D. Redmond drawn game. L. Foley, D. Redmond, S. Mullins replay.

1974
U.C.D.—I. Heffernan, M. Judge, G. O'Reilly, P. Gilroy, F. O'Donoghue, E. O'Donoghue, P. Kerr, K. Kilmurray, B. Gaughran, E. Condron, O. Leddy, J. Walsh, J. P. Keane, D. O'Connor, P. Duggan. (Note: J. Waldron, P. J. O'Halloran, J. O'Keeffe played in drawn game.) Sub: D. O'Connor in drawn match.

Clann na Gael—P. Scullion, K. France, J. O'Hagan, T. Moore, O. Crewe, J. Greene, S. Lavelle, S. O'Hagan, C. McKinstry, M. O'Neill, J. Smyth, T. McCaughey, G. Hamill, N. O. Hagan, P. McGuinness. (Note: J. McKenna and J. Byrne played in drawn game.) Subs: J. McKenna and J. Moore in replay.

1975
U.C.D.—I. Heffernan, M. Judge, G. O'Reilly, C. Moynihan, P. J. O'Halloran, E. O'Donoghue, F. O'Donoghue, M. Carty, P. O'Neill, B. Dunleavy, J. P. Keane, J. Walsh, B. Walsh, P. Duggan, B. Heneghan. Sub: E. Condron.

Nemo Rangers—W. Morgan, J. Corcoran, E. Brophy, D. O'Sullivan, D. Cogan, B. Murphy, D. O'Driscoll, K. Collins, K. Murphy, L. Goode, S. Coughlan, S. Leydon, N. Morgan, J. Barrett, C. Murphy. Subs: Declan Murphy, M. O'Donoghue.

1976
St. Vincent's—N. Bernard, D. Billings, G. O'Driscoll, M. Hennrick, M. Behan, V. Lambe, B. Pocock, B. Mullins, F. Ryder, B. Reddy, T. Hanahoe, M. Whelan, L. Deegan, J. Keaveney, B. Doyle. Sub: P. Reid for M. Hennrick.

Roscommon Gaels—T. O'Connor, P. Kelly, P. Dolan, S. Hunt, M. Menton, M. McNeela, A. de Paoli, J. O'Gara, J. Donlon, J. Martin, M. McNamara, H. Griffin, F. Daly, L. O'Gara, P. Shaughnessy. Sub: M. Moloney for F. Daly.

1977
Austin Stacks—T. Brick, G. Scollard, N. Power, P. Lucey, F. Lawlor, A. O'Keeffe, G. Power, G. O'Keeffe, J. O'Keeffe, F. Ryan, D. Long, T. Sheehan, J. Power, P. McCarthy, M. Sheehy. Sub: C. Mangan.

Ballerin—S. Deighan, E. Moloney, S. McGahan, G. Forrest, V. Moloney, P. Stevenson, B. O'Kane, M. McAfee, J. Scullion, G. O'Connell, G. Keane, J. McAfee, C. Faulkner, S. O'Connell, P. M. Deighan.

1978
Thomond College—L. Murphy, M. Heuston, S. O'Shea, E. Mahon, M. Spillane, B. McSweeney, M. Connolly, T. Harkin, B. Talty, J. Dunne, R. Bell, D. Smyth, M. Kilcoyne, P. Spillane, J. O'Connell. Sub: D. O'Boyle for M. Connolly.

Saint John's—P. McCann, D. McNeill, K. McFerran, G. McCann, J. Rainey, J. McGuinness, J. Donnelly, L. Jennings, P. McGinnitty, K. Gough, H. McRory, A. McCallin, M. Darragh, S. McFerran, P. McFaul. Subs: J. McGranaghan, J. Cunningham.

1979
Nemo Rangers—W. Morgan, F. Cogan, F. Stone, K. Murphy, J. Kerrigan, B. Murphy, D. O'Driscoll, K. Brady, D. Linehan, J. Barrett, D. Allen, T. Dalton, N. Morgan, K. Collins, C. Murphy. Sub: D. Murphy for C. Murphy.

Scottstown—E. Keenan, M. McCarville, G. McCarville, F. Caulfield, D. Stirratt, S. McCarville, J. Treanor, B. Lillis, S. McCrudden, B. Morgan, Seamus McCarville, C. Morgan, J. McCabe, J. Moyna, B. Rice. Sub: R. McDermott for B. Rice.

1980
St. Finbarr's—B. O'Brien, D. O'Grady, E. Desmond, N. Aherne, D. Brosnan, M. Lynch, M. Carey, C. Ryan, D. Philpott, F. Twomey, R. Kenny, F. O'Mahony, J. Barry Murphy, J. Allen, J. O'Callaghan. Sub: D. Barry for D. Philpott.

St Grellan's—W. Devlin, N. Jennings, J. Kelly, J. Boswell, P. Cunningham, E. Flanagan, K. Mitchell, B. Brennan, P. McGettigan, M. Cunningham, J. Manton, G. Gibbons, J. Whelan, C. Loftus, S. Riddell. Subs: P. Ryan, L. White.

1981
St. Finbarr's—B. O'Brien, J. Cremin, M. Healy, E. Desmond, M. Carey, C. Ryan, D. O'Grady, T. Holland, M. Lynch, D. Barry, R. Kenny, F. O'Mahony, J. Barry Murphy, J. Allen, J. O'Callaghan. Sub: J. Barry for T. Holland.

Walterstown—S. Reilly, P. Smith, W. Clarke, M. Sheils, E. Ward, C. Bowens, G. Reynolds, C Reynolds, N. O'Sullivan, E. O'Brien, E. Barry, G. McLaughlin, G. Cooney, O. O'Brien, F. O'Sullivan. Subs: M. Barry for P. Smith, T. Clarke for G. McLaughlin.

1982
Nemo Rangers—D. Bevan, F. Cogan, B. Murphy, A. Keane, D. O'Driscoll, T. Hennebry, J. Kerrigan, M. Niblock, T. Dalton, S. Coughlan, D. Allen, S. Hayes, C. Murphy, E. Fitzgerald, M. Dorgan. Subs: Charlie Murphy for D. Allen, K. Murphy for D. O'Driscoll, D. Linehan for S. Hayes.

Garrymore—M. J. Connolly, P. Nally, D. Conway, J. Nally, P. Flannery, D. Mellett, G. Farraghter, J. Monaghan, P. Mohan, T. Walsh, P. Dixon, D. Dolan, T. Connolly, L. Dolan, B. Fitzpatrick. Subs: P. Monaghan for D. Conway, M. Walsh for P. Nally.

1983
Portlaoise—M. Mulhall, J. Bohane, J. Bergin, M. Kavanagh, C. Browne, M. Lillis, B. Conroy, E. Whelan, M. Dooley, N. Prendergast, L. Scully, P. Critchley, T. Prendergast, J. Keenan, G. Browne. Subs: W. Bohane for J. Keenan, J. Keenan for W. Bohane.

Clan na nGael—J. O'Neill, W. Harney, L. O'Neill, C. Deignan, G. Petitt, M. Keegan, J. McManus, E. McManus, F. Nicholson, E. McManus (Jnr), M. McManus, O. McManus, P. J. Glynn, T. McManus, D. Shine. Subs: L. Dunne for G. Petitt, V. Harney for P. J. Glynn.

1984
Nemo Rangers—D. Bevan, A. Keane, B. Murphy, K. Murphy, J. Kerrigan, M. Lynch, T. Nation, M. Niblock, T. Dalton, S. Coughlan, S. Hayes, C. Murphy, E. Fitzgerald, D. Allen, M. Dorgan. Sub: Charlie Murphy for S. Hayes.

Walterstown—C. Bowen, G. McLaughlin, W. Clarke, P. Smith, P. Carr, E. O'Brien, G. Reynolds, C. Reynolds, N. O'Sullivan, J. Barry, E. Barry, M. Barry, F. O'Sullivan, O. O'Brien, G. Cooney. Subs: O. Clynch for M. Barry, K. McLoughlin for O. Clynch.

1985
Castleisland Desmonds—C. Nelligan, D. Ciarubhain, B. Lyons, W. King, D. Lyons, M. J Kearney, P. Callaghan, M. O'Connor, D. Hannafin, W. O'Connor, C. Kearney, D. Lyne, J O'Connor, D. Buckley, P. Horan. Subs: M. Downey for J. O'Connor, J. Lyons for D. Lyne.

St. Vincent's—N. Bernard, T. Diamond, V. Conroy, S. Wade, R. Hazley, S. Fleming, A. Devlin, P. Canavan, B. Mullins, T. Conroy, B. Jordan, S. McDermott, C. Buffini, M. Loftus, P. McLoughlin. Sub: E. Heery for C. Buffini.

1986
Burren—D. Murdock, B. McKernan, A. Murdock, M. Murdock, K, McConville, W.

McMahon, B. McGovern, T. McGovern, P. O'Rourke, L. Fitzpatrick, J. Treanor, P. McKay, J. McGreevy, V. McGovern, T. McArdle. Sub: C. Doyle for J. McGreevy.

Castleisland Desmonds—C. Nelligan, D. Ó Ciarubhain, B. Lyons, W. King, J. O'Connor, M. J. Kearney, P. O'Callaghan, M. O'Connor, D. Hannafin, W. O'Connor, C. Kearney, D. Lyne, P. Horan, D. Buckley, J. Lordan. Sub: M. Downey for P. Horan.

1987

St. Finbarr's—J. Kerins, J. Cremin, J. Meyler, E. Desmond, M. Carey, K. Scanlon, B. O'Connell, P. Hayes, T. Leahy, K McCarthy, C. Ryan, M. Slocum, T. Power, D. O'Mahony, J Allen. Sub: M. Barry for T. Power.

Clan na Gael—T. Seery, J. Dowling, M. Keegan, J McManus, O. McManus, F. Nicholson, A. McManus, P McManus, E. McManus (Snr), K. Pettit, P. Naughton, E McManus (Jnr), T. Lennon, T. McManus, E. Durney. Subs: H. Moody for P. Naughton, J. Connaughton for M. Petitt.

1988

Burren—D. Murdock, B. McKernan, A. Murdock, M. Murdock, K. McConville, L. Fitzpatrick, B. McGovern, B. Laverty, T. McGovern, T. McArdle, J. Traenor, P. McKay, R. Fitzpatrick, V. McGovern, T. Fegan. Sub: P. Fegan for B. Laverty.

Clan na Gael—T. Seery, J. Dowling, M. Keegan, V. Harney, O. McManus, F. Nicholson, A. McManus, P. McManus, J McManus, J. Connaughton, G. Lennon, E. McManus (Jnr), P. Naughton, T. Lennon, J. McManus. Subs: E. McManus (Snr) for G. Lennon, E. Durney for P. Naughton.

1989

Nemo Rangers—J. O'Mahoney, A. Keane, N. Creedon, M. Lynch, J. Kerrigan, T. Griffin, D. Creedon, D. O'Sullivan, T. Dalton, S. O'Brien, E. O'Mahoney, T. Nation, S. Calnan, D. Allen, M. Dargan. Subs: P. O'Donovan for Dalton, S. Hayes for Calnan.

Clan na nGael—P. Naughton, J. Dowling, J. McManus, D. Rock. O. McManus, J. Lennon, A. McManus, P. McManus, G. Lennon, J. Connaughton, E. McManus (Snr), E. McManus (Jnr), P. Naughton, T. McManus, E. Durney. Subs: L. Dunne for E. Durney, M. Keegan for J. Lennon.

1990

Baltinglass—D. Leigh, S. O'Brien, H. Kenny, T. Donohue, H. Fitzpatrick, P. Murphy, B. Kilcoyne, R. Danne, B. Kenny, P. Kenny, R. McHugh, L. Horgan, C. Murphy, K. O'Brien, T. Murphy. Sub: B. Timmons for P. Kenny.

Clan na nGael—Paul Naughton, D. Rock, M. Keegan, F. Nicholson, J. Connaughton, J. McManus, A. McManus, P. McManus, Eamonn McManus, Eoin McManus, Eamonn McManus (Jnr), E. Durney, Pauric Naughton, T. Lennon, T. McManus. Subs: D. Kenny for Pauric Naughton, D. Nolan for Durney.

1991

Lavey—B. Regan, D. Doherty, A. Scullion, B. Scullion, J. McGurk, H. Downey, Ciaran McGurk, D. O'Boyle, J. Chivers, F. Rafferty, B. McCormack, H. M. McGurk, D. Mulholland, S. Downey, Colm McGurk. Sub: A. McGurk for Colm McGurk.

Salthill—C. McGinley, J. Kilraine, E. O'Donnellan, G. O'Farrell, F. Mitchell, E. O'Donoghue, M. Tarpey, A. Mulholland, M. Gibbs, P. J. Kelly, M. Butler, J. McDonagh, N. Costelloe, P. Comer, N. Finnegan, Subs: C. McGauran for Kelly, M. Ruane for McDonagh.

1992

Dr. Croke's—P. O'Brien, D. Keogh, L. Hartnett, S. Clarke, J. Clifford, J. Galvin, C. O'Shea, C. Murphy, N. O'Leary, C. Doherty, D. Cooper, S. O'Shea, P. O'Shea, V. Casey, G. O'Shea.

Thomas Davis—F. Troy, D. Nugent, J. J. Martin, E. O'Toole; J. Fadian, P. Curran, G. Kilmartin, D. Foran, P. Godson, P. Waldron, P. Nugent, S. Grealis, P. Joyce, L. Adamson, V. Corney. Subs: K. O'Donovon for O'Toole, P. Dwane for Joyce.

1993

O'Donovan Rossa—K. O'Dwyer, J. Evans, J. O'Donovan, F. McCarthy, G. O'Driscoll, A. Davis, I. Breen, D. O'Driscoll, B. O'Donovan, B. Carmody, J. O'Driscoll, D. Davis, N. Murphy, M. McCarthy, P. Davis. Sub: M. McCarthy for G. O'Driscoll. (In drawn game, sub.: D. Whooley for Murphy).

Eire Og—J. Kearns, J. Wynne, R. Moore, J. Dooley, B. Hayden, A. Callinan, N. Fallon, G. Ware, H. Brennan, J. Hayden, J. Morrissey, T. Nolan, J. Murphy, C. Hayden, A. Keating. Sub: D. Moore for Nolan. (In drawn game, D. Wynne at full-back, D. Walker centre half-back.)

1994

Nemo Rangers—D. Bevan; J. Kerrigan, N. Creedon, P. Dorgan; K. Cowhie, T. Griffin, T. Nation; S. Fahy, S. O'Brien; J. Kavanagh, T. Dalton, S. Calnan; P. Lambert, C. Corkery, E. Fitzgerald. Subs: L. Kavanagh for Dorgan, A. Quinlivan for Nation, N. Corkery for Fitzgerald.

Castlebar Mitchels—J. Cuddy; W. Flynn, J. McCabe, A. Waldron; D. Shaw, J. Maughan, D. Noone; R. Ruane, P. Holmes; S. Murphy, T. Reilly, P. Jordan; B. Kilkelly, D. Byrne, K. Lydon. Subs: F. Joyce for Jordan, M. Feeney for Ruane, H. Gavin for Kilkelly.

1995

Kilmacud Crokes—M. Pender; R. Ward, C. Cleary, R. Leahy; J. O'Callaghan, J. Sweeney, P. Burke; M. Dillon, Mick Leahy; P. Dalton, S. Morris, P. Ward; N. Clancy, Maurice Leahy, P.

O'Donoghue. Sub: T. Gunning for Maurice Leahy.

Ballaghy—M. Kearns; S. Birt, P. Downey, P. Diamond; D. Brown, K. Diamond, G. McPeake; D. Quinn, J. Mulholland; L. McPeake, B. Lee, G. Doherty; J. Donnelly, D. Cassidy, E. Cassidy. Subs: C. Scullion for Donnelly, M. Diamond for E. Cassidy.

1996

Laune Rangers—P. Lyons; A. Hassett, P. Sheahan, M. O'Connor; M. Hassett, T. Byrne, S. O'Sullivan; T. Fleming, P. Prendiville; G. Murphy, C. Kearney, J. Shannon; P. Griffin, L. Hassett, B. O'Shea. Subs: B. O'Sullivan for Griffin, J. O'Shea for Prendiville.

Éire Óg—J. Kearns; J. Wynne, D. Wynne, J. Murphy; B. Hayden, D. Moore, A. Callinan; J. Morrissey, H. Brennan; J. Hayden, G. Ware, W. Quinlan; P. McCarthy, C. Hayden, A. Keating. Subs: J. Owens for Morrissey, K. Haughney for McCarthy.

1997

Crossmaglen Rangers—Jarlath McConville; M. Califf, D. Murtagh, P. McKeown; J. Fitzpatrick, F. Bellew, G. McShane; J. McEntee, A. Cunningham; C. Short, A. McEntee, O. McConville; Jim McConville, G. Cumiskey, C. O'Neill. Sub: M. Moley for J. McEntee.

Knockmore—P. Reape; F. Sweeney, C. Naughton, T. Bourke; G. O'Hora, P. Butler, J. Davis; K. Staunton, D. Dempsey; P. Cawley, D. Sweeney, S. Sweeney; K. O'Neill, R. Dempsey, P. Brogan. Subs: T. Holmes for Dempsey, H. Langan for O'Hora.

1998

Corofin—M. McNamara; O. Burke, J. Killeen, J. Lardner; A. Fahy, R. Silke, T. Greaney; G. Burke, A. Donnellan; S. Conlisk, M. Donnellan, T. Burke; M. Kenny, E. Steede, D. Reilly. Subs: K. Newell for Killeen, K. Comer for Kenny, K. Treacy for Steede.

Erin's Isle—T. Quinn; K. Murray, K. Spratt, M. Naughton; D. Collins, M. Deegan, G. O'Connell; K. Barr, J. Barr; E. Barr, P. Cunningham, T. Gorman; C. O'Hare, R. Boyle, N. Crossan. Subs: S. McCormack for Gorman, F. Brown for O'Connell.

1999

Crossmaglen Rangers—P. Hearty, M. Califf, D. Murtagh, C. Dooley, F. Shields, F. Bellew, J. Fitzpatrick, J. McEntee, A. Cunningham, C. Short, T. McEntee, O. McConville, J. McConville, G. Cummiskey, C. O'Neill. Subs: G. McShea for M. Califf, M. Moley for C. O'Neill.

Ballina Stephenites—J. Healy, K. Golden, J. Devenney, D. Leydon, B. Ruane, B. Heffernan, S. Sweeney, L. McHale, D. Brady, B. McStay, D. Coen, M. McGrath, G. Brady, P. McGarry, K. Lynn. Subs: L. Brady for D. Coen, C. Deacy for M. McGrath, P. McStay for B. McStay.

2000

Crossmaglen Rangers – P.Hearty, M.Califf, D.Murtagh, G.McShane, J.Fitzpatrick, F.Bellew, J.Donaldson, J.McEntee, A.Cunningham, C.Shortt, T.McEntee, O.McConville, J.McConville, G.Cumiskey, C.O'Neill. Sub – M.Moley for J.McConville.

Na Fianna – S.Gray, S.McGlinchey, B.Quinn, M.Foley, S.Connell, T.Lynch, P.McCarthy, S.Forde, K.McGeeney, M.Galvin, D.Farrell, K.Donnelly, D.Mackin, J.Sherlock, A.Shearer. Subs – D.Keegan for Forde, I.Foley for Shearer, N.O'Murchu for Foley.

2001

Crossmolina – B.Heffernan, S.Rochford, T.Nallen, C.Reilly, P.Gardiner, D.Mulligan, P.McAndrew, J.Nallen, M.Moyles, J.Keane, K.McDonald, E.Lavelle, P.McGuinness, L.Moffatt, J.Leonard. Subs – G.O'Malley for Leonard, T.Loftus for Keane.

Nemo Rangers – D.Heaphy, L.Kavanagh, N.Geary, I.Gibbons, K.Connolly, S.O'Brien, M.Cronin, D.Kavanagh, K.Cahill, S.O'Brien, L.O'Sullivan, D.Niblock, J.Kavanagh, C.Corkery, A.Cronin. Subs – J.P.O'Neill for Niblock, M.McCarthy for Cahill, A.Morgan for O'Sullivan.

2002

Ballinderry – M.Conlan, K.McGuckin, N.McCusker, J.Bell, P.Wilson, R.McGuckin, D.Crozier, S.Donnelly, B.McCusker, A.McGuckin, C.Gilligan, D.Conway, D.Bateson, E.Muldoon, G.Cassidy. Sub – M.Harney for B.McCusker.

Nemo Rangers – D.Heaphy, L.Kavanagh, Steven O'Brien, Sean O'Brien, G.Murphy, N.Geary, M.Cronin, K.Cahill, D.Kavanagh, D.Meighan, J.P.O'Neill, M.McCarthy, J.Kavanagh, C.Corkery, A.Cronin. Subs – S.Calnan for Meighan, L.O'Sullivan for O'Neill.

2003

Nemo Rangers – D.Heaphy, L.Kavanagh, N.Geary, Sean O'Brien, G.Murphy, M.Cronin, M.Daly, K.Cahill, D.Kavanagh, A.Cronin, Steven O'Brien, M.McCarthy, J.Kavanagh, C.Corkery, W.Morgan. Subs – P.Brophy for Geary, B.O'Regan for Cronin, D.Mehigan for D.Kavanagh, J.P.O'Neill for Steven O'Brien.

Crossmolina – B.Heffernan, S.Rochford, T.Nallen, C.Reilly, P.Gardiner, D.Mulligan, G.O'Malley, G.Walsh, J.Nallen, M.Moyles, C.McDonald, E.Lavelle, L.Moffatt, J.Keane, P.McGuinness. Subs – J.Leonard for Lavelle, P.McAndrew for O'Malley.

2004

Caltra – K.Kilroy, J.Murray, E.Meehan, B.Kilroy, D.Meehan, K.Gavin, O.Kelly, T.Meehan, D.Cunniffe, J.Galvin, B.Laffey, M.Killilea, M.Meehan, N.Meehan, S.Hogan. Subs – C.Kilroy for Laffey, O.Hennelly for Hogan.

An Ghaeltacht – P.Ó hEalaithe, D.MacGearailt, S.MacSithigh, M.Ó Sé, R.Ó Flatharta, T.Ó Sé, B.Breathnach, D.Ó Sé, P.Ó

Cuinn, C.Ó Dubhda, R. MacGearailt, T.Conchúir, C.Ó Cruadhlaoich, D.Ó Cinnéide, A.MacGearailt. Subs – M.MacGearailt for Ó Cruadhlaoich, F.Ó Sé for MacSithigh.

2005

Ballina – J.Healy, J.Devenney, M.Wynne, C.Leonard, B.Ruane, S.Sweeney, S.Melia, R.McGarrity, D.Brady, P.Harte, G.Brady, E.Casey, P.McGarry, L.Brady, S.Hughes. Subs – P.McHale for Melia, E.Devenney for McGarry, A.Tighe for Leonard.

Portlaoise – M.Nolan, T.Fitzgerald, C.Byrne, E.Bland, B.Mulligan, C.Healy, A.Fennelly, M.Delaney, K.Fitzpatrick, B.McCormack, I.Fitzgerald, C.Rogers, P.McNulty, C.Parkinson, B.Fitzgerald. Sub – M.Fennelly for Delaney.

2006

Salthill-Knocknacarra – C.McGinley, R.McTiernan, F.Hanley, C.Begley, M.O'Connell, G.Morley, B.Geraghty, M.Sheridan, B.Dooney, A.Kerins, M.Donnellan, S.Rabbitte, S.Crowe, J.Boylan, S.Armstrong. Subs – A.Callanan for Boylan, D.Burke for Kerins, P.J.Kelly for Callanan, F.McCann for Crowe, A.McDermott for Geraghty.

St.Gall's – R.Gallagher, S.Kennedy, Kieran McGourty, C.Brady, A.Healey, G.McGirr, S.Kelly, M.McCrory, C.McCrossan, P.Gribbin, S.Burns, A.Gallagher, K.Stewart, Kevin McGourty, K.Niblock. Subs – A.McLean for McCrossan, T.O'Neill for Stewart, C.McGourty for Kieran McGourty.

2007

Crossmaglen Rangers – P.Hearty, S.McNamee, F.Bellew, P.Kernan, A.Kernan, J.Donaldson, B.McKeown, D.McKenna, T.McEntee, M.Ahern, J.McEntee, J.Murtagh, M.McNamee, J.Hanratty, O.McConville. Subs – S.Kernan for M.McNamee, S.Clarke for J.McEntee, C.Short for Ahern, A.Finnegan for S.McNamee.

Dr.Crokes – K.Cremin, K.McMahon, L.Quinn, M.Moloney, B.Moriarty, B.McMahon, E.Cavanagh, A.O'Donovan, E.Brosnan, B.Looney, S.Doolan, J.Fleming, C.Cooper, D.Moloney, K.O'Leary. Subs – J.Cahillane for B.McMahon, B.McMahon for Doolan, K.Brosnan for Looney.

*In the drawn encounter for Crossmaglen S.Clarke started for P.Kernan. Dr.Crokes started with the same fifteen. Subs in the drawn game were – Crossmaglen; S.Kernan for Aherne, P.Kernan for Clarke, C.Short for Hanratty, T.Kernan for McNamee. Dr.Crokes; J.Cahillane for McMahon, K.Brosnan for E.Brosnan V.Cooper for Doolan.

2008

St.Vincent's – M.Savage, P.Conlon, E.Brady, H.Gill, T.Doyle, G.Brennan, P.Kelly, H.Coughlan, M.O'Shea, K.Golden, T.Diamond, D.Connolly, B.Maloney, P.Gilroy, T.Quinn. Subs – R.Traynor for Gilroy, C.Brady for Coughlan, R.Fallon for Gill, W.Lowry for O'Shea.

Nemo Rangers – B.Morgan, N.Geary, D.Kavanagh, D.Breen, G.O'Shea, M.Cronin, B.O'Regan, P.Morgan, M.McCarthy, R.Kenny, D.Meighan, A.Cronin, D.Kearney, J.Masters, P.Kerrigan. Subs – S.O'Brien for Kenny, C.O'Brien for O'Shea, D.Niblock for P.Morgan, B.O'Driscoll for A.Cronin.

2009

Kilmacud Crokes – D.Nestor, Ross O'Carroll, Rory O'Carroll, K.Nolan, B.McGrath, P.Griffin, C.O'Sullivan, D.Magee, N.Corkery, L.Og O'hEineachainn, B.Kavanagh, A.Morrisey, M.Vaughan, M.Davoren, P.Burke. Subs – J.Magee for O'hEineachainn, R.Cosgrove for Kavanagh.

Crossmaglen Rangers – P.Hearty, B.McKeown, P.Kernan, P.McKeown, A.Kernan, F.Bellew, J.Donaldson, T.McEntee, D.McKenna, M.McEntee, J.McEntee, T.Kernan, J.Clarke, J.Murtagh, O.McConville. Subs – S.Kernan for M.McEntee, K.Carragher for Murtagh, S.Finnegan for B.McKeown, R.O'Kelly for Donaldson, C.Short for J.McEntee.

CAPTAINS OF WINNING ALL-IRELAND CLUB FOOTBALL TEAMS

1971—M. Gleeson (East Kerry)
1972—T. Scullion (Ballaghy)
1973—W. Morgan (Nemo Rangers)
1974—P. Kerr (U.C.D.)
1975—M. Carty (U.C.D.)
1976—T. Hanahoe (St. Vincent's)
1977—J. O'Keeffe (Austin Stacks)
1978—R. Bell (Thomond College)
1979—B. Murphy (Nemo Rangers)
1980—N. Aherne (St. Finbarr's)
1981—B. O'Brien (St. Finbarr's)
1982—C. Murphy (Nemo Rangers)
1983—L. Scully (Portlaoise)
1984—J. Kerrigan (Nemo Rangers)
1985—B. Lyons (Castleisland Desmonds)
1986—T. McGovern (Burren)
1987—J. Meyler (St. Finbarr's)
1988—V. McGovern (Burren)
1989—Tony Nation (Nemo Rangers)
1990—Brian Fitzpatrick (Baltinglass)
1991—John McGurk (Lavey)
1992—Seán O'Shea (Dr. Croke's)
1993—Mick McCarthy (O'Donovan Rossa)
1994—Steven O'Brien (Nemo Rangers)
1995—Mick Dillon (Kilmacud Crokes)
1996—Gerard Murphy (Laune Rangers)
1997—Jim McConville (Crossmaglen Rangers)
1998—Ray Silke (Corofin)
1999—John McEntee (Crossmaglen Rangers)
2000—A.Cunningham (Crossmaglen Rangers)
2001—T.Nallen (Crossmolina)

2002—A.McGuckin (Ballinderry)
2003—C.Corkery (Nemo Rangers)
2004—N.Meehan (Caltra)
2005—B.Ruane (Ballina)
2006—M.Sheridan (Salthill-Knocknacarra)
2007—O.McConville (Crossmaglen Rangers)
2008—T.Quinn (St.Vincent's)
2009—J.Magee (Kilmacud Crokes)

ALL-IRELAND CLUB FOOTBALL FINAL REFEREES

1971—Jimmy Hatton (Wicklow)
1972—D. Guerin (Dublin)
1973—Mick Spain (Offaly)
1974—Mick Spain (Offaly)
1975—P. J. McGrath (Mayo)
1976—Paddy Collins (Westmeath)
1977—Seamus Aldridge (Kildare)
1978—Seamus Aldridge (Kildare)
1979—Tommy Moran (Leitrim)
1980—Weeshy Fogarty (Kerry)
1981—Seamus Aldridge (Kildare)
1982—Tony Jordan (Dublin)
1983—John Moloney (Tipperary)
1984—Seamus Aldridge (Kildare)
1985—Pat Kavanagh (Meath)
1986—Mickey Kearns (Sligo)
1987—Michael Greenan (Cavan)
1988—D. Guerin (Dublin)
1989—Gerry McGlory (Antrim)
1990—Tommy Sugrue (Kerry)
1991—Tommy Howard (Kildare)
1992—T. McDermott (Cavan)
1993—Jimmy Curran (Tyrone)
1994—Pat Casserly (Westmeath)
1995—Paddy Russell (Tipperary)
1996—Pat McEneaney (Monaghan)
1997—Brian White (Wexford)
1998—Pat Casserly (Westmeath)
1999—John Bannon (Longford)
2000—M.Curley (Galway)
2001—J.Bannon (Longford)
2002—S.McCormack (Meath)
2003—B.Crowe (Cavan)
2004—M.Monahan (Kildare)
2005—B.Crowe (Cavan)
2006—D.Coldrick (Meath)
2007—S.Doyle (Wexford)
Replay—S.Doyle (Wexford)
2008—J.McQuillan (Cavan)
2009—G.Ó Conamha (Galway)

REPRESENTATIVE GAMES

1950—February 26, Croke Park. Ireland 1-12, Combined Universities 2-3
1951—March 4, Croke Park. Ireland 0-10, Combined Universities
1952—March 2, Croke Park. Ireland 2-4, Combined Universities 1-5
1953—March 1, Croke Park. Ireland 4-10, Combined Universities
1954—March 7, Croke Park. Combined Universities 2-8, Ireland 1-8.
1955—March 6, Croke Park. Ireland 1-10, Combined Universities 2-5
1956—March 18, Croke Park. Ireland 2-14, Combined Universities 3-10
1957—March 18, Croke Park. Ireland 3-10, Combined Univsities 3-6
1958—May 4, Croke Park. Combined Universities 0-12, Ireland 0-10
1959—Not played because of re-construction work at Croke Park.
1960—March 20, Croke Park. Ireland 4-5, Combined Universities 3-2
1961—March 12, Croke Park. Combined Universities 2-10, The Army 1-7
1962—March 18, Croke Park. Combined Universities 1-8, Ireland 1-6
1963—March 24, Croke Park. Kerry (All-Ireland Champions) 4-7, Combined Universities 1-7

1950

Ireland—K. Smyth (Meath), J. Bell (Louth), P. O'Brien (Meath), S. Flanagan (Mayo), J. Lyne (Kerry), W. Goodison (Wexford), S. Quinn (Armagh), C. McGrath (Cork), W. McCorry (Armagh), A. Tighe (Cavan), B. Smyth (Meath), V. Sherlock (Cavan), N. Crowley (Clare), P. O'Donohoe (Cavan), B. Garvey (Kerry).

Combined Vniversities—M. O'Malley (UCG), N. Redmond (UCD), W. McQuillan (UCG), J. O'Brien (UCD), P. J. Duke (UCD), P. O'Neill (QUB), C. Garvey (UCG), P. Carney (UCD), W. Kenny (UCG), P. O'Regan (UCC), H. McKearney (UCD), J. Brosnan (UCC), T. L'Estrange (QUB), P. Solan (UCG), E. Carolan (UCD).

1951

Ireland—S. Thornton (Louth), J. Murphy (Kerry), P. O'Brien (Meath), S. Flanagan (Mayo), J. Lyne (Kerry), H. Dixon (Mayo), S. Quinn (Armagh), C. McGrath (Cork), E. Mongey (Mayo), A. Tighe (Cavan), M. Higgins (Cavan), J. McDonnell (Louth), B. Smyth (Meath), T. Langan (Mayo), E. Carolan (Cavan).

Combined Universities—M. O'Malley (UCG), P. Bernard (UCC), N. Redmond (UCD), D. Murphy (UCD), P. Markey (UCD), P. O'Neill (QUB), M. Gould (UCD), S. Purcell (UCG), J. Brosnan (UCC), N. Redmond (UCD), D. Murphy (UCD), P. Markey (UCD), P. O'Neill (QUB), M. Gould (UCD), S. Purcell (UCG), J. Brosnan (UCC), E. Devlin (UCD), H. McKearney (UCD), M. Brosnan (UCC), P. O'Regan (UCC), T. L'Estrange (QUB), P. Solan (UCG).

1952

Ireland—S. Wynne (Mayo), M. O'Brien (Meath), P. Prendergast (Mayo), S. Flanagan (Mayo), L. Lyne (Kerry), R. Beirne (Antrim); C. Hand (Meath), C. Duggan (Cork), E. Mongey (Mayo), S. Purcell (Galway), P. Carney (Mayo), P. Meegan (Meath), M. Flanagan (Mayo), T. Langan (Mayo), M. Higgins (Cavan).

Combined Universities—G. Stack (UCG), J.

O'Brien (UCC), M. Costello (UCG), D. Bernard (UCC), M. Gould (UCD), P. O'Neill (QUB), C. Garvey (UCG), E. Devlin (UCD), J. Galvin (UCC), J. Brosnan (UCC), H. McKearney (UCD), P. Sheehy (UCC), E. Carolan (UCD), T. L'Estrange (QUB), P. Solan (UCG).

1953

Ireland—S. Morris (Cavan), M. O'Brien (Meath), P. O'Brien (Meath), S. Flanagan (Mayo), P. Driscoll (Cork), G. O'Malley (Roscommon), J. Cronin (Kerry), P. Carney (Mayo), V. Sherlock (Cavan), S. Purcell (Galway), M. Higgins (Cavan), P. Meegan (Meath), O. Freaney (Dublin), T. Langan (Mayo), J. McDonnell (Louth).

Combined Universities—P. McGearty (UCD), I. Hanniffy (UCG), J. McArdle (UCD), C. Garvey (UCG), T. Hardy (UCD), S. Gallagher (QUB), K. Mussen (QUB), E. O'Donoghue (UCG), E. Devlin (UCD), J. Cunningham (QUB), R. Buckley (UCC), P. Sheehy (UCC), M. Walsh (QUB), P. Kearns (UCG), P. Brennan (DU).

1954

Combined Universities—A. Brady (UCD), M. Gould (UCD), D. Bernard (UCC), J. McKnight (UCD), T. Hardy (UCD), G. O'Malley (UCG), S. Murphy (UCD), E. Devlin (UCD), P. J. McElroy (UCD), J. Brosnan (UCC), P. Carolan (UCD), E. Donoghue (UCG), O. Freaney (UCD), P. Fenelon (UCD), K. Heffernan (DU).

Ireland—P. McGearty (Meath), E. Morgan (Armagh), T. Conlon (Louth), K. McConnell (Meath), P. Driscoll (Cork), M. O'Hanlon (Armagh), B. Lynch (Roscommon), I. O'Dowd (Sligo), D. Kelleher (Cork), T. Lyne (Kerry), J. J. Sheehan (Kerry), S. White (Louth), T. Langan (Mayo), A. O'Hagan (Armagh), I. Jones (Tyrone).

1955

Ireland—J. Mangan (Galway}, W. Casey (Mayo), P. O'Brien (Meath), D. Murphy (Kerry), P. Casey (Offaly), T. Dillon (Galway), N. Maher Dublin), M. McEvoy (Armagh), I. O'Dowd (Sligo), T. Lyne (Kerry), M. McDonnell (Meath), S. White (Louth), M. Grace (Meath), A. O'Hagan (Armagh), P. Sheehy (Kerry). Subs: J. Teggart (Tyrone) for Lyne, J. Mahon 1Galway) for O'Brien.

Combined Universities—O. R. O'Neill (UCG), J. McCabe (UCC), S. Purcell (UCG), J. McKnight (UCD), S. Murphy (UCD), D. Bernard (UCC), K. Swords (UCG), G. O'Malley (UCG), J. Nangle (UCC), J. Cunningham (QUB), K. Denvir (UCD), O. Freaney (UCD), J. O'Donovan (UCC), P. Carolan (UCD), K. Heffernan (DU). Subs J. McArdle (UCD) For McCabe, P. Kearns (UCG) for Nangle.

1956

Ireland—A. Brady (Roscommon), W. Casey (Mayo), P. Prendergast (Mayo), J. M. Palmer (Kerry), P. Casey (Offaly), J. Crowley (Dublin), E. Moriarty (Mayo), J. Dowling (Kerry), J. Nallen (Mayo), J. McKeever (Derry), M. McDonnell (Meath), T. Lyne (Kerry), D. Ferguson (Dublin), M. Murphy (Kerry), J. Boyle (Dublin). Subs: E. Ryan for Dowling, J. O'Shea for W. Casey.

Combined Universities—O. R. O'Neill (UCG), D. Murray (UCC), T. Lyons (UCD), J. McKnight (UCD), S. Murphy (UCD), J. Mahon (UCG), D. Bernard (UCC), G. O'Malley (UCG), J. McDonnell (UCD), P. Sheehy (UCC), S. Purcell (UCG), J. Cunningham (QUB), S. O'Donnell (UCC), O. Freaney (UCD), K. Heffernan (DU).

1957

Ireland—J. Mangan (Galway), P. Driscoll (Cork), J. Devlin (Tyrone), T. Dillon (Galway), P. Harrington (Cork), J. Rice (Monaghan), G. O'Reilly (Wicklow), S. Moore (Cork), F. Evers (Galway), J. McKeever (Derry), L. McCormack (Kildare), P. McGarty (Leitrim), D. Ferguson (Dublin), F. Stockwell (Galway), D. Kelleher (Cork). Sub: N. Fitzgerald (Cork) for McCormack.

Combined Universities—J. O'Neill (QUB), C. Mallon (QUB), T. Lyons (UCD), C. O'Toole (UCG), S. Murphy (UCD), J. Ryan (UCD), D. Murray (UCG), G. O'Malley (UCG), J. McDonnell (UCD), E. Devlin (UCD), S. Purcell (UCG), M. Stewart (UCG), M. Moroney (UCC), F. Higgins (QUB), K. Keffernan (DU).

1958

Combined Universities—J. O'Neill (QUB), D. Murray (UCC), J. Ryan (UCD), T. Lyons (UCD), S. Murphy (UCD, capt.), J. Mahon (UCG), J. McDonnell (UCD), G. O'Malley (UCG), S. Moore (UCC), H. O'Kane (QUB), S. Purcell (UCG), M. O'Connell (UCC), J. Brady (UCD), K. Heffernan (DU), P. Sheehy (UCC).

Ireland—T. Turbett (Tyrone), P. Driscoll (Cork), T. Conlon (Louth), T. Dillon (Galway), M. Greally (Galway), P. Nolan (Offaly), S. White (Louth), J. McKeever (Derry), E. Ryan (Cork), K. Beahan (Louth), J. Nallen (Mayo), P. McGarty (Leitrim), D. O'Brien (Louth, capt.), F. Stockwell (Galway), F. Donnelly (Tyrone). Sub: J. Boyle (Dublin) for Stockwell.

1960

Ireland—A. Brady (Roscommon), W. Casey (Mayo), G. Hughes (Offaly), P. Rice (Down), K. Mussen (Down), C. O'Leary (Dublin), M. O'Dwyer (Kerry), F. Evers (Galway), D. Foley (Dublin), J. McKeever (Derry), T. Long (Kerry), J. Kenna (Loois), D. McAuliffe (Kerry), J. Joyce (Dublin), C. Flynn (Leitrim).

Combined Universities—J. O'Neill (QUB), F. McKnight (UCD), N. Sheehy (UCC), M. Brewster (QUB), L. O'Neill (QUB), J. Mahon (UCG), E. Curley (UCG), M. O'Connell (UCC), J. McDonnell (UCD), S. O'Neill (QUB), G. O'Malley (UCG), P. Sheehy (UCC), C. Gallagher (UCD), J. Brady (UCD), K. Heffernan (DU). Sub: J. Healy (UCC) for Mahon.

1961

Combined Universities—J. Boyle (QUB), B. O'Callaghan (UCC), F. McKnight (UCD), S.

Murray (UCD), M. Laide (UCG), B. Donaghy (QUB), M. Newell (UCG), G. Glynn (UCG), F. O'Leary (UCD), P. Donnellan (UCG), P. Kelly (UCD), D. Feely (UCG), D. Geaney (UCG), S. Donnelly (UCG), A. Kenny (UCG). Sub: J. Healy (UCD) for O'Leary.

The Army—R. Bennett (CTC), P. McCaffrey (Air Corps), D. Flood (Western), B. Kavanagh (CTC), B. Bardon (AC), J. Harold (Eastern), C. Wrenn (AC), C. O'Leary (Eastern), M. Coughlan (AC), S. Kilgannon (Western), P. Daly (CTC), T. Gunn (Western), N. Fitzgerald (Southern), S. O'Keeffe (AC), H. Donnelly (AC). Sub: C. Leaney (CTC) for Kilgannon.

1962

Combined Universities—J. Finn (UCD), B. O'Callaghan (UCC), F. McKnight (UCD), S. Murray (UCD), K. O'Neill (UCD), G. O'Malley (UCD), M. Newell (UCG), J. McDonnell (UCD), G. B. McDermott (UCG), S. O'Neill (QUB), B. Geraghty (UCG), P. Kelly (UCD), G. Kane (UCD), S. Donnelly (USG), D. Geaney (UCC).

Ireland—J. Culloty (Kerry), J. Lynch (Roscommon), L. Murphy (Down), P. McCormack (Offaly), M. Dwyer (Kerry), D. McCartan (Down), P. Doherty (Down), S. Brereton (Offaly), J. Timmons (Dublin), B. Morgan (Down). Subs: J. Whan (Armagh), E. McCarthy (Cork).

1963

Kerry—J. Culloty, P. O'Donoghue, N. Sheehy, T. Lyons, J. J. Barrett, D. O'Sullivan, J. O'Driscoll, S. Murphy, J. O'Riordan, B. O'Callaghan, S. Roche, W. Doran, T. Long, P. Ahearn.

Combined Universities—S. Gannon (UCG), B. O'Callaghan (UCC), H. McGonigle (UCG), H. Toner (QUB), E. Colleran (UCG), K. Coffey (DU), M. Fleming (UCC), M. O'Shea (UCG), F. McFeeley (UCD), D. Philpott (UCC), E. McGuire (UCC), P. Donnellan (UCG), P. Harte (QUB), B. Brady (UCD), S. Donnelly (UCG).

O'BYRNE CUP FOOTBALL
(Leinster Football)

Kildare (8)—1962, 1968, 1970, 1973, 1976, 1982, 1989, 2003.
Meath (8)—1967, 1974, 1977, 1983, 1992, 2001, 2004, 2006.
Dublin (7)—1956, 1958, 1960, 1966, 1999, 2007, 2008.
Offaly (6)—1954, 1961, 1981, 1993, 1997, 1998.
Laois (5)—1978, 1987, 1991, 1994, 2005.
Wicklow (4)—1955, 1957, 1986, 1996.
Louth (4)—1963, 1980, 1990, 2009.
Westmeath (3)—1959, 1964, 1988.
Longford (2)—1965, 2000.
Wexford (1)—1995.
No competition: 1969, 1971, 1972, 1975, 1979, 1984, 1985.

DR. McKENNA CUP
(Ulster Football)

Monaghan (14)—1927, 1928, 1932, 1935, 1936, 1937, 1948, 1952, 1976, 1979, 1980, 1983, 1995, 2003.
Cavan (11)—1936, 1940, 1943, 1951, 1953, 1955, 1956, 1962, 1968, 1988, 2000.
Down (11)—1944, 1959, 1961, 1964, 1972, 1987, 1989, 1993, 1996, 1998, 2008.
Derry (10)—1947, 1954, 1958, 1960, 1969, 1970, 1971, 1974, 1993, 1999.
Armagh (9)—1929, 1931, 1938, 1939, 1949, 1950, 1986, 1990, 1994.
Tyrone (9)—1957, 1973, 1978, 1982, 1984, 2004, 2005, 2006, 2007.
Antrim (7)—1926, 1941, 1942, 1945, 1946, 1966, 1981.
Donegal (7)—1963, 1965, 1967, 1975, 1985, 1991, 2009.
Fermanagh (4)—1930, 1934, 1977, 1997.

DR. LAGAN CUP
(Ulster Football)

Derry (6)—1945, 1947, 1950, 1953, 1959, 1961.
Down (5)—1949, 1960, 1962, 1963, 1964.
Donegal (4)—1952, 1965, 1966, 1967.
Antrim (3)—1944, 1946, 1948.
Tyrone (3)—1943, 1957, 1958.
Armagh (3)—1954, 1955, 1956.
Monaghan (1)—1951.
(Discontinued)

RAILWAY SHIELD FINALS

1905—Limerick, 11 November. Leinster (Kildare) 1-8, Connacht (Mayo) 0-5
1906—Ennis, 17 February, 1907. Munster (Kerry) 2-10, Connacht (Roscommon) 2-2
1907—Tipperary, 22 September. Munster (Kerry), 1-7, Leinster (Selected) 1-6. (Munster won outright 1907)

GROUNDS TOURNAMENT
(1961-1973)

1961—Tullamore, October 3. Offaly 2-12, Kerry 1-7
Belfast, October 3. Down 0-11, Roscommon 0-7
Croke Park, October 29. Final: Offaly 0-11, Down O-8
1962—Croke Park, October 7. Dublin 0-8, Roscommon 0-7
Croke Park, October 7. Kerry 2-7, Cavan 1-10 (draw)
October 21. Kerry 5-4, Cavan 1-10 (replay)
Croke Park, November 4. Final: Kerry 0-14, Dublin 0-7
1963—Croke Park, October 13. Dublin 1-12, Kerry 2-7
Croke Park, October 13. Galway 0-10, Down 0-8
Croke Park, November 3. Final: Dublin 2-10, Galway 0-8

1964—Croke Park, October 11. Galway 3-10, Cavan 0-9
Croke Park, October 11. Meath 2-7, Cork 0-7 (Meath withdrew and were replaced by Dublin in final)
Croke Park, November 8. Final: Galway 0-13, Dublin 0-10
1965—Croke Park, October 24. Down 0-11, Kerry 1-7
Croke Park, October 24. Galway 2-11, Dublin 1-6
Croke Park, November 7. Final: Down 3-10, Galway 0-7
1966—Croke Park, October 24. Cork 1-14, Meath 1-11
Croke Park, October 24. Galway 2-15, Down 0-10
Croke Park, November 7. Final: Galway 0-15, Cork 1-6
1967—Croke Park, October 22. Mayo 2-9, Cork 1-8
Croke Park, October 22. Cavan 2-8, Meath 1-11 (draw)
November 5. Cavan 1-8, Meath 2-4 (replay)
Croke Park, May 19, 1968. Final: Mayo 1-10, Cavan 1-7
1968—Croke Park, October 6. Galway 2-12, Kerry 1-14.
Croke Park, October 6. Longford 3-9, Down 1-12
Croke Park, November 18. Final: Galway 2-8, Longford 0-7
1969—Croke Park, October 12. Kerry 3-15, Cavan 0-8
Croke Park, October 12. Offaly 2-7, Mayo 0-13 (draw)
Croke Park, October 26. Offaly 3-9, Mayo 2-7 (replay)
Croke Park, November 30. Final: Kerry 2-17, Offaly 1-9
1970—Croke Park, October 11. Derry 2-13, Meath 1-7
Croke Park, October 25. Kerry 3-9, Galway 0-11
Croke Park, November 8. Final:
Kerry 2-6, Derry 1-8
1971—Croke Park, October 24.
Offaly 1-12, Down 0-8
Croke Park, October 24. Galway 2-15, Cork 1-6
Croke Park, November 7. Final:
Offaly 5-7, Galway 1-7
1972—Croke Park, October 22.
Donegal 1-12, Roscommon 1-11
(Offaly qualified by their All-Ireland win over Kerry)
Croke Park, November 5. Final:
Offaly 4-11, Donegal 0-7
1973—Croke Park, November 3.
Offaly 1-8, Cork 0-8
Croke Park, November 4.
Tyrone 0-12, Galway 1-6
Croke Park, November 18. Final:
Offaly 3-9, Tyrone 2-6
(Suspended)

CROKE CUP FINALS
(1896-1915)

1896—Jones's Road, June 1, 1897.
Dublin 0-4, Tipperary 0-3
1897—Jones's Road, May 28, 1899.
Wexford 1-11, Cork 0-2
1898-1901—Cup presented to All-Ireland winners
1902—Jones's Road, February 19, 1905.
Tipperary 0-5, London 0-2
1903—Jones's Road, April 1,1906.
Kildare 1-9, Mayo 0-0
1904-1905—None
1906—Ennis, November 17, 1907.
Kerry 2-6, Mayo 2-3
1907—Jones's Road, November 22, 1908.
Mayo 1-8, Kerry 0-5
1908—Athlone, August 29, 1909.
Kildare 0-7, Mayo 0-4
1909—Limerick, November 14.
Mayo 1-8, Waterford 0-5
1910—Cork, April 23, 1911.
Cork 3-3, Galway 0-1
1911—Jones's Road, May 26, 1912.
Meath 1-4, Waterford 0-3
1912—Jones's Road, February 12, 1913.
Dublin 3-4, Clare 0-1
1913—Croke Park, June 28, 1914.
Louth 2-2, Cork 1-1
1914—Croke Park, February 28, 1915.
Cork 2-1, Louth 0-3
1915—Athlone, April 9, 1916.
Dublin 1-8, Roscommon 2-1

G.A.A. ALL-STAR FOOTBALL TEAMS

1971—P. J. Smyth (Galway); Johnny Carey (Mayo), Jack Cosgrove (Galway), Donie O'Sullivan (Kerry); Eugene Mulligan (Offaly), Nicholas Clavin (Offaly), Pat Reynolds (Meath); Liam Sammon (Galway), Willie Bryan (Offaly); Tony McTague (Offaly), Ray Cummins (Cork), Mickey Kearns (Sligo); Andy McCallin (Antrim), Seán O'Neill (Down), Seamus Leydon (Galway).

1972—Martin Furlong (Offaly); Mick Ryan (Offaly), Paddy McCormack (Offaly), Donie O'Sullivan (Kerry); Brian McEniff (Donegal), Tommy Joe Gilmore (Galway), Kevin Jer O'Sullivan (Cork); Willie Bryan (Offaly), Mick O'Connell (Kerry); Johnny Cooney (Offaly), Kevin Kilmurray (Offaly), Tony McTague (Offaly); Mickey Freyne (Roscommon), Seán O'Neill (Down), Paddy Moriarty (Armagh).

1973—Billy Morgan (Cork); Frank Cogan (Cork), Mick Ryan (Offaly), Brian Murphy (Cork); Liam O'Neill (Galway), Tommy Joe Gilmore (Galway), Kevin Jer O'Sullivan (Cork); John O'Keeffe (Kerry), Denis Long (Cork); Johnny Cooney (Offaly), Kevin Kilmurray (Offaly), Liam Sammon (Galway); Jimmy Barry Murphy (Cork), Ray Cummins (Cork), Anthony McGurk (Derry).

1974—Paddy Cullen (Dublin); Donal

Monaghan (Donegal), Seán Doherty (Dublin), Robbie Kelleher (Dublin); Paddy Reilly (Dublin), Barnes Murphy (Sligo), Johnny Hughes (Galway); Dermot Earley (Roscommon), Paud Lynch (Kerry); Tom Naughton (Galway), Declan Barron (Cork), David Hickey (Dublin); Jimmy Barry Murphy (Cork), Jimmy Keaveney (Dublin), Johnny Tobin (Galway).

1975—Paud O'Mahony (Kerry); Gay O'Driscoll (Dublin), John O'Keeffe (Kerry), Robbie Kelleher (Dublin); Peter Stevenson (Derry), Anthony McGurk (Derry), Ger Power (Kerry); Denis Long (Cork), Colm McAlarney (Down); Gerry McElhinney (Derry), Ken Rennicks (Meath), Mickey O'Sullivan (Kerry); John Egan (Kerry), Matt Kerrigan (Meath), Anton O'Toole (Dublin).

1976—Paddy Cullen (Dublin); Ger O'Keeffe (Kerry), John O'Keeffe (Kerry), Brian Murphy (Cork); Johnny Hughes (Galway), Kevin Moran (Dublin), Ger Power (Kerry); Brian Mullins (Dublin), Dave McCarthy (Cork); Anton O'Toole (Dublin), Tony Hanahoe (Dublin), David Hickey (Dublin); Bobby Doyle (Dublin), Mike Sheehy (Kerry), Pat Spillane (Kerry).

1977—Paddy Cullen (Dublin); Gay O'Driscoll (Dublin), Pat Lindsay (Roscommon), Robbie Kelleher (Dublin); Tommy Drumm (Dublin), Paddy Moriarty (Armagh), Pat O'Neill (Dublin); Brian Mullins (Dublin), Joe Kernan (Armagh); Anton O'Toole (Dublin), Jimmy Smyth (Armagh), Pat Spillane (Kerry); Bobby Doyle (Dublin), Jimmy Keaveney (Dublin), John Egan (Kerry).

1978—Ollie Crinnigan (Kildare); Harry Keegan (Roscommon), John O'Keeffe (Kerry), Robbie Kelleher (Dublin); Tommy Drumm (Dublin), Ollie Brady (Cavan), Paud Lynch (Kerry); Colm McAlarney (Down), Tomás Connor (Offaly); Ger Power (Kerry), Declan Barron (Cork), Pat Spillane (Kerry); Mike Sheehy (Kerry), Jimmy Keaveney (Dublin), John Egan (Kerry).

1979—Paddy Cullen (Dublin); Eugene Hughes (Monaghan), John O'Keeffe (Kerry), Tom Heneghan (Roscommon); Tommy Drumm (Dublin), Tim Kennelly (Kerry), Danny Murray (Roscommon); Dermot Earley (Roscommon), Bernard Brogan (Dublin); Ger Power (Kerry), Seán Walsh (Kerry), Pat Spillane (Kerry); Mike Sheehy (Kerry), Seán Lowry (Offaly}, Joe McGrath (Mayo).

1980—Charlie Nelligan (Kerry); Harry Keegan (Roscommon), Kevin Kehily (Cork), Gerry Connellan (Roscommon); Kevin McCabe (Tyrone), Tim Kennelly (Kerry), Danny Murray (Roscommon); Jack O'Shea (Kerry), Colm McKinstry (Armagh); Ger Power (Kerry), Denis Allen (Cork), Pat Spillane (Kerry); Matt Connor (Offaly), Eoin Liston (Kerry), John Egan (Kerry).

1981—Martin Furlong (Offaly); Jimmy Deenihan (Kerry), Paddy Kennedy (Down), Paud Lynch (Kerry); Páidí Ó Sé (Kerry), Richie Connor (Offaly), Seamus McHugh (Galway); Jack O'Shea (Kerry), Seán Walsh (Kerry); Barry Brennan (Galway), Denis "Ogie" Moran (Kerry), Pat Spillane (Kerry); Mike Sheehy (Kerry), Eoin Liston (Kerry), Brendan Lowry (Offaly).

1982—Martin Furlong (Offaly); Mick Fitzgerald (Offaly), Liam Connor (Offaly), Kevin Kehily (Cork); Páidí Ó Sé (Kerry), Seán Lowry (Offaly), Liam Currams (Offaly); Jack O'Shea (Kerry), Padraig Dunne (Offaly); Peter McGinnity (Fermanagh), Joe Kernan (Armagh), Matt Connor (Offaly); Mike Sheehy (Kerry), Eoin Liston (Kerry), John Egan (Kerry).

1983—Martin Furlong (Offaly); Páidí Ó Sé (Kerry), Stephen Kinneavy (Galway), John Evans (Cork); Pat Canavan (Dublin), Tommy Drumm (Dublin), Jimmy Kerrigan (Cork); Jack O'Shea (Kerry), Liam Austin (Down); Barney Rock (Dublin), Matt Connor (Offaly), Greg Blaney (Down); Martin McHugh (Donegal), Colm O'Rourke (Meath), Joe McNally (Dublin).

1984—John O'Leary (Dublin); Páidí Ó Sé (Kerry), Mick Lyons (Meath), Seamus McHugh (Galway); Tommy Doyle (Kerry), Tom Spillane (Kerry), P. J. Buckley (Dublin); Jack O'Shea (Kerry), Eugene McKenna (Tyrone); Barney Rock (Dublin), Eoin Liston (Kerry), Pat Spillane (Kerry); Mike Sheehy (Kerry), Frank McGuigan (Tyrone), Dermot McNicholl (Derry).

1985—John O'Leary (Dublin); Páidí Ó Sé (Kerry), Gerry Hargan (Dublin), Mick Spillane (Kerry); Tommy Doyle (Kerry), Ciarán Murray (Monaghan), Dermot Flanagan (Mayo); Jack O'Shea (Kerry), Willie Joe Padden (Mayo); Barney Rock (Dublin), Tommy Conroy (Dublin), Pat Spillane (Kerry); Kevin McStay (Mayo), Paul Earley (Roscommon), Eugene Hughes (Monaghan).

1986—Charlie Nelligan (Kerry); Harry Keegan (Roscommon), Mick Lyons (Meath), John Lynch (Tyrone); Tommy Doyle (Kerry), Tom Spillane (Kerry), Colm Browne (Laois); Plunkett Donaghy (Tyrone), Liam Irwin (Laois); Ray McCarron (Monaghan), Eugene McKenna (Tyrone), Pat Spillane (Kerry); Mike Sheehy (Kerry), Damian O'Hagan (Tyrone), Ger Power (Kerry).

1987—John Kearns (Cork); Robbie O'Malley (Meath), Colman Corrigan (Cork), Tony Scullion (Derry); Niall Cahalane (Cork), Tom Spillane (Kerry), Ger Lynch (Kerry); Gerry McEntee (Meath), Brian McGilligan (Derry); David Beggy (Meath), Larry Tompkins (Cork), Kieran Duff (Dublin); Val Daly (Galway), Brian Stafford (Meath), Bernard Flynn (Meath).

1988—Paddy Linden (Monaghan); Bobby O'Malley (Meath), Colman Corrigan (Cork), Mick Kennedy (Dublin); Niall Cahalane (Cork), Noel McCaffrey (Dublin), Martin O'Connell (Meath); Shea Fahy (Cork), Liam Hayes (Meath); Maurice Fitzgerald (Kerry), Larry Tompkins (Cork), Kieran Duff (Dublin); Colm O'Rourke (Meath), Brian Stafford (Meath), Eugene Hughes (Monaghan).

1989—Gabriel Irwin (Mayo), Jimmy Browne (Mayo), Gerry Hargan (Dublin), Dermot Flanagan (Mayo); Connie Murphy (Kerry), Conor Counihan (Cork), Anthony Davis (Cork); Teddy McCarthy (Cork), Willie Joe Padden (Mayo); Dave Barry (Cork) Larry Tompkins (Cork), Noel Durkin (Mayo); Paul McGrath (Cork), Eugene McKenna (Tyrone), Tony McManus (Roscommon).

1990—John Kerins (Cork); Bobby O'Malley (Meath), Stephen O'Brien (Cork), Terry Ferguson (Meath); Michael Slocum (Cork), Conor Counihan (Cork), Martin O'Connell (Meath); Shea Fahy (Cork), Mickey Quinn (Leitrim); David Beggy (Meath), Val Daly (Galway), Joyce McMullan (Donegal); Paul McGrath (Cork), Kevin O'Brien (Wicklow), James McCartan (Down).

1991—Michael McQuillan (Meath); Mick Deegan (Dublin), Conor Deegan (Down), Enon Gavin (Roscommon); Tommy Carr (Dublin), Keith Barr (Dublin), Martin O'Connell (Meath); Barry Breen (Down), Martin Lynch (Kildare); Ross Carr (Down), Greg Blaney (Down), Tommy Dowd (Meath); Colm O'Rourke (Meath), Brian Stafford (Meath), Bernard Flynn (Meath).

1992—Gary Walsh (Donegal); Seamus Clancy (Clare), Matt Gallagher (Donegal), Tony Scullion (Derry); Paul Curran (Dublin), Martin Gavigan (Donegal), Eamonn Heery (Dublin); Anthony Molloy (Donegal), T. J. Kilgallon (Mayo); Anthony Tohill (Derry), Martin McHugh (Donegal), James McHugh (Donegal); Tony Boyle (Donegal), Vinny Murphy (Dublin), Enda Gormley (Derry).

1993—J. O'Leary (Dublin); J. J. Doherty (Donegal), D. Deasy (Dublin), T. Scullion (Derry); McGuirk (Derry), H. Downey (Derry), G. Coleman (Derry); A. Tohill (Derry), B. McGilligan (Derry); Kevin O'Neill (Mayo), Joe Kavanagh (Cork), C. Redmond (Dublin); C. Corkery (Cork), G. Houlihan (Armagh), E. Gormley (Derry).

1994—J. O'Leary (Dublin); M. Magill (Down), S. Quinn (Leitrim), P. Higgins (Down); G. Geraghty (Meath), S. O'Brien (Cork), D. J. Kane (Down); J. Sheedy (Dublin), G. McCartan (Down); Peter Canavan (Tyrone), G. Blayney (Down), J. McCartan (Down); M. Linden (Down), T. Dowd (Meath), C. Redmond (Dublin).

1995—J. O'Leary (Dublin); T. Scullion (Derry), M. O'Connor (Cork), F. Devlin (Tyrone); P. Curran (Dublin), K. Barr (Dublin), S. O'Brien (Cork); B. Stynes (Dublin), A. Tohill (Derry); J. Fallon (Galway), D. Farrell (Dublin), P. Clarke (Dublin); T. Dowd (Meath), Peter Canavan (Tyrone), C. Redmond (Dublin).

1996—F. McConnell (Tyrone); K. Mortimer (Mayo), D. Fay (Meath), M. O'Connell (Meath); P. Holmes (Mayo), J. Nallen (Mayo), P. Curran (Dublin); L. McHale (Mayo), J. McDermott (Meath); T. Giles (Meath), T. Dowd (Meath), J. Horan (Mayo); J. Brolly (Derry), Peter Canavan (Tyrone), M. Fitzgerald (Kerry).

1997—D. O'Keeffe (Kerry); K. Mortimer (Mayo), D. Dalton (Kildare), C. Daly (Offaly); S. Moynihan (Kerry), G. Ryan (Kildare), E. Breen (Kerry); P. Fallon (Mayo), N. Buckley (Kildare); P. Laide (Kerry), T. Giles (Meath), D. McCabe (Cavan); J. Brolly (Derry), B. Reilly (Meath), M. Fitzgerald (Kerry).

1998—M. McNamara (Galway), B. Lacey (Kildare), S. M. Lockhart (Derry), T. Mannion (Galway); J. Finn (Kildare), G. Ryan (Kildare), S. Óg de Paor (Galway); K. Walsh (Galway), J. McDermott (Meath), M. Donnellan (Galway), J. Fallon (Galway), D. Earley (Kildare); K. O'Dwyer (Kildare), P. Joyce (Galway), D. Browne (Tipperary).

1999 – Kevin O'Dwyer (Cork), Mark O'Reilly (Meath), Darren Fay (Meath), Anthony Lynch (Cork), Ciaran O'Sullivan (Cork), Kieran McGeeney (Armagh), Paddy Reynolds (Meath), John McDermott (Meath), Ciaran Whelan (Dublin), Diarmuid Marsden (Armagh), Trevor Giles (Meath), James Horan (Mayo), Philip Clifford (Cork), Graham Geraghty (Meath), Ollie Murphy (Meath).

2000 – Declan O'Keeffe (Kerry), Kieran McKeever (Derry), Seamus Moynihan (Kerry), Michael McCarthy (Kerry), Declan Meehan (Galway), Kieran McGeeney (Armagh), Anthony Rainbow (Kildare), Anthony Tohill (Derry), Darragh Ó Sé (Kerry), Michael Donnellan (Galway), Liam Hassett (Kerry), Oisín McConville (Armagh), Mike Frank Russell (Kerry), Padraig Joyce (Galway), Derek Savage (Galway).

2001 – Cormac Sullivan (Meath), Kieran Fitzgerald (Galway), Darren Fay (Meath), Coman Goggins (Dublin), Declan Meehan (Galway), Francie Grehan (Roscommon), Seán Óg de Paor (Galway), Kevin Walsh (Galway), Rory O'Connell (Westmeath), Evan Kelly (Meath), Stephen O'Neill (Tyrone), Michael Donnellan (Galway), Ollie Murphy (Meath), Padraig Joyce (Galway), John Crowley (Kerry).

2002 – Stephen Cluxton (Dublin), Enda McNulty (Armagh), Paddy Christie (Dublin), Anthony Lynch (Cork), Aidan O'Rourke (Armagh), Kieran McGeeney (Armagh), Kevin Cassidy (Donegal), Darragh Ó Sé (Kerry), Paul McGrane (Armagh), Steven McDonnell (Armagh), Eamonn O'Hara (Sligo), Oisín McConville (Armagh), Peter Canavan (Tyrone), Ray Cosgrove (Dublin), Colm Cooper (Kerry).

2003 – Fergal Byron (Laois), Francie Bellew (Armagh), Cormac McAnallen (Tyrone), Joe Higgins (Laois), Conor Gormley (Tyrone), Tom Kelly (Laois), Philip Jordan (Tyrone), Kevin Walsh (Galway), Sean Cavanagh (Tyrone), Brian Dooher (Tyrone), Brian McGuigan (Tyrone), Declan Browne (Tipperary), Steven McDonnell (Armagh), Peter Canavan (Tyrone), Adrian Sweeney (Donegal).

2004 – Diarmuid Murphy (Kerry), Tom O'Sullivan (Kerry), Barry Owens (Fermanagh), Michael McCarthy (Kerry), Tomas Ó Sé (Kerry), James Nallen (Mayo), John Keane (Westmeath), Martin McGrath (Fermanagh), Sean Cavanagh (Tyrone), Paul Galvin (Kerry), Ciaran McDonald (Mayo), Dessie Dolan (Westmeath), Colm Cooper (Kerry), Enda Muldoon (Derry), Matty Forde (Wexford).

2005 – Diarmuid Murphy (Kerry), Ryan McMenamin (Tyrone), Mike McCarthy (Kerry), Andy Mallon (Armagh), Tomas Ó Sé (Kerry), Conor Gormley (Tyrone), Philip Jordan (Tyrone), Sean Cavanagh (Tyrone), Paul McGrane (Armagh), Brian Dooher (Tyrone), Peter Canavan (Tyrone), Eoin Mulligan (Tyrone), Colm Cooper (Kerry), Stephen O'Neill (Tyrone), Steven McDonnell (Armagh).

2006 – Stephen Cluxton (Dublin), Marc Ó Sé (Kerry), Barry Owens (Fermanagh), Karl Lacey

(Donegal), Seamus Moynihan (Kerry), Ger Spillane (Cork), Aidan O'Mahony (Kerry), Darragh Ó Sé (Kerry), Nicholas Murphy (Cork), Paul Galvin (Kerry), Alan Brogan (Dublin), Alan Dillon (Mayo), Conor Mortimer (Mayo), Kieran Donaghy (Kerry), Ronan Clarke (Armagh).

2007 - Stephen Cluxton (Dublin), Marc Ó Sé (Kerry), Kevin McCloy (Derry), Graham Canty (Cork), Tomas Ó Sé (Kerry), Aidan O'Mahony (Kerry), Barry Cahill (Dublin), Ciaran Whelan (Dublin), Darragh Ó Sé (Kerry), Stephen Bray (Meath), Declan O'Sullivan (Kerry), Alan Brogan (Dublin), Colm Cooper (Kerry), Paddy Bradley (Derry), Thomas Freeman (Monaghan).

2008 – Gary Connaughton (Westmeath), Conor Gormley (Tyrone), Justin McMahon (Tyrone), John Keane (Westmeath), Davy Harte (Tyrone), Tomas Ó Sé (Kerry), Philip Jordan (Tyrone), Enda McGinley (Tyrone), Shane Ryan (Dublin), Brian Dooher (Tyrone), Declan O'Sullivan (Kerry), Sean Cavanagh (Tyrone), Colm Cooper (Kerry), Kieran Donaghy (Kerry), Ronan Clarke (Armagh).

2009 – Diarmuid Murphy (Kerry), Karl Lacey (Donegal), Michael Shields (Cork), Tom O'Sullivan (Kerry), Tomás Ó Sé (Kerry), Graham Canty (Cork), John Miskella (Cork), Dermot Earley (Kildare), Seamus Scanlon (Kerry), Paul Galvin (Kerry), Pearse O'Neill (Cork), Tadhg Kennelly (Kerry), Daniel Goulding (Cork), Declan O'Sullivan (Kerry), Stephen O'Neill (Tyrone).

LEADING AWARD WINNERS

Pat Spillane (Kerry) 9 – 1976-'81, 1984-'86.
Mike Sheehy (Kerry) 7 – 1976, 1978, 1979, 1981, 1982, 1984, 1986.
Jack O'Shea (Kerry) 6 – 1980-'85.
Ger Power (Kerry) 6 – 1975,1976,1978,1979, 1980, 1986.

ALL-TIME ALL-STAR AWARD WINNERS FOOTBALL

1980—Larry Stanley (Kildare).
1981—Tommy Murphy (Laois).
1982—Paddy Moclair (Mayo).
1983—Jim McCullogh (Armagh).
1984—John Dunne (Galway).
1985—J. J. (Purty) Landers and Tim (Roundy) Landers (Kerry).
1986—Alf Murray (Armagh).
1987—Mick Higgins (Cavan).
1988—Kevin Armstrong (Antrim).
1989—Peter McDermott (Meath).
1990—Eddie Boyle (Louth).
1991—Seán Purcell (Galway).
1992—Seán Flanagan (Mayo).
1993—Jimmy Murray (Roscommon).
1994—Bill Delaney (Laois).
Discontinued.

TEXACO FOOTBALLER OF THE YEAR AWARD

The following are the football stars who have been awarded Texaco Trophies by the Sports Editors since the inauguration of the award in 1958. Also listed are the Hall of Fame winners in football since the introduction of this category in 1960.

1958—Jim McKeever, Derry.
1959—Seán Murphy, Kerry.
1960—Jim McCartan, Down.
1961—Jim McCartan, Down.
1962—Mick O'Connell, Kerry.
1963—Lar Foley, Dublin.
1964—Noel Tierney, Galway.
1965—Martin Newell, Galway.
1966—Mattie McDonagh, Galway.
1967—Bertie Cunningham, Meath.
1968—Seán O'Neill, Down.
1969—Mick O'Dwyer, Kerry.
1970—Tom Prendergast, Kerry.
1971—Eugene Mulligan, Offaly.
1972—Willie Bryan, Offaly.
1973—Billy Morgan, Cork.
1974—Kevin Heffernan, Dublin (coach/manager).
1975—John O'Keeffe, Kerry.
1976—Jimmy Keaveney, Dublin.
1977—Jimmy Keaveney, Dublin.
1978—Pat Spillane, Kerry.
1979—Mike Sheehy, Kerry
1980—Jack O'Shea, Kerry.
1981—Jack O'Shea, Kerry.
1982—Martin Furlong, Offaly.
1983—Tommy Drumm, Dublin.
1984—Jack O'Shea, Kerry.
1985—Jack O'Shea, Kerry.
1986—Pat Spillane, Kerry.
1987—Brian Stafford, Meath.
1988—Bobby O'Malley, Meath.
1989—Teddy McCarthy, Cork.
1990—Shay Fahy, Cork.
1991—Colm O'Rourke, Meath.
1992—Martin McHugh, Donegal.
1993—Henry Downey, Derry.
1994—Mickey Linden, Down.
1995—Paul Curran, Dublin.
1996—Martin O'Connell, Meath.
1997—Maurice Fitzgerald, Kerry.
1998—Michael Donnellan, Galway.
1999—Trevor Giles, Meath.
2000—Seamus Moynihan, Kerry.
2001—Padraig Joyce, Galway.
2002—Kieran McGeeney, Armagh.
2003—Peter Canavan, Tyrone.
2004—Colm Cooper, Kerry.

2005—Stephen O'Neill, Tyrone.
2006—Kieran Donaghy, Kerry.
2007—Marc Ó Sé, Kerry.
2008—Seán Cavanagh, Tyrone.
2009—Paul Galvin, Kerry.

HALL OF FAME

1963—John Joe Sheehy (Kerry)
1970—Larry Stanley (Kildare)
1989—Mick Higgins (Cavan)
1992—John Doyle (Tipperary)
1998—Kevin Heffernan (Dublin)

In 1993 Jack Lynch (Cork) was given the Hall of Fame award under the heading Gaelic Sport as he had won five All-Ireland senior hurling medals with Cork (1941-'44 and '46) and one senior football medal in 1945.

ATTENDANCE FIGURES ALL-IRELAND FINALS

2009—Kerry v Cork	82,286
2008—Tyrone v Kerry	82,204
2007—Kerry v Cork	82,126
2006—Kerry v Mayo	82,289
2005—Tyrone v Kerry	82,112
2004—Kerry v Mayo	79,749
2003—Tyrone v Armagh	79,391
2002—Armagh v Kerry	79,500
2001—Galway v Meath	70,482
2001—Kerry v Galway (replay)	64,094
2000—Kerry v Galway	63,349
1999—Meath v Cork	62,989
1998—Galway v Kildare	65,886
1997—Kerry v Mayo	65,601
1996—Meath v Mayo (draw)	65,898
Meath v Mayo (replay)	65,802
1995—Dublin v Tyrone	65,983
1994—Down v Dublin	58,684
1993—Cork v Derry	64,500
1992—Donegal v Dublin	64,547
1991—Down v Meath	64,500
1990—Cork v Meath	65,723
1989—Cork v Mayo	65,519
1988—Meath v Cork (replay)	64,067
1988—Meath v Cork (drawn game) (all-ticket)	65,000
1987—Meath v Cork	68,431
1986—Kerry v Tyrone	68,628
1985—Kerry v Dublin	69,389
1984—Kerry v Dublin	68,365
1983—Dublin v Galway	71,988
1982—Offaly v. Kerry	62,309
1981—Kerry v Offaly	61,489
1980—Kerry v Roscommon	63,854
1979—Kerry v Dublin	72,185
1978—Kerry v Dublin	71,503
1977—Dublin v Armagh (all ticket)	66,542
1976—Dublin v Kerry (new record)	73,588
1975—Dublin v Kerry	66,346
1974—Dublin v Galway	71,898
1973—Cork v Galway	73,309
1972—Offaly v Kerry (record for replay)	66,136
1972—Offaly v. Kerry (drawn game)	72,032
1971—Offaly v Galway	70,798
1970—Kerry v. Meath	71,775
1969—Kerry v Offaly	67,828
1968—Down v Kerry	71,294
1967—Meath v Cork	70,343
1966—Galway v Meath	71,569
1965—Galway v Kerry	77,735
1964—Galway v Kerry	76,498
1963—Dublin v Galway	87,106
1962—Kerry v Roscommon	75,771
1961—Down v. Offaly	90,556
1960—Down v Kerry	87,768
1959—Kerry v Galway	85,897
1958—Dublin v Derry	73,371
1957—Louth v Cork	72,732
1956—Galway v Cork	70,772
1955—Kerry v Dublin	87,102
1954—Meath v Kerry	72,276
1953—Kerry v Armagh	86,155
1952—Cavan v Meath (replay)	62,515
1952—Cavan v Meath (draw)	60,020
1951—Mayo v Meath	78,201
1950—Mayo v Louth	76,174
1949—Meath v Cavan	79,460
1948—Cavan v Mayo	74,645
*1947—Cavan v Kerry	34,941
1946—Kerry v Roscommon	75,771
1945—Cork v Cavan	67,329
1944—Roscommon v Kerry	79,245
1943—Roscommon v Cavan (draw)	68,023
Roscommon v Cavan (replay)	47,193
1942—Dublin v Galway	37,105
1941—Kerry v Galway	45,512
1940—Kerry v Galway	60,824
1939—Kerry v Meath	46,828
1938—Galway v Kerry (draw)	68,950
Galway v Kerry (replay)	47,581
1937—Kerry v Cavan (draw)	52,325
Kerry v Cavan (replay)	51,234
1936—Mayo v Laois	50,168
1935—Cavan v Kildare	50,380
1934—Galway v Dublin	36,143
*1933—Galway v Cavan	45,188

*The 1933 figures set up a new record, the previous highest being an attendance of 43,839 at the 1929 final, in which Kerry defeated Kildare. The 1947 football final between Cavan and Kerry, was played in the Polo Grounds New York.

The attendance of 73,588 at the Dublin-Kerry game in 1976 was the highest at a final since the capacity of Croke Park was reduced with the installation of the seats under the old Cusack Stand in 1966 (the previous best for the altered Croke Park was set in 1973 when 73,308 saw the Cork-Galway final).

Note: The first Cusack Stand was officially opened on August 21, 1938 with 5,000 upperdeck seats. In 1996 seating for 9,000 was installed on the terraces underneath to form the lower deck. This reduced the capacity of Croke Park to 75,000. The first Hogan Stand (capacity 900) was opened in 1924 and replaced with the new structure which was officially opened on June 7, 1959, with accommodation for 16,000. The first phase of the modernisation of the stadium began in October 1993 with the demolition of the Cusack Stand. It was replaced with a 26,000 seater structure, the first in Irish sport to offer corporate boxes and premier seating; it was first in use on July 31, 1994, for the Leinster football final and was offically opened on June 5, 1996. Phase 2 of the re-development – a new stand at the Canal end of the ground – commenced in October 1998. This and the new Hogan Stand were officially opened in March 2003 and the redevelopment was completed in 2005 with the opening of the new HIll 16. This brings the capacity to 83,000.

DUAL ALL-IRELAND SENIOR MEDALLISTS

W. J. Spain (Tipperary):
Hurling 1889. Football (Limerick) 1887.
Bill Mackessey (Cork):
Hurling 1903. Football 1911.
Pierce Grace (Kilkenny):
Hurling 1911, 1912, 1913. Football (Dublin) 1908.
Seán O'Kennedy (Wexford):
Hurling 1910. Football 1915-'17.
Paddy Mackey (Wexford):
Hurling 1910. Football 1915-'18.
Frank Burke (Kildare):
Hurling (Dublin) 1917, 1920. Football (Dublin) 1921 -'23.
Leonard McGrath (Galway):
Hurling 1923. Football 1925.
Jack Lynch (Cork):
Hurling 1941, 1942, 1943, 1944, 1946. Football 1945.
Derry Beckett (Cork):
Hurling 1942. Football 1945.
Ray Cummins (Cork):
Hurling 1970, 1976, 1977, 1978. Football 1973.
Denis Coughlan (Cork):
Hurling 1970 (sub), 1976, 1977, 1978. Football 1973.
Brian Murphy (Cork):
Hurling 1976, 1977, 1978. Football 1973.
Jimmy Barry Murphy (Cork):
Hurling 1976, 1977, 1978, 1984, 1986. Football 1973.
Liam Currams (Offaly):
Hurling 1981. Football 1982.
Teddy McCarthy (Cork):
Hurling 1986, 1990. Football 1989, 1990.
Denis Walsh (Cork):
Hurling 1986. Football 1989 (sub).
Paddy Healy (Cork):
Hurling 1944, 1946. Football 1945 (sub).
Teddy O'Brien (Cork):
Football 1973 (sub). Hurling 1976 (sub).

N.B.: Teddy McCarthy is the only player to win two senior All-Ireland medals in the same year. That record was achieved in 1990 when he was on the victorious Cork hurling and football teams.

COLLEGES
Records

COLLEGES

ALL-IRELAND CHAMPIONSHIPS

HURLING

ROLL OF HONOUR 1944-2009

St. Kieran's, Kilkenny (16)—1948, 1957, 1959, 1961, 1965, 1971, 1975, 1988, 1989, 1990, 1992, 1993, 1996, 2000, 2003, 2004.
St. Flannan's, Ennis (14)—1944, 1945, 1946, 1947, 1958, 1976, 1979, 1982, 1983, 1987, 1991, 1998, 1999, 2005.
St. Finbarr's, Farranferris, Cork (5)—1963, 1969, 1972, 1974, 1984.
North Monastery, Cork (5)—1960, 1970, 1980, 1985, 1994.
St. Peter's, Wexford (4)—1962, 1967, 1968, 1973.
St. Colman's, Fermoy (4)—1977, 1997, 2001, 2002.
Limerick C.B.S. (2)—1964, 1966.
De La Salle, Waterford (2)—2007, 2008.
Kilkenny C.B.S. (1)—1981.
Templemore C.B.S. (1)—1978.
Birr Community School (1)—1986.
St. Raphael's, Loughrea (1)—1995.
Dublin Colleges (1)— 2006.
Thurles C.B.S. (1)— 2009.

Only Leinster and Munster took part, 1944-'48
1944—Thurles, April 23. Final: St. Flannan's (Ennis) 5-5; St. Kieran's (Kilkenny) 3-3.
1945—Croke Park, April 29. Final: St. Flannan's (Ennis) 7-10; St. Joseph's (Marino) 2-3.
1946—Croke Park, May 5. Final: St. Flannan's (Ennis) 5-7; O'Connell Schools (Dublin) 5-2.
1947—Thurles, May 4. Final: St. Flannan's (Ennis) 6-8; St. Joseph's (Roscrea) 3-1.
1948—Croke Park, May 2. Final: St. Kieran's (Kilkenny) 2-12; St. Colman's (Fermoy) 2-2.
1949-1956—Suspended .
1957—Galway, April 7. St. Flannan's (Ennis) 7-4; St. Mary's (Galway) 1-6.
Thurles, April 28. Final: St. Kieran's (Kilkenny) 4-2; St. Flannan's (Ennis) 2-7.
1958—Ennis, March 30. St. Flannan's (Ennis) 6-8; St. Joseph's (Galway) 1-3.
Thurles, April 27. Final: St. Flannan's (Ennis) 3-10; St. Kieran's (Kilkenny) 0-2.
1959—Birr, 15: St. Kieran's (Kilkenny) 8-7; St. Joseph's (Garbally) 6-5.
Thurles, April 19. Final: St. Kieran's (Kilkenny) 2-13; Tipperary C.B.S. 4-2.
1960—Croke Park, March 27. St. Peter's (Wexford) 4-4; St. Marys (Galway) 3-7 (draw).
Croke Park, April 10. St. Peter's (Wexford) 2-5; St. Marys (Galway) 1-4 (replay).
Croke Park—May 8. Final: North Mon. (Cork) 1-9; St. Peter's (Wexford) 1-4.
1961—Thurles, March 26. North Mon. (Cork) 1-8; St. Molaise's (Portumna) 1-1.
Thurles, April 23. Final: St. Kieran's (Kilkenny) 8-8; North Mon. (Cork) 1-4.
1962—Kilkenny, April 1: St. Peter's (Wexford) 4-8; St. Molaise's (Portumna) 1-3.
Thurles, April 15 Final: St. Peter's (Wexford) 0-10; Ennis C.B.S. 2-4 (draw).
Croke Park, May 6. St. Peter's (Wexford) 4-11; Ennis C.B.S. 2-4 (replay).
1963—Limerick, April 7. St. Finbarr's (Cork) 7-9; St. Mary's (Galway) 2-6.
Croke Park, May 5. Final: St. Finbarr's (Cork) 4-8; Ballyfin (Laois) 3-4.
1964—Croke Park, March 8. St. Peter's (Wexford) 8-7; St. Mac Nissis (Garrantower) 2-5.
Birr, April 12. Limerick C.B.S. 4-5; St. Mary's (Galway) 4-2.
Croke Park, April 25. Final: Limerick C.B.S. 6-7; St. Peter's 4-5.
1965—Croke Park, May 2. St. Kieran's (Kilkenny) 5-8; St. Mary's (Galway) 5-7.
Clonmel—May 16. Final: St. Kieran's (Kilkenny) 6-9; Limerick C.B.S. 6-1.
1966—Cavan, April 3. St. Mary's (Galway) 4-5; St. Mary's (Belfast) 1-5.
Nenagh, April 3. Limerick C.B.S. 8-9; St. Kieran's (Kilkenny) 3-9.
Birr, April 24. Final: Limerick C.B.S. 8-9; St. Mary's (Galway) 2-2.
1967—Croke Park, April 9. St. Peter's (Wexford) 7-12; St. Mary's (Belfast) 1-3.
Nenagh, 9 April. Limerick C.B.S. 5-9; St. Marys (Galway) 2-4.
Portlaoise, April 23. Final: St. Peter's (Wexford) 5-13; Limerick C.B.S. 5-13 (draw).
Croke Park, May 7. St. Peter's (Wexford) 5-11, Limerick C.B.S. 3-6 (replay).
1968—Portlaoise, April 7. St. Peter's (Wexford) 4-14; St. Joseph's (Garbally) 2-5.
Clonmel, May 12. Final: St. Peter's (Wexford) 4-3; Col. Chríost Rí (Cork) 3-6 (draw).
Croke Park, May 19. St. Peter's (Wexford) 5-10; Col. Chríost Rí (Cork) 4-5 (replay).
1969—Thurles, April 20. St. Finbarr's (Cork) 9-10; Our Lady's (Gort) 3-1.
Thurles, April 27. Final: St. Finbarr's (Cork) 5-15; St. Kieran's (Kilkenny) 2-1.
1970—Birr, March 22. Kilkenny C.B.S. 3-7; Presentation (Athenry) 1-9.
Dungarvan, April 26. Final: North Mon. (Cork) 2-13; Kilkenny C.B.S. 2-8
1971—Limerick, March 28. St. Finbarr's (Cork) 4-8; Presentation (Athenry) 2-6.
Thurles, May 9. Final: St. Kieran's (Kilkenny) 8-6; St. Finbarr's (Cork) 5-8.
1972—Nenagh, March 26. St. Kieran's (Kilkenny) 7-5; Our Lady's (Gort) 3-1.
Thurles, April 30. Final: St. Finbarr's (Cork) 3-7; St. Kieran's (Kilkenny) 2-5.
1973—Limerick, May 23. Our Lady's (Gort) 4-6; St. Finbarr's (Cork) 2-6.
Thurles, April 8. Final: St. Peter's (Wexford) 2-6; Our Lady's (Gort) 2-6 (draw).
Portlaoise, April 15. St. Peter's (Wexford) 4-15; Our Lady's (Gort) 1-5 (replay).
1974—Nenagh, April 7. St. Kieran's (Kilkenny) 5-

12; Our Lady's (Gort) 1-4.
Dungarvan, April 28. Final: St. Finbarr's (Cork) 2-11; St. Kieran's (Kilkenny) 1-12.
1975—Limerick, March 23. Col. Iognaid Ris (Cork) 8-10; Our Lady's (Gort) 5-2.
Thurles, April 20. Final: St. Kieran's (Kilkenny) 6-9; Col. Iognaid Ris 2-3.
1976—Nenagh, April 4. Presentation (Athenry) 2-11; Kilkenny C.B.S. 2-7.
Nenagh, May 2. Final: St. Flannan's (Ennis) 3-7; Presentation (Athenry) 4-4 (draw).
Nenagh, May 16. St. Flannan's (Ennis) 3-9; Presentation (Athenry) 1-7 (replay).
1977—Nenagh, April 3. St. Colman's (Fermoy) 2-10; Presentation (Athenry) 2-3.
Thurles, May 1. Final: St. Colman's (Fermoy) 2-13; St. Kieran's (Kilkenny) 1-9.
1978—Carlow, April 16. St. Peter's (Wexford) 1-9; Our Lady's (Gort) 0-4.
Kilkenny, May 7. Final: Templemore CBS 2-11; St. Peter's (Wexford) 1-4.
1979—Nenagh, March 21. St. Flannan's (Ennis) 4-15; St. Mary's (Galway) 1-1.
Thurles, April 29. Final: St. Flannan's (Ennis) 3-15; Presentation (Birr) 2-3.
1980—Roscrea, March 30. Birr Community School 0-7; St. Joseph's (Garbally) 1-4 (draw).
Thurles, April 6. Birr Community School 2-15; St. Joseph's (Garbally) 3-4 (replay).
Thurles, April 27. Final: North Mon. (Cork) 5-11; Birr Community 3-7.
1981—Thurles, April 13. North Mon. (Cork) 1-9; Our Lady's (Gort) 0-4.
Waterford, May 10. Final: Kilkenny C.B.S. 3-5; North Mon. (Cork) 1-8.
1982—Thurles, April 25. St. Peter's (Wexford) 1-18; Our Lady's (Gort) 1-9.
Thurles, May 9. Final: St. Flannan's (Ennis) 1-4; St. Peter's (Wexford) 1-4 (draw).
Thurles, May 16. St. Flannan's (Ennis) 2-9; St. Peter's (Wexford) 0-10 (replay).
1983—Cloughjordan, April 24. St. Flannan's (Ennis) 4-7; St. Joseph's (Garbally) 0-11.
Thurles, May 8. Final: St. Flannan's (Ennis) 0-16; Kilkenny C.B.S. 2-4.
1984—Birr, April 15: St. Kieran's (Kilkenny) 3-8; Our Lady's (Gort) 1-5.
Croke Park, May 6: Final: St. Finbarr's (Farrenferris) 1-15, St. Kieran's 0-8.
1985—Limerick, April 22: North Mon. (Cork) 2-11; St. Joseph's (Garbally) 0-7.
Portlaoise, May 12 Final: North Mon. (Cork) 2-7; Birr Community School 3-4 (draw).
Limerick, May 19. North Mon. (Cork) 4-11; Birr Community School 1-5 (replay).
1986—Tynagh, April 13. Birr Community School 2-10; St. Joseph's (Garbally) 1-5.
Portlaoise, April 27. Final: Birr C.S. 5-8; North Mon. (Cork) 1-8.
1987—Athenry, April 12: St. Flannan's (Ennis) 2-15; St. Joseph's (Garbally) 1-5.
Birr, May 10. Final: St. Flannan's (Ennis) 4-11; St. Kieran's (Kilkenny) 1-7.
1988—Portumna, April 24. St. Kieran's (Kilkenny) 3-8; St. Mary's (Galway) 0-4.
Waterford, May 8. Final: St. Kieran's (Kilkenny) 3-10; Midleton C.B.S. 2-7.
1989—Ballinsaloe, April 23. St. Flannan's (Ennis) 1-16, St. Mary's (Galway) 0-5.
Nenagh, May 7. Final: St. Kieran's (Kilkenny) 3-5, St. Flannan's (Ennis) 1-9.
1990—Birr, April 15: St. Kieran's (Kilkenny) 4-7; St. Mary's (Galway) 2-3.
Mitchelstown, May 6. Final: St. Kieran's (Kilkenny) 2-10; St. Flannan's (Ennis) 0-7.
1991—Whitegate, April 13. St. Flannan's (Ennis) 1-7; St. Raphael's (Loughrea) 0-9.
Thurles, April 27. Final: St. Flannan's (Ennis) 1-15; St. Kieran's (Kilkenny) 1-9.
1992—Trim, April 5: St. Colman's (Fermoy) 1-12; St. Patrick's (Maghera) 0-3.
Tullamore, April 12. St. Kieran's (Kilkenny) 4-13; St. Raphael's (Loughrea) 3-3.
Thurles, April 26. Final: St. Kieran's (Kilkenny) 1-7; St. Colman's (Fermoy) 0-8.
1993—Athboy, April 4. St. Kieran's (Kilkenny) 1-15; St. Patrick's (Maghera) 0-3.
Ennis, April 4. Our Lady's (Gort) 1-9; St. Michael's CBS (Limerick) 2-5.
Nenagh, April 25. Final: St. Kieran's (Kilkenny) 3-15; Our Lady's (Gort) 1-10.
1994—Nenagh, April 17. North Mon 1-16; Cross and Passion (Ballycastle) (after extra time).
Birr, April 17. St. Mary's (Galway) 3-13; St. Kieran's (Kilkenny) 1-16.
Nenagh, April 24. Final: North Mon 1-10; St. Mary's 1-6.
1995—Dungarvan, April 24. Midleton CBS 0-10; Good Counsel (New Ross) 0-5.
UCD, April 1. St. Raphael's (Loughrea) 3-27; Cross and Passion (Ballycastle) 0-2.
Limerick, April 30. Final: St. Raphael's (Loughrea) 3-10; Midleton CBS 3-5.
1996—Navan, March 31. St. Kieran's (Kilkenny) 0-18; St. Mary's (Belfast) 0-4.
Nenagh, March 31. St. Colman's (Fermoy) 1-15; St. Raphael's (Loughrea) 2-7.
Croke Park, April 28. Final: St. Kieran's (Kilkenny) 1-14; St. Colman's 2-6.
1997—Tullamore, April 13. St. Colman's (Fermoy) 4-18; St Mary's (Belfast) 1-6.
Nenagh, April 13. Good Counsel (New Ross) 4-10; St. Raphael's (Loughrea) 1-7.
Croke Park, April 27. Final: St. Colman's (Fermoy) 4-20, Good Counsel 0-9.
1998—Drogheda, April 5. St. Raphael's (Loughrea) 2-16; St. Mary's (Belfast) 0-5.
Thurles, April 5. St. Flannan's (Ennis) 1-8; Coláiste Eammain Rís (Callan) 1-6.
Croke Park, May 3. Final: St. Flannan's (Ennis) 2-16; St. Raphael's 1-11.
1999—Nenagh, March 27. St. Flannan's (Ennis) 2-16; Gort CS 0-10.
Parnell Park, March 28. St. Kieran's (Kilkenny) 3-

19; Ulster Colleges 0-6.
Croke Park, April 18. Final: St. Flannan's (Ennis) 2-15; St. Kieran's (Kilkenny) 2-10.
2000—Nenagh, April 2: St.Kieran's (Kilkenny) 2-14, Gort CC 0-11
Nenagh, April 16 Final: St.Kieran's (Kilkenny) 1-10, St.Flannan's (Ennis) 0-9.
2001—April 8: St.Colman's (Fermoy) 2-7, Dublin Colleges 1-5.
Croke Park, May 5, Final: St.Colman's (Fermoy) 2-10, Gort CS 2-7.
2002—St.Colman's (Fermoy) 4-15, Mercy College (Woodford) 0-5.
Thurles, April 28, Final: St.Colman's (Fermoy) 0-11, St.Kieran's (Kilkenny) 2-4.
2003—Boherlahan, April 7: St. Kieran's (Kilkenny) 2-20, Gort CS 0-4.
April 26, Final: St.Kieran's (Kilkenny) 1-15, St.Colman's (Fermoy) 1-4.
2004—The Ragg, April 4: St.Kieran's (Kilkenny) 0-17, St.Flannan's (Ennis) 1-8.
Final: St.Kieran's (Kilkenny) 3-20, St.Raphael's (Loughrea) 1-6.
2005—St.Kieran's (Kilkenny) 5-14, Thurles CBS 2-9.St.Flannan's (Ennis) 2-13, St.Brendan's CS (Birr) 1-14. St.Flannan's (Ennis) 2-15, St.Kieran's (Kilkenny) 2-12.
2006—Quarter-Final: St. Flannan's Ennis 1-16; Gort CC 0-12. Semi Finals: Dublin Colleges 1-13; Midleton CBS 0-10; St. Flannan's Ennis 1-11; Kilkenny CBS 0-13. Final: Dublin Colleges 1-11; St. Flannan's Ennis 0-1.
2007—Quarter-Final: Kilkenny CBS 2-12; St. Flannan's, Ennis 1-14. Semi Finals: Kilkenny CBS 0-19; Gort Cc 1-11; De La Salle Waterford 2-6; Castlecomer CS 1-7. Final: De La Salle Waterford 0-13; Kilkenny CBS 1-9.
2008 —Quarter Final: Thurles CBS 0-22; Kilkenny CBS 0-10. Semi Finals: Thurles CBS 0-12; Dublin Colleges 0-10; De La Salle Waterford 4-14; Gort CC 1-5. Final: De La Salle Waterford 2-12; Thurles CBS 1-15. Final Replay: De La Salle Waterford 2-9; Thurles CBS 2-8.
2009 —Quarter Final: Castlecomer CC 2-9; St. Caimins CS Shannon 1-9. Semi Finals: Thurles CBS 1-16; Castlecomer CC 0-9; Good Counsel, New Ross 1-12; Gort CC 0-11 Final: Thurles CBS 1-17; Good Counsel 1-15.

MUNSTER SENIOR HURLING

DR. HARTY CUP

ROLL OF HONOUR 1918-2009

St. Flannan's, Ennis (21); North Monastery, Cork (20); Limerick CBS (10); St. Colman's, Fermoy (9); St. Finbarr's, Farrenferris (7); Thurles CBS (7); Rockwell College (5); Midleton CBS (3); De La Salle, Waterford (2); Coláiste Chriost Rí, Cork (1); Coláiste Iognáid Rís, Cork (1); Ennis CBS (1); Mount Sion, Waterford (1); St. Munchin's Limerick (1); Tipperary CBS (1); Templemore CBS (1), St. Michael's CBS, Limerick (1).

1918—Rockwell College
1919—North Monastery, Cork
1920—Limerick C.B.S.
1921—None
1922—St. Munchin's, Limerick
1923—Rockwell College
1924—Rockwell College
1925—Limerick C.B.S.
1926—Limerick C.B.S.
1927—Limerick C.B.S.
1928—No Competition
1929—North Monastery, Cork
1930—Rockwell College
1931—Rockwell College
1932—Limerick C.B.S.
1933—Thurles C.B.S.
1934—North Monastery, Cork
1935—North Monastery, Cork
1936—North Monastery, Cork
1937—North Monastery, Cork
1938—Thurles C.B.S.
1939—Thurles C.B.S.
1940—North Monastery, Cork
1941—North Monastery, Cork
1942—North Monastery, Cork
1943—North Monastery, Cork
1944—St. Flannan's, Ennis
1945—St. Flannan's, Ennis
1946—St. Flannan's, Ennis
1947—St. Flannan's, Ennis
1948—St. Colman's, Fermoy
1949—St. Colman's, Fermoy
1950—Thurles C.B.S.
1951—Thurles C.B.S.
1952—St. Flannan's, Ennis
1953—Mount Sion, Waterford
1954—St. Flannan's, Ennis
1955—North Monastery, Cork
1956—Thurles C.B.S.
1957—St. Flannan's, Ennis
1958—St. Flannan's, Ennis
1959—Tipperary C.B.S.
1960—North Monastery, Cork
1961—North Monastery, Cork
1962—Ennis C.B.S.
1963—St. Finbarr's, Farranferris
1964—Limerick C.B.S.
1965—Limerick C.B.S.
1966—Limerick C.B.S.
1967—Limerick C.B.S.
1968—Col. Chríost Rí, Cork
1969—St. Finbarr's, Farranferris
1970—North Monastery, Cork
1971—St. Finbarr's, Farranferris
1972—St. Finbarr's, Farranferris
1973—St. Finbarr's, Farranferris
1974—St. Finbarr's, Farranferris
1975—Col. Iognaid Rís, Cork

1976—St. Flannan's, Ennis
1977—St. Coleman's, Fermoy
1978—Templemore C.B.S.
1979—St. Flannan's, Ennis
1980—North Monastery, Cork
1981—North Monastery, Cork
1982—St. Flannan's, Ennis
1983—St. Flannan's, Ennis
1984—St. Finbarr's, Farranferris
1985—North Monastery, Cork
1986—North Monastery, Cork
1987—St. Flannan's, Ennis
1988—Midleton C.B.S.
1989—St. Flannan's, Ennis
1990—St. Flannan's, Ennis
1991—St. Flannan's, Ennis
1992—St. Colman's, Fermoy
1993—St. Michael's CBS, Limerick
1994—North Monastery, Cork
1995—Midleton CBS, Cork
1996—St. Colman's, Fermoy
1997—St. Colman's, Fermoy
1998—St. Flannan's, Ennis
1999—St. Flannan's, Ennis
2000—St. Flannan's, Ennis
2001—St. Colman's, Fermoy
2002—St. Colman's, Fermoy
2003—St. Colman's, Fermoy
2004—St. Flannan's, Ennis
2005—St. Flannan's, Ennis
2006—Midleton CBS, Cork
2007—De La Salle, Waterford.
2008—De La Salle, Waterford.
2009—Thurles C.B.S.

LEINSTER SENIOR HURLING

ROLL OF HONOUR 1918-2009

St. Kieran's, Kilkenny (49); St. Peter's, Wexford (8); Kilkenny CBS (6); Mount St. Joseph's, Roscrea (4); St. Brendan's, Birr (formerly Presentation College, Birr to 1980 and Birr Community School) (4); Patrician College, Ballyfin (4); Good Counsel, New Ross (3); Coláiste Caoimghin, Dublin (2); O'Connell School, Dublin (2); Dublin Colleges (2); St. Joseph's, Marino, Dublin (1); Blackrock College, Dublin (1); Castleknock College, Dublin (1); Knockbeg College, Carlow (1); Coláiste Eamon Rís, Callan (1); Castlecomer CS (1).

1918—Castleknock College, Dublin
1919—No Competition
1920-'21—Mount St. Joseph's, Roscrea
1922—St. Kieran's, Kilkenny
1923—Mount St. Joseph's, Roscrea
1924—Mount St. Joseph's, Roscrea
1925—St. Kieran's, Kilkenny
1926—St. Kieran's, Kilkenny
1927—St. Kieran's, Kilkenny
1928—St. Kieran's, Kilkenny
1929—St. Kieran's, Kilkenny
1930—Col. Caoimhghin, Dublin
1931—St. Kieran's, Kilkenny
1932—St. Kieran's, Kilkenny
1933—St. Kieran's, Kilkenny
1934—Col. Caoimhghin, Dublin
1935—Blackrock College, Dublin
1936—Kilkenny C.B.S.
1937—St. Kieran's, Kilkenny
1938—St. Kieran's, Kilkenny
1939—St. Kieran's, Kilkenny
1940—St. Kieran's, Kilkenny
1941—St. Kieran's, Kilkenny
1942—Patrician College, Ballyfin
1943—St. Kieran's, Kilkenny
1944—St. Kieran's, Kilkenny
1945—St. Joseph's, Marino, Dublin
1946—O'Connell's School, Dublin
1947—Mount St. Joseph's, Roscrea
1948—St. Kieran's, Kilkenny
1949—St. Kieran's, Kilkenny
1950—St. Kieran's, Kilkenny
1951—St. Kieran's, Kilkenny
1952—Patrician College, Ballyfin
1953—St. Kieran's, Kilkenny
1954—O'Connell Schools, Dublin
1955—Knockbeg College, Carlow
1956—Patrician College, Ballyfin
1957—St. Kieran's, Kilkenny
1958—St. Kieran's, Kilkenny
1959—St. Kieran's, Kilkenny
1960—St. Peter's, Wexford
1961—St. Kieran's, Kilkenny
1962—St. Peter's, Wexford
1963—Patrician College, Ballyfin
1964—St. Peter's, Wexford
1965—St. Kieran's, Kilkenny
1966—St. Kieran's, Kilkenny
1967—St. Peter's, Wexford
1968—St. Peter's, Wexford
1969—St. Kieran's, Kilkenny
1970—Kilkenny C.B.S.
1971—St. Kieran's, Kilkenny
1972—St. Kieran's, Kilkenny
1973—St. Peter's, Wexford
1974—St. Kieran's, Kilkenny
1975—St. Kieran's, Kilkenny
1976—Kilkenny C.B.S.
1977—St. Kieran's, Kilkenny
1978—St. Peter's, Wexford
1979—Presentation, Birr
1980—Birr Community School
1981—Kilkenny C.B.S.
1982—St. Peter's, Wexford
1983—Kilkenny C.B.S.
1984—St. Kieran's, Kilkenny
1985—Birr Community School
1986—Birr Community School
1987—St. Kieran's, Kilkenny
1988—St. Kieran's, Kilkenny
1989—St. Kieran's, Kilkenny

1990—St. Kieran's, Kilkenny
1991—St. Kieran's, Kilkenny
1992—St. Kieran's, Kilkenny
1993—St. Kieran's, Kilkenny
1994—St. Kieran's, Kilkenny
1995—Good Counsel, New Ross
1996—St. Kieran's, Kilkenny
1997—Good Counsel, New Ross
1998—Coláiste Eamon Rís, Callan
1999—St. Kieran's, Kilkenny
2000—St. Kieran's, Kilkenny
2001—Dublin Colleges
2002—St. Kieran's, Kilkenny
2003—St. Kieran's, Kilkenny
2004—St. Kieran's, Kilkenny
2005—St. Kieran's, Kilkenny
2006—Kilkenny C.B.S.
2007—Castlecomer CS.
2008—Dublin Colleges
2009—Good Counsel, New Ross

CONNACHT SENIOR HURLING

ROLL OF HONOUR 1938-2009

St. Mary's, Galway (25); Gort Community School (formerly Our Lady's, Gort) (11); St. Joseph's, Garbally Park, Ballinsloe (7); St. Raphael's, Loughrea (7); Gort CC (5); Presentation, Athenry (4); Roscommon CBS (3); Gort CS (3); St. Molaise's, Portumna (2); De La Salle, Loughrea (1); St. Joseph's P.B.S. Galway (1); Mercy College (Woodford) (1).

1938—Roscommon C.B.S.
1939—Roscommon C.B.S.
1940—St. Mary's, Galway
1941—St. Mary's, Galway
1942—St. Mary's, Galway
1943-'45—None
1946—St. Mary's, Galway
1947—St. Mary's, Galway
1948—De La Salle, Loughrea
1949—St. Mary's, Galway
1950—St. Mary's, Galway
1951—St. Mary's, Galway
1952—St. Mary's, Galway
1953—St. Mary's, Galway
1954—St. Mary's, Galway
1955—St. Mary's, Galway
1956—St. Mary's, Galway
1957—St. Mary's, Galway
1958—St. Joseph's, Galway
1959—St. Joseph's, Gorbally
1960—St. Marys, Galway
1961—St. Molaises', Portumna
1962—St. Molaises', Portumna
1963—St. Mary's, Galway
1964—St. Mary's, Galway
1965—St. Mary's, Galway
1966—St. Mary's, Galway
1967—St. Mary's, Galway
1968—St. Joseph's, Garbally
1969—Our Ladys, Gort
1970—Presentation, Athenry
1971—Presentation, Athenry
1972—Our Lady's, Gort
1973—Our Lady's, Gort
1974—Our Lady's, Gort
1975—Our Lady's, Gort
1976—Presentation, Athenry
1977—Presentation, Athenry
1978—Our Lady's, Gort
1979—St. Mary's, Galway
1980—St. Joseph's, Garbally
1981—Our Ladys, Gort
1982—Our Ladys, Gort
1983—St. Joseph's, Garbally
1984—Our Ladys, Gort
1985—St. Joseph's, Garbally
1986—St. Joseph's, Garbally
1987—St. Joseph's, Garbally
1988—St. Mary's, Galway
1989—St. Mary's, Galway
1990—St. Mary's, Galway
1991—St. Raphael's, Loughrea
1992—St. Raphael's, Loughrea
1993—Our Lady's, Gort
1994—St. Mary's, Galway
1995—St. Raphael's, Loughrea
1996—St. Raphael's, Loughrea
1997—Presentation, Athenry
1998—St. Raphael's, Loughrea
1999—Gort C.S.
2000—Gort C.C.
2001—Gort C.S.
2002— Mercy College, Woodford
2003—Gort C.S.
2004—St. Raphael's, Loughrea
2005—
2006—Gort C.C.
2007—Gort C.C.
2008—Gort C.C.
2009—Gort C.C.

ALL-IRELAND CHAMPIONSHIPS

FOOTBALL

ROLL OF HONOUR 1946-2009

St. Jarlath's, Tuam (12)—1947, 1958, 1960, 1961, 1964, 1966, 1974, 1978, 1982, 1984, 1994, 2002.
St. Colman's, Newry (6)—1967, 1975, 1986, 1988, 1993, 1998.
St. Mel's, Longford (4)—1948, 1962, 1963, 1987.
Coláiste Chríost Ri, Cork (4)—1968, 1970, 1983, 1985.
St. Patrick's, Maghera (4)—1989, 1990, 1995, 2003.
Carmelite College, Moate (3)—1976, 1980, 1981.
St. Patrick's, Navan (3)—2000, 2001, 2004.

St. Brendan's, Killarney (2)—1969, 1992.
St. Patrick's, Dungannon (2)—1997, 2008.
Ard Scoil Ris, Dublin (1)—1979.
Franciscan College, Gormanston (1)—1973.
St. Columb's, Derry (1)—1965.
St. Colman 's, Claremorris (1)—1977.
St. Joseph's, Fairview, Dublin (1)—1959.
St. Mary's CBS, Belfast (1)—1971.
St. Patrick's, Armagh (1)—1946.
St. Patrick's, Cavan (1)—1972.
St. Nathy's, Ballaghaderreen (1)—1957.
St. Fachtna's, Skibbereen (1)—1991.
Intermediate School Killorglin (1)—1996.
Good Counsel, New Ross (1)—1999.
Knockbeg, Carlow (1)—2005.
Abbey CBS (1)—2006.
Omagh CBS (1)—2007.
Coláiste na Scéilge (1)—2009.

1946—Killarney, April 8. St. Jarlath's (Tuam) 2-14, St. Brendan's (Killarney) 2-4.
Cavan, April 8. St. Patrick's (Armagh) 3-7; St. Mel's (Longford) 2-7.
Croke Park, May 5. Final: St. Patrick's (Armagh) 3-11; St. Jarlath's (Tuam) 4-7
1947—Tuam, April 20. St. Jarath's (Tuam) 5-12; St. Brendan's (Killarney) 1-0.
Cavan, April 27. St. Patrick's (Armagh) 3-12; St. Mel's (Longford) 2-6.
Croke Park, May 11. Final: St. Jarlath's (Tuam) 4-10; St. Patrick's (Armagh) 3-8.
1948—Longford, April 18. St. Mel's (Longford) 1-7; Tralee C.B.S. 2-2.
Longford, April 18. St. Patrick's (Cavan) 2-15; Roscommon C.B.S. 0-6.
Croke Park, May 2. Final: St. Mel's (Longford) 4-7; St. Patrick's 3-3.
1949-1956—Suspended .
1957—Navan, March 31. St. Colman's (Newry) 5-4; Presentation (Ballyfin) 1-4.
Killarney, March 31. St. Nathy's (Ballaghadereen) 3-7; Coláiste losagáin (Ballyvourney) 0-4.
Croke Park, April 14. Final: St. Nathy's (Ballaghadereen) 1-7; St. Colman's 0-4.
1958—Croke Park, March 30. Franciscan College (Gormanston) 3-7; St. Colman's (Newry) 1-9.
Tuam, March 30. St. Jarlath's (Tuam) 0-9; De La Salle (Waterford) 1-4.
Croke Park, April 27. Final: St. Jarlath's (Tuam) 1-7; Franciscan College (Gormanston) 2-3.
1959—Sligo, March 22. St. Nathy's (Ballaghaderreen) 2-10; Abbey C.B.S. (Newry) 1-7.
Roscrea, March 22. St. Joseph's (Fairview) 1-7; St. Flannan's (Ennis) 0-7.
Croke Park, April 19. Final St. Joseph's (Fairview) 3-9; St. Nathy's (Ballaghaderreen) 2-8.
1960—Croke Park, April 10. St. Jarlath's (Tuam) 2-10; St. Colman's (Newry) 1-2.
Portlaoise, April 10: St. Finian's (Mullingar) 0-8; Limerick C.B.S. 0-7.
Athlone, May 1. Final: St. Jarlath's (Tuam) 3-10; St. Finian's, Mullingar 3-7.
1961—Croke Park, March 19: St. Mel's (Longford) 1-10; De La Salle (Waterford) 2-7 (draw).
Croke Park, March 26. St. Mel's (Longford) 1-14; De La Salle (Waterford) 3-4 (replay).
Longford, March 26. St. Jarlath's (Tuam) 5-9; St. Patrick's (Cavan) 1-8.
Athlone, April 16. Final: St. Jarlath's (Tuam) 2-8; St. Mel's (Longford) 1-8.
1962—Croke Park, March 24. St. Mel's (Longford) 2-5; De La Salle (Waterford) 2-3.
Athlone, March 24. St. Jarlath's (Tuam) 2-8; St. Patrick's (Cavan) 1-3.
Ballinasloe, April 8. Final: St. Mel's (Longford) 3-11; St. Jarlath's (Tuam) 2-12.
1963—Limerick, April 7. St. Brendan's (Killarney) 1-7; St. Jarlath's (Tuam) 0-8.
Kells, April 7. St. Mel's (Longford) 1-10; St. Colman's (Newry) 2-5.
Croke Park, April 28. Final: St. Mel's (Longford) 1-6; St. Brendan's (Killarney) 2-2.
1964—Tullamore, March 22. St. Jarlath's (Tuam)1-10; De La Salle (Waterford) 1-7.
Clones, March 22. St. Mel's (Longford) 3-10; Newry C.B.S. 3-2.
Athlone, April 19. Final: St. Jarlath's (Tuam) 0-11; St. Mel's (Longford) 1-8 (draw).
Tullamore, May 3. St. Jarlath's (Tuam) 1-10; St. Mel's (Longford) 0-4 (replay).
1965—Ballybay, March 28. St. Columb's (Derry) 3-9; St. Jarlath's (Tuam) 1-11.
Carlow, March 28. Belcamp O.M.I. (Dublin) 2-9; De La Salle (Waterford) 2-8.
Cavan, April 11. Final: St. Columb's (Derry) 0-9; Belcamp O.M.I. (Dublin) 0-9 (draw).
Ballybay, May 9. St. Columb's (Derry) 0-11; Belcamp O.M.I. (Dublin) 1-7 (replay).
1966—Nenagh, April 3. St. Finian's (Mullingar) 1-6; St. Brendan's (Killarney) 0-9 (draw).
Nenagh, April 17. St. Finian's (Mullingar) 3-13, St. Brendan's (Killarney) 3-9 (replay).
Athlone, May 1. Final: St. Jarlath's (Tuam) 1-10; St. Finian's (Mullingar) 1-9.
1967—Drogheda, April 9. St. Colman's (Newry) 2-7; Belcamp O.M.I. (Dublin) 0-4.
Nenagh, April 9. St. Jarlath's (Tuam) 2-13; Col. Chriost Ri (Cork) 3-5.
Mullingar, April 23. Final: St. Colman's (Newry) 1-8; St. Jarlath's (Tuam) 1-7.
1968—Portlaoise, April 7. Col. Chríost Rí (Cork) 1-7; St. Nathy's (Ballaghadereen) 1-7 (draw).
Limerick, April 28. Col. Chríost Rí (Cork) 2-11; St. Nathy's (Ballaghadereen) 0-15 (replay).
Croke Park, April 7. Belcamp O.M.I. (Dublin) 2-7; St. Colman's (Newry) 0-11.
Croke Park, May 5. Final: Col. Chríost Rí (Cork) 3-11; Belcamp O.M.I. (Dublin) 1-10.
1969—Longford, March 30. St. Mary's (Galway) 1-6; St. Colman's (Newry) 0-4.
Thurles, April 20. St. Brendan's (Killarney) 2-6; St. Mel's (Longford) 1-9 (draw).
Thurles, April 27. St. Brendan's (Killarney) 2-8; St. Mel's (Longford) 1-10 (replay).

Thurles, May 4: Final: St. Brendan's (Killarney) 1-13; St. Mary's (Galway) 3-3.
1970—Cavan, May 22. St. Malachy's (Belfast) 4-9; St. Colman's (Claremorris) 2-6.
Thurles, May 22. Col. Chríost Rí (Cork) 1-5; Franciscan College (Gormanstown) 0-6.
Croke Park, April 19. Final: Col. Chríost Rí (Cork) 4-5; St. Malachy's (Belfast) 1-13.
1971—Dundalk, April 4. St. Mary's C.B.S. (Belfast) 2-6; St. Mel's (Longford) 0-4.
Athlone, April 4: Col. Iosagáin (Ballyvourney) 1-10; Summerhill (Sligo) 2-6.
Croke Park, April 25. Final: St. Mary's C.B.S. (Belfast) 1-13; Col. Iosagain (Ballyvourney) 1-7.
1972—Longford, March 26. St. Patrick's (Cavan) 4-6; St. Jarlath's (Tuam) 0-7.
Nenagh, March 26. St. Brendan's (Killarney) 1-12; Franciscan College (Gormanstown) 0-12.
Croke Park, April 16 Final: St.Patrick's (Cavan) 2-11; St. Brendan's (Killarney) 1-5.
1973—Limerick, April 1: St. Jarlath's (Tuam) 2-13; St. Brendan's (Killarney) 2-10.
Ballybay, April 1: Franciscan College (Gormanstown) 1-8; St. Michael's (Enniskillen) 1-6.
Athlone, April 15. Final: Franciscan College (Gormanston) 1-7; St. Jarlath's (Tuam) 0-8.
1974—Limerick, March 24. St. Jarlath's (Tuam) 1-11; St. Brendan's (Killarney) 0-8.
Cavan, March 31. Franciscan College (Gormanston) 1-9; Omagh C.B.S. 1-7.
Athlone, April 7. Final: St. Jarlath's (Tuam) 4-11; Franciscan College (Gormanston) 2-11.
1975—Clones, March 23. St. Colman's (Newry) 1-9; Summerhill (Sligo) 2-4.
Thurles, April 13. Carmelite College (Moate) 0-12; Col. Iognóid Rís (Cork) 1-9 (draw).
Thurles, April 27. Carmelite College (Moate) 1-16; Col. Iognaid Ris (Cork) 1-13 (replay).
Croke Park, May 4. Final: St. Colman's (Newry) 1-7; Carmelite College (Moate) 2-3.
1976—Mullingar, April 4. St. Jarlath's (Tuam) 1-13; St. Colman's (Newry) 1-2.
Nenagh, April 4. Carmelite College (Moate) 1-14; Tralee C.B.S. 1-3.
Roscommon, May 2. Final: Carmelite College (Moate) 1-10; St. Jarlath's (Tuam) 0-11.
1977—Clones, April 3. Carmelite College (Moate) 1-9; St. Patrick's (Maghera) 1-8.
Limerick, April 3. St. Colman's (Claremorris) 1-11; St. Brendan's (Killarney) 3-4.
Roscommon, April 24. Final: St. Colman's (Claremorris) 1-11; Carmelite College (Moate) 1-10.
1978—Limerick, April 16. St. Jarlath's (Tuam) 5-10; Col. Chríost Rí (Cork) 1-6.
Croke Park, April 16. St. Colman's (Newry) 0-13; Carmelite College (Moate) 3-2.
Croke Park, April 30. Final: St. Jarlath's (Tuam) 2-11; St. Colman's (Newry) 2-4.
1979—Cavan, April 8. St. Jarlath's (Tuam) 2-4; St. Colman's (Newry) 1-2.
Cashel, April 8. Ard Scoil Rís (Dublin) 2-8; Col. Chríost Rí (Cork) 1-7.
Tullamore, May 6. Final: Ard Scoil Rís (Dublin) 0-10; St. Jarlath's (Tuam) 0-10 (draw).
Tullamore, May 13. Ard Scoil Rís (Dublin) 2-9; St. Jarlath's (Tuam) 1-10 (replay).
1980—Sligo, March 30. St. Patrick's (Maghera) 2-7; Tuam C.B.S. 1-9.
Carlow, March 30. Carmelite College (Moate) 0-10; Col. Chriost Rí (Cork) 0-6.
Croke Park, April 20. Final: Carmelite College (Moate) 0-12; St. Patrick's (Maghera) 1-8.
1981—Cloughjordan, April 5. St. Colman's (Claremorris) 3-5; Col. Iosagáin (Ballyvourney) 0-10.
Cavan, April 5: Carmelite College (Moate) 1-5; St. Colman's (Newry) 0-6.
Roscommon, May 3. Final: Carmelite College (Moate) 2-2; St. Colman's (Claremorris) 1-4.
1982—Athlone, April 25. St. Jarlath's (Tuam) 2-7; St. Mel's (Longford) 1-8.
Croke Park: St. Fachna's (Skibbereen) 0-15; St. Patrick's (Maghera) 1-9.
Thurles, May 9. Final: St. Jarlath's (Tuam) 1-7; St. Fachtna's (Skibbereen) 1-7 (draw).
Limerick, May 16: St. Jarlath's (Tuam) 1-8; St. Fachtna's (Skibbereen) 0-7 (replay).
1983—Cavan, April 17. St. Jarlath's (Tuam) 1-9; St. Patrick's (Maghera) 0-9.
Cloughjordan, April 17. Col. Chríost Rí (Cork) 2-7; St. Mary's (Mullingar) 1-6.
Croke Park, May 1. Final: Col. Chríost Rí (Cork) 3-6; St. Jarlath's (Tuam) 2-5.
1984—Limerick, April 14. St. Jarlath's (Tuam) 1-14; Col. Chríost Rí (Cork) 1-6.
Cavan, April 15. St. Patrick's (Maghera) 1-5; Portarlington C.B.S. 0-8 (draw).
Cavan, April 21. St. Patrick's (Maghera) 0-15; Portarlington C.B.S. 1-5 (replay).
Croke Park. Final: St. Jarlath's (Tuam) 0-10; St. Patrick's (Maghera) 2-3.
1985—Mullingar, April 21. Summerhill (Sligo) 1-10; Dundalk C.B.S. 0-8.
Croke Park, April 21. Col. Chríost Rí 2-6; St. Patrick's (Maghera) 0-?.
Portlaoise, May 12. Final Col. Chríost Rí 1-9; Summerhill 0-9.
1986—Nenagh, April 13. St. David's (Artane) 0-9; St. Brendan's (Killarney) 1-4.
Mullingar, April 13. St. Colman's (Newry) 1-6; St. Mary's (Galway) 1-5.
Portlaoise, April 27. Final: St. Colman's (Newry) 3-10; St. David's (Artane) 0-7.
1987—Ennis, April 12. St. Mary's (Galway) 0-7; Col. Chríost Rí (Cork) 0-6.
Kells, April 19. St. Mel's (Longford) 0-7; Abbey C.B.S. (Newry) 1-2.
Roscommon, May 3. Final: St. Mel's (Longford) 0-8; St. Mary's (Galway) 1-4.
1988—Portlaoise, April 17. St. Colman's (Newry) 2-14; North Mon. (Cork) 1-5.
April 17. St. Mel's (Longford) 1-9; St. Mary's (Galway) 0-8.
Clones, May 1. Final: St. Colman's (Newry) 1-11; St. Mel's (Longford) 1-7.
1989—Portlaoise, April 23: Col. Chríost Rí (Cork) 4-9; St. Mel's (Longford) 2-6.

Cavan, April 23: St. Patrick's (Maghera) 1-9, Tuam CBS 0-7.
Portlaoise, May 7. Final: St. Patrick's 1-5, Col. Chríost Rí 0-8 (draw).
Longford, May 14. St. Patrick's 2-15; Col. Chríost Rí 1-6 (replay).
1990—Castleblayney, April 22. St. Patrick's Magheral 5-12; St. Mel's (Longford) 1-5.
Emly, April 22. St. Jarlath's (Tuam) 1-13; St. Fachtna's (Skibbereen) 1-8.
Cavan, May 6. Final: St. Patrick's (Maghera) 1-4; St. Jarlath's 0-7 (draw).
Cavan, May 13. St. Patrick's 1-11; St. Jarlath's 0-13 (replay).
1991—Athlone, April 20. St. Patrick's (Navan) 1-14; St. Mary's (Galway) 2-9.
Tullamore, April 21. St. Fachtna's (Skibbereen) 1-11; St. Patrick's (Dungannon) 1-7.
Croke Park, April 28. Final: St. Fachtna's 2-9; St. Patrick's 0-7.
1992—Clonmel, April 5. St. Brendan's (Killarney) 3-10; St. Peter's (Wexford) 3-8.
Longford, April 12: St. Jarlath's (Tuam) 0-8, St. Michael's (Enniskillen) 0-5.
Thurles, April 26. Final: St. Brendan's 0-9, St. Jarlath's 0-5.
1993—Ballinsaloe, April 4. St. Jarlath's (Tuam) 4-12, St. Flannan's (Ennis) 1-3.
Cavan, April 4. St. Colman's (Newry) 1-14, St. Patrick's (Navan) 0-7.
Longford, April 25. Final: St. Colman's 2-10, St. Jarlath's 1-9
1994—Roscommon, April 24. St. Jarlath's (Tuam) 3-9, St. Mel's (Longford) 1-6.
Portlaoise, April 24. St. Patrick's (Maghera) 2-15, St. Brendan's (Killarney) 0-6.
Longford, April 30. Final: St. Jarlath's (Tuam) 3-11, St. Patrick's 0-9.
1995—Ballyshannon, April 1. St. Patrick's (Maghera) 2-11, St. Patrick's (Tuam) 0-9.
Clonmel, April 1. Good Counsel (New Ross) 1-9, St. Flannan's (Ennis) 1-8.
Navan, April 30. Final: St. Patrick's (Maghera) 2-11, Good Counsel 1-6.
1996—Limerick, March 31. Intermediate School (Kilrorglin) 4-12, St. Gerard's (Castlebar) 1-8.
Navan, April 7. St. Patrick's (Maghera) 1-17, Good Counsel (New Ross) 2-5.
Croke Park, April 28. Final: Intermediate School (Killorglin) 4-8, St. Patrick's 1-14.
1997—Tullamore, April 13. St. Patrick's (Dungannon) 5-10, Coláiste Chríost Ri 0-10.
Longford, April 13. St. Gerard's (Castlebar) 1-13, St. Patrick's (Navan) 0-15.
Croke Park, April 27. Final: St. Patrick's (Dungannon) 1-10, St. Gerard's (Castlebar) 0-3.
1998—Thurles, April 5. Coláiste Eoin (Stillorglin) 1-9, Coláiste Chríost Rí 1-8.
Clones, April 5. St. Colman's (Newry) 2-15, Roscommon CBS 1-15 (after extra time).
Croke Park, May 4. Final: St. Colman's (Newry) 2-14, Coláiste Eoin 1-7.
1999—Parnell Park, March 28. Good Counsel (New Ross), 2-10, St. Michael's (Enniskillen) 1-11.
Miltownmalbay, March 28. St. Jarlath's (Tuam) 2-14, Tralee CBS 2-6.
Croke Park, April 18. Final: Good Counsel (New Ross) 1-11, St. Jarlath's 1-7.
2000—Tullamore, April 2: St.Patrick's (Armagh) 2-9, Tralee CBS 0-13.
Longford, April 2: St.Patrick's (Navan) 3-7, St.Jarlath's (Tuam) 0-13.
Breffni Park, April 16, Final: St.Patrick's (Navan) 0-11, St.Patrick's (Armagh) 1-6.
2001—Breffni Park, April 29: St.Jarlath's (Tuam) 0-11, St.Michael's (Enniskillen) 0-10.
Limerick, April 1: St.Patrick's (Navan) 2-7, Colaiste na Sceilige 0-11.
Croke Park, May 5, Final: St.Patrick's (Navan) 2-10, St.Jarlath's (Tuam) 2-8.
2002—St.Michael's (Enniskillen) 1-13, Dundalk Schools 0-11.
St.Jarlath's (Tuam) 0-20, Coláiste na Sceilige (Kerry) 0-20.
Limerick, April 22: St. Jarlath's (Tuam) 2-13, Coláiste na Sceilige (Kerry) 2-12.
Carrick-on-Shannon, April 28, Final: St.Jarlath's (Tuam) 3-13, St.Michael's (Enniskillen) 0-6.
2003—Hyde Park, April 7: St. Jarlath's (Tuam) 0-14, St. Mel's (Longford) 1-6.
Birr, April 7: St. Patrick's (Maghera) 1-14, Coláiste na Sceilige (Kerry) 3-5.
Breffni Park, April 26, Final: St.Patrick's (Maghera) 1-9, St.Jarlath's (Tuam) 2-4.
2004—Nenagh, March 28: St.Patrick's (Navan) 2-8, Col. Chroist Rí (Cork) 1-6.
Markievicz Park, March 28: St.Patrick's (Dungannon) 3-15, St.Mary's (Galway) 1-4.
Final: St.Patrick's (Navan) 1-11, St.Patrick's (Dungannon) 1-10.
2005—St.Mary's (Galway) 1-11, Spioraid Naomh 0-9. Knockbeg College (Carlow) 0-12, Omagh CBS 1-8.
Final: Knockbeg College (Carlow) 2-8, St.Mary's (Galway) 0-11.
2006—Semi Finals: St. Patrick's, Navan 2-15; St. Mary's Galway 0-11. Abbey CBS 1-10; De La Salle Macroom 1-8. Final: Abbey CBS 2-15; St. Patrick's Navan 2-13.
2007—Semi Finals: Tralee CBS 1-13; St. Patrick's, Navan 1-7; Omagh CBS 2-16; St. Jarlath's, Tuam 3-11. Final: Omagh CBS 0-16; Tralee CBS 0-7.
2008—Semi Finals: St. Brendan's Killarney 0-11; St. Jarlath's Tuam 0-6; St. Patrick's Academy Dungannon 0-10; Athlone CC 1-5. Final: St. Patrick's Academy Dungannon 1-9; St. Brendan's Killarney 1-7
2009—Semi Finals: Coláiste na Sceilge 3-10; St. Patrick's, Dungannon 1-6; St. Mary's SS Edenderry 1-12; St. Colman's, Claremorris 1-11. Final: Coláiste na Scéilge 1-9; St. Mary's SS Edenderry 0-10.

MUNSTER SENIOR FOOTBALL

CORN UÍ MHUIRÍ

ROLL OF HONOUR 1928-2009

St. Brendan's, Killarney (17); Tralee C.B.S. (16); Coláiste Chríost Rí, Cork (14); Coláiste Iosagáin, Ballyvourney (7); De La Salle, Waterford (5); Coláiste na Sceilige, Kerry (4); North Monastery, Cork (3); St. Fachtna's, Skibbereen (3); St. Flannan's, Ennis (3); Limerick CBS (2); Coláiste Iognáid Rís, Cork (1); Coláiste na Mumhan, Mallow (1); High School, Clonmel (1); Rochestown College, Cork (1); Intermediate School, Killorglin (1), Spioraid Naomh (1); De La Salle, Macroom (1).

1928—High School, Clonmel
1929—St. Brendan's, Killarney
1930—St. Brendan's, Killarney
1931—Tralee C.B.S.
1932—Tralee C.B.S.
1933—Tralee C.B.S.
1934—Tralee C.B.S.
1935—North Monastery, Cork
1936—North Monastery, Cork
1937—St. Brendan's, Killarney
1938—St. Brendan's, Killarney
1939—Col. na Mumban, Mallow
1940—Tralee C.B.S.
1941—Tralee C.B.S.
1942—Tralee C.B.S.
1943—St. Brendan's, Killarney
1944—Tralee C.B.S.
1945—Tralee C.B.S.
1946—St. Brendan's, Killarney
1947—St. Brendan's, Killarney
1948—Tralee C.B.S.
1949—Col. Iosagáin, Ballyvourney
1950— Rochestown College, Cork
1951—Col. Iosagáin, Ballyvourney
1952—Col. Iosagáin, Ballyvourney
1953—Tralee C.B.S.
1954—Col. Iosagáin, Ballyvourney
1955—Tralee C.B.S.
1956—Limerick C.B.S.
1957—Col. Iosagáin, Ballyvourney
1958—De La Salle, Waterford
1959—St. Flannan's, Ennis
1960—Limerick C.B.S.
1961—De La Salle, Waterford
1962—De La Salle, Waterford
1963—De La Salle, Waterford
1964—De La Salle, Waterford
1965—De La Salle, Waterford
1966—St. Brendan's, Killarney
1967—Col. Chríost Rí, Cork
1968—Col. Chríost Rí, Cork
1969—St. Brendan's, Killarney
1970—Col. Chríost Rí, Cork
1971—Col. Iosagáin, Ballyvourney
1972—St. Brendan's, Killarney
1973—St. Brendan's, Killarney
1974—St. Brendan's, Killarney
1975—Col. Iognáid Rís, Cork
1976—Tralee C.B.S.
1977—St. Brendan's, Killarney
1978—Col. Chríost Rí, Cork
1979—Col. Chríost Rí, Cork
1980—Col. Chríost Rí, Cork
1981—Col. Iosagáin, Ballyvourney
1982—St. Fachtna's, Skibbereen
1983—Col. Chríost Rí, Cork
1984—Col. Chríost Rí, Cork
1985—Col. Chríost Rí, Cork
1986—St. Brendan's, Killarney
1987—Col. Chríost Rí, Cork
1988—North Monastery, Cork
1989—Col. Chríost Rí, Cork
1990—St. Fachtna's, Skibbereen
1991—St. Fachtna's, Skibbereen
1992—St. Brendan's, Killarney
1993—St. Flannan's, Ennis
1994—St. Brendan's, Killarney
1995—St. Flannan's, Ennis
1996—Intermediate School, Killorglin
1997—Col. Chríost Rí, Cork
1998—Col. Chríost Rí, Cork
1999—Tralee C.B.S.
2000—Tralee C.B.S.
2001—Coláiste na Sceilige.
2002—Coláiste na Sceilige
2003—Coláiste na Sceilige
2004—Col. Chroist Rí (Cork)
2005—Spioraid Naomh
2006—De La Salle, Macroom
2007—Tralee C.B.S.
2008—St Brendan's, Killarney
2009—Coláiste na Sceilige

LEINSTER SENIOR FOOTBALL

ROLL OF HONOUR 1920-2009

St. Mel's, Longford (30), St. Finian's, Mullingar (10); Carmelite College, Moate (6); St. Patrick's, Navan (8); Franciscan College, Gormanston (5); Knockbeg College, Carlow (5); Belcamp College, Dublin (4); Coláiste Caoimhghin, Dublin (3); Good Counsel, New Ross (3); St. Joseph's, Fairview, Dublin (2); Ard Scoil Rís, Dublin (1); Franciscan College, Multyfarnham (1); St. Joseph's, Roscrea (1); St. Kieran's College, Kilkenny (1); St. Mary's CBS, Mullingar (1); St. Joseph's, Portarlington (1); Dundalk CBS (1); St. David's, Artane (1); Patrician College, Ballyfin (1); St. Peter's, Wexford (1); St. Thomas' College, Newbridge (1); Coláiste Eoin, Stillorgan, Dublin (1); Dundalk Schools (1); Athlone (1), St. Mary's SS, Edenderry (1).

1920—Knockbeg College, Carlow
1921—Belcamp College, Dublin
1922—St. Kieran's, Kilkenny
1923—St. Thomas' College, Newbridge.
1924—St. Joseph's, Roscrea
1925—St. Finian's, Mullingar
1926—St. Finian's, Mullingar
1927—St. Finian's, Mullingar
1928—St. Mel's, Longford
1929—Col. Caoimhghin, Dublin
1930—Col. Caoimhghin, Dublin
1931—Col. Caoimhghin, Dublin
1932—Knockbeg College, Carlow
1933—St. Mel's, Longford
1934—St. Mel's, Longford
1935—St. Mel's, Longford
1936—St. Mel's, Longford
1937—St. Mel's, Longford
1938—St. Mel's, Longford
1939—St Finian's. Mullingar
1940—St. Mel's, Longford
1941—St. Mel's, Longford
1942—St. Mel's, Longford
1943—St. Mel's, Longford
1944—St. Finian's, Mullingar
1945—St. Mel's, Longford
1946—St. Mel's, Longford
1947—St. Mel's, Longford
1948—St. Mel's, Longford
1949—St. Finian's, Mullingar
1950—St. Finian's, Mullingar
1951—St. Mel's, Longford
1952—Franciscan College, Multyfarnham
1953—St. Finian's, Mullingar
1954—Knockbeg College, Carlow
1955—Knockbeg College, Carlow
1956—St. Joseph's, Fariview
1957—Patrician College, Ballyfin
1958—Franciscan College, Gormanston
1959—St. Joseph's, Fairview
1960—St. Finian's, Mullingar
1961—St. Mel's, Longford
1962—St. Mel's, Longford
1962—St. Mel's, Longford
1963—St. Mel's, Longford
1964—St. Mel's, Longford
1965—Belcamp O.M.I., Dublin
1966—Franciscan College, Gormanston
1967—Belcamp O.M.I., Dublin
1968—Belcamp O.M.I., Dublin
1969—St. Mel's, Longford
1970—Franciscan College, Gormanston
1971—St. Mel's, Longford
1972—Franciscan College, Gormanston
1973—Franciscan College, Gormanston
1974—Franciscan College, Gormanston
1975—Carmelite College, Moate
1976—Carmelite College, Moate
1977—Carmelite College, Moate
1978—Carmelite College, Moate
1979—Ard Scoil Rís, Dublin
1980—Carmelite College, Moate
1981—Carmelite College, Moate
1982—St. Mel's, Longford
1983—St. Mary's, Mullingar
1984—Portarlington C.B.S.
1985—Dundalk C.B.S.
1986—St. David's, Artaine
1987—St. Mel's, Longford
1988—St. Mel's, Longford
1989—St. Mel's, Longford
1990—St. Mel's, Longford
1991—St. Patrick's, Navan
1992—St. Peter's, Wexford
1993—St. Patrick's, Navan
1994—St. Mel's, Longford
1995—Good Counsel, New Ross
1996—Good Counsel, New Ross
1997—St. Patrick's, Navan
1998—Coláiste Eoin, Stillorgan, Dublin
1999—Good Counsel, New Ross
2000—St.Patrick's (Navan)
2001—St.Patrick's (Navan)
2002 – Dundalk Schools
2003—St. Mel's (Longford)
2004—St.Patrick's (Navan)
2005—Knockbeg College (Carlow)
2006—St.Patrick's (Navan)
2007—St.Patrick's (Navan)
2008—Athlone CC
2009—St. Mary's SS, Edenderry

CONNACHT SENIOR FOOTBALL

ROLL OF HONOUR 1929-2009

St. Jarlath's, Tuam (46), St. Mary's, Galway (9); Summerhill College, Sligo (7); Roscommon CBS (5); St. Nathy's, Ballaghaderreen (5); St. Colman's, Claremorris (4); St. Gerard's, Castlebar (3); Tuam CBS (2); St. Patrick's, Tuam (formerly Tuam CBS) (1).

1929—St. Gerard's, Castlebar
1930—Summerhill, Sligo
1931—Summerhill, Sligo
1932—St. Jarlath's, Tuam
1933—St. Jarlath's, Tuam
1934—St. Jarlath's, Tuam
1935—St. Jarlath's, Tuam
1936—St. Jarlath's, Tuam
1937—St. Jarlath's, Tuam
1938—St. Jarlath's, Tuam
1939—St. Jarlath's, Tuam
1940—Roscommon C.B.S.
1941—Roscommon C.B.S
1942—Roscommon C.B.S.
1943—St. Jarlath's, Tuam
1944—St. Jarlath's, Tuam
1945—St. Jarlath's, Tuam
1946—St. Jarlath's, Tuam
1947—St. Jarlath's, Tuam
1948—Roscommon C.B.S.
1949—St. Nathy's, Ballaghaderreen

1950—St. Jarlath's Tuam
1951—St. Jarlath's, Tuam
1952—St. Mary's, Galway
1953—St. Jarlath's, Tuam
1954—Summerhill, Sligo
1955—Summerhill, Sligo
1956—St. Jarlath's, Tuam
1957—St. Nathy's, Ballaghaderreen
1958—St. Jarlath's, Tuam
1959—St. Nathy's, Ballaghaderreen
1960—St. Jarlath's, Tuam
1961—St. Jarlath's, Tuam
1962—St. Jarlath's, Tuam
1963—St. Jarlath's, Tuam
1964—St. Jarlath's, Tuam
1965—St. Jarlath's, Tuam
1966—St. Jarlath's, Tuam
1967—St. Jarlath's, Tuam
1968—St. Nathy's, Ballaghaderreen
1969—St. Mary's, Galway
1970—St. Colman's, Claremorris
1971—Summerhill, Sligo
1972—St. Jarlath's, Tuam
1973—St. Jarlath's, Tuam
1974—St. Jarlath's, Tuam
1975—Summerhill, Sligo
1976—St. Jarlath's, Tuam
1977—St. Colman's, Claremorris
1978—St. Jarlath's, Tuam
1979—St. Jarlath's, Tuam
1980—Tuam C.B.S.
1981—St. Colman's, Claremorris
1982—St. Jarlath's, Tuam
1983—St. Jarlath's, Tuam
1984—St. Jarlath's, Tuam
1985—Summerhill, Sligo
1986—St. Mary's, Galway
1987—St. Mary's, Galway
1988—St. Mary's, Galway
1989—Tuam CBS
1990—St. Jarlath's, Tuam
1991—St Mary's, Galway
1992—St. Jarlath's, Tuam
1993—St. Jarlath's, Tuam
1994—St. Jarlath's, Tuam
1995—St. Patrick's, Tuam
1996—St. Gerard's, Castlebar
1997—St. Gerard's, Castlebar
1998—Roscommon CBS
1999—St. Jarlath's, Tuam
2000 – St.Jarlath's (Tuam)
2001—St.Jarlath's (Tuam)
2002—St.Jarlath's (Tuam)
2003—St.Jarlath's (Tuam)
2004—St.Mary's (Galway)
2005—St.Mary's (Galway)
2006—St.Mary's (Galway)
2007—St.Jarlath's (Tuam)
2008—St.Jarlath's (Tuam)
2009—St. Colman's (Claremorris)

ULSTER SENIOR FOOTBALL

ROLL OF HONOUR 1919-2009

St. Colman's Newry (19); St. Patrick's, Armagh (12); St. Patrick's, Maghera (12); St. Patrick's, Cavan (11); St. McCartan's, Monaghan (7); St. Michael's, Enniskillen (5); Abbey CBS, Newry (5); St. Patrick's, Dungannon (4); Omagh CBS (3); St. Columb's, Derry (2); St. Malachy's, Belfast (2); St. Mary's, Dundalk (2); St. Mary's, Belfast (2).
Note: St. Patrick's, Armagh and St. McCartan's, Monaghan shared the 1934 title.

1919—St. Patrick's, Armagh
1920-'23—None
1924—St. Patrick's, Armagh
1925—Unfinished
1926—St. Patrick's, Armagh
1927—St. Patrick's, Armagh
1928—St. Patrick's, Armagh
1929—St. Malachy's, Belfast
1930—St. McCartan's, Monaghan
1931—St. Patrick's, Armagh
1932—St. McCartan's, Monaghan
1933—St. McCartan's, Monaghan
1934—St. McCartan's, Monaghan, St. Patrick's, Armagh (joint holders)
1935—St. Patrick's, Cavan
1936—St. Patrick's, Cavan
1937—St. Patrick's, Cavan
1938—St. Mary's, Dundalk
1939—St. Patrick's, Covan
1940—St. McCartan's, Monaghan
1941—St. Mary's, Dundalk
1942—St. McCartan's, Monaghan
1943—St. Patrick's, Cavan
1944—St. Patrick's, Armagh
1945—St. Patrick's, Armagh
1946—St. Patrick's, Armagh
1947—St. Patrick's, Armagh
1948—St. Patrick's, Cavan
1949—St. Colman's, Newry
1950—St. Colman's, Newry
1951—St. Patrick's, Cavan
1952—St. McCartan's, Monaghan
1953—St. Patrick's, Armagh
1954—Newry C.B.S.
1955—St. Patrick's, Cavan
1956—St. McCartan's, Monaghan
1957—St. Colman's, Newry
1958—St. Colman's, Newry
1959—Newry C.B.S.
1960—St. Coleman's' Newry
1961—St. Patrick's, Cavan
1962—St. Colman's, Newry
1963—St. Colman's, Newry
1964—Newry C.B.S.
1965—St. Columb's, Derry
1966—St. Columb's, Derry
1967—St. Colman's, Newry

1968—St. Colman's, Newry
1969—St. Colman's, Newry
1970—St. Malachy's, Belfast
1971—St. Mary's C.B.S., Belfast
1972—St. Patrick's, Cavan
1973—St. Michael's, Enniskillen
1974—Omagh C.B.S.
1975—St. Colman's, Newry
1976—St. Colman's, Newry
1977—St. Patrick's, Maghera
1978—St. Colman's, Newry
1979—St. Colman's, Newry
1980—St. Patrick's, Maghera
1981—St. Colman's, Newry
1982—St. Patrick's, Maghera
1983—St. Patrick's, Maghera
1984—St. Patrick's, Maghera
1985—St. Patrick's, Maghera
1986—St. Colman's, Newry
1987—Abbey C.B.S., Newry
1988—St. Colman's, Newry
1989—St. Patrick's, Maghera
1990—St. Patrick's, Maghera
1991—St. Patrick's, Dungannon
1992—St. Michael's, Enniskillen
1993—St. Colman's, Newry
1994—St. Patrick's, Maghera
1995—St. Patrick's, Maghera
1996—St. Patrick's, Maghera
1997—St. Patrick's, Dungannon
1998—St. Colman's, Newry
1999—St. Michael's, Enniskillen
2000—St.Patrick's (Armagh)
2001—St.Michael's (Enniskillen)
2002—St.Michael's (Enniskillen)
2003—St. Patrick's (Maghera)
2004—St.Patrick's (Dungannon)
2005—Omagh CBS
2006—Abbey CBS
2007—Omagh CBS
2008—St. Patrick's, Dungannon
2009—St. Patrick's, Dungannon

HIGHER EDUCATION

Records

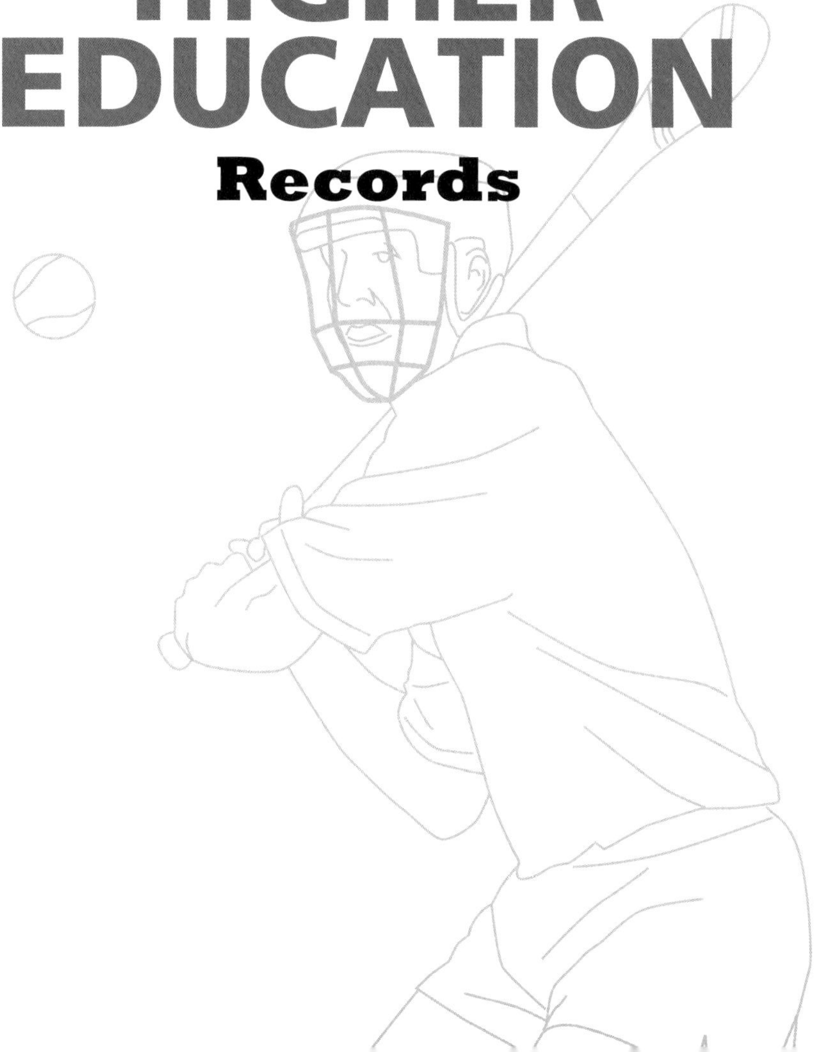

HIGHER EDUCATION

By Donal McAnallen

KEY

UCD – University College Dublin.
UCC – University College Cork.
UCG – University College Galway.
QUB – Queen's University Belfast.
TCD – Trinity College Dublin.
NUU – New University of Ulster (Coleraine), which changed to UUC (University of Ulster, Coleraine) in 1985.
UUJ – University of Ulster, Jordanstown
NIHEL – National Institute of Higher Education, Limerick, which became UL (University of Limerick) in 1990.
TRTC / ITT – Tralee Regional Technical College, which became Institute of Technology, Tralee in 1997.
ARTC / AIT – Athlone Regional Technical College, which became Institute of Technology in 1997.
ITS – Institute of Technology, Sligo.
WRTC / WIT – Waterford Institute of Technology.
GMIT – Galway-Mayo Institute of Technology.
DCU – Dublin City University.
DIT – Dublin Institute of Technology.

FITZGIBBON CUP

The Fitzgibbon Cup, the trophy for the Higher Education Hurling Championship, is named after Dr. Edwin Fitzgibbon, a Capuchin priest who was Professor of Philosophy at University College Cork from 1911 to 1936.

In 1912 Dr. Edwin donated most of his annual salary to present the trophy that bears his name for the hurling championship between the constituent colleges of the NUI.

For the first three decades the competition was dominated by UCC and UCD, with UCG winning occasionally. Queen's, who first entered in 1946, made a singular breakthrough by winning in 1953.

In the 1960s and 1970s three more university colleges entered the competition – Trinity, NUU Coleraine and Maynooth – and the last-named won successive Fitzgibbon Cup titles almost straight away.

An even greater expansion took place in the late 1980s when all teams in Division 1 of the Higher Education League were allowed to participate in the Fitzgibbon Cup and its sister football championship, the Sigerson Cup. As many as twenty colleges participated in the Fitzgibbon Cup in the late 1990s, but the number has since retracted to fewer than a dozen.

Since the event went "open" newer colleges from Limerick and Waterford have quickly become the dominant colleges in the competition. UCC lead the roll of honour with 39 championships, and its eight-in-a-row (1981-88 inclusive) is the longest winning sequence recorded in this competition to date.

In 2000/01 the original Fitzgibbon Cup was decommissioned and a replica was introduced in its place.

RECORDS

ROLL OF HONOUR

UCC (40), UCD (30), UCG (9), WRTC / WIT (8), NIHEL / UL (3), Maynooth (2), QUB (1), LIT (2).

Winners at a Glance
1911/12 – UCD
1912/13 – UCC
1913/14 – UCC
1914/15 – UCD
1915/16 – UCD
1916/17 – UCD
1917/18 – UCC
1918/19 – UCG
1919/20 – UCC
1920/21 – Not played
1921/22 – UCC
1922/23 – UCD
1923/24 – UCD
1924/25 – UCC
1925/26 – UCG
1926/27 – UCD
1927/28 – UCC
1928/29 – UCC
1929/30 – UCC
1930/31 – UCC
1931/32 – UCD
1932/33 – UCC
1933/34 – UCD
1934/35 – UCD
1935/36 – UCD
1936/37 – UCD
1937/38 – UCD
1938/39 – UCC
1939/40 – UCC
1940/41 – UCC
1941/42 – UCG
1942/43 – Not played
1943/44 – UCD
1944/45 – UCG
1945/46 – UCG
1946/47 – UCC
1947/48 – UCD
1948/49 – UCG
1949/50 – UCD
1950/51 – UCD
1951/52 – UCD
1952/53 – QUB
1953/54 – Declared null & void
1954/55 – UCD
1955/56 – UCC
1956/57 – UCC
1957/58 – UCD
1958/59 – UCC
1959/60 – UCD
1960/61 – UCD
1961/62 – UCC

1962/63 – UCC
1963/64 – UCD
1964/65 – UCD
1965/66 – UCC
1966/67 – UCC
1967/68 – UCD
1968/69 – UCD
1969/70 – UCG
1970/71 – UCC
1971/72 – UCC
1972/73 – Maynooth
1973/74 – Maynooth
1974/75 – UCD
1975/76 – UCC
1976/77 – UCG
1977/78 – UCD
1978/79 – UCD
1979/80 – UCG
1980/81 – UCC
1981/82 – UCC
1982/83 – UCC
1983/84 – UCC
1984/85 – UCC
1985/86 – UCC
1986/87 – UCC
1987/88 – UCC
1988/89 – NIHEL
1989/90 – UCC
1990/91 – UCC
1991/92 – WRTC
1992/93 – UCD
1993/94 – UL
1994/95 – WRTC
1995/96 – UCC
1996/97 – UCC
1997/98 – UCC
1998/99 – WIT
1999/00 – WIT
2000/01 – UCD
2001/02 – UL
2002/03 – WIT
2003/04 – WIT
2004/05 – LIT
2005/06 – WIT
2006/07 – LIT
2007/08 – WIT
2008/09 – UCC

FITZGIBBON CUP CHAMPIONSHIP RECORDS

Note: From the start and in most years up to 1948/49 the competition was played on a league basis over one weekend and the college that collected the most league points won the championship.

1911/12 –UCD hosted. All games at Jones' Road. 26 April: UCD 6-0, UCG 1-1. 27 April: UCC 1-3, UCG 1-1. 28 April: UCD 1-0, UCC 0-2.
UCD champions with four league points.
1912/13 – UCG hosted. Galway, 11 April: UCC 6-1, UCG 0-0. 12 April: UCD 2-1, UCG 0-0. 13 April: UCC 5-1, UCD 1-0.
UCC champions with four league points.
1913/14 –UCC hosted. The Mardyke, 20 February: UCD beat UCG. Ballintemple, 21 February: UCC 15-2, UCG 1-2. The Mardyke, 22 February: UCC 4-3, UCD 2-2
UCC champions with four league points.
Note: In the years 1914/15 to 1917/18 UCG did not take part.
1914/15 – UCD hosted. Terenure, 2 March. Final: UCD 6-0, UCC 3-0.
1915/16 – UCC hosted. Cork Athletic Grounds, 27 February. Final: UCD 7-2, UCC 1-2.
1916/17 – UCD hosted. Terenure, 18 February. Final: UCD 3-2, UCC 2-1.
1917/18 – UCC hosted. Date unknown. Final: UCC beat UCD.
1918/19 – UCG hosted. All games at South Park, Galway. 9 May: UCG 3-2, UCC 1-1. 10 May: UCC (23), UCD (22). 11 May: UCD 7-2, UCG 5-3.
UCG champions by conceding fewest scores.
Note: In the years 1919/20 to 1921/22 UCG did not take part.
1919/20 –UCD hosted. Terenure, 12 May. Final: UCC 3-4, UCD 3-3.
1920/21 – Not played.
1921/22 – UCC hosted. The Mardyke, 3 May. Final: UCC 6-1, UCD 3-2.
1922/23 – UCG hosted. Galway, 27 April: UCC 1-6, UCG 1-3. 28 April: UCD 8-3, UCG 3-2. 29 April: UCD 3-2, UCC 2-2.
UCD champions with four league points.
1923/24 – UCD hosted. All games at Terenure. 9 May: UCD 10-4, UCG 3-1. 10 May: UCC 4-3, UCG 0-3. 11 May: UCD 6-2, UCC 4-5.
UCD champions with four league points.
1924/25 – UCC hosted. All games at the Mardyke. 1 May: UCC beat UCG. 2 May: UCD beat UCG. 3 May: UCC 7-1, UCD 2-2.
UCC champions with four league points.
1925/26 – UCG hosted. Galway, 30 April: UCG 4-10, UCC 1-1. 1 May: UCC 3-1, UCD 3-0. 2 May: UCD 2-2, UCG 1-2.
UCG champions with highest aggregate score.
Note: In the years 1926/27 and 1927/28 UCG did not take part.
1926/27 – UCD hosted. Terenure, 8 May. Final: UCD 5-4, UCC 1-3.
1927/28 – UCC hosted. The Mardyke, 26 February. Final: UCC 10-5, UCD 2-0.
1928/29 – UCD hosted. All games at Terenure. 22 February: UCD 5-8, UCG 0-1. 23 February: UCC 7-3, UCG 2-4. 24 February: UCC 8-1, UCD 7-2.
UCC champions with four league points.
1929/30 – UCG hosted. Galway, 28 February: UCC 2-2, UCG 2-1. 1 March: UCD 8-6, UCG 3-3. 2 March: UCC 5-2, UCD 3-1.
UCC champions with four league points.
1930/31 – UCC hosted. All games at the Mardyke. 27 February: UCC 3-3, UCG 1-2. 28

HIGHER EDUCATION

February: UCD 4-3, UCG 0-3. 1 March: UCC 3-1, UCD 0-3.
UCC champions with four league points.
1931/32 – UCD hosted. All games at Terenure: 5 February: UCD 3-8, UCC 1-0. 6 February: UCG 5-4, UCC 2-0. 7 February: UCD 2-8, UCG 2-1.
UCD champions with four league points.
1932/33 – UCG hosted. Galway, 17 February: UCD 7-3, UCG 4-3. 18 February: UCC 3-6, UCG 3-3. 19 February: UCD 5-2, UCC 4-3.
UCC awarded title on objection, after UCD topped league with four points.
1933/34 – UCC hosted. All games at the Mardyke. 23 February: UCC 6-5, UCG 2-4. 24 February: UCD 8-5, UCG 1-2. 25 February: UCD 1-5, UCC 2-2.
UCC and UCD level with three league points each.
Play-off: Limerick, 25 March 1934. UCD 6-1, UCC 2-2.
1934/35 – UCD hosted. All games at Terenure. 22 February: UCD 4-1, UCC 2-3.
23 February: UCG 5-6, UCC 1-6. 24 February: UCD 5-4, UCG 1-2.
UCD champions with four league points.
1935/36 – UCG hosted. Galway, 21 February: UCC 7-3, UCG 4-4. 22 February: UCD 7-3, UCG 2-0. 23 February: UCD 3-2, UCC 1-2.
UCD champions with four league points
1936/37 – UCC hosted. All games at the Mardyke. 12 February: UCC 5-5, UCG 2-3. 13 February: UCD 6-3, UCG 1-0. 14 February: UCC 1-3, UCD 0-4.
UCC champions with four league points.
1937/38 – UCD hosted. All games at Belfield. 25 February: UCD 8-1, UCG 0-3. 26 February: UCC 5-1, UCG 4-1. 27 February: UCD 4-4, UCC 2-1.
UCD champions with four league points.
1938/39 – UCG hosted. Galway, 10 February: UCC 2-3, UCG 2-1. 11 February: UCD 5-5, UCG 1-1. 12 February: UCC 6-2, UCD 0-2.
UCC champions with four league points.
1939/40 – UCC hosted. Douglas, 16 February: UCC 2-5, UCG 0-0. Camp Field, Cork, 17 February: UCD 4-7, UCG 3-2. Camp Field, 18 February: UCC 6-0, UCD 4-3
UCC champions with four league points.
1940/41 – UCD hosted. All games at Belfield. 21 February: UCD 2-8, UCG 2-4. 22 February: UCC 7-6, UCG 2-1. 23 February: UCD 7-10, UCC 3-1.
UCD champions with four league points.
1941/42 – UCG hosted. Galway, 6 February: UCG 3-4, UCD 2-3. 7 February: UCD 5-2, UCC 3-4. 8 February: UCG 4-6, UCC 4-5.
UCG champions with four league points.
1942/43 – Not played.
1943/44 – UCC hosted. All games at the Mardyke. 25 February: UCC 5-7, UCG 1-3. 26 February: UCD 2-10, UCG 2-4. 27 February: UCD 6-5, UCC 4-2.
UCD champions with four league points.
1944/45 – UCD hosted. Belfield, 16 February: UCD 2-6, UCG 3-2. Croke Park, 17 February: UCG 6-4, UCC 2-3. Croke Park, 18 February: UCC 6-1, UCD 3-5.
UCG champions with highest aggregate score.
1945/46 – UCG hosted. Galway Sports Ground, 8 February: UCG 4-4, QUB 2-0; UCC 1-1, UCD 0-4. Fahy's Field, 9 February: UCG 4-4, UCD 3-6; UCC 4-5, QUB 1-1. Fahy's Field, 10 February: UCG 2-4, UCC 0-4; UCD vs. QUB cancelled.
UCG champions with six league points.
1946/47 – UCC hosted. All games at the Mardyke. 28 February: UCC 8-9, UCD 4-1; UCG 7-3, QUB 2-1. 1 March: UCC 2-5, QUB 0-4; UCD 2-14, UCG 2-4. 2 March: UCC 6-5, UCG 0-0; UCD vs. QUB cancelled.
UCC champions with six league points.
1947/48 – UCD hosted. Belfield, 30 January: UCD 4-6, UCG 3-2; UCC 6-0, QUB 1-3. Belfield, 31 January: UCD 13-4, QUB 4-2; UCC 7-6, UCG 2-5. Croke Park, 1 February: UCD 3-5, UCC 2-0; UCG vs. QUB cancelled.
UCD champions with six league points.
Note: From 1948/49 onwards the competition adopted a straight knock-out format.
1948/49 – QUB hosted. Semi-finals at Cherryvale, 29 January: UCG 6-4, QUB 3-5; UCD 5-6, UCC 0-2. Final at Corrigan Park, 30 January: UCG 4-8, UCD 3-1.
1949/50 – UCG hosted. Semi-finals at Galway, 4 February: UCG 9-0, QUB 1-4;
UCD 6-2, UCC 4-3. Final at Galway, 5 February: UCD 4-6, UCG 2-3.
1950/51 – UCC hosted. Semi-finals at the Mardyke, 27 January: UCD 4-8, UCG 1-1; UCC 4-9, QUB 0-1. Final at the Mardyke, 28 January: UCD 2-6, UCC 1-3.
1951/52 – UCD hosted. Semi-finals at Belfield, 26 January: UCD 9-6, QUB 1-1; UCC 3-12, UCG 4-2. Final at Croke Park, 27 January: UCD 2-12, UCC 2-2.
1952/53 – QUB hosted. Semi-finals at Cherryvale, 7 February: QUB 2-5, UCG 1-4; UCD 3-4, UCC 0-4. Final at Corrigan Park, 26 April: QUB 1-3, UCD 0-5.
1953/54 – UCG hosted. Semi-finals at Galway, 13 February: UCG 5-3, UCC 2-1;
UCD 3-6, QUB 1-3. Final at Fahy's Field, 14 February: UCG 5-3, UCD 0-3.
Competition declared null and void
1954/55 – UCC hosted. Semi-finals at the Mardyke, 12 February: UCC 3-6, UCD 3-5; UCG 6-9, QUB 1-4. Final at the Mardyke, 13 February: UCC 7-3, UCG 1-1.
1955/56 – UCD hosted. Semi-finals at Belfield, 25 February: UCD 6-11, UCG 1-6; UCC 14-8, QUB 0-1. Final at Nenagh, 26 February: UCC 4-6, UCD 3-5.
Note: From 1956/57 to 1965/66 (except for 1963/64) the Fitzgibbon Cup competition was played during the first term of the academic year (Michaelmas), chiefly in November and December.

1956/57 – UCG hosted. All games at Fahy's Field. Semi-finals, 17 November: UCC 4-10, UCD 2-5; UCG 8-11, QUB 0-1. Final, 18 November: UCC 3-8, UCG 2-6.
1957/58 – UCC hosted. All games at the Mardyke. Semi-finals, 30 November: UCD 4-6, UCC 1-11; UCG 7-0, QUB 3-3. Final, 1 December: UCD 7-9, UCG 2-1
1958/59 – QUB hosted. Semi-finals at Cherryvale, 15 November: UCD 5-11, UCG 1-6; UCC 10-5, QUB 2-6. Final at Casement Park, 16 November: UCC 4-8, UCD 3-2.
1959/60 – UCD hosted. Semi-finals at Belfield, 28 November: UCD 8-7, QUB 1-0; UCC 4-2, UCG 1-2. Final at Croke Park, 29 November: UCD 4-10, UCC 4-3.
1960/61 – UCG hosted. All games at Pearse Stadium. Semi-finals, 3 December: UCG 1-7, UCC 1-6; UCD 8-9, QUB 1-1. Final, 4 December: UCD 3-6, UCG 3-4.
1961/62 – UCC hosted. Semi-finals at the Mardyke, 18 November: UCC 2-6, UCD 1-6; UCG 7-9, QUB 4-1. Final at the Mardyke, 19 November: UCC 5-9, UCG 1-6.
1962/63 – QUB hosted. Semi-finals at Cherryvale, 17 November: UCC 7-10, QUB 2-1; UCD 6-9, UCG 5-3. Final at Casement Park, 18 November:UCC 3-5, UCD 2-2.
1963/64 – UCD hosted. Semi-finals at Belfield, 7 March: UCC 1-12, UCG 2-6; UCD 7-15, QUB 1-2. Final at Croke Park, 8 March: UCD 4-7, UCC 4-3.
1964/65 – UCG hosted. Semi-finals at Pearse Stadium, 21 November: UCD 1-10, UCC 1-7; UCG 9-3, TCD 0-2. Final at Pearse Stadium, 22 November: UCD 4-8, UCG 4-2.
1965/66 – UCC hosted. Semi-finals at the Farm, 20 November: UCD 2-10, UCG 3-3; UCC 9-7, QUB 3-1. Final at the Mardyke, 21 November: UCC 5-5, UCD 3-3.
Note: From 1966/67 to the present day the Fitzgibbon Cup was played in the second term (Hilary), chiefly in February and March.
1966/67 – TCD hosted. Semi-finals at O'Toole Park, 4 March: UCC 1-11, UCD 1-6; UCG 8-10, TCD 3-6. Final at Croke Park, 5 March: UCC 3-17, UCG 2-5.
1967/68 – QUB hosted. Semi-finals at Malone, 2 March: UCD 8-12, QUB 3-7; UCC 5-11, UCG 1-4. Final at Casement Park, 3 March: UCD 1-15, UCC 2-1.
1968/69 – UCD hosted. Semi-finals at O'Toole Park, 22 February: UCD 3-8, TCD 1-1; UCC 7-9, UCG 0-2. Final at Croke Park, 23 February: UCD 1-12, UCC 1-10.
1969/70 – UCG hosted. Semi-finals at Pearse Stadium, 7 March: UCD 4-8, UCC 1-4; UCG 9-9, QUB 0-2. Final at Pearse Stadium, 8 March: UCG 4-8, UCD 2-12 (a.e.t.).
1970/71 – UCC hosted. Semi-finals at the Mardyke, 27 February: UCC 3-16, UCD 4-11 (a.e.t.); UCG 11-7, QUB 3-11. Final at the Mardyke, 28 February: UCC 2-16, UCG 2-6.
1971/72 – TCD hosted. Semi-finals at O'Toole Park, 11 March: UCG 8-10, QUB 2-6; UCC 7-12, TCD 1-5. Final at Croke Park, 12 March: UCC 3-11, UCG 0-6.
1972/73 – UCG hosted. Semi-finals at Athenry, 10 March: UCG 2-17, UCC 2-11 (a.e.t.); Maynooth 2-18, UCD 2-7. Final at Pearse Stadium, 11 March: Maynooth 2-12, UCG 4-4.
1973/74 – QUB hosted. Semi-finals at Carey, 2 March: UCD 4-9, QUB 3-9; Maynooth 7-16, TCD 1-0. Final at Ballycastle, 3 March: Maynooth 2-10, UCD 1-7.
1974/75 – UCD hosted. Semi-finals at O'Toole Park, 1 March: UCD 3-12, UCC 0-4; Maynooth 2-10, UCG 2-7. Final at O'Toole Park, 2 March: UCD 4-8, Maynooth 2-7.
1975/76 – UCC hosted. Semi-finals at the Mardyke, 21 February 1976: UCC 5-7, UCD 3-11; Maynooth 3-10, UCG 2-7. Final at the Mardyke, 22 February: UCC 3-5, Maynooth 0-10.
1976/77 – Maynooth hosted. Semi-finals at High Field, Maynooth, 5 March: UCG 2-12, UCC 1-6; Maynooth 4-12, UCD 3-12. Final at Maynooth College, 6 March: UCG 1-14, Maynooth 1-12.
1977/78 – QUB hosted. Semi-finals at Malone, 4 March: UCD 5-11, UCG 2-8; UCC 5-7, QUB 2-9. Final at Corrigan Park, 5 March: UCD 3-15, UCC 2-7.
1978/79 – TCD hosted. Semi-finals at O'Toole Park, 24 March: UCC 2-8, Maynooth 1-6; UCG 2-8, UCD 1-9. Final at Croke Park, 25 March: UCD 4-21, Maynooth 1-8.
1979/80 – Semi-finals at Athenry, 1 March: UCC 2-8, Maynooth 1-6; UCG 2-8, UCD 1-9. Final at Galway, 2 March: UCG 0-10, UCC 1-5.
1980/81 – UCD hosted. Semi-finals at O'Toole Park, 28 February: UCC 3-12, UCG 0-5; UCD 7-12, Maynooth 1-9. Final at Croke Park, 1 March: UCC 2-9, UCD 0-8.
1981/82 – UCC hosted. Semi-finals at the Mardyke, 20 February: UCC 5-14, QUB 0-4; UCG 1-10, UCD 2-4. Final at Páirc Uí Chaoimh, 21 February: UCC 0-14, UCG 3-3.
1982/83 – NUU Coleraine hosted. Semi-finals at NUU, 26 February: UCG beat NUU; UCC beat UCD. Final at Bellaghy, 27 February: UCC 3-12, UCG 1-3.
1983/84 – Maynooth hosted. Semi-final at Maynooth College Park, 18 February: UCC 1-15, UCG 1-9. Semi-final at Highfield, Maynooth, 18 February: UCD 3-15, Maynooth 0-6. Final at Highfield, 19 February: UCC 0-7, UCD 0-5.
1984/85 – QUB hosted. Semi-finals at Malone, 2 March: UCC 5-14, UCD 0-7; UCG beat QUB. Final at Malone, 3 March: UCC 1-15, UCG 1-7.
1985/86 – TCD hosted. Semi-finals at Santry, 1 March: QUB 3-7, UCD 1-12; UCC 3-15, UCG 4-11 (a.e.t.). Final at Croke Park, 2 March: UCC 3-10, QUB 0-12.
1986/87 – UCG hosted. Semi-finals at Castlegar, 21 February: UCC 0-12, UCG 0-8; UCD 0-20,

QUB 2-11 (a.e.t.). Final at Castlegar, 22 February: UCC 1-11, UCD 0-11.
1987/88 – UUJ hosted. Semi-final at Jordanstown, 27 February: UCC 3-20, UCD 4-15 (a.e.t.). Semi-final at O'Donovan Rossa's, 27 February: UCG 2-12, QUB 2-9 (a.e.t. – 2 periods). Final at Corrigan Park, 28 February: UCC 1-14, UCG 1-3.
1988/89 – UCD hosted. Semi-finals at Belfield, 25 February: NIHEL 1-9, WRTC 0-7; UCD 1-12, UCC 0-9. Final at Belfield, 26 February: NIHEL 2-9, UCD 1-9.
1989/90 – UCC hosted. Semi-final at Páirc Uí Chaoimh, 17 March: UCC 5-11, UL 2-10. Semi-final at Na Piarsaigh grounds, 17 March: WRTC 2-14, QUB 3-7 (a.e.t.). Final at Páirc Uí Chaoimh, 18 March: UCC 3-10, WRTC 0-12.
1990/91 – QUB & UUJ hosted together. Semi-finals at Jordanstown, 9 March 1991: UCC 4-13, UL 3-3; UCD 1-10, QUB 0-7. Final at Corrigan Park, 10 March: UCC 1-14, UCD 1-6.
1991/92 – UL hosted. Semi-final at UL, 7 March: UL 3-6, UCC 1-11. Semi-final at MICL Grounds, 7 March: WRTC 1-13, UCD 1-12. Final at Limerick Gaelic Grounds, 8 March: WRTC 1-19, UL 1-8.
1992/93 – WRTC hosted. Semi-final at De La Salle, 13 March: UCD 0-12, UL 0-10. Semi-final at Mount Sion, 13 March: UCC 1-16, WRTC 1-9. Final at Walsh Park, 14 March: UCD 2-21, UCC 4-14 (a.e.t.).
1993/94 –UCG hosted. Semi-finals at Castlegar, 12 March: UL 4-9, UCC 3-8 (a.e.t.); WRTC 0-11, UCD 0-7. Final at Clarenbridge, 13 March: UL 2-12, WRTC 1-11 (a.e.t.).
1994/95 – Maynooth hosted. Semi-finals at Clane, 4 March: UCD 2-4, Maynooth 0-4; WRTC 0-11, UL 1-7. Final at Clane, 5 March: WRTC 3-15 UCD 1-4.
1995/96 – UCD hosted. Semi-finals at Belfield, 9 March: UCC 2-19, Maynooth 3-10; UL 1-9, Garda 1-8. Final at Belfield, 10 March: UCC 3-16, UL 0-16.
1996/97 – UCC hosted. Semi-finals at the Mardyke, 1 March: UCC 3-13, DCU 2-3; Garda 1-8, WRTC 1-7. Final at Páirc Uí Rinn, 2 March: UCC 0-14, Garda 1-8
1997/98 – MICL hosted. Semi-finals at Claughaun, 28 February: WIT 1-11, Garda 1-9; UCC 3-11, UCD 0-6. Final at Limerick Gaelic Grounds, 1 March: UCC 2-17, WIT 0-13.
1998/99 – Garda TC hosted. Semi-finals at Templemore, 27 February: WIT 1-17, Garda 2-4; UCC 1-11, UCD 1-8. Final at Templemore, 28 February: WIT 4-15, UCC 3-12.
1999/00 – WIT hosted. Semi-final at Mount Sion, 4 March: WIT 4-20, Limerick IT 0-6. Semi-final at De La Salle, 4 March: UCD 1-15, UCC 0-17. Final at Walsh Park, 5 March: WIT 2-10, UCD 1-6.
2000/2001 –UCD meant to host (until foot-and-mouth outbreak). Semi-final at Ardfinnan, 28 March: UCC 2-13, WIT 1-14. Semi-final at Nenagh, 29 March: UCD 4-15, NUIG 2-16 (a.e.t.). Final at Parnell Park, 11 April: UCD 0-15, UCC 0-15 (a.e.t.). Final replay at Nenagh, 18 April: UCD 2-10, UCC 1-9.
2001/02 – NUIG hosted. Semi-final at Castlegar, 2 March: WIT 2-17, Limerick IT 0-9. Semi-final at Daingean, 2 March: UL 2-11, UCC 0-9. Final at Castlegar, 3 March: UL 2-14, WIT 2-11.
2002/03 – Semi-final at Ardfinnan, 25 February: WIT 1-17, UL 1-13. Semi-final at the Mardyke, 25 February: Cork IT 3-6, UCC 0-8. Final at the Ragg, 1 March: WIT 0-13, CIT 0-7.
2003/04 – AIT hosted. Semi-final at Athlone, 5 March: UCC 0-19, LIT 1-11. Semi-final at Garrycastle: WIT 2-9, UCD 0-13. Final at Athlone, 6 March: WIT 0-11, Cork IT 0-9.
2004/05 – LIT hosted. Semi-finals at LIT, 4 March: UL 4-9, WIT 2-13; LIT 2-15, NUIG 0-8. Final at Limerick Gaelic Grounds, 5 March: LIT 2-13, UL 3-6.
2005/06 – UCC hosted. Semi-finals at the Mardyke, 3 March: UCD 0-13, UCC 1-9; WIT 0-24, NUIG 1-19 (a.e.t.). Final at Páirc Uí Rinn, 4 March: WIT 4-13, UCD 0-8.
2006/07 – IT Carlow hosted. Semi-finals at IT Carlow, 9 March: LIT 1-19, UL 2-9; NUIG 1-11, DIT 2-5. Final at Dr Cullen Park, 10 March: LIT 2-15, NUIG 0-13.
2007/08 – Cork IT hosted. Semi-finals at Cork IT, 29 February: LIT 3-10, GMIT 2-10; WIT 2-14, UCD 1-15. Final at Cork IT, 1 March: WIT 1-29, LIT 1-24 (a.e.t. – 2 periods).
2008/09 – TCD hosted. Semi-finals at Clann na nGael Fontenoy, Ringsend, 6 March: UL 3-20, Cork IT 2-11; UCC 1-18, WIT 2-14. Final at Parnell Park, 7 March: UCC 2-17, UL 0-14.

FITZGIBBON CUP FINAL TEAMS

Note: Although in most years up to 1948/49 there was no Fitzgibbon Cup final per se, the following list includes the runner-up college team where available.

1911/12

U.C.D. – B Hynes, P Salmon, John Ryan (Limerick & Dublin), J O'Keeffe, M O'Hanlon, M Heenan, J Pollard, P D Murphy, Patrick Stokes (Tipperary), D Kennedy, P Fitzpatrick, D Chadwick, J Dwan (capt.), R Hennessy, T F Connolly, C Ryan, Éamon Bulfin (Offaly).

U.C.C. – Peter M Murphy (Cork) (capt.), T Lynch, Jim Reidy (Limerick), Dan Boohan (Limerick), John Hickey (Tipperary), Bill Fitzgerald (Cork), T Kelleher, E Hartnett, D O'Keeffe, T O'Keeffe, William Lehane (Cork), Patrick Joseph Burke (Tipperary), J O'Mullane, Denny Pa Lucey, Jack O'Sullivan, Hugh Whelan, Davy Ring (Cork).

1912/13

U.C.C. (16 players listed) – T O'Keeffe, Jim Reidy (Limerick), T Lynch, Peter M Murphy (Cork) (capt.), Patrick Joseph Burke (Tipperary), J Nunan, Bill Fitzgerald (Cork), Davy Ring (Cork), J Connolly, Tommy Richardson (Cork), J O'Brien, Denny Pa Lucey, Hugh Whelan, D O'Keeffe, P Hayes, George O'Mahoney.

U.C.D. (15 players listed) – John Ryan (Limerick & Dublin) (capt.), Éamon Bulfin (Offaly), P D Murphy, Solomon Lawlor (Kerry & Dublin), J Dwan, M Heenan, R Hennessy, W Chadwick, P Fitzgerald, B Hynes, Pierce Walton (Kilkenny), Frank Burke (Kildare & Dublin), J O'Keeffe, D Fury, J Duffy.

1913/14

U.C.C. – A McGuinness (Cork) (goal), Jim Reidy (Limerick), John Hickey (Tipperary), Charlie O'Riordan (Cork), T Flynn, George Mahony, Dan Boohan (Limerick), Peter M Murphy (Cork), David Coleman, Hugh Whelan, M 'Hawk' O'Brien (Tipperary), Denny Pa Lucey, Cornie O'Neill, T Dwane (Tipperary), Dan Joe Murphy. J Nunan also played over weekend.

U.C.D. – B Hayes, Pierce Walton (Kilkenny), John Ryan (Dublin), M Heenan, P O'Brien, P Fitzpatrick, Eimar O'Duffy (Dublin), N Maher, L Flynn, D Murphy, E Finn, Éamon Bulfin (Offaly), Thomas O'Hickey, Solomon Lawlor (Kerry & Dublin), Frank Burke (Kildare & Dublin).

1914/15

U.C.D. – Éamon Bulfin (Offaly) (capt.), John Ryan (Dublin), E Coogan, Charlie Stuart (Clare), Eimar O'Duffy (Dublin), Pierce Walton (Kilkenny), D Kennedy, Tommy Daly (Clare & Dublin) (goal), Solomon Lawlor (Kerry & Dublin), Brian Joyce (Galway), Thomas O'Hickey, D Sullivan, N Maher, Frank Burke (Kildare & Dublin), T Cummins.

U.C.C. – John Hickey (Tipperary), Dan Boohan (Limerick), Peter M Murphy (Cork), T Dwane (Tipperary), J McCarthy, J Maher, E Dwyer, Harry St. John Atkins (Cork), Davy Ring (Cork), D J O'Sullivan, Dick F O'Brien, M Hurley, George O'Mahoney, Dan O'Driscoll, R B O'Brien, Jack Saunders, J Looney.

1915/16

U.C.D. – John Ryan (Dublin) (capt.), Tommy Daly (Clare & Dublin), Solomon Lawlor (Kerry & Dublin), P Harte, P Cummins, Charlie Stuart (Clare), P O'Brien, Thomas O'Hickey, J P Nolan, Frank Burke (Dublin), E Coogan, W Murphy, N Cooney, D Sullivan.

U.C.C. – team-list not available.

1916/17

U.C.D. – John Ryan (Dublin) (capt.), Tommy Daly (Clare & Dublin) (goal), Solomon Lawlor (Kerry & Dublin), P Harte, Pierce Walton (Kilkenny), E Coogan, P Cummins, D Sullivan, Brian Joyce (Galway & Dublin), Joe Phelan (Kilkenny & Dublin), Frank Burke (Dublin), P J O'Brien, Charlie Stuart (Clare), N Cooney, D Downey.

U.C.C. – Con Lucey (Cork) (capt.), Tim Sheehan (goal), Willie Moore (Kilkenny), T Dwane (Tipperary), R Lahiffe, Donovan, O'Brien, J McCarthy, John Breen, Harry St. John Atkins (Cork), Eugene 'Nudge' Callanan (Tipperary), Jack Falvey (Cork), Christopher T O'Neill, Curran, Murphy.

1917/18

U.C.C. (as listed in a non-Fitzgibbon Cup game) – James G Lahiff, P O'Keeffe, Willie Moore (Kilkenny & Cork), P F Fitzpatrick, J McCarthy, J Meagher, Jack Falvey (Cork), E Lahiff, T Blake, J J Lucy, T O'Driscoll, M C O'Mahony, S Kelleher, C Moloney, William S Nunan. Subs.: C Bastible.

U.C.D. – team-list not available.

1918/19

U.C.G. – Martin Fahy (capt.), J Darcy, M O'Keeffe, M O'Farrell, M Kyne, Leonard? McGrath, Tom Fahy (Galway), Andrew Sexton, Edward Brennan, Arthur de B Joyce, Joseph Sexton, D Clune, G H Joyce, J Jordan, P Fahy (Galway).

U.C.D. – team-list not available.

1919/20

U.C.C. – team-list not available.

U.C.D. – team-list not unavailable.

1920/21 – NO COMPETITION.

1921/22

U.C.C. – J O'Donnell, Maurice O'Brien, William Fortune (Cork), M C O'Mahony, Bernie Flynn (Cork), Harry St. John Atkins (Cork), Wille Cotter (Cork), Eugene 'Nudge' Callanan (Tipperary), R Lahiffe, M Cotter, R Kelly, Con Lucey (Cork), Finian O'Shea (Cork), Pat Nyhan (Cork), Joe Kearney (Cork).

U.C.D. – M O'Brien (goal), J Hogan, J Godfrey, Tommy Daly (Clare & Dublin) (capt.), G Conway, M McManus, Mick D'Arcy (Tipperary & Dublin), J O'Neill, F O'Dea, Tom Pierse (Wexford), J Pierce, Timothy J Kirby, John Kennedy, T Fanning, John Joe Callanan (Tipperary & Dublin).

1922/23

U.C.D. – Tommy Daly (Clare & Dublin) (capt.), Mick D'Arcy (Tipperary), Tom Pierse (Wexford), S Conway, J Pierce, E MacMahon, Joe Phelan (Kilkenny & Dublin), Paul Power (Tipperary), Michael Waldron, Paddy McDonald (Cavan), J O'Neill, T Fanning, John Kennedy, Timothy J Kirby, J Hogan.

U.C.C. – Finian O'Shea (Cork) (capt.), Tom Lee (Tipperary), M O'Sullivan, J O'Sullivan, J Breen, Dan Walsh (Cork), Dinny Barry-Murphy (Cork), M C O'Mahony, J O'Mahony, Michael O'Toole, R Hazel, Seán Forde, B Kelly, M O'Donnell, Pat Nyhan (Cork).

1923/24

U.C.D. – Tommy Daly (Clare & Dublin) (goal) (capt.), William Small (Tipperary & Dublin), Conway, Paddy McDonald (Cavan), Conway, Mick D'Arcy (Tipperary), Flanagan, Paul Power (Tipperary), Myles J Shelly, Joe Phelan (Kilkenny & Dublin), Frank Burke (Dublin), Tom Pierse (Wexford), D Smith, Donovan, D Kennedy.

U.C.C. – Pat Nyhan (Cork) (goal), William Fortune (Cork) (capt.), Maurice O'Brien (Cork), M O'Donnell, John Barry-Murphy (Cork), Dinny Barry-Murphy (Cork), Matt Murphy (Cork), Frank Creedon (Cork), Bernie Flynn (Cork), Donovan, Joe Kearney (Cork), Callaghan, Finian O'Shea (Cork), Dan Walsh (Cork), O'Mahony.

1924/25

U.C.C. – Pat Nyhan (Cork) (goal), Maurice O'Brien (Cork), J Barry (Cork), M O'Donnell, Seán Forde, Dinny Barry-Murphy (Cork), John Barry-Murphy (Cork), Tom Lee (Tipperary) (capt.), Jim Hurley (Cork), M Ryan (Cork), Bernie Flynn (Cork), Dan Walsh (Cork), William Fortune (Cork), J O'Shea, Joe Kearney (Cork).

U.C.D. – Tommy Daly (Clare & Dublin) (goal) (capt.), Mick D'Arcy (Tipperary), J Lowery, Phil Sullivan (Kerry), T Maguire, T Lyng, Michael Waldron (Dublin), Paddy McDonald (Cavan), Denis Finn (Tipperary), Jim Smith (Cavan), Andrew Cooney (Tipperary), Paul Power (Tipperary), J O'Neill, W Ryan.

1925/26

U.C.G. – T O'Grady (capt.), Nicholas J Bodkin, M O'Toole, P J Hanley, P Lenihan, P Kelly, B Roland, P Barry, Andy Kelly (Galway), P Finn, M King (Galway), Peadar Ó Maille, Bernard F S McKiernan, W Keane, D Kelleher, T Cunningham.

U.C.D. – team-list not available.

1926/27

U.C.D. – O O'Neill (capt.), Tommy Daly (Clare & Dublin), William Small (Tipperary & Dublin), Joe Stuart (Clare), Myles J Shelly, Mick D'Arcy (Tipperary & Dublin), Michael Waldron (Dublin), Patrick G Collier, Denis Finn (Tipperary), Andrew Cooney (Tipperary), P O'Meara, Frank Sheehy (Kerry), D Smith, J Gleeson, P Muldowney.

U.C.C. – Donal McCarthy (capt.), Paddy O'Donovan (Cork), Tom Lee (Tipperary), John Barry-Murphy (Cork), B Farrell, William Finlay (Tipperary), Dinny Barry-Murphy (Cork), Bernie Flynn (Cork), Pat Nyhan (Cork), J Dargan, Eugene 'Nudge' Callanan (Cork), T O'Brien, Dan Walsh (Cork), Mossie Donegan (Cork), J Barry (Cork).

1927/28

U.C.C. – Richard Molloy (Cork) (capt.), Donal McCarthy (Cork), Batt Daly, Patrick O'Donnell, R Coughlan, Dinny Barry-Murphy (Cork), John J Dorgan, Mossie Donegan (Cork), Jack Russell (Cork), J Benson, Bernie Flynn (Cork), William Finlay (Tipperary), C Creegan, Paddy O'Donovan (Cork), Tony Hennerty (Cork).

U.C.D. – Denis Finn (Tipperary) (capt.), William Small (Tipperary & Dublin), Joe Stuart (Clare), P Teehan, Frank Sheehy (Kerry), Andrew Cooney (Tipperary), F Fanning, Andrew Quinn (Tipperary), M Quirke, Joseph Canning (Cork), V Corcoran, T Mitchell, T McConnell, Michael Waldron (Dublin), Patrick G Collier.

1928/29

U.C.C. – Paddy O'Donovan (Cork) (capt.), Richard Molloy (Cork), Donal McCarthy (Cork), Batt Daly, Denis W Harvey, William Finlay (Tipperary), Mossie Donegan (Cork), B Farrell, M Queally, J Barry (Cork), Jim O'Regan (Cork), Tony Hennerty (Cork), T Hegarty, Patrick O'Donnell, R Coughlan.

U.C.D. – team-list not available.

1929/30

U.C.C. – Daniel O'Connell Keating (Cork), Patrick O'Donnell (capt.), Richard Molloy (Cork), Batt Daly, William Finlay (Tipperary), Tony Hennerty (Cork), Paddy O'Donovan (Cork), Gus Kelleher (Cork), J A Costelloe, P Condon, D Murphy, C Sheehan, T McCarthy, J Murphy, Jim Hurley (Cork).

U.C.D. – James Flanagan (Tipperary), Frank Sheehy (Kerry) (capt.), P McDonnell, Andrew Quinn (Tipperary), Mick D'Arcy (Tipperary), Joe Stuart (Clare), J Walsh, Michael Falvey (Clare), John Bourke, Thomas Costelloe (Clare), T Mitchell, V Ryan, P Barron, P O'Connor, Kevin McNeill (Dublin).

1930/31

U.C.C. – Richard Molloy (Cork), P Condon, D Murphy, J Murphy, J Casey, Gus Kelleher (Cork), Patrick O'Donnell, Jim Hurley (Cork), William Finlay (Tipperary), Ted Vaughan (Cork), Paddy O'Donovan (Cork), M Teehan, Luke Tully (Cork), T Calthorpe, T O'Neill. Sub.: J A Costelloe.

U.C.D. – James Flanagan (Tipperary), Terry McCarthy (Cork), Michael Falvey (Clare), Mick D'Arcy (Tipperary), Paddy Bresnihan (Limerick), P O'Neill, Martin Waldron, M Walsh, Andrew Quinn (Tipperary), E T Lundren, Jack Walsh,

Thomas Costelloe (Clare), Tom Loughnane (Clare), Joseph Canning (Cork), L G Cooney. John Durkin (Mayo), McMahon & Kenny also played over the weekend.

1931/32

U.C.D. – Jack Walsh (capt.), James Flanagan (Tipperary) (goal), Paddy Bresnihan (Limerick), Tom Loughnane (Clare), Patrick Devaney (Clare), Kevin McNeill (Dublin), T Hogan, W Walsh, Michael Falvey (Clare), Terry McCarthy (Cork), Thomas Costelloe (Clare), J O'Dea, Joseph Canning (Cork), Dennis Madigan (Limerick), W F Dwyer.

U.C.G. – John Langan (capt.), Michael Lee (Galway), H Casey, Christopher McKeown, Joseph Madden, J Harrington (Clare), Michael Kennedy (Tipperary), William Kennedy, Tom Gill, John O'Leary (Clare), Pádraic Fahy, John Bourke, J Sweeney, Seán O'Donovan, Maurice Moynihan. Sub.: J Leydon.

1932/33

U.C.C. (18-man squad) – Richard Cronin (Cork) (capt.), Richard Molloy (Cork), Donal McCarthy (Cork), William Finlay (Tipperary), G Gleeson, Tony Hennerty (Cork), Paddy O'Donovan (Cork), Tom Murphy (Cork), Martin Cronin (Cork), M Franklin, C Ronan, Con McGrath (Cork), Gus Kelleher (Cork), P Nunan, John McCarthy (Cork), Tom O'Reilly (Cork), T O'Neill, P O'Keeffe.

U.C.D. – James Flanagan (Tipperary) (capt.), Tom Loughnane (Clare), Séamus Hogan (Clare), Terry McCarthy (Cork), Michael Falvey (Clare), Colm Boland (Westmeath & Dublin), Dennis Madigan (Limerick), Paddy Bresnihan (Limerick), Kevin McNeill (Dublin), Thomas Costelloe (Clare), Joseph Canning (Cork), Patrick Devaney (Tipperary), J Lynch (Cork), Andrew Quinn (Tipperary), John Durkin (Mayo). T Lee also played over the weekend.

1933/34

U.C.D. (as in first final) – James O'Flanagan (Tipperary), Paddy C Bresnihan (Limerick), Tom Loughnane (Clare), Matt Hawe (Cork), Larry M Hayes (Kilkenny), Séamus Hogan (Clare), Jer Lynch (Cork), Terry McCarthy (Cork), Jimmy Cooney (Tipperary), Tony MacSullivan (Limerick), John T Ryan (Kilkenny), Joseph Canning (Cork & Dublin), Colm Boland (Westmeath & Dublin), Thomas J Butler (Kilkenny), Bill Loughnane (Clare).

U.C.C. (as in first final) – Tom O'Reilly (Cork), P O'Keeffe, Con McGrath (Cork), Martin Cronin (Cork), Tom Murphy (Cork), Donal McCarthy (Cork), John McCarthy (Cork), Paddy O'Donovan (Cork), C Ronan, Joe Roche (Cork), Luke Tully (Cork), D Conroy, Derry Beckett (Cork), Ted Vaughan (Cork), J Sullivan.

1934/35

U.C.D. – Toddy Walsh (Kerry), Mickey Griffin (Clare), Tom Loughnane (Clare), Patrick Devaney (Tipperary), Larry M Hayes (Kilkenny), Paddy C Bresnihan (Limerick), Tony MacSullivan (Limerick), Jimmy Cooney (Tipperary), Seán Feeney (Waterford & Dublin), Dick Foley, Colm Boland (Westmeath & Dublin), Peter Flanagan (Clare), Thomas J Butler (Kilkenny), Bill Loughnane (Clare), John T Ryan (Kilkenny).

U.C.G. – team-list not available.

1935/36

U.C.D. – Toddy Walsh (Kerry), Mickey Griffin (Clare), Tom Loughnane (Clare), Tony MacSullivan (Limerick), Larry M Hayes (Kilkenny), Paddy Bresnihan (Limerick), P Ó Flaithinn, Jimmy Cooney (Tipperary), Seán Feeney (Waterford & Dublin), Dick Foley, Colm Boland (Westmeath & Dublin), Peter Flanagan (Clare), Michael Falvey (Clare), Bill Loughnane (Clare & Dublin), Jim McCarthy (Dublin). M Franklin also played over the weekend.

1936/37

U.C.C. – Tom O'Reilly (Cork), Eddie O'Donovan (Cork), Mícheál Cranitch (Cork), D Gavin (Cork), Tommy Magner (Cork), Tom Murphy (Cork), Jackie Spencer (Cork), Mossie Roche (Limerick), Gus Kelleher (Cork), P J McCarthy, John McCarthy (Cork), Joe Roche (Cork), M Moriarty, Gerry Madden (Limerick), Paddy Reid (Cork). Theo Lynch (Cork) & T O'Sullivan (Cork) also played.

U.C.D. – Toddy Walsh (Kerry), Dave Hurley (Limerick), Frank Lahiffe (Galway), Tony MacSullivan (Limerick), Larry M Hayes (Kilkenny), Seán Feeney (Waterford & Dublin), Mickey Griffin (Clare), T Healy, Jimmy Cooney (Tipperary), Roger Hayes (Limerick), Colm Boland (Westmeath & Dublin), Peter Flanagan (Clare), M Sheehy, Jim McCarthy (Dublin), W Herlihy. Sub.: D Fitzgerald for Boland.

1937/38

U.C.D. – Toddy Walsh (Kerry), W Herlihy, M Sheehy, Frank Lahiffe (Galway), Larry M Hayes (Kilkenny), Dave Hurley (Limerick), Tony MacSullivan (Limerick), Jimmy Cooney (Tipperary), Roger Hayes (Limerick), T Healy (Cork), Bill Loughnane (Clare), Liam White (Kilkenny), T Fitzgerald, Toddy Walsh (Kerry), Jim McCarthy (Dublin).

U.C.C.– Tom O'Reilly (Cork), Mícheál Cranitch (Cork), Seán Houlihan (Laois), Eddie O'Donovan (Cork), Tommy Magner (Cork), Tom Murphy (Cork), Jackie Spencer (Cork), Mossie Roche (Limerick), P J McCarthy (Cork), John McCarthy (Cork), M McGrath. (Only 11 players listed in reports.)

1938/39

U.C.C. – Tom O'Reilly (Cork), James O'Neill (Cork), Seán Houlihan (Laois), Mícheál Cranitch (Cork), Dan Coughlan (Cork), Tom Murphy (Cork), Kevin Flynn (Clare), Jim Young (Cork), McCarthy, Prendergast, Jackie Spencer (Cork), Roche, Peadar Garvan (Cork), Gerry Madden (Limerick), Derry Beckett (Cork).

U.C.D. – team-list not available.

1939/40

U.C.C. – Paddy Moynihan (Cork), James O'Neill (Cork), Mícheál Cranitch (Cork), Jim Duggan (Cork), Tommy Magner (Cork), Tom Murphy (Cork), Dan Coughlan (Cork), Jim Young (Cork), Jackie Spencer (Cork), P J McCarthy (Cork), Paddy Reid (Cork), Joe Roche (Cork), Peadar Garvan (Cork), Gerry Madden (Limerick), Derry Beckett (Cork). Sub.: D O'Mahony.

U.C.D. – T Hennessy, Dave Hurley (Limerick), Jim McCarthy (Limerick), Johnny Wall (Limerick), J / Billy O'Neill (Kilkenny), Kevin Flynn (Clare), Liam White (Kilkenny), Dick Stokes (Limerick), Roger Hayes (Limerick), M Healy (Cork), Bill Loughnane (Clare & Dublin), Fintan Flynn (Clare), Éamonn O'Boyle (Offaly), T Walsh, M Walsh.

1940/41

U.C.D. – Gerry Fitzgerald (Clare), Billy O'Connell (Limerick), Jim McCarthy (Limerick), Johnny Wall (Limerick), Billy O'Neill (Kilkenny), Kevin Jones (Clare), Jimmy Hurley (Tipperary), Luke O'Sullivan (Cork), Dick Stokes (Limerick), J Phelan, Éamonn O'Boyle (Offaly), Fintan Flynn (Clare), Roger Hayes (Limerick), "Jumbo" Maher (Tipperary), Bill Loughnane (Clare & Dublin).

U.C.C. – Paddy Moynihan (Cork), Peadar Garvan (Cork), C Healy, Jim Duggan (Cork), Tom Murphy (Cork), James O'Neill (Cork), Tom Fleming, Jim Young (Cork), Arthur Beckett (Cork), J McCarthy, Derry Beckett (Cork), J Healy (Cork), T Riordan, J O'Mahoney, Luke Tully (Cork).

1941/42

U.C.G. – Tom Nolan (Galway), M Walsh, Donal Flynn (Cork & Galway), Pat Hehir (Galway), Stephen Fahy (Galway), Jimmy Brophy (Kilkenny & Galway), Michael McDermott (Galway), Paddy Donnellan (Galway), Pierce Thornton (Galway), Tommy Doyle (Galway), Bob Forde (Galway), Bill Trayers (Galway), J Lynch, Seán Thornton (Galway), T Donohue. Sub.: Martin Kelly.

U.C.D. – Gerry Fitzgerald (Clare), Seán Doohan (Offaly), Johnny Wall (Limerick), Kevin Jones (Clare), G Fitzgerald (Limerick), Billy O'Neill (Kilkenny), Jimmy Hurley (Tipperary), Dick Stokes (Limerick), Roger Hayes (Limerick), L Keating (Kilkenny), Ned Daly (Waterford), Mickey Feeney (Waterford), Brendan White (Tipperary), Éamonn O'Boyle (Offaly & Dublin), Luke O'Sullivan (Cork).

1942/43 – NO COMPETITION

1943/44

U.C.D. – Peter O'Keeffe (Laois), Seán Doohan (Offaly), Davy Walsh (Kilkenny), Kieran Maloney (Clare), George Frost (Clare), Bob Frost (Clare), Mick Maher (Tipperary), Dick Stokes (Limerick), Mick Hassett (Dublin), ?????, Ned Daly (Waterford), Mickey Feeney (Waterford), Brendan White (Tipperary), Éamonn O'Boyle (Offaly), Frank Commons (Tipperary), McInerney. Luke O'Sullivan also played.

U.C.C. – Paddy Moynihan (Cork), C Healy, J Duggan, Bernie Murphy, Con Murphy, Tom Fleming, J O'Mahony, S/J Keane, D Keating, T Joyce, J Healy, Derry Beckett, A Power, Jim Young (Cork), Liam Moriarty, T Aherne, J McNamara, B Murphy, R Brennan, J Daly. (20-man squad.)

1944/45

U.C.G. – Seánie Duggan (Galway), Seán Thornton (Galway), Pat Hehir (Galway), Tom Hanley (Limerick), Joe Glynn (Galway), Vincent Baston (Waterford & Galway), Paul Murphy (Galway), Pierce Thornton (Galway), Michael "Hockey" Nestor (Galway), Bob Forde (Galway), Tony Dervan (Galway), Michael "Miko" Doyle (Galway), Johnny Scanlon (Galway), Eugene Lee (Clare), Dinny McMahon (Clare). Tim Regan (Galway), Cathal O'Connor (Galway) & Tommy Doyle (Galway) also played over the weekend.

U.C.C. – team-list not available.

1945/46

U.C.G. – Seánie Duggan (Galway), Tom Hanley (Limerick), Donal Flynn (Cork), Pat Hehir (Galway), Joe Glynn (Galway), Jimmy Brophy (Kilkenny & Galway), Paddy Donnellan (Galway), Bob Forde (Galway), Tony Dervan (Galway), Johnny Scanlon (Galway), Josie Gallagher (Galway), Michael "Miko" Doyle (Galway), Vincent Doyle (Galway), Gerry Fahy (Galway), Dinny McMahon (Clare). Sub.: Finian Fahy (Galway).

U.C.D. – Peter O'Keeffe (Laois), Harry Boland (Dublin), Davy Walsh (Kilkenny), Mick Maher (Tipperary), George Frost (Clare), Bob Frost (Clare), Brian McMahon (Clare), Mick Hassett (Dublin), Des Dillon (Clare), Jimmy Kennedy (Tipperary & Dublin), Ned Daly (Waterford), Mickey Feeney (Waterford), Brendan White (Offaly), Dan McInerney (Clare), Frank Commons (Tipperary). Sub.: Kieran Maloney (Clare).

1946/47

U.C.C. – Dinny Houlihan (Kilkenny), Tony Daly (Cork), Ted O'Driscoll (Cork), Frank Coughlan (Cork), Paddy Tyers (Waterford), Bernie Murphy (Cork), Jackie Houlihan (Limerick), Bill Carroll (Tipperary), Paddy Gallagher (Clare), (i.e. Fr. Paddy Gantley (Galway)) Jackie Harris (Tipperary), Michael O'Shaughnessy (Tipperary), Mick Herlihy (Cork), Bill Cahill (Kilkenny), Arthur Beckett (Cork), Derry Beckett (Cork). Nicky Purcell (Kilkenny) and Mick Phelan (Waterford) also played over the weekend.

U.C.D. – Peter O'Keeffe (Laois), Seán Doohan (Tipperary), Davy Walsh (Kilkenny & Dublin), Kieran Maloney (Clare), Mick Maher (Tipperary), Pierce Thornton (Galway), Brian McMahon (Clare), Des Dillon (Clare), Phil Bartley (Limerick), Jimmy Kennedy (Tipperary & Dublin), Ned Daly (Waterford), Willie Harty (Tipperary), Joby Maher (Tipperary), Ned Ryan (Limerick), Frank Commons (Tipperary).

1947/48

U.C.D. – Tadhg Hurley (Kerry), Seán Doohan (Offaly), Davy Walsh (Kilkenny & Dublin), Mick Maher (Boharlahan), Paddy Enright (Clare), Pierce Thornton (Galway & Dublin), Joby Maher (Tipperary), Mick Hassett (Dublin), Phil Bartley (Limerick), Jimmy Kennedy (Tipperary), Ned Daly (Waterford), Mickey Feeney (Waterford), Willie Harty (Tipperary), Ned Ryan (Limerick), Frank Commons (Tipperary & Dublin). Des Dillon (Clare) also played in the tournament.

U.C.C. – Gary Fleming (Cork), Tony Daly (Cork), Ted O'Driscoll (Cork), Frank Coughlan (Cork), Paddy Tyers (Waterford), Bernie Murphy (Cork), Jimmy O'Reilly (Cork), Brendan Hanniffy (Galway), Bill Carroll (Tipperary), Dave O'Connor (Cork), Humphrey O'Neill (Cork), Seán McCarthy (Cork), Mick Fennelly (Kilkenny), Tony Brennan (Kilkenny), B Herlihy (Cork).

1948/49

U.C.G. - Bernie Egan (Galway), Joe Glynn (Galway), Pat Hehir (Galway), Billy Glynn (Galway), Harry Crowley (Galway), Mick Costello (Galway), Paul Murphy (Galway), Joe Salmon (Galway), Michael McInerney (Galway), Frank Duignan (Galway), Dick Leonard (Limerick), Jack O'Brien (Clare), Johnny Scanlon (Galway), John Joe Coyne (Galway), Donal Donovan (Galway). Sub.: Paddy Greally (Galway) for McInerney.

U.C.D. – Tadhg Hurley (Kerry), Seán Doohan (Offaly), Frank Flynn (Galway), Mick Maher (Boharlahan), Finian Fahy (Galway), Dick Stokes (Limerick), Joby Maher (Tipperary), Peter Fitzgerald (Tipperary), Maurice Queally (Waterford), Jimmy Kennedy (Tipperary), Frank Commons (Tipperary & Dublin), Ned Ryan (Limerick), Willie Harty (Tipperary), Harry Murphy (Kilkenny), Gerry Fahy (Galway).

1949/50

U.C.D. – Ray Brennan (Wexford), A McCarthy, Frank Flynn (Galway), Mick Maher (Boharlahan), Finian Fahy (Galway), Maurice Queally (Waterford), Mick O'Shaughnessy (Cork), Des Dillon (Clare & Dublin), Martin Fitzgerald (Tipperary & Dublin), Gerry Kelly (Tipperary & Dublin), M O'Connell, Johnny Ryan (Tipperary), Tim O'Sullivan (Kerry), Harry Murphy (Kilkenny), Danny Mehigan (Cork).

U.C.G. – Bernie Egan (Galway), Joe Glynn (Galway), Ned Quinn (Galway), Billy Glynn (Galway), Paul Murphy (Galway), Mick Costello (Galway), Paddy Daly (Galway), Dick Leonard (Limerick), Joe Salmon (Galway), Kevin Maher (Tipperary), Michael McInerney (Galway), S Murphy, John Joe Coyne (Galway), Donie Murphy (Kerry), Fergie McDonagh (Westmeath). Sub.: Jack O'Brien (Clare) for Daly.

1950/51

U.C.D. – Ray Brennan (Wexford), Martin McDonnell (Wexford), Mick Maher (Holycross), Mick Maher (Boharlahan), Pat Tynan (Kilkenny), Mick O'Shaughnessy (Cork), Maurice Queally (Waterford), Des Dillon (Clare & Dublin), Martin Fitzgerald (Tipperary & Dublin), Danny Mehigan (Cork), Gerry Kelly (Tipperary & Dublin), Joe Conlon (Waterford), Dick O'Neill (Kilkenny), Harry Murphy (Kilkenny), Johnny Ryan (Tipperary).

U.C.C. – John O'Grady (Tipperary), Jimmy Leahy (Tipperary), J J O'Brien (Cork), Paddy Hayes (Cork), Tom Barry (Waterford), Denis McCarthy (Cork), Paddy O'Regan (Cork), Mickey 'Jinx' Ryan (Tipperary), Tom Crotty (Cork), Seán Boyle (Tipperary), Bill Lineen (Waterford), Willie Walsh (Cork), S McSweeney (Cork), Pat O'Grady (Clare), Paddy Horgan (Cork). Subs.: Vilem Steiglitz (Tipperary) for Boyle, Tom Cavanagh (Cork) for O'Regan

1951/52

U.C.D. – Ray Brennan (Wexford), Pat Tynan (Kilkenny), Mick Maher (Holycross), Ted Hurley (Cork), Éamonn 'Ned' Hallahan (Waterford), Jim White (Clare), Maurice Queally (Waterford), Martin Fitzgerald (Tipperary & Dublin), Des Dillon (Clare & Dublin), Gerry Kelly (Tipperary & Dublin), Seán Kennedy (Tipperary), Mick Gardiner (Kilkenny), Johnny Ryan (Tipperary), Dick O'Neill (Kilkenny), Donal Mehigan (Cork)

U.C.C. – John O'Grady (Tipperary), Tom O'Connor (Kilkenny), Ted O'Driscoll (Cork), J J O'Brien (Cork), Paddy Hayes (Cork), Denis McCarthy (Cork), John Joe O'Sullivan (Cork),

HIGHER EDUCATION

Gerry Murphy (Cork), Willie O'Driscoll (Cork), Mickey 'Jinx' Ryan (Tipperary), Tom Barry (Waterford), Vincent Walsh (Waterford), Paddy Horgan (Cork), P Walsh (Waterford), Tom Crotty (Cork).

1952/53

Q.U.B. – Brendan Trainor (Antrim), Vincent Kelly (Antrim), John Butler (Antrim), John Flanagan (Antrim), Danny Gilmartin (Antrim), Des Cormican (Antrim), Paddy Duggan (Antrim), Séamus "Stout" McDonald (Antrim), Jack Savage (Antrim), Ted McConnell (Antrim), Bobby McMullen (Antrim), Brendan McAleenan (Down), Paul Crilly (Antrim), Donal Anglin (Antrim), Gerry Treacy (Antrim).

U.C.D. – Todd Comerford (Kilkenny), Bill English (Tipperary), Éamonn McGrath (Tipperary), Ted Hurley (Cork), Éamonn 'Ned' Hallahan (Waterford), Jim White (Clare), Michael Doyle (Kilkenny), Pat Tynan (Kilkenny), Jim O'Keeffe , Des Dillon (Clare & Dublin), Gerry Kelly (Tipperary & Dublin), Danny Mehigan (Cork), J Buckley, John Daly (Cork), Larry Power (Tipperary). Sub.: P Ryan for O'Keeffe.

1953/54

U.C.G. – Phil Waldron (Clare), Gerry Meehan (Galway), Frank Daly (Cork), John Naughton (Laois), Eddie Kelly (Limerick), Séamus Cullinane (Galway), Tom O'Toole (Galway), Eddie Fallon (Galway), Pádraic Keane (Galway), Eddie Abberton (Galway), Michael McInerney (Galway), Paddy O'Donoghue (Waterford), Séamus Trayers (Galway), Jimmy Haverty (Galway), Noel McMahon (Offaly). Sub.: Máirtín Fallon (Galway) for Cullinane.

U.C.D. – Todd Comerford (Kilkenny), Bill English (Tipperary), Éamonn McGrath (Tipperary), John O'Mahony (Tipperary), Éamonn 'Ned' Hallahan (Waterford), Jim White (Clare), Michael Doyle (Kilkenny), Nicky Stokes (Limerick), Declan O'Sullivan (Westmeath), Ted Hurley (Cork), Des Dillon (Dublin), Bill Hartley (Wexford), Jimmy Barrett (Kilkenny), Bernard Hoey (Clare), Danny Mehigan (Cork). Sub.: Martin Gibbons (Kilkenny) for Mehigan.

1954/55

U.C.C. – Tony Murphy (Cork), Leo Young (Cork), Paddy Maloney (Tipperary), Jim Forrestal (Kilkenny), Tommy Ryan (Tipperary), Liam Shalloe (Waterford), Pat Teehan (Waterford), Donal 'Duck' Whelan (Waterford), Dick Troy (Cork), Mick Hanley (Clare), Cathal Hurley (Cork), Dan Kennefick (Cork), Tom Crotty (Cork), Billy McCarthy (Kerry), Johnny Dwane (Cork).

U.C.G. – Des Nolan (Galway), Tony O'Gorman (Galway), Frank Daly (Cork), Tom Brennan (Waterford), Tom O'Toole (Galway), Séamus Cullinane (Cork), John Hassett (Clare), Mickey Cullinane (Galway), F Fahy (Galway), Séamus Trayers (Galway), Eddie Fallon (Galway), Paddy O'Donoghue (Waterford), Pádraic Cummins (Galway), Niall McInerney (Galway), Noel McMahon (Offaly).

1955/56

U.C.C. – Tony Murphy (Cork), Leo Young (Cork), George O'Sullivan (Cork), Dan Kelleher (Cork), Tom Gallagher (Waterford), Johnny Vaughan (Cork), Seán Browne (Cork), Dick Troy (Cork), Bernie Cotter (Cork), Gerry McCarthy (Cork), Steve Long (Limerick), Seán Moore (Cork), Paddy Horgan (Cork), Kevin Twomey (Cork), Johnny Dwane (Cork). Subs.: Cathal O'Keeffe for Long, Long for O'Keeffe.

U.C.D. – Phil Waldron (Clare), Bill English (Tipperary), Bernard Hoey (Clare), Ted Hurley (Cork), Seán Dunne (Kilkenny), Éamonn McGrath (Tipperary), Jim McDonnell (Tipperary), Gerry Murphy (Cork), Declan O'Sullivan (Westmeath), Nicky Stokes (Limerick), Billy O'Donovan (Tipperary), Dan Delaney (Tipperary), Jimmy Barrett (Tipperary), Mick Cowhig (Cork), Billy McCarthy (Kerry). Sub.: Maurice Begley (Limerick) for Delaney.

1956/57

U.C.C. – Tony Murphy (Cork), Leo Young (Cork), George O'Sullivan (Cork), Dan Kelleher (Cork), Tom Gallagher (Waterford), Seán O'Riordan (Cork), Gerry O'Meara (Tipperary), Dick Troy (Cork), Liam Shalloe (Waterford), Gerry McCarthy (Cork), Jim McGrath (Limerick), Joe Phelan (Limerick), Bernie Cotter (Cork), Joe Rabbitte (Galway), Seán Moore (Cork).

U.C.G. – Alphonsus Tully (Roscommon), Máirtín Nestor (Galway), Tony O'Gorman (Galway), Pádraic Keane (Galway), Owen Lynch (Cork), Tom Brennan (Waterford), John Dunne (Galway), Bobby Curran (Waterford), Jim Hassett (Clare), Dennis McSweeney (Galway), Mickey Cullinane (Galway), Michael Greene (Clare), Pádraic Cummins (Galway), Eddie Fallon (Galway), John White (Cork). Sub.: Paschal Finn (Galway) for Nestor.

1957/58

U.C.D. - Dan Delaney (Tipperary), Roger O'Donnell (Tipperary), Bernard Hoey (Clare), Dan Kelleher (Cork), Billy O'Donovan (Tipperary), Dennis Kelleher (Cork), Mick Cowhig (Cork), Jim McDonnell (Tipperary), Johnny O'Connor (Waterford), Seán Dunne (Kilkenny), Mickey Cullinane (Galway), Donie Nealon (Tipperary), Tommy Ryan (Tipperary), Nicky Stokes (Limerick), Ted Hurley (Cork). Sub.: Ted Carroll (Kilkenny) for Denis Kelleher.

U.C.G. – Enda O'Flaherty (Galway), Máirtín

Nestor (Galway), Tony O'Gorman (Galway), Pádraic Keane (Galway), Owen Lynch (Cork), Tom Brennan (Waterford), John Dunne (Galway), Bobby Curran (Waterford), Jim Hassett (Clare), Dennis McSweeney (Galway), Liam Gilmartin (Offaly), John White (Cork), Richie Queally (Waterford), Jack Daly (Clare), Pádraig Cummins (Galway). Sub.: Donal Murphy (Limerick) for Cummins.

1958/59

U.C.C. – Billy Moroney (Tipperary), Donie Murphy (Cork), Des Kiely (Tipperary), Seán O'Riordan (Cork), Tom Gallagher (Waterford), Liam Shalloe (Waterford), Mickey Horgan (Cork), Noel Gallagher (Cork), Pat O'Shea (Tipperary), Ollie Harrington (Kilkenny), Jim McGrath (Limerick), Pat Henchy (Clare), John Joe Browne (Cork), Tom Riordan (Cork), Steve Long (Limerick).

U.C.D. – Dan Delaney (Tipperary), Harry Hickey (Kilkenny), Billy O'Donovan (Tipperary), Dan Kelleher (Cork), Seán Moore (Cork), Dennis Kelleher (Cork), Ted Carroll (Kilkenny), Jim McDonnell (Tipperary), Seán Dunne (Kilkenny), Donie Nealon (Tipperary), Mick Leahy (Cork), John Joe O'Keeffe (Limerick), Patsy Nealon (Tipperary), Nicky Stokes (Limerick), Billy McCarthy (Kerry).

1959/60

U.C.D. – Dan Delaney (Tipperary), Tom Nolan (Carlow), Dick O'Donnell (Tipperary), Louis Foyle (Tipperary), Brian McDonnell (Tipperary), Ted Carroll (Kilkenny), Seán Kinsella (Wexford), Seán Quinlivan (Clare), Gus Danaher (Tipperary), Pat Henchy (Clare), Jim Kissane (Wexford), Donie Nealon (Tipperary), Mick Leahy (Cork), Owen O'Neill (Limerick), Patsy Nealon (Tipperary). Sub.: R Reynolds for Danaher.

U.C.C. – Ollie Harrington (Kilkenny), Cormac Flynn (Limerick), Des Kiely (Tipperary), Robert Galvin (Cork), Mickey Horgan (Cork), George Walsh (Cork), Jimmy Byrne (Waterford), Pat O'Shea (Tipperary), Noel Phelan (Limerick), Mick Mortell (Cork), John Joe Browne (Cork), Joe Flynn (Cork), Danny McDonnell (Cork), Tom Riordan (Cork), Steve Long (Limerick). Subs.: Donie Cregan (Limerick) for McDonnell, Ciaran Kelly (Cork) for Walsh.

1960/61

U.C.D. – Owen Hurley (Cork), Seán Kinsella (Wexford), Tom Melody (Clare), Louis Foyle (Tipperary), John Joe O'Keeffe (Limerick), Ted Carroll (Kilkenny), Richard Walsh (Kilkenny), Brian McDonnell (Tipperary), Seán Quinlivan (Limerick), Pat Henchy (Clare), Mick Carroll (Kilkenny), Donie Nealon (Tipperary), Patsy Nealon (Tipperary), Owen O'Neill (Limerick), Murt Duggan (Tipperary). Sub.: Dick Dowling (Kilkenny) for Duggan.

U.C.G. – John O'Mahony (Galway), Séamus Hayes (Waterford), Pat Hassett (Clare), Pádraic Keane (Galway), Joe Lyons (Galway), Tony O'Gorman (Galway), Kevin Smyth (Clare), Paddy Fahy (Galway), John Whiriskey (Galway), Séamus Gohery (Galway), Leo Gardiner (Galway), Seán Devlin (Galway), Gerry Gardiner (Galway), Mick Shaughnessy (Galway), E Burke (Galway). Sub.: Séamus Fallon (Galway) for Burke.

1961/62

U.C.C. – John O'Donoghue (Tipperary), Tom Conway (Limerick), Des Kiely (Tipperary), Noel Phelan (Limerick), Jimmy Byrne (Waterford), Dan Kelleher (Cork), John Alley (Laois), Ollie Harrington (Kilkenny), Mick Waters (Cork), John O'Halloran (Cork), Jimmy Blake (Limerick), Mick Mortell (Cork), George Allen (Cork), Donie Flynn (Limerick), Gerry Gleeson (Limerick). Sub.: Mícheál Óg Murphy (Cork) for Mortell.

U.C.G. – John O'Mahony (Galway), Séamus Hayes (Waterford), Paddy Hassett (Clare), Bernie Diviney (Galway), Joe Lyons (Galway), Mick Shaughnessy (Galway), Kevin Smyth (Clare), John Whiriskey (Galway), Tom Gilmore (Galway), P J Qualter (Galway), Leo Gardiner (Galway), Seán Devlin (Galway), M Niland, Tom Brennan (Waterford), Gerry Gardiner (Galway). Subs.: Séamus Fallon (Galway) for Diviney, J Greally for G Gardiner, Diviney for Hayes.

1962/63

U.C.C. – John O'Donoghue (Tipperary), Tom Conway (Limerick), Des Kiely (Tipperary), Mick McCormack (Tipperary), Ollie Harrington (Kilkenny), Jimmy Byrne (Waterford), John Alley (Laois), Mícheál Óg Murphy (Cork), Donie Flynn (Limerick), John O'Halloran (Cork), Jimmy Blake (Limerick), Mick Mortell (Cork), George Allen (Cork), Maurice Fahy (Cork), Donal Murphy (Cork).

U.C.D. – Murt Duggan (Tipperary), Noel Rohan (Kilkenny), Pat Hassett (Clare), Dick Dowling (Kilkenny), Nicky Hanrahan (Kilkenny), Phil Murray (Tipperary), Richard Walsh (Kilkenny), Brian McDonnell (Tipperary), Seán Quinlivan (Clare), Tom Forrestal (Kilkenny), Hugh McDonnell (Tipperary), Donie Nealon (Tipperary), Patsy Nealon (Tipperary), Owen O'Neill (Limerick), Pat Carroll (Kilkenny).

1963/64

U.C.D. – Murt Duggan (Tipperary), Willie Smith (Tipperary), Dick Dowling (Kilkenny), John Dowling (Kilkenny), Michael Browne (Wexford), Phil Murray (Tipperary), Nicky Hanrahan (Kilkenny), Seán Quinlivan (Clare), Tom Barry (Kilkenny), Pat Henchy (Clare),

Donal Walsh (Wexford), Pat Murphy (Limerick), Tony Loughnane (Clare), Tom Forrestal (Kilkenny), Pat Kennedy (Tipperary). Subs.: Pat Hassett (Clare) for Murphy, Eddie Walsh (Wexford) for Browne.

U.C.C. – Jerry O'Callaghan (Cork), Tom Kavanagh (Wexford), Eamonn "Ned" Rea (Limerick), Mick McCormack (Tipperary), Jimmy Byrne (Waterford), Tony O'Brien (Limerick), John Alley (Laois), Mícheál Óg Murphy (Cork), Dermot Mulcahy (Limerick), Donie Flynn (Limerick), John O'Halloran (Cork), Dan Harnedy (Cork), Noel Phelan (Limerick), Jimmy Blake (Limerick), Ollie Harrington (Kilkenny). Subs.: Michael Fahy (Cork) for Phelan, Phelan for Fahy, Jerry Gleeson (Limerick) for Mulcahy.

1964/65

U.C.D. – Murt Duggan (Tipperary), Willie Smith (Tipperary), Eddie Walsh (Wexford), Dick Dowling (Kilkenny), Brian McDonnell (Tipperary), Phil Murray (Tipperary), John Murphy (Wexford), Tom Barry (Kilkenny), Phil Ryan (Tipperary), Peadar Murphy (Wexford), Kevin Long (Limerick), Pat Murphy (Limerick), Tony Loughnane (Clare), Tom Forrestal (Kilkenny), Paudie Kennedy (Tipperary). Subs.: Jimmy Cummins (Tipperary) for Peadar Murphy, Caimin Jones (Clare) for Cummins.

U.C.G. – Pat O'Neill (Galway), Oliver Dolly (Galway), John Egan (Limerick), Michael Walsh (Galway), Coilín McDonagh (Galway), Tom Canavan (Galway), Séamus Fallon (Galway), Frank Coffey (Galway), Ray Gilmore (Galway), Ray Niland (Westmeath & Galway), Richard Pyne (Clare), Jimmy Rabbitte (Galway), Seán Murphy (Galway), Austin Costelloe (Galway), Frank Hassett (Clare). Subs.: Bernie Diviney (Galway) for Walsh, P J Qualter (Galway) for McDonagh, Tom Holton (Galway) for Fallon.

1965/66

U.C.C. – T O'Shea (Kilkenny), Tom Field (Cork), Mick McCormack (Tipperary), Éamonn 'Ned' Rea (Limerick), Ger O'Herlihy (Cork), John O'Keeffe (Cork), Tom Walsh (Waterford), Willie Cronin (Cork), Pat O'Connell (Tipperary), Donal Clifford (Cork), John O'Halloran (Cork), Seánie Barry (Cork), Richard Lehane (Cork), Jimmy Blake (Limerick), Brendan Kenneally (Cork). Sub.: Pierce Dooley (Laois) for Lehane.

U.C.D. – Murt Duggan (Tipperary), Willie Smith (Tipperary), Willie Hoyne (Kilkenny), Jim Furlong (Wexford), Pat Drennan (Kilkenny), Kevin Long (Limerick), John Murphy (Wexford), Pat Kavanagh (Kilkenny), Phil Dillon (Laois), Frank Smith (Tipperary), Jim O'Neill (Wexford), Derry O'Connor (Tipperary), Tony Loughnane (Dublin), Dermot Kavanagh (Kilkenny), Joe Carroll (Limerick). Sub.: Caimin Jones (Clare) for O'Connor.

1966/67

U.C.C. – John Mitchell (Cork), Tom Field (Cork), Mick McCormack (Tipperary), Éamonn 'Ned' Rea (Limerick), Ger O'Herlihy Cork), John O'Keeffe (Cork), Noel Dunne (Cork), Pat O'Connell (Tipperary), Pierce Dooley (Laois), Seánie Barry (Cork), John O'Halloran (Cork), Donal Clifford (Cork), Richard Lehane (Cork), Denis Philpott (Cork), Noel Morgan (Cork). Subs.: Ray Cummins (Cork) for Morgan, Jimmy McCarthy (Cork) for O'Connell.

U.C.G. – Peter Cosgrave (Galway), Tom McGarry (Tipperary), John Egan (Limerick), Bernie Diviney (Galway), Tom Canavan (Galway), Sam Stanley (Galway), John Kenny (Galway), Frank Coffey (Galway), Séamus Hogan (Tipperary), Ray Niland (Galway), Brendan Shaughnessy (Galway), Pádraig Fahy (Galway), Michael Keane (Galway), Gus Costello (Galway), Brendan Barry (Offaly). Subs.: Niall O'Halloran (Galway) for Kenny, Kenny for O'Halloran, O'Halloran for Shaughnessy, Pat Tobin (Tipperary) for McGarry.

1967/68

U.C.D. - Éamonn Kennedy (Tipperary), Willie Smyth (Tipperary), Jim Furlong (Wexford), Jim O'Neill (Wexford), Donal Kavanagh (Kilkenny), Pat Drennan (Kilkenny), Jimmy Rabbitte (Galway), Phil Dillon (Laois), Willie Cronin (Cork), Pat Kavanagh (Kilkenny), Gerry Quinlan (Tipperary), Frank Smyth (Tipperary), Jack Ryan (Tipperary), Nicky Walsh (Wexford), Colm Muldoon (Galway). Subs.: Tony Loughnane (Dublin) for Muldoon, Mattie Ryan (Limerick) for D Kavanagh, Tony Henry (Mayo) for Cronin.

U.C.C. - John Mitchell (Cork), Tom Field (Cork), John Kelly (Tipperary), Simon O'Leary (Cork), Ger O'Herlihy (Cork), Seán O'Keeffe (Cork), Noel Dunne (Cork), Mick Watters (Cork), Pierce Dooley (Laois), Kevin Cummins (Cork), Ray Cummins (Cork), Donal Motherway (Cork), S Meade (Cork), Henry O'Sullivan (Cork), Noel Rochford (Wexford). Subs.: Michael Bond (Galway) for Rochford, Richard Lehane (Cork) for Meade, Mick Murphy (Cork) for Motherway.

1968/69

U.C.D. - Éamonn Kennedy (Tipperary), Jim O'Neill (Wexford), Mattie Ryan (Limerick), Kevin Kehilly (Cork), Donal Kavanagh (Kilkenny), Conor O'Brien (Kilkenny), Tony Henry (Mayo), Phil Dillon (Laois), Tim Delaney (Tipperary), Pat Kavanagh (Kilkenny), Tom Crowe (Clare), Donal Carroll (Limerick), Pat O'Connor (Tipperary), Tony Loughnane (Dublin), Jack Ryan (Tipperary). Sub.: Denis Burke (Tipperary) for Crowe.

U.C.C. – John Mitchell (Cork), Mick McCarthy

(Cork), Pat McDonnell (Cork), Paddy Crowley (Cork), Gabriel Daly (Waterford), Donal Clifford (Cork), Séamus Looney (Cork), Michael Murphy (Cork), Seán Walsh (Kilkenny), Noel Dunne (Cork), Jimmy Barrett (Cork), John O'Halloran (Cork), Noel Morgan (Cork), Henry O'Sullivan (Cork), Tom Buckley (Cork). Subs.: Pat Doherty (Limerick) for Barrett, Mick Dowling (Cork) for Murphy, Murphy for Walsh.

1969/70

U.C.G. – Peter Cosgrave (Galway), Niall McInerney (Clare), Richard Walsh (Wexford), Terry Crowe (Clare), Tom Cloonan (Galway), Éamonn Corcoran (Galway), Jim Goulding (Waterford), Séamus Hogan (Tipperary), Colm O'Flaherty (Tipperary), Seán Ó Broudar (Limerick), Austin Costello (Galway), Paul McNamee (Galway), Tim Burns (Galway), Michael Keane (Galway), Seán Burke (Limerick). Subs.: Des O'Halloran (Galway) for Burns, Pat Sheedy (Tipperary) for McNamee, John O'Donoghue (Clare) for Crowe.

U.C.D. – Éamonn Kennedy (Tipperary), Kevin O'Connell (Cork), Enda Murphy (Wexford), Willie Dwyer (Tipperary), Donal Kavanagh (Kilkenny), Conor O'Brien (Kilkenny), Willie Murphy (Kilkenny), Jack Russell (Wexford), Eugene Moore (Laois), Gerry McCarthy (Kilkenny), Aidan Spooner (Tipperary), Tony Henry (Mayo), Jack Ryan (Tipperary), Phil Ryan (Tipperary), Pat O'Connor (Tipperary). Sub.: Dermot Kavanagh (Kilkenny) for Murphy.

1970/71

U.C.C. – Jer Cremin (Cork), Mick McCarthy (Cork), Pat McDonnell (Cork), Willie Moore (Limerick), Simon Murphy (Cork), John O'Grady (Kerry), Jim Darcy (Tipperary), Mick Dowling (Cork), Donie Walsh (Cork), Mick Crotty (Kilkenny), Séamus Looney (Cork), Seán Twomey (Cork), Pat Lucey (Cork), Henry O'Sullivan (Cork), Éamonn Fitzpatrick (Cork). Subs.: Jim Geoghegan (Waterford) for O'Sullivan, O'Sullivan for Geoghegan, Pat McCarthy for Lucey.

U.C.G. – Frank Fahy (Galway), Niall McInerney (Clare), Richard Walsh (Wexford), Éamonn Corcoran (Galway), Michael Bond (Galway), Donal Ahern (Cork), Jim Goulding (Waterford), Mick O'Shea (Kilkenny), Frank Burke (Galway), Seán Ó Broudar (Limerick), Michael Hanniffy (Galway), Paul McNamee (Galway), Pat Sheedy (Tipperary), Michael Keane (Galway), Seán Burke (Limerick).

1971/72

U.C.C. – Tony Smith (Cork), Mick McCarthy (Cork), Pat McDonnell (Cork), Paddy Geary (Cork), Paddy Crowley (Cork), John Buckley (Cork), Liam Kearney (Cork), Michael Murphy (Cork), John O'Grady (Kerry), Seán Twomey (Cork), Séamus Looney (Cork), Mick Crotty (Kilkenny), Henry O'Sullivan (Cork), Willie Moore (Limerick), Seán Burke (Limerick). Sub.: Éamonn Fitzpatrick (Cork) for O'Sullivan.

U.C.G. – Michael Kennedy (Galway), Luke Glynn (Galway), Tom Cloonan (Galway), John O'Donoghue (Clare), Paul McNamee (Galway), Niall McInerney (Clare), Jim Goulding (Waterford), Séamus Hogan (Tipperary), Joe McDonagh (Galway), Mick O'Shea (Kilkenny), Jody Spooner (Tipperary), Martin Barrett (Galway), Pat Sheedy (Tipperary), John Cremin (Kilkenny), Seán Ó Broudar (Limerick). Subs.: Brendan Forde (Galway) for Cremin, Frank Burke (Galway) for Barrett, Michael Hanniffy (Galway) for Sheedy.

1972/73

Maynooth – Dick Browne (Tipperary), Paddy Barry (Cork), Oliver Perkins (Tipperary), Michael Ryan (Tipperary), Mick Brennan (Galway), Seán Silke (Galway), Seán Stack (Clare), Iggy Clarke (Galway), Andy Fenton (Galway), Willie Fitzmaurice (Limerick), Paudie Fitmaurice (Limerick), Joe Condon (Limerick), Gus O'Driscoll (Cork), Larry Byrne (Wexford), Henry Goff (Wexford). Sub.: Aidan Kerrigan (Wexford) for Stack.

U.C.G. – Frank Fahy (Galway), Luke Glynn (Galway), John O'Donoghue (Clare), Nicky O'Connor (Clare), Mick O'Shea (Kilkenny), Niall McInerney (Clare), Joe McDonagh (Galway), Séamus Hogan (Tipperary), Joe Larkin (Galway), Mattie Murphy (Galway), Jody Spooner (Tipperary), Seán Ó Broudar (Limerick), Pat Sheedy (Tipperary), Frank Burke (Galway), Pat Moroney (Clare). Sub.: John Cremin (Kilkenny) for Larkin.

1973/74

Maynooth – Dick Browne (Tipperary), Paddy Barry (Cork), Oliver Perkins (Tipperary), Joe Clarke (Galway), Seán Stack (Clare), Seán Silke (Galway), Mick Brennan (Galway), Iggy Clarke (Galway), Paddy Ballard (Kilkenny), Henry Goff (Wexford), Paudie Fitzmaurice (Limerick), Fachtna O'Driscoll (Cork), Gus O'Driscoll (Cork), Andy Fenton (Galway), Liam Everard (Tipperary). Sub.: Séamus Fitzgerald (Tipperary) for F O'Driscoll.

U.C.D. – Dave Behan (Waterford), Timmy Cleary (Tipperary), Matt Ryan (Limerick & Laois), Pat Flynn (Clare), Martin Bohan (Tipperary), Dennis Burns (Cork), Eugene Ryan (Tipperary), Tom Barry (Kilkenny), Séamus Ryan (Tipperary), Martin Troy (Tipperary), John O'Leary (Kildare), John Callinan (Clare), Jimmy Duggan (Tipperary), Dick O'Shea (Kilkenny), Seán Liddy (Clare). Sub.: Mick Hennessy (Tipperary) for Duggan.

HIGHER EDUCATION

1974/75

U.C.D. – Jimmy Duggan (Tipperary), Martin Quirke (Tipperary), Matt Ryan (Tipperary), Timmy Cleary (Tipperary), John Killeen (Laois), Tom Walsh (Wexford), Eugene Ryan (Tipperary), Mick Brophy (Tipperary), Séamus Ryan (Tipperary), Matt Ruth (Kilkenny), Mick Reidy (Dublin), Pat White (Kildare), Martin Barrett (Galway), Hugh Dolan (Offaly), Martin Troy (Tipperary). Subs.: Jack Ryan (Tipperary) for Troy.

Maynooth – Fachtna O'Driscoll (Cork), Paddy Barry (Cork), Martin Downey (Laois), Joe Clarke (Galway), Tony Kelly (Galway), Seán Silke (Galway), Seán Stack (Clare), Iggy Clarke (Galway), Christy Kennedy (Offaly), Tony Brennan (Cork), Paudie Fitzmaurice (Limerick), Liam Everard (Tipperary), Gus O'Driscoll (Cork), Henry Goff (Wexford), Tommy Ryan (Tipperary). Sub.: Mick O'Mahoney (Cork) for T Ryan.

1975/76

U.C.C. – Gerry Cronin (Cork), Billy Reidy (Cork), Pat Quigley (Wexford), John Roche (Cork), Andrew O'Regan (Cork), Donal McGovern (Cork), Gerard McEvoy (Cork), Sylvester O'Mahony (Cork), Dave Keane (Cork), John Higgins (Cork), Martin McDonnell (Cork), Brian Waldron (Kilkenny), Tadhg O'Sullivan (Cork), Oliver Cussen (Cork), Patsy O'Keeffe (Waterford). Subs.: Eamonn Coakley (Cork) for McEvoy, Willie Vereker (Kilkenny) for Waldron.

Maynooth – Frank O'Neill (Cork), Anthony Kelly (Galway), Joe Clarke (Galway), Seán Clarke (Offaly), Pat Greene (Tipperary), Seán Silke (Galway), Austin McNamara (Limerick), Seán Stack (Clare), Iggy Clarke (Galway), Liam Everard (Tipperary), Paddy Barry (Cork), Liam Lynch (Monaghan), Tommy Ryan (Tipperary), Gus O'Driscoll (Cork), Fachtna O'Driscoll (Cork).

1976/77

U.C.G. - Brendan Kenny (Clare), Hugh O'Donovan (Cork), Tom Cloonan (Galway), Conor Hayes (Galway), Niall McInerney (Galway), Pat Fleury (Offaly), Pat Leahy (Galway), Joe McDonagh (Galway), Frank Holohan (Kilkenny), Pat Costello (Galway), Martin Quilty (Limerick), Gerry P Fahy (Galway), Jody Spooner (Tipperary), Joe Connolly (Galway), Cyril Farrell (Galway). Subs.: Seán Flaherty (Galway) for Quigley, Alfie Barrett (Galway) for Costello.

Maynooth - Finbarr Crowley (Cork), Tony Kelly (Galway), Joe Clarke (Galway), Austin McNamara (Limerick), Seán Clarke (Offaly), Iggy Clarke (Galway), Con Woods (Clare), Anthony Brennan (Galway), Seán Stack (Clare), Noel Foynes (Laois), Fachtna O'Driscoll (Cork), Dick Marnell (Kilkenny), Tommy Ryan (Tipperary), Gus O'Driscoll (Cork), Liam Everard (Tipperary). Subs.: Willie Allen (Dublin) for Foynes, Henry Goff (Wexford) for Allen.

1977/78

U.C.D. - Jack Ryan (Tipperary), Tom Breen (Wexford), Michael Meagher (Kilkenny), Andy Doyle (Wexford), John Killeen (Laois), John Martin (Kilkenny), Mick Maher (Tipperary), Mick Brophy (Tipperary), Gerry Lohan (Galway), Matt Ruth (Kilkenny), Sylvie Lester (Kilkenny), Pat White (Kildare), Tom Browne (Down), Tom Crowe (Clare), Séamus Burke (Tipperary).

U.C.C. - Matt Shortt (Tipperary), Seán Feehan (Waterford), Martin O'Doherty (Cork), John Roche (Cork), Brian Dineen (Cork), Martin McDonnell (Cork), Timmy O'Callaghan (Cork), Dave Keane (Cork), John Minogue (Clare), Patsy Corbett (Cork), John Higgins (Cork), Brian Waldron (Kilkenny), Terry Brennan (Kilkenny), Theo Cullinane (Cork), Gerard McEvoy (Cork).

1978/79

U.C.D. - Jack Ryan (Tipperary), John Martin (Kilkenny), Michael Meagher (Kilkenny), Andy Doyle (Wexford), Paul Redmond (Cork), Tom Breen (Wexford), Mick Maher (Tipperary), Gerry Lohan (Galway), John Kennedy (Cork), Pat Quigley (Tipperary), Peadar Queally (Tipperary), Pat White (Kildare), Tom Browne (Down), Jim McCarthy (Kilkenny), Séamus Burke (Tipperary).

Maynooth - Jim Doyle (Wexford), Frank O'Neill (Cork), Michael Kennedy (Offaly), Denis Forde (Cork), Pat Greene (Tipperary), Seán Clarke (Offaly), Austin McNamara (Limerick), John Curtis (Wexford), Bill Doherty (Kilkenny), Henry Goff (Wexford), Finbar Crowley (Cork), John Kennedy (Tipperary), Jack Caesar (Tipperary), Fachtna O'Driscoll (Cork), Noel Foynes (Laois). Sub.: Phil Stack for O'Driscoll.

1979/80

U.C.G. - Billy Reilly (Galway), Mick McGuane (Galway), Conor Hayes (Galway), Willie Burke (Limerick), John Costello (Kilkenny), Seánie McMahon (Clare), Pat Ryan (Clare), John Boland (Galway), Ian Barrett (Galway), Leo Quinlan (Clare), Vincent Daly (Clare), Noel Colleran (Clare), Gerry Dempsey (Galway), Seán Forde (Galway), Mick Clohessy (Clare). Subs.: Kevin Menton (Galway) for Clohessy, Billy Loughnane (Clare) for Daly, Éamonn Burke (Galway) for Menton.

U.C.C. – Tom Abernethy (Cork), John Minogue (Clare), John Murphy (Cork), Seán Feehan (Waterford), Noel Wall (Tipperary), Billy Farrell (Cork), Frank Houlihan (Limerick), Kieran White (Cork), Noel Leonard (Limerick), David Boylan (Cork), Jimmy Greally (Cork),

Danny Buckley (Cork), Michael Kelleher (Cork), Pat O'Leary (Cork), Michael Walsh (Waterford). Subs.: Eddie Murphy (Cork) for Walsh, Pat Curran (Waterford) for White.

1980/81

U.C.C. - John Farrell (Tipperary), John Minogue (Clare), Michael Boylan (Cork), Billy Farrell (Cork), Pat O'Leary (Cork), Noel Leonard (Limerick), Brian Dineen (Cork), Mick Lyons (Cork), Maurice O'Donoghue (Kerry), Danny Buckley (Cork), Michael Kilcoyne (Westmeath), Nicholas English (Tipperary), Michael Kelleher (Cork), Ger Motherway (Cork), Tadhg Coakley (Cork).

U.C.D. - Denis Corry (Clare), Tom Hogan (Kilkenny), Michael Meagher (Kilkenny), P J Burke (Galway), Willie Burke (Limerick), Cormac Bonner (Tipperary), Liam Grogan (Offaly), John Kennedy (Cork), Dennis O'Driscoll (Cork), Éamonn O'Shea (Tipperary), Peadar Queally (Tipperary), Pat Quigley (Tipperary), Pat Power (Tipperary), Andy Doyle (Wexford), Mick Kelly (Kilkenny).

1981/82

U.C.C. – John Farrell (Tipperary), John Minogue (Clare), Mick Boylan (Cork), Jim Murray (Cork), Michael Allen (Cork), Noel Leonard (Limerick), Brian Dineen (Cork), Mick Lyons (Cork), Paul O'Connor (Cork), Danny Buckley (Cork), Dennis O'Driscoll (Cork), Nicholas English (Tipperary), Michael Kelleher (Cork), Ger Motherway (Cork), Tim Finn (Cork). Sub.: Tadhg Coakley (Cork) for Finn.

U.C.G. – Billy Reilly (Galway), Michael Morrissey (Galway), Peter Casserley (Galway), Ger Costello (Galway), Dermot Monaghan (Galway), Noel Colleran (Clare), Tom Nolan (Galway), Michael Molyneaux (Limerick), Brian Ryan (Limerick), Leo Quinlan (Clare), Martin Raftery (Galway), Derek Fahy (Galway), Gerry Dempsey (Galway), John Boland (Galway), Brendan Kenny (Clare). Sub.: Albert Moylan (Galway) for Raftery.

1982/83

U.C.C. – John Farrell (Tipperary), Michael Allen (Cork), Mick Boylan (Cork), Jim Murray (Cork), John Grainger (Cork), John O'Connor (Wexford), Kieran White (Cork), Maurice O'Donoghue (Kerry), Mick Lyons (Cork), Paul O'Connor (Cork), Nicholas English (Tipperary), Tadhg Coakley (Cork), Michael Walsh (Waterford), Mick Quaide (Limerick), Tim Finn (Cork).

U.C.G. – Billy Reilly (Galway), Damien Kennedy (Galway), Peter Casserley (Galway), Tom Phillips (Mayo), John Barry (Tipperary), Tom Nolan (Galway), Aidan Bellew (Galway), Alan Cunningham (Clare), John Joe Flaherty (Galway), John Leahy (Galway), Peter Leydon (Clare), Michael Coleman (Galway), Joe Byrne (Galway), Michael Keane (Galway), Anthony Cunningham (Galway).

1983/84

U.C.C. – Ger Cotter (Cork), Mick Boylan (Cork), Richard Browne (Cork), John Grainger (Cork), Oliver Kearney (Cork), Seán O'Gorman (Cork), Tadhg Coakley (Cork), Paul O'Connor (Cork), Ian Conroy (Tipperary), Jerry Sheehan (Limerick), Colm O'Neill (Cork), Nicholas English (Tipperary), Christy Ring (Cork), Mick Quaide (Limerick), John O'Connor (Wexford). Sub.: Rory Dwan (Tipperary).

U.C.D. – Denis Corry (Clare), Austin Finn (Wexford), Richie Healy (Cork), Gerry Morrissey (Kilkenny), Frank O'Donoghue (Galway), Mick Glynn (Clare), Willie Burke (Limerick), Richie Walsh (Waterford), Mick Ronayne (Cork), Brian Slattery (Waterford), Jim Kinsella (Kilkenny), Ed Prendergast (Kilkenny), Danny O'Donoghue (Kerry), Aidan Stafford (Wexford), Gerry Drennan (Kilkenny).

1984/85

U.C.C. – Michael Hartnett (Cork), Mick Quaide (Limerick), Richard Browne (Cork), Rory Dwan (Tipperary), John O'Connor (Wexford), John Grainger (Cork), Pat Hartnett (Cork), Paul O'Connor (Cork), Ian Conroy (Tipperary), Kevin Coakley (Cork), Colm O'Neill (Cork), Nicholas English (Tipperary), Mark Foley (Cork), Mick Crowe (Limerick), Niall Sheehan (Limerick). Sub.: John O'Leary (Cork) for John O'Connor.

U.C.G. – Richard Woulfe (Limerick), Seán Williams (Tipperary), Tony Henderson (Kilkenny), Jim Ryan (Limerick), Michael Nash (Limerick), Michael Coleman (Galway), Joe Byrne (Galway), Alan Cunningham (Clare), Gerry Brennan (Kilkenny), Séamie Kearns (Galway), Paddy Maher (Laois), Dave Cowhig (Kilkenny), Pat Ryan (Limerick), Brian Ryan (Limerick), Anthony Cunningham (Galway). Subs.: Joe O'Rourke (Galway) for Brennan, Damien Kennedy (Galway) for Cowhig, Bobby Power (Clare) for C Ryan.

1985/86

U.C.C. – Ger Cotter (Cork), Andy O'Callaghan (Cork), Shane O'Connell (Cork), John Grainger (Cork), Mick Coakley (Cork), John O'Connor (Cork), Denis O'Mahony (Cork), Paul O'Connor (Cork), Kieran Looney (Cork), Mick Crowe (Limerick), Michael Walsh (Kilkenny), Bill O'Connell (Cork), Martin Everard (Cork), Mark Foley (Cork), Tomás Fitzgibbon (Cork). Sub.: Rory McInerney (Limerick) for O'Connell.

Q.U.B. – Conor McGurk (Derry), Peter Flynn (Antrim), Ciarán Cooper (Antrim), Bernard McKay (Antrim), Colm McGurk (Derry), Pádraig Devlin (Tyrone), Joe McClintock (Derry), Ciarán

Barr (Antrim), Liam Coulter (Down), Joe Cunningham (Meath), David Ross (Down), Henry Downey (Derry), David Maguire (Antrim), Declan McLoughlin (Antrim), John McGurk (Derry).

1986/87

U.C.C. - Ger Cotter (Cork), Andy O'Callaghan (Cork), Shane O'Connell (Cork), John Grainger (Cork), Trevor Cooney (Cork), John O'Connor (Cork), John Considine (Cork), Mick Coakley (Cork), Cathal Casey (Cork), Kieran Looney (Cork), Michael Walsh (Kilkenny), Tomás Fitzgibbon (Cork), Mark Foley (Cork), Mick Crowe (Limerick), Barry Harte (Cork).

U.C.D. - Philly Ryan (Tipperary), Mick Brady (Cork), Liam Kinsella (Kilkenny), John Herbert (Limerick), Séamie O'Shea (Tipperary), Andy Dunne (Laois), Austin Finn (Wexford), Conor Stakelum (Tipperary), Jim Bolger (Wexford), Gerry Drennan (Kilkenny), Joe Walsh (Kilkenny), Tom Callan (Kilkenny), Charlie Purcell (Kilkenny), Éamon Kehir (Kilkenny), Vincent Teehan (Offaly).

1987/88

U.C.C. – Ger Cotter (Cork), Andy O'Callaghan (Cork), Shane O'Connell (Cork), David Quinlan (Tipperary), Trevor Cooney (Cork), John Considine (Cork), Damien Keane (Cork), Cathal Casey (Cork), Anthony O'Sullivan (Cork), Pat Heffernan (Limerick), John O'Connor (Cork), Colm Egan (Tipperary), Mark Foley (Cork), Mick Crowe (Limerick), Tomás Fitzgibbon (Cork). Sub.: Tim Cummins (Cork) for J O'Connor.

U.C.G. – Billy Curley (Waterford), Ken Corless (Galway), Martin Dowd (Galway), John O'Dwyer (Tipperary), Andrew Hanley (Clare), John Lee (Clare), Seánie McCarthy (Clare), Séamus Grealish (Galway), Rory O'Connor (Cork), John Bates (Laois), Fergus Fleming (Kilkenny), Dave Cowhig (Kilkenny), Frank Keane (Cork), Séamie Kearns (Galway), Michael O'Doherty (Galway).

1988/89

N.I.H.E.L. – Paul Brennan (Kilkenny), Shane McManus (Tipperary), Paddy Carter (Limerick), Vincent Morrissey (Waterford), Pádraic Hogan (Tipperary), Eoin O'Shaughnessy (Galway), Daragh O'Neill (Limerick), Dan Tracey (Clare), Dave Quinlan (Tipperary), Brendan Corcoran (Tipperary), Michael Hogan (Clare), Eoin Cleary (Clare), Brian Stapleton (Limerick), Vincent Reddy (Wexford), Brendan Ryan (Tipperary). Sub.: T J O'Dwyer (Tipperary) for M Hogan.

U.C.D. – Philly Ryan (Tipperary), Fergal Finn (Wexford), John Herbert (Limerick), Shane McGuckian (Offaly), Paddy O'Brien (Limerick), Séamie O'Shea (Tipperary), Nicky Farrell (Limerick), Jim Bolger (Wexford), Conal Bonnar (Tipperary), Joe Walsh (Kilkenny), Derek Gaffney (Kilkenny), Conor Stakelum (Tipperary), Gerry Drennan (Kilkenny), Vincent Teehan (Offaly), Charlie Purcell (Kilkenny).

1989/90

U.C.C. – Ger Cotter (Cork), Eddie Burke (Waterford), Brian Murphy (Cork), David Quinlan (Tipperary), Pat Kenneally (Cork), Noel O'Leary (Cork), John Considine (Cork), Cathal Casey (Cork), Derry Murphy (Cork), Brian Cunningham (Cork), Adrian Kelly (Roscommon), Mick Crowe (Limerick), Anthony O'Sullivan (Cork), Niall Aherne (Cork), Kevin Roche (Cork). Sub.: Johnny Ryan (Cork) for Kelly.

W.R.T.C. – Liam Slevin (Kilkenny), Donncha O'Donnell (Cork), Paudie Coffey (Waterford), John Houlihan (Kilkenny), Denis Mullally (Kilkenny), Damien Hernon (Dublin), Ger Crosse (Tipperary), Owen Cummins (Tipperary), Phil O'Callaghan (Wexford), Noel Dalton (Waterford), Kevin Byrne (Wexford), Billy O'Sullivan (Waterford), Ger Scully (Cork), Michael O'Mahony (Waterford), Damien Curley (Galway). Subs.: Anthony Qualter (Waterford) for Byrne, Tony O'Meara (Tipperary) for Dalton, James Aherne (Cork) for Scully.

1990/91

U.C.C. – Pat Looney (Cork), Eddie Burke (Waterford), Garret Kavanagh (Wexford), Noel O'Leary (Cork), John Considine (Cork), Brian Murphy (Cork), Pat Hartnett (Cork), Cathal Casey (Cork), Derry Murphy (Cork), Brian Cunningham (Cork), Adrian Kelly (Roscommon), Brian Kehoe (Wexford), Johnny Ryan (Cork), Pat Heffernan (Limerick), John Magner (Cork). Sub.: Kevin Roche (Cork) for Kehoe.

U.C.D. – Pádraig Delaney (Dublin), Mick Cullen (Wexford), Shane McGuckian (Offaly), Ray Cullinane (Wexford), Dave O'Mahony (Wexford), Pat O'Callaghan (Cork), Nicky O'Farrell (Limerick), John Pilkington (Offaly), Conal Bonnar (Tipperary), Danny Curran (Wicklow), Tom Ryan (Tipperary), Barry O'Brien (Tipperary), Pat Leahy (Tipperary), Ciarán Carroll (Tipperary), Jim Byrne (Wexford). Subs.: Mick Quigley (Tipperary) for Cullen, Brendan Carroll (Tipperary) for Byrne, Niall Murphy (Dublin) for Carroll.

1991/92

W.R.T.C. – Alan Hickey (Cork), John Houlihan (Kilkenny), Paul Lee (Clare), Denis Mullally (Kilkenny), David Beirne (Kilkenny), Ger Crosse (Tipperary), Donncha O'Donnell (Cork), Owen Cummins (Tipperary), Paudie O'Keeffe (Tipperary), Michael Hubbard (Waterford), Pádraic Fanning (Waterford), P J Delaney (Kilkenny), Noel Dalton (Waterford), Seán

Ryan (Kilkenny), James Aherne (Cork).

U.L. – Alan Quirke (Tipperary), Alby Quinlan (Tipperary), Willie Burke (Galway), Mark Kenny (Offaly), Paul Hardiman (Galway), Daragh O'Neill (Limerick), Ger Moroney (Clare), Damien Considine (Clare), Jack Griffin (Tipperary), Ray Dooley (Offaly), John Fitzgerald (Limerick), Pat Maguire (Tipperary), Ger Rodgers (Clare), David O'Driscoll (Limerick), T J O'Dwyer (Tipperary). Subs.: Andrew Ryan (Limerick) for Griffin, Mark Scanlon (Clare) for Fitzgerald.

1992/93

U.C.D. – Jim Conroy (Kilkenny), Pádraig Dolan (Galway), Mick Cullen (Wexford), Paul Finnegan (Galway), Andy Dunne (Laois), Tim Cronin (Cork), Dan O'Neill (Kilkenny), John Pilkington (Offaly), Brendan Carroll (Tipperary), Paul Maher (Tipperary), Joe Walsh (Kilkenny), Colmáin Ó Drisceoill (Dublin), Éamonn Scallan (Wexford), Séamus Hughes (Wexford), Jim Byrne (Wexford). Sub.: Dave O'Mahony (Wexford) for Cronin.

U.C.C. – Pat Looney (Cork), Diarmaid McInerney (Wexford), Andrew Murphy (Cork), Frank Lohan (Clare), Kieran Murphy (Cork), Pat Kenneally (Cork), Colman Dillon (Cork), Johnny Brenner (Waterford), Damien Quigley (Limerick), Declan O'Sullivan (Cork), Alan Browne (Cork), Vincent O'Neill (Cork), Donal O'Mahony (Cork), Tony Doolan (Cork), Gerry Maguire (Tipperary). Subs.: Pat Hartnett (Cork) for O'Sullivan, Tom O'Connell (Kerry) for Dillon, Dillon for O'Connell, O'Sullivan for Murphy, Murphy for Quigley.

1993/94

U.L. – Damien Garrihy (Clare), Brian Lohan (Clare), Willie Burke (Galway), Conor Galvin (Clare), Shane Doyle (Kilkenny), Daragh O'Neill (Limerick), Seán McMahon (Clare), Fergal Hartley (Waterford), Pat Maguire (Tipperary), Colm O'Doherty (Galway), John O'Halloran (Limerick), Pat Divinney (Galway), Darren O'Donoghue (Cork), Alan Quirke (Tipperary), Fionán O'Sullivan (Laois). Subs.: Con Murphy (Clare) for Hartley, Barry White (Cork) for Quirke, Quirke for White, Kevin McCarthy (Cork) for Quirke.

W.R.T.C. – Brendan Cummins (Tipperary), Tomás Keane (Tipperary), Paul Lee (Clare), Brian Flannery (Tipperary), Ollie Moran (Limerick), Fergal McCormack (Cork), Tom Feeney (Waterford), Pádraic Fanning (Waterford), Peter Barry (Kilkenny), Tommy Dunne (Tipperary), Brian O'Meara (Tipperary), Ollie O'Connor (Kilkenny), James Moran (Limerick), Anthony Qualter Waterford), P J Delaney (Kilkenny). Subs.: Paudie O'Keeffe (Tipperary) for O'Connor, Tom Kavanagh (Galway) for Fanning, O'Connor for Kavanagh.

1994/95

W.R.T.C. – Patrick Harnan (Waterford), Brian Kelly (Kilkenny), Paul Lee (Clare), Tom Feeney (Waterford), Colm O'Flaherty (Tipperary), Fergal McCormack (Cork), Patrick Mullally (Kilkenny), Colm Bonnar (Tipperary), Peter Barry (Kilkenny), Tommy Dunne (Tipperary), P J Delaney (Kilkenny), James Moran (Limerick), Barry Walsh (Waterford), Michael Hubbard (Waterford), Ollie O'Connor (Kilkenny). Subs.: Aidan Flanagan (Tipperary) for Mullally, Martin Morrissey (Wexford) for O'Connor, Richie Murphy (Wexford) for Hubbard.

U.C.D. – Myles Byrne (Meath), Dave Larkin (Dublin), John Dowling (Kilkenny), Kevin Harrington (Dublin), Hugh Sisk (Kildare), Barry O'Connell (Limerick), Brendan Bolger (Kilkenny), Dan O'Neill (Kilkenny), Seán Kealy (Kilkenny), Jarlath Bolger (Kilkenny), John Ryan (Tipperary), Noel Carr (Tipperary), Máirtín Óg Corrigan (Cork), Adrian Donoghue (Dublin), John Morris (Dublin). Subs.: Pat O'Keeffe (Cork) for O'Connell, Ciaran Collins (Cork) for Kerrigan.

1995/96

U.C.C. – John O'Brien (Limerick), Denis Twomey (Cork), Frank Lohan (Clare), Niall Murphy (Limerick), Dan Murphy (Cork), Johnny Collins (Cork), Tim Cronin (Cork), Alan Cummins (Cork), Tim Coffey (Cork), Donal O'Mahony (Cork), Eddie Enright (Tipperary), John Enright (Tipperary), Eoin O'Neill (Limerick), Kieran Morrison (Cork), Joe Deane (Cork). Sub.: Richard Woods (Cork) for Cronin.

U.L. – Damien Garrihy (Clare), Michael Healy (Galway), Shane Doyle (Kilkenny), Tom Hickey (Kilkenny), Noel Finnerty (Galway), Seán McMahon (Clare), Conor Hanniffy (Offaly), Pat Divinney (Galway), Rory McCarthy (Wexford), David Forde (Clare), Darren O'Connor (Tipperary), Colm O'Doherty (Galway), Darren O'Donoghue (Cork), Gerry Maguire (Tipperary), Brian O'Driscoll (Cork). Subs.: John Kiely (Limerick) for McCarthy, Niall Hayes (Galway) for Diviney.

1996/97

U.C.C. – Brendan Kelly (Cork), Denis Twomey (Cork), Tom Bambury (Cork), Niall Murphy (Limerick), Dan Murphy (Cork), Richard Woods (Cork), John Browne (Cork), Martin Hayes (Cork), Colm O'Brien (Limerick), Derek McGrath (Waterford), Eddie Enright (Tipperary), Seánie McGrath (Cork), John Enright (Tipperary), Kieran Morrison (Cork), Joe Deane (Cork).

Garda – Cathal Jordan (Galway), Niall O'Donnell (Cork), Séamus McIntyre (Kerry), John Finnegan (Dublin), Kevin Long (Cork), Conor Gleeson (Tipperary), Stephen Hogan (Tipperary), Ollie Baker (Clare), Tommy

Kennedy (Tipperary), Damien Cleere (Kilkenny), Brian O'Dwyer (Tipperary), Tom Kavanagh (Galway), Niall Maloney (Kilkenny), Denis Byrne (Kilkenny), Aidan Flanagan (Tipperary). Subs.: Jimmy Smiddy (Cork) for Flanagan, Séamus Maher (Tipperary) for O'Dwyer, Nigel Carey (Limerick) for Kennedy.

1997/98

U.C.C. – Brendan Kelly (Cork), Pat Mahon (Laois), Tom Bambury (Cork), Luke Mannix (Cork), Mark O'Sullivan (Waterford), Dan Murphy (Cork), Liam Harte (Cork), James Murray (Waterford), Eddie Enright (Tipperary), John Enright (Tipperary), John O'Brien (Limerick), Seánie McGrath (Cork), Dave Bennett (Waterford), Kieran Morrison (Cork), Joe Deane (Cork). Subs.: Seán Ryan (Tipperary) for O'Brien, Colm O'Brien (Limerick) for McGrath, Niall Murphy (Limerick) for E Enright.

W.I.T. – Anthony McCormack (Kilkenny), Cathal Murray (Galway), Michael Kavanagh (Kilkenny), Alan Kelleher (Cork), Brian Forde (Clare), Éamonn Corcoran (Tipperary), Declan Ruth (Wexford), Fergus Flynn (Clare), Colm Cassidy (Offaly), Liam Walsh (Kilkenny), William Maher (Tipperary), Andy Moloney (Tipperary), Chris McGrath (Wexford), Henry Shefflin (Kilkenny), Mark O'Leary (Tipperary). Subs.: Michael O'Dowd (Tipperary) for Ruth, Pádraig Delaney (Kilkenny) for Cassidy, Dara O'Sullivan (Waterford) for McGrath.

1998/99

W.I.T. – Kevin O'Brien (Tipperary), Michael Kavanagh (Kilkenny), Eric Flynn (Clare), Alan Kelleher (Cork), Brian Forde (Clare), Éamonn Corcoran (Tipperary), Colm Cassidy (Offaly), Shane McClaren (Galway), Alan Geoghegan (Kilkenny), Michael Bevans (Tipperary), Andy Moloney (Tipperary), Dave Bennett (Waterford), Neil Ronan (Cork), Henry Shefflin (Kilkenny), Declan Browne (Waterford). Subs.: Derek Lyng (Kilkenny) for Flynn, Alan Ahearne (Kilkenny) for Geoghegan, Pádraig Delaney (Kilkenny) for Forde.

U.C.C. – Jim McDonald (Tipperary), Pat Mahon (Laois), Tom Bambury (Cork), Niall Murphy (Limerick), James Murray (Waterford), John Browne (Cork), Liam Harte (Cork), Stefan Fitzpatrick (Clare), Luke Mannix (Cork), John Enright (Tipperary), Richie Flannery (Tipperary), Eoin Bennett (Waterford), Donagh Sheehan (Limerick), John Kingston (Cork), John Murphy (Cork). Subs.: Shane Killeen (Cork) for Sheehan, Michael Hartigan (Clare) for Mahon.

1999/00

W.I.T. – Damien Young (Tipperary), Cathal Murray (Galway), Paul Curran (Tipperary), Alan Kelleher (Cork), Brian Forde (Clare), Éamonn Corcoran (Tipperary), Michael Kavanagh (Kilkenny), John O'Neill (Kilkenny), Andy Moloney (Tipperary), Alan Geoghegan (Kilkenny), William Maher (Tipperary), Damien Joyce (Galway), Michael Bevans (Tipperary), Henry Shefflin (Kilkenny), Declan Browne (Tipperary). Sub.: Leigh O'Brien (Wexford) for Maher.

U.C.D. – Michael Lyons (Offaly), Brian Walton (Tipperary), Stephen Lucey (Limerick), Cathal Murphy (Offaly), Conor O'Donovan (Galway), David Hegarty (Clare), Hugh Flannery (Tipperary), Seán O'Neill (Limerick), Paul Ormonde (Tipperary), Paddy O'Brien (Tipperary), Noel Murphy (Offaly), Pat Fitzgerald (Waterford), Michael Gordon (Kilkenny), Jim Byrne (Wexford), Brendan Murphy (Offaly). Subs.: Alan Barry (Kilkenny) for O'Donovan, John Berkery (Wicklow) for Byrne.

2000/01

U.C.D. – Matt White (Wexford), Brian Walton (Tipperary), Dave O'Connor (Wexford), Robbie Kirwan (Wexford), Hugh Flannery (Tipperary), David Hegarty (Clare), Colm Everard (Tipperary), Gary Mernagh (Tipperary), Stephen Lucey (Limerick), Pat Fitzgerald (Waterford), Seán O'Neill (Limerick), Redmond Barry (Wexford), John Culkin (Galway), Alan Barry (Kilkenny), Brendan Murphy (Offaly). Subs.: Tim Murphy (Kilkenny) for Lucey, Pat Tennyson (Kilkenny) for Culkin, Paddy O'Brien (Tipperary) for Mernagh. Tim Murphy, Martin Bergin (Kilkenny) and Tennyson all started the first match, and were replaced by Mernagh, O'Neill and Alan Barry respectively. Hugh Gannon (Kilkenny) and Aidan Power (Dublin) also appeared as substitutes in the drawn game.

U.C.C. – Richie O'Neill (Kilkenny), John Browne (Cork), John Crowley (Cork), Alan Kirwan (Waterford), Rory O'Doherty (Cork), Richie Flannery (Tipperary), Jonathan Olden (Cork), Eoin Murphy (Waterford), Eoin Morrissey (Tipperary), Brian Phelan (Kilkenny), Stiofán Fitzpatrick (Clare), Noel Brodie (Clare), Donncha Sheehan (Limerick), John Kingston (Cork), John Murphy (Cork). Subs: Éamonn Collins (Cork) for Kingston, Victor Cusack (Cork) for Sheehan. Tom Kenny (Cork) and Mark O'Connor (Cork) started the first game, and were replaced by Olden and Brodie respectively. David Niblock (Cork), Jim McDonnell (Tipperary), Niall Murphy (Limerick) also appeared as substitutes in the drawn match.

2001/02

U.L.: Timmy Houlihan (Limerick), Brian O'Mahony (Galway), John Devane (Tipperary),

Dermot Gleeson (Tipperary), Colm Forde (Clare), Brian Geary (Limerick), Conor Earley (Clare), Richie Murray (Galway), John Barron (Kilkenny), Conor Fitzgerald (Cork), Niall Moran (Limerick), Eoin Fitzgerald (Cork), David Donohoe (Galway), David Forde (Galway), Donncha Sheehan (Limerick). Sub.: Paul O'Reilly (Limerick) for Gleeson, Mick O'Hara (Offaly) for Donohoe.

W.I.T.: Damien Young (Tipperary), Damien Joyce (Galway), Paul Curran (Tipperary), J.J. Delaney (Kilkenny), Mick Fitzgerald (Cork), Joe Brady (Offaly), John O'Neill (Kilkenny), Alan Geoghegan (Kilkenny), Ger Coleman (Wexford), Mick Jacob (Wexford), Fergus Flynn (Clare), Setanta Ó hAilpín (Cork), Brian Dowling (Kilkenny), Henry Shefflin (Kilkenny), Damien Murray (Offaly). Subs.: Stephen Brown (Offaly) for Dowling, Niall Murphy (Cork) for Flynn.

2002/03

W.I.T. – Damien Young (Tipperary), Brian Lynch (Clare), Paul Curran (Tipperary), J.J. Delaney (Kilkenny), Mick Fitzgerald (Cork), Joe Brady (Offaly), Ken Coogan (Kilkenny), Ollie Moran (Limerick), Fergus Flynn (Clare), Brian Dowling (Kilkenny), Mick Jacob (Wexford), M.J. Furlong (Wexford), Setanta Ó hAilpín (Cork), Conor Phelan (Kilkenny), Damien Murray (Offaly). Subs.: Shane Hennessy (Kilkenny) for Phelan, Rory Jacob (Wexford) for Murray, C. Phelan for Ó hAilpín.

C.I.T. – Martin Coleman (Cork), Brian Murphy (Cork), Jackie Tyrrell (Kilkenny), Michael Prout (Cork), Vincent Hurley (Cork), Ronan Curran (Cork), Pat Sloane (Cork), Stephen O'Sullivan (Cork), John Gardiner (Cork), Garvan McCarthy (Cork), Colin O'Leary (Cork), John O'Connor (Cork), Aidan Fogarty (Kilkenny), Diarmuid O'Riordan (Cork), Kieran Murphy (Cork). Subs.: Paul Tierney (Cork) for O'Leary, Gary McLoughlin (Cork) for O'Riordan, Garvan McCarthy (Cork) for O'Connor.

2003/04

W.I.T. – Philip Brennan (Clare), Chris O'Neill (Kilkenny), Ken Coogan (Kilkenny), J.J. Delaney (Kilkenny), Tommy Holland (Clare), Keith Rossiter (Wexford), Hugh Maloney (Tipperary), David Hayes (Galway), Michael Walsh (Waterford), Conor Phelan (Kilkenny), Peter Garvey (Galway), John Phelan (Kilkenny), Rory Jacob (Wexford), Anthony Owens (Kilkenny), Brian Dowling (Kilkenny). Subs.: P.J. Delaney (Kilkenny) for Rossiter, Conor Burns (Cork) for Owens, Adrian Cullinane (Galway).

U.C.C. – Richie O'Neill (Kilkenny), John Tennyson (Kilkenny), Canice Hickey (Kilkenny), Michael Phelan (Kilkenny), Tom Kenny (Cork), Kevin Hartnett (Cork), Evan Hanley (Tipperary), Tommy Walsh (Kilkenny), Mark O'Connor (Cork), Mark O'Leary (Tipperary), Eoin Conway (Cork), Shane O'Sullivan (Waterford), James 'Cha' Fitzpatrick (Kilkenny), Éamonn Collins (Cork), Noel Moloney (Tipperary). Subs.: Paul O'Brien (Waterford) for Moloney, Donagh O'Sullivan (Limerick) for Conway.

2004/05

L.I.T. – Aidan Ryan (Galway), Enda Collins (Clare), John Coen (Clare), Conor O'Mahony (Tipperary), Shane McGrath (Tipperary), Fergus Flynn (Clare), David Morrissey (Tipperary), Jackie Tyrrell (Kilkenny), John Reddan (Clare), Aengus Callanan (Galway), Barry Nugent (Clare), Iarla Tannian (Galway), Niall Healy (Galway), Eoin Kelly (Tipperary), Kieran Murphy (Cork). Subs.: Donal O'Reilly (Galway) for Murphy.

U.L. – Tadhg Flynn (Kerry), Brendan Bugler (Clare), John Devane (Tipperary), Aidan Murphy (Wexford), Robert Conlon (Clare), Raymond Hayes (Limerick), Ger Flood (Wexford), Niall Moran (Limerick), Barry Coleman (Cork), Paul O'Flynn (Kilkenny), Joe Gantley (Galway), David McCormack (Kilkenny), Brian Carroll (Limerick), David Greene (Galway), Nicky Kenny (Kilkenny). Subs.: Tadhg Healy (Cork) for Coleman, Peter Dowling (Kilkenny) for Gantley, John Heneghan (Waterford) for McCormack.

2005/06

W.I.T. – Philip Brennan (Clare), Keith Rossiter (Wexford), Kevin Moran (Waterford), Alan Kirwan (Waterford), Daniel Hoctor (Offaly), Kevin Brady (Offaly), Hugh Maloney (Tipperary), Ger Mahon (Galway), Michael Walsh (Waterford), Conor Phelan (Kilkenny), Adrian Cullinane (Galway), Eoin Reid (Kilkenny), Brian Dowling (Kilkenny), Willie Ryan (Tipperary), Rory Jacob (Wexford). Subs.: Liam Lawlor (Waterford) for Hayes, Cathal Parlon (Offaly) for Cullinane, Conor O'Brien (Tipperary) for Hoctor, Pat Hartley (Kilkenny) for Walsh, Mark Heffernan (Kilkenny) for Kirwan.

U.C.D. – Mattie White (Wexford), Diarmaid Fitzgerald (Tipperary), Michael Fitzgerald (Cork), Eddie Campion (Kilkenny), David Prendergast (Kilkenny), Éamon Ryan (Tipperary), Seán Cummins (Kilkenny), Bryan Barry (Kilkenny), David Hayes (Galway), Éamon O'Gorman (Kilkenny), John McCarthy (Limerick), Brendan Murphy (Offaly), Andy Smith (Galway), Tommy Fitzgerald (Tipperary), John O'Connor (Wexford). Subs.: Paul Ormond (Tipperary) for Hayes, Stephen Nolan (Wexford) for Fitzgerald, PJ Nolan (Wexford) for O'Connor, Kieran Breen (Limerick) for Nolan.

2006/07

L.I.T. – James Skehill (Galway), Michael Walsh (Cork), Jackie Tyrrell (Kilkenny), Alan Byrne (Tipperary), Shane McGrath (Tipperary), Conor O'Mahony (Tipperary), Maurice O'Brien (Limerick), Jonathan Clancy (Clare), Kieran Murphy (Cork), Eoin Cadogan (Cork), Austin Murphy (Kilkenny), Iarla Tannian (Galway), Aonghus Callanan (Galway), Joe Canning (Galway), James McInerney (Clare). Subs.: Bernard Gaffney (Clare) for Cadogan.

N.U.I.G. – David Woods (Clare), Roderick Whyte (Galway), Martin Ryan (Galway), Liam Geraghty (Galway), James Dunphy (Kilkenny), John Lee (Galway), Enda Barrett (Clare), Colin Ryan (Clare), Stephen Molumphy (Waterford), Peter O'Brien (Cork), David Barrett (Clare), Finian Coone (Galway), David Kenny (Offaly), Darragh Egan (Tipperary), Seán Glynn (Galway). Subs.: Vinny Faherty (Galway) for O'Brien, Pádraic Kennedy (Limerick) for Ryan.

2007/08

W.I.T. – Adrian Power (Waterford), Kevin Lanigan (Tipperary), John Dalton (Kilkenny), Conor Cooney (Clare), Shane Fives (Waterford), Pat Hartley (Kilkenny), Kevin Moran (Waterford), Stephen Lillis (Tipperary), Pat Kelly (Clare), Fintan O'Leary (Cork), TJ Reid (Kilkenny), Ronan Good (Cork), Ray McLoughney (Tipperary), Eoin Reid (Kilkenny), Shane O'Sullivan (Waterford). Subs.: Mark Gorman (Waterford) for Good, Shane Kelly (Cork) for Fives, Gavin Nolan (Kilkenny) for S Kelly, Kieran Grehan (Kilkenny) for Gorman.

L.I.T. – Matthew Ryan (Tipperary), Michael Walsh (Cork), Alan Byrne (Tipperary), Enda Collins (Clare), Gary O'Connell (Clare), Shane Maher (Tipperary), Maurice O'Brien (Limerick), Jonathan Clancy (Clare), Wayne McNamara (Limerick), Willie Hyland (Laois), Cyril Donnellan (Galway), James McInerney (Clare), Paudie O'Brien (Limerick), Joe Canning (Galway), Niall Healy (Galway). Subs.: Blaine Earley (Clare) for P O'Brien, Austin Murphy (Kilkenny) for Clancy, Clancy for Healy, Healy for McInerney.

2008/09

U.C.C.: Anthony Nash (Cork), Shane O'Neill (Cork), Darragh McSweeney (Cork), Conor O'Sullivan (Cork), Richie Foley (Waterford), Joe Jordan (Cork), Kevin Hartnett (Cork), Bryan O'Sullivan (Limerick), Michael Cahill (Tipperary), Don Hanley (Limerick), Bill Beckett (Kilkenny), John Mulhall (Kilkenny), Stephen Moylan (Cork), Shane Burke (Tipperary), Tadhg Óg Murphy (Cork). Subs: Éanna Martin (Wexford) for Hanley, Damien Browne (Clare) for Cahill, William Kearney for C O'Sullivan, Michael Grace (Kilkenny) for O'Neill, Conor O'Driscoll for Burke.

U.L.: Patrick McCormack (Tipperary), Brian Fox (Tipperary), Kieran Joyce (Kilkenny), Michael Verney (Offaly), Jim Bob McCarthy (Tipperary), Tom Stapleton (Tipperary), Martin Walsh (Kilkenny), Séamus Hickey (Limerick), Michael Gleeson (Tipperary), Seán Ryan (Offaly), Ryan O'Dwyer (Tipperary), John Greene (Galway), Brian Carroll (Offaly), Matt Ruth (Kilkenny), Alan Egan (Offaly). Subs used: Noel Ó Murchú (Waterford) for Greene, Shane O'Brien (Clare) for Fox, Dylan Hayden (Offaly) for Stapleton, David Burke (Galway) for O'Dwyer, Kevin Lanigan (Tipperary) for Egan).

FITZGIBBON CUP WINNING CAPTAINS

1911/12 – J Dwan (UCD)
1912/13 – Peter M Murphy (UCC & Cork)
1913/14 – Jim Reidy (UCC & Limerick)
1914/15 – Éamon Bulfin (UCD & Offaly)
1915/16 – John Ryan (UCD, Limerick & Dublin)
1916/17 – John Ryan (UCD, Limerick & Dublin)
1917/18 – (UCC captain's name not available)
1918/19 – Martin Fahy (UCG)
1919/20 – R Lahiffe (UCC)
1920/21 – Not played
1921/22 – (UCC captain's name not available)
1922/23 – Tommy Daly (UCD & Clare & Dublin)
1923/24 – Tommy Daly (UCD & Clare & Dublin)
1924/25 – Tom Lee (UCC & Tipperary)
1925/26 – T O'Grady (UCG)
1926/27 – O O'Neill (UCD)
1927/28 – Richard Molloy (UCC & Cork)
1928/29 – Paddy O'Donovan (UCC & Cork)
1929/30 – Patrick O'Donnell (UCC)
1930/31 – William Finlay (UCC & Tipperary)
1931/32 – Jack Walsh (UCD)
1932/33 – Richard Cronin (UCC & Cork)
1933/34 – Séamus Hogan (UCD & Clare)
1934/35 – Tom Loughnane (UCD & Clare)
1935/36 – Tony MacSullivan (UCD & Limerick)
1936/37 – Mossie Roche (UCD & Limerick)
1937/38 – Jimmy Cooney (UCD & Tipperary)
1938/39 – Jackie Spencer (UCC & Cork)
1939/40 – Jim Young (UCC & Cork)
1940/41 – Billy O'Neill (UCC & Kilkenny)
1941/42 – Pat Hehir (UCG & Galway)
1942/43 – Not played
1943/44 – Dick Stokes (UCD & Limerick)
1944/45 – Michael "Miko" Doyle (UCG & Galway)
1945/46 – Michael "Miko" Doyle (UCG & Galway)
1946/47 – Mick Herlihy (UCC & Cork)
1947/48 – Frank Commons (UCD & Tipperary & Dublin)
1948/49 – Johnny Scanlon (UCG & Galway)
1949/50 – Mick Maher (UCD & Boharlahan, Tipperary)

1950/51 – Martin Fitzgerald (UCD & Tipperary & Dublin)
1951/52 – Des Dillon (UCD & Clare & Dublin)
1952/53 – Ted McConnell (QUB & Antrim)
1953/54 – Declared null & void
1954/55 – Pat Teehan (UCD & Waterford)
1955/56 – Johnny Dwane (UCC & Cork)
1956/57 – Tony Murphy (UCC & Cork)
1957/58 – Bernard Hoey (UCD & Clare)
1958/59 – Steve Long (UCC & Limerick)
1959/60 – Donie Nealon (UCD & Tipperary)
1960/61 – Owen O'Neill (UCD & Limerick)
1961/62 – Jimmy Byrne (UCC & Waterford)
1962/63 – Des Kiely (UCC & Tipperary)
1963/64 – Seán Quinlivan (UCD & Clare)
1964/65 – Murt Duggan (UCD & Tipperary)
1965/66 – Willie Cronin (UCC & Cork)
1966/67 – Seánie Barry (UCC & Cork)
1967/68 – Jim Furlong (UCD & Wexford)
1968/69 – Pat Kavanagh (UCD & Kilkenny)
1969/70 – Séamus Hogan (UCG & Tipperary)
1970/71 – Pat McDonnell (UCC & Cork)
1971/72 – Mick McCarthy (UCC & Cork)
1972/73 – Paudie Fitzmaurice (Maynooth & Limerick)
1973/74 – Paddy Barry (Maynooth & Cork)
1974/75 – Séamus Ryan (UCD & Tipperary)
1975/76 – Donal McGovern (UCC & Cork)
1976/77 – Pat Fleury (UCG & Offaly)
1977/78 – John Martin (UCD & Kilkenny)
1978/79 – Tom Breen (UCD & Wexford)
1979/80 – Vincent Daly (UCG & Clare)
1980/81 – John Minogue (UCC & Clare)
1981/82 – John Farrell (UCC & Tipperary)
1982/83 – Tadhg Coakley (UCC & Cork)
1983/84 – Mick Boylan (UCC & Cork)
1984/85 – Nicholas English (UCC & Tipperary)
1985/86 – Paul O'Connor (UCC & Cork)
1986/87 – John Grainger (UCC & Cork)
1987/88 – Andy O'Callaghan (UCC & Cork)
1988/89 – Dan Treacy (NIHEL & Clare)
1989/90 – Mick Crowe (UCC & Limerick)
1990/91 – Pat Heffernan (UCC & Limerick)
1991/92 – Pádraic Fanning (WRTC & Tipperary)
1992/93 – Jim Byrne (UCD & Wexford)
1993/94 – Daragh O'Neill (UL & Limerick)
1994/95 – Colm Bonnar (WRTC & Tipperary)
1995/96 – Frank Lohan (UCC & Clare)
1996/97 – Kieran Morrison (UCC & Cork)
1997/98 – Eddie Enright (UCC & Tipperary)
1998/99 – Andy Moloney (WIT & Tipperary)
1999/00 – Andy Moloney (WIT & Tipperary)
2000/01 – David Hegarty (UCD & Clare)
2001/02 – Eoin Fitzgerald (UL & Cork)
2002/03 – Paul Curran (WIT & Tipperary)
2003/04 – J.J. Delaney (WIT & Kilkenny)
2004/05 – Eoin Kelly (LIT & Tipperary)
2005/06 – Brian Dowling (WIT & Kilkenny), Hugh Maloney (WIT & Tipperary)
2006/07 – Kieran Murphy (LIT & Cork)
2007/08 – Kevin Moran (WIT & Waterford)
2008/09 – Kevin Hartnett (UCC & Cork)

FITZGIBBON CUP FINAL TOP SCORERS 1949-2009

Note: The competition was played on a league basis up until 1947/48 inclusive.

1948/49 – John L Coyne (UCG & Galway) 2-0
1949/50 – S Murphy (UCG) 2-1
1950/51 – Johnny Ryan (UCD & Tipperary) 1-1
1951/52 – Johnny Ryan (UCD & Tipperary) 1-2
1952/53 – Séamus "Stout" McDonald (QUB & Antrim) 1-1
1953/54 – Paddy O'Donoghue (UCG & Waterford) 2-0; Noel McMahon (UCG & Offaly) 2-0; *result declared void
1954/55 – Mick Hanley (UCC & Clare) 3-1
1955/56 – Dick Troy (UCC & Cork) 1-5
1956/57 – Dick Troy (UCC & Cork) 1-6
1957/58 – Nicky Stokes (UCD & Limerick) 2-4
1958/59 – Tom Riordan (UCC & Cork) 2-0; John Joe Browne (UCC & Cork) 2-0; Donie Nealon (UCD & Tipperary) 2-0
1959/60 – Donie Nealon (UCD & Tipperary) 2-3
1960/61 – Pat Henchy (UCD & Clare) 2-0
1961/62 – Ollie Harrington (UCC & Kilkenny) 1-4
1962/63 – Donie Nealon (UCD & Tipperary) 2-1
1963/64 – Pat Henchy (UCD & Clare) 4-3
1964/65 – Tom Forrestal (UCD & Kilkenny) 3-2
1965/66 – Brendan Kenneally (UCC & Cork) 2-1
1966/67 – Séamus Hogan (UCG & Tipperary) 2-2; Dennis Philpott (UCC & Cork) 2-2
1967/68 – Pat Kavanagh (UCD & Kilkenny) 1-7
1968/69 – Pat Kavanagh (UCD & Kilkenny) 0-7
1969/70 – Gerry McCarthy (UCD & Kilkenny) 1-8
1970/71 – Seán Twomey (UCC & Cork) 1-10
1971/72 – Seán Twomey (UCC & Cork) 1-6
1972/73 – Henry Goff (Maynooth & Wexford) 2-0
1973/74 – Paudie Fitzmaurice (Maynooth & Limerick) 0-7
1974/75 – Matt Ruth (UCD & Kilkenny) 2-2
1975/76 – Gus O'Driscoll (Maynooth & Cork) 0-7
1976/77 – Fachtna O'Driscoll (Maynooth & Cork) 0-9
1977/78 – Dave Keane (UCC & Cork) 2-3
1978/79 – Peadar Queally (UCD & Tipperary) 3-2
1979/80 – Seán Forde (UCG & Galway) 0-4; Gerry Dempsey (UCG & Galway) 0-4
1980/81 – Michael Kelleher (UCC & Cork) 1-2
1981/82 – Nicholas English (UCC & Tipperary) 0-10
1982/83 – Mick Quaide (UCC & Limerick) 3-2
1983/84 – Colm O'Neill (UCC & Cork) 0-4; Jim Kinsella (UCD & Kilkenny) 0-4
1984/85 – Colm O'Neill (UCC & Cork) 0-5
1985/86 – Mick Walsh (UCC & Kilkenny) 2-1
1986/87 – Mark Foley (UCC & Cork) 0-5; Vincent Teehan (UCD & Offaly) 0-5; Jim Bolger (UCD & Wexford) 0-5
1987/88 – Tony O'Sullivan (UCC & Cork) 0-5
1988/89 – Derek Gaffney (UCD & Kilkenny) 1-4
1989/90 – Damien Curley (WRTC & Galway) 0-10

1990/91 – Brian Cunningham (UCC & Cork) 0-5; Johnny Ryan (UCC & Cork) 1-2
1991/92 – Noel Dalton (WRTC & Waterford) 0-9
1992/93 – Jim Byrne (UCD & Wexford) 2-7
1993/94 – Colm O'Doherty (UL & Galway) 1-5
1994/95 – Barry Walsh (WRTC & Waterford) 2-1
1995/96 – John Enright (UCC & Tipperary) 0-7
1996/97 – John Enright (UCC & Tipperary) 0-9
1997/98 – Seánie McGrath (UCC & Cork) 1-4; Henry Shefflin (WIT & Kilkenny) 0-7
1998/99 – John Enright (UCC & Tipperary) 1-7
1999/00 – Henry Shefflin (WIT & Kilkenny) 1-5
2000/01 – Pat Fitzgerald (UCD & Waterford) 0-9
2000/01 replay – John Murphy (UCC & Cork) 0-6; Alan Barry (UCD & Kilkenny) 2-0; Pat Fitzgerald (UCD & Waterford) 0-6
2001/02 – Conor Fitzgerald (UL & Cork) 0-7
2002/03 – Aidan Fogarty (Cork IT & Kilkenny) 0-4
2003/04 – James Fitzpatrick (UCC & Kilkenny) 0-5
2004/05 – Eoin Kelly (LIT & Tipperary) 1-9
2005/06 – Willie Ryan (WIT & Tipperary 3-0
2006/07 – Joe Canning (LIT & Galway) 1-8
2007/08 – Joe Canning (LIT & Galway) 1-16
2008/09 – John Mulhall (UCC & Kilkenny) 1-3
Compiled by Dónal McAnallen

SIGERSON CUP

By Donal McAnallen.

The Sigerson Cup, the trophy for the Higher Education Gaelic Football Championship, was presented by Strabane man, Dr. George Sigerson, a Professor in UCD, in 1911, and has been played for ever since.

Initially, only UCD, UCC and UCG participated in the competition. UCD hold the record number of cup victories (32), having won six titles in seven years in the 1970s as well as two All-Ireland club championships.

UCG are next in line with 22 triumphs. The six-in-a-row achieved by the Galway college in the years 1936-41 inclusive is the longest winning sequence in the competition's history.

Queen's University did not join the Sigerson Cup competition permanently until 1933, having made a brief outing previously in 1923. The Belfast university won its initial title in 1958/59, but did not enjoy its greatest success until the early 1990s, when, along with newcomers St. Mary's and UUJ, they kept the cup in Ulster for six years out of eight.

Trinity College first entered in 1963, Maynooth in 1972, NUU (Coleraine) in 1976, UUJ in 1985, Thomond, NIHE Limerick and St. Mary's, Belfast in 1988. DCU came in in 1990, Athlone RTC in 1991, Sligo RTC in 1992, Cork RTC in 1995 and Tralee RTC in 1996. From 1997 all the new institutes of technology were allowed to take part.

The story of the late 1990s and early 2000s was the dominance of two of these new institutes, IT Tralee and IT Sligo, both winning three titles each. DCU recorded its maiden victory in 2006.

The original Sigerson Cup was retired in the 2000/01 season and a replica was introduced in its stead.

ROLL OF HONOUR:

UCD (32), UCG / NUIG (22), UCC (20), QUB (8), UUJ (5), TRTC / ITT (3), SIT (3), DCU (1), Maynooth (1), St. Mary's (1), Cork IT (1).

Winners at a Glance
1910/11 – UCC
1911/12 – UCG
1912/13 – UCD
1913/14 – UCC
1914/15 – UCD
1915/16 – UCC
1916/17 – UCD
1917/18 – UCD
1918/19 – UCC
1919/20 – UCD
1920/21 – Not played
1921/22 – UCG
1922/23 – UCC
1923/24 – UCD
1924/25 – UCC
1925/26 – UCC
1926/27 – UCD
1927/28 – UCC
1928/29 – UCD
1929/30 – UCD
1930/31 – UCD
1931/32 – UCD
1932/33 – UCD
1933/34 – UCG
1934/35 – UCG
1935/36 – UCD
1936/37 – UCG
1937/38 – UCG
1938/39 – UCG
1939/40 – UCG
1940/41 – UCG
1941/42 – UCG
1942/43 – Not played
1943/44 – UCC
1944/45 – UCD
1945/46 – UCD
1946/47 – UCC
1947/48 – UCD
1948/49 – UCG
1949/50 – UCD
1950/51 – UCG
1951/52 – UCC
1952/53 – UCC
1953/54 – UCD
1954/55 – UCG
1955/56 – UCD
1956/57 – UCD

1957/58 – UCD
1958/59 – QUB
1959/60 – UCD
1960/61 – UCG
1961/62 – UCD
1962/63 – UCG
1963/64 – UCG
1964/65 – QUB
1965/66 – UCC
1966/67 – UCC
1967/68 – UCD
1968/69 – UCC
1969/70 – UCC
1970/71 – QUB
1971/72 – UCC
1972/73 – UCD
1973/74 – UCD
1974/75 – UCD
1975/76 – Maynooth
1976/77 – UCD
1977/78 – UCD
1978/79 – UCD
1979/80 – UCG
1980/81 – UCG
1981/82 – QUB
1982/83 – UCG
1983/84 – UCG
1984/85 – UCD
1985/86 – UUJ
1986/87 – UUJ
1987/88 – UCC
1988/89 – St. Mary's
1989/90 – QUB
1990/91 – UUJ
1991/92 – UCG
1992/93 – QUB
1993/94 – UCC
1994/95 – UCC
1995/96 – UCD
1996/97 – TRTC
1997/98 – ITT
1998/99 – ITT
1999/00 – QUB
2000/01 – UUJ
2001/02 – ITS
2002/03 – NUIG
2003/04 – ITS
2004/05 – ITS
2005/06 – DCU
2006/07 – QUB
2007/08 – UUJ
2008/09 – Cork IT

SIGERSON CUP CHAMPIONSHIP RECORDS

1910/11 – UCD hosted. All games at Jones' Road. 9 May: UCC 1-4, UCD 0-3. 10 May: UCC 4-6, UCG 1-2. 11 May: UCG 6-1, UCD 2-6.
UCC champions with four league points.
1911/12 – UCG hosted. All games at Renmore. 18 February: UCG 2-1, UCD 2-1. 19 February: UCC 1-0, UCD 1-0. 20 February: UCG 1-4, UCC 0-1.
UCG champions with three league points.
1912/13 – UCC hosted. All games at the Mardyke. 25 February: UCG 2-1, UCD 1-4. 26 February: UCG 2-2, UCC 0-5. 27 February: UCD 3-3, UCC 0-2.
UCD champions with highest aggregate score.
1913/14 – UCD hosted. All games at Terenure. 5 May: UCC 1-1, UCG 0-0. 6 May: UCD 2-6, UCG 0-0. 7 May: UCC 1-0, UCD 0-2.
UCC champions with four league points.
1914/15 – UCG hosted. All games at Renmore. 15 January: UCG 1-1, UCD 0-0. 16 January: UCD 1-5, UCC 0-1. 17 January: UCC 1-2, UCG 0-2.
UCD champions by conceding fewest scores.
1915/16 – UCC hosted. All games at Cork Athletic Grounds. 24 February: UCC 0-5, UCG 1-0. 25 February: UCD 3-8, UCG 0-1. 26 February: UCC 2-2, UCD 0-0.
UCC champions with four league points.
1916/17 – UCD hosted. All games at Terenure. 15 February: UCD 1-3, UCC 0-3. 16 February: UCC 4-4, UCG 1-1. 17 February: UCD 5-2, UCG 1-3.
UCD champions with four league points.
1917/18 – UCG hosted. Dates unknown. UCD beat UCG; UCC beat UCD; UCD beat UCG.
1918/19 – UCC hosted. 28 February, The Mardyke: UCC 0-7, UCG 0-1. 1 March, The Mardyke: UCD beat UCG. 2 March, Cork Athletic Grounds: UCC 0-5, UCD 1-0.
UCC champions with four league points.
Note: from 1919/20 to 1925/26 the competition was played as a straight knock-out.
1919/20 – UCD hosted. Semi-final at Terenure, 21 February: UCC 2-3, UCG 0-6 (a.e.t.). Final at Terenure, 22 February: UCD 1-7, UCC 1-4.
1920/21 – No competition.
Note: from 1921/22 to 1966/67 the Sigerson Cup competition was held in the first academic term of the year (Michaelmas), chiefly in November and December.
1921/22 – UCG hosted. 18 December 1921, South Park, Galway: UCC 2-1, UCD 0-3. 19 December, South Park: UCG 0-1, UCC 0-0.
1922/23 – UCC hosted. The Mardyke, 4 February 1923. Final: UCC 3-1, UCD 0-8. (UCG did not take part.)
1923/24 – UCD hosted. Semi-finals at Terenure: 14 December 1923, UCD 3-5, QUB 2-1; 15 December, UCC beat UCG. Final at Terenure, 16 December 1923: UCD 2-4, UCC 0-2.
1924/25 – UCG hosted. Semi-final at Galway, 20 December: UCC 1-1, UCD 0-3. Final at Galway, 21 December: UCC 1-2, UCG 0-2.
1925/26 – UCC hosted. Semi-final at the Mardyke, 12 December: UCD 0-7, UCG 0-3. Final at the Mardyke, 13 December: UCC 4-3, UCD 0-2.

HIGHER EDUCATION

Note: From 1926/27 to 1932/33 the competition reverted to a league format.
1926/27 – UCD hosted. All games at Terenure. 10 December: UCD 3-4, UCC 1-2. 11 December: UCG 2-2, UCC 0-1. 12 December: UCD 0-4, UCG 0-1.
UCD champions with four league points.
1927/28 – UCG hosted. 9 December, Galway: UCC 2-5, UCG 0-2. 10 December, Galway: UCD 2-8, UCG 0-2. 11 December, Galway: UCC 3-3, UCD 1-5.
UCC champions with four league points.
1928/29 – UCC hosted. The Mardyke, 27 January 1929. Final: UCD 5-6, UCC 0-0. (UCG did not take part.)
1929/30 – UCD hosted. All games at Terenure. 6 December: UCD 0-5, UCC 1-2. 7 December: UCC 1-4, UCG 0-1. 8 December: UCD 5-3, UCG 0-0.
UCD champions with highest scoring aggregate.
1930/31 – UCG hosted. 7 December, Galway: UCG 2-3, UCC 2-0. 8 December, Galway: UCD 1-2, UCC 0-1. 9 December, Galway: UCD 2-1, UCG 0-6.
UCD champions with four league points.
1931/32 – UCC hosted. All games at the Mardyke. 4 December: UCD 2-5, UCC 2-5 (a.e.t.). 5 December: UCD 2-4, UCG 0-5. 6 December: UCG 0-8, UCC 1-0.
UCD champions with three league points.
1932/33 – UCD hosted. All games at Terenure. 9 December: UCD 5-7, UCC 0-1. 10 December: UCC 4-2, UCG 0-8. 11 December: UCD 5-6, UCG 1-2.
UCD champions with four league points.
Note: From 1933/34 onwards the competition was played as a straight knock-out.
1933/34 – UCG hosted. Semi-finals at Galway Sports Ground, 8 December: UCG 4-7, QUB 1-6; UCD 2-7, UCC 1-3. Final at Galway Sports Ground, 10 December: UCG 5-6, UCD 2-3.
1934/35 – UCC hosted. All games at the Mardyke. Semi-final, 7 December: UCG 2-3, UCD 1-1. Semi-final, 8 December: UCC 4-2, QUB 0-4. Final, 9 December: UCG 1-6, UCC 0-2.
1935/36 – QUB hosted. Semi-final at Cherryvale, 6 December: QUB 3-5, UCC 0-3. Semi-final at Cherryvale, 7 December: UCD 3-6, UCG 1-5. Final at Corrigan Park, 8 December: UCD 2-3, QUB 0-1.
1936/37 – UCD hosted. Semi-finals at Belfield, 5 December: UCG 5-1, QUB 0-4; UCD 1-3, UCC 0-3. Final at Croke Park, 6 December: UCG 4-6, UCD 1-3.
1937/38 – UCG hosted. All games at Galway Sports Ground. Semi-finals, 4 December: UCD 4-7, UCC 0-0; UCG 6-6, QUB 2-2. Final, 5 December: UCG 0-7, UCD 1-2.
1938/39 – UCC hosted. All games at the Mardyke. Semi-finals, 3 December: UCC 1-5, UCD 1-3; UCG 3-8, QUB 2-2. Final, 4 December: UCG 2-3, UCC 0-0.
1939/40 – QUB hosted. Semi-finals at Cherryvale, 9 December: QUB 6-4, UCC 2-4; UCG 1-3, UCD 0-6. Final at Corrigan Park, 10 December: UCG 1-5, QUB 1-2. 18 February 1940, Galway – 'Replay': UCG 2-6, UCD 1-3.
Note: It was too dark to play extra-time after the UCG vs. UCD drawn semi-final, so the teams agreed that UCG should play Queen's (the other semi-final winners) the next day, on the understanding that if Queen's won, they would become champions. Alternatively, if UCG beat Queen's, then UCG would play UCD for the title in a 'replay' in Galway – and that is what happened.
1940/41 – UCD hosted. Semi-finals at Belfield, 14 December: UCD 1-10, QUB 3-3; UCG 5-3, UCC 3-4. Final at Belfield, 15 December: UCG 3-5, UCD 1-2.
1941/42 – UCG hosted. All games at Galway Sports Ground. Semi-finals, 13 December: UCD 4-5, QUB 2-3; UCG 4-6, UCC 0-3. Final, 14 December: UCG 0-8, UCD 2-1.
1942/43 – Not played.
1943/44 – UCC hosted. Semi-finals at the Mardyke, 27 November: UCD 4-9, UCG 2-1; UCC 3-7, QUB 1-1. Final at the Mardyke, 28 November: UCC 2-5, UCD 3-1.
1944/45 – UCD hosted. Semi-finals at Belfield, 9 December: UCD 7-7, QUB 2-4; UCC 2-8, UCG 1-4. Final, 10 December: UCD 3-8, UCC 0-2.
1945/46 – QUB hosted. Semi-finals at Cherryvale, 24 November: QUB 0-8, UCG 0-4; UCD 2-7, UCC 1-5. Final at Corrigan Park, 9 December: UCD 4-5, QUB 2-6.
1946/47 – UCG hosted. All games at Galway Sports Ground. Semi-finals, 9 December: UCD 4-8, QUB 2-6; UCC 3-6, UCG 3-4. Final, 10 December: UCC 2-3, UCD 0-4.
1947/48 – UCC hosted. All games at the Camp Field. Semi-finals, 22 November: UCC 5-8, QUB 1-1; UCD 3-4, UCG 3-3. Final at the Mardyke, 23 November: UCD 0-3, UCC 0-2.
1948/49 – QUB hosted. Semi-finals at Cherryvale, 13 November: UCD 3-10, UCC 0-0; UCG 2-10, QUB 0-4. Final at Corrigan Park, 14 November: UCG 2-5, UCD 2-4.
1949/50 – UCD hosted. Semi-finals at Belfield, 5 November: UCG 5-7, QUB 0-4; UCD 2-10, UCC 1-6. Final at Croke Park, 6 November: UCD 1-8, UCG 1-7.
1950/51 – UCG hosted. Semi-finals at Fahy's Field, 25 November: UCG 2-11, QUB 0-4; UCC 0-5, UCD 0-4. Final at Galway Sports Ground, 26 November: UCG 1-12, UCC 1-2.
1951/52 – UCC hosted. All games at the Mardyke. Semi-finals, 10 November: UCC 3-8, QUB 1-8; UCG 3-7, UCD 3-4. Final, 11 November: UCC 0-5, UCG 0-3.
1952/53 – QUB hosted. Semi-finals at Cherryvale, 8 November: UCD 4-1, UCG 1-8; UCC 4-4, QUB 3-3. Final at Corrigan Park, 9 November: UCC 3-4, UCD 0-3.

1953/54 – UCD hosted. Semi-finals at Belfield, 28 November: UCD 2-9, QUB 0-5; UCG 2-8, UCC 1-9 (a.e.t.). Final at Croke Park, 29 November: UCD 2-7, UCG 0-4.
1954/55 – UCG hosted. Semi-finals at Galway, 13 November: UCG 2-4, QUB 0-3; UCD 3-10, UCC 2-8. Final at Galway Sports Ground, 14 November: UCG 2-6, UCD 1-9. Final replay at Fahy's Field, 30 January 1955: UCG 1-10, UCD 2-6 (a.e.t.).
1955/56 – UCC hosted. All games at the Mardyke. Semi-finals, 19 November: UCC 4-7, QUB 3-3; UCD 2-5, UCG 3-1. Final, 20 November: UCD 3-5, UCC 2-4.
1956/57 – QUB hosted. Semi-finals at Cherryvale, 1 December: UCD 1-7, UCG 1-2; UCC 2-5, QUB 2-4. Final at Casement Park, 2 December: UCD 1-8, UCC 1-4.
1957/58 – UCD hosted. Semi-finals at Belfield, 23 November: UCD 2-7, QUB 0-4; UCC 2-8, UCG 1-6. Final at Croke Park, 24 November: UCD 0-9, UCC 2-2.
1958/59 – UCG hosted. Semi-finals at Fahy's Field, 22 November: QUB 2-9, UCG 1-7; UCD 3-11, UCC 0-6. Final at Fahy's Field, 23 November: QUB 2-7, UCD 2-7. Final replay at Ballybay, 15 February 1959: QUB 0-10, UCD 0-9.
1959/60 – UCC hosted. All games at the Mardyke. Semi-finals, 6 December: UCD 2-9, QUB 1-5; UCC 2-5, UCG 2-2. Final, 7 December: UCD 3-8, UCC 1-4.
1960/61 – QUB hosted. Semi-finals at Cherryvale, 19 November: UCG 2-9, QUB 2-4; UCD beat UCC. Final at Casement Park, 20 November: UCG 1-9, UCD 2-3.
1961/62 – UCD hosted. Semi-finals at Belfield, 25 November: UCG 1-13, QUB 0-3; UCD 2-11, UCC 1-5. Final at Croke Park, 26 November: UCD 3-7, UCG 2-7.
1962/63 – UCG hosted. Semi-finals at Galway, 24 November: UCC 3-5, UCD 3-4; UCG 0-9, QUB 0-4. Final at Pearse Stadium, 25 November: UCG 1-9, UCC 1-3.
1963/64 – UCC hosted. All games at the Mardyke. Semi-finals, 30 November: UCC 1-11, TCD 1-7; UCG 1-9, UCD 1-5. Final, 1 December: UCG 2-10, UCC 0-5.
1964/65 – QUB hosted. Semi-finals at Cherryvale, 28 November: QUB 3-8, UCC 2-3; UCD 2-5, UCG 1-2. Final at Casement Park, 29 November: QUB 3-5, UCD 0-8
1965/66 – UCD hosted. Semi-finals at O'Toole Park, 4 December: UCC 1-7, UCD 1-6; UCG 2-4, QUB 0-6. Final at Croke Park, 5 December: UCC 3-9, UCG 0-2.
1966/67 – UCG hosted. Semi-finals at Tuam, 26 November: UCC 2-7, UCD 2-5; UCG 1-12, QUB 0-2. Final at Pearse Stadium, 27 November: UCC 0-9, UCG 1-5.
Note: From 1967/68 onwards the Sigerson Cup competition was held during the second term (Hilary), chiefly in February and March.
1967/68 – TCD hosted. Semi-finals at Santry, 27 January: UCD 1-16, TCD 0-4;
UCG 1-13, UCC 1-7. Final at Croke Park, 28 January: UCD 1-10, UCG 0-4.
1968/69 – UCC hosted. Semi-finals at the Mardyke, 1 March: UCC 2-12, UCD 1-6; UCG 2-5, QUB 1-6. Final at the Mardyke, 2 March: UCC 5-12, UCG 0-3.
1969/70 – QUB hosted. Semi-finals at Hilltown, 15 March: UCC 3-5, UCD 0-5; QUB 3-15, TCD 0-1. Final at Newry, 16 March: UCC 1-10, QUB 1-5.
1970/71 – UCG hosted. Semi-finals at Pearse Stadium, 6 March: QUB 2-6, UCG 2-4; UCD 0-14, UCC 2-6. UCD was then ejected from the competition and UCC reinstated. Final at Pearse Stadium, 7 March: QUB 0-7, UCC 0-6.
1971/72 – UCD hosted. Semi-finals at O'Toole Park, 4 March: UCC 3-7, UCD 0-15; UCG 0-13, QUB 1-9. Final at O'Toole Park, 5 March: UCC 5-7, UCG 3-8.
1972/73 – UCC hosted. Semi-finals at the Mardyke, 3 March: Maynooth 2-17, UCC 1-4; UCD 1-12, QUB 2-5. Final at Cork Athletic Grounds, 4 March: UCD 1-9, Maynooth 1-5.
1973/74 – Maynooth hosted. Semi-finals at Naas, 23 February: UCD 2-9, Maynooth 0-7; UCG 3-2, QUB 0-10 (a.e.t.). Final at Newbridge, 24 February: UCD 0-14, UCG 1-5.
1974/75 – QUB hosted. Semi-finals at Corrigan Park, 8 March: QUB 4-9, UCG 0-2; UCD 1-18, UCC 1-7. Final at Corrigan Park, 9 March: UCD 0-18, QUB 0-10.
1975/76 – TCD hosted. Semi-finals at Croke Park, 28 February: Maynooth 1-11, TCD 0-6; UCD 1-12; UCC 0-10. Final at Croke Park, 29 February: Maynooth 2-5, UCD 0-9.
1976/77 – UCG hosted. Semi-finals at Galway, 26 February: UCD 0-8, Maynooth 1-4; UCG 3-6, UCC 1-3. Final at Pearse Stadium, 27 February: UCD 1-8, UCG 1-8. Final replay at Pearse Stadium, 10 April: UCD 1-11, UCG 0-6.
1977/78 – UCD hosted. Semi-finals at O'Toole Park, 25 February: UCD 0-17, UCC 0-8; UCG 1-7, Maynooth 0-7. Final at Croke Park, 26 February: UCD 1-13, UCG 0-7.
1978/79 – UCC hosted. Semi-finals at the Mardyke, 24 February: UCD 1-15, Maynooth 1-4; UCG 1-7, UCC 1-5. Final at Páirc Uí Chaoimh, 25 February: UCD 2-15, UCG 0-2.
1979/80 – NUU Coleraine hosted. Semi-finals at NUU Coleraine, 8 March: UCD 2-11, NUU 1-6; UCG 1-7, Maynooth 0-3. Final at Bellaghy, 9 March: UCG 1-8, UCD 0-7.
1980/81 – Maynooth hosted. Semi-final at Highfield, Maynooth, 21 February:
TCD 1-7, Maynooth 0-7. Semi-final at St. Mary's Park, Maynooth: UCG 1-5, UCC 1-4. Final at Maynooth College, 22 February: UCG 1-12, TCD 0-6.
1981/82 – QUB hosted. Semi-finals at Malone, 27 February: UCG 2-12, TCD 1-3; QUB 1-10,

HIGHER EDUCATION

UCD 0-7. Final at Malone, 28 February: QUB 0-12, UCG 1-7 (a.e.t.).
1982/83 – TCD hosted. Semi-finals at Santry, 19 February: UCG 0-13, TCD 0-6; QUB 2-12, UCC 1-10. Final at Santry, 20 February: UCG 2-8, QUB 2-5.
1983/84 – UCG hosted. Semi-finals at Pearse Stadium, 3 March: UCG 1-5, QUB 1-4; UCC 1-8, UCD 2-4. Final at Pearse Stadium, 4 March: UCG 1-11, UCC 0-6.
1984/85 – UCD hosted. Semi-finals at Belfield, 23 February: UCD 2-10, UCG 2-7; QUB 2-4, UCC 0-5. Final at Croke Park, 24 February: UCD 0-10, QUB 0-5.
1985/86 – UCC hosted. Semi-finals at the Mardyke, 8 March: UUJ 2-10, Maynooth 1-4; UCC 2-6, UCG 0-9. Final at the Mardyke, 9 March: UUJ 1-8, UCC 1-5.
1986/87 – UUC hosted. Semi-finals at UUC, 28 February: UCC 2-12, TCD 0-3; UUJ 0-10, Maynooth 0-6. Final at Bellaghy, 1 March: UUJ 0-6, UCC 0-4.
1987/88 – Maynooth hosted. Semi-finals at Maynooth, 5 March: UCC 1-8, Maynooth 1-6; UCG 1-7, St. Mary's 0-9. Final at Summerhill, 6 March: UCC 0-8, UCG 0-5.
1988/89 – QUB hosted. Semi-finals at Malone, 4 March: UCC 4-13, TCD 3-9 (a.e.t.); St. Mary's 1-7, QUB 1-4. Final at Malone, 5 March: St. Mary's 3-13, UCC 1-5.
1989/90 – TCD hosted. Semi-finals at Santry, 23 February: St. Mary's 1-9, UCC 1-8; QUB 1-5, TCD 0-7. Final at Santry, 24 February: QUB 3-8, St. Mary's 1-9.
1990/91 – No host college. Semi-final at Scotstown, 13 March: UUJ beat ARTC. Semi-final at Walsh Island, 20 March: UCG 2-11, TCD 2-9. Final at Enniskillen, 24 March: UUJ 0-7, UCG 0-6.
1991/92 – UCG hosted. Semi-final at the Prairie, Salthill, 14 March: QUB 0-7, St. Mary's 0-2. Semi-final at Pearse Stadium, 14 March: UCG 1-17, UUJ 1-13 (a.e.t.). Final at Pearse Stadium, 15 March: UCG 2-8, QUB 0-11.
1992/93 – UUJ hosted. Semi-final at Shaw's Road, 20 March: St. Mary's 1-12, UCG 1-7. Semi-final at Casement Park, 20 March: QUB 1-9, UUJ 1-7.
Final at Casement Park, 21 March: QUB 1-12, St. Mary's 0-4.
1993/94 – UCD hosted. Semi-finals at Belfield, 26 February: UCC 0-13, UUJ 0-6; QUB 0-15, UL 1-11. Final at Belfield, 27 February: UCC 1-9, QUB 2-5.
1994/95 – UCC hosted. Semi-finals at the Mardyke, 11 March: UCC 1-17, UUJ 2-5; UCG 2-12, Garda 1-6. Final at Páirc Uí Rinn, 12 March: UCC 0-12, UCG 1-7.
1995/96 – UL hosted. Semi-finals at UL Grounds, 2 March: UCD 3-15, UCC 3-13 (a.e.t.); Garda 1-7, UUJ 0-5. Final at UL Grounds, 3 March: UCD 2-11, Garda 3-5.
1996/97 – UUC hosted. Semi-finals at UUC, 8 March: TRTC 2-10, SRTC 0-10; UL 3-12, UUC 2-4. Final at UUC, 9 March: TRTC 1-13, UL 1-6.
1997/98 – ITT hosted. Semi-final at John Mitchel's, 7 March: UUJ 1-8, QUB 2-3. Semi-final at Kerin's O'Rahilly's, 7 March: ITT 2-12, AIT 0-6. Final at Austin Stack Park, 8 March: ITT 0-10, UUJ 0-8.
1998/99 – QUB hosted. Semi-finals at Malone, 6 March: ITT 0-14, ITS 0-11; Garda 2-9, QUB 1-10. Final at Malone, 7 March: ITT 1-8, Garda 0-7.
1999/2000 – NUIG hosted. Semi-final at Daingean, 26 February: UCD 0-9, NUIG 0-8. Semi-final at the Prairie, Salthill, 26 February: QUB 0-13, UCC 1-7. Final at Maigh Cuilinn, 27 February: QUB 1-8, UCD 0-8 (a.e.t.).
2000/2001 – ITS meant to host (until foot-and-mouth outbreak). Semi-final at Newbridge, 4 April: UUJ 0-15, UCC 0-8. Semi-final at Walterstown, 4 April: UCD 1-12, St. Mary's 0-11. Final at Scotstown, 11 April: UUJ 1-14, UCD 1-9.
2001/02 – ITS hosted. Semi-final at Kent Park, 22 February: ITS 2-4, AIT 1-6. Semi-final at IT Sligo, 22 February: UCC 1-9, UUJ 1-8 (a.e.t.). Final at Markiewicz Park, 23 February: ITS 0-6, UCC 0-5.
2002/03 – UCC hosted. Semi-finals at the Mardyke, 8 March: NUIG 2-14, Maynooth 0-8; UCD 1-10, UUJ 2-6. Final at Páirc Uí Rinn, 9 March: NUIG 1-8, UCD 0-8.
2003/04 – St. Mary's hosted. Semi-final at Rossa Park, 27 February: ITS 0-12, Cork IT 0-8. Semi-final at Sarsfield's Park, 27 February: QUB 1-10, UCD 0-9. Final at Corrigan Park, 28 February: ITS 1-10, QUB 1-7.
2004/05 – Dundalk IT hosted. Semi-finals at Dundalk IT, 25 February: QUB 1-9, UUJ 1-8; ITS 2-12, UCC 0-10. Final at Dundalk IT, 26 February: ITS 0-10, QUB 0-7 (a.e.t.).
2005/06 – DCU hosted. Semi-finals at DCU, 24 February: DCU 0-8, UCC 0-6; QUB 0-10, UUJ 1-6. Final at Parnell Park, 25 February: DCU 0-11, QUB 1-4.
2006/07 – QUB hosted. Semi-finals at Malone, 2 March: QUB 1-11, Cork IT 0-7; UUJ 0-18, ITS 1-11 (a.e.t.). Final at Malone, 3 March: QUB 0-15, UUJ 0-14 (a.e.t.).
2007/08 – IT Carlow hosted. Semi-final at ITC, 8 March: UUJ 2-12, DIT 0-10; semi-final at Páirc Chiaráin, Athlone, 15 April: Garda 2-12, GMIT 1-14 (a.e.t.). Final at ITC, 22 April: UUJ 1-16, Garda 1-14 (a.e.t.).
2008/09 – Cork IT hosted. Semi-finals at Cork IT grounds, Bishopstown, 27 February: DIT 3-8, UCD 1-4; Cork IT 0-14, NUIG 0-13. Final at Cork IT grounds, Bishopstown, 28 February: Cork 1-15, DIT 1-10.

SIGERSON CUP FINAL TEAMS

Note: Although in most years up to 1933/34 there was no Sigerson Cup final per se, the following list includes the runner-up college team where available.

1910/11

U.C.C. - W John Riordan (Cork) (capt.), T Nunan, Charlie Delea, Bill Fitzgerald (Cork), William Lehane (Cork), W O'Brien, J J O'Keeffe, D J Burke, E Hartnett, W Walsh, Tommy Richardson (Cork), D Saunders, Eddie Cotter (Cork), C Collins, T Buckley, D O'Keeffe, J Barry.

U.C.G. – (as listed for a non-Sigerson Cup game) – D Morrin (capt.), J F McDermott, Mick Martin (Galway), T McGowan, J Collins, Toss Heneghan, J Eaton, T Doyle, Brian Cusack, J Devine, F Ronayne, T Curtin, J Doyle, D Flannery, C Farrell, J Sheills, Conor O'Malley (Galway).

1911/12

U.C.G. - Joseph F Donegan (Sligo) (capt.), Mick Martin (Galway), Jack Sheehy, Tom Flannery, Hubert O'Connor, T Goff, Conor O'Malley (Galway), B Barrett, Geoff Collins, J Marron, Michael Keane (Galway), J F McDermott, T McGowan, Tommy Quinn (Galway), Toss Heneghan, P Dempsey, J Doherty.

U.C.D. – team-list not available.

1912/13

U.C.D. - L Murray, J Murray, Solomon Lawlor (Kerry & Dublin), J F Kearney (Kerry), Redihan, Finnegan, Fitzmaurice, Joseph McGrath, Ward, P Fitzpatrick, Kelly, J Marron, Heavey, Éamon Bulfin (Offaly), Finnegan.

U.C.G. – O Leonard (goal), Peter O'Farrell (Roscommon), Joseph F Donegan (Sligo) (capt.), Toss Heneghan, Casey, Michael Keane (Galway), Mick Martin (Galway), Doherty, Conor O'Malley (Galway), Thompson, T Goff, Tom Flannery, J F McDermott, J Marron, Jack Sheehy.

1913/14

U.C.C. - Tom Nunan (Cork) (capt.), Patrick O'Donnell, W John Riordan (Cork), Michael 'Charlie' Troy (Kerry), Tommy Richardson (Cork), William Lehane (Cork), Dick F O'Brien (Cork), James J Mulvihill (Kerry), Jack Lynch (Cork), Jeremiah J Creed (Cork), C Collins, E Hartnett, Denny Pa Lucy, T Brien, M Kelly, T McCarthy, C Delea.

U.C.D. - Éamon Bulfin (Offaly), P Fitzpatrick (capt.), J Ward, Heneghan, Pierce Walton (Kilkenny), J F Kearney (Kerry), Sheehan, Joseph McGrath, Stokes, Ward, James McPhillips, Thomas O'Hickey, J Marron, Solomon Lawlor (Kerry & Dublin), Frank Burke (Kildare & Dublin).

1914/15

U.C.D. - Solomon Lawlor (Kerry & Dublin), Éamon Bulfin (Offaly) (goal), John Ryan (Limerick & Dublin), P Fitzpatrick, Pierce Walton (Kilkenny), T Hassett, P Purcell, Thomas Joyce, Thomas Hickey, M McGuinness, Frank Burke (Kildare & Dublin), James McPhillips, J Marron, J F Kearney (Kerry), P Conway.

U.C.G. (14 players listed) - T Goff, Fred O'Doherty, Peter O'Farrell (Roscommon), O Leonard, Burke, B Barrett, T.P. Flanagan, Jimmy Collins (capt.), J Drury, D Rowland, Tom Flannery, M Whelan, J McEvoy, O'Sullivan.

1915/16

U.C.C. - E/Michael 'Charlie' Troy (goal), P J Moloney, Jack Lynch (Cork), L O'Connor, James Mulvihill (Kerry), R Evans, Willie Moore (Kilkenny), Patrick O'Donnell, Willie Murphy (Cork), William Richardson (Cork), D J O'Sullivan, Jeremiah J Creed (Cork), Con Lucey (Cork), D Mulcahy, Larry O'Brien (Cork), James Murphy-O'Connor (Cork). C Collins also played.

U.C.D. - Solomon Lawlor (Kerry & Dublin) (capt.), Deignan, Young, P McGuinness, Brian Joyce (Galway & Dublin), P Fitzpatrick, Harte, Pierce Walton (Kilkenny), Pat O'Shea, Joe Phelan (Kilkenny & Dublin, P J O'Brien, Fanning, Thomas O'Hickey, John Ryan (Dublin), P Purcell.

1916/17

U.C.D. - Solomon Lawlor (Kerry & Dublin) (capt.), Éamon Bulfin (Offaly) (goal), James P McNulty, Michael 'Charlie' Troy, P Purcell, J Keating, P McGuinness, Brian Joyce (Galway & Dublin), Pierce Walton (Kilkenny), Patrick Concannon, Maurice Collins, Patrick McCarvill (Monaghan), P J O'Brien, Joe Phelan (Kilkenny & Dublin), Frank Burke (Dublin).

U.C.C. - James J Mulvihill (Kerry & Cork) (capt.), Jack Lynch (Cork) (goal), Roger O'Connor (Cork), James Lynch (Cork), Willie Moore (Kilkenny), R Evans, James Carver, D J O'Sullivan, Willie Murphy (Cork), William Richardson (Cork), Andrew McCarthy, Dick F O'Brien (Cork), James Murphy-O'Connor (Cork), Con Lucey (Cork), P O'Sullivan.

1917/18

U.C.D. (16 players listed) - Solomon Lawlor (Dublin) (capt.), Brian Joyce (Galway & Dublin), Frank Burke (Dublin), P Purcell, P McGuinness, Patrick McCarvill (Monaghan), P Fitzpatrick, T Long, P Collins, J Keating, Johnny Keohane, J Cullen, F McGinley, Joe Phelan (Kilkenny & Dublin), J O'Connor, D Healy.

U.C.C. – team-list not available.

1918/19

U.C.C. (16 players listed) - Con Lucey (Cork), Roger O'Connor (Cork), Willie Moore (Kilkenny & Cork), Willie Murphy (Cork), James Murphy-O'Connor (Cork), J Fenton, William S Nunan, Joe Kearney (Cork), Richard O'Brien (Cork), John Kiely (Waterford), Eugene 'Nudge' Callanan (Tipperary), Michael Breen, T O'Sullivan, Jack Murphy (Kerry), Jack Falvey (Cork), F Fitzpatrick.

U.C.D. – team-list not available.

1919/20

U.C.D. - T Long (goal), Tom Pierse (Wexford) (capt.), John A Henry (Mayo), P Lenihan, Joe Phelan (Kilkenny & Dublin), Frank Burke (Dublin), Garrett Scanlan, Patrick Moran (Roscommon), Patrick Caffrey (Dublin), John A Cusack, Mick J Mullen (Mayo), D Purcell, W Doyle, Éamonn N M O'Sullivan (Kerry), T O'Sullivan.

U.C.C. - J Fenton (capt.), C Balty (goal), Roger O'Connor, H Johnson, Jack Murphy (Kerry), William S Nunan, Eugene 'Nudge' Callanan (Tipperary), Willie Murphy (Cork), J Kennedy, T Fitzpatrick, P O'Sullivan, M Bastible (Cork), Con Lucey (Cork), John Kiely (Waterford), Finian O'Shea (Cork).

1920/21 – NO COMPETITION.

1921/22

U.C.G. - W McDonald (capt.), Michael Greene (goal), Fred O 'Doherty, M J Ring, J Scott, J F Glavey, C O'Connor, T Jordan, M Dalton, Arthur de B Joyce, T McDonagh/ld, T Linehan, Michael Dolan, E Moran, C E Flynn.

U.C.C. - Joe Kearney (Cork) (capt.), Willie Moore (Kilkenny & Cork), Willie Cotter (Cork), Frank Creedon (Cork), Tom Nunan (Cork), Michael Breen (goal), Eugene 'Nudge' Callanan (Tipperary), Finian O'Shea (Cork), Donal O'Donoghue (Kerry), John Kiely (Waterford), William Fortune (Cork), R Bastible, J Fenton, Con Lucey (Cork), Harry St. John Atkins (Cork).

1922/23

U.C.C. - Tom Nunan (Cork) (capt.), Michael Breen, Tom Lee (Tipperary), R Mulcahy, Jack Murphy (Kerry), Harry St. John Atkins (Cork), Murphy, Finian O'Shea (Cork), M C O'Mahony, J O'Connor, William Fleming (Cork), T Fitzgerald, E Scanlan, J Kirwan, T Quinlan. Subs.: T Fitzgerald, T O'Toole.

U.C.D. - Éamonn N M O'Sullivan (Kerry) (capt.), Garrett Scanlan, Séamus Gardiner (Tipperary & Dublin), P Groarke, Thomas Gardiner (Clare), T O'Sullivan, James D Grant, Éamonn O'Doherty (Clare), Gerard A Conway, B McGowan, Seán Lavan (Mayo), Tom Pierse (Wexford), John A Henry (Mayo), George Madigan, Éamonn Mongey (Mayo). Subs.: B McDonnell, John Kennedy, Mick D'Arcy (Tipperary).

1923/24

U.C.D. - Séamus Gardiner (Tipperary & Dublin) (captain), Thomas Gardiner (Clare) (goal), Éamonn O'Doherty (Clare), John A Henry (Mayo), James D Grant, Mick Kilcoyne (Sligo), P Mannix, M McQuaide, George Madigan, G Hurlay, Éamonn O'Sullivan (Kerry), Tom Pierse (Wexford), B McGowan, Jim Smith (Cavan), Frank Burke (Dublin).

U.C.C. - Michael Breen (goal), Finian O'Shea (Cork) (capt.), Tom Nunan (Cork), Jack Murphy (Kerry), R Mulcahy, Donal O'Donoghue (Kerry), Tom Lee (Tipperary), Frank Creedon (Cork), Joe Kearney (Cork), William Fleming (Cork), M Murphy, Éamonn Fitzgerald (Kerry), J O'Connor, Harry St. John Atkins (Cork), J Powell.

1924/25

U.C.C. - Michael Murphy (Kerry) (capt.), Jack Murphy (Kerry), J O'Sullivan, Tom Nunan (Cork), Frank Hurley, Donal O'Donoghue (Kerry), Matt Murphy (Cork), Harry St. John Atkins (Cork), Tom Lee (Tipperary), Patrick O'Sullivan, David Barry, Pat Nyhan (Cork), Joe Kearney (Cork), Frank Creedon (Cork), Peter Coughlan (Kerry & Cork). Subs.: Patrick O'Donoghue (Kerry), W McLaughlin, D O'Keeffe.

U.C.G. – J M Treacy, J H Higgins, C E Flynn, W T Hession (Galway), M Moloney, M Mannion (Galway), R Donnellan, E Donnelly, T Jordan, J Walsh (Galway), T Collian, W Croyne, P Molloy, C Macken, D Walshe. Sub.: J P Caffrey.

1925/26

U.C.C. - Seán O'Sullivan (goal), Tom Nunan (Cork), Eugene 'Nudge' Callanan (Tipperary & Cork), Dan Lynch (Cork), William Fleming (Cork), Frank Creedon (Cork), Tom Lee (Tipperary), Donal O'Donoghue (Kerry), M Murphy, David Barry, Patrick O'Sullivan, Peter Coughlan (Kerry & Cork), Michael Powell (Kerry), Joe Kearney (Cork), J O'Connor.

U.C.D. - Drury (goal), Éamonn O'Doherty (Clare), R Mulcahy, Paddy McDonald (Cavan), Brown, Francis Friel, Éamonn Fitzgerald (Kerry), Mick J Mullen (Mayo), Seán Lavan (Mayo), M McQuaid, Balfe, George Madigan, John A Henry (Mayo), T Mullen. Sub.: Daly for Devine.

1926/27

U.C.D. - Paddy McDonald (Cavan) (goal), R Mulcahy, Éamonn O'Doherty (Clare), J Stack, J Duffy, Éamonn Fitzgerald (Kerry), Bernard F Leavy, Joe O'Sullivan (Kerry), Mick J Mullen (Mayo), Seán Lavan (Mayo), Patrick Casey, J/T

O'Connell, T Mullen, Frank Sheehy (Kerry), John A Henry (Mayo).
U.C.G. – team-list not available.

1927/28

U.C.C. - Michael Lane, Tom Nunan (Cork), Seán Russell, Richard Molloy (Cork), Donal McCarthy (Cork), N Matthew, Matt Murphy (Cork), Dennis O'Keeffe, Michael Murphy (Kerry), Mossie Donegan (Cork), Peter Coughlan (Kerry & Cork), Eugene 'Nudge' Callanan (Cork), David Barry, Patrick O'Sullivan, Patrick Moynihan (Kerry). Donal O'Donoghue (Kerry) & Michael Powell (Kerry) also played over weekend.
U.C.D. – team-list not available.

1928/29

U.C.D. - K Mallin, Éamonn O'Doherty (Clare), James J O'Shea, J Duffy, Mick O'Gorman (Monaghan), Joe O'Sullivan (Kerry), Michael 'Al' Moroney (Clare), Mick J Mullen (Mayo), B Quigley, Laurence Marron (Monaghan), Éamonn Fitzgerald (Kerry), Seán Lavan (Mayo), Michael Falvey (Clare), Frank Sheehy (Kerry), T P O'Callaghan.
U.C.C. - Denis W Harvey, Tom Nunan (Cork), Richard Molloy (Cork), Jim O'Regan (Cork), J Murphy, Dennis O'Keeffe, Mossie Donegan (Cork), H O'Leary (Cork), Seán Vaughan (Cork), D Coughlan, Michael Murphy (Kerry & Cork), Donal McCarthy (Cork), Eugene 'Nudge' Callanan (Cork), Donal O'Donoghue (Kerry), Anthony O'Callaghan.

1929/30

U.C.D. - Con O'Leary (goal), Joe O'Sullivan (Kerry), N Devine, Mick J Mullen (Mayo), Jack Walsh (Kerry), Mick O'Gorman (Monaghan), Séamus Duffy, J Quigley, Éamonn Fitzgerald (Kerry), P Jordan, Bernard Higgins, Seán Lavan (Mayo), Patrick Flynn, Michael Falvey (Clare), Peter J Duffy (Monaghan).
U.C.C. – team-list not available.

1930/31

U.C.D. - B Winston (goal), Mick O'Gorman (Monaghan), James J O'Shea, Jack Walsh (Kerry), Joe O'Sullivan (Kerry), John Kennedy, George Powell (Kerry), Éamonn Fitzgerald (Kerry), B Quigley, Bernard Higgins, Patrick Flynn, Johnny O'Donnell (Donegal), B Sullivan, Colm Connolly (Galway), Thomas Walsh.
U.C.G. - Jack Langan (Mayo) (goal), Séamus O'Malley (Mayo), Kelly (Mayo), J Egan, P J Dempsey, John O'Leary (Clare), Paddy Stephens (Galway), Dermot Mitchell (Galway) (capt.), Paddy Quinn (Mayo), Mick Higgins (Galway), Frank Burke (Galway), Michael Naughton (Mayo), Tom Gill (Mayo), John Donnellan (Galway), James P ("Tot") McGowan (Mayo). Sub.: Éamonn "Ned" Murphy (Mayo). B Mannion, T McCarthy & Glynn also played over the weekend.

1931/32

U.C.D. - J Doyle, Mick O'Gorman (Monaghan), Jack Walsh (Kerry), John Kennedy, George Powell (Kerry), J Colleran, Colm Connolly (Galway), Byrne, P Fitzgibbon, J Lynch, Seán Flood (Meath), MacNamara, McGillicuddy, Johnny O'Donnell (Donegal), Mick Casey (Clare).
U.C.G. - Jack Langan (Mayo), Patrick Colleran (Sligo), Tom Gill (Mayo), Séamus O'Malley (Mayo), Paddy Quinn (Mayo), Dermot Mitchell (Galway), Mick Ferriter (Galway), James Patrick ("Tot") McGowan (Mayo), Brian Scanlon (Mayo), Éamonn "Ned" Murphy (Mayo), John O'Leary (Clare), Mick Higgins (Galway), John Egan (Mayo), Michael Naughton (Mayo), Mulvihill.

1932/33

U.C.D. - J Doyle, Mick Casey (Clare), Mick O'Gorman (Monaghan), Jack Walsh (Kerry), James J O'Shea, Stephen Barrett, Toddy Walsh (Kerry), Seán Flood (Meath), Johnny Walsh (Kerry), James J Dore, Maurice McKenna (Kerry), Colm Boland (Westmeath & Dublin), Colm Connolly (Galway), Dermot Bourke (Kildare), George Powell (Kerry & Dublin).
U.C.C. - Daniel Buckley, E O'Mahony (Kerry & Cork), M Lillis (Cork), J / T Connolly (Cork), Luke Flanagan (Cork), Richard Molloy (Cork), M Finnucane (Kerry), Martin Cronin (Cork), Thomas O'Reilly (Cork), B Herlihy, Donal McCarthy (Cork), Gus Kelleher (Cork), Michael Murphy (Cork), J Flanagan, William Finlay (Tipperary).

1933/34

U.C.G. - Mícheál Conneely (Galway), Mick Raftery (Mayo), Paddy Quinn (Mayo), Vinny Kelly (Mayo), Tony Regan (Galway), Séamus O'Malley (Mayo), John O'Leary (Clare), Dinny O'Sullivan (Galway), Mick Higgins (Galway), Mick Ferriter (Kerry), Brendan Nestor (Galway), J Cummins (Mayo), Vincent McDarby (Galway), Brian Scanlon (Mayo), James Patrick ('Tot') McGowan (Mayo). Sub.: James Laffey (Mayo) for Cummins.
U.C.D. - J Doyle, Paddy McMahon (Kerry), James J O'Shea, A Moran, Colm Boland (Dublin), Mick Casey (Clare), George Powell (Kerry & Dublin), Seán Flood (Meath), Patrick M Farrell (Longford), Vincent McGovern (Cavan), Maurice McKenna (Kerry), J Lynham (Dublin), Colm Connolly (Galway), Dermot Bourke (Kildare), T O'Gorman.

1934/35

U.C.G. - Mícheál Conneely (Galway), Mick Raftery (Mayo), Paddy Quinn (Mayo), Ned

HIGHER EDUCATION

Murphy (Mayo), Tony Regan (Galway), Dinny O'Sullivan (Galway), John O'Leary (Clare), Donal McCarthy (Kerry), Diarmaid O'Connell (Cork), James Laffey (Mayo), Hugh Gibbons (Roscommon), Mick Higgins (Galway), Brian Scanlon (Mayo), Vincent McDarby (Galway), Mick Ferriter (Kerry & Galway). Sub.: Andy Laffey (Mayo) for McCarthy.

U.C.C. - Denis W Harvey, Gus Kelleher (Cork), C Ryan (Kerry), H O'Leary (Cork), D Crowley, Thomas O'Reilly (Cork), F O'Donovan (Cork), Michael Geaney, J Sullivan, M Collins, Donal McCarthy (Cork), Joe Roche (Cork), Brendan Flahive, Liam Tierney (Cork), C Greaney.

1935/36

U.C.D. - John "Roger" Horan (Kerry), Gerry O'Leary (Cork), Paddy McMahon (Kerry), Rex Keelaghan (Monaghan), Jack O'Connor (Kerry), Joe Hughes (Galway), Paddy O'Loughlin (Mayo), Patrick Henry (Offaly), George Powell (Kerry & Dublin), J Lynham (Dublin), Kevin Maher (Carlow), Toddy Walsh (Kerry), Éamonn Gavin (Westmeath), Vincent McGovern (Cavan), Peter Carney (Westmeath).

Q.U.B. - Joe McNamee (Antrim), Frank Murray (Antrim), Hugh Albert McCaffrey (Tyrone), Seán Arthurs (Armagh), Felix O'Kane (Antrim), Terence McLornan (Antrim), John A Macaulay (Antrim), Brendan Murray (Armagh), Jimmy Burns (Down), Tom Fee (Fermanagh), Kevin Flynn (Armagh), Larry Higgins (Derry), Phil Bradley (Antrim), Frank Martin (Antrim), Jerry Hicks (Armagh). Sub.: William Steele (Antrim) for Higgins.

1936/37

U.C.G. - Jimmy McGauran (Roscommon), John O'Leary (Clare), Mick Raftery (Mayo & Galway), Joe Salmon (Mayo), Tony Regan (Galway), Henry Kenny (Mayo), Charlie O'Sullivan (Galway), Eugene O'Sullivan (Kerry), Donal McCarthy (Kerry), Joe Fitzgerald (Galway), Hugh Gibbons (Roscommon), Dick Winters (Mayo), Dennis Egan (Mayo), Brian Scanlon (Mayo), Gerry O'Beirne (Roscommon).

U.C.D. - John "Roger" Horan (Kerry), V Moran (Mayo), Gerry O'Leary (Cork), Robert O'Connor (Roscommon), Jack O'Connor (Kerry), Rex Keelaghan (Monaghan), Paddy O'Loughlin (Mayo), Thomas Canning (Cavan), J Lynham (Dublin), M McGahey (Monaghan), Toddy Walsh (Kerry), Paddy McEllin (Mayo), Patrick O'Riordan (Carlow), Vincent McGovern (Cavan), W O'Brien (Kerry).

1937/38

U.C.G. - Jimmy McGauran (Roscommon), John O'Leary (Clare), Mick Raftery (Mayo & Galway), Joe Salmon (Mayo & Galway), Tony Regan (Galway), Henry Kenny (Mayo), Charlie O'Sullivan (Galway), James Laffey (Mayo), Eugene O'Sullivan (Kerry), Con McGovern (Longford & Galway), Hugh Gibbons (Roscommon), Brendan Houlihan (Kerry), Dennis Egan (Mayo), Joe Joe Carney (Mayo), Gerry O'Beirne (Roscommon).

U.C.D. - John "Roger" Horan (Kerry), Dinny Cullinan (Limerick), Gerry O'Leary (Cork), Rex Keelaghan (Monaghan), Jack O'Connor (Kerry), Paddy Lynch (Clare), Robert O'Connor (Roscommon), Paddy Smith (Cavan), Thomas Canning (Cavan), Jim Clarke (Meath), Vincent McGovern (Cavan), Paddy McEllin (Mayo), Patrick O'Riordan (Carlow), Lar McEntee (Meath), Dick Winters (Mayo).

1938/39

U.C.G. - Jimmy McGauran (Roscommon & Galway), Jim Bohan (Leitrim), Mick Raftery (Galway), Joe Salmon (Galway), Charlie O'Sullivan (Galway), John O'Leary (Clare), Hugh Gibbons (Roscommon), Con McGovern (Longford & Galway), Pat Mitchell (Galway), James Laffey (Mayo), Jack Bracken (Mayo), P J Carroll (Mayo), Dennis Egan (Mayo), Joe Joe Carney (Mayo), Gerry O'Beirne (Roscommon).

U.C.C. - Steve O'Donoghue (Kerry), Tim Foley (Kerry), M Murphy (Kerry), D McCarthy (Cork), Jackie Spencer (Cork), T Mangan, Arthur Beckett (Cork), Dick Walsh (Kerry), Jim Young (Cork), P O'Sullivan (Kerry), Johnny Daly (Kerry), Joe Roche (Cork), P Dowling (Kerry), D Cotter (Limerick), Derry Beckett (Cork).

1939/40

N.B. - U.C.G. & U.C.D. listed as in "replay" final, Q.U.B. as in Belfast "final".

U.C.G. - Jimmy McGauran (Roscommon), Jim Bohan (Leitrim), Mick Raftery (Mayo & Galway), Joe Salmon (Mayo & Galway), Hugh Gibbons (Roscommon), Henry Kenny (Mayo), Paddy Dixon (Mayo), Pat Mitchell (Galway), Con McGovern (Galway), James Laffey (Mayo), Seán Mitchell (Leitrim), Dermot McDermott (Roscommon), Joe Joe Carney (Mayo), Jack Bracken (Mayo), Gerry O'Beirne (Roscommon). In the Belfast final, Dan Kavanagh (Kerry) was centre-forward, and Eugene Heavey (Roscommon) no.13.

Q.U.B. - Johnny Tohill (Antrim), John A Macaulay (Antrim), Eddie McLaughlin (Armagh), Paddy O'Neill (Antrim), George Watterson (Antrim), Danny MacRandal (Antrim), T Byrne (Antrim), Gene Thornbury (Antrim), Peter Lenfesty (Antrim), Brian O'Kane (Antrim), Alf Murray (Armagh), Austin Colohan (Armagh), Gerard Quigley (Derry), Hugh Glancy (Armagh), Jarlath Gibbons (Down).

U.C.D. - Aloysius 'Wishie' Lynn (Monaghan), Billy Durkan (Mayo), Gerry O'Leary (Cork), Rex Keelaghan (Monaghan), Cornelius Murphy (Limerick), Paddy Lynch (Clare & Dublin), Joe

O'Leary (Cork), Jim Clarke (Meath), Dinny Cullinan (Limerick), Tom P O'Reilly (Cavan), Vincent White (Cavan), Vincent Duffy (Monaghan), Eugene 'Silky' Smith (Dublin), Robert O'Connor (Roscommon), Seán Mullarkey (Sligo). N.B. - John 'Roger' Horan, U.C.D. goalkeeper in their drawn match against U.C.G. in 1939, died between then and the "replay".

1940/41

U.C.G. - Jimmy McGauran (Roscommon), Jim Bohan (Leitrim), Mick Raftery (Galway), Joe Salmon (Galway), Pat McDonagh (Galway), Henry Kenny (Mayo), Pat Mitchell (Galway), Joe Duggan (Galway), Dan Kavanagh (Kerry), Dermot McDermott (Roscommon), Oliver Clarke (Mayo), Pierce Thornton (Galway), Bernie Egan (Mayo), Tom Walsh (Kerry), Seán Thornton (Galway). Sub.: Evan Kennedy (Galway) for Walsh.

U.C.D. - Aloysius 'Wishie' Lynn (Monaghan), J O'Kane (Clare), Gerry O'Leary (Cork), Rex Keelaghan (Monaghan), Cyril Hayes (Clare), Barney Cully (Cavan), Jim Clarke (Meath), Vincent Duffy (Monaghan), Joe O'Leary (Cork), Eugene 'Silky' Smith (Dublin), Tom P O'Reilly (Cavan), Donal Keenan (Roscommon), Brendan Devlin (Tyrone), Seán Mullarkey (Sligo), Vincent White (Cavan). Sub.: Bernard Burbage (Longford) for Cully.

1941/42

U.C.G. - Jack Morahan (Mayo), Pat McDonagh (Galway), Mick Raftery (Galway), Joe Salmon (Galway), Oliver Clarke (Mayo), Kevin Forde (Roscommon), Paddy Fitzgerald (Galway), Dan Kavanagh (Kerry & Galway), Henry Kenny (Mayo), Vincent Keane (Kerry), Dermot McDermott (Roscommon), Evan Kennedy (Galway), Bernie Egan (Mayo), Pierce Thornton (Galway), Seán Thornton (Galway). Sub.: Séamus Sweeney (Mayo) for Keane.

U.C.D. - John Desmond Benson (Cavan), Jim Bohan (Leitrim), Jack Culleton (Wexford), Dennis O'Driscoll (Cork), Jim Clarke (Meath), Barney Cully (Cavan), Vincent Duffy (Monaghan & Dublin), Seán Brosnan (Kerry), Tom P O'Reilly (Cavan), Eugene 'Silky' Smith (Dublin), Donal Keenan (Roscommon), Murt Kelly (Kerry), Brendan Devlin (Tyrone), Walsh, Bernard Burbage (Longford).

1942/43 - NO COMPETITION.

1943/44

U.C.C. - Dessie Lucey (Kerry), Tom McElligott (Kerry), William Gavin (Tipperary), Jim Carr (Limerick), Paddy Fitzgerald (Limerick), Martin McCarthy (Kerry), Jack Lyne (Kerry), Frank McGovern (Leitrim), Donagh Keating (Cork), Mick Casey (Tipperary), Hugh McNeill, Jim Young (Cork), Paddy O'Keeffe (Cork), George Cashell (Cork), Derry Beckett (Cork). Sub.: Anthony Power (Waterford) for O'Keeffe.

U.C.D. - John Desmond Benson (Cavan), Niall Kennedy (Offaly), Dennis O'Driscoll (Cork), Jack Culleton (Wexford), Tom Staunton (Mayo), Vincent Duffy (Monaghan), Jim Clarke (Meath), Phelim Murray (Roscommon), Tom P O'Reilly (Cavan), Des O'Neill (Wicklow), Tadhg Brennan (Kildare), Donal Keenan (Roscommon), Charlie Brennan (Monaghan), Pearse O'Connor (Tyrone), Dick Stokes (Limerick).

1944/45

U.C.D. - J Greenan, Seán Flanagan (Mayo), Jack Culleton (Wexford), Tom Deignan (Longford), Jim Clarke (Meath), Seán Mitchell (Leitrim), Vincent Duffy (Monaghan), Phelim Murray (Roscommon), Tom Lawlor (Roscommon), Des O'Neill (Wicklow), Frank Kinlough (Roscommon), Donal Keenan (Roscommon), Brendan Devlin (Tyrone), Dick Stokes (Limerick), Charlie Brennan (Monaghan). Subs.: Colm Kelleher (Leitrim), Pierce Thornton (Galway).

U.C.C. - Dessie Lucey (Kerry), J Glynn, Tom McElligott (Kerry), Donagh Keating (Cork), Jack Lyne (Kerry), Martin McCarthy (Kerry), Paddy Fitzgerald (Limerick), Frank McGovern (Leitrim & Cork), Arthur Beckett (Cork), Martin Murtagh (Leitrim), Mick Casey (Tipperary), Jim Young (Cork), Anthony Power (Waterford), Denny Burke (Kerry), Derry Beckett (Cork).

1945/46

U.C.D. - John Shorten (Cork), Seán Flanagan (Mayo), Barney Cully (Cavan), Jim Clarke (Meath), Pádraic Carney (Mayo), Jack Culleton (Wexford), Charlie Coughlan (Kerry), Brendan Lunney (Fermanagh), P J Duke (Cavan), Joe Gilvarry (Mayo), Frank Kinlough (Roscommon), Donal Keenan (Roscommon), Charlie Brennan (Monaghan), Seán Mitchell (Leitrim), Paddy Kelly (Westmeath).

Q.U.B. - Mannix McAllister (Antrim), Colm Murphy (Antrim), Harry McPartland (Armagh), John Joe McKenna (Tyrone), Seán Carey (Down), Brian Gallagher (Fermanagh), Donal Kelly (Antrim), Danny MacRandal (Antrim), John Gallagher (Antrim), Seán Gibson (Antrim), Kevin Armstrong (Antrim), Joe McCallin (Antrim), Harry Greenwood (Antrim), Peter Lenfesty (Antrim), Brendan Mullan (Tyrone).

1946/47

U.C.C. - Tony Daly (Cork), Paddy Fitzgerald (Limerick), Tom McElligott (Kerry), Frank O'Brien (Waterford), Paddy Tyers (Waterford),

HIGHER EDUCATION

James 'Mixie' Palmer (Kerry), Humphrey O'Neill (Cork), Bernie Murphy (Cork), Frank McGovern (Leitrim & Cork), Paddy O'Regan (Cork), Derry Burke (Kerry), Nioclás Mac Craith (Waterford), Jim Young (Cork), Paddy Burke (Kerry), Derry Beckett (Cork).

U.C.D. - Peter Conlon (Roscommon), Pat Walsh (Carlow), Seán Flanagan (Mayo), Christy Garvey (Roscommon), P J Duke (Cavan), Jack Lyne (Kerry), Pádraic Carney (Mayo), Liam Hastings (Mayo), Brendan Lunney (Fermanagh), Paddy Kelly (Westmeath), Pierce Thornton (Galway), Donal Keenan (Roscommon), Frank Kinlough (Roscommon), Seán Mitchell (Leitrim), Augustine Waldron (Mayo). Sub.: Éamonn Quinn (Leitrim) for Kinlough.

1947/48

U.C.D. - Peter Conlon (Roscommon), Jim Fox (Leitrim), John O'Brien (Meath), Éamonn Quinn (Leitrim), Mick Costello (Galway), Paddy Henry (Sligo), John Lynch (Cork), Pádraic Carney (Mayo), P J Duke (Cavan), Mick Flanagan (Mayo), Des McEvoy (Galway & Dublin), Mick McCormack (Monaghan), Edwin Carolan (Cavan), Jimmy Adams (Offaly), Dick Corcoran (Dublin).

U.C.C. - Tony Daly (Cork), Gerry Murray (Cork), Bernie Murphy (Cork), Con Power (Cork), Paddy Tyers (Waterford), James 'Mixie' Palmer (Kerry), Humphrey O'Neill (Cork), Gerald O'Sullivan (Kerry), Steve Gavin (Offaly), P Marron (Cork), Paddy O'Regan (Cork), Brendan Hanniffy (Galway), Gerry Byrne (Kerry), Derry Burke (Kerry), Donal Murphy (Tipperary).

1948/49

U.C.G. - Mick O'Malley (Mayo), Willie McQuillan (Roscommon), Mick Costello (Galway), Donie Murphy (Kerry), Christy Garvey (Roscommon), Pat McAndrew (Mayo), Iggy Hanniffy (Galway), Con McGrath (Cork), Billy Kenny (Mayo), Peadar "Pat" McGowan (Mayo), Brian O'Rourke (Roscommon), Mick Loftus (Mayo), Pat Fenelon (Offaly), Peter Solan (Mayo), John Joe McGowan (Mayo).

U.C.D. - Gerry Gearty (Longford), B Carroll (Monaghan), Nicky Redmond (Wexford), John O'Brien (Meath), Seán F Heslin (Leitrim), P J Duke (Cavan), John Lynch (Cork), Pádraic Carney (Mayo), Des McEvoy (Galway & Dublin), Pat Harrington (Dublin), Eddie Devlin (Tyrone), Mick Flanagan (Mayo), Frank Deady (Kilkenny), Brian Sharkey (Monaghan), Brendan Duffy (Monaghan).

1949/50

U.C.D. - Gerry Gearty (Longford), Jim McDonnell (Louth), Nicky Redmond (Wexford), John O'Brien (Meath), Séamus O'Connor (Monaghan), P J Duke (Cavan), John Lynch (Cork), Pádraic Carney (Mayo), Frank Deady (Kilkenny), Mick Flanagan (Mayo), Hugh McKearney (Monaghan), Tom Hardy (Cavan), Brendan Duffy (Monaghan), Edwin Carolan (Cavan), Anton Rodgers (Donegal).

U.C.G. - Mick O'Malley (Mayo), Willie McQuillan (Roscommon), Mick Costello (Galway), John Trant (Kerry), John Fitzpatrick (Westmeath), Christy Garvey (Roscommon), Iggy Hanniffy (Galway), Billy Kenny (Mayo), Donie Murphy (Kerry), Peadar "Pat" McGowan (Mayo), John Joe McGowan (Mayo), Mick Loftus (Mayo), Mick Greaney (Galway), Peter Solan (Mayo), Tony O'Toole (Mayo).

1950/51

U.C.G. - Mick O'Malley (Mayo), Willie McQuillan (Roscommon), Gerry Stack (Kerry), John Trant (Kerry), Kevin Weir (Westmeath), Christy Garvey (Roscommon), Pat O'Malley (Galway), Seán Purcell (Galway), Mick Loftus (Mayo), Peadar "Pat" McGowan (Mayo), John Joe McGowan (Mayo), Peadar Kearns (Roscommon), Gussie O'Malley (Mayo), Tom O'Toole (Galway), Peter Solan (Mayo).

U.C.C. - Tony Daly (Cork), Tom Cavanagh (Cork), Jim O'Brien (Cork) (i.e. Fr. Jim White), Kevin O'Sullivan (Cork), Mick Brosnan (Kerry), Denis Bernard (Cork), Con Murray (Cork), Jim Galvin (Cork), Jim Brosnan (Kerry), Paddy O'Regan (Cork), Tom Barry (Waterford), Paudie Sheehy (Kerry), Ted Downey (Cork), Mick Galvin (Kerry), Tom Lawlor (Kerry). Sub.: Joe Kelly (Cork) for O'Sulivan.

1951/52

U.C.C. - Ted Downey (Cork), Paddy Tyers (Waterford), Jim O'Brien (i.e. Fr. Jim White) (Cork), Kevin O'Sullivan (Cork), Tom Cavanagh (Cork), Denis Bernard (Cork), Jim Brosnan (Kerry), Jim Galvin (Cork), Tom Barry (Waterford), Tom Lawlor (Kerry), Paddy O'Regan (Cork), Paudie Sheehy (Kerry), Mick Galvin (Cork), Dick Murphy (Cork), John Sugrue (Kerry). Subs.: Tomás Murphy (Kerry) for Lawlor, Justin Graham (Westmeath) for Cavanagh.

U.C.G. - Gerry Stack (Kerry), Pat O'Malley (Galway), Mick Costello (Galway), Seán Downes (Mayo), Joe O'Donoghue (Mayo), Christy Garvey (Roscommon), Brian Mahon (Galway), Mick Loftus (Mayo), Iggy Hanniffy (Galway), Peadar McGowan (Mayo), Peadar Kearns (Roscommon), Liam Hanniffy (Galway), Mick Mellotte (Mayo), Seán Collearry (Mayo), Peter Solan (Mayo). Sub.: T Griffin (Westmeath) for Mellotte.

1952/53

U.C.C. - Pat Dineen (Cork), Jim Bennett (Cork), Denis Bernard (Cork), Paddy Gallagher (Clare) (i.e. Fr. Paddy Gantley (Galway)) Tom

Cavanagh (Cork), John Holland (Mayo), Walter Cleary (Tipperary), Tom Barry (Waterford), Bobby Buckley (Kerry), Jim Brosnan (Kerry), Mick Brosnan (Kerry), Paudie Sheehy (Kerry), Tom Lawlor (Kerry), Tom Connolly (Tipperary), Tomás Murphy (Kerry).

U.C.D. - Gerry Stack (Kerry), Paddy O'Donnell (Donegal), John O'Brien (Meath), Seán Collins (Kerry), Leo Heslin (Leitrim), Mick Gould (Cork), Kieran Mulderrig (Mayo), Jim McArdle (Louth), P J McElroy (Down), Kieran Denvir (Down), Eddie Devlin (Tyrone), Pádraig Gearty (Longford), John McKnight (Armagh), Pat Fenelon (Offaly), Tom Crotty (Cavan).

1953/54

U.C.D. - Pádraig Gearty (Longford), Jim McArdle (Louth), Tim Lyons (Kerry), John McKnight (Armagh), Seán Collins (Kerry), Mick Gould (Cork), Tom Hardy (Cavan), P J McElroy (Down), Eddie Devlin (Tyrone), Tom McEvoy (Monaghan), Paddy Carolan (Cavan), Kieran Denvir (Down), David Sheeran (Longford), Pat Fenelon (Offaly), Mick Murphy (Cork).

U.C.G. - Eoghan Roe O'Neill (Mayo), Iggy Hanniffy (Galway), Colm O'Toole (Mayo), Maurice Hegarty (Galway), Paddy Dockery (Sligo), Christy Garvey (Roscommon), Brian Mahon (Galway), Seán Purcell (Galway), Art Thornberry (Westmeath), Kevin Swords (Mayo), Éamonn O'Donoghue (Roscommon), Con McAuley (Donegal), Peadar Kearns (Roscommon), Séamus "Sam" Breslin (Donegal), Séamus Mannion (Galway).

1954/55 REPLAY

U.C.G. - Eoghan Roe O'Neill (Mayo), Maurice Hegarty (Galway), Colm O'Toole (Mayo), Colm Toland (Donegal), Kevin Swords (Mayo), Christy Garvey (Roscommon), Paddy Hoare (Galway), Mick Hanley (Sligo), Mick Loftus (Mayo), Francis McGovern (Sligo), Peadar Kearns (Roscommon), Peadar "Pat" McGowan (Mayo), Éamonn McTigue (Mayo), Frank Daly (Cork), Aidan Swords (Galway). Sub.: Séamus "Sam" Breslin (Donegal) for Hegarty.

U.C.D. - Pádraig Gearty (Longford), Dan O'Donovan (Limerick), Jim McArdle (Louth), John McKnight (Armagh), Seán Murphy (Kerry), Tom Hardy (Cavan), Paddy Dockery (Sligo), Eddie Duffy (Leitrim), Art Thornberry (Westmeath), Jim McDonnell (Cavan), J Lovett (Kerry), Kieran Denvir (Down), Johnny Maguire (Fermanagh), Paddy Carolan (Cavan), Paul McMurrough (Monaghan). Subs.: Tom Crotty (Cavan) for McMurrough.

1954/55 DRAWN FINAL

U.C.G. - Eoghan Roe O'Neill (Mayo), Maurice Hegarty (Galway), Colm O'Toole (Mayo), Colm Toland (Donegal), Kevin Swords (Mayo), Christy Garvey (Roscommon), Brian Mahon (Galway), Francis McGovern (Sligo), Paddy Hoare (Galway), Peadar 'Pat' McGowan (Mayo), Mick Loftus (Mayo), Éamonn McTigue (Mayo), Peadar Kearns (Roscommon), Tom O'Toole (Galway), Liam Hanniffy (Galway).

U.C.D. - Pádraig Gearty (Longford), Colm O'Shea (Kerry), John McKnight (Armagh), Paddy Dockery (Sligo), Tom Hardy (Cavan), Leo Heslin (Leitrim), Seán Murphy (Kerry), Eddie Duffy (Leitrim), Jim McDonnell (Cavan), Art Thornberry (Westmeath), Kieran Denvir (Down), Johnny Maguire (Fermanagh), Paddy Carolan (Cavan), Paul McMurrough (Monaghan), Jim McArdle (Louth).

1955/56

U.C.D. - Pádraig Gearty (Longford), Felix McKnight (Armagh), Tim Lyons (Kerry), Jim Ryan (Meath), Seán Murphy (Kerry), John McKnight (Armagh), Paddy Dockery (Sligo), Art Thornberry (Westmeath), Jim McDonnell (Cavan), James Brady (Cavan), Kieran Denvir (Down), Séamus Murphy (Kerry), Johnny Maguire (Fermanagh), Colm Swords (Mayo), Tom Crotty (Cavan). Sub.: Mick Murphy (Cork) for Maguire.

U.C.C. - Ted Murphy (Kerry), Dermot O'Sullivan (Cork), Donal O'Sullivan (Cork), Dan Murray (Cork), Séamus O'Donoghue (Kerry), Jack Dowling (Kerry), Liam Coughlan (Kerry), Mick O'Connell (Kerry), Paddy Murphy (Cork), Mick Moroney (Tipperary), Mick Brosnan (Kerry), Tom Costelloe (Kerry), Seán O'Donnell (Mayo), Dave O'Donovan (Cork), Jim O'Donovan (Cork).

1956/57

U.C.D. - Brian O'Reilly (Cavan), Felix McKnight (Armagh), Tim Lyons (Kerry), Dermot O'Sullivan (Cork), Seán Murphy (Kerry), Jim Ryan (Meath), Eddie Duffy (Leitrim), Frank O'Leary (Westmeath), Jim McDonnell (Cavan), Des Keane (Mayo), Kieran Denvir (Down), Paddy Murphy (Cork), Jim Brosnan (Kerry), Colm Swords (Mayo), James Brady (Cavan). Sub.: Séamus Conaty (Cavan) for O'Leary.

U.C.C. - Gerry O'Sullivan (Cork), Tony O'Sullivan (Kerry), Jack Dowling (Kerry), Liam Coughlan (Cork), Liam Shalloe (Waterford), Séamus O'Donoghue (Kerry), Dan Murray (Cork), Tom Stapleton (Limerick), Dick Troy (Cork), Mick Moroney (Tipperary), Pat O'Shea (Kerry), Dennis Corrigan (Cork), Seán O'Donnell (Mayo), John Burke (Kerry), Dan Kennefick (Cork).

1957/58

U.C.D. - Brian O'Reilly (Cavan), Felix McKnight (Armagh), Dermot O'Sullivan (Cork), Joe Fingleton (Laois), Seán Murphy (Kerry), Eddie Duffy (Leitrim), Jim McDonnell (Cavan), Paddy Murphy (Cork), James Brady (Cavan),

Don Feeley (Roscommon), Kieran Denvir (Down), Séamus Murphy (Kerry), Ted Duffy (Monaghan), Colm Swords (Mayo), Cathal Young (Cavan). Sub.: Dennis Brosnan (Kerry) for Young.

U.C.C. - Tom Fitzgerald (Kerry), Noel Mullins (Cork), Tony O'Sullivan (Kerry), Mick Garvey (Limerick), Éamonn Horan (Kerry), Liam Shalloe (Waterford), Éamonn O'Connor (Limerick), Barry Studdart (Cork), Mick Lovett (Kerry), Mick Moroney (Tipperary), Seán Murphy (Cork), Dick Troy (Cork), Pat Whelan (Galway), John Joe Sheehan (Kerry), Dan Corrigan (Cork). Sub.: Frankie Sawyers (Kerry) for Corrigan.

1958/59

Q.U.B. - John O'Neill (Fermanagh), Charles Murphy (Antrim), Mick Brewster (Fermanagh), Christy Mallon (Tyrone), Leo O'Neill (Derry), Brendan Donaghy (Armagh), Peter Smith (Derry), Hugh O'Kane (Antrim), Phil Stuart (Derry), Tom Scullion (Derry), Frank Higgins (Tyrone), Seán O'Neill (Down), Barney McNally (Antrim), Séamus Mallon (Armagh), Kevin Halpenny (Armagh).

U.C.D. (1st game) - Anthony Leavey (Westmeath), Joe Fingleton (Laois), Felix McKnight (Armagh), Seán Murray (Longford), Seán Murphy (Kerry), Jim McDonnell (Cavan), John L'Estrange (Westmeath), Tom Stapleton (Limerick), Frank O'Leary (Westmeath & Mayo), Harry McGann (Longford), Don Feeley (Roscommon), Séamus Murphy (Kerry), Willie McCarthy (Kerry), James Brady (Cavan), Charlie Gallagher (Cavan). Subs.: Plunkett Devlin (Tyrone) for O'Leary, O'Leary for Stapleton.

U.C.D. (replay) - Anthony Leavey, Jim Flynn (Longford), Felix McKnight, John Vesey (Mayo), Seán Murphy, Joe Fingleton, John L'Estrange, Jim McDonnell, Frank O'Leary, Don Feeley, Ted Duffy, Séamus Murphy, Colm Stanley (Dublin), Willie McCarthy, Charlie Gallagher. Sub.: James Brady for O'Leary.

1959/60

U.C.D. - Noel Sammon (Mayo), Felix McKnight (Armagh), Peadar Kealey (Derry), Seán Murray (Longford), Paddy McMenamin (Mayo), Joe Fingleton (Laois), John Vesey (Mayo), Tom Stapleton (Limerick), Frank O'Leary (Mayo), Aidan Swords (Mayo), Charlie Gallagher (Cavan), Kieran O'Malley (Kildare), George Keane (Westmeath), James Brady (Cavan), Paul Kelly (Donegal).

U.C.C. - Tony Guerin (Kerry), Brian O'Callaghan (Tipperary), Mick Brosnan (Kerry), Éamonn O'Connor (Limerick), Mick Crowley (Cork), Liam Shalloe (Waterford), Éamonn Horan (Kerry), Séan Sheehy (Kerry), John Healy (Kerry), Mick O'Sullivan (Cork), Seán Murphy (Cork), Paudie Sheehy (Kerry), Liam Scully (Kerry), John Joe Sheehan (Kerry), Dave Geaney (Kerry). Subs.: 'Jasper' McAuliffe (Kerry) for Shalloe, Bob Honohan (Cork) for Geaney.

1960/61

U.C.G. - Aidan Kilbane (Mayo), Willie Loftus (Mayo), Hubert McGonigle (Sligo), Alan Delaney (Roscommon), Tony Ryan (Galway), Mick Laide (Kerry & Galway), Martin Newell (Galway), George Glynn (Galway), John Kelly (Limerick), Pat Donnellan (Galway), Brian Geraghty (Galway), Des Feeley (Roscommon), Joe Langan (Mayo), Seán Donnelly (Longford), Tony Kenny (Roscommon).

U.C.D. - Anthony Leavey (Westmeath), Paddy McMenamin (Mayo), Felix McKnight (Armagh), Seán Murray (Longford), Éamonn Curley (Roscommon), Johnny Healy (Kerry), Seán Woods (Louth), Frank O'Leary (Mayo), Dave McCarthy (Kerry), Paul Kelly (Donegal), Brendan McFeeley (Donegal), George Keane (Westmeath), Bobby Burns (Longford), Aidan Swords (Mayo).

1961/62

U.C.D. - Jimmy Finn (Tipperary), Connor Maguire (Cavan), Kevin O'Neill (Down), Seán Murray (Longford), Paddy McMenamin (Mayo), Bernard Brady (Donegal), Brian McMahon (Kerry), Frank O'Leary (Mayo), Seán O'Loughlin (Kildare), Paul Kelly (Donegal), Eddie Melvin (Mayo), Mick O'Brien (Cork), George Kane (Westmeath), Seán Cleary (Galway), Leo McEldowney (Derry).

U.C.G. - Aidan Kilbane (Mayo), Willie Loftus (Mayo), Hubert McGonigle (Sligo), Enda Colleran (Galway), Kevin Moyles (Mayo), Bosco McDermott (Galway), Martin Newell (Galway), George Glynn (Galway), John Stafford Kelly (Roscommon), Joe Langan (Mayo), Brian Geraghty (Galway), Pat Donnellan (Galway), Des Feeley (Roscommon), Seán Donnelly (Longford), Tony Kenny (Roscommon). Subs.: Mick O'Shea (Kerry) for Colleran, Pat McGee for Moyles.

1962/63

U.C.G. - Seán Gannon (Galway), Mick Moylett (Mayo), Hubert McGonigle (Sligo), Enda Colleran (Galway), Kevin Moyles (Mayo), Kieran O'Connor (Galway), Martin Newell (Galway), Mick O'Shea (Kerry), Tom Gilmore (Galway), Jimmy Jordan (Louth), Éamonn Slattery (Galway), Pat Donnellan (Galway), Christy Tyrrell (Galway), Seán Donnelly (Longford), Séamus Kilraine (Roscommon).

U.C.C. - John O'Donoghue (Tipperary), Brian O'Callaghan (Tipperary), Jim Harmon (Kerry), Derry Spillane (Kerry), Seánie Condon (Kerry), Jim Blake (Tipperary), Liam Scully (Kerry), Mick Fleming (Kerry), Fergus O'Rourke (Leitrim),

Dave Geaney (Kerry), Eddie Maguire (Mayo), Denis Philpott (Cork), Dan Harnedy (Cork), Frank Heslin (Leitrim), Olly Whitson (Kerry). Subs.: Cillian O'Neill (Clare) for Philpott, Dan Mangan (Kerry) for O'Rourke.

1963/64

U.C.G. - Johnny Geraghty (Galway), John Bonner (Donegal), Kieran O'Connor (Galway), Mick O'Malley (Mayo), Kevin Moyles (Mayo), Enda Colleran (Galway), Ray Niland (Westmeath), Pat Donnellan (Galway), Joe Langan (Mayo), Jimmy Jordan (Louth), Éamonn Slattery (Galway), Pat Sheridan (Mayo), Christy Tyrrell (Galway), Seán Donnelly (Longford), Tony McDevitt (Donegal).

U.C.C. - Gabriel Lohan (Galway), Brian O'Callaghan (Tipperary), Mick McCormack (Tipperary), Derry Spillane (Kerry), Finbarr O'Reilly (Cavan), Jim Blake (Limerick), Seán McCarthy (Kerry), Mick Fleming (Kerry), Frank Cogan (Cork), Dave Geaney (Kerry), John O'Sullivan (Cork), Dan Harnedy (Cork), Éamonn Ryan (Cork), Fergus O'Rourke (Leitrim), Olly Whitson (Kerry). Sub.: Denis Philpott (Cork) for Ryan.

1964/65

Q.U.B. - Des Sharkey (Antrim), Pat Loughran (Armagh), Leonard McEvoy (Armagh), Niall McEnhill (Tyrone), Paddy Diamond (Derry), James McKenny (Down), Phil McCotter (Derry), Terry Gilmore (Antrim), Jimmy Hughes (Tyrone), Oliver McDonald (Armagh), Gerry McCrory (Antrim), Jackie Fitzsimmons (Down), Jimmy Beggs (Tyrone), Seán O'Neill (Down), Éamonn Flanagan (Fermanagh). Subs.: Stephen Fitzpatrick (Antrim) for Loughran.

U.C.D. - Matt McHugh (Cavan), Paddy O'Hanlon (Armagh), Paud O'Donoghue (Kerry), Paul Kelly (Donegal), Peadar McGee (Mayo), Bernard Brady (Donegal), Frank Kennedy (Cavan), Mick O'Shea (Kerry), Mick O'Brien (Cork), Benny Gaughran (Louth), Davy Doris (Mayo), George Kane (Westmeath), Brian Kennedy (Cavan), Jim Hennigan (Mayo), Brendan O'Rourke (Kerry).

1965/66

U.C.C. - Billy Morgan (Cork), Christy O'Sullivan (Kerry), Jerry Lucey (Cork), John McCarthy (Kerry), John O'Halloran (Cork), Mick Morris (Kerry), Frank Cogan (Cork), Mick Fleming (Kerry), Pat Moynihan (Kerry), Pat O'Connell (Tipperary), Éamonn Ryan (Cork), Denis Philpott (Cork), Dan Harnedy (Cork), Dave Geaney (Kerry), Brendan O'Keeffe (Cork).

U.C.G. - Seán Gannon (Galway), Mick O'Sullivan (Galway), Kieran O'Connor (Galway), Mick O'Malley (Mayo), Kevin Moyles (Mayo), Enda Colleran (Galway), Cóilín McDonagh (Galway), Ray Gilmore (Galway), Pat Donnellan (Galway), Christy Tyrrell (Galway), Liam Sammon (Galway), Ray Niland (Westmeath & Galway), Billy Doran (Kerry), Éamonn Maguire (Mayo), Frank Canny (Galway). Sub.: Pat Sheridan (Mayo) for Sammon.

1966/67

U.C.C. - Billy Morgan (Cork), Ger O'Herlihy (Cork), Mick McCormack (Tipperary), Christy O'Sullivan (Kerry), John O'Halloran (Cork), Mick Morris (Kerry), John McGrath (Fermanagh), Mick Fleming (Kerry), Pat Moynihan (Kerry), Éamonn Ryan (Cork), Pat O'Connell (Tipperary), Denis Philpott (Cork), Eric Philpott (Cork), Brian Hurley (Cork), Dick Geaney (Kerry). Subs.: P J Gormley (Tyrone) for Moynihan, Brendan O'Keeffe (Cork) for Geaney.

U.C.G. - Michael Moore (Galway), Martin Flatley (Mayo), Mick Moylett (Mayo), Ray Niland (Galway), Joe Earley (Mayo), Ray Gilmore (Galway), Cóilín McDonagh (Galway), Adrian O'Sullivan (Roscommon), Jimmy Hanniffy (Longford), Christy Tyrrell (Galway), Seán McGhee (Donegal), Pat Sheridan (Mayo), Joe McLoughlin (Galway), Éamonn Maguire (Mayo), Noel McCormack (Galway). Subs.: Jimmy Langan (Mayo) for Magee, Liam Sammon (Galway) for Maguire.

1967/68

U.C.D. - Willie Howlett (Wexford), Jim McElwee (Donegal), Garret O'Reilly (Cavan), Denis Burke (Tipperary), Tom O'Callaghan (Kerry), Gerry Mannion (Roscommon), Anton Carroll (Donegal), Donie O'Sullivan (Kerry), Tom Mulvihill (Longford), Benny Gaughran (Louth), Frank Canavan (Galway), John Purdy (Down), Tony Barrett (Kerry), Mick Gleeson (Kerry), John Kelly (Roscommon).

U.C.G. - Michael Moore (Galway), Seán McGhee (Donegal), Mick Moylett (Mayo), Ray Niland (Galway), Joe Earley (Mayo), Ray Gilmore (Galway), Cóilín McDonagh (Galway), Martin Flatley (Mayo), Adrian O'Sullivan (Roscommon), Kevin Lavelle (Mayo), Joe McLoughlin (Galway), Jimmy Hanniffy (Longford), Alo Conneely (Galway), Liam Sammon (Galway), Lorcan Geoghegan (Galway). Subs.: Jimmy Langan (Mayo) for O'Sullivan, Jerry Conway (Sligo) for Geoghegan.

1968/69

U.C.C. - Jim Carroll (Dublin), Jim Gleeson (Kerry), Moss Keane (Kerry), Jim Coughlan (Kerry), Séamus Looney (Cork), Mick Morris (Kerry), Ted Murphy (Cork), Paddy Doherty (Limerick), Mick Power (Waterford), Brendan Lynch (Kerry), Christy O'Sullivan (Kerry), Richie Bambury (Kerry), Eric Philpott (Cork),

Ray Cummins (Cork), Dick Geaney (Kerry).

U.C.G. - Mick Deegan (Galway), Jimmy Langan (Mayo), Mick Moylett (Mayo), Ray Niland (Galway), Tony Geraghty (Galway), Adrian O'Sullivan (Roscommon), Seán McGhee (Donegal), Christy Scanlan (Galway), Johnny Coughlan (Mayo), Aidan Kelly (Mayo), Joe McLoughlin (Galway), Anthony Canny (Galway), Enda Bonner (Donegal), Johnny Kilbane (Mayo), Colm O'Flaherty (Tipperary). Sub.: Rory Kilfeather (Donegal) for O'Sullivan.

1969/70

U.C.C. - Jim Carroll (Dublin), Jim Gleeson (Kerry), Jim Coughlan (Kerry), Tony Mahon (Roscommon), John O'Grady (Kerry), Moss Keane (Kerry), John O'Halloran (Cork), Paddy Doherty (Cork), Séamus Looney (Cork), Dan Kavanagh (Kerry), Jimmy Barrett (Cork), Richie Bambury (Kerry), Denis Coffey (Kerry), Ray Cummins (Cork), Barry Hanley (Cork). Sub.: Noel Sullivan (Kerry) for Bambury.

Q.U.B. - Ciaran Lewis (Armagh), Liam Murphy (Derry), Séamus Killough (Antrim), Michael P Kelly (Derry), Barney McKibbon (Down), Noel Moore (Armagh), Seán McMullan (Down), Anthony McGurk (Derry), Pat Turley (Down), Fionn Sherry (Fermanagh), Brendan Neeson (Down), Kevin Teague (Tyrone), Paddy Park (Tyrone), Séamus Woods (Tyrone), Aidan Hamill (Antrim). Sub.: Martin McAleese (Antrim) for Neeson.

1970/71

Q.U.B. - Ciarán Lewis (Armagh), Liam Murphy (Derry), Seamus Killough (Antrim), Malachy McDonald (Antrim), Malachy Duffin (Antrim), Maurice Denvir (Down), Kevin Stevenson (Armagh), J J O'Reilly (Fermanagh), Pat Turley (Down), Paddy Park (Tyrone), Kevin Teague (Tyrone), Fionn Sherry (Fermanagh), Martin McAleese (Antrim), Anthony McGurk (Derry), John Rainey (Antrim). Sub.: Séamus Mullan (Derry) for O'Reilly.

U.C.C. - Noel Murphy (Cork), Jim Gleeson (Kerry), Moss Keane (Kerry), Jim Coughlan (Kerry), John O'Grady (Kerry), Séamus Looney (Cork), Tony Mahon (Roscommon), Paudie Lynch (Kerry), Dan Kavanagh (Kerry), Brendan Lynch (Kerry), Richie Bambury (Kerry), Donie Murray (Cork), Billy Field (Cork), Denis Coffey (Kerry), Brendan O'Keeffe (Kerry). Subs.: Tom Looney (Kerry) for O'Keeffe, Seán Kavanagh (Kerry) for Mahon.

1971/72

U.C.C. - Noel Murphy (Cork), Jim Gleeson (Kerry), Moss Keane (Kerry), Mick Scannell (Cork), John O'Grady (Kerry), Séamus Looney (Cork), Tom Looney (Kerry), Flan Groarke (Kerry), Paudie Lynch (Kerry), Brendan Lynch (Kerry), Richie Bambury (Kerry), Donie Murray (Cork), Denis Coffey (Kerry), Dan Kavanagh (Kerry), Billy Field (Cork). Subs.: Pat O'Connell (Tipperary), Mick Fleming (Kerry).

U.C.G. - Paudie O'Mahony (Kerry), Colm O'Flaherty (Tipperary), Bernie Jennings (Mayo), Tony Dolan (Leitrim), Martin Carney (Donegal), Ger O'Keeffe (Kerry), Tony Regan (Roscommon), Jimmy Mannion (Roscommon), Martin Flatley (Mayo), Tommy O'Malley (Roscommon), Dan Ahern (Cork), Aidan Kelly (Mayo), Mark O'Gara (Roscommon), Mick Sweeney (Mayo), John Tobin (Galway). Subs.: Eddie O'Sullivan (Galway) for O'Flaherty, Jimmy Langan (Mayo) for Dolan.

1972/73

U.C.D. - Tom Hunt (Waterford), Joe Waldron (Galway), Alfie Marron (Galway), Jimmy Stafford (Cavan), Frank Donoghue (Galway), Éamonn O'Donoghue (Kildare), Pat O'Neill (Dublin), John O'Keeffe (Kerry), Dave McCarthy (Cork), Paddy Kerr (Monaghan), Kevin Kilmurray (Offaly), Jackie Walsh (Kerry), Enda Condron (Laois), Pat Duggan (Dublin), John P Kean (Mayo). Sub.: Bernie Geraghty (Kildare) for Marron.

Maynooth - Kieran McGovern (Leitrim), Bob Casey (Kerry), John O'Mahony (Mayo), Dan O'Mahony (Mayo), Pat Henry (Sligo), Tony O'Keeffe (Kerry), Louis Walsh (Donegal), Cyril Hughes (Carlow), Seán McCarthy (Cork), Frank Murray (Longford), Peter Burke (Longford), Jimmy Kennelly (Cork), Seán McKeown (Kildare), Mel Flanagan (Roscommon), Frank McCann (Meath). Sub.: Terry McElvanney (Monaghan) for Henry.

1973/74

U.C.D. - Ivan Heffernan (Mayo), Mick Judge (Sligo), Bernie Jennings (Mayo), Gerry McCaul (Dublin), P J O'Halloran (Meath), Éamonn O'Donoghue (Kildare), Paddy Kerr (Monaghan), John O'Keeffe (Kerry), Mick Carty (Wexford), Enda Condron (Laois), Kevin Kilmurray (Offaly), Jackie Walsh (Kerry), John P Kean (Mayo), Oliver Leddy (Cavan), Pat Duggan (Dublin). Sub.: Barry Walsh (Kerry) for Duggan.

U.C.G. - Paudie O'Mahony (Kerry), Joe McDonagh (Galway), Jim Miller (Laois), Christy McCann (Mayo), Jimmy O'Dowd (Roscommon), Martin Carney (Donegal), Tony Regan (Roscommon), Jimmy Mannion (Roscommon), Benny Wilkinson (Sligo), Morgan Hughes (Galway), Michael McNamara (Roscommon), Hugh Griffin (Roscommon), Ger Aherne (Cork), Mick Sweeney (Mayo), Mickey Fox (Westmeath). Sub.: Kevin Clancy (Galway) for Wilkinson.

1974/75

U.C.D. - Ivan Heffernan (Mayo), Con Moynihan (Mayo), Éamonn O'Donoghue (Kildare), Gerry McCaul (Dublin), P J O'Halloran (Meath), Mick Carty (Wexford), Frank Donoghue (Galway), Denis "Ogie" Moran (Kerry), John O'Keeffe (Kerry), Benny Wilkinson (Sligo), John P Kean (Mayo), Jackie Walsh (Kerry), Barry Walsh (Kerry), Pat Duggan (Dublin), Paddy Gray (Meath). Sub.: Finian Mac an Bhaird (Donegal) for McCaul, Brendan Dunleavy (Donegal) for Wilkinson).

Q.U.B. - Gerry Moore (Antrim), Kevin McFerran (Antrim), Canice Woods (Tyrone), John Killen (Down), Seán Sands (Down), Gerry McHugh (Antrim), Joe McGrade (Tyrone), Pat Armstrong (Antrim), Peter McGinnity (Fermanagh), Brendan Kelly (Derry), Paddy Moriarty (Armagh), Con McAllister (Antrim), Kieran O'Toole (Down), Brendan Donnelly (Tyrone), Denis Stevenson (Armagh).

1975/76

Maynooth - Jack Fitzgerald (Cork), Tony O'Keeffe (Kerry), Dan O'Mahony (Mayo), Tom Barden (Longford), Larry Kelly (Kerry), Mick McElvanney (Longford), Francie Henry (Mayo), Éamonn Whelan (Laois), Paddy Henry (Sligo), Donal Brennan (Sligo), Martin Nugent (Offaly), Paddy McGovern (Cavan), Pat Donellan (Galway), John McPartland (Down), Peter Burke (Longford). Sub.: Seán McKeown (Kildare) for McGovern.

U.C.D. - Ivan Heffernan (Mayo), Finian Ward (Donegal), Bernie Jennings (Mayo), Gerry McCaul (Dublin), P J O'Halloran (Meath), Mick Carty (Wexford), Denis 'Ogie' Moran (Kerry), Éamonn O'Donoghue (Kildare), Gerry McEntee (Meath), Colm O'Rourke (Meath), John P Kean (Mayo), Jackie Walsh (Kerry), Barry Walsh (Kerry), Pat Duggan (Dublin), Paddy Gray (Meath). Subs.: Oliver Leddy (Cavan) for O'Rourke, Tony McManus (Roscommon) for Gray.

1976/77 REPLAY

U.C.D. - Ivan Heffernan (Mayo), Dave Billings (Dublin), Bernie Jennings (Mayo), Séamus Hunt (Roscommon), P J O'Halloran (Meath), Mick Carty (Wexford), Pat O'Neill (Dublin), Gerry McEntee (Meath), Denis 'Ogie' Moran (Kerry), Adge King (Cavan), John P Kean (Mayo), Tony McManus (Roscommon), Barry Walsh (Kerry), Tommy Murphy (Wicklow), Pat Duggan (Dublin). Sub.: P J Finlay (Monaghan) for Billings.

N.B. - In the drawn game, Ger Griffin (Kerry) started as No.15, and was substituted by Oliver Leddy (Cavan), and Kean came on as a sub for King. McManus lined out the first day as No.11, Murphy as No.12, and Duggan as No.14.

U.C.G. - Gay Mitchell (Galway), Paddy Tunney (Donegal), Joe McDonagh (Galway), Breandán Ó Callaráin (Galway), John Costello (Kilkenny), M J Reddington (Galway), Tony Regan (Roscommon), Martin McCarrick (Sligo), Martin Carney (Donegal), Paul McGettigan (Donegal), Kevin Clancy (Galway), Tony O'Connor (Mayo), Brendan Dooley (Wicklow), Gay McManus (Galway), John Tobin (Galway). Sub.: Paul Griffin (Kerry) for O'Connor, O'Connor for Griffin.

N.B. - In the drawn match, Frank Morris (Galway) began at full-back, but McDonagh was brought on as a sub in his place. Carney lined out at No.12 that day, while McGettigan was at midfield and O'Connor at No.12. Morgan Hughes (Galway) and Colm Loftus (Sligo) were also used as replacements in the drawn game.

1977/78

U.C.D. - Johnny Murphy (Sligo), Séamus Hunt (Roscommon), Brendan Dunleavy (Donegal), Gerry McCaul (Dublin), Declan Carey (Down), Mick Carty (Wexford), Pat O'Neill (Dublin), Paddy O'Donoghue (Kildare), Vincent O'Connor (Kerry), Tony McManus (Roscommon), Mick Hickey (Dublin), Jackie Walsh (Kerry), Mick Fennelly (Kildare), Tommy Murphy (Wicklow), Mícheál Flannery (Mayo). Sub.: Mickey O'Sullivan (Kerry) for Fennelly.

U.C.G. - Gay Mitchell (Galway), Bernard O'Sullivan (Kerry), Gerry King (Mayo), Breandán Ó Callaráin (Galway), John Costello (Kilkenny), Richie Lee (Galway), Brendan Walsh (Galway), Martin Dolphin (Roscommon), Colm Brogan (Galway), Paul McGettigan (Donegal), Pádraig Mitchell (Galway), Kevin Clancy (Galway), Micksey Clarke (Westmeath), Gay McManus (Galway), Conor Richardson (Dublin).

1978/79

U.C.D. - Johnny Murphy (Sligo), Joe Joe O'Connor (Kerry), Paddy O'Donoghue (Kildare), Séan O'Doherty (Tyrone), Declan Carey (Down), P J Finlay (Monaghan), Barry O'Donoghue (Kildare), Colm O'Rourke (Meath), John Caffrey (Dublin), Andy Roche (Dublin), Tony McManus (Roscommon), Morgan Hughes (Galway), Jimmy Lyons (Mayo), Tommy Murphy (Wicklow), Frank O'Sullivan (Meath). Sub.: Finn McDonagh (Cavan) for Lyons.

U.C.G. - Joe Cuddy (Mayo), Bernard O'Sullivan (Kerry), Gerry King (Mayo), Brendan Colleran (Galway), Seán Luskin (Mayo), Joe Kelly (Galway), John Costello (Kilkenny), Richie Lee (Galway), Seán Forde (Galway), Conor Richardson (Dublin), Pádraig Mitchell (Galway), Martin Joyce (Mayo), Paudie O'Riordan (Laois), Gay McManus (Galway), Mícheál Flannery (Mayo). Subs.: Des Bergin (Kildare) for Forde, Kieran O'Malley (Mayo) for O'Riordan, John Hayes (Galway) for King.

1979/80

U.C.G. - Gay Mitchell (Galway), Joe Kelly (Galway), Christy McCutcheon (Cavan), Seán Luskin (Mayo), John Costello (Kilkenny), Pádraig Monaghan (Mayo), Séamus McHugh (Galway), Richie Lee (Galway), T J Kilgallon (Mayo), Jimmy Ward (Leitrim), Gay McManus (Galway), Pádraig Mitchell (Galway), Micksey Clarke (Westmeath), Seán Forde (Galway), Paudie O'Riordan (Laois). Subs.: Colm Brogan (Galway) for Forde, Kieran O'Malley (Mayo) for Ward, Breandán Ó Callaráin (Galway) for Costello.

U.C.D. - Johnny Murphy (Sligo), Séamus Hunt (Roscommon), Cormac Bonner (Tipperary), Joe Joe O'Connor (Kerry), Declan Carey (Down), Austin Finnegan (Galway), Barry O'Donoghue (Kildare), Gerry McEntee (Meath), Colm O'Rourke (Meath), Jimmy Lyons (Mayo), Tony McManus (Roscommon), Morgan Hughes (Galway), Tony O'Connor (Mayo), Tommy Murphy (Wicklow), Finn McDonagh (Cavan). Sub.: Brian Bonner (Dublin) for T O'Connor.

1980/81

U.C.G. - Éamonn Rodgers (Roscommon), Pádraig 'Oxie' Moran (Galway), Tomás Tierney (Galway), Mick Walsh (Mayo), John Costello (Kilkenny), Des Bergin (Kildare), Séamus McHugh (Galway), T J Kilgallon (Mayo), Anthony Finnerty (Mayo), Pádraig Mitchell (Galway), Gay McManus (Galway), Brian O'Donnell (Galway), Kieran O'Malley (Mayo), Seán Forde (Galway), Paudie O'Riordan (Laois). Subs.: Micksey Clarke (Westmeath) for Forde, Peter Heffernan (Mayo) for O'Donnell.

T.C.D. - John McDonagh (Dublin), G Sheeran (Roscommon), Jimmy O'Callaghan (Laois), Seán McGearty (Cavan), Frank Harte (Dublin), John Bourke (Kerry), Seán McAleese (Antrim), Frank Johnston (Derry), Barry Tierney (Cavan), Hugh Gibbons (London), Joe O'Rourke (Dublin), Terry Smith (Dublin), Liam Adams (Offaly), Mick "Frank" Mescall (Clare), John Farren (Donegal). Subs.: Dave Gilliland (Meath) for Sheeran, Tadhg O'Reilly (Cavan) for Farren.

1981/82

Q.U.B. - Paddy Mahon (Down), Joe Fearon (Armagh), Seán Gordon (Armagh), Donagh O'Kane (Down), Gerard Rodgers (Down), Joey Donnelly (Armagh), Martin Small (Down), John McAleenan (Down), Seán McAuley (Antrim), Brian McErlean (Derry), Dermot Dowling (Armagh), Aidan Short (Armagh), Séamus Leonard (Fermanagh), Greg Blaney (Down), Donal Armstrong (Antrim). Subs.: Eamonn Larkin (Down) for Leonard, Séamus Boyd (Antrim) for McAleenan, John Mackle (Derry) for Mahon.

U.C.G. - James Reidy (Mayo), Pádraig 'Oxie' Moran (Galway), Peter Forde (Mayo), John Hayes (Galway), Jamesie O'Sullivan (Kerry), Tomás Tierney (Galway), Séamus McHugh (Galway), Anthony Finnerty (Mayo), T J Kilgallon (Mayo), Eugene Macken (Mayo), Martin Joyce (Mayo), Richie Lee (Galway), Ciarán O'Malley (Mayo), Micksey Clarke (Westmeath), Michael Brennan (Galway). Subs.: Pádraig 'Dandy' Kelly (Galway) for O'Malley, Peter Heffernan (Mayo) for Macken, O'Malley for Kelly, Tom McWalter (Galway) for Tierney, Paul Carr (Donegal) for Moran.

1982/83

U.C.G. - James Reidy (Mayo), Tom McWalter (Galway), Peter Forde (Mayo), Seán Twomey (Dublin), Jim Egan (Galway), Richie Lee (Galway), Hugh Heskin (Galway), Tomás Tierney (Galway), Michael Brennan (Galway), Pádraig 'Dandy' Kelly (Galway), Brian O'Donnell (Galway), Paul Carr (Donegal), Anthony Finnerty (Mayo), Micksey Clarke (Westmeath), Pádraic Duffy (Mayo).

Q.U.B. - Paddy Mahon (Down), Mark Haran (Tyrone), Paul Mahon (Down), Seán Gordon (Armagh), Gerard Rodgers (Down), Séamus Boyd (Antrim), Donagh O'Kane (Down), John McAleenan (Down), Aidan Short (Armagh), Brian McErlean (Derry), Dermot Dowling (Armagh), Paul McCormack (Derry), Donal Armstrong (Antrim), Greg Blaney (Down), Michael Madine (Down). Subs.: Martin Durkan (Down) for McErlean, Brian Turbett (Tyrone) for Madine.

1983/84

U.C.G. - James Reidy (Mayo), Seán Twomey (Dublin), John Maughan (Mayo), Harry Walsh (Galway), Jim Egan (Galway), Tomás Tierney (Galway), Hugh Heskin (Galway), Tom Carr (Tipperary), Pádraig 'Dandy' Kelly (Galway), Brian O'Donnell (Galway), Michael Brennan (Galway), Peter Heffernan (Mayo), Pádraic Duffy (Mayo), Shay Fahy (Kildare), Anthony Finnerty (Mayo). Subs.: Declan Duke (Roscommon) for Tierney, John Hayes (Galway) for Heskin.

U.C.C. - Mícheál Conacur (Roscommon), Leonard O'Keeffe (Cork), Charles Gilmartin (Mayo), John O'Dwyer (Kerry), John Keane (Listowel), John T O'Sullivan (Kerry), Éamonn Walsh (Kerry), Tom Mannix (Cork), Micheal Keating (Kerry), Barry Coffey (Cork), Seán Liston (Kerry), Martin O'Sullivan (Cork), Colm O'Neill (Cork), John Murphy (Cork), Richard Hickey (Kerry).

1984/85

U.C.D. - Senan McGuire (Westmeath), John Joe McKearney (Monaghan), Seán McGovern (Kildare), Séamus O'Neill (Tipperary), Peter Smith (Westmeath), Noel McCaffrey (Dublin),

Andrew Healy (Tipperary), Bill Sex (Kildare), Mícheál O'Donoghue (Kerry), Seán Ryan (Kildare), Dermot Flanagan (Mayo), Jimmy Lyons (Mayo), Michael Lynam (Westmeath), Niall Clancy (Dublin), Frank McNamee (Longford). Sub.: Séamus Rodgers (Armagh) for Ryan.

Q.U.B. - John Mackle (Derry), Gerard Rodgers (Down), Paul Maxwell (Tyrone), Martin Tully (Derry), Seán McCormack (Antrim), Ciarán Hamill (Antrim), Paul Mahon (Down), Stephen Muldoon (Antrim), Brian Conlon (Down), Paul McCormack (Derry), Greg Blaney (Down), Liam Heaney (Down), Éamon O'Hare (Down), Donal Armstrong (Antrim), Conn Mulholland (Tyrone). Subs.: Patrick J Gallagher (Down) for O'Hare, Alphonsus McConnell (Tyrone) for Hamill.

1985/86

U.U.J. - Fergal Harney (Armagh), D J Kane (Down), Martin Lennon (Armagh), Paul Mahon (Down), Barry Young (Derry), Colin Harney (Armagh), Barry Breen (Down), Cahal Glass (Derry), Stephen Conway (Tyrone), Dermot McNicholl (Derry), Ger Houlahan (Armagh), Enda Gormley (Derry), Stephen Rice (Tyrone), Donal Durkan (Down), Cathal McNicholl (Derry). Subs.: Malachy O'Hare (Down) for Glass, Mark Bohill (Down) for C McNicholl, Donal Armstrong (Antrim) for Durkan.

U.C.C. - Micheal Conacur (Roscommon), John O'Dwyer (Kerry), Charles Gilmartin (Mayo), Éamonn Murray (Kerry), Richard Hickey (Kerry), John Keane (Kenmare), Denis Cremin (Kerry), Barry Coffey (Cork), Tommy Higgins (Galway), Paul McGrath (Cork), Colm O'Neill (Cork), Eoin Moynihan (Kerry), Paul Cahill (Cork), Éamonn Lyons (Cork), John Walsh (Kerry).

1986/87

U.U.J. - Cathal Canavan (Armagh), D J Kane (Down), Pádraig O'Neill (Armagh), Seán Meyler (Tyrone), Barry Young (Derry), Barry Breen (Down), Gary McConville (Tyrone), Stephen Conway (Tyrone), Cahal Glass (Derry), Dermot McNicholl (Derry), Enda Gormley (Derry), Declan Canavan (Armagh), Thomas Maguire (Fermanagh), Cathal McNicholl (Derry), Rory Scullion (Derry). Subs.: Mark Bohill (Down) for D Canavan, Peter Young (Derry) for C McNicholl, Conal Heatley (Antrim) for Maguire.

U.C.C. - Micheal Conacur (Roscommon), John O'Dwyer (Kerry), Marc Healy (Cork), Ralph O'Leary (Cork), Denis Cleary (Cork), John Keane (Kenmare), Tony Griffin (Cork), Mossy Murphy (Cork), Barry Coffey (Cork), John Walsh (Kerry), Anthony O'Sullivan (Cork), Éamonn Lyons (Cork), Eoin Moynihan (Kerry), David Burke (Waterford), Paul McGrath (Cork).

1987/88

U.C.C. - Carl Walsh (Clare), Niall Looney (Cork), Ralph O'Leary (Cork), Michael Crowley (Cork), Barry Duggan (Cork), John Keane (Kenmare), Denis Cleary (Cork), Noel Creedon (Cork), Mossy Murphy (Cork), Paul McGrath (Kerry), John Costelloe (Tipperary), Denis O'Sullivan (Cork), Eoin Moynihan (Kerry), Maurice Fitzgerald (Kerry), Ivan Aherne (Cork). Sub.: Fintan Corrigan (Cork) for Creedon.

U.C.G. - Paul Staunton (Roscommon), David Fitzgerald (Mayo), Tom Greaney (Galway), Harry Walsh (Galway), Seán Twomey (Dublin), Patrick J Guckian (Roscommon), Pádraig Fallon (Galway), Mark Butler (Mayo), Kevin O'Hanlon (Louth), Pat Vaughan (Clare), John Joyce (Galway), Brendan Ryan (Offaly), Aidan O'Keeffe (Clare), Matt Tierney (Galway), Pádraig Kenny (Leitrim). Subs.: Alan Mulholland (Galway) for Ryan, Tomás Kilcummins (Galway) for Kenny, Ryan for Vaughan.

1988/89

St. Mary's - Brendan Tierney (Armagh), Malachy O'Rourke (Fermanagh), Martin McNally (Antrim), Pascal Canavan (Tyrone), John Rafferty (Armagh), Danny Quinn (Derry), Cathal Murray (Down), John Reihill (Fermanagh), Jarlath Burns (Armagh), Séamus Downey (Derry), Oliver Reel (Armagh), Paddy Barton (Derry), Martin Houlihan (Armagh), Fergal McCann (Fermanagh), Iggy Gallagher (Tyrone). Subs.: Conrad McGuigan (Derry) for Gallagher, Éamonn Shannon (Fermanagh) for Houlihan.

U.C.C. - Frank Lyons (Cork), Niall Looney (Cork), Niall Savage (Kerry), Colm O'Donovan (Cork), Denis Cleary (Cork), Tony Griffin (Cork), John Walsh (Kerry), Brian Murphy (Cork), Mossy Murphy (Cork), Denis O'Sullivan (Cork), Pat Kenneally (Cork), Maurice Fitzgerald (Kerry), Eoin Moynihan (Kerry), Mike Finnegan (Kerry), Ivan Aherne (Cork). Subs.: Fintan Corrigan (Cork) for Fitzgerald, Gene O'Donnell (Kerry) for O'Donovan, Peter Creedon (Cork) for Finnegan

1989/90

Q.U.B. - Éamonn Connolly (Down), Shane O'Neill (Armagh), Paul O'Neill (Tyrone), Mark McNeill (Armagh), Fergal Logan (Tyrone), Colm Hanratty (Armagh), Mickey Quinn (Down), Danny Barr (Tyrone), Liam Conneally (Clare), Collie McGurk (Derry), Damien Devine (Tyrone), Paul McErlean (Antrim), Hugh Martin Tohill (Derry), Tony McMahon (Down), James McCartan (Down). Subs.: Keith Quigley (Armagh) for S O'Neill, Declan Conlon (Down) for Tohill, Iggy McGowan (Fermanagh) for McMahon.

St. Mary's - Brendan Tierney (Armagh), Martin Houlihan (Armagh), John Rafferty (Armagh), Conor McQuaid (Tyrone), Pascal Canavan (Tyrone), Malachy O'Rourke (Fermanagh), Cathal Murray (Down), Jarlath Burns (Armagh), Pat Slevin (Tyrone), Séamus Downey (Derry), Oliver Reel (Armagh), Paddy Barton (Derry), Gerry Armstrong (Antrim), Fergal McCann (Fermanagh), Peter Canavan (Tyrone).

1990/91

U.U.J. - Hugh Fitzpatrick (Fermanagh), Aidan Morris (Tyrone), Gareth O'Neill (Armagh), Pádraig O'Neill (Armagh), Gary Lyons (Down), Noel Donnelly (Tyrone), Paddy Tinnelly (Down), Dermot McNicholl (Derry), Gerard Colgan (Down), Laurence Strain (Tyrone), Gary Mason (Down), Conor Burns (Down), Collie Burns (Down), Brian Carty (Fermanagh), Alan Downey (Down). Subs.: Mark Gallagher (Fermanagh) for Strain, Niall McGuinness (Tyrone) for Downey.

U.C.G. - Cathal McGinley (Galway), John Kilraine (Galway), Diarmaid Keon (Donegal), John Donnellan (Cavan), Damien Mitchell (Galway), Kevin McDonagh (Galway), Pádraig Fallon (Galway), Mark Gibbs (Galway), Tony Maher (Laois), Tomás Kilcummins (Galway), Pádraig Oates (Roscommon), Padraig Kenny (Leitrim), Lorcan Dowd (Roscommon), David Farrell (Kerry), Niall Finnegan (Galway).

1991/92

U.C.G. - Brian Morkan (Roscommon), John Kilraine (Galway), Diarmaid Keon (Donegal), Gary Fahy (Galway), John Donnellan (Cavan), Mark O'Connor (Cork), Seán Óg de Paor (Galway), Tony Maher (Laois), Tom Ryan (Roscommon), Don Connellan (Roscommon), Sylvester Maguire (Donegal), Máirtín McDermott (Galway), Lorcan Dowd (Roscommon), Conor McGauran (Galway), Niall Finnegan (Galway). Subs.: Brendan Duffy (Galway) for Connellan, Damien Mitchell (Galway) for McDermott.

Q.U.B. - Éamonn Connolly (Down), Dermot O'Neill (Derry), Brian Burns (Down), Kieran McGeeney (Armagh), Fergal Logan (Tyrone), Noel Donnelly (Tyrone), Keith Quigley (Armagh), Anthony Tohill (Derry), Paul Brewster (Fermanagh), Éamonn Burns (Derry), Cathal O'Rourke (Armagh), Joe Brolly (Derry), Damien Devine (Tyrone), Brian McCormick (Derry), James McCartan (Down). Subs.: Michael Ferguson (Antrim) for Quigley, Patrick McGeeney (Armagh) for Devine.

1992/93

Q.U.B. - Éamonn Connolly (Down), Gareth McGirr (Tyrone), Paddy McGuinness (Fermanagh), Patrick McGeary (Armagh), Stephen Walls (Derry), Kieran McGeeney (Armagh), Paul Brewster (Fermanagh), Anthony Tohill (Derry), Cathal O'Rourke (Armagh), Patrick McGeeney (Armagh), Brian McCormick (Derry), Paul McGrane (Armagh), Dennis Hollywood (Armagh), Paul Greene (Fermanagh), James McCartan (Down). Subs.: John Hanna (Fermanagh) for Hollywood, Paul Burns (Down) for McGrane.

St. Mary's - Mark O'Neill (Tyrone), Conor McQuaid (Tyrone), Brendan Rice (Down), Declan Murtagh (Tyrone), Conor Daly (Tyrone), Paul Donnelly (Tyrone), Garret McFerran (Down), Simon Bradley (Fermanagh), Paul Fitzpatrick (Fermanagh), Conall Sheridan (Tyrone), Brian Gormley (Tyrone), Paddy Tally (Tyrone), Stephen Ramsey (Antrim), Peter Canavan (Tyrone), Séamus McCreesh (Armagh). Sub.: Conor Gallagher (Tyrone) for McCreesh.

1993/94

U.C.C. - Éamonn Scollard (Limerick), John O'Donovan (Cork), Niall Mangan (Kerry), Daire Gilmartin (Dublin), Michael O'Donovan (Cork), Niall Savage (Kerry), Pádraig O'Regan (Cork), Chris Collins (Cork), Paul O'Keeffe (Cork), John Clifford (Cork), Mark O'Sullivan (Cork), John Buckley (Cork), Fergal Keohane (Cork), Niall Fleming (Cork), Jason Whooley (Cork). Sub.: Martin Hayes (Cork) for Clifford.

Q.U.B. - Conor O'Neill (Down), Ronan Hamill (Antrim), Paddy McGuinness (Fermanagh), Gareth McGirr (Tyrone), Andrew McCann (Armagh), Paul Brewster (Fermanagh), Conor Wilson (Armagh), Anthony Tohill (Derry), Mark McCrory (Armagh), Paul Greene (Fermanagh), Cathal O'Rourke (Armagh), J J Kavanagh (Tyrone), Tom Rodgers (Armagh), Éamonn Burns (Derry), Diarmaid Marsden (Armagh). Sub.: Paul McGrane (Armagh) for Greene, Barry Hughes (Armagh) for Rodgers, Terry McGivern (Down) for Wilson.

1994/95

U.C.C. - Éamonn Scollard (Limerick), Conor Murphy (Cork), Ronan McCarthy (Cork), Donie Galvin (Cork), Martin Hayes (Cork), Séamus Moynihan (Kerry), Pádraig O'Regan (Cork), Paul O'Keeffe (Cork), Chris Collins (Cork), John Crowley (Kerry), John Clifford (Cork), John Buckley (Cork), Fergal Keohane (Cork), Mark O'Sullivan (Cork), Jason Whooley (Cork).

U.C.G. - Brian Morkham (Roscommon), Killian Burns (Kerry), Gary Fahy (Galway), Dónal Ó Liatháin (Cork), Declan Meehan (Galway), Hughie Sheehan (Mayo), Paul Cunney (Mayo), Shay Walsh (Galway), Fergal Gavin (Galway), Seán Moffatt (Mayo), Don Connellan (Roscommon), Brendan Duffy (Galway), Gerald Hussey (Kerry), Lorcan Dowd (Roscommon), Maurice Sheridan (Mayo). Subs.: Mick Higgins (Mayo) for Moffatt, Lorcán Ó Callaráin (Galway) for Sheridan.

1995/96

U.C.D. - Brian Morkan (Roscommon), Ultan Keane (Dublin), John Quinn (Kildare), Martin Ryan (Kildare), Daniel Flynn (Down), Trevor Giles (Meath), Joe Coyle (Monaghan), Fachtna Collins (Dublin), Ciarán McManus (Offaly), Brian Dooher (Tyrone), Mick O'Dowd (Meath), Alan Nolan (Roscommon), John Hegarty (Wexford), Anthony Finnerty (Mayo), David Nestor (Mayo). Sub.: Bernie Butler (Roscommon) for O'Dowd.

Garda - Kevin O'Dwyer (Cork), Jason Lynch (Cork), Brian McCarthy (Kerry), Fergal Reynolds (Leitrim), Ollie O'Sullivan (Cork), Kevin McGettigan (Donegal), Colm O'Flaherty (Tipperary), Pádraig Boyce (Galway), Adrian Phelan (Laois), James O'Donoghue (Cork), Brian O'Donovan (Cork), Enda Freaney (Kildare), James O'Shea (Kerry), Fergal O'Donnell (Roscommon), John Barrett (Cork). Subs.: James Kingston (Cork) for Lynch, Christopher Grogan (Roscommon) for Barrett.

1996/97

T.R.T.C. - David Maloney (Kerry), Kenneth Leen (Kerry), Barry O'Shea (Kerry), Mark O'Reilly (Meath), Éamon Ferris (Kerry), Séamus Moynihan (Kerry), Michael O'Donoghue (Kerry), Michael Cloherty (Galway), William Kirby (Kerry), Pádraig Joyce (Galway), John Casey (Mayo), Seán Ó Mathúna (Kerry), Johnny McGlynn (Kerry), Jack Dennehy (Kerry), Genie Farrell (Kerry). Subs.: Brendan Hannafin (Kerry) for O'Mahony, Mark McGauran (Cavan) for Joyce.

U.L. - Diarmaid Murphy (Kerry), Tom Davey (Sligo), Morgan O'Shea (Kerry), Patrick P Kenny (Offaly), Kenneth Cantwell (Meath), Niall Flynn (Louth), Aidan Keane (Cork), Michael O'Sullivan (Cork), Gary McGrath (Kerry), Dara Ó Cinnéide (Kerry), Damien Donlon (Roscommon), Ruairí O'Rahilly (Kerry), Michael F Russell (Kerry), Jonathan McCarthy (Cork), Denis O'Driscoll (Clare). Subs.: Chris Drummond (Kerry) for Cantwell, Fergal O'Brien (Kerry) for Donnellan.

1997/98

I.T.T. - Ger Cremin (Kerry), Barry O'Shea (Kerry), Michael Galvin (Clare), Kenneth Leen (Kerry), Damien Hendy (Kildare), Séamus Moynihan (Kerry), Mark McGauran (Cavan), Michael Cloherty (Galway), William Kirby (Kerry), Jimmy McGuinness (Donegal), Michael Donnellan (Galway), Pa O'Sullivan (Kerry), Jack Ferriter (Kerry), Pádraig Joyce (Galway), Michael F Russell (Kerry). Subs.: Jack Dennehy (Kerry) for Russell, Genie Farrell (Kerry) for Cloherty.

U.U.J. - Michael Conlon (Derry), Fergal Crossan (Derry), Neil Farren (Derry), Paul McGurk (Tyrone), Seánie McGuckin (Derry), Seán Lockhart (Derry), Paul Diamond (Derry), Davitt McElroy (Tyrone), John McEntee (Armagh), Kieran Donnelly (Fermanagh), Tony McEntee (Armagh), Gavin Diamond (Derry), Brian McGuckin (Tyrone), Gerard Colgan (Down), Joe Cassidy (Derry). Sub.: Kevin Madden (Antrim) for Donnelly.

1998/99

I.T.T. - Niall Hobbert (Kerry), Seán Hegarty (Kerry), Éamonn Reddin (Donegal), Damien Hendy (Kildare), Noel Griffin (Clare), Niall Sheehy (Kerry), William Harmon (Kerry), Jimmy McGuinness (Donegal), Noel Garvan (Laois), Noel Kennelly (Kerry), Pa O'Sullivan (Kerry), James Fleming (Kerry), Michael Liddane (Clare), Jack Dennehy (Kerry), Jack Ferriter (Kerry).

Garda - John McCallion (Mayo), Anton McNulty (Dublin), Mícheál O'Donoghue (Kerry), Robbie Doyle (Galway), Colin White (Sligo), Cathal Daly (Offaly), Michael Ryan (Roscommon), John Whelan (Kildare), Don Connellan (Roscommon), Aaron Hoey (Louth), Colin Crowley (Cork), David Earley (Kildare), Declan Lynch (Kerry), Tom Bowe (Laois), Cathal Sheridan (Kildare). Subs.: Mark Moynihan (Kerry) for Hoey, Rory McGrath (Kerry) for Bowe, Seán McDaid (Donegal) for Earley.

1999/00

Q.U.B.: Aidan Quinn (Down), Paddy Campbell (Donegal), Peter Quinn (Fermanagh), Brian Robinson (Tyrone), Simon Poland (Down), Enda McNulty (Armagh), Philip Jordan (Tyrone), Joe Quinn (Antrim), Conall Martin (Tyrone), Tom Brewster (Fermanagh), Cormac McAnallen (Tyrone), Karl Oakes (Down), Paddy McKeever (Armagh), Liam McBarron (Fermanagh), Philip Oldham (Armagh). Subs.: Diarmaid Marsden (Armagh) for Martin, Barry Ward (Donegal) for Oakes, Peter Campbell (Tyrone) for Oldham, Adrian Scullion (Derry) for Poland, Kevin McElvanna (Armagh) for Jordan.

U.C.D. - Cathal Mullin (Westmeath), Breandán Ó hAnnaidh (Wicklow), Noel McGuire (Sligo), John Quinn (Kildare), Declan Meehan (Galway), Cormac Ó Muircheartaigh (Dublin), Peadar Andrews (Dublin), Nigel Crawford (Meath), Ciarán McManus (Offaly), John Lynch (Kerry), Colin Moran (Dublin), Mick O'Keeffe (Dublin), Noel Meehan (Galway), Conor O'Donoghue (Meath), Barry Mooney (Offaly). Subs.: David Hanniffy (Longford) for O'Donoghue, Oisín Ó hAnnaidh (Wicklow) for Mooney, John Hegarty (Wexford) for Moran, Cian McGrath (Meath) for Hegarty, Stephen Lucey (Limerick) for McGuire.

2000/01

U.U.J. – Ronan Gallagher (Fermanagh), Cormac McGinley (Tyrone), Enda McNulty (Armagh), Paul McGurk (Tyrone), Raymond Johnston (Fermanagh), Aidan O'Rourke (Armagh), Declan McCrossan (Tyrone), Liam Doyle (Down), Kevin Hughes (Tyrone), Martin O'Rourke (Armagh), John Toal (Armagh), Michael Walsh (Down), Patrick Bradley (Derry), Jimmy McGuinness (Donegal), Kevin Brady (Antrim). Subs.: Kieran Donnelly (Fermanagh) for Martin O'Rourke, Enda McGinley (Tyrone) for Toal, Ronan Sexton (Down) for Brady.

U.C.D. – Gearóid Mac An Ghoill (Donegal), Breandán Ó hAnnaidh (Wicklow), Maghnus Breathnach (Dublin), Noel McGuire (Sligo), Dara Breen (Wexford), Dara Ó hAnnaidh (Wicklow), Ronan Kelly (Meath), Nigel Crawford (Meath), David Hanniffy (Longford), Stephen Lucey (Limerick), Ciarán McManus (Offaly), Oisín Ó hAnnaidh (Wicklow), Joe Fallon (Westmeath), Brian McDonald (Laois), John Paul Casey (Westmeath). Subs.: John Hanly (Roscommon) for Casey, John Lynch (Kerry) for Fallon, Joe Byrne (Carlow) for Lucey.

2001/02

I.T.S. – Damien Sheridan (Longford), Pat Kelly (Mayo), Aidan Higgins (Mayo), John McKeon (Leitrim), Dermot Higgins (Mayo), Damien Hendy (Kildare), Seán Grimes (Mayo), Brendan Boyle (Donegal), Michael Moyles (Mayo), Paul Finlay (Monaghan), Rory Gallagher (Fermanagh), Dara McGrath (Fermanagh), Nicholas Joyce (Galway), Brian Maloney (Mayo), Gerry Lohan (Roscommon). Subs.: David Barden (Longford) for McGrath, Garret Blake (Donegal) for Joyce.

U.C.C. – Cian Kelleher (Cork), Enda Wiseman (Cork), Paul Hanley (Cork), Stephen Curran (Kerry), Paul Galvin (Kerry), Anthony Lynch (Cork), Damien Reidy (Limerick), Karl O'Keeffe (Waterford), Micheal Ó Sé (Kerry), Tom Kenny (Cork), Conrad Murphy (Cork), Seán O'Brien (Cork), Michael D Cahill (Kerry), Billy Sheehan (Kerry), Ian Twiss (Kerry). Subs.: Conor McCarthy (Cork) for O'Brien, Dylan Mehigan (Cork) for Kenny, Jonathan Olden (Cork) for Twiss.

2002/03

N.U.I.G. – David Morris (Galway), Clive Monahan (Galway), Richie Murray (Galway), Daragh Blake (Clare), Dermot Costello (Mayo), John O'Donoghue (Meath), Karol O'Neill (Sligo), Barry Cullinane (Galway), Lorcán Ó Callaráin (Galway), Breandán Óg Ó Callaráin (Galway), Matthew Clancy (Galway), Rory Donnelly (Clare), Michael Meehan (Galway), Mícheál Keane (Mayo), Colm McFadden (Donegal). Subs.: James Rafter (Mayo) for O'Neill, Gary Flanagan (Westmeath) for Cullinane.

U.C.D. – Gearóid Mac An Ghoill (Donegal), Breandán Ó hAnnaidh (Wicklow), Conor Evans (Offaly), Paul Griffin (Dublin), Stephen Lucey (Limerick), Barry Cahill (Dublin), Ronan Kelly (Meath), Darren Magee (Dublin), Conor Murphy (Dublin), Peter Curran (Meath), John Hanly (Roscommon), Liam Óg Ó hÉineacháin (Dublin), Alan Brogan (Dublin), Raymond Ronaghan (Monaghan), Peter Lawless (Dublin). Subs.: Joe Sheridan (Meath) for Curran, David O'Connor (Wexford) for Ronaghan, Tom O'Connor (Meath) for Murphy.

2003/04

I.T.S. – Paul Durcan (Donegal), Aidan Higgins (Mayo), Éamon McGee (Donegal), Neil McGee (Donegal), Pat Kelly (Mayo), Seán Grimes (Mayo), Kevin Cassidy (Donegal), Brendan Boyle (Donegal), Michael Moyles (Mayo), Christy Toye (Donegal), Paul Finlay (Monaghan), Patrick Harte (Mayo), David Ward (Galway), Nicky Joyce (Galway), Austin O'Malley (Mayo). Subs.: Andy Moran (Mayo) for Boyle.

Q.U.B. – Willie McSorley (Armagh), Niall Bogue (Fermanagh), Daniel McCartan (Down), Chris Rafferty (Armagh), Paul O'Hea (Derry), Eoin Devine (Tyrone), Seán Kelly (Antrim), Martin McGrath (Fermanagh), Dick Clerkin (Monaghan), Aidan Carr (Down), John Clarke (Down), Karl Oakes (Down), Eoin McCartan (Down), Billy Joe Padden (Mayo), Aidan Fegan (Down). Subs.: Gavin Donaghy (Derry) for Oakes, Conall Dunne (Donegal) for Carr, Colm Brady (Antrim) for Bogue.

2004/05

I.T.S. – Paul Durcan (Donegal), Barry McWeeney (Leitrim), Keith Higgins (Mayo), Colm Cafferkey (Mayo), Jamie Murphy (Galway), Éamon McGee (Donegal), Seánie McDermott (Roscommon), Paddy Brady (Cavan), Michael Moyles (Mayo), Michael Doherty (Donegal), Rory O'Connor (Roscommon), Christy Toye (Donegal), Andy Moran (Donegal), Alan Costello (Mayo), David Ward (Galway). Subs.: James Glancy (Leitrim), Donncha Gallagher (Donegal), Paddy O'Connor (Roscommon), Eoin Gallagher (Mayo).

Q.U.B.: John Gibney (Down), Niall Bogue (Fermanagh), Daniel McCartan (Down), Ryan O'Neill (Tyrone), Kevin Gunn (Fermanagh), Gerard O'Kane (Derry), John Turley (Down), Martin McGrath (Fermanagh), Conan O'Brien (Derry), Gavin Donaghy (Derry), Brian Mallon (Armagh), Kevin McGourty (Antrim), Conleth Moran (Derry), James McGovern (Down), Peter Turley (Down). Subs.: Ciarán O'Reilly (Fermanagh), Paul O'Hea (Derry).

2005/06

D.C.U. – Stephen Cluxton (Dublin), Brian O'Reilly (Meath), Kevin Reilly (Meath), Paul Casey (Dublin), Declan Lally (Dublin), Bryan Cullen (Dublin), Gary Mullins (Mayo), Eoin Lennon (Monaghan), Ross McConnell (Dublin), Bernard Brogan (Dublin), Brendan Egan (Sligo), Ronan Flanagan (Cavan), Conor Mortimer (Mayo), Shane Smith (Monaghan), Seán Johnston (Cavan). Subs.: Niall Cooper (Dublin) for Reilly, Liam Moffatt (Mayo) for Smith, Ciaran Hanratty (Monaghan) for Cooper, Cahir Healy (Laois) for O'Reilly.

Q.U.B. – Declan Alder (Down), Ryan Dillon (Derry), Daniel McCartan (Down), Joe O'Kane (Derry), Charlie Vernon (Armagh), Gerard O'Kane (Derry), Kevin Gunn (Fermanagh), Conan O'Brien (Derry), Peter Turley (Down), Miceál O'Rourke (Armagh), Aidan Carr (Down), Kevin McGourty (Antrim), James McGovern (Down), Eoin McCartan (Down), Brian Mallon (Armagh). Subs.: Michael Ward (Tyrone) for O'Rourke, Paul O'Hea (Derry) for Vernon.

2006/07

Q.U.B. – Feargal Murphy (Fermanagh), Hugh Gallagher (Tyrone), Daniel McCartan (Down), Ryan Dillon (Derry), Justin Crozier (Antrim), Gerard O'Kane (Derry), Joe O'Kane (Derry), Paul Courtney (Armagh), Charlie Vernon (Armagh), Kevin McGourty (Antrim), Aidan Carr (Down), Gavin Donaghy (Derry), Paul McComiskey (Armagh), Ciaran O'Reilly (Fermanagh), Miceál O'Rourke (Armagh). Subs.: James McGovern (Down) for Donaghy, Luke Howard (Down) for Dillon, Eoin McCartan (Down) for O'Reilly, Caolan Tierney for O'Rourke, James Loughrey (Antrim) for J O'Kane, O'Rourke for Tierney, J O'Kane for Loughrey, Tierney for E McCartan.

U.U.J. – Michael McAllister (Down), Philip Mooney (Derry), James Conlon (Monaghan), Finian Moriarty (Armagh), Damien McCaul (Tyrone), Peter Donnelly (Tyrone), Rory Murray (Derry), James Colgan (Down), Jonathan Bradley (Derry), Michael Herron (Antrim), John Boyle (Down), Raymond Mulgrew (Tyrone), Paddy Cunningham (Antrim), Colm Cavanagh (Tyrone), Mark Lynch (Derry). Subs.: Darren Hughes (Monaghan) for Conlon, Kevin Dyas (Armagh) for Herron, Michael McCann (Antrim) for Boyle, Brendan Boggs (Tyrone) for Moriarty, Bernard O'Brien (Monaghan) for Cunningham.

2007/08

U.U.J. – Michael McAllister (Antrim), Charles Harrison (Sligo), Damien McCaul (Tyrone), Donal Morgan (Monaghan), Paul McGuigan (Monaghan), Karl Lacey (Donegal), Peter Donnelly (Tyrone), Brendan McKenna (Monaghan), Colm Cavanagh (Tyrone), Darren Hughes (Monaghan), Tomás McCann (Antrim), Raymond Mulgrew (Tyrone), Mark Lynch (Derry), Paddy Cunningham (Antrim), Andy Moran (Mayo). Subs.: James McGovern (Down) for Hughes, Barry Dunnion (Donegal) for Harrison, Ciaran Donnelly (Tyrone) for Moran.

Garda – Pádraig O'Connor (Mayo), Cormac McGill (Meath), Ciaran McGrath (Galway), Anthony Pender (Galway), Graham Dillon (Westmeath), Darren Mullahy (Galway), Éamon Callaghan (Kildare), Aidan O'Mahony (Kerry), Ambrose O'Donovan (Kerry), Seán Buckley (Limerick), Rory Guinan (Offaly), Denis Glennon (Westmeath), John O'Brien (Dublin), Mark Harrington (Cork), Joe Keane (Mayo). Subs.: Barry Brennan (Laois) for Keane, James Martin (Longford) for O'Donovan.

2008/09

CORK I.T.: Liam Sheehan (Kerry), Anthony Fenton (Cork), Ray Carey (Cork), Noel Galvin (Cork), Stephen O'Donoghue (Cork), Aidan O'Sullivan (Kerry), Conor O'Driscoll (Cork), Seán O'Hare (Waterford), Paul O'Flynn (Cork), Gary Sayers (Kerry), Paul Kerrigan (Cork), Shane McCarthy (Cork), Daniel Goulding (Cork), Colm O'Neill (Cork), Seán Cahalane (Cork). Subs: James Fitzpatrick (Cork) for McCarthy, Roy Leahy (Cork) for O'Neill.

D.I.T.: Eoin Somerville (Dublin), Darragh Breathnach (Dublin), Niall O'Shea (Dublin), Michael Burke (Meath), David Hughes (Monaghan), Ross Glavin (Kildare), John Coughlan (Dublin), P O'Neill (Kildare), Martin Reilly (Cavan), Donncha Reilly (Dublin), Kevin McLoughlin (Mayo), Paul Flynn (Dublin), Colin Daly (Dublin), Kevin McManamon (Dublin). Subs: Daniel Graham (Cavan) for Flynn, Niall Coughlan (Dublin) for Daly, Enda Gaffney (Cavan) for Breathnach, Billy O'Loughlin (Laois) for D Reilly, Eoghan Naughton (Kildare) for Hughes.

SIGERSON CUP WINNING CAPTAINS

1910/11 – W John Riordan (UCC & Cork)
1911/12 – Joseph F Donegan (UCG & Sligo)
1912/13 – F J Cronin (UCD)
1913/14 – Tom Nunan (UCC & Cork)
1914/15 – P Fitzpatrick (UCD)
1915/16 – E 'Charlie' Troy (UCC & Kerry)
1916/17 – Solomon Lawlor (UCD & Kerry)
1917/18 – Solomon Lawlor (UCD & Kerry)
1918/19 – Con Lucey (UCC & Cork)
1919/20 – Tom Pierce (UCD & Wexford)
1920/21 – Not played
1921/22 – W McDonald (UCG)
1922/23 – Tom Nunan (UCC & Cork)
1923/24 – Séamus Gardiner (UCD & Tipperary)

1924/25 – Michael Murphy (UCC & Kerry)
1925/26 – Patrick O'Sullivan (UCC)
1926/27 – Éamonn O'Doherty (UCD & Clare)
1927/28 – Peter Coughlan (UCC & Kerry & Cork)
1928/29 – Éamonn O'Doherty (UCD & Clare)
1929/30 – Joe O'Sullivan (UCD & Kerry)
1930/31 – Mick O'Gorman (UCD & Monaghan)
1931/32 – Martin Moloney (UCD & Clare)
1932/33 – Seán Flood (UCD & Meath)
1933/34 – Mick Higgins (UCG & Galway)
1934/35 – Tony O'Regan (UCG & Galway)
1935/36 – Paddy McMahon (UCD & Kerry)
1936/37 – Hugh Gibbons (UCG & Roscommon)
1937/38 – James Laffey (UCG & Mayo)
1938/39 – Gerry O'Beirne (UCG & Roscommon)
1939/40 – Joe Salmon (UCG & Mayo & Galway)
1940/41 – Joe Salmon (UCG & Mayo & Galway)
1941/42 – Dan Kavanagh (UCG & Kerry & Galway)
1942/43 – Not played
1943/44 – William Gavin (UCC & Tipperary)
1944/45 – Jack Culleton (UCD & Wexford)
1945/46 – Seán Flanagan (UCD & Mayo)
1946/47 – Nioclás Mac Craith (UCC & Waterford)
1947/48 – P J Duke (UCD & Cavan)
1948/49 – Billy Kenny (UCG & Mayo)
1949/50 – John O'Brien (UCD & Meath)
1950/51 – Bill McQuillan (UCG & Roscommon)
1951/52 – Jim O'Brien (UCC & Cork)
1952/53 – Paudie Sheehy (UCC & Kerry)
1953/54 – Pat Fenelon (UCD & Offaly)
1954/55 – Eoghan Roe O'Neill (UCG & Mayo)
1955/56 – Kieran Denvir (UCD & Down)
1956/57 – Jim McDonnell (UCD & Cavan)
1957/58 – Felix McKnight (UCD & Armagh)
1958/59 – Hugh O'Kane (QUB & Antrim)
1959/60 – James Brady (UCD & Cavan)
1960/61 – George Glynn (UCG & Galway)
1961/62 – Sean Murray (UCD & Longford)
1962/63 – Hugh McGonigle (UCG & Sligo)
1963/64 – Enda Colleran (UCG & Galway)
1964 /65 – Des Sharkey (QUB & Antrim)
1965/66 – Pat Moynihan (UCC & Kerry)
1966/67 – Denis Philpott (UCC & Cork)
1967/68 – Benny Gaughran (UCD & Louth)
1968/69 – Christy O'Sullivan (UCC & Kerry)
1969/70 – Moss Keane (UCC & Kerry)
1970/71 – Paddy Park (QUB & Tyrone)
1971/72 – Jim Gleeson (UCC & Cork)
1972/73 – Éamonn O'Donoghue (UCD & Kildare)
1973/74 – Paddy Kerr (UCD & Monaghan)
1974/75 – Mick Carty (UCD & Wexford)
1975/76 – Dan O'Mahony (Maynooth & Mayo)
1976/77 – Ivan Heffernan (UCD & Mayo)
1977/78 – Gerry McEntee (UCD & Meath)
1978/79 – Tony McManus (UCD & Roscommon)
1979/80 – Pádraig Monaghan (UCG & Mayo)
1980/81 – Gay McManus (UCG & Galway)
1981/82 – Séamus Boyd (QUB & Antrim)
1982/83 – Richie Lee (UCG & Galway)
1983/84 – Tomás Tierney (UCG & Galway)
1984/85 – Bill Sex (UCD & Kildare)
1985/86 – Colin Harney (UUJ & Armagh)
1986/87 – D.J. Kane (UUJ & Down)
1987/88 – John Keane (UCC & Kerry)
1988/89 – John Reihill (St. Mary's & Fermanagh)
1989/90 – Fergal Logan (QUB & Tyrone)
1990/91 – Noel Donnelly (UUJ & Tyrone)
1991/92 – Seán Óg de Paor (UCG & Galway)
1992/93 – Paul Brewster (QUB & Fermanagh)
1993/94 – Niall Savage (UCC & Kerry)
1994/95 – Paul O'Keeffe (UCC & Kerry)
1995/96 – Fachtna Collins (UCD & Cork)
1996/97 – Éamon Ferris (TRTC & Kerry)
1997/98 – Michael Cloherty (ITT & Galway)
1998/99 – Jimmy McGuinness (ITT & Donegal)
1999/00 – Diarmaid Marsden (QUB & Armagh)
2000/01 – Jimmy McGuinness (UUJ & Donegal)
2001/02 – Aidan Higgins (ITS & Mayo)
2002/03 – Lorcán Ó Callaráin (NUIG & Galway)
2003/04 – Michael Moyles (ITS & Mayo)
2004/05 – Christy Toye (ITS & Donegal)
2005/06 – Bryan Cullen (DCU & Dublin)
2006/07 – Daniel McCartan (QUB & Down)
2007/08 – Peter Donnelly (UUJ & Tyrone)
2008/09 – Paul Flynn (Cork IT & Cork)

SIGERSON FINAL TOP SCORERS 1933-2009

Note: This list starts from 1933/34 because in most years previous there was no final proper.

1933/34 – Vincent McDarby (UCG & Galway) 2-4.
1934/35 – Brian Scanlon (UCG & Mayo) 1-0.
1935/36 – Vincent McGovern (UCD & Cavan) 1-0; Eamonn Gavin (UCD & Westmeath) 1-0.
1936/37 – Dick Winters (UCG & Mayo) 1-1; Joe Fitzgerald (UCG & Galway) 1-1.
1937/38 – Eugene O'Sullivan (UCG & Kerry) 0-4.
1938/39 – Dennis Egan (UCG & Mayo) 1-1.
1939/40 Belfast final – Jack Bracken (UCG & Mayo) 1-2.
1939/40 Replay – Seán Mitchell (UCG & Leitrim) 1-1.
1940/41 – Seán Thornton (UCG & Galway) 3-0.
1941/42 – Walsh (UCD) 2-0.
1942/43 – No competition
1943/44 – Dick Stokes (UCD & Limerick) 1-1.
1944/45 – Charlie Brennan (UCD & Monaghan) 2-0.
1945/46 – Paddy Kelly (UCD & Westmeath) 2-0.
1946/47 – Frank McGovern (UCC & Cork) 1-0, Paddy O'Regan (UCC & Cork) 1-0, Donal Keenan (UCD & Roscommon) 0-3.

1947/48 – Derry Burke (UCC & Kerry), Brendan Hanniffy (UCC & Galway), Mick McCormack (UCD & Monaghan), Pádraic Carney (UCD & Mayo), Des McEvoy (UCD & Dublin) 0-1 each.
1948/49 – Brian O'Rourke (UCG & Roscommon), Peadar McGowan (UCG & Mayo) 0-3 each, Pat Fenelon (UCG & Offaly), Mick Flanagan (UCD & Mayo), Frank Deady (UCD & Kilkenny) 1-0 each.
1949/50 – Pádraic Carney (UCD & Mayo) (0-6).
1950/51 – Peter Solan (UCG & Mayo) 0-5.
1951/52 – Peadar Kearns (UCG & Roscommon) & Paudie Sheehy (UCC & Kerry) 0-5 each.
1952/53 – Jim Brosnan (UCC & Kerry) 3-0.
1953/54 – Kieran Denvir (UCD & Down) 0-5.
1954/55 – Draw: Kieran Denvir (UCD & Down) 0-4, Peadar McGowan (UCG & Mayo) 1-1.
Replay: Peadar McGowan (UCG & Mayo) 1-2, Éamonn McTigue (UCD & Mayo) 0-5.
1955/56 – Colm Swords (UCD & Mayo) 2-1, Seán O'Donnell (UCC & Mayo) 2-1.
1956/57 – Jim McDonnell (UCD & Cavan) 0-4.
1957/58 – Eddie Duffy (UCD & Leitrim) 0-3, Dan Corrigan (UCC & Cork) 1-0, Seán Murphy (UCC & Cork) 1-0.
1958/59 – Draw: Don Feeley (UCD & Roscommon) 2-0. Replay: Charlie Gallagher (UCD & Cavan) 0-5.
1959/60 – Kieran O'Malley (UCD & Kildare) 1-4.
1960/61 – George Kane (UCD & Westmeath) 2-0.
1961/62 – Brian Geraghty (UCG & Galway) 1-2, Seán Cleary (UCD & Galway) 1-2.
1962/63 – Dave Geaney (UCC & Kerry) 1-2.
1963/64 – Christy Tyrrell (UCG & Galway) 2-2.
1964/65 – Seán O'Neill (QUB & Down) 2-2.
1965/66 – Dave Geaney (UCC & Kerry) 2-2.
1966/67 – Eric Philpott (UCC & Cork) 0-6.
1967/68 – Benny Gaughran (UCD & Louth) 1-7.
1968/69 – Brendan Lynch (UCC & Kerry) 0-7, Ray Cummins (UCC & Cork) 2-1.
1969/70 – Barry Hanley (UCC & Kerry) 0-6.
1970/71 – Brendan Lynch (UCC & Kerry) 0-5.
1971/72 – Brendan Lynch (UCC & Kerry) 1-4, Martin Carney (UCG & Donegal) 2-1.
1972/73 – Enda Condron (UCD & Laois) 1-3.
1973/74 – Jackie Walsh (UCD & Kerry) 0-8.
1974/75 – Jackie Walsh (UCD & Kerry) 0-6.
1975/76 – Peter Burke (Maynooth & Longford) 0-4.
1976/77 – Draw: Paul McGettigan (UCG & Donegal) 1-3. Replay: Barry Walsh (UCD & Kerry) 0-5.
1977/78 – Jackie Walsh (UCD & Kerry) 0-7.
1978/79 – Tony McManus (UCD & Roscommon) 0-6.
1979/80 – Micksey Clarke (UCG & Westmeath) 1-2.
1980/81 – Gay McManus (UCG & Galway) 0-6.
1981/82 – Greg Blaney (QUB & Down) 0-5.
1982/83 – Pádraig Duffy (UCG & Mayo) 1-2.
1983/84 – Colm O'Neill (UCC & Cork) 1-4.
1984/85 – Mícheál O'Donoghue (UCD & Kerry) 0-3, Niall Clancy (UCD & Dublin) 0-3.
1985/86 – Enda Gormley (UUJ & Derry) 0-5, Ger Houlahan (UUJ & Armagh) 1-2.
1986/87 – Enda Gormley (UUJ & Derry) 0-3.
1987/88 – Maurice Fitzgerald (UCC & Kerry) 0-3, Paul McGrath (UCC & Cork) 0-3.
1988/89 – Fergal McCann (St. Mary's & Fermanagh) 2-1.
1989/90 – James McCartan (QUB & Down) 1-3.
1990/91 – Niall Finnegan (UCG & Galway) 0-3.
1991/92 – Conor McGauran (UCG & Galway) 1-1, Lorcan Dowd (UCG & Roscommon) 1-1.
1992/93 – Anthony Tohill (QUB & Derry) 0-6.
1993/94 – Mark O'Sullivan (UCC & Cork) 1-2.
1994/95 – Johnny Crowley (UCC & Kerry) 0-4, John Clifford (UCC & Cork) 0-4, Brendan Duffy (UCG & Galway) 0-4.
1995/96 – James O'Shea (Garda & Kerry) 1-2.
1996/97 – Genie Farrell (TRTC & Kerry) 0-4, Dara Ó Cinnéide (UL & Kerry) 0-4.
1997/98 – Jack Ferriter (ITT & Kerry) 0-3, Brian McGuckin (UUJ & Tyrone) 0-3.
1998/99 – Jack Ferriter (ITT & Kerry) 0-3, Noel Kennelly (ITT & Kerry) 1-0, Declan Lynch (Garda & Kerry) 0-3.
1999/00 – Liam McBarron (QUB & Fermanagh) 1-1.
2000/01 – Patrick Bradley (UUJ & Derry) 0-5.
2001/02 – Conrad Murphy (UCC & Cork) 0-4.
2002/03 – Michael Meehan (NUIG & Galway) 1-4.
2003/04 – Paul Finlay (ITS & Monaghan) 0-5, Aidan Fegan (QUB & Down) 0-5.
2004/05 – Brian Mallon (QUB & Armagh) 0-4.
2005/06 – Seán Johnston (DCU & An Cabhán) 0-4, Conor Mortimer (DCU & Maigh Eo) 0-4.
2006/07 – Paddy Cunningham (UUJ & Antrim) 0-6.
2007/08 – Paddy Cunningham (UUJ & Antrim) 1-9.
2008/09 – Daniel Goulding (Cork IT & Cork) 0-9.

Compiled by Dónal McAnallen

HIGHER EDUCATION GAA COMPETITIONS

ROLLS OF HONOUR:

IOMÁNAÍOCHT

SECOND DIVISION HURLING CHAMPIONSHIP (for Corn Uí Riain)
Limerick RTC / IT (5): 1983, 1985, 1988, 1992, 2001.
MICL (4): 1981, 1982, 2006, 2009.
Carlow RTC (3): 1979, 1991, 1993.

Cork RTC (2): 1977, 1989.
DCU (2): 1998, 2002.
IT Sligo (2): 1999, 2005.
St. John's, Cork / C.C.F.E (2): 2000, 2004.
Thomond (2): 1984, 1986.
Tralee RTC / IT Tralee (2): 1997, 2007.
ARTC (1): 1996.
DIT (1): 1994.
Galway RTC (1): 1990.
Garda (1): 1995.
NUI Maynooth (1): 2008.
Tipp. Inst. (1): 2003.
Waterford RTC (1): 1987.

THIRD DIVISION HURLING CHAMPIONSHIP (for the Fergal Maher Cup)
Col. Phádraig (2): 1994, 1996.
Dundalk RTC (2): 1990, 1997.
AIT (1): 2002.
Cadets (1): 1991.
GMIT Castlebar (1): 2004.
IT Tallaght (1): 2007.
King's Inns (1): 2006.
MICL (1): 1995.
Maynooth (1): 2003.
Napier (1): 2008.
Sligo RTC (1): 1993.
Tralee RTC (1): 1989.
UUC (1): 1998.
St Mary's / Belfast Met. (1): 2009.

DIVISION ONE HURLING LEAGUE
UCC (12): 1980/81, 1981/82, 1982/83, 1983/84, 1987/88, 1988/89, 1989/90, 1992/93, 1994/95, 1995/96, 2000/01, 2004/05.
UCD (7): 1970/71, 1972/73, 1974/75, 1975/76, 1978/79, 1979/80, 1984/85.
WRTC / WIT (8): 1985/86, 1986/87, 1991/92, 1996/97, 1997/98, 1999/00, 2001/02, 2005/06.
UL (4): 1990/91, 2002/03, 2003/04, 2006/07.
UCG (3): 1976/77, 1977/78, 1993/94.
Maynooth (2): 1971/72, 1973/74.
Cork IT (1): 1998/99.
LIT (1): 2007/08.
Garda (1): 2008/09.

DIVISION TWO HURLING LEAGUE
Galway RTC (4): 1976/77, 1981/82, 1982/83, 1987/88.
MICL (4): 1979/80, 1984/85, 1985/86, 1996/97.
Cork RTC (3): 1978/79, 1988/89, 1992/93.
Coláiste Phádraig (3): 1977/78, 1980/81, 2004/05.
UUJ (3): 1989/90, 2006/07, 2008/09.
Carlow RTC / IT (2): 1990/91, 2001/02.
DIT (2): 1993/94, 2005/06.
IT Sligo (2): 1998/99, 2000/01.
Limerick IT (2): 2002/03 (shared), 2003/04.
Tipp. Inst. / St Patrick's, Thurles (2): 2002/03 (shared), 2007/08.
ARTC (1): 1995/96.
Garda (1): 1994/95.
GMIT Castlebar (1): 1999/00.
IT Tralee (1): 1997/98.
Marino (1): 1974/75.
NCPE (1): 1973/74.
NIHE Limerick (1): 1986/87.
St Joseph's (1): 1971/72.
WRTC (1): 1983/84.

DIVISION THREE HURLING LEAGUE
MICL (3): 1978/79, 1988/89, 1994/95.
WRTC (3): 1982/83, 1986/87, (WIT III) 1997/98.
Army Apprentice School (2): 1984/85, 1995/96.
ARTC (2): 1980/81, (AIT III) 2006/07.
Carlow RTC (2): 1976/77, 1985/86.
CoACT II / Limerick RTC (2): 1981/82, 1991/92.
Cork RTC (2): 1977/78, (Cork IT III) 2004/05.
UCD III (2): 2002/03, 2003/04.
Cadets (1): 1990/91.
Coláiste Phádraig (1): 1996/97.
CCFE (1): 2001/02.
DIT (1): 1983/84.
GMIT Leitir Fraic (1) : 2007/08.
NIHE Limerick (1): 1979/80.
Sligo RTC (1): 1992/93.
Tralee RTC (1): 1989/90.
TCD (1): 2005/06.
St Mary's/Belfast Met. (1): 2008/09.

FIRST-YEAR HURLING LEAGUE DIVISION ONE (for Corn Uí Mhuirthile)
UCC (9): 1970/71, 1975/76, 1980/81, 1984/85, 1985/86, 1986/87, 1992/93, 2000/01, 2006/07.
WRTC / WIT (9): 1987/88, 1988/89, 1993/94, 1995/96, 1996/97, 1997/98, 1999/00, 2002/03, 2005/06.
UCG / NUIG (7): 1971/72, 1974/75, 1976/77, 1978/79, 1979/80, 1982/83, 2004/05.
UCD (7): 1968/69, 1973/74, 1977/78, 1981/82, 1983/84, 1994/95, 2001/02.
Cork RTC (2): 1990/91, 2001/02.
Limerick IT (2): 2003/04, 2007/08.
GMIT (1): 1998/99.
DIT (1): 2008/09.

FIRST-YEAR HURLING LEAGUE DIVISION TWO
MICL (3): 2001/02, 2004/05, 2006/07.
WIT II (3): 1997/98, 2002/03, 2003/04.
UL II (2): 2007/08, 2008/09
Coláiste Phádraig (1): 2005/06.
Cork IT (1): 2000/01.
DCU (1): 1998/99.
Maynooth (1): 1999/2000.

PEIL

SECOND DIVISION FOOTBALL CHAMPIONSHIP (for the Trench Cup)
Sligo RTC (5): 1981, 1985, 1986, 1990, 1991.
NCPE / Thomond (4): 1976, 1977, 1982, 1988.
DIT (3): 1987, 1995, 1997.
Coláiste Phádraig (3): 2002, 2007, 2009.

Garda (2): 1993, 1994.
IT Tallaght (2): 2001, 2003.
Polytechnic (2): 1980, 1983.
Athlone RTC (1): 1992.
Cadets (1): 2000.
Cork RTC (1): 1979.
Galway RTC (2): 1989, 1996.
Letterkenny IT (1): 2005.
Limerick IT (1): 1999.
MICL (1): 2008.
NIHE Limerick (1): 1984.
St. Joseph's (1): 1978.
St. Mary's, London (1): 2004.
TCD (1): 2006.
UUC (1): 1998.

THIRD DIVISION FOOTBALL CHAMPIONSHIP (for Corn na Mac Léinn)
Marino (3): 2005, 2008, 2009.
Cadets (2): 1990, 1994.
Letterkenny RTC (2): 1993, 1997.
Carlow RTC (1): 1989.
Cavan CFS (1): 1996.
Coláiste Íde (1): 2006.
MICL (1): 1995.
St. Mary's, Strawberry Hill (1): 1998.
Tipp. Inst. / St. Patrick's, Thurles (1): 2007.

DIVISION ONE FOOTBALL LEAGUE
QUB (8): 1971/72, 1972/73, 1983/84, 1984/85, 1991/92, 1993/94, 1998/99, 2006/07.
UUJ (7): 1986/87, 1987/88, 1988/89, 1994/95, 1997/98, 1999/00, 2001/02.
St. Joseph's (5): 1969/70, 1970/71, 1977/78, 1980/81, 1982/83.
NCPE / Thomond (3): 1974/75, 1976/77, 1981/82.
UCD (3): 1975/76, 1979/80, 2003/04.
ITS (3): 2000/01, 2002/03, 2004/05.
UCC (3): 1985/86, 1995/96, 2005/06.
TCD (2): 1989/90, 1990/91.
UCG (2): 1973/74, 1978/79.
ARTC (2): 1992/93, 1996/97.
DCU (1): 2007/08.
Maynooth (1): 1968/69.
Garda (1): 2008/09.

DIVISION TWO FOOTBALL LEAGUE
Coláiste Phádraig (4): 1974/75, 2000/01, 2001/02, 2003/04.
UCD (4): 1969/70, 1971/72, 1979/80, 1988/89.
Maynooth (3): 1970/71, 1983/84, 1997/98.
Sligo RTC (3): 1975/76, 1984/85, 1990/91.
ARTC (2): 1989/90, 1991/92.
BIFHE (2): 2005/06, 2006/07.
Cork RTC (2): 1981/82, 1992/93.
IT Carlow (2): 2002/03, 2007/08.
TCD (2): 1976/77, 1987/88.
MICL (2): 1985/86, 2008/09.
Dundalk RTC (1): 1980/81.
Galway RTC (1): 1996/97.
Inchicore (1): 1998/99.
IT Tallaght (1): 2004/05.
Limerick IT (1): 1999/00.
NIHEL (1): 1986/87.
NCPE (1): 1973/74.
NUU (1): 1982/83.
Polytechnic (1): 1978/79.
QUB II (1): 1977/78.
Tralee RTC (1): 1994/95.
UCG (1): 1993/94.
WRTC (1): 1995/96.

DIVISION THREE FOOTBALL LEAGUE
Cork RTC / Cork IT III (4): 1977/78, 1989/90, (Cork IT III) 2001/02, 2002/03.
Carlow IE (2): 2002/03, 2003/04.
Carlow RTC (2): 1975/76, 1988/89.
Coláiste Phádraig (2): 1976/77, 1994/95.
MICL (2): 1978/79, 1997/98.
UUJ III (2): 1993/94, 1995/96.
ARTC (1): 1983/84.
Carysfort (1): 1980/81.
Coláiste Íde (1): 2007/08.
DIT (1): 1986/87.
Griffith (1): 1996/97.
Inchicore (1): 1992/93.
Law School (1): 2007.
Letterkenny RTC (1): 1981/82.
Limavady CFHE (1): 2006.
Maynooth II (1): 1982/83.
NIHE Limerick (1): 1979/80.
QUB III (1): 1991/92.
Tralee RTC (1): 1985/86.
UCD III (1): 2004/05.
UUC (1): 1990/91.
Warrenstown Agr. College (1): 1973/74.
WRTC (1): 1984/85.
DIT III (1): 2008/09.

FIRST-YEAR FOOTBALL LEAGUE DIVISION ONE (for Corn Mhic Cionnaoith)
UUJ / Polytechnic (14): 1976/77, 1980/81, 1982/83, 1984/85, 1985/86, 1987/88, 1988/89, 1991/92, 1992/93, 1996/97, 1997/98, 1999/00, 2002/03, 2003/04.
QUB (8): 1972/73, 1975/76, 1981/82, 1983/84, 1986/87, 1989/90, 1994/95, 2001/02.
UCG / NUIG (5): 1974/75, 1998/99, 2000/01, 2004/05, 2005/06.
St. Joseph's (4): 1968/69, 1970/71, 1973/74, 1978/79.
UCD (3): 1966/67, 1967/68, 1969/70, 1971/72.
UCC (3): 1967/68, 1995/96, 2008/09.
DCU (2): 2006/07, 2007/08.
Cork RTC (1): 1990/91.
Maynooth (1): 1977/78.
Thomond (1): 1979/80.
UL (1): 1993/94.

FIRST-YEAR FOOTBALL LEAGUE DIVISION TWO

Tralee RTC / IT Tralee (4): 1982/83, 1994/95, 1995/96, 2007/08.
UUJ II (4): 1996/97, 1997/98, 1998/99, 2000/01.
WRTC (3): 1984/85, 1986/87, 1992/93.
Dundalk IT (2): 2003/04, 2004/05.
Sligo RTC (2): 1983/84, 1985/86.
Maynooth (2): 1991/92, 2008/09.
Carlow RTC (1): 1993/94.
Cork RTC (1): 1981/82.
DIT (1): 1989/90.
Galway RTC (1): 1988/89.
Letterkenny RTC (1): 1990/91.
Limerick IT (1): 2006.
MICL (1): 2001/02.
UCD II (1): 2002/03.
UUC (1): 1999/00.

KEY:
BIFHE – Belfast Institute of Further & Higher Education
Carlow IE – Carlow Institute of Education
Cavan CFS – Cavan College of Further Studies
CCFE – Cork Colleges of Further Education
MICL – Mary Immaculate College, Limerick
NCPE – National College of Physical Education (Thomond)
Polytechnic – Belfast / Ulster / NI Polytechnic (previous names for UUJ)
Tipp. Inst. – Tipperary Institute

CAMOGIE

Records

CAMOGIE

The Camogie Association has experienced unprecedented growth in recent years enjoying increased membership, an 11% increase in the number of clubs, growth overseas and a higher profile than ever before.

The first camogie match in public was a practice game in the Phoenix Park, Dublin on July 10th, 1904 played between Dublin selections. That game was followed a week later by a match between Keatings and Cuchulains, both from Dublin, at An Uaimh and was played in conjunction with an Aerideacht in the county Meath town. The celebrations of the founding of the Association in 2004 marked a turning point for the Association, re-energising those involved and bringing people back to the game twho had not been involved in recent years. It also saw the launch of the Camogie Association's Strategic Plan 2004 – 2008 which has been the roadmap for the development of Camogie at all levels.

All Ireland Senior Championship

On the playing fields Tipperary and Cork have dominated the opening years of the new century in terms of the All Ireland senior title.

The Premier County won the O'Duffy Cup for the first time, surprisingly enough, in 1999. They met Cork in an All Ireland senior final for the first time in 2000 and the goal scoring expertise of full forward Deirdre Hughes, who finished with 2-2, was a key factor in enabling Tipperary to regain the title. Tipperary went on to win five All Ireland titles between 1999 and 2004, beaten only by Cork in 2002.

2005 and 2006 saw the return of the Rebels for the All Ireland senior honours but they were stopped short of the three-in-a-row by an inspired Wexford side that captured the 2007 Gala All Ireland senior final, their first since 1975 and only the county's fourth All Ireland title. Wexford brought great excitement and colour to the All Ireland final with a record breaking 34,000 people attending the finals in Croke Park. Sisters Mary (captain) and Una Leacy were instrumental in their side's win and went on to be the first sisters to win All Stars in the same year. Kate Kelly was a powerhouse throughout the championship for Wexford and ended the year as the Gala All Ireland Championships top scorer.

2008 saw Cork win their 23rd Senior Championship in 2008 beating Galway in the final. Mary O'Connor added her sixth All Ireland medal to her collection ensuring her place in history with players such as Noelle O'Driscoll and Sandie Fitzgibbon. Cork draw ever closer to Dublin with a record 26 All Ireland titles.

Junior titles for Dublin, Derry and Clare

In the junior ranks Dublin added a second Junior All Ireland title in 2006 beating Derry before returning to the senior ranks. Derry avenged their 2006 defeat by taking the title in 2007 beating Clare with a last minute goal after six minutes of injury time. Clare took the honours in the 2008 Gala All Ireland Junior Final beating Offaly in a thrilling game. This was Clare's first title since 1986 and captain Deirdre Murphy proudly lifted the New Ireland Cup making up for the disappointments of 2005 and 2007 when she also captained the side.

Kilkenny captured the 2008 Gala All Ireland Intermediate Championship with a win over Cork after needing two attempts to overcome Galway in the semi finals. Meath took its first All Ireland title in 2008 when it won the Gala All Ireland Junior Championship (Nancy Murray Cup) and the Division 4 League title, beating Roscommon in both.

Kilkenny dominate underage scene

Kilkenny have dominated the under-age scene for the last four years. 2008 saw them win their fourth All Ireland U16 title in a row and their third All Ireland Minor title in a row. Offaly's Minor B brought All Ireland honours to the Faithful county when they defeated Waterford in the 2008 final. Derry also succeeded in retaining their U16B All Ireland title defeating Offaly in the final.

The year came to a glittering end with the 2008 Camogie All Stars in association with O'Neills in November. Gemma O' Connor of Cork received her fifth consecutive All Star award while Michaela Morkan (Offaly) and Jane Adams (Antrim) brought the first ever All Stars to their respective counties.

All Ireland Club Championship

St. Lachtain's of Kilkenny dominated the club scene from 2004 to 2006 winning three titles in a row. Cashel of Tipperary won their first title in 2007 defeating Athenry. Jane Adams went on to add an All Ireland Club medal to her collection when she captained her club O'Donovan Rossa to an All Ireland Senior Club title beating Drom and Inch in the final, again in Donaghmore/Ashbourne. Meanwhile Harps of Laois made it three-in-a-row when they beat Kilmaley of Clare for the All Ireland Junior Club title in Nenagh.

The Gael Linn Interprovincial competition was held in the superb Donaghmore/Ashbourne grounds in May of this year. Connacht, which was made up of players from Galway alone, took the honours in the Senior competition while Munster took the Junior grade.

The Coillte U14 Development Squad Day was held in Croke Park in July giving young players from eight counties the opportunity to showcase their talents and skills in front of coaches and family in a fun filled day of games.

Off the field Liz Howard was elected President of the Camogie Association at Congress 2006 and took over the role from Offaly woman Miriam O'Callaghan. 2009 saw the end of her three year term when Uachtarán Tofa Joan O'Flynn took over.

Cumann Camógaíochta na nGael has come a long way since it's centenary year celebrations in 2004. In 2007, dual Cork star Mary O' Connor was appointed Director of Camogie. Along with Mary there are now five full time Regional Development Co-ordinators for the regions of Connacht, North Leinster/South Ulster, Dublin/Kildare, Munster and South Leinster. A 2nd Level Development Co-ordinator was also appointed to oversee 2nd level development throughout the country. Sinéad O'Connor was appointed Ardstiúrthóir in October, 2009 replacing Síle de Bhailís who retired after 22 years with the Association.

CAMOGIE RECORDS

ALL-IRELAND CHAMPIONSHIPS (SENIOR)

ROLL OF HONOUR

Dublin (26)—1932, 1933, 1937, 1938, 1942, 1943, 1944, 1948, 1949, 1950, 1951, 1952, 1953, 1954, 1955, 1957, 1958, 1959, 1960, 1961, 1962, 1963, 1964, 1965, 1966, 1984.
Cork (24)—1934, 1935, 1936, 1939, 1940, 1941, 1970, 1971, 1972, 1973, 1978, 1980, 1982, 1983, 1992, 1993, 1995, 1997, 1998, 2002, 2005, 2006, 2008, 2009.
Kilkenny (12)—1974, 1976, 1977, 1981, 1985, 1986, 1987, 1988, 1989, 1990, 1991, 1994.
Antrim (6)—1945, 1946, 1947, 1956, 1967,1979.
Tipperary (5)—1999, 2000, 2001, 2003, 2004.
Wexford (4)—1968, 1969, 1975, 2007.
Galway (1)—1996.

1932—Dublin 3-2; Galway 0-2
1933—Dublin 9-2; Galway 4-0
1934—Cork 4-3; Louth 1-4
1935—Cork 3-4; Dublin 4-0
1936—Cork 6-4; Louth 3-3
1937—Dublin 9-4; Galway 1-0
1938—Dublin 5-0; Cork 2-3
1939—Cork 6-1; Galway 1-1
1940—Cork 4-1; Galway 2-2
1941—Cork 7-5; Dublin 1-2
1942—Dublin 1-2; Cork 1-2 (draw)
Dublin 4-1; Cork 2-2 (replay)
1943—Dublin 8-0; Cork 1-1
1944—Dublin 5-4; Antrim 0-0
1945—Antrim 5-2; Waterford 3-2
1946—Antrim 4-1; Galway 2-3
1947—Antrim 2-4; Dublin 2-1
1948—Dublin 11-4; Down 4-2
1949—Dublin 8-6; Tipperary 4-1
1950—Dublin 6-5; Antrim 4-1
1951—Dublin 8-6; Antrim 4-1
1952—Dublin 5-1; Antrim 4-2
1953—Dublin 8-4; Tipperary 1-3
1954—Dublin 10-4; Derry 4-2
1955—Dublin 9-2; Cork 5-6
1956—Antrim 5-3; Cork 4-2
1957—Dublin 3-3; Antrim 3-1
1958—Dublin 5-4; Tipperary 1-1
1959—Dublin 11-6; Mayo 1-3
1960—Dublin 6-2; Galway 2-0
1961—Dublin 7-2; Tipperary 4-1
1962—Dublin 5-5; Galway 2-0
1963—Dublin 7-3; Antrim 2-5
1964—Dublin 7-4; Antrim 3-1
1965—Dublin 10-1; Tipperary 5-3
1966—Dublin 2-2; Antrim 0-6
1967—Antrim 4-2; Dublin 4-2 (draw)
Antrim 3-9; Dublin 4-2 (replay)
1968—Wexford 4-2; Cork 2-5
1969—Wexford 4-4; Antrim 4-2
1970—Cork 5-7; Kilkenny 3-2
1971—Cork 4-6; Wexford 1-2
1972—Cork 2-5; Kilkenny 1-4
1973—Cork 2-5; Antrim 3-1
1974—Kilkenny 3-8; Cork 4-5 (draw)
Kilkenny 3-3; Cork 1-5, (replay)
1975—Wexford 4-3; Cork 1-2
1976—Kilkenny 0-6; Dublin 1-2
1977—Kilkenny 3-4; Wexford 1-3
1978—Cork 6-4; Dublin 1-2
1979—Antrim 2-3; Tipperary 1-3
1980—Cork 2-7; Limerick 3-4 (draw)
Cork 1-8; Limerick 2-2 (replay)
1981—Kilkenny 3-9; Cork 3-9 (draw)
Kilkenny 1-9; Cork 0-7 (replay)
1982—Cork 2-7; Dublin 2-6
1983—Cork 2-5; Dublin 1-6
1984—Dublin 5-9; Tipperary 2-4
1985—Kilkenny 0-13; Dublin 1-5
1986—Kilkenny 2-12; Dublin 2-3
1987—Kilkenny 3-10; Cork 1-7
1988—Kilkenny 4-11; Cork 3-8
1989—Kilkenny 3-10; Cork 2-6
1990—Kilkenny 1-14; Wexford 0-7
1991—Kilkenny 3-8; Cork 0-10
1992—Cork 1-20; Wexford 2-6
1993—Cork 3-15; Galway 2-8
1994—Kilkenny 2-11; Wexford 0-8
1995—Cork 4-8; Kilkenny 2-10
1996—Galway 4-8; Cork 1-15
1997—Cork 0-15; Galway 2-5
1998—Cork 2-13; Galway 0-15
1999—Tipperary 0-12, Kilkenny 1-8
2000—Tipperary 2-11; Cork 1-9
2001—Tipperary 4-13; Kilkenny 1-6
2002—Cork 4-9; Tipperary 1-9
2003—Tipperary 2-11; Cork 1-11
2004—Tipperary 2-11; Cork 0-9
2005—Cork 1-17; Tipperary 1-13
2006—Cork 0-12; Tipperary 0-4
2007—Wexford 0-7; Cork 1-8
2008—Cork 2-10; Galway 1-8
2009—Cork 0-15; Kilkenny 0-7

ALL-IRELAND CHAMPIONSHIPS (JUNIOR) New Ireland Cup

ROLL OF HONOUR

Galway (7)—1972, 1979, 1985, 1988, 1994, 1998, 2003.
Cork (7)—1973, 1980, 1983, 1984, 1996, 1999, 2004.
Dublin (5)—1970, 1971, 1975, 2005, 2006.
Derry (4)—1969, 1978, 2000, 2007.
Clare (4)—1974, 1981, 1986, 2008.
Down (3)—1968, 1976, 1991.
Kildare (3)—1987, 1989, 1990.
Limerick (2)—1977, 1995.
Tipperary (2)—1992, 2001.
Louth (1)—1982.
Antrim (1)—1997.

Armagh (1)—1993.
Kilkenny (1)—2002.
Offaly (1)—2009.
1968—Down 2-3; Cork 1-1
1969—Derry 4-2; Cork 2-4
1970—Dublin 4-2; Armagh 3-3
1971—Dublin 2-2; Cork 1-2
1972—Galway 3-6; Wexford 2-1
1973—Cork 4-4; Galway 1-4
1974—Clare 3-2; Dublin 3-0
1975—Dublin 5-0; Down 0-3
1976—Down 3-4; Wexford 3-3
1977—Limerick 2-7; Wexford 3-1
1978—Derry 3-4; Cork 1 -4
1979—Galway 4-3; Cork 3-2
1980—Cork 4-4; Tyrone 1-4
1981—Clare 3-2; Antrim 0-7
1982—Louth 1-7; Cork 1-6
1983—Cork 2-5, Dublin 2-3
1984—Cork 5-8; Cavan 2-2
1985—Galway 8-7; Armagh 3-7
1986—Clare 1-13; Kildare 3-4
1987—Kildare 2-10; Armagh 0-7
1988—Galway 3-4; Limerick 1-5
1989—Kildare 0-15; Galway 2-9 (draw)
Kildare 3-11; Galway 1-3 (replay)
1990—Kildare 2-14; Tipperary 3-7
1991—Down 3-13; Tipperary 2-14
1992—Tipperary 6- 13; Galway 2-7
1993—Armagh 3-9; Galway 3-9 (draw)
Armagh 2-10; Galway 0-6 (replay)
1994—Galway 2-10; Limerick 1-11
1995—Limerick 3-7; Roscommon 4-3
1996—Cork 6-5; Roscommon 2-7
1997—Anrtim 7-11; Cork 2-10
1998—Galway 3-11; Tipperary 2-10
1999—Cork 1-13; Derry 2-9
2000—Derry 3-15; Cork 1-13
2001—Tipperary 4-16; Offaly 1-7
2002—Kilkenny 2-11; Cork 2-8
2003—Galway 3-9; Clare 309
Galway 1-12; Clare 2-5 (replay)
2004—Cork 4-5; Down 2-4
2005—Dublin 1-7; Clare 1-7 (draw)
Dublin 2-9; Clare 1-4 (replay)
2006—Dublin 0-12; Derry 1-7
2007—Derry 3-12; Clare 2-14
2008—Clare 2-8; Offaly 1-10
2009—Offaly 3-14; Waterford 2-8

ALL-IRELAND CHAMPIONSHIPS (INTERMEDIATE)

ROLL OF HONOUR

Cork (3)—2000, 2002, 2006
Clare (2)—1993, 1995
Antrim (2)—2001, 2003
Limerick (2)—1996, 2007
Galway (2)—2004, 2009
Armagh (1)—1994
Tipperary (1)—1997
Down (1)—1998
Dublin (1)—1992
Kilkenny (1)—2008
1992—Dublin 4-11; Down 4-4
1993—Care 1-8; Dublin 1-5
1994—Armagh 7-11; Kildare 3-11
1995—Clare 1-10; Tipperary 1-9
1996—Limerick 2-10; Down 1-6
1997—Tipperary 2-19; Clare 2-12
1998—Down 1-12; Cork -8
1999—Clare 1-8; Antrim 1-3
2000—Cork 3-9; Limerick 0-11
2001—Antrim 3-10; Derry 0-5
2002—Cork 3-6; Antrim 1-10
2003—Antrim 2-9; Tipperary 0-10
2004—Galway 2-5; Tipperary 0-4
2005—No Competition
2006—Cork 2-9; Galway 1-7
2007—Limerick 2-9; Cork 0-6
2008—Kilkenny 5-5; Cork 1-14
2009—Galway 3-10; Cork 1-5

ALL-IRELAND CHAMPIONSHIPS (MINOR)

ROLL OF HONOUR

Cork (13)—1975, 1976, 1978, 1979, 1980, 1983, 1984, 1985, 1998, 1999, 2001, 2002, 2003.
Galway (9)—1977, 1981, 1986, 1987, 1994, 1996, 1997, 2000, 2004.
Kilkenny (8)—1988, 1989, 1991, 2005, 2006, 2007, 2008, 2009.
Tipperary (3)—1990, 1992, 1993.
Down (1)—1974.
Dublin (1)—1982.
Wexford (1)—1995.

1974—Down 3-0; Cork 0-1
1975—Cork 6-2; Galway 0-3
1976—Cork 4-6; Down 2-1
1977—Galway 5-4; Dublin 2-1
1978—Cork 5-1; Dublin 3-4
1979—Cork 5-3; Cavan 3-0
1980—Cork 5-5; Cavan 0-2
1981—Galway 3-4; Antrim 3-3
1982—Dublin 5-2; Galway 2-3
1983—Cork 3-3; Dublin 2-3
1984—Cork 2-12; Galway 5-0
1985—Cork 3-8; Galway 2-3
1986—Galway 2-8; Wexford 1-4
1987—Galway 1-11; Cork 3-3
1988—Kilkenny 5-6; Armagh 2-5
1989—Kilkenny 9-10; Tipperary 3-8
1990—Tipperary 2-11; Kilkenny 3-6
1991—Kilkenny 4-12; Galway 3-7
1992—Tipperary 4-9; Kilkenny 1-3
1993—Tipperary 1-5; Galway 1-5 (draw)
Tipperary 3-10; Galway 2-9 (replay)
1994—Galway 7-13; Tipperary 3-9
1995—Wexford 2-9; Galway 1-7
1996—Galway 3-16; Tipperary 4-11

1997—Galway 2-14; Cork 1-6
1998—Cork 3-18; Derry 1-5
1999—Cork 2-12; Galway 3-8
2000—Galway 2-9; Wexford 0-3
2001—Cork 6-15; Kilkenny 0-7
2002—Cork 1-11; Galway 1-5
2003—Cork 3-12; Galway 1-4
2004—Galway 3-16; Kilkenny 2-6
2005—Kilkenny 4-7; Tipperary 2-7
2006—Kilkenny 4-10; Galway 2-5
2007—Kilkenny 3-12; Cork 0-7
2008—Kilkenny 3-15; Clare 1-7
2009—Kilkenny 5-10; Clare 3-8

NATIONAL LEAGUES (SENIOR)

ROLL OF HONOUR

Cork (14)—1984, 1986, 1991, 1992, 1995, 1996, 1997, 1 998, 1999, 2000, 2001, 2003, 2006, 2007.
Kilkenny (9)—1980, 1982, 1985, 1987, 1988, 1989, 1990, 1993, 2008.
Dublin (3)—1979, 1981, 1983.
Galway (3)—1994, 2002, 2005.
Tipperary (2)—1977, 2004.
Wexford (2)—1978, 2009.

1977—Tipperary 4-2; Wexford 1-3
1978—Wexford 2-5; Cork 0-4
1979—Dublin 0-6; Limerick 0-0
1980—Kilkenny 3-8; Tipperary 1-3
1981—Dublin 1-7; Cork 1-4
1982—Kilkenny 2-5; Cork 1-4
1983—Dublin 4-8; Wexford 1-6
1984—Cork 1-8; Dublin 0-4
1985—Kilkenny 4-7; Dublin 3-6
1986—Cork 3-8; Dublin 1-10
1987—Kilkenny 4-8; Dublin 1-6
1988—Kilkenny 3-10; Dublin 2-4
1989—Kilkenny 6-7; Cork 1-11
1990—Kilkenny 1-10; Wexford 2-4
1991—Cork 2-13; Kilkenny 2-6
1992—Cork 2-17; Wexford 0-11
1993—Kilkenny 4-7; Cork 1-13
1994—Galway 1-13; Tipperary 1-8
1995—Cork 5-16; Armagh 3-4
1996—Cork 3-16; Galway 1-7
1997—Cork 4-12; Kilkenny 0-9
1998—Cork 1-16; Galway 2-9
1999—Cork 9-19; Tipperary 2-7
2000—Cork 3-7; Tipperary 1-10
2001—Cork 6-9; Galway 0-1
2002—Galway 6-6; Limerick 1-7
2003—Cork 3-13; Tipperary 2-12
2004—Tipperary 3-10; Wexford 2-9
2005—Galway 1-6; Cork 0-6
2006—Cork 2-7; Tipperary 2-5
2007—Cork 3-8; Wexford 1-10
2008—Kilkenny 3-11; Galway 0-17
2009—Wexford 2-12; Tipperary 0-11

NATIONAL LEAGUES (JUNIOR)

ROLL OF HONOUR

Dublin (4)—1982, 1983, 1984, 1987.
Armagh (4)—1980, 1988, 1993, 1994.
Kíldare (4)—1986, 1989, 1990, 2004.
Limerick (3)—1991, 1992, 1996.
Galway (3)—1985, 1995, 2003.
Cork (3)—2000, 2001, 2005.
Cavan (2)—1981, 2009.
Antrim (1)—1997.
Down (1)—1998.
Derry (1)—1999.
Offaly (1)—2002.

1980—Armagh 2-5; Kildare 2-3
1981—Cavan 2-4; Louth 1-7 (draw)
Cavan 0-4; Louth 0-2 (replay)
1982—Dublin 6-9; Tyrone 0-2
1983—Dublin 3-9; Westmeath 2-5
1984—Dublin 2-4; Armagh 1-3
1985—Galway 3-10; Kildare 3-3
1986—Kildare 2-3; Dublin 1-4
1987—Dublin 6-4; Kildare 1-7
1988—Armagh 1-9; Down 0-6
1989—Kildare 2-14; Armagh 3-8
1990—Kildare 2-13; Kilkenny 1-3
1991—Limerick 3-13; Roscommon 3-4
1992—Limerick 4-13; Down 2-6
1993—Armagh 3-8; Dublin 2-1
1994—Armagh 1-10; Cork 1-10 (draw)
Armagh 1-18; Cork 1-2 (replay)
1995—Galway 3-8; Down 3-8 (draw)
Galway 4-13; Down 2-9 (replay)
1996—Limerick 5-10; Down 3-7
1997—Antrim 5- 12; Down 3-16
1998—Down 0-20; Cork 0-12
1999—Derry 3-7; Wexford 0-7
2000—Cork 2-12; Kildare 0-4
2001—Cork 3-14; Derry 4-3
2002—Offaly 3-18; Laois 2-6
2003—Galway 1-11; Armagh 2-5
2004—Kildare 2-11; Laois 2-6
2005—Cork 2-10; Galway 2-7
2006—Clare 1-14, Derry 3-7
2007—Waterford 1-18; Down 2-13
2008—Clare 4-8; Derry 3-9
2009—Cavan 0-5; Wicklow 0-4

GAEL LINN SENIOR INTERPROVINCIAL CHAMPIONSHIPS

ROLL OF HONOUR

Leinster (25)—1956, 1957, 1958, 1959, 1960, 1962, 1965, 1968, 1969, 1970, 1971, 1972, 1978, 1979, 1981, 1983, 1984, 1985, 1986, 1987, 1988, 1989, 1991, 1993, 2006.

Munster (20)—1961, 1963, 1964, 1966, 1980, 1982, 1990, 1992, 1994, 1995, 1996, 1997, 1998, 1999, 2001, 2002, 2003, 2004, 2005, 2009.
Connacht (4)—1973, 1974, 2000, 2008.
Ulster (2)—1967, 2007.

1956—Leinster 7-1; Ulster 3-1
1957—Leinster 5-1; Munster 3-1
1958—Leinster 8-2; Ulster 3-3
1959—Leinster 6-0; Ulster 1-3
1960—Leinster 4-9; Munster 3-1
1961—Munster 5-2; Connacht 1-0
1962—Leinster 7-2; Ulster 5-3
1963—Munster 3-2; Leinster 2-2
1964—Munster 2-6; Leinster 3-2
1965—Leinster 4-3; Ulster 4-1
1966—Munster 4-2; Leinster 1-3
1967—Ulster 5-4; Leinster 5-1
1968—Leinster 7-0; Ulster 2-5
1969—Leinster 5-4; Munster 2-2
1970—Leinster 12-2; Ulster 4-1
1971—Leinster 5-4; Ulster 0-5
1972—Leinster 7-7; Connacht 4-2
1973—Connacht 4-4; Leinster 3-3
1974—Connacht 3-7; Munster 3-0
1975-'77—Suspended.
1978—Leinster 4-9; Connacht 2-2
1979—Leinster 1-5; Munster 0-4
1980—Munster 2-5; Leinster 2-1
1981—Leinster 3-10; Ulster 2-4
1982—Munster 3-10; Leinster 2-12
1983—Leinster 2-7; Munster 1-7
1984—Leinster 3-9; Connacht 1-4
1985—Leinster 4-9; Munster 1-6
1986—Leinster 4-6; Munster 1-6
1987—Leinster 8-11; Connacht 0-5
1988—Leinster 2-9; Connacht 2-4
1989—Leinster 5-12; Munster 3-6
1990—Munster 10-10; Ulster 1-2
1991—Leinster 5-13; Munster 0-7
1992—Munster 1-18; Leinster 2-9
1993—Leinster 6-14; Ulster 1-4
1994—Munster 4-11; Ulster 2-7
1995—Munster 4-13; Connacht 3-10
1996—Munster 4-18; Ulster 6-10
1997—Munster 4-18; Leinster 2-11
1998—Munster 6-20; Leinster 1-11
1999—Munster 1-18; Connacht 1-9
2000—Connacht 1-10; Ulster 0-3
2001—Munster 1-18; Connacht 1-9
2002—Munster 7-23; Ulster 0-11
2003—Munster 3-13; Ulster 1-9
2004—Munster 1-16; Connacht 1-9
2005—Munster 3-14; Connacht 2-8
2006—Leinster 2-7; Munster 1-8
2007—Ulster 2-12; Leinster 3-8
2008—Connacht 1-14; Munster 2-10
2009—Munster 0-7; Connacht 0-2

GAEL LINN JUNIOR INTERPROVINCIAL CHAMPIONSHIPS FINALS

ROLL OF HONOUR

Munster (16)—1975, 1977, 1978, 1980, 1983, 1985, 1987, 1988, 1992, 1994, 1996, 1997, 2003, 2004, 2005, 2008, 2009.
Ulster (8)—1979, 1989, 1990, 1991, 1993, 1998, 2000, 2002.
Leinster (7)—1976, 1982, 1984, 1986, 1999, 2001, 2007.
Connacht (4)—1981, 1995, 2006, 2009.

1975—Munster 5-1; Ulster 2-0
1976—Leinster 2-6; Munster 2-3
1977—Munster 3-7; Connacht 3-1
1978—Munster 3-2; Ulster 2-1
1979—Ulster 0-4; Munster 1-0
1980—Munster 1-9; Leinster 3-2
1981—Connacht 2-3; Munster 2-2
1982—Leinster 3-16; Connacht 2-8
1983—Munster 1-12; Leinster 1-11
1984—Leinster 3-6; Ulster 1-3
1985—Munster 1-7; Ulster 2-3
1986—Leinster 1-5; Munster 0-7
1987—Munster 2-6; Ulster 2-5
1988—Munster 4-3; Leinster 3-5
1989—Ulster 1-11; Leinster 2-3
1990—Ulster 5-11; Munster 5-3
1991—Ulster 4-5; Munster 0-6
1992—Munster 6-11; Connacht 3-3
1993—Ulster 4-5; Leinster 1-9
1994—Munster 5-9; Ulster 2-12
1995—Connacht 1-9; Munster 0-10
1996—Munster 3-17; Ulster 1-7
1997—Munster 3-11; Leinster 2-10
1998—Ulster 3-12; Leinster 1-12.
1999—Leinster 3-17; Connacht 4-6
2000—Ulster 1-10; Munster 2-6
2001—Leinster 1-14; Munster 1-11
2002—Ulster 4-11; Leinster 1-13
2003—Munster 4-7; Ulster 0-5
2004—Munster 4-16; Leinster 1-4
2005—Munster 2-14; Ulster 2-4
2006—Connacht 3-12; Ulster 1-7
2007—Leinster 3-16; Munster 0-11
2008—Munster 3-17; Ulster 0-3
2009—Connacht 4-4; Munster 0-2

ALL-IRELAND CLUB CHAMPIONSHIPS

ROLL OF HONOUR

St. Paul's, Kilkenny (8)—1968, 1969, 1970, 1974, 1976, 1987, 1988, 1989.
Buffer's Alley, Wexford (5)—1979, 1981, 1982, 1983, 1984.

Pearses, Galway (5)—1966, 1997, 2000, 2001, 2002.
Glen Rovers, Cork (4)—1986, 1990, 1992, 1993.
Granagh/Balingarry, Limerick (3)—1998, 1999, 2003.
St. Lachtain's, Kilkenny (3)—2004, 2005, 2006.
Austin Stacks, Dublin (2)—1971, 1972.
St. Patrick's, Glengoole, Tipperary (2)—1965, 1966.
Ballyagran, Limerick (1)—1978
Celtic, Dublin (1)—1964.
Croagh-Kilfinny, Limerick (1)—1975.
Eoghan Ruadh, Dublin (1)—1967.
Killeagh, Cork (1)—1980.
Oranmore, Galway (1)—1973.
Athenry, Galway (1)—1977.
Mullagh, Galway (1)—1991.
Crumlin, Dublin (1)—1985.
Lisdowney, Kilkenny (1)—1994.
Rathnure, Wexford (1)—1995.
Cashel, Tippeary (1)—2007.
Rathnure, Wexford (1)—1995.
O'Donovan Rossa, Antrim (1)—2008.

1964—Celtic, Dublin 5-2; Deirdre, Belfast 1-0
1965—St. Patrick's, Glengoole, Tipperary 3-3; Deirdre, Belfast 2-3
1966—St. Patrick's, Glengoole, Tipperary 5-5; St. Paul's, Kilkenny 2-1
1967—Eoghan Ruadh, Dublin 7-3; Oranmore, Galway 1-0
1968—St. Paul's, Kilkenny 7-2; Ahane, Limerick 1-2
1969—St. Paul's, Kilkenny 3-7; Ahane, Limerick 2-1
1970-'71—St. Paul's, Kilkenny 6-5; Bellaghy, Derry 2-0
1971-'72—Austin Stacks, Dublin 5-4; Thurles, Tipperary 2-1
1972-'73—Austin Stacks, Dublin 4-2; Portglenone, Antrim 2-0
1973-'74—Oranmore, Galway 3-2; St. Paul's, Kilkenny 2-3
1974-'75—St. Paul's, Kilkenny 3-3; Oranmore, Galway 1-1
1975-'76—Croagh-Kilfinny, Limerick 4-6; Athenry, Galway 4-5
1976-'77—St. Paul's, Kilkenny 6-3; Athenry, Galway 1-3
1977-'78—Athenry, Galway 10-5; Portglenone, Antrim 1-1
1978—Ballyagran, Limerick 1-3; Buffer's Alley, Wexford 0-1
1979—Buffer's Alley, Wexford 2-6; Athenry, Galway 1-2
1980—Killeagh, Cork 4-2; Buffer's Alley, Wexford 1-7
1981—Buffer's Alley, Wexford 2-6; Killeagh, Cork 1-4
1982—Buffer's Alley, Wexford 3-2; Athenry, Galway 0-2
1983—Buffer's Alley, Wexford 3-7; St. Marys, Kilkerrin-Glenamaddy, Galway 0-6
1984—Buffer's Alley, Wexford 2-4; Killeagh, Cork 1-4
1985—Crumlin, Dublin 4-8; Athenry, Galway 3-2
1986—Glen Rovers, Cork 4-11; St. Paul's, Kilkenny 5-7
1987—St. Paul's, Kilkenny 1-4; Glen Rovers, Cork 0-5
1988—St Paul's, Kilkenny 4-5; St. Mary's, Glenamaddy, Galway 3-7
1989—St. Paul's, Kilkenny 6-10; Mullagh, Galway 4-2
1990—Glen Rovers, Cork 4-13; St. Paul's, Kilkenny 2-7
1991—Mullagh, Galway 4-13; Eglish, Tyrone 0-2
1992—Glen Rovers, Cork 1-9; St. Anne's, Rathnure, Wexford 0-2
1993—Glen Rovers, Cork 6-10; Mullagh, Galway 0-2
1994—Lisdowney, Kilkenny 5-9; Glen Rovers, Cork 1-15
1995—Rathnure, Wexford 4-9; Toomevara, Tipperary 1-5
1996—Pearses, Galway 1-8; Granagh/ Ballingarry, Limerick 2-3
1997—Pearses, Galway 4-6; Lisdowney, Kilkenny 2-5
1998—Granagh/Ballingarry, Limerick 1-19; St. Vincent's, Dublin 1-8
1999 – Granagh/Balingarry, Limerick 2-4; Davitts, Galway 1-3
2000—Pearses, Galway 2-11; Swatragh, Derry 1-3
2001—Pearses, Galway 2-8; Cashel, Tipperary 0-13
2002—Pearses, Galway 2-13; St.Ibar's, Wexford 1-5
2003—Granagh, Balingarry, Limerick 1-10; Davitts, Galway 1-6
2004—St.Lachtain's, Kilkenny 2-8, Granagh/Balingarry, Limerick 0-7
2005—St. Lachtain's, Kilkenny 1-9; Davitt's 1-4
2006—St. Lachtain's, Kilkenny 1-5; O'Donovan Rossa, Antrim 1-3
2007—Cashel, Tipperary 1-18; Athenry, Galway 0-9
2008—O'Donovan Rossa, Antrim 2-15; Drom & Inch, Tippeary 1-12.

LEADING ALL-IRELAND SENIOR MEDAL HOLDERS

Kathleen Mills, Dublin (15): 1942, '43, '44, '48, '50, '51, '52, '53, '54, '55, '57, '58, '59, '60, '61.
Una O'Connor, Dublin (13): 1953, '54, '55, '57 (sub), '58, '59, '60, '61, '62, '63, '64, '65, '66.
Angela Downey, Kilkenny (12): 1974, '76, '77, '81, '85, '86, '87, '88, '89, '90, '91, '94.
Ann Downey, Kilkenny (12): 1974 (sub), '76, '77, '81, '85, '86, '87, '88, '89, '90, '91, '94.
Kay Ryder, Dublin (10): 1955 (sub), '58, '59, '60, '61, '62, '63, '64, '65, '66.
Gerry Hughes, Dublin (9): 1954, '55, '57, '58, '59, '60, '61, '62, '63.
Kay Lyons, Dublin (9): 1957, '58, '59, '61 (sub), '62, '63, '64, '65, '66.

Bridie McGarry, Kilkenny (9): 1974, '76, '77, '81, '85, '86, '87, '89, '90.
Deirdre Malone, Kilkenny (9): 1981 (sub), '85, '86 (sub), '87, '88, '89, '90, '91, '94.
Sophia Brack, Dublin (8): 1948, '49, '50, '51, '52, '53, '54, '55.
Eileen Duffy, Dublin (8): 1949, '50, '51, '52, '53, '54, '55, '57.
Eithne Leech, Dublin (8): 1959, '60, '61,'62,'63 (sub), '64 (sub), '65, '66.
Marion McCarthy, Cork (8): 1970 (sub), '71, '72, '73, '78, '80, '82, '83.
Jo Dunne, Kilkenny (8): 1976, '77, '81, '85, '86, '87,'88,'89 (sub).
Biddy O'Sullivan, Kilkenny (8): 1981, '85, '86, '87, '88, '89, '90, '91.
Kathleen Cody, Dublin (7): 1942, '43, '44, '48, '49, '50, '51.
Annette Corrigan, Dublin (7): 1952, '53, '54, '55, '57, '58, '59.
Pat Moloney, Cork (7): 1970, '71, '72, '73, '78, '80, '82.
Liz Neary, Kilkenny (7): 1974, '76, '77, '81,'85, '86, '87.
Anna Whelan, Kilkenny (7): 1981, '85, '87, '88, '89, '90 (sub).
Marie Fitzpatrick, Kilkenny (7): 1985, '86, '87, '88, '89, '90, '91.
Breda Holmes, Kilkenny (7): 1985, '86, '87, '88, '89, '90, '91.
Lil Kirby, Cork (6): 1934, '35, '36, '39, '40, '41.
Kitty Buckley, Cork (6): 1934 (sub), '35, '36, '39, '40, '41.
Nancy Caffrey, Dublin (6): 1949, '50, '51 (sub), '52, '53, '54.
Brid Reid, Dublin (6): 1950 (sub), '53 (sub), '55, '57, '58, '59.
Ally Hussey, Dublin (6): 1960, '61, '62, '63, '64, '65.
Doreen Rodgers, Dublin (6): 1937, '38, '42, '43, '44, '49.
Mary Ryan, Dublin (6): 1961, '62, '63, '64, '65, '66.
Marion Sweeney, Cork (6): 1972, '73, '78, '80, '82, '83.
Sandie Fitzgibbon, Cork (6): 1982 1sub), '83, '92, '93, '95, '97.
Noelle O'Driscoll, Cork & Kilkenny (6): 1982 (Cork), 1983 (sub, Cork), '88 (sub, Kilkenny), '89 (sub, Kikenny), '90 (sub, Kilkenny), '91 (sub, Kilkenny).
Mary O'Connor (Cork) (6): 1997, 1998, 2002, 2005, 2006, 2008.,

ASHBOURNE CUP

ROLL OF HONOUR

U.C.D. (36)—1915, 1916, 1918, 1921, 1933, 1935, 1938, 1 939, 1940, 1941, 1942, 1946, 1950, 1952, 1953, 1954, 1955, 1958, 1959, 1960, 1961, 1962, 1966, 1969, 1970, 1971, 1980, 1981, 1982, 1983, 1984, 1986, 1987, 1988, 2007, 2008.
U.C.C. (31)—1919, 1922, 1923, 1924, 1925, 1926, 1927, 1929, 1931, 1932, 1934, 1936, 1937, 1944, 1945, 1947, 1951, 1965, 1967, 1972, 1973, 1974, 1975, 1976, 1977, 1985, 1996, 1998, 2000, 2002, 2003.
U.C.G. (15)—1917, 1920, 1928, 1930, 1948, 1949, 1956, 1957, 1964, 1968, 1978, 1979, 1989, 1990, 1994.
U.L. (4)—1995, 2004, 2005, 2006.
U.U.J. (3)—1992, 1993, 1997.
Waterford I.T. (3)—1999. 2001, 2009.
Q.U.B. (1)—1991.

1915—U.C.D.
1916—U.C.D.
1917—U.C.G.
1918—U.C.D.
1919—U.C.C.
1920—U.C.G.
1921—U.C.D.
1922—U.C.C.
1923—U.C.C.
1924—U.C.C.
1925—U.C.C.
1926—U.C.C.
1927—U.C.C.
1928—U.C.G.
1929—U.C.C.
1930—U.C.G.
1931—U.C.C.
1932—U.C.C.
1933—U.C.D.
1934—U.C.C.
1935—U.C.D.
1936—U.C.C.
1937—U.C.C.
1938—U.C.D.
1939—U.C.D.
1940—U.C.D.
1941—U.C.D.
1942—U.C.D.
1943—Not Played.
1944—U.C.C.
1945—U.C.C.
1946—U.C.D.
1947—U.C.C.
1948—U.C.G.
1949—U.C.G.
1950—U.C.D.
1951—U.C.C.
1952—U.C.D.
1953—U.C.D.
1954—U.C.D.
1955—U.C.D.
1956—U.C.G.
1957—U.C.G.
1958—U.C.D.
1959—U.C.D.
1960—U.C.D.
1961—U.C.D.
1962—U.C.D.
1963—Undecided.
1964—U.C.G.

1965—U.C.C.
1966—U.C.D.
1967—U.C.C.
1968—U.C.G.
1969—U.C.D.
1970—U.C.D.
1971—U.C.D.
1972—U.C.C.
1973—U.C.C.
1974—U.C.C.
1975—U.C.C.
1976—U.C.C.
1977—U.C.C.
1978—U.C.G.
1979—U.C.G.
1980—U.C.D.
1981—U.C.D.
1982—U.C.D.
1983—U.C.D.
1984—U.C.D.
1985—U.C.C.
1986—U.C.D.
1987—U.C.D.
1988—U.C.D.
1989—U.C.G.
1990—U.C.G.
1991—Q.U.B.
1992—U.U.J.
1993—U.U.J.
1994—U.C.G.
1995—U.L.
1996—U.C.C.
1997—U.U.J.
1998—U.C.C.
1999—W.I.T. (Waterford Institute of Technology)
2000—U.C.C.
2001—W.I.T.
2002—U.C.C.
2003—U.C.C.
2004—U.L.
2005—U.L.
2006—U.L.
2007—U.C.D.
2008—U.C.D.
2009—W.I.T.

PURCELL CUP

ROLL OF HONOUR

Thomond College, Limerick (7)—1980, 1981, 1985, 1986, 1987, 1988, 1991.
Mary Immaculate, Limerick (5)—1977, 1978, 1983, 1989, 1998.
Athone R.T.C. (3)—1993, 1995, 2007.
U.U.J. (3)—2000, 2003, 2006.
Ulster Polytechnic (2)—1979, 1984.
Waterford R.T.C. (2)—1990, 1992.
Queen's University, Belfast (2)—1997, 2008.
Athlone I.T. (2)—2004, 2009.
U.C.C. (1)—1994.
St. Patrick's, Maynooth (1)—1996.
St. Mary's, Belfast (1)—1982.
Limerick I.T. (1)—1999.
Cork I.T. (1)—2001.
Carlow I.T. (1)—2002.
Garda College (1)—2005.

1977—Mary Immaculate, Limerick
1978—Mary Immaculate, Limerick
1979—Ulster Polytechnic, Belfast
1980—Thomond/N.I.H.E., Limerick
1981—Thomond/N.I.H.E., Limerick
1982—St. Mary's, Belfast
1983—Mary Immaculate, Limerick
1984—Ulster Polytechnic, Belfast
1985—Thomond College, Limerick
1986—Thomond College, Limerick
1987—Thomond College, Limerick
1988—Thomond College, Limerick
1989—Mary Immaculate, Limerick
1990—Waterford R.T.C.
1991—Thomond College, Limerick
1992—Waterford R.T.C.
1993—Athlone R.T.C.
1994—University College, Cork
1995—Athlone R.T.C.
1996—St. Patrick's, Maynooth
1997—Queen's University, Belfast
1998—Mary Immaculate, Limerick
1999—Limerick I.T.
2000—U.U.J.
2001—Cork IT
2002—Carlow IT
2003—U.U.J.
2004—Athlone IT
2005—Garda College
2006—U.U.J.
2007—Athlone IT
2008—Queen's University, Belfast
2009—Athlone IT

CAMOGIE IN THE COLLEGES

ALL-IRELAND COLLEGES SENIOR CHAMPIONSHIP

ROLL OF HONOUR

St. Raphael's, Loughrea (8)—1985, 1986,1987, 1988, 1989, 1990, 1991, 1992.
St. Mary's, Charleville (8)—1996, 1997, 1998, 1999, 2001, 2002, 2004, 2006.
Presentation Kilkenny (3)—1969, 1970, 1995.
Presentation, Athenry (3)—1974, 1975, 1978.
Coláiste Bríde, Enniscorthy (3)—2003, 2004, 2005.
St. Brigid's, Callan (3)—1993, 2008, 2009.
Sacred Heart, Newry (1)—1971.

Presentation, Oranmore (1)—1972.
Presentation, Mountmellick (1)—1973.
St. Aloysius, Cork (1)—1976.
Scoil Mhuire, Cashel (1)—1977.
North Presentation, Cork (1)—1980.
St. Patrick's, Cork (1)—1981.
St. Patrick's, Shannon (1)—1982.
St. John of God, Artane (1)—1983.
Maryfield College, Dublin (1)—1984.
St. Mary's, Nenagh (1)—1994.
St. Mary's, Magherafelt (1)—2007.

1969—Pres., Kilkenny 3-2; St. Aloysius, Cork 1-2.
1970—Pres., Kilkenny 2-3; Sacred Heart, Newry 1-1
1971—Sacred Heart, Newry 3-2; Pres. Mountmellick 2-1
1972—Pres., Oranmore 6-1; St. Louis, Kilkeel 4-4
1973—Pres., Mountmellick 4-2; Pres., Athenry 1-2
1974—Pres., Athenry 3-1; St. Louis, Kilkeel 1-0
1975—Pres., Athenry 7-4; St. Brigid's, Callan 2-4
1976—St. Aloysius, Cork 2-2; Pres., Athenry 0-2
1977—Scoil Mhuire, Cashel 2-2; Pres., Athenry 1-3
1978—Pres., Athenry 2-3; Loreto, Coleraine 2-2
1979—Scoil Mhuire, Cashel 3-3; Pres., Athenry 1-3
1980—North Pres., Cork 4-7; Assumption, Walkinstown 1-1
1981—St. Patrick's, Cork 1-3; Assumption, Walkinstown 0-5
1982—St. Patrick's, Shannon 1-7; St. Raphael's, Loughrea 1-4
1983—St. John of God, Artane 2-6; St. Patrick's, Cork 2-1
1984—Maryfield College, Dublin 2-5; North Pres., Cork 0-5
1985—St. Raphael's, Loughrea 4-7; St. Patrick's, Cork 3-3
1986—St. Raphael's, Loughrea 3-5; F.C.J., Bunclody 0-4
1987—St. Raphael's, Loughrea 3-8; St. Marys, Charleville 0-4
1988—St. Raphael's, Loughrea 2-13; F.C.J., Bunclody 1-5
1989—St. Raphael's, Loughrea 5-9; St. Patrick's, Keady 2-10
1990—St. Raphael's, Loughrea 3-11; Scoil Mhuire, Cashel 2-0
1991—St. Raphael's, Loughrea 3-6; Vocational, Thomastown 0-0
1992—St. Raphael's, Loughrea 7-7; St. Brigid's, Callan 2-4
1993—St. Brigid's, Callan 3-7; St. Mary's, Charleville 1-2
1994—St. Marys, Nenagh 1-10; St. Patrick's, Maghera 1-2
1995—Pres., Kilkenny 3-4; St. Mary's, Charleville 2-4
1996—St. Mary's, Charleville 1-15; St. Raphael's, Loughrea 3-3
1997—St. Mary's, Charleville 2-16; St. Brigid's, Loughrea 4-2
1998—St. Mary's, Charleville 1-11; Coláiste Bríde, Enniscorthy 1-4
1999—St. Mary's, Charleville 3-10; Coláiste Bhríde, Enniscorthy 0-5
2000—St.Mary's, Nenagh 3-6; Seamount, Kinvara 0-7
2001—St.Mary's, Charleville 4-7; Loretto, Kilkenny 0-3
2002—St.Mary's, Charleville 4-19; Portumna CS 1-9
2003—Coláiste Bríde, Enniscorthy 5-7; St.Patrick's, Maghera 1-3
2004—Coláiste Bríde, Enniscorthy 4-7; St.Mary's, Charleville 1-4
2005—Coláiste Bríde, Enniscorthy 1-8; St.Mary's, Charleville 2-3
2006—St.Mary's, Charleville 1-11; Presentation College, Athenry 0-4
2007—St. Mary's, Magherafelt 2-9; Presentation College, Athenry 2-6
2008—St. Brigid's Callan, Kilkenny 3-7; St. Mary's, Charleville 0-6.
2009—St. Brigid's Callan, Kilkenny 1-11; Portumna CS 1-6

ALL-IRELAND COLLEGES JUNIOR CHAMPIONSHIP

ROLL OF HONOUR

St. Mary's, Charleville (9)—1986, 1987, 1994, 1995, 1999, 2001, 2002, 2003, 2006.
St. Raphael's, Loughrea (4)—1984, 1985, 1988, 1989.
Presentation, Athenry (4)—1974, 1976, 1977, 2005.
Scoil Mhuire, Cashel (2)—1975, 1978.
Maryfield College (2)—1980, 1982.
Mercy, Roscommon (2)—1979, 1983.
St. Mary's, Nenagh (2)—1991, 1992.
Coláiste Bríde, Enniscorthy (2)—2000, 2004.
Loreto, Kilkenny (2)—2007, 2009.
St. John of God, Artane (1)—1981.
St. Brigid's, Callan (1)—1990.
F.C.J., Bunclody (1)—1993.
St. Mary's, Magherafelt (1)—1996.
Holy Rosary, Mountbellew (1)—1997.
Seamount, Kinvara (1)—1998.
Cross & Passion, Ballycastle (1)—2008.

1974—Pres., Athenry 3-0; North Pres., Cork 0-0
1975—Scoil Mhuire, Cashel 4-0; Pres., Terenure 1-0
1976—Pres., Athenry 4-2; Scoil Mhuire, Cashel 3-2
1977—Pres. Athenry 4-1; Sacred Heart, Cork 1-3
1978—Scoil Mhuire, Cashel 2-3; Vocational, Bawnboy 0-1

1979—Mercy, Roscommon 1-2; Scoil Pol, Kilfinane 0-1
1980—Maryfield College 2-3; Pres., de la Salle, Hospital 1-5
1981—St. John of God, Artane 4-0; St. Patrick's, Cork 0-2
1982—Maryfield College 3-9; St. Raphael's, Loughrea 4-0
1983—Mercy, Roscommon 7-1; St. Paul's, Kilrea 1-3
1984—St. Raphael's, Loughrea 6-8; St. Patrick's, Shannon 2-1
1985—St. Raphael's, Loughrea 3-4; Colaiste Muire, Ennis 1-0
1986—St Mary's, Charleville 2-6; F.C.J., Bunclody 0-3
1987—St Mary's, Charleville 2-3; St. Raphael's, Loughrea 1-4
1988—St. Raphael's, Loughrea 5-7; St. Mary's, Macroom 1-0
1989—St. Raphael's, Loughrea 5-0; St. Patrick's, Maghera 0-1
1990—St. Brigid's, Callan 5-8; St. Patrick's, Maghera 1-4
1991—St. Mary's, Nenagh 3-9; St. Cuan's, Castleblakeney 1-10
1992—St. Marys, Nenagh 2-6; St. Mary's, Magherafelt 0-8
1993—F.C.J., Bunclody 2-7; St. Mary's, Charleville 1-4
1994—St. Mary's, Charleville 3-6; St. Mary's, Magherafelt 1-5
1995—St. Mary's, Charleville 2-12; St. Mary's, Magherafelt 1-1
1996—St. Mary's, Magherafelt 1-10; F.C.J., Bunclody 0-4
1997—Holy Rosary, Mountbellew 2-4; St. Mary's, Charleville 1-5
1998—Seamount, Kinvara 3-8; St. Mary's, Magherafelt 1-2
1999—St. Mary's, Charleville 2-8; Seamount, Kinvara 0-6
2000—Coláiste Bríde, Enniscorthy 3-5; Seamount, Kinvara 0-8
2001—St.Mary's, Charleville 7-16; St.Mary's, Magherafelt 1-2
2002—St.Mary's, Charleville 4-10; Colaiste Bride, Eniscorthy 4-8
2003—St. Mary's, Charleville 9-9; Portumna Community College 0-3
2004—Colaiste Bride, Enniscorthy 3-10; St.Mary's, Magherafelt 1-2
2005—Presentation College, Athenry 3-10; St.Mary's, Magherafelt 2-3
2006—St. Mary's, Charleville 1-14; Portumna Community College 0-4
2007—Loreto, Kilkenny 0-7; Portumna Community College 0-5
2008—Cross and Passion, Ballycastle 2-8; St. Brigid's, Loughrea 2-5
2009—Loreto, Kilkenny 2-7; St. Patrick's Maghera 0-9.

THE COMPLETE HANDBOOK OF

GAELIC GAMES

LADIES FOOTBALL

Records

LADIES' FOOTBALL

LADIES FOOTBALL CONTINUES TO EVOLVE

2009 saw a changeover at the top in Ladies Football as Pat Quill took over the Presidency from Geraldine Giles. Geraldine served two terms in the position and was a hard working, popular and very well respected representative for the sport. She officially handed the presidency over to Pat at Congress in March but he was no stranger to the role having already served a term from 1985-1988.

The sport has changed to an almost unrecognisable degree in those 20 years, reflected by the role the Association played this year in the launch of an Integration and Inclusion Strategy in tandem with the GAA. Over the last decade or so, Ireland's population demographic has changed beyond and Ladies Football has worked to adapt to that.

The GAA celebrated its 125 year anniversary this year too and the growth and success of Ladies Football is acknowledged as one of the most important landmarks in the GAA's history. Before the association's establishment, women had no real outlet for sport and stood at the background of the GAA. The Ladies Gaelic Football Association now boasts a membership well in excess of 130,000. The fun and enjoyment the sport brings to young girls and women all over Ireland and overseas is the main reason people are involved in the sport.

In 2009, the Association continued to abide by the ambition to offer an inclusive and welcoming environment for everyone and to encourage women and girls of all abilities to play sport for fun and get out and be active. This is proving to be a successful mantra that marks Ladies Football out and contributes to its popularity.

Initiatives to this end have continued to grow and develop through the course of this year, including Gaelic4Girls and Gaelic4Mothers. The first ever Gaelic4Mothers National Blitz was held in Dublin and attracted over 500 players. 43 teams from 25 clubs were involved and the size of the event was a real testament to the ongoing success of the programme.

At a competitive level, Cork continued their run of success, securing a coveted fifth TG4 Senior All-Ireland trophy in a row. A newly revitalised Dublin side came close to knocking the Rebelettes from their mantle, but just fell short. The reappearance of Dublin in the senior All-Ireland Final after five years is encouraging and they contributed to a classic triple header of finals in Croke Park.

Antrim and Limerick played out a storming final at Junior level with last year's beaten semi-finalists Antrim emerging five-point winners against Limerick to secure a place in the 2010 intermediate championship.

At Intermediate level, Clare made up for last year's final heartbreak by capturing the TG4 All-Ireland ladies intermediate football championship crown. The Banner County received a fierce test from first-time finalists Fermanagh but eventually emerged five-point winners to move into the 2010 senior championship. This shows the depth of talent that is emerging across the country and the continuous improvement of standards in the game.

The TG4 All-Ireland Ladies Football Finals again attracted over 22,000 spectators to Croke Park, a remarkable achievement for a stand alone female sports fixture. Moreover, TG4 was the most popular channel in Ireland during its live coverage of the 2009 finals and the Senior Final between Cork and Dublin was watched by one in four television viewers in Ireland that afternoon. It had an average of 169,000 viewers throughout the match, peaking at 230,000, making it TG4's third most popular programme of 2009 to date.

TG4 has continued to be a massive contributor to the development of Ladies Football and at a time of economic difficulty, its support has been unwavering. Ladies Football also secured another dedicated sponsor in Bord Gáis Energy, which sponsored the Ladies National Football Leagues for the first time this year. Like TG4, Lucozade Sport, O'Neills and Pat the Baker, Bord Gáis Energy is a committed and pro-active sponsor and the Association is fortunate to have partners like these on board. They are crucial to the ongoing growth and development of Ladies Football.

Playing Rules

The playing rules of ladies' Gaelic football are similar to that of men's Gaelic football. There are some modifications which are designed mostly to speed up the game and to eliminate unnecessary physical contact which are outlined as follows:

1. A size four football is used in all grades of competition.
2. A player may pick the ball off the ground providing she is in a standing position. (The standing restriction does not apply to the goalkeeper inside the small parallelogram.)
3. A player while on the ground may play the ball away from her but cannot bring it into her possession.
4. All deliberate bodily contact is forbidden. When executing the tackle to dispossess an opponent it must be timed as the ball leaves the hands of the player in possession, i.e. while the ball is being hopped or in the act of soloing or kicking. It may also be knocked from an opponent's hands by flicking it with the open hand.
5. Deliberate use of the shoulder is forbidden.
6. When a free is awarded any player has the option to take it either from the hand or off the ground.
7. A team may use five substitutes during the game.

ALL-IRELAND SENIOR CHAMPIONSHIP

1974—Tipperary 2-3, Offaly 2-2
1975—Tipperary 1-4, Galway 0-0
1976—Kerry 4-6, Offaly 1-5
1977—Cavan 4-3, Roscommon 2-3
1978—Roscommon 2-3, Tipperary 0-5
1979—Offaly 2-6, Tipperary 3-3
1980—Tipperary 1-1, Cavan 0-1
1981—Offaly 1-11, Cavan 4-0
1982—Kerry 1-8, Offaly 1-2
1983—Kerry 4-6, Wexford 1-7
1984—Kerry 0-5, Leitrim 0-3
1985—Kerry 2-9, Laois 0-5
1986—Kerry 1-10, Wexford 0-8
1987—Kerry 2-10, Westmeath 2-2
1988—Kerry 2-12, Laois 3-3
1989—Kerry 1-13, Wexford 1-5
1990—Kerry 1-9, Laois 0-6
1991—Waterford 5-8, Laois 3-7
1992—Waterford 2-10, Laois 3-4
1993—Kerry 4-8, Laois 2-6
1994—Waterford 2-10, Monaghan 0-12
1995—Waterford 4-4, Monaghan 1-5
1996—Monaghan 2-9, Laois 2-9 (draw)
Monaghan 2-11, Laois 1-9 (replay)
1997—Monaghan 2-15, Waterford 1-16
1998—Waterford 1-16, Monaghan 4-7 (draw)
Waterford 2-14, Monaghan 3-8 (replay)
1999—Mayo 0-12, Waterford 0-8
2000—Mayo 3-6, Waterford 0-14
2001—Laois 2-14, Mayo 1-16
2002—Mayo 0-12, Monaghan 1-8
2003—Mayo 1-4, Dublin 0-5
2004—Galway 3-8, Dublin 0-11
2005—Cork 1-11, Galway 0-8
2006—Cork 1-7 Armagh 1-6
2007—Cork 2-11, Mayo 2-6
2008—Cork 4-13, Monaghan 0-11
2009—Cork 1-9, Dublin 0-11

INTERMEDIATE CHAMPIONSHIP

2007—Leitrim 0-17, Wexford 1-10
2008—Tipperary 0-14, Clare 1-08
2009—Clare 3-10, Fermanagh 1-11

JUNIOR CHAMPIONSHIP

1985—Galway 5-7, Cork 0-3
1986—Waterford 4-13, Wexford 0-0
1987—Mayo 4-10, Wexford 4-7
1988—Leitrim 2-8, London 0-5
1989—Dublin 1-8, Clare 2-5
1990—Wicklow 3-3, London 2-1
1991—Clare 0-8, London 1-2
1992—Monaghan 2-8, London 2-6
1993—London 4-8, Donegal 0-3
1994—Meath 5-13, Donegal 1-3
1995—Cork 4-8, Tyrone 3-2
1996—Clare 5-9, Longford 4-9
1997—Longford 2-12, Tyrone 1-11
1998—Louth 4-8, Roscommon 2-9
1999—Tyrone 3-12, New York 2-4
2000—Down 0-14, Galway 1-9
2001—Roscommon 1-18, Kildare 0-8
2002—Galway 2-17, Donegal 2-7
2003—Donegal 3-14, Kildare 0-12
2004—Kildare 2-13, Sligo 3-5
2005—Armagh 0-12, Sligo 0-9
2006—Sligo 0-08, Leitrim 0-04
2007—Kilkenny 3-05, London 2-05
2008—London 5-05, Derry 1-11
2009—Antrim 3-10, Limerick 2-8

UNDER-18 CHAMPIONSHIP

1980—Kerry 10-7, Cavan 2-1
1981—Kerry 3-8, Wexford 2-5
1982—Wexford 1-5, Leitrim 0-6
1983—Wexford 5-8, Leitrim 0-1
1984—Wexford 4-4, Cork 4-2
1985—Cork 2-5, Wexford 2-3
1986—Wexford 3-6, Clare 1-5
1987—Mayo 1-8, Cork 2-4

1988—Cork 3-5, Wexford 0-4
1989—Clare 2-11, Laois 0-7
1990—Clare 2-6, Dublin 0-10
1991—Waterford 6-17, Roscommon 1-3
1992—Laois 4-5, Waterford 2-8
1993—Waterford 4-9, Wexford 1-5
1994—Monaghan 1-14, Wexford 1-14
1995—Kerry 4-8, Wexford 4-3
1996—Waterford 4-10, Mayo 3-9
1997—Waterford 4-10, Mayo 3-9
1998—Monaghan 2-12, Mayo 1-7
1999—Monaghan 4-11, Mayo 3-5
2000—Tyrone 1-6, Waterford 7-12
(Tyrone awarded title as Waterford played 6 subs)
2001—Waterford 6-12, Meath 2-6
2002—Galway 3-20, Monaghan 4-5
2003—Cork 1-15, Mayo 3-5
2004—Cork 4-17, Laois 0-8
2005—Galway 5-8, Donegal 1-8
2006—Cork 1-22, Galway 0-08
2007—Cork 6-08, Dublin 2-10
2008—Dublin 2-18, Tyrone 1-04
2009—Donegal 5-13, Clare 5-5

NATIONAL SENIOR LEAGUE

1978—Tipperary 1-5, Cavan 1-3
1979—Tipperary 1-6, Galway 0-8
1980—Kerry 4-8, Offaly 3-3
1981—Kerry 5-4, Tipperary 1-8
1982—Kerry 5-7, Tipperary 2-4
1983—Kerry 1-9, Leitrim 2-6 (draw)
Kerry 1-4, Leitrim 0-4 (replay)
1984—Kerry 2-10, Laois 1-7
1985—Kerry 5-11, Leitrim 0-1
1986—Wexford 3-2, Laois 0-6
1987—Kerry 6-12, Laois 1-2
1988—Kerry 2-8, Waterford 0-6
1989—Kerry 4-9, Waterford 2-7
1990—Kerry 2-11, Waterford 4-3
1991—Kerry 2-12, Waterford 4-3
1992—Waterford 1-8, Laois 2-3
1993—Laois 1-16, Cork 1-8
1994—Monaghan 2-9, Mayo 1-10
1995—Waterford 3-11, Mayo 4-8 (draw)
Waterford 2-13, Mayo 3-8 (replay)
1996—Monaghan 3-16, Mayo 4-3
1997—Monaghan 4-6, Waterford 1-15 (draw)
Monaghan 4-15, Waterford 3-13 (replay)
1998—Waterford 3-10, Clare 4-6
1999—Monaghan 4-6, Waterford 0-12
2000—Mayo 1-11, Tyrone 2-6
2001—Clare 2-10, Monaghan 1-10
2002—Waterford 2-9, Mayo 1-9
2003—Laois 2-10, Kerry 2-9
2004—Mayo 1-13, Cork 1-11
2005—Cork 2-13, Galway 0-6
2006—Cork 0-14, Meath 0-02
2007—Mayo 1-13, Galway 0-06
2008—Cork 6-13, Kerry 2-10
2009—Cork 1-20, Mayo 0-11

SENIOR CLUB CHAMPIONSHIP

1988—Adamstown (Wexford)
1989—Ballymacarbery (Waterford)
1990—Ballymacarbery (Waterford)
1991—Ballymacarbery (Waterford)
1992—Ballymacarbery (Waterford)
1993—Ballymacarbery (Waterford)
1994—Ballymacarbery (Waterford)
1995—Ballymacarbery (Waterford)
1996—Shelmaliers (Wexford)
1997—Ballymacarbery (Waterford)
1998—Ballymacarbery (Waterford)
1999—Shelmaliers (Wexford)
2000—Monaghan Harps
2001—Donoughmore (Cork)
2002—Carnacon (Mayo)
2003—Donoughmore (Cork)
2004—Ballyboden St.Enda's (Dublin)
2005—Ballyboden St. Enda's (Dublin)
2006—Donaghmoyne (Monaghan)
2007—Carnacon (Mayo)
2008—Carnacon (Mayo)

POST-PRIMARY SCHOOLS SENIOR CHAMPIONSHIP

1985—Ballingeary VS (Cork) 2-1, Adamstown VS (Wexford) 1-1
1986—Mercy Convent, Spanish Pt. (Clare) 1-8, Adamstown VS (Wexford) 2-0
1987—Mercy Convent, Spanish Pt. (Clare) 5-5, Adamstown VS (Wexford) 0-7
1988—Presentation Convent, Portlaoise 2-4, Mercy Convent, Spanish Pt. 2-3
1989—Mercy Convent, Castlerea (Roscommon), 4-2, Tarbert Como. (Kerry) 1-5
1990—Ramsgrange CS (Wexford) 1 -6, Tarbert Como. (Kerry) 1-5
1991—Ballinrobe CS (Mayo) 4-8, Salesian Convent (Clare) 2-8
1992—Ballinrobe CS (Mayo) 2-7, Cahercon CS (Clare) 1-8
1993—Ballinrobe CS (Mayo) 3-13, Bridgetown CS (Wexford) 1-7
1994—Ballinrobe CS (Mayo) 2-10, Col. Bride, Enniscorthy (Wexford) 2-6
1995—Ballinrobe CS (Mayo) 2-18, St. Joseph's Spanish Pt. (Clare) 2-4
1996—St. Joseph's, Spanish Pt. (Clare) 2-9, St. Michael's, Navan (Meath) 1-5
1997—St. Joseph's Spanish Pt. (Clare) 3-11, Scoil Mhuire, Tourmakeady (Mayo) 1-11
1998—Intermediate School, Killorglin (Kerry) 4-10, Eureka, Kells (Meath) 0-6
1999—St. John Bosco, Caherciveen (Kerry) 2-11, St. Leo's (Carlow) 1-8.
2000—St.Louis (Monaghan) 2-8, KIllorglin (Kerry) 1-9

2001—Colaiste na Sceilige (Kerry) 4-15, Colaiste Mhuire Tourmakeady (Mayo) 0-7
2002—Colaiste na Sceilige (Kerry) 2-13, St.Michael's Loreto Navan (Meath) 0-11
2003—Presentation Tuam (Galway) 4-10, Colaiste na Sceilige (Kerry) 2-10
2004—St.Louis (Monaghan) 5-11, Presentation Tuam (Galway) 4-4
2005—St.Louis (Monaghan) 3-19, Colaiste na Sceilige (Kerry) 4-13
2006—St. Louis (Monaghan) 4-08 St Leo's (Carlow) 2-6
2007—St. Leo's (Carlow) 3-09 Loretto SS Fermoy (Cork) 2-10
2008—St Mary's Mallow (Cork) 0-14 St Louis (Monaghan) 1-9
2009—Convent of Mercy (Roscommon) 4-10 Loreto College (Fermoy) 2-7

INTERPROVINCIAL CHAMPIONSHIP

1976—Munster 1-12, Leinster 0-2
1977—Munster 3-5, Connacht 1-3
1978—Connacht 1-8, Leinster 1-5
1979—Connacht 1-4, Leinster 1-0
1980—Munster 5-6, Leinster 3-9
1981—Munster 6-7, Ulster 1-1
1982—Leinster 1-8, Munster 1-6
1983—Leinster 1-9, Munster 0-3
1984—Munster 4-9, Connacht 0-6
1985—Munster 1 -6, Leinster 0-6
1986—Munster 3-7, Leinster 1-5
1987—Munster 2-10, Leinster 0-7
1988—Munster 2-10, Leinster 0-4
1989—Leinster 2-8, Connacht 1-8
1990—Leinster 1-3, Munster 0-4
1991—Munster 4-11, Leinster 3-3
1992—Leinster 2-8, Munster 1-9
1993—Munster 3-8, Leinster 1-5
1994—Leinster 3-7, Munster 0-4
1995—Munster 2-11, Leinster 1-9
1996—Munster 4-8, Colleges 0-9
1997—Connacht 1-10, Colleges 0-11
1998—Leinster 3-14, Connacht 0-12
2000—Connacht 2-13, Leinster 1-11
2001—No Competition due to foot & mouth disease
2002—Ulster 0-19, Connacht 2-8
2003—Munster 2-11, Ulster 2-4
2004—Munster 1-16, Leinster 1-7
2005—Leinster 1-11, Munster 2-6
2006—Leinster 2-12, Ulster 0-09
2007—Munster 2-13, Ulster 2-11
2008—Ulster 6-10, Munster 1-11
2009—Munster 2-6, Leinster 0-8

THE COMPLETE HANDBOOK OF

GAELIC GAMES

HANDBALL
Records

HANDBALL — A GAA Sport for life!

Irish handballers amassed an incredible 36 titles at the World Championships in Portland, Oregon in 2009 and with the nation's hosting of the event in 2012, there are plenty more success stories to look forward to in the future.

Cavan ace, Paul Brady, became the first player in history to collect three consecutive Men's Open Singles titles when he defeated Texan, Allan Garner, in an 11-7 tiebreaker. The Breffni man, who also plays senior inter-county football for Cavan, contested the event with a serious muscle injury but despite this, was in imperious form throughout the event.

Brady's victory over Garner followed his 5-in-a-row US Nationals triumph in June and 6th All-Ireland senior singles success earlier in the year. At 30 years of age, there is no doubt he will already be thinking ahead to a remarkable fourth win in his own country in 2012.

Likewise, Antrim's Fiona Shannon retained her Women's Open title, and was in unstoppable form in the Ladies Open Singles. The Saffron lady overcame a tough challenge from her club colleague, Aisling Reilly, in the final to take her third title in succession. She also made it a rare double when she teamed up sister, Sibeal, to collect the Open Doubles title. In the final, they came from 18-9 down in the second game, having lost the first, to take an 11-3 tie-breaker win against compatriots, Aisling Reilly and Maria Daly.

In the Men's Open Doubles, Dublin's Eoin Kennedy teamed up with Cavan's Michael Finnegan and it proved a winning combination as the duo picked up their second world open doubles titles. Westmeath's Robbie McCarthy and Meath's Brian Carroll showed super form in denying USA number 1 seeds, Alan Garner and Emmet Peixoto, in their quarter-final meeting but in the final were outplayed by their more experienced rivals.

One of the most famous names in Irish handball, Kilkenny's Michael 'Ducksy' Walsh continued his incredible success story with emphatic World Masters Singles and Doubles successes, teaming up with Dublin's Egin Jensen, to win the latter.

Ireland simply blew away the opposition at underage level. In the singles competitions the brilliant Boys 19 & Under Singles triumph of Limerick's Seamus O'Carroll was one of the highlights of the championships, as he defeated highly regarded American, Tyree Bastidas and Mexican, Luis Cordova, to claim the honours.

All-Ireland under 16 singles champion, Martin Mulkerrins, came through a huge draw in the Boys 17 & Under Singles championship before denying Cork's Killian Carroll in the final and he made it a clean sweep in the grade with a doubles title win alongside Kildare's Niall O'Connor.

Monaghan, who had never tasted world championship success until 2009, saw an amazing treble at this year's championships. At 13 & Under, Darren Doherty had a double in 4-wall and one-wall while in 15 & Under Padraig McKenna secured a famous triumph. Both players look real stars of the future. Daniel Curry of Wicklow also displayed amazing form and completed the 40x20 and one-wall 11 & Under double.

In the junior girls events, there were eyecatching 4-wall singles wins for Ciana Ni Churraoin (Gawlay), Lauren O'Riordan (Roscommon), Lorraine Havern (Down) and Shauna Hilley (Wicklow) while Catriona Casey & Aisling O'Keefe (Cork) were crowned Girls 19 & Under Doubles champions and O'Riordan and Martina McMahon (Limerick) picked up the 15 & Under girls doubles honours.

Other highlights in the handball calendar included Mayo's Dessie Keegan and Joe McCann collecting Connacht's first senior title since 1985 when they defeated Cavan duo, Paul Brady and Michael Finnegan in a nail-biting All-Ireland 40x20 Senior Doubles Final. In June, Armagh's Charly Shanks stole the show at the One-Wall Nationals in Mayo, where he was unstoppable in the Men's Open, recording an emphatic win over Keegan in the final. Dublin's Eoin Kennedy had a brilliant year, reclaiming the GAA Hardball Senior crown and then continued his domination of the 60x30 Senior Championships, where he collected his 20th All-Ireland senior title. He also added the Senior Doubles crown, where he partnered Egin Jensen, as they recorded victory over Meath's Tom Sheridan and Brian Carroll. Sheridan and Carroll had captured the Senior hardball doubles honours in July.

ALL-IRELAND 40x20 CHAMPIONSHIPS

SENIOR SINGLES

1975—P. Kirby (Clare)
1976—P. Kirby (Clare)
1977—P. Kirby (Clare)
1978—P. Kirby (Clare)
1979—P. Kirby (Clare)
1980—P. Kirby (Clare)
1981—T. Ryan (Tipperary)
1982—T. Ryan (Tipperary}
1983—T. Ryan (Tipperary)
1984—M. Hennigan (Mayo)
1985—M. Hennigan (Mayo)
1986—Michael Walsh (Kilkenny)
1987—Mickey Walsh (Roscommon)
1988—M. Walsh (Kilkenny)
1989—M. Walsh (Kilkenny)
1990—M. Walsh (Kilkenny)
1991—M. Walsh (Kilkenny)
1992—W. O'Connor (Meath)
1993—E. Corbett (Tipperary)
1994—E. Corbett (Tipperary)
1995—P. McAuley (Louth)
1996—M. Walsh (Kilkenny)
1997—P. McAuley (Louth)
1998—M. Walsh (Kilkenny)
1999—T. Healy (Cork)
2000—T .Healy (Cork)
2001—T. Healy (Cork)
2002—E. Kennedy (Dublin)
2003—P. Brady (Cavan)
2004—T. Healy (Cork)
2005—P. Brady (Cavan)
2006—P. Brady (Cavan)
2007—P. Brady (Cavan)
2008—P. Brady (Cavan)
2009—P. Brady (Cavan)

SENIOR DOUBLES

1975—P. and M. Kirby (Clare)
1976—P. and M. Kirby (Clare)
1977—P. and M. Kirby (Clare)
1978—P. and M. Kirby (Clare)
1979—P. and M. Kirby (Clare)
1980—P. McGee and P. McCormack (Mayo)
1981—P. Delaney and W. Mullins (Offaly)
1982—J. Fleming and P. Cleary (Wexford)
1983—J. Fleming and P. Cleary (Wexford)
1984—J. Fleming and P. Cleary (Wexford)
1985—E. Rabbitt and P. Delaney (Galway)
1986—M. Walsh and M. Reade (Kilkenny)
1987—T. Sheridan and J. McGovern (Meath)
1988—T. Sheridan and J. McGovern (Meath)
1989—M. Walsh and M. Reade (Kilkenny)
1990—T. Sheridan and J. McGovern (Meath)
1991—E. Corbett and J. O'Donoghue (Tipperary)
1992—T. Sheridan and J. McGovern (Meath)
1993—T. Sheridan and J. McGovern (Meath)
1994—M. Walsh and D.J. Carey (Kilkenny)
1995—M.. Walsh and D.J. Carey (Kilkenny)
1996—T. Sheridan and E. Jensen (Meath)
1997—T. Sheridan and E. Jensen (Meath)
1998—M. Walsh and D.J. Carey (Kilkenny)
1999—T. Healy and J. Herlihy (Cork)
2000—T. Sheridan and W.O'Connor (Meath)
2001—T. Healy and S.Palmer (Cork)
2002—T. Sheridan and W.O'Connor (Meath)
2003—P .Brady and M.Finnegan (Cavan)
2004—P. Brady and M.Finnegan (Cavan)
2005—E .Kennedy and E.Jensen (Dublin)
2006—P. Brady and M. Finnegan (Cavan)
2007—P. Brady and M. Finnegan (Cavan)
2008—P. Brady and M. Finnegan (Cavan)
2009—J. McCann and D. Keegan (Mayo)

JUNIOR SINGLES

1975—P. O'Keeffe (Tipperary)
1976—M. Walsh {Roscommon)
1977—P. Morris (Cork)
1978—P. Delaney (Offaly)
1979—Tony Ryan (Tipperary)
1980—G. O'Callaghan (Cork)
1981—J. Fleming (Wexford)
1982—G. Coughlan (Clare)
1983—E. Conneely (Galway)
1984—W. Bourke (Kilkenny)
1985—M. Walsh (Kilkenny)
1986—J. Herlihy (Cork)
1987—P. McAuley (Louth)
1988—W. Silcock (Antrim)
1989—E. Jenson (Meath)
1990—D. J. Carey (Kilkenny)
1991—F. McCann (Sligo)
1992—J. Donlan (Clare)
1993—P. Crothers (Antrim)
1994—D. Moloney (Tipperary)
1995—J. O'Dwyer (Tipperary)
1996—R. Breen (Wexford)
1997—D. Lynch (Kerry)
1998—G. Buggy (Wexford)
1999—J. King (Carlow)
2000—T. Savage (Down)
2001—S. Dormer (Laois)
2002—D. Frawley (Clare)
2003—C. O'Brien (Offaly)
2004—O. Cassidy (Mayo)
2005—E. Burke (Kilkenny)
2006—P. Donovan (Laois)
2007—S. O'Neill (Tyrone)
2008—R. Kelly (Tyrone)
2009—C. Doolin (Roscommon)

JUNIOR DOUBLES

1975—T. Morrissey and E. Farrell (Tipperary)
1976—P. Kealy and W. Mullins (Offaly)
1977—G. Scully and M. Ward (Galway)
1978—M. Aherne and B. O'Brien (Kerry)
1979—E. Rabbitte and J. Callinan (Galway)
1980—M. Hennigan and M. Sweeney (Mayo)
1981—J. Fleming and P. Cleary (Wexford)
1982—G. Coughlan and J. Duggan (Clare)
1983—J. McGovern and M. McGovern (Meath)
1984—W. Bourke and M. Reade {Kilkenny)
1985—P. Hall and D. O'Brien (Dublin)
1986—T. Quish and J. Quish (Limerick)
1987—P. McAuley and M. Maher (Louth)
1988—N. Breen and P. Devanney (RIP) (Clare)
1989—W. Pratt and P. O'Keeffe (Kilkenny)
1990—E. Corbett and J. O'Donoghue (Tipperary)
1991—R. McCarthy and J. Guilfoyle (Westmeath)
1992—J. Donlan and P. Walsh (Clare)
1993—P. Crothers and J. McGarry (Antrim)
1994—D. Moloney and N. Murphy (Tipperary)
1995—F. Coughlan and D. Kirby (Clare)
1996—R. Breen and B. Doyle (Wexford)
1997—D. and A. Lynch (Kerry)
1998—C. and N. Kerr (Tyrone)
1999—P. Madden and P. Coughlan (Clare)
2000—A. Kenny and I.Griffin (Dublin)
2001—A. O'Donnell and M.Tormey (Roscommon)
2002—P .Graham and P.Duffy (Antrim)
2003—D. Kelly and M.Carroll (Tipperary)
2004—P. Conway and O.Conway (Galway)
2005—T. Clifford and M.Clifford (Kilkenny)
2006—B. and. F Manogue (Kilkenny
2007—M. Lennon and P. Quaile (Wicklow)
2008—N. McDermott and N. McGrath (Roscommon)
2009—C. Doolin and A. Cunningham (Roscommon)

MINOR SINGLES

1975—M. Maher (Louth)
1976—M. Maher (Louth)
1977—T. Ryan (Tipperary)
1978—T. Ryan (Tipperary)
1979—W. O'Donnell (Tipperary)
1980—W. Bourke (Kilkenny}
1981—W. Bourke (Kilkenny}
1982—J. Duggan (Clare)
1983—M. Walsh (Kilkenny)
1984—M. Walsh (Kilkenny)
1985—W. O'Connor (Meath)
1986—P. McAuley (Louth)
1987—P. McAuley (Louth)
1988—D. J. Carey (Kilkenny)
1989—D. J. Carey (Kilkenny)
1990—P. Walsh (Clare)
1991—C. Curran (Tyrone)
1992—M. Finnegan (Cavan)
1993—M. Finnegan (Cavan)
1994—M. Finnegan (Cavan)
1995—T. Healy (Cork)
1996—T. Healy (Cork)
1997—K. Kane (Carlow)
1998—P. Brady (Cavan)
1999—Keegan (Mayo)
2000—P. Finnegan (Cavan)
2001—C. Shanks (Armagh)
2002—N. McHugh (Galway)
2003—B. Carroll (Meath)
2004—R. McCarthy (Westmeath)
2005—R. McCarthy (Westmeath)
2006—R. Hogan (Kilkenny)
2007—S. O'Carroll (Limerick)
2008—G. McConnell (Meath)
2009—C. Daly (Tyrone)

MINOR DOUBLES

1975—P. Delaney and S. O'Connell (Offaly)
1976—P. Murphy and D. Neff (Cork)
1977—T. Ryan and G. Walsh (Tipperary)
1978—T. Ryan and M. Dyer (Tipperary)
1979—M. Cantwell and W. Bourke (Kilkenny)
1980—W. Bourke and M. Lawlor (Kilkenny)
1981—W. Bourke and M. Lawlor (Kilkenny)
1982—J. Duggan and P. Clavin (Clare
1983—J. Duggan and P. Clavin (Clore)
1984—M. Walsh and P. O'Keeffe (Kilkenny)
1985—W. O'Connor and T. Sheridan (Meath)
1986—P. McAuley and J. McArdle (Louth)
1987—D. Gough and P. O'Rourke (Meath)
1988—D. J. Carey and E. Law (Kilkenny)
1989—D. J. Carey and E. Law (Kilkenny)
1990—D. King and S. Kavanagh (Carlow)
1991—D. Moloney and N. Murphy (Tipperary)
1992—M. Finnegan and D. Bartley (Cavan)
1993—M. Finnegan and R. Cunningham (Cavan)
1994—M. Finnegan and C. McDonnell (Cavan)
1995—T. and J. Healy (Cork)
1996—T. and J. Healy (Cork)
1997—B. Goff and C. Keeling (Wexford)
1998—E. and B. Kennedy (Dublin)
1999—D. Keegan and B. Hough (Mayo)
2000—M. Gregan and R.Willoughby (Wicklow)
2001—J. McCann and J.Kilcullen (Mayo)
2002—N. McHugh and T.Connaughton (Galway)
2003—D. Martin and R.O'Gara (Roscommon)
2004—R. McCarthy and J.O'Shaughnessy (Westmeath)
2005—R. McCarthy and C.Curley (Westmeath)
2006—R. Hogan and N. Anthony (Kilkenny)
2007—D. Nash and N. Malone (Clare)
2008—S. Ó Carroll and C.J. Fitzpatrick (Limerick)
2009—S. Cooney and I. McLoughlin (Mayo)

INTERMEDIATE 40X20 SINGLES

1995—C. Curran (Tyrone)
1996—G. Sweeney (Mayo)
1997—M. Finnegan (Cavan)
1998—T. Healy (Cork)
1999—P. Brady (Cavan)
2000—S. Palmer (Cork)
2001—R. McCann (Antrim)
2002—D. Keegan (Mayo)
2003—B. Goff (Wexford)
2004—C. Shanks (Armagh)
2005—M. Gregan (Wicklow)
2006—R. McCarthy (Westmeath)
2007—B. Carroll (Meath)
2008—G. Buggy (Wexford)
2009—O. McKenna (Antrim)

INTERMEDIATE 40 X 20 DOUBLES

1995—J. McAlister and S. Madden (Antrim)
1996—T. Hynes and N. Buggy (Wexford)
1997—M. Finnegan and R. Cunningham (Cavan)
1998—K. and T. Kane (Carlow)
1999—D. and A. Lynch (Kerry)
2000—S. Devine and S.O'Tuama (Antrim)
2001—J. Ryan and D.King (Carlow)
2002—D. Keegan and P.Gaffney (Mayo)
2003—C. Brennan and V.Moran (Mayo)
2004—C. Shanks and J.Doyle (Armagh)
2005—M. Gregan and J.Willoughby (Wicklow)
2006—D. Martin and R. O'Gara (Roscommon)
2007—D. Daly and N. Kerr (Tyrone)
2008—C. Jordon and P. Buckley (Cork)
2009—T. Clifford and M. Clifford (Kilkenny)

U.21 40 X 20 SINGLES

1980—T. Ryan (Tipperary)
1981—T. Ryan (Tipperary)
1982—G. Coughlan (Clare)
1983—P. Hall 1Dublin)
1984—P. Hall (Dublin)
1985—E. Jensen (Meath;
1986—E. Jensen (Meath)
1987—E. Corbett (Tipperary)
1988—J. Ryan (Carlow)
1989—D. Gough (Meath)
1990—S. Palmer (Cork)
1991—J. McKeon (Cavan)
1992—A. Benson (Dublin)
1993—D. Moloney Tipperary}
1994—R. Cunningham (Cavan)
1995—M. Finnegan (Cavan)
1996—S. Devine (Antrim)
1997—J. Doyle (Wexford)
1998—R. McCann (Antrim)
1999—P. Buckley (Cork)
2000—C. Browne (Meath)
2001—P. Finnegan (Cavan)
2002—M. Gregan (Wicklow)
2003—J. McCann (Mayo)
2004—J. Willoughby (Wicklow)
2005—G. Coonan (Tipperary)
2006—D. Daly (Tyrone)
2007—G. McCrory (Tyrone)
2008—P. McGlinchey (Tyrone)
2009—C. J. Fitzpatrick (Limerick)

U.21 40 X 20 DOUBLES

1980—P. Cleary and J. Fleming (Wexford)
1981—T. Ryan and W. O'Donnell (Tipperary)
1982—G. Coughlan and J. Duggan (Clare)
1983—J. Herlihy and N. Collins (Cork)
1984—P. Hall and D. O'Brien (Dublin)
1985—J. Kelly and P. Clooney (Cork)
1986—J. O'Donoghue and E. Corbett (Tipperary}
1987—P. O'Keeffe and P. Maher (Kilkenny)
1988—P. O'Keeffe and T. Donegan (Cork)
1989—D. Gough and J. Lynch (Meath)
1990—D. Gough and J. Lynch (Meath)
1991—G. O'Brien and E. Law (Kilkenny)
1992—D. Moloney and N. Murphy (Tipperaryl
1993—D. Moloney and N. Murphy (Tipperary}
1994—G. Kelleher and B. O'Neill (Cork)
1995—M. Finnegan and D. Leggett (Cavan)
1996—S. Devine and S. Ó Tuama (Antrim)
1997—J. Doyle and J. Bergin (Wexford)
1998—C. Jordan and J. Healy (Cork)
1999—B. and A. Marrinan (Clare)
2000—C. Browne and J.Cummins (Meath)
2001—B. Fleming and N.Fleming (Cork)
2002—M. Gregan and S.Willoughby (Wicklow)
2003—O. McKenna and K.Holmes (Antrim)
2004—C. Smyth and M.Cash (Wexford)
2005—M. McGowan and M.Marley (Donegal)
2006—D. Daly and G. McCrory (Tyrone)
2007—J. and C. Cooney (Clare)
2008—C. Hannon and C. Cooney (Clare)
2009—S. O'Carroll and C.J. Fitzpatrick (Limerick)

40 X 20 LADIES SENIOR SINGLES

1990—S. Carey (Kildare)
1991—S. Carey (Kildare)
1991—B. Hennessy (Limerick)
1992—B. Hennessy (Limerick)
1993—B. Hennessy (Limerick)
1994—B. Hennessy (Limerick)
1995—B. Hennessy (Limerick)
1996—B. Hennessy (Limerick)
1997—B. Hennessy (Limerick)
1998—B. Hennessy (Limerick)
1999—F. McKenna (Antrim)
2000—F. McKenna (Antrim)
2001—F. Shannon (Antrim)
2002—S. McKenna (Antrim)
2003—F. Shannon (Antrim)

2004—M. Daly (Kerry)
2005—M. Daly (Kerry)
2006—F. Shannon (Antrim)
2007—F. Shannon (Antrim)
2008—F. Shannon (Antrim)
2009—F. Shannon (Antrim)

40 X 20 LADIES SENIOR DOUBLES

1992—M. Lindsay, M. Armstrong (Antrim)
1993—M. Lindsay, M. Armstrong (Antrim)
1994—
1995—
1996—S. Smith, E. Campbell (Antrim)
1997—J. Keating, C. Maloney (Tipperary)
1998—F. McKenna, B. Kerr MacCorraidh Antrim
1999—F. McKenna, B. Kerr MacCorraidh (Antrim)
2000—F. McKenna, S. McKenna (Antrim)
2001—No championship
2002—A. Wrynn, F. Heal (Kildare)
2003—F. Shannon, S. McKenna (Antrim)
2004—No championship
2005—F. Shannon, S. McKenna (Antrim)
2006—F. Shannon, A. Reilly (Antrim)
2007—F. Shannon, A. Reilly (Antrim)
2008—F. Shannon, S. Gallagher (Antrim)
2009—F. Shannon, S. Gallagher (Antrim)

IRISH NATIONALS

MEN'S SINGLES

1995—D. Chapman (California)
1996—M. Walsh (Kilkenny)
1997—P. McAuley (Louth)
1998—D. Chapman (California)
1999—J. Bike (California)
2000—T. Healy (Cork)
2001—K. Kane (Carlow)
2002—E. Kennedy (Dublin)
2003—E. Kennedy (Dublin)
2004—E. Kennedy (Dublin)
2005—P. Brady (Cavan)
2006—T. Healy (Cork)
2007—T. Healy (Cork)
2008—T. Healy (Cork)
2009—P. Brady (Cavan)

WOMEN'S SINGLES

1995—B. Hennessy (Limerick)
1996—B. Hennessy (Limerick)
1997—B. Hennessy (Limerick)
1998—F. McKenna (Antrim)
1999—F. McKenna (Antrim}
2000—F. McKenna (Antrim)
2001—L. F. Gilmore (Canada)
2002—F. McKenna (Antrim)
2003—F. Shannon (Antrim)
2004—M. Daly (Kerry)
2005—F. Shannon (Antrim)
2006—F. Shannon (Antrim)
2007—F. Shannon (Antrim)
2008—A. Reilly (Antrim)
2007—F. Shannon (Antrim)
2009—F. Shannon (Antrim)

UNIVERSITIES CHAMPIONSHIPS

TEAM COMPETITION

1963—U.C.D.
1964—U.CG.
1965—U.C.D.
1966—U.C.D.
1967—U.C.D.
1968—U.C.D.
1969—U.C.D.
1970—U.C.C.
1971—U.C.G.
1972—U.C.G.
1973—U.C.G.
1974—U.C.D.
1975—U.C.C.
1976—U.C.D.
1977—U.C.D.
1978—U.C.C.
1979—U.C.G.
1980—Q.U.B.
1981—U.C.G.
1982—U.C.G.
1983—U.C.G.
1984—U.C.G.
1985—U.C.G.
1986—U.C.G.
1987—U.C.D.
1988—U.C.G.
1989—U.C.G.
1990—U.C.G.
1991—U.C.G.
1992—U.C.G.
1993—Waterford R.T.C.
1994—U.C.D.
1995—Q.U.B.
1996—U.C.C.
1997—D.I.T.
1998—N.U.I.G.
1999—U.U.J.
2000—D.I.T.
2001—D.I.T.
2002—D.I.T.
2003—Q.U.B.
2004—S.I.T.
2005—D.I.T.
2006—D.I.T.
2007—N.U.I.G.
2008—U.U.J.
2009—not played at time of going to press

MEN'S SINGLES

1975—P. Morris (UCC)
1976—C. Quinn (UCD)
1977—C. Quinn (UCD)
1978—P. Morris (UCC)
1979—M. Shiel (UCG)
1980—M. Patterson (TCD)
1981—G. Coughlan (UCG)
1982—G. Coughlan (UCG)
1983—G. Coughlan (UCG)
1984—J. Duggan (UCG)
1985—J. Duggan (UCG)
1986—J. Duggan (UCG)
1987—E. Jensen (UCD)
1988—E. Jensen (UCD)
1989—W. O'Connor (Dame St.)
1990—W. O'Connor (Dame St.)
1991—E. O'Neill (Garda)
1992—A. Benson (UCD)
1993—C. Curran (St. Mary's)
1994—C. Curran (QUB)
1995—C. Curran (QUB)
1996—C. Curran (QUB)
1997—T. Healy (UCC)
1998—P. Brady (DIT)
1999—T. Healy (UCC)
2000—P. Brady (DIT)
2001—E. Kennedy (DCU)
2002—E. Kennedy (DCU)
2003—E. Kennedy (DCU)
2004—E. Kennedy (DCU)
2005—D. Keegan (DIT)
2006—C. Shanks (QUB)
2007—G. Coonan (UL)
2008—B. Carroll (DIT)
2009—B. Carroll (DIT)

WOMEN'S SINGLES

1994—Y. Gacquin (UCG)
1995—Y. Gacquin (UCG)
1996—J. Keating (Waterford RTC)
1997—L. Campbell (QUB)
1998—B. MacCorraidh (QUB)
1999—A. Wrynn (Maynooth)
2000—F. Healy (Crumlin College)
2001—F. Healy (DIT)
2002—F. Healy (DIT)
2003—S. Gartland (QUB)
2004—M. Daly (UCC)
2005—M. Daly (UCC)
2006—M. Daly (UCC)
2007—M. Daly (UCC)
2008—E. Ní Fhallúin (UCD)
2009—Marianna Rushe (UCD)

60 X 30 MEN'S SINGLES

2002—N. McHugh (SIT)
2003—N. McHugh (SIT)
2004—B. Carroll (DIT)
2005—J. McCann (SIT)
2006—G. Coonan (UL)
2007—R. O'Gara (NUIG)
2008—N. Anthony (WIT)
2009—N. Anthony (WIT)

60 X 30 WOMEN'S SINGLES

2002—F. Healy (DIT)
2003—M. Daly (UCC)
2004—M. Daly (UCC)
2005—M. Daly (UCC)
2006—E. Ní Fhallúin (UCD)
2007—M. Rushe (NUIG)
2008—A. Prendeville (UCC)
2009—A. Prendeville (UCC)

ALL-IRELAND CHAMPIONSHIPS (1925-2009)

SENIOR SOFTBALL SINGLES

1925—M. Joyce (Dublin)
1926—T. Behan (Kilkenny)
1927—W. McGuire (Dublin)
1928—J. McNally (Mayo)
1929—D. Brennan (Kilkenny)
1930—P. Perry (Roscommon}
1931—P. Perry (Roscommon)
1932—P. Perry (Roscommon)
1933—P. Perry (Roscommon)
1934—P. Perry (Roscommon)
1935—P. Perry (Roscommon)
1936—P. Perry (Roscommon)
1937—P. Perry (Roscommon)
1938—J. J. Gilmartin (Kilkenny)
1939—J. J. Gilmartin (Kilkenny)
1940—M. Walsh (Galway)
1941—J. Dunne (Kilkenny)
1942-45—Suspended due to scarcity of softballs
1946—J. J. Gilmartin (Kilkenny)
1947—L. Rowe (Dublin)
1948—J. Bergin (Tipperary)
1949—L. Rowe (Dublin)
1950—J. Bergin (Tipperary)
1951—L. Rowe (Dublin)
1952—J. Ryan (Wexford)
1953—M. Griffin (Cork)
1954—J. Ryan (Wexford)
1955—J. Ryan (Wexford)
1956—J. Ryan (Wexford)
1957—J. Ryan (Wexford)
1958—P. Downey (Kerry)
1959—F. Confrey (Louth)
1960—F. Confrey (Louth)
1961—P. Downey (Kerry)
1962—J. Delaney (Kilkenny)
1963—J. Maher (Louth)

1964—J. Maher (Louth)
1965—R. Lyng (Wexford)
1966—S. McCabe (Monaghan)
1967—S. McCabe (Monaghan)
1968—J. Maher (Louth)
1969—J. Maher {Louth)
1970—J. Maher (Louth)
1971—R. Lyng (Wexford)
1973—P. Murphy (Wexford)
1973—J. Maher (Louth)
1974—P . Kirby (Clare)
1975—P. Kirby (Clare)
1976—P. Kirby (Clare)
1977—P. Kirby (Clare)
1978—R. Lyng (Wexford)
1979—T. O'Rourke (Kildare)
1980—P. Ryan (Dublin)
1981—P. Reilly (Kilkenny)
1982—O. Harold (Kilkenny)
1983—A. Ryan (Tipperary)
1984—T. O'Rourke (Kildare)
1985—M. Walsh (Kilkenny)
1986—M. Walsh (Kilkenny)
1987—M. Walsh (Kilkenny)
1988—M. Walsh (Kilkenny)
1989—M. Walsh (Kilkenny)
1990—M. Walsh (Kilkenny)
1991—M. Walsh (Kilkenny)
1992—M. Walsh (Kilkenny)
1993—M. Walsh (Kilkenny}
1994—M. Walsh (Kilkenny)
1995—M. Walsh (Kilkenny)
1996—M. Walsh (Kilkenny)
1997—M. Walsh (Kilkenny)
1998—W. O'Connor (Meath)
1999—M. Walsh (Kilkenny)
2000—M. Walsh (Kilkenny)
2001—M. Walsh (Kilkenny)
2002—E. Kennedy (Dublin)
2003—T. Sheridan (Meath)
2004—E. Kennedy (Dublin)
2005—E. Kennedy (Dublin)
2006—E. Kennedy (Dublin)
2007—E. Kennedy (Dublin)
2008—E. Kennedy (Dublin)
2009—E. Kennedy (Dublin)

**This was the first open-draw championship.*

SENIOR SOFTBALL DOUBLES

1926—T. Behan and J. Norton (Kilkenny)
1926—J. Whyte and G. Barrett (Galway}
1927—M. Joyce and C. Ryan (Dublin)
1928—J. Flavin and M. Battersby (Waterford)
1929—D. Brennan and J. Lucas (Kilkenny)
1930—M. O'Neill and L. Sherry (Wicklow)
1931—M. O'Neill and L. Sherry (Wicklow}
1932—P. Perry and A. Mullaney (Roscommon)
1933—P. Perry and A. Mullaney (Roscommon)
1934—J. Hassett and E. Hassett (Tipperary)
1935—J. Hassett and E. Hassett (Tipperary)
1936—J. Hassett and E. Hassett (Tipperary)
1937—J. Hassett and E. HasseH (Tipperary}
1938—J. Hassett and E. Hassett (Tipperary)
1939—J. J. Gilmartin and J. Dunne (Kilkenny)
1940—J. J. Gilmartin and J. Dunne (Kilkenny)
1941—J. J. Gilmartin and J. Dunne (Kilkenny)
1942—J. Collins and C. Collins (Tipperary)
1943-45—Suspended
1946—L. Rowe and G. Rowe (Dublin)
1947—J. Bergin and J. O'Rourke (Sligo)
1948—L. Rowe and G. Rowe (Dublin)
1949—J. Bergin and J. Sweeney (Tipperary)
1950—J. Bergin and J. Sweeney (Tipperary)
1951—J. Hassett and J. O'Brien (Kerry)
1952—J. Hassett and J. O'Brien (Kerry}
1953—M. Griffin and W. Walsh (Cork)
1954—C. Delaney and J. Dunne (Kilkenny)
1955—P. Downey and J. O'Brien (Kerry)
1956—P. Downey and J. O'Brien {Kerry)
1957—J. Ryan and J. Doyle (Wexford)
1958—T. McGarry and M. Mullins (Limerick)
1959—T. McGarry and M. Mullins (Limerick)
1960—P. Downey and J. O'Brien (Kerry)
1961—P. Downey and J. O'Brien (Kerry)
1962—P. Downey and J. O'Brien (Kerry)
1963—P. Downey and J. O'Brien (Kerry)
1964—P. Downey and J. O'Brien (Kerry)
1965—J. Delaney and T. Ryan (Kilkenny)
1966—M. Walsh and P. McGee (Mayo)
1967—L. Molloy and D. McGovern (Meath)
1968—T. McEllistrim and M. McEllistrim (Kerry)
1969—P. Lee and J. Cleary (Wicklow)
1970—R. Lyng and S. Buggy (Wexford)
1971—T. McEllistrim and M. McEllistrim (Kerry)
1972—P. Murphy and J. Quigley (Wexford)
1973—M. McEllistrim and N. Kerins (Kerry)
1974—P. Murphy and J. Quigley (Wexford)
1975—R. Lyng and P. Murphy (Wexford)
1976—M. Hogan and P. McGarry (Limerick)
1977—R. Lyng and S. Buggy (Wexford)
1978—D. Kirby and J. Kirby (Clare)
1979—R. Lyng and S. Buggy (Wexford)
1980—P. Reilly and O. Harold (Kilkenny)
1981—A. Greene and P. Hughes (Kilkenny)
1982—R. Lyng and J. Goggins (Wexford)
1983—T. and J. Quish (Limerick)
1984—T. and J. Quish (Limerick)
1985—M. Walsh and E. Downey (Kilkenny)
1986—T. and J. Quish (Limerick)
1987—M. Walsh and E. Downey (Kilkenny)
1988—M. Walsh and E. Downey (Kilkenny)
1989—M. Walsh and E. Downey (Kilkenny)
1990—M. Walsh and E. Downey (Kilkenny)
1991—M. Walsh and E. Downey (Kilkenny)
1992—T. Sheridan and J. McGovern (Meath)
1993—M. Walsh and E. Downey (Kilkenny)
1994—T. Sheridan and J. McGovern (Meath)
1995—M. Walsh and E. Downey (Kilkenny)
1996—M. Walsh and E. Downey (Kilkenny)
1997—M. Walsh and E. Downey (Kilkenny)
1998—T. Sheridan and W. O'Connor (Meath)
1999—T. Sheridan and W. O'Connor (Meath)
2000—T. Hynes and C. Keeling (Wexford)

2001—T. Sheridan and W. O'Connor (Meath)
2002—T. Sheridan and W. O'Connor (Meath)
2003—T. Sheridan and W. O'Connor (Meath)
2004—T. Sheridan and W. O'Connor (Meath)
2005—E. Kennedy and E. Jensen (Dublin)
2006—E. Kennedy and E. Jensen (Dublin)
2007—E. Kennedy and E. Jensen (Dublin)
2008—T. Sheridan and B. Carroll (Meath)
2009—E. Kennedy and E. Jensen (Dublin)

SENIOR HARDBALL SINGLES

1925—W. Aldridge (Kildare)
1926—T. Soye (Dublin)
1927—T. Soye (Dublin)
1928—T. Soye (Dublin)
1929—T. Soye (Dublin)
1930—T. Soye (Dublin)
1931—T. Soye (Dublin)
1932—J. Lucas (Kilkenny)
1933—P. Bell (Meath)
1935—P. Reid (Carlow)
1936—J. J. Gilmartin (Kilkenny)
1937—J. J. Gilmartin (Kilkenny)
1938—J. J. Gilmartin (Kilkenny)
1939—J. J. Gilmartin (Kilkenny)
1940—J. J. Gilmartin (Kilkenny)
1941—J. J. Gilmartin (Kilkenny)
1942—J. J. Gilmartin (Kilkenny}
1943—M. Dowling (Kildare)
1944—A. Clarke (Dublin)
1945—J. J. Gilmartin (Kilkenny)
1946—J. J. Gilmartin (Kilkennyl
1947—J. J. Gilmartin (Kilkenny)
1948—A. Clarke (Dublin)
1949—A. Clarke (Dublin)
1950—R. Grattan (Kildare)
1951—A. Clarke (Dublin)
1952—J. Ryan (Wexford)
1953—J. Ryan (Wexford)
1954—A. Clarke (Dublin)
1955—A. Clarke (Dublin)
1956—J. Ryan (Wexford)
1957—J. Ryan (Wexford)
1958—P. Downey (Kerry)
1959—P. Downey (Kerry)
1960—P. Downey (Kerry)
1961—J. Maher (Louth)
1962—P. Downey (Kerry)
1963—J. Maher (Louth)
1964—J. Maher (Louth)
1965—P. McGee (Mayo)
1966—P. Hickey (Tipperary)
1967—P. McGee (Mayo)
1968—J. Maher (Louth)
1969—J. Maher (Louth)
1970—J. Maher (Louth)
1971—P. Hickey (Tipperary)
1972—P. McGee (Mayo)
1973—P. McGee (Mayo)
1974—P. McGee (Mayo)
1975—P. McGee (Mayo)
1976—P. McGee (Mayo)
1977—P. McGee (Mayo)
1978—C. Winders (Kildare)
1979—P. McGarry (Limerick)
1980—P. McGarry (Limerick)
1981—P. Winders (Kildare)
1982—P. McGee (Mayo)
1983—P. McGee (Mayo)
1984—P. Winders (Kildare)
1985—T. O'Rourke (Kildare)
1986—W. Bourke (Kilkenny)
1987—M. Walsh (Roscommon)
1988—T. O'Rourke (Kildare)
1989—T. O'Rourke (Kildare)
1990—T. O'Rourke (Kildare)
1991—P. McAuley (Louth)
1992—B. Bourke (Kilkenny)
1993—P. McAuley (Louth)
1994—P. McAuley (Louth)
1995—P. McAuley (Louth)
1996—P. McAuley (Louth)
1997—P. McAuley (Louth)
1998—W. O'Connor (Meath)
1999—No Championship
2000—No Championship
2001—W. O'Connor (Meath)
2002—K. Kane (Carlow)
2003—E. Kennedy (Dublin)
2004—E. Kennedy (Dublin)
2005—E. Kennedy (Dublin)
2006—D. Keegan (Mayo)
2007—E. Kennedy (Dublin)
2008—D. Keegan (Mayo)
2007—E. Kennedy (Dublin)
2009—E. Kennedy (Dublin)

SENIOR HARDBALL DOUBLES

1926—J. J. Bowles and S. Gleeson (Limerick)
1927—T. Soye and T. O'Reilly (Dublin)
1928—T. Soye and T. O'Reilly (Dublin)
1929—P. Ormonde and C. Maloney (Tipperary)
1930—T. Soye and G. Brown (Dublin)
1931—P. Ormonde and C. Maloney (Tipperary)
1932—P. Bell and J. Doyle (Meath)
1933—P. Bell and J. Doyle {Meath)
1934—J. Lucas and T. Cherry (Kilkenny)
1935—P. Bell and J. Doyle (Meath)
1936—P. Perry and P. Reid (Roscommon)
1937—J. J. Gilmartin and A. Cullen (Kilkenny)
1938—J. J. Gilmartin and T. Cherry (Kilkenny)
1939—J. J. Gilmartin and T. Jordan (Kilkenny)
1940—J. J. Gilmartin and P. Dalton (Kilkenny)
1941—J. J. Gilmartin and J. Dunne (Kilkenny)
1942—A. Clarke and J. Clarke (Dublin)
1943—W. Walsh and D. Keogh (Cork)
1944—W. Walsh and D. Keogh (Cork)
1945—J. J. Gilmartin and P. Dalton (Kilkenny)
1946—J. J. Gilmartin and P. Dalton (Kilkenny)
1947—J. J. Gilmartin and P. Dalton (Kilkenny)

1948—W. Walsh and T. Morrissey (Cork)
1949—R. Grattan and J. Bolger (Kildare)
1950—A. Clarke and G. Moran (Dublin)
1951—J. Hassett and J. O'Brien (Kerry)
1952—J. Ryan and J. Doyle (Wexford)
1953—J. Hassett and P. Downey (Kerry)
1954—J. Ryan and J. Doyle (Wexford)
1955—J. Ryan and J. Doyle (Wexford)
1956—J. Ryan and J. Doyle (Wexford)
1957—J. Ryan and J. Doyle (Wexford)
1958—J. Ryan and J. Doyle (Wexford)
1959—P. Downey and J. O'Brien (Kerry)
1960—P. Downey and J. O'Brien (Kerry)
1961—J. Delaney and C. Delaney (Kilkenny)
1962—J. Ryan and M. Shanahan (Tipperary)
1963—P. Downey and J. O'Brien (Kerry)
1964—J. Maher and P. Reilly (Louth)
1965—P. McGee and P. Bolingbrook (Mayo)
1966—P. McGee and P. Bolingbrook (Mayo)
1967—P. McGee and P. Bolingbrook (Mayo)
1968—P. Hickey and C. Cleere (Tipperary)
1969—W. Doran and G. Lawlor (Kildare)
1970—S. McCabe and L. Gilmore (Monaghan)
1971—M. Sullivan and J. Doyle (Dublin)
1972—P. Hickey and C. Cleere (Tipperary)
1973—A. Byrne and W. Mullins (Westmeath)
1974—P. McGee and B. Colleran (Mayo)
1974—P. Hickey and J. Cleere (Tipperary)
1976—P. McGee and P. McCormack (Mayo)
1977—G. Lawlor and C. Winders (Kildare)
1978—P. McGarry and J. Bennis (Limerick)
1979—P. McGarry and J. Bennis (Limerick)
1980—P. McGarry and J. Bennis (Limerick)
1981—P. Winders and M. Purcell (Kildare)
1982—Cecil and Pius Winders (Kildarej
1983—Pius and Cecil Winders (Kildare)
1984—Tom and John Quish (Limerick)
1985—Tom and John Quish (Limerick)
1986—Tom and John Quish (Limerick)
1987—Tom and John Quish (Limerick)
1988—T. O'Rourke and P. McCormack (Kildare)
1989—T. O'Rourke and P. McCormack (Kildare)
1990—T. O'Rourke and P. McCormack (Kildare)
1991—B. Bourke and W. Pratt (Kilkenny)
1992—T. Sheridan and W. O'Connor (Meath)
1993—T. Sheridan and W. O'Connor (Meath)
1994—W. O'Connor and D. Gough (Meath)
1995—E. Corbett and N. Ryan (Tipperary)
1996—W. O'Connor and D. Gough (Meath)
1997—None
1998—T. Sheridan and W. O'Connor (Meath)
1999—None
2000 to 2005—No Championship
2006—E. Kennedy and E. Jensen (Dublin)
2007—E. Kennedy and E. Jensen (Dublin)
2008—E. Kennedy and E. Jensen (Dublin)
2009—T. Sheridan and B. Carroll (Meath)

JUNIOR SOFTBALL SINGLES

1928—M. Flannery (Waterford)
1929—P. Berry (Roscommon)
1930—J. Hassett (Tipperary)
1931—P. Delaney (Carlow)
1932—J. Smith (Wexford)
1933—P. Murray (Offaly)
1934—J. Dunne (Kilkenny)
1935—M. McMahon (Tipperary)
1936—P. Phelan (Kilkenny)
1937—W. Delaney (Wexford)
1938—L. Rowe (Dublin)
1939—M. Walsh (Galway)
1940—P. Molloy (Kilkenny)
1941—E. McMahon (Tipperary)
1942-45 Suspended
1946—P. Clarke (Mayo)
1947—J. Ryan (Wexford)
1948—H. Haddock (Armagh)
1949—V. Sherlock (Cavan)
1950—M. Griffin (Dublin)
1951—C. Delaney (Kilkenny)
1952—S. Commane (Kerry)
1953—P. McCarthy (Kerry)
1954—J. Delaney (Kilkenny)
1955—J. Lyng (Wexford)
1956—J. Maher (Louth)
1957—P. Kirby (Clare)
1958—F. Confrey (Louth)
1959—M. Kirby (Clare)
1960—M. O'Brien (Limerick)
1961—D. Walshe (Sligo)
1962—S. McCabe (Monaghan)
1963—R. Lyng (Wexford)
1964—W. Kearins (Kerry)
1965—P. Sheerin (Offaly)
1966—T. McEllistrim (Kerry)
1967—P. McGarry (Limerick)
1968—D. Kirby (Clare)
1969—P. Davin (Tipperary)
1970—M. Conway (Tyrone)
1971—B. Colleran (Mayo}
1972—P. Reilly (Kilkenny)
1973—J. Howlin (Wexford)
1974—P. Ryan (Dublin)
1975—O. Harrold (Kilkenny)
1976—T. O'Brien (Kerry)
1977—J. Roche (Limerick)
1978—J. Scully (Galway)
1979—A. Ryan (Tipperary)
1980—T. Quish (Limerick)
1981—P. Mullins (Tipperary)
1982—W. Bourke (Kilkenny)
1983—M. Sweeney (Sligo)
1984—J. Fleming (Wexford)
1985—D. Doolin (Roscommon)
1986—P. Delaney (Galway)
1987—E. Jensen (Meath)
1988—W. McCarthy (Tipperary)
1989—W. Fitzgibbon (Tipperary)
1990—R. McCarthy (Westmeath)
1991—J. Rossiter (Carlow)
1992—J. Herlihy (Cork)
1993—S. O'Callaghan (Tipperary)
1994—S. O'Connor (Wexford)

1995—N. O'Reilly (Kilkenny)
1996—R. Breen (Wexford)
1997—F. Daly (Dublin)
1998—D. Lynch (Kerry)
1999—E. O'Neill (Limerick)
2000—N. Kerr (Tyrone)
2001—K. Hennessy (Limerick)
2002—S. Dormer (Laois)
2003—A. Johnson (Tipperary)
2004—N. Murphy (Offaly)
2005—N. McInerney (Tipperary)
2006—P. Donovan (Laois)
2007—I. Griffin (Dublin)
2008—O. Conway (Galway)
2009—L. Maughan (Roscommon)

JUNIOR SOFTBALL DOUBLES

1928—T. O'Keeffe and J. McCarthy (Tipperary)
1929—P. Perry and T. Gaughran (Roscommon)
1930—J. Molloy and H. Smith (Cavan)
1931—C. Darcy and J. Cahill (Kildare)
1932—W. Doyle and J. Fleming (Carlow)
1933—T. Cherry and J. O'Brien (Kilkenny)
1934—A. Cullen and P. Power (Kilkenny)
1935—A. Roe and H. Gallagher (Dublin)
1936—J. McDonald and J. Geraghty (Mayo)
1937—J. Bergin and M. O'Gorman (Tipperary)
1938—A. Collins and C. Collins (Tipperary)
1939—W. McDonald and R. Gibbons (Mayo)
1940—D. McDonald and P. Ryan (Carlow)
1941—S. Rice and E. McMahon (Tipperary)
1942—P. Kennedy and J. Gaughran (Roscommon)
1943-45—Suspended
1946—W. Buggy and T. Buggy (Kilkenny)
1947—G. Grogan and C. Donohoe (Dublin)
1948—J. O'Connell and M. O'Keeffe (Kilkenny)
1949—P. Kennedy and D. Carey (Tipperary)
1950—T. McCormack and P. McCormack (Mayo)
1951—P. Downey and T. Commane (Kerry)
1952—J. Byrne and P. Sutherland (Wexford)
1953—P. Munroe and M. Fahy (Dublin)
1954—P. Hackett and J. Moynihan (Limerick)
1955—T. Ryan and S. Lennon (Kilkenny)
1956—E. Connolly and S. Fleming (Mayo)
1957—T. McGarry and M. Mullins (Limerick)
1958—J. Clery and W. McKenna (Wicklow)
1959—T. Reilly and P. Reilly (Louth)
1960—M. O'Brien and S. Walsh (Limerick)
1961—J. Coughlan and G. Barry (Offaly)
1962—M. Walsh and P. McGee (Mayo)
1963—L. Gilmore and J. Gilmore (Cavan)
1964—W. Kerins and P. Moriarty (Kerry)
1965—L. Molloy and D. McGovern (Meath)
1966—T. McElisrim and M. McElistrim (Kerry)
1967—M. Henry and J. Gaffney (Sligo)
1968—R. Doherty and P. Clarke (Roscommon)
1969—N. Cahill and P. Masterson (Dublin)
1970—R. Walsh and J. O'Brien (Dublin)
1971—J. Kirby and M. Hogan (Clare)
1972—P. Reilly and P. Delaney (Kilkenny)
1973—J. Howlin and J. Goggins (Wexford)
1974—E. Hannon and P. Walsh (Sligo)
1975—O. Harold and B. Fitzpatrick (Kilkenny)
1976—G. and D. Sheridan (Cavan)
1977—P. Winders and T. O'Rourke (Kildare)
1978—N. O'Brien and T. Morrissey (Tipperary)
1979—J. B. Molloy and F. Carroll (Meath)
1980—T. and J. Quish (Limerick)
1981—F. McCann and M. Porter (Sligo)
1982—E. Farrell and B. Mullins (Tipperary)
1983—M. Walsh and E. Downey (Kilkenny)
1984—J. Fleming and P. Cleary (Wexford)
1985—P. Donagh and P. Hand (Cavan)
1986—P. Delaney and M. Connors (Galway)
1987—T. Sheridan and J. McGovern (Meath)
1988—W. O'Connor and J. Grant (Meath)
1989—E. Corbett and J. O'Donoghue (Tipperary)
1990—P. Kealey and B. Mullins (Offaly)
1991—J. Donlan and N. Breen (Clare)
1992—T. Derrig and P. McCormack (Mayo)
1993—N. Buggy and T. Hynes (Wexford)
1994—P. Kenny and F. Cunningham (Dublin)
1995—T. and B. O'Brien (Limerick)
1996—P. Ryan and K. Croke (Tipperary)
1997—C. Joyce and R. Charles (Westmeath)
1998—D. King and J. Ryan (Cariow)
1999—E. O'Neill and M. Kiely (Limerick)
2000—P. Mullins and J. Mullins (Tipperary)
2001—M. Lalor and E. Burke (Kilkenny)
2002—K. Hennessy and P. Hedderman (Limerick)
2003—A. Cunningham and D. Rogers (Roscommon)
2004—P. Buckley and C. Jordan (Cork)
2005—T. Clifford and M. Clifford (Kilkenny)
2006—O. Cassidy and P. Flynn (Mayo)
2007—P. Butler and D. Walsh (Waterford)
2008—O. Conway and A. Tierney (Galway)
2009—W. Love and D. Love (Kilkenny)

JUNIOR HARDBALL SINGLES

1928—J. Ryan (Tipperary)
1929—J. O'Mahoney (Cork)
1930—P. Bell (Meath)
1931—J Foley (Kildare)
1932—J. O'Mahoney (Cork)
1933—T. Cherry (Kilkenny)
1934—A. Cullen (Kilkenny)
1935—J. J. Gilmartin (Kilkenny)
1936—P. Murray (Offaly)
1937—W. Butler (Dublin)
1938—T. Jordan (Kilkenny)
1939—M. Butler (Dublin)
1940—P. Molloy (Kilkenny)
1941—M. Dowling (Kildare)
1942—P. Murray (Offaly)
1943—James Gilmartin (Kilkenny)
1944—C. Drumgoole (Wexford)
1945—M. O'Gorman (Tipperary)
1946—G. Ryan (Kildare)

1947—R. Grattan (Kildare)
1948—J. Bolger (Kildare)
1949—P. Kennedy (Tipperary)
1950—M. O'Brien (Kildare)
1951—P. Downey (Kerry)
1952—C. O'Brien (Tipperary)
1953—W. Lawlor (Kildare)
1954—J. Delaney (Kilkenny)
1955—M. Redmond (Kildare)
1956—J. Maher (Louth)
1957—W. Doran (Kildare)
1958—J. Ryan (Tipperary)
1959—D. Downey (Kerry)
1960—J. Donovan (Kerry)
1961—J. Cleary (Tipperary)
1962—P. Hickey (Tipperary)
1963—T. Dowd (Wexford)
1964—P. Bolingbrook (Mayo)
1965—P. Sheerin (Offaly)
1966—T. McEllistrim (Kerry)
1967—M. O'Gara (Roscommon)
1968—A. Byrne (Dublin)
1969—A. McAuliffe (Limerick)
1970—J. Hartnett (Limerick)
1971—J. Quigley (Wexford)
1972—E. Sheeran (Offaly)
1973—M. Purcell (Kildare)
1974—P. McCormack (Mayo)
1975—P. Hughes (Kilkenny)
1976—M. Walsh (Roscommon)
1977—W. McCarthy (Tipperary)
1978—C. Quinn (Mayo)
1979—Noel Ryan (Tipperary)
1980—N. Quigley (Wexford)
1981—W. Pratt (Kilkenny)
1982—W. Bourke (Kilkenny)
1983—E. Lee (Dublin)
1984—N. O'Toole (Cork)
1985—M. Dowling (Kildare)
1986—J. O'Donoghue (Tipperary)
1987—P. McAuley (Louth)
1988—W. O'Connor (Meath)
1989—P. O'Keeffe (Kilkenny)
1990—E. Jenson (Meath)
1991—M. Walsh (Kilkenny)
1992—D. Moloney (Tipperary)
1993—R. McCarthy (Westmeath)
1994—P. Quaile (Wicklow)
1995—A. Campbell (Kildare)
1996—M. Flynn (Tipperary)
1997—V. Moran (Mayo)
1998—K. Kane (Carlow)
1999—E. O'Neill (Limerick)
2000—D. Keegan (Mayo)
2001—S. Dormer (Laois)
2002—D. Ward (Kildare)
2003—J. Doyle (Limerick)
2004—P. O'Donnell (Wicklow)
2005—P .Donovan (Laois)
2006—D. Martin (Roscommon)
2007—G. Coonan (Tipperary)
2008—J. McCann (Mayo)
2009—S O'Carroll (Limerick)

JUNIOR HARDBALL DOUBLES

1928—S. Ryan and S. McInerney (Tipperary)
1929—J. O'Mahoney and D. O'Mahoney (Cork)
1930—N. Gorman and T. Maloney (Tipperary)
1931—J. McGrath and J. O'Connell (Kilkenny)
1932—A. Dalton and C. Baker (Kilkenny)
1933—S. Tormey and P. Bell, Junior (Meath)
1934—A. Cullen and J. Dunne (Kilkenny)
1935—P. Coyne and J. Purcell (Carlow)
1936—G. Ryan and J. Costello (Kildare)
1937—J. Hassett and M. O'Gorman (Tipperary)
1938—J. Hurley and T. Twohill (Cork)
1939—M. Butler and J. Roche (Dublin)
1940—W. Walsh and R. Ward (Cork)
1941—J. McGrath and D. Brennan (Kilkenny)
1942—P. Murray and J. McHugh (Offaly)
1943—James Gilmartin and J. O'Brien (Kilkenny)
1944—C. Drumgoole and J. Duggan (Wexford)
1945—W. Grace and C. Murphy (Kildare)
1946—M. Dalton and J. Dunne (Kilkenny)
1947—J. McGrath and J. Phelan (Kilkenny)
1948—W. McCabe and T. Tormey (Meath)
1949—J. Doyle and P. Doyle (Wexford)
1950—M. O'Brien and R. Maher (Kildare)
1951—S. Monahan and J. Doherty (Kilkenny)
1952—J. Kennedy and M. Heffernan (Tipperary)
1953—W. Lawlor and P. Monahan (Kildare)
1954—M. Gleeson and R. Doyle (Dublin)
1955—M. Redmond and J. Parle (Kildare)
1956—J. Maher and J. McArdle (Louth)
1957—W. Doran and J. Curran (Kildare)
1958—T. Doheny and M. Shanahan (Tipperary)
1959—A. Daly and P. Winders (Kildare)
1960—T Cleere and C. Cleere (Tipperary)
1961—M. Kelly and G. Connolly (Galway)
1962—P. Hickey and T. Breedy (Tipperary)
1963—P. Supple and J. Murphy (Cork)
1964—G. Mahon and K. Fullard (Roscommon)
1965—M. Sullivan and J. Doyle (Dublin)
1966—T. McElistrim and M. McElistrim (Kerry)
1967—G. Lawlor and R. Winders (Kildare)
1968—N. Kerins and T. Fitzgerald (Kerry)
1969—E. Deegan and J. Browne (Kildare)
1970—J. Hartnett and P. Clancy (Limerick)
1971—P. Murphy and J. Quigley (Wexford)
1972—T. Geoghegan and C. Winders (Kildare)
1973—M. Purcell and J. Byrne (Kildare)
1974—M. Brady and T. Hurley (Dublin)
1975—P. Hughes and P. Kennedy (Kilkenny)
1976—G. and D. Sheridan (Cavan)
1977—J. Bennis and V. Moane (Limerick)
1978—E. Rabbitte and G. Scully (Galway)
1979—Tony and Noel Ryan (Tipperary)
1980—T. and J. Quish (Limerick)
1981—P. Cleary and S. McLoughlin (Wexford)
1982—W. Bourke and M. Lawlor (Kilkenny)
1983—E. Lee and R. Walsh (Dublin)
1984—M. Jorden and N. O'Toole (Cork)
1985—P. Hand and P. Donagh (Cavan)
1986—E. Corbett and J. O'Donoghue

(Tipperary)
1987—F. McCann and S. Davey (Sligo)
1988—P. O'Connell and P. Quish (Limerick)
1989—C. McGovern and T. Sheridan (Meath)
1990—E. Jenson and D. Gough (Meath)
1991—M. Walsh and J. Connolly (Kilkenny)
1992—D. Moloney and J. O'Dwyer (Tipperary)
1993—J. Guilfoyle and R. McCarthy (Westmeath)
1994—N. Murphy and M. Carrie (Tipperary)
1995—A. Campbell and T. Winders (Kildare)
1996—M. Kiely and P. Herr (Limerick)
1997—V. Moran and C. Brennan (Mayo)
1998—K. and T. Kane (Carlow)
1999—E. Law and E. Bourke (Kilkenny)
2000—D. Keegan and B. Hough (Mayo)
2001—No Championship
2002—No Championship
2003—P. Conway and O. Conway (Galway)
2004—P. O'Donnell and N. Kealy (Wicklow)
2005—P .Buckley and C. Jordan (Cork)
2006—R. O'Gara and D. Martin (Roscommon)
2007—I. Griffin and C. Donnelly (Dublin)
2008—D. Lynch and J.J. Quirke (Kerry)
2009—S. O'Carroll and C.J. Fitzpatrick (Limerick)

MINOR SOFTBALL SINGLES

1949—J. O'Brien (Kerry)
1950—L. Egan (Kilkenny)
1951—R . Doherty (Roscommon)
1952—R. Doherty (Roscommon)
1953—J. Lyng (Wexford)
1954—E. Horan (Kerry)
1955—T. McGarry (Limerick)
1956—J. Murrary (Kilkenny)
1957—M. Mullins (Limerick)
1958—J. Clery (Wicklow)
1959—J. Clery (Wicklow)
1960—T. Ledwith (Westmeath)
1961—R. Lyng (Wexford)
1962—J. McElistrim (Kerry)
1963—M. Henry (Sligo)
1964—M. Henry (Sligo)
1965—P. Clarke (Roscommon)
1966—P. McCarthy (Limerick)
1967—P. Murphy (Dublin)
1968—P. Bennis (Limerick)
1969—M. Brady (Dublin)
1970—M. Walsh (Roscommon)
1971—S. McLoughlin (Wexford)
1972—S. McLoughlin (Wexford)
1973—T. O'Rourke (Kildare)
1974—D. Doolan (Roscommon)
1975—S. Wafer (Wexford)
1976—M. Maher (Louth)
1977—S. McGovern (Meath)
1978—A. Ryan (Tipperary)
1979—W. Bourke (Kilkenny)
1980—W. Bourke (Kilkenny)
1981—W. Bourke (Kilkemly)
1982—M. Walsh (Kilkenny)
1983—M. Walsh (Kilkenny)
1984—M. Walsh (Kilkenny)
1985—F. Kavanagh (Westmeath)
1986—T. Sheridan (Meath)
1987—P. McAuley (Louth)
1988—P. Galvin (Limerick)
1989—A. Heneghan (Roscommon)
1990—T. Hynes (Wexford)
1991—B. Gilhooly (Wexford)
1992—M. Finnegan (Cavan)
1993—M. Finnegan (Cavan)
1994—M. Finnegan (Cavan)
1995—K. Kane (Carlow)
1996—K. Kane (Carlow)
1997—E. Kennedy (Dublin)
1998—D. Keegan (Mayo)
1999—M. Gregan (Wicklow)
2000—P. Finnegan (Cavan)
2001—N. McHugh (Galway)
2002—N. McHugh (Galway)
2003—G. Coonan (Tipperary)
2004—R. McCarthy (Westmeath)
2005—R. McCarthy (Westmeath)
2006—N. Anthony (Kilkenny)
2007—C. J. Fitzpatrick (Limerick)
2008—Seamus O'Carroll (Limerick)
2009—Stephen Cooney (Mayo)

MINOR SOFTBALL DOUBLES

1938—J. Doran and G. Brogan (Dublin)
1939—A. Kelly and J. Goughran (Roscommon)
1940—P. Kennedy and J. Sweeney (Tipperary)
1941—P. Kennedy and J. Sweeney (Tipperary)
1942-45—Suspended
1946—J. Ryan and A. Power (Wexford)
1947—P. Doherty and M. Mulhern (Meath)
1948—P. Somers and J. O'Keeffe (Kilkenny)
1949—P. Bolingbrook and K. Swords (Mayo)
1950—T. Hughes and J. O'Brien (Mayo)
1951—S. Commane and M. Dennehy (Kerry)
1952—R. Tunney and J. Swords (Mayo)
1953—M. O'Connor and E. Horan (Kerry)
1954—E. Horan and D. Downey (Kerry)
1955—T. McGarry and M. Mullins (Limerick)
1956—M. Sullivan and J. Murray (Kilkenny)
1957—M. Mullins and G. Mitchell (Limerick)
1958—W. Mullen and P. Geelan (Westmeath)
1959—J. Clery and M. Dwyer (Wicklow)
1960—N. Kerins and J. McMullan (Kerry)
1961—R. Lyng and P. Lennon (Wexford)
1962—D. Kirby and J. Kirby (Clare)
1963—H. Ryan and P. Kavanagh (Wexford)
1964—W. Myles and M. Fitzgibbon (Kerry)
1965—W. Myles and M. Fitzgibbon (Kerry)
1966—V. Grimes and C. Grimes (Meath)
1967—P. Murphy and P. Domigan (Dublin)
1968—J. Quigley and J. Sydney (Wexford)
1969—J. Quigley and N. Quigley (Wexford)

1970—M. Quigley and S. McLoughlin (Wexford)
1971—P. McCormack and C. Quinn (Mayo)
1972—D. Doolan and P. J. Moran (Roscommon)
1973—O. Harold and J. Barron (Kilkenny)
1974—P. Hughes and E. Mahon (Kilkenny)
1975—S. Wafer and S. Goggins (Wexford)
1976—J. McGovern and F. Carroll (Meath)
1977—J. and M. McGovern (Meath)
1978—J. and M. McGovern (Meath)
1979—B. Bourke and M. Cantwell (Kilkenny)
1980—W. Bourke and M. Lawlor (Kilkenny)
1981—E. Jensen and C. McGovern (Meath)
1982—M. Walsh and M. Lawlor (Kilkenny)
1983—Michael Walsh and Joe Walsh (Kilkenny)
1984—M. Walsh and P. O'Keeffe (Kilkenny)
1985—T. Sheridan and W. O'Connor (Meath)
1986—T. Sheridan and W. O'Connor (Meath}
1987—K. Lyons and P. Galvin (Limerick)
1988—K. Lyons and P. Galvin (Limerick)
1989—D. J. Carey and G. O'Brien (Kilkenny)
1990—A. and C. Heneghan (Roscommon)
1991—D. Moloney and N. Murphy (Tipperary)
1992—M. Finnegan and R. Cunningham (Cavan)
1993—M. Finnegan and R. Cunningham (Cavan)
1994—M. Finnegan and C. McDonnell (Cavan)
1995—K. Kane and O. Ryan (Carlow)
1996—B. Goff and M. Hillis (Wexford)
1997—B. Goff and C. Keeling (Wexford)
1998—C. Browne and P. Reilly (Meath)
1999—M. Gregan and S. Willoughby (Wicklow)
2000—J. Goggins and T. Gainfort (Wexford)
2001—M. Cash and C. Smyth (Wexford)
2002—R. Walshe and J. Willoughby (Wicklow)
2003—D. Martin and R. O'Gara (Roscommon)
2004—R. McCarthy and J. O'Shaughnessy (Westmeath)
2005—R. Hogan and P. Hogan (Kilkenny)
2006—N. Anthony and K. Greene (Kilkenny)
2007—C. J. Fitzpatrick and S. Carroll (Limerick)
2008—C. J. Fitzpatrick and S. Carroll (Limerick)
2009—S. Cooney and I. McLoughlin (Mayo)

MINOR HARDBALL SINGLES

1953—J. Redmond (Wexford)
1954—E. Horan (Kerry)
1955—J. Ryan (Tipperary)
1956—M. Sullivan (Kilkenny)
1957—P Hickey (Tipperary)
1958—P McGrath (Wexford)
1959—J. Clery (Wicklow)
1960—M. Purcell (Kildare)
1961—J. Brennan (Kilkenny)
1962—P. McLoughlin (Tipperary)
1963—T. Morrissey (Kilkenny)
1964—P. Cody (Cork)
1965—T. Geoghegan (Kildare)
1966—M. O'Gara (Roscommon)
1967—G. Lawlor (Kildare)
1968—J. Quigley (Wexford)
1969—J. Quigley tWexford)
1970—M. Walsh (Roscommon)
1971—P. McCormack (Mayo)
1972—C. Quinn (Mayo)
1973—P. Hughes (Kilkenny)
1974—P. Hughes (Kilkenny)
1975—P. Finnerty (Galway)
1976—J. Dineen (Limerick)
1977—A Ryan (Tipperary)
1978—A Ryan (Tipperary)
1979—W . O'Donnell (Tipperary)
1980—W. Bourke (Kilkenny)
1981—W. Bourke (Kilkenny)
1982—J . O'Donoghue (Tipperary)
1983—J. O'Donoghue (Tipperary)
1984—M. Walsh (Kilkenny)
1985—T. Sheridan (Meath)
1986—W. O'Connor (Meath)
1987—P. McAuley (Louth)
1988—K. Lyons (Limerick)
1989—J. Connoly (Kilkenny)
1990—G. O'Brien (Kilkenny)
1991—D. Moloney (Tipperary)
1992—T. Winders (Kildare)
1993—M. Finnegan (Cavan)
1994—D. Ward (Kildare)
1995—V. Moran (Mayo)
1996—K. Kane (Carlow)
1997—K. Kane (Carlow)
1998—No Championship
1999—No Championship
2000—No Championship
2001—No Championship
2002—D. Martin (Roscommon)
2003—R. McCarthy (Westmeath)
2004—No Championship
2005—No Championship
2006—C.J. Fitzpatrick (Limerick)
2007—S. O'Carroll (Limerick)
2008—C.J. Fitzpatrick (Limerick)
2009—Stephen Cooney (Mayo)

MINOR HARDBALL DOUBLES

1953—J. Redmond and M. Redmond (Wexford)
1954—M. Sullivan and M. Hayes (Kilkenny)
1955—J. O'Neill and M. Keyes (Limerick)
1956—M. Sullivan and J. Murray (Kilkenny)
1957—M. Mullins and J. O'Connell (Limerick)
1958—M. Purcell and R. Winders (Kildare)
1959—C. Cleere and J. Cleary (Tipperary)
1960—M. Purcell and J. Byrne (Kildare)
1961—J. Byrne and J. Browne (Kildare)
1962—P. McLoughlin and A. Murphy (Tipperary)
1963—G. Lawlor and T. Geoghegan (Kildare)
1964—P. Cody and N. O'Brien (Cork)

1965—T. Curley and S. Lynch (Galway)
1966—G. Lawlor and A. Campbell (Kildare)
1967—G. Lawlor and C. Winders (Kildare)
1968—W. McCarthy and S. Halley (Tipperary)
1969—M. Brady and M. Williams (Dublin)
1970—M. Walsh and P. J. Moran (Roscommon)
1971—S. McLoughlin and C. Kehoe (Wexford)
1972—P. Hughes and J. Barron (Kilkenny)
1973—P. Hughes and J. Barron (Kilkenny)
1974—P. Hughes and E. Mahon (Kilkenny)
1975—A. McConnell and J. Reddy (Meath)
1976—F. McCann and M. Porter (Sligo)
1977—T. Ryan and W. O'Donnell (Tipperary)
1978—T. Ryan and W. O'Donnell (Tipperary)
1979—M. McGovern and J. Smith (Meath)
1980—W. Bourke and M. Lawlor (Kilkenny)
1981—W. Bourke and M. Lawlor (Kilkenny)
1982—E. Jensen and R. Morris (Meath)
1983—J. O'Donoghue and E. Corbett (Tipperary)
1984—M. Walsh and P. O'Keeffe (Kilkenny)
1985—T. Sheridan and W. O'Connor (Meath)
1986—T. Sheridan and W. O'Connor (Meath)
1987—P. McAuley and M. McAuley (Louth)
1988—K. Lyons and P. Galvin (Limerick)
1989—G. O'Brien and E. Law (Kilkenny)
1990—D. Maloney and N. Marshall (Tipperary)
1991—D. Moloney and N. Marshall (Tipperary)
1992—M. Carrie and N. Marshall (Tipperary)
1993—M. Finnegan and R. Cunningham (Cavan)
1994—M. Finnegan and N. Doyle (Cavan)
1995—V. Moran and C. Brennan (Mayo)
1996—V. Moran and C. Brennan (Mayo)
1997—K. Kane and D. Dunphy (Carlow)
1998 to 2005 – No Championship
2006—C.J. Fitzpatrick and S. O'Carroll (Limerick)
2007—C.J. Fitzpatrick and S. O'Carroll (Limerick)
2008—C.J. Fitzpatrick and S. O'Carroll (Limerick)
2009—K. Bourke and E. Hennessy (Kilkenny)

INTERMEDIATE SOFTBALL SINGLES

1994—D. Moloney (Tipperary)
1995—B. Gilhooley (Wexford)
1996—M. Finnegan (Cavan)
1997—J. Brennan (Kilkenny)
1998—T. Healy (Cork)
1999—E. Kennedy (Dublin)
2000—B. Goff (Wexford)
2001—D. Lynch (Kerry)
2002—D. Keegan (Mayo)
2003—M. Gregan (Wicklow)
2004—J. McCann (Mayo)
2005—C. Browne (Meath)
2006—R. McCarthy (Westmeath)
2007—P. Mullins (Tipperary)
2008—G. Coonan (Tipperary)
2009—B. Manogue (Kilkenny)

INTERMEDIATE SOFTBALL DOUBLES

1994—S. Ahern and P. Hall (Dublin)
1995—N. Murphy and J. O'Dwyer (Tipperary)
1996—M. Finnegan and R. Cunningham (Cavan)
1997—Pearse O'Keeffe and E. Law (Kilkenny)
1998—K. and T. Kane (Carlow)
1999—D. King and J. Ryan (Carlow)
2000—G. Buggy and B. Goff (Wexford)
2001—E. O'Neill and P. Herr (Limerick)
2002—D. Keegan and V. Moran (Mayo)
2003—M. Gregan and P. Quaile (Wicklow)
2004—J. McCann and C. Brennan (Mayo)
2005—D. Martin and R. O'Gara (Roscommon)
2006—R. McCarthy and L. Cassidy (Westmeath)
2007—E. Burke and M. Clifford (Kilkenny)
2008—G. Coonan and J. McInerney (Tipperary)
2009—N. Anthony and J. Walshe (Kilkenny)

U.21 SOFTBALL SINGLES

1967—P. McGarry (Limerick)
1968—P. McGarry (Limerick)
1969—P. Murphy (Wexford)
1970—J. Delaney (Kilkenny)
1971—M. Walsh (Roscommon)
1972—M. Walsh (Roscommon)
1973—M. Walsh (Roscommon)
1974—None
1975—O. Harold (Kilkenny)
1976—T. O'Brien (Kerry)
1977—D. Doolan (Roscommon)
1978—T. Quish (Limerick)
1979—E. Downey (Kilkenny)
1980—T. Ryan (Tipperary)
1981—T. Ryan (Tipperary)
1982—S. Lyon (Waterford)
1983—P. McCarthy (Wexford)
1984—P. Hall (Dublin)
1985—J. O'Donoghue (Tipperary)
1986—P. O'Keeffe (Kilkenny)
1987—P. O'Keeffe (Kilkenny)
1988—P. O'Keeffe (Kilkenny)
1989—P. Quaile (Wicklow)
1990—J. O'Dwyer (Tipperary)
1991—G. O'Brien (Kilkenny)
1992—B. Gilhooley (Wexford)
1993—N. Murphy (Tipperary)
1994—R. Cunningham (Cavan)
1995—M. Finnegan (Cavan)
1996—T. Winders (Kildare)
1997—V. Moran (Mayo)
1998—E. Kennedy (Dublin)
1999—B. Marrinan (Clare)
2000—D. Keegan (Mayo)
2001—B. Manogue (Kilkenny)
2002—M. Gregan (Wicklow)
2003—J. McCann (Mayo)

2004—D. Martin (Roscommon)
2005—G. Coonan (Tipperary)
2006—G. Coonan (Tipperary)
2007—M. Berry (Wexford)
2008—M. Berry (Wexford)
2009—S. O'Carroll (Limerick)

U.21 SOFTBALL DOUBLES

1967—V. and C. Grimes (Meath)
1968—W. Myles and M. Fitzgibbon (Kerry)
1969—P. McGarry and P. Bennis (Limerick)
1970—P. Murphy and J. Quigley (Wexford)
1971—M. Brady and M. Williams (Dublin)
1972—E. Farrell and J. Ryan (Tipperary)
1973—M. Brady and D. Shanahan (Cavan)
1974—None
1975—P. J. Moran and D. Doolan (Roscommon)
1976—T. O'Rourke and P. Winders (Kildare)
1977—T. O'Rourke and P. Winders (Kildare)
1978—P. Cleary and J. Fleming (Wexford)
1979—F. McCann and M. Porter (Sligo)
1980—P. Cleary and J. Fleming (Wexford)
1981—T. Ryan and W. O'Donnell (Tipperary)
1982—J. and M. McGovern (Meath)
1983—E. MacBholscaidh and D. Lynch (Dublin)
1984—K. Mullins and J. O'Donoghue (Tipperary)
1985—J. O'Donoghue and E. Corbett (Tipperary)
1986—J. O'Donoghue and J. Fitzell (Tipperary)
1987—P. O'Keeffe and P. Maher (Kilkenny)
1988—D. Gough and D. McDonald (Meath)
1989—D. Gough and J. Lynch (Meath)
1990—D. Gough and J. Lynch (Meath)
1991—T. Hynes and P. Carly (Wexford)
1992—D. Moloney and N. Murphy (Tipperary)
1993—D. Moloney and N. Murphy (Tipperary)
1994—G. Kelleher and B. O'Neill (Cork)
1995—M. Finnegan and R. Cunningham (Cavan)
1996—T. Winders and D. Ward (Kildare)
1997—A. and P. Supple (Tipperary)
1998—B. Goff and C. Keeling (Wexford)
1999—C. Meenagh and S. McCullagh (Tyrone)
2000—D. Keegan and B. Hough (Mayo)
2001—P. Finnegan and R. McCormack (Cavan)
2002—M.Gregan and S. Willoughby (Wicklow)
2003—M. Cash and J. Goggins (Wexford)
2004—D. Martin and R. O'Gara (Roscommon)
2005—B. Carroll and D. Maguire (Meath)
2006—R. O'Gara and D. Martin (Roscommon)
2007—M. and J. Berry (Wexford)
2008—P. McGlinchey and B. Donaghy (Tyrone)
2009—S. O'Carroll and C.J. Fitzpatrick (Limerick)

LADIES SENIOR SINGLES

1992—B. Hennessy (Limerick)
1993—B. Hennessy (Limerick)
1996—B. Hennessy (Limerick)
1999—B. Hennessy (Limerick)
2002—A. Wrynn (Kildare)
2007—A. Prendeville (Kerry)
2008—A. Prendeville (Kerry)
2009—B. Hennessy (Limerick)

CLUB Records

CLUBS

COUNTY SENIOR HURLING TITLES WON BY CLUBS FROM START OF CHAMPIONSHIPS TO 2008 (inclusive)

HURLING

ROLL OF HONOUR

CONNACHT

GALWAY

Castlegar (17): 1936, 37, 38, 39, 40, 44, 50, 52, 53, 57, 58, 67, 69, 72, 73, 79, 84.
Ardrahan (11): 1894, 95, 96, 1901, 02, 03, 10, 49, 74, 75, 78.
Turloughmore (8): 1956, 61, 62, 63, 64, 65, 66, 85.
Liam Mellowes (8): 1935, 43, 45, 46, 54, 55, 68, 70.
Athenry (8): 1987, 1994, 1996, 1998, 1999, 2000, 2002, 2004.
Peterswell (7): 1889, 98, 99, 1900, 04, 05, 07.
Sarsfields (6): 1980, 89, 92, 93, 95, 97.
Tynagh (51: 1920, 22, 23, 25, 28.
Craughwell (5): 1909, 15, 18, 30, 31.
Gort (5): 1914, 16, 34, 81, 83.
Kiltormer (5): 1976, 77, 82, 90, 93.
Portumna (4): 2003, 2005, 2007, 2008.
Kilconieron (3): 1908, 12, 19.
Mullagh (3): 1906, 29, 32.
An Cath Gealach (2): 1947, 48.
Woodford (2): 1913, 17.
Fohenagh (2): 1959, 60.
College Road (2): 1892, 93.
Loughrea (2): 1941, 2006.
Meelick (1): 1887.
Killimor (1): 1897.
Derrydonnell (1): 1911.
Tommie Larkin's (1): 1971.
Maree (1): 1933.
Ballinasloe (1): 1951.
Killimordaly (1): 1986.
Abbeyknockmoy (1): 1988.
Clarenbridge (1): 2001.
1942 championship declared void.
There are no championship records for 1890, 1891, 1921, 1924, 1926 and 1927.

LEITRIM

St.Mary's-Carrick-on-Shannon (28): 1953, 1957, 1958, 1960, 1961, 1962, 1967, 1970, 1972, 1976, 1978, 1980, 1982, 1992, 1993, 1994, 1995, 1997, 1999, 2000, 2001, 2002, 2003, 2004, 2005, 2006, 2007, 2008.
Gortletteragh (10): 1983, 1984, 1985, 1986, 1988, 1989, 1990, 1991, 1996, 1998.
St. Finbarrs (Mohill) (9): 1917, 1964, 1965, 1966, 1968, 1969, 1973, 1974, 1979.
Manorhamilton (3): 1935, 1954, 1959.
Aughavas (1): 1956.
St. Brigid's (1): 1971.
Allen Gaels (1): 1975.
Lough Allen Gaels (1): 1977.
Ballinamore (1): 1987.

MAYO

Tooreen (27): 1966, 1972, 1974, 1975, 1978, 1979, 1980, 1981, 1982, 1983, 1984, 1985, 1986, 1987, 1989, 1990, 1991, 1992, 1993, 1994, 1995, 1997, 1998, 1999, 2000, 2001, 2003.
Westport (7): 1927, 1928, 1934, 1962, 1964, 1969, 1970.
Ballina Stephenites (7): 1907, 1925, 1930, 1932, 1933, 1959, 1996.
Swinford (5): 1916, 1917, 1918, 1919, 1956.
Castlebar Dr.Hydes (3): 1904, 1905, 1906.
Ballaghadereen (3): 1923, 1924, 1950.
Ballinrobe (3): 1973, 1976, 1977.
Ballyhaunis (3): 2005, 2006, 2008.
Ballyheane (2): 1929, 1935.
Castlebar Mitchels (2): 1910, 1955.
Manulla (2): 1960, 1961.
Cong (2): 1965, 1967.
Claremorris (2): 1968, 1971.
Castlebar Gaels (1): 1902.
Army-John McBrides (1): 1926.
Moy Slashers-Ballina (1): 1963.
North Mayo (1): 1988.
James Stephens (1): 2007.
1951-54 no records; 1957-58 no records.

ROSCOMMON

Four Roads (26): 1905, 1906, 1907, 1945, 1946, 1948, 1950, 1954, 1958, 1962, 1971, 1977, 1981, 1982, 1983, 1986, 1988, 1991, 1993, 1996, 1997, 2000, 2001, 2002, 2005, 2008.
Athleague (17): 1909, 1910, 1916, 1928, 1929, 1936, 1937, 1949, 1953, 1955, 1957, 1959, 1975, 1978, 2003, 2006, 2007.
Tremane (11): 1956, 60, 63, 68, 72, 73, 74, 76, 79, 80, 95.
Roscommon Town (6): 1913, 14, 1915, 23, 24, 25.
Roscommon Gaels (6): 1961, 64, 65, 66, 69, 70.
Oran (5): 1989, 1990, 1992, 1998, 2004.
Gaels Roscommon (3): 1902, 03, 04.
Roscommon (3): 1931, 35, 38.
St. Coman's Roscommon (3): 1944, 51, 52.
Padraig Pearses (2): 1984, 87.
Ballygar (2): 1930, 85.
St.Dominic's Knockcroghery (2): 1994, 1999.
Patrick's Knockcroghery (1): 1967.
Gael Araghty (1): 1908.
Elphin (1): 1926.
18th Battalion Boyle (1): 1927.

SLIGO

Craobh Rua (19): 1967, 1968, 1970, 1971, 1972, 1973, 1974, 1975, 1976, 1978, 1979, 1980,

1982, 1984, 1987, 1989, 1992, 1993, 1994.
Tubbercurry (13): 1969, 1977, 1995, 1996, 1997, 1998, 1999, 2000, 2001, 2002, 2003, 2004, 2006.
Tourlestrane (7): 1981, 83, 85, 86, 88, 90, 91.
Dromard-O'Growneys (6): 1906, 08, 34-36.
Sligo (3) 1928-30.
Calry/St. Joseph's (3): 2005, 2007, 2008.
Craobh Rua - Grange (2): 1965, 66.
Sligo Wanderers (1): 1905.
Sligo United (1): 1919.
St Columba's (1) 1907.
Note: No championship in 1910-18 and 1931-33.

LEINSTER

CARLOW

St.Mullins (21): 1932, 1949, 1950, 1951, 1952, 1953, 1954, 1957, 1958, 1959, 1960, 1962, 1965, 1966, 1968, 1983, 1984, 1989, 1997, 2000, 2002.
Naomh Eoin Myshall (19): 1974, 1975, 1976, 1978, 1981, 1982, 1985, 1986, 1987, 1990, 1991, 1992, 1993, 1994, 1995, 1997, 1999, 2003, 2005.
Erin's Own (11): 1934, 1935, 1936, 1939, 1940, 1943, 1944, 1945, 1964, 1967, 1970.
Carlow Town (10): 1927, 1937, 1938, 1942, 1961, 1963, 1977, 1979, 1980, 1988.
Bagenalstown (4): 1928, 1929, 1930, 1931.
Naomh Brid (3) – 1996, 2004, 2008.
Courtnellan (2): 1946, 1955.
St. Fintan's (2): 1969, 1971.
Ballinkillen (2) – 1973, 2001.
Mount Leinster Rangers (2): 2006, 2007.
Cooleyhune (1) 1933.
Hacketstown (1): 1947.
Leighlinbridge (1): 1956.
Palatine (1): 1972.

DUBLIN

Faughs (31): 1892, 1900, 1901, 1903, 1904, 1906, 1910, 1911, 1914, 1915, 1920, 1921, 1922, 1923, 1930, 1936, 1939, 1940, 1941, 1944, 1945, 1946, 1950, 1952, 1970, 1972, 1973, 1986, 1987, 1992, 1999.
St. Vincent's (13): 1953-55, 1957, 1960, 1962, 1964, 1967, 1975, 1981-82, 1988, 1993.
Commercials (9): 1895-99, 1905, 1907, 1909, 1916.
O'Tooles (7): 1969,1977,1984, 1990, 1995-97.
Garda (6): 1925-29, 1931.
Young Irelands (6): 1932, 1937, 1942-43, 1949, 1965.
Craobh Chiaráin (6): 1971, 1998, 2001, 2002, 2003, 2006.
Kickhams (4): 1889-90, 1908, 1924.
Raparees (3): 1891, 1894, 1912.
Collegians (3): 1917-19.
Army Metro (3): 1933, 1935, 1938.
Kilmacud Crokes (3): 1974, 1976, 1985.
Cuala (3): 1989, 1991, 1994.
U.C.D. (3): 2000, 2004, 2005.
New Irelands (2): 1958-59.
Ballyboden St. Enda's (2): 2007, 2008.
Metropolitans (1): 1887.
Davitts (1): 1893.
Thomas Davis (1): 1913.
Eoghan Ruadh (1): 1951.
St. Columbas (1): 1956.
Junior Board Sel. (1): 1963.
Crokes (1): 1966.
St. Brendan's (1): 1980.
Erin's Isle (1): 1983.

KILDARE

Clane (16): 1903, 1904, 1905, 1906, 1907, 1908, 1909, 1910, 1911, 1914-1919, 1922.
Ardclough (12): 1968, 1973, 1975, 1976, 1979, 1980, 1981, 1982, 1983, 1985, 2004, 2006.
Éire Óg (10): 1964, 1965, 1966, 1967, 1969, 1970, 1971, 1972, 1977, 1984.
Coill Dubh (10): 1987, 1989, 1990, 1993, 1995, 1996, 1998, 1999, 2000.
Maynooth (5): 1896, 1913, 1924, 1927, 1939.
Killinthomas (5): 1946, 1947, 1949, 1950, 1953.
Curragh Command (5): 1940, 1941, 1942, 1944, 1956.
McDonagh Barracks (4): 1929, 1932, 1934, 1935.
Athy (3): 1928, 1936, 1959.
Moorefield (3): 1944, 1963, 1991.
Military College (3): 1957, 1958, 1962.
Monasterevan (2): 1887, 1889.
St.Conleth's (2): 1901, 1902.
St.Barbara's (2): 1954, 1955.
Broadford (2): 1960, 1961.
Castledermot (2): 1988, 1992.
Naas (2): 2001, 2002.
Celbridge (2): 1921, 2005.
Confey (2): 2007, 2008.
St.Thomas's College (1): 1900.
Goff Barracks (1): 1925.
Eoghan Ruadh (1): 1945.
Suncroft (1): 1974.
Leixlip (1): 1986.

KILKENNY

Tullaroan (20): 1887, 1889, 1895,1897, 1899, 1901, 1902, 1904, 1907, 1910, 1911, 1915, 1924, 1925, 1930, 1933, 1934, 1948, 1958, 1994.
Mooncoin (12): 1888, 1900, 1906, 1908, 1913, 1916, 1926, 1928, 1929, 1932, 1936, 1965.
Bennetsbridge (12): 1890, 1952, 1953, 1955, 1956, 1959, 1960, 1962, 1964, 1966, 1967, 1971.
Ballyhale Shamrocks (12): 1978, 1979, 1980, 1982, 1983, 1985, 1988, 1989, 1991, 2006, 2007, 2008.
James Stephens (8): 1935, 1937, 1969, 1975, 1976, 1981, 2004, 2005.
Carrickshock (7): 1931, 1938, 1940, 1941, 1942, 1943, 1951.
Fenians (5): 1970, 1972, 1973, 1974, 1977.
Glenmore (5): 1987, 1990, 1992, 1995, 1999.

Éire Óg (4): 1939, 1944, 1945, 1947.
Young Irelands-Gowran (3): 1996, 2002, 2003.
Erins Own-City (2): 1905, 1929.
Threecastles (2): 1898, 1903.
St. Lachtain's-Freshford (2): 1961, 1963.
Graigue-Ballycallan (2): 1998, 2000.
Johnstown (1): 1914.
Thomastown (1): 1946.
Graigue (1): 1949.
Slieverue (1): 1954.
John Lockes-Callan (1): 1957.
Rower-Inistiogue (1): 1968.
St. Martin's (1): 1984.
Clara (1): 1986.
Dunnamaggin (1): 1997.
O'Loughlin Gaels (1): – 2001.
No Championships 1891-92, 1912, 1917-18, 1920-22.
Declared Void 1919.

LAOIS

Camross (23): 1959, 1963, 1965-69, 1971, 1973-74, 1976-80, 1985-86, 1988, 1990, 1993-94, 1996, 2007.
Rathdowney (19): 1888-89, 1898-99, 1901-03, 1907-08, 1911-12, 1921-22, 1925-26, 1931, 1936, 1941, 2006.
Clonad (13): 1930, 1933, 1935, 1937, 1946-48, 1950, 1953-54, 1958, 1962, 1992.
Portlaoise (11) – 1928, 1943, 1981, 1982, 1983, 1984, 1987, 1989, 1991, 1998, 2004.
Kilcotton (10): 1904-06, 1909, 1913, 1919-20, 1923-24, 1929.
Abbbeyleix (8): 1927, 1932, 1934, 1939-40, 1944-45, 1949.
Castletown (8): 1995, 1997, 1999, 2000, 2001, 2002, 2003, 2005.
Borris-in-Ossory (6): 1956-58, 1960-61, 1972.
Ballygeehan (5): 1914-18.
Clonaslee (3): 1890, 1910, 1975.
Errill (2): 1938, 1952.
Cullahill (2): 1955, 1964.
Mountrath (1): 1942.
Kyle (1): 1951.
Rathdowney-Errill (1): 2008

LONGFORD

Slasher Gaels (12): 1982, 1983, 1984, 1986, 1987, 1989, 1990, 1991, 1997, 1999, 2000, 2001.
Wolfe Tones (9): 1992, 1993, 1994, 1995, 1996, 1998, 2002, 2004, 2008.
Longford Leo Caseys (5): 1902, 1903, 1904, 1905, 1906.
Granard Slashers (3): 1932, 1933, 1934.
Clonguish (3): 2003, 2005, 2006.
Rathcline (Naomh Chiaráin) (2): 1985, 1988.
Killoe Young Emmets (1): 1907.
Mostrim (1): 2007.
No competition 1935-1981.

LOUTH

Naomh Moninne-Dundalk (19): 1964, 1965, 1973, 1974, 1976, 1978, 1982, 1983, 1984, 1985, 1986, 1987, 1992, 1993, 1995, 1997, 1998, 1999.
Naomh Colmcille Ardee (8): 1955, 1958, 1960, 1962-63, 1966, 1971, 1975.
Wolfe Tones (Drogheda) (7): 1954, 1959, 1988, 1990-91, 1994, 1996.
Knockbridge (7): 2000, 2001, 2003, 2005, 2006, 2007, 2008.
C.B.S. Tredaghs (Drogheda) (6): 1907, 1911-12, 1927, 1934-35.
C.B.S. Shamrocks (Drogheda) (6): 1933, 1936, 1940, 1943-45.
Dundalk Hurling Club (4): 1904, 1917, 1924-25.
Erins Own (Dundalk) (3): 1951-53.
Clan na nGael (Dundalk) (2): 1970, 1972.
Na Piarsaigh (Drogheda) (2) 1968-69.
Cuchulainns (2): 1956-57.
Con Colberts (Dundalk) (2): 1919, 1921.
Pearse Óg (2): 2002, 2004.
Hitchestown (1): 1932.
Gaelic League (Dundalk) (1): 1928.
Ardee St. Mochta's (1): 1926.
John Mitchells (Drogheda) (1): *1918.
Dundalk Recreation Club (1): 1909.
Boyne Emmets (Drogheda) (1): 1908.
Hitchestown (1): 1932.
Shamracks (Dundalk) (1): 1902 (First organised Louth Championship).
Note: 1902-1986 (inclusive) run as Junior Championship. Changed to Senior status in 1987.

MEATH

Kilmessan (29): 1907, 1922, 1924, 1927, 1934, 1937, 1938, 1939, 1943, 1944, 1945, 1946, 1947, 1948, 1961, 1962, 1965, 1969, 1976, 1977, 1978, 1990, 1997, 1998, 1999, 2002, 2003, 2004, 2008.
Trim (26): 1915, 1916, 1918, 1920, 1921, 1935, 1940, 1941, 1942, 1949, 1950, 1952, 1955, 1956, 1957, 1959, 1960, 1987, 1988, 1989, 1992, 1994, 1995, 1998, 2000, 2001.
Athboy (9): 1923, 1926, 1928-29, 1966-68, 1970, 1972.
Killyon (7): 1919, 1979-81, 1984, 1991, 2005.
Boardsmill (6): 1958, 1964, 1971, 1973-75.
Dunboyne (5): 1908, 1911-14.
Young Irelands (4): 1903-06.
Rathmolyon (3): 1993, 1996, 2006.
Kiltale (3): 1982-83, 2007.
Erin's Own (2): 1930-31.
St. Patrick's (2): 1953-54.
Navan O'Mahoneys (2): 1985-86.
Hibernian, Kells (1): 1902.
Longwood (1): 1936.
Kildalkey (1): 1951.
Rathoath (1): 1963.

OFFALY

Coolderry (28): 1899, 1901, 1903, 1904, 1905, 1906, 1910, 1911, 1914, 1916, 1917, 1926, 1931, 1939, 1942, 1945, 1947, 1949, 1953, 1956, 1961, 1962, 1963, 1977, 1980, 1986, 2004.
Birr (22): 1912, 1913, 1915, 1938, 1940, 1943, 1944, 1946, 1948, 1971, 1991, 1994, 1997, 1999, 2000, 2001, 2002, 2003, 2005, 2006, 2007, 2008.
Drumcullen (17): 1908, 1918, 1919, 1924, 1925, 1927, 1928, 1929, 1933, 1941, 1950, 1951, 1952, 1954, 1957, 1958, 1960.
St. Rynagh's (17): 1965-66, 1968-70, 1972-76, 1981-82,1987-88, 1990, 1992-93.
Tullamore (9): 1909, 1932, 1934-37, 1955, 1959, 1964.
Kinnitty (9): 1920, 1923, 1930, 1967, 1978-79, 1983-85.
Sier Kieran (4): 1988, 1995-96, 1998.
Killoughey (3): 1896-97, 1907.
Cadamstown (2): 1900, 1902.
Lusmagh (1): 1989.
Fortal (1): 1898.

WESTMEATH

Brownstown (15): 1938, 1943, 1946, 1947, 1948, 1952, 1977, 1978, 1981, 1983, 1985, 1988, 1989, 1991, 1993.
Castlepollard (14): 1925, 1928, 1933, 1934, 1936, 1937, 1961, 1965, 1966, 1974, 1995, 1997, 2003, 2005.
Castletown-Geoghegan (11): 1923, 1956, 1957, 1958, 1960, 1964, 1979, 1982, 1986, 1990, 2004.
Raharney (11): 1913, 1914, 1919, 1967, 1973, 1984, 1992, 1994, 2006, 2008.
Clonkill (10): 1929, 1930, 1931, 1932, 1939, 1940, 1941, 1969, 2001, 2007.
Ringtown (9): 1906, 1908, 1910, 1915, 1916, 1917, 1942, 1980, 1987.
Lough Lene Gaels (7): 1975, 1976, 1996, 1998, 1999, 2000, 2002.
St. Brigid's (4): 1968, 1970, 1971, 1972.
Athlone (4): 1905, 1907, 1911, 1912.
Delvin (4): 1949, 1950, 1951, 1953.
Mullingar (4): 1903, 1904, 1935, 1944.
Rickardstown (3): 1954, 1959, 1963.
Athlone Military (2): 1926, 1927.
Drumroney (2): 1918, 1921.
Riverstown (1): 1909.
Collinstown (1): 1955.
Mental Hospital (1): 1924.
Pearses (1): 1962.
Columb Rovers (1): 1945.
N.B.: No championships in 1920 or 1922.

WEXFORD

Rathnure (20): 1948, 1950, 1955, 1961, 1967, 1971, 1972, 1973, 1974, 1977, 1979, 1980, 1986, 1987, 1990, 1996, 1998, 2002, 2003.
Buffers Alley (12): 1968, 1970, 1975, 1976, 1982, 1983, 1984, 1985, 1988, 1989, 1991, 1992. 2006.
Adamstown (11): 1926, 1927, 1931, 1932, 1933, 1935, 1936, 1937, 1940, 1941, 1942.
St. Aidan's (Enniscorthy) (9): 1946, 1947, 1952, 1953, 1954, 1956, 1957, 1958, 1959.
Faythe Harriers (5): 1960, 1962, 1965, 1981, 2001.
Blackwater (3): 1889, 1890, 1898.
New Ross United (3): 1943, 1944, 1945.
Cloughbown (3): 1949, 1951, 1993.
Oulart-the-Ballagh (5): 1994, 1997, 2004, 2005, 2007.
Castlebridge (2): 1904, 1919.
Ballymurn (2): 1910, 1911.
Glenbrien (2): 1915, 1916.
Sally Beachers (2): 1928, 1930.
St. Fintan's (2): 1929, 1934.
Shamrocks (2): 1964, 1969.
St.Martin's (2): 1999, 2008.
Slaney Harriers (1): 1903.
Rathgarogue (1): 1912.
New Ross (1): 1913.
Enniscorthy Rapparees (1): 1914.
Crossabeg (1): 1918.
O'Hanrahan's (New Ross) (1): 1939.
Oylegate-Glenbrien (1) 1963.
Geraldine O'Hanrahans (1): 1966.
Raparees (1): 1978.
St.Anne's-Rathangan (1): 2000.

WICKLOW

Carnew (18): 1965, 1967, 1968, 1969, 1973, 1974, 1976, 1978, 1979, 1980, 1981, 1984, 1988, 1991, 2000, 2002, 2004, 2006.
Avondale (14): 1908, 1915, 1931, 1936, 1940, 1941, 1942, 1946, 1947, 1949, 1960, 1964, 1966, 1983.
Barndarrig (12): 1923, 1924, 1955, 1956, 1988.
Rathnew (11): 1906, 1911, 1913, 1925, 1929, 1932, 1933, 1934.
Glenealy (10): 1957, 1958, 1959, 1975, 1986, 1996, 2003, 2005, 2007, 2008.
Kiltegan (8): 1987, 1993, 1995, 1997, 1998, 1999, 2001.
St. Patrick's (Wicklow) (6): 1903, 1916, 1928, 1930 (as Wicklow), 1990, 1992.
Arklow (6): 1970, 1971, 1972, 1977, 1982, 1985.
Arklow Rocks (3): 1917, 1918, 1919.
St. Kevin's (Bray) (2): 1961, 1963.
Ballymoney (1): 1910.
Baltinglass (1): 1927.
Ballinacor (1): 1935.
Bray Emmets (1): 1952.
Avoca (1): 1953.
Forestry College (1): 1962.

MUNSTER

CLARE

Newmarket (22): 1912, 1916, 1925-27, 1930-31, 1936, 1955, 1963-65, 1967-69, 1971-74, 1976, 1978, 1981.
Clarecastle (11): 1943, 1945, 1949, 1970, 1986, 1987, 1991, 1994, 1997, 2003, 2005.
Sixmilebridge (10): 1977, 1979, 1983, 1984, 1989, 1992, 1993, 1995, 2000, 2002.
Tulla (8): 1889, 1896, 1897, 1899, 1905, 1913, 1933, 2007.
Feakle (6): 1935, 1938-40, 1944, 1988.
Éire Óg (6): 1956, 1957, 1966, 1980, 1982, 1990.
O'Callaghans Mills (5): 1904, 1906, 1910, 1918, 1937.
Scarriff (5): 1907, 1917, 1946, 1952, 1953.
Ennis Dalcassians (5): 1914, 1915, 1924, 1929, 1934.
St.Joseph's Doora-Barefield (5): 1954, 1958, 1998, 1999, 2001.
Ruan (5): 1948, 1951, 1959, 1960, 1962.
Kilnamona (3): 1902, 1903, 1908.
Carrahan (2): 1898, 1900.
Ennis (2): 1911, 1941.
Kilkishen (2): 1923, 1932.
Whitegate (2): 1950, 1961.
Kilmaley (2): 1985, 2004.
Wolfe Tones Shannon (2): 1997, 2006.
Clonlara (2): 1919, 2008.
Smith O'Briens-Garranboy (1): 1887.
Ogonnolloe (1): 1888.
Ennis Faughs (1): 1890.
O'C Mills-Fireballs (1): 1909.
Ennis-Clarecastle (1): 1928.
Clooney (1): 1942.
Bodyke (1): 1947.
Brian Borus (1): 1975.

CORK

Blackrock (32): 1887, 1889, 1891, 1893, 1894, 1895, 1897, 1898, 1903, 1908, 1910, 1911, 1912, 1913, 1920, 1924, 1925, 1927, 1929, 1930, 1931, 1956, 1961, 1971, 1973, 1975, 1978, 1979, 1985, 1999, 2001, 2002.
Glen Rovers (25): 1934, 1935, 1936, 1937, 1938, 1939, 1940, 1941, 1944, 1945, 1948, 1949, 1950, 1953, 1954, 1958, 1959, 1960, 1962, 1964, 1967, 1969, 1972, 1976, 1989.
St. Finbarrs (25): 1899, 1904, 1905, 1906, 1919, 1922, 1923, 1926, 1932, 1933, 1942, 1943, 1946, 1947, 1955, 1965, 1968, 1974, 1977, 1980, 1981, 1982, 1984, 1988, 1993.
Midleton (6): 1914, 1916, 1983, 1986, 1987, 1991.
Redmonds (5): 1892, 1900, 1901, 1915, 1917.
Avondhu (3): 1952, 1966, 1996.
Na Piarsaigh (3): 1990, 1995, 2004.
Dungourney (3): 1902, 1907, 1909.
Newtownshandrum (3): 2000, 2003, 2005.
Erin's Own (3): 1992, 2006, 2007.
Sarsfields (3): 1951, 1957, 2008.
University College (2): 1963, 1970.
Imokilly (2): 1997, 1998.
Tower Street (1): 1888.
Aghabullogue (1): 1890.
Ballyhea (1): 1896.
Carrigtwohill (1): 1918.
Éire Óg (1): 1928.
Carberry (1): 1994.

KERRY

Ballyduff (21): 1891, 1955, 1959, 1960, 1961, 1965,1966, 1972, 1973, 1977, 1979, 1984, 1988, 1989, 1991, 1993, 1994, 1995, 2006.
Kilmoyley (21): 1890, 1892, 1894, 1895, 1900, 1901, 1905, 1907, 1910, 1914, 1948, 1962, 1963, 1964, 1970, 1971, 2001, 2002, 2003, 2004, 2008.
Crotta (10): 1939, 1941, 1943, 1944, 1945, 1947, 1950, 1951, 1968, 1999.
Causeway (7): 1932, 1979, 1980, 1981, 1982, 1987, 1998.
Ardfert St. Brendan's (6): 1949, 1952, 1967, 1975, 1986, 1990.
Lixnaw (6): 1933, 1954, 1983, 1985, 2005, 2007.
Tralee Mitchels/Parnells (5): 1908, 1911, 1912, 1918, 1919.
Ballyheigue (5): 1946, 1992, 1996, 1997, 2000.
Abbeydorney (4): 1893, 1896, 1913, 1974.
Austin Stacks (3): 1928, 1929, 1931.
Kilgarvan (3): 1953, 1956, 1958.
Tralee Celtic (2): 1903, 1904.
Pearses (div.) (2): 1937, 1938.
Tullig (1): 1916 (disputed with Kenmare).
Tubrid (1): 1917.
Tralee (div.) (1): 1925.
St. Brendan's (div.) (1): 1936.
Banna (1): 1940.
Killarney (1): 1969.

LIMERICK

Ahane (20): 1931, 1933, 1934, 1935, 1936, 1937, 1938, 1939, 1942, 1943, 1944, 1945, 1946, 1947, 1948, 1955, 1998, 1999, 2001, 2004.
Patrickswell (18): 1965, 1966, 1969, 1970, 1977, 1979, 1982, 1983, 1984, 1987, 1988, 1990, 1993, 1995, 1996, 1997, 2000, 2003.
Claughaun (10): 1914-16, 1918, 1926, 1957, 1958, 1968, 1971, 1986.
Kilmallock (8): 1960, 1967, 1973-75, 1985, 1992, 1994.
Young Irelands (7): 1902, 1910, 1920, 1922, 1928, 1930, 1932.
South Liberties (7): 1888-1890, 1972, 1976, 1978, 1981.
Croom (6): 1908, 1919, 1924, 1929, 1940-41.
Cappamore (5): 1904, 1954, 1956, 1959, 1964.
Caherline (3): 1896, 1905, 1907.
Treaty Sarsfields (3): 1951-53.
Adare (3): 2002, 2007, 2008.
Kilfinane (2): 1897, 1899.
Fedamore (2): 1912, 1927.
Newcastlewest (2): 1917, 1925.

Western Gaels (2): 1961, 1962.
Ballybrown (2): 1989, 1991.
Saints Patrick's (2): 1949, 1950.
Castleconnell (1): 1950.
Murroe (1): 1887.
Treaty Stones (1): 1891.
Saint Michael's (1): 1895.
South Limerick (1): 1893.
Shamrocks (1): 1898.
Sallymount (1): 1900.
Ballingarry (1): 1911.
Killeedy (1): 1980.
Feenagh-Kilmeedy (1): 1963.
Garryspillane (1): 2005.
Bruree (1): 2006.

TIPPERARY

Thurles Sarsfields (21): 1935, 1936, 1938-39, 1942, 1944-46, 1952, 1955-59, 1961-65, 1974, 2005.
Toomevara (21): 1890, 1910, 1912, 1913, 1914, 1919, 1923, 1930, 1931, 1960, 1992, 1993, 1994, 1998, 1999, 2000, 2001, 2003, 2004, 2006, 2008.
Boherlahan (11): 1915-18, 1922, 1924-25, 1927-28, 1941, 1946.
Borris-lleigh (7): 1949-50, 1953, 1981, 1983, 1986-87.
Thurles (7): 1904, 1906-09, 1911, 1929.
Roscrea (6): 1968-70, 1972-73, 1980.
Moycarkey-Borris (6): 1932, 1934, 1937, 1940, 1982, 1984.
Kilruane-McDonaghs (4): 1977-79, 1985.
Tubberadora (3): 1895-96, 1898.
Two Mile Borris (3): 1900, 1903, 1905.
Moycarkey (2): 1889, 1926.
Carrick Davins (2): 1966-67.
Moneygall (2): 1975-76.
Clonoulty-Rossmore (2): 1989, 1997.
Holycross-Ballycahill (2): 1948, 1951.
Holycross (2): 1954, 1990.
Clonoulty (1): 1888.
Drombane (1): 1994.
Suir View (1): 1897.
Horse and Jockey (1): 1899.
Ballytarsna (1): 1901.
Lahorna De Wets (1): 1902.
Éire Óg-Annacarty (1): 1943.
Carrick Swans (1): 1947.
Moyne-Templetuohy (1): 1971.
Cappawhite (1): 1987.
Loughmore (1): 1988.
Cashel King Cormacs (1): 1991.
Éire Óg Nenagh (1): 1995.
Mullinahone (1): 2002.
Loughmore/Castleiney (1): 2007.

WATERFORD

Mount Sion (35): 1938, 1939, 1940, 1943, 1945, 1948, 1949, 1951, 1953, 1954, 1955, 1956, 1957, 1958, 1959, 1960, 1961, 1963, 1964, 1965, 1969, 1972, 1974, 1975, 1981, 1983, 1986, 1988, 1994, 1998, 2000, 2002, 2003, 2004, 2006.
Erin's Own (12): 1927-35, 1942, 1947, 1962.
Ballygunner (10): 1966, 1967, 1968, 1993, 1995, 1996, 1997, 1999, 2001, 2005.
T. F. Meagher (6): 1909-12, 1922, 1924.
Dungarvan (6): 1908, 1917, 1920, 1923, 1926, 1941.
Portlaw (6): 1937, 1970, 1971, 1973, 1976, 1977.
Clonea (4): 1903, 1905, 1907, 1952.
Tallow (4): 1936, 1980, 1984, 1985.
Ferrybank (3): 1915, 1916, 1919.
Lismore (3): 1925, 1991, 1993.
De La Salle (3): 1913, 1914, 2008.
Dunhill (2): 1982, 1987.
Roanmore (2): 1989, 1990.
Ballytruckle (1): 1897.
Ballydurn (1): 1899.
Gracedieu (1): 1904.
Ballyduff Lower (1): 1906.
Éire Óg (1): 1918.
Tourin (1): 1950.
Army (1): 1944.
Ballyduff Upper (1): 2007.

ULSTER

ANTRIM

Ballycastle (17): 1913, 1914, 1933, 1944, 1948, 1950, 1952, 1953, 1954, 1964, 1975, 1978, 1979, 1 980, 1983, 1984, 1986.
Loughgiel (15): 1920, 1924, 1925, 1929, 1938, 1943, 1956, 1963, 1966, 1967, 1 968, 1970, 1971, 1982, 1989.
O'Donovan Rossa (15): 1918, 1919, 1921, 1946, 1949, 1955, 1957, 1958, 1959, 1960, 1972, 1976, 1977, 1988, 2004.
Cushendall (11): 1981, 1985, 1987, 1991, 1992, 1993, 1996, 1999, 2005, 2006, 2008.
Dunloy (10): 1990, 1994, 1995, 1997, 1998, 2000, 2001, 2002, 2003, 2007.
O'Connell's (9): 1927, 1928, 1930, 1 932, 1936, 1940, 1941, 1942, 1945.
St. John's (7): 1934, 1951, 1961, 1962, 1965, 1969, 1973.
Tír na nÓg (5): 1904, 1905, 1922, 1926, 1939.
Carey (3): 1906, 1916, 1923.
Seaghan an Díomais (3): 1908, 1910, 1915.
Seán Mitchel's (3): 1911, 1912, 1947.
Brian Óg (2): 1901, 1909.
Glenariffe (2): 1935, 1937.
O'Neill Crowleys (2): 1903, 1907.
Cushendun (1): 1931.
James Stephen's (1): 1917.
Lámh Dhearg (1): 1902.
Sarsfields (1): 1974.

ARMAGH

Cuchullain's, Armagh (21): 1951, 1952, 1953, 1954, 1961, 1962, 1963, 1964, 1969, 1970, 1971, 1973, 1974, 1979, 1 980, 1 982, 1983,

1984, 1987, 1988, 1989.
Lámh Dhearg, Keady (15): 1949, 1965, 1972, 1975, 1990, 1992, 1993, 1994, 1995, 1996, 1997, 1998, 2005, 2007, 2008.
Middletown (5): 1981, 1985, 1986, 1991, 2006.
Christian Brothers' Armagh Past Pupils' Union (3): 1945, 1946, 1948.
Éire Óg, Keady (3): 1927, 1932, 1933.
Armagh Harps (1): 1905.
Michael Dwyer's, Keady (1): 1906.
St. Malachy's, Portadown (2): 1966, 1967.
Bessbrook (1): 1947.
O'Donnell's, Armagh (1): 1934.
Red Hand's, Armagh (1): 1931.
Hugh Carberry's, Rocks (1): 1950.
Seán an Díomais, Camlough (1): 1907.
Tir na nÓg, Armagh (1): 1904.
Young Ireland's (1): 1928.

CAVAN

Cavan Slashers (8): 1922, 1924, 1927, 1928, 1933-1936.
Bailieboro Shamrocks (5): 1982, 1984, 2005, 2006, 2007.
Ballyhaise (4): 1925, 1926, 1947, 1948.
Woodford Gaels (3): 1986, 1987, 1988.
Mullahoran St. Joseph's (3): 1989, 1990, 2008.
Cavan Gaels (2): 1983, 1985.
Drumbo (1): 1927.
Kill (1): 1930.
Cootehill (1): 1932.
Granard (1): 1950.
(Mullahoran St. Joseph's have been nominated every year since 1990).

DERRY

Kevin Lynch's Dungiven (19) 1972, 1973, 1974, 1975, 1976, 1977, 1979, 1981, 1982, 1984, 1987, 1989, 1996, 1998, 2003, 2004, 2006, 2007, 2008.
Lavey (17):1940, 1944, 1946, 1948, 1962, 1985, 1986, 1988, 1990, 1991, 1992, 1994, 1995, 1997, 1999, 2001, 2002.
Dungiven (14): 1972, 1973, 1974, 1975, 1976, 1977, 1979, 1981, 1982, 1984, 1987, 1989, 2003, 2004.
Slaughtneil (6): 1965, 1966, 1968, 1969, 1993, 2000.
Banagher (3): 2005.
Sarsfields (2): 1933, '34.
St. Patrick's Waterside (2) 1891, 1905.
Banagher (2): 1978, '80.
Kevin Lynch's (2): 1996, 1998.
St. Finbarr's Lough (2): 1963, '64.
Hibernians (1): 1889.
Burt (1): 1930.
Ailech (1): 1937.
Ballinscran (1): 1938.
Mitchells Coleraine (1): 1945.
Note: No championship in 1983.

DONEGAL

Burt (32): 1906, 1956-'57, 1961-'62, '67, 1969-'71, '76, 1978-'79, 1982-'83, 1989, 1991 -'05, 2005, 2006.
Setanta (10): 1980-'81, 1983-'87, 1990, 2007, 2008.
St. Union's Letterkenny (7): 1926, 1932-'33, 1938, 1945, 1953, 1972.
Aodh-Ruadh Ballyshannon (5): 1 924-'25, 1929, 1975, 1977.
Carrowmore (4): 1934-'37.
Carndonagh (3): 1944, 1954, 1959.
Gleann-Eirne (2): 1958, 1960.
Lifford (2): 1958, 1960.
Bundoran (1): 1907.
Finner Camp (1): 1927.
Glen Swilly (1) 1963.

DOWN

Kilclief (23): 1912, 1913, 1914, 1915, 1916, 1917, 1918, 1919, 1920, 1925, 1931, 1932, 1933, 1935, 1939, 1942, 1943, 1944, 1945, 1947, 1954, 1955, 1956.
Ballycran (20): 1949, 1953, 1957, 1960, 1961, 1967, 1972, 1974, 1976, 1977, 1979, 1980, 1984, 1985, 1986, 1987, 1993, 1994, 1995, 2007.
Portaferry (19):1926, 1929, 1938, 1963, 1965, 1968, 1969, 1971, 1978, 1981, 1988, 1989, 1991, 1996, 2000, 2001, 2002, 2003, 2006.
Ballygalget (17): 1959, 1964, 1966, 1970, 1973, 1974, 1975, 1982, 1983, 1990, 1992, 1997, 1998, 1999, 2004, 2005, 2008.
Ballela (7): 1936, 1937, 1940, 1941, 1948, 1951, 1952.
Faugh-an-Bealach, Newry (6): 1903, 1904, 1907, 1908, 1909, 1930.
Clann na Boirce, Newry (2): 1905, 1906.
Clann Uladh, Newry (2): 1934, 1936.
Liatroim (2): 1927, 1928.
Ballyvarley (1): 1910.
*N.B. 1962 final result declared null and void
*Not played in 1911, 1927-24, 1950.

FERMANAGH

Lisbellaw St. Patrick's (21): 1972, 1976-'77, 1982-'83, 1985-'89, 1991'98, 2006, 2007, 2008.
Belleek Erne Gaels (5): 1973, '75, '81, '84.
Enniskillen O'Neill (3): 1904, 1906, 1907.
COA O'Dwyers (3): 1935, 1938-39.
Glasmullagh (3): 1936, 1945-46.
Enniskillen Gaels (2): 1979, 1990.
Ashwood Maguires (2): 1905, 1908.
Lisnaskea Emmets (2): 1980, 2005.
Newtownbutler (1): 1937.
Note: No championship played in 1909-'34, 1940-'44, 1947-'71 and 1978.

MONAGHAN

Clontibret (16): 1966, '69, 1973, '78, 1980-'87, 1990-'91, 1997.

Castleblayney (13): 1943, 1955, 1957, 1962, 1974, '79, 1988-'89, 1992, 2005, 2006, 2007, 2008.
(Note: Castleblayney were known as "Eire Óg" Club in 1962).
Carrickmacross (7): 1914, '45, 1963-'64, '67, 1971, '75.
Monaghan Harps (5): 1956, 1993, 1995-'96, 1998.
Clones (4): 1911, 1950-'51, 1968.
Ballybay (1): 1976.
Note: The championship was unfinished in 1965.

TYRONE

Dungannon (18): 1948, 1951, 1952, 1953, 1955, 1956, 1957, 1961, 1969, 1975, 1978, 1990, 1992, 1993, 1996, 1997, 2005, 2008.
Carrickmore (15): 1974, 1976, 1979, 1980, 1982, 1983, 1984, 1985, 1986, 1987, 1988, 1989, 1998, 2006, 2007.
Killyclogher (6): 1905, 1950, 1977, 1991, 1994, 1995.
Omagh (3): 1967, 1971, 1973.
Strabane (2): 1924, 1926.
Benburb (1): 1966.
Dromore (1): 1949.
Dunamanagh (1): 1981.
*N.B. Competition not played in other years.

COUNTY SENIOR FOOTBALL TITLES WON BY CLUBS FROM START OF CHAMPIONSHIPS TO 2008 (inclusive)

FOOTBALL

ROLL OF HONOUR

CONNACHT

GALWAY

Tuam Stars (24): 1892, 93, 94, 95, 96,1908, 09,11, 42, 43, 47, 52, 54, 55, 56, 57, 58, 59, 60, 62, 84, 88, 89, 94.
Ballinasloe (17): 1913, 14, 15, 16, 17, 18, 19, 22, 23, 25, 28, 29, 39, 44, 45, 79, 80.
Dunmore McHales (15): 1889, 91, 1900, 02, 07, 10, 12, 53, 61, 66, 68, 69, 73, 83.
Corofin (12): 1932, 1946, 1977, 1991, 1993, 1995, 1997, 1998, 2000, 2002, 2006, 2008.
Fr Griffin's (7): 1948, 49, 50, 67, 70, 72, 75.
Killererin (5): 1976, 1978, 1999, 2004, 2007.
Annaghdown (5): 1931, 1982, 1985, 1987, 2001.
Mountbellew/Moylough (4): 1964, 65, 74, 86.
Athenry De Wets (3): 1903, 04, 06.
UCG (3) 1933, 34, 37.
Loughrea (2): 1897, 98.
Army Renmore (2): 1940, 51.
Milltown (2): 1971, 81.
An Cheathru Rua (2): 1996, 1999.
Caherlistrane (1): 1890.
Tuam Krugers (1): 1901.
Tuam St Jarlath's (1): 1905.
Galway Gaels (1): 1930.
Wolfe Tones, Galway (1): 1936.
Oughterard (1): 1938.
Salthill (1): 1990.
Monivea/Abbeyknockmoy (1): 1992.
Calta (1): 2003.
Salthill/Knocknacarra (1): 2005
Championships were not completed in the following years: 1899, 1920, 21, 24, 26, 27, 35.

LEITRIM

Seán O'Heslins (Ballinamore) (20): 1913, 22, 30, 33, 35, 36, 39, 56, 64, 67, 69, 69, 72, 73, 75, 79, 82, 86, 88, 90.
Cloone (11): 1911, 34, 37, 42, 44, 46, 47, 48, 50, 51, 80.
Aughawillan (9): 1923 (Kiltyhugh), 76, 78, 83, 84, 89, 92, 93, 94.
Aughavas (9): 1915, 1940, 1949, 1952, 1954, 1955, 1963, 1966, 2000.
Gortletteragh (5): 1905, 70, 81, 85, 87.
Fenagh (5): 1906, 10 (probable), 12, 19, 32.
Melvin Gaels (5): 1959, 60, 61, 65, 98.
Allen Gaels (5): 1991, 1996, 1997, 2001, 2002.
Mohill (5): 1890, 1914, 1929, 1971, 2006.
Bornacoola (4): 1938, 43, 53, 57.
Gorvagh (4): 1924, 25, 26, 27.
St Mary's (Carrick-on-Shannon) (4): 1958, 1995, 2003, 2007.
Eslin (3): 1891, 1916, 17.
Glencar/Manorhamilton (3): 1977, 1999, 2008.
Annaduff (2): 1928, 2004.
Aughnasheelin (1): 1918.
Drumreilly (1): 1931.
Sheemore Gaels (1): 1974 (St Mary's/Fenagh/ Kiltubrid amalgamation).
Kiltubrid (1): 2005.

MAYO

Ballina Stephenites (35): 1889, 1904, 1905, 1906, 1907, 1908, 1909, 1910, 1911, 1912, 1913, 1914, 1915, 1916, 1918, 1920, 1924, 1925, 1926, 1927, 1928, 1929, 1935, 1938, 1940, 1943, 1947, 1955, 1966, 1985, 1987, 1998, 2003, 2004, 2007.
Castlebar Mitchels (28): 1888, 1903, 30, 31, 32, 33, 34, 41, 42, 44, 45, 46, 48, 50, 51, 52, 53, 54, 56, 59, 62, 63, 69, 70, 78, 86, 88, 93.
Knockmore (8): 1973, 80, 83, 84, 89, 92, 96, 97.
Crossmolina (7): 1949, 1995, 1999, 2000, 2002, 2005, 2006.
Garrymore (6): 1974, 75, 76, 79, 81, 92.
Claremorris (4): 1961, 64, 65, 71.
Ballycastle (3): 1936, 37, 39.
Hollymount (3): 1990, 91, 94.
Ballyhaunis (2): 1919, 58.

East Mayo (2): 1957, 67.
Ballaghaderreen (2): 1972, 2008.
Ballina Commercials (1): 1890.
Charleston Sarsfields (1): 1902.
Lacken (1): 1917.
West Mayo (1): 1960.
North Mayo (1): 1968.
Aughamore (1): 1977.
Charlestown (1): 2001.

ROSCOMMON

Clan na nGael (19): 1961, 66, 70, 76, 77, 79, 81, 82, 84, 85, 86, 87, 88, 89, 90, 91, 93, 95, 96.
Roscommon Gaels (11): 1962, 1972, 1974, 1975, 1978, 1980, 1994, 1998, 1999, 2001, 2004.
Elphin (10): 1889, 1891, 1931, 1932, 1937, 1950, 1951, 1955, 1956, 1957.
Strokestown (10): 1912, 1915, 1916, 1917, 1922, 1926, 1928, 1933, 1992, 2002.
St. Brigid's (9): 1953, 58, 59, 63, 69, 97, 2005, 2006, 2007.
Tarmon (6): 1935, 39, 40, 41, 44, 47.
St. Patrick's (6): 1942, 43, 45, 46, 48, 49.
Kilbride (5): 1907, 1908, 1909, 1914, 2000.
Castlerea St. Kevin's (5): 1967, 1968, 1971, 1973, 2008.
Elphin Wm O'Briens (4): 1902, 03, 04, 05.
Donamon (4): 1918, 19, 20, 1925.
Roscommon (3): 1930, 1936, 1938.
Roscommon "The Blues" (2): 1911, 13.
Tulsk Lord Edwards (2): 1923, 24.
Boyle (2): 1890, 1927.
Fuerty (2): 1929, 1934.
Kilbride Emmets/Elphin (1): 1906.
Tulsk (1): 1910.
St. Coman's Knockcroghery (1): 1952.
St. Coman's Roscommon (1): 1954.
United Stars (Oran/Creggs) (1): 1960.
Shannon Gaels (1): 1964.
St. Faithleachs (1): 1965.
Kilmore (1): 1983.
Castlerea (1): 2003.

SLIGO

Tubbercurry (19): 1890, 1917, 18, 24, 27, 28, 30, 34, 38, 39, 40, 46, 50, 51, 55, 57, 76, 86, 91.
St.Mary's (11): 1972, 1979, 1980, 1981, 1983, 1984, 1985, 1987, 1996, 2001, 2004.
Tourlestrane (7): 1956, 1978, 1982, 1994, 1997, 1999, 2007.
Ballymote (6): 1892, 1905, 13, 25, 26, 48.
Moylough (5): 1919, 20, 21, 22, 23.
St Patrick's (5): 1968, 70, 71, 88, 89.
Easkey (5): 1935, 36, 37, 41, 66.
Ballisodare (5): 1931, 32, 60, 62, 63.
Curry (5): 1889, 1964, 1972, 2003, 2006.
Eastern Harps (5): 1975, 93, 95, 98, 2008.
Sligo Wanderers (4): 1908, 09, 10, 12.
Collooney Harps (4): 1942, 43, 61, 65.
Craobh Rua (4): 1944, 52, 53, 54.
Gurteen (2): 1 906, 07.
Enniscrone (2): 1914, 16.
Knockalassa (2): 1 933, 35.
Skreen (2): 1945, 47.
Sooey (2): 1949, 59.
Collooney/Ballisodare (2): 1967, 69.
Shamrock Gaels (2) 1990, 92.
Bunninadden (2): 1891, 2000.
Coolera-Strandhill (2): 2002, 2005.
Sligo Emmets (1): 1888.
Coolera (1): 1907.
Killavil (1): 1911.
Derroon (1): 1915.
Kilglass (1): 1929.
Mullinabreena (1): 1958.

LEINSTER

CARLOW

Éire Óg (25): 1960, 1962, 1965, 1967, 1968, 1969, 1974, 1976, 1977, 1978, 1980, 1982, 1984, 1987, 1988, 1989, 1992, 1993, 1994, 1995, 1996, 1998, 2005, 2007, 2008.
Tinryland (15): 1934, 1936, 1939, 1940, 1943, 1944, 1946, 1948, 1949, 1950, 1971, 1972, 1975, 1979, 1981.
Graiguecullen (13): 1908, 1909, 1911, 1912, 1913, 1914, 1915, 1918, 1921, 1922, 1923, 1924, 1925.
O'Hanrahans (13): 1931, 1932, 1937, 1942, 1945, 1951, 1954, 1958, 1961, 1999, 2000, 2001, 2003.
Loughmartin Emmetts (5): 1898, 1899, 1900,1901, 1902.
Tullow (5): 1904, 1916, 1959, 1963, 1964.
Palatine (5): 1919, 1920, 1952, 2002, 2006.
Rathvilly (4): 1983, 1985, 1990, 1991.
Carlow Town (3): 1927, 1928, 1930.
Kildavin (3): 1966, 1970, 1973.
Milford (2): 1926, 1933.
Leighlinbridge (2): 1929, 1957.
Ballymurphy (2): 1947, 1953.
Clonmore (2): 1955, 1956.
Carlow Barrow Rangers (1): 1903.
Borris (1) 1910.
Kilbride (1): 1935.
Fighting Cocks (1): 1938.
Naomh Eoin (Myshall) (1): 1986.
Old Leighlin (1): 1997.
Fenagh (1): 2004.
No championship 1905, 7 906, 1907, 1917, 1941.

DUBLIN

St. Vincent's (25): 1949-55, 1957-62, 1964, 1966-67, 1970-72, 1975-77, 1981, 1984, 2007.
O'Tooles (11): 1918-20, 1922-26, 1928, 1931, 1946.
Geraldines (10): 1898-99, 1908, 1910, 191415, 1917, 1940-42.
Keatings (7): 1903-07, 1909, 1911.
U.C.D. (7): 1943, 1963, 1965, 1973, 1974, 2002, 2006.

Garda (6): 1927, 1929, 1933-35, 1948.
Parnells (6): 1913, 1916, 1939, 1945, 1987-88.
Kilmacud Crokes (6): 1992, 1994, 1998, 2004, 2005, 2008.
Young Irelands (5): 1891-94, 1896.
Na Fianna (5): 1969, 1979, 1999, 2000, 2001.
Kickhams (4): 1897, 1904,1907, 1912.
Erin's Hope (4): 1887, 1932, 1965, 1978.
Isles of the Sea (3): 1890, 1895, 1900.
Clan na Gael (3): 1936-37, 1968.
Seán McDermott's (2): 1938, 1947.
Civil Service (2): 1944, 1980.
Ballymun Kickhams (2): 1982, 1985.
Scoil Ui Chonaill (2): 1944, 1980.
Thomas Davis (2): 1989, 1991.
Erin's Isle (2): 1993, 1997.
Feach McHughs (1): 1888.
Faughs (1): 1889.
St. Mary's (1): 1921.
St. Joseph's (1): 1930.
Ballyboden St. Enda's (1): 1995.
St. Sylvesters (1): 1996.
St.Brigid's (1): – 2003.
*No championship in 1902.

KILDARE

Clane (17): 1888, 1892, 1895, 1900-03, 1916, 1963, 1967, 1975,1980, 1984, 1991-92, 1995, 1997.
Sarsfields (12): 1945, 1947, 1950, 1951, 1952, 1982, 1986, 1993, 1994, 1999, 2001, 2005.
Carbury (10): 1940-1941, 1946, 1960, 1965-66, 1969, 1971-72, 1974.
Roseberry (9): 1904-10, 1912, 1915.
Raheens (8): 1935-36, 1943, 1968, 1976, 1978-79, 1981.
Naas (6): 1920, 1922-24, 1928, 1990.
Round Towers (6): 1954, 1959, 1961, 1996, 1998, 2003.
Athy (5): 1933-34, 1937, 1942, 1987.
Moorefield (5): 1962, 2000, 2002, 2006, 2007.
Kilcock (4): 1914, 1955, 1957-58.
Caragh (4): 1918-19, 1921, 1926.
Monasterevin (3): 1890, 1911, 1977.
Maynooth (3): 1896-97, 1913.
Kildare (3): 1927, 1929-30.
Johnstownbridge (3): 1983, 1988-89.
Mountrice (2): 1889, 1891.
Rathangan (1): 1925.
St. Patrick's (1): 1938.
Ellistown (1): 1944.
Curragh (1): 1948.
Ardclough (1): 1949.
Ballymore (1): 1953.
Military College (1): 1956.
Eadestown (1): 1970.
Allenwood (1): 2004.
Celbridge (1): 2008.

KILKENNY

Glenmore (19): 1906, 15, 16, 20, 22, 23, 24, 29, 38, 40, 42, 43, 49, 50, 54, 55, 89, 98.
Railyard (19): 1951, 1952, 1953, 1957, 1958, 1959, 1960, 1961, 1965, 1966, 1967, 1969, 1970, 1971, 1972, 1973, 1978, 1992, 1999.
Tullogher (8). 1930, 31, 34, 36, 37, 41, 44, 62.
Muckalee (8): 1968, 1975, 1977, 1987, 1990, 2001, 2004, 2005.
James Stephens (6): 1988, 1991, 1993, 1995, 1996, 2003, 2008.
Commercials-City (4): 1890, 1893, 1894, 1895.
Lamogue (4): 1902, 03, 04, 05.
Knocktopher (4): 1901, 08, 10, 11.
Thomastown (4): 1981, 83, 84, 85.
Slatequarry Miners (3): 1900, 07, 13.
Shamrocks (3): 1979, 80, 82.
Kilmacow (2): 1887, 88.
Coolagh (2): 1914, 19.
St. John's (2): 1946, 48.
Clann na Gael-City (2): 1963, 64.
Dicksboro (2): 1994, 97.
Erin's Own (2): 2002, 2006.
Ballyhale (1): 1889.
Sevenhouses (1): 1896.
Green Rovers-City (1): 1897.
Callan (1): 1898.
City Rangers (1): 1899.
Coolroe (1): 1909.
Ye Faire City (1): 1925.
Cotterstown (1): 1926.
Owen Roes-Army (1): 1928.
Blacks & Whites (1): 1932.
Moneenroe (1): 1933.
Barrow Rovers-Glenmore/Slieverue (1): 1935.
Northern Junior Selection (1): 1945.
Sarsfields (1): 1947.
Graignamanagh (1): 1956.
St. Kieran's-Mooncoin/Kilmacow (1): 1974.
The Village (1): 1976.
Mooncoin (1): 1986.
Kilmoganny (1): 2000.
Mullinavat (1): 2007.
No championships 1891-92, 1912, 1917-13, 1921.
Declared Void 1927.

LAOIS

Portlaoise (25): 1889, 1897, 1907, 1918, 1964, 1966, 1967, 1968, 1970, 1971, 1976, 1979, 1981, 1982, 1984, 1985, 1986, 1987, 1990, 1991, 1999, 2002, 2004, 2007, 2008.
Stradbally (16): 1905, 1908, 1910, 1911, 1929, 1930, 1932, 1933, 1936, 1937, 1940, 1941, 1997, 1998, 2001, 2005.
The Heath (10): 1891, 1912-13, 1920, 1957-58, 1960-61, 1974, 1993.
St.Joseph's (9): 1973, 1975, 1977, 1978, 1983, 1989, 1994, 1996, 2000.
Abbeyleix (8): 1898-99, 1902-04, 1909, 1916, 1919.
Portarlington (8): 1893, 1921 -22, 1954-55, 1959, 1988, 1995.
Annanough (6): 1924-27, 1951, 1956.
Ballyroan Gaels (6): 1890, 1943, 1948, 1950, 1992, 2006.
Raheenbrogue (2): 1901, 1906.

CLUB

Park (2): 1952-53.
O'Dempseys (2): 1963, 1980.
Moyanna (1): 1892.
Wolfhill (1): 1896.
Timahoe (1): 1969.
Emo (1): 1972.
Arles-Kilcruise (1): 2003.
Note: The 1889, 1897 and 1907 won under the name Maryborough, now Portlaoise.

LONGFORD

Drumlish/Fr.Manning Gaels (15): 1927, 1928, 1932, 1937, 1939, 1940, 1943, 1945, 1951, 1953, 1955, 1996, 1997, 1998, 2001.
Longford Slashers (13): 1954, 1955, 1957, 1959, 1961, 1971, 1975, 1979, 1980, 1989, 1990, 1991, 1994.
Clonguish (12): 1919, 1962, 1963, 1964, 1965, 1968, 1969, 1972, 1973, 1981, 2003, 2004.
St. Marys (Granard) (11): 1929, 1930, 1931, 1933, 1934, 1935, 1941, 1966, 1967, 1970, 1982.
Emmet Óg (Killoe) (9): 1907, 1911, 1912, 1913, 1915, 1960, 1988, 1993, 1995.
Colmcilles (6): 1890, 1938, 1949, 1952, 1958, 2008.
Longford Wanderers (4): 1922, 1923, 1944, 1947.
Cashel (4): 1977, 1983, 1984, 1986.
Ardagh St. Patrick's (4): 1936, 1942, 1978, 1987.
Dromard (4): 1946, 2000, 2005, 2007.
Mostrim (3): 1974, 1985, 1992.
Longford (Leo Casey's) (2): 1904, 1905.
Mullinalachta (2): 1948, 1950.
Abbeylara (2): 1999, 2006.
Longford Shamrocks (1): 1896.
Ballinamuck (1): 1917.
Rathcline (1): 1976.
Ballymahon (1): 2002.

LOUTH

Newtown Blues (19): 1889, 1932, 1933, 1936, 1961, 1962, 1963, 1964, 1966, 1967, 1969, 1970, 1974, 1981, 1986, 1988, 2000, 2001, 2008.
Young Irelands (Dundalk) (11): 1887, 1888, 1905, 1911, 1938, 1940, 1941, 1944, 1947, 1950, 1979.
St. Mary's (Ardee) (11): 1914, 1946, 1948, 1951, 1955, 1956, 1960, 1968, 1972, 1975, 1995.
Cooley Kickhams (9): 1935, 1939, 1971, 1973, 1976, 1977, 1978, 1989, 1990.
Clan na Gael (8): 1923, 1924, 1959, 1985, 1987, 1992, 1993, 1997.
Wolfe Tones (5): 1925,1926, 1929, 1931, 1937.
Geraldines (5): 1913, 1915, 1916, 1920, 1982.
Tredaghs (Drogheda) (4): 1906, 1909, 1910, 1912.
Boyne Rangers (4): 1895, 1921, 1922, 1930.
Gaels (3): 1942, 1945, 1952.
St.Patrick's (3): 2003, 2004, 2007.
Boyne Rovers (2). 1897, 1904.
Dundalk Rovers (2): 1907, 1908.
Drogheda Stars (2): 1917, 1919.
Drogheda Independents (2): 1901, 1902.
O'Rahillys (2): 1918, 1965.
Sarsfields (2): 1927, 1928.
Roche Emmetts (2): 1958, 1980.
St. Fechins (2): 1983, 1984.
Mattock Rangers (2): 2002, 2005.
St. Joseph's (2): 1996, 2006.
Davitts (Drogheda) (1): 1890.
Drogheda (Emmetts) (1): 1896.
Ardee Volunteers (1): 1903.
Glyde Rangers (1): 1934.
St. Bride's (1): 1943.
Naomh Mhuire (1): 1953.
Oliver Plunkett's (1): 1957.
Stabannon Parnells (1): 1999.
No championships 1891-1894, 1898-1900.

MEATH

Navan O'Mahoneys (17): 1953, 1957-61, 1963, 1973, 1979, 1981, 1985, 1987-90, 1997, 2008.
Skryne (11): 1940, 1941, 1944, 1945, 1947, 1948, 1954, 1965, 1992, 1993, 2004.
Navan Gaels (10): 1907, 1924-26, 1929-30, 1933-35, 1938.
Bohermeen (6): 1909, 1910-14.
Castletown (5): 1902, 1904-06, 1908.
Rathkenny (5): 1917-19, 1922-23.
Kilbride (5): 1964, 1967, 1969-71.
Walterstown (5); 1978, 1980, 1982-84.
Summerhill (5): 1974-77, 1986.
Pierce O'Mahoney's (3): 1894-96.
Navan Harps (3): 1915, 1920-21.
Kilmessan (3): 1903, 1936, 1939.
Donaghmore (3): 1927-28, 1942.
Gael Colmcille, Kells (3): 1966, 1968, 1991.
Dunshaughlin (3): 2000, 2001, 2002.
Seneschalstown (3): 1972, 1994, 2007.
St. Peter's, Dunboyne (3): 1998, 1999, 2005.
Dowdstown (2): 1887-88.
Moynalty (21: 1932, 1937.
Julianstown (1): 1889.
Owen Roe's (1): 1897.
Stamullen (1): 1900.
Martry (1): 1931.
Duleek (1): 1943.
Navan Parnells (1): 1946.
North Meath (1): 1950.
St. Vincent's (1): 1955.
Trim (1): 1962.
Dunderry (1): 1995.
Kilmainhamwood (1): 1996.
Blackhall Gaels (1): 2003.
Wolfe Tones (1): 2006

OFFALY

Tullamore (26): 1896, 1897, 1898, 1899, 1908, 1911, 1912, 1913, 1917, 1924, 1925, 1926, 1930, 1932, 1935, 1941, 1946, 1948, 1954, 1956, 1963, 1973, 1977, 2000, 2002, 2007.
Rhode (23): 1900, 1918, 1920, 1923, 1927, 1928, 1929, 1931, 1939, 1940, 1944, 1949, 1955, 1958, 1966, 1967, 1969, 1975, 1998, 2004, 2005, 2006, 2008.

Walsh Island (12): 1933-34, 1937-38, 1942-43, 1978-83.
Ferbane (11): 1914, 1971, 1974, 1976, 1986-90, 1992, 1994.
Edenderry (9): 1936, 1951, 1953, 1957, 1985, 1995, 1997, 1999, 2001.
Geashill (5): 1902, 1904-07.
Clara (5): 1960, 1964, 1991, 1993, 2003.
Gracefield (4): 1961, 1970, 1972, 1984.
Daingean (3): 1909, 1962, 1965.
Killeigh (2): 1915-16.
Cloghan (2): 1903, 1945.
St. Mary's (2): 1947, 1950.
Quarrymount (1): 1901.
Banagher (1): 1910.
Clonmore (1): 1919.
Durrow (1): 1952.
St. Patrick's (1): 1959.
Ballycumber (1): 1968.
Shannonbridge (1): 1996.

WESTMEATH

Athlone (21): 1905, 1909, 1947, 1949, 1955, 1956, 1957, 1958, 1959, 1960, 1965, 1971, 1973, 1977, 1979, 1982, 1984, 1988, 1991, 1998, 1999.
Mullingar Shamrocks (10): 1903, 1964, 1966, 1986, 1987, 1990, 1992, 1993, 1994, 1995.
Riverstown Emmets (9): 1904, 06, 07, 08, 10, 11, 12, 13, 14.
Rosemount (9): 1932, 34, 39, 40, 41, 51, 52, 53, 89.
Moate (9): 1933, 36, 43, 45, 75, 76, 78, 83, 97.
The Downs (9): 1918, 1968, 1969, 1970, 1972, 1974, 1980, 2003, 2005.
Kilbeggan (8): 1919, 21, 24, 26, 27, 30, 31, 35.
Rochfortbridge (4): 1915, 17, 23, 25.
Kinnegad (4): 1916, 29, 44, 46.
St. Mary's (3): 1950, 54, 62.
St. Loman's (3): 1948, 61, 63.
Garrycastle (3): 2001, 2002, 2004.
Tyrrellspass (3): 1999, 2006, 2007.
Athlone Army (2): 1905, 28.
Milltown (2): 1938, 42.
Coralstown-Kinnegad (2): 1996, 2000.
Coralstown (1): 1937.
St. Finian's (1): 1967.
St. Malachy's (1): 1981.
Tubberclair (1): 1985.
Castledaly (1); 2008.
No championship played in 1920 or 1922.

WEXFORD

Volunteers (11): 1895, 1898, 1939, 1940, 1941, 1942, 1943, 1948, 1949, 1953, 1956.
Ballyhogue (10): 1911, 1921, 1924, 1931, 1932, 1962, 1963, 1964, 1971, 1972.
Castletown (9): 1965, 1966, 1969, 1970, 1973, 1976, 1978, 1979, 1981.
Starlights (9): 1927, 1928, 1929, 1933, 1936, 1937, 1983, 2002, 2004.
Duffry Rovers (8): 1986, 1987, 1988, 1989, 1990, 1991, 1992, 1994.
Kilanerin (7): 1974, 1993, 1995, 1997, 1999, 2003, 2008.
Blue and Whites (Wexford) (6): 1889, 1890, 1914, 1916, 1917, 1918.
Rapparees (5): 1907, 1908, 1909, 1912, 1913.
Sarsfields (5): 1934, 1935, 1961, 1967, 1984.
Gusserane (5): 1945,1946,1947,1954,1975.
Gymnasiums (New Ross) (4): 1899, 1900, 1901, 1902.
St. Munn's (Taghmon) (3): 1955, 1957, 1958.
St.Anne's (3): 1968, 2000, 2001.
Young Irelands (Wexford) (2): 1893, 1894.
Slaney Harriers (Enniscorthy) (2): 1903, 1904.
Wexford United (2): 1905, 1926.
New Ross Geraldines (1): 1915.
Faythe Harriers (2): 1959, 1960.
Bunclody (2): 1982, 1985.
St. Fintan's (2): 1930, 1980.
St. Aidan's (Enniscorthy) (2): 1950, 1951.
Horeswood (2): 2005, 2006.
St. Mary's (Rosslare) (1): 1886.
Castlebridge (1): 1887.
St. Patrick's (Wexford) (1): 1896.
Ballymurrin (1): 1897.
Faughs (Wexford) (1): 1910.
Emmetts (Enniscorthy) (1): 1944.
Rathnure (1): 1952.
Wexford District (1): 1977.
Glynn-Barntown (1): 1996.
Fethard (1): 1998.
Clongeen (1): 2007.

WICKLOW

Rathnew (27): 1893, 1896, 1897, 1902, 1904, 1905, 1906, 1909, 1910, 1911, 1921, 1924, 1928, 1932, 1941, 1942, 1943, 1970, 1978, 1996, 1997, 1998, 1999, 2000, 2001, 2002, 2003, 2005.
Baltinglass (21): 1958, 1963, 1965, 1966, 1967, 1971, 1972, 1976, 1979, 1980, 1982, 1985, 1987, 1988, 1989, 1990, 1991, 1992, 1993, 1994, 2007.
St. Patrick's, Wicklow (12): 1890, 1950, 1952, 1953, 1955, 1956, 1959, 1960, 1961, 2006.
Annacurra (8): 1887, 1889, 1892, 1913, 1920, 1925, 1926, 1931.
Donard (6): 1937, 1940, 1944, 1947, 1951, 1957.
Carnew (4): 1916, 1927, 1945, 1973.
Tinahely (3): 1917, 1919, 1984.
Kilcoole (3): 1929, 1939, 1954.
Ballinacor (3): 1946, 1948, 1949.
Blessington (2): 1915, 1983.
Rathdangan (2): 1930, 1936.
Bray Emmets (2): 1934, 1935.
Kilbride (2): 1962, 1968.
Newtown (2): 1964, 1975.
Dunlavin (2): 1977, 1981.
Kiltegan (2): 1986, 2008.

Avondale (1): 1908.
Granabeg (Valleymount) (1): 1923.
Roundwood (1): 1933.
Ashford (1): 1974.
An Tochar (1): 1995.
Annacurra and Clara shared the title in 1888.

MUNSTER

CORK

Nemo Rangers (17): 1972, 1974, 1975, 1977, 1978, 1981, 1983, 1987, 1988, 1993, 2000, 2001, 2002, 2005, 2006, 2007, 2008.
Lees (11): 1887, 1896, 1902, 1903, 1904, 1907, 1908, 1911, 1914, 1923, 1955.
Macroom (10): 1909, 1910, 1912, 1913, 1926, 1930, 1931, 1935, 1958, 1962.
University College (9): 1920, 1927, 1928, 1960, 1963, 1964, 1969, 1973, 1999.
Clonakilty (8): 1939, 42, 43, 44, 46, 47, 52, 96.
St Finbarr's (8): 1956, 57, 59, 76, 79, 80, 82.
Fermoy (7): 1895, 98, 99, 1900, 05, 06, 45.
Beara (6) 1932, 33, 34, 40, 67, 97.
Nils (6): 1894, 1901, 15, 17, 24, 25.
St Nicholas (5): 1938, 41, 54, 65, 66.
Collins (4): 1929 (awarded), 49, 51, 53.
Carbery (4): 1937, 1968, 1971, 2004.
Castlehaven (3): 1989, 1994, 2003.
Midleton (2): 1889, 1990.
Clondrohid (2): 1891, 1892.
Cobh (2): 1918, 19.
Imokilly (2): 1984, 1986.
Duhallow (2): 1990, 1991.
Bantry Blues (2): 1995, 1998.
Dromtarriff (1) 1893.
Dunmanway (1): 1897.
Collegians (1): 1916.
Duhallow West (1): 1936.
Millstreet (1): 1948.
Garda (1): 1950.
Avondhu (1): 1961.
Muskerry (1): 1970.
O'Donovan Rossa (1): 1992.

CLARE

Kilrush (21): 1902, 03, 12, 24, 30, 31, 34, 37, 38, 51, 57, 58, 60, 62, 75, 76, 77, 78, 79, 81, 87.
Doonbeg (17): 1955, 1961, 1967, 1968, 1969, 1972, 1973, 1974, 1982, 1983, 1988, 1991, 1995, 1996, 1998, 1999, 2001.
Milltown (11): 1905, 06, 16, 23, 27, 32, 49, 53, 59, 85, 90.
Cooraclare (11): 1915, 17, 18, 25, 44, 45, 56, 64, 65, 86, 97.
Ennis-Dal gCais (10): 1897, 99, 1904, 07, 09, 10, 11, 13, 14, 29.
Kilkee (7): 1926, 1928, 1942, 1984, 1989, 1992, 2003.
Kilmurry-Ibrickane (6): 1933, 1963, 1966, 1993, 2002, 2008.
Ennis Faughs (4): 1947, 48, 52, 54.
Quilty (3): 1935, 36, 39.
Éire Óg (3): 2000, 2004, 2006.
Coolmeen (2): 1919, 22.
Newmarket (2): 1887, 88.
Kilfenora (2): 1941, 50.
Shannon Gaels (2): 1970, 71.
Kildysart (1): 1889.
Ennis (1): 1890.
Killimer (1): 1896.
Doora (1): 1898.
Labasheeda (1): 1900.
Clarecastle (1): 1908.
Liscannor (1): 1940.
Ennistymon/Kilkee (1): 1940 disq.
O'Currys (1): 1946.
Kilmihill (1): 1980.
Faughs (1): 1994.
St. Senan's (1): 2005.
Lisseycasey (1): 2007.

KERRY

Austin Stacks (11): 1928, 30, 31, 32, 36, 73, 75, 76, 89, 86, 94.
John Mitchels (10): 1929, 37, 47, 52, 59, 60, 61, 62, 63, 66.
Laune Rangers (10): 1889, 90, 92, 93, 1900, 11, 89, 93, 95, 96.
Tralee Mitchels (9): 1896 (shared), 97, 1902, 03, 07, 08, 10, 17, 19.
East Kerry (7): 1965, 1968, 1969, 1970, 1997, 1998, 1999.
Dingle (6): 1938, 40, 41, 43, 44, 48.
Kerins O'Rahillys (6): 1933, 1939, 1953, 1954, 1957, 2002.
Killarney Crokes (5): 1901, 12, 13, 14, 91.
Shannon Rangers (5): 1942, 45, 64, 72, 77.
Ballymacelligott (4): 1891, 94, 95, 1918.
Mid-Kerry (3): 1967, 71, 92, 2008.
West Kerry (3): 1984, 85, 90.
Feale Rangers (3) 1978, 1980, 2007.
South Kerry (3): 2004, 2005, 2006.
Tralee (Div.) (2): 1925, 26.
Killarney (2): 1949, 83.
Kenmare (2): 1974, 87.
An Ghaeltacht (2): 2001, 2003.
Caherciveen (1): 1896 (shared).
Killarney Legion (1): 1946.
Castleisland (1): 1950.
Dick Fitzgeralds (1): 1951.
St Kieran's (1): 1988.
Glenflesk (1): 2000.

LIMERICK

Commercials (16): 1887, 88, 89, 95, 96, 97, 98, 99, 1902, 04, 05, 10, 11, 19, 27.
Claughaun (14): 1955, 59, 67, 69, 70, 71, 82, 84, 86, 88, 89, 93, 95, 90.
Treaty Sarsfields (12): 1946, 48, 49, 50, 51, 52, 56, 57, 63, 73, 74, 75.
Glin (7): 1926, 28, 29, 30, 31, 33, 34.
Abbeyfeale (6): 1914, 15, 32, 41, 42, 47.

Oola (6): 1900, 18, 22, 25, 61, 79.
Ahane (5): 1935, 36, 37, 38, 39.
St Patrick's (5): 1890, 91, 1943, 44, 54.
Drom-Broadford (4): 2001, 2003, 2004, 2008.
Kilmallock (3): 1908, 09, 16.
Askeaton (3): 1965, 66, 72.
St Kieran's (3): 1981, 85, 90.
Ballylanders (3): 1917, 1999, 2007.
Monaleen (3): 1978, 2002, 2005.
Garda (2): 1924, 58.
Western Gaels (2): 1953, 60.
Thomond (2): 1977, 80.
Croom (2): 1976, 83.
Newcastlewest (2): 1987, 92.
Galbally (2): 1994, 1998.
Fr. Casey's (2): 2000, 2006.
Foynes (1): 1907.
Knockaney (1): 1940.
Army (Ninth Desmonds) (1): 1945.
Old Christians (1): 1962.
Ballysteen (1) 1964.
Athea (1): 1968.
Glencurrane Rovers (1): 1991.
University of Limerick (1): 1998.

TIPPERARY

Fethard (21): 1887, 1917, 1918, 1919, 1920, 1922, 1923, 1924, 1927, 1928, 1938, 1942, 1954, 1957, 1978, 1984, 1988, 1991, 1993, 1997, 2001.
Clonmel Commercials (14): 1944, 1948, 1956, 1965, 1966, 1967, 1969, 1971, 1982, 1986, 1989, 1990, 1994, 2002.
Grangemockler (8): 1890, 1903, 04, 05, 06, 07, 09, 31.
Clonmel Shamrocks (8): 1897, 98, 99, 1900, 01, 33, 34, 37.
Loughmore-Castleiney (8): 1940, 1946, 1973, 1977, 1979, 1983, 1987, 2004.
Ardfinnan (8): 1935, 39, 62, 63, 64, 70, 74, 2005.
Arravale Rovers (6): 1894, 95, 96, 99, 1941, 85.
Galtee Rovers (6): 1949, 50, 76, 80, 81, 2008.
Moyle Rovers (6): 1995, 1996, 1998, 1999, 2000, 2007.
Mullinahone (5): 1912, 13, 16, 26, 29.
Kilsheelan (4): 1930, 32, 68, 72.
St Flannan's (North Sel.) (3): 1958, 59, 61.
Loughmore (3): 1955, 88, 92.
Bohercrowe (2): 1888, 89.
Nenagh (2): 1911, 15.
Templemore (2): 1925, 36.
10th Batt. Templemore (2): 1943, 1945.
St Patrick's (Drangan Cloneen) (2): 1947, 53.
Tipperary Town (1): 1902.
Cloneen (1): 1908.
Tipperary O'Learys (1): 1910.
Castleiney (1): 1914.
Ballingarry (1) 1951.
Old Bridge (1) 1952.
Thurles Crokes (1): 1960.
Kilruane McDonaghs (1): 1975.
Cahir (1): 2003.
Aherlow (1): 2006

WATERFORD

Dungarvan (23): 1890, 92, 93, 96, 97, 98, 1908, 16, 26, 27, 28, 29, 30, 37, 38, 45, 46, 47, 48, 56, 90, 91, 92.
Kilrossanty (15): 1888, 1919, 39, 49, 50, 51, 52, 57, 60, 64, 83, 85, 86, 88, 89.
Stradbally (13): 1940, 1941, 1942, 1943, 1944, 1972, 1980, 1982, 1987, 2002, 2003, 2004, 2005.
Rathgormack (10): 1909, 1910, 1911, 1912, 1913, 1918, 1995, 1996, 1999, 2001.
Clashmore (7): 1 903, 04, 05, 06, 07, 20, 25.
The Nire (6): 1993, 1994, 1997, 2000, 2006, 2008
De La Salle (5): 1931, 33, 34, 35, 36.
Mount Sion (5): 1953, 55, 56, 59, 61.
Lismore (4): 1899, 1901, 02, 11.
Kill (4): 1962, 66, 67, 68.
Ballinacourty (4): 1978, 79, 81, 2007.
Aglish (3): 1915, 22, 23.
Kinsalebeg (3): 1886, 91, 1925.
John Mitchels (3): 1970, 73, 76.
Tramore (3): 1969, 71, 84.
Windgap (2): 1894, 95.
Ardmore (2): 1965, 77.
Ballysaggart (1): 1885.
Ballyduff Lower (1): 1887.
Ballyduff Upper (1): 1924.
Dunhill (1): 1925.
Fenor (1): 1932.
Brickey Rangers (1): 1963.
Affane (1): 1974.
St Saviour's (1): 1998.

ULSTER

ANTRIM

St. John's (24): 1945, 1949, 1951,1957,1959, 1960, 1961, 1962, 1963, 1964, 1965, 1969, 1970, 1972, 1975, 1976, 1977, 1978, 1980, 1981, 1984, 1986, 1988, 1998.
O'Donovan Rossa (15) 1920, 1921, 1927, 1930, 1944, 1946, 1950, 1952, 1953, 1955, 1956, 1958, 1973, 1989, 1991.
St.Gall's (13): 1933, 1982, 1983, 1987, 1990, 1993, 2001, 2002, 2003, 2004, 2005, 2007, 2008.
James Stephen's (7): 1914, 1915, 1916, 1917, 1918, 1919, 1922.
Cuchuilain's (6): 1924, 1925, 1926, 1931, 1935, 1936.
Seaghan an Diomais (5): 1903, 1906, 1908, 1909, 1910.
Sarsfield's (4): 1913, 1941, 1967, 1985.
Cargin (4): 1974, 1995, 1999, 2000.
Gaedhail Ulaidh (3): 1938, 1939, 1942.
O'Connell's (3): 1928, 1934, 1947.
St. Paul's (3): 1994, 1996, 1997.
Ollamh Fodhla (2): 1904, 1907.
Mitchel's (2): 1911, 1912.
Ardoyne (2): 1932, 1937.
Kickham's, Randalstown (2): 1943, 1954.
Lámh Dhearg, Belfast (2): 1971, 1992.
Tir na nOg (1): 1902.

O'Neill Crowley's (1): 1905.
Davitt's (1): 1923.
Lámh Dhearg, Toome (1): 1929.
O'Donnell's (1): 1940.
Éire Óg (1): 1948.
Glenravel (1): 1966.
Pearse's (1): 1968
St. Teresa's (1): 1979.
Erin's Own (1): 2006.

ARMAGH

Crossmaglen (37): 1906, 1908, 1911, 1912, 1913, 1923, 1924, 1925, 1926, 1927, 1933, 1936, 1937, 1947, 1960, 1962, 1965, 1966, 1967, 1970, 1975, 1977, 1983, 1986, 1996, 1997, 1998, 1999, 2000, 2001, 2002, 2003, 2004, 2005, 2006, 2007, 2008
Clann na nGael, Lurgan (14): 1949, 1950, 1968, 1969, 1971, 1972, 1973, 1974, 1976, 1980, 1981, 1987, 1993, 1994.
Armagh Harps (13): 1889, 1890, 1891, 1901, 1902, 1903, 1946, 1952, 1955, 1957, 1958. 1989, 1991.
Young Ireland's, Armagh (7): 1917, 1918, 1928, 1930, 1931, 1932, 1934.
Carrickcruppin (4): 1959, 1978, 1979, 1982.
Keady (4): 1938, 1953, 1956, 1984.
Bessbrook (3): 1909, 1916, 1939.
Killeavey (3): 1914, 1915, 1948.
Pearse Og, Armagh (3): 1985, 1989, 1992.
Clann Éireann, Lurgan (2).
Shane O'Neill's, Camlough (2): 1907, 1910.
Tír na nÓg, Armagh (2): 1904, 1935.
St. Michael's, Newtownhamilton (2): 1940, 1941.
St. Malachy's, Armagh (2): 1942, 1945.
Mullaghbawn (2): 1964, 1995.
Whitecross (1): 1905.
Wolfe Tone's, Derrymacash (1): 1943.
St. Peter's Selection (1): 1944.
St. Peter's, Lurgan (1): 1951.
Collegeland (1): 1961.
Sarsfields, Derrytrasna (1): 1990.

CAVAN

Cornafean (19): 1909, 1910, 1912, 1913, 1914, 1915, 1918, l920, 1929, 1932, 1933, 1934, 1936, 1937, 1938, 1939, 1940, 1943, 1956.
Mullahoran (11): 1935, 1942, 1944, 1945, 1947, 1948, 1949, 1950, 1963, 1998, 2006.
Cavan Slashers (10): 1890, 1917, 1922, 1924, 1925, 1927, 1928, 1930, 1931, 1941.
Crosserlough (9): 1958, 1961, 1966, 1967, 1968, 1969, 1971, 1972.
Kingscourt (9): 1921, 1980, 1981, 1986, 1987, 1989, 1990, 1991, 1993.
Cavan Gaels (9):1965, 1975, 1977, 1978, 2001, 2003, 2005, 2007, 2008.
Gowna (8): 1988, 1994, 1996, 1997, 1999, 2000, 2002, 2004.
Bailieboro (5): 1911, 1952, 1957, 1964, 1995.
Drumlane (4): 1903, 1904, 1905, 1907.
Virginia (4): 1916, 1919, 1959, 1962.
Laragh (4): 1979, 1982, 1983, 1984
Cootehill (3): 1953, 1954, 1955.
Ramor (3): 1974, 1985, 1992.
Maghera (2): 1888, 1926.
Templeport (1): 1923.
Mountnugent (1): 1946.
Lavey (1): 1951.
Annagh (Redhills/Belturbet) (1): 1973.
St. Mary's (Castlerahan/Munsterconnaught) (1): 1976.
*N.B. 1960 Championship not finished.

DERRY

Bellaghy (21): 1956, 1958, 1959, 1960, 1961, 1963, 1964, 1965, 1968, 1969, 1971, 1972, 1975, 1979, 1986, 1994, 1996, 1998, 1999, 2000, 2005.
Ballinderry (10): 1927, 1974, 1980, 1981, 1995, 2001, 2002, 2006, 2008.
Newbridge (9): 1937, 1940, 1945, 1948, 1950, 1966, 1967, 1970, 1989.
Lavey (9): 1938, 1943, 1944, 1954, 1977, 1988, 1990, 1992, 1993.
Dungiven (7): 1947, 1951, 1983, 1984, 1987, 1991, 1997.
Magherafelt (5): 1939, 1942, 1946, 1949, 1978.
Ballinascreen (4): 1934, 1935, 1941, 1973.
Glenullin (3): 1928, 1985, 2007.
Éire Óg (2) 1907, 1952.
Ballerin (2): 1957, 1976.
Loup (2): 1936, 2003.
Clann Chonaill (1): 1914.
Sarsfields (1): 1916.
St. Patrick's (1): 1917.
Emmet's (1): 1918.
Derry Guilds (1): 1921.
Buncrana (1): 1930.
Burt (1): 1931.
Desertmartin (1): 1953.
Ballymaguigan (1): 1962.
Slaughtneil (1): 2004.
*N.B. 1982 final result declared null and void.
*N.B. No competitions in pre-1907, 1908-14, 1919-20, 1922-26, 1929 and 1932-33 periods.

DONEGAL

St.Eunan's, Letterkenny (13): 1927, 1948, 1950, 1956, 1960, 1967, 1969, 1972, 1983, 1999, 2001, 2007, 2008.
Aodh Ruadh, Ballyshannon (12): 1929, 1932, 1937, 1939, 1942, 1943, 1951, 1986, 1987, 1994, 1997, 1998.
Gaoth Dobhair (12): 1935, 1938, 1941, 1944, 1945, 1946, 1947, 1949, 1953, 1954, 1955, 1961.
St. Joseph's (Bundoran/Ballyshannon) (8): 1965, 1966, 1968, 1970, 1973, 1974, 1975, 1976.
Dungloe (7): 1930, 1931, 1933, 1936, 1940, 1957, 1958.
MacCumhaill's, Ballybofey (6): 1959, 1962, 1963, 1964, 1971, 1977.
Killybegs (6): 1952, 1988, 1991, 1992, 1995, 1996.
Ardara (6): 1923, 1926, 1928, 1981, 2000, 2004.
Kilcar (5): 1925, 1980, 1985, 1989, 1993.
Four Masters, Donegal (4): 1924, 1982, 1984, 2003.

Bundoran (3): 1920, 1934, 1979.
Killygordon (1): 1921.
Castlefin (1): 1922.
Gleann Choilm Cille (1): 1978.
Naomh Columba (1): 1990.
Naomh Chonaill (1): 2005.
Gweedore (1): 2006.

DOWN

Burren (12): 1966, 1981, 1983, 1984, 1985, 1986, 1987, 1988, 1992, 1996, 1997, 1999.
Bryansford (11): 1939, 1940, 1941, 1942, 1969, 1970, 1971, 1973, 1974, 1977, 2003.
Castlewellan (10): 1924, 1934, 1936, 1950, 1958, 1965, 1979, 1982,1994,1995.
Kilcoo (9): 1917, 1921, 1925, 1926, 1927, 1928, 1932, 1933, 1937.
Clonduff (9): 1930, 1944, 1945, 1947, 1949, 1952, 1957, 1980, 2000.
Mayobridge (9): 1916, 1919, 2001, 2002, 2004, 2005, 2006, 2007, 2008.
Downpatrick (6): 1935, 1972, 1978, 1990, 1991, 1993.
Faugh-an-Bealach (4): 1903, 1906, 1907, 1908.
Newry Shamrocks (4): 1946, 1951, 1956, 1961.
Mitchel's, Newry (4): 1960, 1964, 1967, 1968.
Warrenpoint (3): 1943, 1948, 1953.
Glenn (3): 1959, 1962, 1963.
Liatroim (2): 1905, 1920.
Ballymartin (2): 1938, 1958.
Loughinisland (2): 1975, 1989.
Rostrevor (2): 1976, 1998.
Clann na Banna (1): 1904.
Annsborough (1): 1908.
Clann Uladh (1): 1910.
Rossqlass (1): 1922.
Drumnaquoile (1): 1929.
Rathfriland (1): 1931.
Lisnacree (1): 1954.

FERMANAGH

Teemore (21): 1904, 1905, 1906, 1910, 1911, 1912, 1913, 1914, 1915, 1916, 1917, 1924, 1926, 1929, 1935, 1969, 1971, 1974, 1975, 1983, 2005.
Lisnaskea (20): 1928, 1931, 1936, 1937, 1938, 1939, 1941, 1942, 1943, 1945, 1946, 1947, 1948, 1950, 1951, 1954, 1977, 1980, 1991, 1994.
Enniskillen (15): 1907, 1908, 1909, 1930, 1976, 1978, 1987, 1992, 1998, 1999, 2000, 2001, 2002, 2003, 2006.
Devenish (9): 1963, 1965, 1966, 1967, 1985, 1989, 1990, 1993, 1996.
Newtownbutler (9): 1934, 1940, 1944, 1953, 1959, 1964, 1988, 1997, 2007.
Roslea (8): 1955, 1956, 1957, 1958, 1962, 1982, 1984, 1986.
Erne Gaels, Belleek (3): 1949, 1979, 1981.
Tempo (3): 1970, 1972, 1973.
Irvinestown (2): 1918, 1952.
Wattlebridge (2): 1919, 1920.
Knockninny (2): 1927, 1932.
Derrygonnelly (2): 1995, 2004.
Killyrover (1): 1925.
Belnaleck (1): 1933.
Devenish/Mulleek (1): 1960.
Aughadrumsee (1): 1961.
Ederney (1): 1968.
St. Patrick's (1): 2008.

MONAGHAN

Castleblaney (37): 1907, 1916, 1917, 1924, 1926, 1931, 1932, 1933, 1936, 1937, 1939, 1940, 1941, 1946, 1963, 1964, 1965, 1966, 1967, 1970, 1971, 1972, 1973, 1975, 1976, 1982, 1986, 1988, 1990, 1991, 1995, 1996, 1998, 1999, 2000, 2001, 2003.
Scotstown (14): 1960, 1961, 1974, 1977, 1978, 1979, 1980, 1981, 1983, 1984, 1985, 1989, 1992, 1993.
Clontibret (13): 1949, 1950, 1951, 1952, 1955, 1956, 1958, 1968, 1994, 1997, 2002, 2006, 2007.
Carrickmacross (7): 1908, 1909, 1910, 1913, 1914, 1918, 1919.
Ballybay (7): 1953, 1954, 1957, 1959, 1962, 1969, 1987.
Donaghmoyne (6): 1904, 1906, 1934, 1935, 1942, 1945.
Inniskeen (5) 1888, 1905, 1938, 1947, 1948.
Monaghan (3): 1911, 1922, 1923.
Killeevan (3): 1927, 1929, 1944.
Latton (3): 1930, 2005, 2008.
Magherarney (1): 1915.
North Selection (1): 1925.
Corcaghan (1): 1928.
Clones (1): 1943.
Magheracloone (1): 2004.

TYRONE

Carrickmore (15): 1940, 1943, 1949, 1961, 1966, 1969, 1977, 1978, 1979, 1995, 1996, 1999, 2001, 2004, 2005.
Dungannon (10): 1908, 1925, 1929, 1933, 1935, 1936, 1944, 1947, 1951, 1959.
Coalisland (8): 1904, 1907, 1928, 1930, 1946, 1955, 1989, 1990.
Omagh (7): 1948, 1952, 1953, 1954, 1957, 1963, 1988.
Ardboe (7): 1968, 1971, 1972, 1973, 1984, 1987, 1998.
Clonoe (7): 1958-59, 1960, 1964-65, 1991, 2008.
Trillick (6): 1937, 1974, 1975, 1980, 1983, 1986.
Errigal Ciarán (6): 1993, 1994, 1997, 2000, 2002, 2006.
Moortown (4): 1941, 1942, 1960, 1992.
Augher (3): 1976, 1982, 1985.
Cookstown (2): 1916, 1917.
Ballygawley (2): 1926, 1931.
Fintona (2): 1913, 1938.
Strabane (2): 1905, 1945.
Stewartstown (2): 1924, 1962.
Derrylaughan (2): 1967, 1981.
Moy (1): 1919.
Donaghmore (1): 1927.
Washinghay (1): 1934.
Eglish (1): 1970.
Killyclogher (1): 2003.
Dromore (1): 2007.

COUNTY CHAMPIONS 2009

	Hurling	Football
CONNACHT		
Galway	Portumna/Loughrea	Corofin
Leitrim	St Mary's	Glencar/Manorhamilton
Mayo	Ballyhaunis	Charlestown
Roscommon	Four Roads	Castlerea St Kevin's
Sligo	Calry/St Joseph's	Tourlestrane
LEINSTER		
Carlow	Mt Leinster Rangers	Rathvilly
Dublin	Ballyboden St Enda's	Ballyboden St Enda's
Kildare	Celbridge	St Laurence's
Kilkenny	Ballyhale Shamrocks	Glenmore
Laois	Clough Ballacolla	Portlaoise
Longford	Wolfe Tones	Clonguish
Louth	Knockbridge	Mattock Rangers
Meath	Kildalkey	Seneschalstown
Offaly	Tullamore	Clara
Westmeath	Clonkill	Garrycastle
Wexford	Oulart-the-Ballagh	Horeswood
Wicklow	Carnew	Rathnew
MUNSTER		
Clare	Cratloe	Kilmurry/Ibrickane
Cork	Newtownshandrum	Clonakilty
Kerry	Kilmoyley	South Kerry
Limerick	Adare	Dromcollogher/Broadford
Tipperary	Thurles Sarsfields	Moyle Rovers
Waterford	Ballygunner	Stradbally
ULSTER		
Antrim	Dunloy	St Gall's
Armagh	Middletown	Pearse Óg
Cavan	Mullahoran	Cavan Gaels
Derry	Kevin Lynch's	Loup
Donegal	Burt	St Eunan's
Down	Ballycran	Kilcoo
Fermanagh	Lisbellaw	Derrygonnelly Harps
Monaghan	Carrickmacross	Clontibret
Tyrone	Dungannon	Dromore

GENERAL RECORDS & NOTEWORTHY ACHIEVEMENTS

GENERAL

INTERNATIONAL SERIES (UNDER COMPROMISE RULES)

1984
First Test — Cork, October 21:
Australia 70 pts, Ireland 57 pts.
Second Test — Croke Park, October 28:
Ireland 80 pts, Australia 76 pts.
Third Test — Croke Park, November 4:
Australia 76 pts, Ireland 71 pts.

1986
First Test — Perth, October 11:
Australia 64 pts, Ireland 57 pts.
Second Test — Melbourne, October 19:
Ireland 62 pts, Australia 46 pts.
Third Test — Adelaide, October 24:
Ireland 55 pts, Australia 32 pts.

1987
First Test —Croke Park, October 18:
Ireland 53 pts, Australia 51 pts.
Second Test — Croke Park, October 25:
Australia 72 pts, Ireland 47 pts.
Third Test — Croke Park, November 1:
Australia 59 pts, Ireland 55.

1990
First Test — Melbourne, November 2:
Ireland 47 pts, Australia 38 pts.
Second Test — Canberra, November 20:
Ireland 52 pts, Australia 31 pts.
Third Test — Perth, November 17:
Australia 50 pts, Ireland 44 pts.

1998
First Test — Croke Park, October 11:
Australia 62 pts, Ireland 61 pts.
Second Test — Croke Park, October 18:
Ireland 67 pts, Australia 56 pts.
Ireland won two-game series on aggregate points: 128 to 118.

1999
First Test — Melbourne, October 7:
Ireland 70 pts., Australia 62 pts.
Second Test — Adelaide, October 15.
Ireland 52 pts., Australia 52 pts.
Ireland won two-game series on aggregate points, 122- 114.

2000
First Test — Croke Park, October 8:
Australia 55 pts, Ireland 47.
Second Test – Croke Park, October 15:
Australia 68 pts, Ireland 51.
Australia won the two-game series on aggregate points 123-98.

2001
First Test — Melbourne, October 12:
Ireland 59 pts, Australia 53 pts.
Second Test — Adelaide, October 19:
Ireland 71 pts, Australia 52pts.
Ireland won the two game series on aggregate points 130-105.

2002
First Test — Croke Park, October 13:
Australia 65 pts, Ireland 58 pts.
Second Test — Croke Park, October 20:
Australia 42 pts, Ireland 42 pts.
Australia won the two game series on aggregate points 107-100.

2003
First Test— Perth, October 24:
Australia 56 pts, Ireland 46 pts.
Second Test — Melbourne, October 31:
Ireland 48 pts, Australia 45 pts.
Australia won the two game series on aggregate points 101-94.

2004
First Test — Croke Park, October 17:
Ireland 77 pts, Australia 41 pts.
Second Test v Croke Park, October 24:
Ireland 55 pts, Australia 41pts.
Ireland won the two game series on aggregate points 132-82.

2005
First Test — Perth, October 21:
Australia 100 pts, Ireland 64 pts.
Second Test — Melbourne, October 28:
Australia 63 pts, Ireland 42 pts.
Australia won the two game series on aggregate points 163-106.

2006
First Test — Salthill, October 28:
Ireland 48 pts, Australia 40 pts.
Second Test — Croke Park, November 5:
Australia 69 pts, Ireland 31 pts.
Australia won the two game series on aggregate points 117-71.

2008
First Test — Perth, October 24:
Ireland 45 pts, Australia 44 pts.
Second Test — Melbourne, October 31:
Ireland 57 pts, Australia 53 pts.
Ireland won the two game series on aggregate points 102-97.

INTERNATIONAL SERIES
IRISH CAPS

Player	County	Caps	Year (No of Caps)
Liam Austin	Down	2	1984
Paul Barden	Longford	2	2006 (2)
Keith Barr	Dublin	1	1990
Pat Barrett	Limerick	1	1990
Des Barry	Longford	1	1990
Colm Begley	Laois	4	2006 (2) 2008 (2)
Joe Bergin	Galway	8	2002 (2) 2003 (2) 2004 (2) 2006 (2)
Greg Blaney	Down	7	1984 (2) 1986 (3) 1987 (2)
Paddy Bradley	Derry	2	2008
Paul Brewster	Fermanagh	2	1998
Alan Brogan	Dublin	4	2004 (2) 2006 (2)
Eoin Brosnan	Kerry	2	2004 (1) 2005 (1)
Colum Browne	Laois	1	1987
Declan Browne	Tipperary	1	2004
Niall Buckley	Kildare	4	1998 (1) 1999 (2) 2001 (1)
P.J. Buckley	Dublin	3	1984
Brian Burke	Tipperary	1	1990
Peter Burke	Mayo	1	2002
Niall Cahalane	Cork	5	1986 (3) 1987 (2)
Peter Canavan	Tyrone	6	1998 (2) 1999 (2) 2000 (2)
Graham Canty	Cork	12	2001 (2) 2002 (2) 2003 (2) 2004 (2) 2005 (2) 2008 (2)
Tommy Carr	Dublin	1	1990
Joe Cassells	Meath	1	1984
Sean Cavanagh	Tyrone	8	2004 (2) 2005 (2) 2006 (2) 2008 (2)
Ger Cavlan	Tyrone	3	1998 (1) 2000 (2)
Paddy Christie	Dublin	3	2002 (1) 2003 (2)
Ronan Clarke	Armagh	3	2005 (2) 2006
Stephen Cluxton	Dublin	3	2002 (1) 2004 (2)
Pat Comer	Galway	3	1990
Matt Connor	Offaly	1	1984
Richie Connor	Offaly	1	1984
Colm Cooper	Kerry	2	2005
Colin Corkery	Cork	1	2003
Ray Cosgrove	Dublin	2	2002
John Costello	Laois	1	1984
Benny Coulter	Down	10	2003 (2) 2004 (2) 2005 (2) 2006 (2) 2008 (2)
Gary Cox	Roscommon	1	2003
Martin Crossan	Donegal	2	2000
John Crowley	Kerry	2	2001
Bryan Cullen	Dublin	6	2004 (2) 2005 (2) 2008 (2)
Finbar Cullen	Offaly	6	1998 (2) 1999 (2) 2000 (2)
Paul Curran	Dublin	3	1990
Cathal Daly	Offaly	1	2003
Martin Daly	Clare	1	1998
Val Daly	Galway	8	1986 (3) 1987 (2) 1990 (3)
Brendan Devenney	Donegal	3	1998 (1) 2001 (2)
Dessie Dolan	Westmeath	8	1999 (1) 2002 (2) 2003 (2) 2004 (2) 2005 (1)
Kieran Donaghy	Kerry	3	2006 (1) 2008 (2)
Plunkett Donaghy	Tyrone	2	1984
Michael Donnellan	Galway	6	1998 (2) 1999 (2) 2001 (2)
Brian Dooher	Tyrone	2	2005
Kieran Duff	Dublin	2	1987
Tom Dwyer	Carlow	1	1984
Dermot Earley	Kildare	8	1999 (2) 2000 (2) 2001 (2) 2006 (2)
Paul Earley	Roscommon	1	1987
Kevin Fagan	Dublin	1	1990
Michael Fagan	Westmeath	8	1986 (3) 1987 (3) 1990 (2)
Shea Fahy	Kildare	3	1984
Jarlath Fallon	Galway	4	1998 (2) 1999 (2)
Darren Fay	Meath	8	1998 (2) 1999 (2) 2000 (2) 2001 (2)
Paul Finlay	Monaghan	1	2008
Kieran Fitzgerald	Galway	1	2006
Bernard Flynn	Meath	4	1987 (1) 1990 (3)
Derry Foley	Tipperary	3	1998 (2) 1999 (1)
Mattie Forde	Wexford	4	2004 (2) 2005 (2)
Thomas Freeman	Monaghan	1	2003
Martin Furlong	Offaly	1	1984
David Gallagher	Meath	2	2008
Paul Galvin	Kerry	4	2004 (2) 2006 (2)
Martin Gavigan	Donegal	3	1990
Graham Geraghty	Meath	9	1999 (1) 2000 (2) 2001 (2) 2002 (2) 2006 (2)
Trevor Giles	Meath	6	1999 (2) 2000 (2) 2002 (2)
Leighton Glynn	Wicklow	2	2008
Coman Goggins	Dublin	1	2001
Eoin Gormley	Tyrone	1	2000
Francie Grehan	Roscommon	1	2001
John Grimley	Armagh	2	1990
Mark Grimley	Armagh	2	1990
Finian Hanley	Galway	2	2008
Gerry Hargan	Dublin	4	1986 (2) 1987 (2)
Liam Hayes	Meath	3	1984 (1) 1987 (2)
David Heaney	Mayo	4	2004 (2) 2005 (2)
Eamon Heary	Dublin	2	1990
Joe Higgins	Laois	2	2003
Mick Holden	Dublin	1	1986
Colin Holmes	Tyrone	1	2002
James Horan	Mayo	1	1999
Kevin Hughes	Tyrone	2	2003
Philip Jordan	Tyrone	1	2005
Pádraig Joyce	Galway	11	2000 (1) 2001 (2) 2002 (2) 2003 (2) 2004 (2) 2005 (2)
Joe Kavanagh	Cork	2	1999
John Keane	Westmeath	2	2008
Evan Kelly	Meath	2	2002
Stephen Kelly	Limerick	2	2003
Tom Kelly	Laois	8	2003 (2) 2004 (2) 2005 (2) 2006 (2)
Tadhg Kennelly	Kerry	8	2001 (2) 2002 (2) 2004 (2) 2006 (2)
John Kenny	Offaly	2	1998
Aaron Kernan	Armagh	2	2008
Jimmy Kerrigan	Cork	6	1984 (3) 1986 (3)
Stephen King	Cavan	1	1987
Karl Lacey	Donegal	1	2006
Eoin Liston	Kerry	3	1984 (2) 1990 (1)
Sean Marty Lockhart	Derry	16	1998 (2) 1999 (2) 2000 (2) 2001 (2) 2003 (2) 2004 (2) 2005 (2) 2006 (2)
Anthony Lynch	Cork	6	2002 (2) 2003 (2) 2005 (2)

Ger Lynch	Kerry	3	1987 (3)
John Lynch	Tyrone	1	1987
Ciarán Lyng	Wexford	1	2008
Mick Lyons	Meath	9	1984 (3) 1986 (3) 1987 (3)
Diarmuid Marsden	Armagh	1	1998
Mick Martin	Leitrim	2	1984
Cormac McAnallen	Tyrone	6	2001 (2) 2002 (2) 2003 (2)
Dermot McCabe	Cavan	2	1998
James McCartan	Down	2	1990 (2)
Teddy McCarthy	Cork	1	1986
Finbar McConnell	Tyrone	2	1998
John McDermott	Meath	4	1998 (2) 1999 (2)
Brian McDonald	Laois	2	2003
Ciarán McDonald	Mayo	4	2004 (2) 2005 (2)
Steven McDonnell	Armagh	7	2003 (2) 2004 (1) 2006 (2) 2008 (2)
Jonathan McGee	Dublin	1	2000
Kieran McGeeney	Armagh	10	1998 (1) 2000 (1) 2001 (2) 2002 (2) 2003 (2) 2006 (2)
Brian McGilligan	Derry	6	1986 (3) 1987 (3)
Enda McGinley	Tyrone	2	2008
Peter McGinnity	Fermanagh	1	1984
Paul McGrane	Armagh	5	2000 (2) 2002 (1) 2003 (2)
Martin McGrath	Fermanagh	3	2004 (2) 2008 (1)
Brian McGuigan	Tyrone	4	2004 (2) 2005 (2)
Seamus McHugh	Galway	8	1984 (3) 1986 (2) 1987 (3)
Ciarán McKeever	Armagh	2	2008
Fran McMahon	Armagh	2	1984
Joe McMahon	Tyrone	2	2008
Justin McMahon	Tyrone	2	2008
Colm McManamon	Mayo	3	1998 (1) 2000 (2)
Ciarán McManus	Offaly	14	1999 (2) 2000 (2) 2001 (2) 2002 (2) 2003 (2) 2004 (2) 2005 (2)
Ryan McMenamin	Tyrone	1	2005
Joe McNally	Dublin	3	1986
Dermot McNicholl	Derry	9	1984 (3) 1986 (3) 1987 (3)
Michael McVeigh	Down	2	2005
Declan Meehan	Galway	2	2002
Michael Meehan	Galway	3	2005 (1) 2008 (2)
John Miskella	Cork	2	2008
Colin Moran	Dublin	1	2000
Anthony Moyles	Meath	2	2006 (2)
Seamus Moynihan	Kerry	9	1998 (2) 1999 (2) 2000 (1) 2001 (2) 2002 (2)
Alan Mulholland	Galway	3	1990
Eoin Mulligan	Tyrone	1	2005
Ross Munnelly	Laois	1	2005
Enda Murphy	Kildare	2	2003
Nicholas Murphy	Cork	1	2006
Ciarán Murray	Monaghan	6	1986 (3) 1987 (3)
James Nallen	Mayo	6	1998 (2) 1999 (2) 2004 (2)
Charlie Nelligan	Kerry	1	1984
Setanta Ó hAilpín	Cork	1	2004
Kevin O'Brien	Wicklow	4	1990 (3) 1998 (1)
Stephen O'Brien	Cork	2	1990
Pat O'Byrne	Wicklow	8	1986 (3) 1987 (2) 1990 (3)
Sean Ó Domhnaill	Galway	1	1998
Brian O'Donnell	Galway	3	1984
John O'Driscoll	Cork	3	1986
Odran O'Dwyer	Clare	1	2003
Damien O'Hagan	Tyrone	2	1986
Eamon O'Hara	Sligo	4	2001 (2) 2002 (2)
Declan O'Keeffe	Kerry	2	1999
John O'Leary	Dublin	7	1984 (1) 1986 (3) 1987 (3)
Aidan O'Mahony	Kerry	4	2006 (2) 2008 (2)
Robbie O'Malley	Meath	3	1987
Pearse O'Neill	Cork	1	2008
Stephen O'Neill	Tyrone	2	2005
Colm O'Rourke	Meath	4	1984 (3) 1986 (1)
Darragh Ó Sé	Kerry	4	2001 (2) 2002 (2)
Marc Ó Sé	Kerry	2	2006 (2)
Tomas Ó Sé	Kerry	4	2002 (2) 2005 (2)
Jack O'Shea	Kerry	9	1984 (3) 1986 (3) 1990 (3)
Brendan Jer O'Sullivan	Cork	3	2001 (1) 2002 (2)
Ciarán O'Sullivan	Cork	2	1999
Sean Óg Ó hAilpín	Cork	4	2004 (2) 2005 (2)
Sean Óg de Paor	Galway	7	1998 (1) 1999 (2) 2000 (2) 2001 (2)
Tom Parsons	Mayo	1	2008
Mark Plunkett	Offaly	1	1990
Seamus Quinn	Leitrim	1	2000
Alan Quirke	Cork	2	2006
Anthony Rainbow	Kildare	5	2000 (2) 2001 (2) 2002 (1)
Jim Reilly	Cavan	3	1987
Larry Reilly	Cavan	2	2000
Kevin Reilly	Meath	4	2006 (2) 2008 (2)
Noel Roche	Clare	10	1984 (3) 1986 (2) 1987 (3) 1990 (2)
Barney Rock	Dublin	3	1984
Mike Frank Russell	Kerry	1	2001
Glen Ryan	Kildare	5	1998 (2) 1999 (2) 2000 (1)
Shane Ryan	Dublin	3	2003 (2) 2006
Derek Savage	Galway	2	2002
Tony Scullion	Derry	4	1987 (1) 1990 (3)
Bill Sex	Kildare	4	1987 (2) 1990 (2)
Eoin Sexton	Cork	2	2000
Pat Spillane	Kerry	4	1986 (1) 1987 (3)
Tom Spillane	Kerry	8	1984 (3) 1986 (2) 1987 (3)
Brian Stynes	Dublin	6	1998 (2) 1999 (2) 2000 (2)
Jim Stynes	Dublin	3	1990
Cormac Sullivan	Meath	4	2000 (2) 2001 (2)
Liam Tierney	Longford	2	1984
Anthony Tohill	Derry	8	1998 (2) 1999 (2) 2000 (2) 2001 (2)
Sean Walsh	Kerry	2	1984
Ciarán Whelan	Dublin	4	1999 (2) 2000 (1) 2001 (1)
Killian Young	Kerry	1	2008

LEADING CAP WINNERS

16	Seán Marty Lockhart (Derry)
14	Ciarán McManus (Offaly)
12	Graham Canty (Cork)
11	Pádraig Joyce (Galway)
10	Benny Coulter (Down)
	Noel Roche (Clare)
	Kieran McGeeney (Armagh)

AUSTRALIAN CHAMPIONSHIPS

(1971-2009 inclusive)

HURLING

1971—Victoria
1972—None
1973—New South Wales
1974—New South Wales
1975—New South Wales
1976—Victoria
1977—Victoria
1978—Victoria
1979—New South Wales
1980—New South Wales
1981—Victoria
1982—New South Wales
1983—New South Wales
1984—None (Tour of Ireland)
1985—New South Wales
1986—New South Wales
1987—New South Wales
1988—New South Wales
1989—Victoria
1990—New South Wales
1991—Victoria
1992—New South Wales
1993—New South Wales
1994—New South Wales
1995—New South Wales
1996—None (Tour of Ireland)
1997—Auckland
1998—New South Wales
1999—New South Wales
2001—New South Wales Country
2003—New South Wales Coast
2004—New South Wales
2005—New South Wales
2006—New South Wales
2007—New South Wales City
2008—Victoria
2009—New South Wales

FOOTBALL

1971—South Australia
1972—None
1973—South Australia
1974—Victoria
1975—Victoria
1976—New South Wales
1977—Victoria
1978—West Australia
1979—New South Wales
1980—New South Wales
1981—West Australia
1982—New South Wales
1983—South Australia
1984—None
1985—Victoria
1986—Victoria
1987—West Australia
1988—Victoria
1989—Victoria
1990—New South Wales
1991—Victoria
1992—Auckland
1993—New South Wales
1994—Victoria
1995—Victoria
1996—None
1997—Auckland
1998—New South Wales
1999—New South Wales
2001—Victoria
2002—Victoria
2003—New South Wales
2004—New South Wales
2005—New South Wales
2006—Western Australia
2007—New South Wales
2008—Victoria
2009—Victoria

**The minor football championship, inaugurated in 1978, has been won by Victoria (9) in 1980-'84, 1986, 1988, 1992-'93; Auckland (5) 1989-'91, 1995, 1997; South Australia (4) 1978-'79, 1985, 1987; West Australia 1994 and Queensland 1998. The Queensland victory was the first championship for that State in any grade. The ladies' football competition began in 1995 and has been won by New South Wales in 1995 and 1998 and Auckland in 1997.*

NORTH AMERICAN BOARD CHAMPIONSHIPS

(1959-2009 inclusive)

HURLING

1959—San Francisco
1960—Los Angeles
1961—Montreal
1962—Galway (Boston)
1963—Shannon Rangers (Chicago)
1964—Galway (Boston)
1965—Garryowen (Toronto)
1966—Harry Bolands (Chicago)
1967—Galway (Boston)
1968—Galway (Boston)
1969—Harry Bolands (Chicago)
1970—Garryowen (Toronto)
1971—Harry Bolands (Chicago)
1972—Harry Bolands (Chicago)
1973—Galway (Boston)
1974—Garryowen (Toronto)
1975—St. Michael's (Toronto)
1976—Harry Bolands (Chicago)
1977—Limerick (Chicago)
1978—St. Michael's (Toronto)
1979—St. Vincent's (Chicago)
1980—Harry Bolands (Chicago)
1981—Cork (Boston)
1982—Cork (Boston)
1983—Harry Bolands (Chicago)

1984—Harry Bolands (Chicago)
1985—Gaels (San Francisco)
1986—Tipperary (Boston)
1987—Fr. Tom Burkes (Boston)
1988—Gaels (San Francisco)
1989—Harry Bolands (Chicago)
1990—Na Fianna (San Francisco)
1991—Na Fianna (San Francisco)
1992—Tipperary (Boston)
1993—Harry Bolands (Chicago)
1994—Cork (Boston)
1995—Cu Chulainn (Chicago)
1996—Harry Bolands (Chicago)
1997—N. Padraig (San Francisco)
1998—Harry Bolands (Chicago)
1999—Information not available
2001—Cork (Boston)
2002—Tipperary (Boston)
2003—Galway (Boston)
2004—Fr. Tom's (Boston)
2005—Tipperary (Boston)
2006—Harry Bolands (Chicago)
2007—Cu Chulainn (Chicago)
2008—Chicago Limerick
2009—Wexford (Boston)

FOOTBALL

1959—Los Angeles
1960—San Francisco
1961—San Francisco
1962—St. Patrick's (Cleveland)
1963—Galway (Boston)
1964—St. Patrick's (Cleveland)
1965—St. Patrick's (Cleveland)
1966—St. Patrick's (Cleveland)
1967—Hartford
1968—St. Patrick's (Chicago)
1969—Detroit
1970—Galway (Boston)
1971—Tyrone (Philadelphia)
1972—St. Brendan's (Chicago)
1973—Connemara Gaels (Boston)
1974—Tyrone (Philadelphia)
1975—Tyrone (Philadelphia)
1976—St. Patrick's (Boston)
1977—Tyrone (Philadelphia)
1978—Wolfe Tones (Chicago)
1979—Gaels (San Francisco)
1980—Wolfe Tones (Chicago)
1981—St. Brendan's (Chicago)
1982—Wolfe Tones (Chicago)
1983—St. Brendan's (Chicago)
1984—St. Patrick's (Boston)
1985—Wolfe Tones (Chicago)
1986—Galway (Boston)
1987—John McBrides (Chicago)
1988—Wolfe Tones (Chicago)
1989—Galway (Boston)
1990—Donegal (Philadelphia)
1991—Wolfe Tones (Chicago)
1992—Donegal (Philadelphia)
1993—Donegal (Philadelphia)
1994—Cusacks (San Francisco)
1995—Wolfe Tones (Chicago)
1996—Wolfe Tones (Chicago)
1997—Wolfe Tones (Chicago)
1998—McAnespies (Boston)
1999—Information not available
2001—Wolfe Tones (Chicago)
2002—Wolfe Tones (Chicago)
2003—Cork (Boston)
2004—St. Brendan's (Chicago)
2005—Ulster (San Francisco)
2006—Wolfe Tones (Chicago)
2007—St.Brendan's (Chicago)
2008—McAnespies (Boston)
2009—St. Christopher's (Boston)

CHAMPIONSHIPS OF BRITAIN

HURLING

1963—Brian Boru (London)
1967—Cuchulains (London)
1968—St Chad's (Warwickshire)
1969—Brian Boru (London)
1970—John Mitchell's (Warwickshire)
1971—Brian Boru (London)
1972—Brother Pearse (London)
1973—St Gabriel's (London)
1974—St Gabriel's (London)
1975—Brian Boru (London)
1976—St Gabriel's (London)
1977—St Gabriel's (London)
1978—St Gabriel's (London)
1979—Brian Boru (London)
1980—Brian Boru (London)
1981—St Gabriel's (London)
1982—Brian Boru (London)
1983—Desmonds (London)
1984—St Gabriel's (London)
1985—Desmonds (London)
1986—St Gabriel's (London)
1987—Glen Rovers (Hertfordshire)
1988—Desmonds (London)
1989—Desmonds (London)
1990—St Gabriel's (London)
1991—Seán Treacy's (London)
1992—Desmonds (London)
1993—Seán Treacy's (London)
1994—Seán Treacy's (London)
1995—St Gabriel's (London)
1996—St Gabriel's (London)
1997—St Gabriel's (London)
1998—Brother Pearse (London)
1999—St.Gabriel's (London)
2000—Fr.Murphy's (London)
2001—Fr.Murphy's (London)
2002—Seán Treacy's (London)
2003—Fr.Murphy's (London)
2004—Robert Emmets (London)
2005—Fr.Murphy's (London)

2006—Robert Emmets (London)
2007—Brother Pearse (London)
2008—Robert Emmets (London)

FOOTBALL

1967—St Mary's (London)
1968—Parnell's (London)
1969—Parnell's (London)
1970—Garryowen (London)
1971—Seán Treacy's (London)
1972—Seán McDermott's (Warwickshire)
1973—Seán McDermott's (Warwickshire)
1974—De La Salle College (Lancashire)
1975—Seán McDermott's (Warwickshire)
1976—An Ríocht (London)
1977—An Ríocht (London)
1978—An Ríocht (London)
1979—An Ríocht (London)
1980—Tara (London)
1981—Parnell's (London)
1982— Hugh O'Neill's (Yorkshire)
1983—Tír Conaill Gaels (London)
1984—Parnell's (London)
1985—An Ríocht (London)
1986—An Ríocht (London)
1987—An Ríocht (London)
1988—John Mitchell's (Warwickshire)
1989—An Ríocht (London)
1990—Tír Conaill Gaels (London)
1991—Parnell's (London)
1992—Tír Conaill Gaels (London)
1993—Tír Conaill Gaels (London)
1994—Oisin's (Lancashire)
1995—Tara (London)
1996—Tír Conaill Gaels (London)
1997—Tír Conaill Gaels (London)
1998—Tír Conaill Gaels (London)
1999—Hugh O'Neills (Yorkshire)
2000—Tir Conaill Gaels (London)
2001—Tir Conaill Gaels (London)
2002—St.Brendan's (London)
2003—Tara (London)
2004—Kingdom Kerry Gaels (London)
2005—Tír Conaill Gaels (London)
2006—St.Brendan's (London)
2007—Tír Conaill Gaels (London)
2008—Tír Conaill Gaels (London)

INTERNATIONAL COMPETITIONS

TAILTEANN GAMES

Many of the greatest players of earlier decades lined out in the Tailteann Games of 1924, 1928 and 1932 and the distinction of playing for Ireland in international matches became a prize of great distinction for those honoured.

For the record then, here are the teams that contested those historic games:

1924 - HURLING

Ireland—J. Humphreys (capt.), W. Ryan, W. Gleeson, D. Murnane (Limerick), J. Kennedy, D. Ring (Cork), J. J. Hayes, J. D'Arcy, Michael D'Arcy (Tipperary), T. Kelly (Laois), J. O'Mahony (goal), B. Gibbs, M. Derivan (Galway), G. Howard, Jim Walsh (Dublin).

United States—W. Finn (capt.), D. Kelly (goal), P. Aylward, M. Kenney, P. Kelly, M. Kavanagh, C. McCarthy, M. Flanagan, R. Stokes, J. Deegan, J. Murphy, P. Cox, J. Galvin, P. J. Grimes, J. Ryan.

1924 - FOOTBALL

Ireland (v. England)—J. McDonnell, P. Carey, J. Norris (Dublin), J. P. Murphy, T. P. Masterson, P. Smyth (Cavan), C. Brosnan, J. Bailey, P. Sullivan (Kerry), J. Doyle (Carlow), L. McGrath (Galway), P. Kilroy (Wexford), T. Shevlin (Roscommon), J. Byrne (Louth), J. Martin (Leitrim).

1928 - HURLING

Ireland—T. Daly (goal), J. Walsh, M. Gill, M. Power, G. Howard (Dublin), Seán Óg Murphy, Jas. O'Regan, E. Coughlan (Cork), P. Cahill, M. Kennedy (Tipperary), M. King, M. Derivan (Galway}, J. Kinnane (Limerick), E. Tobin (Laois), T. Considine (Clare).

America—J. Dermody (goal), J Keoghan, H. Meagher, S. Fitzpatrick, J. Grey, P. Fitzgibbon, P. Delany, C. Clohane, J. Galvin, J. Halligan, J. Horan, A. Cordial, W. Ryan, J. Burke, T. Hickey. (Included natives of Kilkenny, Laois, Cork, Offaly, Clare and Tipperary.)

1928 - FOOTBALL

Ireland—J. McDonnell (goal), P. McDonnell, M. O'Brien (Dublin), J. Barrett, C. Brosnan, P. Russell (Kerry), J. Higgins, M. Goff, P. Doyle, F. Malone (Kildare), T. Shevlin (Roscommon), J. Smith (Cavan), P. Colleran (Sligo), J. Shanley (Leitrim), M. O'Neill (Wexford).

America—E. Roberts (goal), A. Furlong, P. Ormsby, M. Ormsby, J. Tuite, M. Moloney, T. Armitage, M. Gunn, P. Lenihan, J. Stynes, M. Cody, W. Landers, J. Moriarty, T. Flynn, J. McGoldrick. (Waterford, Wexford, Mayo, Louth, Clare, Tipperary, Cork, Kildare, Kilkenny, Kerry and Leitrim were represented on this team.)

1932 - HURLING

Ireland—E. O'Connell (capt.), J. O'Regan, J. Hurley, D. B. Murphy, M. Ahern (Cork), T. O'Meara (goal), P. Purcell (Tipperary), C. McMahon, J. Walsh (Dublin), J. J. Doyle (Clare), M. Cross (Limerick), E. Byrne, M. Power (Kiikenny), M. King (Galway), D. O'Neill (Laois).

America—J. Holligan (capt.), J. Costigan (goal), J. Burke, W. Fox, J. Horan, P. Leamy, T. Delany, B. Dooley, T. Cooney, J. Smee, G. Fitzpatrick, W. Spearin, R. Purcell, J. Duane, J. Kenny. Sub: P. Loughman.

1932 - FOOTBALL

Ireland—J. Barrett (capt.), D. O'Connor, P. Whitty, J. Ryan (Kerry), J. Higgins, P. Martin (Kildare), J. Fane, M. O'Neill, N. Walsh (Wexford), J. Delaney (Laois), J. McDonnell (Dublin, goal), J. Smith (Cavan), T. Leetch (Galway), L. Colleran (Sligo), G. Courell (Mayo).

America—T. Armitage (capt.), J. Curran (goal), M. Maloney, A. Furlong, M. Kelleher, P. Landy, J. McGoldrick, J. Tuite, M. Shanahan, W. Landers, M. Mahon, M. Ormsby, T. Keogh, W. Mangan, J. Stynes. Sub: M. Spillane.

ST. BRENDAN CUP FINALS

New York v National League Winners 1954-1960

HURLING

1954—Polo Grounds, October 31. Cork 7-8, New York 3-10
1955—Croke Park, October 9. Tipperary 4-17, New York 4-7
1957—Polo Grounds, October 20. Tipperary 2-14, New York 4-4
1958—Croke Park, Septembr 14. New York 3-8, Wexford 3-7
1959—Gaelic Park, September 20. Tipperary 4-11, New York 1-5
1960—Croke Park, October 9. Tipperary 5-18, New York 4-4

FOOTBALL

1954—Polo Grounds, October 31. New York 0-10, Mayo 2-3
1955—Croke Park, October 9. Dublin 2-9, New York 0-10
1957—Polo Grounds, October 20. Galway 3-13, New York 3-8
1958—Croke Park, October 5. Dublin 2-6, New York 1-7
1959—Gaelic Park, October 18. Kerry 2-11, New York 1-8
1960—Croke Park, October 9. Down 2-8, New York 0-6

WORLD CHAMPIONSHIP CUP

HURLING

New York v All-Ireland Champions

1967—Gaelic Park, September 17. Kilkenny 1-12, New York 1-10. September 24. New York 2-13, Kilkenny 0-23 (aet). Aggregate score: Kilkenny 1-35, New York 3-23.
1968—Wexford Park, September 29. Wexford 1-17, New York 3-5.
1969—Gaelic Park, October 5. New York 3-13, Kilkenny 1-7. October 12. New York 1-11, Kilkenny 3-5. Aggregate score: New York 4-24, Kilkenny 4-12.

FOOTBALL

New York v All-Ireland Champions

1967—Croke Park, October 1. Meath 0-13, New York 1-6.
1968—Gaelic Park, October 13. New York 1-9, Down 1-8. October 20. Down 2-11, New York 1-9. Aggregate score: Down 3-19, NewYork 2-18.
1969—Croke Park, October 25. Kerry 4-13, New York 0-7.

AN POC FADA

Craohh Na hÉireann

THE Poc Fada All-Ireland Final, inaugurated in 1961, takes place each year on August Bank Holiday Monday on Ath na Bearna Mountain in Cooley, County Louth. The mountain lies on the border between Armagh and Louth.

An Poc Fada has grown in recent times to have an established status all its own in GAA competitions and some famous hurlers like Pat Hartigan (Limerick), Ollie Walsh (Kilkenny) and Ger Cunningham (Cork) figure in the Roll of Honour of those who have won the crown (the Corn Cuailnge). The occasion of the final has been graced by the President of the GAA, Joe McDonagh who has not hidden his admiration for its unique place in the Irish mythology and in the skill it demands of the contestants.

Poc Fada na hÉireann has its roots in the saga of the Táin Bó Cuailgne. The tale of Setanta driving his sliothar from Dun Dealgan to Eamhan Macha gave rise to speculation among a group of young Dundalk hurlers, back in the Sixties, as to how many pocs it would take to drive a sliothar between two points on the Cooley Mountains in County Louth. They were overheard by Fr. Pól Mac Seoin a founder member of Naomh Moninne Hurling Club – and he decided to find out. The result was Poc Fada na hÉireann.

The course is almost 5 km long and the winner is the man who can cover it in the least pocs. Each hurler has a team of four, the Feighlí Scóir, who stay with the hurler and record his score.

The All-Ireland Final has been sponsored by M. Donnelly & Co., Dublin and Ennis.

The winner of the All-Ireland Poc Fada is presented with the Corn Cuailgne trophy.

ROLL OF HONOUR

The following are the winners of the Poc Fada All-Ireland title:

2009—Gerry Fallon (Ros Comáin)
2008—Brendan Cummins (Tiobraid Árann)
2007—Brendan Cummins (Tiobraid Árann)
2006—Brendan Cummins (Tiobraid Árann)
2005—Albert Shanahan (Luimneach)
2004—Brendan Cummins (Tiobraid Árann)
2003—Paul Dunne (An Lú)
2002—David Fitzgerald (An Clár)
2001—Albert Shannon (Luimneach)
2000—Colin Byrne (Cill Mhantáin)
1999—Davy Fitzgerald (An Clár)
1998—Albert Kelly (Uibh Fháilí)
1997—Colin Byrne (Cill Mhaintain)
1996—Michael Shaughnessy (Gaillimh)
1995—Michael Shaughnessy (Gaillimh)
1994—Michael Shaughnessy (Gaillimh)
1993—Albert Kelly (Uibh Fháilí)
1992—Albert Kelly (Uibh Fháilí)
1991—Tommy Quaid (Luimneach)
1990—Ger Cunningham (Corcaigh)
1989—Ger Cunningham (Corcaigh)
1988—Ger Cunningham (Corcaigh)
1987—Ger Cunningham (Corcaigh)
1986—Ger Cunningham (Corcaigh)
1985—Ger Cunningham (Corcaigh)
1984—Ger Cunningham (Corcaigh)
1983—Pat Hartigan (Luimneach)
1982—Gerry Goodwin (Tír Eoghain)
1981—Pat Hartigan (Luimneach)
Note—No competition between 1970 and 1980.
1969—Liam Tobin (Port Láirge)
1968—Fionbarr Ó Néill (Corcaigh)
1967—Fionbarr Ó Néill (Corcaigh)
1966—Fionbarr Ó Néill (Corcaigh)
1965—Denis Murphy (Corcaigh)
1964—Oliver Gough (Cill Chainnigh)
1963—Three way tie—Ollie Walsh (Cill Chainnigh), Tom Geary (Port Láirge), Dinny Donnelly (An Mhí).
1962—Ollie Walsh (Cill Chainnigh).
1961—Vincent Godfrey (Luimneach).

COMORTAS BEIRTE (PAIRS) CHAMPIONSHIP

The winners are the pair with the least number of combined pocs. The Corn Setanta and Corn na Craoibhe Rua Cups are presented to the winners.
2009— Gerry Fallon (Ros Comáin) and Brendan Cummins (Tiobraid Árann)
2008—Brendan Cummins (Tiobraid Árann) and Brendan McNamara (An Clár)
2007—Pat Mullany (Laois) and Shane O'Connor (Uíbh Fhailí)
2006—Brendan Cummins (Tiobraid Árann) and Eoin Kelly (Tiobraid Árann)
2005—Davy Fitzgerald (An Clár) and Damien Fitzhenry (Loch Garman).
2004—Brendan Cummins (Tiobraid Árann) and Albert Shannon (Luimneach).
2003—Paul Dunne (An Lú) and Tom Finn (Cill Mhantáin).
2002—Graham Clark (An Dún) and Davy Fitzgerald (An Clár).
2001—Liam Shinners (Tiobraid Árann) and Albert Shannon (Luimneach).
2000—Richie Burke (Gaillimh) and Christy O'Connor (An Clár).
1999—Ian Scallan (Loch Garman) and Brendan Cummins (Tiobraid Árann).
1998—Seamus McMullan (Aontroim) and Davy Fitzgerald (An Clár).
1997—Colin Byrne (Cill Mhantáin) and Kevin Coulter (An Dún).
1996—Paul Dunne (An Lú) and Niall Linnane (Gaillimh).
1995—Liam Shinners (Tiobraid Árann) and Michael Shaughnessy (Gaillimh).
1994—Johnny Masterson (An Mhí) and Michael Shaughnessy (Gaillimh).
1993—Davy Fitzgerald (An Clár) and Michael Shaughnessy (Gaillimh).
1992—Michael Shaughnessy (Gaillimh) and Albert Kelly (Uíbh Fhailí).
1991—Tommy Quaid (Luimneach) and Michael Shaughnessy (Gaillimh).
1990—Des Donnelly (Aontroim) and Tommy Quaid (Luimneach).
1989—John Conway (Ciarraí) and Michael Shaughnessy (Gaillimh).
1988—Vincent Moore (Cill Dara) and Michael Shaughnessy (Gaillimh).
1987—Des Donnelly (Aontroim) and Christy Ryan (An Clár).
1986—John Kelly (Uíbh Fhaili) and Tommy Quaid (Luimneach).
1985—Ger Cunningham (Corcaigh) and Donal O'Brien (Nua Eabhrach).
1984—Justin McCarthy (Corcaigh) and Michael Shaughnessy (Gaillimh).
1983—Joe Shortt (Ard Mhacha) and Tommy Quaid (Luimneach).

AN POST/GAA TEAMS OF THE MILLENNIUM

In 1999 An Post in conjunction with the GAA arranged for a special panel comprising well-known GAA writers and broadcasters and former GAA Presidents to select the official Football Team of the Millennium.

The panel comprised: Raymond Smith (Sunday Independent), Donal Carroll (Sunday Independent), Jim O'Sullivan (The Examiner), Paddy Downey (Irish Times), Mick Dunne (RTÉ), Micheál Ó Muirheartaigh (RTÉ) and Paddy

O'Hara (BBC), also former Presidents, John Dowling, Dr. Mick Loftus and Jack Boothman. The teams chosen after long deliberations was:

Football: Dan O'Keefe (Kerry), Enda Colleran (Galway), Joe Keohane (Kerry), Seán Flannagan (Mayo), Sean Murphy (Kerry), John Joe Reilly (Cavan), Martin O'Connell (Meath), Mick O'Connell (Kerry), Tommy Murphy (Laois), Seán O'Neill (Down), Seán Purcell (Galway), Pat Spillane (Kerry), Mick Sheehy (Kerry), Tom Langan (Mayo), Kevin Heffernan (Dublin).

Hurling: Tony Reddan (Tipperary), Bobby Rackard (Wexford), Nick O'Donnell (Wexford), John Doyle (Tipperary), Brian Whelahan (Offaly), John Keane (Waterford), Paddy Phelan (Kilkenny), Lory Meagher (Kilkenny), Jack Lynch (Cork), Jim Langton (Kilkenny), Mick Mackey (Limerick), Christy Ring (Cork), Jimmy Doyle (Tipperary), Ray Cummins (Cork), Eddie Keher (Kilkenny).

TEAMS OF THE CENTURY AND CENTENARY TEAMS

In the Centenary Year of 1984 the Sunday Independent/Irish Nationwide/GAA Teams of the Century in Hurling and Football were selected by a special panel, after the Sunday Independent had carried out a national poll of its readers.

Hurling: Tony Reddan (Tipperary), Bobby Rackard (Wexford), Nick O'Donnell (Wexford), John Doyle (Tipperary), Jimmy Finn (Tipperary), John Keane (Waterford), Paddy Phelan (Kilkenny), Lory Meagher (Kilkenny), Jack Lynch (Cork), Christy Ring (Cork), Mick Mackey (Limerick), Jimmy Langton (Kilkenny), Jimmy Doyle (Tipperary), Nick Rackard (Wexford), Eddie Keher (Kilkenny).

Football: Danno Keefe (Kerry), Enda Colleran (Galway), Paddy O'Brien (Meath), Seán Flanagan (Mayo), Seán Murphy (Kerry), John Joe O'Reilly (Cavan), Stephen White (Louth), Mick O'Connell (Kerry), Jack O'Shea (Kerry), Seán O'Neill (Down), Seán Purcell (Galway), Pat Spillane (Kerry), Mike Sheehy (Kerry), Tom Langan (Mayo), Kevin Heffernan (Dublin).

SPECIAL SELECTIONS

Also in 1984 the Sunday Independent/Irish Nationwide/GAA Centenary Teams, comprising players who had never won an All-Ireland Senior Championship medal, were selected by a special panel.

Hurling: Seán Duggan (Galway), Jim Fives (Waterford), Noel Drumgoole (Dublin), J. J. ("Goggles") Doyle (Clare), Seán Herbert (Limerick), Seán Stack (Clare), Colm Doran (Wexford), Joe Salmon (Galway), "Jobber" McGrath (Westmeath), Josie Gallagher (Galway), Martin Quigley (Wexford), Kevin Armstrong (Antrim), Jimmy Smith (Clare), Christy O'Brien (Laois), Mick Bermingham (Dublin).

Football: Aidan Brady (Roscommon), Willie Casey (Mayo), Eddie Boyle (Louth), John McKnight (Armagh), Gerry O'Reilly (Wicklow), Gerry O'Malley (Roscommon), Seán Quinn (Armagh), Jim McKeever (Derry), Tommy Murphy (Laois), Seán O'Connell (Derry), Pakie McGarty (Leitrim), Michael Kearns (Sligo), Charlie Gallagher (Cavan), Willie McGee (Mayo), Dinny Allen (Cork).

ALL-IRELAND TROPHIES

Liam McCarthy Cup—The Trophy for the All-Ireland senior hurling championship commemorates the memory of Liam McCarthy who was prominently associated with the GAA in London. He was born in London in 1851 to a Bruff (Co. Limerick) mother and Ballygarvan (Co. Cork) father. When the first County Board was formed in London in 1895 he was appointed treasurer and he became president of the board three years later. In 1921 a trophy in his honour was presented to the Central Council and the first winners were Limerick who beat Dublin in the delayed final played in May 1923. This cup was "retired" in 1992 to be replaced by an exact replica which was first won by Kilkenny who beat Cork in the final.

Sam Maguire Cup—A native of Dunmanway, Co. Cork, where he was born in 1879, Maguire at 20 years of age took a position with the postal service in London. There he was prominent in GAA affairs as a member of the Hibernians club and played with London in the All-Ireland football finals of 1900, 1901 (captain) and 1902. He was active in the Irish Republican Brotherhood and he initiated Michael Collins into that organisation. In December 1924 he returned to Dunmanway and died there three years later. The trophy in his name was presented to the GAA by a group of friends and former colleagues in 1928 and the first winners were Kildare who beat Cavan in the final. It was taken out of circulation in 1988 and the replacement first won by Meath when they beat Cork in that year's final.

Andy Merrigan Cup—The All-Ireland Club championships began in 1971, but the first winners of this trophy presented for the football championship to the association by the Wexford Co. Board were U.C.D. in 1974. The cup is named after Andy Merrigan a former Wexford footballer from the Castletown club who was tragically killed in a farming accident.

Tommy Moore Cup—A native of Ballyragget, Co. Kilkenny, Tommy Moore was prominently associated with the Faughs club in Dublin for most of his adult life. He was chairman and treasurer for 40 years until he stepped down in 1969, but was immediately elected president. Following his death in May 1973 the club president presented the trophy in his honour to the Central Council of the GAA.

THE MAJOR STADIA

Croke Park—The stadium stands on land once known as "Butterly's Field" as the property of 21 acres, one rood was bought in 1864 by Maurice Butterly who 30 years later sold it to a company called the City & Suburban Racecourse Amusements Ground. It was then used mainly for sports meetings and whippet racing and was frequently rented to the GAA who first used it for All-Ireland finals on March 15, 1896 (Tipperary-Meath and Tipperary-Kilkenny). In 1908 the property was bought by Frank B. Dineen, who was both General Secretary and President of the GAA in the 1800s, and he held it until such time as the Association had sufficient funds. Eventually they paid £3,641 to Dineen and on September 17, 1914, GAA Ltd. was incorporated as owners of the ground.

Hill 16 was put in place in 1917 with rubble from O'Connell St. (Dublin) in the aftermath of the Easter Rising, the Hogan Stand, commemorating Tipperary footballer Michael Hogan shot at the Park during a challenge between Tipperary and Dublin on November 21, 1920, Bloody Sunday – was built for the first Tailteann Games in 1924, the Cusack Stand was opened in 1938 and the Nally Stand in 1952. The new Hogan Stand was opened in 1959, a new Hill 16 in 1989.

In the early nineties, the GAA drew up plans for a complete re-building of the stadium. The first phase of this was a new Cusack Stand which was opened in 1994 and construction of a new stand at the Canal end commenced in October 1998. Phase 3 of the redevelopment was the erection of a third Hogan Stand. By 2001 the Canal End had been completed followed by the Hogan Stand. Both of those phases were officially opened in 2003.

The final phase of the redevelopment, the Hill 16 and Nally End, were completed in time for the 2005 championships season.

New floodlights were officially switched on in early February 2007. Tyrone and Dublin subsequently met in the opening round of the Allianz National Football League before an attendance of 81,678. Tyrone won the game by 011 to 0-10.

Semple Stadium—In 1901 a Thurles merchant sold 11 acres to the local Agricultural Show Committee who used it for their various shows for nine years, but then sold it to the GAA committee. One of the committee members was Tom Semple who had captained the Thurles Blues to win the All-Ireland hurling championships of 1906 and 1908 for Tipperary and also served as chairman of the Tipperary County Board (1915-'17) as well as treasurer of the Central Council. He was later president of the Thurles Sarsfields club before his death in April 1943. The first Munster hurling final played there was the 1914 game between Cork and Clare with Tom Semple the referee. The Sportsfield was one of the first to be selected by Bórd na bPairc in the 1960s for redevelopment and with the completion of the first phase in 1968 the arena was renamed Semple Stadium. Further modernisation was completed in the early eighties with a new stand and terracing in time for the staging of the Centenary All-Ireland hurling final (Cork v Offaly) attended by 59,814 in 1984. Floodlights were officially switched on during 2009.

Páirc Uí Chaoimh—Sports meetings were frequently staged in the area now occupied by the Cork stadium even before the foundation of the GAA, but by the end of the 1800s the Cork Co. Board were permitted by the Cork Agricultural Company, the leaseholders, to enclose a portion of the site for Gaelic games. Soon a new stadium was constructed there and in September 1904 it was opened with the staging of the delayed 1902 All-Ireland finals (Dublin v London, football, Cork v London, hurling). Known now as the Cork Athletic Grounds it was used for several sports, but from 1906 only Gaelic games were played in the ground.

Over the years some development was carried out, but in 1974 the ground was demolished to make way for a totally new stadium to be named to commemorate Pádraig Ó Caoimh, who was secretary of the Cork Board from 1920 until his election as general secretary of the GAA in 1929, a position he held until his death in 1964. The modern stadium was opened on June 6, 1976, by president Con Murphy, who as county secretary had been a prime mover in the redevelopment. Cork played Kilkenny and Kerry in the first games on opening day. The capacity was increased dramatically and the biggest crowd following the development was 49,691 at the Cork-Tipperary Munster Hurling Final of 1985.

The stadium has a seated capacity of 10,000.

Tuam Stadium—The proper name of the ground "St. Jarlath's Park" has never been in common usage although it was dedicated to the patron saint of the archhiocese when officially opened on May 21, 1950. Previously football games in Tuam were staged at Parkmore, close to the racecourse, among them All-Ireland semifinals of 1927, '31 and '34. But severe overcrowding at the Cavan-Galway game of 1934 convinced officials in the town of the urgent need for a more suitable venue and seven acres were bought from the Racecourse Company. However, difficulties soon arose with this site and new land was purchased in 1946 with development work beginning two years later. For the formal opening Cavan played Mayo and Galway took on Dublin.

St. Tiernach's Park—Clones has long been associated as the venue for Ulster finals. Between 1944 and 2003 all but ten finals were played at the County Monaghan venue. The 2004 and 2005 finals were played at Croke Park.

It was only in the 1940s that the field which is now the foremost venue in the province came into possession of the GAA. This field was owned by Samuel Keary and after some unsuccessful attempts the local club eventually persuaded him to sell the land in 1944. The purchase price was £700 and a further £500 was spent on levelling, resodding and other work before the opening was scheduled for August 6, 1944. In the meantime the Ulster Council fixed that year's provincial final (Monaghan v Cavan) for the ground, so a major game was staged at the venue a week before the official opening which went ahead as planned with Monaghan playing Antrim and a second game between North Monaghan and East Fermanagh.

The stadium was completely modernised with uncovered seating (replacing the famous "hill") and a stand erected and a new pitch laid in time for the Ulster football final of 1993, but further work had to be carried out on the playing surface subsequently because of damage caused that day by torrential rains. The stadium is named after the patron saint of the locality whose grave is in a nearby cemetery.

Fitzgerald Stadium—The Killarney ground is named after one of Kerry's greatest footballers, Dick Fitzgerald, who won five All-Ireland medals and captained the winning teams of 1913 and '14. He was held in such high regard that when he died on September 26, 1930, two days before Kerry were due to play Monaghan in the All-Ireland final, the Kerry Board called an emergency meeting to consider whether they should go ahead with the final. It was only after a second meeting held on the Saturday, with officials aware of many hundreds of supporters already on their way to Dublin, that the decision was made that the Kerry team should travel. Soon afterwards the decision was taken to find a suitable site for a stadium to commemorate Fitzgerald's memory and a field close to the Killarney mental hospital was acquired mainly through the efforts of the late Dr. Eamonn O'Sullivan, the medical officer at the hospital and for many years trainer of Kerry teams. The official opening on May 31, 1936, was marked by a game between Kerry and Mayo and a parade of all past Kerry players.

Hyde Park—Connacht finals and All-Ireland semi-finals were staged in Roscommon town on many occasions, but the venue was St. Coman's Park (known locally as "the Lough") in the centre of the town. However, this was prone to flooding and when it was eventually decided that it couldn't be successfully drained, a field on the Athlone Road was purchased for £3,000 in 1969. Rafferty's field, a 14-acre plot, had been used for Gaelic games in the past, most notably the 1930 All-Ireland semi-final between Kerry and Mayo, but now it was to be developed by a park committee as a ground to be named aher Dr. Douglas Hyde, the first president of Ireland. It was ready for the first Connacht championship game on June 20, 1971, when Sligo gained their first victory over Roscommon since 1937. The game also marked the first appearance of prominent soccer players in a county game since the abolition of the "Ban" two months earlier as the Sligo team included David Pugh and Gerry Mitchell of Sligo Rovers. In recent years Hyde Park has been further modernised.

McHale Park—The Castlebar stadium was once the property of Lord Lucan which had been handed over at one period for development as a racecourse. However, when the plans never came to fruition the site was bought by the Castlebar Mitchels club in April 1930 for £650. It was named aher Rev. Dr. John McHale, who was Archbishop of Tuam (1834-'81) and was officially opened on May 24, 1931, when 4,000 attended for a football game between Mayo and Kerry. After development work was carried out in the early Fifties it was re-opened by the then president of the GAA, Vin O'Donoghue, in June 1952. A stand was built in 1990 and further improvements were later carried out at the venue to bring the capacity to 35,000, which is all-seated making it unique in Ireland.

Páirc Uí Rinn—Cork County Board purchased Flower Lodge Stadium, a well established soccer ground, in 1989 and development work on the grounds commenced in 1991.

The Stadium, finished to the most modern standards, was officially opened in 1993. The Stadium, known as Páirc Uí Rinn, is a monument to one of the greatest hurlers of all time, Christy Ring.

Floodlighting was established at the stadium some years ago and competitive inter-county games have been played there under lights. It has a capacity of 16,500.

Pearse Stadium—Pearse Stadium was opened in June 1957 and Galway beat Tipperary in hurling and Kerry in football to mark the occasion. The Stadium served Gaelic Games well down the years.

In December 1995 at a meeting under the auspices of the County Board moves were set in motion to redevelop the Stadium.

Eventually the magnificent new 34,000 capacity Pearse Stadium was officially opened on May 2003, providing Galway with an ultra-modern stadium and a major asset in meeting the testing challenges of the future.

Casement Park—Corrigan Park in Belfast was opened in 1927 and went on to contribute to the advancement of the games in the county.

However, in the early forties it was decided that a new ground was required and steps were initiated that eventually resulted in the opening of Casement Park in June 1953. The Ulster final was played there that year and Casement Park has hosted seven provincial finals since then, the last in 1971.

Big improvements have been carried out at the venue in recent times with the construction of extensive terracing.

COUNTY COLOURS

Antrim	Saffron and white trim
Armagh	Orange and white trim
Carlow	Red, yellow and green
Cavan	Royal blue and white trim
Clare	Saffron, blue hoop
Cork	Red and white trim
Derry	White, red hoop and red trim
Donegal	Green, gold and white trim
Down	Red and black trim
Dublin	Navy and sky blue
Fermanagh	Green and white trim
Galway	Maroon and white trim
Kerry	Green, gold hoop and white trim
Kildare	White with black numbers
Kilkenny	Black and amber vertical stripes and white trim
Laois	Blue, white hoop and white trim
Leitrim	Green and yellow trim
Limerick	Green and white trim
Longford	Royal blue and gold trim
Louth	Red and white trim
Mayo	Green, red hoop and white trim
Meath	Green and gold trim
Monaghan	White and blue trim
Offaly	Green, white and gold hoops
Roscommon	Primrose and royal blue trim
Sligo	Black with white trim
Tipperary	Blue and gold hoop
Tyrone	White and red trim
Waterford	White and blue trim
Westmeath	Maroon and white trim
Wexford	Purple and gold
Wicklow	Royal blue and gold trim

NOTEWORTHY ACHIEVEMENTS

IN THIS SECTION WE LIST SOME NOTEWORTHY AHIEVEMENTS THAT HAVE WON A SPECIAL PLACE IN THE HISTORY OF THE NATIONAL GAMES.

It would not be possible to list everything of marked achievements or cover all that was achieved back to the inauguration of the senior championships in 1887 but we feel that what we have recorded here will give permanence to individual achievements that have a lasting place in any book of records.

The list can be added to in future editions of this book as further research unearths more outstanding feats of distinction.

Cork stars lead the way with an impressive list from the record created in the 1940s by former Taoiseoch, Jack Lynch, down to Teddy McCarthy, as we have seen, opening the 199Os by becoming the only player to date in GAA history to win two senior All-Ireland medals in the same year.

CHRISTY RING THE GREATEST OF ALL TIME

Christy Ring is reckoned by many great judges to have been THE greatest hurler in the history of the national game. Certainly, few exerted the same dominance over opposing defences or made such an amazing impact over a period of close on a quarter of a century in the Cork colours while his achievements for Munster in the Railway Cup and for his club Glen Rovers added still further to the lustre with which he adorned the scene.

He first wore the Cork colours as a sub on the minor team that triumphed over Kilkenny in the 1937 All-Ireland final, was at right-wing back on the 1938 Leeside winning team and first donned the colours in senior grade in 1939, though he did not make the side that lost to Kilkenny in the famous "Thunder and Lightning" All-Ireland final of same year.

From 1940 to the 1903 season he was an automatic choice, captaining his county to three All-Ireland titles (1946, '53 and '54) as he won in all eight All-Ireland senior medals on the field of play.

He was 46 years old when he played for Glen Rovers against Mount Sion in the 1966 Munster Club final. Paddy Downey, writing in the Irish Times at the time that, "while he revealed his age when the spurt to the ball was more than ten yards, otherwise he gave us the whole gamut of his enormous skill the dazzling stickwork, the lightning stroke, the dainty pass, all the artistry that would not have surprised us twenty years earlier, but which enchanted with its very magic every soul in the 9,000 attendance at the Limerick Gaelic Grounds".

"Zenith of his Career"

Paddy Purcell of the Irish Press wrote after the 1951 Munster final, that although Ring was on the losing side that day as the boys in the Blue and Gold completed the three-in-a-row in the South (and went on to do likewise in the All-Ireland final), he "never again saw him dominate a game so completely" and he concluded that it was for him "the zenith of Ring's hurling career".

Yet, five years later in the 1956 Munster Final in Thurles, he was held until five minutes from the end and then in a truly amazing burst, he grabbed three goals that put paid to a gallant Limerick effort. "The Shannonsiders might have won were it not for the fate that made Christy Ring a Corkman", wrote Val Dorgan in the Cork Examiner.

John D. Hickey wrote in the Irish Independent of "the splendour of Ring in fashioning victory over St. Vincent's (4-8 to 2-7) at Croke Park in March 1954" and concluded that on this day for him there was no doubt that Ring was "a man apart on the hurling field". He pointed to the extraordinary point he scored midway through the second half and noted: "What a pity that his great effort overall was not filmed so that posterity could see hurling at its greatest".

Jack Lynch's Tribute

One could go on pinpointing other tributes like these from selected matches. Suffice it, to quote Jack Lynch at the graveside of Ring: "As long as young men will match their hurling skills against each other on Ireland's green fields, so long as young boys swing their camáns for the sheer thrill of the tingle in their fingers of the impact of the ash with leather, as long as hurling is played, the story of Christy Ring will be told – and that will be forever".

He was buried in St. Colman's Cemetery in his native village of Cloyne on a day in March, 1979. He is commemorated in Cork by a bridge over the Lee (near the Opera House) and also by the stadium, Páirc Christóir Ui Rinn, which was formally opened and named by Jack Lynch. And, of course, there is a lifesize memorial to him in Cloyne.

THE FABULOUS RING RECORD

- All-Ireland Senior Hurling Medals (8): 1941, '42, '43, '44, '46, '52, '53, '54.
- All-Ireland Runners-Up (2): 1947-1956.
- All-Ireland Minor Hurling Medal (1): 1938.
- National Hurling League Medals (4): 1940, '41, '48, '53.

- Railway Cup Medals (18): 1942, '43, '44, '45, '46, '48, '49, '50, '51, '52, '53, '55, '57, '58, '59, '60, '61, '63.
- Cork County Senior Hurling Medals (14) (with Glen Rovers): 1941, '44, '45, '48, '49, '50, '53, '54, '58, '59, '60, '62, '64, '67.
- Cork County Senior Hurling Medals (Runners-Up) (4): 1946, '51, '55, '56.
- Cork County Senior Football Medal (1) (with St. Enda's): 1954.
- Cork County Minor Hurling Medal (1) (with St. Nicholas's): 1938.
- Cork County Junior Hurling Medal (1) (with Cloyne): 1939.
- Munster Club Championship: 1965.
- Texaco Awards: 1959.
- Texaco Hall of Fame Award: 1971.
- Rest of Ireland Team: 1952, '53, '55, '56, '57, '58, '60, '62.
- Selector and Captain of Cork's 1946 All-Ireland winning team.
- Selector on Cork's All-Ireland winning teams 1976, '77, '78.
- Played on Cork Senior Hurling Team 1939-1963.
- Played on Munster Railway Cup Team: 1941-1963.
- Played on Glen Rovers Senior Hurling Team: 1941 -1967.
- Captained 3 Cork Teams to win All-Ireland: 1946, '53, '54.

THE RECORD JOHN DOYLE SHARES WITH RING

John Doyle shares with Christy Ring the distinction that they were the only two players in the history of the national game to win eight All-Ireland senior hurling championship medals on the field of play.

The powerful Tipperary defender won his eight medals in 1949, '50, '51, '58, '61, '62, '64 and '65. He played in two losing All-Ireland finals 1960 and '67.

He first wore the Blue and Gold of his county in senior grade in 1949 – at the age of 19 – and had the proud record of never having retired in a championship game during an inter-county career that spanned the seasons from 1949 to 1967 when he had his "Last Hurrah" in Croke Park. There were suggestions that Christy Ring might have made the 1966 Cork panel but Ring would never have dreamt of a situation where he would have picked up a ninth as a sub in order to go ahead of Doyle. And Doyle himself would never have done the same to get ahead of the Maestro from Cloyne. What had to be done in forging records that would be incomparable would have to be done on the field of play. Pride and respect dictated that.

John Doyle won eleven National League medals in 1949, '50, '51, 54, '55, '57, '59, '60,'61, '64 and '65.

In addition his tally of Oireachtas medals came to six in a period when this competition produced some tremendous contests. He won them in 1949, '60, '61, '63, '64 and '65.

And he won in all eight Railway Cup medals – in 1951, '52, '53, '55, '60, '61, '63 and '65. He won Tipperary County Senior Championship medals with Holycross-Ballycahill in 1948, '51 and '54.

He made the Hurling Team of the Century in 1984 with Christy Ring.

He was given the supreme accolade of being inducted in the Hall of Fame in 1962, thus joining Mick Mackey (1961) and Christy Ring (1971).

And in 1999 he was honoured with a Civil Reception by Tipperary South Riding County Council.

He created a lasting impact as a left-corner back in the line comprising also Mickey (The Rattler) Byrne and Tony Brennan in front of the incomparable Tony Reddan in epic matches against Cork and later his partners were Michael Maher and Kieran Carey. He switched for a time to left-half back and formed a tremendous bulwark with Jimmy Finn (who also made the Team of the Century) and Tony Wall.

His inspiational clearances could lift a team to new heights. He was a man for the big stage and there is little doubt that his contribution will always be remembered and cherished in the homes of Tipperary. In some ways he was right out of Kickham's Knocknagow.

His eldest son Michael followed in his footsteps by wearing the Blue and Gold of his county in senior grade and, having been unlucky to have been on the losing end against Cork in the epic Munster final at Semple Stadium in the Centenary Year in 1984, he played a notable role in the defeat of Tipperary's traditional rivals in the marathon Munster final replay in Killarney in 1987.

JACK LYNCH'S UNIQUE RECORD

Jack Lynch is the only player to win six consecutive senior All-Ireland medals. Hurling 1941 to 1944 and 1946, football 1945.

Brian Murphy is the only player to have won All-Ireland medals in minor, under 21 and senior grades in both hurling and football. He has also won All-Ireland medals with Coláiste Chríost Rí and Nemo Rangers.

Martin O'Doherty won All-Ireland medals in minor, under 21, senior and club in hurling, as well as minor and junior in football.

Jimmy Barry-Murphy holds All-Ireland medals in minor, under 21, senior and club in hurling, minor, senior and club in football, as well as National League medals in both codes (hurling

1974, 1980; football 1980). Jimmy was a dual All-Star in 1976.

He won five in a row of Munster senior hurling medals – TWICE – 1975-1979 and 1982-1986.

He shares with **Ray Cummins** and **Denis Coughlan** the distinction of winning 12 senior Munster Championship medals. Denis won 8 hurling and 4 football. Ray won 9 hurling and 3 football and Jimmy won 10 hurling and 2 football Ray and Jimmy are two of the six players, all Corkmen, who have won National League medals in hurling and football. The other four are: Eamon Young, hurling 1941; football 1952. Christy Ryan, hurling 1980; football 1980. Teddy McCarthy, football 1989; hurling 1993. Denis Walsh (St. Catherine's), football 1989; hurling 1993. Seán Óg Ó hAilpín, hurling 1998; football 1999.

Ray Cummins is the only player to have won eleven consecutive Munster senior titles, a feat achieved in the years 1969-1979. He won hurling titles in 1969-1970-1972 and 1975-1979 inclusive, and football titles in 1971-1973 and 1974. He also won another hurling medal in 1982. Ray was a dual All-Star in 1971.

Simon Murphy won All-Ireland medals in senior (1), under 21 (1), minor (1) and club (1) in hurling, and under 21 (1) and minor (1) in football, together with 2 National Hurling League and 12 Munster Championship medals - all between 1966-1972 before his playing career was cut short by injury.

Seamus Looney won All-Ireland medals in senior (1), under 21 (3) and club (1) in hurling, and under 21 (2), minor (2) and colleges (1) in football together with 15 Munster Championships between 1967 and 1972. Only player with 5 under 21 medals.

Tony O'Sullivan has All-Ireland medals for senior, minor and colleges in hurling and minor and under 21 in football.

Mick Malone is the only player to win four All-Ireland under 21 hurling medals. He also won one All-Ireland minor and two All-Ireland senior medals.

Four player have won four All-Ireland junior football medals: London's **Patsy McKenna, Joe Harrison, Malachy Nally** and **Kieran Creed** (Clondroichid).

Tadhg Murphy has All-Ireland medals for minor, under 21, senior and colleges in hurling as well as minor and junior in football.

Caleb Crone won All-Ireland football medals with Dublin in 1942 and Cork in 1945, and Railway Cup medals with Leinster in 1944 and Munster in 1946.

Teddy McCarthy, from Glanmire, in Cork, has the distinction of being the only man to win All-Ireland senior hurling and football medals in the one year.

He achieved that unique distinction in September 1990 when he returned to action from an ankle injury.

The injury kept him out of both Munster finals that year and it is a tribute to his bravery, dedication and skill that he battled back so well to earn a place apart in the annals of Gaelic Games.

McCarthy made four appearances in hurling and two in football on the way to the double. He was at left midfield in the side that beat Galway in the hurling final and left half forward in the football final success over Meath.

A year earlier McCarthy became the fifteenth player to win All-Ireland medals in both codes. He was right half forward in the 1986 All-Ireland senior hurling title winning team and at midfield in 1989 when Cork beat Mayo in the Sam Maguire Cup tie.

JIMMY DOYLE'S FABULOUS RECORD

Tipperary's star names, like their Cork counterparts, stitched many noteworthy achievements into the annals of our games and none more so than Jimmy Doyle, stylist supreme of Thurles Sarsfields who was so admired by Christy Ring that he made a special point of calling to him more than once in Thurles.

Jimmy Doyle won nine out of thirteen All-Irelands between 1954 and 1971. He played in four All-Ireland minor finals, losing out in 1954, but winning in 1955, '56 and '57. He won his first senior in 1958, lost in 1960, won 1961, '62, '64 and '65, lost in 1967 and '68, and won his sixth in 1971.

He had the distinction also of being the youngest player to play in an All-Ireland minor hurling final when he manned the goal position in 1954 against Dublin (Dublin 2-7, Tipperary 2-3) at the age of 14. He was captain when he won his third minor medal in 1957.

He captained Tipperary to victory in senior grade in the All-Irelands of 1962 and 1965, though he did not receive the Liam McCarthy Cup in '62. He was injured eleven minutes into the second half and had to retire. The cup was accepted by Tony Wall.

Jimmy Finn was the youngest player to captain a winning Tipperary senior hurling All-Ireland team at 19 years of age, when he led the county to victory over Wexford in 1951. He was only 18 when he won his first All-Ireland senior hurling medal against Kilkenny in 1950.

Pat Fox was 18 years when he won the first of three under 21 All-Ireland in 1979. Although later he came to be recognised as one of the best corner-forwards in the game, he played centre-field in 1979 ond corner-back in 1980 and '81.

THE HENDERSONS, THE BONNARS AND THE LEAHYS

The **Hendersons** of Johnstown, Co. Kilkenny were the first family in which three members received All-Star awards – Pat (1973-'74), Ger (1978, '79, '82, '83, '87) and John (1983).

The **Bonnars** also had three All-Stars, Colm (1988), Cormac and Conal (1989 and 1991).

Cormac Bonnar won All-Irelands in three decades, under 21 in 1979 and 1980, senior in 1989 and 1991. He also has two All-Star awards and two Fitzgibbon Cup medals with U.C.C. in 1976 and 1977.

The **Leahys** can rightly claim to be one of the most famous of all hurling families in Tipperary, four of them having won All-Ireland senior hurling medals. Johnny and Paddy were successful in 1916 and 1925. Another brother, Mick, won an All-Ireland with Cork in 1928. The fourth member, Tommy, won his All-Ireland in 1930. The father of the family, Mike, was on the Moycarkey selection which took part in the first great Cork-Tipperary clash in August 1886. And their uncle, Thomas Leahy of Tubberadora Mill, was President of the famous Tubberadora team which brought All-Irelands to Tipperary in 1895, '96 and '98.

Johnny Leahy captained two All-Ireland winning teams in 1916 and 1925.

SEVEN FOR SHEFFLIN

Henry Shefflin and **Eddie Brennan** each won a seventh All-Ireland Senior hurling medal in 2009. Their earlier successes were in 2000, 2002, 2003, 2006, 2007 and 2008.

BABS A DUAL STAR

Babs Keating was a noted dual star in the blue and gold colours and also played in both codes for Munster. He won Railway Cup honours in hurling in 1968, '70 and in football in 1972.

Keating and **Willie Nolan** of Roscrea hold an unenviable distinction. Both played unsuccessfully in three minor hurling All-Ireland finals, in 1960, '61, '62. Nolan was No. 10 and Keating No. 11 in all three finals.

DOUBLE CAPTAINS

Philip Kennedy (Éire Óg, Nenagh) was the first to lead his county to two All-Ireland under-21 wins in 1980 and 1981 in hurling.

Peter Canavan led Tyrone to their All-Ireland under-21 football titles of 1991 and 1992—the first to captain two title winning teams in the grade in football.

Cormac McAnallen equalled that distinction by leading Tyrone to their 2000 and 2001 All-Ireland under-21 football titles.

Tadhg O'Connor (Roscrea) captained Tipperary to an All-Ireland senior hurling title in 1971 and an All-Ireland Masters in 1992. In the latter year his son, Tadhg, led Roscrea to a county under 14 hurling title.

Declan O'Sullivan was the first to be twice presented with the new Sam Maguire Cup. He led Kerry to their All-Ireland Senior Football Final wins in 2006 and 2007.

Brian Dooher equalled that feat in 2008 when he captained Tyrone to the title, he first led the northern county to All-Ireland Senior Football glory in 2005.

The new Sam Maguire cup was first presented in 1988 when Meath beat Cork in a replay.

FOURTEEN OF THE BEST!

Tony Brennan played full-forward for Tipperary in the 1945 All-Ireland and full-back in the 1949, '50 and '51 teams. He was victorious on all four occasions.

Mickey ("The Rattler") Byrne (Thurles Sarsfields) won four All-Ireland senior medals with Tipperary in 1949, '50, '51 and '58 and was a sub in 1945. His chief record is to have won 14 county senior hurling finals in 1944, '45, '46, '52, '55, '56, '57, '58, '59, '61, '62, '63, '64, '65.

When **Paul Byrne** came on as a substitute in the 1971 All-Ireland he became the first son of a Tipperary All-Ireland hurler to win an All-Ireland medal on the field of play.

Tom Ryan (Killenaule), who won All-Ireland senior hurling medals with Tipperary in 1961 and 1962, was a member of the Clare team defeated by Tipperary in the 1967 Munster senior hurling final and also played with Galway.

The three **Kenny brothers** of Borris-Ileigh won All-Ireland senior hurling medals: Seán and Paddy in 1949, '50 and '51 and Philly (or Phippie) in 1950.

Timmy Ryan (Borris-Ileigh) won senior All-Irelands in 1949, '50 and '51. His sons; Bobby and Aidan, won senior medals in 1989 and 1991.

Denis Walsh (Tubberadora and Boherlahan) won five All-Irelands. He must be unique because 21 years separated his first in 1895 from his fifth in 1916. In between he was successful in 1896, 1898, 1899.

SIX IN SUCCESSION

Tipperary enjoy the distinction of being the only county to appear in six successive National Hurling League finals between 1952 and 1957. They were beaten in two of them, by Cork in 1953 and by Wexford in 1956.

Limerick played in the league finals of 1933, 1934 (won) and 1938 (won) and they won the title in 1935, 1936 and 1937 when the league was played on a one-division system.

The biggest winning margin in a National League final was in 1952 when **Tipperary** beat New York by a margin of 21 points on a scoreline of 6-14 to 2-5.

The biggest gap between sides at half-time in a National League final was in 1940 between **Cork** and **Tipperary** in the Athletic Grounds. Cork held a 21 points lead, 6-8 to 1-2.

Mayo wion six National Football League titles in succession between 1934 and 1939. They did not compete in the 1939-40 series but returned to win the 1940-41 series—or seven League titles in seven successive attempts.

DONNELLAN RECORD

The **Donnellan** family of Dunmore, Co. Galway, have a unique record. All-Ireland senior football medals were won by three generations in direct line – Mick (grandfather) in 1925; John (father) in 1964, '65 and '66 and Michael (son) in 1998.

John Donnellan was captain of the All-Ireland winning team of 1964. He did not learn that his father Mick had died during the match until after he received the Sam Maguire Cup.

His son Michael was named "Young Footballer of the Year" for 1998 and made a lasting imprint in the All-Ireland final against Kildare and in 2001 against Meath.

GOALKEEPER SUPREME

Danno O'Keeffe, selected in goal on the Team of the Century in 1984, was Kerry goalkeeper in seven All-Ireland senior football finals won by the Kingdom between 1931 and 1947 and in all he participated in thirteen finals, including three replays. He must be the record-holder in the number of football medals won as in addition to his seven All-Ireland senior medals, he collected one junior All-Ireland medal, fifteen Munster senior medals (between 1931 and 1948) and one junior Provincial medal, two Railway Cup medals, one National League medal, two Kerry championship medals, besides several medals and trophies won on American tours and in tournament games. He was a native of Fermoy, Co. Cork. In 1999 he was chosen as goalkeeper on the Gaelic Football Team of the Millennium.

FAMILY RECORDS

The family record for All-Ireland senior medals goes to the **Doyles of Mooncoin** who hold eighteen among them. Dick won seven, Eddie six and Mick five.

Among the wearers of the Tipperary blue and gold were the **Walsh brothers** who among them won sixteen All-Ireland medals. Denis Walsh put up a record of his own by winning the 1895 Championship with Tubberadora and twenty one years later turning out to help Boherlahan win the All-Ireland under the leadership of Johnny Leahy.

The **Graces of Tullaroan** also have fifteen All-Ireland medals among their plate, but six were gained in football.

Then line out the **Mahers of Tubberadora** generated fifteen hurling medals; the **Coughlans of Blackrock** amassed eleven; the **Ahearnes** of Blackrock nine. The **Landers of Tralee** won twelve All-Ireland senior football medals.

YOUNG STARS

It is doubtful if any player can better the record of **Johnny Walsh** of Tipperary who, at the age of twenty-three won his fifth All-Ireland senior hurling medal. Tubberadora born, he won his first medal in 1896 and his fifth six years later.

Another record was that made by **Seán Murphy of Kerry,** who had All-Ireland medals in all three grades – minor, junior and senior, to his credit before his twenty-second birthday. Strangest feature of his performance was the fact that his junior All-Ireland success came before the minor one.

Brendan Considine must have been one of the youngest players to win an All-Ireland senior medal, when at seventeen, he helped Clare in their 1914 triumph. Three years later he was with the Dublin Collegians side that won the 1917 title.

John Joe (Jobie) Callanan, who assisted Dublin to victory in the 1920 All-Ireland hurling final, was captain of the Tipperary team in the 1930 decider and refereed the 1940 All-Ireland final.

Mick Cummins, Ballylucas, Wexford, helped Leinster to win the Railway Shield double in hurling and football in Limerick in 1907, and three years later won an All-Ireland senior hurling title with Wexford. He hurled in this first All-Ireland final in 1901 and he was captain of the Wexford team beaten by Limerick in the 1918 final.

HAT-TRICK

Tom Collins of St Brendan's Club, Ardfert, Co. Kerry, had the remarkable distinction of playing in three Munster finals on the same evening. It was 29 July 1956 at Fitzgerald Stadium, Killarney, when Tom helped Kerry junior hurlers to a great success - the Kingdom's first big hurling success for over sixty years; later collecting his second Munster medal of the evening and scoring 2-3 in the junior football decider. And, to cap it all, he came on as a sub in the closing quarter of the Munster Senior Football final replay against Cork, which the Leesiders won by a point, 1-8 to 1-7.

Denis O'Sullivan of Kerry was the first man to play in All-Ireland finals in minor, under 21, junior and senior football, completing this feat in 1964.

Pat (Cocker) Daly, a member of the Dublin winning sides of 1901, 1902 and 1908 – perfect kicker of points, left and right – was still a fine footballer when he retired in 1926, at the age of fifty-three. His was a record surely for long service.

Five Ryans played for Tipperary and five **Cushions** played for Laois in the 1889 All-Ireland football final.

Seven Wexford men – **Jim Byrne, Gus Kennedy, Tom Doyle, Paddy Mackey, Tom Murphy, Martin Howlett and Aidan Doyle** – played in six All-Ireland football finals in a row between 1913 and 1918.

FIVE FINALS

Mick Flannelly, when on eighteen-year-old member of the Mount Sion club, Waterford, had the distinction of taking part in five Waterford county finals in one season: minor, junior and senior hurling, minor and junior football. He won senior and minor hurling and minor football medals.

The family record for **Railway Cup** medals is held by the **Delaneys of Laois**, who between them won seventeen – Jack (7), Bill 15), Chris (4) and Mick (1). In hurling Christy Ring won eighteen Railway Cup medals.

Mick Crowe, a native of Ballysimon, Limerick, refereed nine All-Ireland finals – seven in hurling and two in football – between 1906 and 1913.

Miko Doyle of Kerry had won four senior All-Ireland medals – 1929 to 1932 – with Kerry before his twenty-first birthday.

Des Foley helped Dublin win All-Ireland minor football honours in 1956. Three years later, whilst still a schoolboy and playing with St Joseph's, Marino, he was selected on the Leinster Railway Cup football team and collected his first of six interprovincial medals - three each in hurling (1962, 1964 and 1965) and in football (1959, 1961 and 1962).

The only person to win two All-Ireland senior hurling medals in the same year was **Mick Gill** in 1924. He helped Galway triumph over Limerick in the 1923 final played on 14 September 1924 and he was on the Dublin team that beat Galway in the 1924 final which was decided on 14 December 1924.

The **Grace brothers of Tullaroan** between them won seven senior football medals with Dublin. Jack was on the victorious Metropolitan teams of 1901, 1902, 1906, 1907 and 1909, and Pierce joined him on the 1906 and 1907 sides. Pierce later returned to Kilkenny and won hurling medals in 1911, 1912 and 1913. Jack is the only man to have captained All-Ireland sides in both hurling and football. He played for Dublin in three All-Ireland finals within a space of four Sundays – 3rd to 24th July 1904.

Garret Howard of Croom won All-Ireland hurling medals with Limerick in 1921, 1934 and 1936, whilst he was also on the 1924 and 1927 Dublin All-Ireland winning sides. Garret also won Railway Cup honours with Leinster in 1927 and with Munster in 1931.

Des Foley of Dublin became the first player to win Railway Cup hurling and football medals on the same day and in the same year when, playing at midfield, he helped Leinster to capture both titles on St Patrick's Day, 1962.

P. T. Treacy became the first Fermanagh man to play on a winning Railway Cup team when he figured at full-forward on the Ulster side that won the title in 1963.

Jim Barry of Cork trained fourteen All-Ireland winning senior teams. They were Cork hurlers in 1926, 1928, 1929, 1931, 1941, 1942, 1943, 1944, 1946, 1952, 1953 and 1954; Cork footballers in 1954 and Limerick hurlers in 1934.

Mick Kenny of Callan captained Kilkenny against Tipperary in the 1950 All-Ireland senior hurling final. Subsequently when domiciled in Clonmel, Kenny captained Tipperary to victory in the All-Ireland junior hurling final of 1953 and later played on the Tipperary side, winning with them a National League hurling medal in 1954, before returning to the black and amber colours to win a senior All-Ireland medal in 1957. He got an All-Ireland junior medal eleven years earlier.

Bobby Beggs won All-Ireland football medals with Galway in 1938 and Dublin in 1942 and Railway Cup football medals with Leinster in 1935 and Connacht in 1937.

Carrigtwohill-born **Billy O'Neill**, who captained Cork to All-Ireland junior hurling success in 1950, helped Galway beat the Rebel County boys in the 1956 All-Ireland senior football final. He also figured with Galway in the All-Ireland senior hurling deciders of 1953 and 1955. In the All-Army final of the latter year he scored a goal from a puck out for his team, Western Command.

Peter McDermott holds the unique record of participation in six All-Ireland senior finals between 1949 and 1954 in two contrasting roles — player and referee. First of all, he was on the great winning Meath side of 1949, the initial great breakthrough of the Meath men. Two years later he was again in the Meath colours in an All-Ireland final but this time they lost to Mayo. In 1952 he was on the side that drew with Cavan but lost the replay (two finals). The following year he appeared in a different category, when he refereed the Kerry v Armagh All-Ireland decider. But 1954 saw his real day of glory when he captained Meath to their second great All-Ireland triumph.

Josie Munnelly won a senior football All-Ireland medal with Mayo in 1936 and a junior football one with them twenty-one years later in 1957.

Mayo-born **John Nallen** played senior football for Mayo, Galway and Meath. He starred on the victorious Connacht Railway Cup teams of 1957 and 1958 and played for Ireland against the Combined Universities in 1956 and 1959. His last inter-county appearance was in junior ranks with Cavan.

Seán McKeown of Antrim began hurling at the beginning of the century. He played for Antrim in 1908 and was still a member of the county side into the late 1930s.

SPECIAL TRAIN

Clare chartered a special train – an engine and one carriage – to bring one of their stars – **Jim Houlihan** from Dublin to Thurles on 28 May 1933 for their Munster championship game with Limerick. He had played earlier that day with his club, Army Metro, in a Dublin championship game. The effort was all in vain. **Christy O'Brien** (Limerick} also travelled on the train.

Kilrush-born **P. J. O'Dea,** who figured with distinction for his county and in the Munster colours, was probably the most travelled player of all, for he played both hurling and football with clubs as far apart as San Francisco, Los Angeles, Toronto, Chicago, New York, London and Birmingham, as well as in Dublin, Cork, Limerick and his home county.

Tom McGrath, who helped Clare win the All-Ireland senior hurling title in 1914, opened his hurling account with the Banner County on 8 August 1909. Afterwards, a founder member of the Army Athletic Association, he played his last hurling game in an Army competition in 1944 - a record playing span of thirty-five years.

Pat (Fowler) McInerney won an All-Ireland medal with Clare in 1914 and again played for them in the 1932 All-Ireland final and in between won a medal with Dublin in 1927.

Paddy Phelan, the great Kilkenny defender, who was chosen at left-wing back on the Hurling Team of the Century in 1984, had played in goal for Kilkenny in the Autumn of 1929 in a tournament game. He did play in goal for Leinster in 1930 when the selected goalie had to play outfield and Paddy had only travelled to watch the game. He was again to play in goal in the 1942 Leinster final which Kilkenny lost to Dublin 4-8 to 1-4. He moved to his usual half-back position for the second half. It was his last game for the Noresiders. Incidentally, he was grand-uncle of D. J. Carey.

Eddie Keher is the only player to figure in the Senior and Minor All-Ireland finals in the same year. He was on the Minor team which lost the 1959 All-Ireland to Tipperary. The Senior final between Kilkenny and Waterford ended in a draw and Eddie was added to the panel for the replay. He came on in the second half, scoring two points.

FIRST BROADCAST

Michael O'Hehir made his first broadcast at Mullingar in 1938, the occasion was the All-Ireland senior football semi-final between Galway and Monaghan. Michael was born in Dublin but his father Jim hailed from Clare and trained the Dalcassian side that won its first All-Ireland senior hurling title in 1914.

The "man with the hat", identified Dublin's great goalkeeper of the 1920s and early 1930s – **Johnny McDonnell**, who always wore a black felt hat when playing. His brother, Paddy, also played with him on many great O'Toole's and Dublin teams.

From Croke Park in 1922 to Killarney in 1937 – that was the All-Ireland senior hurling trail of the renowned Matty Power, during which he played in eleven All-Ireland finals, including replays, winning five – four with Kilkenny in 1922, 1932, 1933 and 1935 and one with Dublin in 1927.

Mattie McDonagh of Ballygar, in 1953 played for Galway against Roscommon in the Connacht minor football championship and the following Sunday legally played for Roscommon against Galway in the Connacht minor hurling championship. At the period Ballygar minor footballers were affiliated to Galway and the minor hurlers to Roscommon.

Mick and John Mackey won 15 Limerick Senior Hurling medals and five Senior Football medals each.

Mick Fennelly (Mount Sion) has 15 Waterford Senior Hurling medals.

The **Spillanes** of Kerry hold the record number of All-Ireland Senior medals won in either hurling or football with 19. The Doyles of Mooncoin won 18 on the field while the Spillanes won 17 on the field of play. Mick Spillane was a sub in 1980 and Tom was a sub in 1981. The total of 19 is thus completed: Pat (8), Mick (7), Tom (4). The Graces of Tulleroan have 15 – Dick (5 hurling), Jack (5 football) with Dublin, and Pierce (3 hurling and 2 football).

THREE-TIMES CAPTAINS

The following players captained 3 All-Ireland winning teams: **Mickey Maher** (Tipperary) 1895, 1896, 1898; **Dick "Drug" Walsh** (Kilkenny): 1907, 1909, 1913; **Christy Ring (Cork)**: 1946, 1953, 1954. Only Christy Ring got his hands on the McCarthy Cup.

The following players captained 3 All-Ireland winning football teams and both were the same names: **John Kennedy (Dublin): 1891,**

1892, 1894; John (Seán Óg) Kennedy (Wexford): 1915, 1916, 1917. None of them got the Sam Maguire.

Bill ("Squires") Gannon of Kildare had the honour of being the first player to hold the Sam Maguire Cup high in triumph at Croke Park in All-Ireland. That was in 1928 - the year it first went up for competition and the Lily Whites beat Cavan by 2-6 to 2-5 in the final.

John Joe Sheehy (Kerry), 1926 and 1930, and **Seán Óg Sheehy**, 1962, are the only father and son to captain All-Ireland winning teams in either hurling or football.

The first All-Ireland Minor hurling final (1928) was not played until 1 September 1929 as a curtain raiser to the 1929 Senior final between Cork and Galway. **Johnny Kenneally** (Cork) was eligible to play in the minor final but had to forego the chance as he was on the Senior team. The Minor final ended in a draw and the replay took place in the Mardyke (Cork) on October 27. Although he had a Senior All-Ireland medal the Minor selectors did not call upon him for the Minor final replay which Cork won.

Tom Murphy (Threecastles) who won an All-Ireland medal in 1905 when he came on as a sub holds the record for the longest puck. He drove the ball 129 yards in Jones' Road (now Croke Park) in 1906. This feat is recorded in the Guinness Book of Records.

Patrick O'Keeffe (Cork) 1893 and **John O'Keeffe** (Cork) in 1919 were the first father and son to win All-Ireland medals in either hurling or football on the field of play.

THREE GENERATIONS

Three generation All-Ireland Senior medal winners: **Matt Gargan** 5 hurling with Kilkenny: 1907, 1909, 1911, 1912 and 1913; his son **Jack Senior** hurling with Kilkenny: 1939; his grandson, **Frank Cogan**, football with Cork 1972.

Jackie Power, Senior Hurling with Limerick: 1936, 1940; his son **Ger,** 7 Football with Kerry: 1975, 1978, 1980, 1981, 1984, 1985, 1986; and his grandson **Stephen McNamara** hurling with Clare 1995.

Christy Walsh (Kilmoyley) is the only Kerry man to win a Railway Cup Hurling medal on the field of play. He came on as a sub for the second half in the Munster victory of 1992.

Eamon Murray (Wicklow and London) has 2 All-Ireland intermediate Hurling medals with London 1967 and 1968 (sub), 4 All-Ireland Junior Hurling medals - 1959, 1960, 1963 (all with London), 1971 (with Wicklow); 3 All-Ireland Intermediate runners-up medals - 1961, 1964 and 1965 with London; 2 All-Ireland Junior Hurling runners-up with London - 1956 and 1957. He also won a Leinster Junior medal with Wicklow in 1954, won a Kerry Cup Intermediate medal with Avoca in 1995 at the age of 62. Played with Bros. Pearses Intermedite Football team in 1991. Also on the team was his grandson who was thirteen years of age at the time.

SCULLION AN EVER PRESENT

Tony Scullion of Derry helped to make history in a grand scale in the Railway Cup in football, now the M. Donnelly interprovincial championship.

Ulster beat Munster at Ennis in 1994 to complete the first-ever sequence of five titles in a row.

Scullion's role in the history-making achievement is strongly illustrated by the fact that he was chosen as left full back in every game and had not to retire once during a match.

He was also the only player to appear in every game in the record-making run.

Scullion also joined the ranks of title winning captains during the run, as he led the province to the 1991 championship

Sean O'Neill (Down) made 26 appearances with Ulster between 1960 and 1975 and won a record eight Railway Cup medals.

In the early fifties Leinster became the first province to win four interprovincial titles in a row in football—1952 to 1955 inclusive.

Ollie Freaney (Dublin) and **Stephen White (Louth)** were the only players to appear in all eight games and neither had to retire in any engagement.

Freaney was on duty as a forward, while White's versatility is underlined by the fact that he appeared as a defender, midfielder and forward during the history-making series.

Kevin Mussen led Down from right half back to an historic double in the All-Ireland senior football championship in 1960. The Mourne County won their first title that year and also became the first county to bring the Sam Maguire Cup across the Border.

Centre half back **Henry Downey** led Derry to their first All-Ireland senior football title in 1993 and Kieran McGeeney captained Armagh when they captured the trophy for the first time in 2002.

Peter Canavan joined the ranks of first-time winning captains when he led Tyrone to their initial All-Ireland senior crown in 2003.

FOUR-IN-A-ROW

In 2009 **Kilkenny** equalled Cork's long standing record of four All-Ireland Senior Hurling titles in succession from 1941 to 1944 incluisive.

Kilkenny played eighteen games on the way to their record-equalling feat.

Henry Shefflin was their top scorer with 6-149 (167 points).

SHEFFLIN JOINS RECORD MAKERS

Henry Shefflin joined the All Stars record-makers by winning his ninth award in 2009. He collected his first in 2000 and has now won eight in succession.

He joins Pat Spillane (Kerry), football, and fellow kilkenny man, D.J. Carey, on top of the roll of honour.

LEADING ALL-IRELAND SENIOR MEDAL WINNERS

FOOTBALL

Páidí Ó Sé (Kerry) 8: 1975, 1978, 1979, 1980, 1981, 1984, 1985, 1986
Denis "Ogie" Moran (Kerry) 8: 1975, 1978, 1979, 1980, 1981, 1984, 1985, 1986
Pat Spillane (Kerry) 8: 1975, 1978, 1979, 1980, 1981 (in as sub), 1984, 1985, 1986
Ger Power (Kerry) 8: 1975, 1978, 1979 (sub), 1980, 1981, 1984, 1985, 1986
Mike Sheehy (Kerry) 8: 1975, 1978, 1979, 1980, 1981, 1984 (sub), 1985, 1986
Dan O'Keeffe (Kerry) 7: 1931, 1932, 1937, 1939 1940, 1941, 1946
Jack O'Shea (Kerry) 7: 1978, 1979, 1980, 1981, 1984, 1985, 1986
John O'Keeffe (Kerry) 7: 1969 (sub), 1970, 1975, 1978, 1979, 1980, 1981
Charlie Nelligan (Kerry) 7: 1978, 1979, 1980, 1981, 1984, 1985, 1986
Sean Walsh (Kerry) 7: 1978, 1979, 1980, 1981, 1984, 1985, 1986
Mick Spillane (Kerry) 7: 1978, 1979, 1980 (sub), 1981, 1984, 1985, 1986.
Darragh Ó Sé (Kerry): 6: 1997, 2000, 2004, 2006, 2007, 2009.

HURLING

Noel Skehan (Kilkenny) 9: 1963 (sub), 1967 (sub), 1969 (sub) 1972, 1974, 1975, 1979, 1982, 1983
Christy Ring (Cork) 8: 1941, 1942, 1943, 1944, 1946, 1952, 1953, 1954
John Doyle (Tipperary) 8: 1949, 1950, 1951, 1958, 1961, 1962, 1964, 1965
Frank Cummins (Kilkenny) 8 1967 (sub), 1969, 1972, 1974, 1975 1979, 1982, 1983
Jack Rockford (Kilkenny) 7: 1904, 1905, 1907, 1909, 1911-'13
Dick Walsh (Kilkenny) 7: 1904, 1905, 1907, 1909, 1911-'13
Sim Walton (Kilkenny) 7: 1904, 1905, 1907, 1909, 1911-'13
Dick Doyle (Kilkenny) 7: 1904, 1905, 1907, 1909, 1911-'13.
Jimmy Doyle (Tipperary) 6: 1958, 1961, 1962, 1964, 1965, 1971 (in as sub).
Eddie Brennan (Kilkenny) 6: 2000, 2002, 2003, 2006, 2007, 2008.
Noel Hickey (Kilkenny) 6: 2000, 2002, 2003, 2006, 2007, 2008.
Michael Kavanagh (Kilkenny) 6: 2000, 2002, 2003, 2006, 2007, 2008.
James McGarry (Kilkenny) 6: 2000, 2002, 2003, 2006, 2007, 2008.
Henry Shefflin (Kilkenny) 6: 2000, 2002, 2003, 2006, 2007, 2008.

Note: John Doyle and Christy Ring share the record of being the only two players in hurling history to have won eight All-Ireland medals playing the full duration of each All-Ireland final.

Jack Lynch's Distinction

Jack Lynch (Cork) had the distinction of winning six All-Ireland senior championship medals in a row, five in hurling (1941-'44 and 1946) and one in football, 1945.

HIGHEST SCORERS IN ALL-IRELAND FINALS

HURLING:

60 minutes: 19 points—Michael "Gah" Ahearne (Cork) 5-4 v Galway 1928.

12 points—Bob McConkey (Limerick) 4-0 v Dublin 1921

12 points—Dave Clohessy (Limerick) 4-0 v Dublin 1934. REPLAY.

70 minutes: 18 points – Nicholas English (Tipperary) 2-12 v Antrim 1989.

13 points—Eddie Keher (Kilkenny) 2-7 v Galway in 1975.

13 points—Eamonn Cregan (Limerick) v Galway 1-7 in 1980.

80 minutes: 17 points – Eddie Keher (Kilkenny) 2-11 v Tipperary 1971.

15 points—Eddie Keher (Kilkenny) 2-9 v Cork in 1972.

14 points—Eddie Keher (Kilkenny) 1-11 v Limerick in 1974.

13 points—Eoin Kelly (Tipperary) 0-13 v Kilkenny 2009.

OTHER HIGH SCORERS IN CHAMPIONSHIP GAMES:

28 points – Nick Rackard (Wexford) 7-7 v Antrim, All-Ireland semi-final, 1954 – 60 minutes.

25 points – Andy "Doric" Buckley (Cork) 7-4 v Kilkenny in Home final, 1903 – 60 minutes.

22 points Nick Rackard (Wexford) 6-4 v Dublin, Leinster final, 1954 – 60 minutes.

22 points – Jimmy Smith (Clare) 6-4 v Limerick, Munster championship, 1954 – 60 minutes.

21 points: Nicky Horan (Meath) 2-15 v Kildare, Leinster championship, 2001—70 minutes.

19 points - Nick Rackard (Wexford) 5-4 v Galway, All-Ireland semi-final, 1956 – 60 minutes.

19 points – Mick Kennedy (Kilkenny) 6-1 v Wexford, Leinster final, 1916 – 60 minutes.

19 points – Paddy Molloy (Offaly) 5-4 v Laois, Leinster quarter-final, 1969 – 60 minutes.

19 points: Eugene Cloonan (Galway) 4-7 v Down, All-Ireland Qualifier, 2004—70 minutes.

19 points—Eoin Kelly (Waterford) 2-13 v Offaly, All-Ireland Qualifier 2008.

18 points – Babs Keating (Tipperary) 2-12 v Galway, All-Ireland semi-final, 1971 – 80 minutes.

18 points – Tull Considine (Clare) 6-0 v Galway, All-Ireland semi-final, 1932 – 60 minutes.

18 points – Mick Mackey (Limerick) 5-3 v Tipperary, Munster final, 1936.

18 Points—Joe Cooney (Galway) 2-12 v Cork 2008 All-Ireland Qualifier.

17 points – Eddie Keher (Kilkenny) 0-17 v Galway, All-Ireland semi-final, 1972 – 80 minutes.

17 points – Mark Corrigan (Offaly) 3-8 v Kilkenny, Leinster final, 1989 – 70 minutes.

17 points – Jimmy Kelly (Kilkenny) 5-2 v Cork, All-Ireland replay, 1905 – 60 minutes.

17 points – Eugene Cloonan (Galway) 2-11 v Derry, All-Ireland Quarter-Final, 2001—70 minutes.

17 points – Henry Shefflin (Kilkenny) 2-11 v Galway, All-Ireland Qualifier, 2004—70 minutes.

17 points – Henry Shefflin (Kilkenny) 2-11v Offaly, Leinster Championship 2005—70 minutes.

17 Points—Hernry Shefflin (Kilkenny) 1-14 v Waterford, 2009 All-Ireland Semi-Final.

16 points – Daragh Coen (Galway) 1-13 v Roscommon, Connacht Championship, 1998—70 minutes.

16 points – Eugene Cloonan (Galway) 2-10 v Clare, All-Ireland Quarter-Final Replay 1999—70 minutes.

16 points – Tom Carew (Kildare) 0-16 v Meath, Leinster Championship 2001—70 minutes.

16 points – Niall Gilligan (Clare) 2-10 v Laois All-Ireland Qualifier, 2002—70 minutes.

16 points: Brian McFaul (Antrim) 3-7 v London, Ulster championship, 2003—70 minutes.

Note: Some reports had P. J. Riordan (Tipperary) scoring the team's entire total (6-8) v Kilkenny in the 1895 All-Ireland final – 60 minutes.

FOOTBALL:

60 Minutes: 11 points—Frank Stockwell (Galway) 2-5 v Cork 1956.

9 points—Cyril Dunne (Galway) 0-9 v Kerry 1964.

9 points—Josie Munnelly (Mayo) 2-3 v Laois 1936.

70 minutes: 12 points—Jimmy Keaveney (Dublin) 2-6 v Armagh 1977.

12 points—Michael Sheehy (Kerry) 2-6 v Dublin 1979.

11 points—Eoin Liston (Kerry) 3-2 v Dublin 1978.

11 points—Peter Canavan (Tyrone) 0-11 v Dublin 1995.

80 minutes: 10 points—Mick Fay (Meath) 0-10 v Kerry 1970.

10 points—Brendan Lynch (Kerry) 1-7 v Offaly 1972 (Draw).

10 points—Tony McTague (Offaly) 0-10 v Kerry 1972 (Replay).

Note: What added special distinction to Frank Stockwell's feat was that all his scores came from play – a record in itself.

OTHER HIGH SCORES IN CHAMPIONSHIP GAMES:

19 Points—Declan Darcy (Leitrim) 2-13 v London, Connacht Championship, 1997—70 minutes.

18 points—Johnny Joyce (Dublin) 5-3 v Longford, Leinster championship, 1960—60 minutes.

18 points—Rory Gallagher (Fermanagh) 3-9 v Monaghan, Ulster Championship, 2002—70 minutes.

17 points—Mattie Hoey (Sligo) 3-8 v London, Connacht championship, 1978 – 70 minutes.

16 points—Brendan Hayden (Carlow) 3-7 v Kilkenny, Leinster championship, 1962 – 60 minutes.

16 points – John McCarthy (Dublin) 3-7 v Carlow, Leinster championship, 1978 – 70 minutes.

16 points—Matty Forde (Wexford) 2-10 v Offaly All-Ireland Qualifier, 2004—70 minutes.

16 points—Ian Ryan (Limerick) v Meath 2008 All-Ireland Qualifier.

15 points—Peter Nolan (Offaly) 4-3 v Laois, Leinster championship, 1958 – 60 minutes.

15 points—Matt Connor (Offaly) 2-9 v Kerry, All-Ireland semi-final, 1980 – 70 minutes.

15 points—Conor Mortimer (Mayo) 1-12 v New York, Connacht Championship, 2004—70 minutes.

Note: Connor's feat is regarded as a record for an All-Ireland semi-final.

PRESIDENTS OF THE G.A.A.

1884—Maurice Davin (Tipperary)
1887—E. M. Bennett (Clare)
1888—Maurice Davin (Tipperary)
1889—Peter J. Kelly (Galway)
1895—Frank B. Dineen (Limerick)
1898—Michael Deering (Cork)
1901—James Nowlan (Kilkenny)
1921—Daniel McCarthy (Dublin)
1924—P. D. Breen (Wexford)
1926—W. P. Clifford (Limerick)
1928—Seán Ryan (Dublin)
1932—Seán McCarthy (Cork)
1935—Robert O'Keeffe (Laois)
1938—Padraig McNamee (Antrim)
1943—Seamus Gardiner (Tipperary)
1946—Dan O'Rourke (Roscommon)
1949—Michael Kehoe (Wexford)
1952—M. V. O'Donoghue (Waterford)
1955—Seamus McFerran (Belfast)
1958—Dr. J. J. Stuart (Dublin)
1961—Hugh Byrne (Wicklow)
1964—Alf Murray (Armagh)
1967—Seamus O'Riain (Tipperary)
1970—Pat Fanning (Waterford)
1973—Dr Donal Keenan (Roscommon)
1976—Con Murphy (Cork)
1979—Paddy McFlynn (Down)
1982—Paddy Buggy (Kilkenny)
1985—Dr Mick Loftus (Mayo)
1988—John Dowling (Offaly)
1991—Peter Quinn (Fermanagh)
1994—Jack Boothman (Wicklow)
1997—Joe McDonagh (Galway)
2000—Seán McCague (Monaghan)
2003—Seán Kelly (Kerry)
2006—Nickey Brennan (Kilkenny)
2009—Christy Cooney (Cork)

ARD STIÚRTHÓIRÍ

1884-'85—Michael Cusack (Clare)
1884-'85—John McKay (Cork)
1884-'87—John Wyse Power (Kildare)
1885-'87—J. B. O'Reilly (Dublin)
1885-'89—Timothy O'Riordan (Cork)
1887-'88—James Moore (Louth)
1888-'89—William Prendergast (Tipperary)
1889-'90—P. R. Cleary (Limerick)
1890-'92—Maurice Moynihan (Kerry)
1891-'94—Patrick Tobin (Dublin)
1894-'95—David Walsh (Cork)
1895-'98—Richard T. C. Blake (Meath)
1898-1901—Frank B. Dineen (Limerick)
1901-'09—Luke J. O'Toole (Dublin)
1929-'64—Padraic Ó Caoimh (Cork)
1964-'79—Seán Ó Síocháin (Cork)
1979-2007—Liam Ó Maolmhichíl (Longford)
2008- Pauric Ó Dufaigh (Monaghan)

Maurice Davin (1942-1927); president 1884-1887 and 1888-1889.

Edward Bennet (1845-1910); president 1887.

Peter Kelly (1843-1908); president 1889.

Frank Dineen (1862-1916); president 1895-1898.

Michael Deering (1858-1901); president 1898-1901.

James Nowlan (1855-1924); president 1901-1921.

Daniel McCarthy (1883-1957); president 1921-1924.

Patrick Breen (1893-1949); president 1924-1926.

Liam Clifford (1877-1949); president 1926-1928.

Seán Ryan (1895-1963); president 1928-1932.

Seán McCarthy (1890-1974); president 1932-1935.

Robert O'Keeffe (1881-1949); president 1935-1938.

Pádraig MacNamee (1896-1975); president 1938-1943.

Séamus Gardiner (1895-1976); president 1943-1946.

Dan O'Rourke (1887-1968). president 1946-1949.

Micheál Kehoe (1899-1977); president 1949-1952.

Vincent O'Donoghue (1900-1972); president 1952-1955.

Séamus MacFerran (1917-1968); president 1955-1958.

Doctor Joseph Stuart (1904-1980); president 1958-1961.

Aodh Ó Broin; president 1961-1964.

Alf Ó Muirí; president 1964-1967.

Séamus Ó Riain; president 1967-1970.

Pádraig Ó Fainín; president 1970-1973.

Dr. Donal Ó Cianáin; president 1973-1976.

Conchur Ó Murchú; president 1976-1979.

Pádraig Mac Floinn; president 1979-1982.

Pádraig Ó Bogaigh; president 1982-1985.

Micheál Ó Lochlainn; president 1985-1988

Séan Ó Dúllaing president 1988-1991

Peadar Ó Coinn president 1991-1994

Séan Boothman president 1994-1997

Seosamh Mac Donncha president 1997 -2000

Séan Mac Thaidhg president 2000-2003

Séan Ó Ceallaigh president 2003-2006

Nioclás Ó Braonáin president 2006-2009

Christóir Ó Cuana president 2009-

GAA 125 –The Seven Founders

By John Arnold

The meeting that led to the formation of the Gaelic Athletic Association was held in Miss Hayes' Commercial Hotel in Thurles on November 1st, 1884. We can be certain that at least seven people attended the Association's inauspicious beginning but there may have been more – there is no doubt however that Cusack, Davin, Wyse Power, McKay, McCarthy and Ryan do deserve the title of the GAA's Founding Fathers and they deserve to be remembered and honoured in this, the 125th Anniversary year of the Association.

Michael Cusack.

Born in Carron, Co. Clare on September 20th 1847 – one hundred and sixty two years ago today! He qualified as a teacher and worked in schools in Connacht, Ulster and Leinster before setting up his own Private Academy in Dublin in 1877. With Maurice Davin, Cusack was the inspirational force behind the summoning of the Thurles meeting. Cusack served as GAA secretary from 1884 until 1896. He was narrowly beaten on a 19/17 vote in 1901 when he attempted to regain the position of GAA Secretary. Michael Cusack died in Whitworth Hospital in Dublin on November 27th, 1906. He is buried in Glasnevin Cemetery.

Maurice Davin.

A native of Deerpark, Carrick-on-Suir, Maurice Davin was born on June 29, 1842. An all-round athlete Maurice and his brother Pat were National and International stars at various athletic pursuits. These included hammer and weight throwing, shot putting and long and high jumping. Davin advocated that Athletics in Ireland should not be governed by English rules. He was appointed first President of the GAA in 1884. Though he resigned in 1887 he returned to the GAA the following year to help heal the split after the stormy Thurles Convention. The 1904 All Ireland Hurling Final between Kilkenny and Cork was played on the Davin farm at Deerpark. Maurice Davin died on January 26, 1927 and was buried in Dysert-Churchtown Cemetery.

John McKay.

A native of Co. Down, John McKay was a reporter and journalist. He worked with the Cork Examiner newspaper and along with Cusack was one of the first joint Secretaries of the GAA. He later moved to London. In 1934, when the GAA celebrated it's 50th Anniversary and again in Centenary Year, 1984 extensive efforts were made to try and find out more information about McKay's latter life- all to no avail. Recently due to the research of Donal McAnallen it has been established that John McKay died in London in 1923. He is buried in a London Cemetery in an unmarked grave and Cumann Lúthchleas Gael plan to erect a suitable memorial.

J.K.Bracken.

Joseph Kevin Bracken was born in Templemore. A stonemason and building contractor by trade, Bracken was very involved in athletics. He was a member of the IRB and at the 1886 GAA convention was elected National Vice President. He became the first chairman of Templemore UDC. The Bracken family moved to Kilmallock Co. Limerick in 1904 and two years later J.K. Bracken died. He is buried at Tankardstown Cemetery near Kilmallock.

John Wyse Power.

John Wyse Power was born in Waterford. He was a member of the Fenian Movement and a journalist by profession. He worked for the Leinster Leader and the Freeman's Journal. He was the official GAA athletics handicapper for several years. He also served as Honorary Secretary of the GAA and Dublin GAA Board Chairman. His wife Jenny was an elected member of Seanad Éireann. He died on May 29th, 1926 and is buried in Glasnevin Cemetery.

Joseph Patrick Ryan.

Joseph P. Ryan was born in Carrick-on-Suir in April, 1857. Having qualified as a Solicitor he practised in Callan and Thurles. He would have known Maurice Davin well and that friendship was possibly the reason he attended the meeting in 1884. In 1899 Ryan emigrated to Canada. He settled in Cranbrook, British Columbia where he became inmmersed in local life – the Board of Trade, the Mining Industry and as a Police Magistrate as well as becoming a prominent journalist. He died in March, 1918 and is buried in Cranbrook.

Thomas St. George McCarthy.

The longest surviving GAA founder, Thomas St. George McCarthy was born in Bansha, Co. Tipperary in June 1862. Like his father George, Thomas St. John joined the Royal Irish Constabulary. He joined Michael Cusack's Academy in Dublin and it was Cusack who prepared him for his Cadetship Examination in 1882. At the time of the November, 1884 meeting McCarthy was stationed in Templemore. He retired from the RIC in 1912 and lived in the Ranelagh area of Dublin. He died on March 12th, 1943 at the Linden Convalescent Home in Stillorgan. He is buried in Deansgrange Cemetery in an unmarked grave. Cumann Lúthchleas Gael intend to erect a fitting memorial shortly.